Trent Holden, Anna Kaminski, Vesna Maric, Kate Morgan, Isabella Noble, Leonid Ragozin, Kevin Raub, Andrea Schulte-Peevers, Greg Ward

Contents

PLAN YOUR TRIP

ON THE ROAD

KIRK FISHER/SHUTTERSTOCK ©

RHODES P342

Contents

NAXOS P212

RANDREI/SHUTTERSTOCK ©

Contents

ON THE ROAD

HORA (MYKONOS) P190

Contents

UNDERSTAND

SURVIVAL
GUIDE

SPECIAL
FEATURES

Welcome to the Greek Islands

The Greek islands ignite the imagination and satisfy the soul with a history laced in mythical tales and told through ancient, sun-bleached ruins.

Satisfy Your Appetite

Island hopping is a culinary adventure and a tour of regional cuisine. Discover traditional dishes featuring unique local products including cheeses, olive oils, wild greens, honey, wines and spirits. Zone in on harbourside tavernas serving up the daily catch fresh from fishing nets, and look for people collecting wild produce on the hillsides. On many islands, you'll encounter the Italian legacy of pasta with a Greek slant, like rich sauces with mussels steamed in ouzo. On others, the Ottoman past surfaces in spiced sweets and pastries.

Travel Through Time

Surround yourself with the ruins of Delos or wander through the reconstructed Minoan Palace of Knossos and you can almost sense the Ancient Greeks moving alongside you. Step through a window into times past as you explore the medieval walled city of Rhodes or the ruins of Ancient Thira on Santorini. Beyond these celebrated sites are the quieter ruins scattered on nearly every island, filled with mystery and often overgrown with wildflowers – from the enormous marble statues of Naxos to the colourful 2nd-century mosaics on Kos. Greek ruins are as impressive as they are numerous.

Get Active

Greece's islands are an active traveller's adventure playground. Meander along cobbled Byzantine footpaths, hike into volcanoes, kayak beside dolphins, watch for sea turtles and cycle through lush forests. The Greek islands also offer some of the world's top kitesurfing, diving and rock-climbing locations. With blue skies and a vast and varied landscape that begs to be conquered, it's easy to understand how so many myths of gods and giants originated here.

Experience Island Life

Sink your toes deep into the sand and listen to the warm Aegean waters lap the shore like you have nowhere else to be. This is island life. Swoon at the majestic beauty of Santorini or indulge in the pulsing nightlife of Mykonos. Wander through lush wildflowers in spring on Skopelos. Become acquainted with the melancholy throb of *rembetika* (blues songs) and the tang of homemade tzatziki. The days melt from one to the next, filled with miles of aquamarine coastline blessed with some of Europe's cleanest beaches. No wonder many travellers settle down here and never go home.

Why I Love the Greek Islands

by Kate Armstrong, Writer

Greek island hopping is thrilling. Sure, the exhilaration comes in discovering each island's 'best' tiny beach cove and off-the-radar turquoise waters, but it's far more profound than that. Every time I disembark a ferry, it's like encountering a new country: the aromas of wild herbs (the sage of Ikaria, the thyme of rugged Kalymnos), the taste of a *tyropita* (cheese pie) on Alonnisos, the blue and white churches of Sifnos, the streetscapes of Nisyros, the archaeological treasures of Crete. And then there's the proud, welcoming islanders themselves.

For more about our writers, see p624

Above: Shipwreck Beach (p547), Zakynthos

Greek Islands

Adriatic Sea

TIRANA ✪

NORTH MACEDONIA

Kilkis

Serres

Drar

MACEDONIA

ALBANIA

Florina

Edessa

Thessaloniki

Veria

Halkidiki

Kastoria

Kozani

Katerini

Gulf of Kassandra

Corfu
Byzantine, Venetian, French and British influences (p510)

Konitsa

Lake Aliakmonas

Mt Olympus ▲

Kassandra Peninsula

ITALY

Corfu

Corfu Town (Kerkyra)

Igoumenitsa

Ioannina

Kalambaka

Lake Kremasta

Trikala

Larissa

THESSALY

Volos

Pelion Peninsula

EPIROS

Parga

Karditsa

GREECE

Skiathos Town

Alonnis

Ionian Sea

Arta

Karpenisi

Lamia

Skiathos

Skopelo

Sporades

Preveza

STEREA ELLADA

Agios Konstantinos

Istiea

Lefkada Town

Mytikas

Mt Iti ▲

Lefkada

Agrinio

Mt Parnassos ▲

Evia

Assos

Ithaki

Nafpaktos

Delphi

Thiva (Thebes)

Marathon

Sami

Messolongi

Patra

Gulf of Corinth

Mt Parintha ▲

ATHENS ▲

Argostoli

Kefallonia

Egio

Piraeus ✪

ATTIC

IONIAN ISLANDS

Aegina Town

Lav

Agios Nikolaos

Kyllini

Amaliada

Mycenae

Aegina

Saron Gulf

Zakynthos Town

Argos

Nafplio

Poros

Zakynthos

Pyrgos

Olympia

Tripoli

Poros Town

Poros Town

Hydra Town

Megalopoli

PELOPONNESE

Spetses

Hydra

MEDITERRANEAN SEA

Kyparissia

Sparta

Kalamata

Crete
Unique culture, cuisine and customs (p281)

Pylos

Gythio

Monemvasia

Areopoli

Neapoli

Lakonian Gulf

Myrtoön Sea

Kythira

Samaria Gorge
Magnificent canyon rich in wildflowers and wildlife (p324)

Antikythira

Kissamos

Paleohora

ELEVATION

	4000m
	3000m
	2000m
	1000m
	500m
	0

0 — 100 km
0 — 50 miles

BULGARIA

Edirne
Orestiada
Didymotiho

THRACE
Xanthi
Komotini

İstanbul

Sea of Marmara

Kavala
Alexandroupoli
Thasos
Thracian Sea

The Dardanelles

Samothraki
Gallipoli Peninsula
Imvros (Gökçeada)
Çanakkale

Myrina
Limnos

TURKEY
Akçay

NORTHEASTERN AEGEAN ISLANDS
Bozcaada

Agios Efstratios

Ayvalık

Lesvos
Mytilini Town

Lesvos
Rolling olive groves and cool pine forests (p451)

Skyros

Psara
Chios

Aegean Sea

Chios Town
Çeşme
İzmir

Santorini
Spectacular clifftop sunsets (p238)

ea Styra
Karystos

Gavrio
Andros

Kuşadası

Vathy (Samos)
Samos

Kea
Tinos
Hora (Mykonos)

Ikaria

Fourni Islands
Patmos

Rhodes' Old Town
Magical, walled medieval town (p345)

Ermoupoli
Syros

Mykonos
Delos

Milas

Leros

Bodrum

Kythnos
CYCLADES
Serifos
Parikia
Antiparos
Hora (Naxos)
Donousa

Kalymnos
Kos Town
Kos

Datça Peninsula
Marmaris

Sifnos
Paros
Naxos
Little Cyclades
Amorgos

Datça

Symi

Kimolos
Sikinos
Ios
Astypalea

Nisyros

Milos
Folegandros

Tilos

Rhodes Town

Kastellorizo (Megisti)

Fira
Anafi

Halki
Rhodes

Karpathian Sea
Santorini (Thira)

Aegean Sea
DODECANESE

Lindos
Kattavia

MEDITERRANEAN SEA

Preveli Beach
Palm-fringed sands overlooked by a monastery (p312)

Saria

Olympos
Karpathos
Pigadia

Sea of Crete

Crete

Kasos

ania
ethymno
Plakias

Iraklio
Knossos
Moni Arkadiou
Sitia

Knossos
Restored Minoan palace (p294)

Agia Galini

Agios Nikolaos
Ierapetra

Gavdos

Greek Islands'
Top 15

Rhodes' Old Town

1 Getting lost in Rhodes' Old Town (p345) is a must. Away from the crowds, you'll find yourself meandering down twisting, cobbled alleyways with soaring archways and lively squares. In these hidden corners your imagination will take off with flights of medieval fancy. Explore the ancient Knights' Quarter, the old Jewish Quarter or the Hora (Turkish Quarter). Hear traditional live music in tiny tavernas or dine on fresh seafood at atmospheric outdoor restaurants. Wander along the top of the city's walls, with the sea on one side and a bird's-eye view into this living museum.

Nisyros Volcano

2 Legend has it that during the battle between the gods and Titans, Poseidon ripped a chunk off Kos and used it to trap the giant Polyvotis deep beneath. That rock became Nisyros and the roar of the volcano (p384) is Polyvotis' angered voice. It may have last erupted 25,000 years ago but this volcano is officially classified as dormant rather than extinct. Make your way into the island's hollow caldera, a vast and otherworldly plain where ancient, ruined agricultural terraces climb the walls, while cows graze amid sci-fi-set rocks.

LITTLEKIDMOON/SHUTTERSTOCK ©

ZLATAMARKA/SHUTTERSTOCK ©

Cretan Cuisine

3 Waistlines be damned: Crete (p281) is the perfect place to indulge. The island's Mediterranean diet is known for its health benefits but the farm-fresh produce, aromatic herbs, straight-from-the-ocean seafood, soft, tangy cheese and some of the world's best virgin olive oil make it legendary. Whether it's a bowl of snails, fresh artichokes, mussels or figs, the essence of this rustic cuisine is a balance of flavours. It's hard to beat traditional hand-spun filo, a salad of *horta* (wild greens) picked from a backyard garden, and red mullet just hauled in.

Knossos

4 Rub shoulders with the ghosts of the mighty Minoans. Knossos (p292) was their Bronze Age capital more than 4000 years ago; from here they attained an astonishingly high level of civilisation and ruled vast parts of the Aegean. After mysteriously disappearing less than a thousand years later, their extraordinary wealth of frescoes, sculptures, jewellery and structures lay buried under the Cretan soil until the site's excavation in the early 20th century. Despite a controversial partial reconstruction, Knossos remains one of the most important archaeological sites in the Mediterranean.

Corfu

5 The story of Corfu (p510) is written across the handsome facades of its main town's buildings. This is a place that crams a remarkable mix of architecture into its small circumference. Stroll past Byzantine fortresses, neoclassical 19th-century British buildings, Parisian-style arcades, Orthodox church towers and the narrow, sun-dappled streets of the Venetian Old Town. Beyond the town, Corfu is lush green mountains, rolling countryside and dramatic coastlines. And if the architecture and scenery aren't enough, come to enjoy the Italian-influenced food.

Lefkada

6 Lefkada may be connected to mainland Greece by a narrow causeway road, but it remains surprisingly unaffected by tourism. Lefkada Town (p528) is charming while the soaring mountains of the interior still conceal timeless villages and wild olive groves, and the rugged west coast holds some amazing beaches, such as delightful Mylos. Speed through the east coast's overdeveloped enclaves to discover stunning little bays and inlets in the island's south such as Poros, and the windy conditions that make this the ideal location for kite and windsurfing.

Experiencing the Acropolis

7 Regal on its hilltop, the elegant Acropolis (p148) remains the quintessential landmark of Western civilisation. Explore it early in the morning or soak up the view from a dinnertime terrace; no matter how you experience the Acropolis, you will be mesmerised by its beauty, history and sheer size. The Parthenon is the star attraction, but don't overlook the exquisite Temple of Athena Nike and the Theatre of Dionysos. Nearby, the state-of-the-art Acropolis Museum provides a close-up look at the surviving treasures of the site.

Cutting-Edge Capital

8 Life in Athens (p68) is a magnificent mash-up of both the ancient and the contemporary. Beneath the majestic facades of the many venerable landmarks, the city is teeming with life and creativity. Galleries and clubs hold the exhibitions, performances and installations of the city's booming arts scene. Street art is all around. Fashionable restaurants and humble tavernas rustle up plate after plate of satisfying fare. Soulful *rembetika* (blues songs) serenade the cobbled streets, while cocktail bars and nightclubs abound and swing deep into the night.

Skopelos

9 You may not of heard of Skopelos (p492) but if you've seen the 2008 movie *Mamma Mia!* you'll certainly recognise this handsome island that's part of the Northern Sporades. The gorgeous whitewashed Old Town is considered a Traditional Settlement of Outstanding Beauty and there are over 360 churches and chapels on the island. Pine forests, olive groves, rippling vineyards and orchards of plums and almonds cover the countryside. The southeast coast harbours a string of beautiful sand-and-pebble beaches, while the northwest coast offers high jagged cliffs – perfect for adventure activities.

Lesvos

10 Bulky and imposing, Lesvos (p451) does its size justice with tremendously varied landscape. Rolling olive groves and cool pine forests stretch into grassy plains, where one of the world's few petrified forests stands. The island's coast is lined with beaches, many hardly touched by tourism. Lesvos' capital, Mytilini, is energised by a large student population and a busy cafe and bar scene aided by fine local ouzo and wine. Some exploration will reveal a medieval castle town and two exquisite Byzantine churches. The only thing you may be short of here is time.

Easter Festivities on Patmos

11 The Greek calendar is chock-full of festivals and holidays, but the biggest event of the Greek Orthodox Church is Easter. One of the best places to experience it is on Patmos (p410) in the Dodecanese. The island comes to life with fireworks, dancing in the streets, goats roasted outdoors and plenty of ouzo. Begin by witnessing the moving, candlelit processions of flower-filled biers through the capital, marking the start of the celebration on Good Friday. By Saturday night you'll be shouting *Hristos Anesti* (Christ is Risen) and cracking vibrant red-dyed eggs.

Island Hopping in the Cyclades

12 From the spirited nightlife and celebrity hideaways of Mykonos and Ios, to the isolated sandy coasts of tiny, far-flung specks such as Anafi, hopping through the Cyclades (p173) is a Greek experience not to be missed. Peppered with ancient ruins (try Delos), mystical castles (head to Naxos), lush scenery and dramatic coastlines (visit Milos), the islands are spread like Greek jewels across the sea. Speed over the Aegean on catamarans and sway on old-fashioned ferry boats.

Samaria Gorge

13 The dramatic gorge of Samaria (p324) is the most-trodden canyon in Crete – and with good reason. Starting near Omalos and running down through an ancient riverbed to the Libyan Sea, it's home to soaring birds of prey and a dazzling array of wildflowers in spring. It's a full-day's walk (about six hours down) but the jaw-dropping views make it worth every step. To get more solitude, try lesser-known Imbros Gorge, which runs roughly parallel to Samaria and is around half the length.

Hydra

14 Everyone approaches Hydra (p162) by sea. There is no airport, there are no cars. The white-gold houses of the tiny island's stunningly preserved stone village fill a natural cove and hug the edges of the surrounding mountains. Below, sailboats, caïques (little boats) and megayachts fill Hydra's quays while locals and vacationers fill the harbourside cafes. Here, a mere hour and a half from Athens, you'll find a great cappuccino, rich naval and architectural history, and the raw sea coast beckoning you for a swim.

Preveli Beach

15 With its heart-shaped boulder lapped by the bluest waves just offshore, Crete's Preveli Beach (p312) is one of Greece's most iconic. Bisected by a freshwater river and flanked by cliffs concealing sea caves, Preveli is a thick ribbon of soft sand on the Libyan Sea, with clear pools of water along its palm-lined riverbank that are perfect for cool dips. The beach lies under the sacred gaze of a magnificent monastery perched high above. Once the centre of anti-Ottoman resistance and later a shelter for Allied soldiers, this building offers magnificent views.

What's New

The Greek Islands may be a destination packed with ancient sites but that doesn't mean it's stuck in the past. From new and expanded museums in Athens and elsewhere, to vegan eats on Mykonos and alternative tourism initiatives in the Dodecanese, there's plenty of new stuff going on across the country to impress first-time and repeat visitors alike.

Wine Tourism

Greece's ancient tradition of winemaking is being increasingly celebrated in many of the country's great wine regions. Check out Evia's wineries, Manousakis Winery (p316) on Crete, and the Paneri Winery (p507) on Skyros.

Archaeological Museum

Reopened after many years of restoration, this Corfu Town institution (p513) houses a fine collection including a massive gorgon pediment from the Temple of Artemis.

Acropolis Museum

A new section of the museum (p84) provides access to 4000 sq metres of archaeological excavations beneath the building so you can see up close the remains of an ancient Athenian neighbourhood.

Basil & Elise Goulandris Foundation

Works by leading Greek artists share wall space with the likes of Van Gogh and Picasso at this new museum (p105) that houses a top flight private collection.

Local Tourism in the Dodecanese

On Kastellorizo (p543), Kalymnos (p403) and Nisyros (p384), new businesses run by passionate, younger locals are offering some great cultural and alternative experiences, other than those for which the islands might be known.

LOCAL KNOWLEDGE

WHAT'S HAPPENING IN GREECE

Simon Richmond, Lonely Planet writer

A decade on from the economic crisis that forced Greece to implement severe austerity in exchange for remaining within the European Union (EU), the country appears to be turning a corner. There's a long way to go to full recovery, but key economic indicators are looking positive, with tourism, in particular, going gangbusters – a record 33 million people visited the country in 2018, making Greece one of the most popular destinations in the world. The downside is that Greece's loveliest and most iconic locations are also now struggling with the scourge of overtourism.

For Santorini, in particular, the exponential growth in visitor numbers (in peak season anywhere between 10,000 and 18,000 people a day were disembarking mammoth cruise ships for tours of the island) has created havoc. The island's electricity and water supply resources have been pushed to their limits, while the amount of rubbish generated over the last five years has doubled. In 2019 Santorini capped daily cruise ship passenger arrivals at 8000.

Vegan Mykonos

This Cyclades hot spot for hedonistic partying is also developing into a haven for vegetable lovers, with vegan menus being offered by the likes of Reeza (p201), Bowl (p201) and Nice n Easy (p194).

Casa Romana

Also recently reopened, this archaeological site (p389) provides enormous insight into how a wealthy Koan official and his family lived.

Cultural & Conference Center of Heraklion

This new facility (p291) is Crete's most important cultural and events venue and includes a gorgeous 800-seat auditorium hosting a variety of performances.

Atlantis Oia

The first diving outfit (p248) in Greece to be part of Cousteau Divers is committed to marine conservation and is campaigning to create a protected marine reserve around Santorini.

Chios Mastic Museum

This imaginatively designed museum (p449) has its own mastic garden and a good souvenir shop for the island's premier export.

Museum of Ancient Eleutherna

This modern facility (p306) exhibits treasures unearthed from the ruins of Eleutherna on Crete with pieces from the early Iron Age to the Byzantine eras.

LISTEN, WATCH & FOLLOW

For inspiration and up-to-date news, visit www.lonelyplanet.com/greece/travel-tips-and-articles.

Rembetika: Songs of the Greek Underground 1925–1947 Classic songs still performed in the country's bars and clubs.

Ekathimerini.com (www.ekathimerini.com) English-language edition of daily Greek newspaper Kathimerini.

Greek to Me (Mary Norris; 2019) Passionate Hellenophile and New Yorker magazine copy editor on her love of the Greek language and travels in the country.

FAST FACTS

Food trend Gourmet souvlaki

National drink Ouzo

Number of refugees 67,100

Population 1.54 million

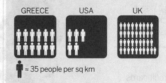

GREECE   USA   UK

≈ 35 people per sq km

Need to Know

For more information, see Survival Guide (p589)

Currency
Euro (€)

Language
Greek

Visas
Generally not required for stays of up to 90 days; however, travellers from some nations may require a visa, so double-check with the Greek embassy.

Money
Debit and credit cards are accepted in cities, but elsewhere it's handy to have cash. Most towns have ATMs, but they may be out of order.

Mobile Phones
Local SIM cards can be used in unlocked phones. Most other phones can be set to roaming. US and Canadian phones need to have a dual- or tri-band system.

Time
Eastern European Time (GMT/UTC plus two hours)

When to Go

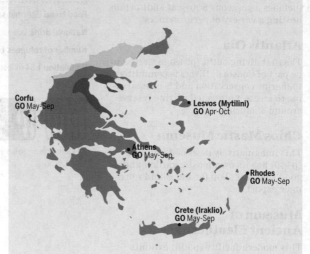

- Dry climate
- Warm summer, mild winter
- Mild summer, very cold winter

Corfu
GO May-Sep

Lesvos (Mytilini)
GO Apr-Oct

Athens
GO May-Sep

Rhodes
GO May-Sep

Crete (Iraklio)
GO May-Sep

High Season
(Jun–Aug)

➡ Sights, tours and transport are running full tilt.

➡ Accommodation prices can double.

➡ Crowds swell and temperatures soar.

Shoulder
(Apr & May, Sep & Oct)

➡ Accommodation prices can drop by up to 20%.

➡ Temperatures are not as blazing.

➡ Internal flights and island ferries have reduced schedules.

Low Season
(Nov–Mar)

➡ Many islands shut up their tourist infrastructure and ferry schedules are skeletal.

➡ Accommodation rates can drop by as much as 50%.

➡ Expect chilly, wet weather; Athens and Crete may even see snow.

Useful Websites

EOT (Greek National Tourist Organisation; www.visitgreece.gr) Concise tourist information.

Greeka (www.greeka.com) Plenty of planning advice, photos and booking services.

Greek Travel Pages (www.gtp.gr) Access to ferry schedules and accommodation.

Lonely Planet (www.lonelyplanet.com/greece) Destination information, hotel bookings, traveller forum and more.

Ministry of Culture (www.culture.gr) Cultural events and sites.

Odysseus (http://odysseus.culture.gr) Portal for info on ancient sites and for booking tickets.

Important Numbers

In Greece, the area code must be dialled for ordinary numbers, meaning you always dial the full 10-digit telephone number. Emergency numbers are shorter, as detailed in the table below.

Country code	✆30
International access code	✆00
Ambulance	✆166
Police	✆100
Tourist police	✆171

Exchange Rates

Australia	A$1	€0.61
Canada	C$1	€0.67
Japan	¥100	€0.81
New Zealand	NZ$1	€0.58
UK	£1	€1.13
US	US$1	€0.88

For current exchange rates see www.xe.com.

Daily Costs

Budget: Less than €100

➡ Dorm bed and domatio (Greek B&B): less than €60

➡ Meal at markets and street stalls: less than €15

Midrange: €100–180

➡ Double room in midrange hotel: €60–150

➡ Hearty meal at a local taverna: around €20

➡ Entrance fee for most sights: less than €15

Top End: More than €180

➡ Double room in top hotel: from €150

➡ Excellent dining, some accompanied by Michelin stars: €60–100

➡ Activity such as diving certification: around €400

➡ Cocktail: around €12

Opening Hours

The following are high-season hours; hours decrease significantly for shoulder and low seasons, and some places close completely.

Banks 8.30am–2.30pm Monday to Thursday, 8am–2pm Friday

Restaurants 11am–11pm

Cafes 10am–midnight

Bars 8pm–late

Clubs 10pm–4am

Post Offices 7.30am–2pm Monday to Friday (rural); 7.30am–8pm Monday to Friday, 7.30am–2pm Saturday (urban)

Shops 8am–2pm Monday, Wednesday and Saturday; 8am–2pm and 5pm–9pm Tuesday, Thursday and Friday

Arriving in Greece

Eleftherios Venizelos International Airport (Athens) Express buses (€6, one hour) operate 24 hours between the airport, city centre and Piraeus. Half-hourly metro trains (€10, 50 minutes) run between the city centre and the airport from 5.30am to 11.30pm. Taxis to the city centre cost €38 (€50 at night) and take about 45 minutes.

Makedonia International Airport (Thessaloniki) Buses X1, N1, 45 & 79 (€2, 50 minutes) connect to the city every half hour around the clock. Taxis to the city centre cost €30.

Nikos Kazantzakis International Airport (Iraklio, Crete) Buses run to the city centre from 6am to midnight (€1.20, every 15 minutes). Taxis to the city centre cost €15.

Diagoras Airport (Rhodes) Buses run to Rhodes Town from 6.40am to 11.15pm (€2.60, 25 minutes). Taxis cost €25.

Getting Around

Air Domestic flights are abundant. In high season, flights fill up fast so book ahead.

Boat Ferries, including catamarans, well-equipped modern ferries and overnight boats with cabins, link the islands to each other and the mainland. Schedules change annually and can be announced as late as May. In high season it's smart to book ahead.

Bus Generally air-conditioned, frequent, and as efficient as traffic allows; good for travel between major cities.

Car & Motorcycle Rentals are reasonably priced and found on all but the tiniest islands. They give you the freedom to explore the islands, but some islands are becoming overrun with hire vehicles.

For much more on **getting around**, see p598

First Time Greek Islands

For more information, see Survival Guide (p589)

Checklist

➡ Check your passport is valid for at least six months past your arrival date

➡ Make reservations for accommodation and travel, especially in high season

➡ Check airline baggage restrictions, including for regional flights

➡ Inform credit-/debit-card company of your travel plans

➡ Organise travel insurance

➡ Check if you'll be able to use your mobile (cell) phone

What to Pack

➡ International driving licence, if you don't hold an EU one

➡ Phrasebook

➡ Diving qualifications

➡ Phone charger

➡ Power adaptor

➡ Lock/padlock

➡ Lightweight raincoat

➡ Seasickness remedies for ferry trips

➡ Mosquito repellent

➡ Swimwear, snorkel and fins

➡ Clothes pegs and laundry line

Top Tips for Your Trip

➡ In late spring or early autumn, the weather is softer and the crowds are slimer.

➡ Visit a few out-of-the-way villages to find traditional culture. Rent a car and explore. Stop for lunch, check out the local shops and test out your Greek.

➡ Go slowly. Greece's infrastructure doesn't befit a fast-paced itinerary. Visit fewer places for longer.

➡ Many sites (including the ancient sites in Athens) offer free entry on the first Sunday of the month, except in July and August.

What to Wear

Athenians are well groomed and the younger crowd is trendy, so keep your most stylish clothes for the city. Nevertheless, in Athens and other big cities such as Rhodes and Iraklio, you'll get away with shorts or jeans and casual tops. Bars or high-end restaurants require more effort – the scene is fashionable rather than dressy. Think tops and trousers rather than T-shirts and cut-offs. In out-of-the-way places you can wear casual clothing; in summer, the heat will make you want to run naked so bring things such as quick-drying tank tops and cool dresses. Sturdy walking shoes are a must for the cobbled roads and ruins.

Sleeping

If travelling in high season, reserve accommodation well in advance. Many hotels on islands are closed during winter.

Hotels Greece ranks all accommodation from one to five stars depending on how they meet 'minimum standards' (this includes allowances for guests in wheelchairs). As such, the stars may reflect the services offered, rather than quality.

Domatia The Greek equivalent of the British B&B, minus the breakfast. Many have equipped kitchens.

Campgrounds Found in the majority of regions and islands and often include hot showers, communal kitchens, restaurants and swimming pools.

Money

ATMs are widespread in tourist areas, and can usually be found in most towns large enough to support a bank. Most are compatible with MasterCard or Visa, while Cirrus and Maestro users can make withdrawals in major towns and tourist areas. If travelling to smaller islands, you may want to take a backup supply of cash, as many ATMs can lose their connection or (in remote areas) run out of cash at the end of the day!

It's always wise to notify your bank of your travel plans before you leave, to avoid them blocking the card as an antifraud measure after your first withdrawal abroad.

Bargaining

Bargaining is acceptable in flea markets and markets, but elsewhere you are expected to pay the stated price.

Tipping

Restaurants Tipping is not traditionally the culture in Greece, though it is appreciated. Locals tend to leave a few coins. Depending on where you are, you can round it up or leave around 10%.

Taxis Round up the fare. There's a small fee for handling bags; this is an official charge, not a tip.

Bellhops Bellhops in hotels appreciate a small gratuity of around €1.

Language

Tourism is big business in Greece and being good businesspeople, many Greeks have learned the tools of the trade: English. In cities and popular towns, you can get by with less than a smattering of Greek; in smaller villages or out-of-the-way islands and destinations, a few phrases in Greek will go a long way. Wherever you are, Greeks will hugely appreciate your efforts to speak their language.

 Does this ferry go to (Rhodes)?
Πηγαίνει αυτό το φέρι στη (Ρόδο)
pi·ye·ni af·to to fe·ri sti (ro·tho)

With over a hundred islands, it would be a shame not to get out there and explore.

 What is the local speciality?
Ποιες είναι οι τοπικές λιχουδιές
pies i·ne i to·pi·kes li·khu·thies

Most areas and islands in Greece have a local dish – and the locals love to talk food.

 Do you speak English?
Μιλάς Αγγλικά
mi·las ang·gli·ka

Given the tourist-oriented nature of Greece, the chance is the answer will be 'yes', but it's always polite to ask.

 I'd like to hire a car.
Θα ήθελα να ενοικιάσω ένα αυτοκίνητο
tha i·the·la na e·ni·ki·a·so e·na af·to·ki·ni·to

For some of the more remote areas and islands, travelling around is easier by car.

5 **What time does it open?**
Τι ώρα ανοίγει
ti o·ra a·ni·yi

Avoid the crowds – especially if a cruise ship is in port – by getting to sites and museums as they open.

Etiquette

Eating Meals are commonly laid in the table centre and shared. Always accept a drink offer as it's a show of goodwill. Don't insist on paying if invited out; it insults your hosts. In restaurants, service might feel slow; dining is a drawn-out experience and it's impolite to rush waitstaff.

Photography In churches, avoid using a flash or photographing the main altar, which is considered taboo. At archaeological sites, you'll be stopped from using a tripod which marks you as a professional and thereby requires special permissions.

Places of worship If you visit churches, cover up with a shawl or long sleeves and a long skirt or trousers to show respect. Some places will deny admission if you're showing too much skin.

Body language 'Yes' is a swing of the head and 'no' is a curt raising of the head or eyebrows, often accompanied by a 'ts' click-of-the-tongue.

If You Like...

Ancient History

Ancient Agora Athens' civic, political and commercial centre in ancient times, beautifully preserved. (p88)

Ancient Thira Largely intact remains of a phenomenal ancient city in a stupendous mountaintop location overlooking Santorini. (p250)

Kos Town Explore the once-impregnable Castle of the Knights, check out 3rd century AD mosaics and rest under the plane tree where Hippocrates taught his students. (p387)

Knossos Crete's marquee Minoan site; ideally paired with Heraklion Archaeological Museum. Thanks to its restoration, today's Knossos is one of the easiest ruins for your imagination to take hold of. (p581)

Beaches

Elafonisi Turquoise water and long pink sand dunes await sun worshippers on Crete's southwest coast. Wade through the water or stroll across a thin, sandy isthmus to Elafonisi Islet. (p327)

Lefkada's West Coast Wide stretches of uninterrupted soft sand on a little island that's off the beaten track. Some of the best-known beaches were badly damaged by the 2015 earthquake, but others remain intact and beautiful. (p531)

Loutra Edipsou At this truly therapeutic beach the bay is fed by warm, thermal sulphur water. The spa resort is the most visited spot in northern Evia - and for good reason. (p485)

Santorini Beautiful beaches of red and black volcanic sand are easily reached and surprisingly quiet. (p238)

Myrtos Beach Scrappy car park aside, this strip of sand on Kefallonia is breathtakingly beautiful. (p540)

Arts & Crafts

Byzantine & Christian Museum The exquisite, gold-hued creations in this Athens museum are simply beautiful. (p104)

Art Space Showcasing top current artists, this atmospheric gallery is housed in the wine caverns of one of Santorini's oldest vineyards. Enjoy the paintings and scultures while indulging in a vintage wine tasting. (p250)

Museum of Islamic Art Mesmerising collection of over 8000 pieces of Islamic art, from tiles to carvings and prayer rugs. (p101)

Fish & Olive In the heart of Naxos, this gallery showcases ceramics by renowned local artists Katharina Bolesch and Alexander Reichardt. (p221)

Corfu Museum of Asian Art This amazing collection ranges from prehistoric bronzes to Graeco-Buddhist figures and Japanese Noh masks. (p512)

The Great Outdoors

Crete's gorges Hikers flock to the spectacular Samaria Gorge; its nearby cousins, the Imbros and Agia Irini Gorges, are equally breathtaking and less crowded. (p324)

Homer's Ithaki Hike through dramatic island scenery and past archaeological sites in Odysseus' homeland. (p541)

Skopelos Wander deep into pine forests, through olive groves and clifftop plum and almond orchards. (p492)

Museums

Heraklion Archaeological Museum Most famous for its Minoan collection, including the gob-smacking frescoes from Knossos. This museum is one of the largest and most important in all of Greece. (p285)

Acropolis Museum Sculptures and other finds from the Acropolis shine in this spacious, superbly designed gem. (p84)

Andros Archaeological Museum Holds an exquisite 2nd century BC marble copy of the bronze Hermes of Andros by Praxiteles. (p178)

Chios Mastic Museum State of the art hilltop museum documenting the cultivation of the mastic tree and the processing of its resin. (p449)

Religious Buildings

Moni Hozoviotissis This 1017 monastery clings to a cliff face high above the pounding sea. (p233)

St George's Cathedral One of the country's most significant Catholic churches, a legacy of the Venetian occupation. (p185)

Moni Evangelistrias Greek Independence was first declared at this Skiathos monastery. (p490)

Church of Panagia Kera This tiny triple-aisled church shelters Crete's best-preserved Byzantine frescoes. (p333)

Beth Shalom Synagogue Athens' main synagogue is a handsome white marble building dating to 1935. (p105)

PLAN YOUR TRIP IF YOU LIKE...

Top: Monastery of Moni Hozoviotissis (p233), Amorgos

Bottom: Heraklion Archaeological Museum, Iraklio (p285)

Month by Month

January

Most islands go into hibernation during winter. However, the capital and surrounding mainland welcome visitors with festivals that aren't really aimed at tourists. Expect local insight and warmth from hospitality (rather than the sun).

✯✯ Feast of Agios Vasilios (St Basil)

The first day of January sees a busy church ceremony followed by gifts, singing, dancing and feasting. The *vasilopita* (golden glazed cake for New Year's Eve) is cut; if you're fortunate enough to get the slice containing a coin, you'll supposedly have a lucky year.

✯✯ Epiphany (Blessing of the Waters)

The day of Christ's baptism by St John is celebrated throughout Greece on 6 January. Seas, lakes and rivers are all blessed, with the largest ceremony held at Piraeus.

February

While February is an unlikely time to head to Greece, if you like a party and can time your visit with Carnival, which starts three weeks before Lent, it's well worth it.

✯✯ Carnival Season

Minor events from as early as late February lead to a wild weekend of costume parades, floats, feasting and traditional dancing. There are regional variations: Patra's Carnival is the largest, while Skyros features men and their male 'brides' dressed in goatskins.

March

The islands are sleepy but the weather is warming up, making March a relaxed time to visit. Although the national calendar is quiet, there are countless religious festivals celebrated with great gusto in towns.

✯✯ Clean Monday (Shrove Monday)

On the first day of Lent (a day which is referred to as Kathara Deftera), people take to the hills throughout Greece to enjoy picnicking and kite-flying.

✯✯ Independence Day

The anniversary of the hoisting of the Greek flag by independence supporters at Moni Agias Lavras is celebrated with parades and dancing on 25 March. This act of revolt marked the start of the War of Independence.

April

A great month to visit with the scent of orange blossom heavy in the air. Easter weekend is busy with vacationing Greeks; reserve accommodation well in advance. Some businesses shut up shop for the week.

✳ Orthodox Easter

Communities commemorate Jesus' crucifixion with candlelight processions on Good Friday and celebrate his resurrection at midnight on Easter Saturday. Feasting follows on Easter Sunday.

✳ Festival of Agios Georgios (St George)

The feast day of Greece's patron saint is celebrated on 23 April, but if this falls during Lent then it moves to the first Tuesday following Easter. Expect dancing, feasting and a general party atmosphere.

May

If you're planning to go hiking, May is a great time to hit Greece's trails. Temperatures are relatively mild and wildflowers create a huge splash of colour. Local produce fills Greek kitchens.

✳ May Day

The first of May is marked by a mass exodus from towns for picnics in the country. Wildflowers are gathered and made into wreaths to decorate houses. It's a day associated with workers' rights, so recent years have also seen mass walkouts and strikes.

✳ Naxos Festivals

Between May and September various festivals take place on Naxos. Classical concerts are held in the Venetian kastro, art exhibitions are staged at the Bazeos Tower and celebrations of traditional food and music are held in several different venues.

June

For festival-goers looking for contemporary acts rather than traditional village parties, June is hopping on the mainland. Top national and international performers fill atmospheric stages with dance, music and drama.

✳ Navy Week

Celebrating their long relationship with the sea, fishing villages and ports throughout the country host historical reenactments and parties in early June.

✳ Feast of St John the Baptist

The country is ablaze with bonfires on 24 June as Greeks light up the wreaths they made on May Day.

☆ Athens & Epidaurus Festival

The most prominent Greek summer festival features local and international music, dance and drama at the ancient Odeon of Herodes Atticus on the slopes of the Acropolis in Athens and the world-famous Theatre of Epidavros in the Peloponnese. Events run from June to August. (p109)

✳ Miaoulia Festival

Hydra ignites in celebration of Admiral Miaoulis and the Hydriot contribution to the War of Independence. Witness a spectacular boat burning, fireworks, boat racing and folk dancing, usually held the third weekend of June.

July

Guaranteed sunshine as temperatures soar and life buzzes on the islands' beaches. Outdoor cinemas and giant beach clubs draw visitors to Athens' nightlife.

☆ Rockwave Festival

Rockwave has major international artists (with an emphasis on metal, most years) and is held over several weekends at Terra Vibe, a parkland venue on the outskirts of Athens in Malakasa. (p109)

☆ Skopelos Rembetika Festival

Held in Skopelos Town in mid-July, this musical jamboree is a three-day showcase for local folk-blues musicians. (p495)

August

Respect the high heat of August – do a little bit less and relax a little more fully. If you're travelling midmonth, reserve well ahead as Greeks take to the roads and boats in large numbers.

✳ August Moon Festival

Under the year's brightest moon, historical venues in Athens open with free moonlit performances. Watch theatre, dance and music at venues such as the Acropolis or Roman Agora. The festival is also celebrated at other towns and sites around Greece; check locally for details. (p109)

Top: Patra's Festival celebrations in the Peloponnese might lure you from the islands to the mainland.

Bottom: Independence Day, Athens (p72)

✯ Feast of the Dormition

Also called Assumption and celebrated with family reunions on 15 August; the whole population is seemingly on the move on either side of the big day. Thousands also make a pilgrimage to Tinos to its miracle-working icon of Panagia Evangelistria.

✯ XLSIOR

One of the LGBT+ pride season's biggest party events is this week-long festival held on Mykonos at the end of the month. See https://xlsiorfestival.com for the full line-up.

♟ Wine & Culture Festival

Held at Evia's coastal town of Karystos during the last week of August and the first week of September, this festival includes theatre, traditional dancing, music and visual-art exhibits as well as a sampling of every local wine imaginable. (p486)

September

The sun is high though less and less blazing, especially on the islands. The crowds begin to thin and some ferry schedules begin to decline midmonth. Fresh figs and grapes are in season and plentiful.

✯ Gennisis Tis Panagias

The birthday of the Virgin Mary is celebrated throughout the country on 8 September with religious services and feasting.

October

While most of the islands start to quieten down, the sunny weather often holds in October. City life continues apace.

✯ Ohi Day

A simple 'no' (*ohi* in Greek) was Prime Minister Metaxas' famous response when Mussolini demanded free passage through Greece for his troops on 28 October 1940. The date is now a major national holiday with remembrance services, parades, feasting and dance.

December

The islands may be quiet but Athens is still in full swing. Expect cooler temperatures and a chilly sea. With fewer tourists, you're likely to meet more locals and not have to push through crowds at the major sights.

✯ Christmas

Celebrated on 25 December and traditionally marking the end of a 40-day fast. Expect to see Christmas trees, children carolling and fishing boats decorated with lights. Families gather for a Christmas Day feast including a roasted hog and honey cookies.

Itineraries

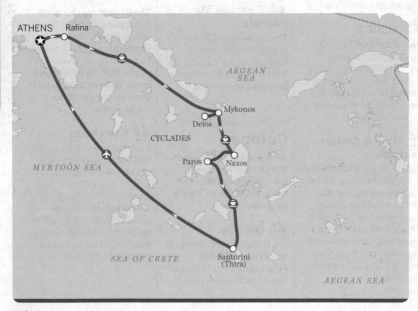

 10 DAYS **Athens & the Cyclades**

Perfect for the time-pressed, this island-hopping itinerary includes magnificent Athens, a few popular, bustling islands, and chilling out in quieter havens. Transport between these islands and the mainland is plentiful.

Spend a couple of days in **Athens**, visiting the Acropolis, exploring the Ancient Agora and wandering through the Acropolis and archaeological museums. There's also the capital's excellent contemporary art and food scenes as well as brilliant nightlife.

Catch a ferry from **Rafina** to spend a day or two on chic **Mykonos** and enjoy the colourful harbour, vibrant bars and beaches full of sun worshippers. Take a day trip to sacred **Delos** and explore ancient ruins. Hop on a ferry to **Naxos**, the greenest of the Cyclades with its hilltop, Venetian-walled Old Town, quaint villages and sugar-soft beaches. Move on to **Paros**, whose cobbled capital is filled with trendy boutiques and excellent dining. Head to the seaside village of Naoussa for excellent seafood.

Lastly, visit spectacular **Santorini**, aka Thira, for stunning sunset views. Explore excellent wineries and volcanic beaches, along with the truly impressive Minoan site of Akrotiri. From here, catch a flight back to Athens.

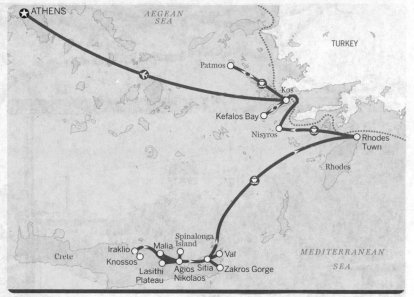

 Crete & the Dodecanese

Eastern Crete offers a tranquil side of the island with relaxed resorts and impressive sights. From here it's a short hop to the neighbouring Dodecanese, with their wealth of culture and speedy catamaran services that make island hopping a breeze.

Begin in **Iraklio**, taking in the excellent archaeological museum. Make a day trip to the captivating Minoan ruins of **Knossos** before sampling fine vintages in the Iraklio Wine Country, a mosaic of shapely hills, sun-baked slopes and lush valleys.

From Iraklio head east along the northern coast to the relaxed resort town of **Agios Nikolaos**, which radiates charm and chilled ambience. This makes a great base for exploring the surrounding region. Explore the massive Venetian fortress on **Spinalonga Island**, a leper colony until 1957 and just a short ferry ride across the Gulf of Mirabello. Visit the surrounding Minoan ruins, such as the **Palace of Malia**, still filled with mysteries, and rent a bike to explore the tranquil villages of the fertile **Lasithi Plateau**, lying snugly between mountain ranges and home to Zeus' birthplace.

Continue on to **Sitia**, from where you can head for the clear water and white sand of **Vaï**, Europe's only natural palm-forest beach. You can also head south from here to Zakros to hike through the dramatic, cave-honeycombed **Zakros Gorge** to Kato Zakros and its Minoan palace.

From Sitia, get settled on a twice-weekly, 12-hour ferry ride to **Rhodes**. Spend a couple of days exploring the atmospheric, walled medieval Old Town and checking out its burgeoning nightlife. Visit some of the surrounding beaches and stunning Acropolis of Lindos. Catch a catamaran to lush **Nisyros** to explore atop the alarmingly thin crust of its caldera and then carry on to **Kos** to spend a couple of days on gorgeous, sandy **Kefalos Bay** and to sip coffee and cocktails in Kos Town's lively squares. There still may be time to squeeze in a quick trip to **Patmos** to experience its artistic and religious vibe, and to visit the cave where St John wrote the Book of Revelations, before backtracking to Kos from where you can catch onward flights to **Athens**.

Top: Corfu (p510)

Bottom: Santorini (p238)

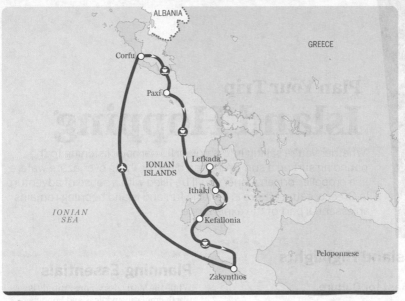

10 DAYS The Ionians

The Ionian Islands offer beautiful architecture, scrumptious food, flour-soft beaches and dramatic scenery. There are also plenty of outdoor activities to enjoy in this island group. Both the start and end of this itinerary are reachable by short, scenic flights from Athens.

Begin your tour in **Corfu**, where you can easily spend a couple of days wandering through the amazing blend of Italian, French and British architecture in Corfu Old Town, set between two spellbinding fortresses. The arcaded promenade is a hive of cafes, boutiques and restaurants where you can indulge in gourmet cuisine that packs a heavy Italian influence. Take in the island's world-class museums, such as the Corfu Museum of Asian Art, and its fortresses – the views from the Byzantine stronghold of Angelokastro on the west coast are unforgettable. Explore picturesque coastal villages and lounge on fantastic sandy beaches. If you want to expend a bit more energy, Corfu is also a great place for windsurfing, or try biking in the island's mountainous interior.

From Corfu, hop on a ferry to tiny **Paxi**, where ancient olive groves and windmills dot the interior while tranquil coves beckon from the coastline. Snorkel in the crystalline water and dine on seafood in colourful, Venetian-style harbour towns that beg you to stay. Drag yourself away to the west-coast beaches of **Lefkada**, where you can take water taxis to isolated stretches of sand and turquoise water. Head to the southern tip to windsurf before carrying on to sleepy **Ithaki,** where you can walk the paths of Homer and feel inspired by ancient Byzantine churches and monasteries.

Hop over to neighbouring **Kefallonia**; overnight in the picturesque village of Fiskardo, with its top restaurants. Kayak to isolated golden beaches and sample the island's unique, well-regarded local wine. Explore the Paliki Peninsula with its red clay cliffs, hilltop villages and powdery beaches. Catch a boat south to **Zakynthos** to take in the fabulous Byzantine Museum, then head for the verdant southern cape to escape the crowds. This island is the nesting ground of the endangered loggerhead turtle. From here you can grab a flight back to Corfu or on to Athens.

Plan Your Trip
Island Hopping

Whether you're sailing into a colourful harbour, listening to the pounding surf on a sun-drenched deck, or flying over azure waters in a propeller-driven plane, you'll be filled with a sense of adventure. In Greece, getting there is half the fun and island hopping remains an essential part of the experience.

Island Highlights

Best for Culture

Delos (p201) A stunning archaeological site.

Rhodes (p344) Explore the (literally) multilayered history of the Old Town.

Patmos (p410) See the cave where St John wrote the Book of Revelations.

Best for Low Season

Hydra (p162) Escape from Athens.

Corfu (p510) Venetian and French architecture.

Amorgos (p228) Hike the rugged trails.

Best for Drinking & Dining

Ikaria (p421) Have your fill of fresh lobster.

Crete (p281) Savour herb-rich Cretan specialities.

Samos (p432) Sample the famous sweet wine.

Best for Outdoors

Kefallonia (p532) Kayak to a remote cove or beach.

Lesvos (p451) Hike in a 20-million-year-old petrified forest.

Kos (p386) Ride bikes to long stretches of sand.

Planning Essentials

While the local laissez-faire attitude is worth emulating while island hopping, a little bit of planning can take you a long way. Deciding where and when you want to go and getting your head around routes and schedules before you go will take the work out of your holiday.

Be flexible Your travels will be that much more enjoyable when you leave wiggle room in your itinerary. Transportation schedules are *always* vulnerable to change. Everything from windy weather to striking workers mean planes and boats are regularly subject to delays and cancellations at short notice.

Double check timetables Ferry and airline timetables change from year to year and season to season, with ferry companies often being awarded contracts to operate different routes annually. When island hopping, it's important to remember that no timetable is iron-clad.

Fast ferries are not always best Fast ferries have a reputation for lateness, because if they are late to one place, particularly in high season, things tend to snowball. Santorini and Naxos can be particularly bad because of congestion at their ports.

Consider local boats Planning websites never cover absolutely every ferry or boat service. While you don't want to rely on it, be aware that there may also be local boats shuttling between islands, including day excursion boats that may work for your itinerary. Check with contacts on an island (the hotel where you are staying for example) for up-to-date information.

GETTING YOUR SEA LEGS

Even those with the sturdiest stomachs can feel seasick when a boat hits rough weather. Here are a few tips to calm your tummy.

➡ Gaze at the horizon, not the sea. Don't read or stare at objects that your mind will assume are stable.

➡ Drink plenty and eat lightly. Many people claim ginger biscuits and ginger tea settle the stomach.

➡ Don't use binoculars.

➡ Sit towards the back of the boat, this is marginally more stable.

➡ If possible stay in the fresh air – don't go below deck and avoid hydrofoils where you are trapped indoors.

➡ Try to keep your mind occupied.

➡ If you know you're prone to seasickness, take seasickness medication and/or invest in acupressure wristbands before you leave.

When to Go

High Season

➡ Lots of ferries and transport links but book ahead.

➡ Water temperature is warm enough for swimming.

➡ The *meltemi* (dry northerly wind) blows south across the Aegean, sometimes playing havoc with ferry schedules.

Shoulder Season

➡ Transport is less frequent but still connects most destinations.

➡ Water temperature is still warm in September and early October, so great for diving.

➡ The best time for sea-life spotting begins in May and runs through to September.

Low Season

➡ Planning ahead is essential as transportation can be limited.

➡ Swimming in the sea is only for those immune to cold water.

➡ Most businesses offering water sports are closed for the winter.

Travelling by Sea

With a network covering every inhabited island, the Greek ferry system is vast and varied. The slow rust buckets that used to ply the seas are nearly a thing of the past. You'll still find slow boats, but high-speed ferries are increasingly common and cover most of the popular routes. Local ferries, excursion boats and tiny, private fishing boats called caïques often connect neighbouring islands and islets. You'll also find water taxis that will take you to isolated beaches and coves. At the other end of the spectrum, hydrofoils and catamarans can drastically reduce travel time. Hydrofoils have seen their heyday but continue to link some of the more remote islands and island groups. Catamarans have taken to the sea in a big way, offering more comfort and coping better with poor weather conditions.

For long-haul ferry travel, it's still possible to board one of the slow boats chugging between the islands and to curl up on deck in your sleeping bag to save a night's accommodation. Nevertheless, Greece's domestic ferry scene has undergone a radical transformation in the past decade and these days you can also travel in serious comfort and at a decent speed. Of course, the trade-off is that long-haul sea travel can be quite expensive. A bed for the night in a cabin from Piraeus to Rhodes can be more expensive than a discounted airline ticket.

Ticketing

As ferries are prone to delays and cancellations, for short trips it's often best not to purchase a ticket until it has been confirmed that the ferry is leaving. During high season, or if you need to reserve a car space, you should book in advance. High-speed boats such as catamarans tend to sell out long before the slow chuggers. For overnight ferries it's always best to book in advance, particularly if you want a cabin

Shipwreck Beach (p547), Zakynthos

or particular type of accommodation. If a service is cancelled you can usually transfer your ticket to the next available service with that company.

Many ferry companies have online booking services or you can purchase tickets from their local offices and most travel agents in Greece. Agencies selling tickets line the waterfront of most ports, but rarely is there one that sells tickets for every boat, and often an agency is reluctant to give you information about a boat it doesn't sell tickets for. Most have timetables displayed outside; check these for the next departing boat or ask the *limenarhio* (port police).

Fares

Ferry prices are determined by the distance of the destination from the port of origin, and the type of boat. The small differences in price you may find at ticket agencies are the results of some agencies sacrificing part of their designated commission to qualify as a 'discount service'. (The discount is seldom more than €0.50.)

High-speed ferries and hydrofoils cost about 20% more than traditional ferries, while catamarans are often 30% to 100% more expensive than their slower counterparts. Caïques and water taxis are usually very reasonable, while excursion boats can be pricey but useful if you're trying to reach out-of-the-way islands. Children under five years of age travel for free while those aged between five and 10 are usually half price.

Classes

On smaller boats, hydrofoils and catamarans, there is only one type of ticket available and these days, even on larger vessels, classes are largely a thing of the past. The public spaces on the more modern ferries are generally open to all. What does differ is the level of accommodation that you can purchase for overnight boats.

A 'deck-class' ticket typically gives you access to the deck and interior, but no overnight accommodation. Aeroplane-type seats give you a reserved, reclining seat in which you will hope to sleep. Then come various shades of cabin accommodation: four-berth, three-berth or two-berth interior cabins are cheaper than their equivalent outside cabins with a porthole. On most boats, cabins are very comfortable, resembling a small hotel room with private bathroom. However, light sleepers should note that you are likely to be woken in the middle of the night by announcements over the loud speakers in each of the cabins.

ISLAND FINDER

ISLAND	FOOD	FAMILY FRIENDLY	OFF THE BEATEN TRACK	NIGHTLIFE	BEACHES	CULTURE	ACTIVITIES	EASY ACCESS
Aegina						X		X
Alonnisos			X			X	X	
Amorgos			X			X	X	
Andros			X			X	X	X
Chios	X	X			X	X	X	X
Corfu	X	X			X		X	X
Crete	X	X			X	X	X	X
Evia			X			X	X	X
Fourni Islands			X		X	X		
Hydra		X		X		X		X
Ios	X			X	X		X	X
Kalymnos		X		X		X	X	X
Karpathos			X			X	X	
Kefallonia	X	X			X		X	X
Kos		X		X	X	X	X	X
Lefkada					X	X	X	X
Leros		X	X			X	X	
Lesvos	X	X				X	X	X
Milos		X			X	X	X	X
Mykonos	X			X	X			X
Naxos	X	X		X	X	X	X	X
Paros	X	X		X	X	X	X	X
Patmos	X	X			X	X	X	X
Paxi			X			X		X
Rhodes	X	X		X		X		X
Samos	X	X			X	X	X	X
Samothraki			X		X	X	X	
Santorini	X			X	X	X		X
Sifnos			X			X	X	
Skiathos				X	X		X	X
Skopelos	X	X			X	X	X	X
Skyros	X				X	X	X	X
Small Cyclades			X		X		X	
Symi						X		X
Thasos		X			X	X	X	X
Tilos			X		X		X	
Zakynthos					X	X		X

Unless you state otherwise, you will automatically be given deck class when purchasing a ticket.

Taking a Car

While almost all islands are served by car ferries, they are expensive and, to ensure boarding, you'll generally need to secure tickets in advance. A more flexible way to travel is to board as a foot passenger and hire a car on each island. Hiring a car for a day or two is relatively cheap and possible on virtually all islands.

Resources

The comprehensive weekly list of departures from Piraeus put out by the EOT (known abroad as the GNTO, the Greek National Tourist Organisation) in Athens is as accurate as possible. While on the islands, the people with the most up-to-date ferry information are the local *limenarhio* (port police), whose offices are usually on or near the quayside.

You'll find lots of information about ferry services on the internet and many of the larger ferry companies have their own websites. Always check online schedules, or with operators or travel agencies for up-to-the-minute information.

A few useful websites:

➡ **Danae Travel** (www.danae.gr) A good site for booking boat tickets.

➡ **Ferries.gr** (www.ferries.gr) Listing all the information for all the boats.

➡ **Greek Travel Pages** (www.gtp.gr) Has a useful search program and links for ferries.

➡ **Greekferries.gr** (www.greekferries.gr) Allows you to search ferry schedules from countless providers, including accommodation options and multileg journeys.

➡ **My Ship Tracking** (www.myshiptracking. com) Tracks boats in real time; a way to keep tabs on chronically late ferries.

➡ **Open Seas** (www.openseas.gr) A reliable search engine for international ferry routes and schedules.

Day Trip Boats

At some mainland ports you'll find boats offering day trips to the islands (and vice versa), and there are also interisland day trips. Usually, you cannot use such day-tripping boats for a one-way journey – you have to return on the same boat the same day. If it's an island-to-island trip, some boats are permitted to drop off passengers and pick them up for the return leg on another day.

Some excursion boats, however, are also permitted to offer a 'one-way' trip, such as the *Kasos Princess*, a cruiser that runs day trips between Kasos and Kalymnos and can also drop people off in Kalymnos – useful on the days the ferries don't run. Make careful enquiries at boat booking offices before purchasing tickets.

Travelling by Air

A flight can save you hours at sea and offers extraordinary views across the island groups. Flights between the islands tend to be short and aeroplanes small, often making for a bumpy ride. The vast majority of domestic flights are handled by the merged Olympic Air and Aegean Airlines, offering regular domestic services and competitive rates. In addition to these national airlines, there are a number of smaller outfits running seaplanes or complementing the most popular routes.

Ticketing & Fares

The easiest way to book tickets is online, via the carriers themselves. You can also purchase flight tickets at most travel agencies in Greece. Olympic Air has offices in the towns that flights depart from, as well as in other major towns. There are discounts for return tickets when travelling midweek (Monday to Thursday), and bigger discounts for trips that include a Saturday night away. You'll find full details and information on timetables on the airlines' websites.

Resources

Up-to-date information on flight timetables is best found online. Airlines often have local offices on the islands.

➡ **Aegean Airlines** (https://en.aegeanair.com) Domestic flights.

➡ **Astra Airlines** (www.astra-airlines.gr) Thessaloniki-based carrier with domestic flights.

➡ **Olympic Air** (www.olympicair.com) Aegean Airline's subsidiary with further domestic flights.

➡ **Sky Express** (www.skyexpress.gr) Domestic flights based out of Crete.

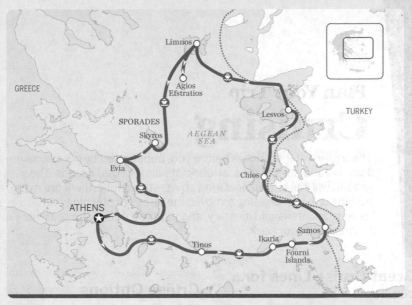

3 WEEKS Island-Hopping Itinerary

For intrepid travellers without a tight time schedule, Greece's northeastern islands offer languid coasts, lush scenery and divine beaches, as well as some amazing historic sights. Scheduled ferries are regular but not always very frequent – thankfully you won't be in any hurry to leave.

From Athens, hop a ferry for **Tinos** (p179) to visit the sacred Church of the Annunciation and explore marble-ornamented villages dotted across the terraced hillsides and misty mountaintops. Head east via Mykonos and Syros to **Ikaria** (p421) for isolated stretches of soft sand. Join in the island culture of dancing, drinking and feasting during summer *panigyria* (all-night celebrations held on saints' days across the island). Afterwards take a short hop to the serene **Fourni Islands** (p430), a former pirates' lair with surreal sunsets.

Ferry north to **Samos** (p432) where you can hike through lush forests to secluded waterfalls and laze on idyllic beaches. From Samos, head to **Chios** (p441) and get lost in the labyrinth of stone alleyways in the southern village of Mesta before venturing into the interior to hike through citrus groves under the shade of towering mountain peaks.

The next stop is **Lesvos** (p451), birthplace of the poet Sappho and producer of some of Greece's finest olive oil and ouzo. Mytilini, the island's capital and port, offers a fantastic modern-art gallery as well as great eating and drinking. Also check out the well-preserved Ottoman-era town of Molyvos and the hilltop Byzantine monastery of Moni Ypsilou. Lesvos' landscape, with salt marshes, gushing hot springs, dense forests and variety of beaches, is as diverse as its cultural offerings.

From Lesvos, hop to **Limnos** (p463) to dine on the day's catch at Myrina's waterside seafood restaurants. Carry on to secluded **Agios Efstratios** (p468) to stretch out on volcanic-sand beaches. The village, flattened by an earthquake in 1968 and rebuilt by uninspired junta, draws few tourists meaning the beaches are all yours.

Continue to **Skyros** (p502) for its cobble-stoned village, Byzantine-Venetian fortress and many artist studios; if lucky, you may also spot an endangered Skyrian wild horse. Hop a ferry to **Evia** (p482) for a therapeutic dip in the thermal-fed bay at Loutra Edipsou before catching a final boat to Rafina on the mainland and returning to **Athens** (p68).

Plan Your Trip
Cruising

The azure water stretches before you, punctuated by occasional dolphins and an endless scattering of palm-fringed islands. The Aegean will call to your seafaring spirit – thankfully, there are many cruising options. Cruising removes the stress of planning and booking an interisland itinerary, and gets you out on the sea with the breeze at your back.

Great Cruise Lines for...

Culture
Silversea (www.silversea.com) Runs exclusive tours with language and cooking classes, guest lectures and entertainment from local ports.

Freedom
Azamara (www.azamaraclubcruises.com) Offers cruises at a slower pace, with top service and few organised activities.

Luxury
Seadream Yacht Club (https://seadream.com) Ultrapampering with nearly as many crew as guests.

Small & Personalised Trips
Variety Cruises (www.varietycruises.com) Has a maximum of 50 guests and the sea as its swimming pool.

Unconventional Trips
Star Clippers (www.starclipperscruises.com) Runs cruises on the world's largest fully rigged tall ships.

Cruise Options

Ship Size

Forget what you've heard, size does matter – at least when you're choosing a cruise ship. A ship's size says a lot about the experience it's offering: megaships can seem more like floating resorts, with a few thousand people on board, while tiny liners cater to fewer than 50 passengers.

Large or Megaships

➡ Accommodate 1000-plus people.

➡ Nonstop activities and complete amenities.

➡ Casinos, restaurants, spas, theatres, children's clubs, discos, bars, cafes and shops.

➡ Often unable to squeeze into some of the smaller islands' harbours and so visit the largest, most popular ports.

➡ Can seem to dwarf an island, with its passengers more than doubling the destination's population.

Medium or Midsized Ships

➡ Cater for 400 to 1000 passengers.

➡ Usually more focused on the destination, with more port stops, more excursions and fewer on-board activities.

➡ Spa, pool, restaurants and bars.

➡ More often able to dock in small island harbours.

Small Ships

➡ Itineraries tend to be more varied as they can stop at small, out-of-the-way ports.

➡ Often concentrate on a particular cruise niche, such as luxury or activity-based adventure.

➡ Don't expect a pool, spa, large cabin or plethora of dining options.

Local Cruise Lines

International cruises tend to visit Greece in combination with ports from other countries – usually Italy, Turkey and Croatia, often beginning at one port and ending at another. Greece-based cruises usually focus solely on ports within Greece and offer round-trips. These cruises are often more destination-focused, with one or two stops each day. The crew are usually Greek, adding to the feel of authenticity, and cuisine and entertainment is more locally based with a bit of international flavour thrown in.

Among Greek-based cruise lines worth checking out are Golden Star, Variety Cruises and Celestyal Cruises.

Excursions

Excursions are often what make cruises worthwhile and are designed to help you make the most of your sometimes-brief visits ashore. They are generally most valuable when sights are not near the port or if a cultural expert is leading the tour. Where all the sights are near the harbour, it's often just as worthwhile and more relaxing to go exploring on your own. If you plan to explore alone, it's worth double-checking before you book; some larger cruise boats dock at distant ports and it's difficult to reach the island's sights or main towns independently.

Excursions are usually booked before you depart or when you first board the ship. They are offered on a first-come, first-served basis and are generally very popular, so if you're choosing your cruise based on the excursions on offer, it's important to book as soon as possible. Tours generally range from €40 to €60 for a half-day, or €80 to €120 for a full day. Activity-based tours such as mountain biking or kayaking tend to be more, with a half-day around €100. Ensure that you factor in the cost of excursions from the get-go.

Budgeting

Cruise prices vary greatly depending on the time of year. Booking during the low season will get you good deals but it means you will probably only have the opportunity to visit the largest and busiest ports, as smaller islands virtually close out of season.

Budget cruises (€) can be anywhere from €100 to €200 per day, midrange (€€) from €200 to €400, and luxury liners (€€€) begin at around €400 and go up to as much as €650 per day. Prices on cruises include meals, on-board activities, entertainment, port fees and portage but there are sometimes additional fuel charges. You also need to budget for airfare, tips, alcohol, pre- and post-cruise accommodation and excursions. Deals to look out for include two-for-one offers, airfare- or hotel-inclusive deals, and early-bird rates.

Booking

If you know what you want from your cruise, booking online can be a straightforward option, and certainly worth it for the virtual tours and reviews. But a knowledgeable travel agent can help you through the plethora of options available and advise you on extra excursion charges and surcharges that you may miss when booking online.

There are often great rates for booking early and this allows you more choice in choosing cabins, excursions, dining options and so forth. While you can get great last-minute deals, you need to be willing to be flexible about dates and options. Booking your airfare through the cruise line may also mean you're collected at the airport and taken to the ship and if your flight or luggage is delayed, they will wait or transport you to the first port.

Choosing a Cabin

Standard cabins are akin to very small hotel rooms, with fully equipped en suites, a double bed and somewhere to unpack. The cheapest option is an 'inside cabin' (ie no window). If you get claustrophobic, you can pay significantly more for an 'outside cabin' where you get either a window or

Top: Santorini (p238)

Bottom: Yachting to Thira Old Port, Santorini

CRUISING INDEPENDENTLY

Yachting offers the freedom to visit remote and uninhabited islands – but what if you can't afford to buy a yacht? The answer is yacht charter companies and there are several options:

Bareboat If two of your party have sailing certificates, you can hire a boat without a crew. Prices start at around €2000 per week; check out Bare Boat Yacht Charters (www.moorings.com).

Crewed yachts If you'd rather have someone else do the sailing for you, Odyssey Sailing (www.odysseysailing.gr) will add a skipper to your bare-bones boat for around an additional €150 per day.

Cabin cruises Book a cabin on a crewed yacht and sit back and enjoy the ride. However, on these trips you'll be tied into a generally pre-set itinerary. Offering all types of yachting experience is Yacht Cruising Holidays (www.we-yachting.com) known as World Expeditions in Greece.

Hellenic Yachting Server (www.yachting.gr) has general information on sailing around the islands and lots of links, including information on chartering yachts.

The sailing season is from April to October, although July to September is most popular. Unfortunately, it also happens to be when the *meltemi* (dry northerly wind) is at its strongest. This isn't an issue in the Ionian Sea, where the main summer wind is the *maïstros*, a light to moderate northwesterly that rises in the afternoon and usually dies away at sunset.

porthole. Prices tend to climb with each floor on the ship but so does the ship's movement. If you suffer from seasickness, choose a lower deck where it's less rocky.

Cabin pricing is for double occupancy; if you're travelling solo you pay a surcharge, and if you're travelling as a group of three or four and willing to share a cabin, you can receive substantial discounts. Bunks are referred to as upper and lower berths, otherwise there is a double bed or twin beds that can be pushed together to make a double. Family rooms are sometimes available via connecting cabins.

Things to check are how close your cabin is located to the disco and, if you're paying extra for a window, whether or not your view is likely to be blocked by a lifeboat.

Life on Board
Embarking: What to Expect

➡ Check-in time will be two or three hours before sailing.

➡ Your passport will be taken for immigration processing.

➡ The first day's program and a deck map can be found in your cabin.

➡ You'll be offered a tour of the ship.

➡ A safety drill is legally required on all ships.

➡ You'll be able to set up an on-board credit account.

➡ Your dining-room table will be assigned.

Meals

Set mealtimes and seating assignments are still the norm on most ships and you will be able to choose your preferred dinnertime and table size when you book. Many ships continue to have formal dining evenings with dress codes. Some smaller ships have an all-casual policy, while others have alternative dining options for those not interested in attending the formal evenings.

Tipping

Firstly, don't tip the captain or officers; it would be akin to tipping your dentist or airline pilot. On the final day of your cruise, you'll likely find tipping guidelines in your cabin, usually around €8 per person per day. Tipping is not required but makes up a huge part of the wage of service staff, and is expected.

CRUISE COMPANIES

COMPANY	CONTACT	SHIP SIZE	CRUISE LENGTH	DESTINATIONS	PRICE RANGE
Azamara	www.azamara clubcruises. com	medium	7-10 days	Greece, Turkey, Italy	€€€
Celebrity Cruises	www.celebrity cruises.co.uk	mega	10-13 days	Greece, Italy, Turkey, Croatia, France	€€
Celestyal Cruises	www.celestyal cruises.uk	medium	3-7 days	Greece, Cyprus	€€
Costa Cruise Lines	www.msc cruises.co.uk	large	7-9 days	Greece, Italy, Turkey, Croatia, Israel	€
Crystal Yacht Cruises	www.crystal cruises.com	small	9-15 days	Greece, Italy, Turkey, Spain, Portugal	€€€
Cunard Line	www.cunard. com	large	7-14 days	Greece, Croatia, Italy, Turkey, France, Spain	€
Golden Star	www.golden-star-cruises. com	medium	3-8 days	Greece, Turkey	€
Holland America Line	www.holland america.com	large	6-12 days	Greece, Italy, Spain, Croatia	€
MSC	www.msc cruises.co.uk	large	7-10 days	Greece, Turkey, Croatia, Italy, Egypt	€
Oceania Cruises	www.oceania cruises.com	medium	10-12 days	Greece, Turkey, France, Italy, Spain	€€
Ponant	https:// en.ponant.com	small & medium	8-9 days	Greece, Croatia, Italy, Montenegro, Turkey	€€€
Princess Cruises	www.princess. com	large & mega	7-21 days	Greece, Italy, Turkey	€€
Regent Seven Sea Cruises	www.rssc.com	medium	7-21 days	Greece, Italy, Turkey, France	€€€
Seabourn	www.seabourn. com	medium	7-26 days	Greece, Italy, Spain, Portugal, France, Israel, Jordan, Oman, UAE	€€€
Seadream Yacht Club	https://sea dream.com	small	6-13 days	Greece, Turkey, Italy, Croatia	€€€
Silversea	www.silversea. com	small & medium	7-12 days	Greece, Spain, Turkey, Italy	€€€
Star Clippers	www.star clipperscruises. com	small	7-14 days	Greece, Turkey, Italy	€€€
Voyages to Antiquity	www.voyages toantiquity.com	small	13-27 days	Greece, Italy	€€
Windstar	www.windstar cruises.com	small & medium	7-51 days	Greece, Turkey, Italy, Spain, Portugal, France, Croatia	€€€

Plan Your Trip

Escaping the Crowds

Greece is attracting record numbers of visitors – which means at the most popular attractions and locations you'll be elbowing your way through a scrum of fellow tourists. However, with planning and a willingness to go off the beaten track, it is still entirely possible to dodge the crowds.

What's the Problem?

Since 2010, the number of tourists heading to Greece each year has more than doubled, with a record 33 million people choosing to visit the country in 2018. However, as anyone who has braved the Acropolis, or the super-popular Cycladic islands of Santorini or Mykonos, at the height of summer can attest, some of the country's most iconic locations have been blighted by overtourism.

It's no fun elbowing your way past crowds to take your holiday snaps of a famous view, lining up for hours for entrance to an overcrowded tourist sight, or laying down on a beach that is more suntan lotion and human flesh than sand. And yet, despite the fact that Greece has far more than its fair share of wonderful places to visit (some 6000 islands, of which 277 are inhabited) many of us continue to do just that. Read on for our advice on where best to go and what you can do to not be part of the problem.

Need to Know

When to go Visit early in spring or late in autumn to avoid the worst of the crowds and the scorching heat, while still being able to take advantage of

Best Alternatives

Instead of the Acropolis

Hike up to the summit of nearby Filopappou Hill (p76) which provides a spectacular perch to view the Acropolis, the city and the sunset.

Instead of Santorini

Sail to quietly beautiful Folegandros (p258), home to clifftop Hora, one of the most appealing villages in the Cyclades.

Instead of Hora (Mykonos)

Spend a day exploring the Unesco World Heritage Site of Delos (p201), one of the most important archaeological sites in Greece.

Instead of Preveli Beach (Crete)

Spread your towel at the more remote and palm-fringed Vaï (p336) where even at the height of summer you should be able to find space on the sand.

Instead of the Cyclades

Explore Evia and the four Sporades islands (p480) which remain largely off the beaten track. Evia in particular offers lovely inland landscapes, vineyards and secluded bays.

SOLOMAKHA/SHUTTERSTOCK ©

Top: Achata beach, Karpathos (p364)

Bottom: Skiathos Town (p488)

more frequent ferry schedules and lower prices for accommodations. Be aware that between late October and early April much of the Greek islands' tourist infrastructure shuts up shop.

Go remote Rent a car, scooter or bicycle and head away from the main resorts and island towns to more remote villages and beaches. More active visitors can find splendid hiking routes across quiet island interiors.

Go cruising Really escape the crowds and reach remote spots by chartering a yacht or joining a cruise (p43).

Go slowly Visit fewer places for longer. Connect with locals by lingering in a non-touristy *kafeneio* (coffee house), or a humble seafood taverna with a sea view.

Go early and midweek Free entry on the first Sunday of the month to ancient sites may be tempting but can mean even bigger crowds. Instead visit sites as soon as they open – or head to them towards the end of the day once the tour-bus crowds have departed.

Go online Avoid ticket lines for ancient sites by buying tickets online at https://etickets.tap.gr. You can also avoid the ticket-booth lines at the Acropolis by buying the €30 combo ticket at one of the other ancient sites it covers in Athens.

Athens & Saronic Gulf Islands

First the good news: Athens is a year-round city so while it's obviously more pleasant to visit in the warmer months (though note that June to August can be uncomfortably hot) it's fine to head here in, say, April, September and October and not have to battle with the peak density of crowds at top sights.

This said, save for the winter, you're pretty much always going to encounter congestion at the Acropolis (p78). Set your alarm clock to arrive here as soon as the site opens, or wait until towards the end of the day when crowds have thinned. There are plenty of other superb archaeological sites in the capital and surrounds – the Ancient Agora (p88) and Kerameikos (p101) are among our favourites – and they too can be blissfully quiet first thing in the morning or towards sunset. The pine-clad slopes of Filopappou Hill (p76) provide a

prime vantage point for photographs of the Acropolis.

As easy getaways for Athenians, the Saronic Gulf islands can also get crowded, particularly over weekends and public holidays. On Aegina (p154) head for the quaint fishing village of Perdika (p157) or hop across to nearby Angistri (p158). Poros Town (p160) on Poros is also a fine alternative to super-popular Hydra (p17).

Cyclades

Should you not wish to party with the throngs on Mykonos (p188) or watch the sunset with a cast of thousands on Santorini (p238), there are plenty of alternatives.

Of course, Santorini is breathtaking but it's worth remembering that you can catch the sunset without the crowds from almost anywhere along the island's western cliff edge – not just the hotspots of Fira and Oia. Another great alternative is to rise at dawn and face east for some fairly stunning sunrises. Sikinos (p255) and Anafi (p254), islands both within easy reach of Santorini, are quiet, charming and uncommercial.

Mykonos' beaches, once the pride of Greece, are now mostly jammed with umbrellas and backed by rowdy beach bars. Make your escape by hiring a decent 4WD and heading to Fokos or Mersini on the northeast coast.

Elsewhere in the Cyclades consider Milos (p262) and nearby Kimolos (p267), which has an atmospheric Old Town and an impressive beach. Dozens of little-visited villages and isolated beaches are scattered around Andros (p175), the second-largest of the Cyclades islands. Pack your hiking boots and take to one of its 19 wonderful waymarked trails, which range in duration from 30 minutes to six hours.

Crete

If the mass of sunbathers at Elafonisi (p495) or Preveli (p312) is putting you off Crete as a beach destination, fear not – the largest and most populous of the Greek islands still has plenty of off-the-beaten-track options. Try **Agios Pavlos** (Αγιος

Παυλοσ) – even when it's busy on the main strip of sand you'll find quieter beaches nearby behind Cape Melissa. There's also solitude and natural beauty along the dozen or so beaches lining the remote southeastern Xerokambos region.

Crete's rugged interior is spectacular and Zakros Gorge (p337) packs in all that's best in gorge walking, without the crowds of the more famous Samaria Gorge (p324). You can also use Crete as a jumping-off point for Gavdos Island (p323), the southernmost spot in Europe, where there's little do except swim, walk and relax.

To beat the crowds and avoid the heat at Knossos (p581) arrive for the 8am opening or later in the afternoon when it's cooler and the light is good for photographs. Or, skip Knossos and delve into Crete's ancient past while trekking to Hellenistic, Roman and Byzantine ruins at **Lissos** on a 13km hike through lovely coastal scenery between Paleohora and Sougia.

Dodecanese

Karpathos (p364) may be one of Greece's least commercialised islands but its key sight – the pastel-coloured mountainside village of Olymbos (p368) – can easily be overwhelmed by tourists. As usual, aim to arrive early or late in the afternoon to have the place to yourself. Otherwise, the villages at the south of the island, within easy reach of sandy beaches, have reinvented themselves as small-scale resorts. The hills inland here are crisscrossed by scenic walking tracks.

The gentle landscape of Tilos (p378) makes it an ideal walking and birdwatching location – with around 54km of trails on the island you're sure to find yourself enjoying solitude. Tilos' northwestern end offers several attractive beaches including the generally deserted Eristos Beach, lapped by sapphire-hued waters and great for swimming.

If you're really fed up with the package crowds, head to far-flung Astypalea (p395), great for walking, camping and history. Tourist infrastructure and ferry connections remain minimal, and most visitors are Greek. The tiny islands of Agathonisi, Arki and Maratha (p416) are magical and barely discovered beyond

an eclectic mix of yachties, artists and the occasional backpacker.

Evia & the Sporades

Evia (p482) is off the mainstream tourist trail in general even though it's Greece's second-largest island after Crete. Evia's more remote eastern beaches facing the Aegean Sea have fine sand and clear waters while inland there are picturesque mountain villages such as Steni (p501).

Skiathos (p487) is by far the most touristed of the Sporades and can get very busy in July and August. However, with 65 beaches to pick from you're sure to find somewhere that's not too crowded: try Mandraki Beach, which is graced by dunes and pines and boasts a good taverna.

On Skopelos (p492) head for less visited Perivoliou Beach or Cape Amarandos (p496), where you can walk along the cliffs and jump straight into the sea at a location where some of *Mamma Mia!* was filmed.

Alonnisos (p497) is much less touristed than Skopelos and Skiathos (because it's one step further on the ferry), but still equally beautiful. Skyros (p502) is also less touristed than the other Sporades, but just as appealing. Its beaches are not so great, but still good and there's a chance while on the island to see endangered Skyrian horses.

Ionians

Large parts of the coastline of Corfu (p510) have been scarred by mass tourism, but fortunately there are still some places where you can find undeveloped beaches. Head to the island's far northeast where a coastal path leads from the port village of Agios Stefanos to the long windsurfing beach of Avlaki.

Tiny Paxi (p523), lacking an airport, has been spared overdevelopment. Explore the island's unspoiled coves, accessible only via motorboat, and hike through its rolling hills and centuries-old olive groves.

Despite being connected to the mainland by a narrow causeway, much of Lefkada (p526) remains unaffected by tourism. Head to the south of the island to find unspoiled Poros Beach (also known as

Ikaria Island (p421)

Mikros Gialos). Halfway up the west coast, the village of Kalamitsi has a narrow road leading down to a series of gorgeous white-pebble beaches.

Kefallonia (p532), the largest of the Ionian Islands, offers the best range of options for escaping the crowds. Hike through Ainos National Park (p536) to gain astounding views from the summit of Mt Ainos, or drive out to the more remote Paliki Peninsula, stopping off at the postcard-perfect village of Assos (p541) where there's a hidden beach around the cove.

Northeastern Aegean Islands

The one group of Greek islands where you are currently unlikely to encounter mass numbers of tourists are those in the northeastern Aegean. That's because a whole other category of travellers – refugees – have arrived in these islands from nearby Turkey. Refugee camps remain a tragic feature, particularly on Lesvos and Samos, where regular tourism has taken a big hit as a result. Don't be put off: these islands still all offer wonderful accommodation, eating and cultural experiences and remain worth visiting.

There's also some great hiking on offer for independent, activity-driven travellers. On Ikaria (p421), Fanari is the starting point for a fairly easy, two-hour circular trek (p426) that offers breathtaking views of the sea and surrounding islands. On Samos (p432), the southern part of the island west of Pythagorio offers sparsely populated and beautiful mountainous terrain.

To really get away from it all, head to Agios Efstratios (p468), south of Limnos, for remote beaches and quiet beauty.

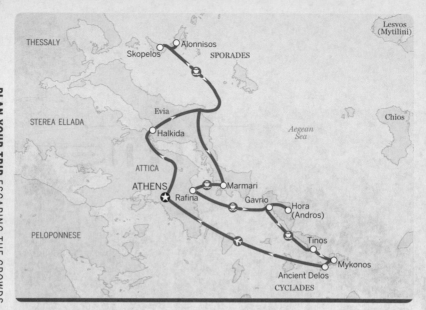

 Escaping the Crowds Itinerary

Get off the beaten track in some gorgeous places that are just as beautiful as headline acts such as Santorini, but with hopefully a fraction of the crowds, particularly if you travel early in spring or in autumn before the islands shut up shop.

In **Athens** (p68) set your alarm for an early-morning visit to the Acropolis or simply admire the ancient monuments at one remove from Filopappou Hill. Take a bus or train to Halkida, the gateway to **Evia** (p482) and spend a couple of days exploring this island. Board a ferry to **Skopelos** (p492), spend a day there and another on **Alonnisos** (p497). Return to Evia and make your way to Marmari for the ferry hop to Rafina where you can connect to another ferry to **Andros** (p175). Explore the main town, Hora, which has a great contemporary art museum, and go hiking for a couple of days.

Next up is **Tinos** (p179), famous for its tradition of marble sculpting and its glorious countryside. If it's all getting too laid-back for you, a night of partying on **Mykonos** (p188) is sure to spark you back into action. Regain serenity on a day trip to **Ancient Delos** (p202), then fly back to Athens.

Plan Your Trip

Eat & Drink Like a Local

Greeks love eating out, sharing impossibly big meals with family and friends in a drawn-out, convivial fashion. Whether you're eating seafood at a seaside table or sampling contemporary Greek cuisine under the floodlit Acropolis, dining out in Greece is never just about what you eat, but the whole sensory experience.

Food Experiences

Take a cue from the locals and go straight to the source, heading to seaside fishing hamlets for fresh fish or mountain villages for local meat. Seek out tavernas that produce their own vegetables, wine and oil, where the fried potatoes are hand-cut and recipes are passed down through generations.

Meals of a Lifetime

Marco Polo Cafe (p351) Idyllic garden courtyard with an ever-changing menu of delicious Greek and Italian-influenced dishes in Rhodes.

Peskesi (p290) Crete's finest culinary moment with dishes made from heirloom produce, organic meats and olive oil from the owner's farm.

Lauda (p249) Santorini fine dining that's a destination in its own right.

Yevsea (p384) In Nisyros and run by two former Masterchef contestants cooking gourmet cuisine, using local ingredients.

Taverna Mylos (p407) In a sublime setting in Leros this charming place is up there on the world's gastronomic scale.

Karamanlidika tou Fani (p120) Athens corner deli, reimagined as a casual restaurant serving delicious small plates of food.

Year in Food

Spring

Artichokes and other fresh vegetables abound while cheesemaking kicks into gear. Easter is celebrated with *tsoureki* (brioche-style bread flavoured with cherry kernels and mastic) and dyed-red hard-boiled eggs.

Summer

Watermelon, cherries and other fruit jam-pack markets. In August, Skala Kaloni on Lesvos celebrates its sardine festival, while in the Peloponnese you can attend Leonidio's Aubergine Festival in the same month.

Autumn

Nuts and figs are harvested and raki (Cretan firewater) is distilled. Aegina's pistachio industry celebrates Fistiki Fest mid-September. Raki or tsikoudia festivals are held in Voukolies and Cretan villages in November, when olive oil is produced.

Winter

Olive harvest peaks. Honey cookies are eaten at Christmas to end fasting. On New Year's Day, the golden-glazed cake vasilopita is shared.

EATING PRICE RANGES

The following price ranges refer to the average cost of a main course (not including service charges).

€ less than €10

€€ €10–20

€€€ more than €20

Cheap Treats

Souvlaki Greece's favourite fast food, both the *gyros* (meat cooked on a vertical rotisserie) and skewered meat versions wrapped in pitta bread, with tomato, onion and lashings of tzatziki.

Pies Bakeries make endless variations of *tyropita* (cheese pie) and *spanakopita* (spinach pie), plus other pies.

Street food Includes *koulouria* (fresh pretzel-style bread) and seasonal snacks such as roasted chestnuts or corn.

Cooking Courses

Well-known Greece-based cooking writers and chefs run workshops on several islands and in Athens, mostly during spring and autumn.

Glorious Greek Kitchen Cooking School (www.dianekochilas.com) Diane Kochilas runs week-long courses (from US$3750) on her ancestral island, Ikaria, in spring and summer, as well as culinary tours to Athens, Nemea and Nafplion (from US$1560).

Kea Artisanal (www.aglaiakremezi.com/kea-artisanal) Aglaia Kremezi and her friends open their kitchens and gardens on the island of Kea for cooking workshops.

Crete's Culinary Sanctuaries (www.cookingincrete.com) Nikki Rose combines cooking classes, organic-farm tours and cultural excursions around Crete.

The Greek Kitchen (www.greekkitchenathens.com) Runs half-day hands-on cooking classes in Athens (adult/concession €59/29) as well as food tours of the city's main market.

Other courses include **Selene** (22860 22249; www.selene.gr; Pyrgos; cooking class €85-100) on Santorini, FindinGreece (p234) in Amorgos, **Rodialos** (28340 51310; www.rodialos.gr; Vassilis Damvoglou) on Crete and Sifnos Farm Narlis on Sifnos.

Cook It at Home

Leave room in your baggage for local treats (customs and quarantine rules permitting) such as olives and extra virgin olive oil from small, organic producers; aromatic Greek thyme honey; dried oregano, mountain tea and camomile flowers; or a jar of spoon sweets (fruit preserves).

The Greek Kitchen

The essence of traditional Greek cuisine lies in seasonal homegrown produce. Dishes are simply seasoned. Lemon juice, garlic, pungent Greek oregano and extra virgin olive oil are the quintessential flavours, along with tomato, parsley, dill, cinnamon and cloves.

Mayirefta Home-style, one-pot, baked or casserole dishes. Prepared early, they are left to cool to enhance the flavours. Well-known *mayirefta* include *mousaka* (eggplant, minced meat, potatoes and cheese), *yemista* (vegetables stuffed with rice and herbs), *lemonato* (meat with lemon and oregano) and *stifadho* (sweet stewed meat with tomato and onion).

Grills Greeks are masterful with grilled and spit-roasted meats. Souvlaki – arguably the national dish – comes in many forms, from cubes of grilled meat on a skewer to pitta-wrapped snacks with pork or chicken *gyros* done kebab-style on a rotisserie. *Païdakia* (lamb cutlets) and *brizoles* (pork chops) are also popular.

Fish and seafood Fish is often grilled whole and drizzled with *ladholemono* (lemon and oil dressing). Smaller fish such as *barbounia* (red mullet) or *maridha* (whitebait) are lightly fried. Octopus is grilled, marinated or stewed in wine sauce. Popular seafood dishes include *soupies* (cuttlefish), calamari stuffed with cheese and herbs, and *psarosoupa* (fish soup). The best way to avoid imports is to seek out tavernas run by local fishing families.

Mezedhes These small dishes (or appetisers) are often shared. Classics include tzatziki (yoghurt, cucumber and garlic), *melidzanosalata* (aubergine), *taramasalata* (fish roe), fava (split-pea puree with lemon juice) and *saganaki* (fried cheese). Also watch for *keftedhes* (meatballs), *loukaniko* (pork sausage), grilled *gavros* (white anchovies) and dolmadhes (rice wrapped in marinated vine leaves).

Greek salad This ubiquitous salad (*horiatiki* or 'village salad') is made of tomatoes, cucumber, onions, feta and olives; however, it's often garnished with local greens, peppers, capers or nuts. Feta is sometimes replaced by a local cheese. Beetroot salad is also popular, often served with walnuts and cheese.

Cheese Greece's regions produce many different types of cheese, most using goat's and sheep's milk, with infinite variations in taste. Apart from feta, local cheeses include *graviera* (a nutty, mild Gruyere-like sheep's-milk cheese), *kaseri* (similar to provolone), *myzithra* (ricotta-like whey cheese) and *manouri* (creamy soft cheese from the north).

Traditional sweets These include baklava, *loukoumadhes* (spherical doughnuts drizzled with honey and cinnamon), *kataïfi* (chopped nuts inside angel-hair pastry), *ryzogalo* (rice pudding) and *galaktoboureko* (custard-filled pastry). *Ghlika kutalyu* (syrupy fruit preserves, also known as 'spoon sweets') are served on tiny plates as a welcome offering but are also eaten over yoghurt.

Local Specialities

From cheese and olive oil to the raw ingredients on your plate, you will find many regional variations and specialities on your travels.

Crete is a popular foodie destination with distinct culinary traditions, but the islands and mainland offer their own culinary treats.

Be sure to ask about local dishes, cheese and produce.

Northern Greece Influenced by eastern flavours, there's more butter, peppers and spices in this region's dishes, along with a strong *mezes* (small-plate) culture and Ottoman sweets.

Peloponnese Known for its herb-rich, one-pot dishes and *ladhera* (vegetarian, peasant-style dishes).

Cyclades A traditional reliance on beans and pulses led to the popularity of fava (split-pea puree) and *revythadha* (chickpea stew); you'll also find spaghetti with lobster and a strong sausage tradition.

Ionian Islands The Venetian influence is found in spicy braised beef, rooster *pastitsadha* (red-sauce pasta) and *sofrito* (braised veal with garlic and wine sauce).

Crete Herb-rich dishes include *anthoi* (stuffed zucchini flowers), *soupies* (cuttlefish) with wild fennel and *hohlioi bourbouristoi* (snails with vinegar and rosemary).

What to Drink

Coffee

The ubiquitous *kafeneio* (coffee house) is a time-honoured tradition, with older Greeks stationed over a cup of coffee, intensely debating local politics, football or gossip. They're often small and unchanged for generations, and it's well worth visiting at least one. The trendy cafes serving delicious iced coffees (*frappé*) are the modern answer to the *kafeneia* and are usually packed with a younger crowd.

Greek coffee is traditionally brewed in a *briki* (narrow-top pot), on a hot-sand apparatus called a *hovoli*, and served in a small cup. Order a *metrio* (medium, with one sugar) and sip slowly until you reach the mud-like grounds (don't drink them).

Ouzo & Other Spirits

Ouzo – Greece's famous liquor – has come to embody a way of eating and socialising, enjoyed with *mezedhes* (small plates) during lazy, extended summer afternoons. Sipped slowly and ritually to cleanse the palate between dishes, ouzo is usually served in small bottles or *karafakia* (carafes) with a bowl of ice cubes to dilute it (turning it a cloudy white).

Ouzo is made from distilled grapes with residuals from fruit, grains and potatoes, and flavoured with spices, primarily aniseed, giving it that liquorice flavour. The best ouzo is produced on Lesvos.

Tsipouro is a distilled spirit, similar to grappa, that is produced only in Greece. It's made using the leftover must from pressing wine and is usually enjoyed as an aperitif. *Tsikoudia*, also known as *raki*, is essentially the Cretan version of *tsipouro*.

If all of the above are too harsh a shot of alcohol for your tastes, you may well prefer the sweet sweet liqueur *mastika*, made with mastica resin grown on Chios. It's an excellent digestive.

Greek Wine

Greece's wine industry benefits from some age-old indigenous varietals with unique character. The contemporary generation of winemakers are producing great, award-winning wines from Greece's premier wine regions, including Nemea in the Peloponnese, the vineyards of Santorini, the Iraklio Wine Country on Crete and Naoussa in the Cyclades.

Greek white varieties include *moschofilero, asyrtiko, athiri, roditis, robola* and *savatiano;* the popular reds include *xinomavro, agiorgitiko* and *kotsifali.*

House or barrel wine varies dramatically in quality (white is the safer bet), and is ordered by the kilo/carafe or glass.

Greek dessert wines include excellent muscats from Samos, Limnos and Rhodes, Santorini's Vinsanto, Mavrodafni wine (often used in cooking) and Monemvasia's Malmsey sweet wine.

Retsina, white wine flavoured with the resin of pine trees, became popular in the 1960s and retains a largely folkloric significance with foreigners. It's something of an acquired taste but some winemakers make a modern version. It's popular in Thessaloniki (where the main brand, Malamatina, is made) and it goes great with salty *mezedhes* (share plates) and seafood.

How to Eat & Drink

When to Eat

Greece doesn't have a big breakfast tradition, unless you count coffee and a cigarette, and maybe a *koulouri* (pretzel-style bread) or *tyropita* (cheese pie) eaten on the run. You'll find English-style breakfasts in hotels and tourist areas.

While changes in working hours are affecting traditional meal patterns, lunch is still usually the big meal of the day, starting around 2pm.

Greeks eat dinner late, rarely sitting down before sunset in summer. This coincides with shop closing hours, so restaurants often don't fill until after 10pm. Get in by 9pm to avoid the crowds. Given the long summers and mild winters, al fresco dining is central to the dining experience.

Most tavernas open all day, but some upmarket restaurants open for dinner only.

Vegetarian Friendly

Vegetarians are well catered for, since vegetables feature prominently in Greek cooking – a legacy of lean times and the Orthodox faith's fasting traditions. The more traditional a restaurant you go to, the more vegetable options you get, because they follow more of these fasting rules. If you come during Lent, it's a vegan bonanza at these places.

Look for popular vegetable dishes such as *fasolakia yiahni* (braised green beans), *bamies* (okra), *briam* (oven-baked vegetable casserole) and vine-leaf dolmadhes. Of the nutritious *horta* (wild greens), *vlita* (amaranth) is the sweetest, but other common varieties include wild radish, dandelion, stinging nettle and sorrel.

Festive Food

The 40-day Lenten fast spawned *nistisima*, foods without meat or dairy (or oil if you go strictly by the book). Lenten sweets include *halva*, both the Macedonian-style version made from tahini (sold in delis) and the semolina dessert often served after a meal.

Red-dyed boiled Easter eggs decorate the *tsoureki*, a brioche-style bread flavoured with *mahlepi* (a species of cherry with very small fruit and kernels with an almond flavour) and mastic (the crystallised resin of the mastic tree). Saturday night's post-Resurrection Mass supper includes *mayiritsa* (offal soup), while Easter Sunday sees whole lambs cooking on spits all over the countryside.

A *vasilopita* (golden-glazed cake) is cut at midnight on New Year's Eve, giving good fortune to whoever gets the lucky coin inside.

Where to Eat

Steer away from tourist restaurants and go where locals eat. As a general rule, avoid places on the main tourist drags, especially those with touts outside and big signs with photos of food. Be wary of hotel recommendations, as some have deals with particular restaurants.

Tavernas are casual, good-value, often family-run (and child-friendly) places, where the waiter arrives with a paper tablecloth and plonks cutlery on the table.

Top: Plaka district of Athens (p70)

Bottom: Greek cuisine

ETIQUETTE & TABLE MANNERS

➡ Greek tavernas can be disarmingly and refreshingly laid-back. The dress code is generally casual, except in upmarket places.

➡ Service may feel slow (and patchy), but there's no rushing you out of there either.

➡ Tables generally aren't cleared until you ask for the bill, which in traditional places arrives with complimentary fruit or sweets or a shot of liquor. Receipts may be placed on the table at the start and during the meal in case tax inspectors visit.

➡ Greeks drink with meals (the drinking age is 16), but public drunkenness is uncommon and frowned upon.

➡ Book for upmarket restaurants, but reservations are unnecessary in most tavernas.

➡ Service charges are included in the bill, but most people leave a small tip or round up the bill; 10% to 15% is acceptable. If you want to split the bill, it's best you work it out among your group rather than ask the server to do it.

➡ Greeks are generous and proud hosts. Don't refuse a coffee or drink – it's a gesture of hospitality and goodwill. If you're invited out, the host normally pays. If you are invited to someone's home, it is polite to take a small gift (flowers or sweets), and remember to pace yourself, as you will be expected to eat everything on your plate.

➡ Smoking is banned in enclosed public spaces, including restaurants and cafes, but this rule is largely ignored, especially on distant islands.

Don't judge a place by its decor (or view). Go for places with a smaller selection (where food is more likely to be freshly cooked) rather than those with impossibly extensive menus.

Restaurant Guide

Taverna The classic Greek taverna has a few specialist variations – the *psarotaverna* (serving fish and seafood) and *hasapotaverna* or *psistaria* (for chargrilled or spit-roasted meat).

Mayirio (cookhouse) Specialises in traditional one-pot stews and *mayirefta* (baked dishes).

Estiatorio Serves upmarket international cuisine or Greek classics in a more formal setting.

Mezedhopoleio Offers lots of *mezedhes* (small plates).

Ouzerie In a similar vein to the *mezedhopoleio*, the *ouzerie* serves a usually free round of *mezedhes* with your ouzo. Regional variations focusing on the local firewater include the *rakadhiko* (serving *raki*) in Crete and the *tsipouradhiko* (serving *tsipouro*) in the mainland north.

Menu Advice

➡ Menus with prices must be displayed outside restaurants. English menus are fairly standard but off the beaten track you may encounter Greek-only menus. Many places display big trays of the day's *mayirefta* (ready-cooked meals) or encourage you to see what's cooking in the kitchen.

➡ Bread and occasionally small dips or nibbles are often served on arrival (you are increasingly given a choice as they are added to the bill).

➡ Don't stick to the three-course paradigm – locals often share a range of starters and mains (or starters can be the whole meal). Dishes may arrive in no particular order.

➡ Salads and other side dishes can be large – if you're a single diner, it's usually alright to ask for half portions.

➡ Frozen ingredients, especially seafood, are usually flagged on the menu (an asterisk or 'kat' on Greek menu).

➡ Fish is usually sold per kilogram rather than per portion, and is generally cooked whole rather than filleted. It's customary to go into the kitchen to select your fish (go for firm flesh and glistening eyes). Check the weight (raw) so there are no surprises on the bill.

Plan Your Trip
Outdoor Activities

Greece is graced with blue water, warm winds, undersea life, dramatic cliff faces, flourishing forests and ancient walkways – making it perfect terrain for outdoor activities. If you're a novice kitesurfer or avid cyclist, if you want to hike deep gorges or ski from lofty heights, opportunities abound.

Water Activities

Diving & Snorkelling

Snorkelling can be enjoyed just about anywhere along the coast of Greece and equipment is cheaply available. Especially good spots to don your fins are Monastiri on Paros, Paleokastritsa on Corfu, Xirokambos Bay on Leros and anywhere off the coast of Kastellorizo (Megisti). Many dive schools also use their boats to take groups of snorkellers to prime spots.

Greek law insists that diving be done under the supervision of a diving school in order to protect the many antiquities in the depths of the Mediterranean and Aegean Seas. Until recently dive sites were severely restricted, but many more have been opened and diving schools have flourished. You'll find schools on the islands of Corfu, Evia, Leros, Milos, Mykonos, Paros, Rhodes, Santorini, Skiathos, Crete, in Glyfada near Athens, and in Parga and Halkidiki in northern Greece.

The Professional Association of Diving Instructors (PADI; www.padi.com) has lots of useful information, including a list of all PADI-approved dive centres in Greece.

Windsurfing

Windsurfing is a very popular water sport in Greece. Hrysi Akti on Paros and Vasiliki on Lefkada vie for the position of the best windsurfing beach.

Best Outdoors

Hiking
Samaria Gorge (p324) Trek among towering cliffs and wildflowers.

Andros (p175) Follow well-worn footpaths across hills to deep valleys.

Nisyros (p384) Hike amid lush foliage and down into the caldera.

Samos (p432) Wander through woods and swim under waterfalls.

Experts
Santorini (p238) Enjoy a pathway of canyons and swim-through sand caverns for divers.

Kalymnos (p404) Climb towering limestone cliffs.

Paros (p204) Shangri-La for kitesurfing.

Novices
Vasiliki (p530) Learn how to windsurf.

Santorini (p251) Dive schools catering to first-timers.

Poros (p162) Waterskiing beginners.

Paxi (p523) Walks through ancient olive groves.

Kalafatis Beach (p197), Mykonos

There are numerous other prime locations around the islands and many water-adventure outlets rent equipment. Check out Kalafatis Beach on Mykonos, Agios Georgios on Naxos, Mylopotas Beach on Ios, Cape Prasonisi in southern Rhodes, around Tingaki on Kos, Kokkari on Samos and Kouremenos Beach on Crete's east coast.

You'll find sailboards for hire almost everywhere. Hire charges range from €15 to €30, depending on the gear and the location. If you are a novice, note that most places that rent equipment also give lessons. Sailboards can be imported into Greece freely (one per passenger) provided they will be taken out of the country on departure, but always check customs regulations for your country.

Kitesurfing & Surfing

With near-constant wind and ideal conditions, Paros' Pounta Beach is a magnet for kitesurfing's top talent, attracting both the Professional Kiteboard Riders Association and the Kiteboard Pro World Tour. With a shallow side, this is also a great place to learn surfing. Mikri Vigla on Naxos is also an excellent spot, with courses off the gorgeous white-sand beach.

Waterskiing

Given the relatively calm and flat waters of most island locations and the generally warm waters of the Mediterranean, water-skiing is a very pleasant activity. August is sometimes a tricky month, when the *meltemi* (dry northerly wind) can make conditions difficult in the central Aegean. Poros is a particularly well-organised locale, with Passage (p162) hosting a popular school and slalom centre.

White-Water Rafting

The popularity of white-water rafting and other river-adventure sports has grown rapidly in recent years as more and more urban Greeks, particularly Athenians, head off in search of a wilderness experience. While spring and autumn are the best times, with high water levels and decent weather, many operators offer trips year-round on the larger rivers.

Athens Extreme Sports (www.athens extremesports.com) offers rafting on several rivers including the Nestos and Lusios Alfios. Also check out the rafting trips organised by Trekking Hellas (https://trek king.gr) and **No Limits** (☑6944751418; www. facebook.com/nolimits.rafting).

Land Activities

Hiking

Much of mainland Greece is mountainous and, in many ways, a hiker's paradise. Popular routes are well walked and maintained; however, the EOS (p106) is underfunded and consequently many lesser-known paths are overgrown and inadequately marked. **Hania** (EOS; ☑28210 44647; www.eoshanion.gr; Tzanakaki 90; ☺9-11pm Mon-Fri) and Halkida (p482).

Northern Greece has plenty of rugged hiking terrain, especially around the Zagorohoria in the Pindos Mountains and the hill trails around Prespa Lakes. Beyond the mainland, the Lousios Gorge and the Mani, both in the Peloponnese, are two of the best places in Greece to explore on foot. Crete's Samaria Gorge is rightly a global favourite, but western

Crete boasts many gorges suitable for hikers of different skill levels. If you're headed to Tilos, pick up a copy of *Exploring Tilos: a Walkers' Guide to the Island* by Jim Osborne.

On small islands you will encounter a variety of paths, including *kalderimia,* which are cobbled or flagstone paths that have linked settlements since Byzantine times. Other paths include *monopatia* (shepherds' or monks' trails) that link settlements with sheepfolds or link remote settlements via rough unmarked trails. Shepherd or animal trails can be very steep and difficult to navigate.

If you're venturing off the beaten track, a good map is essential. Most tourist maps are inadequate; the best hiking maps for the islands are produced by Anavasi (www.anavasi.gr) and Terrain (www.terrainmaps.gr), both Greece-based companies. Be realistic about your abilities. Always inform

TOP ISLAND HIKES

DESTINATION, ISLAND GROUP	SKILL LEVEL	DESCRIPTION
Alonnisos, Sporades	easy	A network of established trails that lead to pristine beaches
Hydra, Saronic Gulf Islands	easy	A vehicle-free island with a well-maintained network of paths to beaches and monasteries
Paxi, Ionian Islands	easy	Paths along ancient olive groves and snaking drystone walls; perfect for escaping the crowds
Samaria Gorge, Crete	easy to medium	One of Europe's most popular hikes with 500m vertical walls, countless wildflowers and endangered wildlife (impassable mid-October to mid-April)
Zakros & Kato Zakros, Crete	easy to medium	The trail through Zakros Gorge (also known as Gorge of the Dead) leads to a remote Minoan palace site
Tragaea, Naxos, Cyclades	easy to medium	A broad central plain of olive groves, unspoiled villages and plenty of trails
Sifnos, Cyclades	easy to medium	Monasteries, beaches and sprawling views abound on this network of trails, covering 200km of island terrain
Tilos, Dodecanese	easy to medium	Countless traditional trails along dramatic clifftops and down to isolated beaches; a bird-lover's paradise
Dimosari Gorge, Evia	easy to medium	A 10km trek through a spectacular gorge of shady streams and cobbled paths ending at a small bay
Ithaki, Ionian Islands	easy to medium	Mythology fans can hike between sites linked to the Trojan War hero Odysseus
Samos, Northeastern Aegean Islands	easy to medium	Explore the quiet interior of this island with its mountain villages and the forested northern slopes of Mt Ambelos
Nisyros, Dodecanese	medium to difficult	A fertile volcanic island with hikes that lead down steep cliffs to reach steaming craters
Steni, Evia	medium to difficult	Day hikes and more serious trekking opportunities up Mt Dirfys, Evia's highest mountain

your guesthouse or local hiking association of your planned route before setting out.

Spring (April to June) is the best time for hiking; the countryside is green and fresh from the winter rains, and carpeted with wildflowers. Autumn (September to October) is another good time, but July and August, when temperatures rise to around 40°C (104°F), are not much fun. Whatever the season, come equipped with a good pair of walking boots to handle the rough, rocky terrain, a wide-brimmed hat, a water bottle and a high-UV-factor sunscreen.

A number of companies run organised hikes. The biggest is Trekking Hellas (https://trekking.gr), which offers a variety of hikes ranging from a four-hour stroll through the Lousios Valley to a week-long hike around Mt Olympus and Meteora. The company also runs hikes in Crete and the Cyclades. Many of the treks require a minimum number of participants or the price hike is steeper than the trail. Also look into the Greece hiking offerings of UK-based On Foot Holidays (www.onfoot holidays.co.uk).

Long-Distance Hikes

Menalon Trail (https://menalontrail.eu) Along this 75km route, hikers can choose between short walks or the five-day trek along the Lousios Gorge, Mt Menalon's western slopes and scenic villages galore.

Corfu Trail (www.thecorfutrail.com) Crosses the whole island from Kavos to Agios Spyridon and can be completed in between eight and 12 days, offering a fantastic mix of scenery on the way.

E4 European long-distance path staring in Portugal that also makes it way through mainland Greece and Crete on its way to Cyprus. A great resource if you plan to follow this challenging route is *Trekking in Greece: The Peloponnese and Pindos Way* by Tim Salmon and Michael Cullen.

Cycling

Greece has recently established itself as a cycling destination both for mountain bikers and novices yearning to take a spin on its coastal roads. Bicycles can usually be taken on trains for free, though you may need a ticket. On ferries, mention your bike when booking tickets.

Much of Greece is very remote. Be sure to carry puncture-repair and first-aid kits with you. Motorists are notoriously fast and not always travelling in the expected lane; extra caution on corners and narrow roads is well warranted. In July and August most cyclists break between noon and 4pm to avoid sunstroke and dehydration.

CycleGreece (www.cyclegreece.gr) Runs road- and mountain-bike tours across most of Greece for various skill levels including some sail-and-cycle tours.

Hooked on Cycling (www.hookedoncycling. co.uk/greece) Offers boat – and bike – trips through the islands plus tours of the mainland.

Cyclists Welcome Hellas (http://cyclists welcomehellas.blogspot.com/) Local business network supporting the needs of cyclists and tourists on bicycles.

Plan Your Trip

Family Travel

While Greece doesn't cater to kids the way that some countries do, children will be welcomed and included wherever you go. Greeks generally make a fuss over children, who may find themselves receiving many gifts and treats. Teach them some Greek words and they'll feel even more appreciated.

Children Will Love...

Ruins & Palaces

Palace of Knossos (p292) Spot dolphins on the frescos in the Queen's room at this imaginatively reconstucted Minoan complex.

Rhodes Town (p344) Explore the Old Town, a medieval time capsule behind a double ring of high walls and a deep moat.

Pandeli Castle (p406) Take in 360-degree views from the 14th century walls of this hilltop ruin on Leros.

Fun Museums

Acropolis Museum (p84) A great way to educate kids on the glories of ancient Greece.

Herakleidon Museum (p77) Split across two buildings this quirky Athens museum includes an exhibition on ancient types of robots and warships.

Volcanological Museum (p385) Learn about the history, mythology and environmental impact of Nisyros' volcano.

Noesis (Science Museum; ☑2310 483 000; www. noesis.edu.gr; Km 6 Thessaloniki–Thermi Rd; adult/child combined ticket €12/8; ☺10.30am-3pm Tue-Fri, 6.30-9.30pm Sat & Sun; P🚗) Fascinating museum of science and technology outside of Thessaloniki, that includes a planetarium and a giant-screen cinema.

Keeping Costs Down

Accommodation

Many hotels let small children stay for free and will squeeze an extra bed or cot in the room. Larger hotels and resorts often have package deals for families.

Sightseeing

There are free or half price tickets for children and teens at most sights. Save time queuing at major sites such as the Acropolis by prepurchasing tickets online.

Eating

Ordering lots of *mezedhes* (small dishes) lets your children try the local cuisine and find their favourites. You'll also find lots of kid-friendly options such as pizza and pasta, omelettes, chips, bread, savoury pies and yoghurt.

Transport

Travel on ferries, buses and trains is free for children under four. For those up to age 10 (ferries) or 12 (buses and trains) the fare is half. Full fares apply otherwise. On domestic flights, you'll pay 10% of the adult fare to have a child under two sitting on your knee. Kids aged two to 12 travel with half-fare.

PLANET.LV/GETTY IMAGES ©

Butterfly Valley, Rhodes island (p359)

Wildlife Encounters

Saloon Park (☎22370 24606; www.saloonpark.gr; Karpenisi–Prousos; ⊕9am-midnight; 🛜🚗) Wild West theme park where all the family can enjoy horse riding.

Valley of the Butterflies (p359) Visit this top Rhodes attraction between mid June and September to wander through a forest alive with colourful butterflies.

Mouries Farm (p596) Call ahead to book tours, take riding lessons and dine at this breeding farm for rare Skyrian horses.

Aqua Adventures

Limni Vouliagmenis (p144) Have your feet tickled by tiny fish in the mineral rich and warm waters of this lake on the Apollo Coast.

Acqua Plus This Crete-based waterpark is good for a few hours of splashy fun.

Creta Semi-Submarine (☎28410 24822, 6936051186; www.semi-submarine.gr; adult/child €16/10; ⊕11am, 1pm & 3pm; 🚗) This yellow submarine in Crete allows all the family to go deep sea marine life spotting without getting wet.

Tasty Treats

Yemista Veggies (usually tomatoes) stuffed with rice.

Pastitsio Buttery macaroni baked with minced lamb.

Kolokithokeftedes Freshly made courgette (zucchini) fritters.

Loukoumadhes Ball-shaped doughnuts served with honey and cinnamon.

Galaktoboureko Custard-filled pastry.

Politiko pagoto Constantinople-style (slightly chewy) ice cream made with mastic.

Region by Region

Athens

With superb park playgrounds such as the ones at Stavros Niarchos Park (p143) and Flisvos Park (p91), ruins to clamber over and child-geared sights to explore, Athens is great for kids. Many museums make an effort to appeal to kids. Older children may like the War Museum (p106), where they can climb into the cockpit of a WWII plane and other aircraft. Come summer, there's no shortage of outdoor cinemas for evening entertainment.

Crete

The island's beaches are long and sandy, Knossos (p292) ignites kids' imaginations, and you can explore from a single base, side-stepping the need to pack up and move around.

Dodecanese

The magical forts and castles, glorious beaches, laid-back islands, and speedy catamarans linking the Dodecanese daily make it ideal for families. And the Italian influence means an abundance of kid-friendly pasta dishes. Rhodes, the largest island, is particularly good for family holidays.

Northern Greece

Offers slightly lower summertime temperatures, Ottoman patisseries and Halkidiki's beaches. Laid-back Ioannina makes a great base and Parga is popular with families. Sithonia is less crowded but also less family-friendly than the rest of Halkidiki.

Good to Know

Look out for the ⊞ icon for family-friendly suggestions throughout this guide.

Pre-trip study Lots of younger children enjoy stories of Greek gods and Greek myths while slightly older kids will enjoy movies like *Mamma Mia*, *300* or *Lara Croft: Tomb Raider* for their Greek settings. You can also find children's books about life in Greece that include a few easy phrases that your kids can try out.

When to Go The shoulder seasons (April to May and September to October) are great times to travel with children because the weather is milder and the crowds thinner.

Pushchairs (strollers) Unless they are the sturdy, off-road style, pushchairs can be a struggle in towns and villages with slippery cobblestones and high pavements. Consider a sturdy carrying backpack for your little ones instead.

Baby needs Fresh milk is available in large towns and tourist areas, but harder to find on smaller islands. Supermarkets are the best place to look. Formula is available almost everywhere, as is heat-treated milk. Disposable nappies are also available everywhere, although it's wise to take extra supplies of all of these things to out-of-the-way islands in case of local shortages.

Useful Resources

Lonely Planet (www.lonelyplanet.com/family-holidays) Articles, products, destinations and more. For an entertaining guide packed with information and tips, turn to Lonely Planet's *Travel with Children* book.

Santorini Dave (https://santorinidave.com/greece-with-kids) For plenty of recommendations and hearty discussion on visiting Greece with kids.

Travel Guide to Greece (www.greektravel.com) Matt Barrett's website has lots of useful tips for parents.

Greece 4 Kids (www.greece4kids.com) Matt Barrett's daughter Amarandi has put together some tips of her own.

Kids' Corner

Say What?

Hello.	Γειά σας. ya·sas
Goodbye.	Αντίο. an·di·o
Please.	Παρακαλώ. pa·ra·ka·lo
Thank you.	Ευχαριστώ. ef·ha·ri·sto
My name is ...	Με λένε ... me le·ne ...

Did You Know?

- There are 114 Greek Islands with people living on them.
- Greece's currency is the euro.

Have You Tried?

Souvlaki
Greece's favourite fast food

Regions at a Glance

If you're after knockout sites, Crete, the Dodecanese, the Ionians and the Cyclades have atmospheric architecture and ancient ruins that draw crowds. If you fancy getting active, these same regions offer diving, surfing, rock climbing, hiking and kayaking. They're well set up for tourists – and receive lots.

For a beach scene, head to Corfu, Mykonos or Kos. Thankfully, isolated pockets of sandy bliss can be found within almost all of the island groups, but to really escape, make a beeline for the northeastern Aegean.

Some island groups, including the Dodecanese and Cyclades, have strong transport links that zip you easily from one harbour to the next. Others, such as the northeastern Aegean Islands, require you to take more time and be more intrepid in manoeuvring to and from.

Athens & Around

Ancient Ruins
Museums
Nightlife

Ancient Greece

The Acropolis is a must but there are many other superb ruins to visit; in Athens don't miss the Odeon of Herodes Atticus and the Ancient Agora, then head out to the dramatic Temple of Poseidon on Cape Sounion.

Greek Music & Clubs

This city refuses to snooze, with glamorous beachside clubs, intimate *rembetika* (blues songs) bars and everything in between.

Cultural Treasures

From the eclectic Benaki Museum to the ultra-modern Acropolis Museum, Athens is a major contributor to the world's museum scene. Regardless of your interests, you're sure to find one to wow you.

p68

Saronic Gulf Islands

Outdoor Activities
Architecture
Museums

Diving & Hilltops

Encounter dolphins, sunken pirate ships and caves when diving. On dry land, Poros, Hydra and Spetses have forests to explore and hilltops to climb.

Traditional Buildings

Hydra is picture-perfect, with tiers of ochre-coloured buildings sweeping down to the harbour. Spetses' Old Harbour shows off traditional boatbuilding, while mansions are scattered across the island.

Nautical Collections

See fully restored mansions, eclectic naval collections, gold-crusted ecclesiastic paraphernalia, traditional seafarers' homes and a museum of sea craft with caïques and yachts.

p152

Cyclades

Ancient Ruins
Cuisine
Nightlife

Sacred Relics

The sacred relics of Delos are protected on their own strictly regulated island. Ancient Thira on Santorini is a melange of Hellenistic, Roman and Byzantine ruins.

Local Food

Smoked eel and ham, Mykonian prosciutto, soft cheeses and wild mushrooms are gathered locally and fill the menus on Mykonos and Paros with creative, modern takes on traditional food.

Raising the Roof

Mykonos' nightlife is glamorous and LGBT+ friendly. Ios is less swanky but very full-on, with wall-to-wall clubs and nonstop beach parties. Quieter Santorini has cocktail bars over the caldera with unparalleled sunset views.

p173

Crete

Ancient Ruins
Outdoor Activities
Beaches

Minoan Sites

Splendid Minoan ruins grace the island. The impressive, restored Palace of Knossos is the star, with its famous labyrinth.

Canyons & Mountains

A footpath winds down between the steep, long canyon walls of Samaria Gorge, one of Crete's most popular draws. There are quieter, equally dramatic gorges for trekking and rock climbing and a mountainous interior concealing hermit caves and a 'haunted' woodland.

Superb Sands

Crete has some of Greece's top beaches: palm-fringed stretches of powder-soft sand. Others are lapped by the crystal-clear Libyan Sea or backed by charismatic old towns.

p281

Dodecanese

Architecture
Outdoor Activities
Cuisine

Churches & Castles

Architectural eye candy galore, with fairy-tale castles, frescoed Byzantine churches and a walled medieval city. Find mountain villages hidden from pirates, ancient temple ruins and Italian-inspired harbour towns.

Outdoor Action

World-class rock climbing, kitesurfing, beachcombing, diving and walking are all here. Follow ancient footpaths, hike into the caldera of a smoking volcano or surf the waves.

Italian Influence

Traditional Greek cuisine stirred up with an Italian influence equals scrumptious results. Expect creative pizzas, pastas, stews, stuffed veggies and lots of fresh cheeses.

p340

Northeastern Aegean Islands

Outdoor Activities
Cuisine
Beaches

Great Outdoors

Dive into the clear water that laps these islands. You'll be beckoned by waterfalls, rivers and old-growth forests to explore by foot or cycle.

Fresh Seafood

Dining daily on fresh seafood is a way of life here. Venus clams, sea urchins, crayfish, grilled cod and lobster are all washed down with ouzo and Samos' sweet wine.

Hidden Coves

From the remote, white-pebbled coast on Ikaria to hidden coves on the Fourni Islands, pristine sandy stretches on Chios and seaside resorts on Samos, you're never far from a beach gently lapped by the Aegean.

p419

Evia & the Sporades

Outdoor Activities
Cuisine
Nightlife

Water Sports

Soak in thermal waters, watch for dolphins as you tour a marine park, and hike through olive groves. This region's watery depths are renowned for scuba-diving, with opportunities for beginners and pros.

Local Produce

Try the local *elatos* (fir) and *pefko* (pine) honeys and the amazingly fresh fish – choose it from the nets and dine on the dock. Locally grown veggies and pressed olive oil enhance every dish.

Live Music

Nightlife here is about listening to some of the country's top bouzouki players and watching the sun sink over the horizon from low-key wine bars.

p480

Ionian Islands

Architecture
Outdoor Activities
Cuisine

Mansions & Windmills

Corfu Town is a symphony of pastel-hued Venetian mansions, French arcades and British neoclassical architecture. Neighbouring islands have traditional white-washed villages and ancient windmills.

Kayaking & Rambling

Kayak to remote coves, windsail across the deep-blue Aegean and trek through the mountains. The gorgeous coastline and quiet interiors lure the adventurous here.

Corfiot Flavours

Soft-braised meat, plenty of garlic, home-made bread, seafood risottos and hand-rolled pasta allude to an Italian influence.

p508

On the Road

Ionian Islands
p508

Evia & the Sporades
p480

Northeastern Aegean Islands
p419

Athens & Around
p68

Saronic Gulf Islands
p152

Cyclades
p173

Dodecanese
p340

Crete
p281

Athens & Around

Best Places to Eat

➡ Karamanlidika tou Fani (p120)

➡ Mavro Provato (p124)

➡ Seychelles (p121)

➡ Sushimou (p119)

➡ Ellevoro (p118)

Best Places to Stay

➡ Grande Bretagne (p113)

➡ InnAthens (p113)

➡ Athens Was (p112)

➡ City Circus (p113)

➡ Perianth Hotel (p114)

Why Go?

With equal measures of grunge and grace, Athens is a heady mix of ancient history and contemporary cool. Cultural and social life plays out amid, around and in ancient landmarks. The magnificent Acropolis, visible from almost every part of the city, reminds Greeks daily of their heritage and the city's many transformations.

Although individuals have endured difficult circumstances since the start of the economic crisis in 2009, the city is on the rise. There is crackling energy in galleries, political debates and even on the walls of derelict buildings. This creates a lively urban bustle, but at the end of the day, Athenians build their own villages in the city, especially in open-air restaurants and bars where they linger for hours.

Beyond Athens, down the Attica peninsula, are more spectacular antiquities, such as the Temple of Poseidon at Sounion, as well as very good beaches, such as those near historic Marathon.

When to Go
Athens

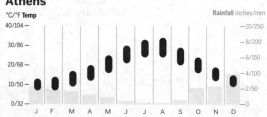

May Perfect weather for sight-seeing and open-air attractions such as cinemas and restaurants.

Jun–Aug The Athens & Epidaurus Festival lights up venues with drama and music.

Sep & Oct Weather cools and the social scene heats up as residents return from the islands.

Athens Highlights

1 **Acropolis** (p78) Visiting the awe-inspiring ancient site.

2 **Acropolis Museum** (p84) Enjoying the majesty of the Parthenon sculptures.

3 **Ancient Agora** (p88) Strolling in the historic centre.

4 **Benaki Museum** (p104) Admiring superb antiquities and cultural artefacts.

5 **National Archaeological Museum** (p96) Exploring the finest collection of Greek antiquities.

6 **Odeon of Herodes Atticus** (p81) Watching a performance in this ancient amphitheatre.

7 **Stavros Niarchos Foundation Cultural Center** (p145) Feeling the sea breeze at this wonderful arts hub and park.

8 **Panathenaic Stadium** (p105) Revelling in ancient feats of strength.

NEIGHBOURHOODS AT A GLANCE

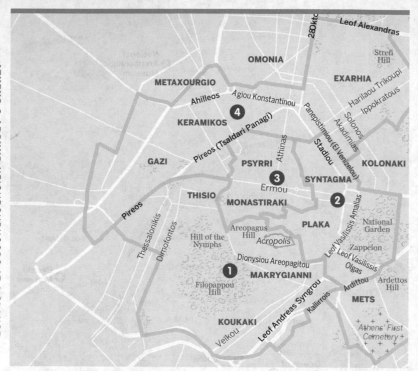

❶ Acropolis, Filopappou Hill & Thisio (p76)

Athens' crown is the Acropolis and its jewel is the Parthenon. This epic monument soars above the city, and on the hill's southern slopes, a fabulous modern museum holds its treasures. A pedestrian promenade links the two – it's a tourist throughway, but also a favourite spot for locals to enjoy a sunset stroll.

Further south, the neighbourhoods of Makrygianni and Koukaki deliver a slice of residential Athens life and offer reliable hotels, hip bars and restaurants, and cool craft shops and boutiques. Filopappou Hill offers eye-level views of the Acropolis, as well as some welcome green space. Just beyond, the sedate Thisio neighbourhood is cut through with two fine pedestrian routes, around which a pleasant cafe precinct flourishes.

❷ Syntagma & Plaka (p77)

Syntagma is the heart of modern Athens, a business and bar district with Plateia Syntagmatos (Syntagma Sq) its historical meeting point, political centre and transport hub.

Adjacent to the square is the National Garden; a short stroll southwest is Plaka, the heart of old Athens, virtually all that existed when the city was declared the new Greek nation's capital in 1834. With narrow streets winding by neoclassical mansions, Byzantine churches and telegenic tavernas, Plaka is ground zero for Athens tourism. Lifelong residents and splashes of graffiti keep its soul strong.

0 — 1 km
0 — 0.5 miles

Lykavittos Hill

Leof Vasilissis Sofias

⑤

Leof Vasileos Konstantinou

PANGRATI

❸ Monastiraki & Psyrri (p94)

Monastiraki's busy square is one of Athens' key hubs. To the south, the Ancient Agora was the city's original civic meeting place and remains a wonderful site to explore. And to the north and west, Psyrri is the city's liveliest quarter, where restaurants and bars coexist with warehouse conversions and workshops.

❹ Gazi, Keramikos & Exarhia (p101)

Gazi's story is a typical contemporary urban one: abandoned industry – here, a former gasworks – is revived by artists and bar owners.

A decade passes, the edge becomes the centre, and the transformation continues in the adjacent areas of Keramikos and Metaxourgio, where new scruffy-cool bars, theatres and cafes are popping up, alongside derelict mansions, moped dealerships and Chinese wholesalers. Come to this area at night, certainly, but also by day for the ancient cemetery of Kerameikos, as well as a couple of good museums.

Exarhia is famous for its squat scene and its vocal anarchists, but also offers a fascinating mix of students (it's near the universities), creative types, immigrants, families, old lefties and intellectuals, against a backdrop of graffiti, street art and ever-present riot police.

❺ Kolonaki, Mets & Pangrati (p104)

Kolonaki is an adjective as much as a district: chic, stylish, elite.

The area, which stretches from near Syntagma to the slopes of Lykavittos Hill, is where old money mixes with the nouveau riche and wannabes. The location of several excellent museums, the cool, tree-shaded streets here make a lovely retreat after walking around sun-blasted ruins.

The attractive residential districts of Mets and Pangrati surround the Panathenaic Stadium, built into Ardettos Hill.

ATHENS

AΘHNA

♪ 21 / POP CITY 664,000;
WIDER MUNICIPALITY 3.1 MILLION

History

Early History

The archaeological record of Athens' early years is patchy. What is known is that the hilltop site of the Acropolis, with two abundant springs, drew some of Greece's earliest Neolithic settlers. When a peaceful agricultural existence gave way to war-orientated city-states, the Acropolis provided an ideal defensive position.

By 1400 BC the Acropolis had become a powerful Mycenaean city. It survived a Dorian assault in 1200 BC but didn't escape the dark age that enveloped Greece for the next 400 years. Then, in the 8th century BC, during a period of peace, Athens became the artistic centre of Greece, excelling in ceramics.

By the 6th century BC, Athens was ruled by aristocrats and generals. Labourers and peasants had no rights until Solon, the harbinger of Athenian democracy, became *arhon* (chief magistrate) in 594 BC and improved the lot of the poor by establishing a process of trial by jury. Continuing unrest over the reforms created the pretext for the tyrant Peisistratos, formerly head of the military, to seize power in 560 BC.

Peisistratos built a formidable navy and extended the boundaries of Athenian influence. A patron of the arts, he inaugurated the Festival of the Great Dionysia, the precursor to Attic drama, and commissioned many splendid works, most of which were later destroyed by the Persians.

In 528 BC, he was succeeded by his son, Hippias, no less an oppressor. With the help of Sparta in 510 BC, Athens rid itself of him.

Athens' Golden Age

After Athens finally repulsed the Persian Empire at the battles of Salamis (480 BC) and Plataea (479 BC) – again, with the help of Sparta – its power knew no bounds.

In 477 BC Athens established a confederacy on the sacred island of Delos and demanded tributes from the surrounding islands to protect them from the Persians. The treasury was moved to Athens in 461 BC and Pericles, ruler from 461 BC to 429 BC, used the money to transform the city. This period has become known as Athens' golden age.

Most of the monuments on the Acropolis today date from this period. Drama and literature flourished due to such luminaries

as Aeschylus, Sophocles and Euripides. The sculptors Pheidias and Myron and the historians Herodotus, Thucydides and Xenophon also lived during this time.

Rivalry with Sparta

Sparta didn't let Athens revel in its newfound glory. Cooperation gave way to competition and the Peloponnesian Wars, which began in 431 BC and dragged on until 404 BC. Sparta gained the upper hand and Athens never returned to its former glory. The 4th century BC did, however, produce three of the West's greatest orators and philosophers: Socrates, Plato and Aristotle.

In 338 BC Athens, along with the other city-states of Greece, was conquered by Philip II of Macedon. After Philip's assassination, his son Alexander (soon to be known as the Great) favoured Athens over other city-states. But after Alexander's untimely death, Athens passed in quick succession through the hands of his generals.

Roman & Byzantine Rule

The Romans defeated the Macedonians, and in 86 BC attacked Athens after it sided against them in a botched rebellion in Asia Minor. They destroyed the city walls and took precious sculptures to Rome. During three centuries of peace under Roman rule, known as the 'Pax Romana', Athens continued to be a major seat of learning. The Romans adopted Hellenistic culture: many wealthy young Romans attended Athens schools and anyone who was anyone in Rome spoke Greek. The Roman emperors, particularly Hadrian, graced Athens with many grand buildings.

In the late 4th century AD, Christianity became the official religion of Athens and worship of the 'pagan' Greek gods was outlawed. After the subdivision of the Roman Empire into east and west, Athens remained an important cultural and intellectual centre until Emperor Justinian closed its schools of philosophy in 529. Athens declined and, between 1200 and 1450, was continually invaded – by the Franks, Catalans, Florentines and Venetians, all preoccupied with grabbing principalities from the crumbling Byzantine Empire.

Ottoman Rule & Independence

Athens was captured by the Turks in 1456, and nearly 400 years of Ottoman rule followed. The Acropolis became the home of the Turkish governor, the Parthenon was converted to a mosque and the Erechtheion became a harem.

ATHENS IN...

Two Days

Climb to the glorious **Acropolis** (p78) in the early morning, then wind down through the **Ancient Agora** (p88). Explore Plaka, looping back to the **Acropolis Museum** (p84) for the Parthenon masterpieces. Complete your circuit along the pedestrian promenade, then up to **Filopappou Hill** (p76) and the cafes of Thisio before dinner at a restaurant with Acropolis views – or grab a souvlaki and head to an outdoor movie.

On day two, watch the **changing of the guard** (p80) at Syntagma Sq before heading through the gardens to the **Temple of Olympian Zeus** (p77) or the **Panathenaic Stadium** (p105). Spend the afternoon at the **National Archaeological Museum** (p96), then head to the Plateia Agia Irini area in Monastiraki for dinner and nightlife.

Four Days

Take your pick from the **Benaki Museum** (p104), the **Museum of Cycladic Art** (p105) and the **Byzantine & Christian Museum** (p104) before lunch in Kolonaki. Take the *teleferik* (funicular railway) or climb **Lykavittos Hill** (p105) for panoramic views. Hit a *rembetika* club in winter, or bar-hop around Exarhia in summer.

On day four spend the morning exploring the Varvakios Agora and Kerameikos, then head in the afternoon to the **Stavros Niarchos Foundation Cultural Center** (p145), finishing the day with a show at the **Greek National Opera** (p130). Alternatively, trip along the coast to Cape Sounion's **Temple of Poseidon** (p147), saving some energy for nightlife at Glyfada's beach bars.

On 25 March 1821, the Greeks launched the War of Independence, declaring independence in 1822. Fierce fighting broke out in the streets of Athens, which changed hands several times. Britain, France and Russia eventually stepped in and destroyed the Turkish–Egyptian fleet in the famous Battle of Navarino in October 1827.

Initially the city of Nafplio was named Greece's capital. After elected president Ioannis Kapodistrias was assassinated in 1831, Britain, France and Russia again intervened, declaring Greece a monarchy. The throne was given to 17-year-old Prince Otto of Bavaria, who transferred his court to Athens. It became the Greek capital in 1834, though was little more than a sleepy town of about 6000, as so many residents had fled after the 1827 siege. Bavarian architects created imposing neoclassical buildings, tree-lined boulevards and squares.

Otto was overthrown in 1862 after a period of power struggles, including the British and French occupation of Piraeus, aimed at quashing the 'Great Idea' – Greece's doomed expansionist goal. The imposed sovereign was Danish Prince William, crowned as Prince George in 1863.

The 20th Century

Throughout the latter half of the 19th century and the beginning of the 20th, Athens grew steadily – and then quite suddenly in 1922 and 1923, when more than a million refugees arrived in the city, first from the burning of Smyrna (Izmir), then due to the population exchange mandated by the Treaty of Lausanne the next spring.

During the German occupation of WWII, Athens suffered appallingly. More Athenians died from starvation than were killed by the enemy. The suffering only continued during the bitter civil war that followed.

A 1950s industrialisation programme, launched with the help of US aid, brought another population boom, as people from the islands and mainland villages moved to Athens in search of work. The colonels' junta (1967–74) tore down many of the old Turkish houses of Plaka and the neoclassical buildings of King Otto's time, but failed to tackle the chronic infrastructure problems resulting from the rapid growth of the 1950s. The elected governments that followed didn't do much better, and by the end of the 1980s the city had a reputation as one of the most traffic-clogged, polluted and dysfunctional in Europe.

In the 1990s, as part of an initial bid to host the Olympics, authorities embarked on an ambitious program to drag the city into the 21st century. Athens finally won the competition to host the 2004 Olympics, a deadline that fast-tracked infrastructure projects.

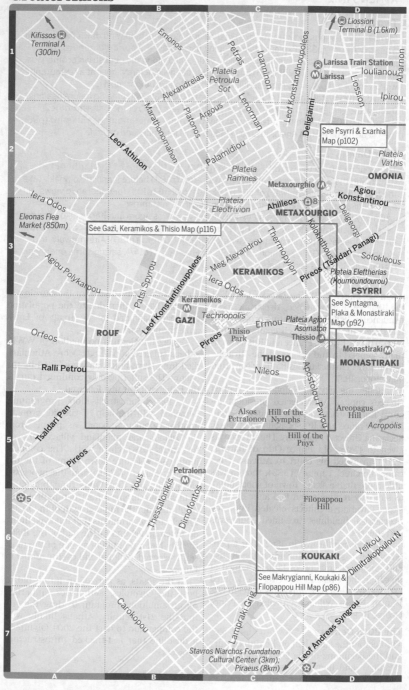

Kifissos Terminal A (300m)

Liossion Terminal B (1.6km)

Larissa Train Station

Larissa

Emonos

Petras

Ioanninon

Plateia Petroula Sot

Leof Konstandinoupoleos

Ioulianou

Liossion

Ipirou

Aharnon

Alexandreias

Platoros

Argous

Lenorman

Deligianni

See Psyrri & Exarhia Map (p102)

Marathonomahon

Leof Athinon

Palamidiou

Plateia Ramnes

Plateia Vathis

OMONIA

Agiou Konstantinou

Metaxourghio

Ahilleos

8

Deligeorgi

Iera Odos

Eleonas Flea Market (850m)

Plateia Eleotrivion

METAXOURGIO

Kolokithous

Plateia (Tsaldari Panagi)

Sofokleous

See Gazi, Keramikos & Thisio Map (p116)

Thermopylon

Pireos (Tsaldari Panagi)

Meg Alexandrou

Agiou Polykarpou

Pafsi Spyrou

Leof Konstantinoupoleos

KERAMIKOS

Iera Odos

Plateia Eleftherias (Koumoundourou)

PSYRRI

Kerameikos

See Syntagma, Plaka & Monastiraki Map (p92)

Orfeos

ROUF

GAZI

Technopolis

Ermou

Plateia Agion Asomaton

Thissio

Pireos

Thisio Park

Ralli Petrou

THISIO

Nileos

Apostolou Pavlou

Monastiraki

MONASTIRAKI

Areopagus Hill

Acropolis

Tsaldari Pan

Alsos Petralonon

Hill of the Nymphs

Hill of the Pnyx

Pireos

5

Petralona

Filopappou Hill

Thessalonikis

Dimofontos

KOUKAKI

Veikou

Dimitrakopoulou N

See Makrygianni, Koukaki & Filopappou Hill Map (p86)

Carokopou

Lampraki Grig

Stavros Niarchos Foundation Cultural Center (3km); Piraeus (8km)

Leof Andreas Syngrou

7

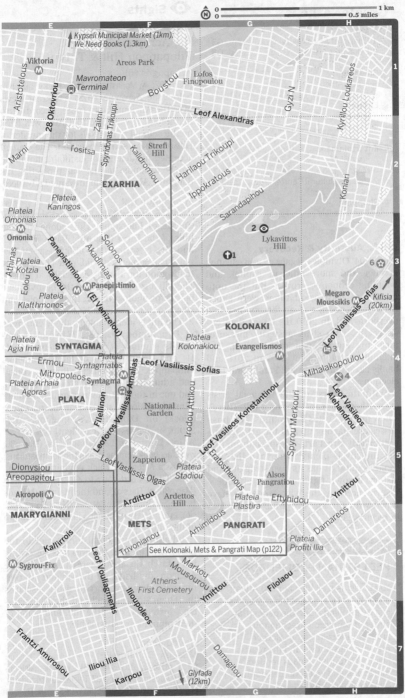

0 1 km
0 0.5 miles

Kypseli Municipal Market (1km);
We Need Books (1.3km)

Viktoria Ⓜ

Areos Park

Mavromateon
Terminal

Lofos
Finopoulou

Boustou

Leof Alexandras

Gyzi N

Kyrillou Loukareos

Aristotelous

28 Oktovriou

Zaimi

Spyridonas Trikoupi

Kallidromiou

Strefi
Hill

Harilaou Trikoupi

Ippokratous

Koniari

Marni

Tositsa

EXARHIA

Plateia
Kaningos

Solonos

Akadimias

Sarandapihou

2 ◎

Lykavittos
Hill

Plateia
Omonias

Omonia Ⓜ

Panepistimiou

✝1

6 ☆

Athinas

Plateia
Kotzia

Eolou

Stadiou

Panepistimio
(El Venizelou) Ⓜ

Megaro
Moussikis

Leof Vasilissis Sofias

Kifisia
(20km)

Plateia
Klafthmonos

KOLONAKI

Plateia
Agia Irini

SYNTAGMA

Plateia
Syntagmatos

Plateia
Kolonakiou

Evangelismos Ⓜ

3 🖭

Ermou

Leof Vasilissis Sofias

Mitropoleos

Syntagma

Mihalakopoulou

4 ✕

Plateia Arhaia
Agoras

PLAKA

Fillelinon

Leoforos Vasilissis Amalias

National
Garden

Leof Vasileos
Alehandrou

Spyrou Merkouri

Dionysiou
Areopagitou

Akropoli Ⓜ

MAKRYGIANNI

Leof Vasilissis Olgas

Zappeion

Plateia
Stadiou

Irodou Attikou

Leof Vasileos Konstantinou

Eratosthenous

Alsos
Pangratiou

Eftyhidou

Ymittou

Kallirrois

Ardittou

Ardettos
Hill

Arhimidous

Plateia
Plastira

Damareos

Sygrou-Fix Ⓜ

METS

Trivonianou

PANGRATI

Plateia
Profiti Ilia

See Kolonaki, Mets & Pangrati Map (p122)

Markou
Mousourou

Leof Vouliagmenis

Athens'
First Cemetery

Ymittou

Filolaou

Frantzi Amvrosiou

Iliou Ilia

Illoupoleos

Karpou

Glyfada
(12km)

Damagitou

E F G H

N

Greater Athens

Crisis, Austerity & Recovery

The 2004 Olympics legacy was a cleaner, greener and more efficient capital, and booming economic growth. But the optimism and fiscal good times were short-lived, as it became clear the country had overborrowed. In 2010 the Greek debt crisis set in, with strict austerity measures including cutting pensions by half. The unemployment rate hit 28% in 2014 and banks closed briefly in 2015 amid dramatic elections.

With the worst of the financial crisis over, Athens appears to be on a roll. There's a new mayor, Kostas Bakoyannis, new businesses are starting up and the arts scene – particularly street art – is especially on fire. But the city is plenty more than the next trendy capital. It has its own struggles and history, its own fight-the-power attitude – as evidenced by the way Athenians have coped with the massive influx of refugees in recent years.

LOCAL KNOWLEDGE

PEDESTRIAN PROMENADE

You could skip all the sights in Athens and still feel you've got the city's pulse just by strolling along the pedestrian street of Dionysiou Areopagitou around sundown. Lights glow on the Acropolis above, and the road is filled with tourists, snack vendors, musicians and local couples out for an arm-in-arm promenade.

◉ Sights

◉ Acropolis, Filopappou Hill & Thisio

Areopagus Hill   PARK

(Map p92; Ⓜ Monastiraki) This rocky outcrop below the Acropolis (p78) has great views over the Ancient Agora (p88). According to mythology, it was here that Ares was tried by the council of the gods for the murder of Halirrhothios, son of Poseidon. The council accepted his defence of justifiable homicide on the grounds that he was protecting his daughter, Alcippe, from unwanted advances.

Filopappou Hill   PARK

(Map p86; Ⓜ Akropoli) Also called the Hill of the Muses, Filopappou Hill – along with the hills of the **Pnyx** (Map p116; Thisio; Ⓜ Thissio) and the **Nymphs** (Map p116; Thisio; Ⓜ Thissio) – is a somewhat wild, pine-shaded spot that's good for a stroll, especially at sunset. The hill also gives some of the best vantage points for photographing the Acropolis, and views to the Saronic Gulf.

The hill is identifiable by the **Monument of Filopappos** (Map p86; Ⓜ Thissio) crowning its summit; it was built between AD 114 and 116 in honour of Julius Antiochus Filopappos, a prominent Roman consul and administrator. The marble-paved path, laid out in the 1950s by modernist architect Dimitris Pikionis, starts near the *periptero* (kiosk) on Dionysiou Areopagitou. After 250m, it passes the excellent **Church of Agios Dimitrios Loumbardiaris** (Map p86; www.facebook.com/agiosdimitriosloumpardiaris; Ⓜ Thissio, Akropoli), which contains fine frescoes. There's a detour to **Socrates' prison** (Map p86; Ⓜ Thissio), and the main path leads to the **Shrine of the Muses** (Map p86; Ⓜ Thissio), cut into the rock face just below the top of the hill.

Inhabited from prehistoric times to the post-Byzantine era, the area was, according to Plutarch, the area where Theseus and the Amazons did battle. In the 4th and 5th centuries BC, defensive **fortifications** – such as the Themistoclean wall and the Diateichisma – extended over the hill, and some of their remains are still visible.

Herakleidon Museum Building B   MUSEUM

(Map p116; 📞 210 346 1981; www.herakleidonart.gr; Apostolou Pavlou 37, Thisio; adult/student/child €7/5/free; ⊙ 10am-6pm Wed-Sun; Ⓜ Thissio)

ℹ COMBINED TICKETS & ENTRY HOURS

➡ A €30 combo ticket covers entry to the Acropolis and Athens' other main ancient sites: the Ancient Agora, the Roman Agora, Hadrian's Library, Kerameikos, the Temple of Olympian Zeus and Aristotle's Lyceum. It pays off if you're planning to see the Acropolis (€20 alone) and at least two other sites. The ticket is valid for five consecutive days and can be purchased at any of the included sites.

➡ For museums, a €15 ticket covers the National Archaeological Museum, the Byzantine & Christian Museum, the Epigraphic Museum and the Numismatic Museum. It's valid for three days.

➡ A €25 pass covers entry to all branches of the Benaki Museum and is valid for three months.

➡ Hours for many sites and museums cut back in winter, closing sometimes as early as 1pm. Additionally, budget cuts occasionally curtail opening times. Double-check hours before making a special trip. Ticket offices close 15 to 30 minutes before the sites close.

➡ Check www.culture.gr for free-admission holidays.

This eclectic private museum, split over two locations, examines the interrelation of art, mathematics and philosophy, explored through rotating exhibits on such diverse subjects as ancient robotic and computer technology, and shipbuilding. Building B focuses on weapons of war, including triremes, the ancient warships that allowed the Greeks to conquer the Persians at the Battle of Salamis.

Around the corner in a restored mansion, the smaller **Building A** (Map p116; ☑ 210 346 1981; www.herakleidon-art.gr; Iraklidon 16, Thisio; adult/student/child €7/5/free; ☺ 10am-6pm Wed-Sun; Ⓜ Thissio) has an exhibition on automata, featuring an ancient type of robot including one of a moving servant girl. The museum also holds one of the world's biggest collections of MC Escher artworks (though it is not always on view).

Athens Pinball Museum   MUSEUM
(Map p86; ☑ 210 924 5958; www.facebook.com/ AthensPinballMuseum; Makri 2, Makrygianni; adult/student/child €10/7/free; ☺ 10am-10pm Mon-Fri, 9am-11pm Sat & Sun; Ⓜ Akropoli) Not so much a museum as an all-bleeping, flashing games arcade where you play pinball to your heart's content. It has more than 100 working pinball machines, with the oldest dating back to 1957; the fanciest is a gold-plated version of an *Addams Family*–themed machine.

**Melina Merkouri
Cultural Centre**   MUSEUM
(Map p116; ☑ 210 345 2150; www.cityofathens.gr/ node/676; Iraklidon 66, Thisio; ☺ 10am-8pm Tue-Sat, to 2pm Sun; Ⓜ Thissio) FREE For anyone who loves the Greek tradition of *karagiozi* (shadow puppets), this free museum is a treat, packed with the creations of master puppeteer Haridimos (Sotiris Haritos). There's very little English signage, but the displays tell their own stories. Upstairs is a mock street scene of 'old Athens', with shop windows of the typesetter, the photo studio, the barber and more.

**National Museum
of Contemporary Art**   MUSEUM
(EMST; Map p86; ☑ 211 101 9000; www.emst.gr; Kallirrois & Frantzi, Koukaki-Syngrou; Ⓜ Syngrou-Fix) Set in the former Fix Brewery, this contemporary museum opened in 2015 but was closed for prolonged renovations at the time of research. In the past, it has exhibited Greek and international art in all media, from painting to video to experimental architecture.

◎ Syntagma & Plaka

★ **Temple of Olympian Zeus**   TEMPLE
(Olympieio; Map p92; ☑ 210 922 6330; http://odysseus.culture.gr; Leoforos Vasilissis Olgas, Plaka; adult/student/child €6/3/free; ☺ 8am-3pm Oct-Apr, to 8pm May-Sep; Ⓜ Akropoli, Syntagma) A can't-miss on two counts: it's a marvellous temple, once the largest in Greece, and it's smack in the centre of Athens. Of the temple's 104 original Corinthian columns (17m high with a base diameter of 1.7m), only 15 remain – the fallen column was blown down in a gale in 1852.

⊙ TOP SIGHT
ACROPOLIS

The Acropolis is the most important ancient site in the Western world. Crowned by the Parthenon, it's visible from almost everywhere in Athens. Its marble gleams white in the midday sun and takes on a honey hue as the sun sinks, then glows above the city by night. A glimpse of this magnificent sight cannot fail to exalt your spirit.

Parthenon

The Parthenon (p85) is the monument that more than any other epitomises the glory of Ancient Greece. It is dedicated to Athena Parthenos, the goddess embodying the power and prestige of the city. One of the largest Doric temples ever completed in Greece, it was designed by Iktinos and Kallicrates to be the pre-eminent monument of the Acropolis and was completed in time for the Great Panathenaic Festival of 438 BC.

Columns

The Parthenon's fluted Doric columns achieve perfect form. The eight columns at either end and 17 on each side were ingeniously curved to create an optical illusion: the foundations (like all the 'horizontal' surfaces of the temple) are slightly concave and the columns are slightly convex, making both appear straight. Supervised by Pheidias, the sculptors worked on the architectural detail of the Parthenon, including the pediments, frieze and metopes, which were brightly coloured and gilded.

DON'T MISS

➡ Parthenon
➡ Erechtheion
➡ Porch of the Caryatids
➡ Propylaia
➡ Temple of Athena Nike
➡ Beulé Gate and Monument of Agrippa
➡ Theatre of Dionysos
➡ Asclepieion and Stoa of Eumenes
➡ Odeon of Herodes Atticus

PRACTICALITIES

➡ Map p92; Ⓜ Akropoli
➡ ☏ 210 321 4172
➡ http://odysseus. culture.gr
➡ adult/concession/child €20/10/free
➡ ⊙ 8am-8pm May-Sep, reduced hours in winter, last entry 30min before closing

Pediments

The temple's pediments (the triangular elements topping the east and west facades) were filled with elaborately carved three-dimensional sculptures. The west side depicted Athena and Poseidon in their contest for the city's patronage, the east Athena's birth from Zeus' head. See their remnants and the rest of the Acropolis' sculptures and artefacts in the Acropolis Museum (p84).

Metopes & Frieze

The Parthenon's metopes, designed by Pheidias, are square carved panels set between channelled triglyphs. The metopes on the eastern side depicted the Olympian gods fighting the giants, and on the western side they showed Theseus leading the Athenian youths into battle against the Amazons. The southern metopes illustrated the contest of the Lapiths and centaurs at a marriage feast, while the northern ones depicted the sacking of Troy. The internal cella was topped by the Ionic frieze, a continuous sculptured band depicting the Panathenaic Procession.

Erechtheion

The Erechtheion, completed around 406 BC, was a sanctuary built on the most sacred part of the Acropolis: the spot where Poseidon struck the ground with his trident, and where Athena produced the olive tree. Named after Erechtheus, a mythical king of Athens, the temple housed the cults of Athena, Poseidon and Erechtheus. This supreme example of Ionic architecture was ingeniously built on several levels to compensate for the uneven bedrock.

Porch of the Caryatids

The Erechtheion is immediately recognisable by the six majestic maiden columns, the Caryatids (415 BC), that support its southern portico. Modelled on women from Karyai (modern-day Karyes, in Lakonia), each figure is thought to have held a libation bowl in one hand, and to be drawing up her dress with the other. Those you see are plaster casts. The originals (except for one removed by Lord Elgin, now in the British Museum) are in the Acropolis Museum.

Temple of Poseidon

Poseidon's cella, the Erechtheion's northern porch, is accessible by a small set of stairs against the boundary wall. It consists of six Ionic columns; the fissure in the floor is supposedly left either by Poseidon's trident in his contest with Athena, or by Zeus' thunderbolt when he killed the mythical king Erechtheus.

TOP TIPS

➡ Visit at 8am or late in the day.

➡ Large bags must be checked in the cloakrooms – you'll find them at both entrances.

➡ Wheelchairs access the site via a cage lift; call ahead to arrange it (210 321 4172).

➡ Tickets can be bought online at https://etickets.tap.gr.

➡ Also avoid the ticket-booth lines at the Acropolis by buying the €30 combo ticket at other covered ancient sites.

➡ Check www.culture.gr for free-admission holidays and changing opening hours.

➡ Big tour groups tend to use the main entrance. The southeast entrance can be less crowded.

QUICK TOUR

It's possible to tour the site in about 90 minutes towards the end of the day. Enter from the less busy southeast entrance, and make a beeline up to the Parthenon. Site clearance starts up here about 45 minutes before closing time; then you can start making your way back down along the south slope, a little ahead of the exiting crowds.

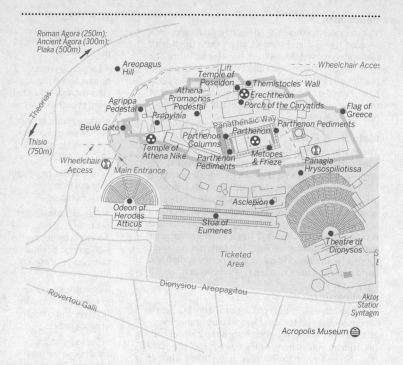

Themistocles' Wall

Crafty general Themistocles (524–459 BC) hastened to build a protective wall around the Acropolis and in so doing incorporated elements from archaic temples on the site. When you're down the hill in Monastiraki, look for the column drums built into the wall on the north side of the Erechtheion.

Propylaia

The monumental entrance to the Acropolis, the Propylaia was built by Mnesicles between 437 BC and 432 BC, and consists of a central hall with two wings on either side. In ancient times its five gates were the only entrances to the 'upper city'. The middle gate opens onto the Panathenaic Way. The ceiling of the central hall was painted with gold stars on a dark-blue background. The northern wing was used as a *pinakothiki* (art gallery).

Temple of Athena Nike

This tiny but exquisitely proportioned Pentelic marble temple was designed by Kallicrates and originally built around 425 BC; it has been restored three times, most recently in 2003. The internal cella housed a wooden statue of Athena as Victory (Nike), and the exterior friezes illustrated scenes from mythology, the Battle of Plataea (479 BC) and Athenians fighting Boeotians and Persians. Parts of the frieze are in the Acropolis Museum, as are some relief sculptures, including the beautiful depiction of Athena Nike fastening her sandal.

Beulé Gate & Monument of Agrippa

Just outside the Propylaia lies the Beulé Gate, named after French archaeologist Ernest Beulé, who uncovered it in 1852. The 8m pedestal halfway up the zigzagging ramp to the Propylaia was once topped by the Monument of Agrippa. This bronze statue of the Roman general riding a chariot was erected in 27 BC to commemorate victory in the Panathenaic Games.

Theatre of Dionysos

Originally, a 6th-century-BC timber theatre was built here, on the site of the Festival of the Great Dionysia. During Athens' golden age, the theatre (Map p92; Dionysiou Areopagitou) hosted productions of the works of Aeschylus, Sophocles, Euripides and Aristophanes. Reconstructed in stone and marble between 342 and 326 BC, the theatre held 17,000 spectators (spread over 64 tiers, of which only about 20 tiers survive) and an altar to Dionysos in the orchestra pit.

The ringside Pentelic marble thrones were for dignitaries and priests. The grandest, with lions' paws, satyrs and griffins, was reserved for the Priest of Dionysos. The 2nd-century-BC reliefs at the rear of the stage depict the exploits of Dionysos. The two hefty men (who still have their heads) are *sileni*, worshippers of the mythical Silenus, the debauched father of the satyrs, whose favourite pastime was charging up mountains with his oversized phallus in lecherous pursuit of nymphs.

Asclepieion & Stoa of Eumenes

Above the Theatre of Dionysos, steps lead to the Asclepieion (Map p92), a temple built around a sacred spring. The worship of Asclepius, the physician son of Apollo, began in Epidavros and was introduced to Athens in 429 BC at a time when plague was sweeping the city: people sought cures here.

Beneath the Asclepieion, the Stoa of Eumenes is a colonnade built by Eumenes II, King of Pergamum (197–159 BC), as a shelter and promenade for theatre audiences.

Odeon of Herodes Atticus

The path continues west from the Asclepieion to the magnificent Odeon of Herodes Atticus (Herodeon; Map p92; ☎210 324 1807; Ⓜ Akropoli), known as the Herodion. It was built in AD 161 by wealthy Roman Herodes Atticus in memory of his wife Regilla. The theatre was excavated in 1857–58 and completely restored between 1950 and 1961. Performances of drama, music and dance are held here during the Athens & Epidaurus Festival (p109).

GREEK FLAG

The one modern detail on the Acropolis (aside from the ever-present scaffolding and cranes) is the large Greek flag at the far east end. In 1941 early in the Nazi occupation, two teenage boys climbed up the cliff and raised the Greek flag; their act of resistance is commemorated on a brass plaque nearby.

STATUE OF ATHENA PARTHENOS

The statue for which the temple was built – the Athena Parthenos (Athena the Virgin) – was considered one of the wonders of the ancient world. It was taken to Constantinople in AD 426, where it disappeared. Designed by Pheidias and completed in 432 BC, it stood almost 12m high on its pedestal and was plated in gold. Athena's face, hands and feet were made of ivory, and the eyes fashioned from jewels.

ATHENS & AROUND ACROPOLIS

The Acropolis

A WALKING TOUR

Cast your imagination back in time, two and a half millennia ago, and envision the majesty of the Acropolis. Its famed and hallowed monument, the Parthenon, dedicated to the goddess Athena, stood proudly over a small city, dwarfing the population with its graceful grandeur. In the Acropolis' heyday in the 5th century BC, pilgrims and priests worshipped at the temples illustrated here (most of which still stand in varying states of restoration). Many were painted brilliant colours and were abundantly adorned with sculptural masterpieces crafted from ivory, gold and semiprecious stones.

As you enter the site today, elevated on the right perches one of the Acropolis' best-restored buildings: the diminutive **❶ Temple of Athena Nike**. Follow the Panathenaic Way through the Propylaia and up the slope towards the Parthenon – icon of the Western world. Its **❷ majestic columns** sweep up to some of what were the finest carvings of their time: wrap-around **❸ pediments, metopes and a frieze**. Stroll around the temple's exterior and take in the spectacular views over Athens and Piraeus below.

As you circle back to the centre of the site, you will encounter those renowned lovely ladies, the **❹ Caryatids** of the Erechtheion. On the Erechtheion's northern face, the oft-forgotten **❺ Temple of Poseidon** sits alongside ingenious **❻ Themistocles' Wall**. Wander to the Erechtheion's western side to find Athena's gift to the city: **❼ the olive tree**.

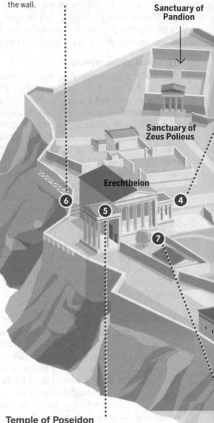

Themistocles' Wall
Crafty general Themistocles (524–459 BC) hastened to build a protective wall around the Acropolis and in so doing incorporated elements from archaic temples on the site. Look for the column drums built into the wall.

Sanctuary of Pandion

Sanctuary of Zeus Polieus

Erechtheion

Temple of Poseidon
Though he didn't win patronage of the city, Poseidon was worshipped on the northern side of the Erechtheion, which is said to bear the mark of his trident-strike. Imagine the finely decorated coffered porch painted in rich colours, as it was in the past.

ALEXTRAVELERPHOTOGRAPHER/ GETTY IMAGES ©

TOP TIP

The Acropolis is a must-see for every visitor to Athens. Avoid the crowds by arriving first thing in the morning or late in the day.

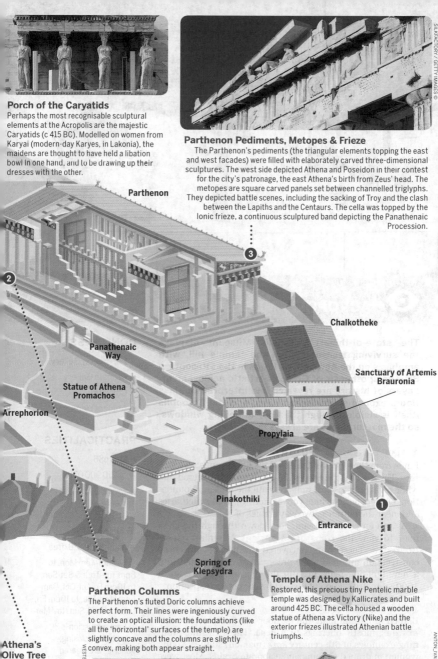

Porch of the Caryatids
Perhaps the most recognisable sculptural elements at the Acropolis are the majestic Caryatids (c 415 BC). Modelled on women from Karyai (modern-day Karyes, in Lakonia), the maidens are thought to have held a libation bowl in one hand, and to be drawing up their dresses with the other.

Parthenon Pediments, Metopes & Frieze
The Parthenon's pediments (the triangular elements topping the east and west facades) were filled with elaborately carved three-dimensional sculptures. The west side depicted Athena and Poseidon in their contest for the city's patronage, the east Athena's birth from Zeus' head. The metopes are square carved panels set between channelled triglyphs. They depicted battle scenes, including the sacking of Troy and the clash between the Lapiths and the Centaurs. The cella was topped by the Ionic frieze, a continuous sculptured band depicting the Panathenaic Procession.

Parthenon

Chalkotheke

Panathenaic Way

Sanctuary of Artemis Brauronia

Statue of Athena Promachos

Arrephorion

Propylaia

Pinakothiki

Entrance

Spring of Klepsydra

Temple of Athena Nike
Restored, this precious tiny Pentelic marble temple was designed by Kallicrates and built around 425 BC. The cella housed a wooden statue of Athena as Victory (Nike) and the exterior friezes illustrated Athenian battle triumphs.

Parthenon Columns
The Parthenon's fluted Doric columns achieve perfect form. Their lines were ingeniously curved to create an optical illusion: the foundations (like all the 'horizontal' surfaces of the temple) are slightly concave and the columns are slightly convex, making both appear straight.

Athena's Olive Tree
The flourishing olive tree next to the Erechtheion is meant to be the sacred tree that Athena produced to seize victory in the contest for Athens.

SILKFACTORY / GETTY IMAGES ©
WESTEND61 / GETTY IMAGES ©
ANTON_IVANOV / SHUTTERSTOCK ©

TOP SIGHT
ACROPOLIS MUSEUM

The state-of-the-art Acropolis Museum displays the surviving treasures from the temple hill, with emphasis on the Acropolis as it was in the 5th century BC, the apotheosis of Greece's artistic achievement. Layers of history are revealed and interpreted: glass floors expose subterranean ruins, and the Acropolis itself is visible through the floor-to-ceiling windows, so the masterpieces are always in context.

Entry Gallery & Ruins

Finds from the slopes of the Acropolis fill the entryway gallery. The floor's slope echoes the climb up to the sacred hill, while giving glimpses of ruins beneath the museum foundation. Objects here include votive offerings from sanctuaries and, near the entrance, two clay statues of Nike.

As you enter the museum, look down through the glass floor to view the ruins of an ancient Athenian neighbourhood. These were uncovered during the museum's construction and had to be preserved and integrated into a new building plan. In 2019 the museum opened up a 4000-sq-metre section of these ruins for closer inspection.

Archaic Gallery

Bathed in natural light, the 1st floor is a veritable forest of statues, mostly offerings to Athena. These include stunning examples of 6th-century *kore* (maiden) statues: young women in draped clothing and elaborate braids. Most were recovered from a pit on the Acropolis, where the Athenians buried them after the Battle of Salamis. The youth bearing a calf, from 570 BC, is one of the rare male statues discovered.

DON'T MISS

➡ Parthenon Gallery
➡ Archaic Gallery
➡ Caryatids
➡ Ancient ruins

PRACTICALITIES

➡ Map p86
➡ ☎ 210 900 0900
➡ www.theacropolis museum.gr
➡ Dionysiou Areopagitou 15, Makrygianni
➡ adult/child €10/free
➡ ⊙ 8am-4pm Mon, to 8pm Tue-Thur & Sat-Sun, to 10pm Fri Apr-Oct, 9am-5pm Mon-Thu, to 10pm Fri, to 8pm Sat & Sun Nov-Mar
➡ Last admission is 30 mins before closing; galleries are cleared 15 mins before closing, starting from the top floor
➡ Ⓜ Akropolis

The Archaic Gallery also houses **bronze figurines** and interesting finds from temples predating the Parthenon, which were destroyed by the Persians. These include elaborate pedimental sculptures of Hercules slaying the Lernaian Hydra and a lioness devouring a bull.

On the mezzanine of the 1st floor are the five grand **Caryatids**, the world-famous maiden columns that held up the porch of the Erechtheion. (The sixth is in the British Museum.)

Parthenon Gallery

The museum's crowning glory, this top-floor glass atrium is built in alignment with the **Parthenon** (Map p92) (visible through the wraparound windows) and showcases the Parthenon's pediments, metopes and 160m frieze. When the museum opened in 2009, it marked the first time in more than 200 years that the frieze was displayed in sequence, depicting the full Panathenaic Procession. Interspersed between golden-hued originals are white plaster replicas of missing pieces – the controversial Parthenon Marbles taken to Britain by Lord Elgin in 1801.

Acropolis History

The earliest temples on the Acropolis were built during the Mycenaean era, in homage to the goddess Athena. People lived on the Acropolis until the late 6th century BC, but in 510 BC the Delphic oracle declared it the sole province of the gods.

In the 4th century BC Pericles transformed the Acropolis into a city of temples, which has come to be regarded as the zenith of Classical Greece. It was a showcase of lavishly coloured buildings and gargantuan statues, some of bronze, others of marble plated with gold and encrusted with precious stones.

Foreign occupation, inept renovations, visitors' footsteps, earthquakes and, more recently, acid rain and pollution have all taken their toll on the surviving monuments. The worst blow was in 1687, when the Venetians attacked the Turks, opening fire on the Acropolis and causing an explosion in the Parthenon – where the Turks had been storing gunpowder – and damaging all the buildings. And in 1801, Thomas Bruce, Earl of Elgin, spirited away a portion of the Parthenon frieze, which is still on display in the British Museum, despite Greece's ongoing campaign for its return.

The Acropolis became a World Heritage–listed site in 1987. Major restoration programs are ongoing. Most of the original sculptures and friezes have been moved to the Acropolis Museum, so what you see now on the hill are replicas.

TOP TIPS

➡ Buy tickets online at www.theacropolismuseum.gr to skip the queue.

➡ EU students and under-18s enter free; non-EU students and youth, plus EU citizens over 65, get reduced admission. Bring ID.

➡ Leave time for the fine museum shop (ground floor) and the film describing the history of the Acropolis (top floor).

➡ You can visit the restaurant on the 2nd floor without paying, but you must get a special ticket at the desk. The ground-floor shop and cafe are open without admission.

TAKE A BREAK

For the splendid view it provides of the Acropolis, the museum's **restaurant** (Map p86; ☑ 210 900 0915; www.theacropolismuseum.gr; Dionysiou Areopagitou 15, Makrygianni; mains €8-34; ⊗ 8am-4pm Mon, until 8pm Tue-Thu, Sat & Sun, until midnight Fri; 🛜; Ⓜ Akropoli) is already a winner. Even better is that the food, made using local seasonal ingredients, is excellent and very reasonably priced, given its location. Breakfast dishes are served up until noon, then a lunch menu continues until the end of the day.

Makrygianni, Koukaki & Filopappou Hill

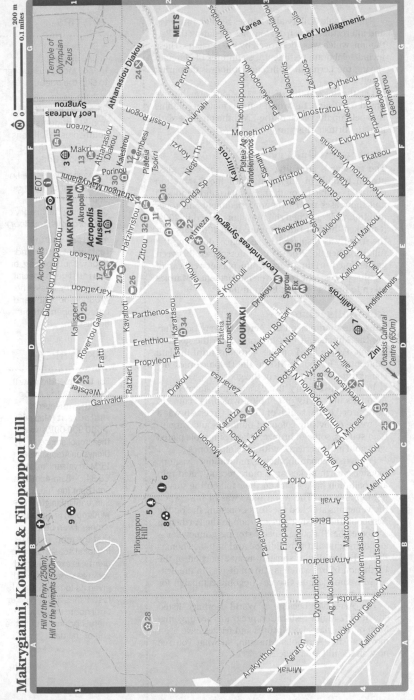

0 — 200 m
0 — 0.1 miles

Makrygianni, Koukaki & Filopappou Hill

Begun in the 6th century BC by Peisistratos, the temple was abandoned for lack of funds. Various other leaders took a stab at completing it, but it was left to Hadrian to finish the job in AD 131, thus taking more than 700 years in total to build. In typically immodest fashion, Hadrian built not just a colossal statue of Zeus, but an equally large one of himself.

Admission to the site is included with the Acropolis combo ticket (€30), which permits entry to the Acropolis and six other sites (including this one) within five days.

Final admission is 30 minutes before closing.

★ **Hadrian's Arch** MONUMENT
(Map p92; cnr Leoforos Vasilissis Olgas & Leoforos Vasilissis Amalias, Plaka; M Akropoli, Syntagma) FREE The Roman emperor Hadrian had a great affection for Athens. Although he did his fair share of spiriting its Classical artwork to Rome, he also embellished the city with many temples and infrastructure improvements. As thanks, the people of Athens erected this lofty monument of Pentelic marble in 131 AD. It now stands on the edge of one of Athens' busiest avenues.

★ **National Garden** GARDENS
(Map p122; ☏ 210 721 5019; www.cityofathens.gr; ☉ 7am-dusk; M Syntagma) FREE The former royal gardens, designed by Queen Amalia in 1838, are a pleasantly unkempt park that makes a welcome shady refuge from summer heat and traffic. Tucked among the trees are a cafe, a playground, turtle and duck ponds, and a tiny (if slightly dispiriting) zoo. The main entrance is on Leoforos Vasilissis Sofias, south of Parliament; you can also enter from Irodou Attikou to the east, or from the adjacent Zappeion (p91) to the south.

★ **Museum of Greek Popular Instruments** MUSEUM
(Map p92; ☏ 210 325 4119; Diogenous 1-3, Plaka; ☉ 10am-2pm Tue & Thu-Sun, noon-6pm Wed; M Monastiraki) FREE A single avid ethnomusicologist collected almost 1200 folk instruments; the best are on display in three floors of this house-turned-museum. Headphones let visitors listen to the *gaïda* (Greek goatskin bagpipes) and the wood planks that priests on Mt Athos use to call prayer times, among other distinctly Greek sounds. Musical performances are held in the lovely garden in summer.

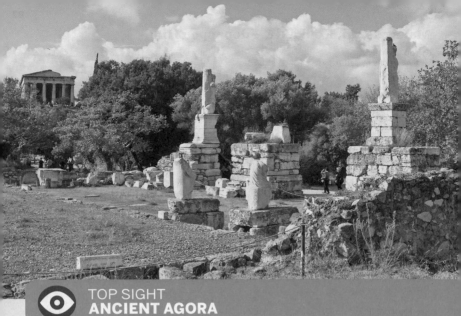

TOP SIGHT
ANCIENT AGORA

Starting in the 6th century BC, this area was Athens' commercial, political and social hub. Socrates expounded his philosophy here, and St Paul preached here. The site today has been cleared of later Ottoman buildings to reveal only classical remains. It's a green respite, with a well-restored temple, a good museum and a Byzantine church.

Stoa of Attalos

In architectural terms, a stoa is a covered portico, but the ancient model, this stoa built by King Attalos II of Pergamum (159–138 BC), was essentially an ancient shopping mall. The majestic two-storey structure, with an open-front ground floor supported by 45 Doric columns, was filled with storefronts. (Today, Greek still uses the word *stoa* for a shopping arcade.) The building, which was restored in the 1950s, holds the site museum.

Housed on both floors of the Stoa of Attalos is a museum (Map p92; ☑ 210 321 0185; http://odysseus.culture.gr; Adrianou 24, Monastiraki; admission included with Ancient Agora ticket; ⊙ 10am-3.30pm Mon, from 8.30am Tue-Sun; Ⓜ Monastiraki), which can get uncomfortably crowded when tour groups come through. Inside, you'll find neat relics that show how the *agora* was used on a daily basis: ancient voting ballots, coins, terracotta figurines and more. Some of the oldest finds date from 4000 BC. If the crowds get too much, head to the upper part of the building, which provides panoramic views over the site.

DON'T MISS

➡ Stoa of Attalos and Agora Museum

➡ Temple of Hephaistos

➡ Council House and Tholos

➡ Church of the Holy Apostles

PRACTICALITIES

➡ Map p92

➡ ☑ 210 321 0185

➡ http://odysseus. culture.gr

➡ Adrianou 24, Monastiraki

➡ adult/student/child €8/4/free

➡ ⊙ 8am-8pm Apr-Oct, to 3pm Nov-Mar

➡ Ⓜ Monastiraki

Temple of Hephaistos

On the opposite (west) end of the agora site stands the best-preserved Doric temple in Greece. Built in 449 BC by Iktinos, one of the architects of the Parthenon, it was dedicated to the god of the forge and surrounded by foundries and metalwork shops. It has 34 columns and a frieze on the eastern side depicting nine of the Twelve Labours of Hercules. In AD 1300 it was converted into the Church of Agios Georgios, then deconsecrated in 1934. In 1922 and 1923 it was a shelter for refugees from Asia Minor; iconic photos from that period show families hanging laundry among the pillars and white tents erected along the temple's base.

Stoa Foundations

Northeast of the Temple of Hephaistos are the foundations of the Stoa of Zeus Eleutherios, one of the places where Socrates spoke. Further north are the foundations of the Stoa of Basileios, as well as the Stoa Poikile, or 'Painted Stoa', for its murals of battles of myth and history, rendered by the leading artists of the day.

Council House & Tholos

Southeast of the Temple of Hephaistos, archaeologists uncovered the New Bouleuterion (Council House), where the Senate (originally created by Solon) met, while the heads of government met to the south at the circular Tholos.

Church of the Holy Apostles

This charming little Byzantine church, near the southern site gate, was built in the 11th century to commemorate St Paul's teaching in the *agora*. Following the style of the time, its external brick decorations mimic Arabic calligraphy. During the period of Ottoman rule, it underwent many changes, but between 1954 and 1957 it was stripped of its 19th-century additions and restored to its original form. It contains several fine Byzantine frescoes, which were transferred from a demolished church.

ATHENS & AROUND ANCIENT AGORA

TOP TIPS

➡ The main (and most reliable) entrance is on Adrianou; the south entrance is open only at peak times.

➡ The Temple of Hephaistos is a key photo op: it's well preserved, and you can get quite close to it.

➡ Site clearing starts 30 minutes before closing, from each end. Late in the day, visit the Temple of Hephaistos and the Stoa of Attalos first, then more central spots.

➡ If you're interested in birds, come early: the many trees here harbour a lot of life.

➡ Hours change. Call ahead to check.

PANATHENAIC FESTIVAL

The biggest event in ancient Athens was the Panathenaic Procession, the climax of the Panathenaic Festival held to venerate the goddess Athena. The route cut through the whole city, including the Ancient Agora. Scenes of the procession are vividly depicted in the 160m-long Parthenon frieze in the Acropolis Museum (p84).

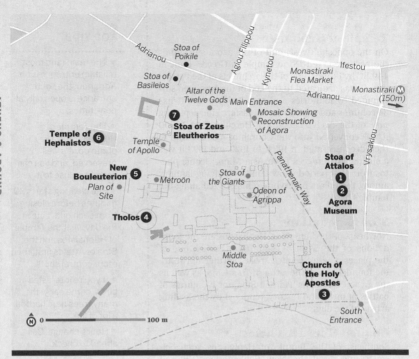

Sight Tour
Ancient Agora

START STOA OF ATTALOS
END STOA OF ZEUS ELEUTHERIOS
LENGTH TWO HOURS

As you enter the Agora, make your way first to the magnificent ❶ **Stoa of Attalos**, a two-storeyed portico, replete with columns, built by the king of Pergamum in the 2nd century BC as a shopping arcade. Originally its facade was painted red and blue. People gathered here to watch the Panathenaic Procession. The ❷ **Agora Museum**, inside the stoa, holds some of the site's best finds, and illustrates how the area was used. It is surrounded by ancient statues of the gods.

Continue to the southern side of the site to the charming ❸ **Church of the Holy Apostles**. The exterior brick patterns are an imitation of Islamic Kufic-style decoration, showing the cross-pollination of style in this period. Inside, it's decorated with 17th-century frescoes.

Walking northwest across the site, you'll pass the circular ❹ **Tholos**, where the heads of government met, and what was the ❺ **New Bouleuterion** (Council House), where the Senate met.

On the *agora*'s western edge is the striking ❻ **Temple of Hephaistos**, god of the forge, which was surrounded by foundries and metalwork shops. It was one of the first buildings of Pericles' rebuilding programme. The last service held there was in 1834, to honour King Otto's arrival in Athens.

Northeast of the temple, you'll pass the foundation of the ❼ **Stoa of Zeus Eleutherios**, one of the places where Socrates expounded his philosophy.

ATHENS WITH CHILDREN

Athens is short on playgrounds, but between ice cream and street musicians and stray cats, there's plenty to keep kids amused. It helps too that children are welcome everywhere; at casual restaurants they're often encouraged to run off and play together while the adults eat.

The shady National Garden (p87) has a playground, duck pond and small (if somewhat dismal) zoo; immediately south, **Zappeion** (Map p122; Leoforos Vasilissis Amalias; Ⓜ Syntagma) **FREE** also has an enclosed, shaded playground. Beside the coast there are much bigger facilities at Stavros Niarchos Park (p145) and **Flisvos Park** (☑210 988 5140; https://parkoflisvos.gr; Palaio Faliro; ☺24hr; ⛟; 🚊 Parko Flisvou) **FREE**.

The **Museum of Greek Children's Art** (Map p92; ☑210 331 2621; www. childrensartmuseum.gr; Kodrou 9, Plaka; €3; ☺10am-2pm Tue-Sat, 11am-2pm Sun; Ⓜ Syntagma) has a room set aside where children can learn about Ancient Greece. The **Hellenic Children's Museum** (Map p122; ☑210 331 2995; www.hcm.gr; Leoforos Vasileos Georgiou B 17-19, Athens Conservatoire; ☺11am-7pm Wed, to 3pm Thu-Sun; ⛟; Ⓜ Evangelismos) **FREE** is a good place to meet Greek kids. Older children may like the War Museum (p106), where they can climb into the cockpit of a WWII plane and other aircraft.

Younger children may enjoy Greece's traditional shadow-puppet tradition. Shows are in Greek, but are slapstick, with lots of music. In summer, visit **Theatro Skion Tasou Konsta** (☑210 322 7507; www.fkt.gr; Flisvos Park, Palaio Faliro; €3.50; ☺8.30pm Fri-Sun Jun-Sep; ⛟; 🚊 Park Flisvou); in winter, check the Melina Merkouri Cultural Centre (p77).

Anafiotika
AREA

(Map p92; Stratonos, Plaka; Ⓜ Monastiraki, Akropoli) Clinging to the north slope of the Acropolis, the tiny Anafiotika district is a beautiful, architecturally distinct subdistrict of Plaka. In the mid-1800s, King Otto hired builders from Anafi to build a new palace. In their homes here, they mimicked their island's architecture, all whitewashed cubes, bedecked with bougainvillea and geraniums. The area now is a clutch of about 40 homes, linked by footpaths just wide enough for people and stray cats.

It's easy to completely miss the entrances to the district. On the west side, head uphill near the Church of the Metamorphosis on Theorias. On the east side, zigzag up Stratonos. On the way, you'll pass a surprise olive grove/local park.

Church of Agioi Anargyroi
CHURCH

(Metochi of the Holy Sepulchre; Map p92; ☑210 322 5810; https://jerusalem-patriarchate.info; Erechtheos 18, Plaka; Ⓜ Akropoli) Tucked away in Plaka, this 17th-century church is worth visiting any time for its peaceful courtyard and beautiful interior decoration. On the evening of Easter Saturday, a 'holy flame' is flown from the mother Church of the Holy Sepulchre in Jerusalem, and in ritual said to be over a millennium old, the faithful pack out the church to light their candles from it.

Plateia Syntagmatos
SQUARE

(Syntagma Sq; Map p92; Syntagma; Ⓜ Syntagma) Generally considered the centre of Athens, this square is a transport hub and general hang-out spot, especially on warm summer evenings when young people and families lounge around the central fountain. Parliament, where the *syntagma* (constitution) was granted in 1843, is directly across the road, so the square is also the epicentre for any demonstrations or strikes.

National Historical Museum
MUSEUM

(Map p92; ☑210 323 7617; www.nhmuseum. gr; Stadiou 13, Syntagma; adult/child €3/free; ☺9am-2pm Tue-Sun; Ⓜ Syntagma) This grand collection of swords, ship figureheads and portraits of moustachioed generals is a bit short on signage, and is best for people who already know something about modern Greek history and the many battles of the 19th century that built the nation. This includes the battle of Messolongi, where Lord Byron fought; the museum owns the camp bed on which he died of malaria, among other effects – though they are often out on loan.

Syntagma, Plaka & Monastiraki

Sarri
Nika
Ogygou
Agathartou
Agion Anargyron
Aristofanous
Eshylou
Lepeniotou
Taki
Plateia
Iroön
Pallados
Plateia
Karamanou
Vyssis
Agathonos
57
Nikiou
Leokoriou
Ivis
Navarhou Apostoli
Avliton
Mikonos
Esopou
Histokopidou
Plateia
Iroön
Protogenous
Athinas
41
Voreou
Limbona
Vasilikis
48
61
79

Arionos
Karaïskaki
Pittaki
Agias Theklas
Agias Eleousis
Maouli
PSYRRI
Avramiotou
82
Karori
Eolou
Plateia
Agia Irini
80
60

Ermou

99
Thisiou
Astingos
Agiou Filippou
Kynetou
Plateia
Avyssinias
69
54
101
76
TAF
8
102
Plateia
Monastirakiou
Plateia
Dimopratiriou
Ermou
58
62
Adrianou
105
Ifestou
97
93
100
Pandrosou
Histopoulou

35
2 ◉ **Ancient
Agora**
11
Vrysakiou
Nisou
Monastiraki
26
Adrianou
22
28
MONASTIRAKI
Kolonou
Kapnikareas

Kladou
Areos
Dexippou
Adrianou
Plateia Arhaia
Agoras
Kalogrioni
**Museum of Greek
Popular Instruments**
4
Peikilis
Epaminonda
Pelopida

7
Roman Agora
37
Markou Aureliou
Kyrristou
15
Minisikleous
Polygnotou
Panos
Lyssiou
Dioskouron
Mitroou
29
Tholou
Thrasyvoulou
Theorias
84 Erotokri
18
Prytaniou
Aretousas
Klepsydras
24

Areopagus
Hill
13
Theorias
Theorias
12
ANAFIOTIKA

21
1 ◉ **Acropolis**
16
32
6 ◉ **Parthenon**
34
10

5 ◉ **Odeon of
Herodes Atticus**
33

36

Apostolou Pavlou
Dionysiou Areopagitou
Rovertou Galli
Filopappou
Hill

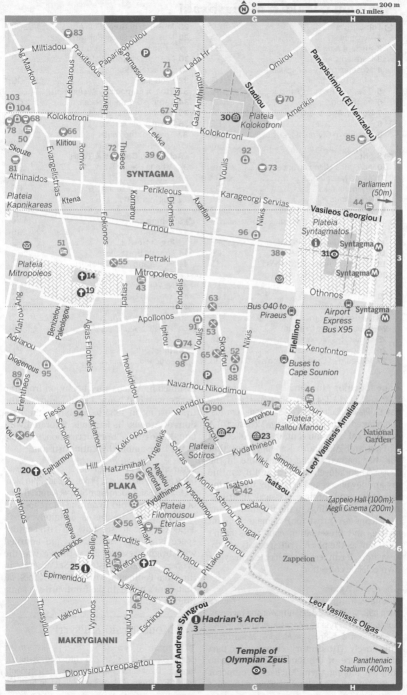

Syntagma, Plaka & Monastiraki

◉ Top Sights

◉ Sights

◉ Activities, Courses & Tours

◉ Sleeping

◉ Eating

Kanellopoulos Museum
MUSEUM

(Map p92; ☑ 210 324 4447; https://pacf.gr; Theorias 12, Plaka; adult/child €4/2; ⊘ 8am-3pm Tue-Sun, reduced hours in low season; Ⓜ Monastiraki) A neoclassical mansion contains the collection of Paul and Alexandra Kanellopoulos that was bequeathed to the Greek state in the 1970s. There's lovely classical and Byzantine art and jewellery, and especially transfixing terracotta and bronze classical figurines. Also note the ceilings in the Byzantine wing (the icons are great too). Signage is a bit sparse, and preservation conditions aren't ideal, but as the place is often empty of other visitors, it can feel like you're touring your own eclectic collection.

Church of Agios Nikolaos Rangavas
CHURCH

(Map p92; ☑ 210 322 8193; http://enoria-ragkavas. blogspot.com; Prytaniou 1, cnr Epiharmou, Plaka; ⊘ 8am-noon & 5-8pm; Ⓜ Akropoli, Monastiraki) This lovely 11th-century church was part of the palace of the Rangavas family, who counted among them Michael I, emperor of Byzantium. The church bell was the first installed in Athens after liberation from the Turks (who had banned them), and was the first to ring in 1833 to announce the freedom of Athens. Its facade is decorated with faux-Kufic Arabic brick decoration, in vogue at the time among Byzantine artisans.

Church of Agia Ekaterini
CHURCH

(Map p92; Lysikratous 3, Plaka; ⊘ 8am-2pm Mon-Fri, to noon Sat, 7.30am-11pm Sun; Ⓜ Akropoli) One of the few very old Byzantine churches that is open regularly, this is definitely worth a peek inside to see how an 11th-century space is still in vibrant use and adorned with bright frescoes. For a time it was the property of the Monastery of St Catherine in the Sinai Peninsula, which is how it took on that saint's name. In the front yard are some Roman ruins.

◉ Monastiraki & Psyrri

★ Roman Agora
HISTORIC SITE

(Map p92; ☑ 210 324 5220; http://odysseus.culture.gr; Dioskouron, Monastiraki; adult/student/child €6/3/free; ⊘ 8am-3pm Mon-Fri, to 5pm Sat

& Sun, mosque from 10am; Ⓜ Monastiraki) This was the city's market area under Roman rule, and it occupied a much larger area than the current site borders. You can see a lot from outside the fence, but it's worth going in for a closer look at the well-preserved **Gate of Athena Archegetis**, the propylaeum (entrance gate) to the market, as well as an Ottoman mosque and the ingenious and beautiful **Tower of the Winds** (Map p92), on the east side of the site.

The gate, formed by four Doric columns, was financed by Julius Caesar and erected sometime during 10 BC. To the right of the entry, look also for the outlines of what was a 68-seat public latrine. Squatting atop one wing of the *agora* is the 17th-century **Fethiye Mosque**, now restored and housing temporary exhibitions. The mosque's interior frescoes have been lost – except for a tiny patch high on the back wall.

Admission to the site is included with the Acropolis combo ticket (€30), which permits entry to the Acropolis and six other sites (including this one) within five days.

Museum Alex Mylona   MUSEUM
(Map p102; ☑ 210 321 5717; http://mouseioalex mylona.blogspot.com; Plateia Agion Asomaton 5, Psyrri; adult/concession €4/2; ⏱ 11am-7pm Tue, Wed, Fri & Sat, to 10pm Thu, to 4pm Sun; Ⓜ Thissio, Monastiraki) The permanent collection here is superminimalist sculpture and paintings by Athenian grande dame Alex Mylona, who died in 2016. The creatively refurbished mansion also hosts contemporary shows, and often includes dynamic video and sculpture by Alex's daughter, Eleni. Make sure you go to the roof for a great view of the area. Entrance is on Lepeniotou.

Museum of Greek Folk Art   MUSEUM
(Map p92; ☑ 210 322 9031; www.mnep.gr; Adrianou & Areos, Monastiraki; Ⓜ Monastiraki) This museum closed in 2015 to begin its transition to this new site at Adrianou. When it reopens in 2020, it will display secular and religious folk art, mainly from the 18th and 19th centuries, including Greek traditional costumes, embroidery, pottery, weaving and puppets, and a reconstructed traditional village house with paintings by Theophilos.

TOP SIGHT
NATIONAL ARCHAEOLOGICAL MUSEUM

The **National Archaeological Museum** houses the world's finest collection of Greek antiquities. The enormous 19th-century neoclassical building holds room upon room filled with more than 10,000 examples of sculpture, pottery, jewellery, frescoes and more. You simply can't appreciate it all in one go – but whatever you do lay eyes on will be a treat.

Prehistoric Collection & Mycenaen Antiquities

Directly ahead as you enter the museum is the prehistoric collection, showcasing some of the most important pieces of Mycenaean, Neolithic and Cycladic art, many in solid gold. The fabulous collection of Mycenaean antiquities (gallery 4) is the museum's tour de force.

A highlight is the great death mask of beaten gold is commonly known as the Mask of Agamemnon, the king who, according to legend, attacked Troy in the 12th century BC – but this is hardly certain. Heinrich Schliemann, the archaeologist who set to prove that Homer's epics were true tales, and not just myth, unearthed the mask at Mycenae in 1876. But now some archaeologists have found the surrounding grave items date from centuries earlier. And one researcher even asserts that Schliemann, a master of self-promotion, forged it completely.

The exquisite Vaphio gold cups, showing scenes of men taming wild bulls, are regarded as among the finest surviving examples of Mycenaean art. They were found in a *tholos* (Mycenaean tomb shaped like a beehive) at Vaphio, near Sparta.

DON'T MISS

→ Mask of Agamemnon
→ Vaphio gold cups
→ Sounion Kouros
→ Artemision Bronze
→ Varvakeion Athena
→ Artemision Jockey
→ Antikythera Mechanism

PRACTICALITIES

→ Map p102
→ ☎ 213 214 4800
→ www.namuseum.gr
→ Patision 44, Exarhia
→ adult/child €10/free mid-Apr–Oct; €5/free Nov–mid-Apr
→ ☉ 8am-8pm Wed-Mon, 12.30pm-8pm Tue mid-Apr–Oct, reduced hours Nov–mid-Apr
→ ☐ 2, 3, 4, 5 or 11 to Polytechneio, Ⓜ Viktoria

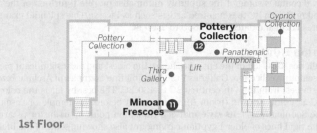

1st Floor

- *Cypriot Collection*
- *Pottery Collection*
- **Pottery Collection** 12
- *Panathenaic Amphorae*
- *Thira Gallery*
- *Lift*
- **Minoan Frescoes** 11

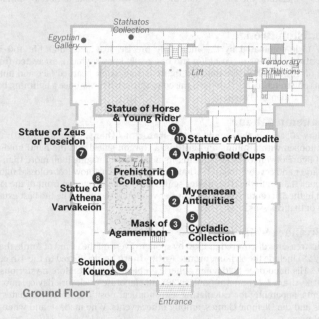

Ground Floor

- *Stathatos Collection*
- *Egyptian Gallery*
- *Lift*
- *Temporary Exhibitions*
- **Statue of Horse & Young Rider** 9
- **Statue of Zeus or Poseidon** 7
- **Statue of Aphrodite** 10
- **Vaphio Gold Cups** 4
- *Lift*
- **Prehistoric Collection** 1
- **Statue of Athena Varvakeion** 8
- **Mycenaean Antiquities** 2
- **Mask of Agamemnon** 3
- **Cycladic Collection** 5
- **Sounion Kouros** 6
- *Entrance*

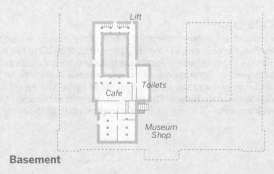

Basement

- *Lift*
- *Toilets*
- *Cafe*
- *Museum Shop*

Cycladic Collection

Gallery 6 contains some of the superbly minimalist marble figurines of the 3rd and 2nd millennia BC that inspired artists such as Picasso. One splendid example measures 1.52m and dates from 2600 to 2300 BC.

Sounion Kouros

The galleries to the left of the entrance house the oldest and most significant pieces of the sculpture collection. Galleries 7 to 13 exhibit fine examples of Archaic *kouroi* (male statues) from the 7th century BC to 480 BC. The best by far is the colossal 600 BC Sounion Kouros (room 8), which stood before the Temple of Poseidon at Cape Sounion (p147). Its style marks a transition point in art history, starting with the rigid lines of older Egyptian carving but also showing some of the lifelike qualities – including the smile – that the Greeks would come to develop in later centuries.

Artemision Bronze

Gallery 15 is dominated by the incredibly precise, just-larger-than-life 460 BC bronze statue of Zeus or Poseidon (no one really knows which), excavated from the sea off Evia in 1928. The muscled figure has an iconic bearded face and holds his arms outstretched, his right arm raised to throw what was once a lightning bolt (if Zeus) or trident (if Poseidon).

Varvakeion Athena

In Gallery 20, admire the details on the statue of Athena, made in 200 AD: the helmet topped with a sphinx and griffins, a Gorgon shield and the hand holding a small figure of winged Nike (missing its head). Now imagine it all more than 10 times larger and covered in gold – that was the legendary, now-lost colossal figure of Athena (11.5m tall) that the master sculptor Pheidias erected in front of the Parthenon in the 5th century BC. This daintier version is thought to be the best extant replica of that colossus.

Antikythera Shipwreck

Precious treasures discovered in 1900 by sponge divers off the island of Antikythera (gallery 28) include the striking bronze Antikythera Youth, forged in the 4th century BC. His hand once held some spherical object, now lost. More mysterious is the Antikythera Mechanism (gallery 38), an elaborate clockwork device, now in fragments, apparently for calculating astronomical positions as well as dates of eclipses and the Olympic Games, among other events. Who made it, and when, is still unknown.

Egyptian Collection

The two-room (40 and 41) gallery presents the best of the museum's significant Egyptian collection, the only one in Greece. Dating from 5000 BC to the Roman conquest, artefacts include mummies, Fayum portraits and bronze figurines.

The bulk of the museum's Egyptian collection was donated in the late 19th and early 20th centuries by two wealthy Greek residents of Egypt. The Egyptian government also donated nine mummies. The relics provide critical historical context for Ancient Greek art, some of which took early inspiration from the culture just across the sea.

Attic black-figured pottery

ottery Collection

e superb pottery collection (galleries 49 to 56) traces the velopment of ceramics from the Bronze Age through the otogeometric and Geometric periods, to the famous **Attic ack-figured pottery** (6th century BC), and **red-figured ttery** (late 5th to early 4th centuries BC). Other uniquely henian vessels are the **Attic White Lekythoi**, slender vases picting scenes at tombs.

In the centre of gallery 56 are ceramic vases presented to e winners of the Panathenaic Games. Each one contained from the sacred olive trees of Athens; victors might have ceived up to 140 of them. The vases are painted with scenes om the relevant sport (wrestling, in this case) on one side and armed Athena *promachos* (leading warrior) on the other.

ockey of Artemision

Gallery 21 is a find from the shipwreck off Evia excavat- in 1928. This delicately rendered **bronze horse and rider** tes from the 2nd century BC; only a few parts were found at st, and it was finally reassembled in 1972. Opposite the horse e several lesser-known but equally exquisite works, such as e **statue of Aphrodite** showing the demure nude goddess uggling to hold her draped gown over herself.

DON'T MISS

ART GALLERIES

Athens has a dynamic and vibrant contemporary arts scene. Download the **Athens Contemporary Art Map** (http://athensartmap.net) or pick up a paper copy at galleries and cafes around town. The following are some of our favourite spaces.

TAF (The Art Foundation; Map p92; ☑ 210 323 8757; http://theartfoundation.metamatic.gr; Normanou 5, Monastiraki; ☺ noon-9pm Mon-Sat, to 7pm Sun, cafe-bar open late; Ⓜ Monastiraki) Whether you want a shot of art, a clever design morsel or a refreshing drink, stop in at TAF, a just-barely updated complex of 1870s brick buildings. The central courtyard is a cafe-bar that fills with an eclectic young crowd, and the surrounding rooms act as galleries, DJ space and an excellent souvenir shop. Events are usually free.

A.antonopoulou.art (Map p102; ☑ 210 321 4994; www.aaart.gr; 4th fl, Aristofanous 20, Psyrri; ☺ 2-8pm Wed-Fri, noon-4pm Sat; Ⓜ Monastiraki) One of the original galleries to open in Psyrri's warehouses, this impressive art space hosts exhibitions of contemporary Greek and international art, including installations, video art and photography.

Bernier/Eliades (Map p116; ☑ 210 341 3935; www.bernier-eliades.gr; Eptachalkou 11, Thisio; ☺ 10.30am-6.30pm Tue-Fri, noon-4pm Sat; Ⓜ Thissio) This gallery, established in 1977 and occupying this grand old home since 1999, showcases prominent Greek artists and an impressive list of international artists, from abstract American impressionists to British pop. Shows change roughly every six weeks and tend towards the minimalistic.

The Breeder (Map p74; ☑ 210 331 7527; http://thebreedersystem.com; Iasonos 45, Metaxourgio; ☺ noon-8pm Tue-Fri, to 6pm Sat; Ⓜ Metaxourghiou) Press the buzzer to gain entry to this hip concrete warehouse-style art gallery that displays a variety of works over two levels. Every year they reinvent the exterior design of the gallery as an art project.

Allouche Benias Gallery (Map p122; ☑ 210 338 9111; http://allouchebenias.com; Kanari 1, Kolonaki; ☺ 11am-8pm Tue-Fri, until 5pm Sat; Ⓜ Syntagma) Occupying the beautifully restored 1882 Deligeorgis Mansion, designed by Ernst Ziller, this gallery made a splash on the local art scene when it opened in 2018. There's usually a couple of different shows a year with contemporary pieces in all media by both international artists and local talents such as Filippos Kavakas and Elias Kafouros.

CAN (Map p122; ☑ 210 339 0833; www.can-gallery.com; Anagnostopoulou 42, Kolonaki; ☺ noon-3pm & 5-8pm Mon-Fri, noon-4pm Sat; Ⓜ Syntagma) This fresh entry on the Kolonaki gallery scene, founded by art specialist Christina Androulidaki, has a stable of emerging and midcareer contemporary Greek and international artists. In August it's open by appointment only.

Zoumboulakis Gallery (Map p122; ☑ 210 363 4454; www.zoumboulakis.gr; Kriezotou 6, Kolonaki; ☺ 10am-3pm Mon & Wed, to 8pm Tue, Thu & Fri, to 4pm Sat; Ⓜ Syntagma) An excellent selection of limited-edition prints and posters by leading Greek artists, including Yannis Tsarouchis, Dimitris Mytaras and Alekos Fassianos, plus other decorative objects. The curators also have a contemporary space on the *plateia* (square) in Kolonaki.

The museum has two annexes currently open: **22 Panos** (Map p92; ☑ 210 321 4972; www.mnep.gr; Panos 22, Plaka; adult/child €2/free; ☺ 8am-3pm Tue-Sun) and the **Bath House of the Winds** (Map p92; ☑ 210 324 4340; www.mnep.gr; Kyrristou 8, Plaka; adult/child €2/free; ☺ 8am-3pm Wed-Mon). It also manages the **Mosque of Tzistarakis** (Map p92; ☑ 210 324 2066; www.mnep.gr; Areos 1, Monastiraki), which is occasionally open for temporary exhibitions.

Church of Agios Eleftherios   CHURCH
(Little Metropolis; Map p92; Plateia Mitropoleos, Monastiraki; Ⓜ Monastiraki) This 12th-century church, dedicated to both Agios Eleftherios and Panagia Gorgoepikoos (Virgin Swift to Hear), is Athens' religious history in one tiny building. The cruciform-style marble church was erected on the ruins of an ancient temple and its exterior is a mix of medieval beasts and ancient gods in bas-relief, and columns appropriated from

older structures. It was once the city's cathedral, but now stands in the shadows of the much larger **new cathedral** (Map p92; ☎210 322 1308; http://iaath.gr; ⊙7am-7pm).

Hadrian's Library   RUINS

(Map p92; ☎210 324 9350; http://odysseus. culture.gr; Areos 3, Monastiraki; adult/child €4/ free; ⊙8am-3pm; Ⓜ Monastiraki) These are the remains of the largest structure erected by Hadrian (2nd century AD). Not just a library, it also held music and lecture rooms. It was laid out as a typical Roman forum, with a pool in the centre of a courtyard bordered by 100 columns. The library's west wall, by the site entrance, has been restored. Beyond are only traces of the library, as well as two churches, built in the 7th and 12th centuries.

◉ Gazi, Keramikos & Exarhia

★Kerameikos   HISTORIC SITE

(Map p116; ☎210 346 3552; http://odysseus.culture. gr; Ermou 148, Keramikos; adult/child incl museum €8/free; ⊙8am-8pm, reduced hours in low season; Ⓜ Thissio) This lush, tranquil site is named for the potters who settled it around 3000 BC. It was used as a cemetery through the 6th century AD. The grave markers give a sense of ancient life; numerous marble *stelae* (grave markers) are carved with vivid portraits and familiar scenes.

The site was uncovered in 1861 during the construction of Pireos St; it once sat on the clay-rich banks of the Iridanos River. There's an excellent small **museum** here.

★Museum of Islamic Art   MUSEUM

(Map p116; ☎210 325 1311; www.benaki.org; Agion Asomaton 22, Keramikos; adult/student/ child €9/7/free; ⊙10am-6pm Thu-Sun; Ⓜ Thissio) While not particularly large, this museum houses a significant collection of Islamic art. Four floors of a mansion display, in ascending chronological order, exceptionally beautiful weaving, jewellery, porcelain and even a marble-floored reception room from a 17th-century Cairo mansion. Informative signage provides the detail on what you're seeing. In the basement, part of Athens' ancient Themistoklean wall is exposed. The rooftop cafe, with a great view of Keramikos, has a lovely mural: *Imagine a Palm Tree* by Narvine G Khan-Dossos.

Benaki Museum
at 138 Pireos St   MUSEUM

(Map p116; ☎210 345 3111; www.benaki.org; Pireos 138, Rouf; adult/concession from €6/3; ⊙10am-6pm Thu & Sun, until 10pm Fri & Sat, closed Aug; Ⓜ Kerameikos) While the main Benaki Museum of Greek Culture (p104) displays the classical and traditional, this annexe focuses on modern and inventive. Apart from a few canvases by contemporary painters that are portraits of founder Antonis Benakis, there are no permanent exhibitions here, rather several rotating temporary exhibits, which can be excellent. Also check the schedule of musical performances in its atrium courtyard. It has a pleasant cafe and an excellent gift shop.

OFF THE BEATEN TRACK

KYPSELI

Kypseli, a 15-minute walk north of Exarhia, was once one of the most desirable residential areas of Athens, on a par with Kolonaki. It's not so ritzy today, even though if you keep an eye out there's still the odd pretty neoclassical mansion or art deco block to be found among the dense streets of identikit five-storey Athens apartment blocks.

The neighbourhood's social centre is the Fokionos Negri pedestrian strip of park, lined with cafes. Here you'll find an interesting new development at the **Kypseli Municipal Market** (https://athens.impacthub.net/dimotiki-agora-kypselis; Fokionos Negri 42, Kypseli; ⊙8am-8pm Mon-Fri, until 2pm Sat; Ⓜ Victoria). The 1935 modernist building now houses a range of social projects including the first physical store for the nonprofit business **Wise Greece** (www.en.wisegreece.com), which sells some 2500 good-quality food products from across the country. For every product sold, a percentage of the profit goes into a fund to buy food for people in need.

The NGO **We Need Books** (https://weneedbooks.org; Evias 7, Kypseli) has also set up nearby. This free library, play space and social integration centre has been set up to help marginalised and vulnerable people, including refugees in Athens. They welcome donations of books and they sometimes host discussions and events in English.

Psyrri & Exarhia

A | B | C | D

Ag Pavlou
Sahini
Paleologou K
Tremper
Hiou
Iliou
P Saron
Liosson
Mayer
Aharnon
Kapnokoptiriou
Aristotelous
Marni
Polytehniou
Stournari

Akominatou
Tarella
Sonierou
Mezonos
Mayer
Solomou

Pouqueville
Favierou
Mayer
Marni
Plateia
Vathis
Kapodistriou

Victor Hugo
Halkokondyli
OMONIA

Deligianni
Karolou
Veranzerou
Xouthou

Metaxourghio
Ierotheou
Nikiforou
Satovrianidou
Sokratous
28 Oktovriou

Plateia
Karaiskaki
Koumoundourou
Menandrou
3 Septemvriou
Dorou
Gladstonos

Agiou Konstantinou
34
Plateia Agiou
Konstantinou
Plateia
Omonias

Meg Alexandrou
Kallergi
Vilara
Geraniou
Omonia

Leonidou
Keramikou
Delgeorgi
Voulgari
Zinonos
Eolou

Kolokinthous
Kolonou
Agisilaou
6
Anaxagora
Menandrou
Geraniou
Night Bus 500
to Piraeus
14
Lykourgou

Akadimou
Iasonos
Pireos (Tsaldari Panagi)
30
Sofokleous
Klisthenous
Sokratous
Athinas
Efpolidos
Plateia
Kotzia
Kratinou
Stavrou
Georgiou

Sapfous
Plateia
Theatrou
Theatrou
19
Armodiou
13
Sofokleous

Plateia
Eleftherias
(Koumoundourou)
Korinis
Epikourou
24
Diplari
Theatrou
23
Aristogitonos
39
45

Buses to
Elefsina
Sahtouri
Evripidou
37
17
Eshylou
Agiou Dimitriou
Kalamida
9
42
Evripidou

Dipylou
Kranaou
Sarri
10
Aristofanous
1
Polykliitou

Kriezi
PSYRRI
Plateia Agion
Anargyron
Plateia
Karamanou
Hrysospiliotissis

Tombazi
12
Sarri
Agion Anargyron
Plateia
Iroon
Pallados
Vyssis
Ag Markou
Miltiadou

Leoloriou
Oxygou
Taki
Mikonos
7
18
Protogenous
Athinas
Voreou
Nikiou
Eolou

Asomaton
Agion
Lepeniotou
Ivis
Navarhou Apostoli
Hristokopidou
16
Esopou
20
26
Agias Theklas
Miaouli
Aramindou
Karori
Plateia
Agia Irini

Plateia
Agion
Asomaton
3
Aviiton
Arionos
Karaiskaki
Pittaki
41
Agias Irinis
Plateia
Agia Irini
Kalamiotou

Thissio
Erm23ou
Protogenous

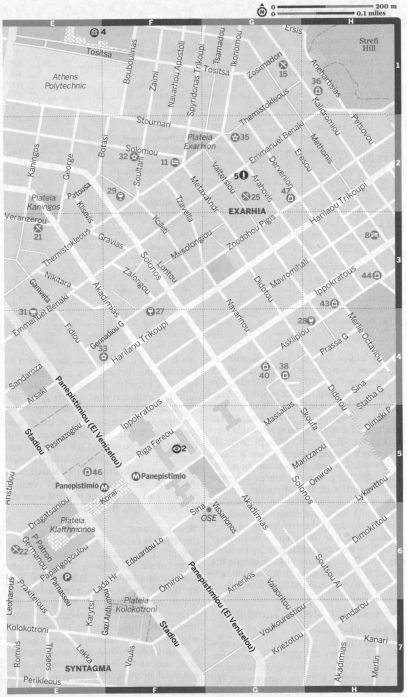

Strefi
Hill

Athens
Polytechnic

Plateia
Exarhion

EXARHIA

Plateia
Kaningos

Veranzerou

Plateia
Klafthmonos

Stadiou

Panepistimio

Panepistimiou (El Venizelou)

Riga Fereou

OSE

Plateia
Kolokotroni

Stadiou

Panepistimiou (El Venizelou)

SYNTAGMA

Psyrri & Exarhia

◎ Sights
1	A.antonopoulou.art	B6
2	Athens University	F5
3	Museum Alex Mylona	A7
4	National Archaeological Museum	E1
5	No Land For the Poor Mural	G2
6	Praying Hands Mural	B4

⬤ Sleeping
7	18 Micon Street	B7
8	Athens Quinta Hostel	H3
9	Cecil	C6
10	City Circus	B6
11	Exarchion	F2
12	Foundry Hotel	A6
13	Fresh Hotel	C5
14	Grecotel Pallas Athena	C4

✖ Eating
15	Ama Lachei stis Nefelis	G1
16	Atlantikos	B7
17	Avli	C6
18	Bougatsadiko Thessaloniki	B7
19	Diporto Agoras	C5
20	Gostijo	B7
21	I Kriti	E3
22	Kalderimi	E6
23	Karamanlidika tou Fani	C5
24	Telis	B5

25	Yiantes	G2

◎ Drinking & Nightlife
26	Little Kook	B7
27	Lotos	F4
28	Nabokov	H4
29	Revolt	F2
30	Romantso	C4
31	Taf Coffee	E4

⬤ Entertainment
32	AN Club	F2
33	Feidiou 2 Music Cafe	F4
34	National Theatre	B3
35	Vox	G2

⬤ Shopping
36	Exarhia Weekly Market	H1
37	Fotsi	C6
38	Free Thinking Zone	G4
39	Fruit & Vegetable Market	C5
40	Koukoutsi	G4
41	Melissinos Art	C7
42	Pan-Pol	C6
43	Plastikourgeio	H3
44	Redo	H3
45	Varvakios Agora	C5
46	Xylouris	E5
47	Zacharias	G2

Industrial Gas Museum   NOTABLE BUILDING
(Technopolis; Map p116; ☑ 210 347 5535; https://gasmuseum.gr; Pireos 100, Gazi; adult/child €1/free; ⊙ 10am-8pm Tue, Wed, Fri & Sat, to 9pm Thu & Sun mid-Oct–mid-Apr, to 6pm Tue, Wed, Fri & Sat, to 9pm Thu & Sun mid–Apr–mid-Oct; Ⓜ Kerameikos) It's fascinating to follow the walking route that runs through the old **gasworks** (Map p116; ☑ 210 346 7322; www.technopolis-athens.com; Pireos 100, Gazi; Ⓜ Kerameikos) in Gazi, in operation from 1862 until 1984. The preserved complex of furnaces and industrial buildings from the mid-19th century appear like giant art installations. Photos and interactive elements provide an idea of what the works were like when in operation. Make sure you go up the watchtower of the New Watergas building for a panoramic city view. There's is also a pleasant cafe on-site as well as a kids' playground. Note that the site is often used for music and other events.

◎ Kolonaki, Mets & Pangrati

★ **Benaki Museum of Greek Culture**   MUSEUM
(Map p122; ☑ 210 367 1000; www.benaki.org; Koumbari 1, cnr Leoforos Vasilissis Sofias, Kolonaki; adult/student/child €9/7/free, 6pm-midnight Thu free; ⊙ 10am-6pm Mon, Wed, Fri & Sat, to midnight Thu, to 4pm Sun; Ⓜ Syntagma, Evangelismos) In 1930 Antonis Benakis – a politician's son born in Alexandria, Egypt, in the late 19th century – endowed what is perhaps the finest museum in Greece. Its three floors showcase impeccable treasures from the Bronze Age up to WWII. Especially gorgeous are the Byzantine icons and the extensive collection of Greek regional costumes, as well as complete sitting rooms from Macedonian mansions, intricately carved and painted. Benakis had such a good eye that even the agricultural tools are beautiful.

★ **Byzantine & Christian Museum**   MUSEUM
(Map p122; ☑ 213 213 9500; www.byzantinemuseum.gr; Leoforos Vasilissis Sofias 22, Kolonaki; adult/student/child €8/4/free; ⊙ 12.30-8pm Tue, from 8am Wed-Sun Apr-Oct, reduced hours Nov-Mar; Ⓜ Evangelismos) This outstanding museum, based in the 1848 Villa Ilissia, offers exhibition halls, most of them underground, crammed with religious art. The exhibits go chronologically, charting the gradual and fascinating shift from ancient traditions to Christian ones, and the flourishing of a distinctive Byzantine style. Of course there are icons, but also del-

icate frescoes (some salvaged from a church and installed on floating panels) and more personal remnants of daily life.

⭐ Museum of Cycladic Art   MUSEUM
(Map p122; ☑ 210 722 8321; https://cycladic.gr; Neofytou Douka 4, Kolonaki; adult/child €7/free, Mon €3.50, special exhibits €10; ⏱ 10am-5pm Mon, Wed, Fri & Sat, to 8pm Thu, 11am-5pm Sun; Ⓜ Evangelismos) The 1st floor of this exceptional private museum is dedicated to the iconic minimalist marble Cycladic figurines, dating from 3000 BC to 2000 BC. They inspired many 20th-century artists, such as Picasso and Modigliani, with their simplicity and purity of form. Most are surprisingly small, considering their outsize influence, though one is almost human size. The rest of the museum features Greek and Cypriot art dating from 2000 BC to the 4th century AD.

Lykavittos Hill   LANDMARK
(Map p74; www.lycabettushill.com; Kolonaki; Ⓜ Evangelismos) The 277m summit of Lykavittos – 'Hill of Wolves', from ancient times, when it was wilder than it is now – gives the finest panoramas of the city and the Attic basin, *nefos* (pollution haze) permitting. Perched on the summit is the little **Chapel of Agios Georgios**, floodlit like a beacon over the city at night. Walk up the path from the top of Loukianou in Kolonaki, or take the 10-minute funicular railway (p139) from the top of Ploutarhou.

⭐ Basil & Elise Goulandris Foundation   MUSEUM
(Map p122; ☑ 210 725 2895; https://goulandris.gr; Eratosthenous 13, Pangrati; Ⓜ Akropoli) Opened in October 2019, this new museum showcases the collection of modern and contemporary artworks belonging to shipping magnate Basil Goulandris and his wife Elise. Alongside pieces from the likes of top European artists including Cézanne, Van Gogh, Picasso and Giacometti are works from pioneering Greek painters such as Parthenis, Vasiliou, Hadjikyriakos-Ghikas, Tsarouchis and Moralis.

⭐ Panathenaic Stadium   HISTORIC SITE
(Kallimarmaro; Map p122; ☑ 210 752 2985; www.panathenaicstadium.gr; Leoforos Vasileos Konstantinou, Pangrati; adult/student/child €5/2.50/free; ⏱ 8am-7pm Mar-Oct, to 5pm Nov-Feb; 🚌 2, 4, 10, 11 to Stadio, Ⓜ Akropoli, 🚋 Zappeio) With its serried rows of white Pentelic marble seats built into a ravine next to Ardettos Hill, this ancient-turned-modern stadium is a draw both for lovers of classical architecture and sports fans who can imagine the roar of the crowds from millennia past. A ticket gets you an audio tour, admission to a tiny exhibit on the modern Olympics (mainly eyecandy games posters) and the opportunity to take your photo on a winners' pedestal.

Numismatic Museum   MUSEUM
(Map p122; ☑ 210 363 2057; www.nummus.gr; Panepistimiou 12, Kolonaki; adult/student €6/3;

JEWISH ATHENS

The Jewish community of Athens numbers nearly 3000 today but its roots go back thousands of years, perhaps even to before the 5th century BC: some archaeologists believe there was a synagogue in Ancient Agora (p88). You can find out about the community's history at the **Jewish Museum** (Map p92; ☑ 210 322 5582; www.jewishmuseum.gr; Nikis 39, Plaka; adult/student/child €6/3/free; ⏱ 9am-2.30pm Mon-Fri, 10am-2pm Sun; Ⓜ Syntagma), beginning with the Romaniotes of the 3rd century BC, through to the arrival of Sephardic Jews in the 15th century and beyond the Holocaust.

There are two synagogues in Athens – the small **Ets Hayim** (Map p116; ☑ 210 325 2875; https://athjcom.gr; Melidoni 8, Keramikos; ⏱ 8.30am-1.30pm Mon-Fri by appointment only; Ⓜ Thissio) **FREE**, a Romaniote synagogue built in 1904, and the larger **Beth Shalom** (Map p116; ☑ 210 325 2875; https://athjcom.gr; Melidoni 5, Keramikos; ⏱ 8.30am-1.30pm Mon-Fri by appointment only; Ⓜ Thissio) **FREE**, dating from 1935; they stand opposite each other. A fascinating tour of the synagogues is by appointment only: send an email with a photocopy of your passport to sec@athjcom.gr.

Outside Beth Shalom look for the metal book memorial to the Righteous Gentiles – Greeks who helped save Jews during the Nazi German occupation of WWII. Nearby, shaded by trees next to Keramikos, is the city's **Holocaust Memorial** (Map p116; cnr Melidoni, Ermou & Evvoulou, Keramikos; Ⓜ Thissio), a Star of David made of large sculpted fragments of marble. Finish your tour of Jewish Athens with a hearty meal at the good kosher restaurant Gostijo (p120), part of the city's Chabbad centre.

⊙ 8.30am-3.30pm Tue-Sun; Ⓜ Panepistimio, Syntagma) The collection of coins here, dating from ancient through to modern times, is excellent, but of more general interest is the dazzling 1881 mansion in which it's housed. Built by architect Ernst Ziller, it was the home of Heinrich Schliemann, the archaeologist who excavated Troy; fittingly, its mosaic floors and painted walls and ceilings are covered in classical motifs.

War Museum
MUSEUM

(Map p122; ☏ 210 725 2975; www.warmuseum.gr; Rizari 2, cnr Leoforos Vasilissis Sofias, Kolonaki; adult/child €4/2; ⊙ 9am-7pm Apr-Oct, to 5pm Nov-Mar; Ⓜ Evangelismos) This relic of the junta years is a stark architectural statement of the times. But its displays of weapons, maps, armour and models from the Mycenaean civilisation to the present day make an interesting break from the classics and there are some impressive pieces of kit parked around it, including fighter jets and an exact copy of the 1912 *Daedalus,* Greece's first military aircraft.

🏃 Activities

Hammam
SPA

(Map p116; ☏ 210 323 1073; www.hammam.gr; Melidoni 1, cnr Agion Asomaton, Keramikos; 1hr €25, bath-scrub combos from €45; ⊙ 11am-10pm Mon-Fri, 10am-10pm Sat & Sun; Ⓜ Thissio) The marble-lined steam room may be a bit small, but thanks to the attention to detail throughout, this Turkish-style place is the best of the three major bathhouses in central Athens. Amenities include proper-size water bowls, and hot tea and Turkish delight in the lounge afterwards. For the full effect, reserve ahead for a full-body scrub.

Adidas Runbase
RUNNING

(Map p86; ☏ 210 924 4073; www.adidas.gr/adidasrunners; Falirou 16, Koukaki; ⊙ runs 6am-9pm; Ⓜ Akropoli) **FREE** Sign up online and join free guided runs around Athens starting from this showroom for the latest in the brand's trainers (which you can road test for free if you haven't brought your own running shoes with you). The runs are between 5km and 6km.

EOS
HIKING

(Greek Alpine Club; Map p92; ☏ 210 321 3255; www.eosathinon.gr; 1st fl, Lekka 23-25, Syntagma; Ⓜ Syntagma) The EOS runs weekly hiking trips outside the city (information in Greek only) and maintains trails on Mt Hymettos and around Attica. It's not really geared to tourists, but it is the place to ask for advice on longer trips and lesser-known trails. Find their office on the 1st floor inside the shopping arcade.

🏃 City Walk
Central Athens

START PLATEIA SYNTAGMATOS
END MONASTIRAKI FLEA MARKET
LENGTH 3.5KM; TWO HOURS

Start in ❶ **Plateia Syntagmatos** (p91). The square has been a favourite place for protests ever since the rally that led to the granting of a constitution on 3 September 1843. In 1944 the first round of the civil war began here after police, under British direction, opened fire on a communist rally.

The ❷ **Grande Bretagne** (p113), the most illustrious of Athens' hotels, was built in 1862. During WWII, the Nazis made it their headquarters; the British moved in afterwards. Resistance fighters laid dynamite to blow up the entire building but the operation was halted when Winston Churchill arrived unexpectedly; the fighters weren't willing to assassinate him.

On the north side of the square is a section of the ❸ **Peisistratos aqueduct**, which was unearthed during metro excavations. Across the road, in front of ❹ **Parliament** (p80), the much-photographed *evzones* (presidential guards) stand sentinel at the ❺ **Tomb of the Unknown Soldier** (Map p122; Plateia Syntagmatos, Syntagma; Ⓜ Syntagma) The changing of the guard takes place every hour on the hour.

Walk through the lush ❻ **National Garden** (p87) and exit to the ❼ **Zappeio Hall** (Map p122; ☏ 21 0322 3509; www.zappeion.gr; Leoforos Vasilissis Amalias; Ⓜ Syntagma), opened in 1888 in preparation for the first modern Olympic Games in 1896, for which part was used as a fencing venue.

Walk back along the south edge of the gardens to the striking ❽ **Temple of Olympian Zeus** (p77), the remains of the largest temple ever built. Teetering on the edge of the traffic alongside the temple is ❾ **Hadrian's Arch** (p87), erected to mark the boundary of Hadrian's Athens.

Cross Leoforos Vasilissis Amalias and head right towards Lysikratous, where you turn left into Plaka. Ahead on your right, below street level, is the a ❿ **Church of Agia Ekaterini** (p94), with the ruins of a Roman monument in the forecourt.

Ahead on the left is the ⓫ **Lysikrates Monument** (Map p92; cnr Sellei & Lysikratous, Plaka; Ⓜ Akropoli, Syntagma) **FREE**, built in 334 BC, the only remaining example of the

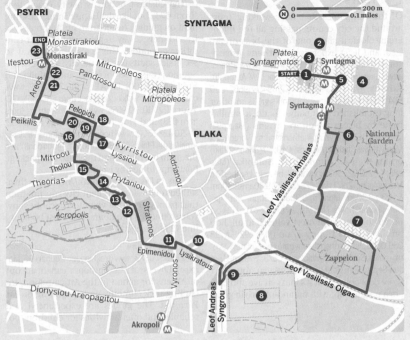

monuments that once lined this street to the Theatre of Dionysos, site of dramatic contests. The monument commemorates one chorus' victory, with reliefs showing Dionysos battling the Tyrrhenian pirates, transformed into dolphins. It's the earliest known monument using Corinthian capitals externally, a style imitated in many modern monuments. Later, the monument was made into a Capuchin convent library, where Lord Byron stayed in 1810–11 and wrote *Childe Harold*.

Facing the monument, turn left and then right into Epimenidou. At the top of the steps, turn right into Stratonos. Just ahead you'll see the **12 Church of St George of the Rock**, which marks the entry to **13 Anafiotika** (p91). This picturesque maze of whitewashed houses is the legacy of stonemasons from the Cycladic island of Anafi who were brought to build the king's palace after Independence in the mid-19th century. It's a peaceful spot, with brightly painted olive-oil cans brimming with flowers in the tiny gardens in summer.

Continue past the tiny **14 Church of Agios Simeon**. The street looks like a dead end but persevere and you'll emerge at the Acropolis road. Turn right, then left into Prytaniou, veering right after 50m into Tholou. The yellow-ochre building at Tholou 5 is the **15 old Athens University** (1837–41). Built by the

Venetians, it was used by the Turks as public offices; it's now a missable history museum.

Continue down to the ruins of the **16 Roman Agora** (p94). Jog right on Kyrristou to see the **17 Bath House of the Winds** (p100), a historical (but nonfunctional) Turkish *hammam*. On the next corner, Diogenous, the **18 Museum of Greek Popular Instruments** (p87) is a three-storey mansion filled with more than a thousand ways to make music. Turning on to Pelopida, skirting the edge of the Roman Agora, you'll see on the right the gate of a 1721 madrasa. It's a short walk across the road to the **19 Tower of the Winds** (p95), a classical weather station which was repurposed as a Sufi meeting house in the Ottoman period. Ahead on the left, the 17th-century **20 Fetiye Mosque** is inside the fence of the Roman Agora.

Follow the road around the *agora* to the ruins of **21 Hadrian's Library** (p101). Next to them is the 1759 **22 Mosque of Tzistarakis** (p100); after Independence it lost its minaret and was used as a prison – it is now occasionally open as a museum.

You're now in Monastiraki, the colourful, chaotic square teeming with street vendors. To the left down Ifestou is **23 Monastiraki Flea Market** (p132).

☞ Tours

Of the companies that offer walking tours around the city centre, passing all the major archaeological sites, one of the best organised, and least expensive, is **Athens Adventures** (Map p86; ☑ 210 922 4044; www.athens-adventures.gr; Veïkou 3a, Makrygianni; Ⓜ Akropoli). **Athens Walking Tours** (☑ 6945859662, 210 884 7269; www.athenswalkingtours.gr) is another long-established company. To do a similar route by bike, try **Roll in Athens** (Map p92; ☑ 6974231611; www.rollinathens.tours; Voreou 10, Monastiraki; half-day tours €40; Ⓜ Monastiraki) or, for the ease of an e-bike, **Solebike** (Map p86; ☑ 210 921 5620; www.solebike.eu; Lembesi 11, Makrygianni; 2hr/1 day €28/36; ⊙ 9.30am-2.30pm & 4.30-8.30pm Mon-Fri, 9.30am-4.30pm Sat Apr-Oct, shorter hours Nov-Mar; Ⓜ Akropoli). If you prefer to sit and not exert yourself at all, hop on the **Athens Happy Train** (Map p92; ☑ 213 039 0888; www.athenshappytrain.com; Plateia Syntagmatos, Syntagma; adult/child €5/3; ⊙ 9am-11pm Jun-Sep, to 9pm Oct-May; Ⓜ Syntagma). You won't score cool points, but it's inexpensive and covers a useful loop, with on-and-off privileges.

The cushiest option is a city coach tour (from €78), but like the Happy Train, these are light on guiding (aside from an Acropolis visit) and more a way to get oriented in air-conditioned comfort. This is also an easy way to see major sights outside the city, such as Cape Sounion (€49), Delphi (€93), and Nafplio and Epidavros (€100). **CHAT** (☑ 210 323 0827; www.chat-tours.com; walking/bus tour from €39/55), **GO Tours** (☑ 210 921 9555; www.gotours.com.gr; tours from €38) and **Hop In Sightseeing** (Map p92; ☑ 210 428 5500; www.hopin.com; Leoforos Vasilissis Amalias 44, Plaka; ⊙ 6.30am-10pm; Ⓜ Akropoli) are the main operators, and they also run package boat trips to nearby islands.

This Is My Athens (http://myathens.thisisathens.org) is an excellent city-run program that pairs you with a volunteer local to show you around for two hours. You must book online 72 hours ahead.

Trekking Hellas   OUTDOORS
(☑ 210 331 0323; www.trekking.gr; Gounari 96, Marousi) Lovers of the outdoors can head out of Athens for action in the Attica region, including rock climbing and canyoning on Mt Parnitha. The guides are experienced and reliable, and offer activities for children too.

FROM GRAFFITI TO STREET ART

The one thing you cannot miss in Athens, apart from the Acropolis, is how much graffiti there is across the city. It's not just walls that are blighted by tagging and general spray-paint scribbling, but practically any part of the urban fabric from trains to park benches. There's an age-old tradition to all this; the word 'graffiti' comes from the Ancient Greek word '*graphi*' meaning 'to write'.

The 2008 financial crisis was a particular spur to people venting their economic and political frustrations in spray-paint slogans and images. Recently, though, there has been a civic effort to work more creatively with street artists, so as to add some beauty and form to the general visual chaos. Projects such as Urban Act (https://urbanact.gr) have bequeathed Athens some giant and very impressive murals.

Particularly notable are the murals by INO (http://ino.net), who can be recognised by his trademark monotone paintings with splashes of vivid light blue. One of his most impressive creations, on the Pireos side of the **Old OSY Depot** (Map p116; www.osy.gr/ethelsite/pages/gazi_amax.php; Ermou, Keramikos; Ⓜ Keramikos), is a homage to famous Leonardo da Vinci images: take note of the rioter and policeman reflected in the Mona Lisa's eyes.

Manolis Anastasakos and Pavlos Tsakonas, along with students from the Athens School of Fine Arts (ASKT), are responsible for the giant **Praying Hands Mural** (Map p102; Pireos 20, Omonia; Ⓜ Omonia). Inspired by Albrecht Dürer's image, the hands have been inverted so that it appears that it is the Lord praying for the people rather than the other way around.

Exarhia is so plastered with graffiti that spotting the better pieces of street art can be a challenge. Standing out is the splendidly executed mural **No Land For the Poor** (Map p102; http://wdstreetart.com; Emmanuel Benaki 84, Exarhia; Ⓜ Omonia) of a sleeping homeless man, by Indonesian-born and Athens-based artist Wild Drawing. See the map on his website for the locations of more of his works around the city.

If you'd like to discover more prime pieces of street art, **Alternative Athens** (☑ 211 012 6544; www.alternativeathens.com; tours from €40) offers an excellent themed walking tour.

DON'T MISS

PARLIAMENT & THE CHANGING OF THE PRESIDENTIAL GUARD

Designed by Bavarian architect Friedrich von Gärtner, Greece's **Parliament** (Map p122; www.hellenicparliament.gr; Plateia Syntagmatos, Syntagma; ⊗ tours 3pm Mon & Fri Jun, Jul & Sep; M Syntagma) **FREE** was originally the royal palace. From its balcony, the *syntagma* (constitution) was declared on 3 September 1843, and in 1935 the palace became the seat of parliament. For history and politics geeks, the building is open by guided tour a few months of the year; book at least five days ahead.

In front of Parliament, the traditionally costumed *evzones* (presidential guards) stand by the tomb and change every hour on the hour. On Sunday at 11am, a whole platoon marches down Vasilissis Sofias to the tomb, accompanied by a band. The *evzones* uniform of the *fustanella* (white skirt) and pom-pom shoes is based on the attire worn by the klephts, the mountain fighters of the War of Independence. You can also see *evzones* outside the **Presidential Guard** (Map p122; 10 Irodou Attikou, Syntagma) and nearby Presidential Palace. It's interesting to see them here, alone and away from tourist cameras, going through their ritual pomp even in the dead of night.

Pyrgos Vasilissis Winery   WINE
(Map p146; ☎ 210 231 3607; www.pyrgos vasilissis.gr; 67 Dimokratias Ave, Ilion; adult/child €27/13.50; ⊗ by appointment) Crops were first planted at this winery back in the 1850s. The stately property offers organic wines and one-to two-hour tours around the castle tower, vineyards, gardens and the winery itself; the tour concludes with wine tasting. Reserve in advance. For more information on the region's wineries, see www.winesofathens.com, which has a downloadable map. **Cycle Greece** (☎ 210 921 8160; www.cyclegreece.com) runs day-trip bike rides to some regional wineries.

★★ Festivals & Events

Athens &
Epidaurus Festival   PERFORMING ARTS
(Hellenic Festival; ☎ 21092 82900; www.greek festival.gr; ⊗ Jun-Aug) The ancient **Theatre of Epidavros** (☎ 27530 22009; http://odysseus. culture.gr; adult/concession/child €12/6/free; ⊗ 8am-8pm Apr-Aug, reduced hours Sep-Mar) and Athens' Odeon of Herodes Atticus (p81) are the headline venues for Greece's annual cultural festival, running since 1955 and featuring a top line-up of local and international music, dance and theatre.

August Moon Festival   PERFORMING ARTS
A reward for enduring the hottest month in Athens: on the night of the full moon, major historical sites such as the Acropolis and the Roman Agora are open all night and host musical performances.

Athens International Film Festival   FILM
(☎ 210 606 1413; www.aiff.gr; ⊗ Sep) Features retrospectives, premieres and international art films and documentaries.

Athens Pride   PARADE
(☎ 697 418 7383; www.athenspride.eu) Athens Pride is an annual LGBTQ event, usually celebrated in early June, culminating in a parade that usually starts on Syntagma.

Athens Biennale   ART
(☎ 210 523 2222; http://athensbiennale.org; ⊗ Oct-Dec) Every odd-numbered year, the Athens Biennale showcases top local and international artists across a range of media and locations around the capital.

Athens Technopolis Jazz Festival   MUSIC
(☎ 213 010 9300; www.technopolisjazzfestival.com; ⊗ late May-early Jun) Week-long jazz festival at Technopolis (p104), the converted gasworks in Gazi, as well as at the Onassis Cultural Centre (p131).

Athens Street
Food Festival   FOOD & DRINK
(☎ 210 963 6489; https://athensstreetfoodfestival. gr) Athenians have embraced this event with gusto since the first one in 2016. Over three weekends in May, the former tram depot next to the Kerameikos (p101) archaeological site is crammed with every delicious snack the capital has to offer. A great place to sample both traditional and supercreative parts of the food scene.

Rockwave Festival   MUSIC
(☎ 210 882 0426; www.rockwavefestival.gr; ⊗ Jul) Annual international rock festival (with an emphasis on metal, most years) held over several weekends at Terra Vibe, a parkland venue on the outskirts of Athens in Malakasa. Special buses run from town. Sometimes cheap camping is offered.

ADRIANA IACOB/SHUTTERSTOCK ©

1. Architectural details, Church of Eleftherios **2.** Moni Kaisarianis
3. Church of the Holy Apostles **4.** Mosaic, Moni Dafniou

Byzantine Athens

The city is dotted with churches that just happen to be a thousand years old, dating from the high point of the Byzantine Empire. Few churches open regularly, but the ones that do are gold-bedecked portals to the past. Don't miss the outstanding Byzantine & Christian Museum (p90), as well as the great icons at the Benaki Museum (p89).

Moni Dafniou

The area's most important Byzantine building is the World Heritage–listed 11th-century **Moni Dafniou** (☑210 581 1558; http://whc.unesco.org/en/list/537; Dafni; ☺9am-2pm Tue & Fri; 🚌811, 866 or A16 to Psychiatreion) FREE at Dafni, 10km northwest of Athens. Many of the church's elaborate mosaics, wrought by artisans from Constantinople, have been beautifully restored and more work is underway. The octagonal structure incorporates part of a wall from a 6th-century church.

Moni Kaisarianis

Nestled on the slopes of Mt Hymettos, 5km east of Athens, beautiful 11th-century **Moni Kaisarianis** (Monastery of Kaisariani; ☑210 723 6619; Mt Hymettos; adult/child €2/free; ☺8.30am-2.45pm, grounds to sunset, Tue-Sun) is a peaceful walled sanctuary. The domed *katholikon* (main church), supported by four columns from an ancient temple, has well-preserved frescoes from the 17th and 18th centuries.

Church of the Holy Apostles

One of the oldest churches in Athens is the 11th-century Church of the Holy Apostles in the Ancient Agora (p77), a tribute to the place where St Paul once taught. It bears decorative details that are now seen as Islamic but were a product of artisans who worked across the eastern Mediterranean.

Church of Eleftherios (Little Metropolis)

Look closely at this 12th-century **church** (Plateia Mitropoleos, Monastiraki), and you'll see it's a historical collage of medieval stonework and ancient Pentelic marble. Its facade sports both medieval lions and Classical athletes, a portion of a delicate ancient marble frieze. It was even built on the ruins of an ancient temple.

🛏 Sleeping

Athens' lodging covers the full range, from one- to five-star hotels plus plenty of short-term rental accommodation. In recent years there's been a mini-explosion of chic boutique developments, most with only a handful of rooms. To be sure your ideal choice is available, make bookings at least a couple of months ahead; for July and August, ideally aim for four months ahead.

🛏 Acropolis, Filopappou Hill & Thisio

Marble House Pension PENSION €
(Map p86; ☎ 21092 34058; www.marblehouse.gr; Zini 35a, Koukaki; d/tr/q from €45/55/69; ✳@🛜; Ⓜ Sygrou-Fix) Tucked into a quiet cul-de-sac is one of Athens' best-value budget hotels. Rooms are well maintained, all with a fridge and a ceiling fan; some have small balconies. If you use the air-con it's €5 extra per night. It's a 15-minute walk to the Acropolis (p78), but close to the metro. Breakfast available (€5).

Athens Backpackers HOSTEL €
(Map p86; ☎ 21092 24044; www.backpackers.gr; Makri 12, Makrygianni; dm incl breakfast from €27; ✳@🛜; Ⓜ Akropoli) The popular rooftop bar with cheap drinks and Acropolis (p78) views is a major draw at this modern and friendly Australian-run backpacker favourite. There's a courtyard, a well-stocked kitchen and a busy social scene. Spotless dorms with private bathrooms and lockers have bedding, but towel use costs €1.

Management also runs the nearby, well-priced **Athens Studios** (Map p86; ☎ 21092 35811; www.athensstudios.gr; Veïkou 3a, Makrygianni; apt from €90; @🛜).

Chameleon Youth Hostel HOSTEL €
(Map p116; ☎ 21034 28053; www.chameleon youthhostel.com; Nileos 25, Thisio; dm/d with private bathroom €19/40; ✳🛜; Ⓜ Thissio) This friendly, colourful hostel is a homey place with a comfy lounge, useful kitchen and laundry facilities as well as a nice rooftop terrace for chilling. It's a short walk from the main entrance to the Acropolis (p78); trendy Petralona is also not far away.

Tony APARTMENT €
(Map p86; ☎ 210 923 0561; www.hoteltony.gr; Zaharitsa 26, Koukaki; studios from €65; ✳@🛜; Ⓜ Sygrou-Fix) Hotel Tony offers spacious, clean and modern studios, all with kitch-enette, split across two buildings. Great for groups; for instance, the 'superior family room' has three balconies. It's about 1km southwest of the Acropolis (p78) and has a great view of the monument from its roof terrace.

★ Be My Guest Athens HOTEL €€
(Map p116; ☎ 213 044 9929; www.bemyguest athens.gr; Nileos 33, Thisio; d/tr/ste incl breakfast €102/126/150; ✳🛜; Ⓜ Thissio) Opened in 2017, this 14-room hotel is for those seeking calm: the minimalist monotone-and-turquoise colour scheme is soothing, and its residential location (about 15 minutes' walk to the Acropolis (p78)) is quiet. The cheapest double rooms don't have balconies, but it's not much to upgrade. The suites have kitchens, and there's a handy grocery store downstairs.

Hera Hotel BOUTIQUE HOTEL €€
(Map p86; ☎ 210 923 6682; www.herahotel.gr; Falirou 9, Makrygianni; d/ste incl breakfast from €145/280; ✳@🛜; Ⓜ Akropoli) Behind its elegant neoclassical facade, this boutique hotel has been totally rebuilt. But the formal interior design stays true to exterior style, with lots of brass and dark wood. It's a short walk to the Acropolis (p78) and Plaka. North-side rooms, away from an adjacent music bar, are preferable. The rooftop Peacock restaurant and bar have fine views and good service.

★ Athens Was BOUTIQUE HOTEL €€€
(Map p86; ☎ 210 924 9954; www.athenswas.gr; Dionysiou Areopagitou 5, Makrygianni; d/ste incl breakfast from €390/465; ✳@🛜; Ⓜ Akropoli) The location, a two-minute walk to the east gate of the Acropolis (p78), couldn't be better. Staff are friendly, adding a warm touch to the minimalist decor, and standard rooms have big balconies overlooking the pedestrianised street. Breakfast is excellent and the terrace has a magnificent view. Suites on the 5th and 6th floors also have Acropolis views.

Herodion HOTEL €€€
(Map p86; ☎ 210 923 6832; www.herodion.gr; Rovertou Galli 4, Makrygianni; d incl breakfast from €195; ✳@🛜; Ⓜ Akropoli) At this pleasant, contemporary hotel, rooms are small but have super-comfortable beds and a not-trying-too-hard minimalist style. The roof terrace and two outdoor Jacuzzi baths have great Acropolis (p78) views.

Syntagma & Plaka

★ Phaedra
HOTEL €

(Map p92; ☑ 210 323 8461; www.hotelphaedra.com; Herefontos 16, Plaka; s/d/tr from €60/80/90; ✻ @ ☎; Ⓜ Akropoli) Almost all the 21 rooms at this family-run hotel have balconies overlooking a church or the Acropolis (p78). The rooms are basic and range from small to snug; a few have private bathrooms across the hall. Given the superb rooftop terrace, the friendly staff and the unbeatable location, it's one of the best deals in Plaka.

★ InnAthens
BOUTIQUE HOTEL €€

(Map p92; ☑ 210 325 8555; www.innathens.com; Souri 3, Syntagma; d incl breakfast €150; ✻ @ ☎; Ⓜ Syntagma) This 37-room hotel is minutes from Syntagma, but you'd never know it once you're inside its cocoon, down the end of a shopping arcade. Most rooms look on to a pretty interior courtyard, and the restfulness is reinforced with soothing grey-and-white decor and excellent beds.

Home and Poetry Hotel
BOUTIQUE HOTEL €€

(Map p92; ☑ 210 322 3204; www.homeandpoetry.com; Lysikratous 10, Plaka; d incl breakfast from €150; ✻ ☎; Ⓜ Akropoli) A lovely neoclassical mansion has been converted to create this elegant and excellently located property. The 16 rooms – all with wooden floors and classical furnishings – come in a range of different sizes. A plus is the rooftop dining terrace with the all-important Acropolis (p78) views.

Alice Inn
GUESTHOUSE €€

(Map p92; ☑ 210 323 7139; www.jjhospitality.net; Tsatsou 9, Plaka; d/tr/ste from €100/170/220; ✻ ☎; Ⓜ Akropoli, Syntagma) On a blessedly quiet block, this big old town house fulfils the fantasy that you live in Athens, in old-time elegance: high ceilings, fans, marble floors, plus a shared kitchen and a comfy living room where you're welcome to crank up the gramophone. In addition to the three main suites, there is a cosy budget double.

★ Grande Bretagne
LUXURY HOTEL €€€

(Map p92; ☑ 210 333 0000; www.marriott.com; Vasileos Georgiou I 1, Syntagma; r/ste from €515/838; P ✻ @ ☎ ☲; Ⓜ Syntagma) If you aspire to the best, *the* most prestigious place to stay in Athens is – and always has been – the Grande Bretagne, right on Syntagma Sq. Built in 1862 to accommodate visiting heads of state, it was renovated some years ago, but still retains enough old-world grandeur.

Ergon House
BOUTIQUE HOTEL €€€

(Map p92; ☑ 210 010 9090; https://house.ergon-foods.com; Mitropoleos 23, Syntagma; d from €195; P ✻ @ ☎; Ⓜ Syntagma) Having created a sleek boutique hotel above their stylish deli and restaurant (p119), Ergon House offers communal kitchens in its hallways so you can prepare meals with all the goodies you can buy on the ground floor. The cheapest rooms are compact but are appealingly decorated with breeze (Besser) blocks, grey marble and wooden fittings in minimalist style.

NEW Hotel
DESIGN HOTEL €€€

(Map p92; ☑ 210 327 3000; www.yeshotels.gr; Filellinon 16, Plaka; d from €239; P ✻ @ ☎; Ⓜ Syntagma) Brazilian designers the Campana brothers melded their signature scraps-to-art style with Greek-folk touches and old Athens photos, creating a hip space that's full of fun eye candy. More practically, the rooms are cushy (lots of pillow options) and there's a good roof lounge and restaurant. Location is prime but can be noisy; upper floors are better.

Monastiraki & Psyrri

★ City Circus
HOSTEL €

(Map p102; ☑ 213 023 7244; www.citycircus.gr; Sarri 16, Psyrri; dm/d incl breakfast from €27/72; ✻ @ ☎; Ⓜ Thissio, Monastiraki) With its jaunty, colourful style and helpful staff, City Circus lifts the spirit more than most budget hostels. Its bright, well-designed rooms have modern bathrooms; some have kitchens. Book on its website for free breakfast at the chic bistro Zampano downstairs.

Cecil
HOTEL €

(Map p102; ☑ 210 321 7079; www.cecilhotel.gr; Athinas 39, Monastiraki; s/d/tw/tr/q incl breakfast €60/75/85/120/155; ✻ @ ☎; Ⓜ Monastiraki) This charming old hotel on busy Athinas has beautiful high moulded ceilings, polished timber floors and an original cage-style lift. The simple rooms are tastefully furnished, but don't have fridges. Two connecting rooms with a shared bathroom are ideal for families.

Small Funny World
HOSTEL €

(Map p92; ☑ 210 324 7167; www.sfwhostel.com; Kalamiotou 25, Monastiraki; dm €17; ✻ @ ☎; Ⓜ Monastiraki) Located in the most happening corner of Monastiraki, this laid-back hostel is an excellent budget option with 14 beds in each of the four large tiled dorm rooms. The communal kitchen is a plus and so is

APARTMENT RENTALS

Athens is awash with short-term apartment rentals of the likes offered by Airbnb. You'll pay a premium the closer you are to the Acropolis. Pleasant and generally safe areas of the city to look for rentals include Plaka, Kolonaki, Mets and Pangrati.

Book ahead with **Boutique Athens** (☑ 6985083556; www.boutiqueathens.com; 1-/2-/4-bedroom apt from €40/59/134; ❄ 🛜) for a superbly renovated, spacious apartment or whole house. Prime locations around the centre offer excellent value for the amenities. In Psyrri, for example, one apartment's massive roof garden with Acropolis views has sunbeds, a barbecue and a beer fridge. There is a two-night minimum.

the rooftop terrace, a casual meeting place decorated with cushioned wooden sofas and mismatched tables facing out to the urban skyline.

18 Micon Street
BOUTIQUE HOTEL €€

(Map p102; ☑ 210 323 5307; www.18miconstr.com; Esopou 14, Psyrri; d/ste incl breakfast €138/151; ❄🛜; Ⓜ Monastiraki) An old warehouse has been sprinkled with interior-designer fairy dust to emerge as this chic 14-room boutique hotel. Cement, wood and brick are the foundation blocks of the interior design, with pops of colour and pattern from wall art and tiles. Rooms also come equipped with smart phones for full internet access in and out of the hotel.

★ Foundry Hotel
APARTMENT €€€

(Map p102; ☑ 211 182 4602; www.thefoundryhotelathens.com; Sarri 40, Psyrri; apt incl breakfast from €170; ❄🛜; Ⓜ Thissio) An old metalwork factory provides the base and inspiration for this industrial-chic apartment hotel. Rooms, which all have mini-kitchens, sport thematic steel-and-wood decor and favour analogue features such as books and vinyl LP players rather than TVs. Choose a wine from the wine cellar and enjoy it up on the beautiful roof garden.

★ Perianth Hotel
DESIGN HOTEL €€€

(Map p92; ☑ 210 321 6660; https://perianth-hotel.com; Limbona 2, Monastiraki; d/ste from €198/351; ❄@🛜❄; Ⓜ Monastiraki) Athens designers K-Studio have done a splendid job modernising this 1930s building into a gorgeous 38-room hotel, using natural materials such as marble, wood and metal alongside choice pieces of contemporary art. Splash out on the two-bedroom penthouse suite which includes a private Jacuzzi and swimming pool on a wrap-around roof terrace with stunning Acropolis (p78) views.

Zillers
BOUTIQUE HOTEL €€€

(Map p92; ☑ 210 322 2277; www.thezillersathenshotel.com; Mitropoleos 54, Monastiraki; r incl breakfast from €180; ❄@🛜; Ⓜ Monastiraki) This boutique hotel offers just 10 rooms in a handsomely converted neoclassical building right beside the metropolitan cathedral (p101). Six of the rooms overlook the Acropolis (p78) (the rest get light from an atrium). Breakfast is served at the excellent rooftop restaurant and bar, which is worth a visit even if you aren't staying at the hotel.

🛏 Gazi, Keramikos & Exarhia

★ Athens Quinta Hostel
HOSTEL €

(Map p102; ☑ 213 030 5322; www.facebook.com/athensquinta; Methonis 13, Exarhia; dm/d with shared bathroom €25/55; 🛜; Ⓜ Panepistimio) Set in an old mansion, complete with velvet sofas and patterned tile floors, this friendly place is pleasantly homey and a nice change from slicker, busier hostels. There's a leafy backyard for lounging.

The House
PENSION €

(Map p116; ☑ 210 345 7765; www.thehouseathens.com; Iakchou 7, Gazi; d from €70; ❄@🛜; Ⓜ Kerameikos) If you want to be close to the Gazi nightlife, then this place hits the sweet spot. It bills itself as a boutique hotel, but in reality the rustic furnishings, whitewashed walls and mock stone-flagged floors give it the feel of a Greek island pension. Some rooms have small kitchenettes, and the vibe is relaxed and youthful.

Exarchion
HOTEL €

(Map p102; ☑ 210 380 0731; www.exarchion.com; Themistokleous 55, Exarhia; s/d/tr €45/58/70; ❄🛜; Ⓜ Omonia) What this 1960s high-rise hotel lacks in character, the surrounding neighbourhood of Exarhia makes up for. Rooms are clean and comfortable; some have balconies. There's a rooftop cafe-bar and the management is friendly. There are numerous nearby dining and entertainment options.

Grecotel Pallas Athena
DESIGN HOTEL €€

(Map p102; ✆210 325 0900; www.grecotelpallasathena.com; Athinas 63, Syntagma; d from €168; ❄️@🛜; Ⓜ Omonia) The designers have brought a playful touch to the rooms of this 63-room boutique hotel, filling them quirky, colourful pieces of contemporary art, decor and furnishings. Kids will love the superheroes and other cartoon characters that feature in some of the wall murals.

Fresh Hotel
BOUTIQUE HOTEL €€

(Map p102; ✆210 524 8511; www.freshhotel.gr; Sofokleous 26, Omonia; r incl breakfast from €144; ❄️🛜🏊; Ⓜ Omonia) A hip hotel in the gritty south-of-Omonia area, this groovily designed place offers modern rooms freshly renovated in 2019 with new mock bleached-wood floors and splashes of colour on the walls. Pluses include a fantastic Acropolis-view rooftop with small pool, bar and restaurant. Front rooms have balconies, but can be noisy if you sleep with the window open.

🛏 Kolonaki & Around

⭐ Coco-Mat Athens Jumelle
BOUTIQUE HOTEL €€

(Map p122; ✆210 723 0000; www.cocomatathens.com; Ypsilandou 2, Kolonaki; s/d incl breakfast from €150/165; ❄️@🛜; Ⓜ Evangelismos) Coco-Mat, the luxury mattress and bedding company that has branched out into hotels, has another winner on its hands with this property. It cleverly combines a neoclassical mansion with a modern block, linked by a corridor with a cascading wall of water. There's a gorgeous wooden staircase and rooftop terrace for breakfast. The entrance is on Irodotou.

St George Lycabettus
BOUTIQUE HOTEL €€€

(Map p122; ✆210 741 6000; www.sglycabettus.gr; Kleomenous 2, Kolonaki; s/d from €221/235; ❄️@🛜🏊; Ⓜ Evangelismos, Syntagma) A high-end clientele bunks here for excellent service and posh rooms. Newer 'eco-chic' rooms have organic bedding and comfy Coco-Mat beds; other floors are styled to focus on young Greek fashion designers, photography and local composers. Up the hill in Kolonaki, it's a bit remote, but this pays off in views of the city (Lycabettus greenery isn't bad either).

Periscope
BOUTIQUE HOTEL €€€

(Map p122; ✆210 729 7200; www.yeshotels.gr; Haritos 22, Kolonaki; d/ste incl breakfast from €318/393; ❄️@🛜; Ⓜ Evangelismos) On a quiet street lined with tiny, chic boutiques, this sleek grey-tone hotel is the essence of new Kolonaki. Rooms are minimalist but have great beds and neat aerial shots of the city on the ceilings or walls. Complimentary snacks are available all day in the lounge.

Hilton Athens
BUSINESS HOTEL €€€

(Map p74; ✆210 728 1000; www.hiltonathens.gr; Leoforos Vasilissis Sofias 46, Hilton; r from €196; ❄️@🛜🏊; Ⓜ Evangelismos) Swathes of polished marble greet you both in the lobby and rooms of the Hilton, occupying an iconic 1963 modernist building that's worth a look in its own right for its clean lines and facade relief mural by Yiannis Moralis, inspired by Greek themes. Rooms are spacious, many with splendid views, and there are plenty of facilities.

🍴 Eating

Eating, drinking and talking is the main entertainment for Athenians. The vibrant restaurant scene is marked by a delightful culture of casual, convivial al fresco dining. *Ouzeries* and *mezedhopoleia,* both serving small plates with drinks, are popular for those with limited budgets. Some of the best food is found in just-slightly modernised tavernas that showcase fresh produce and regional ingredients.

Acropolis, Filopappou Hill & Thisio

Gevomai kai Magevomai
TAVERNA €

(Map p116; ✆210 345 2802; Nileos 11, Thisio; mains €4-13; ⊘1pm-midnight Tue-Sun; 🛜; Ⓜ Thissio) Stroll off the pedestrian way to find this small corner taverna with marble-topped tables. Neighbourhood denizens know it as one of the best for home-cooked, simple food with fresh ingredients – a boon in this high tourist-traffic area.

Veganaki
VEGAN €

(Map p86; ✆210 924 4322; www.facebook.com/VeganakiGR; Athanasiou Diakou 38, Kynosargous; mains €3.50-6.50; ⊘8.30am-11.30pm; 🍴; Ⓜ Akropoli) A fine addition to Athens' vegan dining options, this convivial spot may occupy a spot overlooking a busy road, but inside all is calm as customers enjoy falafel wraps and plates, sandwiches and traditional Greek pies, some of which are also gluten free. Also served here, a great cup of fair trade organic coffee.

Gazi, Keramikos & Thisio

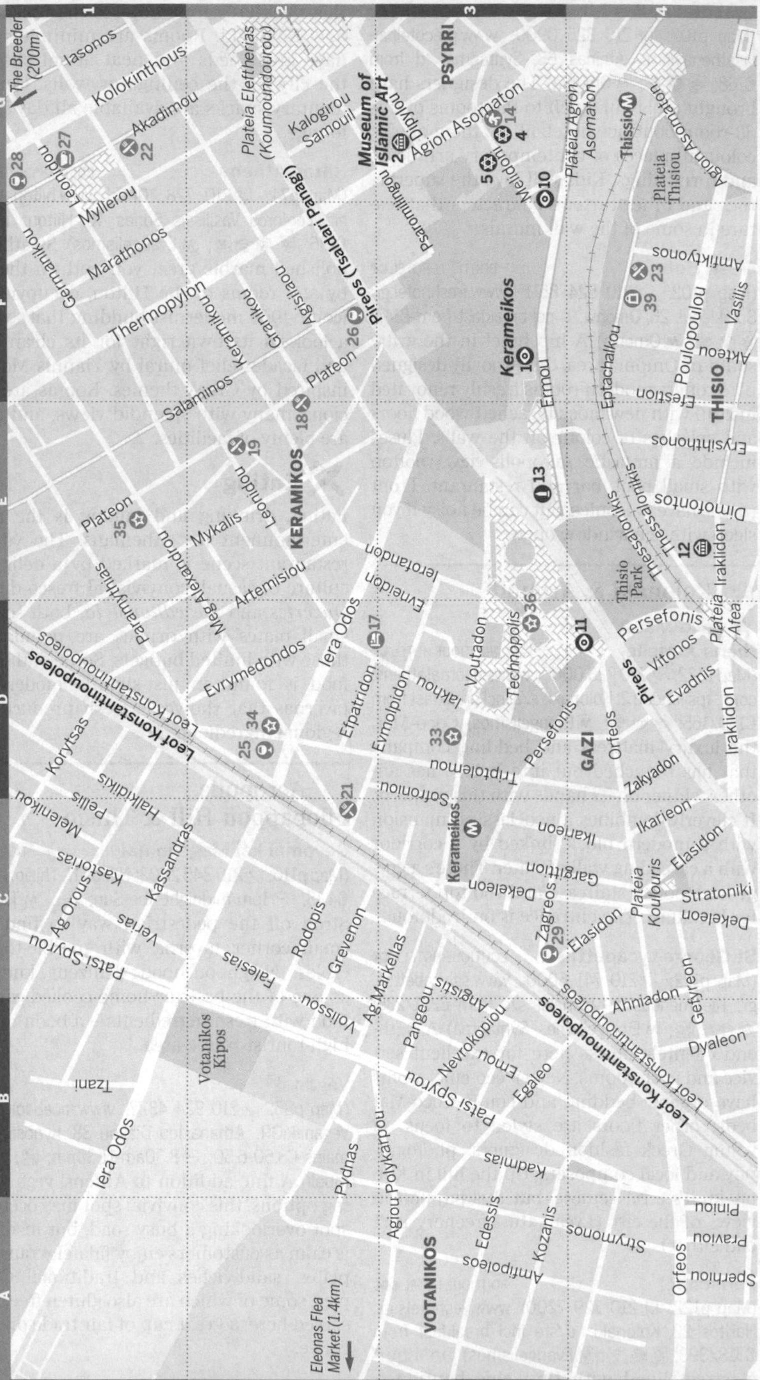

Museum of Islamic Art

PSYRRI

KERAMIKOS

THISIO

GAZI

VOTANIKOS

The Breeder (200m)

Eleonas Flea Market (1.4km)

Plateia Eleftherias (Koumoundourou)

Kalogirou Samouil

Plateia Agion Asomaton

Plateia Thisiou

Thisio Park

Votanikos Kipos

200 m
0.1 miles

Gazi, Keramikos & Thisio

★ **Ellevoro** GREEK €€

(Map p86; ☎ 210 924 6256; www.facebook.com/el-levoro; Rovertou Galli 2, Makrygianni; mains €17-28; ⊙2pm-midnight Mon-Sat, 1-9pm Sun; 🛜; Ⓜ Akropoli) Three generations of a family work at this romantic homestyle restaurant that's decorated with wood beams, lacy white tablecloths, twinkling candles and chandeliers. Traditional Greek dishes – such as fava beans with smoked eel, and slow oven-baked lamb *kleftiko* – are superbly prepared and presented. A nice touch is the welcoming amuse bouche of a small cup of soup.

★ **Steki tou Ilia** TAVERNA €€

(Map p116; ☎ 210 345 8052; Eptachalkou 5, Thisio; mains €6-30; ⊙noon-1am, to 7pm Sun; Ⓜ Thissio) If there's a line to dine at this no-frills *psistaria* (restaurant serving grilled food), it's worth joining. The payoff is succulent lamb and pork chops, barrel wine and simple dips, chips and salads. In summer, the operation moves across the street into a hidden garden over the train tracks.

Fabrika tou Efrosinou GREEK €€

(Map p86; ☎ 210 924 6354; Zini 34, Koukaki; mains €14-18.50; ⊙1-11pm Sun & Tue-Thu, to midnight Fri & Sat; Ⓜ Sygrou-Fix) Named for the patron saint of cooks, this 'factory' is really a two-level restaurant focusing on good ingredients and rarer Greek recipes. When everything is swinging, it's the perfect combination of bountiful, healthy food, including organic vegetables and farmstead cheeses, excellent Greek wines and great atmosphere. Book ahead on weekends.

Mani Mani GREEK €€

(Map p86; ☎ 210 921 8180; www.manimani.com.gr; Falirou 10, Makrygianni; mains €12-23; ⊙2-11pm; Ⓜ Akropoli) Head upstairs to the relaxing, elegant dining rooms of this delightful modern restaurant, which specialises in herb-filled cuisine from the Mani region in the Peloponnese. Standouts include the ravioli with Swiss chard, the tangy sausage with orange, and the chicken stuffed with mushrooms and pecorino cheese.

Strofi GREEK €€

(Map p86; ☎ 210 921 4130; www.strofi.gr; Rovertou Galli 25, Makrygianni; mains €16-19; ⊙noon-1am, closed Mon Nov-Apr; Ⓜ Akropoli) Book ahead for a Parthenon (p85) view from the rooftop of this exquisitely renovated town house. Food is simple grilled meats and fish, but the setting, with elegant white linen and excellent service, elevates the experience to romantic levels.

Hytra MEDITERRANEAN €€€

(Map p74; ☎ 217 707 1118, 210 331 6767; www.hytra.gr; Onassis Cultural Centre, Leoforos Syngrou 107-109, Neos Kosmos; mains €34-39, 8-course tasting menu €62; ⊙restaurant 8pm-midnight Sun-Thu, to 1am Fri & Sat, bar to 3am; ☒10, 550 to Panteio, Ⓜ Sygrou-Fix) Hytra offers exquisitely presented Greek food with a hypermodern twist. Though portions can be small, the flavours and cooking techniques are spot on, which is how it earned its Michelin star. There's a 10-course vegetarian tasting menu (€58), and a lighter, more casual menu (mains €20 to €25) served in the bar area.

✕ Syntagma & Plaka

Damigos TAVERNA €

(Map p92; ☎ 210 322 5084; www.mpakaliarakia.gr; Kydathineon 41, Plaka; mains €9-12; ⊙2pm-midnight; Ⓜ Akropoli) Hidden away and with an intimate feel, this traditional place, in business since 1865, specialises in *bakaliaros*, toothsome cod fried in pillow-light batter and spiked with garlicky sauce. Everything else is solid too, aided by quality house wine, naturally chilled in barrels set in the bedrock. A real treat in Plaka.

Avocado VEGETARIAN €

(Map p92; ☎ 210 323 7878; www.avocadoathens.com; Nikis 30, Plaka; mains €9-14; ⊙noon-11pm Mon-Fri, 11am-11pm Sat, noon-7pm Sun; 🛜🍽; Ⓜ Syntagma) This popular cafe offers a full array of vegan, gluten-free and organic treats with an international spin. Next to an organic market, and with a tiny front patio, here you can enjoy everything from sandwiches to quinoa with aubergine, or mixed-veg coconut curry. Juices and mango lassis are all made on the spot.

Kalderimi TAVERNA €

(Map p102; ☎ 210 331 0049; P022; Pleatia Agion Theodoron, Panepistimio; mains €6-12; ⊙11am-8pm Mon-Thu, to 10pm Fri & Sat; 🛜; Ⓜ Panepistimio) This downtown taverna offers Greek food at its most authentic. Everything is freshly cooked and delicious: you can't go wrong. Hand-painted tables edge a pedestrian street, providing for a feeling of peace in one of the busiest parts of the city. (It helps that it closes just before nearby bars get rolling.)

Glykys MEZEDHES €

(Map p92; ☎ 210 322 3925; www.glykys.gr; Angelou Geronta 2, Plaka; mezedhes €4-8; ⊙10am-1am; Ⓜ Akropoli) In a quiet corner of Plaka, this low-key place with a shady front yard is mostly frequented by students and locals. It has a tasty selection of mezedhes, including traditional dishes such as *briam* (oven-baked vegetable casserole, only available in the evening) and cuttlefish in wine.

★**Ergon House Agora** GREEK €€
(Map p92; ☑ 210 010 9090; https://house.ergonfoods.com; Mitropoleos 23, Syntagma; mains €8-11.50; ⊙ 7.30am-midnight; 🛜; Ⓜ Syntagma) A superb addition to Athens' culinary landscape is this deli, cafe and restaurant occupying a gorgeously designed atrium space flooded with light. There are separate areas for a greengrocer, fishmonger, butcher and bakery, plus shelves packed with top-quality Greek products sourced from small-scale producers around the country. You'll dine well here and, most likely, leave laden down with goodies.

Birdman JAPANESE €€
(Map p92; ☑ 210 321 2800; www.facebook.com/birdmanathens; Skoufou 2, Syntagma; skewer €2.50-4, mains €15; ⊙ 6pm-midnight Mon-Fri, from 1pm Sat; 🛜; Ⓜ Syntagma) This part of Syntagma offers a cluster of Japanese restaurants, among which Birdman, which specialises in yakitori (charcoal-grilled skewers of meat) is a gem. The main ingredients – free-range organic chicken, grass-fed beef – are top quality, the cooking by Japanese chefs is totally authentic and the ambience relaxed and contemporary.

Cherche la Femme GREEK €€
(Map p92; ☑ 210 322 2029; Mitropoleos 46, Syntagma; mains €7.50-12.50; ⊙ 9am-11.30pm, until midnight Fri & Sat; Ⓜ Syntagma) Leafy wallpaper, a twinkling chandelier and Parisian brasserie-style furniture and bar set the chic tone for this all-day cafe. The atmosphere may scream France but the menu, with traditional dishes such as *mousakas* and *skioufichta* (a local pasta), is very much homegrown. It's a perfect spot to graze on mezedhes with a glass of wine or beer.

Nolan FUSION €€
(Map p92; ☑ 210 324 3545; www.nolanrestaurant.gr; Voulis 31-33, Syntagma; mains €8.50-13; ⊙ 1pm-midnight Mon-Sat; 🛜; Ⓜ Syntagma) It's a good idea to make a reservation for this casual, chic and popular restaurant. Chef Sotiris Kontizas has incorporated some Asian ingredients and influences into his fresh and flavoursome menu with dishes such as soba noodles with smoked salmon, and NFC (Nolan Fried Chicken). Everything is designed to be shared.

Palia Taverna tou Psara TAVERNA €€
(Map p92; ☑ 210 321 8734; www.psaras-taverna.gr; Erehtheos 16, Plaka; mains €12-24; ⊙ noon-1am; Ⓜ Akropoli) A little above the main bustle of Plaka, this taverna fills tables cascading across the street and down the stairs. It's touristy, but respected by locals as one of the best seafood tavernas in the area. If fish (€65 per kilogram) isn't your thing, they have plenty of other dishes to choose from.

★**Sushimou** JAPANESE €€€
(Map p92; ☑ 211 407 8457; www.sushimou.gr; Skoufou 6, Syntagma; set menu €50-60; ⊙ 6.30-10.30pm; 🛜; Ⓜ Syntagma) Sushi in Athens doesn't get any better than this. Tell Antonis Drakoularakos, the Tokyo-trained chef who holds court behind the counter, your budget and he'll prepare a feast of local seafood sliced up as sashimi (raw fish) and nigiri (atop vinegared rice). It's a tiny place so book ahead at least a month to be sure of a spot.

Monastiraki & Psyrri

★**Diporto Agoras** TAVERNA €
(Map p102; ☑ 210 321 1463; Sokratous 9 & Theatrou, Psyrri; plates €5-7; ⊙ 7am-7pm Mon-Sat, closed 1-25 Aug; Ⓜ Omonia, Monastiraki) This charming old taverna is an Athens gem. There's no signage – look for two sets of doors leading to a rustic cellar. There's no printed menu, just a few dishes that haven't changed in years. Order the house speciality *revythia* (chickpea stew) and follow up with grilled fish, paired with wine from one of the giant barrels lining the wall.

Hoocut GREEK €
(Map p92; ☑ 210 324 0026; https://hoocut.com; Plateia Agia Irini 9, Monastiraki; souvlaki from €2.50; ⊙ noon-1am; Ⓜ Monastiraki) The five Athenian chefs behind this upmarket snack joint have focused on the quality of the ingredients to create 'haute cuisine' souvlaki with a choice of meats beyond pork and chicken. The portions are a little smaller and the prices slightly higher than your run-of-the-mill *gyros*, but with the meat grilled to perfection it's totally worth it.

Bougatsadiko Thessaloniki PIES €
(Map p102; ☑ 210 322 2088; Plateia Iroön 1, Psyrri; pita €2; ⊙ 7am-2am Sun-Thu, 24hr Fri & Sat; Ⓜ Monastiraki) Unexpected for its location on a key nightlife square in Psyrri, this place makes excellent *pites* (pies), with filo crust that's 'opened' (rolled out by hand) every day – you

WORTH A TRIP

TRENO STO ROUF

Look for the glowing headlight on a steam locomotive behind Rouf station. Attached is **Treno sto Rouf** (Map p116; ☑21052 98922; https://totrenostorouf. gr; Leoforos Konstantinoupoleos, Rouf; ☺7.30pm-1am Tue-Sun; ☐21 or B16 to Rouf, Ⓜ Kerameikos), a string of old train cars converted into a restaurant, bar-cafe, music club and theatre. Even on a night when nothing's scheduled, it's a cool place to have a drink and a snack (€6 to €15) and imagine yourself on the *Orient Express* of old. Check online for slightly different hours from June to October.

can watch the baker at work. *Bougatsa* (filo with custard) is great for breakfast, the meat pies are a treat after drinks and *spanakopita* (spinach pie) hits the spot anytime.

Feyrouz
TURKISH €

(Map p92; ☑213 031 8060; www.feyrouz.gr; Karori 23, Monastiraki; sandwiches from €3; ☺noon-10pm Mon-Thu, to 11pm Fri & Sat; ☑; Ⓜ Monastiraki) *Lahmajoun* (flatbread topped with spiced meat and rolled up with vegetables) is the focus at this jewel box of a Turkish-Lebanese snack shop. The vegetarian option is a treat, with chewy whole-grain bread; there's also excellent lentil soup and bountiful salads. It's on a pedestrian street with benches, so you can eat outside if the tiny place is jammed.

Kostas
GREEK €

(Map p92; ☑210 323 2971; Plateia Agia Irini 2, Monastiraki; sandwich €2.20; ☺9am-6pm; Ⓜ Monastiraki) On a pleasant square opposite Agia Irini church, this old-style virtual hole-in-the-wall joint grills up tasty souvlaki and *bifteki* (Greek-seasoned hamburger), served on pitta with a signature spicy tomato sauce. Go before the lunch rush, as it may close early if it runs out of meat.

Avli
MEZEDHES €

(Map p102; ☑210 321 7642; Agiou Dimitriou 12, Psyrri; dishes €5-13; ☺1pm-midnight; Ⓜ Monastiraki) Cheap, cheerful and borderline chaotic on weekend nights, Avli requires you to squeeze down a narrow hall to get in; you'll probably wait for service if it's busy. The whitewashed walls and outdoor seating give you an island feel in the city, and the

keftedhes (fried meatballs) and the special omelette, filled with fries and sausage, are excellent drinking food.

★ Atlantikos
SEAFOOD €€

(Map p102; ☑213 033 0850; Avliton 7, Psyrri; mains €6-13; ☺1pm-midnight; Ⓜ Monastiraki, Thissio) Tucked down a little lane, this small, hip fish restaurant is easy to miss – look for happy people chatting over heaps of shrimp shells. The atmosphere is simple and casual, with low prices to match – but there's excellent-quality seafood, whether it's fried or grilled.

★ Karamanlidika tou Fani
GREEK €€

(Map p102; ☑210 325 4184; www.karamanlidika. gr; Sokratous 1, Psyrri; dishes €6-15; ☺11am-midnight; Ⓜ Monastiraki) At this modern-day *pastomageireio* (combo tavern-deli) tables are set alongside the deli cases, and staff offer complimentary tasty morsels while you're looking at the menu. Beyond the Greek cheeses and cured meats, there's good seafood, such as marinated anchovies, as well as rarer wines and craft beers. Service is excellent, as is the warm welcome, often from Fani herself.

Fouar
ASIAN €€

(Map p92; ☑210 321 1381; http://fouar-athens.gr; 1st fl, 6 Hristopoulou, Monastiraki; mains from €10; ☺7pm-3am Tue-Fri, 1pm-3am Sat & Sun; Ⓜ Syntagma) Fouar is a central meeting point for Athens' fashionable crowd. The casual-stylish restaurant serves international cuisine with a strong Asian influence. Start with a signature cocktail at the bar, check out the running exhibition in the gallery, enjoy your meal under the atrium greenery and dance in the club (open only some nights) until the early hours.

Gostijo
JEWISH €€

(Map p102; ☑210 323 3825; www.gostijo.gr; Esopou 10, Psyrri; mains €8.50-17; ☺1-10.30pm Sun-Thu Apr-Oct, from 4pm Nov-Mar; ☎; Ⓜ Monastiraki) Convivial Israeli expat Ricky Vidal is the force of nature running this fully kosher restaurant that occupies a modern, pleasantly decorated space on the ground floor of Jewish outreach organisation Chabbad. Dishes are both traditional Sephardic and Mediterranean; the menu includes options such as beef stew with wine and prunes; falafel; and Moroccan chicken. Reservations are recommended.

Café Avissinia
MEZEDHES €€

(Map p92; ☑210 321 7047; https://cafeavissinia. net; Kynetou 7, Monastiraki; mains €10-16; ⊙11am-1am Tue-Sat, to 7pm Sun; ⓂMonastiraki) This antiques-bedecked place on Plateia Avyssinias, in the middle of the antique dealers, has been legendary since the 1980s for its live music and varied mezedhes. It's great for a midday break from the market (p132), or for a late supper on a weekend night. In summer, snag fantastic Acropolis (p78) views upstairs from their terrace.

Kuzina
GREEK €€

(Map p92; ☑210 324 0133; www.kuzina.gr; Adrianou 9, Monastiraki; mains €16-36; ⊙1pm-midnight; ⓂThissio) This comfortably elegant restaurant does chic Greek, with creations such as fried dumplings filled with feta and olives. It's cosy in winter, as light streams in, warming the crowded tables. In summer, book ahead for a rooftop-terrace table for views all around. A fine second choice is an outside table on the pedestrian street.

Telis
TAVERNA €€

(Map p102; ☑210 324 9582; Evripidou 86, Psyrri; meal with salad €13; ⊙noon-midnight Mon-Sat; ⓂThissio) A fluorescent-lit beacon of good food and kind service on a grimy block, Telis has been serving up simplicity since 1978. There's no menu, just a set meal: a small mountain of charcoal-grilled pork chops atop chips, plus a side vegetable. Greek salad is optional, as is beer or rough house wine.

Gazi, Keramikos & Exarhia

★Ama Lachei stis Nefelis
GREEK €

(Map p102; ☑210 384 5978; https://restaurant-47828.business.site; Kalidromiou 69, Exarhia; mezedhes €5.50-11.50; ⊙1pm-12.30am Thu-Sun, from 6pm Tue & Wed; ☒2, 5, 9, 11 to Polytechneio) This modern *mezedhopoleio* (restaurant specialising in mezedhes) is a minor hike up Exarhia's hill, but you're rewarded with a lovely setting – an old school building, with tables outside in the vine-shaded playground – and super-savoury small plates that go well with drinks. Think pickled octopus, meatballs flavoured with cinnamon and cloves, and lamb kebabs.

Elvis
GREEK €

(Map p116; ☑210 345 5836; Plateon 29, Keramikos; skewers €1.70; ⊙noon-3am, to 5am Fri & Sat; ⓂKerameikos or Thissio) This souvlaki joint is mobbed, and not just because the counter staff slide you a shot of booze while you're waiting. The meat quality is high, the prices are right and the music is great. Every skewer comes with good chewy bread and fried potatoes.

★Seychelles
GREEK €€

(Map p116; ☑210 118 3478; www.seycheles.gr; Keramikou 49, Metaxourgio; mains €8.50-14.50; ⊙2pm-12.30am Sun-Thu, until 1am Fri & Sat; ⓂMetaxourghiou) Gutsy fresh food, an open kitchen, friendly service, a handwritten daily menu and rock on the soundtrack: Seychelles may be the Platonic ideal of a restaurant. Dishes can look simple – meaty pan-fried mushrooms with just a sliver of sheep's cheese, say, or greens with fish roe – but the flavours are excellent. Go early or book ahead; it's deservedly popular.

★Athiri
GREEK €€

(Map p116; ☑210 346 2983; www.athirirestaurant. gr; Plateon 15, Keramikos; mains €17-20; ⊙7-11.30pm Tue-Sat, plus 1-5pm Sun Oct-May; ⓂThissio) Athiri's lovely garden courtyard is a verdant surprise in this pocket of Keramikos. The small but innovative menu plays on Greek regional classics, with seasonal specialities. This might include Santorini *fava* (split-pea dip) and hearty beef stew with *myzithra* (sheep's-milk cheese), and handmade pasta from Karpathos.

Kanella
TAVERNA €€

(Map p116; ☑210 347 6320; www.kanellagazi. gr; Leoforos Konstantinoupoleos 70, Gazi; dishes €8.50-14; ⊙1pm-midnight Mon-Fri, to 1am Sat & Sun; ⓂKerameikos) Housemade village-style bread, mismatched retro crockery and brown paper on the tabletops set the tone for this modern taverna serving regional Greek cuisine. Friendly staff offer daily specials such as lemon lamb with potatoes, and an excellent zucchini and avocado salad.

★I Kriti
CRETAN €€

(Map p102; ☑210 382 6998; Veranzerou 5, Omonia; mains €6-12; ⊙noon-midnight Mon-Sat; ☎; ⓂOmonia) There is no shortage of Cretan restaurants in Athens, but this is the one that Cretans themselves recommend, especially for rare seasonal treats such as stewed snails, bittersweet pickled *volvi* (wild bulbs), and tender baby goat with nuts and garlic. It occupies several storefronts inside the arcade; on weekends it's a good idea to reserve.

Kolonaki, Mets & Pangrati

Lykavittos Hill
(1.25km via road)

Chapel of Agios Georgios
(150m via cable car)

200 m
0.1 miles

Doras D'Istria

Aristippou

Aristodimou

Sina

Skoufa

Lykavittou

Evelpidos Rogakou II

Stratiotikou Syndesmou

Kleomenous

Plateia
Dante

Solonos

Omirou

27

35

Fokylidou

Anagnostopoulou

Xanthippou

17

Dinokratous

38

Xenokratous

Souidias

Plateia Agiou
Dionysiou

24

Akadimias

Dimokritou

Al Soutsou

Voukourestiou

Tsakalof

31

Plateia
Dexameni

28

Aheou

19

Spefsipou

29

40

39

KOLONAKI

Glykonos

Haritos

16

Patriarhou Ioakeim

20

Marasli

Amerikis

Valaoritou

Pindarou

Iraklitou

Xanthou

Levendi

23

Alopekis

Patera I

8

Panepistimiou
(El Venizelou)

41

42

Kriezotou

Zalokosta

33

34

Akadimias

Merlin

Sekeri

Kanari

37

Plateia
Kolonakiou

Neofytou
Vamva

Neofytou
Douka

Loukianou

Ploutarhou

Karneadou

Plateia
Megalis tou
Genous Sholi

Syntagma

11

9

Benaki Museum of
Greek Culture
2

Koumbari

Leof Vasilissis Sofias

Irodotou

Kapsali

Ypsilandou

Evangelismos

Plateia
Syntagmatos

4

15

Museum of
Cycladic Art

Leof Vasilissis Sofias

12

Rizari

10

Mourouzi

Byzantine &
Christian
Museum

3

Hilton Athens (250m);
Vezené (400m);
Megaron (1km)

Leoforos Vasilissis
Amalias

Lykiou

Stisihorou

Rigilis

5

National
Garden

Irodou Attikou

Leof Vas Georgiou

Meleagrou

7

Leof Vasileos Konstantinou

Plateia
Trouman

Leof Vas Georgiou

22

36

Isiodou

Fokianou

Amynda

21

13

Arktinou

Ironda

Telesilis

Paisaniou

Polemonos

Ptolemeou

Ptolemokratous

Arnelaou

Hironos

30

14

Arrianou

Ellanikou

Fedrou

1

Basil & Elise
Goulandris
Foundation

Efronos

Eratosthenous

Aristoxenou

Ippodamou

Athanasias

Nikosthenous

Alsos
Pangratiou

Leof Vasilissis Olgas

Plateia
Stadiou

Agras

6

Panathenaic
Stadium

Ardettos
Hill

Plateia
Plastira

Eftyhidou

Ardittou

26

Polydamandos

Krisila

Pasitelous

Effranoros

Piga M

Theotoki

Markou Mousourou

Protagora

Arhimidous

Ferekydou

18

Proklou

Vryaxidos

Sophokleous

Sorvolou

Fotiadou

Balanou K

Trivonianou

Dikearhou

Embedokleous

Plateia
Varnava

Melissou

PANGRATI

Plateia
Profitiou
Ilia

Aristonikou

Gorgiou

Voulgareos Evg

Longinou

METS

Parmenidou

Kyniskas

Stilponos

25

Edesiou

32

Anapafseos

Miniati

Balanou K

Alsos
Longinou

Stratigou Domboli

Ymittou

Kolonaki, Mets & Pangrati

★ **Yiantes** TAVERNA €€
(Map p102; ☎210 330 1369; www.yiantes.gr; Valtetsiou 44, Exarhia; mains €9-15; ⊙1pm-midnight; ⚲; ⓂOmonia) This lovely restaurant with a central courtyard garden is up-market for Exarhia, but the food is superb and made with largely organic produce. Expect interesting seasonal greens such as *almirikia* (sea beans), perfectly grilled fish or delicious mussels and calamari with saffron.

✕ **Kolonaki, Mets & Pangrati**

Kalamaki Kolonaki GREEK €
(Map p122; ☎210 721 8800; Ploutarhou 32, Kolonaki; souvlaki from €5; ⊙1pm-midnight; ⓂEvangelismos) Order your pork or chicken by the *kalamaki* (skewer), add some salad and pittas, and you have great quick bites at this standout souvlaki joint. It's small, but there's pavement seating for the requisite people-watching. And, because it's Kolonaki, it's just a little more chic than average.

Filippou TAVERNA €
(Map p122; ☎210 721 6390; www.filippou.gr; Xenokratous 19, Kolonaki; mains €5-10; ⊙1-5pm & 7.30pm-midnight Mon-Fri, 1-5pm Sat; ⓂEvangelis-

mos) Why mess with what works? Filippou has been dishing out Greek goodness – hearty meats, long-stewed vegetables – since 1923, and it's still a go-to for the neighbourhood. You can get this food elsewhere, but here you get white linen and a gracious, older, long-lunching clientele, in the heart of Kolonaki.

Ohh Boy CAFE €
(Map p122; ☎211 183 8340; www.facebook.com/ohhboygr; Archelaou 32, Pangrati; sandwiches €6.50; ⊙8.30am-midnight, from 9am Sat & Sun; ⚲⚲; ⓂEvangelismos) Whitewashed tables and chairs nestle beneath olive trees at this cool cafe that has plenty of healthy eating options, including vegan cakes. It's a great spot for sandwiches and a coffee.

Colibri PIZZA €
(Map p122; ☎210 701 1011; Embedokleous 9-13, Pangrati; pizzas €6.50-14, mains €7-9; ⊙1pm-12.30am; ⬜2, 4, 11 to Plateia Plastira) Locals go here for the alleged best pizza in Athens. The pies range from classic Italian to creative vegetarian (seriously, the yoghurt works). Burgers and salads are also excellent. It's one of several fine eateries on a quiet tree-lined street.

★ **Mavro Provato** MEZEDHES €€

(Black Sheep; Map p122; 210 722 3466; www.tomauroprovato.gr; Arrianou 31-33, Pangrati; dishes €6-17.50; 1pm-1am Mon-Sat, to 7pm Sun; Evangelismos) Book ahead for this wildly popular modern *mezedhopoleio* in Pangrati, where tables line the footpath and delicious small (well, small for Greece) plates are paired with regional Greek wines.

★ **Philos Athens** INTERNATIONAL €€

(Map p122; 210 361 9163; www.facebook.com/philos.athens; Solonos 32, Kolonaki; mains €8-16; 9am-5pm Mon-Fri, from 10am Sat & Sun; Panepistimio, Syntagma) Distressed walls, a beautiful old tiled floor and a cascade of paper cranes dangling from the tall ceiling set the shabby-chic tone for this delightful cafe. It's a lovely spot to browse style magazines while grazing on breakfast or lunch dishes such as macrobiotic bowls or bolognese ragu over pasta.

★ **Oikeio** MEDITERRANEAN €€

(Map p122; 210 725 9216; www.facebook.com/oikeio; Ploutarhou 15, Kolonaki; mains €10-12; 12.30pm-midnight Mon-Thu, to 1am Fri & Sat, to 6pm Sun; Evangelismos) With excellent homestyle cooking, this modern taverna lives up to its name (meaning 'homey'). It's decorated like a cosy bistro, and tables on the footpath allow people-watching without the usual Kolonaki bill. Pastas, salads and international fare are tasty, but try the daily *mayirefta* (ready-cooked meals), such as the excellent stuffed zucchini. Book ahead on weekends.

Benaki Museum Cafe GREEK €€

(Map p122; 210 367 1000; www.benaki.org; Koumbari 1, Kolonaki; mains €10-24; 10am-6pm Mon, Wed, Fri & Sat, to midnight Thu, to 4pm Sun; Evangelismos) Traditional Greek food gets dressed up to match the museum (p104) setting, with an open dining room and terrace with a view of the National Garden (p87) and the Acropolis (p78). It feels a bit clubby, with older locals meeting for lunch, and it's open as late as the museum is, so you can have dinner or even just a late drink here.

★ **Spondi** MEDITERRANEAN €€€

(Map p122; 210 756 4021; www.spondi.gr; Pyrronos 5, Pangrati; mains €48-60, set menus from €79; 8-11.45pm; 209 to Plateia Varnava, 2, 4 or 11 to Plateia Plastira) Athenians frequently vote two-Michelin-starred Spondi the city's best restaurant, and its Mediterranean haute cuisine, with a strong French influence, is indeed

excellent. It's a lovely dining experience, in a relaxed setting in a charming old house with a bougainvillea-draped garden. Book ahead.

Vezené GREEK €€€

(Map p74; 210 723 2002; http://vezene.gr; Vrasida 11, Hilton; mains €25-40; 7pm-2am Mon-Sat, 1-5.30pm Sun; ; Evangelismos) One of Athens' best modern Greek bistros, Vezené is a relaxed affair where the waiters will bring to the table the catch of the day and glistening cuts of prime steak to explain the provenance and what goes into each dish. The wood-oven-baked pies are very good, as is the signature, deconstructed *pastitsio*, a kind of Greek lasagne.

🍷 Drinking & Nightlife

In Athens the line between cafe and bar is blurry. Most places segue from coffee to drinks, and maybe music and a DJ, at night. There is almost always food – although places that serve only drinks are more common in the economic crisis (in which case, you can bring your own snacks). The smoking ban is often ignored.

⬡ Acropolis, Filopappou Hill & Thisio

★ **Little Tree Book Cafe** CAFE

(Map p86; 210 924 3762; www.facebook.com/littletreebooksandcoffee; Kavalloti 2, Makrygianni; 8am-11pm Tue-Thu, until 11.30pm Fri, 9am-11.30pm Sat & Sun; Akropoli) This friendly social hub is much beloved by neighbourhood residents, who go for books (they stock a small selection of translated Greek authors here), but also excellent coffee, cocktails and snacks.

★ **The Underdog** COFFEE

(Map p116; 213 036 5393; www.underdog.gr; Iraklidon 8, Thisio; 9am-11pm; ; Thissio) Far from underdogs, the championship-winning baristas here really know how to make a decent cup of coffee. This speciality coffee roaster and cafe-bar occupies a roomy location with a shaded courtyard to the rear and industrial fittings throughout. If coffee isn't your thing, they also serve craft beers and have a decent brunch-style menu.

Drupes & Drips CAFE

(Map p86; 6970300404; www.facebook.com/drupesdrips; Zitrou 20; 7am-4pm Mon, until 10pm Tue-Fri, until 11pm Sat; Akropoli) A coffee to speed your step up to the Acropolis (p78) in the morning, or an Aperol spritz or glass of wine to soothe you into the evening on the way down – that's what this pocket-sized cafe/wine bar is all about. Pair your drink with a small plate of something, usually involving the bread from Takis Bakery across the way.

Bel Rey
CAFE

(Map p86; ☎ 213 032 6450; http://belraybar.gr; Falirou 88, Koukaki; ☺10am-2am; Ⓜ Sygrou-Fix) Occupying the triangular corner of a former car workshop, this is the go-to hang-out of Koukaki's hipsters. It's a buzzy, casual scene that works equally well for a quiet morning coffee or late-night drinks against the background sounds of chatter and a DJ.

★ Upopa Epops
BAR

(Map p116; ☎ 212 105 5214; www.facebook.com/upupaepopsthebar2016; Alkminis 7, Kato Petralona; ☺10am-2am, to 3am Fri & Sat; Ⓜ Petralona) This lovely bar-restaurant is one of the reasons Petralona is considered a just-the-right-amount-of-cool neighbourhood. It has numerous rooms filled with vintage furniture and a pretty courtyard, the food and drinks are great and there's often a DJ, but there's always a place to have a conversation. And the name? Latin for the hoopoe bird.

Sin Athina
CAFE

(Map p116; ☎ 210 345 5550; www.sinathina.gr; Iraklidon 2, Thisio; ☺8am-1am, until 2am Fri & Sat; Ⓜ Thissio) Location, location, location! This cafe-bar sits at the junction of the two pedestrianised cafe strips and has a sweeping view up to the Acropolis (p78). The real magic is on the rooftop – though the menu up here is more elaborate and slightly higher priced.

🍷 Syntagma & Plaka

★ The Clumsies
BAR

(Map p92; ☎ 210 323 2682; www.theclumsies.gr; Praxitelous 30, Syntagma; ☺10am-2am Sun-Thu, to 4am Fri & Sat; Ⓜ Syntagma) Look for the red neon in the hallway of this discreet bar that fills your coffee and creative cocktail needs. Founded by three award-winning bartenders, it's very serious about its drinks, but the atmosphere is definitely fun, and full of slick, handsome types on the weekends. From 6pm to 10pm you can order their degustation of four cocktails for €20.

★ Baba Au Rum
COCKTAIL BAR

(Map p92; ☎ 211 710 9140; www.babaaurum.com; Klitiou 6, Syntagma; ☺7pm-3am Sun-Fri, 1pm-4am Sat; Ⓜ Syntagma, Monastiraki) As the name implies, the focus here is on rum drinks, with an

excellent selection of rarer Caribbean rums and a whole range of cocktails, from classic tiki drinks to new inventions. This is just one of a handful of good little bars on this strip.

★ Yiasemi
CAFE

(Map p92; ☎ 213 041 7937; www.yiasemi.gr; Mnisikleous 23, Plaka; ☺10am-3am; Ⓜ Monastiraki) Proof that Plaka is still very much a Greek neighbourhood despite the tourists, Yiasemi attracts a good mix of young Athenians, who set up for hours in the big armchairs or out on the scenic steps. It's better by day (especially for the great veg breakfast buffet) and on weeknights, when it's not overwhelmed by the scene at nearby restaurants.

L'Audrion
WINE BAR

(Map p92; ☎ 210 324 1193; https://laudrion.gr; Plateia Filomousou 3 & Farmaki 1, Plaka; ☺5pm-1am; Ⓜ Akropoli, Syntagma) Something of an oasis of Gallic calm in the midst of touristy Plaka, L'Audrion is a classy French wine bar and restaurant that sports more than 100 different labels in its cellar. As well as bottles you can order by the glass. The food is excellent. An added bonus is live music from 7.30pm on Wednesday.

Zonars
CAFE

(Map p92; ☎ 210 325 1430; Voukourestiou 9, Syntagma; ☺9am-3am, to 4am Fri & Sat; Ⓜ Syntagma) It's worth coming here for a coffee (from €4) or cocktail (€13) just to lounge in the sumptuous interior of this famous cafe, all velvet and brass and walnut panelling. In the 1950s and '60s, it claimed patrons such as Simone de Beauvoir and Sophia Loren; following a 2016 renovation, it still hosts a distinctly elegant scene.

Ippo
BAR

(Map p92; ☎ 213 005 4715; Thiseos 11, Syntagma; ☺7.30pm-2am Sun-Thu, to 4am Fri & Sat; Ⓜ Syntagma) This great little place caters to the slightly more mature bar-crawler, with pinball, David Bowie and old soul on the sound system, and better-than-average bar snacks. The bathrooms are a whole other world.

Barley Cargo
BAR

(Map p92; ☎ 210 323 0445; www.facebook.com/BarleyCargo; Kolokotroni 6, Syntagma; ☺11am-3am, from 5pm Sun; Ⓜ Syntagma) If you think Greek beer begins and ends with Alfa, head here to learn more. The big open-front bar stocks the products of many Greek microbreweries, as well as more than 100 international beers. Live music is a bonus.

Galaxy
BAR

(Map p92; ☎210 322 7733; www.facebook.com/GalaxyBarAthens; Stadiou 10, Syntagma; ⊙1pm-2am Mon-Sat; ⓂSyntagma) Once upon a time (1972 to be exact), this was a modern bar – the sort with an actual European-style *bar*. Now it's a worn-at-the-edges but atmospheric time capsule with gallant bartenders who respect the spirit of the place, which can be summarised in the framed photos of the Rat Pack and Franz Kafka. It's at the end of the arcade.

Brettos
BAR

(Map p92; ☎210 323 2110; https://brettosplaka.com; Kydathineon 41, Plaka; ⊙10am-2am; ⓂAkropoli) Plaka is short on bars in general, but Brettos, both a bar and a distillery, makes up for it. More than a century old, its walls glow with stacks of multicoloured bottles and huge barrels. Sample its home brands of wine, ouzo, brandy and other spirits.

Kaya
COFFEE

(Map p92; Voulis 7, Syntagma; ⊙7am-6pm Mon-Fri, 8am-3pm Sat; ⓂSyntagma) Serving the best coffee in the Syntagma area, Kaya is in an odd triangle of real estate, with just enough room for the baristas. Order to go, or sip your flat white while standing at the small counter by the window. It's at the back of the shopping arcade.

Kiki de Grece
WINE BAR

(Map p92; ☎210 321 1279; www.facebook.com/kikidegrece; Ipitou 4, Syntagma; ⊙noon-1am, to 2am; ⓂSyntagma) Man Ray's muse, Kiki de Montparnasse, declared that in hard times, all she needed was bread, an onion and a bottle of red wine. This pedestrian-street bar also takes her as its muse, and offers plenty more than a bottle of red. There's a huge range from Greece's vintners, paired with seasonal dishes from various regions in Greece.

Gin Joint
COCKTAIL BAR

(Map p92; ☎210 321 8646; Christou Lada 1, Syntagma; ⊙6pm-2am Tue-Thu & Sun, 7pm-3am Fri & Sat; ⓂSyntagma) Just what the name promises: there's an impressive 180 gins (but only one produced in Greece) as well as other fancy beverages to sample, some with historical notes on their origin. It's a tiny place but, like so many downtown bars, the crowd can expand into the adjacent arcade.

Melina
CAFE

(Map p92; ☎210 324 6501; Lyssiou 22, Plaka; ⊙9am-2am; ⓂAkropoli, Monastiraki) A tribute to the great Mercouri, this cafe-bar is decorated with images of the actress and politician who lobbied for the repatriation of the missing Parthenon marbles. Mercouri's most famous for the film *Never on Sunday*, but in fact that's a great day to come, when it's very busy and prime outdoor seats offer a view of the Plaka parade.

🍷 Monastiraki & Psyrri

★Couleur Locale
BAR

(Map p92; ☎216 700 4917; www.couleurlocaleathens.com; Normanou 3, Monastiraki; ⊙10am-2am Sun-Thu, to 3am Fri & Sat; ⓂMonastiraki) Look for the entrance to this rooftop bar down a narrow pedestrian lane, then inside the arcade. From there, an elevator goes to the 3rd floor and its lively all-day bar-restaurant. It's a go-to spot for Athenians who love a chill coffee or a louder evening, all in view of their beloved Acropolis (p78).

★Noel
BAR

(Map p92; ☎211 215 9534; https://noelbar.gr; Kolokotroni 59b, Monastiraki; ⊙10am-2am Sun-Thu, to 4am Fri & Sat; ⓂMonastiraki) One of the best of Athens' breed of maximalist-designed cafe-bars, Noel's slogan is 'where it's always Christmas' – meaning the candlelit cocktail-party kind of Christmas, no Santa suits required. Under softly glimmering chandeliers, smartly suited bartenders serve some of the most creative cocktails in town. Music is a mix of 1980s, '90s and jazz.

★Six d.o.g.s.
BAR

(Map p92; ☎210 321 0510; https://sixdogs.gr; Avramiotou 6-8, Monastiraki; ⊙10am-late; ⓂMonastiraki) The core of this super-creative events space is a rustic, multilevel back garden, a great place for quiet daytime chats over coffee or a relaxed drink. From there, you can head in to one of several adjoining buildings to see a band, art show or other generally cool happening.

Senios
CAFE

(Map p92; ☎210 331 8778; www.facebook.com/seniosathens; Kalamiotou 15, Monastiraki; ⊙10am-midnight; 🐾; ⓂMonastiraki) This chic cafe-bar with double-height ceilings is as fine a spot for a seriously good coffee (they roast their own beans on the premises daily) as it is for a late-night cocktail.

Orea Hellas CAFE
(Map p92; ☑ 210 321 3023; Pandrosou 36, Monastiraki; ⊙ 8.30am-11pm; 🌐; Ⓜ Monastiraki) This lovely old-style coffee house is a perfect place to take a break from shopping on the Monastiraki strip. Head upstairs for a seat on an open balcony overlooking Mitropoleos, or, in cooler weather, an indoor spot with an Acropolis (p78) view. Pair your Greek coffee with sweets or a range of solid snacks and salads.

Little Kook CAFE
(Map p102; ☑ 210 321 4144; www.facebook.com/littlekookgr; Karaïskaki 17, Psyrri; ⊙ 10am-midnight Mon-Fri, from 9am Sat & Sun; 🖼; Ⓜ Monastiraki) Nominally, this place sells coffee and cake. But it's really about its dazzling decor, which conjures up childhood fantasies. Precisely which one depends on the season, as the theme changes regularly. Everywhere are dolls, props, paintings and table decorations. You'll know you're getting close when you see party streamers over the street. Kids will be dazzled; Instagrammers will swoon.

Playhouse CAFE
(Map p92; ☑ 210 382 1200; www.playhouse.gr; Skouze 3, Monastiraki; ⊙ 10am-midnight Sun-Thu, until 2am Fri & Sat; 🌐🖼; Ⓜ Monastiraki) A great way to spend a rainy day with the kids once you've exhausted the museums is at this brightly decorated cafe that specialises in board games. The choice of some 500 different games is impressive, with expert staff on hand to explain rules if needed.

Booze Cooperativa BAR
(Map p92; ☑ 211 405 3733; http://boozecooperativa.com; Kolokotroni 57, Monastiraki; ⊙ 11am-3am, until 4am Fri & Sat; 🌐; Ⓜ Monastiraki) By day this art mansion is full of young Athenians playing chess and backgammon and

---

LGBT+ ATHENS

Athens' LGBT+ scene is lively and increasingly becoming an international drawcard. Athens Pride (p109), held in June, is an annual event; there's a march and a concert on Syntagma.

For nightlife, Gazi is Athens' LGBT+ hub. Gay and gay-friendly clubs around town are also in Plateia Agia Irini, Metaxourgio and Exarhia. For more information, check out http://athens-real.com and www.athensinfoguide.com.

Rooster (Map p92; ☑ 210 322 4410; www.roostercafe.gr; Plateia Agia Irini 4, Monastiraki; ⊙ 9am-3am; 🌐; Ⓜ Monastiraki) This always-busy LGBT+ cafe on lively Plateia Agia Irini is straight-friendly too, and so fills with chatting locals across the rainbow spectrum.

Loukoumi (Map p92; ☑ 210 323 4814; https://en.loukoumibar.gr; Plateia Avyssinias 3, Monastiraki; ⊙ 10am-3am Sun-Thu, to 4am Fri & Sat; Ⓜ Monastiraki) This creative, gay-friendly cafe and arts space occupies two buildings facing each other across Plateia Avyssinias. It covers everything from daytime coffee and snacks to night-time DJs to drag queens, plus a vintage shop and gallery space.

Shamone (Map p116; ☑ 210 345 0144; www.shamone.gr; Leoforos Konstantinoupoleos 46, Gazi; entry after midnight €8; ⊙ 10.30pm-6am Fri & Sat; Ⓜ Kerameikos) Since it opens a bit earlier than other Gazi LGBT bars and clubs, this is usually where the rainbow dance-and-party crowd starts off the night. Check their Facebook page (www.facebook.com/shamoneclub) for details of events.

BeQueer (Map p116; ☑ 213 012 2249; www.facebook.com/bequeerathens; Keleou 10, Keramikos; ⊙ midnight-6am Fri & Sat; Ⓜ Kerameikos) Gazi's gay bar and club scene can be a little homogenous, but this quirkier, more casual club breaks that mould. The vibe is friendly and open, and there are occasional theme and drag nights.

Beaver Collective (Map p116; ☑ 211 210 3540; www.facebook.com/collectivebeaver; Vasiliou tou Megalou 46, Rouf; ⊙ 1.30pm-2am Mon-Thu, to 3am Fri & Sat, 11.30am-midnight Sun; Ⓜ Kerameikos) This women-run cooperative cafe is of course lesbian-friendly, but also just generally friendly. Sunday brunch gets a good crowd and cocktails flow freely.

Myrovolos (Map p116; ☑ 210 522 8806; Giatrakou 12, Metaxourgio; ⊙ noon-4am Mon-Fri, 11am-4am Sat & Sun; Ⓜ Metaxourghiou) Popular lesbian cafe-bar-restaurant on a somewhat unkempt square, with a motorcycle clubhouse (unrelated) upstairs. Archetypal Metaxourgio, in other words.

working on their laptops. Later it transforms into a happening bar that rocks till late. The basement hosts art exhibitions and there's a theatre upstairs.

Gazi, Keramikos & Exarhia

★ Blue Parrot
CAFE

(Map p116; ☎211 012 1099; Leonidou 31, Metaxourgio; ⊙9am-2am Sun-Thu, until 3am Fri & Sat; Ⓜ Metaxourghiou) Lashes of hanging greenery and a laid-back vibe, both inside and outside, make the Blue Parrot one of the area's most pleasant spots to hang out over a drink.

★ Romantso
CLUB

(Map p102; ☎216 700 3325; www.romantso.gr; Anaxagora 3, Omonia; ⊙9am-1am Mon-Fri, from 10am Sat & Sun; Ⓜ Omonia) Based in the former offices of famous, but now defunct, magazine *Romantso,* this diamond of a creative hub has multiple facets. It's an all-day cafe-bar, there are DJ dance parties pretty much every weekend and they stage regular exhibitions, live music events and activities such as social yoga and fun hula-hoop classes (hoopit.gr).

Bios
ROOFTOP BAR

(Map p116; ☎210 342 5335; www.bios.gr; Pireos 84, Keramikos; ⊙11am-2am Sun-Thu, until 4am Fri & Sat; Ⓜ Thissio) Occupying a Bauhaus apartment building, this multilevel warren has a great rooftop bar, restaurant, basement club and tiny art-house cinema. Expect live performances, art and new-media exhibitions, or at the very least a solid DJ and fab Acropolis view. In colder months, most activity is in Tesla, the ground-floor bar.

Lotos
BAR

(Map p102; ☎210 380 1380; Zoodohou Pigis 5; ⊙3pm-3.30am; Ⓜ Panepistimio) This urban bar with an exotic feel is hidden in a backstreet of the laid-back Exarhia neighbourhood. Loved by a younger crowd and students, it's one of the few bars in Athens that's packed every weeknight until the early hours – not coincidentally it serves the cheapest alcohol in the city. There are different DJs and music genres every night.

Nabokov
BAR

(Map p102; ☎211 111 0432; Asklipiou 41, Exarhia; ⊙noon-2am Mon-Thu, to 3am Fri & Sat, 7pm-2am Sun; Ⓜ Panepistimio) Just what you'd expect in an Exarhia bar: literary leanings, retro music, a bit of food and customers who treat it like their lifelong haunt, even though it only opened in 2017. There's even a pinball machine in the corner.

Taf Coffee
COFFEE

(Map p102; ☎210 380 0014; www.cafetaf.gr; Emmanuel Benaki 7, Omonia; ⊙7am-8pm Mon-Fri, 8am-5pm Sat; Ⓜ Omonia) One of the best of Athens' third-wave coffee roasters, with distribution around the country and a bit abroad. Sip a pour-over here, or grab a quick espresso at the front bar. A nice touch are tasting notes (in English) of the daily coffee blends.

Revolt
BAR

(Map p102; ☎210 380 0016; Koletti 25-27 Exarhia; ⊙10am-2am, to 3am Fri & Sat; Ⓜ Omonia) This small, simple bar with tables spilling out onto a pedestrian street anchors a few solid blocks of good nightlife. The vibrant murals out front are super. Start here and explore down Koletti as far as Mesolongiou, and the pedestrian blocks there.

Kolonaki, Mets & Pangrati

Chelsea Hotel
BAR

(Map p122; ☎210 756 3374; Arhimidous 1, Pangrati; ⊙8am-4am; 🛜; 🚌2, 4, 11 to Plateia Plastira) When people talk about the cool-but-mellow scene in Pangrati, they're probably thinking of this busy cafe-bar on Plateia Plastira. By day it's about coffee and people reading or working on their laptops. When the sun sets every seat, inside and out, is filled with young Athenians aspiring to be as artistic and bohemian as residents of the bar's NYC namesake.

★ To Tsai
TEAHOUSE

(Map p122; ☎210 338 8941; www.tea.gr; Alexandrou Soutsou 19, Kolonaki; ⊙9am-9pm Mon-Sat; 🛜; Ⓜ Syntagma) Get a Zen vibe as you sip from a vast range of teas from around the world at this minimalist tearoom and shop that's a calm respite in the midst of Kolonaki. Keep an eye on your blonde-wood table, though, as they rest on trestles and can shift about a bit unexpectedly.

ⓘ SUMMER CLUBBING

In summer, much of the city's serious nightlife moves to glamorous, enormous seafront clubs radiating out from Glyfada (p143). Many sit on the tram route, which runs to 2.30am on Friday and Saturday. If you book for dinner you don't pay cover; otherwise admission ranges from €10 to €20 and includes one drink. Glam up to get in.

Jazz in Jazz BAR

(Map p122; ☑ 210 722 5246; https://jazzinjazz. business.site; Dinokratous 4, Kolonaki; ⓢ 8pm-3am; Ⓜ Syntagma, Evangelismos) A good cool-weather destination, this cosy bar glows with candles and vintage brass instruments, and stays warm with the sounds of New Orleans bebop and neighbours chatting over a glass of wine or whisky.

Filion CAFE

(Map p122; ☑ 210 361 2850; www.filioncafe.com; Skoufa 34, Kolonaki; ⓢ 7am-12.30am; ☎; Ⓜ Syntagma) Holding strong against Kolonaki's modern glitz, Filion is a pleasantly old-school cafe-bar, frequented by older members of the intellectual establishment and the occasional younger artist or writer.

☆ Entertainment

Athenians consider every musical event an opportunity for a singalong, which can make the most formal concert venues feel wonderfully chummy (even if you don't know the words yourself). Options vary seasonally: most indoor venues close or scale back programming in the summer, when the open-air theatres and cinemas take over.

For comprehensive events listings, with links to online ticket-sales points, try the following.

www.thisisathens.org Athens tourism site

www.athensculturenet.com English listings of events and performances

www.viva.gr Major ticket vendor, including for the Athens & Epidaurus Festival

www.ticketservices.gr Range of events.

Cinema

One of the delights of Athens is the enduring tradition of open-air cinema, where you can watch the latest Hollywood or art-house flick in the warm summer air. The settings are old-fashioned gardens and rooftops, with modern sound and projection. Cinemas start up in early May and usually close in September.

★ Cine Paris CINEMA

(Map p92; ☑ 210 322 2071; www.cineparis.gr; Kydathineon 22, Plaka; adult/child €8/6; ⓢ May-Oct; Ⓜ Syntagma) The Paris was established in the 1920s and it's still a magical place to see a movie. On a rooftop in Plaka, it offers great views of the Acropolis from some seats.

SPORTING ATHENS

Greece's top football teams are the Athens-based Panathinaikos (www. pao.gr) and AEK (www.aekfc.gr), and Piraeus-based Olympiacos (www. olympiacos.org), all three of which are in the European Champions League. Check club websites, English-language press or www.ticketmaster.gr.

'Basket' (basketball) is one of Athens' most popular sports, with a number of men's and women's pro teams in Athens (Panathinaikos and AEK are the biggest) and Piraeus (Olympiacos). For schedules, see the website of the Hellenic Basketball Federation (EOK; www.basket.gr). Games are often held at the 18,000-seat stadium at the **Athens Olympic Complex** (OAKA; Map p146; ☑ 210 683 4777; www. oaka.com.gr; Marousi; Ⓜ Irini).

Thission CINEMA

(Map p116; ☑ 210 342 0864; www.cine-thisio.gr; Apostolou Pavlou 7, Thisio; tickets €6-8; ⓢ May-Oct; Ⓜ Thissio) Across from the Acropolis (p78), this is a lovely old-style outdoor cinema in a garden setting. Sit towards the back if you want to catch a glimpse of the glowing edifice. Tickets are the lower price if you attend Monday to Wednesday shows.

Aegli Cinema CINEMA

(Map p122; ☑ 210 336 9300; www.aeglizappiou.gr; Zappeio Gardens; adult/child €8.50/6.50; ⓢ screenings at 9pm & 11pm May-Oct; Ⓜ Syntagma) This historical open-air cinema showed its first film in 1903. Set in the verdant Zappeion, it's a little quieter than others.

Cine Dexameni CINEMA

(Map p122; ☑ 210 362 3942; www.cinedexameni. gr; Plateia Dexameni, Kolonaki; adult/child €8/5; ⓢ screenings around 9pm; Ⓜ Evangelismos) This classic open-air cinema is in a lovely spot in the quieter reaches of Kolonaki, adjacent to a very good all-day cafe and the ancient cistern of Hadrian's aqueduct. Settle in for the film in a deck chair, with a little table to rest your beer on. A wall of cascading bougainvilleas rounds out the view.

Vox CINEMA

(Map p102; ☑ 210 381 0727; www.facebook.com/ vox.athens; Themistokleous 82, Exarhia; adult/ child €7/6, Tue €5; ⓢ 7.30pm-1am; Ⓜ Omonia) Vox open-air cinema on Exarhia's main square has been around since 1938, and fortunately has received historic-building designation.

Still, it has the rough-and-ready vibe you'd expect in this neighbourhood. Arrive early and have a drink at the ground-floor cafe.

Greek Film Archive
CINEMA
(Tainiothiki tis Ellados; Map p116; ☑ 210 360 9695; www.tainiothiki.gr; Iera 48, Keramikos; tickets €7; ⊙varies; Ⓜ Kerameikos) There are two auditoriums at this art-house cinema. Check the website for special film series and festivals.

Live Music

★Gazarte
LIVE MUSIC
(Map p116; ☑ 21034 60347; www.gazarte.gr; Voutadon 32-34, Gazi; tickets from €10; Ⓜ Kerameikos) At this respected arts complex, you'll find largely mainstream music and a trendy 30-something crowd. A ground-level theatre hosts live performances and there's also a rooftop bar and restaurant.

★Half Note Jazz Club
JAZZ
(Map p122; ☑ 21092 13310; www.halfnote.gr; Trivonianou 17, Mets; tickets €10-25; ⊙varies; Ⓜ Akropoli) Athens' most serious jazz venue is a stylish place that hosts Greek and international musicians. Check the schedule ahead of your trip, as it's not open every night and closes entirely in summer.

Perivoli tou Ouranou
TRADITIONAL MUSIC
(Map p92; ☑ 21032 35517; www.facebook.com/toperivolitououranou; Lysikratous 19, Plaka; ⊙ 9pm-late Fri & Sat, noon-6pm Sun Oct-Jun; Ⓜ Akropoli) A favourite Plaka music haunt with dinner (mains €18 to €29).

Fuzz Club
LIVE MUSIC
(Map p74; ☑ 21034 50817; www.fuzzclub.gr; Patriarchou Ioakim 1, Moschato Tavros; tickets from €10; Ⓜ Petralona, Ⓡ Tavros) One of the best midsize music venues in Athens, this place is a little out of the centre, but worth the trip for a band you like (they host plenty of international acts) and probably with cheaper admission than the equivalent venue in your home city. It also has occasional club nights.

Steki Pinoklis
TRADITIONAL MUSIC
(Map p116; ☑ 21057 77355; www.facebook.com/pinoklis; Megalou Alexandrou 102, Keramikos; ⊙5pm-3am Mon-Sat, 2pm-1am Sun; Ⓜ Kerameikos) Although this taverna opened in 2017, its musical taste and style skews much older. This is an excellent place to hear *rembetika* (blues) songs from Smyrna plus other traditional Greek music, with a band playing most nights (starting at 10pm) and Sunday afternoons (usually from 4pm). Food is average, but not expensive.

Feidiou 2 Music Cafe
LIVE MUSIC
(Map p102; ☑ 21033 00060; www.facebook.com/Feidiou2; Fidiou 2, Exarhia; ⊙ 8am-2.30am Mon-Sat, from 5pm Sun; Ⓜ Omonia) Cosy little space on the edge of Exarhia. Traditional music, usually *rembetika* and other heartfelt tunes, starts around 10pm most nights, when there's a minimum charge of €8 for food and drinks. Attracts a nice mixed crowd of all ages.

AN Club
LIVE MUSIC
(Map p102; ☑ 21033 05056; www.anclub.gr; Solomou 13-15, Exarhia; tickets from €6; Ⓜ Omonia) A small spot with a long history of live rock, featuring lesser-known international and local bands, especially metal.

Theatre & Performing Arts

Greek National Opera
OPERA
(Ethniki Lyriki Skini; ☑ 21036 62100; www.nationalopera.gr; Leoforos Syngrou 364, Kallithea; tickets €10-90; ☎; ☐550 to Onasseio, 10 to Epaminonda) Having settled into state-of-the-art digs within the Stavros Niarchos Foundation Cultural Center, the Greek National Opera is going from strength to strength. The season runs from November to June. Its main 1400-seat auditorium is a stunning space with superb sight lines throughout.

The season includes classic works, quirkier new ones and big international coproductions. Performances are top quality and tickets prices are very reasonable.

As well as the opera, the Greek National Ballet, Orchestra and Choirs perform here. The complex also includes the **Alternative Stage**, a flexible space that accommodates up to 450 people for more experimental and intimate productions.

During the Athens Festival (p109) each summer, the GNO stages performances at the Odeon of Herodes Atticus (p81).

Megaron
PERFORMING ARTS
(Athens Concert Hall; Map p74; ☑ 21072 82333; www.megaron.gr; Kokkali 1, cnr Leoforos Vasilissis Sofias, Ilissia; tickets from €7; ⊙ box office 10am-6pm Mon-Fri, to 2pm Sat, later on performance days; Ⓜ Megaro Mousikis) The city's premier performance hall presents an impressive program of entertainments, including classical concerts, opera, theatre and dance shows, featuring world-class international and Greek performers. There's often some sort of art exhibition on here, and between June and September concerts are also staged outdoors in the complex's back garden.

Onassis Cultural Centre
ARTS CENTRE

(Map p74; ☑ info & tickets 21090 05800; www.sgt. gr; Leoforos Syngrou 107-109, Neos Kosmos; ☏; ☐ 10 or 550 to Panteio, Ⓜ Sygrou-Fix) Housed in an eye-catching piece of architecture that livens up the dull urbanity of Leoforos Syngrou, this visual- and performing-arts centre is well worth a visit. Cloaked in a striped cage of white marble, the building glows at night when it hosts big-name productions, installations and lectures. Check the schedule for free events.

★ National Theatre
THEATRE

(Map p102; ☑ 21052 88100; www.n-t.gr; Agiou Konstantinou 22-24, Omonia; Ⓜ Omonia) One of the city's finest neoclassical buildings hosts contemporary theatre and ancient plays. The organisation also supports performances in other venues around town and, in summer, in ancient theatres across Greece. Happily for tourists, some of the productions are surtitled in English, and tickets are reasonably priced.

Dora Stratou Dance Theatre
DANCE

(Map p86; ☑ 21092 14650; www.grdance.org; Filopappou Hill, Thisio; adult/child €15/5; ☺ performances 9.30pm Wed-Fri, 8.15pm Sat & Sun late May-Sep; Ⓜ Petralona, Akropoli) Every summer this company of 75 singers and dancers performs Greek folk dances, showing off the rich variety of regional costume and musical traditions. Performances are held at its open-air theatre on the western side of Filopappou Hill. It also runs folk-dancing workshops.

🛍 Shopping

Central Athens is the city's original commercial district, and still one big shopping hub, with an eclectic mix of stores. The area is still organised roughly by category – lace and buttons on one block, light bulbs on the next. The main (if generic) shopping street is pedestrianised Ermou, running from Syntagma to Monastiraki.

🛍 Acropolis & Around

★ Athena
Design Workshop
FASHION & ACCESSORIES

(Map p86; ☑ 21092 45713; www.athenadesignworkshop.com; Parthenonos 30, Makrygianni; ☺ 11.30am-7pm Mon-Fri, until 5pm Sat; Ⓜ Akropoli) You can often find Krina Vronti busy woodblock printing her appealing graphic designs on T-shirts, cushion covers and paper at this combined studio and shop. The images are often inspired by ancient and classical themes but are given a contemporary twist.

★ Underflow
MUSIC

(Map p86; ☑ 21140 39926; http://underflow.gr; Kallirrois 39, Kynosargous; ☺ 11am-9pm Mon-Thu, until 1am Fri, 4pm Sat; Ⓜ Sygrou-Fix) Specialising in Greek avant-garde rock and obscure sounds, this is one of Athens' top record shops. It stocks a wide range of music genres on vinyl and CD, both new and secondhand. It's also an art gallery, cafe and, on Friday nights, a performance space – check the website to see who's playing.

El.Marneri Galerie
JEWELLERY

(Map p86; ☑ 21086 19488; www.elenimarneri. com; Lembesi 5-7, Makrygianni; ☺ 11am-8pm Tue, Thu & Fri, to 4pm Wed & Sat; Ⓜ Akropoli) Sample rotating exhibitions of local modern art and some of the best jewellery in the city. Handmade, unusual and totally eye-catching.

Me Then
FASHION & ACCESSORIES

(Map p86; ☑ 6947520477; https://methenathens. com; Odissea Androutsou 36, Koukaki; ☺ 5-8pm Tue, Thu & Sat, 1-5pm Fri; Ⓜ Sygrou-Fix) There's a relative dearth of local designers creating contemporary menswear in Athens, so it's nice to see George Soumpasis filling in the gap at this boutique. Many of his designs are actually unisex; offerings include shirts with bold Matisse-style prints, structural jackets and trousers.

Mon Coin
CERAMICS

(Map p86; ☑ 6976800244; www.facebook.com/ moncoin.athens; Erehthiou 16, Koukaki; ☺ 10am-2.30pm Mon-Fri, also 5-8pm Tue, Thu & Fri, 10am-6pm Sat; Ⓜ Sygrou-Fix) This branch of the ceramics, homewares and accessories boutique set up by former French lawyer Eleonore Trenado-Finetis stocks a traditional – but very appealing – range of designs from across Greece.

There's a second, larger branch in **Monastiraki** (Map p92; ☑ 6976800244; www.facebook.com/moncoin.athens; 7 Thisiou, Monastiraki; ☺ 10am-3pm Mon, until 8pm Tue-Fri, until 6pm Sat; Ⓜ Monastiraki) that carries more contemporary designs.

Fabrika + Sonja Blum
FASHION & ACCESSORIES

(Map p86; ☑ 6946463657; https://fabrika-sonjablum.tumblr.com; Veïkou 9, Makrygianni; ☺ 10.30am-2pm Tue-Fri, also 5-8pm Tue & Thu, 11am-4pm Sat; Ⓜ Akropoli) Sonja Blum's fabric mobiles, kids' clothes and knitted scarves in the shape of foxes are the star attractions in this cute little accessories boutique. It also stocks jewellery and artworks by a collective of other designers and artists.

LOCAL KNOWLEDGE

FLEA MARKETS

Athens' flea markets are not for everyone. The city's trash-pickers prefer the **Eleonas Flea Market** (Pazari; Agias Annis, Eleonas; ☉ dawn-2pm Sun; Ⓜ Eleonas). In this industrial part of town, junk dealers, sellers of vegetables, new clothes and bulk items lay out their wares in several warehouses and parking lots. The brave of heart can find some bargains, collectables and kitsch delights among the junk. You may need to scout around a bit to find it. When you get out at the metro stop, walk south until you see parked cars and a church in a traffic circle. Vendors are usually set up in warehouses nearby.

The central **Monastiraki Flea Market** (Map p92; Plateia Avyssinias, Monastiraki; ☉ daily May-Oct, Sun-Wed & Fri Nov-Apr; Ⓜ Monastiraki) is easy to locate. Ifestou is signed as the 'Athens flea market', but the street mostly has souvenir shops. The true flea feel is on Plateia Avyssinias and in nearby small streets, where dusty *palaiopoleia* ('old-stuff sellers') rule. For the best rummaging, come Sunday mornings, when the bric-a-brac explodes out onto the pavements, including on Astingos and even across Ermou in Psyrri.

Lovecuts   CLOTHING
(Map p86; ☑ 215 501 1526; Veïkou 2, Makrygianni; ☉ 11am-8.30pm Mon-Fri, until 4pm Sat; Ⓜ Akropoli) Greek designer Maria Panagiotou makes all the cute, affordable cotton clothing here, such as reversible hoodies, skirts and blouses in fun prints. It's one of several creative small-scale boutiques on this street.

🏠 Syntagma & Plaka

★ **Alexis Papachatzis**   JEWELLERY
(Map p92; ☑ 210 325 4064; www.alexisp.gr; Erehtheos 6, Plaka; ☉ 10am-4pm Mon, Wed & Fri, to 7pm Tue, Thu & Sat; Ⓜ Monastiraki, Syntagma) This charming jewellery store is a delight before you even enter: turn the handle on the window display and watch as gears and pulleys animate the scene. Papachatzis' designs have a storybook quality: small figures, clouds and animals rendered in sterling silver and enamel.

★ **Forget Me Not**   GIFTS & SOUVENIRS
(Map p92; ☑ 210 325 3740; www.forgetmenotathens.gr; Adrianou 100, Plaka; ☉ 10am-9pm Apr & May, until 10pm Jun, Sep & Oct, until 11pm Jul & Aug, until 8pm Nov-Mar; Ⓜ Syntagma, Monastiraki) This impeccable small store (two shops, one upstairs and one down around the corner) stocks super-cool gear, from fashion to housewares and gifts, all by contemporary Greek designers. Great for gift shopping – who doesn't want a set of cheerful 'evil eye' coasters or some Hermes-winged beach sandals?

Flâneur   DESIGN
(Map p92; ☑ 210 322 6900; www.facebook.com/flaneursouvenirsandsupplies; Adrianou 110, cnr Flessa, Plaka; ☉ 11am-8pm; Ⓜ Syntagma, Monastiraki) This cute shop has a tightly curated collection of souvenirs and travel gear. Get your hand-stamped 'φλανέρ' (that's 'flâneur' spelled in Greek) notebooks and your feta-tin patches and pins here. Even stocks vinyl by Greek indie bands.

Anavasi   MAPS
(Map p92; ☑ 210 321 8104; www.anavasi.gr; Voulis 32, cnr Apollonos, Syntagma; ☉ 9.30am-5pm Mon & Wed, to 8.30pm Tue, Thu & Fri, 10am-4.30pm Sat; Ⓜ Syntagma) Great travel bookshop with an extensive range of Greece maps and walking and activity guides.

Korres   COSMETICS
(Map p92; ☑ 210 321 0054; www.korres.com; Ermou 4, Syntagma; ☉ 9am-9pm Mon-Fri, to 8pm Sat; Ⓜ Syntagma) Many pharmacies stock some of this popular line of natural beauty products, but you can get the full range at the company's original location, where it grew out of a homeopathic pharmacy.

Amorgos   ARTS & CRAFTS
(Map p92; ☑ 210 324 3836; www.amorgosart.gr; Kodrou 3, Plaka; ☉ 11am-8pm Mon-Fri, to 7pm Sat; Ⓜ Syntagma) Charming store crammed with wooden toys, *karagiozi* (shadow puppets), ceramics, embroidery and other Greek folk art, as well as carved wooden furniture made by the owner.

Matalou at Home/Blanc FASHION & ACCESSORIES
(Map p92; ☑ 211 184 5416; www.facebook.com/matalouathome; Ipitou 5, Syntagma; ☉ noon-9pm Tue, Thu & Fri, until 5pm Wed & Sat; Ⓜ Syntagma) Two designers share the space here. Matalou at Home creates an appealing range of affordable bags and accessories from leather, cotton and natural fibres, with the designs inspired by Athens. Blanc (www.blanc.gr) is all about handmade hats.

Chat to the owner for recommendations and tips on other local designers and hip hang-outs, covered twice a year in their free *By Local* map.

Aristokratikon
FOOD

(Map p92; ☑210 322 0546; www.aristokratikon. com; Voulis 7, Syntagma; ☺8am-9pm Mon-Fri, to 4pm Sat; Ⓜ Syntagma) This shop has been making fine chocolates since 1928. One of its specialities is dried fruits and candied citrus peel dipped in dark chocolate.

Aidinis Errikos
ARTS & CRAFTS

(Map p92; ☑210 323 4591; www.facebook.com/ Errikos.Aidinis; Nikis 32, Syntagma; ☺10am-5pm Mon, Wed & Sat, to 8.30pm Tue, Thu & Fri; Ⓜ Syntagma) Artisan Errikos Aidinis' unique metal creations are made in his workshop at the back of this charming store, including small mirrors, candlesticks, lamps, aeroplanes and his signature bronze boats.

Xylouris
MUSIC

(Map p102; ☑210 322 2711; http://xilouris.gr; Stoa Pesmatzoglou, Panepistimiou 39, Panepistimio; ☺9am-4pm Mon, Wed & Sat, to 8pm Tue, Thu & Fri; Ⓜ Panepistimio) Set in an arcade with several other music shops, this treasure trove is run by the family of legendary Cretan composer Nikos Xylouris. They can guide you through the comprehensive range of Greek music CDs and DVDs, as well help with a new bouzouki purchase.

Monastiraki & Psyrri

★ Shedia
ARTS & CRAFTS

(Map p92; ☑213 023 1220; www.shediart.gr; Nikiou 2, Monastiraki; Ⓜ Monastiraki) Meaning 'raft', *Shedia* is Greece's version of street-vendor magazines such as the *Big Issue*. Unsold copies are now being upcycled into an appealing range of homewares and accessories including papier-mâché lampshades and bowls, and dainty earrings and necklaces. The space beneath their editorial offices has been reimagined as a shop and stylish cafe-bar.

★ Varvakios Agora
MARKET

(Athens Central Market; Map p102; Athinas, btwn Sofokleous & Evripidou, Psyrri; ☺7am-6pm Mon-Sat; Ⓜ Panepistimio, Omonia) A wonderful sight in its own right, this huge old wrought-iron market hall is dedicated to fish and meat, especially row upon row of lamb carcasses, hanging in just-barely EU-compliant glass cases. Tavernas within the market, many open 24/7, are an Athenian institution for hangover-busting *patsas* (tripe soup).

West across Athinas is the **fruit and vegetable market** (Map p102; Athinas, btwn Sofokleous & Evripidou, Psyrri; ☺7am-6pm Mon-Sat; Ⓜ Omonia, Monastiraki). In the surrounding streets are olives, cheeses and spices.

To Rodakio & Fotagogos
BOOKS

(Map p92; ☑210 383 9355; www.facebook.com/To-Rodakio; Kolokotroni 59b, Monastiraki; ☺11.30am-9pm Mon-Sat; Ⓜ Monastiraki) This charming bookshop and gallery, run by Julia Tsiakiris and hidden at the back of cafe-bar Noel (p126), is a wonderful find. Browse locally published books and magazines (some in English), and quirky pieces of art.

Pan-Pol
HATS

(Map p102; ☑210 321 1431; Athinas 36, Monastiraki; ☺10am-5pm Mon, Wed & Sat, to 7pm Tue, Thu & Fri; Ⓜ Monastiraki) Whether you want a moss-green fedora or a nontouristy Greek fisherman's cap, this shoebox of a shop will have it, along with many other felt hats in lovely colours and classic shapes. Most of the stock comes from a workshop upstairs, and prices start at just €10.

Fotsi
FOOD

(Map p102; ☑210 321 7131; www.fotsi.gr; Evripidou 39, Psyrri; ☺8am-5pm Mon-Sat; Ⓜ Monastiraki) Evripidou is Athens' traditional street for spices, a couple of highly aromatic blocks of Mediterranean herbs and imported seeds, barks and other wonders. Three generations of the same family have run Fotsi, the most picturesque of half a dozen shops here, all overflowing with hundreds of ways to add flavour and fragrance to your life.

Yiannis Samouelian
MUSICAL INSTRUMENTS

(Map p92; ☑210 321 2433; www.musiceshop.gr; Ifestou 36, Monastiraki; ☺11am-8pm; Ⓜ Monastiraki) Wedged between more-modern, generic shops on Ifestou, this shop is the place to buy the bouzouki of your dreams; handmade ones cost around €180. It has been dealing in musical instruments from around the world since 1928.

Martinos
ANTIQUES

(Map p92; ☑210 321 2414; www.martinosart.gr; Pandrosou 50, Monastiraki; ☺10am-3pm Mon, Wed & Sat, to 6pm Tue, Thu & Fri; Ⓜ Monastiraki) This Monastiraki landmark opened in 1890 and has an excellent, sometimes museum-quality selection of Greek and European antiques and collectables, including painted dowry chests, icons, coins, glassware, porcelain and furniture.

ⓘ WEEKLY FOOD MARKETS

Most Athens neighbourhoods have a weekly *laïki agora*, a street market for fruit, veg, fish, olives, honey, handmade products and flowers. Even if you're not interested in grocery shopping, they are wonderful street theatre and very photogenic. Good ones include those in **Kolonaki** (Map p122; www.laikesagores. gr; Xenokratous, Kolonaki; ⊙7am-2pm Fri; MEvangelismos) and **Exarhia** (Map p102; Kalidromiou, Exarhia; ⊙6am-2pm Sat; ▣026, MOmonia).

Center of Hellenic Tradition   ARTS & CRAFTS
(Map p92; ✔210 321 3023; Pandrosou 36, Monastiraki; ⊙10am-6pm Tue-Sat; MMonastiraki) This organisation collects excellent traditional craftwork and stocks its shop with ceramics, sculpture and handicrafts from around the country.

It shares an upstairs space with the old-style coffee house Orea Hellas (p127) that makes a nice break from the Monastiraki shopping frenzy.

Monastic Art   HOMEWARES
(Map p92; ✔210 324 5034; http://monasticart. gr; Pandrosou 28, Monastiraki; ⊙10am-7pm Mon-Sat; MMonastiraki) All of the products in this store are made by monks on Mt Athos: olives, wine, beauty products from wild and cultivated herbs, and beautiful gold and silver icons. Prices range from €5 to well over €25,000.

Olgianna Melissinos   SHOES
(Map p92; ✔210 331 1925; www.melissinos-sandals.gr; Normanou 7, Monastiraki; ⊙10am-6pm Wed, Sat & Sun, to 8pm Tue, Thu & Fri; MMonastiraki) A scion of the legendary poet/sandalmaker Stavros Melissinos – along with brother Pantelis, who has a separate shop (p134) – Olgianna has a line of custom-fitted sandals as well as smart belts and bags. She can also make designs to order.

Melissinos Art   SHOES
(Map p102; ✔210 321 9247; www.melissinos-art. com; Agias Theklas 2, Psyrri; ⊙10am-8pm Tue-Sun May-Sep, to 6pm Oct-Apr; MMonastiraki) Pantelis Melissinos continues the sandal-making tradition started by his grandfather in 1920 and made famous by his poet/cobbler father Stavros, who built his reputation crafting Classical-inspired shoe designs for Hollywood stars and VIPs. The shop can get a bit crowded, as people come for charming Pantelis himself. Prices are reasonable – especially as the shoes are adjusted to your feet.

🛍 Exarhia

★ Free Thinking Zone   BOOKS
(Map p102; ✔210 361 7461; www.freethinkingzone. gr; Skoufa 64, Exarhia; ⊙10am-9pm Mon-Fri, to 8pm Sat, noon-5pm Sun; MPanepistimio) Billing itself as Greece's first activist bookshop, the Free Thinking Zone specialises in books on LGBT issues, refugees, violence in society and so on. However, rather than being earnest, it's quite a fun and creative place. It has a cafe and sells locally made souvenirs such as their multilingual board game Beat the Book Bug.

★ Zacharias   FASHION & ACCESSORIES
(Map p102; www.zacharias.es; Zoodohou Pigis 55, Exarhia; ⊙10am-5pm Mon-Sat; MOmonia) A Greek-Spanish duo specialising in silk-screen designs inspired by classical motifs. Especially nice are their leather notebooks, wallets and more, where black ink on the natural hide echoes the colours of ancient pottery. Some of their work shows up in museum shops, but this storefront and workspace has the best selection.

Koukoutsi   FASHION & ACCESSORIES
(Map p102; ✔210 361 4060; www.koukoutsi.net; Skoufa 81, Exarhia; ⊙10am-5pm Mon, Wed & Sat, until 8.30pm Tue, Thu & Fri; MPanepistimio) Niko and Taso design the simple, elegant Athens-and Greece-inspired graphics that adorn the T-shirts, accessories and art prints sold in this tiny shop. Their products are available in a few other boutiques and gift shops around the city, but this one has the largest selection in a full range of sizes and colours.

Plastikourgeio   GIFTS & SOUVENIRS
(Map p102; ✔213 044 3356; http://plastikourgeio. com; Asklipiou 51, Exarhia; ⊙10.30am-3.30pm Mon & Wed, until 7pm Tue, until 8pm Thu & Fri; MPanepistimio) In a time when the world is worried about single-use plastics and waste, this store is there to help; it stocks products made from recycled plastic or goods that help avoid the use of plastic in the first place. There are a few nice local craft products to browse.

Redo   FASHION & ACCESSORIES
(Map p102; ✔215 501 7280; www.redo.gr; Asklipiou 67, Exarhia; ⊙3-8pm Mon-Fri, 11am-3pm Sat;

Panepistimio) Cork fabric from Portugal and Italian leather are used for the striking range of handbags and backpacks made at this atelier by designer Maria Mavroudi. Come here to see the full range and have your bag customised as you like.

Kolonaki, Mets & Pangrati

Lemisios
SHOES
(Map p122; ☎ 210 361 1161; Lykavittou 6, Kolonaki; ⊙ 9am-3pm Mon, Wed & Sat, to 8.30pm Tue, Thu & Fri; M Syntagma, Panepistimio) An Athens classic, open since 1912, with classic designs – T-straps, ballet flats, elegant Oxfords (their only style for men) – all custom-fit just for you. Bespoke designs are also possible. Considering the level of craft, this place is surprisingly affordable with shoes starting at €100.

Katerina Ioannidis
JEWELLERY
(Map p122; ☎ 6932375717; www.katerinaioannidis. com; Anagnostopoulou 15, Kolonaki; ⊙ 10am-4pm Mon, Wed & Sat, to 9pm Tue, Thu & Fri; M Syntagma) From a family of goldsmiths, Ioannidis merges Greek and other global folkloric elements into jewellery that is light, bohemian and sometimes even a little funny: a pendant of, say, a gold-plated sheep's head set on a fuzzy black pompom, or a bean-shaped charm.

Mastiha Shop
FOOD
(Map p122; ☎ 210 363 2750; www.mastihashop. com; Panepistimiou 6, Kolonaki; ⊙ 9am-8pm Mon & Wed, to 9pm Tue, Thu & Fri, to 5pm Sat; M Syntagma) Mastic (*mastiha* in Greek), the medicinal resin from rare trees only found on the island of Chios, is the key ingredient in everything in this store, from natural skin products to a liqueur that's divine when served chilled.

Kombologadiko
FASHION & ACCESSORIES
(Map p122; ☎ 212 700 0500; www.kombologadiko. gr; Amerikis 9, Kolonaki; ⊙ 10am-4pm Mon, Wed & Sat, to 9pm Tue, Thu & Fri; M Syntagma) If you're in the market for a very special set of that old-school Greek accessory, *komboloï* (worry beads), check this oh-so-elegant showroom. It stocks ready-made designs, some from industrial materials as well as semiprecious stones and amber, starting from as little as €7. They can also string custom sets from their collection of beads.

Apivita
COSMETICS
(Map p122; ☎ 210 364 0560; www.apivita.com; Solonos 6, Kolonaki; ⊙ 10am-9pm Tue, Thu & Fri, to 5pm Mon, Wed & Sat; M Syntagma) Honey, propolis and other bee-made stuff are the wonder ingredients in many of Apivita's natural beauty products. You can also try Greek herbal teas or head upstairs to the hairdressers, barber shop and spa (which is closed Monday).

★ Hallelujah
FASHION & ACCESSORIES
(Map p122; ☎ 210 723 5210; www.hallelujahdesign. gr; Archelaou 32, Pangrati; ⊙ 10.30am-2.30pm & 5.30-9pm Tue, Thu & Fri, 11am-6pm Wed & Sat; M Evangelismos) Eleftheria Domenikou is the young designer whose minimalistic, elegant yet comfortable clothes and accessories are stocked here. She cooperates with jewellery designers and stocks some other cute accessories and gifts.

ℹ Information

DANGERS & ANNOYANCES
Since the financial crisis, crime has risen in Athens. But this is a rise from almost zero, and violent street crime remains relatively rare. Nonetheless, travellers should be alert. Stay aware of your surroundings at night, especially in streets southwest of Omonia and parts of Metaxourgio, where prostitutes and drug users gather.

EMERGENCY
If you are using a foreign mobile phone in Greece, the only three-digit emergency number that works is the main one (☎ 112).

Greece's country code	☎ 30
Emergency Assistance	☎ 112
Police	☎ 100 or ☎ 21077 05711
Tourist Police	☎ 171 or ☎ 21092 00724
Ambulance	☎ 116

MEDICAL SERVICES
Check pharmacy windows for details of the nearest duty pharmacy, or call 1434 (Greek only). There's a 24-hour pharmacy at the airport (p136).

SOS Doctors (☎ 210 821 2222, 1016; www.sosiatroi.gr; ⊙ 24hr) Pay service with English-speaking doctors who make house (or hotel) calls.

MONEY
Major banks have branches around Syntagma. ATMs are plentiful enough in commercial districts, but harder to find in more residential areas.

National Bank of Greece (210 334 0500; cnr Karageorgi Servias & Stadiou, Syntagma; M Syntagma) Has a 24-hour automated exchange machine.

Onexchange Currency and money transfers. Branches include **Syntagma** (210 331 2462; www.onexchange.gr; Karageorgi Servias 2, Syntagma; 9am-9pm; M Syntagma) and **Monastiraki** (210 322 2657; www.onexchange.gr; Areos 1, Monastiraki; 9am-9pm; M Monastiraki).

POST

The Greek postal system is not entirely reliable and tends to be slow. Larger post offices sell boxes and the like for shipping.

Athens Central Post Office (Map p102; 210 321 6024; www.elta.gr; Eolou 100, Omonia; 7.30am-8.30pm Mon-Fri, to 2.45pm Sat; M Omonia)

Parcel Post Office (Map p92; 210 321 8143; www.elta.gr; Mitropoleos 60, Monastiraki; 7.30am-8.30pm Mon-Fri; M Monastiraki)

Syntagma Post Office (Map p92; 210 324 5970; www.elta.gr; Mitropoleos 2, Syntagma; 7.30am-8.30pm Mon-Fri, to 2.45pm Sat, 9am-1pm Sun; M Syntagma)

TOURIST INFORMATION

Athens City Information Kiosk (Map p92; www.thisisathens.org; Plateia Syntagmatos, Syntagma; 9am-6pm; M Syntagma) Dishes out leaflets and advice. Also has a branch at the **airport** (210 353 0390; www.athensconventionbureau.gr/en/content/info-kiosk-athens-international-airport; Eleftherios Venizelos International Airport; 8am-8pm; M Airport).

Athens Contemporary Art Map (http://athensartmap.net) Download a PDF of art spaces and events; alternatively, pick up a paper copy at galleries and cafes around town.

EOT (Greek National Tourism Organisation; Map p86; 210 331 0347, 210 331 0716; www.visitgreece.gr; Dionysiou Areopagitou 18-20, Makrygianni; 8am-8pm Mon-Fri, 10am-4pm Sat & Sun May-Sep, 9am-7pm Mon-Fri Oct-Apr; M Akropoli) Free Athens map, current site hours, and bus and train information. Also has a branch at the airport (9am to 5pm Monday to Friday, 10am to 4pm Saturday).

❶ Getting There & Away

AIR

Athens' **airport** (ATH; Map p146; 210 353 0000; www.aia.gr), at Spata, 27km east of Athens, is a manageable single terminal with all the modern conveniences, including 24-hour luggage storage in the arrivals hall (from €3.50 for six hours), a children's playroom and even a small archaeological museum above the check-in hall for passing the time.

It's served by many major and budget airlines as well as high-season charters, including **easyJet** (211 198 0013; www.easyjet.com).

Between Aegean Airlines and Olympic Air (which have merged but still run separate routes), there are flights to all islands with airports.

Aegean Airlines (https://en.aegeanair.com)

Astra Airlines (801 700 7466, 2310 489 390; www.astra-airlines.gr) Thessaloniki-based, but with a few flights from Athens to Kozani/Kastoria, Chios and Samos.

Olympic Air (801 801 0101, 21035 50500; www.olympicair.com)

Sky Express (GQ; 215 215 6510; www.skyexpress.gr)

BOAT

Most ferry, hydrofoil and high-speed catamaran services to the islands leave from the massive port at Piraeus (p142), southwest of Athens. Purchase tickets online at **Greek Ferries** (281 052 9000; www.greekferries.gr), over the phone or at booths on the quay next to each ferry. Travel agencies selling tickets also surround each port; there is no surcharge.

BUS

Athens has two main intercity bus stations, plus a small bay for buses bound for south and east Attica. Pick up timetables at the tourist office (p136), or see the relevant KTEL operator's website; find a master list of KTEL companies at www.ktelbus.com. **KTEL Attikis** (210 880 8000; http://ktelattikis.gr) covers the Attica peninsula; **KTEL Argolida** (275 202 7423; www.ktelargolida.gr) serves Epidavros, with dedicated buses during the summer festival season.

Advance tickets for services from **Kifissos Terminal A** (210 515 0025; Drakontos 76, Peristeri; M Agios Antonios) can be purchased at the **ticket office** (210 523 3810; Sokratous 59, Omonia; 7am-5.15pm Mon-Fri; M Omonia) near Omonia.

For international buses (from Bulgaria, Turkey etc), there is no single station; some come to Kifissos, while others stop between Plateia Karaïskaki and Plateia Omonias. **Tourist Service** (www.tourist-service.com) is one operator from Piraeus and Athens to Bulgaria.

TRAIN

Intercity (IC) trains to central and northern Greece depart from the central **Larissi train station** (Stathmos Larisis; €1 per 1 min 6am-11pm 14511; www.trainose.gr; M Larissa), about 1km northwest of Plateia Omonias.

For the Peloponnese, take the **suburban rail** (Proastiakos; ☑14511; www.trainose.gr) to Kiato and change for a bus there. The Patra train line is chronically closed for repairs, so OSE buses, via Kiato, replace its services. Because of this, it's easier to just take a bus from Athens' Kifissos Bus Terminal A (p136) to your ultimate destination.

Domestic schedules/fares should be confirmed online or at **OSE** (☑210 362 1039; www.trainose.gr; Sina 6, Panepistimio; ◷8am-3pm Mon-Fri; Ⓜ Panepistimio), where tickets can also be purchased.

For tips on international trains, consult www.seat61.com; all trains in and out of Greece go via Thessaloniki. International tickets must be purchased in person at the train station.

DESTINATION	DURATION (HOURS)	FARE (€)	FREQUENCY
Alexandroupoli	14	38	1 daily (overnight, via Thessaloniki)
Alexandroupoli (IC)	15	63	1 daily (via Thessaloniki)
Corinth (suburban rail)	1	9	hourly
Kalambaka (for Meteora)	5	18	1 daily direct, 5 via Paleofarsalos (€32)
Kiato (suburban rail)	80mins	12	hourly
Thessaloniki	6	25	1 daily (overnight)
Thessaloniki (IC)	5½	45	5 daily
Volos (IC)	5	35	4 daily (via Larissa)

CAR & MOTORCYCLE

Attiki Odos (Attiki Rd), Ethniki Odos (National Rd) and various ring roads facilitate getting in and out of Athens.

The airport (p136) has all major car hire companies, and the north end of Leoforos Syngrou, near the Temple of Olympian Zeus (p77), is dotted with firms. Expect to pay €45 per day, less for three or more days.

Avis (☑210 322 4951; www.avis.gr; Leoforos Syngrou 23, Makrygianni; ◷7.30am-9pm; Ⓜ Akropoli)

Budget (☑210 922 4200; www.budget.gr; Leoforos Syngrou 23, Makrygianni; ◷7.30am-9pm; Ⓜ Akropoli)

Hertz (☑210 922 0102; www.hertz.gr; Leoforos Syngrou 12, Makrygianni; ◷8am-9pm; Ⓜ Akropoli)

Kosmos (☑210 923 4695; www.kosmos-car-rental.com; Leoforos Syngrou 5, Makrygianni; ◷8am-8.30pm; Ⓜ Akropoli)

Motorent (☑210 923 4939; www.motorent.gr; Kavalloti 4, Makrygianni; ◷9am-5pm Tue-Fri, 9.30am-2pm Sat; Ⓜ Akropoli) From €20 per day; must have motorcycle licence (and nerves of steel).

Nationwide roadside assistance is available through **ELPA** (Flliniki Leschi Aftokinitou kai Periigiseon; ☑24hr roadside assistance 10400).

❶ Getting Around

Central Athens is compact and good for strolling, with narrow streets and a lovely pedestrian promenade. From Gazi in the west to the Byzantine & Christian Museum in the east, for example, takes only about 45 minutes – so you may find you need a transit pass very little or not at all. In summer, however, take the punishing sun into consideration.

TO/FROM THE AIRPORT
Bus

Express buses operate 24 hours between the airport (p136) and key points in the city. At the airport, buy tickets (€6; not valid for other forms of public transport) at the booth near the stop.

Plateia Syntagmatos Bus **X95** (Map p92; tickets €6; ◷24hr), one to 1½ hours, every 20 to 30 minutes. The Syntagma stop is on Othonos St.

Kifissos Terminal A and **Liossion Terminal B bus stations** Bus X93, one hour (terminal B) to 1½ hours (terminal A), every 20 to 30 minutes (60 minutes at night).

Piraeus Bus X96, 1½ hours, every 20 minutes. To Plateia Karaïskaki.

Metro

Metro line 3 goes from the airport (p136) to the city centre. Trains run every 30 minutes, leaving the airport between 6.30am and 11.30pm, on the hour and half-hour. Coming from the centre, trains leave Monastiraki between 5.40am and 11pm; some terminate early at Doukissis Plakentias, so disembark and wait for the airport train (displayed on the train and platform screen).

Tickets from the airport are priced separately from the rest of the metro. The cost is €10 per adult or €18 return (return valid seven days). A €22 pass, good for three days, includes round-trip airport service and all other transit in the centre.

Suburban Rail

Suburban rail (p137) (one hour) is an option to the centre, if you're headed near Larisis train

ATHENS & AROUND GETTING AROUND

station (p136) (after a change at Ano Liosia) or a stop on metro line 1 (change at Neratziotissa). It's the same price as the metro. Trains to Athens run every 15 minutes from 5.10am to 11.30pm; to the airport (p136), from 6am to midnight.

Suburban rail also goes from the airport to Piraeus (change trains at Neratziotissa) and Kiato in the Peloponnese (via Corinth).

Taxi

From the airport to the centre, fares are flat day/night €38/54 rates; tolls are included. The ride takes 30 to 45 minutes. For Piraeus (one hour), expect day/night €50/60.

To the airport, drivers will usually propose a flat fare of €40 from the centre. You can insist on the meter, but with all the legitimate add-ons – tolls, airport fee, luggage fees – it usually works out the same.

To prebook a taxi, contact **Welcome Pickups** (www.welcomepickups.com), at the same flat rate as regular taxis.

BICYCLE

Even experienced cyclists might find Athens' roads a challenge, with no cycle lanes, often reckless drivers and loads of hills – but some hardy locals do ride. A bike route runs from Thisio to the coast. A few outfits offer bicycle hire, such as **Funky Ride** (☑ 211 710 9366; www.funkyride.gr; Dimitrakopoulou 1, Makrygianni; 3hr/day €7/15; ☺ 10.30am-3.30pm & 5.30-8.30pm Mon-Fri, 10.30am-4pm Sat; Ⓜ Akropoli) and Solebike (p108).

CAR & MOTORCYCLE

Athens' notorious traffic congestion, confusing signage, impatient drivers and narrow one-way streets make for occasionally nightmarish driving.

Contrary to what you see, parking is actually illegal alongside kerbs marked with yellow lines, on footpaths and in pedestrian malls. Paid parking areas require tickets available from kiosks.

ⓘ PIRAEUS BUSES

The metro is preferable, but after it stops at midnight, you can still get to Piraeus on the bus:

From Syntagma Bus 040 (Map p92). On Filellinon just south of Syntagma to Akti Xaveriou (every 10 to 20 minutes from 6am to midnight, half-hourly after).

From Omonia Bus 500 (p138) Opposite the town hall south of Omonia to Plateia Themistokleous (hourly from midnight to 5am, starting in Kifisia).

PUBLIC TRANSPORT

Tickets & Passes

The transit system uses the unified Ath.ena Ticket, a reloadable paper card available from ticket offices and machines in the metro. You can load it with a set amount of money or buy a number of rides (€1.40 each; discount when you buy five or 10) or a 24-hour/five-day travel pass for €4.50/9.

Children under six travel free; people under 18 or over 65 are technically eligible to pay half fare, but you must buy the Ath.ena Ticket from a person at a ticket office. If you're staying a while, you may want the sturdier plastic Ath.ena Card, also available at ticket offices; you must load at least €4.50 to start.

Swipe the card at metro turnstiles or, on buses and trams, validate the ticket in the machine as you board, and keep it with you in case of spot-checks. One swipe is good for 90 minutes, including any transfers or return trips.

Bus & Trolleybus

Local express buses, regular buses and electric trolleybuses operate every 15 minutes from 5am to midnight. In lieu of maps, use Google Maps for directions or the trip planner on the website of the bus company, **OASA** (Athens Urban Transport Organisation; ☑ 11185; www.oasa.gr; ☺ call centre 6.30am-10.30pm Mon-Fri, from 7.30am Sat & Sun) (click 'Telematics'). The most useful lines for tourists are trolleybuses 2, 5, 11 and 15, which run north from Syntagma past the National Archaeological Museum (p96). For all buses, board at any door; swipe your ticket on validation machines.

Express buses from the airport (p136) run 24 hours, and also require a dedicated ticket, purchased from a kiosk by the stop.

Buses to Cape Sounion (Map p92; www.ktelattikis.gr)

Buses to Elefsina (Map p102)

Buses to Moni Kaisarianis depart from beside the **Athens University** (Map p102; www.uoa.gr; Omonoia 30, Panepistimio; ☺ closed to public; Ⓜ Panepistimio) building at Panepistimio.

Metro

The metro works well and posted maps have clear icons and English labels. Trains operate from 5.30am to 12.30am, every four minutes during peak periods and every 10 minutes off-peak. On Friday and Saturday, lines 2 and 3 run till 2.30am. Get information at www.stasy.gr. All stations have wheelchair access.

Line 1 (Green) The oldest line, Kifisia–Piraeus, known as the Ilektriko, is slower than the others and above ground. After hours, a **night bus** (Map p102) (500, Piraeus–Kifisia) follows the route, stopping outside the metro stations.

Line 2 (Red) Runs from Agios Antonios in the northwest to Agios Dimitrios in the southeast.

Line 3 (Blue) Runs northeast from Egaleo to Doukissis Plakentias, with airport trains continuing on from there. Transfer for line 1 at Monastiraki; for line 2 at Syntagma.

Train

Suburban rail (p137) is fast, but not commonly used by visitors – though it goes to the airport and as far as Piraeus and the northern Peloponnese. The airport–Kiato line (€14, 1½ hours) connects to the metro at Doukissis Plakentias and Neratziotissa. Two other lines cross the metro at Larisis station.

A short **funicular railway** (Teleferik; ☑210 721 0701; www.lycabettushill.com; Aristippou 1, Kolonaki; return/one way €7.50/5; ☺8.30-2.30am) runs up Lykavittos Hill.

Tram

Athens' trams are slow but can make for very picturesque journeys, particularly once you're following the lines along the coast to either Glyfada or Piraeus. There are three lines:

Line 1 (Red) Connects Kasomoule with Piraeus.

Line 2 (Green) Connects Kasomoule and Glyfada.

Line 3 (Blue): Connects Piraeus with Glyfada.

Trams run from 5.30am to 1am Sunday to Thursday (every 10 minutes), and to 2.30am on Friday and Saturday (every 40 minutes). Ticket-vending machines are on the platforms.

TAXI

Athens' taxis are excellent value and can be the key for efficient travel on some routes. But it can be tricky getting one, especially during rush hour. Thrust your arm out vigorously... you may still have to shout your destination to the driver to see if he or she is interested. Make sure the meter is on. It can be much easier to use the mobile app **Beat** (www.thebeat.co/gr) or **Taxiplon** (☑210 277 3600, 18222; www.taxiplon.gr) – you can pay in cash. Or call a taxi from dispatchers such as **Athina 1** (☑210 921 0417, 210 921 2800; www.athens1.gr), **Enotita** (☑6980666720, 18388, 210 649 5099; www.athensradiotaxienotita.gr) or **Parthenon** (☑210 532 3300; www.radiotaxi-parthenon.gr). For day trips, **Athens Tour Taxi** (☑6932295395; www.athenstourtaxi.com) comes recommended.

If a taxi picks you up while already carrying passengers, the fare is not shared: each person pays the fare on the meter minus any diversions to drop others (note what it's at when you get in). Short trips around central Athens cost about €5; there are surcharges for luggage and pick-ups at transport hubs. Nights and holidays, the fare is about 60% higher.

ATHENS PORTS

Piraeus

POP 163,688

Ten kilometres southwest of central Athens, Piraeus is dazzling in its scale, its seemingly endless quays filled with ferries, ships and hydrofoils. It's the biggest port in the Mediterranean (more than 20 million passengers pass through annually), the hub of the Aegean ferry network, the centre of Greece's maritime trade and the base for its large merchant navy. While technically its own city, it melds into the Athens sprawl, with close to half a million people living in the greater area.

Shabby and congested, central Piraeus is not a place where visitors normally choose to linger. Beyond its shipping offices, banks and public buildings are a jumble of pedestrian precincts, shopping strips and rather grungy areas. The most attractive quarter lies east around **Zea Marina**, **Pasalimani** and **Mikrolimano** harbours. The latter is lined with cafes, restaurants and bars filled with Athenians, locals and visitors.

⊙ Sights

Electric Railways Museum MUSEUM

(Map p140; ☑210 414 7552, 210 412 9503; www.museum-synt-isap.gr; Loudovikou 1; ☺9am-2pm Mon-Fri; MPiraeus) FREE Tucked inside the Piraeus station, this museum is a trove of old switches, nifty models and cool machinery, including a gleaming old wooden train car. It's a passion project of a former railway employee, and he and the other staff are full of interesting facts.

Piraeus Archaeological Museum MUSEUM

(Map p140; ☑210 452 1598; http://odysseus.culture.gr; Harilaou Trikoupi 31; adult/child €4/free; ☺8am-3pm Tue-Sun; MPiraeus) The museum's star attraction is the magnificent statue of Apollo, the *Piraeus Kouros,* the larger-than-life, oldest hollow bronze statue yet found. It dates from about 520 BC and was discovered buried in rubble in 1959. Other important finds from the area include fine tomb reliefs from the 4th to 2nd centuries BC.

Hellenic Maritime Museum MUSEUM

(☑210 451 6264; http://hmmuseum.gr; Akti Themistokieous, Plateia Freatidas, Zea Marina; €4; ☺9am-2pm Tue-Sat; MPiraeus) As nautical museums go, this isn't one of the best, despite Greece's long maritime history. Still, it does have all the requisite models of ancient and modern ships, seascapes by

Piraeus

Piraeus

⊙ Sights
1 Electric Railways Museum.....................C1
2 Piraeus Archaeological Museum..........D4

🛏 Sleeping
3 Hotel Triton...D2
4 Phidias Piraeus......................................D4

5 Piraeus Dream City Hotel.....................D3

✖ Eating
6 General Market.......................................C2
7 Mandragoras...D2
8 Rakadiko..D2
9 Yperokeanio..A4

leading 19th- and 20th-century Greek painters, guns, flags and maps, and even part of a submarine.

🛏 Sleeping

If you're catching an early ferry, it can make sense to stay in Piraeus instead of central Athens. The area closer to Pasalimani has the newer and more elegant hotels.

Phidias Piraeus
HOTEL €

(Map p140; ☎ 210 429 6480; www.hotelphidias.gr; Kountouriotou 189, Zea Marina; s/d/tr from €50/80/120; ❋ @ ☎; ⛽ 040 to Terpsithea) A far

cry from standard Piraeus grunge, this place is also a bit far from the metro (20-minute walk) and the ferry port. But it runs a free shuttle and you're close to the prettier leisure port, for an evening's stroll. Rooms are simple and new, with cute wallpaper. Full breakfast is an extra €7.

Piraeus Dream City Hotel
HOTEL €

(Map p140; ☎ 210 411 0555; www.piraeusdream.gr; Notara 78; d/tr from €75/95; ❋ @ ☎; Ⓜ Piraeus) About a 10-minute walk from the metro, this modern hotel has spacious rooms in whites and creams. Quiet rooms start on the 4th floor. It has a rooftop restaurant.

Hotel Triton
HOTEL €€

(Map p140; ☑ 210 417 3457; www.htriton.gr; Tsamadou 8; s/d/tr from €58/94/95; ❄ @ 🛜; Ⓜ Piraeus) This simple, conveniently located hotel with helpful staff is a treat compared to some of the other run-down joints in Piraeus. Some rooms overlook the bustling market square (p141). There's one family suite (€148) with a large terrace.

✕ Eating & Drinking

The Great Harbour is backed by lots of gritty cafes and fast-food joints; better food and ambience hide away in the backstreets or further afield around Mikrolimano, Zea Marina and along the waterfront promenade at Freatida.

★ Yperokeanio
MEZEDHES €

(Map p140; ☑ 210 418 0030; Marias Hatzikiriakou 48; dishes €6-12; ⊙ noon-11.30pm) Grab a cab to this fantastic seafood *mezedhopoleio,* where you can tuck into small plates of grilled sardines or steamed mussels. For dessert there's *kaimaki* ice cream – an old Asia Minor recipe made chewy with *sahlep* (orchid root) and flavoured with Chios mastic. Book ahead if possible; it's often packed.

★ Mandragoras
DELI €

(Map p140; ☑ 210 417 2961; Gounari 14; ⊙ 7.45am-4pm Mon, Wed & Sat, to 8pm Tue, Thu & Fri; Ⓜ Piraeus) This superb delicatessen and spice shop offers a fine selection of gourmet cheeses, ready-made mezedhes, olive oils, Greek honey and preserved foods. It's a veritable museum of regional Greek foodstuffs and fantastic for snacks and food gifts.

General Market
MARKET €

(Map p140; Dimosthenous; ⊙ 6am-4pm Mon-Fri; Ⓜ Piraeus) With the sea breezes blowing over the morning hustle and bustle, the Piraeus market is an excellent slice of life. There's a broad range of food and bric-a-brac, as well as cheap bars and cafes around the periphery, especially in the back alley behind.

To Kapileio Tou Zaxou
TAVERNA €€

(☑ 210 481 3325; Komotinis 37; mains from €15; ⊙ noon-1am; ☐ 16) It may be a bit inland, but this family-run Greek fish taverna still conveys the spirit of the sea. Choose from grilled catches of the day, calamari and octopus. House wine comes from the big barrels shelved above the tables, as it ought to in a traditional place. A favourite among locals for its reasonable prices and generous portions.

Margaro
SEAFOOD €€

(☑ 210 451 4226; Marias Hatzikiriakou 126; mains €6-21; ⊙ noon-midnight Mon-Sat, to 5.30pm Sun Sep-Jul; ☐ 904) This port restaurant is the picture of simplicity, with a menu that comprises exactly three things: salad, fried shrimp and fried red mullet. Although it's tucked away by the naval academy, it's no secret, and can be very crowded on weekends. Take the bus here from the Piraeus metro, or a taxi.

Rakadiko
TAVERNA €€

(Map p140; ☑ 210 417 8470; www.rakadiko.gr; Karaoli kai Dimitriou 5, Stoa Kouvelou; mains €7-18; ⊙ noon-midnight Mon-Sat, 1-6pm Sun; Ⓜ Piraeus) A spot of calm: head into this renovated old shopping arcade to dine under grapevines on mezedhes or classic dishes from all over Greece. There's live *rembetika* on weekends. If you're not hungry for a full meal, stop at the adjacent sweets shop for ice cream or very good orange-blossom-scented fried *loukoumadhes* (ball-shaped doughnuts served with honey and cinnamon).

★ Varoulko
SEAFOOD €€€

(☑ 210 522 8400; www.varoulko.gr; Akti Koumoundourou 52, Mikrolimano; mains €45-65; ⊙ 1pm-1am; ☐ Nautiko Omilos) Chef Lefteris Lazarou, a Piraeus native, has been shaping Greek tastes since the 1980s, when he brought fish to the fine-dining menu. For years he had a Michelin-starred restaurant in Athens, but moved back to his roots in 2014. Michelin still approves, and his cooking remains elegant and creative. The setting in Mikrolimano, where sailboats bob, is lovely.

Mary Pickford
ROOFTOP BAR

(☑ 210 412 3308; Akti Koumoundourou 54-56, Mikrolimano; ⊙ 7pm-late; 🛜; ☐ Nautiko Omilos) This seaside rooftop bar in the Mikrolimano district offers a bit of Hollywood style and views that stretch past the harbour towards the Acropolis and Lykavittos Hill. The drinks menu is just as expansive with six categories of cocktails; try the Days of Summer, a mix of Greek grape spirits and rosemary and lemon liqueurs.

ⓘ Information

There are luggage lockers at the metro station (€3 for 24 hours, maximum 15 days). ATMs and moneychangers line the Great Harbour.

Alpha Bank (☑ 210 412 1721; Ethnikis Antistasseos 9; ⊙ 8am-2pm Mon-Fri)

National Bank of Greece (☑ 210 414 4311; cnr Antistaseos & Makras Stoas; ⊙ 8am-2.45pm Mon-Fri)

ATHENS & AROUND PIRAEUS

❶ Getting There & Away

The metro and suburban rail from Athens terminate at the **E7 gate** (Map p140) of the Great Harbour on Akti Kalimassioti. A few ferry departure points are just across the road; for further gates, you'll need a port-run bus (free) or a taxi (cheap). The best place to catch the **airport bus X96** (Map p140; adult/child under 6 €6/free) is in front of the church, Agios Dionysios, four blocks north on Papastratou.

The Athens tramway is extending its line from Faliro to the harbour, with a terminus just south of the metro stop; it's expected to be completed in 2020.

BOAT

Piraeus is the busiest port in Greece, with daily service to most island groups. The exceptions are the Ionians, with boats only to Kythira (for the other islands, sail from Igoumenitsa) and the Sporades, plus Kea (Tzia) and Andros in the Cyclades (which sail from Rafina and Lavrio). Piraeus ferries also serve the Peloponnese (Methana, Ermioni, Porto Heli, Monemvasia and Gythio).

Always check departure docks with the ticketing agent.

For Crete, ferries for Iraklio and Hania leave from the western end of Akti Kondyli (Gates **E2** (Map p140) and E3).

Schedules & Tickets

Ferry schedules are reduced in April, May and October, and radically cut in winter, especially to smaller islands. Find schedules and buy tickets online (www.greekferries.gr, www.openseas.gr, www.ferries.gr or company websites), or buy in person at travel agents or at each ferry company's kiosk in front of the boat (open about two hours before sailing). **Piraeus Port Authority** (Map p140; ☑ 210 455 0000, €0.89 per 1min 14541; www.olp.gr) also has schedule information.

BUS

The X96 Piraeus–Athens Airport Express (p142) stops in front of Agios Dionysios on Papastratou. It runs around the outside of the port also, but stops rarely, so it's better to take the inside-port shuttle to your gate. **Bus 040** (Map p140) goes to Athens from Lambraki at the corner of Vasileos Georgiou II. Arriving, you'll come down Polytehniou; get off at Plateia Koraï.

METRO

The fastest and most convenient link between the Great Harbour and Athens is the metro (€1.40, 30 minutes, every 10 minutes, 5am to midnight), near the ferries at the northern end of Akti Kalimassioti.

You can get the metro to/from the airport (p136) all the way to Piraeus, changing at Monastiraki station.

SUBURBAN RAIL

Piraeus is connected to the suburban rail – the terminus is next to the metro station. To get to the airport or to Kiato in the Peloponnese, you need to change trains at Kato Acharnai.

❶ Getting Around

The port is massive, so a free shuttle bus runs regularly along the quay inside the port from gate E7 to E1; cross over from the metro and you'll see it. For gate E9, look for buses outside the port, with route numbers starting with 8.

The Piraeus city buses most likely to interest travellers are 904 and 905 between Zea Marina and the metro station.

Athens tramway and metro extensions are under way (not completed at the time of research), and have made the port area a zoo of blocked streets and redirected traffic.

Rafina

POP 13,091

Rafina, on Attica's east coast, is a port town with passenger ferries to the northern Cyclades. If this is your destination, it's a good alternative to Piraeus, as it's smaller (hence, less confusing), and fares are about 20% cheaper. It's also a pleasant place to spend a night if ferry schedules require it.

🛏 Sleeping & Eating

Avra   HOTEL €€

(☑ 22940 22780; www.hotelavra.gr; Arafinidon Alon 3; d from €75; ❇ ☎) Set on one end of Rafina's pretty crescent port, Avra is a big and functional hotel that helps make this town a pleasant stop midtransit. (It also runs a free shuttle to the airport, about 30 minutes away.) Rooms are modern and comfortable, with balconies for watching the ships come in.

Ta Kavouria Tou Asimaki   GREEK €

(☑ 22940 24551; Akti Andrea Papandreou; mains from €8; ⏰ 9am-midnight) One of Rafina's oldest and most loved restaurants, this place sits right on the port and is handy for those waiting to catch a ferry. The food is excellent; fish is fresh and simply prepared, and there are delicacies such as sea-urchin salad. The grilled squid is tender and fragrant. Super-friendly service.

❶ Getting There & Away

Rafina is close to Athens airport (p136), so if you're headed to the northern Cyclades (Mykonos, Naxos etc), consider coming here directly, bypassing Athens and Piraeus completely.

BOAT

Rafina Port Authority (☑ 22940 28888; www.rafinaport.gr; Akti Andrea Papandreou 10) and www.openseas.gr have information on ferries.

Fast Ferries and Golden Star ferries go to Andros (2½ hours, €19, four to six daily) and Mykonos (4½ hours, €29, two to three daily). Seajets has a high-speed service to Mykonos (2¼ hours, €33, two daily). Golden Star takes you to Ios (six hours, €48, six weekly). Golden Star and Seajets provide a high-speed service to Naxos (four hours, €33, three daily). Fast Ferries gets you slowly to Naxos (six hours, €30, six weekly). Golden Star takes you to Santorini (Thira; 6¾ hours, €48, one daily). Get to Tinos by high-speed Seajets (two hours, €39, two daily) and regular service with Fast Ferries and Golden Star (3¾ hours, €27, six to nine daily).

BUS

Frequent KTEL buses (p136) run from Athens to Rafina (€2.60, one hour) between 5.45am and 10.30pm, departing from Athens' Mavromateon bus terminal. Buses from Athens airport (p136) (€3, 45 minutes) leave from in front of the arrivals hall near the Sofitel, between 4.40am and 10.20pm; buy tickets on the bus. Both stop on the Rafina quay.

Lavrio

POP 10,370

Lavrio, on the coast 60km southeast of Athens, is the port for ferries to Kea and Kythnos, and high-season catamarans to the western Cyclades. It is, unfortunately, not an exciting place to spend the night. The long beach north of the ferry port is a bit of a windsurfing scene, but that same wind is somewhat wearing if you're not on the water. It has a grand industrial past – from silver mining in antiquity to massive late-19th-century steam-powered mining works – but there's not much happening overall.

The sprawling ruins of the more recent industry are awesome, but open only to Athens Technical University students.

Other minor sights include the **Mineralogical Museum** (☑ 22920 26270; Iroön Polytechniou; adult/child €2/free; ⊙ 10am-noon Fri-Sun) with limited opening hours and a small **Archaeological Museum** (☑ 22920 22817; http://odysseus.culture.gr; cnr Agias Paraskevis & Leoforos Souniou; adult/child €2/free; ⊙ 8am-3pm Tue-Sun).

For food, **Pezodromos** (☑ 22920 22670; Ermou 40; mains from €8; ⊙ noon-midnight; ⚲),

located in the old centre of Lavrio, is a popular fish and seafood tavern – try the octopus in vinegar or stuffed squid. There are also meat dishes, such as spit-roast lamb, and a variety of salads and wild greens for vegetarians.

🛈 Getting There & Away

BOAT

Lavrio Port Authority (☑ 22920 25249; Akti Andrea Papandreou) and www.openseas.gr have ferry information.

BUS

KTEL buses (p136) to Lavrio (€5.30, two hours, every 30 minutes) run from the Mavromateon terminal in Athens. Airport buses leave from the front of the arrivals hall near the Sofitel; you must change buses at Markopoulo. Both stop on the Lavrio quay.

TAXI

Taxi Posidon (☑ 22920 24200; www.taxiposeidon.gr) can run you to the airport (day/night €38/55, 30 minutes) and central Athens (€55/87, one hour); fares are higher for pick-up in Athens or the airport. Lavrio to Cape Sounion is €12.

AROUND ATHENS

An agricultural region with several large population centres, the southern Attica peninsula has some fine beaches, particularly along the Apollo Coast and at Shinias, near Marathon. It's also known for its wine production.

Until the 7th century, Attica was home to a number of smaller kingdoms, such as those at Eleusis (Elefsina; p150), Ramnous (p148) and Brauron (Vravrona). In pure visual terms, the remains of these cities pale alongside the superb Temple of Poseidon (p147) at Cape Sounion, but any of them can be nice to visit simply because you'll probably have the place to yourself.

Apollo Coast

Glyfada, about 17km southeast of Athens, is an upscale suburb of Athens that marks the beginning of the Apollo Coast (sometimes called the Athenian Riviera), a 48km stretch down to Cape Sounion of fine beaches, resorts and summer nightlife. It's a great place to get out of overheated Athens in summer, and easily reached by bus.

The coast road (Poseidonos Ave, often just called *Paraliaki*) leads from Glyfada to **Voula**, **Kavouri** and then bustling and popular **Vouliagmeni** and ritzy Astir Beach. The coast is a bit expensive, but the further south you go, the cheaper and less built-up it becomes. Of note are the natural mineral waters at **Limni Vouliagmenis**, and the gay and nudist beaches tucked in the rocky coves at **Limanakia**.

There's better (free) swimming northeast and east of Athens, at Shinias, Marathon and Vravrona; these take longer to get to and are best reached by car.

Activities

Most of the Apollo Coast beaches are privately run and charge admission (€5 to €15 per adult). They're usually open from 8am to dusk, May to October (later during heatwaves), and have sunbeds and umbrellas (additional charge in some places), changing rooms, children's playgrounds and cafes.

Limni Vouliagmenis
SWIMMING

(Map p146; ☑210 896 2239; www.limnivouliagmenis.gr; Leoforos Vouliagmenis; adult/child Mon-Fri €13/6, Sat & Sun €14/7; ⊘7.30am-8pm; ⊕; ☐114, 115 or 149, ☐A2 or E2) This slightly salty lake, at the base of a huge cliff, is connected to the sea underground and fed by mineral-rich warm springs; its temperature never falls below 21°C. This makes it a friendly habitat for fish that nibble the dead skin from your feet – an exfoliating treat for some, or a nightmare for the ticklish.

The loyal clientele of bathing-cap-clad elderly citizens tout the water's healing properties. There's a modern spa-cuisine cafe (lunch from €12) at the edge, where you can eat without paying the lake admission, plus sunbeds, a playground and showers. Take the A2 bus (E2 express in summer) to Plateia Glyfada (aka Plateia Katraki Vasos), then take bus 114, 115 or 149.

Limanakia
BEACH

(Map p146; ☐117, 122) The rocky coves below the bus stop at Limanakia B (near Varkiza) are a popular nudist hang-out with a slight gay slant. Take the tram or A2/E2 express bus to Glyfada, then bus 117 or 122 to the Limanakia B stop.

Asteras Beach
BEACH

(☑210 894 1620; www.asterascomplex.com; Glyfada; adult/child Mon-Fri €6/3, Sat & Sun €7/3; ⊘beach 8.30am-8pm; ☐790 from Syntagma, ☐T5 to Asteria) Swanky Asteras, convenient

to Glyfada and the tram, is a resort without the hotel: a complex of waterfront cafes, play zones, bars and the see-and-be-seen Balux (p146) restaurant. If the megabeach with sunloungers for thousands isn't enough, there's also a pool.

The restaurants are expensive for Greece (coffee €4.50, mains from €15), but if you don't take a seat, you can order from a basic menu of coffee, water and toasted sandwiches for less than €2.

Astir Beach
BEACH

(☑210 890 1621; Apollonos 40, Vouliagmeni; adult/child Mon-Fri €18/10, Sat & Sun €28/15 mid-Jun–mid-Sep, reduced prices rest of year; ⊘beach 8am-9pm, restaurants to midnight; ☐114 from Glyfada or Voula tram stops) Astir is the most exclusive summer beach playground (giveaway: there's a helipad, for the most elite Athenian commuters). It has all the water sports, shops and restaurants you could want (plus, oddly, a TGI Fridays). It's 19.5km south of Athens, 7.5km south of Glyfada. If it all gets too flashy for you, there's a nice public beach across the road.

Yabanaki
BEACH

(☑210 897 2414; www.yabanaki.gr; Varkiza; adult/child Mon-Fri €5/3.50, Sat & Sun €6/3.50; ⊘8am-7pm Jun-Aug, 9am-5pm May; ☐122) Slightly less flashy than the beach clubs near Glyfada, Yabanaki (21km south of Syntagma) nonetheless has a full complement of entertainment options, from a restaurant to beach volleyball. Great if you're travelling with kids.

Akti tou Iliou
BEACH

(☑210 985 5169; www.aktitouiliou.gr; Leoforos Poseidonos, Alimos; adult/child Mon-Fri €5/3, Sat & Sun €6/3; ⊘8am-8pm; ☐Zefyros) Relatively laid-back, with a slew of sunloungers and some reed-roofed beach bars. It's one of the closer beaches to Athens (just 7.5km south).

🛏 Sleeping

Villa Orion
HOTEL €

(☑210 895 8000; www.villaorionhotel.gr; Ioanni Metaxa 4, Voula; d/tr incl breakfast €73/85; ✳☎; ☐A1, A2, 122, ☐Asklipiio Voulas) This simple hotel has been dressed up with a bit of creative interior decor, but the real attraction is its great value. It's a few blocks inland, yes, but convenient to all the beaches. Rooms have little balconies and breakfast is served outside in a small garden. Prices go down off-season.

WORTH A TRIP

STAVROS NIARCHOS FOUNDATION CULTURAL CENTER

Sitting beneath an artificial slope above Faliro Bay, and shaded by a 'Magic Carpet' roof covered with solar panels, is the **Stavros Niarchos Foundation Cultural Center** (SNFCC; Map p146; 21680 91001; www.snfcc.org; Leoforos Syngrou 364, Kallithea; 550 to Onasseio, 10 to Epaminonda) FREE. This stunning Renzo Piano–designed building, completed in 2016, is home to the Greek National Opera (p130) and the main branch of the **National Library** (21680 91000; www.nlg.gr; Pisistratou 172, Kallithea; public areas 6am-midnight, exhibition fl 9am-10pm, library 9am-5pm Mon-Fri; 550 to Onasseio, 10 to Epaminonda) FREE.

Covering a hill that incorporates SNFCC's roof is the 21-hectare and sustainably designed **Stavros Niarchos Park** (21680 91000; www.snfcc.org; Leoforos Syngrou 364, Kallithea; 6am-midnight Apr-Oct, to 8pm Nov-Mar; 550 to Onasseio, 10 to Epaminonda) FREE with paths cutting through plantings of lavender, olive trees and other Mediterranean flora. There are also kids' play areas, an outdoor gym and much more. A variety of free activities are laid on, but you can simply sit in a chair and soak up the sunshine.

In addition to regular public transport, you can also use a free shuttle bus, departing from Syntagma at Ermou. It runs several times a day on weekdays, and every 30 minutes from 9.30am to 9.30pm on weekends.

Palmyra Beach Hotel
HOTEL €€

(www.palmyra.gr; Leoforos Poseidonos 70, Glyfada; d incl breakfast from €125; P❄🛜🏊) The Palmyra has large, sleek and modern rooms with balconies, plus big breakfasts and a swimming pool in a verdant garden. It's also super close to Glyfada beach and the marina.

Hotel Vouliagmeni Suites
HOTEL €€€

(210 896 4901; www.vouliagmenisuites.com; Panos 8, Vouliagmeni; s/d incl breakfast from €172/183; 122 to Agia Pantelimon) This posh pad a bit back from the beach has quirkily decorated luxe rooms, some with sea views.

🍴 Eating

Yi
VEGAN €

(210 964 8512; Grigoriou Lambraki 69, Glyfada; mains €8-10; 8.30am-midnight; 🛜🐾; A3 to Omiroi, 171 to Lambraki) Breezy, elegant Yi is a mostly open-air, all-raw vegan cafe where the food is bursting with colour and life. Go with a friend to share one of the delicious plates for two (€18), such as falafel in a flaxseed wrap, spiced with tahini-mustard sauce. Delectable vegan cheesecakes too.

Family
AMERICAN €€

(21210 43411; www.family-voula.gr; Vasileos Pavlou 74, Voula; mains €9-15; 9am-2am; Asklipiio Voulas) Affectionate service and a nice homey atmosphere in an old mansion. There is a wide-ranging family-friendly menu: eggs, burgers, pizzas and plenty more. It's on Voula's pleasant little downtown strip, calmer than Glyfada. It's about a 20-minute walk from the last tram stop.

Trigono
TAVERNA €€

(22990 48540; Athinon 36, Kalyvia; mains €8-15; lunch & dinner) At this casual grill house, the pork chops are flawless and flow nonstop – thanks to an in-house butcher, a rare feature in Greece. As it's just off the highway back to Athens, it's a popular family pit stop on weekend afternoons. Go early to avoid the epic post-lunch lull, when it feels like an army has just marched out.

Kohylia
ASIAN €€€

(Map p146; 22910 76000; www.lagonissiresort. gr; Grand Resort Lagonissi, Km 40 Athens-Sounion Rd; mains €20-62; 8pm-1.30am Tue-Sun; P❄🛜🐾; Lagonissi 122) Kohylia offers a romantic, upmarket dining experience with elegant tables spread over a seaside veranda at the exclusive Grand Resort Lagonissi. The menu adds its own exotic touch in the form of Polynesian and Japanese cuisine; tasteful mains include the baked black-cod fillet with red miso sauce.

🍷 Drinking & Nightlife

Malabar
LOUNGE

(210 892 9160; www.themargi.gr; Margi Hotel, Litous 11, Vouliagmeni; 11am-2am; 122 to Laimos, Elliniko) Drop in for a drink at the cushy poolside bar at the boutique hotel Margi (doubles from €441).

The hotel's restaurant, Patio, is known for its haute Greek food, with ingredients from the hotel's own organic farm, inland near Kalyvia.

Attica

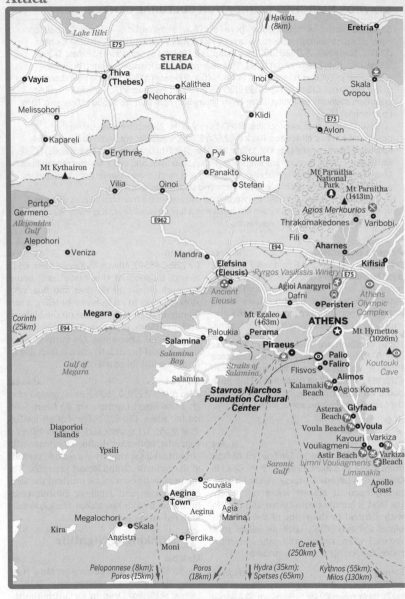

Akanthus CLUB

(☑ 21096 80800; www.akanthus.gr; Leoforos Poseidonos, Alimos; ☺ 8am-late; ☐ Zefyros) Typical of the Glyfada day–night beach clubs, this restaurant-cafe has a DJ at night. It's part of the Akti tou Iliou (p144) beach complex, at the south end. Dress smartly.

Balux LOUNGE

(☑ 210 894 1620; www.baluxcafe.com; Leoforos Poseidonos 58, Glyfada; ☺ 10am-late; ☎; ☐ T5 to Asteria) This glamorous club-restaurant-lounge right on the beach must be seen to be believed, with poolside chaises and four-poster beds with flowing nets.

Island CLUB

(☏ 210 965 3563; www.islandclubrestaurant.gr; Km 27, Athens-Sounion Rd, Varkiza; ⊙ 9pm-4am; 🚌 117 or 122 to Camping Varkizas, Ⓜ Elliniko) Dreamy, classic summer club-restaurant at the seaside, with superb island decor. A bit more grown-up than the clubs in Glyfada.

❶ Getting There & Away

The Athens tram (p139) runs all the way to Voula, via Glyfada. For Vouliagmeni and beyond, you can take buses from the end of the tram line or (faster but less scenic) buses direct from Athens.

To avoid heavy traffic on weekends in summer, set out by 9am; without much traffic, the drive from Glyfada to Sounion should take about an hour.

Cape Sounion
Ακρωτήριο Σούνιο

The Ancient Greeks knew how to choose a site for a temple. At Cape Sounion, 70km south of Athens, the **Temple of Poseidon** (Map p146; ☏ 22920 39363; http://odysseus.culture.gr; Cape Sounion; adult/child €8/4; ⊙ 9am-sunset) stands on a craggy spur that plunges 65m to the sea. Built in 444 BC – same year as the Parthenon – of marble from nearby Agrilesa, it is a vision of gleaming white columns. Sailors in ancient times knew they were nearly home when they saw the first glimpse of white; views from the temple are equally impressive.

On a clear day you can see Kea, Kythnos and Serifos to the southeast, and Aegina and the Peloponnese to the west.

It is thought that the temple was built by Iktinos, the architect of the Temple of Hephaistos in Athens' Ancient Agora. Sixteen of the slender Doric columns remain. The site also contains scant remains of a propylaeum, a fortified tower and, on a lower hill to the northeast, a 6th-century temple to Athena.

As with all major sites, it's best to visit first thing in the morning, or head there for sunset to enact Byron's lines from *Don Juan*: 'Place me on Sunium's marbled steep/ Where nothing save the waves and I/May hear our mutual murmurs sweep.'

Byron was so impressed by Sounion that he carved his name on one of the columns (sadly, many other not-so-famous travellers followed suit).

Akrotiri CLUB

(☏ 210 985 9147; www.akrotirilounge.gr; Vasileos Georgiou II 5, Agios Kosmas, Alimos; ⊙ 10pm-4am; 🚌 2nd Aghios Kosma) This massive beach club holds 3000 people in bars, a restaurant and lounges over different levels. Superbusy party nights bring top resident and visiting DJs.

ⓘ APOLLO COAST TOP TIPS

➡ To avoid heavy traffic on weekends in summer, set out by 9am; without much traffic, the drive from Glyfada to Sounion should take about an hour.

➡ Beaches closest to Glyfada can be reached from Athens by tram. To get further south, change in Glyfada or Voula for a coastal bus.

➡ There are free beaches and rocky coves near Palaio Faliro (Edem), Kavouri, Glyfada and south by Varkiza. Look for areas where locals have parked their cars by the side of the road.

➡ Many beaches morph into summer nightclubs as well; pack evening wear in your beach bag.

There is a decent cafe-restaurant at the site, and from the parking lot at the Athena temple, a steep path leads down to a small beach. If you want more room or variety, you'll need a car, or a short bus ride, to reach the nearby bigger beaches and tavernas. There is a pretty, if busy, beach near the site to the west, plus some nice wilder areas along the west-coast road towards Sounio town.

The site is a common package day trip from Athens; this is the easiest way to visit. KTEL also runs frequent buses from the Mavromateon terminal in Athens; the buses also stop near Syntagma. The ride along the coast road takes about two hours.

Mt Parnitha   Πάρνηθα

Mt Parnitha, about 25km north of Athens, comprises a number of smaller peaks, the highest of which is Karavola (1413m), tall enough to get snow in winter. The forest was badly burned in 2007 but has rebounded well. There are many caves and much wildlife, including red deer. The park is criss-crossed by hiking trails, with two large, full-featured hiking lodges. It's popular for mountain biking as well.

The easiest way to explore is on the path (about a 45-minute walk) through Tatoi, the 40-sq-km grounds of the former summer palace (closed); follow Tatoi Rd out of Varibobi and look for a small trail sign on the right. For other common trails, see 'Activities' on the park website, or contact EOS

(p106) in Athens for current advice (the site is not well maintained).

For a meal with a view, wind past the posh country estates of Varibobi and up the foothills of Mt Parnitha to reach busy taverna **Agios Merkourios** (Map p146; ✆210 816 9617; Varibobi; starters €4-6, lamb per kg €33; ⊙1pm-midnight Tue-Sun). Weekends, it's packed with Athenians making the pilgrimage for a big family meal. You'll see all sorts of meat on the menu, but charcoal-grilled lamb chops are the order of the day.

Marathon & Around

The town of Marathon, northeast of Athens, may be small and unremarkable but, in 490 BC, the surrounding plain was the site of the Battle of Marathon, one of the most celebrated battles in world history. All over the area, you can see traces of the event – even in the road signs that mark the historic route of Pheidippides, the courier who ran to Athens to announce victory, and thus gave the name to the 42km race. The Marathon **battlefield** (Map p146; ✆22940 55155; http://odysseus.culture.gr; site & archaeological museum adult/child €6/3; ⊙8am-3pm Tue-Sat), directly south of town, is where the **Athens Marathon** begins (www.athensauthenticmarathon.gr).

⊙ Sights & Activities

Marathon Archaeological Museum   MUSEUM
(Map p146; ✆22940 55155; http://odysseus.culture.gr; Plataion 114; museum & Marathon Tomb site adult/child €6/3; ⊙8.30am-3pm Tue-Sat) South of Marathon town, this excellent museum displays local discoveries from various periods, including Neolithic pottery from the Cave of Pan and finds from the Tomb of the Athenians. The showpieces are several larger-than-life statues from an **Egyptian sanctuary** in nearby **Brexiza**. Next to the museum is a **prehistoric grave circle site**, which has been preserved under a hangar-like shelter, with raised platforms and walkways. Another hangar on the road to the museum contains an early Helladic **cemetery site**.

The admission fee covers entrance to the Marathon battlefield & tomb (p148) area, a few kilometres southeast.

Ramnous   RUINS
(Map p146; ✆22940 63477; http://odysseus.culture.gr; adult/child €4/2; ⊙8.30am-3pm Tue-Sun)

The evocative, overgrown and secluded ruins of the ancient port of Ramnous, about 10km northeast of Marathon, stand on a picturesque plateau overlooking the sea. Among the ruins are the remains of the Doric **Temple of Nemesis** (435 BC). Another section of the site leads 1km down a track to a clifftop with the relatively well-preserved town **fortress** and the remains of the city, a temple, a gymnasium and a theatre. There is no public transport to the site.

Nemesis was the goddess of divine retribution and mother of Helen of Troy. There are also ruins of a smaller 6th-century **temple** dedicated to Themis, goddess of justice.

Shinias BEACH
A long gold-sand beach, Shinias is backed by a brushy pine forest. There are sunloungers and a taverna, but no other major developments around, making it the most relaxed and prettiest place to swim in this part of Attica. It's very popular at weekends.

🛏 Sleeping & Eating

Ramnous Camping CAMPGROUND **€**
(📋 22940 55855; www.ramnous.gr; Leoforos Poseidonos 174, Shinias; camp sites per adult/child €6/4; ⊙ Apr-Oct; P 🐾) About 1km south of Shinias Beach, this is the most pleasant campground in Attica, with sites nestled among shrubs and trees. Long-stay residents maintain a calm atmosphere. There's a minimarket, playground, laundry and a nice bar-restaurant, **Octopus** (mains €4 to €14). Casual campers can rent a tent (€6 per night). Buses to Athens go right by out front.

Isidora SEAFOOD **€€**
(Map p146; 📋 22940 56467; www.isidora.com. gr; Paralia Marathonos, Pesodromos Perikleous, Παραλία Μαραθώνος, Πεζόδρομος Περικλέους; mains from €12; ⊙ noon-midnight) Right on Marathon Beach, Isidora has beachfront tables and fresh fish and seafood – do check prices per kilo before ordering fish, as it can be quite expensive. Try the marinated anchovies or sardines in season, and enjoy the views.

❶ Getting There & Away

Given that most of the traces of ancient Marathon are spread around the area, it is easiest to visit by car (and you can also pass by the large dam at Lake Marathon). But the tomb (p148) and museum (p148), at least, are a short walk from bus stops. Service is hourly (half-hourly in the afternoon), from Athens' Mavromateon terminal (€4.10, 1¼ hours).

Vravrona Βραυρώνα

The **Sanctuary of Artemis** (Archaeological Museum at Brauron; Map p146; 📋 22990 27020; http://odysseus.culture.gr; Vravron, Markopoulou; adult/child €6/free; ⊙ 8am-2.45pm Tue-Sun), a partially restored temple to the goddess of the hunt, dates from approximately 420 BC, with some earlier remains. Most remarkable is an ancient stone bridge over the river (now rerouted), cut through with wagon-wheel tracks. Entrance is via a very good museum, which shows remarkable votive gems and statues of children (Artemis was their protector). Then a pleasant path leads to the site through lush marshland with lots of birds. Another path leads to a quiet stretch of beach.

From Athens, take metro line 3 to Nomismatikopio, then bus 304 to Artemis (Vravrona). It's a 10-minute taxi ride from there.

Peania Παιανία

Vorres Museum MUSEUM
(📋 210 664 2520; www.vorresmuseum.gr; Parodos Diadohou Konstantinou 4; adult/child €5/ free; ⊙ 10am-2pm Sat & Sun; 🚌 125 or 308 to Koropi-Peania, Ⓜ Nomismatikopio) This hodgepodge of a museum is on a 32-hectare estate, once the home of Ion Vorres. Vorres migrated to Canada as a young man, but built his home here in 1963 and began collecting contemporary art, furniture, artefacts, textiles and historical objects from around Greece to preserve the national heritage. Like many personal collections, it's a bit erratic, but a pleasant place to spend some time. Take bus 125 or 308 to Koropi-Peania from Athens' Nomismatikopio metro station.

Koutouki Cave CAVE
(Σπήλαιο Κουτούκι Παιανίας; Map p146; 📋 210 664 2910; http://odysseus.culture.gr; adult/child €2/free; ⊙ 8.30am-3pm Mon-Fri, to 2.30pm Sat & Sun) This cave is not particularly large, but the winding path goes past some interesting formations and the whole place is tinged rust-red from iron deposits. The guided tour (included in entry) takes about half an hour.

The cave is best visited by car. Buses 125 and 308 from outside Athens' Nomismatikopio metro station can take you as far as Peania, but it's a further 4.5km to the cave. Best use your own wheels.

MONI DAFNIOU

Lovers of mosaics will be dazzled by the glittering gold scenes in the 11th-century main church here, a listed Unesco site. The work was likely done by craftspeople from Constantinople, showing the fluidity of styles between here and what would become the Islamic Empire. In the apse are portions of geometric decoration of the kind popular in Islamic buildings further east – just as, say, the Umayyad Mosque in Damascus features Byzantine-style gold-backed mosaic scenes.

Restoration work is nearly complete. When the Ministry of Culture takes control of the finished project (at an unknown future date), the site is expected to be open six days a week, with an admission fee. Confirm details with the tourism office before you leave Athens.

It's possible to combine a visit to the monastery with one to Elefsina, as they are on the same A16 bus line (departs from Agia Marina metro stop); you can also take the 866 or 811 from Koumoundourou. On the access road to the monastery are a decent cafe and a free, shady botanical garden.

Elefsina

POP 29,902

Rusting hulks of ships and the chuffing towers of an oil refinery greet you on the quay in Elefsina.

This port town west of Athens is gearing up to be the European Capital of Culture in 2021, but apart from the Ancient Eleusis-ruins and the Old Oil Mill, a rejuvenated industrial building that's now a rough-and-ready arts centre, a visitor might find Elefsina a little underwhelming.

Once an old soap factory, the Old Oil Mill features an outdoor theatre (Eleusis was the home town of Aeschylus, father of tragedy); it hosts artistic performances and a **festival** (☑ 21055 65613; https://aisxylia.gr) in June and July.

Elefsina is also home to a small pebble beach right off the *plateia* (main square) and an open-air cinema with interesting screenings.

◉ Sights

Ancient Eleusis RUINS
(Map p146; ☑ 21055 46019; Sotiriou Gkioka; adult/child €6/free; ⊗ 8am-8pm Tue-Sun; 🚌 876 from Agia Marina metro, Ⓜ Agia Marina) Eleusis occupies a great site on the slopes of a low hill, close to the shore of the Saronic Gulf. Although little has been restored, the scale of its construction is impressive, as enormous pieces of columns and building blocks are scattered all over. The core of the site is the **Sanctuary of Demeter**, dating to Mycenaean times, when the god-dess's cult was one of the most important in Ancient Greece.

By Classical times, until the 4th century AD, Demeter was celebrated with a huge annual festival that attracted thousands of pilgrims seeking initiation to the Eleusinian mysteries.

They walked in procession from the Acropolis (p78) to Eleusis along the Sacred Way, which was lined with statues and votive monuments. Initiates were sworn to secrecy on punishment of death; during the 1400 years that the sanctuary functioned, its secrets were never divulged.

The **museum**, at the back of the site, with a good view of the bay, has models of the old city as well as some excellent marble statuary, including a caryatid bust that's great to see at eye level.

✖ Eating & Drinking

Rakoun GREEK €
(☑ 21055 47910; Nikolaidou 66; mezedhes from €4; ⊗ 9am-2am) This excellent *tsipoura-dhiko* (*ouzerie* in the north) hugely popular with locals, serves good Greek mezedhes and specialises in *tsipouro* and raki. Traditional music is played here. The terrace overlooks the ruins of Ancient Eleusis and stays busy until the small hours. If you're visiting on a Sunday or during public holidays, book a table in advance.

Kapaki GREEK €
(☑ 210 554 4126; Plateia Iroon 2; mains from €6; ⊗ 9am-2am) Right on Elefsina's main

square, this popular taverna serves a fantastic fava-bean puree, grilled sardines and chilled wine on a terrace under a canopy of trees. There's also a variety of other traditional Greek dishes. Finish up with a Greek coffee and a baklava.

Gazoza CAFE
(☎ 210 554 5494; Nikolaidou 82; ☺ 9am-midnight) This pleasant cafe and bar on Nikolaidou is busy with families and youngsters who spend hours enjoying their cappuccinos under the shady canopies. Sit here and people-watch while overlooking the Ancient Eleusis ruins.

☆ Entertainment

Old Oil Mill ARTS CENTRE
(Palaio Elaiourgeio; Kanellopoulou 1, Paralia Elefsinas; ☺ 5-9pm Mon-Fri, 10.30am-7pm Sat & Sun) **FREE** Elefsina's current culture revolves around this vast ruined soap factory, a space constantly in flux as various arts and performance groups adapt it to their uses. The big event of the year is the summer Aeschylia Festival; it's also a venue for some events in the Athens & Epidaurus Festival (p109).

❶ Getting There & Away

From Athens, take bus 876 from Agia Marina metro, the last stop on line 3.

Saronic Gulf Islands

Best Places to Eat

➡ On the Verandah (p172)

➡ Techne (p169)

➡ Oraia Hydra (p167)

➡ Aspros Gatos (p162)

➡ Miltos (p158)

➡ Akrogialia (p172)

Best Places to Stay

➡ Poseidonion Grand Hotel (p171)

➡ Hydra Hotel (p166)

➡ Rosy's Little Village (p158)

➡ Orloff Resort (p171)

➡ Sirene Blue Resort (p162)

Why Go?

The Saronic Gulf Islands dot the waters nearest Athens and offer a fast track to Greek island life. As with all Greek islands, each of the Saronics has a unique feel and culture, so you can hop between classical heritage, resort beaches, exquisite architecture and remote escapism.

Aegina is home to a spectacular Doric temple (p157) and ruined Byzantine village (p158), while nearby pine-clad Angistri feels protected and peaceful outside of the booming midsummer months. Further south, Poros, with its beautiful old town and forested hinterland, curves only a few hundred metres from the Peloponnese. The Saronic showpiece, Hydra, is a gorgeous car-free island with a port of carefully preserved stone houses rising from a chic, history-charged harbour. Deepest south of all, pine-scented Spetses also has a vibrant nautical history and pretty town architecture, plus myriad aqua coves only minutes from the Peloponnese.

When to Go
Hydra

Apr & May The islands awake after winter; come for flower-filled Easter.

Jun Celebrate Miaoulia in Hydra with sparkling waters and warm weather.

Sep Enjoy the clear skies, thinning crowds and Spetses' Armata celebration.

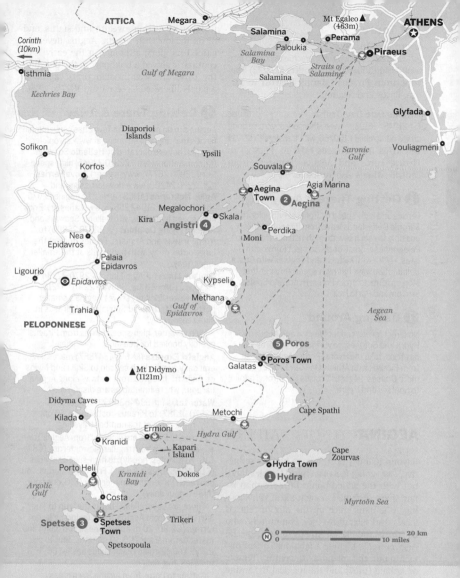

Saronic Gulf Islands Highlights

1 Hydra (p162) Taking in the gorgeous port, with its excellent museums and stylish scene, and the island's deserted trails and ubiquitous swimming rocks.

2 Aegina (p154) Delving into ancient history at the beautiful Temple of Aphaia and the Byzantine village of Paleohora, then sipping seaside cocktails.

3 Spetses (p169) Taste-testing your way through top restaurants, tracing the region's history in Spetses Town's museums, or cycling the island's ring road to dip into sparkling bays.

4 Angistri (p158) Getting away from it all in the low season, when the beaches are at their most tranquil.

5 Poros (p159) Exploring the peaceful, forested interior and wandering the colourful narrow lanes of Poros Town.

☞ Tours

Evermore Cruises CRUISE
(☑ 21118 82220; www.evermorecruises.com; cruise adult/child €100/60, with transfers €112/72) Day trips from Piraeus (Marina Flisvos) to Hydra, Poros and Aegina.

Athens One Day Cruise CRUISE
(☑ 21045 16106; www.athensonedaycruise.com; cruise adult/child €100/60, with transfers €112/72) Day trips from Piraeus (Marina Flisvos) to Hydra, Poros and Aegina. Transfers from central Athens also available.

❶ Getting There & Away

Ferries and high-speed hydrofoil services for the Saronic Gulf Islands leave from Piraeus. It's also possible to reach several of the islands from the Peloponnese. Small boats connect Poros with Galatas, Hydra with Metochi and Spetses with Costa. Hellenic Seaways has high-speed services that stop en route to/from Poros, Hydra and Spetses in Ermioni and Porto Heli.

❶ Getting Around

No direct ferries connect Aegina and Angistri with Hydra and Spetses; go via Piraeus or Poros. For day trips, take the Hydra–Poros–Aegina cruise from Piraeus with Athens One Day Cruise or Evermore Cruises. Pegasus Cruises goes from Nafplio to Spetses and Hydra.

AEGINA ΑΙΓΙΝΑ

POP 13,056

Beyond its busy port, Aegina has the seductive, easy-going feel of a typical Greek island, but with the added bonus of more than its fair share of famed ancient sites. Weekending Athenians spice up the mix of relaxed locals and island-dwelling commuters who use the island like an Athens suburb. Special Aegina treats include a fabulous sort of pistachio nut, the splendid 5th-century Temple of Aphaia (p157) and the magical Byzantine Paleohora (p158) ruins.

History

Aegina was the leading maritime power of the Saronic Gulf during the 7th century BC, when it grew wealthy through trade and political might. The island made a major contribution to the Greek victory over the Persian fleet at the Battle of Salamis in 480 BC. Despite this solidarity with the Athenian state, the latter invaded in 459 BC out of

jealousy of Aegina's wealth and status, and of its liaison with Sparta. Aegina never regained its glory, although in the early 19th century it played a bold part in the defeat of the Turks and was the temporary capital of a partly liberated Greece from 1827 to 1829.

❶ Getting There & Away

Aegina's main port, Aegina Town, has conventional ferries that are booked online at www.saronicferries.gr. They are operated by **Hellenic Seaways** (☑ conventional ferry 22970 22945, high-speed ferry 22970 26777; www.hsw.gr), **Nova Ferries** (☑ 22970 24200; www.novaferries.gr) and **Agios Nektarios** (ANES Ferries; ☑ Aegina 22970 25625, Piraeus 21042 25625; www.anes.gr). Book high-speed hydrofoils with Hellenic Seaways and **Aegean Flying Dolphins** (☑ 22970 25800) to/from Piraeus and Angistri. Ferries dock at the large outer quay, with hydrofoils at the smaller inner quay.

Evoikos Lines (☑ Agia Marina 22970 32234, Piraeus 21048 21002, Souvala 22970 52210; www.evoikoslines.gr) serves Aegina's smaller ports Agia Marina and Souvala, and Piraeus in high season only.

Even in winter, high-speed ferries from Piraeus get fully booked for weekends: book ahead.

Angistri Express (☑ 6934347867) makes several daily trips in high season to Skala and Mylos on Angistri. It leaves from midway along Aegina harbour, where timetables are displayed.

Water taxis (☑ 6944535659, 6972229720, 22970 91387) to Piraeus cost about €40 one way, regardless of the number travelling.

Ferries to Piraeus are plentiful from Aegina Town all year, ranging from regular, slower ferries (€8 to €10, 70 minutes, hourly), to high-speed services (€14, 40 minutes, six daily). From Agia Marina, you can reach Piraeus in summer only (€10, one hour, three to four daily).

There are several daily boats that run to Angistri's Skala from Aegina Town, including large ferries (€2.80, 20 minutes, one to two daily) and faster catamarans (€6, 10 minutes, four to six daily). You can also reach Mylos easily (€6, 10 minutes, five daily).

Getting to Poros from Aegina Town is easy (€8.50, one hour and 50 minutes, two to three daily).

Note that there are no direct ferries to Hydra from Aegina; you must go back to Piraeus and take a Hydra-bound ferry from there.

❶ Getting Around

BUS

Buses from Aegina Town run several times a day on three routes across the island. Departure times are displayed outside the ticket office on

Aegina & Angistri

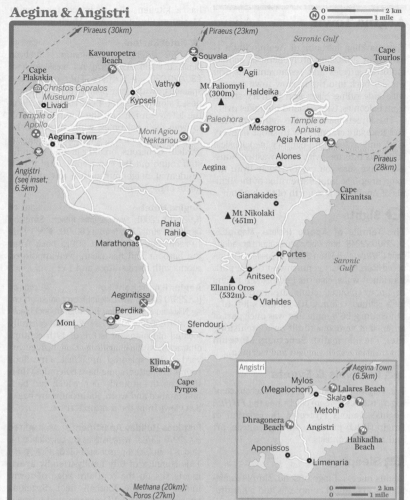

Plateia Ethnegersias (Ethnegersias Sq); you must buy tickets there. Visit www.aeginagreece.com for details.

Agia Marina (€2, 30 minutes) via Paleohora (€2, 15 minutes) and Temple of Aphaia (€2, 25 minutes)

Perdika (€1.80, 15 minutes)

Vagia (€1.80, 25 minutes) via Souvala (€1.80, 20 minutes)

CAR, MOTORCYCLE & BICYCLE

Numerous outfits hire out vehicles. Prices start from €35 per day for cars, €17 for a 50cc motorcycle and €8 for bicycles.

Karagiannis Travel (☑ 22970 28780; www.aeginatravel.gr; Pan Irioti 44; ⊘ 9am-2pm & 5-9pm) Rents vehicles and arranges tours and tickets.

Sklavenas Rent A Car (☑ 22970 22892; Kazantzaki 5; ⊘ 9am-2pm & 5-9pm) For cars, 4WDs, scooters, quads and bikes. In Aegina Town, located on the road near the Temple of Apollo (p156). Also has a branch in **Agia Marina** (☑ 22970 32871; Agia Marina; ⊘ 9am-2pm & 5-9pm).

Taxi (☑ Aegina Town 22970 22010, Agia Marina 22970 32107) Taxis around Aegina island.

Aegina Town   Αίγινα

POP 8905

The sparkling harbour of Aegina Town is backed by a buzzing promenade of people, motorbikes, cafes and restaurants. As you wander back into the narrow town streets, with kids riding bikes and laundry strung from balconies, Greek island life takes over.

The streets backing the harbour, Irioti and Rodi, are crammed with shops of every kind and a few 19th-century neoclassical buildings intermix with whitewashed houses – make sure you explore away from the main drag. The impressive ruins of the Temple of Apollo are just north of the harbour.

◉ Sights

The Temple of Apollo (Kolona; Map p155; ☑ 22970 22248; http://odysseus.culture.gr; adult/child €3/free; ⊙ 8.30am-3pm Tue-Sun May-Oct, reduced hours Nov-Apr) is northwest of the port. Its ruined walls, cisterns and broken pillars in honey-coloured stone are lorded over by a solitary column. It's all that's left of a 5th-century-BC temple that was once part of an ancient acropolis (built on a prehistoric site). The informative **Sanctuary Museum** has translations in English and German.

✯✦ Festivals & Events

The **Aegina Fistiki Fest** (www.facebook.com/AeginaFistikiFest; ⊙ Sep) celebrates the *Fistiki*, Aegina's famous Protected Designation of Origin (PDO) pistachio through music, art and culinary contests.

⌷ Sleeping

Aegina offers a range of solid, simple guesthouses, apartment complexes and a handful of hotels. Book ahead at weekends.

Electra Pension   PENSION €
(☑ 22970 26715; www.aegina-electra.gr; Leonardou Lada 25; r from €45; ☀ ◈) There are no views from this small whitewashed pension, but rooms are impeccable in a quiet corner of the town centre. It outclasses nearby hotels by a long way. Rates go down off-season.

Marianna Studios   PENSION €
(☑ 22970 25650; Kiverniou 16-18; s/d €35/40, d/tr with kitchen €40/45; ☀) Simple, basic rooms and very friendly owners create a top-notch budget choice. Some rooms have balconies or overlook a quiet, leafy garden alongside an interior courtyard. One room

has a kitchen. Not to be confused with Marianna Studios in Agia Marina.

★ Hotel Rastoni   HOTEL €€
(☑ 22970 27039; www.rastoni.gr; Stratigou Dimitriou Petriti 31; d/tr/q incl breakfast from €80/120/130; P ☀ @ ◈) The rooms are spacious, with four-poster beds and exposed-stone walls. Top-floor rooms overlook the lovely garden and the Temple of Apollo from their balconies, while those on the ground floor open straight onto the fragrant garden. Generous breakfasts and friendly staff round out the experience. Find it in a residential neighbourhood a few minutes north of the harbour.

Aegina Hotel   HOTEL €€
(☑ 22970 28501; www.aeginahotel.gr; Stratigou Dimitriou Petriti 23; d/tr from €60/70; ☀ ◈) This 19-room hotel sits about 500m back from the harbour and has clean, well-appointed rooms with refrigerators and TVs.

Aeginitiko Archontiko   PENSION €€
(☑ 22970 24968; www.aeginitikoarchontiko.gr; cnr Ag Nikolaou & Thomaidou 1; s/d/tr/ste incl breakfast from €50/60/70/100; ☀ ◈) This centrally located old mansion is full of 19th century character, with a charming salon, lush courtyard and a splendid breakfast. First-floor rooms are better (some have balconies) than those on the ground floor, which can be a bit cramped and worn. Bathrooms are basic. Sea views from the rooftop terrace.

Fistikies Holiday Apartments   APARTMENT €€
(☑ 22970 23783; www.fistikies.gr; Logiotatidou 1; studios from €90, 4-person apts €120; P ☀ ◈ ☀) This complex of tidy family-friendly apartments sits on the southern edge of town, inland from the football field. Spacious apartments have DVD players, and terraces overlooking the pool.

✕ Eating

The harbourfront restaurants make for lazy world-watching, but are not particularly outstanding, unless you hit the unvarnished *ouzeries* (serving ouzo and light snacks).

Aegina's pistachio nuts are on sale everywhere (from €7 for 500g, depending on quality).

Gelladakis   MEZEDHES €
(☑ 22970 27308; Pan Irioti 45; dishes €7-12; ⊙ lunch & dinner) Ensconced behind the noisy midharbour fish market, this vibrant joint is thronged with people tucking into

charcoal-fired octopus or sardines, plus other classic mezedhes. Arrive early for a table.

Elia
MEDITERRANEAN €

(☎ 22975 00205; Koumoundourou 4; mains €6-9; ⊗ noon-4pm & 6-11pm, reduced winter hours) Burrow into the backstreets for this excellent restaurant that's popular with locals. Orignial, fresh specialities include Aegina's pistachio pesto and the *pites* (pies) of the day.

Tsias
TAVERNA €

(☎ 22970 23529; Dimokratias 47; mains €7-10; ⊗ lunch & dinner) Harbourside eating at its best (mind the buzzing scooters rushing past). Try shrimps with tomatoes and feta, the *horta* (wild greens) and sardines, or one of the daily specials.

Kriton Gefsis
CRETAN €€

(☎ 22970 26255; www.facebook.com/kritongefsis; cnr Pan Irioti & Damanos; dishes €5-15; ⊗ 10am-2am) Cretan ingredients and flavours are the order of the day at this lively taverna featuring fresh seafood. Also has live music.

Bakalogatos
MEZEDHES €€

(☎ 22975 00501; cnr Pan Irioti & Neoptolemou; mains €7-13; ⊗ lunch & dinner Tue-Sun) Marked out by a canopy of colourful umbrellas suspended above the entrance, Bakalogatos has fresh, well-crafted mezedhes in an elegant setting, with faux-finished tables and traditional products on the walls.

🍷 Drinking & Nightlife

Tortuga
BAR

(☎ 6983437913; www.facebook.com/tortugaegina; Pan Irioti 43; ⊗ 10am-midnight) This lovely one-room bar, full of artistic knick-knacks, spills onto the busy Irioti street. This is the place for good coffee in the day and cocktails in the evening. There is live music too.

International Corner
BAR

(☎ 22970 26564; cnr I Katsa & S Rodi; ⊗ noon-late) Get off the main strip and head to this bohemian wood-panelled bar room. The gregarious owner takes requests, from top 40 to fantastic Greek music.

ⓘ Information

Aegina has no tourist office. Check Karagiannis Travel (p155) for car hire, tours and non-Aegina boats.

ⓘ Getting There & Away

Aegina's main port is located in Aegina Town: it's served by both conventional ferries (book online at www.saronicferries.gr) and high-speed hydrofoils operated by Hellenic Seaways (p154) and Aegean Flying Dolphins (p154).

ⓘ Getting Around

There is a hub of local buses and water taxis at the main port.

Around Aegina

⊙ Sights

Aegina is lush and wildflower-laden in spring, and year-round offers some of the best Archaic sites in the Saronic Gulf. The hills and mountains add drama to the small island, but beaches are not its strongest suit. The east-coast town of **Agia Marina** is the island's main package resort. It has a shallow-water beach that is ideal for families, but it's backed by a fairly crowded main drag. A few thin, sandy beaches, such as **Marathonas**, line the roadside between Aegina Town and Perdika.

★ Temple of Aphaia
TEMPLE

(Map p155; ☎ 22970 32398; http://odysseus.culture.gr; adult/child €4/free; ⊗ 9.30am-4.30pm, museum 10.30am-1.30pm Tue-Sun) This impressive temple stands proudly on a pine-covered hill with far-reaching views over the Saronic Gulf. Built in 480 BC, it celebrates a local deity of pre-Hellenic times. The temple's pediments were originally decorated with splendid Trojan War sculptures, most

---

WORTH A TRIP

PERDIKA

The quaint fishing village of Perdika lies about 9km south of Aegina Town on the southern tip of the west coast and makes for a relaxed sojourn.

Perdika's harbour is very shallow; for the best swimming, catch one of the regular caïques (little boats; return adult/child €5/free) to the small island of **Moni**, a few minutes offshore. A nature reserve, it has a tree-lined beach and summertime cafe.

On Perdika's raised harbourfront, sultry sunset relaxation makes way for buzzing nightlife when late-night music bars rev into gear during summer.

of which were stolen in the 19th century and now decorate Munich's Glyptothek. Panels throughout the site are also in English.

Aphaia is 10km east of Aegina Town. Infrequent buses to Agia Marina stop here (20 minutes); taxis cost about €12 one way.

★ Paleohora   CHURCH

(Παλαιοχώρα; Map p155) FREE This enchanting remote hillside is dotted with the remains of a Byzantine village. More than 30 surviving **churches** punctuate the rocky heights of the original citadel, and several have been refurbished. They are linked by a network of paths, carpeted with wildflowers in spring. The ancient town of Paleohora was Aegina's capital from the 9th century and was only abandoned during the 1820s.

It is is 6.5km east of Aegina Town, near enormous modern monastery **Moni Agiou Nektariou** (Map p155; ✆22970 53800; ☉hours vary). Buses from Aegina Town to Agia Marina stop at the turn-off to Paleohora (10 minutes); taxis cost €8 one way.

Christos Capralos Museum   MUSEUM

(Map p155; ✆22970 22001; Nikou Kazantzaki/ Coast Rd, Livadi; €2; ☉10am-2pm & 6-8pm Tue-Sun Jun-Oct, 10am-2pm Fri-Sun Nov-May) The home and studio of acclaimed sculptor Christos Capralos (1909–93), on the coast near Livadi, 1.5km north of Aegina Town, is a museum displaying many of his fluid, powerful works. Monumental sculptures include the 40m-long *Pindus Frieze*.

🛏 Sleeping & Eating

Villa Rodanthos   APARTMENT €

(✆22970 61400, 6944250138; www.villarodanthos. com; Perdika; studios from €55; ❋🐾) A gem of a place with a charming owner. Each room has its own colourful decor and a small kitchen, and there's an excellent roof terrace for afternoon drinks with sea views.

O Thanasis   SEAFOOD €

(✆22970 31348; Seafront, Portes; mains €7-8; ☉lunch & dinner, reduced hours winter) On the east coast of the island in Portes, 13km northeast of Perdika, a family welcomes you to a seafront terrace raped with flowerpots. It serves up top seafood and Greek classics.

★ Miltos   SEAFOOD €€

(✆22970 61051; Perdika; mains €12-15; ☉noon-4pm & 6pm-late) The most locally popular of Perdika's quayside tavernas, known for the highest-quality seafood and Greek staples.

Aeginitissa   SEAFOOD €€

(Map p155; ✆22970 61546, 6944651699; mains €6-15; ☉noon-late May-Sep) Plan for a sunset meal at this simple seafood taverna, 1.5km north of Perdika (6km south of Aegina Town). It's a favourite with locals for its beautiful waterfront setting. If ordering fish, have it weighed first to avoid sticker shock when you get the bill.

ANGISTRI   ΑΓΚΙΣΤΡΙ

POP 1142

Tiny Angistri lies a few kilometres off the west coast of Aegina and, out of high season, its mellow lanes and azure coves make a rewarding day trip or a worthwhile longer escape.

◉ Sights

The port-resort village of **Skala** is crammed with small hotels, apartments, tavernas and cafes, but life still ticks along gently. A right turn from the quay leads to the small harbour beach and then to a church on a low headland. Beyond lies the island's best beach (it's unnamed), which is packed during July and August. Turning left from the quay at Skala takes you south along a dirt path through the pine trees to the pebbly and clothing-optional **Halikadha Beach**.

About 1km west from Skala, Angistri's other port, **Mylos** (Megalochori), has an appealing traditional character, rooms and tavernas, but no beach.

Aponissos has turquoise waters, a small offshore island and a reliably tasty taverna. **Limenaria** has deeper green waters. The island as a whole gets sleepy in low season.

🛏 Sleeping

Book ahead, especially for August and summer weekends. A board on Skala's quay lists a range of small guesthouses and hotels.

Alkyoni Inn   PENSION €

(✆22970 91378; www.alkyoni-agistri.com; Skala; s/d/maisonettes from €30/45/60; ☉Easter-Sep; ❋🐾) This elegant pension offers some sea-facing rooms with unobstructed views. Two-storey family maisonettes sleep up to four. Its taverna is very popular.

★ Rosy's Little Village   PENSION €€

(✆22970 91610; www.rosyslittlevillage.com; Skala; s/d/tr/q from €65/73/83/108; ❋🐾) A complex of simple Cycladic-style cubes steps gently down to the sea, a short way east of Skala's quay. Full of light and colour, with built-in couches and tiny balconies with sea views, Rosy's also offers mountain bikes, summer courses, weekly picnics and live-music evenings. Its restaurant emphasises organics.

Eating

Toxotis GREEK €
(☑ 22970 91283; Skala; mains from €7; ☺ lunch & dinner) A popular restaurant in Skala, with good meat and fish dishes, a decent wine selection and a busy terrace.

Petite Restaurant GREEK €€
(☑ 22970 91610; www.rosyslittlevillage.com; Rosy's Little Village; mains €8-18; ☺ lunch & dinner; ☑) Part of Rosy's Little Village, this small restaurant focuses on organic produce and vegan and vegetarian options, in addition to the traditional Greek staples. Vegetarians and vegans should try the excellent tabbouleh and stuffed tomatoes, while meat and fish eaters can have fish roe salad, fresh fish or baked lamb with rosemary.

Alkyoni Inn TAVERNA €€
(☑ 22970 91378; www.alkyoni-agistri.com; Skala; mains €7-15; ☺ 8am-10pm Easter-Sep; ✳☎☷) The welcoming, family-run Alkyoni is a 10-minute stroll southeast of Skala's quay. The popular taverna dishes up well-prepared fish and meat, while the elegant pension offers sea-facing rooms and family maisonettes.

❶ Information

Visit www.agistri.com.gr for island information.

❶ Getting There & Away

Fast Aegean Flying Dolphins (p154) and Hellenic Seaways (p154) hydrofoils and car ferries (www.saronicferries.gr) come from Piraeus (hydrofoils €14.50, 55 minutes; ferry €10.90, 1½ hours) via Aegina (hydrofoils €6, 10 minutes, four to six daily; ferry €2.80, 20 minutes, one to two daily) to either Skala or Mylos. Angistri Express (p154) serves Aegina several times daily, Monday to Saturday. Water taxis (p154) cost €45 one way between Aegina and Angistri.

❶ Getting Around

Several **buses** (☑ 6973016132, 22970 91244; Skala) a day during summer run from Skala and Mylos (Megalochori) to Limenaria and Dhragonera Beach. It's worth hiring a scooter (€15) or sturdy bike (€7) to explore the coast road.

You can also follow tracks from Metohi overland through cool pine forest to reach Dhragonera Beach. Take a compass; tracks divide often and route-finding can be frustrating.
Kostas Bike Hire (☑ 22970 91021; Skala)
Takis Rent a Bike & Bicycles (Logothetis; ☑ 22970 91001; www.agistri.com.gr/logothetis; Mylos)
Taxi (☑ 6977618040, 22970 91455; Skala)

POROS ΠΟΡΟΣ

POP 3800

Poros is separated from the mountainous Peloponnese by a narrow sea channel, and its protected setting makes the main settlement of Poros Town seem like a vibrant lakeside resort. The sight of its pastel-hued houses stacked up on the hillside around a clock tower is as romantic as it gets.

Poros is made up of two land masses connected by a tiny isthmus: Sferia, which is occupied mainly by the town of Poros; and the much larger, forested Kalavria, where the island's beaches and seasonal hotels are scattered along its southern shore. Poros still maintains a sense of remoteness in its sparsely populated, forested interior.

The Peloponnesian town of Galatas lies on the opposite shore, making Poros a useful base from which to explore the ancient sites of the Peloponnese.

❶ Getting There & Away

Daily ferries (www.saronicferries.gr; €11.50 to €14, 2½ hours, two to three daily) or zippy catamarans (€24.50, one hour, four to five daily) connect Piraeus to Poros in summer (reduced timetable in winter). High-speed Hellenic Seaways (p154) ferries continue south to Hydra (€13.50, 30 minutes, two to five daily), Spetses (€16, 1½ hours, four daily), Ermioni and Porto Heli. Conventional ferries connect Aegina (€8.50,1¼ hours, two to five daily) to Poros and Methana on the mainland.. Travel agents (p161) sell tickets.

Caïques shuttle constantly between Poros and Galatas (€1, five minutes). They leave from the quay opposite Plateia Iroön, the triangular plaza near the main ferry dock in Poros Town. Hydrofoils dock about 50m north of here. Car ferries to Galatas (per person/car €1/6, from 7.30am to 10.40pm) leave from the dock several hundred metres north again, on the road to Kalavria.

You can also do a one-way rental between branches of **Pop's Car** (☑ in Galatas 22980 42910; www.popscar.gr) at Athens Airport and Galatas (or Ermioni).

Poros

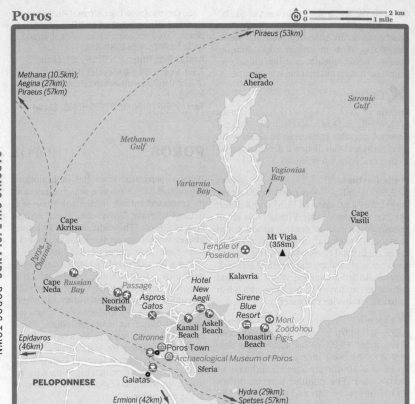

Piraeus (53km)

Methana (10.5km);
Aegina (27km);
Piraeus (57km)

Cape
Aherado

Saronic
Gulf

Methanon
Gulf

Vagionias
Bay

Variarnia
Bay

Cape
Vasili

Cape
Akritsa

Mt Vigla
(358m)

Temple of
Poseidon

Kalavria

Cape
Neda

Russian
Bay

Passage

Hotel
New
Aegli

Sirene
Blue
Resort

Neorion
Beach

Aspros
Gatos

Moni
Zoödohou
Pigis

Epidavros
(46km)

Citronne

Kanali
Beach

Askeli
Beach

Monastiri
Beach

Poros Town

Archaeological Museum of Poros

Sferia

PELOPONNESE

Galatas

Hydra (29km);
Spetses (57km)

Ermioni (42km)

SARONIC GULF ISLANDS POROS TOWN

ⓘ Getting Around

BOAT

Caïques go to beaches around the island during summer.

BUS

A bus (€3) operates mid-June to October every hour from 7am until midnight from the **Galatas KTEL Bus Station** (☑ 22980 42480; www.ktel argolida.gr; Galatas) on a route that starts next to the kiosk at the eastern end of Plateia Iroön. It crosses to Kalavria and goes east along the south coast for 10 minutes as far as Moni Zoödohou Pigis, then turns around and heads west to Neorion Beach (15 minutes). Buy tickets from the kiosk.

MOTORCYCLE & BICYCLE

Several places on the road to Kalavria rent out bicycles, scooters and all-terrain vehicles (ATVs; per day from €6/20/30).
Moto Fotis (☑ 22980 25873; http://motor entalfotis.com.gr; Kanali; ☉ 9am-9pm) Rents bicycles, motorbikes and ATVs.

Moto Stelios (☑ 22980 23026; www.motos telios.gr; Harbour, Poros Town; ☉ 9am-9pm) Rents ATVs, scooters and bicycles in Poros Harbour and Askeli Beach.

TAXI

Fares are posted at the main stand on the quay.
Taxi (Poros) (☑ 22980 23003)
Taxi (Galatas) (☑ 22980 42888)

Poros Town   Πόρος

POP 3651

Poros Town's lively harbour area faces the narrow channel at Galatas and the shapely mountains of the Peloponnese, giving it a dynamic atmosphere – sailing boats bob along the quay, while ferries glide through the channel and smaller vessels scurry about. Behind the harbour, *plateies* (squares) and tavernas hide from view and a rocky bluff rises to a crowning clock tower. The colourful alleyways and slightly dilapidated houses are a true delight.

◉ Sights

Archaeological Museum of Poros   MUSEUM
(Map p160; ☑22980 23276; http://odysseus.culture.gr; Harbourfront, Plateia Koryzi; €2; ⊙8.30am-3pm Tue-Sun) This small museum on the waterfront shows a beautiful collection of classic Greek sculpture from the area.

Citronne   GALLERY
(Map p160; ☑22980 22401; www.facebook.com/citronne.athens.poros; Leoforos Papadopoulou; ⊙10am-3pm Mon-Sat Jun-Aug) This bright and cheerful local gallery shows artists from around Greece.

🛏 Sleeping

Poros Town offers the gamut: simple business-style hotels and charming old-school hotels on the waterfront, and rooms for rent set back on tiny lanes.

★ Seven Brothers Hotel   HOTEL €
(☑22980 23412; www.7brothers.gr; Poros Harbour; s/d/tr €50/55/60; ❄ 🗟) This charming hotel has bright, comfy rooms with antique details and neat bathrooms. Some have small balconies, some sea views. There is also a patio overlooking the small square in the front. It's conveniently close to the hydrofoil quay.

Georgia Mellou Rooms   PENSION €
(☑22980 22309; http://porosnet.gr/gmellou; Plateia Georgiou; d/tr €40/45; ❄ 🗟) Simple old-fashioned rooms are tucked into the heart of the old town, next to the cathedral, high above the harbour. The charming owner keeps everything shipshape. Book ahead for fantastic views from west-side rooms.

Sto Roloi   APARTMENT €€
(☑22980 25808, 6932427267; www.storoloi-poros.gr; studio/apt/houses from €65/110/170; ❄) Roloi is a good source for stylish, tidy apartments and houses around Poros Town.

🍴 Eating

Taverna Karavolos   TAVERNA €
(☑22980 26158; Dalakou; mains €6-12; ⊙7-11pm) Karavolos means 'big snail' and snails are indeed a house speciality at this quaint backstreet eatery. Friendly owners also offer classic Greek meat dishes and some fish, as well as **rooms** (double/triple €37/45) upstairs.

Poseidon   SEAFOOD €€
(☑22980 23597; www.poseidontaverna.gr; Harbourfront; mains €7-15; ⊙9.30am-12.30am Easter-Oct) A quayside favourite for delicious seafood, friendly service and Greek dancing.

Dimitris Family Taverna   TAVERNA €€
(☑22980 23709; www.dimitrisfamily-poros.gr; Giannousi; mains €6-14; ⊙6-10pm or 11pm) Renowned for its meat, this taverna's owners have a butchers, meaning cuts are of the finest quality. It's up the hill in the centre of town; ask a local for directions.

ℹ Information

Poros has no tourist office. Harbourfront agencies arrange accommodation, car hire, tours and cruises.

Askeli Travel (☑22980 23743; www.family tours.gr; Harbourfront; ⊙9am-2pm & 5-10pm) Arranges studios for rent.

Family Tours (☑22980 23743; www.family tours.gr; Harbourfront; ⊙9am-2pm & 5-10pm) Sells conventional-ferry tickets.

Marinos Tours (☑22980 23423; www.marinostours.gr; Harbourfront; ⊙7am-9.30pm Apr-Oct, to 7pm Nov-Mar) Across from the hydrofoil quay; sells hydrofoil tickets.

Around Poros

◉ Sights

Temple of Poseidon   RUINS
(Map p160; ☑22980 23276; ⊙8.30am-3pm) FREE There's very little left of this 6th-century temple. Once it was a magnificent building giving sanctuary to fugitives and wrecked sailors, but in the 18th century it was mostly dismantled and the materials used to build a monastery on Hydra. Still, the walk or drive to the site gives superb views of the Saronic Gulf and the Peloponnese.

With your own wheels, from the road near Moni Zoödohou Pigis, head inland to reach the ruins. Then you can continue along the road and circle back to the bridge onto Sferia. It's about 6km in total.

The free **Moni Zoödohou Pigis** (Map p160; ⊙9am-noon & 2.30-6pm), an 18th-century 'Monastery of the Life-giving Spring', is well signposted 4km east of Poros Town and has a beautiful gilded iconostasis (a screen bearing icons) from Asia Minor.

🏃 Activities

Poros' best beaches include the pebbly **Kanali Beach**, on Kalavria islet 1km east of the bridge, and the long, sandy **Askeli Beach**, about 500m further east.

Neorion Beach, 3km west of the bridge, has waterskiing, and banana-boat and air-chair rides. The best beach is at **Russian Bay**, 1.5km past Neorion.

Passage (Map p160; ☑ 22980 42540; www.passage.gr; Neorion Bay; lesson from €45) is a popular waterskiing school and slalom centre. Beginner lessons are available.

🛏 Sleeping & Eating

⭐ **Sirene Blue Resort**　　　RESORT €€
(Map p160; ☑ 22980 22741; Monastiri Beach; d incl breakfast from €140; 🅿🎬🛜🏊) Sirene Blue Resort offers a deluxe seaside vacation, from the sparkling pool to crisp linens. Find it at Monastiri Beach, near Moni Zoödohou Pigis.

Hotel New Aegli　　　HOTEL €€
(Map p160; ☑ 22980 22372; www.newaegli.com; Askeli Beach; d from €95; ⊙ Apr-Oct; 🅿@🛜🏊) Poros' best beaches include the long, sandy Askeli Beach. Hotel New Aegli, across the road from the beach, is a decent resort-style hotel and offers good modern rooms, many with sea views.

⭐ **Aspros Gatos**　　　SEAFOOD €€
(Map p160; ☑ 22980 24274; Labraki 49; mains €6-15; ⊙ noon-11pm Easter-Oct) A short walk from town, 400m west of the bridge on the road to Neorion Beach, Poros' best seafood taverna sits smack out over the water. Watch the local kayaking team do its thing as the jolly owner provides anything from bolognese to the catch of the day.

HYDRA　　　　ΥΔΡΑ

POP 1966

Breathtaking Hydra is one of the only Greek islands that is car and scooter free. Just tiny marble-cobbled lanes, donkeys, rocks and sea. Artists (Brice Marden, Nikos Chatzikyriakos-Ghikas, Panayiotis Tetsis), musicians (Leonard Cohen), actors and celebrities (Melina Mercouri, Sophia Loren) have all been drawn to Hydra over the years. In addition to the island's exquisitely preserved stone architecture, divine rural paths and clear, deep waters, you can find a good cappuccino along the perfect harbour.

History

Hydra was sparsely populated in ancient times and is just mentioned in passing by Herodotus. There is some evidence of settlement dates from Mycenaean times. But in the 16th century, Hydra became a refuge for people fleeing skirmishes between the Venetians and the Ottomans. Many hailed from the area of modern-day Albania.

By the mid-1700s the settlers began building boats and took to the thin line between maritime commerce and piracy with enthusiasm. They travelled to Egypt and the Black Sea, and ran the British blockade (1803–15) during the Napoleonic Wars. As a result of steady tax paying, the island was largely left alone by the Ottoman Empire. By the 19th century, Hydra was a full-blown maritime power, and wealthy shipping merchants had built most of the town's grand mansions. At its height in 1821, the island's population reached 28,000. It supplied 130 ships for a blockade of the Turks during the Greek War of Independence, and the island bred such leaders as Admiral Andreas Miaoulis, who commanded the Greek fleet, and Georgios Koundouriotis, president of Greece's national assembly from 1822 to 1827.

🛈 Getting There & Away

High-speed **Hellenic Seaways** (www.hsw.gr) ferries link Hydra with Poros, Piraeus and Spetses, and Ermioni and Porto Heli on the Peloponnese. Service is greatly reduced in winter. Buy tickets from **Hydreoniki Travel** (☑ 22980 54007; Port; ⊙ 7am-10pm or around ferry departures), up the lane to the right of the Alpha Bank in Hydra Town.

Freedom (Map p164; ☑ 6944242141, 6947325263; www.hydralines.gr) boats run between Hydra and Metohi (little more than a car park) on the mainland (€6.50, 15 minutes, five to 11 daily). The schedule is posted on the quay and online.

High-speed catamarans run to Piraeus throughout the year (€28, 1¾ hours, four to six daily), stopping at Poros on the way (€13, 30 minutes, four to six daily). You can also get to Spetses (€11.50, 40 minutes, four to six daily).

🛈 Getting Around

Generally, people get around Hydra by walking.

The island is vehicle-free, and mules and donkeys are the main means of heavy transport. Donkey owners are clustered around the port; they transport luggage to the hotels and provide quick donkey rides around the port. Note that animal rights groups urge people to consider

Hydra

whether the animals are maltreated before deciding to take a ride.

In summer, caïques from Hydra Town go to the island's beaches. **Water taxi** (Map p164; ☑ 22980 53690) fares are posted on the quay (Kamini €10, Vlyhos €15).

Hydra Town   Υδρα
POP 1900

Hydra town's sparkling boat-filled harbour and the bright light striking the tiers of carefully preserved stone houses make for an unforgettable scene. The harbour in high season is an ecosystem of its own, with yachts, caïques and water taxis zipping in and out. The marble quay is a surging rhythm of donkeys, visitors, cafe denizens and boat-taxi hawkers. By night it becomes a promenade: grab a chair, buy a drink and watch the world go by.

Head back into the warren of portside houses, to the steep slopes banking away from the town centre and get a different view on Hydriot life. By the deep-blue-and-white houses and quiet lanes, grandmothers chat about what's for dinner, and roads peter out into dirt paths to the mountains.

◉ Sights

★ Kimisis Tis Theotokou Cathedral   CHURCH

(Metropolis; Map p164; Harbour; ⊙ 7am-7pm) Within the peaceful monastery complex on the harbour, this lovely cathedral dates from the 17th century and has a Tinian-marble bell tower. Its **Ecclesiastical Museum** (Map p164; ☑ 22980 54071; www.imhydra.gr/mouseio_main.htm; Harbour; adult/child €2/free; ⊙ 10am-5pm Tue-Sun Apr-Nov) contains a collection of icons and vestments. The monastery complex is also known as Faneromeni. Dress appropriately (covered shoulders, long skirts or trousers) to enter.

★ Deste Foundation   GALLERY

(Map p163; ☑ 21027 58490; www.deste.gr; Harbour; ⊙ 11am-1pm & 7-10pm Wed-Mon Jun-Sep) **FREE** Deste Foundation hosts an annual Hydra exhibit at the small former slaughterhouse on the sea.

★ Lazaros Koundouriotis Historical Mansion   MUSEUM

(Map p164; ☑ 22980 52421; www.nhmuseum.gr; adult/child €3/free, Sun free; ⊙ 10am-4pm Tue-Sun Mar-Oct) Hydra's star cultural attraction is this handsome ochre-coloured *arhontiko* (stone mansion) high above the harbour. It was the home of one of the major players

Hydra Town

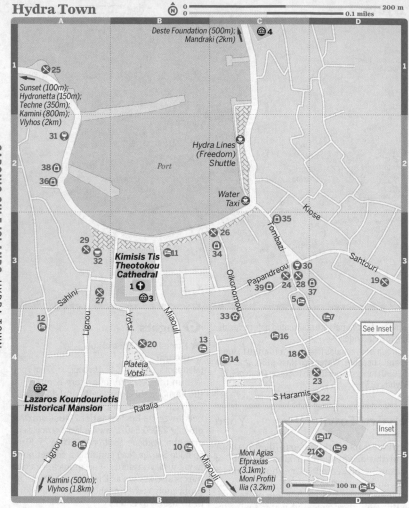

in the Greek independence struggle and is an exquisite example of late-18th-century traditional architecture. It features original furnishings, folk costumes, handicrafts and a painting exhibition.

Historical Archives Museum of Hydra
MUSEUM
(Map; ☏ 22980 52355; www.iamy.gr; Harbour; adult/child €5/3; ⏰ 9am-4pm) This fine harbourfront museum houses an extensive collection of portraits and naval artefacts, with an emphasis on the island's role in the War of Independence. It hosts temporary exhibitions in summer, and concerts on the rooftop terrace.

🏃 Activities

Vasilis Kokkos, (☏ 6977649789; bkokkos@yahoo.com) proprietor of **Caprice** (Map; ☏ 22980 52454; Sahtouri; mains €9-15; ⏰ 6pm-midnight Apr-Oct) restaurant and boat captain, rents speedboats (per day €80 to €250) and a sailing boat (by prior arrangement; one-week minimum from €900). Licence required.

Hydra Town

◎ Top Sights
1 Kimisis Tis Theotokou Cathedral B3
2 Lazaros Koundouriotis Historical
  Mansion.. A4

◎ Sights
3 Ecclesiastical Museum......................... B3
4 Historical Archives Museum of
  Hydra... C1

🛏 Sleeping
5 Amaryllis Hotel...................................... C3
6 Angelica Hotel....................................... B5
7 Bratsera Hotel.. D4
8 Cotommatae A5
9 Greco... D5
10 Hotel Miranda.. B5
11 Hotel Sophia.. B3
12 Hydra Hotel.. A4
13 Leto Hotel.. B4
14 Mastoris Mansion.................................. C4
15 Nereids... D5
16 Pension Alkionides C4
17 Piteoussa D5

✖ Eating
18 Barba Dimas... C4
  Bratsera .... (see 7)

19 Caprice..D3
20 Flora's...B4
21 Giasemi...D5
22 Gitoniko..D4
23 Il Casta...D4
24 Ke Kremmidi...C3
25 Omilos.. A1
26 Oraia Hydra..C3
27 Ostria...A3
28 Paradosiako C3
29 Psarapoula A3

🍷 Drinking & Nightlife
30 Amalour C3
31 Papagalos...A2
32 Pirate..A3

🎭 Entertainment
33 Cinema Club of Hydra.............................C4

🛍 Shopping
34 Elena Votsi...C3
35 Kashish C3
36 Sirens...A2
37 Sugarfree..D3
38 Svoura..A2
39 Turquoise...C3

👉 Tours

Harriet's Hydra Horses (☑ 6980323347; www.harrietshydrahorses.com; 1/2/8hr tour €30/55/175) is run by Harriet, a friendly bilingual British-Greek local, who guides licensed horse-riding tours (anywhere from one to eight hours) around the island, to the monasteries and to the beaches. Note that the eight-hour tour is not available between May and September because of the heat.

🎉 Festivals & Events

The **Melina Mercouri Exhibition Hall** and Deste Foundation (p163) host high-season art shows.

Miaoulia Festival   CULTURAL
(⊙ weekend around 21 Jun) Celebration of Admiral Miaoulis and the Hydriot role in the War of Independence, with boat burning (with fireworks) in Hydra harbour.

Easter   RELIGIOUS
(⊙ Mar/Apr) Week-long extravaganza including a famous parade of a flower-festooned epitaph into the harbour at Kamini.

🛏 Sleeping

Accommodation in Hydra is of a high standard, but you pay accordingly. Most owners will meet you at the harbour and organise luggage transfer.

Piteoussa   PENSION €
(Map; ☑ 22980 52810; www.piteoussa.com; Kouloura; d €50-85; ❋ 🛜) Jolly owners maintain beautiful rooms in two buildings on a quiet, pine-tree-lined street. Rooms in the restored corner mansion drip with character and also have all the modern amenities you need; the upstairs rooms in the second building have a contemporary feel, tea and coffee-making facilities and balconies.

Hotel Sophia   BOUTIQUE HOTEL €€
(Map; ☑ 22980 52313; www.hotelsophia.gr; Harbourfront; d incl breakfast €85-115; ⊙ Apr-Oct; ❋ 🛜) Gorgeous small rooms sit right on the harbour; some have balconies. Each has been outfitted with all the mod cons, and bathrooms are luscious marble. Some rooms are spread over two storeys.

Angelica Hotel   BOUTIQUE HOTEL €€
(Map; ☑ 22980 53202; www.angelica.gr; Miaouli; d/tr/q incl breakfast from €130/180/220; ❋ 🛜) An attractive boutique hotel in a quiet lo-

cation, the Angelica is popular for its comfortable, luxurious rooms and spacious, impeccable bathrooms. Superior rooms have balconies. Relax in the spa or courtyard.

Greco HOTEL €€
(Map p164; ☑ 22980 53200; www.grecohotel.gr; Kouloura; d incl breakfast from €90; ❄ ⓢ) Set in a former bakery, this atmospheric hotel has a gorgeous garden, big breakfasts and comfortable, simply designed rooms. The reception area has exposed-stone walls and antique furnishings, and there is a small library for reading in the lush garden.

Mastoris Mansion BOUTIQUE HOTEL €€
(Map p164; ☑ 22980 29631; www.mastoris-hydra.gr; off Oikonomou; d/tr from €100/150; ❄ ⓢ) This renovated stone building in the centre of town offers plush doubles and triples, with exposed stone walls and colourful decor. While convenient to harbour action, rooms don't have views.

Amaryllis Hotel HOTEL €€
(Map p164; ☑ 22980 53611; www.amarillishydra.gr; Tombazi 15; s/d €50/65, with balcony €70; ❄ ⓢ) Simple rooms, a friendly owner and a super location right in the heart of town make this a safe midrange bet. Good views can be had from the roof terrace. Shared kitchen and laundry.

Pension Alkionides PENSION €€
(Map p164; ☑ 22980 54055; www.alkionidespension.com; off Oikonomou; d/studio €70/85; ❄ ⓢ) Hidden in a central, peaceful cul-de-sac, rooms here are smart (some are quite small) and have tea- and coffee-making facilities. There's a pretty courtyard. One studio has a private terrace.

Nereids PENSION €€
(Map p164; ☑ 22980 52875; www.nereids-hydra.com; Kouloura; d from €70; ❄ ⓢ) This carefully restored stone house contains rooms of exceptional value and quality. Spacious, peaceful and with elegant decor, they have open views to Hydra's rocky heights; top-floor rooms have sea views.

Hotel Miranda HOTEL €€
(Map p164; ☑ 22980 52230; https://mirandahotel.gr; Miaouli; d/tr/apt incl breakfast from €130/145/260; ☺ Mar-Oct; ❄ ⓢ) Pretend you're a 19th-century sea captain in this antique-laden jewel with spacious, lush rooms. Public spaces are decked out in vintage prints, carved woodwork and rotating exhibitions. Gaze at your inlaid ceilings or,

in the higher-end rooms, from your balcony. Apartments are available, too.

★ Cotommatae BOUTIQUE HOTEL €€€
(Map p164; ☑ 22980 53873; www.cotommatae.gr; d/f incl breakfast from €170/250; ❄) This restored mansion has retained the character and some of the memorabilia of the home's original family while adding impeccable modern touches. There's a wonderful sense of understated luxury throughout. Some suites have private terraces or a Jacuzzi.

★ Hydra Hotel APARTMENT €€€
(Map p164; ☑ 22980 53420, 6985910717; www.hydra-hotel.gr; Petrou Voulgari 8; studio incl breakfast €175-265, maisonettes €255; ❄ ⓢ) Climb high on the south side of the port to swishy, top-of-the-line apartments in an impeccably renovated ancient mansion with kitchenettes and sweeping views. Get room 202 for a tiny balcony with panoramas to die for.

Leto Hotel HOTEL €€€
(Map p164; ☑ 22980 53385; www.letohydra.gr; Rigillis 8; d/ste from €177/485; ❄ ⓢ) This hotel is family-owned with formal, comfortable rooms and all the services. It also offers a rarity in Greece: a wheelchair-accessible room, served by ramps from the harbour.

Bratsera Hotel HISTORIC HOTEL €€€
(Map p164; ☑ 22980 53971; www.bratserahotel.com; off Kouloura; d incl breakfast €173-290, ste from €290; ❄ @ ⓢ ❄) The Bratsera is Hydra's most venerable hotel, filling a renovated sponge factory with a complex of quaint rooms, a conference hall and a swimming pool, plus a well-regarded **restaurant** (Map p164; ☑ 22980 53971; www.bratserahotel.com; Tombazi; mains €9-30; ☺ 7am-11pm Apr-Oct).

✖ Eating

Tavernas and restaurants in Hydra Town line the harbour and dot the backstreets of town. The emphasis is on Greek fare, with a couple of excellent Italian options as well.

★ Flora's SWEETS €
(Anemoni; Map p164; ☑ 22980 53136; Plateia Votsi; sweets from €1; ☺ 9am-late) Flora's sweets shop on inland Plateia Votsi makes *galaktoboureko* (custard slice), rice pudding and ice cream from local goat's milk.

Ke Kremmidi GREEK €
(Map p164; ☑ 22980 53099; Tombazi; gyros €2.50, mains €6-9; ☺ noon-late) This friendly souvlaki joint has tables spilling out onto a busy pe-

LEONARD COHEN IN HYDRA

Hydra's pull on the artistic soul is well documented, but there is no more famous former inhabitant of this mesmerising island than the bard of the bedsit himself, Leonard Cohen (1934–2016).

Depressed by the cold weather of his native Canada and adopted UK, Cohen made his way to Greece, after allegedly asking a man in the street where he got his tan – the man answered: 'Greece!' Prompted by artistic expats already living on the island, the 26-year-old Cohen landed on Hydra, and bought a house only a few days later. The five-room house, which sits in **Kamini**, was whitewashed, dishevelled and charming; Cohen published the poetry collection *Flowers for Hitler* (1964), and the novels *The Favourite Game* (1963) and *Beautiful Losers* (1966) while living and writing there.

Young, and not quite the star he became later, Cohen shared his home with Marianne Ihlen, whom he met on the island; Ihlen is the subject of his classic 'So Long, Marianne'.

Some say that the years on Hydra were Cohen's most productive and tranquil – and no wonder, considering the beauty and simplicity of life that must have surrounded him. He wrote the poem 'The Days of Kindness' about his days in Hydra.

Cohen loved the Greek way of life, and the port cafe, Rolo, then known as the Kafenion o Katsikas, is apparently where he held his first public performance for just a few friends.

Cohen left Hydra for pastures new in the mid-1960s but kept returning whenever life and stardom, and increasingly ill health, allowed him. The house remains the property of his two sons. Cohen fans go to leave offerings and read his poetry at the door to this day; ask for directions locally if you want to find it for yourself.

SARONIC GULF ISLANDS HYDRA TOWN

destrian way and offers up good salads and grilled-meat plates as well.

Ostria
TAVERNA €
(Stathis & Tassoula; Map p164; ☑ 22980 54077; off Lignou; mains €5-8; ☺ noon-4pm & 6.30pm-late) Often referred to by just the gregarious owners' names 'Stathis and Tassoula' – Tassoula is the larger-than-life hostess – this year-round taverna serves only what's fresh: put the menu to one side and ask. You might be served grilled fish, or fava-bean or zucchini balls. Stathis catches his own sweet and delicious calamari.

Giasemi
GREEK €
(Map p164; ☑ 22980 52221; Kouloura; mains from €6; ☺ lunch & dinner) Newly opened in 2019, Giasemi comes highly recommended by locals. It has a nice canopied terrace and a decent range of Greek staples – from fava-bean puree to aromatic meatballs.

★ Oraia Hydra
GREEK €€
(Map p164; ☑ 22980 52556; Harbourfront; mains €9-25; ☺ noon-midnight) Oraia Hydra translates as 'Beautiful Hydra' and this small bistro lives up to its name. You'll dine on the harbour with sailboats bobbing alongside and enjoy Greek dishes elevated by top ingredients and creative twists – try the sea urchin pasta or orzo with shrimp and mussels.

★ Il Casta
ITALIAN €€
(Map p164; ☑ 22980 52967; Tombazi; mains €10-22; ☺ noon-11pm) Dine al fresco and enjoy authentic Italian food like owner Pietro's Neapolitan grandmother used to make. Menus change daily. Reserve in high season.

★ Sunset
MEDITERRANEAN €€
(☑ 22980 52067; Kamini path; mains €9-25; ☺ noon-11pm Easter-Oct) Famed for its splendid panoramic spot near the cannons to the west of the harbour, Sunset also has fine, fresh cuisine. Tasty salads, inventive pastas and local fish are prepared with flair.

Gitoniko
TAVERNA €€
(Map p164; ☑ 22980 53615; Haramis; mains €7-25; ☺ noon-3pm & 6-11pm Easter-Oct) Having recently changed owners, Gitoniko remains popular for its broad range of good Greek dishes, and its (pricey) fresh fish. The setting, on a lovely alley, is particularly atmospheric and relaxing.

Paradosiako
TAVERNA €€
(Map p164; ☑ 22980 54155; Tombazi; mains €5-15; ☺ noon-11.30pm Easter-Nov) This little street-side spot is traditionally Greek. Sit on the corner terrace to watch the people parade as you dig into classic mezedhes – perhaps beetroot salad with garlic dip – or meats and seafood such as fresh, filleted and grilled sardines.

Psarapoula
TAVERNA €€

(Map p164; ☑ 22980 52630; Harbourfront; mains €7-14; ⊗ noon-late) Look just above the quay, near the Pirate (p168) bar and main bakery, to find this reliable taverna with lovely harbour views. Visitors and locals dig into daily specials at this historical eatery, which was established in 1911.

Barba Dimas
MEZEDHES €€

(Map p164; ☑ 22980 52967; Tombazi; small dishes €4-12; ⊗ 6-11pm) Tables line a small lane back from the portside, and dishes run the gamut of Greek mezedhes, from tender calamari to greens picked from the mountains.

Omilos
MEDITERRANEAN €€€

(Map p164; ☑ 22980 53800; www.omilos-hydra. com; Seafront, Kamini path; mains €16-25; ⊗ noon-late Easter-Oct) This chic, all-white waterside restaurant is Hydra Town's gourmet entry. It turns into a night-time dance venue.

🍷 Drinking & Nightlife

Prices are high, but lively people-watching comes with your coffee or cocktail. The harbour revs up after midnight.

★ Pirate
CAFE

(Map p164; ☑ 22980 52711; https://thepiratebar. gr; Harbourfront; ⊗ 8am-late) Friendly Wendy and Takis and their kids run this cafe with first-rate coffee, delicious breakfasts and home-cooked lunches (9am to 5pm), then morph it into a raging party place at night. Music changes with the crowd's mood.

★ Hydronetta
BAR

(☑ 22980 54160; www.facebook.com/hydronetta; Kamini path; ⊗ noon-11pm Easter-Oct) You can't beat this gorgeous waterfront location on the swimming rocks to the far west of the harbour. Brothers Andreas and Elias provide snazzy cocktails and lunch (high season only) with a smile.

Papagalos
BAR

(Map p164; ☑ 22980 52626; Harbourfront; ⊗ 9am-late) Papagalos is just that bit away from the madding crowd, on the quieter side of the harbour. By day, it offers coffee and basic food, and by night, cocktails and a clear view of the moonrise.

☆ Entertainment

Head to Cinema Club of Hydra (Map p164; ☑ 22980 53105; http://cineclub hydras.blogspot.com; Oikonomou) in July and August for blockbusters and indie flicks on its open-air cinema screens. It also organises excursions to plays at the ancient theatre of Epidavros (p109).

🛍 Shopping

Kashish
CLOTHING

(Map p164; ☑ 22984 00774; https://kash ish.gr; Tombazi 8; ⊗ 9.30am-midnight May-Sep, reduced hours rest of year) Kelly Fotopoulou designs women's and kids' clothing, jewellery and kaftans – perfect for the beach and summer lounging – using Indian colourful block printing and traditional Greek motifs.

Sirens
CLOTHING

(Map p164; ☑ 22980 53340; Harbourfront; ⊗ 10am-10pm Easter-Oct) Charming owner Elena offers unique island-friendly, high-end fashion and Greek-designed jewellery.

Sugarfree
CLOTHING

(Map p164; ☑ 22980 53352; www.sugar freeshops.com; Tombazi; ⊗ 11am-11pm May-Nov) Youthful beach and loungewear created by Greek designers fill this shop just back from Amalour (Map p164; ☑ 22980 53800; Tombazi; ⊗ 7pm-late Jun-Aug, reduced hours Sep-May), on the way to the Bratsera Hotel (p166). Prices are reasonable; the colours dazzling.

Svoura
ARTS & CRAFTS

(Map p164; ☑ 22980 29784; Harbourfront; ⊗ 10am-11pm Apr-Oct) Ceramics from all over Greece and a smattering of fashion make this one of Hydra's top shops.

Elena Votsi
JEWELLERY

(Map p164; ☑ 22980 52637; www.facebook.com/ ElenaVotsiOfficial; Harbourfront; ⊗ 10am-11.30pm) Hydra native Votsi is famous in New York and London for her bold jewellery designs using exquisite semiprecious stones. She designed the Athens Olympic Games medal. A souvenir to remember Hydra by.

Turquoise
FASHION & ACCESSORIES

(Map p164; ☑ 22980 54033; www.turquoise.gr; off Tombazi; ⊗ 10am-10pm Jun-Aug, reduced hours Sep-May) Local designer Dimitris creates an annual line of womenswear and accessories using intricate Indian block prints.

❶ Getting There & Away

Hydra Town is the main port on the island; all ferries (p162) dock here.

Around Hydra

Hydra's coastal road turns into a partially cobbled, beautiful trail about 1.5km west of the port, after **Kamini**. Kamini has a tiny fishing port, good tavernas, swimming rocks and a small pebble beach. In fact, Hydra's shortcoming – or blessing – is its lack of sandy beaches to draw the crowds. People swim off the rocks, but if you go as far as tiny hamlet **Vlyhos**, 1.5km after Kamini, you'll find two slightly larger pebble beaches (one called Vlyhos and the other, the more pristine, **Plakes**), tavernas and a restored 19th-century stone bridge.

The coastal road leads 2.5km east from the port to a pebble beach at **Mandraki**.

Boats run from the harbour to all of these places, and you need them to reach **Bisti Bay** or **Agios Nikolaos Bay**, in the southwest, with their remote but umbrella-laden pebble beaches and green waters.

Walking & Hiking

Hydra's mountainous interior makes a robust but peaceful contrast to the clamour of the quayside. A useful map for walkers is Anavasi's *Hydra* map. One is posted on the quay, and marked trails extend across the island. Once you leave the villages there are no services. Take plenty of water. Springtime is perfect for flower-strewn hillside walks.

An unbeatable experience is the long haul up to **Moni Profiti Ilia**. The wonderful monastery complex contains beautiful icons and boasts endless, dramatic views. It's a solid hour or more through zigzags and pine trees to panoramic bliss on top.

A smaller monastery run by nuns, **Moni Agias Efpraxias**, sits just below Profiti Ilia.

Other paths lead to **Mt Eros** (588m), the island's highest point, and east and west along the island spine, but make sure to get reliable directions from locals.

Eating

To Pefkaki   SEAFOOD €
(✆6973535709; Kamini; dishes €5-10; ⊙noon-4pm & 6.30-10pm Thu-Tue Easter-Oct) Worth the short walk along the coast to Kamini for a laid-back lunch of mezedhes and fresh seafood (delicious fried anchovies).

★Techne   INTERNATIONAL €€
(✆22980 52500; www.techne-hydra.com; Coast Rd, Avlaki; mains €13-23; ⊙10am-midnight) Spread across several terraces and over-looking a broad sweep of sea and sunset, this elegant cafe and restaurant serves lighter fare by day and full, well-conceived, delicious and thoughtfully served meals at night. Book ahead on weekend evenings to nab a table, perfect for date night.

Four Seasons   TAVERNA €€
(✆22980 53698; www.fourseasonshydra.gr; Plakes Beach; mains €6-15; ⊙noon-10pm Easter-Oct; ☞) This tasty seaside taverna offers a different face of Hydra: the sound of the breeze and the waves instead of the portside buzz. Don't miss the *taramasalata* (fish-roe dip) with bread. It has handsome suites (from €240, including breakfast).

Christina   TAVERNA €€
(✆22980 53516; Kamini; mains €6-12; ⊙noon-4pm & 6-10pm Thu-Tue Easter-Oct) Just inland from the port in Kamini, Mrs Christina and her kids dish out some of the island's best Greek dishes and fresh fish.

Enalion   TAVERNA €€
(✆22980 53455; www.enalion-hydra.gr; Vlyhos; mains €6-12; ⊙noon-10pm Easter-Oct) Perhaps the best seaside option at Vlyhos Beach, with traditional Greek fare. Try the fried shrimps, *horta* and a Greek salad.

Pirofani   INTERNATIONAL €€
(✆22980 53175; www.pirofani.com; Kamini; mains €10-16; ⊙7.30pm-midnight Wed-Sun late May-Sep) Gregarious Theo creates an eclectic range of dishes, from a beef fillet with rose-pepper sauce to a spicy Asian curry.

Castello   MEDITERRANEAN €€€
(✆22980 54101; www.castellohydra.gr; Kamini; snacks €7-15, mains €15-30; ⊙8am-1am Jun-Sep) In a renovated 18th-century bastion and spilling onto the beach, Castello offers snacks at its daytime beach bar, gourmet seaside dining at its refined restaurant and sunset cocktails at its bar. Amazing views.

SPETSES   ΣΠΕΤΣΕΣ
POP 4027

Spetses stands proudly just a few kilometres from mainland Peloponnese, but there is a stronger sense of carefree island Greece here than in other Saronic Gulf destinations. The lively, historical old town is the only village on the island; the rest, ringed by a simple road, is rolling hills, pine forests and crystal-clear coves. Relaxed Spetses Town,

Spetses

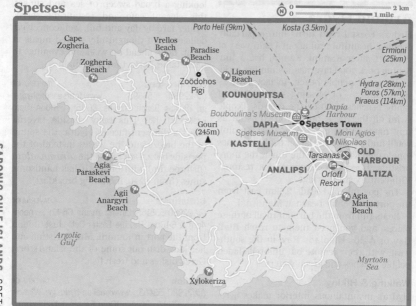

though not as picturesque as other towns on the Saronic Gulf, has great nightlife, some of the best restaurants and gorgeous, easily accessible swimming spots. With a rich naval history, it is still incredibly popular with yachties, and its vibrant culture attracts artists, intellectuals and lovers of a good party.

History

In Spetses Town there's evidence of early Helladic settlement near the Old Harbour and around the Dapia Harbour. Roman and Byzantine remains have been found in the area behind Moni Agios Nikolaos, halfway between the two.

From the 10th century, Spetses is thought to have been uninhabited for almost 600 years, until the arrival of Albanian fleeing fighting between Turks and Venetians.

Spetses, like Hydra, grew wealthy from shipbuilding. Captains busted the British blockade during the Napoleonic Wars and joined the Greek fleet during the War of Independence. In the process they immortalised one local woman (albeit originally from Hydra), Laskarina Bouboulina, ship commander and fearless fighter.

The island's hallmark forests of Aleppo pine, a legacy of the far-sighted philanthropist Sotirios Anargyros, have been devastated by several fires in the past 20 years. The trees are steadily recovering.

◉ Sights

Bustling Spetses Town stretches along a waterfront encompassing several quays and beaches. The main **Dapia Harbour**, where ferries arrive, and the area around adjacent Plateia Limenarhiou and inland Plateia Orologiou (Clocktower Sq) teem with chic tourist shops and cafes.

Inland on the quieter lanes – or left along the harbourfront road of Sotiriou Anargyriou, past the town beach and Plateia Agiou Mama – impressive old *arhontika* illustrate Spetses' historical (and ongoing) wealth.

Passing the church of **Moni Agios Nikolaos**, you arrive at the attractive **Old Harbour** (Palio Limani) and the interesting **Baltiza** yacht anchorage and boatbuilding area.

From the north side of Dapia Harbour, a promenade and road lead through the seafront **Kounoupitsa** area.

Bouboulina's Museum MUSEUM
(Map p170; ☎ 22980 72416; Spetses Town; adult/child €6/2; ⊙10.30am-6pm Apr-Oct) The mansion of Spetses' famous daughter, the 19th-century seagoing commander Laskarina Bouboulina, has been converted into a museum. Entry is via 40-minute guided

tours (billboards around town advertise starting times, also posted online). The museum hosts concerts. There's an impressive statue of Bouboulina on the harbour, opposite the Poseidonion Grand Hotel.

Spetses Museum
MUSEUM

(Map; ☑ 22980 72994; http://odysseus.culture.gr; Spetses Town; adult/child €3/free; ⊙ 8am-3pm Tue-Sun) Small, fascinating collections are housed in the mansion of Hatzigiannis Mexis (1754–1844), a shipowner who became the island's first governor. They include artefacts, traditional costumes and portraits of the island's founding fathers.

🎇 Festivals & Events

The sensational week-long celebration of Armata (⊙ early Sep) culminates on 8 September in a commemoration of Spetses' victory over the Turks in a key 1822 naval battle, with an enormous waterborne re-enactment and fireworks.

🛏 Sleeping

Spetses has high-quality lodgings, with many chic, small hotels, a grand historical hotel and many pensions. Most places offer discounts outside August.

Villa Christina Hotel
PENSION €

(☑ 22980 72218; www.villachristinahotel.com; Dapia; s/d/tr/f incl breakfast from €50/55/70/90; ❄🛜) About 200m uphill on the main road inland from the harbour, these well-kept rustic rooms and garden are back from the worst traffic noise. A great budget choice.

Villa Marina
PENSION €

(☑ 22980 72646; www.villamarinaspetses.com; Agios Mamas; d €55-60; ❄🛜) Basic, clean rooms have refrigerators; there's is a well-equipped communal kitchen downstairs. Just to the right of Plateia Agiou Mama.

Economou Mansion
PENSION €€

(☑ 22980 73400; www.economouspetses.gr; Spetses Town; d incl breakfast from €130; ❄🛜🏊) This beautiful pension on the ground floor of a restored captain's mansion sits right on the waterfront, about 500m north of Dapia Harbour. It combines antique decor and modern amenities such as swimming pool, TV, hairdryer and safe. Breakfast is bountiful.

Kastro Hotel
APARTMENT €€

(☑ 22980 75319; www.kastrohotel-spetses.gr; Spetses Town; studios/4-person apt incl breakfast €120/165; ❄🛜🏊) A private complex encloses these studios and apartments near the centre of town. Low-key decor and modern amenities combine with large terraces. A cancellation deposit is paid when booking.

Klimis Hotel
HOTEL €€

(☑ 22980 73725; www.klimishotel.gr; Dapia Harbour; s/d/apt incl breakfast from €75/95/170; ❄🛜) Sleek rooms, some with seafront balconies, at this standard hotel sit above a ground-floor cafe-bar and patisserie. Breakfast is served in the downstairs bar.

★ Poseidonion Grand Hotel
LUXURY HOTEL €€€

(☑ 22980 74553; www.poseidonion.com; Dapia Harbour; d/ste incl breakfast from €280/670; ❄🛜🏊) Live like a wealthy dame or gent in the roaring '20s. Every inch of this grand old hotel, from the chic rooms to the lobby bar and fabulous pool, drips with luxury. Oh, and it also has two of the island's best restaurants, including On the Verandah.

★ Orloff Resort
BOUTIQUE HOTEL €€€

(Map; ☑ 22980 75444; www.orloffresort.com; Old Harbour; d/studios/apt incl breakfast from €210/225/410; ⊙ Mar-Oct; ❄🛜🏊) On the edge of town, along the road to Agia Marina and near the old port, pristine Orloff hides behind high white walls. Enjoy stylish rooms, private patios and a crystal-clear pool.

Zoe's Club
APARTMENT €€€

(☑ 22980 74447; www.zoesclub.gr; Spetses Town; studio incl breakfast from €220; ❄🛜🏊) Free-standing spacious apartments surround a decadent pool and courtyard. It's behind a high stone wall in the central part of town, near the Spetses Museum.

Nissia
APARTMENT €€€

(☑ 22980 75000; www.nissia.gr; Dapia; studio incl breakfast from €245; ⊙ Apr-Oct; ❄@🛜🏊) Studios and maisonettes are arranged around a spacious courtyard with swimming pool and soothing greenery in this exclusive seafront oasis. It has a fine restaurant.

🍴 Eating

★ Nero tis Agapis
MEDITERRANEAN €€

(☑ 22980 74009; https://ntarestaurant.com; Kounoupitsa; mains €9-22; ⊙ 11am-midnight) The sweetly named 'Water of Love' offers gourmet meat as well as fish dishes. The crayfish tagliatelle is worth every bite, as is the *zarzuela* (fish stew) and selection of creative salads. Book ahead for the romantic tables with the best sea views.

Akrogialia
TAVERNA €€

(☑22980 74749; Kounoupitsa; mains €9-17; ☉11am-midnight) On the Kounoupitsa seafront, Akrogialia matches its delicious food with friendly service and a bright setting. Tasty options include oven-baked *melidzana rolos* (eggplant with cream cheese and walnuts). Enjoy the fish risotto or a choice steak. All are accompanied by a thoughtful selection of Greek wines. Book ahead on weekends.

Patralis
SEAFOOD €€

(☑22980 75380; www.patralis.gr; Kounoupitsa; mains €7-15; ☉10am-midnight Jan-Oct) Operating for more than 70 years and known for its outstanding seafood, Patralis sits smack on the seafront in Kounoupitsa.

★ On the Verandah
MEDITERRANEAN €€€

(☑6957507267; www.poseidonion.com/en/On-the-Verandah; Poseidonion Hotel; 4-course dinner €38; ☉7.30pm-midnight Jul & Aug, reduced hours May, Jun & Sep) One of the Saronic Gulf's top dining experiences, the Verandah at the Poseidonion Grand Hotel is the dining space for the refined, high-concept cuisine of chef Stamatis Marmarinos. Ingredients comprise exquisitely presented creative Mediterranean dishes. Book ahead.

★ Tarsanas
SEAFOOD €€€

(Map p170; ☑22980 74490; www.tarsanas restaurant.com; Old Harbour; mains €17-26; ☉11am-midnight) A hugely popular *psaro-taverna* (fish taverna) on the water at the Old Harbour, this family-run place deals almost exclusively in fish dishes. It can be pricey, but the fish soup (€7) alone is a delight and other starters, such as anchovies marinated with lemon, start at €6.

🍷 Drinking & Nightlife

Head straight for the Old Harbour–Baltiza area, the epicentre of Spetses' vibrant nightlife. Bars and clubs rise and fall in popularity, but the party's always here. Most bars are open May to October only.

Bar Spetsa (☑22980 74131; www.barspetsa.org; Agios Mamas; ☉8pm-late Mar-Oct) is one of life's great little bars and this Spetses institution never loses its easy-going atmosphere. Find it 50m beyond Plateia Agiou Mama, on the road to the right of the kiosk.

🛍 Shopping

Sox Art Shop (☑22980 77166; https://soxart shop.com; Agora; ☉10.30am-2pm & 6-10pm, Apr-Nov) is a great little boutique selling Greek-made arts and crafts, jewellery, sculptures and paintings, plus the specially designed Armata festival (p171) posters.

ℹ Information

Municipal Information Kiosk (www.spetses. com.gr; Dapia Harbour; ☉10am-9pm May-Sep) On the quay; seasonal staff provide answers to general questions about the island.

Bardakos Tours (☑22980 73141; hswbarda@ yahoo.gr; Dapia Harbour; ☉8am-9pm Jun-Aug, reduced hours Sep-May) Sells ferry tickets and assists with other arrangements.

ℹ Getting There & Away

High-speed ferries link Spetses with Hydra, Poros and Piraeus, and Ermioni and Porto Heli on the Peloponnese. In summer, caïques (per person €4) and a car ferry (€2) go from the harbour to Kosta. Note: only local's cars are allowed on Spetses. Park yours in Kosta. Get tickets at Bardakos Tours.

There are high-speed services to Piraeus (€38.50, two hours and 10 minutes, five daily), Hydra (€11.50, 40 minutes, four to five daily) and Poros (€16, 1½ hours, four to five daily).

ℹ Getting Around

BICYCLE

Bike Center (☑22980 72209; http://spet sesbikecenter.blogspot.com; Dapia Harbour; ☉10am-3.30pm & 5.30-10pm) Behind the fish market; rents out bikes (per day €8), including baby seats.

BOAT

In summer, caïques serve the island's beaches (return €13). **Water taxi** (☑22980 72072; Dapia Harbour; ☉24hr) fares are displayed on a board at the quay. All leave from the quay opposite Bardakos Tours.

BUS

Two routes start over Easter and increase in frequency to three or four daily from June to September. Departure times are displayed on boards at bus stops and around town.

One goes from Plateia Agiou Mama in Spetses Town to Agia Paraskevi (€6, 40 minutes), travelling via Agia Marina and Agii Anargyri.

The other leaves from in front of Poseidonion Grand Hotel (p171), going to Vrellos (€4) via Ligoneri.

CAR & MOTORCYCLE

Only locally owned cars are allowed on Spetses. The transport of choice tends to be scooters. Motorbike- and quad-bike-hire shops abound (per day €15 to €35). Taxis are another option.

Cyclades

Best Places to Eat

➡ Salt (p237)

➡ Enalion (p266)

➡ Armeni (p249)

➡ Reeza (p201)

➡ Kalokeri (p211)

➡ Omega 3 (p272)

Best Places to Stay

➡ Rocabella (p200)

➡ Traditional Castle House (p218)

➡ Paradise Design Apartments (p176)

➡ Iconic Santorini (p244)

➡ Francesco's (p236)

Why Go?

On a quest to find the Greek islands of your dreams? Start, here, in the Cyclades. Rugged, sun-drenched outcrops of rock, anchored in azure seas and liberally peppered with snow-white villages and blue-domed churches, this is Greece straight from central casting, with stellar archaeological sites and dozens of postcard-worthy beaches. Throw in a blossoming food scene, some renowned party destinations and a good dose of sophistication, and you really do have the best of Greece's ample charms.

The biggest surprise may be the variety found within this island group. Chase hedonism on Mykonos or Ios, history on Delos, hiking trails on Andros or Amorgos. Want a romantic break? Try Santorini. To escape reality? Pick Donousa or Anafi. You can ferry-hop to your heart's content, enjoy long, lazy lunches at waterside tavernas, or simply lay claim to a sunbed by a spectacular beach. You're living the dream.

When to Go
Mykonos Town

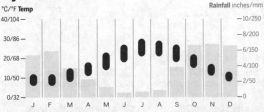

Apr–Jun Catch early-season sun without overheating, and boats without overcrowding.

Jul & Aug Pros: sun, sea, sand, balmy nights and lively company. Cons: peak crowds and prices.

Sep & Oct Quieter beaches, warm seas, the sweet scent of herbs and walks on island hills.

Mt Parnitha (1413m)

ATTICA

Petalia Gulf

Aegean Sea

Evia

Andros

Saronic Gulf

Cape Sounion

Kea

Giaros

Tinos 7

Ikaria

Syros

Mykonos

Ikarian Sea

Samos (100km)

Kythnos

Delos

2 Ancient Delos

Serifos

10

Myrtoön Sea

4 Naxos

Donousa

Astypalea (60km); Rhodes (230km)

Antiparos

Paros

Koufonisia

9

Sifnos

Schinousa

6 Amorgos

Kimolos

Iraklia

8

Small Cyclades

Kos (120km)

Milos 5

Sikinos

Ios

Folegrandros 3

Anydros

Astypalea (30km)

Thirasia

1 Santorini (Thira)

Anafi

Sea of Crete

0 ———— 50 km
0 ———— 25 miles

Iraklio (Crete) (50km)

Cyclades Highlights

1 Santorini (Thira) (p238) Mesmerised by ramatic volcanic cliffs and epic sunsets.

2 Ancient Delos (p201) Immersing yourself in this spellbinding archaeological site.

3 Folegandros (p258) Wandering the leafy streets of atmospheric Hora.

4 Naxos (p212) Exploring traditional villages then reclining on the fine white sand.

5 Milos (p262) Sunning yourself on stone cliffs or lazing in sandy coves.

6 Amorgos (p228) Marvelling at the dazzling monastery that clings to a cliffside, and hiking rugged trails.

7 Tinos (p179) Exploring beautiful marble villages and strolling through gorgeous dovecote valleys.

8 Small Cyclades (p222) Discovering the unique character and hidden beaches of four tiny islands.

9 Sifnos (p268) Admiring the juxtaposition of natural beauty with classic Cycladic architecture.

10 Serifos (p274) Seeking out remote beaches, then gazing over the landscape from the heights of the ancient capital.

History

The Cyclades have been inhabited since at least 7000 BC. Around 3000 BC a Cycladic civilisation emerged, bound together by sea-going commerce. During the Early Cycladic period (3000–2000 BC), the Cycladic marble figurines, mainly representations of the naked female form, were sculpted.

In the Middle Cycladic period (2000–1500 BC), many of the islands were occupied by the Minoans. At Akrotiri, on Santorini, a town has been excavated, and artefacts have all the beauty of those from Crete's Minoan palaces. By the Late Cycladic period (1500–1100 BC), the islands came under the influence of the Mycenaeans of the Peloponnese, who were supplanted by Dorians in the 8th century BC.

By the mid-5th century BC the Cyclades were part of the Athenian empire. In the Hellenistic era (323–146 BC), they were governed by Egypt's Ptolemaic dynasties, and later by the Macedonians. In 146 BC the islands became a Roman province, and trade was established across the Mediterranean.

The division of the Roman Empire in AD 395 resulted in the Cyclades being ruled from Byzantium (Constantinople), but after its fall in 1204, they came under a Venetian authority that doled out the islands to aristocrats. The most powerful was Marco Sanudo, who acquired a dozen of the larger islands – including Naxos, Paros, Ios, Sifnos, Milos, Amorgos and Folegandros – introducing a Venetian architectural gloss that remains today.

The Cyclades came under Turkish rule in 1537, although the empire had difficulty protecting them. Frequent pirate raids led to many villages being moved to hidden inland sites. They survive as the 'Horas' (capitals, also often written as 'Chora') and remain a highlight of the islands. Ottoman neglect, piracy and shortages of food and water led to the depopulation of more remote islands, and in 1563 only five islands were still inhabited.

The Cyclades played a minimal part in the Greek War of Independence, but became havens for people fleeing Turkish massacres on other islands. Italian forces occupied the Cyclades during WWII. After the war, the islands emerged more economically deprived than ever. There was deep poverty and many gave up the struggle and headed for the mainland, or to America and Australia.

Tourism has helped since the 1970s, but the challenge remains of finding other sustainable economies that will not mar the beauty of these remarkable islands.

ℹ️ Information

Terrain (http://terrainmaps.gr) maps are an invaluable resource for travellers wishing to get off the beaten track in the Cyclades and do some exploring on foot or on wheels. History, myths, sights, geography and walking trails are covered, and the maps are regularly updated. Available in most bookshops and souvenir stores.

ℹ️ Getting There & Away

AIR

Of the 24 Cyclades islands, six have airports – Mykonos, Syros, Paros, Naxos, Santorini and Milos – all with daily links to Athens. Some have direct links with European cities in summer (charter flights, plus scheduled services to Mykonos and Santorini). There are rarely direct links between islands, so to fly from Mykonos to Santorini, you'll almost certainly need to go via Athens.

BOAT

The key to sculpting an itinerary through the islands is knowing which ferries go where – and when they're going. The peak ferry services run in July and August, but in winter services are reduced or nonexistent on some routes.

Companies offer connections throughout the Cyclades. They depart from the ports of Attica: Piraeus (the largest, with services to most islands), Rafina (particularly good for Mykonos, Andros and Tinos) and Lavrio (for Kythnos and Kea).

Three extremely useful websites are:

ferries.gr (http://ferries.gr) For checking dates and times, and buying tickets online.

Ferries in Greece (www.ferriesingreece.com/live-boat-traffic.htm) See ferry locations in real time and check if they are likely be on time.

Vessel Finder (www.vesselfinder.com) If you know your ferry's name, check here to see where it is in real time.

ANDROS   ΑΝΔΡΟΣ

POP 9220

The second-largest island of the Cyclades, Andros has a proud seafaring tradition and, conversely, is a walker's paradise. Its wild mountains are cleaved by fecund valleys with bubbling streams and ancient stone mills. Springs are a feature of each village, and waterfalls cascade down hillsides. Get out to the footpaths, many of them stepped and cobbled, which lead you through majestic landscapes and wildflowers and archaeological remnants. The main town of Hora, also known as Andros, is packed with neoclassical mansions.

ⓘ Getting There & Away

Gavrio is the island's ferry port. Up to four boats a day head to Andros from the mainland port of Rafina (€19 to €25, two hours), continuing south to Tinos (€13 to €16, 1½ hours) and Mykonos (€15 to €35, 2¼ hours). In the high season there are also direct boats to Naxos (€38, 3¼ hours, daily) and Paros (€35, 2½ to four hours, two daily). See www.ferries.gr for details.

ⓘ Getting Around

KTEL Andros (☑ 22820 22316; www.ktelandrou.webnode.gr) has at least four buses a day linking Gavrio and Hora (€4, 55 minutes) via Batsi (€2, 15 minutes), at least two between Gavrio and Korthi (€5, 1¼ hours) and at least two on weekdays between Hora and Korthi (€4, 40 minutes). Schedules are posted at the bus stops in Gavrio and Hora; services are much more frequent in the high season.

Taxis (☑ Batsi 22820 41081, Gavrio 22820 71561, Hora 22820 22171) from Gavrio to Batsi cost about €12, and to Hora €40.

Roads can be rough and narrow, but many walking paths and sights are only accessible by car. **Escape in Andros** (☑ 22820 29120; www.escapeinandros.gr) can arrange to meet you at the port with a rental car. Scooters and quad bikes can be hired from **Dino's Rent-a-Bike** (☑ 22820 41003; www.rent-bike-andros.gr; per day from €16; ◷ 9am-9pm) in Batsi.

Gavrio   Γαύριο

POP 810

Gavrio is the main ferry port of Andros and often resembles an oversized car park. The waterfront is lined with services (ATMs, ticket agencies, car and scooter hire), but it's not the most attractive part of the island to stay.

🛏️ Sleeping & Eating

Standard tavernas and lacklustre cafes line Gavrio's waterfront.

Andros Camping   CAMPGROUND €
(☑ 22820 71444; www.campingandros.gr; camp site per adult/tent/car €7.50/4/2; ◷ May-Sep; ☞ ☲) This rustic site is set among olive trees about 400m behind the harbour. It's not huge, but the attractive pool area is a major bonus. Follow the signs from the road to Batsi, turning at the Escape in Andros agency.

Perrakis   HOTEL €€
(☑ 22820 71456; www.hotelperrakis.com; Kipri; s/d from €68/76; ❋ ☞ ☲) Across the road from the blissful sweep of Kipri Beach, about 3km south of Gavrio, this resort-style hotel offers super views and swell rooms, some with big balconies. A dive centre is also based here.

★ **O Kossis**   GRILL €
(Map p177; ☑ 6972002975; mains €7.50-12; ◷ 2-11pm daily Jun-Sep, Fri-Sun Oct-May; ☞) Renowned as the island's best 'meatery', O Kossis is located in the middle of nowhere, in the hills above Gavrio, signposted beyond Epano Fellos. This family-run taverna's speciality is melt-in-your-mouth lamb chops, though diners swear by its other meaty delights as well.

ⓘ Information

Kyklades Travel (☑ 22820 72363) and **Batis Travel** (☑ 22820 71489) sell ferry tickets and can arrange accommodation.

ⓘ Getting There & Away

In low season, buses from Hora and Batsi are timed to meet the ferries. By May there are four daily and up to nine in high season. There are also buses to Korthi (two to three daily, one hour).

Batsi   Μπατσί

POP 1010

The island's main resort town lies 6km southeast of Gavrio around a handsome bay with a golden-sand beach. There's a vibrant stretch of restaurants, cafes and bars that rev up from May. There are also small bays a short walk south, including sandy Anerousa.

🛏️ Sleeping

Cavo D'Oro   GUESTHOUSE €
(☑ 22820 41776; www.andros-cavodoro.gr; d €50; ℗ ❋ ☞) Tucked above a popular waterfront restaurant, these four pleasant en suite rooms are excellent value. Each has a balcony with views over the beach, which is across the road.

★ **Paradise Design Apartments**   BOUTIQUE HOTEL €€
(☑ 22820 41328; www.paradisedesignapartments.gr; r/ste from €75/131; ❋ ☞) Tastefully decorated rooms and suites gaze out to sea from this elegant block, above a cafe at the southern end of the waterfront strip. All have multinozzle showers, smart TVs and balconies.

Cape Kampanos

Cape Fasa

Hartes

Amolohos

716m

Vitali Beach

Vitali

Vori Beach

Gulf of Vitali

O Kossis

Fellos Bay

Agios Petros Beach

Gavrio

Kipri

Ateni

Onar Residence

Cape Gria
Ahla Beach

Rafina (65km)

Golden Beach

Batsi

Remata

Vourkoti

Katakilos

Arni

Stenies

Aerousa Beach

Stivari

Apikia

Gialia Beach

Niborio Beach

Paraporti Beach

Mt Petalo (910m)

Mesathouri

Hora (Andros)

Menites

Mesaria

Paleopoli Bay

Paleopoli

Pitrofos

Sineti

Dipotamata Gorge

Mesa Vouni

Exo Vouni

Kochilou

Halkolimionas

Piskopio

Kapparia

Ormos Korthiou

Cape Orginos

Batsilianos

Aidonia

Korthi

Pera Horio

Piso Meria

Mousionas

648m

Syros (30km);
Tinos (30km);
Mykonos (45km)

Cape Steno

Tinos

Aegean Sea

0 — 10 km
0 — 5 miles

Krinos Suites Hotel BOUTIQUE HOTEL €€€
(22820 42038; www.krinoshotel.com; s/d from €140/200; Jun-Sep;) One of Andros' most luxurious options, this former silk-weaving school on the slopes above the waterfront has nine suites; some have sea-view balconies.

Eating

Oti Kalo SEAFOOD €€
(6939844603; www.facebook.com/OtiKaloAndros; mains €9.50-16; noon-midnight;) Watch the sunset at the covered terrace of this relaxed restaurant, just up from the harbour. There are a couple of meaty mains, but the focus is mainly on seafood: grilled sea bass, octopus carpaccio, stuffed and grilled squid, seafood risotto and prawn linguine.

Stamatis Taverna TAVERNA €€
(22820 41283; www.facebook.com/stamatistavern; mains €7-18; noon-11pm;) Founded in 1965, Batsi's oldest eatery is a charming time

warp, with tables spilling out onto a lane above the harbour. The food is authentic, with specialities such as goat *kleftiko* (slow-cooked in paper), beef *sofrito* (slow-cooked in a white-wine sauce), Andros *chilopita* (a type of pasta) and lobster spaghetti.

Getting There & Away

Buses between Gavrio and Hora pass through Batsi (up to nine daily).

Hora (Andros)
Χώρα (Ανδρος)

POP 1430

Andros' classy capital perches dramatically on a rocky peninsula and has views through the neoclassical mansions to large sandy bays on either side. The old town owes its pretty pastel mansions and squares to both its Venetian heritage and the shipowners who came to inhabit it. Hora's cultural pedigree is burnished by an impressive archaeological museum and art gallery, and several important churches.

The rarefied ambience is let down somewhat by the abandoned hotel and shabby development lining Niborio Beach to the north. You're best to turn in the other direction towards gorgeous Paraporti Beach, where green hills provide a much more pleasant backdrop.

◉ Sights

★ Andros Archaeological Museum MUSEUM
(☑ 22820 23664; Plateia Kaïri; adult/child €4/free; ◷ 8.30am-4pm Wed-Mon) The highlight of this excellent museum is an exquisite 2nd-century BC marble copy of the bronze *Hermes of Andros* by Praxiteles, the handsome life-size god standing naked but for a robe draped over one shoulder. A Roman-period marble Artemis manages to be extraordinarily dynamic in her shimmering dress despite being headless and nearly limbless.

Museum of Contemporary Art GALLERY
(☑ 22820 22444; www.moca-andros.gr; Vasili & Elizas Goulandri; Jul-Sep €5, Oct-Jun €3; ◷ 11am-3pm & 6-9pm Wed-Sun, 11am-3pm Mon Jul-Sep, 10am-2pm Wed-Mon Apr-Jun & Oct, 10am-2pm Sat-Mon Nov-Mar) Split across two buildings, MOCA has a reputation for its outstanding summer exhibitions of famous artists, including the likes of Picasso, Matisse, Toulouse-Lautrec and Miró. The sculpture gallery features prominent Greek artists, and a summertime sea-view cafe offers homemade sweets.

Venetian Fortress RUINS
The picturesque ruins of this fortress, built by Venice's doge (duke) Enrico Dandolo in the early 13th century, stand on an island linked to the tip of the headland by the worn remnants of a steeply arched stone bridge. Don't attempt to scramble over like the locals do.

🛏 Sleeping

Anemomiloi Andros APARTMENT €€
(☑ 22820 29067; www.anemomiloi.gr; apt from €86; ◷ Mar-Nov; ✳ 🛜 🌊) This popular complex of bright, spic-and-span studios, split between two buildings, sits at the southern end of town enjoying views over green fields. There's helpful service from the owners, and a quiet poolside patio. Off-peak rates drop considerably.

Micra Anglia BOUTIQUE HOTEL €€
(☑ 22820 22207; www.micra-anglia.gr; Ml Goulandri 13; r/ste from €129/286; ◷ Apr-Oct; 🅿 ✳ 🛜 🌊)

Five-star 'Little England' has a raft of amenities and stylish decor in neutral shades, as well as Hora's most imaginative restaurant. The clear-sided plunge pool is particularly impressive.

🍴 Eating

Ta Skalakia TAVERNA €
(☑ 22820 22822; 28 Oktovrio 1940; mains €8-9; ◷ 6-11pm; 🛜) Tables spill down the eponymous stairs from this charming strewn taverna run by a mother-and-daughter team on a fairy-lit lane. There's a short, tasty menu offering the likes of Greek salad, tzatziki, oregano-flavoured pork, meatballs and fennel pie.

Endochora MEDITERRANEAN €€
(☑ 22820 23207; www.endochora.com; G Empirikou; mains €9-18; ◷ 6pm-1am Mon-Thu, 1pm-1am Fri-Sun May-Oct, 1pm-1am Fri-Sun Nov, Dec, Mar & Apr; 🛜) Endochora is a stylish hotspot on the main drag, offering a fresh twist on Greek and Italian classics and a great vantage point for people-watching. Salads showcase prime local produce like capers, tomatoes, figs and cheeses. The pearl barley with mushrooms is a vegetarian showstopper.

Dolly's Bar & Restaurant MEDITERRANEAN €€
(☑ 22820 22207; www.micra-anglia.gr; Ml Goulandri 13; mains €13-20; ◷ 7-11pm; ✳ 🛜) Poolside, at the rear of the Micra Anglia hotel, Dolly's is both stylish and relaxed, delivering a menu rich in Cycladic, mainland Greek and Italian influences. Go for the impeccably grilled steak or try the lamb, vegetable and cheese pie. It's open at lunchtime but only for snacks.

ℹ Information

Ploes Travel (☑ 22820 29220; G Empirikou) Sells ferry tickets and arranges guided hikes and vehicle rental.

ℹ Getting There & Away

Buses run to Gavrio via Batsi (at least four daily) and Korthi (at least two on weekdays). Timetables are at the bus station, up from Plateia Goulandri.

Around Andros

It's well worth renting a car or scooter to explore Andros' panorama-filled mountain roads and picturesque villages. The north of the island, with the lush watershed around Arni, gives way to raw, windswept hills as the road zigzags to Vourkoti and Agios Nikolaou with its sweeping views.

The island is cleaved by a sweeping agricultural valley, and loads of small villages with springs, often marked by marble lions' heads and the like, surround Hora. The road winds through Apikia, Stenies, Mesathouri, Strapouries and Menites – all fun to explore.

In the south, visit quaint agricultural villages like Livadia, Kochilou, Piskopio and Aidonia, which has ruined tower houses. The area's charming landscape of fields and cypresses encircle Ormos Korthiou, a relaxed beach town with a picturesque church.

◉ Sights & Activities

Beaches

There are some excellent large and accessible beaches on the main road between Gavrio and Batsi, including built-up Agios Petros (St Peter's), popular Golden Beach (Hrisi Ammos) and long, sandy Kipri.

Halkolimionas – with grey sand and a tiny church – sits 2km down a stone-terraced valley near the junction for Hora. A beach bar sets up here in summer. Nearby are the clear waters of gorgeous Gialia.

Many of the best beaches, such as Ahla, Vori and Vitali (all in the northeast), are only reached by 4WD, ATV or boat. Boat trips can usually be arranged (or boats hired) from Batsi and from Hora's Niborio beach.

Walking

There are 19 wonderful waymarked trails criss-crossing Andros, marking walks that range in duration from 30 minutes to six hours, labelled in difficulty level from easy to average. Wear hiking boots and trekking pants, as there are some (shy) snakes.

The best investment you can make is the *Andros Hiking Map* (€6) published by the marvellous Andros Routes (www.androsroutes.gr) project, in conjunction with the Anavasi mapping company. The Andros Routes website outlines the paths they maintain, with good advice for hiking.

The areas north of Hora have great walks, including the villages of Stenies and Apikia. For a short walk, Pithara is a shady glade of streams accessed from Apikia. For a longer ramble, hike up the dramatic Dipotamata Gorge, signposted as you drive inland, after Sineti (southeast of Hora). The trail is cobbled and leads past ancient bridges and water mills and through vivid foliage.

Better yet, book a guided walk with Trekking Andros ([📞]22820 61368; www.trekkingan

dros.gr; guided walk from €25), a company that guides a menu of activities on the island, including hiking, mountain biking, boat trips, diving, rock climbing and more.

🛏 Sleeping & Eating

Onar Residence   COTTAGE €€€
(Map p177; [📞]21180 02912; www.onar-andros.gr; Ahla Beach; house from €260; ⊙May-Oct; ❄🤏)
🍴 These ecofriendly, unique and luxurious secluded cottages are hidden within wetlands behind the gorgeous remote beach at Ahla. It's really in the middle of nowhere, so the organic onsite restaurant is a lifesaver. Details on how to reach the resort are on the website (access road is 4WD only; transfers can be arranged).

Sea Satin Nino   MEDITERRANEAN €€
([📞]22820 61196; www.facebook.com/Sea.Satin.Nino.Andros; Ormos Korthiou; mains €7-16; ⊙9am-late; 🤏) On a tiny leafy square, this trendy cafe-cum-bistro uses local ingredients to great effect. Homemade pasta, fish dishes and a smattering of beautifully done *mezedes* (snacks) grace the short but sweet menu. Excellent coffee and French toast with bacon make it the island's best breakfast choice, too.

Gialia   GREEK €€
([📞]22820 24452; mains €8-15; ⊙noon-10pm Apr-Oct; 🤏) A few kilometres from Hora is the delightful crystal-clear blue of Gialia Beach, where this excellent restaurant serves snacks and Greek classics to beachgoers or island explorers. Try the delicious (and ample) Andros salad topped with local *kopanisti* cheese.

TINOS   ΤΗΝΟΣ

POP 8640

Tinos is one of those sleeper hit islands. It's known widely for its Greek Orthodox pilgrimage site: the Church of the Annunciation (p181), in the port and main town, Hora.

But as soon as you leave the throngs in town, Tinos is a wonderland of natural beauty, with more than 40 marble-ornamented villages found in hidden bays, on hillsides and atop misty mountains. Also scattered across the brindled countryside are countless ornate dovecotes, a legacy of the Venetians.

There's a strong artistic tradition on Tinos, especially for marble sculpting, as in the sculptors' village of Pyrgos in the north, near the quarries. The food, made from local produce (cheeses, sausage, tomatoes and wild artichokes), might be the best in Greece.

Tinos

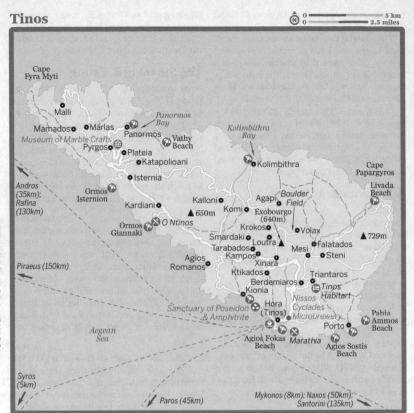

ⓘ Getting There & Away

Year-round ferries serve the mainland ports of Rafina (€27 to €36, two to four hours, up to eight daily) and Piraeus (€52, 5¾ hours, daily) and the islands of Syros (€4.50 to €8.50, 50 minutes, up to two daily), Andros (€13 to €16, 1½ hours, up to four daily) and Mykonos (€8 to €15, 30 minutes, up to nine daily). Summer high-speed services include Tinos on their passage south from Rafina to major islands such as Paros, Naxos, Ios and Santorini; see www.ferries.gr for details.

Hora has two ferry departure quays. The New (or Outer) Port is located 300m to the north of the main harbour and serves conventional and larger fast ferries. The Old (or Inner) Port, at the northern end of the town, serves smaller fast ferries. Check which quay your ferry is leaving from.

ⓘ Getting Around

Between May and September, **KTEL Tinos** (☑ 22830 22440; www.kteltinou.gr) has at least two buses a day from Hora to nearby Kionia (€1.80, 10 minutes), and northwest to Panormos (€4.50, one hour) via Kampos (€1.80, 15 minutes) and Pyrgos (€3.60, 50 minutes). Services are much more frequent in July and August. The Hora bus station is on the harbour near the port. Buy tickets on board.

The best way to explore the island is with your own wheels; you can see a lot with a one-day rental. **Vidalis Rent a Car & Bike** (☑ 22830 23400; www.vidalis-rentacar.gr; Leoforos Stavrou Kionion) has four outlets in Hora.

Alternatively, phone for a **taxi** (☑ 22830 22470).

Hora (Tinos)   Χώρα (Τήνος)

POP 4760

Hora (also known as Tinos) is the island's modest capital and port. For the nondevout, its most appealing aspect is the little warren of narrow lanes, peppered with bars and cafes, set back from the waterfront. However, the town's biggest drawcard by far is the Church of the Annunciation, one of the most important Orthodox pilgrimage sites in Greece.

Two main streets lead up to the church. Evangelistria is lined with shops and stalls crammed with souvenirs and religious wares, while Leoforos Megalocharis has a carpeted strip down the side, used by pilgrims crawling towards the church and pushing long candles before them. Religion takes centre stage here; woe betide the unwitting tourist looking for a room on one of the main feast days.

◉ Sights

Church of the Annunciation CHURCH
(Panagia Evangelistria; ☑ 22830 22256; www.panagiatinou.gr; Leoforos Megalocharis; ⊙ 8am-8pm) FREE Tinos' religious focus is this large church and its icon of Our Lady of Tinos. It was uncovered in 1823 in the ruins of a chapel beneath the current church, after a nun, now St Pelagia, received visions from the Virgin instructing her where to find it.

As you enter the church, the icon is to the left of the aisle, almost completely obscured by jewels. Hundreds of silver lamps hang from the ceiling, each dangling an offering: a ship, a cradle, a heart, a pair of lungs, a chainsaw.

The Renaissance-style church, built in 1830 of marble from the island's Panormos quarries, lies within a courtyard flanked by cool arcades. A disconcerting amount of graffiti is etched into the marble balustrades, some of it dating back over 100 years. Beneath the church is a baptistery of three vaulted chapels, where the famous icon was discovered.

The complex has views all around and museums (with variable hours) that house collections of religious artefacts, icons and art. Respectful attire must be worn.

Cultural Foundation of Tinos GALLERY
(☑ 22830 29070; www.itip.gr; Akti G. Drosou; adult/child €3/free; ⊙ 9am-3pm Mon-Fri) This excellent cultural centre in a neoclassical building on the waterfront houses a superb permanent collection of the work of famous Tinian sculptor Yannoulis Chalepas (1851–1938). A second gallery has rotating exhibitions. Musical events are staged here in summer.

Sanctuary of Poseidon & Amphitrite ARCHAEOLOGICAL SITE
(Map p180; ☑ 22830 22670; Kionia; €2; ⊙ 8.30am-3pm Wed-Mon) From the 4th century BC to the 3rd century AD, the area adjacent to the beach at Kionia (3km northwest of central Hora) was a major religious sanctuary devoted to sea god Poseidon and his wife Amphitrite. Now all that remains are the excavated foundations of temples, altars, fountains and

baths. To make sense of it you really need the pamphlet that comes with admission.

Also helpful is the scale model at the **Tinos Archaeological Museum** (☑ 22830 29063; Leoforos Megalocharis; adult/child €2/free; ⊙ 8.30am-3.30pm Wed-Mon).

☞ Tours

Poseidon Travel BUS
(☑ 22830 22440; www.poseidontravel-tinos.com; Leoforos Stavrou Kionion; full-day tour €12; ⊙ Jun-Aug) In summer, ask at the bus station about the daily tour that takes in St Pelagia's Convent and the villages of Volax, Loutra, Pyrgos, Panormos and Tarambados. It's a great way to see the sights in a day. Tours depart at 11am, returning around 5.30pm.

Nissos Cyclades Microbrewery BREWERY
(Map p180; ☑ 22830 26333; www.nissos.beer; Tinou-Agiou Ioanni Porto, Vagia; tour €6; ⊙ 5pm & 6pm Tue & Thu, 10am, 11am & noon Sat mid-Jun–mid-Sep) Join a tour of this microbrewery to familiarise yourself with the mysteries of brewing and to sample four Nissos beers.

🛏 Sleeping

Nikoleta Rooms GUESTHOUSE €
(☑ 22830 25863; www.nikoletarooms.gr; Kapodistriou 11; r/apt from €45/60; ⊙ Mar-Nov; ❋ 🎱) Little Nikoleta is one of Hora's best-value options, tucked away in a side street down the southern end of town. There's a lovely garden, and some rooms have kitchens.

Voreades GUESTHOUSE €€
(☑ 22830 23845; www.voreades.gr; Nikolaou Foskolou 7; s/d/apt from €63/78/123; ❋ 🎱) Just up from the port, this friendly place offers plenty of local character both in terms of the building (internal courtyard, mosaic, marble fanlights) and the personalities of the Greek mother-and-son team who run it (he speaks good English, she speaks French). While the decor's a little old-fashioned, the rooms are comfortable and spotless.

Studios Eleni II APARTMENT €€
(☑ 22830 24352; www.studio-eleni.gr; Ioannou Plati 7; d/tr €90/120; ❋ 🎱) A stone's throw from the main church, this beautiful complex has whitewashed walls, pale linen and a supremely photogenic Cycladic courtyard. Eleni also runs Studios Eleni I, which is of an equally high standard at the southern end of town, close to Agios Fokas Beach. Port transfer is offered by both properties.

Altana Hotel
BOUTIQUE HOTEL €€

(☑22830 25102; www.altanahotel.gr; Leoforos Stavrou Kionion; r/ste from €85/125; ☉May-Sep; P❋☎☒) Located about a 10-minute walk northwest of the town centre, en route to Kionia Beach, this hotel has a modernist Cycladic style, with snow-white walls and cool interiors incorporating distinctive Tinian motifs.

✖ Eating

Marathia
GREEK €€

(Map p180; ☑22830 23249; www.marathiatinos. gr; Iroon Polytechneiou, Agios Fokas; mains €10-25; ☉8.30am-midnight; ☎☑) Grilled fish with spicy zucchini; slow-cooked octopus with giant beans; a glass of crisp white; waves lapping at the beach – pretty flawless, as far as combinations go. Fresh ingredients, family recipes and an appreciation for Tinian cuisine make this stylish contemporary restaurant on Agios Fokas Beach a special place indeed.

Itan Ena Mikro Karavi
MEDITERRANEAN €€

(☑22830 22818; www.mikrokaravi.gr; Trion Ierarchon; mains €12-19; ☉noon-11.30pm; ☎) Named for the opening line of a well-known children's tale ('There was a little boat...'), this elegant indoor-outdoor eatery serves Greek fare with creative Mediterranean flair. Slow-cooked veal and rabbit ravioli are made with local ingredients, and the internal-courtyard setting and service are first class.

San To Alati
TAVERNA €€

(☑22830 29266; www.facebook.com/santoalati; Iroon Polytechneiou, Agios Fokas; mains €10-20; ☉noon-midnight; ☎) Meaning 'like salt', this cute seaside taverna takes its name from a royal-themed fairy tale. The place lives up to its Aegean cuisine label, with extensive use of local produce, from local cheeses to artichoke pie, marinated anchovies and just-out-of-the-sea *kalamari*, octopus and fish.

❶ Getting There & Away

Malliaris Travel (☑22830 24242; www.malliaris travel.gr; ☉9am-9pm) Sells ferry tickets.

Buses depart from the harbourside bus station and serve numerous destinations around the island.

Around Tinos

The countryside of Tinos is a glorious mix of broad terraced hillsides, mountaintops crowned with crags, unspoilt villages, fine beaches and architecture that includes picturesque dovecotes. Rent wheels to see it all.

North of Hora, beautiful **Ktikados** perches in a hanging valley, with a good taverna and a skyline punctuated by a blue-domed church with an elegant campanile.

Kampos sits atop a scenic hill surrounded by fields and is home to the **Costas Tsoclis Museum** (☑22830 51009; www.tsoclismuseum. gr; Kampos; ☉10am-6pm Wed-Mon Jun-Sep) FREE, displaying works by the contemporary artist.

Don't miss **Tarabados**, a maze of small streets roamed by village dogs and decorated with marble sculptures, leading to a breezy valley lined with dovecotes.

About 17km northwest of Hora, lovely **Kardiani** perches on a steep cliff enclosed by greenery. Narrow lanes wind through the village, and the views are exhilarating.

The gorgeous church-dotted settlement of **Pyrgos** is the highlight of Tinos and one of the prettiest of all the Cyclades towns. Narrow whitewashed lanes wind towards a perfect little square lined with cafes. Marble has been quarried from the encircling hills for millennia, and during the late 19th and early 20th centuries the town was the centre of a remarkable sculpture enclave. A trio of interesting museums celebrates this legacy.

Further north of Pyrgos the main road ends at **Panormos**, a popular excursion destination for its photogenic fishing harbour lined with fish tavernas.

About 12km north of Hora on the north coast is emerald **Kolimbithra**, where surfers take to the breaks at two excellent beaches.

A worthwhile detour inland takes you to **Agapi**, a pretty village set in a lush valley of dovecotes. Ethereal and romantic, it lives up to its name (meaning 'love' in Greek).

Pass eye-catching **Krokos**, with its enormous Catholic monastery, to reach **Volax**, about 6km directly north of Hora. This hamlet sits at the heart of an amphitheatre of low hills festooned with hundreds of giant, multi-coloured boulders. The ruins of the Venetian fortress of **Exobourgo** lie 2km south of Volax, on top of a mighty 640m rock outcropping.

The northeast coast beach at **Livada** is spectacular, but the ones east of Hora, like Porto and Pahia Ammos, can seem built-up.

Museum of Marble Crafts (Map p180; ☑22830 31290; www.piop.gr; Pyrgos; adult/child €4/2; ☉10am-5pm Wed-Mon) On the slopes above Pyrgos, this outstanding, modern, well-curated complex explains the quarrying and sculpting techniques that have been used on the island since antiquity. It includes beautifully illustrated displays with English translations, along with examples of artefacts and architectural features shaped from Tinian marble. The films of the last traditional quarrymen plying their trade are fascinating.

Museum House of Yannoulis Chalepas (Pyrgos; adult/child €3/free; ⏱11am 6pm Thu-Sun Apr–mid-Oct) This absorbing museum lets you see the troubled sculptor's rooms and workshop as they once were. The ticket includes admission to the neighbouring Museum of Panormos Artists.

🛏 Sleeping & Eating

⭐ Tinos Habitart   COTTAGE €€€
(Map p180; 📞 22830 41675; www.tinos-habitart. gr; Triantaros; house €180-400; P ✳ 🛜 🌊) This cleverly designed complex lies in a village 6km northeast of Hora, and gives you a taste of traditional island life. The seven houses incorporate local stone and marble and are fully equipped with kitchen, living spaces and outdoor areas (most with private pool). Our favourite is the dovecote irresistibly transformed into a three-bedroom villa.

⭐ O Ntinos   TAVERNA €€
(Map p180; 📞 22830 31673; Ormos Giannaki; mains €9-22; ⏱12.30-11.30pm Apr-Sep; 🛜) Set on a sunny terrace overlooking Giannaki Bay, this friendly taverna offers superlative homecooked island specialities, including a particularly good selection of mezedhes (appetisers); try the mackerel in oil with basil and fennel, or the eggplant with spicy Tinian cheese. Complimentary fish soup and homemade ice cream often bookend the meal.

Drosia   TAVERNA €€
(📞 22830 21807; www.facebook.com/taverna.drosia. tinos; Ktikados; mains €9-13; ⏱noon-3pm & 6-10pm Easter-Oct; 🛜) Dine on fish or lamb and take in the magnificent views.

SYROS   ΣΥΡΟΣ

POP 21,500

Endearing little Syros merges traditional and modern Greece. One of the smallest islands of the Cyclades and relatively rural outside the capital, it nevertheless has the highest population since it's the legal and administrative centre of the entire archipelago. It's also the ferry hub of the northern islands and home to Ermoupoli, the grandest of all Cycladic towns,

with an unusual history. As the Cyclades' capital, it pays less heed to tourism, and its beaches never get as crowded as those of the neighbouring islands. It buzzes with life year-round, has great eateries and showcases the best of everyday Greek life.

History

The island has been inhabited since at least the Neolithic era, with an early Cycladic fortified settlement and burial ground at Kastri in the island's northeast dating from 2800 to 2300 BC.

The Venetians seized control from the Byzantines in 1204 and remained until 1522, during which time most of the Greek islanders adopted Catholicism. Even during the centuries of Ottoman rule that followed, the island maintained a largely Catholic identity.

During the War of Independence, thousands of Orthodox refugees from islands ravaged by the Turks fled to Syros. They brought an infusion of Greek Orthodoxy and an entrepreneurial drive that made Syros the commercial, naval and cultural centre of Greece during the 19th century. Syros' position declined in the 20th century, but you still see shipyards, textile manufacturing, horticulture, a sizeable administrative sector, a university campus and a continuing Catholic population.

ℹ Information

A useful website for general info on the island is www.syrosisland.gr.

ℹ Getting There & Away

AIR

Sky Express (www.skyexpress.gr) flies from Athens (€109, 35 minutes) to **Syros Island National Airport** (JSY; Map p184; 📞 22810 81900), 5km south of Ermoupoli. There's no public transport but taxis congregate around flight times.

BOAT

As the island group's capital, Syros theoretically has fair to good year-round ferry links with all the Cyclades islands, and to Piraeus on the mainland. High season services to Ermoupoli include Piraeus (€27 to €33, two to 3¾ hours, three daily), Kythnos (€9, 2¼ hours, three daily), Naxos (€29 to €35, 1¼ hours to 2¾ hours, three daily), Mykonos (€20, 40 minutes, three daily) and Tinos (€4.50 to €8.50, 50 minutes, two daily); see www.ferries. gr for details.

Syros

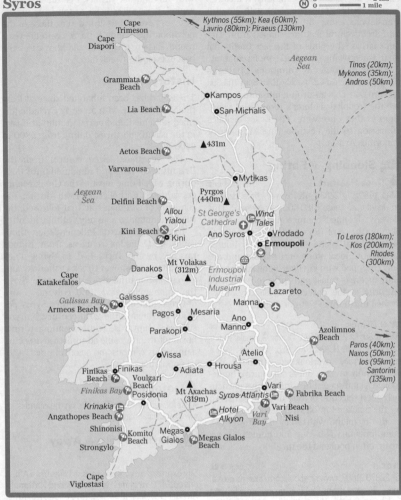

N
0 ——————— 2 km
0 ——————— 1 mile

Kythnos (55km); Kea (60km);
Lavrio (80km); Piraeus (130km)

Cape Trimeson

Cape Diapori

Aegean Sea

Tinos (20km);
Mykonos (35km);
Andros (50km)

Grammata Beach

Kampos

Lia Beach

San Michalis

Aetos Beach

▲431m

Varvarousa

Mytikas

Aegean Sea

Pyrgos (440m) ▲

Delfini Beach

Allou Yialou

St George's Cathedral

Wind Tales

Kini Beach

Ano Syros

Vrodado

Kini

Ermoupoli

To Leros (180km);
Kos (200km);
Rhodes (300km)

Mt Volakas (312m) ▲

Danakos

Ermoupoli Industrial Museum

Cape Katakefalos

Lazareto

Galissas Bay

Galissas

Manna

Armeos Beach

Pagos

Mesaria

Ano Manno

Parakopi

Azolimnos Beach

Vissa

Atelio

Paros (40km);
Naxos (50km);
Ios (95km);
Santorini (135km)

Finikas Beach

Finikas

Adiata

Hrousa

Voulgari Beach

Vari

Fabrika Beach

Finikas Bay

Posidonia

Mt Axachas (319m) ▲

Syros Atlantis

Vari Beach

Krinakia

Hotel Alkyon

Nisi

Angathopes Beach

Vari Bay

Shinonisi

Komito Beach

Megas Gialos

Megas Gialos Beach

Strongylo

Cape Viglostasi

ⓘ Getting Around

BUS

KTEL Syros (☎ 22810 82575; www.ktel-syrou.
gr) buses loop from Ermoupoli bus station beside the ferry quay, taking in Galissas, Finikas,
Posidonia, Megas Gialos, Vari and Azolimnos.
The full loop takes an hour, and buses run in
both directions (at least three daily, increasing
to hourly in the peak season), with a maximum
fare of €1.70.

Three to five buses also go to Kini (€1.60, 20
minutes), some of which join the main island
loop.

There are also regular minibuses to Ano Syros
(€1.60, 15 minutes) from the waterfront end of El
Vanizelou street.

CAR & MOTORCYCLE

You can hire cars and scooters at agencies such
as Vassilikos (p187) on the Ermoupoli waterfront.
Avoid driving in central Ermoupoli, as there are
lots of stairs, pedestrian-only lanes and one-way
streets.

TAXI

From the port, taxis charge around €4 to Ano
Syros, €12 to Galissas and €12 to Vari.

Ermoupoli Ερμούπολη

POP 11,400

As you sail into striking Ermoupoli (literally Hermes' City, named after the messenger god), its two hilltops emerge, each topped by a dazzling church, with even taller hills rising behind. Buildings spread in a pink and white cascade in between, and the centre is a maze of stepped lanes and shopping streets all radiating out from the grand main square.

Catholic Ano Syros (Upper Syros) was the original hilltop settlement; bus to the top and stroll down through its hive of churches, monasteries and whitewashed houses.

During the Greek Revolution, Orthodox refugees from the Turkish-held islands founded the modern town on the flat, spreading up Vrondado, the other hill, and capping it with their own grand church. In the 19th century, Ermoupoli was Greece's principal port. The wealth of its shipowners is evident when wandering through Vaporia, a neighbourhood of palm-lined squares and elegant mansions.

⊙ Sights

Church of the Dormition CHURCH
(Map p186; Proiou; ⊙ hours vary) After being badly bombed during WWII, it's a wonder anything survived in this stately 1820s Orthodox church – which made the discovery, in 1983, of a signed icon painted by El Greco even more extraordinary. The work dates from the 1560s, before the artist left his native Crete to become a leading light of the Spanish Renaissance. It's now proudly displayed in the porch, to the right of the main door.

St George's Cathedral CHURCH
(Map p184; Agios Georgios, Ano Syros; ⊙ 8.30am-9.30pm) Proudly capping the medieval hilltop settlement of Ano Syros, this cathedral is the mother church of the Cyclades' Roman Catholic minority. Call in to admire the pastel-hued interior and star-fretted barrel roof.

Plateia Miaouli SQUARE
(Map p186) This great square is perhaps the finest urban space in the Cyclades. Once situated immediately upon the seashore, today it sits well inland and is dominated by the dignified neoclassical town hall (Map p186; Plateia Miaouli). Flanked by palm trees and lined along all sides with cafes and bars, the square and accompanying statue are named for Hydriot naval hero Andreas Miaoulis.

Ermoupoli Industrial Museum MUSEUM
(Map p184; ☑ 22810 84762; www.ketepo.gr; Georgiou Papandreou 11; adult/child €2/1.50; ⊙ 10am-3.30pm Sun-Fri, 10am-3.30pm & 6-8pm Sat Apr-Aug, 9am-5pm Mon, Tue, Thu & Fri, 9am-2pm Sun Sep-Mar) This excellent chronicle of Syros' industrial and shipbuilding traditions occupies a restored factory packed with more than 300 well-labelled items relating to sewing, printing, spinning, engines, ships and more. Ask if the neighbouring Aneroussis lead shot factory is open – it's fascinating. The museum is opposite the hospital, on the southwestern edge of town.

Syros Archaeological Museum MUSEUM
(Map p186; ☑ 22810 88487; Benaki; adult/child €2/1; ⊙ 8.30am-4pm Wed-Mon) The town's small archaeological museum is housed in the rear of the town hall (enter from the side). Founded in 1834 and one of the oldest in Greece, it houses a modest collection of ceramic and marble vases, grave *stelae*, a black-granite Egyptian statuette from 730 BC, and some very fine Cycladic figurines.

🛏 Sleeping

Most budget options cluster above the ferry quay, while boutique hotels in renovated mansions dot the Vaporia district. Much accommodation is open year-round, with discounts in low season.

Hermoupolis Rooms GUESTHOUSE €
(Map p186; ☑ 6937135880; www.hermoupolis-rooms.gr; Kosma; r €50; ❄️ 🛜) There's a cheerful welcome at these well-kept, self-catering en-suite rooms, a short climb from the waterfront. Front rooms open onto tiny, bougainvillea-cloaked balconies.

Wind Tales B&B €€
(Map p184; ☑ 6946771400; www.windtales.gr; Agiou Aloisiou 4, Ano Syros; r from €96; ❄️ 🛜) If you wish to linger after the madding crowd has gone and wander Ano Syros' labyrinthine lanes at your leisure, then try the Wind Tales' four gorgeous, individually designed rooms, one of them carved into natural rock. The service is wonderfully personalised, breakfast makes extensive use of local produce, and sipping cocktails on the terrace overlooking Ermoupoli is pure magic.

Lila Guesthouse B&B €€
(Map p186; ☑ 22810 82738; www.guesthouse.gr; Kosma; r/ste from €90/126; ❄️ 🛜) In the former French consulate, these elegantly renovated rooms and suites are kitted out with modern

Ermoupoli

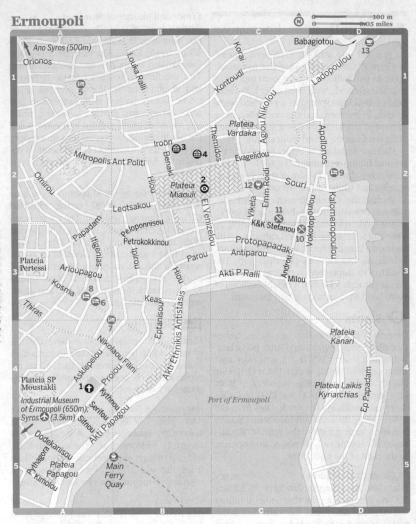

decor and top-notch bathrooms. Suites are spacious, with dining tables and antiques. A bumper breakfast is served in the airy common area. Port pickups available.

1901 Hermoupolis Maison
B&B €€

(Map p186; ☑ 6959990275; www.1901.gr; Palaion Patron Germanou 37-39; r/ste from €90/229; ❋ ❂) Occupying a 19th-century house, this delightful place comprises just five rooms with supercomfortable beds, Molton Brown toiletries and quirky objects scattered throughout – antique telephones, an olive press, a Singer sewing machine. Terrific breakfast, too.

Ethrion
HOTEL €€

(Map p186; ☑ 22810 89066; www.ethrion.gr; Kosma 24; apt/r/ste from €66/73/109; ❋ ❂) The eight rooms, suites and apartments at this family-run hotel are comfortable and well equipped; opt for a sea view if you can. The ground-floor studio is on the dark side but it's priced accordingly and has a kitchenette.

Ploes
BOUTIQUE HOTEL €€€

(Map 186; ☑ 22810 79360; www.hotelploes.com; Apollonos 2; d/ste from €220/600; ⊙ Apr-Oct; ❋ ❂) Elegance and attention to detail are hallmarks of this boutique beauty, inside a 19th-century mansion. Soaring ceilings, Venetian chande-

Ermoupoli

liers, original artworks and designer furniture make the seven rooms here shine, and there's a private pavilion with direct sea access.

✕ Eating

Restaurants and cafe-bars throng the waterfront, especially along the buzzing Akti Petrou Ralli. A great area for dining is the bougainvillea-garlanded lanes of Emmanouil Roidi and Klonos & Kyparissou Stefanou.

★ Kouzina
MEDITERRANEAN €€

(Map p186; ☑ 22810 89150; www.facebook.com/kouzinasyros; Androu 5; mains €10-28; ⊙7-11pm Thu-Tue; 🛜🌿) In an intimate dining room and spilling out onto Ermoupoli's main eat street, Kouzina uses fresh local ingredients to construct creative Mediterranean cuisine, from slow-cooked osso buco on parmesan risotto to smoked *mousakas*. There's a decent wine list, craft beer and excellent service to boot.

Seminario
MEDITERRANEAN €€

(Map p186; ☑ 22813 01339; www.seminariosyros.wixsite.com/seminariosyros; Klonos & Kyparissou Stefanou 7; mains €8.80-16; ⊙noon-midnight Fri-Wed, from 6pm Thu; 🛜🌿) Friendly and fun, this street taverna with a minty interior serves tasty traditional grills and seafood dishes alongside pasta, risotto and burgers. Vegetarians will find plenty of joy in the likes of the delicious Cycladic fennel pie, and the vegan-friendly baked eggplant topped with *fava* puree and smoked paprika.

▣ Drinking & Nightlife

Kouchico
COCKTAIL BAR

(Map p186; ☑ 22813 00880; www.facebook.com/kouchico; Ioannou Lavrentiou Ralli 15; ⊙7am-3am Mon-Fri, from 9am Sat & Sun; 🛜) A cool spot to sip a coffee by day, Kouchico turns into a buzzy cocktail bar at night, with a hip young crowd spilling out of its doors.

Sta Vaporia
CAFE

(Map p186; ☑ 22810 76486; www.facebook.com/StaBaporia; Athanasiou Krinou 2; ⊙10am-3am; 🛜) Down a set of stairs behind St Nicholas' Church, this perfectly positioned all-day cafe/restaurant offers postcard panoramas and a menu of coffee, cocktails, homemade lemonade and snacks, large and small. Down below are popular seaside swimming platforms (so bring your swimsuit).

ⓘ Information

Vassilikos (☑ 22810 84444; www.vassilikos.gr; Akti Papagou 10; ⊙9am-9pm) Sells ferry tickets and tours, and rents cars.

ⓘ Getting There & Away

The island's **main ferry quay** (Map p186) is right in front of the town.

From the nearby **bus station** (☑ 22810 82575), buses loop around Galissas, Finikas, Posidonia, Megas Gialos, Vari and Azolimnos (at least three daily in each direction). There are also buses to Kini (20 minutes, at least three daily). Services are much more frequent (usually hourly) in summer.

Around Syros

Outside Ermoupoli, Syros comprises a series of hills and valleys folding down to small bays and beaches, most well served by buses.

Kini, on the west coast, is a sandy beach in a horseshoe bay with a small strip of bars and tavernas. Families love its shallow waters.

Galissas has an appealing beach, a smattering of white-and-blue-trim Cycladic buildings, good tavernas and a cute little white church on the headland. On the other side of the church is **Armeos**, a pebbly nudist beach.

Further south, **Finikas** sits on a large bay with a marina at one end and a strip of pebbles and sand. It's more built up than most of

SAN MICHALIS

If you have your own wheels, don't miss the drive along the spine of Syros to the northern village of **San Michalis,** with spectacular views of unspoilt valleys and neighbouring islands on either side. Famous for its cheese, San Michalis is a small hamlet of stone houses and vineyards.

Walk the winding rock path to St Michael's Catholic Church and stop for Syran food at its best at atmospheric **Plakostroto** ([☎]22813 06727; www.plakostroto.com; San Michalis; mains €9-16; ⊙lunch & dinner Jun-Sep, Sat & Sun Oct-May; [🛜]). It serves local cheese plus rooster, lamb or rabbit grilled on the open wood fire. Views sweep down the hillside to Kea, Kythnos and beyond.

the others, with a somewhat shabby feel. Further along the bay is **Voulgari Beach**, near the village of **Posidonia**. South of the headland is tiny but popular **Agathopes Beach**, with calm waters and a taverna. Another 10-minute walk south brings you to **Komito**, a sheltered bay backed by olive groves.

The south-coast town of **Megas Gialos** has a couple of beaches hard up against the main road. Gorgeous (and sheltered) **Vari**, further east, is the better bet with its sandy beach, though the waterfront and tavernas get packed with families in high season.

🛏 Sleeping & Eating

Krinakia　　　　　　　　　APARTMENT €
(Map p184; [☎]22810 42375; www.krinakia.gr; Agathopes Beach, Posidonia; apt from €55; ⊙Apr-Oct; [P][❄][🛜]) These eight quiet, spacious, well-equipped apartments occupy a classic blue-trimmed white block overlooking Agathopes Beach. Each sleeps up to four people in two bedrooms, making it popular with families.

★**Syros Atlantis**　　　　　　HOTEL €€
(Map p184; [☎]22810 61454; www.syrosatlantis.com; Vari; r €110; ⊙Apr-Oct; [P][❄][🛜]) Professionally run by a charming pair of brothers, this hotel on a quiet lane near Vari Beach has 15 spacious and spotless rooms, each with a terrace or balcony. Some can be joined together for family use. Delicious Greek-style breakfasts are served in the garden courtyard, featur-

ing homemade pies, dolmadhes (stuffed vine leaves), jams and sweets.

Hotel Alkyon　　　　　　　HOTEL €€
(Map p184; [☎]22810 61761; www.alkyonsyros.gr; Megas Gialos; r from €60; ⊙Apr-Oct; [P][❄][🛜][🏊]) Set back from the water about 1.5km from Megas Gialos, this peaceful hotel is run by a charming French-Greek couple and has a large pool and spotless rooms. The hosts arrange seminars and activities (usually in French) that include painting and philosophy.

Allou Yialou　　　　　　　SEAFOOD €€
(Map p184; [☎]22810 71196; www.allouyialousyros.gr; Kini; mains €11-24; ⊙noon-10pm Easter-Sep; [🛜]) Tops for eats on Kini Beach, this elegant waterfront restaurant focuses mainly on seafood (the prawns in ouzo are worth trying), along with the odd meat dish such as lamb and pork chops. It's a prime spot to watch the sunset.

MYKONOS　　　ΜΥΚΟΝΟΣ

POP 10,100

Mykonos is the great glamour island of Greece and flaunts its sizzling St-Tropez-meets-Ibiza style and party-hard reputation. The high-season mix of hedonistic holiday-makers, cruise-ship crowds, buff gay men and posturing fashionistas throngs Mykonos Town (aka Hora), a gorgeous whitewashed Cycladic maze, delighting in its cubist charms and its chi-chi cafe-bar-boutique scene.

The island is maxed out with cashed-up (or spendthrift) visitors, hip hotels, beach bars and restaurants. There are a few provisos about visiting here. Come only if you are prepared to pay. And are intent on jostling with street crowds. And sitting bum cheek to cheek with oiled-up loungers at the main beaches. Oh, and partying relentlessly. Out of season, devoid of gloss and preening celebrities, Hora basically closes, with nothing but the odd person and pelican wandering the empty streets.

Mykonos is the jumping-off point for the archaeological site of nearby Delos (p201).

ℹ Getting There & Away

AIR

Mykonos Airport (JMK; Map p189; [☎]22890 79000; www.mykonos-airport.com), 3km southeast of Hora, has flights year-round from Athens with Aegean and Olympic Air (who also offer seasonal flights from Thessaloniki). Numerous airlines offer seasonal flights from May

Mykonos

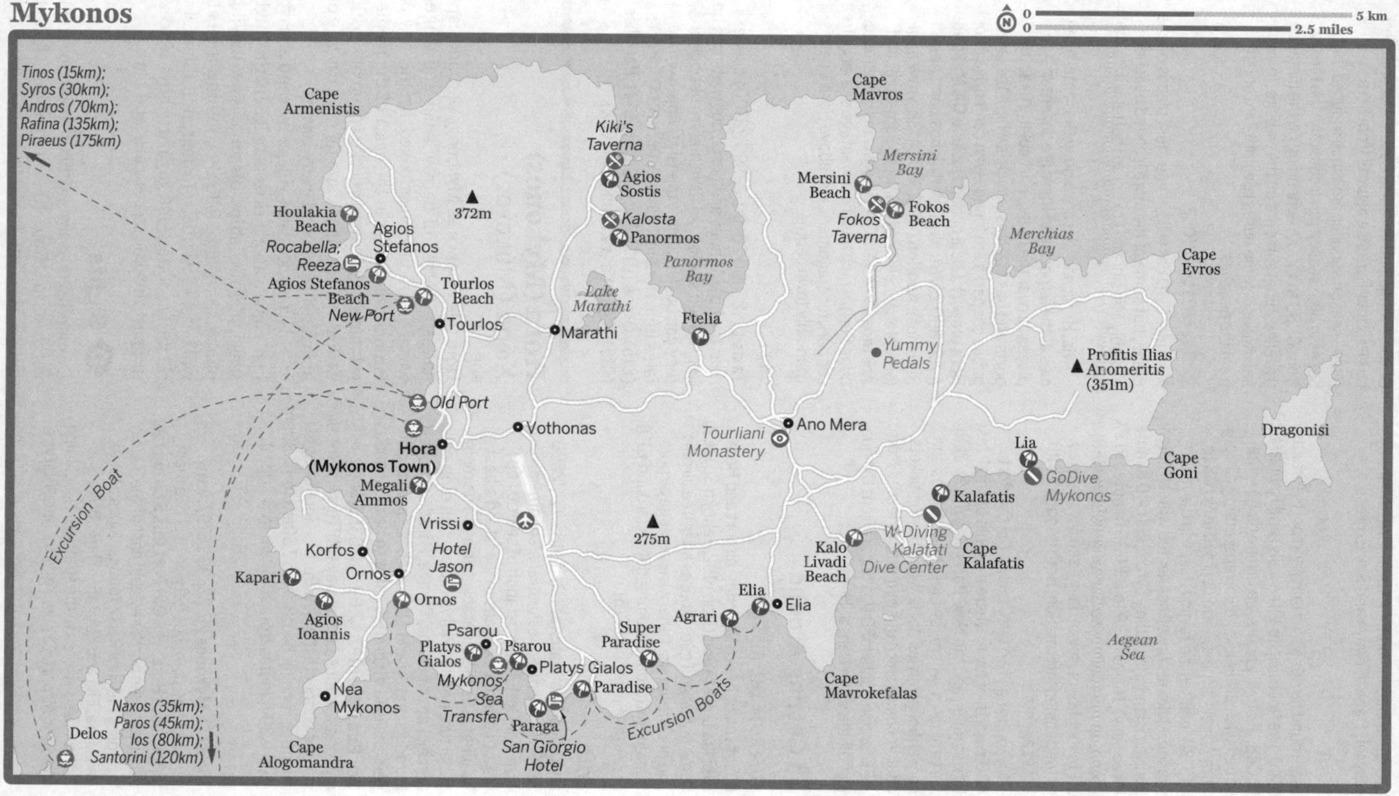
0 5 km
0 2.5 miles
Tinos (15km); Syros (30km); Andros (70km); Rafina (135km); Piraeus (175km)
Cape Armenistis
Houlakia Beach
Agios Stefanos
Rocabella; Reeza
Agios Stefanos Beach
New Port
Tourlos Beach
Tourlos
372m
Kiki's Taverna
Agios Sostis
Kalosta
Panormos
Panormos Bay
Lake Marathi
Marathi
Ftelia
Cape Mavros
Mersini Beach
Mersini Bay
Fokos Taverna
Fokos Beach
Merchias Bay
Cape Evros
Yummy Pedals
Profitis Ilias Anomeritis (351m)
Dragonisi
Old Port
Vothonas
Hora (Mykonos Town)
Tourliani Monastery
Ano Mera
Lia
GoDive Mykonos
Cape Goni
Kalafatis
Megali Ammos
Vrissi
275m
Excursion Boat
Korfos
Kapari
Ornos
Hotel Jason
Ornos
W-Diving Kalafati Dive Center
Kalo Livadi Beach
Cape Kalafatis
Agios Ioannis
Psarou
Platys Gialos
Psarou
Platys Gialos
Mykonos Sea Transfer
Super Paradise
Agrari
Elia
Elia
Paradise
Paraga
San Giorgio Hotel
Excursion Boats
Nea Mykonos
Delos
Naxos (35km); Paros (45km); Ios (80km); Santorini (120km)
Cape Alogomandra
Cape Mavrokefalas
Aegean Sea

to September, including Alitalia, British Airways, easyJet, Qatar Airways and Sky Express.

BOAT

Year-round ferries serve mainland ports Piraeus (€40, five hours, up to three daily) and Rafina (€29 to €48, 2½ hours to 4½ hours, up to nine daily) – the latter is usually quicker if you are coming directly from Athens airport – and nearby Tinos (€8 to €15, 30 minutes, up to nine daily). In the high season, Mykonos is well connected with all neighbouring islands, including Syros (€20, 40 minutes, three daily), Naxos (€29 to €39, 30 minutes to 1¾ hours, up to 11 daily) and Santorini (€52 to €68, 1¾ to four hours, seven daily); see www.ferries. gr for detailed information. Hora is loaded with ticket agents.

Mykonos has two ferry quays: the Old Port, 400m north of town, where a couple of small fast ferries dock, and the **New Port** (Map p189), 2km north of town, where the bigger fast ferries and conventional ferries dock. When buying tickets, double-check which quay your ferry leaves from.

Excursion boats for Delos depart from the quay just off the waterfront at Hora.

🛈 Getting Around

TO/FROM THE AIRPORT

Buses run between Mykonos' airport and Hora's **Fabrika bus station** (Map p192; Fabrika Sq) (€2). Some hotels and guesthouses offer free airport and port transfers. Otherwise, arrange airport transfer with your accommodation (around €10) or take a taxi (around €15).

BOAT

Mykonos Sea Transfer (Map p189; ☑ 22890 23995; www.mykonosseatransfer.com; ☺ 8am-7pm Apr-Oct) An association of sea-taxi operators offering services to the island's best beaches; see the timetables online. The main departure point is Platys Gialos, with drop-offs and pickups at Ornos, Paraga, Paradise, Super Paradise, Agrari and Elia beaches. Cruises and personalised itineraries can also be arranged.
Sea Bus (Map p192; ☑ 6978830355; www. mykonos-seabus.gr; one way €2) This water-taxi service connects the New Port to Hora in eight minutes, running hourly from 7.30am to 10.30pm (every 30 minutes from 10.30am to 6.30pm).

BUS

The **KTEL Mykonos** (☑ 22890 26797; www. mykonosbus.com) bus network has two main terminals in Hora. The **Old Port Bus Station** has services to the northwest and east of the island, including the New Port/Tourlos, Agios Stefanos, Ano Mera, Elia and Kalafatis. The Fabrika Bus Station has services to the southwest, including Mykonos Airport, Ornos, Agios Ioannis, Platys Gialos, Paraga and Paradise Beach. The shuttle bus to Super Paradise departs from here.

Low-season services are much reduced, but buses in high season run frequently; the fare is from €1.80 to €2.30, depending on the distance travelled; timetables are on the website. In July and August, some buses run until 2am or later from the beaches.

CAR & MOTORCYCLE

A regular 2WD car will get you most places on the island, but some of the more isolated beaches (notably Mersini and Fokos) are better with a 4WD or ATV.

Avis, Hertz and Sixt are among the rental agencies at the airport, and there are dozens of hire places all over the island, particularly near the ports and bus stations (which is where the large public car parks are found – you can't drive into Hora proper). Local options include **OK Mykonos** (☑ 22890 23761; www.okmykonos.com; Agios Stefanos), **Apollon** (☑ 22890 24136; www.apollonrentacar.com; Periferiaki; ☺ 9am-8pm) and **Anemos** (☑ 22890 24607; www.mykonosrentcar. com; Peri), which has the advantage of a large free car park for customers, just above Hora's pedestrian-only town centre.

TAXI

Taxis (☑ 22890 22400, 22890 23700) queue near the bus stations and ports, but waits can be long in high season. All have meters but beware: they can be fiendishly expensive. Approximate fares from Hora include New Port (€14), airport (€15), Ornos (€12), Platys Gialos (€14), Paradise (€15), Kalafatis (€22) and Elia (€22).

Hora (Mykonos)
Χώρα (Μύκονος)
POP 3780

Hora (also known as Mykonos), port and capital, is a warren of narrow lanes and white-washed buildings overlooked by the town's famous windmills. In the heart of the medieval maze tiny flower-bedecked churches jostle with glossy boutiques, and there's a cascade of bougainvillea around every corner.

This 'Greek-island village by central casting' comes at a price, people. In the high season, cruise ships disgorge slow-moving phalanxes of flag followers, joining the catwalk cast of wannabe Instagram influencers, celebrity spotters and gay party boys squeezing past the chic stores, cafes and bars.

👁 Sights

Despite its tiny size, without question, you'll get lost in Hora. It's entertaining at first, but can become frustrating amid throngs of equally lost people and fast-moving locals. For quick-fix navigation, head to the water and trace around the periphery of the maze before diving back in – even if there's a more direct route. It's also worth familiarising yourself with Plateia Manto Mavrogenous (Taxi Sq), and the three main streets of Matogianni, Enoplon Dynameon and Mitropoleos, which form a horseshoe through the centre.

Megali Ammos
BEACH

(Map p189) The best beach within walking distance of the centre of town, Megali Ammos has a couple of upmarket resorts and an excellent taverna right on the golden sands. It's a 10-minute walk south from the windmills.

Rarity Gallery
GALLERY

(Map p192; ☑22890 25761; www.raritygallery.com; Kalogera 20-22; ⊙10am-11pm) **FREE** This excellent little gallery is well worth a peek for its temporary exhibitions that showcase contemporary paintings, sculpture and photography.

Windmills
WINDMILL

(Map p192; off Plateia Alefkandra) Constructed in the 16th century by the Venetians for the milling of wheat, seven of Mykonos' iconic windmills are picturesquely situated on a small hill overlooking the harbour.

Archaeological Museum of Mykonos
MUSEUM

(Map p192; ☑22890 22325; Agiou Stefanou; adult/child €4/2; ⊙9am-4pm Sun, Mon & Wed, to 9pm Thu-Sat Apr-Oct, 9am-4pm Tue-Sun Nov-Mar) A headless, almost limbless 2nd-century BC statue of Hercules in Parian marble is the highlight of this small, well-presented collection. Otherwise it's very heavy on pottery and funerary *stelae* (carved monuments), much of it sourced from Delos and the neighbouring island of Rineia, which served as its cemetery. Periodic exhibitions incorporate contemporary art and design into the displays.

Panagia Paraportiani
CHURCH

(Map p192; Paraportianis) Built between the 15th and 17th centuries, Mykonos' most famous church comprises four small chapels – plus another on an upper storey reached by an exterior staircase. It's usually locked, but the fabulously photogenic whitewashed, rock-like exterior is the drawcard.

Aegean Maritime Museum
MUSEUM

(Map p192; ☑22890 22700; www.aegean-maritime-museum.gr; Enoplon Dynameon 10; adult/student €4/2; ⊙10.30am-1pm & 6.30-9pm Apr-Oct) Amid the barnacle-encrusted amphorae, ye olde nautical maps and navigation instruments, there are detailed models of famous sailing ships and paddle steamers. You can also learn the difference between an Athenian trireme, a Byzantine dromon and an ancient Egyptian seagoing ship. There's an enormous Fresnel lighthouse lantern in the courtyard.

🛏 Sleeping

In July and August, a midrange double room with a private bathroom costs anything from €110 (for something fairly average) to €250. The sky's the limit for the top-end category. It's best not to arrive in July or August without a reservation. Many places insist on a minimum stay during the peak period.

MyCocoon
HOSTEL €

(Map p192; ☑22890 78924; www.hostelmykonos.com; Kaminaki; dm/q €72/320; ⊙May-Sep; ❄🛜🍴) A lot of thought has gone into this stylish hostel including custom-made bunks, which are like Cycladic houses in miniature, allowing dorm dwellers some privacy. The 46-person dorm is tightly packed, though, and it's extremely pricy for a hostel but, hey, this is Mykonos, baby! It's a block from the Old Port.

With-Inn
B&B €€

(☑6945188656; www.with-inn.myconos-hotels.com; Tourlos; r from €234; 🅿❄🛜) On a hillside between the New and Old Port, this guesthouse consists of nine spotless rooms. Price includes an excellent cooked breakfast, and pickups and drop-offs. Hora is a 20-minute walk away.

Portobello Boutique Hotel
BOUTIQUE HOTEL €€

(Map p192; ☑22890 23240; www.portobello-hotel.gr; Agios Georgiou; s/d/ste from €160/220/560; ⊙Easter-Oct; 🅿❄🛜🍴) In an elevated location on the edge of Hora, overlooking a ruined windmill, this welcoming hotel is a prime sunset-viewing spot. The delicious breakfast includes homemade yoghurt, and the staff are more than happy to help you plan your stay.

Mykonos Town Suites
APARTMENT €€

(Map p192; ☑22890 23160; www.mykonostownsuites.com; apt from €240; ⊙Apr-Oct; ❄🛜) This hidden complex of bright, high-beamed studios and whole houses (the largest sleeping six in two bedrooms) makes for a splendid choice. Each has a well-equipped kitchen and sunny outdoor space. There's no staffed reception; directions are provided when you book.

Hotel Rochari
HOTEL €€

(Map p192; ☑22890 23107; www.rochari.com; Periferiaki; r/ste from €162/510; ⊙Easter-Oct;

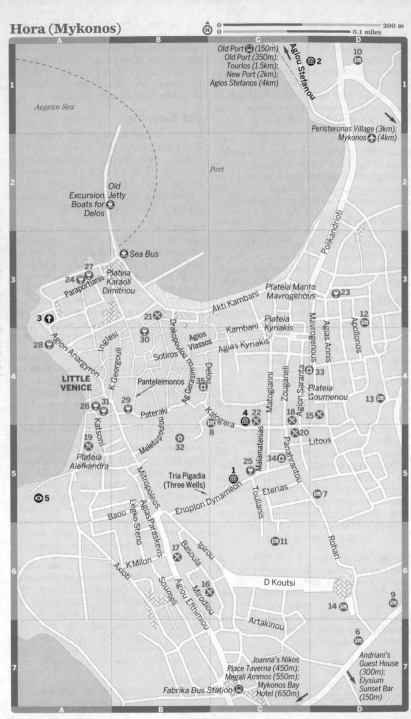

0   200 m
0   0.1 miles

Aegean Sea

Port

Old Port (150m);
Old Port (350m);
Tourlos (1.5km);
New Port (2km);
Agios Stefanos (4km)

Agiou Stefanou

10

2

Peristeronas Village (3km);
Mykonos (4km)

Old
Excursion Jetty
Boats for
Delos

Polikandrioti

Sea Bus

27
24
Paraportianis

Plateia
Karaoli
Dimitriou

Plateia Manto
Mavrogenous

23

21
3
30

Akti Kambani

12
Apollonos

Agios Arnis

28
Agion Anargyron

Inglesi

K Georgouli

Drakopoulou

Ag Gerasimou

Delou

Sotiros

Agios
Vlassos

Kambani

Agias Kyriakis

Plateia
Kyriakis

Mavrogenous

33

Plateia
Goumenou

13

LITTLE
VENICE

Panteleimonos

Pateraki

29

32

Meletou

Kalogera

8

4
22

35

Matogianni

Zouganeli

Agion Saranta

18
15

Panahrantou

20

Litous

26
31
19
Katsoti

Plateia
Alefkandra

Mitropoleos

Agias Paraskevis

Legko Steno

Baou

25

Malamatenias

34

Tria Pigadia
(Three Wells)

1

Enoplon Dynamion

Toulianis

Eterias

7

5

Ipirou

11

Rohari

17
Basoula

K Milon

Axioti

Soumeli

Agiou Efthimiou

Mirodiou

16

D Koutsi

Artakinou

14

9

6

Joanna's Nikos
Place Taverna (450m);
Megali Ammos (550m);
Mykonos Bay
Hotel (650m)

Fabrika Bus Station

Andriani's
Guest House
(300m);
Elysium
Sunset Bar
(150m)

Hora (Mykonos)

P ❄ 🛜 ☕) Founded in 1976 by the present managers' parents, this well-established hotel has kept up with the times. Quietly stylish, it offers comfortable rooms, excellent breakfast spreads, attentive staff and an irresistible swimming pool. It's on the main peripheral road, just up the hill from the centre, so the free transfers will drop you right to the door.

Andriani's Guest House GUESTHOUSE €€
(📞 22890 23091; www.andrianis.com.gr; School of Fine Arts District; s/d from €88/118; ☀ Easter-Sep; ❄ 🛜) 🅟 This clutch of typical Cycladic rooms and studios sits a short but steep walk from the heart of Hora. Relax after your exertions in the peaceful garden.

Pension Joanna APARTMENT €€
(Map p192; 📞 22890 27117; www.pensionjoanna.com; Apollonas 9; apt from €212; ❄ 🛜) Veteran traveller Kostas used to run neighbouring Hotel Lefteris, but has moved directly next door and now owns this striking white-and-plum complex of apartments, each sleeping four to six people. The decor is no-frills but comfy, and there's a roof terrace.

Fresh BOUTIQUE HOTEL €€
(Map p192; 📞 22890 24670; www.hotel-freshmykonos.com; Kalogera 31; s/d from €145/150; ☀ Easter-Oct; ❄ 🛜) In the heart of town, with a lush and leafy garden and highly regarded on-site restaurant, Kalita, Fresh has compact

and stylishly minimalist rooms with a bit of design attitude.

Carbonaki Hotel BOUTIQUE HOTEL €€
(Map p192; 📞 22890 24124; www.carbonaki.gr; Panahrantou 23; s/d from €170/178; ☀ Easter-Oct; ❄ 🛜 ☕) This family-run boutique hotel is a pleasant garden oasis with bright but comfortable rooms (of various price categories). Some open directly onto the sunny central courtyard, with its Jacuzzi and plunge pool.

Mykonos Bay Hotel RESORT €€€
(📞 22890 23338; www.mykonosbay-hotel.com; Megali Ammos; r/ste from €252/666; ☀ Apr-Oct; P ❄ 🛜 ☕) Sitting right on the Megali Ammos Beach, 10 minutes' walk south of Mykonos Town, this whitewashed hotel curves around a saltwater pool, with outdoor whirlpool tubs and risqué art in the rooms and suites.

**Bill & Coo Suites
& Lounge** BOUTIQUE HOTEL €€€
(📞 22890 26292; www.bill-coo-hotel.com; Megali Ammos; ste from €990; ☀ Easter-Oct; P ❄ 🛜 ☕) Consisting of 32 luxuriously styled suites overlooking the dramatic infinity pool, this intimate boutique hotel woos romancing couples. The on-site gourmet restaurant crafts multicourse seasonal menus, the spa offers an extensive range of treatments and the personalised service is among the best on the island.

Belvedere Hotel
LUXURY HOTEL €€€

(Map p192; ☑ 22890 25122; www.belvederehotel.com; Periferiaki; r/ste from €585/900; ☺ Easter-Oct; ❋ 🛜 ⛱) Effortlessly chic but extravagantly expensive, the Belvedere offers charming service, a first-class on-site restaurant (taken over in summer by culinary superstar Nobu Matsuhisa) and a magazine-worthy pool area. It's the kind of place where cocktails cost the equivalent of a nice meal and the honeymoon room has its own private plunge pool.

Semeli Hotel
HOTEL €€€

(Map p192; ☑ 22890 27466; www.semelihotel.gr; Rohari; r/ste from €315/567; ☺ Jan-Nov; ❋ 🛜 ⛱) Expansive grounds, a glamorous restaurant terrace and swimming pool, and dozens of stylish, contemporary rooms combine to make this one of Mykonos' loveliest top-end hotels. It's open nearly all year, too.

🍴 Eating

Mykonos Town has an excellent dining scene, with high-end and fusion restaurants sitting alongside tavernas serving Greek standards and souvlaki shops feeding the partygoers.

Gioras Wood Bakery
BAKERY €

(Map p192; ☑ 22890 27784; Agiou Efthimiou; items €1-3; ☺ 7am-3pm) When the wood ovens first fired up in this bakery, the Byzantines still ruled Constantinople and Christopher Columbus' father was a toddler. Founded in 1420 and operated by the same family for the last 200 years, it's a great place to stock up on mini spinach pies, baklava and all manner of traditional biscuits. Avoid the coffee, though.

Sakis Grill House
GRILL €

(Map p192; ☑ 22890 24848; www.sakisgrill.com; Kalogera 7; mains €3.80-13; ☺ noon-2am) An alternative to Mykonos' pricey restaurants, Sakis is perpetually crammed with people tucking into heaped portions of pork or chicken souvlaki, or *gyros* spilling out of pita bread.

Taste Diaries
CRÊPES €

(Map p192; ☑ 22890 29117; www.facebook.com/TheTasteDiaries; Akti Kambani; mains €5.80-11; ☺ 8am-3am May, Jun, Sep & Oct, 24hr Jul & Aug; 🛜) If you've got a craving for sweet or savoury crêpes, waffles or creamy yoghurt this is the place to come. It's a satisfying breakfast option, and it also serves sandwiches and salads.

Joanna's Nikos Place
TAVERNA €€

(☑ 22890 24251; Megali Ammos; mains €9-16; ☺ 10am-11pm; 🛜) Overlooking the beach just a few minutes' walk south of the windmills, this taverna focuses on Greek standards and it does them very well, particularly the zucchini fritters, Mykonian egg and fennel pie, *mousakas* and the mixed grill.

Nice n Easy
CAFE €€

(Map p192; ☑ 22890 25421; www.niceneasy.gr; Plateia Alefkandra; mains €15-23; breakfasts €9-15; ☺ 10am-12.30am; 🛜 🍴) With a great view of Mykonos' windmills from its terrace, this Athenian outpost is Mykonos' best brunch option, serving eggs Benedict and healthier avocado on toast, egg-white omelettes, quinoa salad and vegan offerings. As the day progresses, burgers, sandwiches and quesadillas vie with traditional Greek fare.

Eva's Garden
GREEK €€

(Map p192; ☑ 22890 22160; www.evas-garden.gr; Plateia Goumenou; mains €12-25; ☺ 6.30pm-midnight; 🛜) Its patio shaded by hanging grapevines, this tempting corner of Eden focuses on traditional Greek home cooking, such as 'Mama's *soutzoukakia*' (oblong meatballs in a tomato sauce), *spanalcopita* (spinach pie), *mousakas* and plenty of grilled fish.

⭐ Funky Kitchen
EUROPEAN €€€

(Map p192; ☑ 22890 27272; www.funkykitchen.gr; Ignatiou Basoula 40; mains €21-26; ☺ 6pm-late May-Oct; 🛜) The open kitchen of this contemporary restaurant brings forth beautifully presented dishes marrying Mediterranean flavours with French techniques. Dishes such as octopus carpaccio with pink peppercorns, grilled fish in a *buerre blanc* sauce, and seared tuna with smoky baba ganoush might tempt you back. The chocolate nirvana is heavenly.

M-Eating
MEDITERRANEAN €€€

(Map p192; ☑ 22890 78550; www.m-eating.gr; Kalogera 10; mains €24-42; ☺ 7pm-1am; 🛜) Attentive service, soft lighting and relaxed luxury are the hallmarks of this restaurant specialising in fresh Greek produce prepared with flair. Options might include the likes of Cycladic fish soup, tuna cakes served on mashed *fava* beans and sous vide lamb, but save room for the dessert of Mykonian honey pie.

To Maereio
GREEK €€€

(Map p192; ☑ 22890 28825; Kalogera 16; mains €17-30; ☺ 7pm-1am; 🛜) With a well-judged menu of Mykonian favourites, this cosy place is popular with locals and foodies in the know. It's heavy on meat – try the meatballs, local ham and spicy sausage. No reservations.

🍷 Drinking & Nightlife

Night starts around 11pm and warms up by 1am. From posh cocktail spots to the colourful bars of Hora's Little Venice (where there are also some hip clubs), Hora has the lot. Another prime spot is the Tria Pigadia (Three Wells) area on Enoplon Dynameon.

★ JackieO' GAY
(Map p192; ☑ 22890 77298; www.jackieomykonos.com; Old Harbour; ⊙ sunset-sunrise) The mainstay of Mykonos' gay party scene, this waterside bar is wall-to-wall writhing bodies after 11.30pm, with the waitstaff shimmying around them delivering drinks with considerable panache. It's a lot of fun, with drag shows adding to the chaos in peak season.

Lola Bar GAY
(Map p192; ☑ 22890 78391; Zanni Pitaraki 4; ⊙ 8pm-3.30am; 🛜) Screen divas line the walls, tasselled lampshades shimmy along to torch songs, and a dragged up mannequin stares endlessly into a mirror at Mykonos' best gay cocktail bar. The vibe is relaxed and friendly, and the staff couldn't be more charming. It's the perfect post-dinner, pre-dancefloor rehydration station. If you can find it within the Mykonos maze.

@54 GAY
(Map p192; ☑ 22890 28543; www.facebook.com/at54Club; Plateia Manto Mavrogenous; ⊙ 9pm-4am; 🛜) With mirror balls cascading from the ceiling and an artsy jungle theme to the decor, this large upstairs space is a stylish spot for an early evening cocktail or a late night boogie. Smokers hog the coveted front balcony, enjoying views along the waterfront.

Cosi BAR
(Map p192; ☑ 22890 27727; www.facebook.com/cosi.gr; Enopion Dynameon; ⊙ 10am-6am; 🛜) This, erm, cosy nook is a stylish cafe by day, with a few al fresco tables. By night it morphs into a lively little bar with occasional DJ sets.

Semeli COCKTAIL BAR
(Map p192; ☑ 22890 26505; www.semelithebar.gr; Little Venice; ⊙ 9am-late) This slick cocktail bar in the heart of Little Venice draws the bold and the beautiful with its signature cocktails and DJ sets.

Babylon GAY
(Map p192; ☑ 22890 25152; www.facebook.com/babylonmyk; Akti Kambani; ⊙ 7.30pm-6am) When JackieO' next door looks set to burst at the seams, the overflow heads here. In summer there are regular drag shows.

Katerina's Bar COCKTAIL BAR
(Map p192; ☑ 22890 23084; www.katerinaslittlevenicemykonos.com; Agion Anargyron 8; ⊙ 9am-3am; 🛜) Katerina's makes no effort to be glamorous or, heaven forbid, cool – INXS is likely to be played at some point in the night – but it consequently manages to have more fun than most places in Little Venice. What is unbelievably cool is that it's owned by the first female Greek naval captain. Plus there's an ace little balcony.

Elysium Sunset Bar GAY
(☑ 22890 23952; www.elysiumhotel.com; School of Fine Arts District; ⊙ 6-10pm Apr-Oct) Attached to the 'straight-friendly' Hotel Elysium, this poolside bar is the first port of call for the gay party crowd. Handsome barstaff flirt shamelessly, perhaps to distract from the hefty drink prices. Drag queens perform nightly from mid-May to September, although the real star of the show is the sun sinking over the horizon.

Galleraki COCKTAIL BAR
(Map p192; ☑ 22890 27188; www.galleraki.com; Little Venice; ⊙ 10am-5am; 🛜) Choose plum waterfront seating or the upstairs balcony

DON'T MISS

LGBT+ MYKONOS

Mykonos is one of the most popular beach-holiday destinations in the world for gay men. Days are spent at glitzy Super Paradise (p197) or cruisy Elia Beach (p196) before heading back to Hora for a disco nap and a costume change. The first stop of the evening is traditionally Elysium Sunset Bar for views, extortionately priced drinks and hit-and-miss drag shows before hitting the bars in town: Lola for camp and cocktails, or Porta for flattering lighting and a more blokey vibe. Everyone inevitably ends up wiggling their hips at JackieO' (but don't think of arriving before 11pm), switching to Babylon or @54 occasionally for a change of scene.

Party people should visit in late August for XLSIOR (www.xlsiorfestival.com), a huge gay clubbing festival that draws some 30,000 revellers.

CYCLADES HORA (MYKONOS)

at this cafe-bar, and order one of its fresh-fruit cocktails (like the signature 'katerinaki', made with melon) or a classic champagne concoction.

Porta   GAY

(Map p192; ☎22890 27807; www.porta bar-mykonos.com; Ioanni Voinovich 5; ☺10pm-5am) The black sheep of the gay herd, Porta's cruisey ambience fills small-scale rooms bedecked in Tom of Finland imagery. Things get crowded and close towards midnight.

☆ Entertainment

Need a break from the bars and clubs? Seek out the gorgeous open-air cinema Cine Manto (Map p192; ☎22890 26165; www.cinemanto.gr; Meletopoulou; adult/child €9/7; ☺9pm & 11pm Jun-Sep) in a garden setting. There's a cafe here, too. Movies are shown in their original language; view the programme online.

🛍 Shopping

Fashion boutiques and art galleries vie for attention. Mavrogenous St is good for art, Matogianni is best for luxe brands and Greek designers, while the streets of Little Venice mix fashion with jewellery and tat. Most stores close in the winter (November to Easter).

True Image   FASHION & ACCESSORIES

(Map p192; ☎22890 78588; www.trueimage.gr; Kalogera 11; ☺10am-11pm) Digitally print images onto T-shirts and Converse sneakers while you wait – from the store's vast digital library or bring in your own image. A unique pair of Converse high or low tops will cost you €99.

Art & Soul   ART

(Map p192; ☎22890 27244; www.mykonosgallery. com; Mavrogenous 18; ☺10am-11pm) Run by the Rousounelos family for over 30 years, this gallery is for serious collectors. On display you'll find sculpture and paintings by renowned Greek artists, each sold with a certificate of authenticity.

HEEL Athens Lab   FASHION & ACCESSORIES

(Map p192; ☎22890 77166; www.heel.gr; Panahrantou; ☺11am-2am Apr-Oct) 🌱 Ecologically friendly women's garments made from organic cotton and other sustainable fibres, as well as one-of-a-kind jewellery made from recycled materials.

Muse   GIFTS & SOUVENIRS

(Map p192; ☎22890 77370; Dilou 8; ☺11am-3pm & 5-11pm) Pick up a fluoro Greek god, a marble figurine modelled on the blank-faced Cycladic

originals or a replica of the classical art, jewellery and ceramics that fill the museums.

ℹ Information

Mykonos has no tourist office; visit travel agencies instead. Online, visit **Mykonos Traveller** (☎69869 93013; www.mykonostraveller.com). www.inmykonos.com and www.mykonos.gr for more information.

Delia Travel (☎22890 22322; www.facebook. com/delia.travel.mykonos; Akti Kambani; ☺9am-9pm) Sells ferry and Delos tickets, and books accommodation and hire cars.

Sea & Sky (☎22890 28240; www.seasky.gr; Akti Kambani; ☺8.30am-9.30pm) Information, aeroplane, ferry and Delos tickets.

ℹ Getting There & Away

Hora is the transport hub of the island. The Old Port Bus Station (p190) has services to the northwest and east of the island, while the airport and beaches to the southwest are served by the Fabrika Bus Station (p190).

There are various car-rental agencies around town, including Apollon (p190) and Anemos (p190).

Excursion boats for Delos (Map p192) leave from the pier directly in front of the town; tickets can be purchased from a nearby kiosk (p203).

Around Mykonos

Located in the centre of Ano Mera is **Tourliani Monastery** (Map p189; Ano Mera; €1; ☺10am-1pm & 3.30-7pm), the island's other main settlement. This castle-like monastery (founded in 1537 but rebuilt in 1767) has a gorgeous domed church with an ornate, gilded iconostasis, and a small museum displaying vestments, historic documents and icons.

🏖 Beaches

Mykonos' golden-sand beaches in their formerly unspoilt state were the pride of Greece. Now most are jammed with umbrellas and backed by beach bars, but they do make for a hopping scene that draws floods of beachgoers. Moods range from the simply hectic to the outright snobby, and nudity levels vary.

Without your own wheels, catch buses from Hora or boats from Ornos and Platys Gialos to further beaches. Mykonos Sea Transfer (p190) has an online timetable.

Elia   BEACH

(Map p189) This beautiful stretch of golden sand has craggy cliffs on either side and an excellent waterfront restaurant. It's backed by some large resorts and rows of recliners line the sand. A rainbow flag down the western end (to the right facing the water) marks the gay section. Just past here is the beginning of the nude area; most of the guys head to a tiny cove a little further along the path.

Buses head here, via Ano Mera, from the Old Port station.

Agios Sostis
BEACH

(Map p189) This gorgeous, wide strip of golden sand receives far fewer visitors than the south coast. There's no shade and only limited parking but there's a popular taverna with a little sheltered cove directly below it.

Paradise
BEACH

(Map p189) Clear waters and golden sands mean it's completely lined with noisy beach bars and rows of umbrellas, but the service (particularly at Tropicana) is friendly and attentive. There's a camping resort here, a dive centre, an excellent Indian restaurant and the island's most highly rated club.

Regular buses head here from Hora's Fabrika station.

Super Paradise
BEACH

(Map p189) Flashy and great for people-watching – Super Paradise is Mykonos' most popular gay-friendly beach. The action is split between the glitzy JackieO' Beach Club on the southern headland and the Super Paradise beach bar on the sands.

During the season, a private bus service connects the beach to Hora's Fabrika station.

Paraga
BEACH

(Map p189) This beautiful crescent-shaped cove became popular in the hippy era and is still known for its beach parties. There's a good selection of tavernas, plus a party hostel, a small gay section and a nudist area.

Buses travel from Hora's Fabrika station.

Agrari
BEACH

(Map p189) There's lots of free sand to spread out on at this lovely sandy cove, and a beach bar to retreat to if you get parched. There are no buses but it's easily reached via a short walk from Elia Beach.

Panormos
BEACH

(Map p189) A chunk of this gorgeous sandy beach is given over to a pretentious beach-bar complex, but that still leaves a large expanse of golden sand to spread out on. There's a good taverna here as well.

Kapari
BEACH

(Map p189) Scooped out of the surrounding cliffs, this appealing sandy cove is reached via a short walk along an unpaved track from the western end of Agios Ioannis (Map p189).

Platys Gialos
BEACH

(Map p189) One of Mykonos' most popular beaches, this broad stretch of white sand is lined with restaurants and has an excellent water sports centre.

Buses come from Hora's Fabrika station.

Psarou
BEACH

(Map p189) A long stretch of white sand and teal waters, favoured by local cognoscenti. It's a short walk from Platys Gialos.

🏃 Activities

There's good diving to be had around Mykonos, with wrecks, caves and walls to explore, and scuba diving operators on Paradise, Kalafatis (Map p189) and Lia (Map p189) beaches. Kalafatis and Ftelia (Map p189) beaches are good for windsurfing, while Platys Gialos (p197) is the place to try flyboarding or rent a stand-up paddleboard or kayak.

GoDive Mykonos
DIVING

(Map p189; 📱6942616102; www.godivemykonos. com; Lia Beach; 1-/2-tank dives €80/130; ⊘9.30am-6pm; 🛝) This highly professional operator is based on Lia Beach and offers a full range of activities below the waves, from multiday scuba safaris to night dives, PADI courses, snorkelling trips and Bubblemaker inductions for kids over seven.

Mykonos Diving Centre
DIVING

(📱22890 24808; www.dive.gr; Paradise Beach; 1-/2-tank dive €75/120; 🛝) Based at Paradise Beach, this reputable operator offers a range of PADI courses, as well as night dives, guided snorkelling (€50), Discover Scuba outings (€120), and Bubblemaker for kids over eight (€120).

Platis Gialos Watersports
WATER SPORTS

(📱6977279584; www.mykonoswatersports.gr; Platys Gialos Beach; ⊘9am-9pm Mon-Fri) This operator specialises in adrenalin-packed water sports and arranges flyboarding, wakeboarding, wakeskating, waterskiing and wakesurfing sessions. It also rents sea kayaks and stand-up paddleboards.

Mykonos On Board
BOATING

(📱69324 71055; www.mykonosonboard.com) Highly recommended private or small-group yachting excursions around Mykonos and to nearby islands Delos and Rineia.

MILA ATKOVSKA/SHUTTERSTOCK ©

1. Ancient Delos (p202)
Once home to a magnificent city, Delos is now one of Greece's most important archaeological sites.

2. Anafi (p254)
Tuck into some local dishes on this secluded and rugged island.

3. Oia (p248), Santorini
Postcard-perfect Cycladic scenery.

4. Paros (p204)
Diving in spectacular, clear blue waters in Paros.

W-Diving Kalafati Dive Center   DIVING
(Map p189; ☑22890 71677; www.mykonos-diving.com; Kalafatis Beach; 1-tank dive €65; ⊙8am-4pm)
Full range of diving courses and packages from a 'discover scuba diving' session (€80) to 10 boat dives with full gear (€470).

🧭 Tours

A world away from the beach bars, multilingual Dimitra offers mountain-biking tours through the backroads of Mykonos with **Yummy Pedals** (Map p189; ☑22890 71883; www.yummypedals.gr; 4hr tour from €50). The duration and route is personalised to fit differing skill levels, but may take in farms, villages and quiet beaches (with swimming and snacking stops). Tours begin and end at Dimitra's family's vineyard, with the option of food and wine.

The vineyard is located outside Ano Mera. See the website for directions, or arrange to be picked up from Ano Mera bus stop.

🛏️ Sleeping

Mykonos Town may have the greatest variety of accommodation, but hotels, apartments and domatia are scattered throughout popular locations, such as Platys Gialos and Ornos. Paraga and Paradise Beach have party hostels.

Hotel Jason   HOTEL €€
(Map p189; ☑22890 23481; www.hoteljason-mykonos.gr; Glastros; s/d from €65/120; P❄🛜🏊) This midpriced hotel, with spotless, tiled rooms is within a half hour's walk of Hora and three beaches (Ornos, Psarou and Platys Gialos) and there's a bus stop nearby. Doubles are nicer than the triple rooms.

Artemoulas Studios   APARTMENT €€
(☑22890 25501; www.artemoulas-mykonos.gr; Platys Gialos; apt from €180; ⊙May-Sep; P❄@🛜🏊) With a hillside location a short walk from two of Mykonos' most popular beaches, these self-contained apartments are a solid midrange choice. Options range from studios with kitchenettes to two-bedroom apartments.

★ Rocabella   BOUTIQUE HOTEL €€€
(Map p189; ☑22890 28930; www.rocabella-hotel-mykonos.com; Agios Stefanos; r/ste from €361/532; ⊙Easter-Oct; P❄🛜🏊) Nothing screams relaxation more than the day beds projecting over the sea-gazing pool at this sophisticated retreat, 3km north of Hora. Rotary telephones and tiny Marshall speakers bring a retro element to the otherwise contemporary decor of the 21 rooms, all of which have decks with sea views, and some have Jacuzzis.

Nissaki   BOUTIQUE HOTEL €€€
(☑22890 27666; www.hotelnissaki.gr; Platys Gialos; d/ste from €485/502; ⊙Apr-Oct; P❄🛜🏊) With its pool overlooking the bay, this is one of Mykonos' loveliest retreats. Whitewashed rooms are livened up with touches of contemporary art, floor-to-ceiling windows let in plenty of light, and suites come with hot tubs. A spa, romantic dining and the pearly light dancing on the water make this an ideal place to canoodle with your sweetie.

Branco Mykonos   RESORT €€€
(☑22890 25500; www.brancohotel.com; Platys Gialos; r/ste from €900/1070; ⊙Apr-Sep; ❄🛜🏊) Ambient beats from the beachfront DJ station drift over the deckchairs and pool of this modern hotel that has commandeered the eastern half of Platys Gialos Beach. All rooms come with sea views, the restaurant serves contemporary Greek dishes and an excellent range of water sports is on offer.

Palladium   BOUTIQUE HOTEL €€€
(☑22890 25925; www.hotelpalladium.gr; Psarou; d/ste from €520/690; ⊙Easter-Oct; P❄🛜🏊) Equidistant from Psarou and Platys Gialos beaches, this intimate five-star hotel is all elegant Cycladic curves and whitewashed, airy rooms and suites (some with private pools). Excellent on-site dining, extensive breakfast, vast main pool and wonderfully helpful service add to the appeal.

San Giorgio Hotel   BOUTIQUE HOTEL €€€
(Map p189; ☑22890 27474; www.sangiorgio-mykonos.com; Paraga Beach; r from €410; ⊙May–mid-Oct; ❄🛜🏊) Let your biggest holiday dilemma be where to recline: by the pool at this luxe, laid-back hotel, at Paradise Beach (seven minutes' walk) or at Paraga Beach (three minutes' walk).

🍴 Eating

Indian Palace   INDIAN €€
(☑22890 78044; www.jaipur-palace.gr; Paradise Beach; mains €8.60-16; ⊙1-11pm; 🛜🍴) An offshoot of Athen's renowned Jaipur Palace, this breezy place overlooks Paradise Beach, offering a fresh and fragrant take on the greatest hits of Indian cuisine. Given the location, ordering the fish curry is a no-brainer.

Bowl CAFE €€

(☑ 22890 77659; www.bowlmykonos.co; Nea Periferiaki, Ornos; mains €9-25; ☺ 9am-6pm Mon-Sat, daily Jul & Aug; ☑) A big pink sequinned disk provides an Instagrammable backdrop to this breezy health-focused cafe, especially popular with those who will later be dancing at the beach clubs in the skimpiest bikinis. Options include delicious breakfast bowls, açai berry smoothies, 'health' shots and plenty of 'superfood', raw and vegan dishes. The coffee's top-notch; the barista even has a topknot.

Kiki's Taverna TAVERNA €€

(Map p189; ☑ 69407 59356; Agios Sostis; mains €10-25; ☺ 1-7pm; ☜) Every day around noon, customers begin lining up outside Kiki's, helping themselves to complimentary cask wine as they wait. Their prize? Enormous portions of simple local food off the grill: marinated pork chops, chewy octopus, swordfish or cheese, accompanied by salads and served beneath a shady vine trellis on a terrace overlooking the sea.

Kalosta MEDITERRANEAN €€

(Map p189; ☑ 22890 78589; www.facebook.com/KalostaRestaurantPanormos; Panormos Beach; mains €12-22; ☺ noon-10pm; ☜) Drunk with sunshine and skin tangy with sea salt, beachgoers make their way up to Kalosta's terrace overlooking Panormos Beach. Bask in the afterglow of a long, lazy day and feast on the seafood-heavy selection of Greek and Italian dishes.

Fokos Taverna TAVERNA €€

(Map p189; ☑ 6944644343; www.fokosmykonos.com; Fokos Beach; mains €9-22; ☺ 1-7pm; ☜) The smell of grilled lamb chops, sizzling burgers and grilled calamari wafts down from this long-standing taverna and over Fokos Beach. It's been attracting locals and visitors alike with its creative take on local dishes, including imaginative salads, along with a few exotic touches (ceviche, 'Oriental' rice). You'll need an ATV to brave the rutted road.

Nikolas Taverna TAVERNA €€

(☑ 22890 25264; www.nikolas-taverna.com; Agia Anna Beach; mains €8-17; ☺ 10am-10pm; ☜) ✪ This seaside taverna has been run by the same family for three generations. The current proprietor, Nikolas, goes fishing for fresh catch of the day to go with the locally sourced meats and vegetables from the family farm.

★Reeza MEDITERRANEAN €€€

(☑ 22890 28930; www.rocabella-hotel-mykonos.com; Agios Stefanos; mains €18-38) Sophisticated yet deceptively simple contemporary Greek cuisine is served poolside at this exceptional restaurant attached to the Rocabella Hotel. Playful takes on classics include 'crab vs dolmas' and 'prawn carpaccio *saganaki*', and there's a range of set tasting menus if you're in the mood to splurge (€55 to €125). Vegans have a couple of options, too.

🍷 Drinking & Nightlife

JackieO' Beach Club GAY

(☑ 22890 77298; www.jackieomykonos.com; Super Paradise) Occupying the western headland of Super Paradise Beach, this slick puppy is wall-to-wall buffed bodies in itsy-bitsy swimsuits, posing and prancing around the swimming pool – in other words, priceless people-watching. Prices are high, but there's free parking, a restaurant and drag shows in the peak season.

Super Paradise Beach Club CLUB

(☑ 6985919002; www.superparadise.com.gr; ☺ 9am-late; ☜) Dominating its namesake beach, this beach bar and club is synonymous with hedonism. Celebrity sightings, a crush of scantily clad young bodies heaving to the DJs' beats, cocktails by the sea – yep, it's got all that. Music kicks off in the afternoons and pumps until the wee hours. Numerous free shuttle buses from Hora.

Paradise Beach Club CLUB

(☑ 6973016311; www.paradiseclubmykonos.com; Paradise Beach; ☺ 4pm-5am Apr-Oct) By day it's a place to sip cocktails around a saltwater pool but afternoon parties kick off at 4pm, with the second shift starting from 10pm. Big-name international DJs such as Tiësto and Erick Morillo have played here.

Cavo Paradiso CLUB

(☑ 22890 26124; www.cavoparadiso.gr; Paradise Beach; ☺ 11.30pm-7am) The only Mykonos venue to appear in DJ Mag's international Top 100 Clubs list, this open-air clifftop megaclub (capacity 3000) consistently showcases top international DJs. Look out for its regular Full Moon parties.

DELOS ΔΗΛΟΣ

POP 24

The Cyclades fulfil their collective name (*kyklos* means circle) by encircling the sacred island of Delos. The mythical birthplace of twins Apollo and Artemis, splendid Ancient Delos was a shrine turned sacred treasury

SANCTUARIES OF THE FOREIGN GODS

Delos was a place of worship for many cultures beyond the Greeks, and their temples are concentrated in the area called the **Sanctuaries of the Foreign Gods** (p203) on the slope of Mt Kynthos. The remains of a 1st-century BC synagogue have also been uncovered near the stadium.

Samothrakeion (Map p203) The Kabeiroi, a mysterious group of Samothracian deities, were worshipped here.

Sanctuary of the Syrian Gods (Map p203) Built in around 150 BC, this complex was dedicated to the Syrian gods Atargatis and Hadad, who were popular in the Greek world.

Sanctuary of the Egyptian Gods (Map p203) Honoured deities including Serapis and Isis.

and commercial centre. This Unesco World Heritage Site is one of the most important archaeological sites in Greece.

The island, just 5km long and 1300m wide, offers a soothing contrast to Mykonos, its main access point. Overnight stays are forbidden, so visits are at the mercy of boat schedules. Aside from the museum, there's very little shelter; a hat, sunscreen and walking shoes are sensible precautions.

There is no cafe operating on the island; it pays to bring water and food.

History

Delos has a special place in Greek mythology. When Leto was pregnant with Apollo and Artemis, she was relentlessly pursued by vengeful Hera, before finally finding sanctuary and giving birth to the twins on the island.

Delos was first inhabited in the 3rd millennium BC. From the 8th century BC it became a shrine to Apollo, and the oldest temples on the island date from this era. The dominant Athenians had full control of Delos – and thus the Aegean – by the 5th century BC.

In 478 BC Athens established an alliance known as the Delian League, which kept its treasury on the island. A cynical decree ensured that no one could be born or die on Delos, thus strengthening Athens' control over the island by expelling the natives.

Delos reached the height of its power in Hellenistic times, becoming one of the three most important religious centres in Greece and a centre of commerce. Many of its inhabitants were wealthy merchants, mariners and bankers from as far away as Egypt and Syria. They built temples to their homeland gods, but Apollo remained the principal deity.

The Romans made Delos a duty-free port in 167 BC. This brought even greater prosperity, due to a slave market that sold up to 10,000 people a day. During the next century, as ancient religions diminished and trade routes shifted, Delos began to delcine. By the 3rd century AD there was remained only a small Christian settlement, and in the following centuries it was a hideout for pirates who looted many of its antiquities.

Fresh discoveries are still unearthed though: in recent years a gold workshop was uncovered alongside the Terrace of the Lions.

◉ Sights

★ **Ancient Delos**   ARCHAEOLOGICAL SITE
(Map p203; ☑ 22890 22259; museum & site adult/concession €12/6; ☉ 8am-8pm Apr-Oct, to 2pm Nov-Mar) The ancient town that sprang up here was a commercial centre as well as shrine. Within the extensive ruins of this Unesco World Heritage Site, it's not difficult to imagine Ancient Delos in all its original splendour.

On the island, the ticket office sells Delos guidebooks but there are also information boards scattered around the site. Visitors are given a map with three walking routes marked on it, taking from 1½ to five hours.

While many significant finds from Delos are in the National Archaeological Museum in Athens, the island's museum retains an interesting collection.

The key areas to explore are the **Sanctuary of Apollo**, the spiritual heart of the complex, to the left of the ferry dock. Two large stoas (colonnaded porticos) lined the Sacred Way leading to the **Propylaea**, the monumental entrance to a complex of magnificent temples and treasuries. Three temples to Apollo stood side by side, facing a colossal 9m-high statue of the god. Also within the compound is the **Artemision**, containing the Temple of Artemis. Beyond here is the much-photographed **Terrace of the Lions**. These proud marble beasts were offerings from the people of Naxos, presented to Delos in the 7th century BC to guard the **Sacred Lake** (drained since 1925 to prevent malarial mosquito-breeding) where Leto gave birth to her twins.

Ancient Delos

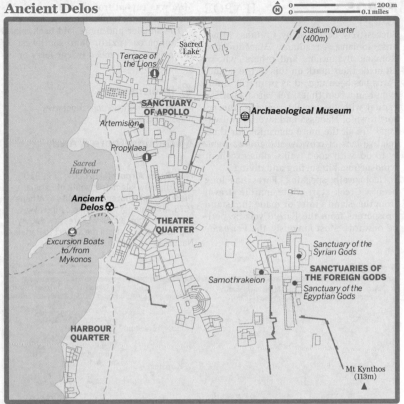

0 —————— 200 m
0 —————— 0.1 miles

Stadium Quarter
(400m)

Sacred
Lake

Terrace of
the Lions

**SANCTUARY
OF APOLLO**

Artemision

Propylaea

Sacred
Harbour

**Ancient
Delos** ⊗

Excursion Boats
to/from
Mykonos

**THEATRE
QUARTER**

Archaeological Museum

Sanctuary of the
Syrian Gods

**SANCTUARIES OF
THE FOREIGN GODS**

Samothrakeion

Sanctuary of the
Egyptian Gods

**HARBOUR
QUARTER**

Mt Kynthos
(113m)
▲

CYCLADES DELOS

To the right of the dock is the **Theatre Quarter**, where Delos' wealthiest inhabitants lived in houses built around peristyle courtyards, with intricate, colourful mosaics. Beyond this are the **Sanctuaries of the Foreign Gods** and the path leading up **Mt Kynthos** (113m); it's worth the steep climb for the terrific views of the encircling islands.

★ **Archaeological Museum**   MUSEUM
(Map p203; ⊘ 8am-8pm mid-Apr–Oct) **FREE** A vast haul of artefacts has been protected from the elements and displayed in this must-see museum, including the originals of many of the frescoes, mosaics and statues that were removed from the site and replaced with replicas in situ. In the left-hand hall, look for the eye-opening cabinet of erotic items including large stone phalluses.

ⓘ **Information**

Information boards make it easy to do without one, but licensed guides can help provide context

to the neighbourhoods and buildings. An added bonus is that they can sometimes speed you past the queues at the entrance gates. Guided tours, including the boat trip and site admission, cost €50 – an extra €18 than if you were going it alone.

ⓘ **Getting There & Away**

Boats (Map p189) for Delos leave Hora (Mykonos) at 9am, 10am, 11.30am and 5pm from May to October, returning at noon, 1.30pm, 3pm and 7.30pm. On Mondays throughout the year, and daily from November to April, only the 10am boat operates, returning at 1.30pm. The journey takes 30 minutes. Tickets are sold from the **Delos Boat Ticket Kiosk** (☑ 22890 28603; www.delostours.gr; adult/child return ticket €20/10), located at the foot of the jetty at the southern end of Mykonos' old harbour. When buying tickets, find out which boat you can return on.

PAROS ΠΑΡΟΣ

POP 12,853

Successively occupied by Cretans, Minoans, Ionians, Arcadians, Macedonians, Romans, Byzantians and others, who've all made their mark on this fertile island, Paros has been tagged as primarily a ferry hub in recent times. Yet Paros' bustling capital with its ancient remains, the resort town of Naoussa and sweet rural villages are all the more charming for their relative lack of crowds, and there's plenty to do, with good walks, plus excellent windsurfing, kitesurfing and diving.

Geologically speaking, Paros has long been a Greek star; white marble drawn from the island's interior made the island prosperous from the Early Cycladic period onwards. Most famously, the *Venus de Milo* was carved from Parian marble, as was Napoleon's tomb.

The smaller and more laid-back island of Antiparos (p210), 1km southwest of Paros, is easily reached by car ferry or excursion boat.

ⓘ Information

For further information, check out www.parosweb.com.

ⓘ Getting There & Away

AIR

From **Paros Airport** (Map p204; ☎ 22840 44070), a few kilometres south of Parikia, there are half a dozen daily flights to Athens (€75, 40 minutes) with Olympic Air (www.olympicair.com) and Sky Express (www.sky-express.gr). Taxis from the airport to Parikia/Naoussa cost around €20/35.

Paros & Antiparos

Ⓝ 0 —————— 5 km
0 —————— 2.5 miles

Syros (35km);
Piraeus (160km)

Mykonos (45km);
Rafina (140km)

Naxos (10km); Ios (50km); Small Cyclades (50km);
Amorgos (75km); Santorini (90km); Astypalea (130km)

Cape Korakas

Paros Park

Cape Agias Marias

Cine Enastron

Monastiri
Lageri

Plastira Bay
Kolimbythres

Santa Maria

Aegean Sea

Kamares

Naoussa

Tao's Center

Kokou Riding Centre

Cape Agios Fokas

Krios

Livadia

Agios Fokas

Ambelas
Ambelas Beach

Marathi

Marble Quarries

Kostos

Parikia

Serifos (45km);
Sifnos (45km);
Milos (80km)

Excursion Boat

Paros Bay
Parasporos

Camping Antiparos

Paros

Lefkes

Marmara

Cape Antikefalos

Molos

Sunset

Antiparos

Glysidia

Prodromos

Pounta

Marpissa

Panaghia

Piso Livadi

Paros Airport

Mt Profitis Ilias
(770m) ▲

Logaras
Pounda

Antiparos

Glyfa

Kamari

Hrysi Akti

Dryos

Restaurant Anna

Hrysi Akti (Golden Beach)

Captain Sargos Boat Trips

Cave of Antiparos

Angeria

Captain Pipinos

Apandima

Aliki

Glyfa

Agios Georgios

Soros

Cape Fanos

Despotiko

Cape Skilos

BOAT

Boat services from Paros are as follows:

DESTINATION	DURATION	FARE (€)	FREQUENCY
Aegiali (on Amorgos)	3¼-5½ hrs	13-21.50	5 weekly
Anafi	7 hrs	16	2 weekly
Astypalea	5 hrs	37	4 weekly
Donousa	2¼-2½ hrs	11-17.50	5 weekly
Folegandros	3½-6¼ hrs	9-60	1-2 daily
Ios	50 mins	11-27	3-5 daily
Iraklia	1¼-6 hrs	11-17	4 weekly
Iraklio	4-6½ hrs	55-75	2-4 daily
Katapola (on Amorgos)	2-6 hrs	13-32	1-3 daily
Koufonisia	1¼-3¼ hrs	19-35	2-3 daily
Mykonos	40mins-1¼ hrs	18-32	6-8 daily
Naxos	30mins-1½ hrs	6-24	5-7 daily
Piraeus	3¼-5¼ hrs	33-40	3-6 daily
Rafina	3¼-6¼ hrs	31-46	3 daily
Santorini	2-3½ hrs	20-46	4-5 daily
Schinousa	2¾ hrs	7-35	1-2 daily
Syros	1½-2¼ hrs	7-35	1-2 daily
Tinos	1½-2½ hrs	34-39	4-5 daily

ⓘ Getting Around

BOAT

Sea taxis leave from the Parikia quay for beaches around Paros and to Antiparos. Tickets range from €8 to €15 and are available on board.

BUS

Parikia is the island's bus hub, and frequent **buses** (☑ 22840 21395; http://ktelparou.gr) link Parikia and Naoussa. It's also easy to reach popular destinations such as the Golden Beach, Prodromos and Marmara from both towns. Buses also link Parikia to Pounta (for the Antiparos ferry) and the airport.

Tickets are bought from machines at bus terminals, and at kiosks and minimarkets island-wide, or from the driver at a higher rate.

CAR & MOTORCYCLE

There are numerous rental outlets along the waterfront in Parikia, Naoussa and all around the island. In peak season the minimum cost is about €45 per day for car hire, €30 for a quad and €20 for a scooter. A good outfit is **Acropolis** (Map p206; ☑ 22840 21830; www.acropolisparos.com; Waterfront, Parikia).

TAXI

Taxis (☑ 22840 21500) gather beside the roundabout in Parikia. Fares include €20 to the airport, €15 to Naoussa, €13 to Pounta, €15 to Lefkes and €24 to Piso Livadi. Add €1 if going from the port. There are extra charges for booking ahead, and for luggage.

Parikia   Παροικιά

POP 3000

For its small size, Parikia packs a punch. Its labyrinthine Old Town is pristine and filled with boutiques, cafes and restaurants. You'll also find a handful of impressive archaeological sites, a waterfront crammed with tavernas and bars, first-class accommodation, and sandy stretches of beach – particularly popular is Livadia, a short walk north of town.

⊙ Sights & Activities

★**Panagia Ekatontapyliani**   CHURCH
(Map p206; www.ekatontapyliani.gr; Ekatondapylianis; ⊙ 8am-9pm) The Panagia Ekatontapyliani, which dates from AD 326, is one of the finest churches in the Cyclades. The building is three distinct churches: Agios Nikolaos, the largest, with columns of Parian marble and a carved iconostasis in the east of the compound; the ornate Church of Our Lady; and the ancient Baptistery. The name translates as Our Lady of the Hundred Doors. The **Byzantine Museum** (Map p206; Ekatondapylianis; €2; ⊙ 9am-10pm Apr-Oct), is within the compound.

★**Archaeological Museum**   MUSEUM
(Map p206; ☑ 22840 21231; €2; ⊙ 8am-3pm Wed-Mon) This museum harbours a 5th-century BC Nike and a 6th-century BC Gorgon, as well as the first known Greek depiction of a seated figure (8th century BC). A major exhibit is a slab of the 264 BC Parian Chronicle, which lists the most outstanding personalities and events of Ancient Greece.

Frankish Kastro   RUINS
(Map p206) Check out the outer walls of this fortress, built by the Venetian Duke Marco Sanudo of Naxos in AD 1260. Built with the stones from ancient buildings that once stood on this site, you can find remnants from the archaic temples of Athena and an Ionic temple from the 5th century BC.

Parikia

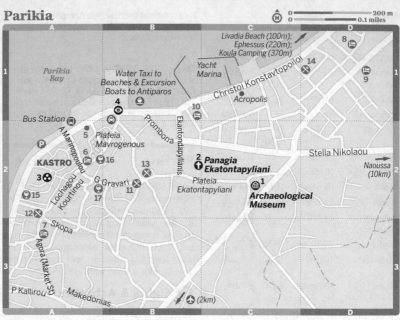

Parikia

Paros Hikes HIKING
(☑ 6972288821; www.paroshikes.com) Christoforos and Lambos guide ecotours to explore the lesser-known sides of Paros and Antiparos, ranging from countryside walks to mountain hiking adventures. Tours can be tailor-made, or you can join them for scheduled walks. Events are outlined on the website, along with route details, departure info and prices. There are also Bike & Hike and Sail & Hike combos.

🛏 Sleeping

★ Pension Sofia PENSION €€
(Map p206; ☑ 22840 22085; http://pension-sofia.gr; d/tr €80/120; ☉ Apr-Oct; ❄ 🛜) A few blocks behind the waterfront, Sofia's verdant garden alone makes it worth the stay. Rooms are immaculate, and some are decorated with the owner's artwork. Breakfast is available for €8. Sofia is inland, 400m east of the ferry quay.

★ Paros Bay RESORT €€
(Map p204; ☑ 22840 21140; www.parosbay.com; s/d/tr from €100/119/140; ❄ 🛜 🏊) A five-minute drive from town yet with all the seclusion and comfort of a beach resort, Paros Bay consists of airy, whitewashed rooms surrounding a saltwater pool and fringed by lush grounds. There's a good Mediterranean restaurant and bar on-site if you want to stay put.

Hotel Dina
HOTEL €€

(Map p206; ✆22840 21325; www.hoteldina.com; Agora (Market St); s/d/tr €80/90/120; ☺May-Oct; ❋☎) Smack-bang in the heart of the Old Town, these eight family-run rooms are a find. They have whitewashed walls and wrought-iron beds, and are spotless and comfortable. Each room has a small balcony, some looking out over Market St, with shared courtyards and verandas in the traditional building's centre. Hostess Dina is a mine of information.

Rooms Mike
PENSION €€

(Map p206; ✆22840 22856; http://roomsmike. com; studio €100; ❋☎) A popular and friendly place, Mike's has a great location within view of the ferry quay. Your only option here are recently renovated, self-contained, two-person studios with kitchens. Mike's sign is easy to spot from the quay – away to the left.

La Selini
GUESTHOUSE €€

(Map p206; ✆22840 23106; www.laselini.com; s/d/tr €75/95/120; ☺Apr-Oct; ❋☎) La Selini shines under the care of its North American owner, Lou Ann. A short walk from Livadia Beach, the cheerful complex offers bright, comfy rooms and studios sleeping up to four. Upper rooms have a sea view.

Argonauta Hotel
BOUTIQUE HOTEL €€

(Map p206; ✆22840 21440; www.argonauta. gr; Plateia Mavrogenous; d/tr/ste incl breakfast €128/135/275; ☺Apr-Oct; ❋☎) Right on the main town square, the Argonauta offers snug rooms, airy suites with balconies and boutique stylings, plus some downright lovely common areas. See the website for nearby studios and apartments. A top location with its own restaurant and cafe, plus the attractions of Market St are just out the front door.

✗ Eating

★ Cafe Distrato
CAFE €

(Map p206; ✆22840 25175; G Gravari; mains €5-12; ☺8am-late) Dine outside under a leafy canopy at this friendly place that will draw you back. This casual cafe exudes wholesomeness, and is attached to a shop selling local food products. The crowd-pleasing menu lists crêpes, sandwiches, burgers, pastas and salads, plus superb milkshakes, cocktails and local wines. Look for the huge tree over the street.

Symposium
CAFE €

(Map p206; ✆22840 24147; http://cafesymposium. gr; mains from €8; ☺9am-3.30pm & 6pm-midnight) A gorgeous location under a massive bougainvillea tree adds to the delicious light meals, sophisticated atmosphere and tasteful jazz and classical music to make this a top place to hang out in Parikia. Head into the back of town to find this haven away from the full-on hustle and bustle. The salads are wonderful.

★ Trata Fish Taverna
SEAFOOD €€

(Map p206; ✆22840 24651; mains €12-20; ☺noon-3am) A five-minute walk from the port, this family-run place has been going strong for two decades. You come here for one thing only: some of the best fish and seafood on Paros, from octopus stew and crispy fried prawns, eaten in their shells, to freshly grilled squid and catch of the day.

Ephessus
GREEK €€

(✆22840 22520; www.parosweb.com/ephessus; Livadia Beach; mains €8-15; ☺10am-late) Sit in the beachfront, lantern-filled garden, then dig into a dish of Greek or Anatolian cuisine from Ephessus' wood-fired oven, and you'll understand why this restaurant is so popular. Try the *manti* (Anatolian ravioli), the *peinirli* (traditional pizza) or take a look at the specials the chef has cooked up for the day.

Levantis
GREEK €€

(Map p206; ✆22840 23613; www.levantisrestaurant. com; Agora (Market St); dishes €13-22; ☺7-11pm May-Oct) A vine-covered courtyard and whitewashed interior with splashes of modern art create a polished setting for some of the Cyclades' finest contemporary Greek cuisine. Savour inspired combinations like chicken and pistachio dolmadhes; slow-braised honey-spiced lamb and fennel; and orange risotto with garlic prawns. Book ahead.

♑ Drinking & Nightlife

★ Sativa Music Bar
COCKTAIL BAR

(Map p206; ✆22840 28307; www.facebook.com/ sativaparos; G Gravari; ☺10am-3am) On the main pedestrian street in Old Town, this bustling cafe and brunch spot by day transforms into a popular cocktail bar by night, with the sultry Moroccan decor providing the ideal backdrop for original cocktails and live music.

★ Bebop
BAR

(Map p206; ✆22840 28075; ☺9am-4am) Climb the steps up to this waterfront spot beneath the *kastro* with its outdoor areas, including a sunset-primed rooftop terrace. Go for one of the original cocktails such as Spicy Clown (bergamot liqueur, cucumber juice, pink peppercorns) or come for brunch and coffee. Enjoy the live-music events, especially jazz.

Koukoutsi
BAR

(Map p206; 6933020592; Plateia Mavrogenous; ☺8am-late) On the inland back corner of the main square, this traditional hangout is a gem. Small and lively, with walls covered in posters and wooden benches filled with cushions, come here to mix with older locals, nibble on mezedhes and sip juices, coffees, beer or a shot of ouzo.

ℹ️ Information

On the waterfront opposite the bus terminal, **Travel to Paros** (Map p206; ☎22840 24245; http://traveltoparos.gr) sells ferry tickets, can advise on accommodation and car hire, and has luggage storage. You can also book various tours here.

Naoussa   Νάουσα

POP 2850

Naoussa has gradually turned from a quiet fishing village into an stylish resort and visitor destination. Perched on the shores of the large Plastira Bay, there are good beaches nearby, excellent restaurants and a number of chic beachside hotels, cafes and bars. Behind the waterfront is a maze of narrow, whitewashed streets, dotted with bars, cafes and intimidating fashion boutiques in stark white.

◉ Sights & Activities

The fun of Naoussa is to get lost wandering the streets of Old Town, and admire the crumbling remains of the 15th-century Venetian *kastro* guarding the port area.

The best beaches in the area are **Kolimbythres**, set among fabulous rock formations, and **Monastiri**, which has some good snor-

kelling. Low-key **Lageri** is also worth seeking out. **Santa Maria**, on the other side of the eastern headland, is ideal for windsurfing. They can be reached by road, but caïques run from Naoussa during July and August.

★ Moraitis Winery
WINE

(☎22840 51350; www.moraitiswines.gr; tastings €6-8; ☺10am-3pm, to 10pm Jun-Sep) Pressing grapes since 1910, the Moraitis family has it down to a fine art. Sidle up to the bar for a taste of six or more wines out of 15. Their bestseller is the Paros White, made with the island's indigenous grape, Monemvasia. It's an easy walk southeast of the centre.

Michael Zeppos
BOATING

(☎6947817125; www.mzeppos.gr) Operating primarily from Naoussa (and also from Aliki), this company offers three full-day sailing itineraries taking in the beaches of Paros, Antiparos and potentially calling in at Naxos. There are also fishing options. See the website for details; prices depend on numbers.

Kokou Riding Centre
HORSE RIDING

(Map p204; ☎22840 51818; www.horseridingparos.com) The well-established Kokou has 2½-hour morning rides (€60), venturing into the sea, and 1½-hour evening rides (€40). Pickup is available from Naoussa's main square for €5.

🛏️ Sleeping

★ Sea House
GUESTHOUSE €€

(☎22840 52198; r €107; ✻🛜) Secluded enough to be away from Naoussa's bustle yet only a stroll away, the aptly named Sea House sits right on the water. Rooms are decked out in classic Cycladic blue-and-white, come with

---

WORTH A TRIP

LEFKES

Lovely Lefkes clings to a natural amphitheatre amid hills whose summits are dotted with old windmills. Siesta is taken seriously here and the village has a general air of serenity. Just 9km southeast of Parikia on the cross-island road, it was the capital of Paros during the Middle Ages. The village's main attraction is wandering through its pristine alleyways. Consider walking here on the Byzantine path east to Marpissa.

The **Cathedral of Agia Triada** is an impressive structure with unique bell towers. On the square in front of the cathedral is **Kafeneio tis Marigos** (☎22840 44014; Lefkes; snacks from €4; ☺9am-late), a delightfully retro cafe run by Kostas serving up mama-made meatballs and cakes. For more substantial, creative Cycladic mains that use homegrown herbs and veggies, swing by **Aranto** (☎22840 44070; Lefkes; mains €10-15; ☺1pm-midnight; 🍽️), near the entrance to the village.

Out on the main road, the **Lefkes Ceramic Workshop** (☎22840 43255; ☺11.30am-10pm) features Kostas Fifas and his award-winning crackle-style ceramics. The style, passed down by Kostas' father, is unique and you can watch him at work and purchase his finished products.

rain showers and – best of all – seafront terraces for sunset-watching.

Katerina Mare
APARTMENT €€

(☎22840 51642; www.katerinamare.com; d/tr incl breakfast €120/140, apt from €160; ❄☎) In a word: lovely. Light-filled suites pristine, each with a great view and every convenience, including kitchenettes. Service is stellar. It's on a hillside southwest of the town centre.

★ Mr & Mrs White
BOUTIQUE HOTEL €€€

(☎22840 55207; https://mrandmrswhiteparos. com; d/q from €180/220; ❄☎🏊) On a hillock overlooking Naoussa from a short distance and surrounded by three pools, this wonderful boutique place combines spacious, airy, whitewashed rooms with quirky wicker features with contemporary Cycladic design and personalised service. A tranquil retreat.

★ Lilly Residence
BOUTIQUE HOTEL €€€

(☎22840 51377; www.lillyresidence.gr; ste incl breakfast €331-873; ⊙May-Oct; P❄☎🏊) Naoussa's most stylish hotel, where stone, wood and wicker combine to great effect and white is the unifying theme. The place is discreetly luxurious (eg Hermes toiletries) and grownup (no kids under 12). Just back from the water, all 11 suites have sea views (and some have private plunge pools or Jacuzzis), or you can enjoy the eye-candy pool area.

✗ Eating

There's plenty of waterfront dining and a superbly convivial atmosphere just inches from moored boats or the beach. The streets of Old Town offer more imaginative options than traditional tavernas, as well as *gyros* joints.

★ Sousouro
CAFE €

(☎22840 53113; www.facebook.com/Sousouro-CafeBar; breakfast €4-6; ⊙9am-3am) Occupying a small corner in Old Town, this cafe is big on flavour. One of the islands' best breakfast menus awaits: superfood smoothies and shakes, a selection of homemade granola with sheep's-milk yoghurt and thyme honey, and toast topped with smashed avocado or cacao hazelnut butter and banana. At night the wholesomeness makes way for killer cocktails.

★ Souvlakia Kargos
KEBAB €

(☎22840 53503; www.facebook.com/KargasParos; mains from €3; ⊙noon-1am) This souvlaki joint is a model of its kind: the pork and chicken *gyros* meat rotates enticingly on their respective spits, the pitas are filled with chips as well as the nicely seasoned meat, and there are nice Greek salads to boot. Sit in the tiny alleyway or get the food to go.

To Paradosiako
SWEETS €

(loukoumadhes €4-5; ⊙6pm-midnight) An essential evening stop for a serve of To Paradosiako's legendary fresh doughy balls of goodness known as *loukoumadhes* (Greek doughnuts). It's a self-service operation: add honey, chocolate sauce and/or ice cream.

★ Tao's Center
THAI €€

(Map p204; ☎22840 28882; www.taos-greece.com; Ambelas; mains €10-14; ⊙Apr-Dec; ☎) ✎ This wellness retreat and meditation centre has an excellent restaurant open to nonguests, serving Thai curries courtesy of the Thai chef, plus pan-Asian dishes, such as gyoza.

The centre is reached by turning off the main road to Ambelas and then following signs along a mainly surfaced track.

Taverna Glafkos
MEDITERRANEAN €€

(☎22840 52100; mains €9-18; ⊙1pm-midnight) With tables practically on the sand on Agios Dimitrios Beach, this tucked-away place specialises in Mediterranean seafood with global touches. Try steamed mussels and grilled calamari, or dig into shrimp *saganaki* or black risotto with cuttlefish – all are great paired with local white wine.

🍷 Drinking & Nightlife

★ Santé
COCKTAIL BAR

(☎22840 51747; www.santecocktailbar.com; ⊙10am-3.30am) Several tiny blocks south of the waterfront, in the shade of a huge eucalyptus tree, Santé is a good spot for coffee during the day, but things only really kick off come nightfall. Come for the signature Aegean Mist of Caramel Passion, expertly mixed from high-quality ingredients, and chill out to a soundtrack of mellow beats.

★ Sommaripa Consolato
BAR

(☎22840 55233; www.facebook.com/Sommaripa-Consolato; ⊙9.30am-3am) The owner opened this elevated cafe-bar in the former home of his grandparents – how fortunate that it's right in the hub of Naoussa's small port (above Mario's restaurant), making for great people-watching from the terraces. First-class drinks, snacks and service, too.

To Takimi
BAR

(Music Cafe; ☎22840 55095; www.facebook.com/takimiparos; ⊙5pm-late) Just south of the main square, this is where locals come to drink beer or ouzo and listen to live music, often played on the traditional string instruments waiting on the walls. Everything from *rembetika* (blues) to rock goes down here.

ℹ️ Information

Erkyna Travel (☑ 22840 53180; www. erkynatravel.com) Sells ferry tickets and can help with accommodation, car hire, excursions, water sports and boat trips to other islands. It's on the main road into town.

ℹ️ Getting There & Away

Naoussa is 8km north of Parikia. Frequent buses (p205) link the two towns directly (€2). The **bus stop** is some way inland from the waterfront, where there's a large public car park (most of the Old Town area is pedestrian-only). Old Town is east of here.

If you've got rental wheels, there is free public parking on the way into town.

Around Paros

On the southeast coast is Paros' top beach, **Hrysi Akti (Golden Beach)** (Map p204), with good swimming, windsurfing and diving operations.

Paros' west coast, around **Pounta**, is the hub for top water sports activities: a long shallow-water shoreline and perfect side-shore wind conditions make it perfect for all skill levels of kiteboarder or windsurfer.

Paros is moderately popular with hikers. **Paros Park** (Map p204; ☑ 22840 53573; www.parospark.com; Agios Ioannis Detis Peninsula) is an 80-hectare park north of Naoussa that features impressive rock formations, caves, hidden coves and gorgeous beaches. There's three walking trails, a museum, monastery, an ancient theatre that now hosts festivals and the extremely popular open-air **Cine Enastron** (Map p204; ☑ 22840 53573; www.parospark.com/cine-enastron; Paros Park; ⊙ 9.30pm Jul-Sep). The park is a 10-minute drive west, then north from Naoussa on the Agios Ioannis Detis Peninsula.

🏃 Activities

Force7 Surf Centre   WINDSURFING
(☑ 22840 41789; www.force7paros.gr) Force7 Surf Centre is a well-run centre on Hrysi Akti (Golden Beach) offering windsurfing lessons (€40 per hour; kids' classes available) and rental (€16 per hour), plus kayak (€15 per hour), stand-up paddleboard (€20 per hour) and catamaran (€50 per hour) rentals.

Paros Kite   KITESURFING
(☑ 22840 93018; www.paroskite.com; 90min intro €90) At this slick, professionally run complex at Pounta it's all about the wind: kitesurfing and windsurfing instruction (four-hour beginner course costs €250) and gear rental are offered, plus there's a surf shop, beach bar-cafe, massage and yoga.

Aegean Diving College   DIVING
(☑ 22840 43347; shore dive from €80; ⊙ 9.30am-7pm) At Hrysi Akti (Golden Beach), the Aegean Diving College has been well established since the 1990s and offers a range of dives. Dive courses are also available.

🛏️ Sleeping

The **Golden Beach Hotel** (☑ 22840 41366; www.goldenbeach.gr; Hrysi Akti; d incl breakfast €130, 4-person apt €260; ⊙ Apr–mid-Oct; ❋ 🛜) right on Hrysi Akti (Golden Beach), is a top spot that offers simple, appealing rooms and apartments in pastel colours. More important is what's outside the rooms: a splendid grassy lawn down to the shore, plus restaurant, beach bar and oodles of beach activities. Lots of fun to be had on Paros' east coast. Two-night minimum in August.

ANTIPAROS ΑΝΤΙΠΑΡΟΣ
POP 1211

Antiparos lies dreamily offshore from Paros. As soon as your ferry docks, there's a distinct slowing down in the pace of things. The main village and port (also called Antiparos) are relaxed. There's a touristy gloss around the waterfront and main street, but the village runs deep inland to quiet squares and alleyways that give way suddenly to open fields.

The rest of the island runs to the south of the main settlement through quiet countryside. There are several decent beaches, especially at Psaralyki near town, and further south at Glyfa and Soros, plus one of Greece's most celebrated caves. Antiparos has recently acquired a 'secret getaway' factor that puts it on the radar of those who don't like to be disturbed: Euro royalty, Hollywood stars and A-list rock stars holiday here.

👁️ Sights

★ **Cave of Antiparos**   CAVE
(Map p204; http://antiparos.gr; adult/child €6/3; ⊙ 10am-5pm Jul & Aug, to 3pm Apr-Jun & Sep) Signposted off the main coastal road some 10km

south of the port, this huge and atmospheric cave remains impressive despite much looting of stalactites and stalagmites in the past. In December 1673, Marquis de Nointel held Christmas Mass here. He and other luminaries (including King Otto and Queen Amalia of Greece) have left their graffiti on the rock formations over the centuries. Descending the 400-plus steps will give you thighs of steel. A bus runs here from the port (€1.80).

★ Antiparos Town
VILLAGE

The long pedestrianised main street of this enchanting village is lined with stylish boutiques, bars and restaurants. Follow it to the end, to the distinctive, giant plane tree of Plateia Agios Nikolaou. From here, a narrow lane leads to the remnants of the old Venetian *kastro*, entered through an archway. This old fortified settlement – defence against pirates – dates from the mid-15th century; the surviving keep is a terrific place for sunset-viewing.

Anti Art Gallery
GALLERY

(⌨ 22840 61544; www.antiartgallery.gr; ⊘ 7pm-12.30am Jun-Sep) The 'anti' Art Gallery by the *kastro* entrance has an excellent run of exhibitions, including cutting-edge photography. The brainchild of curator Mary Chatzaki, it plays an entertaining, educational role in island life. In July, the gallery takes over the *kastro* and hosts an outdoor photo exhibition.

🏃 Activities

Captain Sargos Boat Trips
BOATING

(Map p204; ⌨ 6973794876; www.sargosantiparos.gr; per person €30) Operating out of Agios Georgios, Yorgos runs three- to four-hour boat trips that include a visit to the archaeological site on nearby Despotiko Island, time to swim or laze on the island's spectacular beach, and a cruise through local sea caves. Also available for local charters.

Blue Island Divers
DIVING

(⌨ 22840 61767; www.blueisland-divers.gr; 1-/2-tank dive €65/85, PADI certification from €240) On the northern waterfront, this well-regarded operator and its knowledgeable, enthusiastic instructors introduce you to the wrecks, reefs and caves of Antiparos. Fun dives, night dives and all manner of PADI courses on offer.

🛏 Sleeping

Camping Antiparos
CAMPGROUND €

(Map p204; ⌨ 22840 61221; www.camping-antiparos.gr; campsite per adult/child/tent €8/4/3;

⊘ May-Sep; 🗺) This chilled-out beachside campground is planted with bamboo 'compartments' and cedars. There's a restaurant and minimarket and Greece's first nudist beach is just a few minutes' away. It's a 10-minute walk north of the port (pickup is available).

★ Casa Flora
GUESTHOUSE €€

(⌨ 6937970452; https://casaflora.gr; s/d/apt €63/70/90; 🗺) Near the Kastro, an Athenian couple run a clutch of spotless, spacious rooms and studios. Their knowledge of the island and its history is superb (Flora is a historian) and as a bonus (if you love felines), they look after 16 beautiful cats.

★ Artemis Hotel
HOTEL €€

(⌨ 22840 61460; www.artemisantiparos.com; r incl breakfast €100-110, apt €200; ⊘ Apr–mid-Oct) The family-run, elegant, marble-lined rooms at Artemis (at the northern end of the harbour) are compact but well priced, and have lovely private terraces (a bit extra for a sea-view room). The common areas are stylishly appealing, and the apartments sleep a family of four.

🍴 Eating

Taverna Yorgis
GREEK €

(⌨ 22840 61362; mains €7-12; ⊘ noon-10pm) To locals, this food speaks of quintessential Greek cooking: classic recipes executed with flair and attention to detail. The crisp, fresh Greek salad, topped with a herb-sprinkled slab of feta, is exemplary, and you'll find yourself chasing the last morsels of the *pasticcio* (Greek lasagne) around your plate with a sigh of pleasure. On the main street.

5F Taverna
KEBAB €

(⌨ 22840 61347; www.facebook.com/Taverna.5F; mains from €3; ⊘ noon-2.30am) Run with love and attention by Yorgis and Chrysoula, this souvlaki joint is Antiparos' finest. The pillow-soft pitta bread stuffed with smoky, moreish pork *gyros* is deeply satisfying, the souvlaki is on the right side of spiced, crisped meat and you can fill your boots for under €10.

★ Kalokeri
GREEK €€

(⌨ 22840 63037; mains €14-20; ⊘ 6.30-11.30pm) This imaginative restaurant on the main street executes modern Greek dishes with flair and seasonal ingredients. There's the tang of red mullet tartare with the pop-pop-pop of tobiko roe, the high notes of lemon against the earthiness of the dolmadhes and

Naxos potatoes stuffed with Paros Gruyère and Andros' smoked ham.

Captain Pipinos TAVERNA €€

(Map p204; ☑ 22840 21823; http://captainpipi nos.com; mains €8-15; ⊙ 11am-10pm) In the island's south, right on the water at Agios Georgios and with vies of neighbouring uninhabited Despotiko, Captain Pipinos is an old-school fish taverna. Octopus dishes are a top pick (you'll see them drying), as is anything with fresh fish (sold by the kilo).

ℹ Getting There & Away

In summer, frequent small passenger boats depart for Antiparos from Parikia (€5), and numerous operators offer day cruises taking in the beaches of both islands, departing from Parikia, Pounta, Aliki and Naoussa.

There's also a regular car ferry that runs from Pounta on the west coast of Paros to Antiparos (one way €1.20, per scooter €1.60, per car €6, one or two services hourly from 7am until midnight, 10 minutes). You can take a vehicle rented on Paros to Antiparos on this ferry.

ℹ Getting Around

Oliaris Tours (☑ 22840 61231; www.antiparos travel.gr) runs a bus service from the port to the cave, and another to the east-coast beaches as far as Agios Georgios; tickets cost €3 one way. The schedule varies with the season; in theory, buses run from April to September.

Wheels can be hired from **Aggelos** (☑ 22840 61626; http://antiparosrentacar.com; ⊙ 9am-8pm), the first office as you come from the ferry quay. Cars start at about €50 per day (high season), scooters €20 and bicycles €5 to €10.

Dimitris (☑ 22840 61286; ⊙ 8am-8pm) rents new mountain bikes (€5), electric bikes (€12), plus scooters (from €15) and ATVs (from €20).

NAXOS ΝΑΞΟΣ

The largest of the Cyclades, Naxos packs a lot of bang for its buck. Its main town of Hora has a gorgeous waterfront and steep cobbled alleys below its hilltop *kastro* and Venetian mansions. You'll also find isolated beaches, atmospheric mountain villages, ancient sites and marble quarries.

Naxos was a cultural centre of Classical Greece and Byzantium, and Venetian and Frankish influences also left their mark. Its mountains form rain clouds, and consequently Naxos is more fertile and green than most of the other Cyclades islands. It produces olives, grapes, figs, citrus fruit, corn and potatoes. Mt Zeus (also known as Mt Zas; 1004m) is the Cyclades' highest peak and home to enchanting villages such as Halki and Apiranthos.

ℹ Getting There & Away

BOAT

Like Paros, Naxos is something of a ferry hub in the Cyclades, with conventional and fast ferries making regular calls to/from Piraeus, plus links to/from the mainland port of Rafina via the northern Cyclades. Boat services from Naxos.

DESTINATION	DURATION	FARE (€)	FREQUENCY
Aegiali (on Amorgos)	2¼-5hrs	12	1-2 daily
Anafi	7½hrs	13	2 weekly
Astypalea	4hrs	20	3 weekly
Donousa	1¼-3¾hrs	7	8 weekly
Folegandros	2¾-3¼hrs	11-43	2-3 daily
Ios	45mins-1¾hrs	16-43	2-3 daily
Iraklia	1-5hrs	7	1-2 daily
Iraklio	4hrs	78	daily
Katapola (on Amorgos)	1¼-3¼hrs	11-30	2-3 daily
Koufonisia	45mins-2½hrs	8-26	2-4 daily
Milos	2¼-6hrs	17-42	3-4 daily
Mykonos	35mins-1½hrs	28-39	6-10 daily
Paros	45mins-1½hrs	6-23	6-8 daily
Piraeus	4-8½hrs	37-57	4-8 daily
Rafina	3½-5hrs,	42-46	4-6 daily
Santorini	1¼-2¼hrs	22-44	5-7 daily
Schinousa	1¼-1¾hrs	7	8 weekly
Sikinos	3hrs	7	3 weekly
Syros	1¼-3hrs	9-35	2-3 daily
Tinos	1¼-2½hrs	35-42	4-5d d

AIR

There are several daily flights to/from Athens (around €81, 40 minutes) with Olympic Air (www. olympicair.com) and Sky Express (www.skyex press.gr).

Naxos

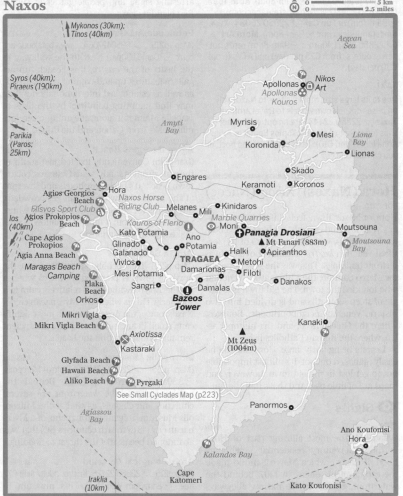

Map labels:
- Mykonos (30km); Tinos (40km)
- Aegean Sea
- Syros (40km); Piraeus (190km)
- Apollonas; Nikos Art; Apollonas Kouros
- Amyti Bay
- Myrisis
- Mesi; Liona Bay
- Koronida; Lionas
- Parikia (Paros; 25km)
- Engares
- Skado
- Keramoti; Koronos
- Hora; Agios Georgios Beach
- Naxos Horse Riding Club
- Flisvos Sport Club
- Ios (40km)
- Agios Prokopios Beach
- Melanes; Mili; Kinidaros
- Marble Quarries
- Kouros of Flerio
- Moni
- Panagia Drosiani
- Moutsouna
- Cape Agios Prokopios
- Kato Potamia
- Ano Potamia
- Mt Fanari (883m); Moutsouna Bay
- Agia Anna Beach
- Glinado; Galanado
- Halki; Apiranthos
- Maragas Beach Camping
- Vivlos; TRAGAEA; Metohi
- Danakos
- Mesi Potamia; Damarionas; Filoti
- Plaka Beach
- Sangri; Damalas
- Orkos; Bazeos Tower
- Mikri Vigla
- Mikri Vigla Beach
- Kanaki
- Axiotissa; Mt Zeus (1004m)
- Kastaraki
- Glyfada Beach
- Hawaii Beach
- Aliko Beach; Pyrgaki
- See Small Cyclades Map (p223)
- Agiassou Bay
- Panormos
- Ano Koufonisi Hora
- Kalandos Bay
- Iraklia (10km)
- Cape Katomeri
- Kato Koufonisi

Scale: 0 — 5 km / 0 — 2.5 miles

❶ Getting Around

TO/FROM THE AIRPORT

The **airport** (JNX; Map p213; www.naxos.net/airport) is 3km south of Hora. There's no shuttle bus, but buses to Agios Prokopios Beach and Agia Anna pass close by. A taxi costs around €15; luggage costs extra.

BUS

Frequent buses run to Agios Prokopios Beach (€1.80) and Agia Anna (€1.80) from Hora. Seven buses daily serve Filoti (€2.50) via Halki (€2.2); five serve Apiranthos (€3.30) via Filoti and Halki; and at least two serve Apollonas (€6.40), Pyrgaki

(€2.50) and Melanes (€1.80). There are less frequent departures to other villages.

Buses leave from the end of the ferry quay in Hora; timetables are posted outside the bus information office (p219), diagonally left and across the road from the bus stop. You have to buy tickets from the office or from the machine outside (not from the bus driver).

CAR & MOTORCYCLE

Rates for hire cars during peak season range from about €45 to €65 per day, quad bikes from €30 and scooters from €20. Hire from **Naxos Auto Rent** (☏ 22850 41350; http://naxosautorent.com; ☉ 9am-7pm), **Rental Center** (☏ 22850 23395; www.rentalcenter.com.gr;

Aristidi Protopapadaki; ⊙9am-8pm), **Auto Tour** (☑22850 25480; www.naxosrentacar.com; ⊙9am-7pm) or **Fun Car** (☑22850 26084; www.funcarandrides.com; ⊙9am-8pm). **Moto Art** (☑22850 23511; Kiprou; ⊙9am-8pm) rents out new scooters (from €25 per day) and ATVs (from €30 per day).

TAXI

Due to its large size, most visitors to Naxos rely on buses or their own wheels to travel around. **Taxis** (☑22850 22444) are an option for shorter trips (eg Hora to Agios Prokopios Beach or Agia Anna for around €10). Taxis cluster at the port, or you can call one.

Hora (Naxos) Χώρα (Νάξος)

POP 7070

Hora, or Naxos Town, feels different from other Cycladic island capitals. It's bigger and busier, for starters, with the remnants of the fortified Venetian *kastro* looming above the waterfront buildings. This was the seat of power for Marco Sanudo, the 13th-century Venetian who founded the town. The old town is a tangle of steep footpaths and is divided into two historic Venetian neighbourhoods: Bourgos, where the Greeks lived, and the hilltop Kastro, where the Roman Catholics lived.

Despite being fairly large, Hora can still be easily managed on foot. It's almost impossible not to get lost in the old town, however, and maps are of little use. And that's half the fun.

◉ Sights

★ Kastro   AREA

(Map p215) The most alluring part of Hora is the 13th-century residential neighbourhood of Kastro, which Marco Sanudo made the capital of his duchy in 1207. Behind the waterfront, get lost in the narrow alleyways scrambling up to its hilltop location. Venetian mansions survive in the centre of Kastro, as do the remnants of the castle, the **Tower of Sanoudos** (Map p215). To see the Bourgos area of the old town, head into the winding backstreets behind the northern end of Paralia.

★ Temple of Apollo   ARCHAEOLOGICAL SITE

(The Portara; ⊙24hr) FREE From Naxos Town Harbour, a causeway leads to the Palatia islet and the striking, unfinished Temple of Apollo, Naxos' most famous landmark (also known as the Portara or 'Doorway'). Simply two marble columns with a crowning lintel, it makes an arresting sight, and people gather at sunset for splendid views.

Petalouda Art Gallery   GALLERY

(Map p215; ☑6950427064; www.petalouda-art.com; ⊙10am-11.30pm) Next to the walkway to the heart of the *kastro*, this French-run art gallery features up-and-coming young artists, as well as established international ones. You may find haunting paintings by the likes of Isabelle Malmezat alongside antique ceremonial masks from Gabon and the Congo.

Agios Georgios Beach   BEACH

(Map p215) Conveniently located just south of the waterfront is sandy Agios Georgios, Naxos' town beach. It's backed by hotels and tavernas at the town end (where it can get crowded), but it runs for some way to the south, where you can spread out a little. Its shallow waters make it great for families.

Grotta Beach   BEACH

(Map p215) This pebbly, stony beach to the north of town is pounded by waves when a northerly is blowing, but is relatively calm in a southerly. This is where the Mycenaean city of Naxos, one of the Aegean region's most significant, stood in ancient times. There are ancient remains underwater off the beach.

Mitropolis Museum   MUSEUM

(Map p215; ☑22850 24151; Plateia Mitropolis; ⊙8.30am-3pm Wed-Mon) FREE Behind the northern end of the waterfront are several churches and chapels, as well as the Mitropolis Museum. It features fragments of a Mycenaean city (13th to 11th centuries BC) that was abandoned because of the threat of flooding.

Archaeological Museum   MUSEUM

(Map p215; ☑22850 22725; Kastro; adult/child €3/free; ⊙8am-3pm Wed-Mon) This museum in Kastro is housed in the former Jesuit school where novelist Nikos Kazantzakis was briefly a pupil. It contains fascinating finds from the Ionic and Doric eras, plus Mycenaean vases, but the most startling are the splendid Early Cycladic marble figurines.

Folk Museum Collection   MUSEUM

(Map p215; ☑22850 25561; Old Market St; €3; ⊙10am-2pm & 7-10pm) This small, well-curated, privately owned collection gives a digestible account of elements that make Naxos' history special: succinct displays cover farming, beekeeping, weaving, bread-making, winemaking and cheese production.

Hora (Naxos)

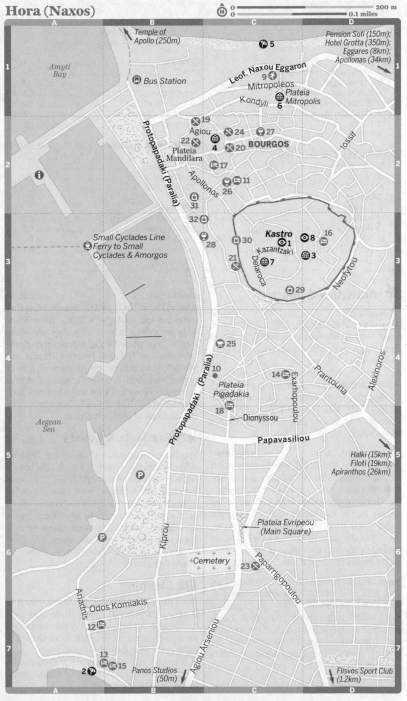

Hora (Naxos)

🏃 Activities & Tours

⭐ **Naxos Bike** CYCLING
(Map p215; ☎6932795125, 22850 25887; www.
naxosbikes.com; bike hire per day from €10) Get all
your equipment at this place near the port,
from electric (€35 per day), road, mountain
and trekking bikes to children's seats. Local
expert Giannis knows everything there is to
know about bikes, and can set you up with
maps to get you exploring. He also leads
three-hour tours (per person €30, minimum
two people).

Flisvos Sport Club WINDSURFING
(Map p213; ☎22850 24308; www.flisvos-sportclub.
com; Agios Georgios Beach) Well-organised beach
club offering a range of windsurfing courses
(one-hour private lesson from €50, three-day
course €225), catamaran sailing (one-hour
rental from €48) and mountain-bike rental
(from €18 per day). It also has a cool cafe, accommodation and the option of beach volleyball, a fitness centre and yoga.

Naxos Horse Riding Club HORSE RIDING
(Map p213; ☎6948809142; www.naxoshorseriding.
com; 2/3hr ride €50/60; ⊙Mon-Sat) Organises
daily morning, afternoon and sunset horse
rides inland and on beaches. Staff can arrange
pickup and return to and from the stables. Beginners, young children and advanced riders
are all catered for.

Naxos Tours TOURS
(Map p215; ☎22850 24000; www.naxostours.net;
island bus tour adult/child €30/15; ⊙8am-10pm)
This waterfront agency organises an island
tour by bus, guided walks in more remote villages such as Melanes, Potamia, Tragaia and
Moni (prices depend on number of participants) plus daily cruises. There are frequent
excursion boats to Delos and Mykonos, Santorini, and Iraklia and Koufonisia, plus sailing
explorations of southern Naxos.

🎉 Festivals & Events

Special evening cultural events are held inside the Venetian Castle in June for the hugely
popular **Domus Festival** (☎22850 22387; www.
naxosfestival.com; Kastro; event admission varies;
⊙June). Posters around town advertise what's
on the horizon. It may be traditional music
and dance concerts, classical piano recitals,
bouzouki, or jazz and blues. There may even
be screenings of *Zorba the Greek*. There's an
inside venue on the off-chance it rains.

🛏 Sleeping

Hora has plenty of accommodation (much of
it open year-round), particularly midrange
hotels and studios, including numerous options backing the town beach, Agios Georgios.
Book early for July and August.

The best campgrounds are at the beaches
south of Hora (Agia Anna and Plaka); minibuses meet the ferries.

★**Venetian Suites** APARTMENT €€
(Map p215; ☑ 22850 23057, 6906389291; venetian-suites.naxos@gmail.com; apt €125; ❄️🛜) Hidden in the maze of tiny medieval streets, these are among the most atmospheric of Naxos' lodgings. In spite of the heavy wooden beams, these studio apartments seem light and bright, and bedroom nooks are accessed through medieval stone arches. Mod cons abound, including rain showers and fully equipped kitchenettes.

★**Hotel Grotta** HOTEL €€
(☑ 22850 22215; www.hotelgrotta.gr; off Kontoleontos; d incl breakfast €125; ❄️🛜) Located on high ground overlooking the *kastro* and main town, this excellent family-run hotel has immaculate rooms in soothing creams and baby blues, great sea views from the front, spacious public areas and a cool indoor Jacuzzi area. It's made even better by the cheerful, attentive atmosphere. A rooftop garden bar and private terraces are extra boons.

★**Panos Studios** HOTEL €€
(☑ 22850 26078; www.studiospanos.com; d/tr/apt/ste €115/155/160/250; ⊙ May-Oct; ❄️🛜) Decked out in chic whites and charcoals, these stylish, well-equipped rooms and apartments sit a block back from Agios Georgios Beach and come with undulating headboards and mirrors, as well as kitchenettes and balconies. There are free port and airport transfers and a friendly welcome, including complimentary welcoming wine from the barrel at reception.

Hotel Glaros BOUTIQUE HOTEL €€
(Map p215; ☑ 22850 23101; www.hotelglaros.com; Agios Georgios Beach; d/ste from €70/225; ⊙ Apr-Oct; ❄️@🛜) Edgy yet homey, simple yet plush, this well-run and immaculate 13-room hotel has a seaside feel in its boutique fit-out. Service is thoughtful, there's an indoor Jacuzzi, the beach is only a few steps away and it's adults only. Breakfast is €10. Two-night minimum in July and August.

Pension Sofi PENSION €€
(☑ 22850 23077; www.pensionsofi.gr; d/tr from €70/90; ❄️🛜) Run by members of the friendly Koufopoulos family, guests at Pension Sofi are met with family-made wine or cake and immaculate rooms, each with a renovated bathroom and a basic kitchen. Sofi is a short walk back from the waterfront. Let them know your arrival details for a complimentary pickup at the port. Rates halve out of high season.

Nikos Verikokos Studios HOTEL €€
(Map p215; ☑ 22850 22025; www.nikos-verikokos.com; d/tr €100/130; ❄️🛜) Friendly Nikos maintains immaculate rooms in the heart of the old town, and is handy to everything. Some have balconies and sea views, all have little kitchenettes. It offers port pickup with prearrangement. A rooftop veranda provides further vistas.

Xenia Hotel HOTEL €€
(Map p215; ☑ 22850 25068; www.hotel-xenia.gr; Plateia Pigadakia; s/d/tr incl breakfast from €92/117/125; ❄️🛜) Sleek and minimalist, this hotel is in the heart of the action in the old town, close to everything, and the staff are attentive. While the neutral tones and blonde-wood furnishings are not exactly unique, balconies overlook the old town and thick glass keeps the noise out. Superb central location. Restaurants and cafes are right outside the front door.

Hotel Galini HOTEL €€
(Map p215; ☑ 22850 22114; www.hotelgalini.com; s/d incl breakfast from €70/120; ❄️🛜) A nautical theme lends this superfriendly, family-run place loads of character. Updated, spacious

CYCLADES HORA (NAXOS)

OFF THE BEATEN TRACK

DINING OFF THE BEATEN TRACK

Parikia and Naoussa don't have the monopoly on Paros' best dining. It's worth travelling to the tiny villages of **Prodromos** and **Dryos** to seek out the best in traditional local cooking, with most ingredients sourced from the families' own farms and there being plenty of inexpensive barrel wine to wash it down with.

Taverna Tsitsanis (☑ 22840 41375; www.facebook.com/tavernatsitsanis; Prodromos; mains €8-14; ⊙ noon-3pm & 6.30-10pm) 🍴 is Paros' oldest tavern, going strong since 1969 and serving terrific meatballs, cuttlefish stewed in wine and more.

Restaurant Anna (Map p204; ☑ 22840 41015; http://restaurant-anna.com; Dryos; mains €8-13; ⊙ noon-3pm & 6.30-11pm; ☑) 🍴 cooks up goat with lemon sauce, as well as rabbit casserole, artichoke stew, or whatever happens to be fresh from the family farm.

LOCAL KNOWLEDGE

DRINKING IN THE HISTORY

It was on Naxos that an ungrateful Theseus is said to have abandoned Ariadne after she helped him escape the Cretan labyrinth. She didn't pine long, and was soon entwined with Dionysos, the god of wine and ecstasy, and the island's favourite deity. Naxian wine has long been considered a useful antidote to a broken heart (though it's not easy on the palate unless you love vinegar).

rooms have small balconies, plus some rooms have creative decor fashioned from seashells and driftwood. The location is first rate – close to the old town and the beach – and the breakfast is hearty. Prices drop significantly outside high season.

Despina's Rooms   PENSION €€
(Map p215; ☑ 22850 22356; www.despinarooms.gr; Kastro; s/d €60/70; ❋ 🐾) Fronted by a sign featuring a buxom mermaid, Despina has been renting simple, comfy rooms for more than 50 years, and they're a steal. Tucked away in the heart of Kastro (reached with a climb), some have sea views. Rooms on the roof terrace are popular despite their smaller size. There's a communal kitchen.

★**Traditional Castle House**   RENTAL HOUSE €€€
(Map p215; ☑ 6986686493; house €160; 🐾) There are few more atmospheric lodgings in Naxos than this beautifully restored Venetian house, right in the heart of the *kastro*. The heavy wooden beams, exposed stone wall and heavy dark-wood furniture blend seamlessly with modern conveniences, the fully equipped kitchen, nautically themed paintings and a playful scattering of traveller paraphernalia.

There are two bedrooms (plus loft bed).

Nissaki Beach Hotel   HOTEL €€€
(Map p215; ☑ 22850 25710; www.nissaki-beach.com; Agios Georgios Beach; d/ste incl breakfast from €285/355; ❋ 🐾 ≋) Hard to beat on the island for luxury, Nissaki Beach Hotel offers up a seaside restaurant and gorgeous pool area right on Agios Georgios Beach. The rooms are elegant, with colourful splashes of contemporary art; the suites have large sea-view terraces. A very good breakfast is included in the rates.

 Eating

Hora has fantastic, varied dining. For the freshest seafood, head to the tavernas on the waterfront. Naxian cheeses, sausages and potatoes are also well worth taste-testing and are found in menus of traditional tavernas and fusion restaurants alike.

★**Maro's Tavern**   GREEK €
(Map p215; ☑ 22850 25113; mains €7-16; ⊙ lunch & dinner) There's no sea view or old-town romance here, but the locals don't care. They're too busy tucking into mammoth portions of delicious, good-value food. The zucchini balls (fritters) are tasty, and the *mousakas* and *pastitsio* (layers of buttery macaroni and seasoned minced lamb) will get you through a siege. It's just south of Plateia Evripeou.

★**Doukato**   GREEK €€
(Map p215; ☑ 22850 27013; www.facebook.com/doukatonaxos; Old Town; mains €9-17; ⊙ 6pm-1am May-Oct, weekends only rest of year) One of the Cyclades' best eating experiences, in a magical setting that was once a monastery, church and a school, Doukato is deserving of accolades. Owner Dimitris grows much of the produce, or sources it locally. The result? Naxian specialities such as *gouna* (sun-dried mackerel), *kalogeras* (beef, eggplant and cheese) and the delicious Doukato 'Special' souvlaki.

★**L'Osteria**   ITALIAN €€
(Map p215; ☑ 22850 24080; www.facebook.com/osterialenuovestorie; mains €11-18; ⊙ 6.30pm-1am Tue-Sun) This authentic Italian eatery is tucked away in a small alley uphill from the harbour, beneath the *kastro* walls. Grab a table in the cute courtyard and prepare to be impressed with the likes of gnocchi stuffed with goat's cheese and pork cheek and octopus with mash and red lentils. Excellent wine list, plus delectable antipasti and Greek craft beer.

Metaxi Mas   GREEK €€
(Map p215; ☑ 22850 26425; mains €8-14; ⊙ 12.30pm-2am) Sit on the tiny, vine-shaded terrace or in the wood-and-stone interior, and join the locals for a feast of flash-fried catch of the day, tender, slow-cooked veal with lemon sauce, local cheeses and heaped portions of superlative *mousakas* and *pastitsio*. Near the northern entrance to the old town.

Lucullus   GREEK €€
(Map p215; ☑ 22850 22569; Palia Agora; mains €9-14; ⊙ 11am-11pm) Tucked into a tiny,

vine-shaded lane off Old Market St, Lucullus has been around since 1908 and claims to be Naxos' oldest taverna. Greek staples are the way to go, with excellent versions of veal *limonata* (on mashed potatoes in a lemon sauce), lamb *kleftiko* (backed with cheese) and octopus *stifado* (stewed with onions and sauce).

Labyrinth   GREEK €€
(Map p215; ✆ 22850 22253; www.facebook.com/ Labyrinth.Naxos; mains €11-18; ☺ 6pm-midnight) It's a toss-up as to which is more welcoming here: the warm interior or pretty, private courtyard. Munch through marinated vegies with grilled *manouri* (soft cheese from northern Naxos), swordfish with herbs, or seafood risotto with ouzo sauce. The name is apt: it has a sign, but is easiest to find if you enter the winding alleys from the north.

🍸 Drinking & Nightlife

There are a few large clubs at the southern end of the waterfront, and some lovely, mellow bars offering big views and cocktails from upper floors in the *kastro* neighbourhood.

★ La Vigne   WINE BAR
(Map p215; ✆ 22850 27199; www.lavignenaxos.com; ☺ 7pm-1am) The only true wine bar in Naxos is hidden in a tiny alley just behind Plateia Mandilara. It's run by two congenial French ladies who'll tell you about their carefully selected wines (mostly from around Greece and France). Excellent fusion food, too.

★ Rum Bar   BAR
(Map p215; ✆ 6948592718; www.facebook.com/ therumbarnaxos; ☺ 8pm-4am) Perched upstairs above Hora's busy waterfront, this sleek place has lovely sunset views. Open year-round, Rum Bar plays rock classics and live music. Original cocktails are the name of the game here – try the Isla Tropical, which includes a healthy dose of Naxos *kitron* (liqueur made from the leaves of the citron tree).

Naxos Cafe   BAR
(Map p215; ✆ 22850 26343; Old Market St; ☺ 8pm-2am) This atmospheric, traditional bar is small and candlelit and spills into the cobbled Bourgos street. Drink wine with the locals and listen to the occasional live music.

Kitrón   CAFE
(Map p215; ✆ 22850 27055; Protopapadaki; ☺ 8am-late) Begin your day here, with coffee and a harbour view, and end it with one of the wonderful cocktails featuring *kitron* from Halki's distillery (p221). Try the *kitron* sour or the one with Prosecco and strawberries.

🛍 Shopping

★ Antico Veneziano   ANTIQUES
(Map p215; ✆ 22850 22702; Dellaroca; ☺ 10am-1pm & 5-9pm) Inside the *kastro*, this remarkable antique shop hides inside a restored 800-year-old Venetian mansion. You'll salivate at the treasure trove of Veneziana inside, the ancient temple pillars that prop up the shop are worth the visit alone.

★ Octopus Naxos   CLOTHING
(Map p215; Palia Agora; ☺ 10am-10pm) If you're looking for something uniquely Naxian, you could do worse than these colourful T-shirts, designed in Naxos since 1988. The octopus appears in various guises.

Kohili Jewels   GIFTS & SOUVENIRS
(Map p215; ✆ 22850 22557; ☺ 10am-11pm) Hidden in the maze of small streets behind the waterfront, this is a good spot to purchase jewellery made from the Eye of Naxos, the hard shell that develops in the hole of a shellfish. The eye in the rings, necklaces, earrings and bracelets is said to bring good luck.

Papyrus   BOOKS
(Map p215; ✆ 22850 23039; ☺ 10am-2pm & 6-10pm) What began as a box of books left by a traveller has turned into a shockingly organised collection of over 10,000 secondhand books, covering multiple languages and genres. It's uphill from the port, behind Meze 2.

ℹ Information

Information Booth (Map p215; ☺ hours vary) At the ferry quay in summer. Opens when ferries arrive.

Handy online resources include www.naxos.gr.

Naxos Tours (✆ 22850 24000; www.naxostours.net; Paralia; ☺ 8am-10pm) Sells ferry tickets and organises excursions and car hire.

Zas Travel (✆ 22850 23330; www.zastravel.com; ☺ 9am-9pm) Ferry tickets, tours and car hire. Located on the harbourfront.

ℹ Getting Around

Hora is the bus hub for the island, with regular departures for various villages and beaches from the **bus station** (Map p215; ✆ 22850 22291; www.naxosdestinations.com; Harbour) next to the port.

ⓘ **ROAD TRIP**

Naxos is a big island. If you have limited time and want to see it all, we recommend renting some wheels and heading out on a road trip. It's feasible to visit Halki, Filoti, Apiranthos and Melanes in a big loop in a day, and even head further afield to Apollonas or Lionas.

The North

Heading north along the coast from Hora, the road winds and twists past the Tower of Ayia, the majestic ruins of a castle with a spectacular ocean backdrop, passing through Engares, where the Engares Olive Press (☏22850 62021; www.olivemuseum.com; ☺10am-6pm May-Sep) FREE is a worthwhile stop. Further north, the road eventually takes you to the fishing village of Apollonas. Signposted in an ancient quarry on the hillside is a colossal 7th-century BC kouros (Map p213; ☺24hr), much larger and easier to find than the Kouros of Flerio (Map p213).

Apollonas' pebble-and-sand beach is decent and tavernas line the waterfront serving fresh fish. Swing by Nikos Art (Map p213; ☏22850 67202; ☺10am-6pm May-Sep) for reasonably priced ceramics in Japanese Raku style.

Take the main road south from Apollonas towards Apiranthos and you pass a turnoff to Lionas, where a scenic 8km drive past old emery mines leads you to a lovely stony beach and a couple of tavernas, including superfriendly Delfinaki (☏22850 51290; www.delfinaki.gr; mains €8-14), serving up great home cooking and farm- and sea-fresh ingredients.

Further south of the Lionas turnoff, the road splits in two at Stavros Keramotis church; take the right fork to Moni, with its woodcarving workshops, stellar views of Mt Zeus, and the 7th-century Panagia Drosiani (Map p213; Halki–Moni Rd; entry by donation; ☺10am-7pm) that attracts pilgrims.

From Moni you can return to Hora via the marble quarries on the road between Kinidaros and Melanes, and the Kouros of Flerio, two marble statues dating back to the 7th and 6th centuries BC, signposted in an ancient marble-working area near Mili.

Southwest Beaches

Beaches south of Agios Georgios (Hora's town beach) include beautiful Agios Prokopios, which is sandy and shallow and lies in a sheltered bay to the south of the headland of Cape Mougkri. It merges with Agia Anna, a stretch of shining white sand, quite narrow but long enough to feel uncrowded towards its southern end. Development is fairly solid at Prokopios and the northern end of Agia Anna.

Sandy beaches continue as far as Pyrgaki, passing the turquoise waters of the long, dreamy Plaka Beach and gorgeous sandy bays (some popular with naturists) punctuated with rocky outcrops. You'll find plenty of restaurants, accommodation and bus stops along this stretch – it's an idyllic place for a chilled-out beach stay. Maragas Beach Camping (Map p213; ☏22850 42552; www.maragascamping.gr; Agia Anna Beach; camp sites per adult/tent €9/3, d/studio from €55/€80) has a good setup across from a long sandy strand south of Agia Anna: camping, studios and rooms, a supermarket and a taverna. There's a regular bus from Hora that stops out front.

At Mikri Vigla (http://mikrivigla.com), golden granite slabs and boulders divide the beach into two. This beach is becoming an increasingly big fish on the kitesurfing scene, with reliable wind conditions. Flisvos Kite Centre (☏6945457407; www.flisvos-kitecentre.com; equipment rental per day/week €90/350) offers kite- and windsurfing classes and rents equipment to certified surfers, as does Naxos Kitelife. You can stay next door at Orkos Beach Hotel (☏22850 75194; www.orkosbeach.gr; r/tr/f incl breakfast €81/95/126; ☺mid-May–Sep; ❄☏🖥), where rooms are clean and comfy.

There is more windsurfing and kitesurfing action in Pyrgaki, south of Mikri Vigla, reachable via an unpaved road past the Aliko promontory. Look out for Hawaii Beach and its blue waters, just north of the promontory.

Heading back home via Kastaraki and Vivlos villages, stop by the Axiotissa (Map p213; ☏22850 75107; www.facebook.com/Axiotissa; Kastraki–Vivlos Rd; mains €7-14; ☺2-11pm) taverna for one of the best meals on the island.

Halki   Χάλκη

POP 500

This village is a vivid reflection of historic Naxos, with the handsome facades of old villas and tower houses a legacy of its wealthy past as the island's long-ago capital. Today it's home to a small but fascinating collection of shops and galleries. Halki lies at the heart of the Tragaea mountainous region, about 20 minutes' drive (15km) from Hora.

The main road skirts Halki, with parking areas near the entry (from Hora) and exit of town (by the schoolyard). Pedestrian lanes lead off the main road to the picturesque square at the heart of Halki.

Paths radiate from Halki through olive groves and flower-filled meadows. The atmospheric 11th-century **Church of St Georgios Diasorites** lies a short distance to the north of the village. It contains splendid frescoes.

◉ Sights

★ Fish & Olive
GALLERY

(☑ 22850 31771; www.fish-olive-creations.com; ☺ May–mid-Oct) This gallery displays the exquisite work of Naxian potter Katharina Bolesch and her partner, artist and jewellery designer Alexander Reichardt. Each piece of work reflects ancient Mediterranean themes of fish and olives, motifs that grace the blue-and-white plates, elegant jugs, bowls and platters, and appear on Alex's prints and his delicate silver tiepins, pendants and earrings. The artists' work has been exhibited nationally and internationally. There's also a boutique selling their works a few metres from the gallery.

★ Vallindras Distillery
DISTILLERY

(☑ 22850 31220; www.facebook.com/vallindras.kitrondistillery; ☺ 10am-10pm Jul & Aug, to 5pm Apr-Jun, Sep & Oct) The Vallindras Distillery on Halki's main square has been distilling the *kitron* liqueur in the same way since 1896, passing from one generation to the next. It's made from the eponymous citrus fruit that looks like a large, lumpy lemon, and the distillery makes three varieties varying in colour and strength, as well as a spice-infused liqueur. While the exact recipe is top secret, visitors can check out the museum-like facilities, sample the wares and stock up on supplies.

The cafe/bar that specialises in *kitrón*-based cocktails is a couple of minutes' walk down a side street.

Phos Gallery
GALLERY

(☑ 22850 31118; www.phosgallery.gr; ☺ 11am-4pm May-Oct) See the island through the lens of talented photographer Dimitris Gavalas. Stunning black-and-white landscapes – mostly of Naxos – grace the walls of this gallery, along with witty conceptual prints.

✗ Eating

Dolce Vita
BAKERY €

(☑ 6981467240; snacks €3-7; ☺ 9am-8pm) Cool and inviting, with dark wood and a gramophone daring to be wound, this is the place to lounge over the amazing orange cake, coffee and ice cream.

Giannis Taverna
TAVERNA €

(☑ 22850 32294; www.yannistavern.gr; dishes €7-14; ☺ 12.30-10pm) With tables filling Halki's pretty central square under a trellis of vine leaves, Giannis is well known for traditional fare. Try *moussakas*, pork souvlaki, *pasticcio* (macaroni pie) or village sausage.

🛍 Shopping

The know-how has been passed down to **Penelope** (☑ 22850 31754) through at least

---

TRAGAEA & MT ZEUS

Naxos' lovely inland Tragaea region is a vast plain of olive groves and unspoilt villages high in the mountains, harbouring numerous little Byzantine churches. The Cyclades' highest peak, Mt Zeus (1004m; also known as Mt Zas), dominates the landscape. Filoti, on the slopes of Mt Zeus, is the region's largest village.

To climb Mt Zeus from Filoti, walk 40 minutes up to Aria Spring, a verdant fountain and picnic area, carry on another 20 minutes to the Cave of Zeus, and then climb to the summit in another hour for 360-degree views of the Cyclades.

Alternatively, if you have own wheels and want to shorten the walk, there's a junction signposted to Aria Spring and Zeus Cave, about 800m up from Filoti on the main road. This side road ends after 1.3km. From the road-end parking it's a very short walk to Aria Spring, and you can carry on to the cave and summit from there.

An option for the descent, if you hike up via the cave, is to walk down via the little chapel of Agia Marina to Filoti. You can walk down this route on waymarked track Number 2 in about 1½ hours.

Make sure to take good walking shoes, water and sunscreen.

four generations – one of two such families of weavers in Halki. Watch her incorporate traditional designs into hats, scarves, bags and tablecloths to make fab souvenirs. You'll notice a lot of red and blue – the traditional colours of Naxos.

ⓘ Getting There & Away

Halki can be visited by public bus (€2), but if you want to explore the mountainous regions of central Naxos, you're better off renting wheels.

Apiranthos   Απείρανθος

POP 711

Apiranthos seems to grow out of the stony flanks of rugged Mt Fanari (883m), about 25km east of Hora (or 10 winding kilometres from Halki). The village's unadorned stone houses and marble-paved streets reflect a rugged individualism that is matched by the villagers themselves. Many of them are descendants of refugees who migrated from Crete, and today the village's distinctive form of the Greek language has echoes of the 'Great Island'. Apiranthos people are known for their spirited politics and populism, and the village has produced a remarkable number of academics. These days, the village is famous for its crafts and excellent tavernas.

◉ Sights

Natural History Museum of Apiranthos   MUSEUM
(☑ 22850 61725; €2.50; ⊗ hours vary) This museum specialises in local flora and fauna and has a marvellous collection of shells. One section focuses on the sea, the other on the land. It's signposted off the pedestrian street.

Archaeological Museum of Apiranthos   MUSEUM
(☑ 22850 61725; ⊗ hours vary) FREE This museum is part-way along the main street. It has a marvellous collection of small Cycladian artefacts collected by mathematics professor Michael Bardani and donated to the museum.

Geological Museum of Apiranthos   MUSEUM
(☑ 22850 61725; €2; ⊗ hours vary) The Geological Museum is near the village entrance and exhibits over 2500 rare rocks from the villages of Naxos, the Cyclades, the rest of Greece and around the world.

✕ Eating

Taverna O Platanos   GREEK €
(☑ 22850 61192; mains €8-15; ⊗ 11.30am-10pm) Set beneath the shade of its namesake plane tree, this lively family restaurant is deserving of its Aegean Cuisine certification. The chunky hamburger comes filled with gooey Naxian Gruyère, the Naxian potato fries are moreish and the *platanos* (grilled pork chunks) come with a back note of oregano and thyme, and with a side of valley views.

★ Lefteris   GREEK €€
(☑ 22850 61333; mains €10-22; ⊗ noon-10pm May-Oct) With an outdoor terrace, this charming, well-regarded family taverna has the feel of an old country kitchen and serves the best food in the village. Grilled meats are a speciality here (try the lamb, cheese-stuffed burger or homemade sausages), along with moreish cheese pie, and seasonal greens with lemon.

🔒 Shopping

Gun-metal amphorae with a twinkle of mica line the street by ceramics shop **Apiranthos Art** (⊗ 10am-8pm May-Oct) on the main pedestrian drag. They are locally made, as are the beautiful utilitarian dishes of varying styles that you find inside. Also on display are a few select pieces and masks by Giannis Nanouris, a renowned artist who happens to live nearby.

ⓘ Getting There & Away

There are five daily public buses from Naxos Town to Apiranthos (€3.10), but if you are keen to explore the mountainous regions of central Naxos, you're best off renting your own wheels.

SMALL CYCLADES
ΜΙΚΡΕΣ ΚΥΚΛΑΔΕΣ

The six tiny islands that lie between Naxos and Amorgos have gone through millennia of civilisation and upheaval, from being densely populated trading centres in the days of antiquity and then fortified Venetian outposts to pirate havens and impoverished fishing backwaters during WWII before recently re-emerging in the spotlight as fashionable getaways. Today, only four have permanent populations – Iraklia, Schinousa, Ano Koufonisi (Koufonisia) and Donousa – and they remain very distinct

Small Cyclades

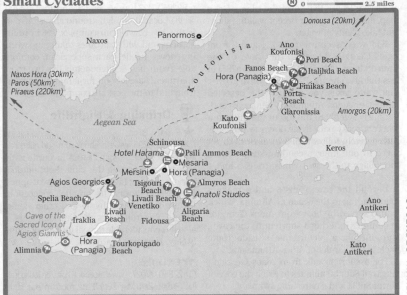

from one another with Koufonisia welcoming sun-worshippers, Schinousa and rugged Donousa appealing to hikers, and Iraklia famous for its cave pilgrimage.

Donousa is the northernmost of the group and the furthest from Naxos; the others are near the larger island's southeast coast.

❶ Information

Terrain (http://terrainmaps.gr) has an excellent map titled *Minor Cyclades*, which covers all the islands, including walking tracks.

❶ Getting There & Away

There are several connections a week between Piraeus and the Small Cyclades via Naxos, and daily connections to/from Naxos to Koufonisia (less frequent to the other islands). For ferry schedules, visit http://ferries.gr.

Blue Star Ferries (www.bluestarferries.gr) serves the Small Cyclades year-round from Piraeus via Paros and Naxos. From Naxos, three times a week the ferry calls at Donousa, then Amorgos (Aegiali) and terminates at Astypalea (in the Dodecanese). Three times a week, from Naxos the ferry stops at Iraklia, Schinousa and Koufonisia before terminating at Amorgos (Katapola).

The Small Cyclades Line runs the mainstay service, weather permitting in winter. Its sturdy *Express Skopelitis* leaves from Naxos in the afternoon daily Monday to Saturday, and calls at the Small Cyclades and Amorgos (often to both Aegiali and Katapola), returning to Naxos early the following morning.

Iraklia   Ηρακλειά

POP 150

Sparsely inhabited, Iraklia only shakes off its soporific air in July and August, when yachts dot the island's sheltered Livadi Bay and the village grows lively. Sitting amid the olive groves, ruins of Hellenic-era temples, Venetian fortifications and mysterious *speires* (spiral petroglyphs, believed to be markers of pirate treasure) are memorials of the island's long and venerable history.

Iraklia rewards hikers who explore its hilly topography on foot with secluded bays and thyme-scented solitude. There are also a couple of excellent beaches.

The port and main village of Iraklia is **Agios Georgios**. It has an attractive covelike harbour, complete with a sandy beach.

◉ Sights & Activities

A surfaced road leads off to the left of the ferry quay, and after about 1km you'll reach **Livadi**, the island's best beach. A steep 2.5km further on is **Hora** (also called Panagia). From Hora, a road carries on to **Tourkopigado Beach**.

There are seven well-marked hiking trails of varying length that cover the island. Get a map, make sure to wear decent walking shoes and take plenty of water.

Follow consecutive trails 7, 4 and 3 from Agios Georgios to get to the **Cave of the Sacred Icon of Agios Giannis** (Map p223) in less than two hours. Passing by olive groves, this route takes you through the deserted hamlet of Agios Athanasios before ascending fairly steeply to the top of the hill, from where a rocky path leads down to the cave. Alternatively, follow trail 3 from Hora to get there in one hour, ascending steeply from the village to the spot where trails 3 and 4 meet.

Beyond the cave, trails 5 and 6 make a loop, leading to the beach at Alimina, which is also served by boat from Agios Georgios in summer (offering a shortcut to the cave), and offering a picturesque seaside route back to the hamlet of Agios Athanasios.

For a shorter walk from Agios Georgios, take trail 8 for 30 minutes to reach the cove of Vorini Spilla and a refreshing swim.

🛏 Sleeping

Maïstrali GUESTHOUSE €
(☑ 22850 71807; r/apt €50/85; 🛜) Up the main road through the village from the port, Maïstrali offers a range of simple, good-value rooms and apartments with rates that tumble to €30 out of high season. It also features a shady terrace taverna that has all the Greek standards covered and is open for breakfast, lunch and dinner. A good budget option.

★ Alexandra Studios GUESTHOUSE €€
(☑ 22850 71482; http://alexandrarooms.blogspot.com; r €80; ✴🛜) Spotless, snug studios on the crest of the hill, with epic sunset views of the village and the bay from the terraces in front of each room. The convivial owner will pick you up from the port; otherwise it's a seven-minute uphill walk through Agios Georgios in the direction of Livadi Beach.

Speires Hotel BOUTIQUE HOTEL €€
(☑ 22850 77015; www.speires.gr; d/tr/ste incl breakfast €66/96/112; ☺May-Oct; ✴🛜) This stylish boutique is a short walk uphill from the port, with white decor and flash bathrooms with all the mod cons. Superior double rooms can fit a family. The terrace at the elegant on-site cafe and wine bar is a fine place to begin your immersion in Greek wine.

Anna's Place PENSION €€
(☑ 22850 74234; www.annasplace.gr; d/apt €65/90; ✴🛜) Located on high ground above the port is this lovely, well-run complex, set in pretty gardens and with balconies taking in sweeping views. Inside, each superclean, comfortable room has a kitchenette; the two-room apartments are a boon for families. Transfers from and to the port are complimentary.

🍷 Drinking & Nightlife

★ Surfin Bird COCKTAIL BAR
(☑ 6936000295; www.facebook.com/surfinbird.irakleia; Livadi Beach; ☺4pm-2am) A favourite gathering spot at sunset, this chilled-out outdoor bar overlooking Livadi Beach has great appeal for cocktail lovers: its original concoctions feature homemade thyme and other herbal syrups, plus fruit juices and Greek liqueurs. It also has considerable appeal for fans of 'Family Guy'. Have you heard…?

★ En Lefko CAFE
(☑ 22850 77027; www.facebook.com/en.leuko.iraklia; ☺8am-2am May-Sep) This rooftop bar right on top of Perigiali Supermarket is lovingly run by local couple Nikos and Anna. There are brunch menus plus cocktails, drinks and snacks until the wee hours. One of few options in Iraklia if you want a late night.

ℹ Getting There & Away

Ferry services are significantly reduced out of season. Differences in journey durations are because of routing or vessel type.

Ferry services from Iraklia:

DESTINATION	DURATION	FARE (€)	FREQUENCY
Aegiali (on Amorgos)	2¼-3¾hrs	9	4 weekly
Donousa	2¼hrs	8	4 weekly
Katapola (on Amorgos)	1¾-4¾hrs	8	1-2 daily
Koufonisia	50mins	5	1-2 daily
Naxos	1-5hrs	7	1-2 daily
Paros	1¼-6hrs	11-17.50	4 weekly
Piraeus	8hrs	20	3 weekly
Schinousa	10mins	4	9 weekly

ℹ Getting Around

There are buses in July and August only linking Agios Georgios, Livadi Beach and Hora. You can also hire **scooters** (☑ 6972755850, 6977168139; scooters/ATVs per day from €20/30; ☺hours vary) in summer.

Schinousa Σχοινούσα

POP 256

The hilly topography of small, laidback Schinousa is a palimpsest of fields, secluded coves, ancient stone walls, Byzantine chapels, and ruins of Venetian fortifications, reflecting the ebb and flow of many civilisations. During three centuries of Turkish rule, the island sheltered pirates from the Mani, but these days it attracts sunseekers after a slower pace of life, and due to the sheer number of beaches, it doesn't feel as crowded as its neighbours. The main settlement, Hora (Panagia), has a long, narrow main street lying along the breezy crest of the island. Ferries dock at the fishing harbour of Mersini. Hora is a steepish 1km walk uphill from there.

◉ Sights & Activities

Dirt tracks lead from Hora to 16 beaches all over the island. The nearest are sandy Tsigouri (Map p223; seven-minute walk) and the wide sweep of Livadi (Map p223; 15-minute walk), both south of Hora and uncrowded outside August. A 20-minute walk southeast and downhill brings you to the smaller, sand-and-pebble bays of Aligaria and Almyros with its shallow water. Thirty minutes' walk, just east of Mesaria in the north is the sheltered cove of Psili Ammos. Tsigouri, Livadi and Almyros have tavernas and/or beach bars; Hotel Harama (Map p223; ☑22850 76015; r €65; ❄☀☎) provides sustenance to beachgoers at Psili Ammos.

Aeolia   BOATING
(☑6979618233, 6982002327; boat trip €20-40) From June to September, Captain Manolis runs various daily trips on the *Aeolia*, including around the beaches of the island (€20), or to Iraklia (€20) and Keros and Koufonisia (€40). Private trips can also be arranged. Ask about the schedule where you are staying.

⌂ Sleeping & Eating

There are rooms at Mersini (the port), several hotels and domatia in Hora, and a handful of excellent options in remoter locations (near Almyros, Livadi, Tsigouri and Psili Ammos beaches). Domatia owners meet ferries from about May and will always meet booked guests. Book ahead in July and August.

Anatoli Studios   HOTEL €€
(Map p223; ☑6932371036; www.anatolistudio. com; Almiros Beach; r €100; ❄☀☎) In the southeast part of the island and reachable via a 20-minute walk from Hora, this delightful, family-run property consists of a neat cluster of airy, whitewashed rooms with mozzie nets and kitchenettes, surrounding the pool and looking out over the undulating coastline. Four beaches are an easy walk away and the restaurant serves terrific sea urchin spaghetti.

Meltemi   PENSION €€
(☑22850 71947; www.pension-meltemi.gr; d €75-85; ❄☎) Genuinely warm hospitality is the hallmark of this family run pension and restaurant in the heart of Hora. Rooms are comfy and simple. You have a choice between older rooms in the Meltemi 1 building or newer rooms in Meltemi 2. Both are good. The on-site restaurant serves up delicious homemade meals. Free port and beach transfers, too.

Iliovasilema   HOTEL €€
(☑22850 71948; www.iliovasilemahotel.gr; Hora; d incl breakfast €90; ⊙mid-May–Sep; ❄☎) In Hora, but perched at the port end of town with king-of-the-castle sunset views ('*iliovaselima*' means sunset), rooms here are small, simple and spotless. The views out towards Iraklia from the balconies are fab, and the service is warm. Rates include a good buffet breakfast.

★ Deli Bistro-Bar   GREEK €€
(☑22850 74278; mains €13-25; ⊙noon-11pm Mar-Oct) Deli consists of a top-notch restaurant with views out to Ios and Iraklia, plus a cool ground-floor cafe-bar. The Cretan owner-chef's menu is the most inventive in Schinousa, with Schinousa cheese in filo pastry with tomato marmalade and slow-cooked prawns with ouzo sitting alongside Greek-style fish carpaccio. Excellent Greek wine list and a fine selection of craft beers, too.

Fish Tavern & Rooms Mersini   SEAFOOD €€
(☑22850 71159; www.mersini.gr; mains €9-20; ⊙May-Sep; ❄☎) Down at the port, 'Aegean Cuisine' flag bearer Mersini woos diners in a garden setting with great harbour views and traditional Greek dishes and seafood (particularly lobster spaghetti and local squid) with a contemporary twist, and hand-picked wild herbs and organic vegetables from its own garden.

The five chic all-white rooms behind the taverna are some of the nicest on the island (double €85 to €110) and are a great option.

❶ Information

Paralos Travel (☑ 22850 71160; ⊙ hours vary) Sells ferry tickets and also doubles as the post office on the main street in Hora.

❶ Getting There & Away

Ferry services are significantly reduced out of season. Differences in journey durations are due to routing or vessel type.

Destinations are: Aegiali on Amorgos (€8.50, 3½ hours, six weekly), Katapola on Amorgos (€8, 1½ to 4½ hours, one to two daily), Donousa (€8, two hours, three weekly), Iraklia (€4, 10 minutes, nine weekly), Koufonisia (€4, 30 minutes, one to three daily), Naxos (€14.50, 1¼ to 1¾ hours, eight weekly), Paros (€14.50, 2¾ hours, four weekly) and Piraeus (€37,50, 6½ hours, three weekly).

❶ Getting Around

There are buses in July and August only, linking the port, Hora and the main beaches. Otherwise, walk or hire a scooter or ATV in summer from **Faros Bikes** (☑ 6977366853, 22850 71920; Hora; scooter/ATV €20/30 per day; ⊙ hours vary).

Koufonisia   Κουφονήσια

POP 399

At the heart of a mighty Cycladic civilisation in millennia past, and an impoverished backwater following the Axis occupation during WWII, the smallest of the inhabited Cyclades has been transformed into a fashionable destination – a place to wind down after the frenetic action of Mykonos and Santorini.

It's made up of three main islands, two of which, Kato Koufonisi and Keros, are uninhabited. You'll arrive at the populated, low-lying **Ano Koufonisi**. It sees a flash flood of tourism each summer season thanks to its superb beaches, good hotels and chic restaurants, and its narrow, bougainvillea-fringed main street is a joy to wander along.

◉ Sights

Koufonisia's only settlement spreads out behind the ferry quay. The older part of town, the **Hora**, sits along a low hill above the harbour, parallel to the coast, and consists of a small grid of whitewashed streets dotted with restaurants, lodgings and cafes.

At the western end of the main street, you'll reach **Loutro**, with a stony cove, small boatyard, windmill and whitewashed church.

🏖 Beaches

The village has the white-sand **Ammos Beach**, though there are nicer beaches further east and south. A 1.2km (15-minute) walk along the coast road east of the settlement brings you to the sandy **Finikas Beach** (Map p223), with calm waters and a taverna. **Fanos Beach** (Map p223), a five-minute walk east around the headland, has a beach bar and some shade. Another five minutes along the coast is **Italihda Beach** (Map p223), a favourite with naturists (though nudity becomes more overt the further east you go).

Beyond Italihda, the path skirts another headland and passes several rocky swimming places, including the deep and clear **Piscina** (10-minute walk), a swimming hole surrounded by rock that is linked to the sea. From there it's another 10 minutes to the yacht-dotted bay at **Pori** (Map p223), where a long crescent of sand slides effortlessly into the clear sea and there's a taverna and a cafe. Pori can also be reached by an inland road from Hora.

🧭 Tours

Prasinos Boat Tours   BOATING
(☑ 22850 71438, 6945042548; www.roussetoshotel. gr; ⊙ May-Sep) Hop on Captain Kostas' boat to transfer to/from various beaches around the island (€3 to €5 return depending on the beach) and Kato Koufonisi (€5 return). In peak season there's a dozen or so departures per day. There's a ticket kiosk at the port, or enquire at Prasinos travel agency.

Koufonissia Tours   BOATING
(☑ 22850 74435; www.koufonissiatours.gr) Based on the main street (and also at Villa Ostria), Koufonissia Tours organises recommended sailing, diving and sea-kayaking trips around Koufonisia and the rest of the Small Cyclades.

🛏 Sleeping

⭐ **Apollon Studios**   GUESTHOUSE €€
(☑ 22850 74464; www.apollonkoufonisia.gr; r from €60; ❄ 🛜) Decked out in blues and whites, these whitewashed, round-edged Cycladic cubes sit uphill from the port and come with small kitchenettes and little terraces overlooking the sea, and shaded by bamboo awnings. The proprietor makes guests feel at home.

⭐ **Ermis Rooms**   PENSION €€
(☑ 6972265240, 22850 71693; www.koufonisia. gr/?page_id=1255&lang=en; d €75-85; ❄ 🛜) These

immaculate rooms are in a quiet location, behind a pretty white-and-lilac exterior and a flowering garden. Ask Sofia for a balcony with sea view. At the port end of the beach, take the road uphill. Ermis Rooms is next to the pale green post office, also run by Sofia.

Villa Ostria HOTEL €€
(☑ 22850 71671; www.ostriavilla.gr; r/studio from €85/120; ❇ 🛜) On the high ground east of the town beach, the flowering, creeper-clad Cycladic cubes of Ostria hide attractive rooms and studios with quirky decor made from seashells and driftwood. Rooms have kitchenettes; spacious studios have kitchens. Take the first left after the bike-rental sign at the eastern end of the beach and climb the hillock.

Anna Villas PENSION €€
(☑ 22850 71697; www.annavillas.gr; d incl breakfast €100; ❇ 🛜) These fresh, bright studios with kitchenettes are charming and run with warmth. All have balconies overlooking either the town beach or the countryside. It's a family-friendly spot, with a lovely reading nook and summertime cafe. Take the first left after the bike-rental sign at the eastern end of the beach and climb the hill.

✖ Eating

★ Kalamia CAFE €
(☑ 22850 74444; www.facebook.com/kalamiabar; mains €7-12; ⊘ 9am-4am; 🛜) A chilled-out cafe and lively bar, Kalamia does many things well. Grab a seat under the thatched roof and dig into eggs florentine for brunch, epic burgers and quesadillas the rest of the day, and wash them down with award-winning Greek craft beers (Voria stout, 56 Isles pilsner, Chios smoked porter...). On the main street up from town beach.

★ Mikres Cyclades GREEK €€
(☑ 22850 74500; https://mikrescyclades.com; mains €10-15; ⊘ 5pm-1am; 🛜 🐾) Showcasing the best of Cycladic produce with pride, Mikres serves a short and sweet menu of mezedhes, fish and meat dishes under a stylish bamboo awning on the main street. The Schinousa *fava* is earthy and moreish, the cheese selection spans Naxos, Syros and Sifnos, and the seafood tastes as if it just leapt out of the water.

Capetan Nikolas SEAFOOD €€
(☑ 22850 71690; Loutro; mains €7-25; ⊘ dinner May-Oct) A local seafood institution, this cheerful restaurant overlooks the harbour at Loutro. Bearded Captain Nikolas may greet you at the door – you may have seen him

spearfishing around the island. The lobster salad is famous and the seafood pasta delicious. Locally caught fish, such as red mullet and sea bream, are priced by the kilo.

❶ Information

Prasinos (☑ 22850 71438; ⊘ 7am-11pm Jun-Aug) sells tours and ferry tickets on Hora's main street.

❶ Getting There & Away

Koufonisia has a growing number of July and August high-speed connections to plenty of Cyclades islands.

Ferry services from Koufonisia:

DESTINATION	DURATION	FARE (€)	FREQUENCY
Amorgos	20mins-3½hrs	7-14	2-4 daily
Donousa	1¼hrs	6	3 weekly
Folegandros	2½hrs	70	6 weekly
Iraklia	50mins	5	1-2 daily
Milos	3-4hrs	69	1-2 daily
Mykonos	2¼hrs	56	daily
Naxos	45mins-2½hrs	9-26	2-4 daily
Paros	1¼-8½hrs	19-35	1-3 daily
Piraeus	4¼-8½hrs	38-70	2-4 daily
Santorini	2hrs	47	daily
Schinousa	30mins	4	1-3 daily
Serifos	5½hrs	65	daily
Sifnos	4-5hrs	65	2 daily

❶ Getting Around

Bike hire (☑ 6973354991; www.thoosa.gr; per day €5-10; ⊘ 9am-9pm Jun-Aug) is available from a shop at the eastern end of the town beach. Koufonisia is largely flat and cycling is easy. The island is also small enough to be easily walkable.

An hourly bus (€2, 10am to 8pm) operates between Hora and Pori Beach via Finikas Beach in July and August only.

Donousa Δονούσα

POP LESS THAN 150

According to Greek mythology, it was here that Dionysus, the god of wine, brought Ariadne to hide her from Theseus. As well he might – Donousa is still wonderfully out-on-a-limb and the remotest of the Small Cyclades. Stavros is Donousa's main settlement and port – a cluster of whitewashed buildings around a handsome church, overlooking the ferry quay and a decent sandy beach.

Crowds of holiday-making Greeks and sun-seeking northern Europeans arrive in late July and August, but out of season, fresh air fiends are likely to have the sandy beach coves and the rocky trails that traverse the hilly, arid landscape all to themselves.

◎ Sights

Kedros, 1.25km southeast of Stavros, reached by a steep, stepped track, is a large, gorgeous sandy crescent with a seasonal taverna, free camping and calm cerulean waters. Limenari, a 40-minute walk along the coast from Kedros, is a more secluded cove; both Kedros and Limenari are popular with naturists. Accessible both from the hamlet of Messaria (Charavgi) via a 25-minute hike and the largest village of Mersini via a steep, 25-minute descent, the white-sand sweep of **Livadi** sees even fewer visitors.

At the end of the road on the northeast coast, the tiny village of **Kalotaritissa** has three little beaches – two pebble beaches closest to the village and a sandy cove a 10-minute hike away. Get here by minibus, hike, or on the boat *Margissa* in summer.

⌂ Sleeping

★ **Argalios Guesthouse**   GUESTHOUSE €
(☏ 22850 79008, 6982953374; www.argaliosguesthouse.gr; r €50; ☎) 🏊 This delightful guesthouse higher up in the village consists of four snug, individually styled apartments, all with heavy wooden beams, characterful reclaimed furniture and superior Cocomat mattresses. Your hosts, Iliad and Ploumissa, are committed to sustainable living and can organise traditional loom weaving classes.

★ **Makares**   APARTMENT €€
(☏ 22850 79079; www.makares-donoussa.gr; r & apt €80-140; ☻ May-Oct; ❄ ☎) Loukas is an excellent host at Makares, a clutch of self-catering studios and apartments at the far end of Stavros Bay (across the beach from the port). It's a short walk to the village hub, the views are fabulous, the decor simple and elegant, and the feeling of seclusion is first-rate. Pickup offered from the port.

✗ Eating

★ **Avli**   GREEK €€
(☏ 22850 51557; www.facebook.com/avlidonoussa; mains €10-15; ☻ noon-late) There's a lot to love about this innovative little restaurant above

the quayside, run by a Greek-Czech couple: the sea views, Donousa's best wine list, plus classy Aegean cuisine (black-eyed pea salad, sardines stuffed with parsley and garlic, calamari stuffed with *graviera* cheese).

★ **I Kori tou Mihali**   TAVERNA €€
(☏ 6984618807; Mersini; mains €9-18) At this welcoming taverna in Mersini village, 6km from Stavros by road, Koula conjures up excellent Greek cuisine with a modern twist: wild goat from the island, pork in honey and yoghurt, and smoky eggplant dip. The knockout views are a bonus.

ℹ Information

Sigalas Travel (☏ 22850 51570; ☻ hours vary Mon-Sat) sells ferry tickets and is open in the mornings and evenings on ferry days, plus 40 minutes before ferry arrivals.

ℹ Getting There & Away

Ferry services are significantly reduced out of season. Differences in journey durations are due to routing or vessel type.

Destinations from Donousa are: Aegiali on Amorgos (€7, 45 minutes to 1¼ hours, seven weekly), Katapola on Amorgos (€7, 2¼ to 4¾ hours, three weekly), Astypalea (€15, 2¾ hours, four weekly), Iraklia (€8, 2¼ hours, four weekly), Koufonisia (€6, 1¼ hours, three weekly), Naxos (€7, 1¼ to 3¼ hours, eight weekly), Paros (€11 to €18, 2¼ to 2½ hours, five weekly), Piraeus (€30, 8¼ hours, four weekly) and Schinousa (€8, two hours, three weekly).

ℹ Getting Around

There are no cars or scooters for hire. A minibus connects Stavros with the tiny hamlet of Kalotaritissa on the far side of the island via Donousa's only road (€2, early June to late August).

Bicycle hire should be up and running in the near future and the island is very walkable.

The island's only **taxi** (☏ 6971774696) can drop you off in Kalotaritissa (€13) and elsewhere.

The small boat *Margissa* takes visitors to island beaches (€5) from June to September with a schedule based on weather and wind direction.

AMORGOS   ΑΜΟΡΓΟΣ

POP 2000

Dramatic Amorgos is shaped like a seahorse swimming its way east towards the Dodecanese, while the ribbon of road that winds its way along the long ridge of mountains, con-

Amorgos

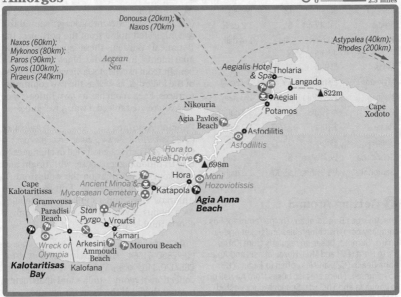

0 ———— 5 km
0 ———— 2.5 miles

Donousa (20km);
Naxos (70km)

Naxos (60km);
Mykonos (80km);
Paros (90km);
Syros (100km);
Piraeus (240km)

Astypalea (40km);
Rhodes (200km)

Aegean
Sea

Aegialis Hotel
& Spa
Tholaria
Langada
Aegiali
▲822m
Potamos
Cape
Xodoto

Nikouria
Agia Pavlos
Beach
Asfodilitis
Asfodilitis

Hora to
Aegiali Drive
▲698m

Hora
Moni
Hozoviotissis

Ancient Minoa &
Mycenaean Cemetery
Katapola
Agia Anna
Beach

Cape
Kalotaritissa
Gramvousa
Paradisi
Beach
Ston
Pyrgo
Arkesini
Vroutsi
Kamari
Arkesini
Ammoudi
Beach
Mourou Beach
Wreck of
Olympia
Kalotaritisas
Bay
Kalofana

necting the main villages, is among the most beautiful drives in the Cyclades.

Amorgos remains relatively off the beaten track – even the fast ferry from Athens takes seven hours to get here! Free-diving aficionados and fans of Luc Besson's cult classic *The Big Blue* come to play in the Aegean, while walkers spend days exploring the numerous trails that zigzag across the rugged terrain, leading to secluded beaches, cutting across hillsides and abandoned stone terraces and meandering past ruined Cycladic windmills and remnants of ancient settlements.

Of the three main settlements, Katapola is more favoured by families, while Aegiali attracts a younger crowd and the enchanting capital of Hora is all maze-like, marble-paved alleyways and tumbling bougainvillea.

ⓘ Information

Three good websites on the island are www.amorgos.gr, www.amorgos.guide and www.amorgos-island-magazine.com.

ⓘ Getting There & Away

Connections from Naxos are good, with the Small Cyclades Line (www.ferries.gr/smallcycladeslines) operating each day (except Sunday), connecting Naxos with the two Amorgos ports by way of the Small Cyclades.

Blue Star Ferries (www.bluestarferries.gr) has three useful routes: two run regularly from Piraeus via Paros, Naxos and the Small Cyclades, ending at either Aegiali or Katapola port. The third route sails weekly from Piraeus to Katapola and eastwards to Patmos, Leros, Kos and Rhodes.

Purchase your tickets from **Nautilos** (☑ Aegiali 22850 73032, Katapola 22850 71201), a ticket agency with offices close to both harbours.

Boat services from Aegiali:

DESTINATION	DURATION	FARE (€)	FREQUENCY
Astypalea	1¾hrs	13	4 weekly
Donousa	45mins-1¼hrs	7	7 weekly
Iraklia	2¼-3¾hrs	9	4 weekly
Koufonisia	2½hrs	7	3 weekly
Naxos	2¼-5hrs	12	1-2 daily
Paros	3½hrs	13-21	5 weekly
Schinousa	3½hrs	8.50	6 weekly
Syros	5¼hrs	16	weekly

Boat services from Katapola (continued over page):

DESTINATION	DURATION	FARE (€)	FREQUENCY
Donousa	2¼-4¾hrs	7	3 weekly
Folegandros	2¼hrs	70	daily

DESTINATION	DURATION	FARE (€)	FREQUENCY
Ios	3hrs	12	weekly
Iraklia	1¾-4½hrs	8	1-2 daily
Koufonisia	40mins-3½hrs	7-14	2-4 daily
Milos	5½hrs	70	daily
Mykonos	2¼hrs	55	3 weekly
Naxos	1¼-3¼hrs	11-30	2-3 daily
Paros	4-4¼hrs	13-29	1-2 daily
Piraeus	5-10hrs	33-70	1-2 daily
Rhodes	8½hrs	33	weekly
Schinousa	1½-4¼hrs	8	1-2 daily
Santorini	1½-3¼hrs	12-50	1-2 daily

❶ Getting Around

The Amorgos Bus Company (http://amorgosbus company.com) has timetables and ticket prices online. Summer buses go regularly from Katapola to Hora (€2) and Moni Hozoviotissis and Agia Anna Beach (€2), and less often to Aegiali (€3, 45 minutes). There are also buses from Aegiali up to Langada and Tholaria. Schedules are posted at the main stop in each village.

Without doubt, the easiest way to get around is with your own wheels. Cars, ATVs and scooters are available for hire from **Thomas Rental** (☑ Aegiali 22850 73444, Katapola 22850 71777; www.thomas-rental.gr) or **Evis Cars** (☑ 22850 71066; www.eviscars.gr; Aegiali). Expect to pay from €40/30/20 per day for a car/ATV/scooter in August; less the rest of the year. There are only two petrol stations: one 1.5km inland from Katapola, the other in Aegiali.

Katapola   Κατάπολα

POP 634

Katapola sprawls round the curving, yacht-filled shoreline of a picturesque bay in the most verdant part of the island. It's a bustling port, divided into three villages: Katapola on the port, Rahidhi in the centre and Xylokeratidhi on the north side of the bay.

The remains of the ancient city of **Minoa** lie above the port and can be easily reached by footpath or a steep concrete road; although there is no information by the ruins, the views are magnificent. Amorgos has also yielded many Cycladic finds: the largest figurine in the National Archaeological Museum in Athens was found in the vicinity of Katapola.

🛏 Sleeping

⭐ Big Blue   GUESTHOUSE €€
(☑ 22850 73471; www.thebigblue.gr; apt €91-120; ❄️🛜) Located uphill from the port, past the Botanical Garden, these spacious studio apartments in Cycladic blues and whites benefit from excellent sea views – from most of the lodgings, as well as the two communal terraces. Each room has its own little terrace and you're guaranteed a warm welcome.

Pension Amorgos   PENSION €€
(☑ 22850 71013; www.pension-amorgos.com; d €80; ❄️🛜) There's a good deal of character in this traditional guesthouse, with bright and well-kept rooms right on the waterfront. It has the same owner as Emprostiada in Amorgos' Hora, and a similarly high quality. As a bonus, Katapola's tavernas are only a short stumble away.

Villa Katapoliani   PENSION €€
(☑ 22850 71664; www.villakatapoliani.gr; d/tr/f €85/120/140; ❄️🛜) Villa has a high-quality collection of rooms, studios and apartments, located behind the waterfront and ferry quay. The balconies at Villa 1 overlook a garden filled with bougainvillea and the scattered ruins of the ancient temple of Apollo. Or scoot upstairs to the rooftop terrace for sea views. Apartments sleep up to four.

Minoa Hotel   HOTEL €€
(☑ 22850 74055; www.hotelminoa.gr; s/d/tr €55/85/95; ❄️🛜) Near the waterfront, this family-run place couldn't be more convenient for ferries. Service is friendly, and the sweet, neat rooms have tidy bathrooms and balconies overlooking a tree- and bird-filled garden. The foyer shares space with the family's Sweets by Pothiti cafe and patisserie.

🍴 Eating

Tavernas and cafes line the waterfront. Most serve traditional seafood and Greek standards, but there are more imaginative options in Xylokeratidhi, on the opposite side of the bay from Katapola port.

Honey & Cinnamon   BAKERY €
(☑ 22850 71485; snacks from €3; ⏱ 9am-11pm) Look for the bright red window shutters and follow your nose. This tiny patisserie, a block back from the waterfront, bakes up cakes, pastries and lots of local cookies. Try the ones made with the local liquor, *psimeni raki*, or simply grab a coffee or a gelato.

⭐ **Youkali** GREEK €€
(☑22850 71838; www.facebook.com/youkaliamorgos; mains €8-14; ⊘noon-2am; 🅙) Wander over to the opposite side of the bay from the port for Katapola's most imaginative cooking. That ingredients are fresh and locally sourced goes without saying; try them in combos such as orzo with beetroot and zucchini, meatballs with leek sauce, and linguine with shrimps. Friendly service, beautiful presentation.

Mouragio SEAFOOD €€
(☑22850 71011; mains €10-19; ⊘11am-1am) An 'Aegean Cuisine' label bearer, this port-side tavern has been going strong since 1980. Fish soup and lobster spaghetti are specialities here, along with grilled catch of the day.

ℹ Getting There & Away

Boats dock right on the waterfront. The **bus station** is a few minutes' walk along the water. From Katapola, buses run to Aegali (€3, one hour, five times daily), Chora (€2, 20 minutes, 16 times daily) and Agia Anna Beach (€2, 30 minutes, eight times daily) from mid-June until the end of August; less frequently the rest of the year.
N Synodinos (☑22850 71201; synodinos@nax. forthnet.gr) Sells ferry tickets and has a money exchange on the waterfront.

Hora (Amorgos)
Χώρα (Αμοργός)

POP 414

Capped by a 13th-century *kastro* (castle) and guarded by **windmills** that stand sentinel on the hill above it, the historic capital of Hora is a wonderfully atmospheric village. Wandering the timeless streets is a joy, and there's a touch of sophistication in the handful of fashionable bars, clothing and offbeat jewellery stores run by local designers along the pedestrian main drag that enhance Hora's appeal without eroding its timelessness.

The bus stop is on a small square at the edge of town. There's an ATM next to a minimarket right at the entrance to Hora, and local preserves and tipples for sale along the main street.

⊙ Sights

Hora's free **Archaeology Collection** (⊘9am-1pm & 6-8.30pm Tue-Sun) has some interesting pieces excavated on the island, including remnants of the Minoan civilisation that existed on Amorgos more than 4000 years ago. It's signposted off the main pedestrian street.

🛏 Sleeping

⭐ **Emprostiada** GUESTHOUSE €€
(☑22850 71814; https://emprostiada.com; d €110, ste €140-160; ⊘Mar-Nov; ❄🛜) There's charm in abundance at this traditional guesthouse, where characterful suites are housed in an old merchant's home. It's a picture-perfect scene in a peaceful setting at the back of the village. Choose from spacious doubles, maisonettes and suites. Doubles are a bargain €60 outside the July and August peak. Free port transfers are available from Katapola or Aegiali.

Pension Ilias PENSION €€
(☑22850 71277; www.iliaspension.gr; d/apt €60/100; ❄🛜) Tucked away amid a jumble of traditional houses not far from the bus stop is this friendly, family-run place with pleasant, comfortable rooms. The apartments can accommodate four people. Two-night minimum stay in July and August.

🍴 Eating

⭐ **Kastanis** GREEK €
(☑22850 72048; mains €7-13; ⊘noon-late; 🅙) In the shade of some trees on the main street, this family-run taverna excels at traditional dishes, such as *patatato* (lamb with potatoes in tomato sauce), *fava* with capers, superlative Greek salad topped with local cheese, and seasonal specialities, such as boiled local greens with a squirt of lemon.

Jazzmin CAFE €
(☑22850 74017; breakfast €6.50-13, snacks €3-6; ⊘9am-2am) Down some steps from the main pedestrian street, Jazzmin spreads through the cosy rooms of a traditional home. Perch in a window seat or lounge on the roof deck. Breakfast choices are good, as are smoothies, juices and herbal teas. The list of cocktails is impressive, and jazz and other smooth tunes provide a chilled-out soundtrack.

Triporto CAFE €
(☑22850 73085; www.facebook.com/3porto; breakfast from €8, snacks €3-5; ⊘8am-4am) Once the village bakery, this hip cafe doubles as a breakfast joint and a mellow late-night bar. Create an omelette from ingredients like olive sauce and hot paprika cream, snack on salads, sandwiches and sweets, or nurse a glass of wine while talking to the friendly owner – a virtual encyclopaedia of local knowledge.

ⓘ Getting There & Away

The **Amorgos Bus Company** (📞 6936671033; http://amorgosbuscompany.com) has timetables and ticket prices online. Buses link Katapola to Hora (€2) and onwards to Aegiali (€2).

Some accommodation options offer free port transfers to/from Katapola and Aegiali. Check when you book.

Picking up a rental car, scooter or ATV at either of the ports is a good option. Or rent a car from Evis Cars (p230).

Aegiali
Αιγιάλη
POP 430

Amorgos' second port sees fewer yachts and more of a younger traveller scene. A sweep of white sand lines the inner edge of the bay on which the village stands, and it's a good place for water sports. Walkers use it as a base for hiking up to the lovely villages of Langada and Tholaria that nestle amid the craggy slopes above the town, each about 3km away, and linked both to each other and other parts of the island by walking trails. On the far side of the bay, a path leads over headlands to three sand-and-pebble beaches, the furthest popular with naturists.

🏃 Activities

Enthusiastic and friendly instruction can be had at the well-run beach-front centre **Amorgos Diving Center** (📞 6932249538, 22850 73611; www.amorgos-diving.com). Dives (with equipment) start at €55, with night dives, wreck dives and PADI courses available. It also has a Bubblemaker class for kids, snorkelling tours (€25), and rents SUPs and kayaks.

🛏 Sleeping

Apollon Studios　　　　　　　　GUESTHOUSE €
(📞 22850 73297; www.apollon-amorgos.com; studio d/tr €55/66; ❄🛜) With a nautically themed entrance, this guesthouse in the heart of the village has studios with well-equipped kitchens and harbour-view balconies. Rooms aren't fussy, but they're comfortable and reasonably priced. This place draws lots of repeat guests and families. Lots of places to eat right out the front door.

Yperia　　　　　　　　　　　　HOTEL €€
(📞 22850 73084; www.yperia.com; incl breakfast d €135-145, f €188; ⊘Apr-Oct; ❄🛜🏊) Yperia's modern rooms have warm, artsy touches, handmade wood-and-iron furnishings, big bathrooms and excellent sea views (pay €10 extra). The pool overlooks the ocean, and the hotel is just a block from the beach. Staff are friendly and accommodating.

Aegialis Hotel & Spa　　　　　　HOTEL €€€
(Map p229; 📞 22850 73393; www.amorgos-aegialis. com; d/ste from €222/548; ❄🛜🏊) High on a hill and with magical views over Aegiali Bay and village, this is the island's only five-star hotel. Rooms are classic Cycladic minimalism with a modern art accent, but it's the facilities that make this place shine: pool and pool bar, a bliss-out day spa, restaurants – oh, and did we mention the view? Decent off-peak rates; book online.

🍴 Eating

Amorgis　　　　　　　　　　　　CAFE €
(📞 22850 73606; mains €4-10; ⊘9am-late; 🛜) On the steps leading up from the ferry quay, Amorgis is all pastel colours and hanging pot

---

> **DON'T MISS**

WALKING ON AMORGOS

Amorgos is a very popular walking destination, and the island has over a dozen hiking trails, eight of them numbered and well marked. Check these routes out online at www. amorgos.gr. Cartography company Terrain (http://terrainmaps.gr) produces an excellent hiking map for Amorgos. The most scenic trails include the following:

#1 (13.4km; four to five hours) The longest trail runs from Hora, going down to Moni Hozoviotissis, then ascending and meandering among the hills before descending to Aegiali.

#2 (3.5km, one hour) Scenic descent from Hora to Katapola.

#3 (14km; five hours) Relatively demanding trail from Katapola to Kato Kampos, via the coastal ruins of Minoa and Arkesini, plus the village of Vroutsi and Aghia Triada tower.

#4 (8km; three hours) Horseshoe-shaped trail that starts and ends in Aegiali, connecting it to the lovely villages of Langada and Tholaria, with a gentle walk between the two.

plants overlooking the bay. Good at any time – for fresh juices, classic cocktails and light bites such as tortillas, salads and baguettes.

★ **Taxidi Gefsis Apo Ti Kriti Sto Aivali** CRETAN €€
(☑22850 73342; mains €7-15) Near the south end of the beach, this Cretan restaurant is exceptional in terms of hospitality and the quality of its homemade dishes. Slow-cooked goat, shrimp *saganaki*, Cretan pasta and mixed *mezedhes* are all on the menu, served to a mellow jazz soundtrack.

★ **Falafel** INTERNATIONAL €€
(☑6936808038; dishes €6-14; ⊙11am-1am) Up an alley from the waterfront, grab a seat at a communal table or perch on a stool to dig into *shakshuka* or a falafel wrap for brunch, and a grab-bag of world cuisines (spring rolls, curries) the rest of the day. The carbonara comes with home-smoked Cretan pork and there are Ora microbrews to quench your thirst.

To Limani TAVERNA €€
(☑22850 73269; http://tolimani.weebly.com; mains €8-18; ⊙8am-midnight) This popular restaurant, up from the main street, carries its traditional atmosphere comfortably. Using homegrown produce, the cooks whip up hefty portions of great local dishes: try the fish soup, *patatato* (lamb with potatoes in tomato sauce), or anything with local cheese. And save room for some homemade orange pie.

🍷 Drinking & Nightlife

★ **Embassa Bar** COCKTAIL BAR
(☑6932547187; ⊙8am-4am) Facing the tiny quayside windmill, this skull-emblazoned bar is arguably Amorgos' best cocktail bar. Sip a cucumber martini with a side of killer sunset or come for a morning coffee to mix with the all-night crowd.

❶ Information

If you're interested in organised walking holidays, try the Special Interest Holidays website, www.walkingingreece.com. It's run by Paul and Henrietta Delahunt-Rimmer, an English couple who have written the excellent resource *Amorgos: A Visitor's and Walker's Guide*, copies of which can be found at an Aegiali gift shop.

Aegialis Tours (☑22850 73393; http://amorgos-aegialis.com/services), based at Aegialis Hotel & Spa, can help arrange local tours and experiences (hiking, cultural excursions, cooking classes etc).

❶ Getting There & Away

There are fewer boat departures from Aegiali than from the other port of Katapola; check the schedule ahead of time.

There are several car/scooter/ATV rental places on the waterfront.

The Amorgos Bus Company links Aegiali with Katapola (€3, 45 minutes) via Hora (five daily), Langada (€2, 10 minutes, six daily) and Tholaria (€2, 10 minutes, six daily) from mid-June until late August; less often the rest of the year.

Around Amorgos

◉ Sights

★ **Kalotaritisas Bay** BEACH
(Map p229) On the western tip of the island, this is Amorgos' loveliest beach. Yachts and fishing boats bob on the cerulean waters of the protected bay. In July and August, boat trips (€4) run from this sand-and-pebble stretch to the uninhabited island of Krambousa.

★ **Agia Anna Beach** BEACH
(Map p229) Agia Anna Beach is tiny and rocky, but with calm waters for swimming and rocks to leap off. It's popular for its starring role in the French film *The Big Blue,* and is known for its dramatic location and photogenic whitewashed chapel. On the other side of the car park there's a larger, sandy beach.

Moni Hozoviotissis MONASTERY
(Μονή της Χοζοβιώτισσας; Map p229; donations appreciated; ⊙8.30am-1pm & 5-7pm) This iconic 11th-century monastery is a dazzling white structure embedded into the cliff face high above the sea on the east coast below Hora. It's also high above the car park, with 350 steps to get to it. With any luck, a custodian will be there to explain the significance of the monastery and its icons. The dress code is strict. No shorts, no miniskirts, no bare shoulders and no women in trousers. No exceptions.

Tholaria VILLAGE
A 3km ride along the looping road or a 30-minute hike from Aegiali, the mountain village of Tholaria sits near the **ruins of ancient Aegiali**, with millennia-old ruins of the yet-to-be-excavated settlement an easy 10-minute walk away. Stop by Kali Kardia (p234) for the best meatballs in the Cyclades and stargaze at night at the Seladi (p234)

cocktail bar. There's a good hike from Tholaria to Langada across the valley, too.

Asfodilitis
VILLAGE

(Map p229) Reachable via a paved, steep and narrow road from the main Hora–Aegiali road, the slate houses in this hamlet seem deserted. Then you spot the single taverna, the Greek Communist Party flag, the odd battered vehicle. It's a silent place, ideal for watching the sunrise, and a handy spot for breaking up the Hora–Aegiali hike. The turnoff for Asfodilitis is around 6km southwest of Aegiali.

Langada
VILLAGE

Some 3km east of Aegiali, the small village of Langada is a picturesque maze of narrow whitewashed streets. There are several excellent tavernas here, plus shops selling beautiful, locally produced ceramics. Stop by FindinGreece to learn about walking and cultural tours of the island. It takes around 30 minutes to hike up from Aegiali, though there are buses as well.

Activities & Tours

★ Hora to Aegiali Drive
SCENIC DRIVE

(Map p229) It's well worth driving the 16km between Hora and Aegiali – among the most scenic roads in the Cyclades. The road zigzags with the scrubland-covered mountains looming to one side and the land falling away gradually towards the sea on the other, where uninhabited Nikouria and Grabonisi sit.

★ FindinGreece
WALKING

(☑6944326036; www.findingreece.com; Langada; ☺9am-8pm) In Laghada village, Alix and Semeli are enthusiastic operators who offer walking tours of Amorgos, as well as all manner of cultural activities – whether you want to take part in ceramic classes, learn about local wild herbs, go scuba diving or learn to cook the local way. Get in touch in advance.

Sleeping & Eating

Pagali Hotel
HOTEL €€

(☑22850 73310; www.pagalihotel-amorgos.com; Langada; s/d/tr €64/73/135; ❋🛜) Pagali Hotel is tucked away in Langada village, and has superb views. Rooms and studios are comfortable, and the year-round hotel offers alternative agritourism activities like grape or olive harvesting and winemaking, as well as activities including rock climbing, hiking, yoga and art workshops.

The hotel sits in a cute family-run pocket of Langada, next to the excellent Nikos Taverna and Vassalos Bakery.

★ Ston Pyrgo
TAVERNA €

(Map p229; ☑22850 72258; Arkesini; mains €7-12; ☺11am-10pm) Turn off from the village of Arkesini towards the signposted Tower of Agia Triada (also well worth a visit) and you find this traditional *mezedhopoleio* (cafe-restaurant specialising in mezedhes), run by young chef Vangelitsa. Terrific home-cooked food, from *patatato*, boiled local greens with lemon, and grilled catch of the day, all shine here.

★ Kali Kardia
GREEK €

(☑22850 73347; Tholaria; mains €5-8; ☺8am-10pm) On the tiny square next to the church, this wonderful, family-run place, decorated with family photos and retsina jugs, cooks up the best meatballs in the Cyclades, plus hearty portions of other Greek classics.

Drinking & Nightlife

★ Seladi Cafe-Bar
COCKTAIL BAR

(☑22850 73197; Tholaria; ☺10am-2pm & 6pm-2am) Its cosy terrace overlooking the valley, Seladi is a just a short walk from the ruins of the ancient settlement. It's a mellow place for a coffee and brunch, while in the evenings it morphs into an intimate cocktail bar. On clear nights, you can stargaze through its telescope.

IOS
ΙΟΣ

POP 1754

Ios' image has long been linked to holiday sun, sea and sex, with a reputation for nonstop, booze-fuelled partying. It's partly true: there's no denying that from June to August, the island is the much-loved stomping ground of youth and hedonism. But it's so much more – if you want it to be – and the partying doesn't infiltrate every village or beach.

Explore the winding footpaths of the traditional hilltop old town or relax on a sandy beach. Discover the isolated interior or sandy beaches such as Manganari in the south, or hike the little-trodden trails to the island's hilltop monasteries. Or visit in the shoulder season for a quieter pace, when Ios draws families and the more mature. It's pretty easy to escape the crowds: simply rent some wheels and venture into the countryside of goat farms, honey boxes and dramatic views.

Ios

⊙ Sights

★Panagia Gremiotissa
VIEWPOINT

(Map p235; Hora) Head up the alleyway behind Sally's Rooftop Garden and then proceed upwards, along cracked steps and through ancient archways, and eventually you'll emerge by the top of Hora, next to the Panagia Gremiotissa church, with its sunset views. For even better views, climb for a few minutes more to the three small chapels above it.

Homer's Tomb
ARCHAEOLOGICAL SITE

(Map p235) A remote and beautiful 13km drive northeast of Hora lies what is locally believed to be the final resting place of Homer, Greece's greatest poet, who wrote the epics *Odyssey* and *Iliad*. While there are various legends surrounding Homer's Ios connections, and the Dutch archaeologist Pasch van Krienen declaring this tomb to be Homer's in 1771 may have little historical evidence behind it, Hellenic coins from Ios do bear Homer's likeness and name. And the drive is stunning.

Skarkos
ARCHAEOLOGICAL SITE

(The Snail; Map p235; €4; ⊘ 8am-3pm Tue-Sun May-Sep) Crowning a low hill just north of Hora, this Early Bronze Age settlement is one of the Aegean's most significant prehistoric sites. There are restored walled terraces that follow the relief of the hill and the low ruins of several Cycladic-style buildings to explore; visiting the Archaeological Museum in Hora first is good for context. If driving, take the signed turnoff between Ormos and Hora, or walk the traditional stone footpath from the back of Hora (15 minutes). Great views.

Archaeological Museum
MUSEUM

(📞 22860 91246; Hora; €2; ⊘ 8.30am-4pm Wed-Mon) This musuem, on the main road that passes by Hora, is a must for those interested in antiquity. It displays a wealth of finds from the early Bronze Age settlement of nearby Skarkos, from ceramics and marble figurines to obsidian wares, bone tools and funereal *stelae*, providing an illuminating glimpse into the early Cycladic civilisation.

Beaches

Ios is well known for its beaches. Those reachable by paved road include **Manganari** – a wide sweep of white sand on the south coast, reached by your own wheels (45 minutes from Hora), bus or by caïque in summer. **Mylopotas** is equally beautiful and is a major water sports centre as well. **Agia Theodoti** has the bluest of blue water and is favoured by Greek families. Nearby **Psathi** is quieter with a popular taverna and is an ace windsurfing venue. Plenty of other fine beaches are only accessible by caïque.

Activities

Ios is a major water sports centre. Mylopotas Beach has the best selection for anything from waterskiing and windsurfing to paddleboarding, scuba diving, and kayaking.

Mylopotas Watersports & New Dive
WATER SPORTS

(☑22860 92340; http://mylopotas-watersports.gr; Mylopotas Beach; ⊙May–mid-Oct) A thousand ways to fill your day: try a discover scuba-diving session (€55) or more intensive PADI courses from €270. There are also wreck dives and night dives. Join a three-hour boat snorkelling trip for €35, take a tube ride or rent all the gear: windsurfing kit, kayaks, paddleboards, sailboats and more. Friendly staff, too.

Meltemi Watersports & Dive Centre
WATER SPORTS

(☑6980386990; www.meltemiwatersports.com; Mylopotas) Based at the **Far Out Beach Club** (☑22860 91468; www.faroutclub.com; camp site per person €12, dm €20, glamp tent €40, d/q €100/190; @🅰🅰), with a ready flow of keen customers, Meltemi has a smorgasbord of ways to get wet: try a diving sampler (€55) or full PADI courses, then check out wreck, cave and night dives. Learn to windsurf, waterski, wakeboard or paddleboard, join a canoe safari or even a Hell Ride (tube ride; €18).

🛏 Sleeping

Ormos has the fewest pensions/hotels. Hora has a wide range of lodgings, from a legendary hostel to guesthouses and boutique hotels on the outskirts, with some places close to the centrally located bars and clubs. There are camp sites, dorms and private villas around Mylopotas. Book early for July and August.

★ Windmill
GUESTHOUSE €

(☑22860 91482; r from €50; 🅰🅰) Sadly, not inside one of Hora's beautiful yet somewhat dilapidated windmills, this guesthouse is the next best thing to it: right at the top of Hora, with great views of said windmills and the village. Simple, spotless rooms are attentively run by the father-and-son team Pavlos and Giorgios, and you're a couple of minutes' walk from the nightlife.

Avra Pension
PENSION €

(☑22860 91985; www.avrapension.gr; Ormos; s/d €40/50; ⊙Apr–mid-Oct; 🅰🅰) Down a lane behind the yacht marina at the port, Katerina runs this delightful guesthouse with warmth and efficiency, and at bargain prices (outside the short summer peak, rooms fall to €30). Colourful potted plants, a restful terrace, homey common areas and fresh, appealing rooms add up to super value.

★ Francesco's
HOSTEL €€

(☑22860 91223; www.francescos.net; Hora; dm/s/d/tr from €20/65/80/120; ⊙Apr–mid-Oct; 🅰@🅰🅰) Former backpackers are now sending their own 18-year-olds to Francesco's, which is still going strong. Rooms are spotless, hillside views are great and it's within stumbling distance of Hora's nightlife. There's a roll call of happy-traveller features: bar, pool, cheap breakfast, free entry to Blue Note. From the square near Astra Bar, head up and left. It's near Midnight Cafe.

★ Kritikakis Village Hotel
HOTEL €€

(☑22860 91100; www.kritikakis.gr; d/tr/q €120/140/158; 🅰🅰🅰) Set back from the port and next to the steps leading up to Hora, this multi-levelcluster of Cycladic cubes attracts mostly young, hip travellers who like the extra comfort of the large whitewashed studios with brick accents, and perks such as the two pools, on-site bar and welcome drink.

Aegeon Hotel
HOTEL €€

(☑22860 91007; www.ios-aegeon.com; Mylopotas; r €105-115; 🅰🅰🅰) Providing a higher level of comfort to a younger crowd than surrounding beachside places, this smart little hotel offers simple whitewashed rooms alongside such perks as a pool, hot tub and hammocks to laze in. A place to relax rather than to party; head down the street for the latter.

Yialos Ios Hotel HOTEL €€
(☑22860 91421; www.yialosioshotel.gr; Ormos; incl breakfast s/d from €90/105, studio from €210; ☺May-Sep; ❄@🅿🏊) Just a block back from the port, this 200-year-old stone building feels like the home you wish you had. Crisp, characterful rooms, wood-beamed ceilings, traditional beds and a flower-filled poolside give it the edge. The owners are attentive, and the breakfast room is just like your Greek grandma's kitchen. Off-peak rates are excellent (doubles around €50).

★**Liostasi** BOUTIQUE HOTEL €€€
(☑22860 92140; www.liostasi.gr; Hora; d/ste incl breakfast from €160/295; ☺May-Sep; ❄@🅿🏊) Step into the foyer of this place and you may never want to leave. This contemporary, on-point place is an effortless blend of chic and comfort. The on-site spa, restaurant and pool area are top quality, and the rooms are crisp with splashes of colour and gorgeous sea views. Service is impeccable. It's halfway between Ormos and Hora.

🍴 Eating

★**Hellenic Social** CAFE €
(☑22860 92663; www.facebook.com/HellenicSocial; mains €6-12; ☺11am-midnight) On any given morning, this place is filled mostly with visitors to Ios, some slumped over their poached eggs, others perkily downing filled bagels, green smoothies and blended juices. Hellenic Social is very hipster, very now, with organic kombucha and dishes involving chia seeds and smashed avo. Evening events and parties frequently break out. It's off the main road.

Katogi MEZEDHES €
(☑6983440900; www.facebook.com/katogios; Hora; dishes €5-12; ☺dinner) Entering Katogi feels like you've walked into a party in someone's quirky house, full of hidden nooks and plants and clamour. The original cocktails hit the spot, while the meze can be hit and miss: the grilled *talagani* cheese with figs and pasta purses filled with cheese and pear rock, while the *saganaki* meatballs are merely okay. Great atmosphere, though.

★**Salt** FUSION €€
(☑2286092217; www.facebook.com/SaltRestaurantBar; Mylopotas; mains €10-14; ☺9am-2am; 🛜) One of those restaurants that get everything right, Salt is a light-filled, breezy outdoor space under a canopy of whitewashed bamboo overlooking the beach. Service is friendly and prompt, the dishes – from fish tartare and

shrimp-and-leek risotto to slow-roasted spare ribs and salted caramel banoffee – are spot on, and it's wallet-friendly to boot.

★**Lord Byron** MEDITERRANEAN €€
(☑22860 92125; dishes €7-14; ☺dinner) Near the main square in Hora, coming here is like entering a curiosity shop, filled with masks, vintage ads, and other quirky items from the owner's travels. The dishes tap into a global smorgasbord of delights, from bacon-wrapped scallops and a Caesar salad to bouillabaisse and Moroccan-Mexican quesadilla crossovers. Service gets five stars.

★**Harmony Ios** MEXICAN €€
(☑22860 91613; https://harmonyios.com; mains €9-13; ☺9am-2am; 🛜) Harmony wears many hats and we like all of them. It's a mellow spot for pancakes, coffee and avo on toast in the morning, a place to laze about in a hammock or on giant cushions while nursing a frozen margarita at sunset, or an al fresco dinner venue for consuming nachos, tacos and quesadillas, accompanied by decent live music.

☆ Entertainment

The lovely **Cine Liostasi** (☑22860 92140; www.liostasi.gr/cine-liostasi; ☺hours vary), outside the Liostasi Hotel & Suites, between Ormos and Hora, hosts a nightly outdoor cinema. The aim is to be the top outdoor cinema in Greece and, indeed, this spot is hard to beat. Watch classic and modern

---

IOS' TOP NIGHTLIFE

Astra (☑6976953624; www.facebook. com/Astra.ios.greece; ☺10pm-3.30am) Scandi-cool decor with fresh fruit-based cocktails.

Blue Note Club (☑22860 92271; www. facebook.com/bluenoteofficial; ☺11.15pm-late May-Oct) Legendary venue pumping out Top 40 tracks.

Coo Bar (☑6982063864; www.facebook. com/CooBarIos; ☺11pm-5.30am) R'n'B beats, cave-like decor, original cocktails.

Free Beach Bar (☑22860 28357; http://freebeachbar.gr; ☺10am-1am May-Sep) DJ sets and pool parties.

Orange Bar (☺8pm-4am) Originally flavoured shots and a rock and alternative soundtrack.

movies in loungers while sipping cocktails with gorgeous views in the background.

❶ Information

Acteon Travel (☑ 22860 91343; www.acteon. gr; ⊙ 8am-10pm) Buy your onward ferry tickets at the port.

❶ Getting There & Away

Boat services from Ios. Differences in journey durations are because of routing or vessel type.

DESTINATION	DURATION	FARE (€)	FREQUENCY
Anafi	3½hrs	9	2 weekly
Folegandros	1¼-1¾hrs	6-45	3-5 daily
Iraklio	3hrs	70	5 weekly
Katapola (on Amorgos)	3hrs	12	weekly
Kimolos	3hrs	11	3 weekly
Milos	3-4hrs	16-50	2-3 daily
Mykonos	1¾-2½hrs	48-54	2-3 daily
Naxos	45mins-1¾hrs	16-34	2-4 daily
Paros	50mins-5¼hrs	11-27	3-5 daily
Piraeus	45mins-6hrs	39-60	3-4 daily
Santorini	30mins-1½hrs	7-39	4-9 daily
Serifos	5-6hrs	14-60	1-2 daily
Sifnos	4½-5¼hrs	12-55	1-2 daily
Sikinos	25mins	4	4 weekly
Syros	6¾hrs	16	4 weekly

❶ Getting Around

In summer crowded **buses** (☑22860 92015; www.ktel-ios.gr) run between Ormos, Hora and Mylopotas Beach (all fares €2) every 20 minutes. Schedules are posted at the main village bus stops and online. In summer, additional buses run frequently to Koubara, and less so to beaches at Agia Theodoti, Psathi and Manganari. For taxis call **Ios Taxi Service** (☑6977760570); it's €5 from the port to Hora and €5 from Hora to Mylopotas.

Summertime caïques travel from Ormos to Manganari via Mylopotas and cost about €12 per person for a return trip.

Ormos, Hora and Mylopotas Beach all have multiple car, motorcycle and 4WD rental outlets.

SANTORINI ΣΑΝΤΟΡΙΝΗ

POP 11,400

If you approach Santorini from the water, you will be awed by the sheer cliffs that soar above a turquoise sea, by the fact that you're sailing in an immense crater of a drowned volcano and that before you lies an island shaped by an ancient cataclysmic eruption.

High above, the main villages of Fira and Oia are a snowdrift of white Cycladic houses that line the clifftops and spill like icy cornices down the terraced rock. And then there are the sunsets, with crowds applauding as the sun disappears below the horizon.

In peak season, Santorini becomes a playground for the very wealthy, and while this has resulted in some stellar restaurants and superb wineries, the strain on the infrastructure is a concern. Still, there's relative seclusion found at the island's ancient sites, on hiking trails and beneath the waves.

History

Minor eruptions have been the norm in Greece's earthquake-prone history, but Santorini has a definite history of overachieving – eruptions here were so earth-shattering and wrenching they changed the shape of the island several times.

Dorians, Venetians and Turks occupied Santorini, but its most influential early inhabitants were Minoans. They came from Crete some time between 2000 BC and 1600 BC, and the settlement at Akrotiri dates from the peak years of their great civilisation.

The island was circular then and was called Strongili (Round One). Thousands of years ago, a volcanic eruption caused the centre of Strongili to sink, leaving a caldera with towering cliffs along the east side – a truly dramatic sight. The latest theory, based on carbon dating of olive-oil samples from Akrotiri, places the event 10 years either side of 1613 BC.

Santorini was recolonised during the 3rd century BC, but for the next 2000 years sporadic volcanic activity created further physical changes that included the formation of the volcanic islands of Palia Kameni and Nea Kameni at the centre of the caldera.

As recently as 1956, a major earthquake devastated Oia and Fira, yet by the 1970s the islanders had embraced tourism as tourists embraced the island, and today Santorini is a destination of truly spectacular global appeal. Chinese bridal parties love the island (in part due to the success of *Beijing Love Story*, filmed partly on Santorini).

For better or worse, Santorini and Mykonos have become the poster children for the Greek islands. As well as bigger crowds, that also means considerably higher prices.

Getting There & Away

AIR

Santorini Airport (JTR; Map p240; ☎22860 28400; www.santoriniairport.com) has flights year-round to/from Athens (from €60, 45 minutes) with Olympic Air (www.olympicair.com), Ryanair (www.ryanair.com) and Sky Express (www.skyexpress.gr). Seasonal European connections are plentiful with some budget carriers from London, Rome, Geneva, Milan and Toulouse.

Give yourself plenty of time when flying back out as tourism infrastructure hasn't kept up with the island's growing popularity and the small airport terminal can be mayhem.

BOAT

There are plenty of ferries each day to and from Piraeus and many Cyclades islands.

Santorini's main port, Athinios, stands on a cramped shelf of land at the base of sphinx-like cliffs. It's a scene of marvellous chaos (that works itself out), except when ferries have been cancelled and arrivals and departures merge. Advice? Be patient. It clears, eventually. Buses (and taxis) meet all ferries and then cart passengers up the towering cliffs through an ever-rising series of S-bends to Fira. Accommodation providers can usually arrange transfers (to Fira per person is around €10 to €25).

Ferries from Santorini:

DESTINATION	DURATION	FARE (€)	FREQUENCY
Amorgos	1½-4hrs	50	1-2 daily
Anafi	1½hrs	8	4 weekly
Folegandros	45mins-3¼hrs	7-45	3-4 daily
Ios	30mins-1½hrs	7-39	4-8 daily
Iraklio	1¾hrs	60	2 daily
Kimolos	4¼hrs	15	3 weekly
Kos	4½hrs	37	4 weekly
Koufonisia	2hrs	47	daily
Milos	2-4hrs	18-59	3-4 daily
Mykonos	2-3½hrs	45-69	5-7 daily
Naxos	1¼-2¾hrs	22-43	5-6 daily
Paros	2-3½hrs	20-46	4-5 daily
Piraeus	4¾-9hrs	38-80	6-8 daily
Rafina	5¾-9½hrs	35-45	2 daily
Rhodes	8½-17¾hrs	39	5 weekly
Serifos	3½-7¼hrs	19-60	2-3 daily
Sifnos	3-7hrs	14-68	2-3 daily
Sikinos	2hrs	7.50	3 weekly
Tinos	3½-5hrs	42-58	7 weekly

Getting Around

TO/FROM THE AIRPORT

There are frequent bus connections between Fira's bus station and the airport, located 5km east of Fira (€1.80, 20 minutes, 5.30am to 10.15pm). Most accommodation providers will arrange paid transfers.

BUS

KTEL Santorini Buses (Map p242; ☎22860 25404; http://ktel-santorini.gr; Mitropoleos) has a good website with schedules and prices. Tickets are purchased on the bus. Fira is the island's bus hub, with departures for most villages, as well as the airport and ferry port.

CAR & MOTORCYCLE

Having your own wheels is the most convenient way to explore the island during high season, when buses are overcrowded and you'll be lucky to get on one at all. Be very patient and cautious when driving – the narrow roads and heavy traffic, especially in and around Fira, can be a nightmare.

There are representatives of all the major international car-hire outfits, plus dozens of local operators in all tourist areas. Good local hire outfits include **Damigos Rent a Car** (☎6979968192, 22860 22048; www.santorini-carhire.com; 25 Martiou, Fira) and **Tony's Rent a Car** (☎22860 22863; Firostefani; scooter/ATV rental per day from €20/30; ⏲8am-8pm). You'll pay from around €50 per day for a car and €25/30 for a scooter/four-wheeler in high season, but shop around. Note: scooter hire requires you to have an appropriate licence, while four-wheelers require a regular car licence. Check this website for details: www.santorini.com/rentals/motorbikes.

TAXI

Fira's **taxi stand** (Map p242; ☎22860 22555, 22860 23951) is on Dekigala just around the corner from the bus station. A taxi from the port of Athinios to Fira costs €10 to €15, and a trip from Fira to Oia about €15. Expect to add €2 if the taxi is booked ahead or if you have luggage. A taxi to Kamari is about €15, to Perissa €18 and to Ancient Thira about €25 one way.

Santorini Transport (☎6984637383; www.santorinitransport.com) is a good option for arranging fixed-price transfers to/from the airport or Athinios port.

Santorini (Thira)

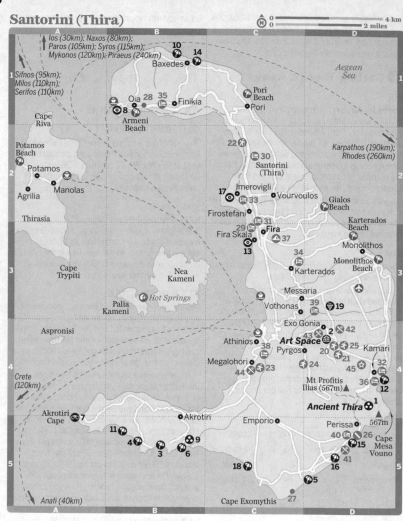

N 0 ———— 4 km
0 ———— 2 miles

Ios (30km); Naxos (80km); Paros (105km); Syros (115km); Mykonos (120km); Piraeus (240km)

Sifnos (95km); Milos (110km); Serifos (110km)

Aegean Sea

Cape Riva

10

14

Baxedes

Oia 28 35 • Finikia

8

Armeni Beach

Pori Beach
Pori

Karpathos (190km); Rhodes (260km)

Potamos Beach

Potamos

Manolas

Agrilia

Thirasia

22

30

Santorini (Thira)

17 Imerovigli
33 • Vourvoulos

Firostefani

31

29 Fira

Fira Skala

13

37

Gialos Beach

Karterados Beach

Monolithos

34

Karterados

Monolithos Beach

Cape Trypiti

Nea Kameni

Palia Kameni

Hot Springs

Messaria

Vothonas

39 19

Aspronisi

Exo Gonia

Art Space 43 2 42

Athinios

38

Pyrgos 20 25 Kamari

21

Megalohori

44 23

24

45 32

36

12

Crete (120km)

Mt Profitis Ilias (567m) ▲

Ancient Thira 1

567m

Akrotiri Cape 7

11

4

3

9

6

• Akrotiri

Emporio

Perissa

40 26

15

Cape Mesa Vouno

18

41

16

5

27

Cape Exomythis

Anafi (40km)

Fira   Φήρα

POP 1900

Santorini's main town of Fira is a vibrant place, having bounced back since the 1956 earthquake. Its caldera edge is layered with swish hotels, cave houses and infinity pools, all backed by a warren of narrow streets packed with shops, more bars and restaurants. And people.

Admittedly, the admiring masses cannot diminish the impact of Fira's stupendous landscape beyond. Views over the multicoloured cliffs are breathtaking, and come sunset, crowds gather at the caldera edge for the greatest free show on earth. Behind the cliffs, however, the prices of fame are exposed: frenetic vehicular activity, meandering pedestrians along the roads (there are few pavements), and frenzied development.

Fira sprawls north and merges into two more villages: **Firostefani** (about a 15-minute walk from Fira) and posher **Imerovigli** (about a half-hour walk from Fira).

◉ Sights

★ **Museum of Prehistoric Thera**   MUSEUM
(Map p242; ☎ 22860 22217; www.santorini.com/museums; Mitropoleos; adult/under 18 €6/3; ☺ 8.30am-

Santorini (Thira)

3pm Wed-Mon) Opposite the bus station, this well-presented museum houses extraordinary finds excavated from Akrotiri, which has been settled since neolithic times. Check out the wealth of wall paintings, ceramics with a heavy Minoan influence and the glowing gold ibex figurine, dating from the 17th century BC and in mint condition. Also look for fossilised olive tree leaves from within the caldera, which date back to 60,000 BC.

It's worth visiting this museum first, before heading out to Ancient Akrotiri (p251).

Skaros Rock   LANDMARK
(Map p240) From Imerovigli, a sign points west for the track to Skaros, the conical peninsula jutting out into the caldera. Not only geologically interesting, it is also historically important, as it was the first of five *kasteli* (fortresses) built on Santorini in the 15th century to protect the islanders from pirate attacks. Earthquakes put an end to that, however, and the inhabitants moved to Fira. Walk out for great views and a perfectly situated church, but expect plenty of steps.

Old Port   PORT
(Map p240) Sitting 220m below Fira – three minutes by cable car, or 587 steps by foot – the Old Port, also known as Fira Skala, is now mainly used by cruise ship passengers visiting Fira for the day. They generally arrive in the morning, then head back in the afternoon. The little port has restaurants, tavernas and small shops, and presents a stunning view from the foot of the caldera cliffs.

Gyzi Megaron   MUSEUM
(Map p242; ☑22860 23077; www.megarogyzi.gr; Erythrou Stavrou; adult/child €3/free; ☺10am-9pm Mon-Sat, 10.30am-4.30pm Sun May-Oct) At the north end of Fira, this museum displays fascinating before-and-after photographs of the 1956 earthquake, along with centuries-old maps of the Cyclades, paintings, striking photography by Christos Simatos and 15th-century manuscripts.

Fira

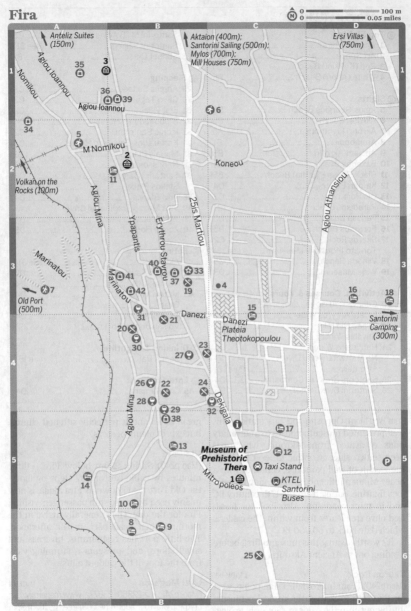

Anteliz Suites (150m)

Aktaion (400m); Santorini Sailing (500m); Mylos (700m); Mill Houses (750m)

Ersi Villas (750m)

Agiou Ioannou

Volkan on the Rocks (100m)

Old Port (500m)

Danezi

Danezi Plateia Theotokopoulou

Santorini Camping (300m)

Museum of Prehistoric Thera

Taxi Stand

KTEL Santorini Buses

🏃 Activities

Santorini Cable Car   CABLE CAR

(Map p242; https://scc.gr/cablecar.htm; one way €6; ⊙7am-9.20pm May-Sep, reduced hours Oct-Apr) Fira's efficient cable car links the caldera-top town with the Old Port (p241), 220m below, in three minutes. It can be totally swamped with cruise ship passengers coming up in the morning and heading back down in the afternoon. One option: walk the 587 steps down, then come back up by cable car.

Fira

CYCLADES FIRA

The Steps WALKING
(Map p242; Marinatou) Fira and the Old Port (p241) are linked by 587 steps down the cliff face and make a fun walk...down. You can also head back by cable car.

🛏 Sleeping

There are plenty of upmarket and midrange boutique hotels in Fira; be prepared to pay a premium for a caldera view. Budget places without views are on the eastern side of town and offer some great deals out of the high season. Book well ahead, especially for July and August.

★**Aroma Suites** BOUTIQUE HOTEL €€
(Map p242; ☑ 22860 24112; www.aromasuites.com; Mitropoleos; d/ste from €240/280; ❋ 🛜) Overlooking the caldera at the quieter southern end of Fira, and more accessible than similar places, this boutique hotel has charming service and six cave house rooms and suites. Built into the side of the caldera, the traditional interiors are paired with monochrome decor, stone bathrooms and sea-view balconies. Breakfast is an extra €12 per person.

Ersi Villas HOTEL €€
(Map p240; ☑ 22860 24719; www.ersivillassantorini.com; Agiou Athanasiou 19, Firostefani; d/tr €120/150; ❋ 🛜 🌊) Friendly and spotless, this wallet-friendly hotel clusters around an appealing dipping pool. Simple rooms come with terraces and the owner is always around to offer guidance, and will arrange transport from the port for late arrivals.

Kavalari Hotel HOTEL €€
(Map p242; ☑ 22860 22455; www.kavalarihotel-santorini.com; Ypapantis; s/d from €145/202; ❋ 🛜) One of Fira's top-value hotels, Kavalari is at the heart of the action and offers standard rooms (which are nothing special) and atmospheric cave rooms and apartments. The central location and views make this a desirable option when surrounding hotel rates are taken into consideration. An excellent breakfast is included.

Pension Petros PENSION €€
(Map p242; ☑ 22860 22573; www.hotelpetros-santorini.gr; r/tr from €172/226; ❋ 🛜 🌊) Three hundred metres east of the square in Fira, Petros offers decent rooms at good rates, but no caldera views. This is an ultrafriendly, family-run

operation and makes an affordable option, especially outside high season, when rates are less than half. Cute Grecian-Roman pool, too.

Villa Soula HOTEL €€
(Map p242; ☎22860 23473; www.santorini-villasoula.gr; Fira; d/tr/apt from €125/160/180; ❄📶🏊) Cheerful and spotless, this hotel is a great deal. Rooms aren't large but come with small, breezy balconies. Colourful public areas and a small, well-maintained undercover pool give you room to spread out a little. It's a short walk from the town centre.

Keti Hotel HOTEL €€
(Map p242; ☎22860 22324; www.hotelketi.gr; Agiou Mina, Fira; d/ste from €198/261; ❄📶) Hotel Keti is one of the smaller 'sunset view' hotels in a peaceful caldera niche. Its attractive traditional rooms are carved into the cliffs, half of which have Jacuzzis. Two-night minimum in high season.

Pelican Hotel HOTEL €€
(Map p242; ☎22860 23113; www.pelicanhotel.gr; Danezi; d/tr incl breakfast €125/155; ❄📶) There's no caldera view, but you're just metres from the heart of the action in this long-standing, good-value hotel with a homey feel. The handy adjoining restaurant next door has a delightful garden setting.

Villa Roussa HOTEL €€
(Map p242; ☎22860 23220; www.villaroussa.gr; d/tr/q from €135/171/216; ❄📶🏊) This place is all about location. Minutes from the caldera (without the prices to match) and seconds from the bus station, it has fresh, immaculate rooms and helpful staff.

★Iconic Santorini BOUTIQUE HOTEL €€€
(Map p240; ☎22860 28950; www.iconicsantorini.com; Imerovigli; r €545, ste €650-1245; ❄📶🏊) This five-star cave hotel is something special, with great attention paid to tiny details. Terraces look out over the caldera, the Cliff Suite comes with a gorgeous grotto pool, all suites are endowed with private hot tubs, and the saltwater infinity pool seems to melt into the horizon. Spa and exceptional service are among the perks. Over 14s only.

★Cavo Tagoo BOUTIQUE HOTEL €€€
(Map p240; ☎22890 20100; www.cavotagoo.com/santorini; Imerovigli; ste €1180-1600 mid-Apr–Oct; ❄📶🏊) If money is no object or you're celebrating a once-in-a-lifetime occasion, it's hard to do better than these sleek, monochromatic suites with copper accents, all with secluded terraces and private plunge pools (though you can lounge by the infinity pool for a change of scenery). Terrific restaurant on-site.

★Anteliz Suites BOUTIQUE HOTEL €€€
(Map p240; ☎22860 28842; www.anteliz.gr; d/ste from €310/665; ❄📶🏊) North of Fira on the path that runs to Firostefani, Anteliz offers an amazing pool, sun terrace and, oh, those views. Relax in the open-air hot tub and take it all in. The suites feature marble floors, the pool suites come with private plunge pools and the Anteliz master suite is a masterpiece of luxurious minimalism.

Aria Suites BOUTIQUE HOTEL €€€
(Map p242; ☎22860 28650; http://ariasuites.com; ste/villa from €635/1000; ❄📶🏊) With a mix of individually styled villas (some with private plunge pools or cave house Jacuzzis) and suites, Aria Suites is one of the top spots to stay in Fira. Just south of the Orthodox Cathedral, it is quiet, yet close enough to the action. Dazzling Cycladic white walls, superb pool, sun terrace and views. Two-night minimum.

Cosmopolitan Suites BOUTIQUE HOTEL €€€
(Map p242; ☎22860 25632; www.cosmopolitan-santorini.com; ste from €699; ❄📶🏊) This is about as good as it gets in the heart of Fira, with a spectacular, undulating infinity pool overlooking the caldera. This member of the Small Luxury Hotels of the World group consists of 10 understated, individually furnished suites, with plenty of natural light, a neutral colour palette and doorways of rough-hewn stone. Perfect location to boot.

Aigialos Niche Residences & Suites BOUTIQUE HOTEL €€€
(Map p242; ☎22860 25191; www.aigialos.gr; r/ste from €339/587; ❄📶🏊) This luxury place features a hotel, residences and suites, and boasts awards from Historic Hotels of Europe such as Most Romantic Historic Hotel. Expect five-star comfort, fine dining and views over the caldera in these 15 renovated cave houses that once belonged to rich sea captains.

Mill Houses BOUTIQUE HOTEL €€€
(☎22860 27117; www.millhouses.gr; Firostefani; d/ste incl breakfast from €399/497; ❄📶🏊) Built right into the side of the caldera at Firostefani, down a long flight of steps, these superb studios and suites are chic and plush. Lots of white linen and whitewashed walls fill them with light. King-sized beds and private patios or shared terraces looking out over the Aegean are just a few of the lavish touches.

✗ Eating

Fira has plenty to offer in terms of traditional Greek cuisine and stellar fusion food, though overpriced, indifferent food geared towards tourists is still present.

There's a price hike for a caldera view, while cheap eats surround the central square. For smart places, book ahead in July and August.

Lucky's Souvlaki   GREEK €

(Map p242; ☑ 22860 22003; gyros from €3; ⊙ 11am-11pm) Λ top spot for cheap eats on Fira's main street. Perch on a bar stool and demolish a tasty *gyros* pitta (pork, chicken or lamb), or attack a plate of souvlaki, fries and tomatoes for €11. Quality inconsistent and service irascible.

Aktaion   TAVERNA €€

(Map p240; ☑ 22860 22336; www.aktaionsantorini. com; Firostefani; mains €13-23; ⊙ 1pm-midnight; 🖉) Just off the tiny Firostefani square, this taverna has been around since 1922 and specialises in traditional island recipes, such as octopus with *fava* and capers, *skordomakarona* (homemade pasta with garlic), steamed seasonal greens and *mousakas*. Sit in the atmospheric cavern or on the outside terrace.

Volkan on the Rocks   CAFE €€

(Map p240; ☑ 22860 28360; https://ergonfoods. com; mains €10-13; ⊙ 9am-midnight May-Oct; 🛜) With a breezy clifftop terrace overlooking the caldera, this cafe is the home of Volkan craft beer, which is nicely paired with Santorini's fire in the sky. Come for breakfast, swing by for the selection of imaginative hot and cold mezedhes, or visit in the evenings for the open-air movie screenings.

Parea Traditional Greek
Restaurant   GREEK €€

(Map p242; ☑ 22860 25444; https://parearestaurant.gr; mains €9-15; ⊙ 12.30-11pm) There's nothing fancy about Parea, which pairs traditional, wallet-friendly, home-cooked Greek dishes with rooftop dining and views out to the eastern coast of Santorini. The seared octopus has bite to it without being rubbery, and when you peel the parchment paper back from the lamb *kleftiko*, the meat is wonderfully tender.

Fanari   GREEK €€

(Map p242; ☑ 22860 25107; www.fanari-restaurant. gr; dishes €8-40) On the steps down to the Old Port, Fanari offers a mix of traditional Greek dishes, plus pastas and pizzas, with a

CYCLADES FIRA

SANTORINI ON A BUDGET

Santorini is not a cheap destination, but it needn't completely blow your budget. Here are some tips to make your euros go further.

➡ If you don't need caldera views from your room, consider staying in Perissa on Santorini's southeast coast, or taking advantage of inexpensive lodgings in Fira, such as **Santorini Camping** (Map p240; ☑ 22860 22944; www.santorinicamping.gr; Fira; dm/d €25/80, camp site per person €15; ⊙ Mar-Nov; ❄ 🛜 ☱) or **Fira Backpackers Place** (Map p242; ☑ 22860 31626; www.firabackpackers.com; dm/d €49/218; 🛜), or staying in Katerados Caveland Hostel.

➡ Take the frequent public buses. Prices range from €1.80 to €2.40 and the buses will get you to most places of interest. For more remote locations, renting a car for a day (€40 to €50) is reasonable if there's three or four of you.

➡ Ancient Thira (p250), Akrotiri (p251), the **Archaeological Museum** (Museum of Akrotiri; Map p242; ☑ 22860 22217; M Nomikou; adult/concession €6/3; ⊙ 8.30am-4pm Wed-Mon), the Museum of Prehistoric Thera (p240) and the Collection of Icons and Ecclesiastical Artefacts at Pyrgos all sell a five-in-one ticket that allows discounted entry to the five sites for €14.

➡ Boat tours of the caldera cost as little as €20 for three hours, and snorkelling excursions start from €30, so you needn't deprive yourself of aquatic adventure.

➡ Eat cheaply. There are inexpensive tavernas and *gyros* joints in most locations, including Fratzeskos Fish Tavern (p253) in Perissa, Lucky's Souvlaki in Fira and PitoGyros (p249) in Oia.

➡ Take advantage of happy hours in the many bars and pubs; many do two-for-one drinks specials between certain hours.

free helping of superlative views of the caldera. The mixed seafood platter is a good bet, plus there are local dessert favourites such as Santorini pudding and *meletinia,* made of skimmed-milk cheese and scented with mastic and vanilla.

Theoni's Kitchen   GREEK €€
(Map p242; ☑ 22860 25680; www.facebook. com/theoniskitchen17; Dekigala; mains €10-24; ⊙noon-midnight) Theoni's isn't fancy and you won't be gazing out over the caldera, but this 'mumma's kitchen' restaurant does its thing with grace, humour and enthusiasm. Expect decent-sized portions of Greek classics, such as *mousakas,* grilled mackerel and grilled white Santorini aubergine with feta. The Greek salad here is exceptional.

Camille Stefani   GREEK €€
(Map p242; ☑ 22860 22762; www.camillestefani. com; Erythrou Stavrou; mains €10-20; ⊙noon-11pm) This old-school rooftop restaurant with views across to the east coast, has perfected its craft since the late '70s. Its authentic, traditional atmosphere matches its meals. Dig into countless mezedhes like *saganaki* and stuffed vine leaves or opt for *mousakas,* chicken souvlaki or swordfish fillet. This place is as popular with locals as it is with tourists.

★ Ovac   FUSION €€€
(Map p240; ☑ 22860 27900; http://ovac.gr; Imerovigli; mains €35-52; ⊙1pm-midnight) Helmed by one of Greece's hottest chefs, this Greek-Asian fusion place is all rough slate-grey rock and caldera views. The flavour combinations are bold and the presentation is impeccable; try the beetroot salmon tartare with roasted fennel or the bao buns with chilli jam. The original cocktails are terrific but the wine list is only for those with deep pockets.

★ Idol Restaurant Bar   FUSION €€€
(Map p242; ☑ 22860 23292; https://idolsantorini. gr; Ypapantis; mains €22-35; ⊙11am-11pm) This caldera-edge, three-level restaurant and bar serves up stupendous views and intelligent dishes full of depth, fire and vivacity. The chef dares combine squid with kimchi, raisins and chickpeas, alongside the more classic slow-cooked pork belly with sweet potato puree. And what could be more Greek than *mastika* (mastic liqueur) ice cream?

Excellent wine list, too; perfect for a romantic sunset dinner.

★ Mylos   GREEK €€€
(☑ 22860 25640; www.mylossantorini.com; Firostefani; mains €24-29; ⊙5.30pm-midnight) Located in a converted windmill on the caldera edge in Firostefani, this uber-glam venue has upscale food that's ambitious in its techniques and beautifully presented. Try crispy fish 'covered with sea snow', or lamb with Greek coffee and shellfish powder. Book ahead.

★ Koukoumavlos   GREEK €€€
(Map p242; ☑ 22860 23807; www.koukoumavlos.com; mains €28-36; ⊙7pm-late Apr–Oct) Award-winning fresh, modern Aegean cuisine (including a worthwhile degustation at €82), with caldera views from the terrace. Daring pairings of ingredients include sea bass with passionfruit and Jerusalem artichoke, and tiramisu with white Santorini aubergine. Excellent selection of local wines. It's located 30m north of the cathedral.

🍷 Drinking & Nightlife

After midnight, Erythrou Stavrou fires up as the clubbing caldera of Fira, while Marinatou is lined with chic cocktail bars and beer bars. The real action in clubs kicks off late and some places party all the way until morning.

MoMix Bar Santorini   BAR
(Map p242; ☑ 6974350179; www.momixbar.com; Agiou Mina; ⊙8pm-3am) MoMix is short for Molecular Mixology. This popular party spot offers innovative cocktails (to help your mind travel), cool interior colours in its cave-like bar and stunning caldera views outside.

Kira Thira   BAR
(Map p242; ☑ 22860 22770; Erythrou Stavrou; ⊙8pm-3am daily) The oldest bar in Fira and one of the best. Dark wood and vaulted ceilings give it an intimate, cave-like atmosphere, with smooth cocktails and smoother jazz, and there's a huge viola hanging on the ceiling, this tiny bar is so popular it often gets swamped, especially when there is live music.

Crystal Cocktail Bar   COCKTAIL BAR
(Map p242; ☑ 22860 22480; www.crystal-santorini. gr; Marinatou, Loucas Hotel; ⊙10am-1am) Relax at Crystal, and its views to die for, with coffee in the morning and cocktails as your day evolves. This is one of those spots that you won't want to leave. Part of Loucas Hotel, Crystal is a top spot, with stupendous sunsets.

Two Brothers Bar BAR
(Map p242; ☑ 22860 23061; www.2brothersbar-santorini.com; Dekigala; ☺10am-6am) Originally started by brothers Dimitris and Giannis in 1983, this cave bar is now run by their sons. Expect a party vibe and, later, little room to move. Two-for-one cocktails from 4pm to 7pm and 9pm to midnight.

PK Cocktail Bar COCKTAIL BAR
(Map p242; ☑ 22860 22430; http://paliakameni.com; ☺10am-late) Open year-round and into its fifth decade of business, PK Cocktail Bar offers outdoor terraces on which to nurse your cocktail while admiring the sunsets over the caldera rim. Cocktails made with fresh fruit are the speciality here. Opposite the cathedral.

Tango COCKTAIL BAR
(Map p242; ☑ 6947453999; www.tangosantorini.gr; Marinatou; ☺8pm-5am) Edge-of-the-caldera stuff, with stupendous views, sumptuous cocktails – its champagne cocktails are a speciality – a fashionable crowd and brilliant tunes that get louder and funkier as the sun goes down. Come for sunset and stay for hours and hours – or until your wallet is empty.

Tropical BAR
(Map p242; ☑ 22860 23089; Marinatou; ☺11am-4am May-Oct) Nicely perched just before the caldera edge, Tropical draws a vibrant traveller crowd with a long list of classic (and some original) cocktails, distinguished by their fresh fruit content. Try the strawberry daiquiri or the Jean Genie against a rock music backdrop, plus unbeatable balcony views. It's on the steps down to the Old Port.

☆ Entertainment

Fira's popular *Greek Wedding Show* is a hit with visitors at the **White Door Theatro** (Map p242; ☑ 22860 21770; www.whitedoorsantorini.com; €55; ☺9pm May, Sep & Oct, 9.30pm Jun-Aug) and features lots of traditional music, dance and audience participation. Small plates (mezedhes) and local wine are included in the ticket, which should be booked online. The show is in an atmospheric open-air courtyard surrounded by whitewashed buildings.

🔒 Shopping

★**Ergon Deli** FOOD & DRINKS
(Map p242; ☑ 22860 28360; www.ergonfoods.com; Erythrou Stavrou; ☺9.30am-9pm) Not only do these guys produce some of Santorini's hottest craft beer (Volkan, served at their caldera-edge cafe, p245), but this deli is also a terrific place to shop for island edibles (superb olive oil, preserves, pickled caper leaves) and drinkables, including Vinsanto dessert wine.

★**Ceramic Art Studio** CERAMICS
(Map p242; ☑ 22860 24750; next to the conference centre; ☺9am-9pm) Ceramics artist Andreas Alefragkis has been perfecting his craft over the course of three decades and the results are striking. Behold the hanging amphorae in an aquamarine or artfully cracked cream glaze and the one-of-a-kind vases, as well as utility drinking vessels and platters.

★**Eduart Gjopalaj Gallery** ART
(Map p242; ☑ 69424 39225; www.facebook.com/gjopalajeduart; Agiou Ioannou; ☺10am-9pm) This gallery is filled with the surreal woodwork of Albanian-born sculptor Eduart Gjopalaj: delicate, lattice-like platters, serene faces seemingly floating out of undulating waves of wood. You might even catch the artist at work.

★**Mati Art Gallery** ART
(Map p242; ☑ 22860 23814; www.matiartgallery.com; Cathedral Plateau; ☺10am-9.30pm) The shark-head installation piece outside is sure to catch your attention. This is the main exhibition space of Yorgos Kypris, an internationally celebrated artist who takes much of his inspiration from Santorini and the sea. From the larger pieces featuring bright silver darts of sardine shoals to glass-and-metal denizens of the deep, his work is striking and unique.

**Tzamia-Krystalla
Art Gallery Santorini** ART
(Map p242; ☑ 22860 21226; www.tzamia-krystallagallery.gr; Marinatou; ☺10am-10pm) Near the top of the steps leading down to the Old Port, this gallery specialises in Greek contemporary art, both from established artists and up-and-coming talent. All the ceramic sculptures – including ones inspired by Santorini's volcanic origins and created for this gallery – are made by Manousos Chalkiadakis, one of the most distinguished ceramic artists in Greece.

Theta 8 FASHION & ACCESSORIES
(Map p242; ☑ 22866 72935; Marinatou; ☺9am-midnight) This chic boutique in a white-cave shop on the steps down to the Old Port is a friendly family business. It offers colourful leather bags handmade in Greece (including some made to look like snakeskin). Owned and operated by the designer and her partner; expect friendly smiles and service.

Orion Art Gallery
ART

(Map p242; ☑22860 21616; www.artoftheloom. gr; Kamares; ☻9am-10pm) This gallery next to the Megaro Gyzi Cultural Centre (p241) at the northern end of town displays gorgeous pieces by some of the island's top artists. Expect everything from fusion glass to modern bronze statues, jewellery and ceramics.

AK
ART

(Map p242; ☑22860 23041; www.ak-galleries.com) Just north of the Orthodox Cathedral, Santorini's first art gallery (and a former flour mill) was founded in 1980 by local painter Christophoros Asimis and his wife, sculptor Eleni Kolaiti. On display are Santorini landscapes by Christophoros and more abstract paintings by his son Katonas, as well as jewellery and sculpture by Eleni.

the White, Santorini
FASHION & ACCESSORIES

(Map p242; ☑22860 36217; www.thewhitesantorini. com; Ypapantis; ☻9am-10pm) This small fashion boutique, run by designer Sophia Hatzigeorgiou, draws inspiration from Santorini's unique landscapes, colours and lifestyle. The clothing is hand-sewn in Greece and, as the name suggests, collections feature plenty of options in white. There's a second store out at Kamari Beach.

Art of the Loom
ARTS & CRAFTS

(Map p242; ☑22860 21190; www.artoftheloom.gr; Nomikou; ☻9am-10pm) A block north of the cable car, this gallery features colourful glasswork from the prioprietor, Mary, as well as silver jewellery, paintings and ceramics by some of the island's top artists.

ℹ Information

Information Kiosk (Map p242; Dekigala; ☻9am-8pm Mon-Fri May-Sep) Seasonal information.

Dakoutros Travel (☑22860 22958; www. dakoutrostravel.gr; Fira; ☻8.30am-midnight Jul & Aug, 9am-9pm Sep-Jun) Helpful travel agency and de facto tourist office on the main street, just before Plateia Theotokopoulou. It sells ferry and air tickets, and provides assistance with excursions, accommodation and transfers.

ℹ Getting There & Away

There are frequent bus connections between Fira's bus station and the airport, located 6km east of Fira. The first leaves Fira around 5.30am and the last leaves around 10.15pm (€1.80, 20 minutes).

In summer buses leave Fira twice hourly for Oia (€1.80), Akrotiri/Red Beach (€2), and Kamari

(€1.80), plus Perissa and Perivolos Beach (€2.40) and Kamari via Messaria (€1.80).

Buses leave Fira for the port of Athinios (€2.30, 30 minutes) seven times per day, but it's wise to check times in advance.

Oia   Οία
POP 1550

Perched on the northern tip of the island, this once centre of trade in antiquity reflects the renaissance of Santorini after the devastating earthquake of 1956. Restoration work has restored the beauty overwhelmingly enjoyed by visitors, though signs imploring visitors to be quiet and respectful remind you that for some, Oia is home year-round and a functioning village. You will struggle to find a more stunning spot in the Cyclades. Built on a steep slope of the caldera, many of its dwellings nestle in niches hewn into the volcanic rock.

Not surprisingly, Oia draws enormous numbers of tourists, and overcrowding is the price it pays for its good looks. Try to visit in the morning or spend the night here; afternoons and evenings often bring busloads from the cruise ships moored in the bay. At sunset the town feels like a magnet for every traveller on the island.

◉ Sights & Activities

Ammoudi
PORT

(Map p240) This tiny port of colourful fishing boats lies 300 steps below Oia. It's a steep haul down and up again but well worth it for the views of the blood-red cliffs, the harbour and back up at Oia. Once you're down there, have lunch at one of the excellent, if pricey, fish tavernas right on the water's edge.

In summer, boats and tours go from Ammoudi to Thirasia daily; check with travel agencies in Fira for departure times.

Maritime Museum
MUSEUM

(☑22860 71156; €3; ☻10am-2pm & 5-8pm Wed-Mon) This museum is located along a narrow lane that leads off north from Nikolaou Nomikou. It's housed in a renovated and converted 19th-century mansion and has endearing displays on Santorini's maritime history. Oia's prosperity was based on its merchant fleet, which serviced the eastern Mediterranean, especially between Alexandria and Russia.

★ Atlantis Oia
DIVING

(☑22860 71158; https://atlantisoia.com; 1 dive €70, PADI course from €230; ☻8am-10pm) Helmed by stellar diving instructor Apostolos, this five-star diving outfit has been going strong for years and is the first of its kind – a member of Cousteau Divers – in all of Greece. Its deep commitment to marine conservation and enthusiastic, professional divemasters make Atlantis Oia a top pick for all manner of dives. Snorkelling outings also (€45). Off main road.

Apostolos works closely with Pierre Cousteau, the son of legendary marine biologist Jacques Cousteau, in a bid to try to convince the Greek government to create a protected marine reserve around Santorini.

🛏 Sleeping

Oia is known for its proliferation of luxury villas and suites cascading down the caldera. Book well ahead. There are several midrange options, but if you're on a budget, consider staying elsewhere.

Maria's Place　　　　　HOTEL **€€**
(Map p240; ☎22860 71221; www.mariasantorini. com; d studio €200; ❋🛜🏊) This cluster of snug studio apartments, some split-level and all with outdoor spas for sunset viewing, is inland from town on the road to Finikia and a 10-minute walk to the caldera. Peaceful (no kids under 16), great hosts and a lovely pool. Three-night minimum in July and August.

Marcos Rooms　　　　HERITAGE HOTEL **€€**
(☎22860 71012; www.marcosrooms.com.gr; r €140–165; 🛜) This traditional cave house is among the very few midrange options in Oia. Run by hospitable Marcos, it consists of an atmospheric subterranean double and studio apartment, as well as a couple of cosy standard rooms with partial sea views. A decent Greek breakfast is thrown in and you're a couple of minutes' walk from the caldera rim.

★Zoe Aegeas　　　　APARTMENT **€€€**
(☎22860 71466; www.zoe-aegeas.gr; studio/4-person cave house €351/504; ❋@🛜) Traditional, split-level cave houses built into the caldera's edge with home comforts. They boast classy decor, amazing views and unrivalled hospitality. Book ahead. Each suite is different; some (including the private villa) can sleep up to six.

★Chelidonia
Traditional Villas　　　APARTMENT **€€€**
(☎22860 71287; www.chelidonia.com; Nikolaou Nomikou; studio €324, villa from €450; ❋🛜) Traditional cliffside dwellings that have been in the owner's family for generations. It offers beds in cosy alcoves, mod cons offset with traditional wooden furniture, and private patios with uninterrupted caldera views.

✕ Eating

PitoGyros　　　　　　KEBAB **€**
(☎22860 71119; https://pitogyros.com; mains €3–11; ⊙11am-11pm) You'll rarely find 'cheap' and 'Oia' in the same sentence, yet both apply to this souvlaki joint, a model of its kind. Go for a pitta filled with smoky, crisped meat with notes of tangy tzatziki and the crunch of onion, or fill your belly with a mixed grill platter, washed down with a Donkey craft beer. Near the bus station.

★Armeni　　　　　　SEAFOOD **€€**
(☎22860 71053; http://armenisantorinirestaurant. gr; mains €13-27; ⊙10am-11pm) With the seashore literally at your table, this gem of a tavern is worth the steep ascent on foot to Armeni Bay (though you can also catch a boat from Amoudi Bay). This is an altar to seafood with a short and brilliantly executed menu of grilled sardines, calamari stuffed with local cheese, and fresh catch seared on the grill.

Karma　　　　　　　GREEK **€€**
(☎22860 71404; www.karma.bz; mains €13-18; ⊙dinner) With fountains, flickering candles, golden-coloured walls and wine-coloured cushions, this courtyard restaurant feels rather royal and august. The food is traditional and hearty (eg *fava* beans with caramelised onions and grilled sea bream with capers), and what you lack in caldera views you make up for with reasonable prices.

★Lauda　　　　　MODERN GREEK **€€€**
(☎22860 72182; www.laudarestaurant.com; mains €48-135; ⊙1-4.30pm & 6.30-10pm) One of the top fine dining experiences in Santorini – natch, in Greece! – Lauda morphed from Oia's humble first restaurant into a destination in its own right. Chef Emmanuel Renaut combines local produce with international cooking techniques, with stellar results. Splurge on a tasting menu or go for fish marinated with caper leaves, or slow-cooked lamb with gnocchi.

★To Krinaki　　　　　TAVERNA **€€€**
(☎22860 71993; Finikia; mains €17-27; ⊙noon-late) All-fresh, all-local ingredients, such as wild greens, white aubergine, hand-crushed *fava*, caper leaves and wild asparagus go into topnotch taverna dishes at this homey spot in tiny Finikia, just east of Oia. Local beer and wine made from grape varieties grown in Santorini since antiquity, plus a sea (but not caldera) view looking north to Ios.

Catch

FUSION €€€

(☑ 22860 72063; https://catchrestaurant.gr; mains €26-39; ☺ 6.30pm-2am) This new kid on the block stands out among Oia's other fusion offerings because it gets everything right. Service is efficient, ingredient-driven dishes – from sea bass tartare and grilled asparagus with Myconian cheese to wild mushroom risotto – are spot on, with beautiful presentation. There are terrific original cocktails, divided into four elements, plus sunset views from the terrace. Near the bus station.

1800

GREEK €€€

(☑ 22860 71485; www.oia-1800.com; Nikolaou Nomikou; mains €15-38; ☺ noon-midnight) Housed in a restored sea captain's mansion, the artistically prepared modern Greek cuisine has won this restaurant accolades for years. Sea bass with an aromatic spell of quinoa, artichoke and fennel puree or grilled lamb with sweet-and-sour green apple sauce give you a glimpse at the creative menu. Dine inside or on the caldera-view rooftop. Book ahead.

🛍 Shopping

★ Atlantis Books

BOOKS

(☑ 22860 72346; www.atlantisbooks.org; Nikolaou Nomikou; ☺ 11am-8pm) Follow quotes and words that wind their way down the steep stairs into a little cavern with floor-to-ceiling shelves of books: fiction, philosophy, history, art and more. Staff are knowledgeable, and musicians are hosted on the rooftop.

B.Loose

CLOTHING

(☑ 22860 27309; https://b-loose.gr; Pliarchon; ☺ 10am-9pm) Going strong for almost a decade, this is the Oia outlet of the Athens casual fashion label that specialises in comfortable, loose-fitting streetwear handmade from high-quality cotton and linen.

❶ Information

Travel agencies such as **NS Travel** (☑ 22860 71199; www.nst-santorinitravel.com; ☺ 9am-9pm) are found by the bus area; purchase ferry tickets here.

❶ Getting There & Away

In summer, buses leave Fira twice-hourly for Oia, with more services pre-sunset (€1.80). From the bus terminal, head left and uphill to reach the rather stark central square and the beautiful marble-lined main street, Nikolaou Nomikou, which skirts the caldera.

It takes around three hours to walk (p252) from Fira to Oia on a spectacular, well-trodden path along the top of the caldera.

Around Santorini

Santorini is not all about the caldera edge. The island slopes gently down to sea level on its eastern and southern sides and here you'll find black beaches of volcanic sand at resorts such as Kamari and Perissa.

Inland lie charming traditional villages such as **Vourvoulos**, to the north of Fira, and **Megalohori**, **Pyrgos** and the 'ghost village' of **Exo Gonia** to its south. Pyrgos, in particular, is worth visiting and a good alternative to Oia, with fabulous restaurants and stunning views (see www.santorinipyrgos.com). Ancient sites round out a comprehensive package.

◉ Sights

★ Ancient Thira

ARCHAEOLOGICAL SITE

(Map p240; ☑ 22860 25405; http://odysseus.culture.gr/h/3/eh351.jsp?obj_id=2454; adult/child €4/free; ☺ 8am-3pm Tue-Sun) First settled by the Dorians in the 9th century BC, Ancient Thira consists of Hellenistic, Roman and Byzantine ruins and is a rewarding site to visit. The ruins include temples, houses with mosaics, an *agora* (market), a theatre and a gymnasium. Views are splendid. If you're driving, take the narrow, switchbacked road from Kamari for 3km. From Perissa, a hike up a dusty path takes a bit over an hour to reach the site.

★ Art Space

GALLERY

(Map p240; ☑ 22860 32774; www.artspace-santorini.com; Exo Gonia; ☺ 11am-sunset Apr-Oct) **FREE** This atmospheric gallery is on the way to Kamari, in Argyros Canava, one of the oldest wineries on the island. The walls and niches of the wine caverns feature paintings and sculptures by some 30 contemporary Greek artists, one of them from Santorini. Winemaking is still in the owner's blood, and part of the complex produces some stellar vintages under the Art Space Wines label (only available for purchase at the gallery). Tastings (from €10) enhance the experience.

Akrotiri Lighthouse

VIEWPOINT

(Map p240) If you want to watch the greatest free show on earth (the sunset!) in seclusion, well, you're out of luck. Word is out, and you will be joined at the tip of this promontory by dozens of sunset-gazers. Still, there's plenty of room for everybody and it lacks Oia's crowds.

Tomato Industrial Museum MUSEUM
(Map p240; 22860 85141; www.tomatomuseum.
gr; Vlihada; €5; 10am-6pm Tue-Sun) Tomato
processing was a major industry on the island
before the earthquake of 1952, and this is a
unique look inside an old tomato factory in
Vlihada. The video interviews of elderly former factory workers are interesting and the
museum is part of the cool **Santorini Arts
Factory** (www.santoriniartsfactory.gr), which
hosts exhibitions, concerts and theatre shows;
check its programme online.

Wine Museum WINERY
(Map p240; 22860 31322; www.winemuseum.gr;
€10; 10am-5pm Apr-Oct, 9am-4.30pm Mon-Sat
Nov-Mar) At the Koutsoyannopoulos Winery
en route to Kamari, this slightly kitsch but
fun museum in a traditional *canava* (winery)
depicts the traditional winemaking process
through a series of cheesy dioramas. Admission includes tastings of four wines; none are
exceptional, though Koutsoyannopoulos Winery is the only one to produce a very palatable
Kamaritis dessert wine from red grapes.

Ancient Akrotiri ARCHAEOLOGICAL SITE
(Map p240; 22860 81366; http://odysseus.culture.
gr/h/3/eh351.jsp?obj_id=2410; adult/concession
€12/6; 8am-8pm May-Sep, to 3pm Oct-Apr) In
1967, excavations in the southwest of Santorini uncovered an ancient Minoan city
buried deep beneath volcanic ash from the
catastrophic eruption of 1613 BC. Housed
within a protective structure, wooden walkways allow you to pass through the city. Peek
inside three-storey buildings, and see roads,
drainage systems and stashes of pottery.

Activities

There's more than just the spectacular caldera
and sunset views to keep visitors busy on Santorini. Head out to visit impressive ancient
sites, black-sand beaches, wineries (and a
brewery), take a boat tour to an active volcanic island in the caldera or explore Santorini's
underwater topography.

Navy's Waterworld Dive Center DIVING
(Map p240; 22860 28190; https://navyswater
world.gr; Kamari Beach; 2-tank dive €95; 8am-
10pm) This five-star PADI operator does a
range of diving excursions, from exploring
lava caves and wreck diving to discovery dives
for beginners and full PADI certification.

Santorini Dive Center DIVING
(Map p240; 22860 83190; www.divecenter.gr; Perissa; 1-/2-tank dive €60/90; 9am-8pm) Reputable diving outfit in Perissa, offering standard

CYCLADES AROUND SANTORINI

DON'T MISS

SANTORINI'S BEACHES

Santorini's best beaches are on the east and south coasts. Some of the beaches have
no facilities at all, whereas others come fully equipped with sunbeds, beach bars and the
odd water-sports operator.

The long stretches of black sand, pebbles and pumice stones at **Perissa** (Map p240),
Perivolos and **Agios Georgios** (Map p240) are backed by bars, tavernas, hotels and
shops and remain fairly relaxed. Perissa has a 24-hour bar that plays DJ sets on summer
nights, so that's the place if you're looking to party.

Red (Kokkini) Beach (Map p240), near Ancient Akrotiri in the south, has particularly
impressive red cliffs. Caïques from **Akrotiri Beach** can take you there and on to the
sheltered cove of **White (Aspri) Beach** (Map p240) and the sunbed-studded sand at
the **Black (Mesa Pigadia) Beach** (Map p240) for about €5 return. Mesa Pigadia has a
beachside tavern, and there are several restaurants up from Kokkini Beach.

Vlihada, also on the south coast, has a **beach** (Map p240) backed by weirdly eroded
cliffs as well as tavernas; it also has a photogenic fishing harbour with an excellent
restaurant above it. The further along the beach you go, the less clothes you see; it's a
favourite with naturists.

Kamari is Santorini's best-developed resort, with a long **beach** (Map p240) of black
sand. The beachfront road is dense with restaurants and bars, and things get extremely
busy in high season. Boats connect Kamari with Perissa in summer.

On the north coast, a short drive from Oia, there is the long, narrow stretch of sand
that is the **Baxedes Beach** that flows seamlessly into **Paradisos Beach**. There are
no facilities there, and the water isn't as sheltered for swimming as their brethren on the
south coast, but there are relatively few people as well.

dives as well as a range of PADI course, and snorkelling outings (€30).

Fira to Oia Hike
WALKING

(Map p240) Head north from Fira to Firostefani and Imerovigli along the caldera-edge pathway for sensational views. It's about a 30-minute walk one way. Keep walking and you can eventually reach Oia, but be aware that this is no small undertaking, especially in the heat of the day. It's about 9km and three hours' walk one way.

Santorini Brewery Company
BREWERY

(Map p240; ☎22860 30268; www.santorinibrewingcompany.gr; Messaria–Kamari Rd; ⏰11am-5pm Mon-Sat summer, shorter hours rest of the year) The home of the island's in-demand Donkey beers is well worth a stop. Sample the Yellow Donkey (hoppy golden ale), Red Donkey (amber ale), the Crazy Donkey (IPA), the White Donkey (wheat with a touch of orange peel), plus the Lazy Ass lager. All are unfiltered, unpasteurised and extremely palatable. There are free tastings, plus cool merchandise.

In August, look out for the seasonal Slow Donkey, matured in oak barrels from the nearby Argyros Estate after its used them for fermenting its Vinsanto dessert wine.

Tours

★ Santorini MTB Adventures
CYCLING

(Map p240; ☎6980289453; www.santoriniadventures.gr; Agios Georgios; mountain bike/e-bike rental €25/50 per day) This up-and-coming operator rents out e-bikes for an ecofriendly way of exploring the island and also runs highly regarded tours (€120 to €150) that either take in the highlights of the south coast or truly put you through your paces if you have experience of technical downhills. Full-day cycling and sailing adventures also available.

🛏 Sleeping

Away from these main villages, the biggest concentration of midrange and budget rooms can be found in and around Kamari, Perissa and Messaria.

Zorzis Hotel
BOUTIQUE HOTEL €

(Map p240; ☎22860 81104; www.santorinizorzis.com; Perissa; d incl breakfast from €99; ❄🅿🏊) Behind a huge bloom of geraniums on Perissa's main street, Hiroko and Spiros (a Japanese-Greek couple) run an immaculate 10-room hotel. It's a pastel-coloured sea of calm (no kids), with a delightful garden, pool and an eye-catching mountain backdrop.

CRUISES

Boat and catamaran cruises are a must-do activity on Santorini and are a terrific way of appreciating the island's dramatic topography and equally dramatic sunsets.

There are three types of cruises to choose from: half-day (five/six hours) boat/catamaran cruises that typically depart around 10am, half-day sunset cruises that leave at 3.30pm, and full-day (nine hour) boat cruises.

Half-day and sunset boat/catamaran cruises typically take in the caldera's volcanic islands of Nea Kameni and Palia Kameni, including a stop at the former's crater and the latter's hot springs. Catamaran cruises stop for swimming at the hot springs but don't dock at the crater, and most sail past the lighthouse and along the Red and White beaches of the south coast. Lunch and refreshments are included in the price.

Full-day tours may call at Thirasia, and/or a port below Oia.

Departures are either from Fira Skala, below Fira, Oia's Ammoudi Bay or the Vlychada marina on the south coast. Rule of thumb is: the cheaper the tour, the more crowded the boat and the less time at any one location. Quick three-hour sails around the caldera with **Caldera's Boats** (Map p242; ☎22860 24355; www.santorini-sea-excursions.com; 25is Martiou, Fira; half-/full-day cruise from €20/44) cost just €20, but it's well worth paying more for a longer tour and better service. Before booking, ask exactly what's included.

The most relaxed sailing tours are the semiprivate (or private, if you can spare the cash) small-group catamaran tours; **Santorini Sailing** (Map p240; ☎22860 21380; www.santorinisailing.com; St Gerasimos, Firostefani; per person €105-165), **Sunset Oia** (Map p240; ☎22860 72200; https://sailing-santorini.com; 5hr catamaran tour €145-190; ⏰9am-10pm) and **Spiridakos Sailing Cruises** (Map p242; ☎22860 23755; www.santorini-yachts.com; 25is Martiou, Fira; cruises from €95; ⏰8am-10pm) are among the top operators.

Karterados Caveland Hostel HOSTEL €
(Map p240; ☑ 22860 22122; www.cave-land.com; Karterados; dm from €39, d incl breakfast €129; ☺ Mar-Oct; ❀ 🕸 🖢) This fabulous, chilled-out hostel is based in an old winery complex in Karterados about 2km from central Fira (see website for directions). Dorms (four, six and 10 beds) are in the big old wine caves, all of them with creative, colourful decor and good facilities. (Warning: claustrophobes might find the tiny windows problematic.) The garden swimming pool tops it off.

Narkissos Hotel HOTEL €
(Map p240; ☑ 22860 34205; www.narkissoshotel. com; Kamari; s/d/tr incl breakfast €88/96/122; ☺ Apr-Nov; ❀ 🕸) A decent budget option at the southern end of Kamari, close to the beach and with well-kept rooms. Outside the summer peak, room prices tumble (€35).

Stelios Place HOTEL €
(Map p240; ☑ 22860 81860; www.steliosplace.com; Perissa; d/tr/q €80/100/120; ❀ @ 🕸 🖢) This small, family-run hotel has a great position set back from the main drag in Perissa, one block from the beach. Well-equipped rooms sparkle with cleanliness, as does the swimming pool. Breakfast is available. Free airport or port transfers for those staying three nights or longer; note that off-peak rates fall to a bargain €35.

Villa Mezzo Traditional Cave House APARTMENT €€
(Map p240; ☑ 6977322712; Vothonas; apr €170; 🕸) In the middle of the countryside, not far from the Wine Museum, this cave house gives you a chance to experience Santorini's traditional dwellings (even if there's no caldera view). It's run by friendly and helpful host Luke and there's a fully equipped kitchen for self-caterers. At night, stargaze from the terrace and enjoy the silence.

Hippocampus Hotel HOTEL €€
(Map p240; ☑ 22860 32050; www.hippocampus-hotel.gr; Kamari; d/tr/q €138/145/185; ☺ May-Oct; ❀ 🕸 🖢) 🍴 Just steps from Kamari's beachfront, this friendly place has a sparkling collection of rooms and studios, with hand-painted murals and a commitment to ecopractices. Good family-sized studios, too.

★ Villa Blanca VILLA €€€
(Map p240; ☑ 22860 81860; http://villablanca-santorini.com; Megalohori; villa €275; ☺ Jun-Sep; P ❀ 🕸) A superb option away from the crowds amid Megalohori's vineyards, 6km south of Fira. Villa Blanca is a luxury villa built in traditional Cycladic style, featuring two bedrooms, living room, kitchen and balcony with a lovely Jacuzzi and ocean view out to the southeast. Perfect for a family, sleeping up to five; you'll need own wheels.

🍴 Eating

Brusco CAFE €
(☑ 22860 30944; Pyrgos; mains from €8) In Pyrgos, Brusco offers coffee, wine and local flavours in a sweet rustic cafe-deli with plenty of outdoor space. Stop by for the warm welcome, homemade cakes (including baklava) and platters of great Santorini produce (*fava*, tomatoes, aubergines, capers and more).

★ Tzanakis GREEK €€
(Map p240; ☑ 22860 81929; http://tavernatzanakis. com; Megalohori; mains €8-14; ☺ noon-midnight) A local institution into its third decade, this family-run taverna uses vegetables and herbs grown in its garden and meat and fish sourced from farmer and fisher friends to cook up such classics as tomato balls, courgette fritters, goat with lemon sauce, *domadakia* (stuffed vine leaves) and more.

★ Aroma Avlis MODERN GREEK €€
(Map p240; ☑ 22860 33794; www.artemiskaramolegos-winery.com; Messaria–Kamari Rd; mains €13-48; ☺ 1-11pm) 🍴 Part of the Artemis Karamolegos winery, this terrific restaurant does wonderful things with local ingredients with brilliance and flourish. Go for the smoked white aubergine mousse, *chloro* (fresh Santorinian goat's cheese), local sausages or *orzotto* with king crab and speck from Crete. Eat on the vine-covered terrace and don't miss out on the extensive selection of local wines.

★ Metaxi Mas CRETAN €€
(Map p240; ☑ 22860 31323; www.santorini-metaximas.gr; Exo Gonia; mains €9-21; ☺ 2pm-midnight Apr-Oct) The raki flows at this convivial taverna near the church, a favourite among locals and authenticity-seeking travellers. It serves a delicious menu of local and Cretan specialities (the owner-chef is from Crete), such as grilled pork belly, oven-baked asparagus with Cretan *graviera* and more. Enjoy sweeping views, too. Book ahead.

Fratzeskos Fish Tavern SEAFOOD €€
(☑ 22860 83488; www.facebook.com/fishtavern-frageskos1; Perissa; mains from €8; ☺ noon-11.30pm) This superb waterfront taverna specialises in

fresh fish, from grouper to sea bream, expertly grilled with the high notes of lemon. There's lobster spaghetti for two, shrimp *saganaki* and other crowd-pleasers.

Apollon Taverna   GREEK €€

(Map p240; ☑ 22860 85340; Perissa; mains €9-14; ⊙ 10am-midnight) This marvellous taverna sits just across the road from the beach, about 400m along the Perissa waterfront from the bus stop. Try the mouthwatering seafood platter for two (€30) or pick from the likes of smoked Santorini aubergine and traditional pies from the full-on menu.

⭐ **Selene**   MODERN GREEK €€€

(☑ 22860 22249; www.selene.gr; Pyrgos; mains restaurant €32-50, bistro €14-21; ⊙ restaurant 7-11pm, bistro noon-11pm) This is one of Santorini's most celebrated restaurants. Dishes such as *pasticcio* stuffed with pork cheek and Aegean codfish with smoked aubergine are pleasing to the eye and to the palate, and the wine list is superb. That said, the more moderately priced Meze & Wine Bistro downstairs is just as satisfying and creative but without the price tag.

🍷 Drinking & Nightlife

Beach Bar   BAR

(Map p240; www.thebeachbar.gr; ⊙ 24hr; 🛜) Round-the-clock fun in season on the black-sand beach on the Perissa waterfront. The Beach Bar does it all, from breakfast, lunch and dinner offerings, sunbeds and umbrellas, cocktails and beers, right through to live bands and DJ sets. The water is only a step or two away once you've overheated!

⭐ **CineKamari**   CINEMA

(Map p240; ☑ 22860 33452; www.cinekamari. gr; Kamari; €10; ⊙ 9.30pm) On the road into Kamari, this tree-surrounded, open-air cinema screens movies in their original language throughout the summer. Pull up a deckchair, request a blanket if you're feeling chilly, and relax. Drinks and snacks available.

ANAFI   ΑΝΑΦΗ

POP 271

Though Anafi lies a mere 22km east of Santorini, its rugged, hilly landscape, dotted with prickly pears and a few hardy olive trees and overlooked by Kalamos (or Monastery Rock, 463m) – believed to be the second-largest in the Mediterranean after the Rock of Gibraltar – is among the least visited in the Cyclades.

Myth has it that it once served as a refuge for the exhausted Argonauts, revealed to them by Apollo only after they'd spent hours battling a tempest. A refuge it remains – from the crowds that descend on the neighbouring islands – so if seclusion and great hiking is what you're after, you've hit the jackpot.

The port of **Agios Nikolaos** is on the south coast, with the main town of **Hora** a steep 2km by road above to the north.

⊙ Sights

There is a string of lovely beaches along the south coast, starting near Agios Nikolaos. **Klissidi**, an 800m (10-minute) walk east of the port, is the closest and most popular. Around 2.4km (40-minute walk) further east, past the Katsouni, Phlamourou, Exo Roukounas and Mikros Roukounas coves, is the broad sweep of **Roukounas**, a sandy beach backed by dunes and home to the superb Roukounas taverna. Further still, the trail meanders past the delightful **Katalimatsa** cove and passes by three more small beaches before climbing up to the monastery from the pebble beach of **Prasies**.

Zoodochos Pigi Monastery   MONASTERY

Incorporating the ruins of the temple of Apollo (allegedly built by the Argonauts) into its building, monastery Zoodochos Pigi is 9km from Hora by road, or reached by a 7km walk along the south-coast trail. Not open to visitors, the monastery lies in the east of the island, on the isthmus connecting Anafi to the imposing 463m Kalamos (or Monastery Rock), which has the uninhabited Kalamiotissas Monastery at its peak.

🛏 Sleeping

Most lodgings are in Hora and consist of self-catering apartments and B&Bs. There's a beach resort west of Hora and a couple of options overlooking Klissidi Beach. Many of the rooms on Hora's main street have good views across Anafi's hills, the sea and the summit of Kalamos. Book early for July and August.

Ostria   GUESTHOUSE €

(☑ 22860 61375; studio from €30; 🛜) Run by a welcoming local couple (little English spoken), this sweet guesthouse consists of several spotless rooms with kitchenettes, with great views down to the port from the hillside from its location in the quiet, southern part of Hora. Accessible via some steps down from the end of the ring road.

★ **Margarita's Rooms** PENSION €€
(☑ 22860 61237; www.margarita-anafi.gr; d from €70; 🛜) Just above Klissidi Beach, these simple, beloved family-run rooms hark back to the Greek island life of quieter times. Nothing luxurious here, but it's an affordable island escape next to a lovely beach, with an excellent restaurant attached – Margarita's taverna. It's a tad isolated, so renting some wheels is a good idea. Port transfers included.

Apollon Village Hotel APARTMENT €€
(☑ 22860 28739; http://apollonvillagehotel.com; d/studio/bungalow/ste from €100/150/160/180; ☺ May-Sep; ❋🛜) Rising in tiers above Klissidi Beach, these individual rooms, studios and apartments with glorious views are each named after a Greek god and remain outstanding value. The Blue Cafe-Bar is a cool adjunct to the hotel, with homemade sweets and pastries. It's not in Hora, so can feel a little isolated without your own wheels.

✖ Eating

★ **Roukounas** TAVERNA €
(☑ 22860 61206; Roukounas Beach; mains €5-8; ☺ 10am-midnight late May-Oct) A little way up from Roukounas Beach, this delightful family-run taverna hides amid a lush garden. A great place to sample simple, hearty dishes such as oven-baked lamb and rabbit casserole, as well as local cheese and seasonal greens.

★ **Margarita's** TAVERNA €
(☑ 22860 61237; www.margarita-anafi.gr; Klissidi; mains €6-12; ☺ 9am-10pm Jun-Sep; 🛜) This standard-bearer of the 'Aegean Cuisine' label has a sunny little terrace overlooking the bay at Klissidi. Margarita's fresh-baked bread, handmade pasta and meatballs are staples; goat stew, shrimp risotto with Anafi crocus and cheese pies are all full of local flavour. There are rooms (see above) here, too.

★ **Liotrivi** TAVERNA €
(☑ 22860 61209; www.facebook.com/liotrivi.rest; mains €7-10; ☺ noon-11pm May-Oct) An old-school taverna on the main street in Hora, where fresh fish is brought in from the family's boat, while the eggs, vegetables and honey come from their garden. Come into the kitchen and choose from the likes of lemon and dill rice with mussels, *mousakas* and catch of the day.

Armenaki TAVERNA €€
(☑ 22860 61234; mains €8-16; ☺ noon-10pm Jun-Sep) Fresh fish dishes are the go-to staples at this traditional taverna in Hora, enhanced by an airy terrace, splendid views and occasional live music. Head down the small street opposite the bakery in central Hora to find it.

ℹ Getting There & Away

Anafi is remote, and reached by fewer ferry services than most of the Cyclades. In inclement weather, ferries may have trouble landing, since Anafi lacks a sheltered bay. Plan ahead, especially outside the high season, and consult http://ferries.gr for up-to-date ferry information.

Buy ferry tickets at **Roussou Travel** (☑ 22860 61220; ☺ 10am-1pm & 6-8pm), in the village or on the harbourfront, an hour before ferries are due.

Boat services from Anafi:

DESTINATION	DURATION	FARE (€)	FREQUENCY
Folegandros	5¼hrs	11	2 weekly
Ios	3½hrs	9	2 weekly
Karpathos	6¾hrs	17	2 weekly
Milos	6¼hrs	21	2 weekly
Naxos	7½hrs	13	2 weekly
Paros	7hrs	16	2 weekly
Piraeus	11½hrs	38	2 weekly
Rhodes	13½hrs	29	2 weekly
Santorini	1½hrs	8	2 weekly
Sikinos	4¼hrs	11	2 weekly
Syros	15½hrs	19.50	2 weekly

ℹ Getting Around

The island's port is Agios Nikolaos. From here, the main village, Hora, is a 10-minute bus ride (€2) up a winding road, or a 2km hike up a less winding but steep walkway. Between May and September, free buses run from the **bus stop**, arriving at the port one hour before scheduled boat departures. Three buses daily run down to the port at 11am, 2pm and 6pm, departing from Hora for the monastery 10 minutes later and returning from the monastery at 11.25am, 2.25pm and 6.25pm (€3).

Summertime caïques serve various beaches and nearby small islands (price depends on distance and number of passengers).

In Hora, **Manos** (☑ 22860 61430; www.rentaca ranafi.gr) hires cars, scooters and four-wheelers for rent; some lodgings do so also.

SIKINOS ΣΙΚΙΝΟΣ

POP 300

Legend has it that Thoas, the king of Lemnos, fled to Sikinos to escape his island's womenfolk who rose up and slaughtered all the men. A succession of Mycenaeans, Ionians, Dorians, Venetians and Turks followed, while in

---

LOCAL KNOWLEDGE

WALKING ON ANAFI

The four main (relatively well-marked) walking trails are the following:

#1: Klisidi Beach to Zoodochos Pigi Monastery (7km, around 2½ to three hours one way) Takes in the south coast and around 10 beaches and coves, including the ancient harbour of Katalimatsa.

#2: Milies to Zoodochos Pigi Monastery via the Kastelli ruins (7.5km, around 3½ hours one way) Beginning from a farmhouse in the hamlet of Milies, this moderately tough trail passes the ruins of the ancient Kastelli and Kastelli peak (325m), from where the ancient Sacred Way leads to the former Temple of Apollo (now a monastery).

#3: Zoodochos Pigi Monastery to Moni Kalamiotissas (2.5km, around an hour one way) The island's most famous (and steepest) hike to the top of the Kalamos rock, with staggering views from the summit.

#4: Hora to Aghia Irini (7km, 2½ hours one way) A gentle ramble through the countryside, past the chapel of Stavros, and a descent to the Aghia Irini chapel through some old estates.

---

the late 1930s, the island was a place of exile for communists and socialists.

With a tiny population, Sikinos is still quiet and remote, the place to come if you want to experience traditional island life at its least commercial. With a charming old town and terraced hills that offer terrific hiking terrain, Sikinos is the antithesis of neighbouring Ios.

The main clusters of habitation are the port of Alopronia and the linked inland villages of Horio and Kastro (known as the Hora).

July and August see lots of Greek visitors turn up, but if you arrive before mid-May, don't expect there to be much going on.

◎ Sights

The beach at the port of **Alopronia** is lovely – sandy, with some shade and a children's playground. It looks straight out at Santorini.

A narrow, dramatic bay with a small sandy patch, **Agios Nikolaos Beach** is a 20-minute walk through the countryside from the port. To find it, follow signs to Dialiskari. A path leads further on to **Agios Georgios**, or you can reach it by sealed road (7km).

Summertime caïques (about €6) run to beaches, including **Maltas** (Map p257) in the north (which has ancient ruins on the hill above) and **Kara** in the south.

★Moni Zoödohou Pigis   MONASTERY
(Map p257; ☑ 6975743928; ⊙ 11.30am-1.30pm Tue-Sun) FREE A flight of whitewashed steps leads to the fortified monastery of Moni Zoödohou Pigis, high above the Kastro. Originally built as a women's monastery in 1690, this is where the nuns and villagers would hide out during

pirate attacks. The monastery has recently opened to the public, and you can go into the church and the visitors' room, or check out the amazing views. Don't miss the nuns' emergency escape route, by rope down the cliffs out the back.

Kastro   VILLAGE
A Venetian fortress that stood here in the 13th century gave Kastro its name. Today it is a charming, lived-in place, with winding alleyways between brilliant white houses. At its heart is the main square and the Church of Pantanassa. Check out the buildings surrounding the church, which were homes to the town's wealthy merchants: two-storey affairs with remnants of ornate stonework around the windows.

Moni Episkopis   MONASTERY
(Map p257) FREE From the saddle between Kastro and Horio, a surfaced road leads southwest for 5km to Moni Episkopis, under renovation during research time. The remains here are believed to be those of a 3rd-century AD Roman mausoleum that was transformed into a church in the 7th century and a monastery 10 centuries later. A couple of excellent hiking trails start here and one bus per day runs here on summer evenings.

★ Activities

Sikinos is popular with walkers, and the island has set up seven **Paths of Culture**, a network of well-signposted paths all over the island. Keen walkers should purchase Terrain's (http://terrainmaps.gr) excellent hiking map for Sikinos.

On the road to Moni Episkopis, family-run **Manalis Winery** (Map p257; ☑6932272854; www.manaliswinery.gr; ⊙6pm-late Jun-Sep) produces Sikinos wine using traditional, self-sustaining methods. The friendly owner can give you a taste and the on-site restaurant serves traditional island dishes (mains €10 to €15). The food won't blow your mind, but the view of the vineyard and coast from the terrace will. The bus stops here summer evenings.

🛏 Sleeping

The dozen or so options in Alopronia, near the beach, range from simple pensions and self-catering studios to three-star hotels. Atmospheric Hora (Kastro) has only a couple of places to stay: a pension and a clutch of apartments. Book early for July and August.

⭐Kastellos Apartments GUESTHOUSE €
(☑6972377729; www.kastellos-sikinos.gr; studios €50; ❄🖥🛜) Spotless, spacious and well-equipped with little kitchenettes, these three individually designed studio apartments with splashes of colour are near the port and have tiny balconies looking out to sea. The friendly owner will help you with your luggage.

Porto Sikinos Hotel HOTEL €€
(☑22860 51220; www.portosikinos.gr; Alopronia; s/d/f incl breakfast €75/90/120; ⊙May-Oct; ❄🛜) The sweet rooms here are traditional tile-and-marble affairs with pastel-coloured accents and balconies. This central, whitewashed complex is the closest thing to a standard hotel on Sikinos and it's well run and appealing, with an on-site cafe.

Stegadi Apartments APARTMENT €€
(☑22860 51305; www.stegadi.com; Kastro; apt €110; ❄🖥🛜) Near the heart of Kastro, these four beautiful, traditional apartments sleep up to four and are individually decorated with modern furnishings and splashes of vibrant colour. The balconies are small oases with views across to the sea.

Ostria Studios PENSION €€
(☑22860 51062; www.ostriastudios-sikinos.gr; Alopronia; d from €110; ❄🖥🛜) These comfy rooms and studios are lovingly decorated. Margarita has three sets of rooms – Ostria Studios Spilia, Agnanti and Molos; Spilia is on the far side of the bay from the ferry quay. The rooms are right on the water, and you can swim below your room. They have sea-view balconies and plenty of natural light.

🍴 Eating

⭐Anemelo CAFE €
(☑22860 51216; Kastro; mains €5-9; ⊙10am-3pm & 5pm-late) This is Kastro's most atmospheric place to grab a local tea, beer or simple crêpe-and-salad lunch. Locals chat at the tables over chess games or lounge over coffee at the tables outside. Take the *tiny* spiral staircase up to the terrace for ace views. The killer Traditional Sandwich (€6) features olive paste, feta, capers and tomato. In the evenings, this place is really hopping!

Kapari GREEK €
(☑22860 51070; Kastro; mains €7.50-11; ⊙12.30-3pm & 6pm-1am) Your go-to place if you arrive out of season or are staying at Alopronia and absolutely nothing is open. This 'Aegean Cuisine' standard bearer is on the main road in Hora, and Evgenia cooks up solid Greek staples, including her own 'beer salad' with local sausage, spicy meatballs and veal cooked in beer.

ℹ Getting There & Away

Ferry tickets can be bought at the port at **Kountouris Travel** (Map p257; ☑22860 51232, 6981594106). Out of high season, boat services are skeletal.

Destinations are: Folegandros (€5, 45 minutes, two weekly), Ios (€4.50, 25 minutes, three weekly), Kimolos (€9, two to 2½ hours, four weekly), Milos (€12.50, 3¼ hours, three weekly), Naxos (€7, three hours, three weekly), Paros (€8, 4¼ hours, three weekly), Piraeus (€40, 10¼ hours, three weekly), Serifos (€13, 4½ hours, two weekly), Sifnos (€10.50, 4¾ hours, three weekly), Santorini (€7.50, 2¼ to 2½ hours, three weekly) and Syros (€13, 5½ to six hours, three weekly).

ℹ️ Getting Around

The local bus meets ferry arrivals and runs between Alopronia and Horio/Kastro (€1.80) every half-hour in August, 10 times daily the rest of summer from 7.45am to 10.45pm, and less frequently at other times. A timetable is posted at the terminus, just inland from the port. One bus daily continues from Kastro to Agios Georgios, and a 7.15pm bus runs to the Manalis Winery (p257), making the return journey at 8.45pm.

If you're out of season and nothing is going on, talk to English-speaking Flora in the minimarket at Alopronia, and she'll help you figure out your options. Her son also runs the petrol station, so she's the person to call if it's closed.

There is a branch of **RaC** (☎ 21040 80300; www.rentacar-sikinos.gr), the Cyclades-wide agency, at the port, hiring out cars and fairly decrepit scooters; **Kostis** (☎ 6981751555) is a better bet for scooter hire.

FOLEGANDROS
ΦΟΛΕΓΑΝΔΡΟΣ

POP 760

Folegandros lies on the southern edge of the Cyclades, with the Sea of Crete sweeping away to its south. The island has a quiet beauty, amplified by the clifftop Hora, one of the most appealing villages in the Cyclades.

The hilly topography, with terraced fields sloping down to the sea, verdant countryside dotted with chapels and ruins and numerous beaches to explore – some reachable via strenuous slogs – make Folegandros a favourite with hikers. The island is barely 12km by 4km

and both the little harbour of **Karavostasis** on the east coast and the village of **Ano Meria** are easily walkable from Hora.

You'll find no signs of it today, but Folegandros shoulders a somewhat dark past. The remoteness and ruggedness of the island made it a place of exile for political prisoners from Roman times to the 20th century, as late as the military dictatorship of 1967–74.

ℹ️ Getting There & Away

Folegandros has good connections (at least from May/June to September) with Piraeus through the western Cyclades route. It has routes to Santorini and is part of an Ios–Sikinos–Folegandros link, with regular ferries passing through.

Boat services from Folegandros:

DESTINATION	DURATION	FARE (€)	FREQUENCY
Amorgos	2½hrs	70	daily
Ios	1¼-1¾hrs	6-45	2-4 daily
Kimolos	1½hrs	6	weekly
Koufonisia	3½hrs	70	daily
Milos	1hr	34-40	3 daily
Mykonos	2¾-3¾hrs	49	2 daily
Naxos	2¾-3¼hrs	11-43	2-3 daily
Piraeus	4¼-4½hrs	63-70	2-3 daily
Santorini	45mins-3¼hrs	7-45	3-4 daily
Serifos	2½hrs	50	2 daily
Sifnos	2hrs	46-50	3 daily
Sikinos	45mins	5	2 weekly
Syros	5-6½hrs	13.50	3 weekly

LOCAL KNOWLEDGE

WALKING ON FOLEGANDROS

Folegandros is popular with walkers and there are six main, signposted walking trails. These include:

#1: Hora to Agios Nikolaos Beach via Angali (4.5km, 1½ hours one way) A descent through the countryside followed by a coastal ramble.

#3: Ano Meria to Agios Georgios (2.6km, 1¼ hours) Gorgeous descent along a cobbled path from the north end of the village to the seaside chapel.

#5: Ano Meria to Livadaki Beach (5.7km, 2¼ hours) Loop hike that starts near the windmills in Ano Meria, descends to the beach and climbs steeply through the countryside to the north end of the village.

#6: Hora to Katergo Beach (6.4km, 2½ hours) Relatively demanding trail that passes by Folegandros' highest peak and Petousis village before descending steeply to the beach.

Check out the detailed information at www.folegandros.com/footpaths.asp. Terrain (http://terrainmaps.gr) produces an excellent Folegandros map.

Folegandros

❶ Getting Around

The local bus meets all ferry arrivals and takes passengers to Hora (€1.80, 3km). From Hora there are buses to the port one hour before ferry departures. Buses from Hora run hourly in summer to Ano Meria (€1.80) and divert to Angali Beach (€2.20).

There is a **taxi service** (☑6944693957) on Folegandros. Fares to the port are about €7 to €10, to Ano Meria €10 and to Angali Beach €10 to €14.

You can hire cars/ATVs/motorbikes from a number of outlets in high season for about €60/40/25 per day. Rates can drop by half outside high season. **Donkey Scooters** (☑22860 41628; www.donkeyscooters.gr; scooter/ATV hire per day from €20/30; ⊙9.30am-8.30pm May-Oct) and **Tomaso** (☑22860 41600; www.tomaso.gr; ⊙9am-9pm) in Hora are good options.

In summer, small boats regularly run between beaches.

Karavostasis Καραβοστάσις

POP LESS THAN 100

Folegandros' port is centred on a pebble beach, with another – sand-and-pebble Vardia – just across the small headland. A 15-minute walk south along the coast, past the pebble coves of Vitsentzou and Pountaki, is the family-friendly beach of Livadi, with its calm waters. In high season, boats leave Karavostasis for beaches further afield, such as Katergo (also reachable by steep hike).

🛏 Sleeping & Eating

There are a dozen or so waterside lodgings here, from hotels to self-catering studios, but Folegandros' Hora is the most atmospheric place to stay. Book early for July and August.

Aeolos Beach Hotel   HOTEL €€
(☑22860 41205; www.aeolos-folegandros.gr; s/d/ste from €80/100/240; ⊙May-Sep; ❄🐾) Settle in right on the beach here at Aeolos. Rooms have sea or mountain views and are each unique, with varying degrees of character. There's a minimum three-night stay in July and August; breakfast costs €8.50.

★Anemi   LUXURY HOTEL €€€
(☑22860 41610; www.anemihotel.gr; d/ste incl breakfast from €385/649; ⊙late May-Sep; ❄🐾🏊) Set back from the road towards Hora and oh so modern and entirely luxurious, this is a place for pampering. Rooms are spacious, minimalist and full of natural light, with welcome touches like modern artworks that double as headboards. Besides the infinity pool, there are holistic wellness options, and kids are kept busy in the playground.

Meltemi
TAVERNA €

(☎ 22860 41287; mains €8-12; ☺ 9am-late Apr-Oct)
Perched above the port with lovely views,
Meltemi stands out with its lovely terrace
with blue balustrades. This is a mama's cooking, family-run place with Greek staples, seafood and grilled meats.

❶ Getting There & Around

Karavostasis is the port for all ferries arriving and
leaving the island.

The local bus that meets ferries links Karavostasis with Hora (€2, 3km). A taxi to Hora will set you
back €7 to €10. Alternatively, you can walk (3.5km
uphill) or rent a scooter or ATV from one of the
waterfront rentals.

Hora (Folegandros)
Χώρα (Φολέγανδρος)

POP 450

Sitting on a plateau that abruptly gives way
to a cliff edge, this pedestrianised maze of
tiny streets lined with houses and churches
in Cycladic white and blue, draped in blazing
bougainvillea, is among the most charming
villages in the Cyclades. Its pedestrianised
main street meanders between the five adjacent leafy squares, where al fresco tables
buzz with diners. Towards the east end of the
village, pass through a low archway to enter
the *kastro* neighbourhood, made up of two-
storey houses and dating from when Marco
Sanudo ruled the island in the 13th century.

◉ Sights & Activities

Given the tough-to-access nature of many
beaches, a popular excursion is the six-hour
boat trip around the island (adult/child
€50/25). The price includes lunch and at
least four swimming stops. The tour, booked
through Diaplous Travel (p262), leaves Karavostasis at 11am. Private and shorter boat trips
can also be arranged.

★ Panagia
CHURCH

(Map p259; ☺ 6-9pm) From Plateia Pounta, a
zigzag path leads up to the large Church of
the Virgin, Panagia, which sits perched on the
side of a hill above the town and acts as a magnet for sunset-watchers (though it's equally
lovely at sunrise). It's an easy 15-minute walk
without steps, with spectacular views down to
Hora and the islands of Milos and Sifnos.

★ Sea U Dive Centre
DIVING

(☎ 22860 41624; https://sea-u.com; 1-/2-tank dive
€55/80; ⧉) Based at the edge of Hora, Spyros
and his team are enthusiastic, professional
divemasters who run all manner of aquatic
outings at a dozen dive sites around the island
– from standard dives to Bubblemaker intros
for kids and full PADI courses. They also do
private boat tours of the island.

Local Path
FOOD

(☎ 22860 41624; www.local-path.com; ☺ 9am-9pm)
Based in Hora, these guys run small-group
tours of the island, ranging from gastronomic
(Taste Local Flavours) that have you exploring

WORTH A TRIP

BEACHES AROUND FOLEGANDROS

For **Livadi Beach**, 1.2km southeast of Karavostasis, take the 'bypass' road just past the
Anemi Hotel and follow it around the coast. There is camping here (see www.folegan-
dros.org).

Katergo Beach is on the southeastern tip of the island and is reached either by fairly
demanding hike or by boat from Karavostasis. Boats leave regularly (weather permitting) and cost €8 return.

The sandy and pebbled **Angali Beach**, on the central coast opposite Hora, is a popular spot. There are some rooms here and reasonable tavernas; buses run here regularly
in summer from Hora. About 750m west of Angali along a coastal footpath is **Agios
Nikolaos**, a clothes-optional beach with a summer restaurant and taverna.

A number of beaches can be reached from where the road ends beyond Ano Meria:
Livadaki Beach is a 1.5km hike from the bus stop near the church of Agios Andreas
at Ano Meria. **Agios Georgios Beach** is north of Ano Meria and requires another demanding walk (about 40 minutes). Have tough footwear and sun protection – and, because most beaches have no shops or tavernas, make sure you take food and water.

Boats connect some west-coast beaches in high season: excursion boats make
separate round trips from Angali to Agios Nikolaos (€5), and from Angali to Livadaki
Beach (€10).

Folegandros' cuisine, to rambles across the countryside. Book in advance; price based on the number of participants.

🛏 Sleeping

Accommodation ranges from simple domatia to boutique hotels; in July and August, most lodgings will be full, so book well in advance. Free port transfers (3km to the port) are generally included.

★ Ampelos   BOUTIQUE HOTEL €€
(☑ 22860 41544; http://ampelosresort.com; s/d/tr €100/110/120; ☺ May-Oct; ✳ 🛜 ⛱) Theo and Areti's place is a gorgeous family-run operation with a sparkling pool, tasteful colours and lovely rooms. It's an easy six-minute stroll into the centre of Hora from just south of town. There are free port transfers, complimentary coffee, rates that halve outside the peak season and friendly smiles.

Hotel Odysseus   HOTEL €€
(☑ 22860 41276; www.hotelodysseus.com; s/d/studio €100/120/155; ☺ mid-May-Sep; ✳ 🛜 ⛱) Tucked away in a quiet corner of town with some dramatic views and colourful green doors, Odysseus has pretty, compact rooms with sweet terraces, and a lovely pool area that's shared with Aria Boutique Hotel next door. Low-season prices are ace (doubles €65) but breakfast is an additional €12.

Folegandros Apartments   APARTMENT €€
(☑ 22860 41239; www.folegandros-apartments.com; d from €135; ☺ May-Sep; ✳ 🛜 ⛱) This lovely complex of studios and apartments (the largest can sleep seven) is set in well-kept gardens around a pristine pool just above Plateia Pounta in Hora. It's only a couple of minutes' stroll into the village.

Anemomilos Apartments   HOTEL €€€
(☑ 22860 41309; www.anemomilosapartments.com; apt incl breakfast from €310; ☺ May-Sep; ✳ 🛜 ⛱) A prime clifftop location just above Plateia Pounta in Hora grants awesome views from this stylish complex and its lovely terraces. Rooms are elegant and embellished with antiques. The clifftop pool is shaded by eucalyptus trees, and the service is warm.

Blue Sand Boutique
Hotel & Suites   BOUTIQUE HOTEL €€€
(Map p259; ☑ 22860 41042; www.bluesand.gr; r/ste from €180/350; ☺ May-Oct; ✳ 🛜) This luxury boutique hotel sits above lovely Angali Beach, a 10-minute drive from Hora. Of the spacious and minimalist rooms decked out in creams

and whites, those with sea views come with little private terraces overlooking the clear Aegean waters below. The on-site bar and restaurant is top-notch and open all day.

🍴 Eating

Cafe Mikro   CAFE €
(☑ 22860 27644; mains from €8; ☺ 9am-11pm Jun-Sep) On a tiny dead-end street off Plateia Maraki, this thimble-sized cafe is popular all day long. Enjoy pancakes and coffee in the morning, or nurse a predinner Aperol spritz at sunset while cuddling up to Paoki the rescue cat.

Chic   GREEK €€
(☑ 22860 41515; Piatsa; mains €7-14; ☺ 7-11pm Easter-Oct; ☑) On an enchanting little square, Chic is perfectly placed for watching the passing parade. But what's more impressive is the flavoursome food: with the menu indicating gluten-free, dairy-free and vegan options (a rarity in Greece). Veggie dishes are plentiful; carnivores should plump for goat and lamb from the owners' farm.

Pounta   TAVERNA €€
(☑ 22860 41063; www.pounta.gr; Plateia Pounta; mains €7-14; ☺ 8am-3pm & 6pm-midnight Easter–mid-Oct) A family business, Pounta is the work of a creative Danish-Greek couple – dishes are served on Lisbet's handmade ceramics (also for sale) in a large, lush garden. The menu ranges from breakfast yoghurt to grilled octopus by way of rabbit *stifadho* and baked eggplant. Right on Plateia Pounta in Hora.

★ Blue Cuisine   FUSION €€€
(☑ 22860 41665; www.bluecuisine.gr; mains €14-25; ☺ 7pm-midnight) The short and sweet menu at this adventurous place near Hora's southern entrance takes you on a culinary journey, with ingredients from across Greece interacting in surprising combinations. Seafood meets citrus and fennel, the sharpness of pickled melon alleviates the saltiness of Cypriot *lountza* ham and smoky goat souvlaki is enhanced by the sweetness of tomato chutney. Book ahead.

Eva's Garden   MEDITERRANEAN €€€
(☑ 22860 41110; mains €12-27; ☺ 7pm-midnight late May-Sep) Eva's is a sophisticated spot that puts a gourmet spin on Greek cuisine. The menu mixes classic and bold flavour combinations, with crayfish risotto and rib-eye steak sitting alongside baked onions stuffed with veal, pine nuts and raisins and octopus carpaccio. Book ahead. Turn left after Plateia Piatsa.

🍷 Drinking & Nightlife

Overlooking a vineyard, **Wine Bar Merkouri** (📞6977272373; www.facebook.com/merkouriwinefolegandros; ⏲7pm-3am) is a must for wine lovers with over 40 Greek vintages by the glass. Talk to the owner about oenology and sample some of his own wine. The dishes – such as the beef carpaccio – are as good as the tipples.

ℹ Information

Travel agencies are good sources of information. There's information (and a downloadable app) at www.folegandros.com.

Diaplous Travel (📞22860 41158; www.diaploustravel.gr; Plateia Pounta; ⏲9am-1.30pm & 6.30-9pm) Sells ferry tickets and arranges boat trips. The office at Karavostasis opens half an hour before ferry departures.

Folegandros Travel (📞22860 41273; www.folegandros-travel.gr; Plateia Dounavi; ⏲9.30am-1pm & 6-9pm) Sells ferry tickets and exchanges money. There's also an office at the port.

ℹ Getting There & Away

The local bus meets all ferry arrivals at Karavostasis port and takes passengers to Hora (€2, 3km). From Hora buses connect with arriving ferries at least three times daily (8am, 2pm and 6.30pm) and with Ano Meria at least four times daily (8.30am, 1.10pm, 2.45pm and 8pm; calling at Angali Beach in summer). The **bus station** is at the entrance to Hora from the south, behind the post office.

There is a taxi service on Folegandros. Fares to the port are about €7 to €10, to Ano Meria €10 and to Angali Beach €10 to €14.

Donkey Scooters (p259) rents 125cc scooters and ATVs and will drop them at designated places around the island if you request it in advance.

Ano Meria   Ανω Μεριά

POP 240

Ano Meria is a spread-out string of tiny hamlets that stretches along the road for several kilometres, on the crest of the island. Several excellent hiking trails start here: one leads down to the Agios Georgios chapel on the north coast from Sinadisi restaurant, while Livadaki Beach can be reached from the imposing windmills in the centre of Ano Meria or from the trail that leads past the Agii Anargiri church from the far end of the village.

🍴 Eating

Sinadisi   TAVERNA €
(📞22860 41208; mains from €7; ⏲noon-10pm May-Sep) Also known as Maria's, Sinadisi is at the far end of the strung-out village. With pale blue colours, it was originally opened in 1920 by the proprietor's grandfather. This is a great spot to try *matsata* and Greek salad with local Folegandros cheese.

★ Pane e Vino   ITALIAN €€
(📞22860 41531; www.facebook.com/PaneVinoFolegandros; mains from €10; ⏲1pm-midnight Jun-Sep; 🍴) At the far end of Ano Meria, Folegandros' only Italian restaurant is run by an Italian couple who settled here after visiting the island. Expect authentic pizzas, tiramisu and caprese salad with buffalo mozzarella.

ℹ Getting There & Away

Buses from Hora run hourly in summer to Ano Meria (€2). Taxis cost around €10, but things are a lot easier if you explore with your own wheels.

MILOS   ΜΗΛΟΣ

POP 4980

Volcanic Milos arches around a central caldera and is ringed with coastal landscapes of colourful and surreal rock formations. The island's most celebrated export, the *Venus de Milo,* is far away in the Louvre, but dozens of beaches (the most of any Cycladic island) and a series of picturesque villages contribute to its current, compelling, attractions.

The island has a fascinating history of mineral extraction dating from the Neolithic period when obsidian was exported to the Minoan world of Crete. Today Milos is the biggest source of bentonite and perlite in the EU.

A substantial western chunk of Milos (and part of the east coast) is off-limits to rental vehicles due to bad roads and a proliferation of the Milos viper, but the beaches are reachable by boat tours.

ℹ Getting There & Away

AIR

Milos National Airport (MLO) is 4km southwest around the bay from Adamas. Sky Express (www.skyexpress.gr) and Olympic Air (www.olympicair.com) both fly here from Athens.

BOAT

Adamas, the island's main port, is on the main western Cyclades ferry route. In the high season, destinations include Piraeus (€40 to €58, 2¾ to 6½ hours, six daily), Serifos (€8 to €18, one to two hours, five daily), Sifnos (€7 to €16, one hour, seven daily), Folegandros (€29 to €40, one hour, four daily) and Santorini (€39 to €53, two hours, four daily). Services are reduced in winter; see www.ferries.gr for detailed information.

There are also ferries from Pollonia to Kimolos.

ⓘ Getting Around

Adamas is the main hub for bus services, operated by **Milos Buses** (www.milosbuses. com). In the peak season there are buses to the airport and Achivadolimni Camping (five daily), Triovasalos/Plaka/Catacombs/Trypiti (hourly), Pollonia (10 daily), Paleohori (seven daily) and Sarakiniko (four daily). In winter services reduce to four buses a day to Triovasalos/ Trypiti and two to Pollonia. Check the website for detailed schedules.

Cars can be hired from the airport, Adamas and Pollonia. Options include **Giourgas Rent a Car** (☑ 22870 22352; www.giourgasrent. com) and **Milos Rent** (☑ 22870 41473; www. milosrent.gr).

From Adamas, **taxis** (☑ 22870 22219) charge around €13 to the airport, €8 to Plaka and €15 to Pollonia.

Adamas Αδάμας

POP 1350

Ferries to Milos are greeted by the classic Cycladic sight of a tight cluster of white houses spreading up a hill towards a picture-perfect, blue-domed church. At the base of the compact old town is a broad, attractive, waterfront promenade lined with shops, travel agencies, cafes, bars, ice-cream parlours and restaurants. A short walk in either direction will bring you to sandy beaches, or you can book a trip to otherwise inaccessible coves from the boats moored along the quay.

⊙ Sights

Ecclesiastical Museum of Milos   MUSEUM
(☎22870 22252; www.ecclesiasticalmuseum.org; ⊙9.15am-1.15pm & 6.15-10.15pm May-Sep) **FREE**
Housed in the venerable Holy Trinity Church, built in the 9th century, this collection has rare artefacts and icons, including works by acclaimed 17th-century Cretan father-and-son team, Emmanuel and Antonios Skordilis.

Milos Mining Museum   MUSEUM
(☎22870 22481; www.milosminingmuseum. gr; adult/child €5/3; ⊙10am-2pm Sun Jan-Mar, daily Apr & May, 10am-2pm & 5.30-9pm Jun-Sep, 10am-2pm Tue-Sun Oct) This mildly interesting museum details Milos' mining history, starting with the quarrying of obsidian on the island in 7000 BC. It's located on the waterfront, about 650m east of the centre.

Ask here about the Miloterranean Geo Experience (www.miloterranean.gr), a series of seven maps that outline great half-day 'geo walks' through Milos. The maps highlight the island's geology and volcanic origin, mining history and natural environment (€3 each).

🛏 Sleeping

★Konstantinos   HOTEL €€
(Map p263; ☎22870 22104; www.milos-konstantinos.gr; r from €110; ⊙Easter-Oct; P ❄ 🛜) Sitting on its own within the fields on the eastern edge of Adamas, this friendly, family-run hotel offers spacious, stylish rooms with balconies, some with sea views. It's a 20-minute walk from town but they'll pick you up from the port. Breakfast is available for €8 extra.

Tassoula Rooms   GUESTHOUSE €€
(☎22870 22674; r from €86; P ❄ 🛜) Run by a friendly family, this place is good value. Some of the spacious, bright rooms have tiny balconies overlooking the flowering inner courtyard, and the owner is decidedly helpful.

Aeolis Hotel   HOTEL €€
(☎22870 23985; www.hotel-aeolis.com; s/d from €130/148; P ❄ 🛜) Inland from the harbour, this sweet, neat 12-room hotel is peaceful and calm, its white rooms given a pop of colour here and there. It's open year-round, with prices diving in the low season (double €45).

Villa Helios Studios   APARTMENT €€
(☎22870 22258; www.studioshelios.com; apt €90-100; ⊙May-Oct; ❄ 🛜) Rising high above the port, these five large self-catering studios are

neat as a pin and decorated in an attractive traditional style, with sea-view balconies.

✕ Eating & Drinking

Artemis   BAKERY €
(items €2-2.50; ⊙6am-11pm; 🛜) Set on a side street next to the main free car park, this excellent bakery serves lip-smacking *spanakopita* (spinach pie), pizza slices, sandwiches and all manner of biscuits and cakes. There are little round tables decorated with potted carnations at the front, if you want to relax somewhere over a coffee.

O! Hamos   TAVERNA €€
(Map p263; ☎22870 21672; www.ohamos-milos. gr; Papikinou Beach; dishes €8.20-14; ⊙noon-11pm Apr-Oct; 🛜) Located just across from the beach, 1.2km southeast of the centre, this rustic taverna delivers a delicious array of traditional recipes, such as *pitarakia tis Giagias* (Grandma's cheese pies), *agriokatsiko sti hovoli* (slow-roasted wild goat and potatoes) and *portokaloglyko* (a cake-like orange-and-chocolate filo pie). Everything is served with warmth and flair, alongside craft beers and local wines.

Akri   COCKTAIL BAR
(☎22870 22064; www.akrimilos.gr; ⊙7pm-late Easter-Oct; 🛜) Tucked up above the port, this classy little bar serves cocktails and coffee on a beautiful terrace with views over the water. In summer, themed party nights continue into the wee small hours.

ℹ Information

Milos Travel (☎22870 22000; www.milostravel. gr; ⊙9am-3.30pm & 6.30-9.30pm Mon-Fri, 9am-2pm & 6.30-9.30pm Sat & Sun) Ferry tickets, excursions and car rental.

Riva Travel (☎22870 24024; www.rivatravel.gr; ⊙9am-9pm) Car hire and ferry tickets.

Tourist Information Office (☎22870 22445; www.milos.gr; ⊙9am-5pm & 7-11pm Jun-Sep) Helpful kiosk opposite the quay, with maps and general info.

ℹ Getting There & Away

In the peak season there are buses to Triovasalos/ Plaka/Catacombs/Trypiti (hourly), Pollonia (10 daily), Paleohori (seven daily) and Sarakiniko (four daily). In winter services reduce to four buses a day to Triovasalos/Trypiti and two to Pollonia.

Cars can be hired from various agencies around town, including Giourgas Rent a Car (p263) and Milos Rent (p263).

Plaka, Trypiti & Triovasalos

Πλάκα, Τρυπητή & Τριοβάσαλος

POP 2130

The bulk of Milos' population lives in this cluster of nearly conjoined towns in the north of the island. This was the site of the great ancient city of Melos, which lasted from around the 9th-century BC until the 7th-century AD before falling into decline.

Charming Plaka embodies the Cycladic ideal, with its white houses and labyrinthine lanes perched along the edge of an escarpment. The courtyard of Panagia Korfiatissa church (built in 1840) offers spectacular views west over the water and gets packed out at sunset during the high season. A little further down the hill is Trypiti, a pleasant village with a backdrop of churches and windmills. Triovasalos is the workaday part of the settlement, with shops and authentic tavernas catering mainly to the local population.

◎ Sights & Activities

Ancient Theatre & Catacombs RUINS

(⊘24hr) FREE Clinging to a lonely patch of hillside just below Trypiti, this large Roman-era theatre entertained the citizens of Ancient Melos from the 1st to the 4th century AD. It was rediscovered in 1735 but only around a tenth of the structure has been uncovered and partially restored, including part of the carved marble facade of the stage that once faced an audience of up to 8000 people.

The path to the theatre is well signposted, just up from the car park for the catacombs. The flattened oval area beside the road was the site of an ancient stadium. To the right of the path, look out for an information board marking the site near where, in 1820, a farmer discovered an exquisite 2m-high armless Parian marble statue of Aphrodite (c120 BC), still standing in her own niche. She was promptly packed off to the Louvre in Paris, where she's now better known as the *Venus de Milo*. A campaign has been launched to bring her home (www.takeaphroditehome.gr).

Archaeological Museum of Melos MUSEUM

(☑22870 21620; Plaka; adult/child €2/1; ⊘9am-10pm Sun, 8.30am-4pm Mon, Wed, Thu & Sat, 2-10pm Fri) This neoclassical building contains some riveting exhibits, including a plaster cast of local lass, the *Venus de Milo*, who now resides in the Louvre. The enigmatic clay goddess and perky little herd of tiny bull figurines in the adjoining rooms were already ancient when the famous statue was carved. Recovered from a shrine in Phylakopi, they date from between 1400 and 1100 BC.

Catacombs of Melos MONUMENT

(☑22870 21625; adult/child €4/2; ⊘9am-7pm Tue-Sun Apr-Sep, to 2pm Oct-Mar) Greece's only Christian catacombs, on the slopes below Trypiti, date from the 1st century and were the burial site for some of the earliest believers. Over 2000 people were interred within the 183m network of tunnels, which range from 1m to 5m in width and 1.6m to 2.5m in height. Entry is via a 15-minute guided tour to lit alcoves within two main chambers.

Kastro FORTRESS

(Plaka; ⊘24hr) FREE Signs mark the path climbing to Plaka's hilltop fortress, built by the Venetians on the ancient acropolis. Little of the structure remains, but the views from the top stretch right over the island. On the way up, call into the old church of Panagia Thalassitra to admire its gilded iconostasis.

Syrmata ARCHITECTURE

Tiny, photogenic Klima clings to the beach-front cliff face below Trypiti. It offers the best example of Milos' *syrmata* (traditional fishers' huts), where the downstairs, with brightly painted doors, are used for boat storage, and the upstairs are used for family life. The homes are incorporated into the rocks. A unique experience is to rent *syrmata* for your stay; some are available via home-sharing services. You'll need your own wheels.

Sea Kayak Milos KAYAKING

(☑6946477170; www.seakayakgreece.com; Triovasalos; sea kayak trip per person €75; ⊘9am-5pm Apr-Oct) Kayaking is a superb way to explore the coastline, and Aussie Rod and his team lead day trips, with no experience required. Itineraries depend on weather conditions.

⌂ Sleeping

Studios Betty APARTMENT €€

(☑22870 21538; www.studiosbetty-milos.com; Plaka; apt from €141; ❈ ☞) Enjoy glorious sunset views from this complex of four simple studios at Plaka's cliff edge.

Mimallis Houses RENTAL HOUSE €€€

(☑22870 21094; www.mimallis.gr; Plaka & Klima; apt €186-290; ⊘Apr-Oct; ❈ ☞) Mimallis rents two small houses in Plaka (sleeping two), and one right on the water in Klima (sleeping up to five) – each is comfortable and packed with amenities. The Klima house comes with a canoe and fishing equipment, but no air-conditioning. Low-season discounts are excellent.

Vaos Windmill
RENTAL HOUSE €€€

(☑ 26103 21742; Trypiti; apt from €180; 🛜) A footpath behind and above Trypiti's main church leads to this windmill, converted into a two-bedroom house, sleeping up to four people. There's a fully equipped kitchen a couple of steps out the front door, and the views from the terrace are nothing short of stupendous. Booking.com handles the reservations.

✖ Eating

Bakalikon Galanis
MEZEDHES €

(☑ 22870 28163; Triovasalos; dishes €4-12; ⊙ 11am-1am Mon-Sat) Retro shop stock (tinned goods, matchboxes, pantyhose etc) line the walls of this atmospheric *mezedhopoleio* (mezedhes bar), a local favourite. Tick off your selections on the printed menu – *saganaki* (fried cheese), *soutzouki* (spicy sausage), *siglino* (smoked pork), *kavourmas* (pork with spices) – and settle in for a long night; the kitchen closes at 1am but the venue stays open later.

Barrielo
GREEK €€

(☑ 6984218360; www.barriello.com; Trypiti; mains €12-18; ⊙ 6.30pm-12.30am Apr-Sep, 7.30pm-1am Thu-Sat Oct-Mar; 🛜) 🍴 Every evening, diners are lured to the little square below Trypiti's church by the smells of sizzling meat on the grill. It's all raised on the owner's farm.

ℹ Getting There & Away

In summer there are hourly buses on the Adamas–Triovasalos–Plaka–Catacombs–Trypiti route. In winter the only services are from Trypiti and Triovasalos to Adamas (four daily) and Pollonia (two daily). Most fares are €1.80.

Pollonia
Πολλώνια

POP 272

Pollonia (sometimes called Apollonia), on the north coast, is a low-key fishing village with clear waters and a sandy beach. In summer it completely transforms into a chic (albeit petite) resort, with the island's best accommodation and dining options.

The town is also the jumping-off point for Kimolos.

🛏 Sleeping

Zoe
GUESTHOUSE €€

(☑ 22870 41235; www.zoe-milos.gr; r/apt from €109/154; ⊙ May-Oct; ❄🛜) This little guesthouse has decent-sized rooms and studio apartments (with kitchenettes), all of which have balconies or terraces; some have sea views. An breakfast spread is included.

Nefeli Sunset Studios
HOTEL €€€

(☑ 22870 41466; www.milos-nefelistudios.gr; r/ste from €160/220; ⊙ Apr-Oct; ❄🛜) Whitewashed cubes combine modern design with traditional touches in this bay-front property at the northern edge of the village. All of the rooms have terraces or balconies with a sea view.

Salt
BOUTIQUE HOTEL €€€

(☑ 22870 41110; www.salt-milos.com; d/ste from €200/250; ⊙ Easter-Oct; ❄🛜) Set on a pebbly shoreline, this upmarket hotel offers sophistication, luxury and sea views. The decor is strikingly minimal: mainly white with natural wood accents. Low-season rates drop by nearly half.

✖ Eating

★ Enalion
GREEK €€

(☑ 22870 41415; www.enalion-milos.gr; mains €10-17; ⊙ noon-midnight; 🛜🍴) The finest Greek produce is showcased at this wonderful little restaurant. Grab a seat on the waterfront terrace and let the switched-on staff guide you through their top-notch selection of PDO (Protected Designation of Origin) olives, wine and cheese. Locally caught seafood features prominently on the menu, including a delicious *stifado* (stew) featuring octopus, tomatoes, onions, wine and Milos honey.

Gialos
SEAFOOD €€

(☑ 22870 41208; www.gialos-pollonia.gr; mains €8.50-26; ⊙ noon-11pm Apr-Oct; 🛜) Bustling Gialos has a creative modern menu bursting with fresh local and international flavours and techniques – everything from prawn ravioli to tuna tataki. Seafood is the focus but the meat dishes are also good, including a tender and delicious beef *tagliata* (sliced steak) marinated in olive oil and rosemary.

Armenaki
GREEK €€

(☑ 22870 41061; www.armenaki.gr; mains €9-18; ⊙ noon-11pm Apr-Oct; 🛜) Armenaki is revered for its fishy business – this place is all about seafood (in fact, there's little else on the menu). Seafood in all its guises is cooked to perfection, and service is first-rate (including the filleting of fish at your table). There's an extensive wine list.

Hanabi
FUSION €€€

(☑ 22870 41180; www.facebook.com/hanabicock-tailsandsushi; mains €16-26; ⊙11am-midnight Apr-Oct; 🛜) You'll find everything from sushi to burgers at this stylish Japanese-inspired restaurant, but the kitchen's at its best when delivering creative fusion dishes such as tagliatelle with baby vegetables, sea urchin and orange ouzo. Grab a seat on the waterside terrace and enjoy the friendly service.

ℹ️ Information

Travel Me to Milos (☑ 22870 41008; www.travelmetomilos.com) Books activities, excursions, accommodation and ferry tickets, as well as car hire.

ℹ️ Getting There & Away

In the height of summer there are 10 buses a day to Adamas. In winter these narrow to two, but they continue on to Trypiti and Triovasalos.

Pollonia is also the main port for ferries to Kimolos.

Around Milos

👁️ Sights

The ancient Minoan town of **Phylakopi** (Map p263; ☑ 22870 41290; adult/child €2/1; ⊙8am-3pm Tue, Fri & Sat Easter-Oct) in the island's northeast (on the main road en route to Pollonia but poorly signed) was one of the earliest settlements in the Cyclades. Now it's mostly rubble but the seaside setting is attractive.

🏖️ Beaches

Milos and its islets have more than 70 splendid beaches garnished in different-coloured sands and stone. You'll need to rent a vehicle to visit most of them; a 4WD or ATV is required to reach those on the rugged west coast. In the case of remote Kleftiko in the southwest, the only access is by boat.

Paleohori
BEACH

One of the island's most beautiful beaches, the long arch of Paleohori is backed by banded cliffs and has tavernas, beach bars, water sports and patches of hot sand, thanks to thermal springs in the area. It's reached by a good sealed road, and buses from Adamas head here seven times a day in summer.

Sarakiniko
BEACH

Sarakiniko's meringue-like rock formations and caves attract scores of budding photographers, even in winter. The sandy beach is tiny but there's a deep channel that's perfect for swimming, and room to spread out on the rocks. It's reached by a good sealed road, with parking at the end. Buses head here from Adamas in summer (four daily).

Kyriaki
BEACH

Kyriaki is a lovely long sandy beach on the south coast, backed by otherworldly grey-, rose- and rust-coloured cliffs. There's a taverna at one end and a good restaurant up in the hills. The road is fine with a 2WD.

Plathiena
BEACH

Sitting at the end of a valley beyond Plaka in the north of the island, this pebble-strewn sandy beach is exceptionally pretty. The water is a vivid aquamarine and there are limestone formations at each end. There's not much development here apart from a single flash house and a summertime beach bar. The road is good, although there's limited parking.

Nerodafni & Trachilas
BEACH

From Firopotamas, an unsealed but well-maintained wide road (fine with a 2WD, although it gets a little bumpy towards the end) leads past active quarries to these remote pebble and rock beaches, separated from each other by a headland. Nerodafni is slightly easier to access, but Trachilas is distinguished by tiny islets with rock arches just offshore.

Mandrakia
BEACH

Village cats form the welcoming committee at this tiny fishing harbour, with brightly coloured boat sheds, cute wee cottages and a little whitewashed church. There are small shingle beaches on either side and, to the east, a large expanse of rocky shelves to spread out on.

Firopotamos
BEACH

The road is sealed all the way to Firopotamos, a picturesque little cove embraced by craggy limestone cliffs and lined with *syrmata* (boathouse dwellings). There's a lovely little blue-trimmed church on the headland and the remains of a quarry nearby, with car parking.

KIMOLOS   ΚΙΜΩΛΟΣ

POP 910

Little Kimolos, perched off the northeast tip of Milos, feels like a step back in time. Few visitors take the opportunity to explore its tiny old town, sparkling bays and picturesque *syrmata* (boat houses). It's an easy day trip from Milos; consider taking a car, bike or scooter on the ferry to make it easier to get around.

Sights

The boat (from Pollonia in Milos' north) docks at **Psathi**, where there's a gravelly beach and a smattering of cafes and tavernas. The pretty capital, **Hora**, is about 800m up the hill. At the centre of its network of atmospheric little lanes is the *kastro,* a crumbling square-shaped castle dating from the 14th to 16th centuries. In among the rubble is the tiny whitewashed **Church of the Nativity**; built in 1592, it's the oldest of Hora's 16 churches. Nearby is the petite **Folk & Maritime Museum** (☑ 22870 51118; ⊙ hours vary) FREE.

Caïques from Psathi buzz out to beaches, the best of which is magnificent, white-sand **Prassa** (also reachable along a partially sealed road). You can walk there from Hora in about an hour.

Sleeping

Domatia, tavernas, cafes and bars pepper Hora and Psathi. There's development at the southern beaches of Aliki and neighbouring Bonatsa, as well as several boutique properties. Aria Hotels (www.ariahotels.gr)has three boutique hotels and five holiday homes on Kimolos, including a converted windmill.

Meltemi Studio Rooms   HOTEL €
(☑ 22870 51360; www.kimolos-meltemi.gr; r from €55; P ❋ ☎) This set of compact rooms is perched on the edge of Hora, with views to the sea. The in-house restaurant specialises in Kimolian cuisine.

Windmill Kimolos   BOUTIQUE HOTEL €€€
(☑ 22870 51677; www.kimoloshotel.com; r from €165; ⊙ May-Sep; P ❋ ☎) The most atmospheric abode in Kimolos, this converted windmill looks down on the island from its hilltop position. The whitewashed rooms are comfortable, and there's a cafe and bar on-site.

Eating

Raventi   CAFE €
(☑ 22870 51212; snacks €3.50-7.50; ⊙ 9am-late; ☎) On the beach at Psathi, this trendy cafe has a comfy terrace and a counter full of drool-inducing cakes, tarts and ice cream. In the high season it also serves the likes of

eggs Benedict and sandwiches, and is open late for cocktails.

Kali Kardia Bohoris   TAVERNA €
(☑ 22870 51495; mains €5-8; ⊙ 6am-10pm) Set on a picturesque street leading up from the *kastro* at the centre of Hora, this humble-looking place serves good local specialities such as roast goat, cheese pies and *mousakas*.

To Kyma   TAVERNA €€
(☑ 22870 51001; mains €7-20; ⊙ noon-11pm Apr-Oct; ☎) The name means 'The Wave' and this taverna, right on the beach at Psathi, is good for seafood and local specialities like *ladenia* (pizza, topped with tomatoes and onions).

Information

Kimolos Travel (☑ 22870 51219; Hora; ⊙ 9am-1pm & 4-8pm) Sells ferry tickets.

Getting There & Away

A small **car ferry** (☑ 6948308758; www.kimolos-link.gr; per adult/child/scooter/car €2.20/1.10/1.80/8.80) connects Pollonia (Milos) with Psathi (Kimolos) up to eight times daily in high season, three times in low season (30 minutes).

In the high season, larger long-distance ferries head to destinations including Piraeus (€36, seven hours, five weekly), Serifos (€9, two hours, daily), Sifnos (€6.50, one hour, daily), Paros (€11, 4¼ to 6¼ hours, three weekly) and Folegandros (€6, 1½ hours, three weekly).

Getting Around

Buses connect Psathi and Hora in high season only; infrequent services also visit beaches. Some rental agencies in Kimolos offer cars, scooters and ATVs. Otherwise **taxis** (☑ 6945464093) from Psathi are around €5 to Hora and €10 to Prassa.

SIFNOS   ΣΙΦΝΟΣ

POP 2625

Sifnos has a dreamlike quality. Three whitewashed villages, anchored by the capital Apollonia, sit like pearls on a string along the crest of the island. The changing light kisses the landscape, and as you explore the slopes of the central mountains you'll discover abundant terraced olive groves, almond trees, oleander and aromatic herbs. Each of the island's bays offers aqua waters and breathtaking vistas.

During the Archaic period (from about the 8th century BC), Sifnos was enriched by its gold and silver deposits, but by the 5th century BC the mines were exhausted. Sifnos is now known for pottery, basket weaving and cookery. Visitors flock to the southern half of the island, served by good bus links, but it's worth getting your own wheels and driving to the remote beaches of the north, where the main road culminates in a church.

❶ Getting There & Away

Sifnos is on the Piraeus to western Cyclades ferry route, with good summer connections to destinations including Piraeus (€36 to €52, 2½ to 5½ hours, six daily), Serifos (€6.50 to €15, 50 minutes, four daily), Paros (€5 to €60, 50 minutes to three hours, one or two daily), Folegandros (€9 to €50, 1¾ hours, three daily) and Milos (€7 to €16, one hour, seven daily). Services reduce in winter; see www.ferries.gr for details.

❶ Getting Around

Bus timetables are posted around the island, and frequent buses connect Kamares with Apollonia and Artemonas. Buses also link Apollonia with Kastro, Vathy, Faros and Platys Gialos. Fares are generally €1.80 (maximum €2.30).

For car and scooter rental, try **Apollo Rental** (☑ 22840 33333; www.automotoapollo.gr; ☺ 9am-9pm Apr-Oct) in Apollonia or **1° Moto Car Rental** (☑ 22840 33791; www.protomotocar.gr) in Kamares.

There are only 10 **taxis** (☑ 6932403485, 6944761210) on Sifnos, so you're best to book in the high season. You'll find a list of taxi numbers posted at bus stops.

Kamares   Καμάρες

POP 245

Scenically hemmed in by steep mountains, the port of Kamares has a holiday feel, with waterfront cafes, tavernas and shops, a good range of accommodation, and a beautiful large beach of its own. The water's very shallow, making it ideal for families with toddlers but less so if you're after a decent swim.

🛏 Sleeping

★ **Morpheas Pension**   GUESTHOUSE €
(☑ 22840 33615; www.morpheas.gr; r/apt from €50/80; P ✳ 🛜) Named after the Greek god of dreams, this friendly family-run place does its best to ensure that yours will be pleasant ones. It's set back from the beach in a classic Cycladic-style building, albeit with pistachio trim rather than blue. The simple but well-kept rooms all have bathrooms, fridges and

Sifnos

Serifos (25km); Kythnos (80km); Piraeus (170km)

kettles, while the two one-bedroom apartments have full kitchens.

Makis Camping   CAMPGROUND €
(☑ 6945946339; www.makiscamping.gr; site per adult/child/tent €8/4/4, r from €70; ☺ May-Nov; P ✳ 🛜) Pitch your tent behind the beach in a well-run lot with shady trees, or hire tents with mattresses for €30. There are well-equipped rooms and apartments (sleeping up to five), a cafe, barbecue, communal kitchen, minimarket and laundry.

Aglaia Studios   GUESTHOUSE €€
(☑ 22840 31513; www.aglaiastudios.gr; Agia Marina; r/apt from €77/154; ✳ 🛜) In the evenings, you can sit on your balcony and watch the lights of Kamares across the bay. By day, a few steps take you down to the swimming platform, from which you can launch yourself into the Aegean. The rooms themselves are snug and comfortable. Free port pickups are included.

Stavros Hotel   HOTEL €€
(☑ 22840 33383; www.sifnostravel.com; r from €80; ✳ 🛜) Grapevines curl over the balconies of this main street hotel that offers good service and excellent, spacious studios with kitchenettes and sea views. A bonus: flexible rooms work to accommodate families. The info desk downstairs can help with car hire.

CYCLADES KAMARES

Eating

Absinthe
FUSION €€

(☑ 22840 31202; www.absinthe-sifnos.gr; mains €15-23; ☺May-Oct) On a terrace above the main street, Absinthe takes inspiration from historic Smyrna, incorporating Greek, Anatolian, Ottoman and Asian elements, and pairing them with fresh local ingredients. Smrynaian meatballs sit alongside *hünkâr beğendi* (veal stew on a spicy eggplant puree) and a stand-out goat coconut curry on rice.

Folie
INTERNATIONAL €€

(☑ 22840 31183; www.foliesifnos.gr; Agia Marina; mains €4-16; ☺10am-late; ☎) Advertising itself as an 'all-day bar restaurant', this beachside terrace allows you to slip from morning coffee to a salad lunch, a lazy sunlounger G&T and then on to dinner, and finally cocktails. The menu covers a lot of territory, too: omelettes, pancakes, pasta, risotto, burgers, tortillas, spring rolls and octopus on *fava* puree.

Shopping

Of Sifnos' many ceramics stores, **Peristeriona** (☑ 22840 32121; www.handmadepotteryart.com; ☺10am-2pm & 5-9.30pm Mon-Sat, 5-9.30pm Sun) is the most stylish. Bright glazes and rainbow stripes decorate tumblers, plates and casserole dishes, while large platters display motifs lifted from traditional fabric designs.

ℹ Information

Aegean Thesaurus (☑ 22840 33151; www.thesaurus.gr; ☺8.45am-8.30pm Mon-Sat, 8.45am-12.30pm & 3-5pm Sun) Books ferry tickets, tours and rental cars, and sells a €3 Sifnos welcome pack (hiking info, bus timetables, map and more).
Municipal Tourist Office (☑ 22840 31977; www.sifnos.gr) On the little square near the ferry dock, this office only opens in high season, and the hours vary with boat arrivals. It's helpful with ferry tickets, accommodation and bus timetables.

ℹ Getting There & Away

Kamares is Sifnos' main ferry port.

From Easter there are five buses a day to Apollonia (€1.80, 20 minutes), with services every 30 minutes in the peak season and one direct bus daily carrying on to Kastro and another to Platys Gialos (€2.30). Otherwise, change in Apollonia.

Cars, scooters and ATVs can be hired from 1° Moto Car Rental (p269), which has a booking office by the port and a main base near the beach. The nearest petrol station is in Apollonia.

Apollonia   Απολλωνία
POP 869

Labyrinthine, church-studded Apollonia comes alive in summer as well-dressed Athenians strut their stuff along Odos Prokou, known as the Steno (meaning 'narrow'). Bars, clubs, shops and restaurants buzz with life.

The main road cuts right through the centre of town, but park at the large free car park downhill from the village and walk up and into the warren of streets. At the central junction you'll find all the services: banks, post office, pharmacy, bookshop, taxis and so on.

From Apollonia, the string of houses continues north into the conjoined village of Ano Petali and then to Artemonas, with its grand mansions, churches, cafes and tavernas. The 20-minute walk along the pedestrian lane heading up behind Mamma Mia restaurant offers unforgettable views over Apollonia's white houses and blue-domed churches.

🛏 Sleeping

Pension Nikoletta Geronti
GUESTHOUSE €

(☑ 22840 31473; www.gerontisifnos.gr; Ano Petali; s/d from €50/55; ❄☎) Opposite Petali Village Hotel, on the walkway between Apollonia and Artemonas, is this gem of a pension, with spotless rooms, sweeping views, sweet hosts and excellent rates.

Eleonas Apartments & Studios
APARTMENT €€

(☑ 22840 33383; www.sifnostravel.com; apt from €85; ❄☎) An idyllic complex tucked away in an olive grove, Eleonas offers two-bedroom apartments that sleep six, with kitchen, living space and terrace. Studios are slightly smaller, but still spacious. It feels peaceful and rural, but it's just minutes' from the Steno.

Petali Village Hotel
HOTEL €€

(☑ 22840 33024; www.petalihotel.gr; Ano Petali; d/ste from €145/238; ❄☎🏊) Suspended on a walking street between Apollonia and Artemonas, this terraced array of rooms and suites has views to Apollonia and the sea, and an inviting kidney-shaped pool. Low-season discounts are decent; port pickup is offered.

Eating

Cayenne
GREEK €€

(☑ 22840 31080; www.facebook.com/CayenneRestaurantSifnos; mains €12-25; ☺1pm-late; ☎🌿) Shaded by a fig tree and drowning in a riot of herbs just off the Steno, this modern Greek restaurant affirms its strong commitment to Cycladic ingredients through dishes such as lemon-caper risotto, Byzantine meat patties and smoked eel with Santorini *fava* beans.

Drimoni   MEDITERRANEAN €€
(☑22840 31434; www.drimoni.gr; mains €8.50-14; ☺6pm-late May-Sep; 🛜) Look out over the countryside or lounge by the pool (yes, pool!) at this bright and contemporary restaurant. Chef Giorgos Patriarchis does the Sifnian culinary tradition proud with the likes of *mastelo* (goat slow-cooked in wine with rosemary and dill), imaginative salads, risottos and pastas.

ℹ Information

The €3 info pack from Thesaurus Travel, on main square, is a great investment. It includes the terrain map of Sifnos, an overview of the island's walking trails, plus the current bus and ferry timetables.

Xidis Travel (☑22840 32373; www.xidis.com.gr; ☺9am-9pm) Books ferry tickets.

ℹ Getting There & Away

From Easter, there are buses from Apollonia to Kamares (five daily, 20 minutes), Faros (three daily, 20 minutes), Kastro (three daily, 20 minutes), Platys Gialos (four daily, 30 minutes) and Vathi (three daily, 50 minutes). Services are much more frequent in the peak season; all routes cost €1.80.

Cars can be hired from Apollo Rental (p269).

Kastro   Κάστρο

POP 118

Dramatically positioned on a crag with sheer drops to the crystalline waters below and terraced valleys all around, Kastro is Sifnos' most magical settlement. Until 1836 it was the island's capital but now it's a sleepy place, with only a single excellent taverna and a couple of seasonal cafes as its main signs of life.

People have lived here continuously since 1000 BC and the remains of an **acropolis** can still be seen at the very top, where a temple to a female goddess (Athena or Artemis, no one's sure) once stood. The Romans left several large stone **sarcophagi**, which can be easily spotted as you walk up the steep lanes.

The small port and pebble beach of **Seralia** is nestled below.

◎ Sights

Church of the Seven Martyrs   CHURCH
From the seaward end of town, a steep but sturdy path leads down the cliff to this tiny blue-domed church, set on its own little promontory surrounded by startlingly green

water. The church is usually locked but it's the exceptionally beautiful setting that's the draw, especially in spring when the path is lined with yellow and mauve flowers. At its base, people swim naked from the rocks.

Archaeological Museum of Sifnos   MUSEUM
(☑22840 31022; €2; ☺8am-3pm Tue-Sun) This small museum in the heart of Kastro houses archaeological remains from the ancient town. It's sometimes inexplicably closed.

🍴 Sleeping & Eating

Antonis Rooms   GUESTHOUSE €
(☑22840 33708; www.sifnosholidays.gr; r from €40; ✳🛜) On the road as it winds up to Kastro, these simple, spotless rooms beckon. They're terrific value, with a communal kitchen and a terrace with splendid valley views. It's open year-round.

Aris & Maria Traditional Houses APARTMENT €
(☑22840 31161; www.arismaria-traditional.com; apt from €46; ✳🛜) For an authentic Kastro experience, rent one of these six traditional Sifnian houses. Some have sea views.

Leonidas   TAVERNA €€
(☑22840 31153; www.facebook.com/leonidastavern; mains €9-15; ☺noon-10pm Easter-Sep; 🛜) At the northern entrance to the village, this popular tavern offers tasty local dishes, including Sifnian appetisers like chickpea croquettes and cheese patties with honey and sesame seeds.

ℹ Getting There & Away

From Easter there are buses from Apollonia to Kastro (€1.80, three daily, 20 minutes). Services are much more frequent in peak season.

Around Sifnos

On the southeast coast, the fishing hamlet of **Faros** has tavernas and nice beaches nearby, including **Fasolou**, reached up steps and over the headland from the bus stop.

Platys Gialos, 10km south of Apollonia, has a generous sandy beach entirely backed by tavernas, hotels and shops. **Vathy**, on the southwest coast, is a low-key resort village on an almost circular bay of aquamarine beauty.

◎ Sights

Moni Chrysopigi   MONASTERY
(Map p269; Chrysopigi) Perched on a tiny islet connected to the shore by a tiny footbridge, this handsome whitewashed monastery is

CYCLADES KASTRO

considered to be the protector of Sifnos. Built in 1650, it's dedicated to the Life-giving Spring, a representation of the Mother of Christ in the Orthodox tradition. Inside the darkened church there's a carved wooden iconostasis and an boat-shaped metal candelabra.

Beautiful, azure Chrysopigi Beach is home to two excellent tavernas.

Acropolis of Agios Andreas MONUMENT
(Map p269; ☑ 22840 31488; adult/child €2/1; ☺ 8.30am-3pm Tue-Sun) At the heart of the island, about 2km south of Apollonia, this well-excavated hilltop acropolis dates from the Mycenaean period (13th century BC). Take in extensive views of interior valleys and neighbouring Paros from above the intact defensive wall. The adjacent **St Andrew's Church** dates from about 1700.

🛏 Sleeping

Aerides Boutique Rooms GUESTHOUSE €€
(Map p269; ☑ 22840 36093; www.aerides-sifnos. com; Vathy; s/d from €59/67; ✹🛜) Run by a friendly young couple and artfully decorated with bits of flotsam and jetsam, this converted *syrma* (boat shed) comprises four spacious rooms. The sea is right under your window.

Windmill Bella Vista BOUTIQUE HOTEL €€
(Map p269; ☑ 22840 33518; www.windmillbellavista. gr; apt from €128; P✹🛜☲) A Cycladic windmill is the atmospheric pick of the spacious, high-beamed apartments and studios at this small hotel, clustered around an infinity pool on the road from Artemonas to Poulati.

Hotel Efrosini HOTEL €€
(☑ 22840 71353; www.hotel-efrosini.gr; Platys Gialos; r €80-90; ☺ May-Sep; P✹🛜) This well-kept, family-run hotel is one of the best on the Platys Gialos strip. Small balconies overlook a leafy courtyard with the sea lapping in front.

Verina Suites APARTMENT €€€
(☑ 6976867641; https://verinahotelsifnos.com; Platys Gialos; d/apt from €190/220; ☺ Easter-Sep; ✹🛜☲) Effortlessly chic, Verina rents minimalist suites and villas at outposts in Platys Gialos, Vathy and above Poulati (north of Kastro). Verina Suites lies behind the beach at Platys Gialos, but try dragging yourself from the gorgeous pool and cafe-bar area.

🍴 Eating

★ Omega 3 SEAFOOD €€
(☑ 22840 72014; www.facebook.com/omega3greece; Platys Gialos; mains €12-15; ☺ noon-11pm

Easter-Sep) The cute name (Ω3) hints at the treats on offer at this small, casual 'fish and wine bar'. There's a fishy menu of which grabs techniques from around the globe (sashimi, ceviche) while still staying true to its roots with marinated octopus and orzo pasta with crayfish. Showstoppers include punchy fish soup and a fish tartare with pickled zucchini.

To Limanaki SEAFOOD €€
(☑ 22840 71425; Faros; mains €14-22; ☺ noon-10pm) It's well worth detouring to the village of Faros just to dine at this seafront taverna, where fisherman and owner, Giorgios, cooks up the sea's bounty using his mother's recipes. You can't go wrong with grilled catch of the day or orzo pasta with lobster.

SERIFOS ΣΕΡΙΦΟΣ

POP 1420

Serifos has a raw, rugged beauty, with steep mountains plunging to broad ultramarine bays. Relatively deserted outside the quaint hilltop capital of Hora or the dusty, Wild West–feeling port of Livadi down below, the island feels like it's gone beautifully feral. All that you find are the occasional remnants of past mining enterprises (rusting tracks, cranes) and the whoosh of the wind (which can be fierce). Rent wheels to make the most of it. Serifos is one of the few islands where locals drink the water.

In Greek mythology, Serifos is where Perseus grew up, bringing back Medusa's head to save his mother from the unwanted romantic attentions of Polydectes, and where the Cyclopes were said to live.

The island can be explored via a network of 10 signposted trails of varying lengths and difficulty; see the 'hiking' page of www.serifos-greece.com for detailed information.

ℹ Getting There & Away

Serifos is on the Piraeus to western Cyclades ferry route and has reasonable summer connections. High-season services include Piraeus (€31 to €48, two to 4½ hours, five daily), Kythnos (€8, 1¼ hours, daily), Sifnos (€6.50 to €15, 50 minutes, four daily), Milos (€8 to €18, one to two hours, five daily) and Syros (€8.50, 2¼ hours, daily). See www.ferries.gr for detailed information.

ℹ Getting Around

Buses connect Livadi and Hora (€1.80, hourly, 15 minutes); the timetable is posted at the bus stop by the yacht quay. In high season, a circular bus route takes in Panagia, Galani, Kendarhos and Agios Ioannis Beach (up to six daily), with a couple of daily buses to Megalo Livadi and Koutalas.

Rent cars, scooters and quads at **Blue Bird** (☑ 22810 51511; www.rentacar-bluebird. gr), **Poseidon Rent a Car** (☑ 22810 52030, 6974789706; www.serifosisland.gr/poseidon) or **Serifos Tours** (☑ 22810 51463; www.serifos-tours.gr) in Livadi.

Taxis (☑ 6932431114, 6944473044) from Livadi to Hora cost €8, Psili Ammos €8, Platys Gialos €20, Sykamia €23 and Megalo Livadi €23.

Livadi Λιβάδι

POP 605

Serifos' main port and biggest town has a large marina that's popular with touring yachties, and a surprisingly buzzy strip of waterfront tavernas and bars. This, along with its proximity to some excellent beaches, make it an excellent base for exploring the island.

◎ Sights & Activities

Livadakia DEACH
Just over the headland that rises from the ferry quay, this gorgeous tamarisk-fringed beach has a long swoop of coarse golden sand and a rustic taverna.

Ramos BEACH
Just past Livadakia, Ramos is a small sandy beach backed with grapevines and a smattering of flash holiday apartments.

Serifos Scuba Divers DIVING
(☑ 6932570552; www.serifosscubadivers.gr; 1-tank dive/snorkelling €50/30) This recommended scuba operator takes divers to a dozen sites around the island, including wrecks and more. Day-long snorkelling trips can be arranged in July and August, and it also rents boats and arranges adrenalin-packed flyboard sessions.

⌂ Sleeping

Alexandros-Vassilia GUESTHOUSE €
(☑ 22810 51119; www.alexandros-vassilia.gr; Livadakia Beach; r/ste from €55/160; ◷ Apr-Oct; 🕸🗺) Best known for its beachfront taverna in a flowering garden, this friendly Livadakia compound also has a big range of rustic rooms and apartments. They range from decent-value economy rooms (no sea view) to family-sized, sea-view suites.

Marousa's APARTMENT €€
(Map p273; ☑ 22810 51807; www.serifosapartments. gr; Ramos; apt from €65; ◷ Easter-Oct; 🅿🕸🗺)

Up above Ramos Beach, this inviting complex offers 11 simple but well-equipped one- and two-bedroom apartments. The couple who run it put on a delicious breakfast spread including homemade jams, olives and capers from their own garden. It's a steep 1km walk southwest of town, above Ramos Beach; best with your own wheels. The wi-fi is terrible.

Studios Niovi APARTMENT €€
(Map p273; ☑ 22810 51900; www.studiosniovi.gr; apt €90-140; 🅿🕸🗺) On the furthest eastern curve of Livadi's bay, about a 15-minute walk from the centre, these immaculate apartments look over the broad expanse of the bay, bustling Livadi, towering Hora and the mountains beyond. The owner makes a super breakfast. Good low-season rates.

✖ Eating

To Bakakaki TAVERNA €
(☑ 22810 51010; mains €8.30-10; ◷ 1pm-late; 🗺) Named after a small native frog, this chilled-out *kreatotaverna* (meat tavern) on the waterfront is known for its grilled and slow-roasted meat, but it also serves delicious traditional snacks such as *tirokafteri* (spicy cheese-and-red-pepper spread) and *sfakiopita* (cheese filo pie topped with honey).

DON'T MISS

BEACHES OF SERIFOS

The island's most strikingly beautiful beach, **Agios Sostis**, is a 40-minute walk northeast of Livadi. It occupies a sandy spit terminating in a headland topped with a blue-vaulted church and craggy golden rock formations. On each side are gravelly golden beaches abutting crystal-clear waters, perfectly framing views of distant islands. It's best reached on foot as the access road is rough and there's only limited parking.

Next up is pretty little **Psili Ammos**, tucked below the main road, offering good swimming and a couple of tavernas. Reached by a steep side road, **Platys Gialos** in the north has gravelly sand and a seasonal taverna. Near the turnoff, look out for the **Monastery of the Taxiarches** (a title referring to the archangels Michael and Gabriel), built in 1572 and fortified to protect it from pirates and other raiders. If it's open, it's worth exploring.

Sykamia is one of the island's best beaches, with a dramatic approach along a steep, windy, sealed road through terraced hills. There's a good taverna set back from its pebble-strewn, grey-brown sands.

Tiny **Megalo Livadi**, on the southwest coast, is interesting for its crumbling neoclassical buildings (remnants of the mining era) and seaside tavernas but the beach is a little muddy and rocky. The cave where the Cyclops was said to dwell is near here.

The best beaches on the south coast tend to be broad and sandy. It's a wild landscape, punctuated by derelict mining machinery. Three of them share a large sheltered bay: **Koutalas**, a small fishing village with a pebble-strewn beach; **Ganema**, a tamarisk-edged beach with vivid green waters giving way to deep-blue depths; and, best of all, **Vagia**, a horseshoe of golden sand and shingle embracing iridescent waters.

★**Kali's**　　　　　　　　SEAFOOD €€
(🖉 22810 52301; www.kaliseafood.gr; mains €7-18; ⊙noon-11pm Mar-Oct; 🖥🖉) Slather zingy seafood spread onto bread and get messy with mussels *saganaki* (in a rich broth, with feta) and scampi on orzo (pasta) at this water's edge restaurant. Funny aiters play show and tell with the day's fresh fish, to be grilled whole.

Metalleio　　　　　MEDITERRANEAN €€
(🖉 22810 51755; www.facebook.com/Metalleio; mains €10-16; ⊙7.30pm-late Easter-Oct; 🖥) On the road behind the waterfront, Metalleio dishes up quality cuisine from a short menu emphasising local products, such as risotto with goat's cheese, veal *tagliata* (sliced steak) and ice cream with homemade sweets.

🍷 Drinking & Nightlife

Livadi's original waterfront cafe-bar **Yacht Club Serifos** (🖉 22810 51888; www.facebook. com/YachtClubSerifos; ⊙7.30am-late; 🖥), which dates back to 1938, maintains a cheerful buzz, delivering good music, light meals, coffee and cocktails under the shade of large tamarisks. It stays open really late, too – until 5am in the peak season.

ⓘ Information

Kondilis (🖉 22810 52340; www.kondilis.gr; ⊙9am-9pm) Sells ferry tickets.
Serifos Tours (p273) Sells ferry tickets, books excursions and rents cars and bikes.

ⓘ Getting There & Around

From the bus stop by the yacht quay, buses run to Hora and, less frequently, to other main villages.

Car rental agencies include Poseidon Rent A Car (p273) and Blue Bird (p273).

Hora (Serifos)
Χώρα (Σέριφος)
POP 364

This tiny town cascades down the summit of the rocky mountain above Livadi, putting it among the most dramatically striking of all the Cycladic capitals. The bus terminus and main car park are on its upper side, near some windmills. From there, steps climb into the maze of Hora proper and lead to the main square, watched over by neoclassical **town hall** and a blue-domed church.

From the square, narrow alleys and more steps lead upwards to the acropolis and the scant remnants of the 15th-century **Venetian Kastro** (castle), offering spectacular views over the water to distant Sifnos. Just below the summit, the barrel-vaulted **Church of St John the Theologian** is carved into the rock on the site of an ancient temple to Athena.

◎ Sights

Archaeological Collection of
Serifos   MUSEUM
(☑ 22810 52611; adult/child €2/1; ☺ 9am-4pm Wed-Mon) This modest museum displays fragments of mainly Hellenic and Roman sculpture excavated from the *kastro*. Panels in Greek and English retell the legend of Perseus, the mythic hero who washed ashore on Serifos as a baby. The building's not well signed; look for it near the upper bus stop.

🛌 Sleeping & Eating

Anemoessa Studios   APARTMENT €€
(☑ 22810 51132; www.serifos-anemoessa.gr; apt €100; ☀🛜) Six pretty, modern studios each sleep four in whitewashed Cycladic style.

Stou Stratou   CAFE €
(☑ 22810 52566; www.stoustratou.com; Plateia Agiou Athanasiou; dishes €3-10; ☺ 9am-late Easter-Oct) Sitting postcard-pretty in the sun-baked main square, Stou Stratou has a menu full of art and poetry (literally), plus it serves good breakfasts and light snacks such as Cretan wild fennel pie or a mixed plate of cold cuts and cheese. Cocktails and coffee, too.

Aloni   TAVERNA €€
(Map p273; ☑ 22810 52603; www.facebook.com/alwni1; mains €7-15; ☺ 7pm-late Jun-Oct, Sat & Sun Nov-May) Halfway up the hill between Livadi and Hora, signposted on the right, Aloni offers splendid panoramas and an upscale feel. Islanders rate it among Serifos' best, with local produce (roasted meat, rabbit in lemon sauce, fennel pie) proudly showcased.

❶ Getting There & Away

If you're coming from Livadi, consider catching the bus up and walking back down. Hourly buses (€1.80) run between Livadi and Hora in the high season; fewer in low season. A scenic 2.5km, vehicle-free walking path (route 1A) winds down through Hora to Livadi.

KYTHNOS   ΚΥΘΝΟΣ

POP 1460

Low-key Kythnos (also known as Kithnos or Thermia) is a series of rolling hills punctuated by stone huts and bisected by ancient walls, green valleys and wonderful beaches. Port life in Merihas and village life in beautiful Hora and Dryopida are easygoing, and tourists are few, although the marina at Loutra brings with it an international buzz in summertime. Ease of access from Athens sees Greek travellers filling the beaches on sunny weekends.

❶ Getting There & Away

In the high season, ferries connect Kythnos to various destinations including Piraeus (€25, three hours, four daily), Lavrio (€16, two hours, two daily), Kea (€6.90, 1¼ hours, daily), Syros (€9, 2¼ hours, three daily) and Serifos (€8, 1¼ hours, daily). Services between the islands are reduced in winter; see www.ferries.gr for information.

❶ Getting Around

In the high season, five buses per day run in each direction on the Merihas–Hora–Loutra and Merihas–Dryopida–Kanala routes; fares range from €1.40 to €2. In the low season, the best way to see the island is by car or scooter. Rentals are available at **Nikitos** (☑ 22810 31419; www.kythnosrentalcar.gr) and Larentzakis Antonis (p276), among other places.

Taxis (☑ 6944271609) from Merihas charge about €10 to Hora and €8 to Dryopida. A water taxi to/from the beaches in summer is €10.

Merihas   Μέριχας

POP 369

Little Merihas is home to much of the island's low-season life. Cafes and restaurants line the small harbour, and rooms for let dot its hills. The beach is uninspiring but good beaches are within walking distance, north of the quay at Martinakia and Episkopi.

◎ Sights

Episkopi   BEACH
(Map p276) This wide swathe of coarse grey sand is a 30-minute walk north of the harbour. There's a popular beach bar at one end and a tiny church at the other.

Martinakia   BEACH
Although you can swim in the centre of town, you're better off walking 10 minutes north to this pretty little cove.

Kythnos

Sleeping & Eating

Kontseta　　　　　　　　　APARTMENT €€
(☑ 22810 33024; www.kontseta.gr; r €100-120; ☺ Apr-Oct; ❄ 🛜) Easily the nicest option in town, these modern studio apartments are a cut above, with fresh decor and fine views. They are high above the ferry quay, with steps signposted next door to the Alpha Bank.

Molos　　　　　　　　　　　　GRILL €
(☑ 22810 32455; mains €2.50-12; ☺ 2-11pm) Quick, delicious souvlaki, kebabs, burgers stuffed with cheese, grilled haloumi and salads, served from an unassuming waterfront location near where the ferries dock.

Ostria　　　　　　　　　　SEAFOOD €€
(☑ 22810 33017; mains €9-20; ☺ 10.30am-midnight; 🛜) Seafood is the main attraction here: grilled snapper, scorpion fish, grouper, calamari and lobster spaghetti all get the thumbs up. Stop by earlier for an omelette and coffee on the terrace overlooking the water.

ⓘ Information

Larentzakis Antonis (☑ 22810 32104; www. rentacarkythnos.gr; ☺ 9am-9pm) Sells ferry tickets, arranges accommodation, and hires ATVs, scooters and cars.
Anerousa Travel (☑ 22810 32372; ☺ 9am-9pm) Sells ferry tickets.

ⓘ Getting There & Away

Between early June and September, buses from Merihas serve Hora (15 minutes), Loutra (30 minutes), Dryopida (30 minutes) and Kanala (45 minutes) five times daily; fares range from €1.40 to €2. Agencies along the waterfront rent scooters, ATVs and cars.

Hora (Kythnos)
Χώρα (Κύθνος)

POP 561

Behind its workaday outskirts, the island's capital, Hora (also known as Kythnos or Messaria), hides a network of lanes branching off a long alley lined with white churches, cafes, tavernas, and ceramics shops. The town has held on to its inherent character as a largely agricultural community. Grannies string out their laundry above the whitewashed lanes, farmers trot by on donkeys and, come Easter, the village kids amuse themselves on a traditional wooden swing bedecked with flowers.

Sleeping & Eating

Filoxenia Studios　　　　APARTMENT €€
(☑ 22810 31644; www.filoxenia-kythnos.gr; d €70; ❄🛜) These well-priced, fully equipped apartments and studios are behind a terrace filled with palms and flowering shrubs. It's on the square just before the pedestrian part of town.

Messaria　　　　　　　　　GREEK €€
(☑ 22810 31620; www.messaria.gr; mains €8.50-11; ☺ 1-10pm; 🛜) Set on the small square at the edge of the pedestrian part of Hora, this restaurant specialises in traditional island dishes, such as rooster cooked in wine, baked chickpeas and rabbit stew.

ⓘ Getting There & Away

Hora is 7km from Merihas by road. During high season there are five daily buses to Merihas and Loutra (€1.40).

BEACHES & VILLAGES OF KYTHNOS

The island's most famous beaches are in the northwest. **Apokrousi** (Map p276) is a wide strip of gravelly sand with a couple of tavernas, a popular beach bar and ample parking. From Apokrousi, a rough, rutted road leads over the hill to the exquisite double bay of **Kolona** (Map p276), a narrow sun-blasted strip of sand anchoring a hilly headland to the main island. In summer it gets jam-packed, and the seasonal cafe does a brisk trade. In low season it's a favourite anchorage for yachts; although the road to the spit is often gated when the cafe is closed, you can still access the first beach and swim to the spit. It's easiest to reach Kolona via water taxi from Merihas, or else by ATV or a hot 30-minute walk from Apokrousi.

At the centre of the island is Kythnos' prettiest village, **Dryopida**. Clinging to either side of a ravine, this collection of red-tiled roofs and winding, car-free lanes has a cluster of cafes, tavernas and small museums gathered around its impressive church.

From Dryopida, the main road runs all the way south to **Agios Dimitrios**, a stone-strewn, grey-sand beach with placid waters. Of the half-dozen east-coast beaches, the most accessible (and loveliest) is the sandy cove next to **Kanala** village. This substantial seaside settlement is also notable for its church, which contains a beloved icon of the Virgin and Child, and for the excellent traditional trattoria, **Archipelagos** (Map p276; ☑ 22810 32380; www.archipelagos-kythnos.gr; Kanala; mains €6.80-20; ⊙ 1-10pm; ☎).

If you're after a hike, it's well worth walking the minor roads from Dryopida down to the less-visited **Lefkes**, **Kato Livadi** and **Liotrivi** beaches. Another worthwhile ramble is the picturesque 90-minute track from Loutra to **Kastro Orias** (Map p276), on Cape Kefalos. These beautifully situated ruins are all that remains of a medieval city of around 5000 people.

Loutra Λουτρά

POP 81

This low-key fishing village, 3km north of Hora, sits on a windy bay, its large marina full of yachts and its harbour front lined with high-standard restaurants, cafes and bars. In summer it's a popular destination for sailing tours and the liveliest spot on the island in which to base yourself.

Maroula, a short coastal walk north, is the site of ancient Mesolithic-era graves.

🏃 Activities

Aqua Team DIVING
(☑ 22810 31333; www.aquakythnos.gr; 1-/2-tank dive €50/90; 🛥) With more than 30 dive sites to choose from, from wrecks and caves to drift dives, Kythnos is a great spot for underwater explorers. This crew offers boat dives, snorkelling trips and diving courses, including Discover Scuba sessions for beginners.

Hot Springs HOT SPRINGS
`FREE` Loutra's unusual claim to fame is its thermal waters, which bubble along a culvert to the beach where they're detained in a large

rock pool before seeping out to sea. It's a popular spot for a soak, any time of the year.

🍴 Sleeping & Eating

★**Kythnos Bay Hotel** HOTEL €€
(☑ 22810 31218; www.kythnosbay.gr; r €70-80; ⊙ Easter-Sep; 🅿❄☎) Drifted in on a summer breeze, this beachy hotel is Loutra's most up-market choice, with an elegantly bleached colour palate and artfully hung driftwood in reception. Well-equipped rooms, friendly staff and a delicious breakfast buffet compensate for the slow wi-fi.

Sofrano INTERNATIONAL €€
(☑ 22810 31436; www.sofrano-yachtingclub.gr; mains €10-19; ⊙ 9am-late; ☎) The mainstay of the Loutra waterfront is this schmick restaurant serving a selection of traditional mezedehes, grilled fresh fish and unusual dishes such as beef tenderloin in a spicy chocolate sauce.

ℹ Getting There & Away

In the high season there are five daily buses in each direction on the Merihas–Hora–Loutra route; fares range from €1.40 to €2.

KEA

POP 2460

Kea has plenty of natural appeal with craggy cliffs, a spectacular coastline and fertile valleys filled with orchards, olive groves and oak trees, as well as interesting historical sights and walking routes. It's also the closest island to Attica, making it a popular destination for wealthy Athenians.

ⓘ Getting There & Away

Kea's only mainland service is to Lavrio; boats get packed on weekends. In the off season, connections to other islands are few. High-season destinations include Lavrio (€12.40, one hour, three daily), Kythnos (€6.90, 1¼ hours, daily), Syros (€11, four hours, three weekly), Tinos (€12, 3½ hours, weekly) and Andros (€9.30, 5½ hours, weekly); see www.ferries.gr for details.

ⓘ Getting Around

In July and August, regular buses go from Korissia to Vourkari, Otzias, Ioulida and Pisses; fewer services run out of season. **Taxis** (☑ 22812 00158) to Ioulida cost around €10, Otzias €8 and Pisses €25.

Leon Rent A Car (☑ 22880 21898; www.renta-carkea.gr) rents cars and scooters from an office very near the ferry terminal.

Korissia   Κορησσία

POP 711

The little port of Korissia may not be quite as picturesque as the island's capital, but it has a lively strip of waterfront bars and tavernas. The north-facing beach tends to catch the wind, but you're only about a 15-minute walk from small but popular **Gialiskari Beach**.

⌂ Sleeping

Koralli Studios   APARTMENT €€
(☑ 22880 21268; www.kea-rooms.gr; s/d from €58/63; P ❄ ☎) These bougainvillea-clad studios are just 150m from the beach but they don't have the most salubrious view, overlooking a boat yard. The owner can meet the ferry and goes out of his way to assist his guests.

Red Tractor Farm   FARMSTAY €€
(☑ 22880 21346; www.redtractorfarm.com; r/studio from €98/132; ❄ ☎) ✎ Set among vineyards and olive groves, this organic agritourism farm offers rooms, studios and whole cottages in a range of beautiful Cycladic buildings. Hosts Kostis and Marcie know the best hiking

routes; they also produce olive oil, wine, marmalade and chutney, plus acorn cookies.

Aegean View   GUESTHOUSE €€
(☑ 22880 22046; www.roomsinkea.gr; r from €71; ⊙ Mar-Dec; ❄ ☎) On the harbourfront, this guesthouse has modern rooms and studios with en suite bathrooms. Some have private balconies; all share a lovely communal deck.

✕ Eating

Rolando's   GREEK €€
(☑ 22880 29129; mains €8-17; ⊙ noon-midnight; ☎) One of the humbler tavernas on the waterfront strip, Rolando's serves tasty rustic food such as meatballs, *katsiki* (kid goat), an excellent *mousakas*, fresh fish and rabbit stew.

Magazes   MEDITERRANEAN €€
(☑ 22880 21104; www.kearestaurant.gr; mains €9-20; ⊙ noon-midnight Easter-Sep; ☎ ✎) Run by Greek-Californian Stefanos, Magazes serves high-quality local dishes in a stylishly restored warehouse on the waterfront. It's recommended for its fresh seafood, including lobster pasta, and tasty vegetarian options such as zucchini fritters and stuffed eggplant.

ⓘ Information

Stegadi (☑ 22880 21435; www.praktoreiokeas. gr) Sells ferry tickets and has good information on Kea's hiking trails on its website.

ⓘ Getting There & Away

Korissia is the island's main ferry port. Leon Rent A Car rents vehicles from an office right by the port. Buses run to Ioulida, Otzias and Pisses several times daily.

Ioulida   Ιουλίδα

POP 633

Ioulida is Kea's gem, its pretty scramble of narrow lanes, churches and houses draping themselves across two hilltops in the island's mountainous heart. Once one of Kea's four ancient city-states, it's been the administrative capital since late Roman/Byzantine times. It's now a thoroughly pleasant place to wander around, with enough interesting sights, tavernas and cafes to detain you for a few hours.

◉ Sights

★ **Ancient Lion of Kea**   MONUMENT
The enigmatic 8m-long Kea Lion, chiselled from schist sometime between the 9th and

6th century BC, lies along the ridge beyond the last of Ioulida's houses. The 15-minute walk to reach it is fantastic: follow small wooden signs reading Αρχαίος Λέων from the top of the main street until the path leads you out of town. The footpath curves past a cemetery, and the lion, with its smooth-worn haunches and Cheshire-cat smile, is reached through a gate on the left.

Archaeological Museum of Kea MUSEUM
(📞 22880 22079; adult/child €2/1; ⊗ 8.30am-3.30pm Wed-Mon) The most intriguing arte-facts displayed at this museum were ancient even before Kea's four archaic city-states were formed. The 13 terracotta figurines of bare-breasted women recovered from a temple at Agia Irini (Vourkari Bay) date from be-tween 3300 and 1100 BC. .

🛌 Sleeping

Hotel Serie HOTEL €€
(📞 22880 22355; www.serie.com.gr; r from €110; P ❄ 🛜) Just a few minutes' walk from laby-rinthine Ioulida, this compact hotel offers a cluster of light, brightly painted rooms with hilly views from the balconies.

Kea Village HOTEL €€
(📞 6972243330; www.keavillas.gr; ste from €140; ⊗ Mar–mid-Nov; P ❄ 🛜 ☂) Gorgeously situat-ed at the highest point of Ioulida, this com-plex with sweeping views offers suites and villas that sleep you and up to nine of your dearest friends in style. All have a veranda and either a kitchenette or a full kitchen.

🍴 Eating

⭐ **To Steki** TAVERNA €
(📞 22880 22088; www.facebook.com/tostekikea; mains €8-9.50; ⊗ 12.30pm-midnight daily Jun-Sep, 7pm-midnight Fri & Sat, 12.30-4pm Sun Oct-May; 🛜) Regular taverna fare is taken to the next level at this attractive place tucked beside St Spyridon's Church, with terrace seating over-looking the valley. Expect the likes of goat in lemon sauce, rabbit, mushroom pie, zucchini pie and delicious *dolmadhes* served warm in an olive oil and lemon emulsion.

O Paparounas TAVERNA €€
(📞 22880 22583; www.facebook.com/Paparounas. Kea; mains from €8.50; ⊗ 10am-midnight; 🛜) Oc-cupying a terrace on the corner of the main square, this friendly little taverna serves local favourites such as Greek salad, taboul-eh, grilled sardines, fried anchovies and eat-

whole fried bait fish. Local farmers drop by around 10am for their morning coffee or *raki* shot; the kitchen gets going at midday.

To Spiti Sti Hora GREEK €€€
(📞 22880 29101; www.tospitistihora.gr; mains €18-27; ⊗ noon-3pm & 7-11pm Jun-Sep; 🛜) Set on ter-races with views over the town to the sea, this restaurant prepares elaborate takes on Kea dishes, with local ingredients put to excellent use. Expect the likes of goat spaghetti, cuttle-fish risotto, octopus stew and sunset views over Ioulida to go with your cocktails.

🍸 Drinking & Nightlife

Large windows and a small terrace showcase extraordinary valley views at the bright and cheery little cafe **To Panorama** (📞 22880 22341; ⊗ 9am-2pm Mon & Thu, 5.30-9pm Fri, 9am-9pm Sat & Sun; 🛜). Thankfully, the coffee's good, too – and there's a good selection of pastries, cakes, waffles, crêpes, omelettes and sandwiches, should you get peckish.

ℹ Getting There & Away

During the mid-June to September high season there are regular buses (every 40 minutes) to Korissia; fewer in the off season.

DIVING KEA

Kea has some of the best diving in Greece, with more than a dozen varied and challenging dive sites that include walls, ship and plane wrecks and underwater caves. Vourkari-based **Kea Divers** (☑ 6973430860; www.keadivers.com; Vourkari; 1/2 dives incl equipment €50/90) is a reputable scuba-diving outfit that also runs snorkelling trips.

Around Kea

The beach road from Korissia leads past golden-sand **Gialiskari Beach** to the marina at **Vourkari**, where the waterfront is lined with yachts, restaurants, bars and cafes.

Four kilometres to the northeast, **Otzias** has a large, sandy beach in an often windy, bay. From Otzias, a 12km road runs inland to Ioulida, connected to the east coast's finest beach, **Spathi**. There's not much here aside from a large beach bar and a few of holiday homes, and there's not much shade.

Eight kilometres southwest of Ioulida is the unfortunately named **Pisses** (also spelt Poisses), a pebble-strewn sandy beach with a taverna and beach bar, backed by rugged hills. Four kilometres south along the coast is **Koundouros**, a playground for moneyed Athenians, with a succession of small sandy coves. A little further south, **Kampi** is an inviting little swimming spot with a taverna.

☉ Sights

★ **Karthaia**   RUINS
(Map p279) From the 8th century BC until the 7th century AD, this remote twin cove was the site of the ancient city of Karthaia, one of Kea's four historic city-states. Now the partly uncovered ruins sit in splendid isolation, only accessible by boat or on foot. Three hiking trails lead here, with the easiest being route 6: a 40-minute walk down from the parking area at the bottom of a narrow lane, signposted from the main road at Stavroudaki.

The small, craggy acropolis has the remains of the **Temple of Apollo Pythios** on its lower level and the **Temple of Athena** at the top, dating from 530 to 500 BC. Down below is a **theatre** that once seated 880 people, and the remains of a Roman-era **bathhouse**.

Kastrianis Monastery   MONASTERY
(Map p279; ☉ sunrise-sunset Jun-Sep) From Otzias, a spectacular coastal road runs for 6.5km to this clifftop, 18th-century monastery, offering extraordinary views to the surrounding islands. A peacock-blue dome caps the baby-blue church and, inside, the walls are covered with frescoes of saints.

🛏 Sleeping & Eating

Anemousa Studios   APARTMENT €€
(Map p279; ☑ 22880 21335; www.anemousa.gr; Otzias; apt from €95; ☉ Apr-Oct; ❋ 🛜 ☎) Surrounded by well-maintained gardens, these comfortable and spacious apartments curve around an attractive pool, 50m inland from the beach in Otzias. Breakfast and drinks can be ordered from the poolside bar, and there's a BBQ, plus a playground for kids.

Seirios   SEAFOOD €€
(☑ 22880 28280; www.facebook.com/seirios.kea; Vourkari; mains €12-20; ☉ 11am-late; ☎) The best of Vourkari's waterfront restaurants delivers a concise but appealing seafood-focused menu including marinated anchovies and delicately battered squid, but the main focus is on whole grilled fish, presented for your appraisal.

I Strofi tou Mimi   SEAFOOD €€
(☑ 22880 21480; www.facebook.com/istrofitoumimi; Vourkari; mains €9-20; ☉ noon-midnight daily Jun-Aug, Sat & Sun Apr, May, Sep & Oct; ☎) On the far side of Vourkari Bay, this waterfront restaurant focuses mainly on seafood, particularly grilled fish, with a few meaty dishes offered as well. In the summer, the glassed-in terrace opens up to let in the sea breezes.

🍷 Drinking & Nightlife

Kea's hippest bar by far, **Zeus Faber** (☑ 6987410707; Vourkari; ☉ 8pm-4am; ☎), sits up above the waterfront tavernas, with a deck gazing over the water and a dimly lit interior furnished with wooden benches, driftwood, candles, old records and interesting art.

Crete

Best Places to Eat

➡ Peskesi (p290)

➡ To Skolio (p327)

➡ Hope (p332)

➡ Garden Arkoudenas (p305)

➡ Milia (p326)

Best Places to Stay

➡ Villa Ippocampi (p300)

➡ Elounda Heights (p332)

➡ Thalori Retreat (p299)

➡ Dalabelos Estate (p308)

Why Go?

Crete (Κρήτη) is the culmination of the Greek experience. There's something undeniably artistic in the way its landscape unfolds, from the sun-drenched beaches in the north to the rugged canyons spilling out at the cliff-lined southern coast. In between, valleys cradle moody villages, and round-shouldered hills are the overture to often snow-dabbed mountains. Take it all in on a driving tour, trek through Europe's longest gorge or hike to the cave where Zeus was born. Leave time to plant your footprints on a sandy beach, and boat, kayak or snorkel in the crystalline waters. Crete's natural beauty is equalled only by the richness of its history. The Palace of Knossos is but one of many vestiges of the mysterious ancient Minoan civilisation. Venetian fortresses, Turkish mosques and Byzantine churches bring history alive all over Crete, but nowhere more so than in charismatic Hania and Rethymno. Foodies too will be in heaven in Crete, where 'locavore' is not a trend but a way of life.

When to Go
Crete (Iraklio)

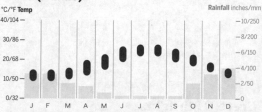

Jul & Aug High season. Queues at big sights, busy beaches. hot days, balmy evenings, warm waters.

Apr–Jun & Sep–Oct Moderate temperatures, smaller crowds. Best time for outdoor activities.

Nov–Mar Low season. Sights and restaurants scale back hours. Beach resorts close. Major sights uncrowded.

Piraeus
(230km)

Piraeus
(240km)

Antikythira (25km);
Kythira (70km);
Gythio (145km);
Piraeus (260km)

Rodopos
Peninsula

Balos
Gramvousa
Peninsula
Kalyviani

Falasarna
Polyrrina

Milia

HANIA

Agia Irini

Elafonisi

Paleohora

Elafonisi
Islet

Spilia

Bay of
Kissamos

Kissamos

Fournes
Meskla
Lakki
Omalos

Mt Volakias
(2116m)

Sougia

Lissos

Gulf of
Hania

Stavros

Hania

Souda

Theriso

Samaria Gorge
National Park

Mt Pachnes
(2454m)

Aradena
Anopoli

Agia
Roumeli

Imbros

Loutro

Hora
Sfakion

Frangokastello

Akrotiri
Peninsula

Souda
Bay

Cape Drapano

Vryses

Georgioupolis

Almyros
Bay

Rethymno

Kournas
Lake

Episkopi

Komitades

Panormo

Adele

RETHYMNO

Selia

Myrthios

Lefkogia

Plakias

Moni
Preveli

Triopetra

Bali

Perama

Ancient
Eleftherna

Moni Arkadiou

Spili

Myrthios

Mt Kedros
(1777m)

Agios
Pavlos

Mesara
Gulf

Anogia

Mt Psilor
(2456m)

Amari

Amari
Valley

Agia
Galini

Tymbaki

Agia Triada

Matala

Paximadia
Islands

Cape
Lithino

Zaros

Vori

Phaest

Gavdopoula

Sarakiniko
Beach

Karabe

Gavdos

Libyan Sea

Crete Highlights

1 **Palace of Knossos** (p292)
Rubbing shoulders with
Europe's oldest civilisation, the
ancient Minoans.

2 **Rethymno** (p300) Getting
lost in the charismatic jumble
of Venetian buildings sprinkled

with exotic features from the
Ottoman period.

3 **Heraklion Archaeological
Museum** (p285) Marvelling
at the treasures unearthed
during the excavation of
ancient sites on the island.

4 **Samaria Gorge** (p324)
Following an old riverbed to the
Libyan Sea on a trek through
Europe's longest canyon.

5 **Elafonisi** (p327) Counting
the colours of the sea while

Sea of
Crete

Santorini
(70km)

0 ────────────── 50 km
0 ────────────── 25 miles

Kasos (55km);
Karpathos (100km);
Halki (185km);
Rhodes (250km)

Cape
avros

Dia

Iraklio
Bay

Iraklio 3

Gournes   Hersonisos   Plaka   Cape Agios
                                            Ioannis
sos   9 **Spinalonga Island**
Palace   Skalani   *Palace*   Elounda   Kolokytha Peninsula
of Knossos 1   *of Malia*   Cape Sideros
odele   Malia Neapoli   *Gulf of*   Mon
Arhanes 7 Myrtia   **Agios**   *Mirabello*   Toplou   Vaï
Iraklio Wine   Peza   Tzermiado   **Nikolaos**   Sitia Palekastro
Country Alagni   *Lato* Kri-Kri   Mohlos
                  Psyhro   Agios   Kritsa Istron
Agia   Arkalokhorion **Dikteon** Georgios   **Gournia**   **LASITHI** Zakros
Varvara   **Cave** 10 ▲ Mt Dikti   Kato
Gortyna   **IRAKLIO**   (2148m) Kalamafka   Ziros   Zakros
                  Ano Viannos   Xerokampos
                         Anatoli   **Ierapetra**   **Koutsouras**
ndas   **Pyrgos**
                 Arvi   **Myrtos**   Koufonisi

                    Gaïdouronisi
                    (Hrysi)

relaxing on this glorious pink-
tinged sandy beach.

6 **Hania** (p313) Wandering
the historic city's romantic old
town and Venetian harbour.

7 **Iraklio Wine Country**
(p296) Sampling fine

vintages on a tour of this
vine-blanketed sylvan
landscape.

8 **Moni Arkadiou** (p306)
Being moved by the bloody
tragedy of this isolated
monastery.

9 **Spinalonga Island** (p329)
Feeling the history of this
former leper colony.

10 **Dikteon Cave** (p339)
Making the pilgrimage to the
birthplace of Zeus, king of the
gods.

History

Although inhabited since Neolithic times (7000–3000 BC), Crete is most famous for being the cradle of Europe's first advanced civilisation, the Minoan. Traces of this enigmatic society were uncovered in the early 20th century, when British archaeologist Sir Arthur Evans discovered the palace at Knossos and named the civilisation after its ruler, the mythical King Minos.

Minoans migrated to Crete in the 3rd millennium BC. Their extraordinary artistic, architectural and cultural achievements culminated in the construction of huge palace complexes at Knossos, Phaestos, Malia and Zakros, which were all levelled by an earthquake around 1700 BC. Undeterred, the Minoans built bigger and better ones over the ruins, while settling more widely across Crete. Around 1450 BC, the palaces were mysteriously destroyed again, possibly by a tsunami triggered by a volcanic eruption on Santorini (Thira). Knossos, the only palace saved, finally burned down around 1400 BC.

Archaeological evidence shows that the Minoans lingered on for a few centuries in small, isolated settlements before disappearing as mysteriously as they had come. They were followed by the Mycenaeans and the Dorians (around 1100 BC). By the 5th century BC, Crete was divided into city-states but did not benefit from the cultural glories of mainland Greece; in fact, it was bypassed by Persian invaders and the Macedonian conqueror Alexander the Great.

By 67 BC Crete had become the Roman province of Cyrenaica, with Gortyna its capital. After the Roman Empire's division in AD 395, Crete fell under the jurisdiction of Greek-speaking Constantinople – the emerging Byzantine Empire. Things went more or less fine until 824, when Arabs appropriated the island. In 961, though, Byzantine general emperor Nikiforas Fokas (912–69) won Crete back following a nine-month siege of Iraklio (then called El Khandak by the Arabs). Crete flourished under Byzantine rule, but with the infamous Fourth Crusade of 1204 the maritime power of Venice received Crete as part of its 'payment' for supplying the Crusaders' fleet.

Much of Crete's most impressive surviving architecture dates from the Venetian period, which lasted until 1669 when Iraklio (then called Candia) became the last domino to fall after a 21-year Ottoman siege. Turkish rule brought new administrative organisation, Islamic culture and Muslim settlers. Cretan resistance was strongest in the mountain strongholds but all revolts were put down brutally, and it was only with the Ottoman Empire's disintegration in the late 19th century that Europe's great powers expedited Crete's sovereign aspirations.

Thus, in 1898, with Russian and French consent, Crete became a British protectorate. However, the banner under which future Greek Prime Minister Eleftherios Venizelos and other Cretan rebels were fighting was Enosis i Thanatos (Unity or Death) – unity with Greece, not mere independence from Turkey. Yet it would take the Greek army's successes in the Balkan Wars (1912–13) to turn Crete's de facto inclusion in the country into reality, with the 1913 Treaty of Bucharest.

Crete suffered tremendously during WWII, due to being coveted by Adolf Hitler for its strategic location. On 20 May 1941 a huge flock of German parachutists quickly overwhelmed the Cretan defenders. The Battle of Crete, as it would become known, raged for 10 days between German and Allied troops from Britain, Australia, New Zealand and Greece. For two days the battle hung in the balance until the Germans captured the Maleme Airfield, near Hania. The Allied forces fought a valiant rearguard action, enabling the British Navy to evacuate 18,000 of the 32,000 Allied troops. The harsh German occupation lasted throughout WWII, with many mountain villages bombed or burnt down and their occupants executed en masse.

IRAKLIO PROVINCE

Iraklio is Crete's most dynamic region, home to almost half the island's population and its top-rated tourist site, the Minoan Palace of Knossos. Priceless treasures unearthed here, and at the many other Minoan sites around Crete, have catapulted the archaeological museum in the capital city of Iraklio onto the world stage.

Admittedly, the coastal stretch east of Iraklio is one continuous band of hotels and resorts. But a few kilometres inland, villages sweetly lost in time provide pleasing contrast. Taste the increasingly sophisticated tipple produced in the Iraklio Wine Country, walk in the footsteps of painter El Greco and writer Nikos Kazantzakis, and revel in the rustic grandeur of remote mountain villages such as Zaros.

On the quieter southern coast, the ex-hippie hangout of Matala is the only developed resort, while in the charming villages the laid-back life unfolds much the way it has since time immemorial.

Iraklio Ηράκλειο

POP 140,730

Crete's capital, Iraklio (also called Heraklion), is Greece's fifth-largest city and the island's economic and administrative hub. It's also home to Crete's blockbuster sights: the must-see Heraklion Archaeological Museum and the nearby Palace of Knossos, which both provide fascinating windows into Crete's ancient past.

Though not pretty in a conventional way, Iraklio definitely grows on you if you take the time to explore its layers and wander its backstreets. You'll discover a low-key urban sophistication with a thriving cafe and restaurant scene, good shopping and bustling nightlife. A revitalised waterfront invites strolling, and the pedestrianised historic centre is punctuated by bustling squares flanked by buildings from the time when Christopher Columbus first set sail.

◎ Sights

★Heraklion Archaeological Museum MUSEUM

(Map p286; www.heraklionmuseum.gr; Xanthoudidou 2; adult/concession/child €10/5/free, combined ticket with Palace of Knossos adult/concession €16/8; ⊗ 8am-8pm Mon & Wed-Sun, 10am-8pm Tue mid-Apr–Oct, 8am-4pm Nov–mid-Apr) This state-of-the-art museum is one of the largest and most important in Greece. The two-storey revamped 1930s Bauhaus building makes a gleaming showcase for artefacts spanning 5500 years from Neolithic to Roman times, including a Minoan collection of unparalleled richness. The rooms are colour coded and displays are arranged both chronologically and thematically, and presented with descriptions in English. A visit here will greatly enhance your understanding of Crete's rich history. Don't skip it.

The museum's treasure trove includes pottery, jewellery and sarcophagi, plus famous frescoes from the sites of Knossos, Tylissos, Amnissos and Agia Triada. The pieces are grouped into comprehensive themes such as settlements, trade, death, religion and administration. Along with clear descriptions, these bring to life both the day-to-day functioning and the long-term progression of societies in Crete and beyond. Allow at least two hours for this extraordinary collection.

★Koules Fortress FORTRESS

(Rocca al Mare; Map p286; http://koules.efah.gr; Venetian Harbour; adult/concession €2/1; ⊗ 8am-8pm May-Sep, to 4pm Oct-Apr) After six years of restoration, Iraklio's 16th-century fortress, called Rocca al Mare by the Venetians, reopened in August 2016 with a brand-new exhibition. It tells the story of the building, zeroes in on milestones in city history, and displays ancient amphorae, Venetian cannons and other finds recovered from shipwrecks around Dia Island by Jacques Cousteau in 1976.

The presentation is insightful and atmospheric thanks to muted light filtering in through the old cannon holes. Visits conclude on the rooftop, with panoramic views over the sea and the city.

★Historical Museum of Crete MUSEUM

(Map p286; www.historical-museum.gr; Sofokli Venizelou 27; adult/concession €5/3; ⊗ 9am-5pm Mon-Sat, 10.30am-3pm Sun Apr-Oct, to 3.30pm daily Nov-Mar) If you're wondering what Crete's been up to for the past, say, 1700 years, a spin around this engagingly curated museum is in order. Exhibits hopscotch from the Byzantine to the Venetian and Turkish periods, culminating with WWII. Quality English labelling, interactive stations throughout and audio guides (€3) in five languages greatly enhance the experience.

The Venetian era receives special emphasis and there's even a huge model of the city c 1650 prior to the Turkish occupation. Start in the introductory room, which charts the major phases of history through maps, books, artefacts and images. First-floor highlights include the only two El Greco paintings in Crete (1569's *The Baptism of Christ* and 1570's *View of Mt Sinai and the Monastery of St Catherine*), 13th- and 14th-century frescoes, exquisite Venetian gold jewellery, and embroidered vestments. A historical exhibition charts Crete's road to independence from the Turks in the early 20th century. The most interesting rooms on the 2nd floor are the recreated study of Cretan-born author Nikos Kazantzakis and those dramatically detailing aspects of the WWII Battle of Crete in 1941, including the Cretan resistance and the role of the Allied Secret Service. The top floor features an outstanding folklore collection.

CRETE IRAKLIO

Iraklio Bay

Old Harbour

Central Taxi Stand

Plateia 18 Anglon

Sofokli Venizelou

Mitsotaki

5

Talos Plaza (600m); Amoudara (4km)

2 **Historical Museum of Crete**

Theotokopoulou

Chronaki

Lahana

Vyronos

Epimenidou

25 Avgoustou

Koroneou

16

Kalimeraki

Grevenon

Hortatson

9
10

Theotokopoulou

Almirou

13

Paleologou

17

El Greco Park

Arkoleondos

Plateia Agiou Titou

Agiou Titou

12

1878

Handakos

Agiostefaniton

Psaromiligkon

Plateia Venizelou

6
4 **7**

15

Milatou

Idaiou Antrou

20

Perdikari

Korai

21

18

19

Station B (750m)

Kalokerinou

i Info Point

Dedalou

22

Dikeosynis

Monis Odigitrias

Katehaki

1821

Odos 1866

23

Evans

Koziri

Zogratou

Agiou Mina

Cultural and Conference Center of Heraklion (500m); Grave of Nikos Kazantzakis (900m)

P Theseus Parking

14

8

Bembo Fountain (100m)

Merastri (500m); Nikos Kazantzakis Open-Air Theatre (500m)

P

Iraklio

◎ Top Sights
1 Heraklion Archaeological Museum	E5
2 Historical Museum of Crete	A3
3 Koules Fortress	E1

◎ Sights
4 Agios Markos Basilica	C5
5 Monastery of St Peter & St Paul	B3
6 Morosini Fountain	C5
7 Municipal Art Gallery	C5

🛏 Sleeping
8 Crops Suites	B7
9 Hotel Mirabello	B4
10 Kastro Hotel	B4
11 Lato Boutique Hotel	E3
12 Olive Green Hotel	D5
13 So Young Hostel	C4

✴ Eating
14 Athali	B7
15 Kritikos Fournos	C5
16 Parasties	A4
17 Peskesi	B4
18 Phyllo Sofies	C5

◎ Drinking & Nightlife
19 Bitters Bar	B5
20 Crop	D5
21 Xalavro	D6

🛍 Shopping
22 Aerakis Music	D6
23 Iraklio Central Market	C7
24 Zalo	E5

Monastery of St Peter & St Paul RUINS
(Map p286; Sofokli Venizelou 19; admission by donation; ⊙10am-2.30pm May-Sep) One of Iraklio's most striking ruins, this 13th-century Dominican monastery has been rebuilt and repackaged (mosque, movie theatre) numerous times throughout the centuries. Unusually located right on the sea wall, the monastery contains some beautiful 15th-century frescoes, as well as a modern mosaic exhibition by Loukas Peiniris that is well worth checking out.

Excavations in the surrounding area have uncovered graves dating to the 2nd Byzantine period. Monastery caretakers can be quite pushy for a donation.

Municipal Art Gallery GALLERY
(Map p286; cnr 25 Avgoustou & Plateia Venizelou; ⊙9am-3pm) **FREE** The three-aisled 13th-century **Agios Markos Basilica** (Map p286; was reconstructed many times and turned

into a mosque by the Turks. Today it's an exhibit space showcasing the work of Greek and foreign artists.

Morosini Fountain
FOUNTAIN

(Lion Fountain; Map p286; Plateia Venizelou) Four water-spouting lions make up this charming fountain, the town's most beloved Venetian vestige. Built in 1628 by Francesco Morosini, it once supplied Iraklio with fresh water.

Flanked by bustling cafes and fast-food joints, it's a fun spot to spend an hour resting and people-watching.

🏃 Activities

Get in touch with your inner Tyrannosaurus rex at **Dinosauria Park** (📞 28103 32089; www.dinosauriapark.com; International Exhibit Centre, Gournes; adult/child €10/8; ⊙10am-6pm) , a fun and educational theme park. You enter a time tunnel (with explanations on the way) and exit into a Jurassic universe complete with moving, roaring, life-size animatronic beasts.

🛏 Sleeping

So Young Hostel
HOSTEL €

(Map p286; 📞6978871355; www.facebook.com/soyoungheraklion; Almirou 22; dm/d from €21/40; ❄🛜) One of Iraklio's best central hostels, So Young, opened in 2018, earns high marks for its wonderful guest kitchen and even better rooftop terrace. Dorms come in both female and mixed varieties, with four-to-six- and eight-bed configurations, good mattresses and particle-board lockers. Interestingly, showers are co-ed.

Hotel Mirabello
HOTEL €

(Map p286; 📞28102 85052; www.mirabello-hotel.gr; Theotokopoulou 20; s/d from €40/50; ❄@🛜) Despite its dated, plain-Jane looks, this friendly and low-key hotel offers excellent value for money. Assets include squeaky-clean rooms with modern bathrooms, beds with individual reading lamps, a fridge and a kettle, plus a location close to, well, everything. The nicest units have a balcony.

★ Crops Suites
APARTMENT €€

(Map p286; 📞6974320857; www.cropssuites.com; Thiseos 3; apt incl breakfast €65; ❄🛜) Smack in the town centre, these stylish one-bedroom apartments will leave you feeling like a local hipster. Featuring canary-yellow cabinetry, plush grey sofas and light hardwoods throughout, they come with full kitchens stocked with coffee, olive oil, raki and more.

🏃 Museum Tour
Heraklion Archaeological Museum

LENGTH: TWO HOURS

Start on the ❶ **ground floor**, where rooms I to III focus on the Neolithic period to the Middle Bronze Age (7000–1700 BC), showing life in the first settlements in Crete and around Knossos. In room II, don't miss the pectoral ❷ **golden pendant with bees** from Malia, a jeweller's masterpiece depicting two bees depositing a drop of honey into a honeycomb; the finial sceptre handle in the shape of panther; and the extensive jewellery collection. The standout in room III is the elaborately embellished ❸ **Kamares tableware** of red, black and white clay, including a 'royal dinner service' from Phaestos, but don't rush past the extraordinary painted miniature plaques showcasing elaborate architectural details and the wooden scale model of Phaestos.

Rooms IV to VI illustrate life in the Late Bronze Age (1700–1450 BC). This is when Minoan culture reached its zenith, as reflected in the elaborate architecture, prolific trading practices and founding of new palaces. Not surprisingly, these are among the most visited rooms and the collection here is vast. Highlights include the ❹ **small clay house from Arhanes**, a stunning ❺ **ivory-and-crystal inlaid draughts board** and a scale model of Knossos. Most visitors home in on the ❻ **Phaistos disc**, a stunning clay piece embossed with 45 signs that has never been deciphered. Nearby, the massive ❼ **copper ingots** from Agia Triada and Zakros Palace demonstrate important units of economic exchange. Other gems include the ❽ **bull-leaping fresco** and the incredible ❾ **bull-leaper sculpture** (room VI) that show daring sporting practices of the time.

Rooms VII and VIII reveal the importance of Minoan religion and ideology, with cult objects and figurines. Don't miss the stone bull's head and the gorgeous limestone lioness vessels (said to be used for libations). Room VII houses the ❿ **chieftain's cup** from Agia Triada, which portrays two men, one holding a staff, the other a sword. In room VIII, the ⓫ **snake goddesses** and ⓬ **stone bull's head** (inlaid with seashell

HERAKLION ARCHAEOLOGICAL MUSEUM

Ground Floor

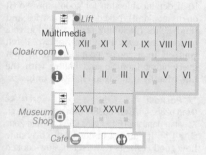

First Floor

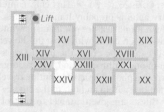

and crystal) are two stunning ceremonial items from Knossos.

Rooms IX and X are dedicated to the palace of Knossos and its emergence as a centralised state (after the administrative collapse of other palaces) along with evidence of the Mycenaeans. **13 Linear B clay tablets** reveal the first 'Greek' script and indicate Knossos' complex administrative system and bureaucratic processes. In room X, look for the extraordinary **14 boar's-tusk helmet** (complete with cheek guards) and the **15 gold-handled swords**, displaying the importance of the aristocratic warrior status.

Rooms XI and XII highlight settlements, sanctuaries and graves of the Late Bronze Age, including visual representations of death. The extraordinary **16 sarcophagus** from Agia Triada (room XII) is presumed to be that of a ruler, given its detailed, honorific fresco-style scenes, including the sacrifice of a bull (you can just make out the horror in his eyes).

On the **17 1st floor**, room XIII showcases Minoan frescoes (1800–1350 BC), including recreations by archaeologist **18 Sir Arthur Evans**, the British amateur journalist and adventurer who spent 30 years excavating the area around Knossos. The paintings, including the **19 Prince of the Lilies**, the **20 Ladies in Blue**, the **21 Cupbearer**, **22 La Parisienne** and the **23 Dolphin Fresco**, reflect the interest in art and nature at the time.

Rooms XV to XIX focus on the Geometric and Archaic periods (10th to 6th century BC), the transition to the Iron Age and the formation of the first Greek cities. The **24 Apollonian Triad**, bronze statues from Deros, are the earliest known Greek hammered-bronze statues, while the **25 bronze shields of the Ideon Cave** are extravagant votive offerings to Zeus.

Rooms XX to XXII move to the Classical, Hellenistic and Roman periods (5th to 4th century BC), where utensils, figurines and stunning mosaic floors and amphorae set the scene for the foundation of the autonomous Greek city-states, followed by civil wars and, finally, the Roman period. The huge **26 Phalagari hoard of silver coins** (room XXI) is thought to be a military or state fund. The cemetery finds of these periods are especially fascinating: look out for the bronze skull with the gilded clay wreath (room XXII).

Room XXIII exhibits two private collections donated to the museum.

Back on the **27 ground floor (part II)**, rooms XXVI and XXVII (7th to 4th century BC) house the museum's sculpture collection. Architectural reliefs from Gortyna demonstrate the role of Crete in the development of monumental sculpture, while Roman sculptures and copies of heroes and gods of the preceding Classical era showcase art from the Roman period.

Spacious balconies with city views are perfect for a glass of crisp white wine at sunset and/or a cuppa at daybreak.

Provocative signage keeps things fun. Yiannis and Anthi are fabulous and friendly as well.

★ Olive Green Hotel HOTEL €€
(Map p286; ☑ 28103 02900; www.olivegreenhotel. com; cnr Idomeneos & Meramvellou; d incl breakfast €109-126; ✴ ❂ 🖨) ✎ This chic, contemporary hotel is probably Iraklio's hippest digs. Clean rooms feature minimalistic white and olive-green decor, with separate shower and toilet (as opposed to the usual Greek-style all-in-one bathroom), and feature large, impressive photographs of tempting travel destinations within an hour of the city.

Guests are given a tablet to control electronic room features, and the bread, olive-oil and raki treatment from check-in. Club rooms are especially spacious, with espresso machines and larger terraces. Solar panels and low-impact building materials give the place an eco edge, and there's a cool cafe that spills out into the plaza.

★ Lato Boutique Hotel BOUTIQUE HOTEL €€
(Map p286; ☑ 28102 28103; www.lato.gr; Epimenidou 15; d incl breakfast from €80; ✴ @ 🖨) Iraklio goes Hollywood – with all the sass but sans the attitude – at this mod boutique hotel overlooking the old harbour, recognisable by its jazzy facade. With 79 rooms, it's hardly boutique, but smallish rooms are styled with rich woods and warm reds and have pillow-top mattresses and a playful lighting scheme. A newer annexe across the street is even more modern.

Kastro Hotel HOTEL €€
(Map p286; ☑ 28102 84185; www.kastro-hotel. gr; Theotokopoulou 22; s/d/tr incl breakfast from €50/80/95; ✴ 🖨) Clearly, plenty of thought has gone into the design of the smartly renovated Kastro, with rooms accented in airy, seafaring colours like turquoise and aqua. Good-quality mattresses, strong hot showers, a good breakfast buffet and the rooftop terrace are all welcome aspects of this central city hotel.

🍴 Eating

Phyllo Sophies CAFE €
(Map p286; www.phyllosophies.gr; Plateia Venizelou 33; mains €3.50-12.50; ❂ 6am-midnight; 🖨) With tables sprawling towards the Morosini Fountain, this is a great place to sample *bougatsa* (creamy semolina pudding wrapped in a pastry envelope and sprinkled with cinnamon and sugar). The less-sweet version is made with *myzithra* (sheep's-milk cheese).

Kritikos Fournos CAFE €
(Map p286; www.kritikosfournosgeuseis.gr; Plateia Kallergon 3; snacks €1-5; ❂ 6am-midnight; 🖨 ✎) This fun cafe-bakery is a Cretan chain, and it's a dependable stop for good espresso (it opens at 6am!), baked goods, pastries and sandwiches (including tasty vegan focaccia options) and even a craft beer or two. Perch yourself in a choice people-watching spot overlooking Lion Sq and banter with the hip, friendly staff. Signed in Greek only.

★ Peskesi CRETAN €€
(Map p286; ☑ 28102 88887; www.peskesicrete.gr; Kapetan Haralampi 6-8; mains €9-14; ❂ 1pm-2am; 🖨 ✎) ✎ It's almost impossible to overstate how good Peskesi's resurrected, slow-cooked Cretan dishes are, nor the beauty of the revamped Venetian villa in which you'll partake of them: this is Crete's finest culinary moment. Nearly everything is forged from heirloom produce and organic meats and olive oils from the restaurant's own farm.

★ Merastri CRETAN €€
(☑ 28102 21910; www.facebook.com/merastri; Chrisostomou 17; mains €5-13; ❂ 6pm-midnight Tue-Sun Jun-Aug, 6pm-midnight Tue-Sat, noon-midnight Sun Sep-May; 🖨) Enjoying one of the most authentic Cretan meals in town, served in this stunning home (a former music building), is a highlight of dining in Iraklio. The family of owners is passionate about its products (including oil and wine), and will conjure up everything from slow-cooked lamb to porterhouse steak with wine and sage.

★ Parasties GREEK €€
(Map p286; ☑ 28102 25009; www.parastiescrete. gr; Handakos 81; mains €9-43; ❂ noon-1am; 🖨) Parasties' owner, Haris, is genuine about serving great-quality local produce and top Cretan wines. And his passion shows in his gourmet menu of inventively updated traditional fare, including a daily special. Grab a seat under an annexe with a bar, in the roomy dining area or on the side patio with sea views.

Athali CRETAN €€
(Map p286; ☑ 28152 00012; www.athali.gr; Karterou 20; mains €8.50-15.50; ❂ noon-midnight; 🖨)

This colourful, crowd-pleasing restaurant is a true family affair: Dad oversees a massive central open fire, roasting spits of succulent lamb and pork for hours, while Mum handles traditional hearty stews such as rustic chicken, rooster and *youvetsi* (baked lamb with tomatoes and *kritharaki* pasta served with *anthotiro* cheese) in the kitchen and their three personable daughters serve.

🍷 Drinking & Nightlife

⭐ **Xalavro**   COCKTAIL BAR
(Map p286; www.facebook.com/xalavro; Milatou 10; ⊙10am-3am; 🛜) This rather idyllic open-air bar gets a whole lot right, with charming servers slinging creative cocktails to a diverse crowd of holidaymakers and locals in the ruins of an archaeologically protected roofless stone house. It exudes *Ef Zin* – the Greek art of living well.

⭐ **Solo Brewery**   MICROBREWERY
(www.solobeer.gr; Kointoirioti 35; ⊙noon-5pm; 🛜) Norwegian brewer Kjetil Jikiun started Norway's first craft brewery (Nøgne Ø) before he founded Crete's first craft brewery (he's clearly a man of firsts). There's no taproom per se, but drinking here is a worthwhile excursion for beer connoisseurs. A wealth of IPAs, stouts and porters, and hoppy saisons across five taps and numerous bottles await for makeshift front-patio consumption.

Bitters Bar   COCKTAIL BAR
(Map p286; www.thebittersbar.com; Plateia Venizelou; ⊙8pm-3am Mon-Thu, to 5am Fri-Sun; 🛜) The indisputable frontrunner of Iraklio's mixology scene is this den of Prohibition-inspired decadence centred on a retail alcove just off Lion Sq. Throwback cocktails dominate the classics on the list, but let the bartenders shine with creations such as Bitters House (gin, ginger syrup, pink-grapefruit and lemon juice, cardamom bitters) and Attaboy (vodka, mango puree, lemon juice, aromatic bitters).

Crop   CRAFT BEER
(Map p286; www.crop.coffee; Aretousas 4; ⊙7am-1am; 🛜) Crop divides its focus equally between two vices: caffeine and craft beer. At the time of writing it was Iraklio's only craft-focused bar, with five independent taps (including Crete's own Solo Brewing and Brewdog, and 25 or so bottled; beers cost €4 to €6). It's also a highly recommended roastery specialising in Third Wave coffee preparations such as V60 and Chemex.

☆ Entertainment

The **Cultural and Conference Center of Heraklion** (☑28102 29618; Plastira 10) is a new and modern five-building complex, opened in 2019, is Crete's most important cultural and events venue. It includes the gorgeous 800-seat Andreas and Maria Kalokairinou Hall, designed for theatre, opera and classical-music performances.

🛍 Shopping

⭐ **Zalo**   GIFTS & SOUVENIRS
(Map p286; www.zalo.gr; Papa Aleksandrou 2; ⊙9am-9pm Mon-Sat, to 4pm Sun) This recommended shop specialises in the kinds of souvenirs that won't embarrass you a year down the track: designer art prints, jewellery, notebooks, frameable postcards, funky handbags and the like, all 100% made in Greece from a network of cutting-edge, contemporary artists and designers.

Aerakis Music   MUSIC
(Map p286; ☑28102 25758; www.aerakis.net; Korai 14; ⊙9am-9pm Mon-Fri, to 5pm Sat) An Iraklio landmark since 1974, this little shop stocks an expertly curated selection of Cretan and Greek music, from old and rare recordings to the latest releases, many on its own record labels, Cretan Musical Workshop and Seistron.

Iraklio Central Market   MARKET
(Map p286; Odus 1866; ⊙hours vary) An Iraklio institution, if slightly touristy these days, this busy, narrow *agora* (market), along Odos 1866 between the Meidani crossroads and Plateia Kornarou, is one of the best in Crete and has everything you need to put together a delicious picnic.

ℹ Information

Info Point (Map p286; ☑28134 09777; www.heraklion.gr; Plateia Venizelou; ⊙8.30am-2.30pm Mon-Fri) The municipality's official tourist-info point.

Tourist Police (☑28104 409500, emergency 171; Dikeosynis 10; ⊙7am-10pm) In the suburb of Halikarnassos, near the airport.

University Hospital of Heraklion (☑28103 92111; www.pagni.gr; Stavrakia; ⊙24hr) In the area of Stavrakia, some 8km south of central Iraklio, this is one of Greece's largest public hospitals and is affiliated with the adjacent school of medicine.

❶ Getting There & Away

AIR

Nikos Kazantzakis Heraklion International Airport (HER; ☑ 2810 397800; www.ypa.gr/en/our-airports/kratikos-aerolimenas-hrak-leioy-n-kazantzakhs) About 5km east of the city centre, the airport has a bank, ATMs, duty-free shops and cafe-bars.

BOAT

The **ferry port** (☑ 28103 38000; www.porth-eraklion.gr) is 500m east of Koules Fortress and the old harbour. Iraklio is a major port for access to many of the Greek islands, though services are spotty outside high season. Tickets can be purchased online or through travel agencies, including central **Paleologos** (☑ 28103 46185; www.paleologos.gr; 25 Avgoustou 5; ⊙ 9am-8pm Mon-Fri, to 3pm Sat). Daily ferries from Iraklio's port include services to Piraeus and faster catamarans to Santorini and other Cycladic islands. Ferries sail east to Rhodes via Sitia, Kasos, Karpathos and Halki.

BUS

KTEL Heraklion Lassithi Bus Station (☑ 28102 46530; www.ktelherlas.gr; Leoforos Ikarou 9; 🛜) Near the waterfront east of Koules Fortress, this depot serves major destinations in eastern and western Crete, including Hania, Rethymno, Agios Nikolaos, Sitia and the Lassithi Plateau. Buses to Knossos leave from the adjacent local bus station.

Bus Station B (Chanioporta Station; ☑ 28102 55965; Machis Kritis 3; 🛜) Just beyond Hania Gate, west of the centre, this station serves the traditional village of Anogia. There's a ticket office inside Restaurant Chanioporta across the street.

Buses to Knossos (Map p286; Plateia Eleftherias) Handy stop for bus 2 to Knossos.

LONG-DISTANCE TAXI

For destinations around Crete, you can order a cab from **Crete Taxi Services** (☑ 6970021970; www.crete-taxi.gr; ⊙ 24hr) or **Crete Cab** (☑ 6955171473; www.crete.cab). There are also long-distance cabs waiting at the airport, at Plateia Eleftherias (outside the Capsis Astoria hotel) and at KTEL Heraklion Lassithi Bus Station. Sample fares for up to four people include Agios Nikolaos €84, Hersonisos €40, Malia €50, Matala €86 and Rethymno €101.

❶ Getting Around

TO/FROM THE AIRPORT

Bus 1 to Airport (Map p286; Plateia Eleftherias) Central stop for bus 1, linking the city with the airport.

CAR & MOTORCYCLE

Iraklio's streets are narrow and chaotic, so it's best to drop your vehicle in a car park (between €5 and €12 per day), and explore on foot; though not the cheapest option, it doesn't get much more central than **Theseus Parking** (www.facebook.com/theseusparking; Thiseos 18; 1st hour €4.80, per additional hour €.80, overnight €12). All the international car-hire companies have branches at the airport. Local outlets line the northern end of 25 Avgoustou and include **Caravel** (☑ 28103 00150; www.caravel.gr; 25 Avgoustou 39; ⊙ 8am-11pm), **Hertz** (☑ 28103 00744; www.hertz.gr; 25 Avgoustou 17; ⊙ 7am-9pm), **Motor Club** (☑ 28102 22408; www.motorclub.gr; Plateia 18 Anglon 1; car per day/week incl insurance from €35/180, scooter from €25/100; ⊙ 8am-10pm), **Loggetta Cars** (☑ 28102 89462; www.loggetta.gr; 25 Avgoustou 20; ⊙ 9am-1.30pm & 4.30-8.30pm) and **Sun Rise** (☑ 28102 21609; www.sunrise-cars.com; 25 Avgoustou 46; ⊙ 8am-9pm May-Oct, 8am-2pm & 5-9pm Mon-Sat Nov-Apr).

TAXI

There are small taxi stands all over town, but the main ones are at the Regional Bus Station, on **Plateia Eleftherias** (Map p286) and at the northern end of **25 Avgoustou** (Map p286; Venizelou). You can also phone for one on 28140 03084.

Useful taxi apps include Aegean Taxi (www.aegeantaxi.com).

Knossos   Κνωσσός

⭐ **Palace of Knossos**   ARCHAEOLOGICAL SITE (http://odysseus.culture.gr; Knossos; adult/concession €15/8, incl Heraklion Archaeological Museum €16/8; ⊙ 8am-8pm Apr-Sep, to 7pm Oct, to 3pm Nov-Mar; 🅿; 🚊2) Crete's most famous historical attraction is the Palace of Knossos, the grand capital of Minoan Crete, located 5km south of Iraklio. The setting is evocative and the ruins and recreations impressive, incorporating an immense palace, courtyards, private apartments, baths, lively frescoes and more. Excavation of the site started in 1878 with Cretan archaeologist Minos Kalokerinos, and continued from 1900 to 1930 with British archaeologist Sir Arthur Evans, who controversially restored parts of the site.

Evans' reconstructions bring to life the palace's most significant parts, including the columns, which are painted deep brown-red with gold-trimmed black capitals and taper gracefully at the bottom. Vibrant frescoes add dramatic flourishes. The advanced

Palace of Knossos

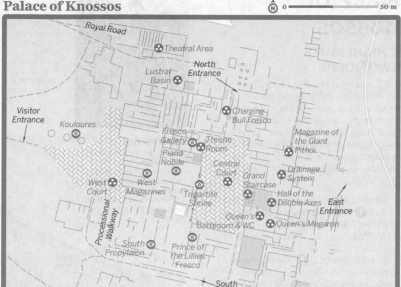

Royal Road
Theatral Area
North Entrance
Lustral Basin
Visitor Entrance
Kouloures
Charging Bull Fresco
Fresco Gallery
Throne Room
Magazine of the Giant Pithoi
Piano Nobile
Central Court
Drainage System
West Court
West Magazines
Grand Staircase
Tripartite Shrine
Hall of the Double Axes
East Entrance
Queen's Bathroom & WC
Queen's Megaron
Processional Walkway
South Propylaion
Prince of the Lillies Fresco
South Entrance

drainage system and a clever floor plan that kept rooms cool in summer and warm in winter are further evidence of Minoan society's sophistication.

There is no prescribed route for exploring the palace, but the following one takes in all the highlights. Entering from the **West Court**, which may have been a marketplace or the site of public gatherings, you'll note a trio of circular pits on your left. Called *kouloures*, they were used for grain storage. From here, continue counterclockwise, starting with a walk along the **Processional Walkway** that leads to the **South Propylaion**, where you can admire the **Cup Bearer Fresco**. From here, a staircase leads past giant storage jars to an upper floor that Evans called the **Piano Nobile** because it reminded him of Italian Renaissance palazzi and where he supposed the reception and staterooms were located. On your left, you can see the **west magazines** (storage rooms), where giant *pithoi* (clay jars) once held oil, wine and other staples.

The restored room at the northern end of the Piano Nobile houses the **Fresco Gallery**, with replicas of Knossos' most famous frescoes, including the *Bull Leaper*, the *Ladies in Blue* and the *Blue Bird*. The originals are now in the Heraklion Archaeological Museum (p285). From the balcony, a great view

unfolds of the **Central Court**, which was hemmed in by high walls during Minoan times. Rooms facing the western side of the courtyard had official and religious purposes, while the residential quarters were on the opposite side.

Follow the stairs down to the courtyard and then turn left to peek inside the beautifully proportioned **Throne Room**, with its simple alabaster seat and walls decorated with frescoes of griffins (mythical beasts regarded by the Minoans as sacred). To the right of the stairs is a three-sectioned room that Evans called the **Tripartite Shrine**. Areas behind it yielded many precious finds, including the famous *Snake Goddess* statue.

Crossing the Central Court takes you to the east wing, where the **Grand Staircase** drops down to the royal apartments. Get there via the ramp off the southeastern corner, but not without first popping by the south entrance to admire a replica of the **Prince of the Lilies fresco**. Down below you can peek inside the **queen's megaron** (bedroom), with a copy of the *Dolphin* fresco, one of the most exquisite Minoan artworks. The small adjacent chamber (behind plexiglass) may have been the **queen's bathroom**, with some sort of toilet. Continue to the king's quarters in the **Hall of the Double Axes**; the latter takes its name from

Palace of Knossos

THE HIGHLIGHTS IN TWO HOURS

The Palace of Knossos is Crete's busiest tourist attraction, and for good reason. A spin around the partially and imaginatively reconstructed complex (shown here as it was thought to be at its peak) delivers an eye-opening glimpse into the remarkably sophisticated society of the Minoans, who dominated southern Europe some 4000 years ago.

From the ticket booth, follow the marked trail to the ❶ **North Entrance** where the Charging Bull fresco gives you a first taste of Minoan artistry. Continue to the Central Court and join the queue waiting to glimpse the mystical ❷ **Throne Room**, which probably hosted religious rituals. Turn right as you exit and follow the stairs up to the so-called Piano Nobile, where replicas of the palace's most famous artworks conveniently cluster in the ❸ **Fresco Room**. Walk the length of the Piano Nobile, pausing to look at the clay storage vessels in the West Magazine. Circle back and descend to the ❹ **South Portico**, beautifully decorated with the Cup Bearer fresco. Make your way back to the Central Court and head to the palace's eastern wing to admire the architecture of the ❺ **Grand Staircase** that led to what Sir Arthur Evans imagined to be the royal family's private quarters. For a closer look at some rooms, walk to the south end of the courtyard, stopping for a peek at the ❻ **Prince of the Lilies Fresco**, and head down to the lower floor. A highlight here is the ❼ **Queen's Megaron** (Evans imagined this was the Queen's chambers), playfully adorned with a fresco of frolicking dolphins. Stay on the lower level and make your way to the ❽ **Giant Pithoi**, huge clay jars used for storage.

PLANNING

To beat the crowds and avoid the heat, arrive bang on opening or two hours before closing. Budget one or two hours to explore the site thoroughly.

JOHN COPLAND/SHUTTERSTOCK ©

Fresco Room
Take in sweeping views of the palace grounds from the west wing's upper floor, the Piano Nobile, before studying copies of the palace's most famous artworks in its Fresco Room.

South Portico
Fine frescoes, most famously the Cup Bearer, embellish this palace entrance anchored by a massive open staircase leading to the Piano Nobile. The Horns of Consecration recreated nearby once topped the entire south facade.

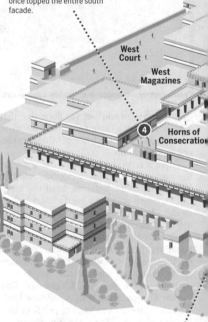

West Court

West Magazines

❹ Horns of Consecration

MICHAEL RUNKEL/GETTY IMAGES ©

Prince of the Lilies Fresco
One of Knossos' most beloved frescoes was controversially cobbled together from various fragments and shows a young man adorned in lilies and peacock feathers.

Throne Room
Sir Arthur Evans, who began excavating the Palace of Knossos in 1900, imagined the mythical King Minos himself holding court seated on the alabaster throne of this beautifully proportioned room. However, the lustral basin and griffin frescoes suggest a religious purpose, possibly under a priestess.

North Entrance
Bulls held a special status in Minoan society, as evidenced by the famous relief fresco of a charging beast gracing the columned west bastion of the north palace, which harboured workshops and storage rooms.

Grand Staircase
The royal apartments in the eastern wing were accessed via this monumental staircase sporting four flights of gypsum steps supported by columns. The lower two flights are original. It's closed to the public.

Piano Nobile

Central Court

Royal Apartments

❶ ❷ ❸ ❺ ❻ ❼ ❽

Giant Pithoi
These massive clay jars are rare remnants from the Old Palace period and were used to store wine, oil and grain. The jars were transported by slinging ropes through a series of handles.

Queen's Megaron
The queen's room is among the prettiest in the residential eastern wing thanks to the playful Dolphin Fresco. The adjacent bathroom (with clay tub) and toilet are evidence of a sophisticated drainage system.

the double axe marks *(labrys)* on its light well, a sacred symbol to the Minoans and the origin of the word 'labyrinth'.

Beyond, you can admire the Minoans' surprisingly sophisticated water and drainage system, pop by a stonemason's workshop and check out more giant storage jars before jogging around to the palace's north side for a good view of the partly reconstructed north entrance, easily recognised by the Charging Bull fresco. Walking towards the exit, you pass the theatral area, a series of shallow steps whose function remains unknown. It could have been a theatre where spectators watched acrobatic and dance performances, or the place where people gathered to welcome important visitors arriving by the Royal Road, which leads off to the west and was flanked by workshops and the houses of ordinary people.

Unlike at other ruins around Iraklio, visitors make their way through the site on platform walkways, which can get very crowded. This makes it all the more important to time your visit for outside the tour-bus onslaught. Avoid ticket lines by buying in advance through the Archaeological Resources Fund e-Ticketing System (www.etickets.tap.gr).

WORTH A TRIP

NIKOS KAZANTZAKIS MUSEUM

This **museum** (⚹ 28107 41689; www. kazantzaki.gr; Myrtia; adult/concessions €5/3; ⊙ 9am-5pm daily Apr-Oct, 10am-3pm Mon-Fri & Sun Nov-Mar) is housed in a modern building overlooking the *kafeneia*-flanked central plaza of author Nikos Kazantzakis' ancestral village, this well-curated museum zeroes in on the life, philosophy and accomplishments of Crete's most famous writer. Watch a short documentary, then use one of the wireless audio guides (€1) to add more meaning to the exhibits, which include movie posters, letters, photographs and various personal effects. Upstairs rooms present an overview of Kazantzakis' best-known works, including, of course, *Zorba the Greek*.

Don't miss the interesting 20-minute video (in 10 languages); ask staff to turn it on if it's not playing.

Myrtia is some 15km southeast of Iraklio.

Iraklio Wine Country

Winemaking in the Iraklio Wine Country dates back to Minoan times, some 4000 years ago, as evidenced by the oldest stomping vat in the world, found at the ruins of Vathypetro. Unfortunately, today's vineyards are a lot younger, as a mighty bout of phylloxera (plant louse) in the 1970s nearly wiped out everything. But Cretan wine rebounded and today about 70% of the wine produced on the island comes from this region. Almost two dozen wineries are embedded in a harmonious landscape of round-shouldered hills, sunbaked slopes and lush valleys. Winemakers cultivate many indigenous, nearly extinct Cretan grape varietals – be sure to introduce your nose and taste buds to Kotsifali, Mandilari, Malvasia and Liatiko, among others – while many estates offer tours, wine museums and wine tastings.

🏃 Activities

★ **Diamantakis Winery** WINE
(⚹ 6949198350; www.diamantakiswines.gr; Kato Asites; tastings €3-5; ⊙ by appointment 9am-4pm Mon-Fri) This winery's Petali Liatiko red has a great story: it was produced as a table wine, but then experts tasted it and said, 'Whoa! Bottle this right now!' Diamantakis is one of a mere handful who make a Liatiko today, and tasting it on the extraordinary property between olive trees (there's no tasting room), surrounded by vineyards, is a remarkable experience.

★ **Lyrarakis** WINE
(⚹ 6981050681; www.lyrarakis.gr; Alagni; tastings €10-60; ⊙ 11am-7pm Mon-Sat Apr-Oct, by appointment rest of year) One of Crete's most visitor-friendly wineries, Lyrarakis should be your go-to if you must pick only one. It rakes in awards and is known for reviving three nearly extinct white varietals (Dafni, Plyto and Melissaki). It was also the first to produce a single-vineyard Mandilari red (a move ridiculed as 'absurd' – but it went on to become one of its bestsellers).

Digenakis Winery WINE
(⚹ 28103 22846; www.digenakis.gr; Katakouzinon 7, Kaloni; tastings €7; ⊙ by appointment 10am-5pm) Opened in 2017, this modern winery marches to a different drum, both in its design and in its winemaking. The striking edifice features poured concrete and glass,

offset by colourful tapestry art. Its 2017 single-vineyard Kotsifali was produced from the fruit of 35-year-old vines – some of the few to escape the 1970s phylloxera outbreak that devastated Crete's vineyards.

Idaia Winery WINE
(📞 28107 92156; www.idaiawine.gr; Kiparissou 90, Venerato; tasting €5; ⊙ 11am-4pm Mon-Fri, to 2pm Sat) This tiny winery is hyper-focused on local varietals. Be on the lookout for its Ocean Thrapsathiri white (one of the best for pairing with seafood), its barrel-matured Liatiko and its sun-dried Liatiko dessert wine. The modern tasting room is small but one of the nicest.

☞ Tours

Made in Crete (📞 6975626830; www.tours.madeincrete.com; €100) is a Belgian-run agency leads the most highly recommended wine-tasting tours around Iraklio Wine Country. Tours take in two wineries as well as lunch at **Bakaliko** (www.bakalikocrete.com; Plateia Eleftheriou Venizelou, Arhanes; mains €7.50-9.50; ⊙ 10am-11pm Apr-Oct, 5-10pm Fri, 10am-10pm Sat & Sun Nov-Mar; 🐾) 🍴 in Arhanes. The price includes transport, tastings (olive oil in addition to wine) and lunch paired with four wines. Pierre, a former journalist and chef, leads tours in French or English.

ⓘ Information

Check Wines of Crete (www.winesofcrete.gr) for tourist info. Look for the burgundy-red road signs directing you to local wineries.

ⓘ Getting There & Away

The majority of wineries are within 20km of Iraklio, beginning just south of Knossos (the industry is headquartered in Peza). Besides an organised tour, having your own wheels is definitely a necessity to fully partake in a proper day of wine tasting: the wineries are spread out and not otherwise served directly by any public transport.

Zaros Ζαρός

POP 2120

At the foot of Mt Psiloritis, Zaros is famous for its natural spring water, which is bottled here and sold all over Crete. But Zaros also has some fine Byzantine monasteries, excellent walking and delicious farm-raised trout, served up in tavernas around town and on emerald-green Lake Votomos (actually a reservoir). The lake is also the kick-off point for the 5km trail through the mighty Rouvas Gorge, a major lure for hikers, birders and naturalists.

Part of the E4 European Path, the Rouvas Gorge hike leads to a protected swathe of forest, home to some of the oldest oak trees in Crete. It's an especially lovely walk in springtime, when hooded helleborine orchids, poppies, irises and other wildflowers give the landscape the vibrancy of an impressionist painting, but is recommended any time from April to November. It's a 10km up-and-back trek from the main trailhead at Lake Votomos north of Zaros village. The trail is mostly signed in Greek (and mostly referring to churches), but small red and white circles painted onto the rocks and trees lead the way.

🛏 Sleeping & Eating

Studios Keramos PENSION €
(📞 28940 31352; www.studiokeramos-zaros.gr; s/d/tr incl breakfast €35/50/65; ❄🐾) Close to the village centre, this friendly, old-style pension is decorated with Cretan crafts, weaving and family heirlooms. Many of the rooms and studios pair antique beds and furniture with TV and kitchenette (the more modern four-room annexe is fine but lacks character). Katerina is up early preparing an absolutely fantastic traditional breakfast.

★ Vegera CRETAN €
(all-you-can-eat buffet €12; ⊙ 11am-11pm Apr–mid-Nov; 🐾) The vivacious Vivi has a knack for turning farm-fresh local produce into flavourful and creative dishes based on traditional recipes. Her philosophy is to 'cook the way we cook in our house' and indeed her cute place quickly feels like home. Allow ample time to savour the generous buffet of salads, cheese and olives, cooked mains, pastries and freshly baked bread. With notice, you can also visit the family farm.

ⓘ Getting There & Away

Zaros is about 46km southwest of Iraklio. The most scenic approach is by turning west off the main road at Agia Varvara. There's also a smaller road heading north from Kapariana just east of Mires (turn north at the small road between a bakery and Kafeneio i Zariani Strofi; look for the little sign). One daily bus heading from Iraklio's KTEL Heraklion Lassithi Bus Station to Kamares passes through Zaros (€5.20, one hour, 1.30pm). Alternatively, take one of the more frequent buses to Mires (€6, 75 minutes) and cab it to Zaros from there (around €16).

BEYOND KNOSSOS: CRETE'S BEST ANCIENT SITES

Phaestos (http://odysseus.culture.gr; Iraklio-Phaestos Rd; adult/concession €8/4; ⊙8am-8pm May-Aug, shorter hours rest of year; Ⓟ) Phaestos was the second-most-important Minoan palace-city after Knossos (p292) and enjoys an awe-inspiring setting with panoramic views of the Messara Plain and Mt Psiloritis. It was built around 1700 BC atop an older, previously destroyed palace, and laid out around a central court. In contrast to Knossos, it had fewer frescoes, as its walls were likely covered with white gypsum. Phaestos was defeated by Gortyna (p298) in the 2nd century BC. Good English panelling and graphics stationed in key spots help demystify the ruins.

Palace of Malia (adult/concession/child €6/3/free; ⊙8am-8pm Tue-Sun May-Nov, to 3pm Tue-Sun Dec-Apr) The Palace of Malia, 3km east of Malia, was built at about the same time as the great Minoan palaces of Phaestos and Knossos. The First Palace dates back to around 1900 BC and was rebuilt after the earthquake of 1700 BC, only to be levelled again by another tremor around 1450 BC. Most of what you see today are the remains of the Second Palace, where many exquisite Minoan artefacts, including the famous **gold bee pendant**, were found.

Gortyna (Γόρτυνα; Iraklio-Phaestos Rd; adult/concession €6/3; ⊙8am-8pm Apr-Oct, to 4pm Nov-Mar) Gortyna (also Gortyn or Gortys) has been inhabited since Neolithic times but reached its pinnacle after becoming the capital of Roman Crete from around 67 BC until the Saracens raided the island in AD 824. At its peak, as many as 100,000 people may have milled around Gortyna's streets.

There are two sections, bisected by the highway. Most people only stop long enough to investigate the fenced area on the north side of the road past the entrance. However, several more important temples, baths and other buildings are scattered south of the road.

Agia Triada (adult/concession €4/2; ⊙8.30am-4pm; Ⓟ) In an enchanting spot 3km west of Phaestos, Agia Triada encompasses vestiges of an L-shaped royal villa, a ramp once leading out to sea, and a village with residences and stores. Built around 1550 BC, Agia Triada succumbed to fire around 1400 BC but was never looted. This accounts for the many Minoan masterpieces found here, most famously the Agia Triada Sarcophagus, now a star exhibit at the Heraklion Archaeological Museum (p285).

Matala Μάταλα

POP 70

In mythology, Matala is the place where Zeus swam ashore with the kidnapped Europa on his back before dragging her off to Gortyna and getting her pregnant with the future King Minos. The Minoans used Matala as their harbour for Phaestos and under the Romans it became the port for Gortyna.

More recently, Matala became legendary thanks to the scores of hippies flocking here in the late 1960s to take up rent-free residence in cliffside caves once used as tombs by the Romans. Joni Mitchell immortalised the era in her 1971 song 'Carey'.

On summer days the village feels anything but peaceful, thanks to coachloads of day trippers. Stay overnight or visit in the low season, though, and it's still possible to discern the Matala magic: the setting along a crescent-shaped bay flanked by headlands is simply spectacular, especially at sunset.

◉ Sights

Matala's sightseeing credentials are limited to the famous **Matala Caves** (Roman Cemetery; €2; ⊙10am-7pm Mar-Oct, 8am-3pm Nov-Apr) caves where hippies camped out in the 1960s and 1970s. Hewn into the porous sandstone cliffs in prehistoric times, they were actually used as tombs by the Romans.

🛏 Sleeping & Eating

Hotel Fantastic Matala HOTEL € (☑ 28920 45262; www.fantastic-matala.com; s/d/tr €45/50/60; Ⓟ❖🛜) Quirky host Natasa (and father) woos guests with her mystical Matala magic at this budget-friendly hotel, be it via motherly doting, morning *tiropites* (cheese pies) or Greek coffee. Whatever the method, you'll feel like one of the family. Rooms, across two traditional, partly stone buildings, are smallish, with frustrating showers (those pesky curtains!), but the hospitality trumps the grumps.

Hotel Nikos HOTEL €€
(www.matala-nikos.com; s/d/q €55/65/110;
P ❄ 🛜) A standout on hotel row, family-run
Nikos has 17 modernised rooms, many with
small kitchens, a terrace and snazzy bathrooms, on two floors flanking a flower-filled
courtyard. The nicest is the top-floor room
24, with cave views. Breakfast is €7.50.

★ **George's Yard** GREEK €€
(📞 69488 78600; mains €7.50-24.50; ⏱ 5-11.30pm
May-Oct; 🛜) George (Giorgos) was the lone
local who dug in with the invading hippies
in the 1970s, coining Matala's motto: 'Today
is life. Tomorrow never comes.' His home is
now occupied by a Greek-German couple,
who along with their Athenian chef are aces
of hospitality at Matala's best restaurant.
Service and culinary creativity are next level.

★ **Scala Fish Tavern** SEAFOOD €€
(📞 69813 88135; mains €7-19; ⏱ 10am-11pm Apr-
Oct; 🛜) Past all the bars at the easternmost
end of the beach, this dramatically perched,
multitiered pit stop is Matala's best seafood
restaurant. It's been in the family for over
30 years, so it's doing something right. Top
marks for its fresh fish, superior service and
fabulous desserts – try the *tzizkeik* (cheese-
cake). The cave views are especially nice at
sunset. Reservations recommended.

❶ Getting There & Away

Two KTEL buses daily leave Iraklio's KTEL Heraklion Lassithi Bus Station for Matala (€8.50, two
hours, 7.30am and 12.45pm). Buses to Iraklio
from Matala leave from a **stop** 800m east of the
main village. There's free roadside parking and a
beach car park that charges €2.

Hersonisos Χερσόνησος

POP 26,700

Hersonisos, about 25km east of Iraklio, has
grown from a small fishing village into one
of Crete's largest and busiest tourist towns.
The main thoroughfare is lined with sprawling hotels, apartment buildings and loud
bars, cafes, tourist shops, clubs, fast-food
eateries, travel agencies and quad-hire places. Its best stretch of sand is the quaint Sa-
randaris Beach.

To escape the bustle, base yourself uphill
in one of three adjoining villages: Koutouloufari, Piskopiano or Old Hersonisos.
Although touristy, these are nonetheless
appealing and have some excellent tavernas
and accommodation options.

OFF THE BEATEN TRACK

KAPETANIANA

In the heart of the Asteroussia mountain
range that runs along the entire
southern coast of Iraklio, and clinging
to the slopes of the highest peak,
Kapetaniana is a remote hamlet that's
a mecca for rock climbers and hikers.
The last 8km of road corkscrews up
into the mountains, making it one of
the most exciting drives in Crete. One
of the best places to stay around here
is **Thalori Retreat** (📞 28930 41762;
www.thalori.com; Kapetaniana; studios/apt
from €70/85; ❄ 🛜 ☒), a cluster of 22
renovated stone cottages.

◉ Sights & Activities

★ **Lychnostatis
Open Air Museum** MUSEUM
(www.lychnostatis.gr; adult/child €6/2; ⏱ 9am-
2pm Sun-Fri Apr-Oct) In a lovely seaside setting
at Hersonisos' eastern edge, this open-air
folklore museum recreates a traditional Cretan village with commendable authenticity.
The various buildings, including windmill,
schoolhouse and farmer's home, were rescued around Crete and moved here. Elsewhere there are weaving workshops, ceramics and plant-dying demonstrations, olive-oil
pressing and raki distilling, orchards and
herb gardens, and a theatre that hosts music
and dance performances. Guided tours and
audio guides (€2) are available, as is a cafe.

🛏 Sleeping & Eating

Skip the identikit tourist tavernas in Hersonisos proper and opt for a more authentic
culinary experience uphill in Koutouloufari
and Piskopiano. A table full of traditional
mezedhes is what's for dinner.

Balsamico Suites APARTMENT €€
(📞 28970 23323; www.balsamico-suites.gr; Old
Hersonisos; ste incl breakfast from €89; P ❄ 🛜 ☒)
This stone complex fuses old-world charm
with smart TVs and hairdryers. Seventeen
well-proportioned suites are decked out in
rich, dark wood and come with balconies.
Two newer rooms have outdoor whirlpool
baths but lack privacy, and you'll forgo much
of the traditional stonework and character.

★**Villa Ippocampi**   APARTMENT €€€
([☎]28970 22316; www.ippocampi.com; 4g Seferi,
Koutouloufari; apt €150-190; [P][❄][📶][🏊]) This
relaxing Dutch-Greek retreat exudes style
and will mesmerise you from the moment
you step past its lavender bushes and pool.
Once you're ensconced in your apartment
(all are decorated in a strong blue-and-white
theme), it'll be hard to go past two choices
– laze by the pool or chat to the charming
owners, Lydia and Nikos.

★**David Vegera**   CRETAN €
(Piskopiano; mezedhes €4.50-10; ⊙5pm-midnight
Mon-Sat; [📶]) A fabulous spot housed in a former *kafeneio* (coffee house), this place has a
buzzy vibe due to the scores of Greeks and
tourists who descend on it from opening
time. David Vegera started this gig in 1954,
and his great-grandson helps run the show
today. It serves old-time mezedhes, efficiently and without fuss.

❶ Getting There & Away

Buses from KTEL Heraklion Lassithi Bus
Station (p292) run at least every 30 minutes
to Hersonisos (€3.30, 40 minutes). Heading
back, catch buses at **stop 19 (west)** by (Palio
EO Iraklio-Agios Nikolaos) heading west along
the main road. Buses heading east to Malia and
Agios Nikolas stop at **stop 19 (east)**, which is
(Palio EO Iraklio-Agios Nikolaos) on the opposite side of the road.

There's a **taxi stand** on Sanoudaki just off
the main drag. Parking uphill in Old Hersonisos, Koutouloufari and Piskopiano is mayhem,
but there's a free **car park** just behind the main
thoroughfare in Hersonisos proper.

RETHYMNO PROVINCE

Wild beauty Rethymno is peppered with
historic sites and natural wonders. Ribbons
of mountain road wind through the timeless interior, passing fields of wildflowers
and traditional hamlets cradled by olive
groves. Descend into the spooky darkness of
grotto-like caves; explore steep, lush gorges; and rest in the shade of lofty Mt Psiloritis, Crete's highest peak. Visit enduring
monasteries, Minoan tombs and Venetian
strongholds. Rethymno is also a magnet for
artists, many practising age-old trades with
modern twists.

The eponymous capital on the northern
coast is a bustle of atmosphere-soaked cobbled lanes, laden with shops, restaurants
and bars and flanked by a wide, sandy
beach. The southern coast is graced with
bewitching beaches in seductive isolation.
Weave your way through this spellbinding
land from shore to shore.

Rethymno   Ρέθυμνο
POP 35,000
Basking between the commanding bastions
of its 15th-century fortress and the glittering azure waters of the Mediterranean,
Rethymno is one of Crete's most enchanting settlements. Its Venetian-Ottoman
quarter is a lyrical maze of lanes draped in
floral canopies and punctuated with graceful wood-balconied houses, ornate monuments and the occasional minaret.

Crete's third-largest centre has lively
nightlife thanks to its sizable student population, some excellent restaurants and
a worthwhile sandy beach right in town.
The busier beaches, with their requisite resorts, line up along a nearly uninterrupted
stretch all the way to Panormo, some 22km
away.

◉ Sights

★**Fortezza**   FORTRESS
(Map p302; adult/concession/family €4/3/10;
⊙8am-8pm Apr-Oct, 10am-5pm Nov-Mar; [P])
Looming over Rethymno, the star-shaped
Venetian fortress cuts an imposing figure
with its massive walls and bastions but was
nevertheless unable to stave off the Turks
in 1646. Over time, an entire village took
shape on the grounds, most of which was
destroyed in WWII. Views over the town,
the Mediterranean and mountains are fabulous up here and it's fun to poke around the
ramparts, palm trees and remaining buildings, most notably the **Sultan Bin Ibrahim
Mosque** with its huge dome.

Head inside the mosque to admire its
impressive mosaic ceiling, with wonderful
acoustics that are perfect for the occasional
musical event held here. A few other buildings (like the twin buildings of the Bastion of
Agios Nikolaos) are also used to showcase art
exhibits. Pick up a free map from the ticket
office, which offers useful info on the site.

Last entry is 45 minutes before closing.

★ **Archaeological
Museum of Rethymno**   MUSEUM
(Map p302; ☑ 28310 27506; www.archmuseum
reth.gr; Argiropoulon; adult/concession €2/1;
☺ 10am-6pm Wed-Mon) Set inside the atmospheric Venetian-built Church of St Fran-
cis, this well-curated museum features a
stunning collection of well-preserved relics
unearthed from major archaeological digs
around Rethymno Province. Its collection
offers a comprehensive snapshot (without
leaving you overwhelmed) that predominantly covers pieces from the Minoan,
Byzantine and Venetian periods. Highlights
include exquisite hand-painted Minoan ceramics, a 9000-year-old limestone deity statue and a bronze lamp from the Hellenistic
period (1st century BC) depicting Dionysus
riding a panther.

Venetian Harbour   LANDMARK
(Map p302) Rethymno's compact histor-
ic harbour is chock-a-block with tourist-
geared fish tavernas and cafes. For a more
atmospheric perspective, walk along the
harbour walls, past the fishing boats to the
prominent **lighthouse** (Map p302), built in
the 19th century by the Egyptians.

Agios Spyridon Church   CHAPEL
(Kefalogiannidon) FREE Built right into the
cliff beneath the Venetian fortress, tiny Agios Spyridon has enough atmosphere to fill
a cathedral. This Byzantine chapel is filled
with richly painted icons, swinging bird
candleholders and the sound of the nearby
pounding surf. You'll see pairs of slippers,
baby shoes and sandals in crevices in the
rock wall, left as offerings for the sick. Find
the chapel at the top of a staircase on the
fortress' western side. Opening hours are
erratic.

Museum of Contemporary Art   MUSEUM
(Map p302; ☑ 28310 52530; www.cca.gr; Mesologhiou 32; adult/concession/student €3/1.50/
free, Thu free; ☺ 9am-2pm & 7-9pm Tue-Fri, 10am-
3pm Sat & Sun May-Oct, reduced hours Nov-Apr)
The cornerstone of the permanent collection
of this well-curated modern-art museum,
founded in 1992, is the oils, drawings and
watercolours of local lad Lefteris Kanakakis,
but over time it has amassed enough works
to present the arc of creative endeavour in
Greece since the 1950s. Temporary exhibits
keep things dynamic. The entrance is off
Mesologhiou.

Rimondi Fountain   FOUNTAIN
(Map p302) Another vestige of Venetian rule
is this small fountain where water spouts
from three lions' heads into three basins
flanked by Corinthian columns. Above the
central basin you can make out the Rimondi
family crest. It was built in 1626 by city rec-
tor Alvise Rimondi. Located off Paleologou.

🏃 Activities

Paradise Dive Center   DIVING
(☑ 28310 26317; www.diving-center.gr; Petres
Geraniou; 2 dives incl equipment from €100,
open-water certification €400) Runs diving
trips for all grades from its base at Petres,
14km west of Rethymno. Its most popular
dive is to the underwater Elephant Cave,
where fossilised remains of elephants were
discovered in 1999. Paradise also offers night
dives and PADI courses for beginners. Book
through travel agencies, phone or website.

★ **Happy Walker**   HIKING
(Map p302; ☑ 28310 52920; www.happywalker.
com; Iombazi 56; guided day walks €32; ☺ 10am-
2pm Apr-Oct) In operation for over a quarter
of a century, this congenial Dutch-run outfit
takes up to 16 global ramblers on day hikes
to gorges, ancient shepherd trails and traditional villages. It's ideal for solo travellers.
Rates include transport to and from trailheads and an English-speaking guide, but
coffee and a vegetarian lunch with wine are
an extra €12.

Eco Events   TOURS
(Map p302; ☑ 6946686857, 28310 50055; www.
ecoevents.gr; Eleftheriou Venizelou 39; tours €18-
70; ☺ 10am-9pm) This outfit specialises in
small-group English-language tours that get
you in touch with land, people and culture.
Options include the Eco Tour, on which
you'll meet a baker, a weaver and a wood-
carver before sampling charcoal-grilled
lamb in a traditional shepherd's shelter in
the mountains. Cooking classes, wine and
olive-oil tastings, and hiking trips are also
part of the lineup.

🛏 Sleeping

★ **Rethymno Youth Hostel**   HOSTEL €
(Map p302; ☑ 28310 22848; www.yhrethymno.
com; Tombazi 41; dm €12-14; ☺ reception 8am-
1pm & 5-11pm Sep-May, 8am-midnight Jun-Aug; 🛜)
Centrally located in a quiet street, this cheerful and professionally run hostel sleeps six
to 12 people in clean, well-presented dorms
(one is for women only). Dorms have comfy

Rethymno

CRETE RETHYMNO

Rethymno

mattresses, personalised power points and good-size lockers, and it's a nice place to relax, with a sociable patio, a bar and a flowering garden. Offers excellent travel info for Crete and beyond.

Facilities include a communal kitchen, free snorkelling and beach gear, a book exchange and Chromecast TV. Cheap drinks keep things social, and breakfast is available for €3.

★**Atelier Frosso Bora**　　　　　　PENSION **€**
(Map p302; ☎ 28310 24440; www.frosso-bora.com; Chimaras 25; d €35-60; ☺ Mar-Nov; ✹ ☎) Run by local artist Frosso Bora and located above her pottery studio, these four spotless, ambience-laden rooms with exposed stone walls, small flat-screen TVs, modern bathrooms and kitchenettes are a superb budget pick. Two units have small balconies facing the old town, while the other two sport Venetian architectural features and a beamed ceiling.

Casa Moazzo　　　　　　BOUTIQUE HOTEL **€€**
(Map p302; ☎ 28310 36235; www.casamoazzo.gr; 57 Tombazi; r incl breakfast €85-180; ✹ ☎) Occupying the former home of Venetian nobles, these 10 newly renovated rooms are elegant and bright. Just a stone's throw from the harbour, they're nonetheless very private. Each room is unique, combining wallpaper, exposed stone and wooden beams for a classy Italian feel. Some have balconies, claw-foot tubs and kitchenettes, and all have king-size beds and an option for goose-down pillows.

Sohora　　　　　　BOUTIQUE HOTEL **€€**
(Map p302; ☎ 28313 00913; www.sohora.net; Plateia Iroön Politechniou 11; studios €50-70, d €60-75, apt €100; ✹ ☎) Extremely comfortable and slightly quirky, the rooms with kitchenette in this 200-year-old home are named after the seasons and incorporate original architectural features alongside upcycled vintage furnishings. A solar water heater, organic bath products and a hearty, homemade breakfast (€6) provide eco-cred. Service is both friendly and professional.

Palazzino di Corina　　　　BOUTIQUE HOTEL **€€**
(Map p302; ☎ 28310 21205; www.corina.gr; Damvergi 9; d €70-170; ✹ ☎ ✹) This regal Venetian mansion is an elegant place to unpack. Fine furniture, exposed stone walls and timber vaulted ceilings create a plush period ambience. You'll also find a good dose of mod cons, including Jacuzzi tubs. In the courtyard, a small, deep pool begs you to dive in, while the lounge is overflowing with antiques – from gramophones to sewing machines. Its attached restaurant is a similarly stylish affair.

★**Hamam**
Oriental Suites　　　　　　BOUTIQUE HOTEL **€€€**
(Map p302; ☎ 28310 50378, 6981649377; www.hamamsuites.com; Nikiforou Foka 86; r incl breakfast €135-230) In a quiet alleyway in the old quarter is this former Venetian-Ottoman bathhouse that, after several reincarnations, has undergone an elegant refit to open as a boutique hotel. Each of its five atmospheric rooms is unique – some feature striking mosaics, domed ceilings, original stone walls and steam rooms or Jacuzzis – but all are lavishly decorated with period furnishings and antiques.

✗ Eating

★**Raki Baraki**　　　　　　CRETAN **€**
(Map p302; ☎ 28310 58250; www.facebook.com/1600rakibaraki; Arampatzoglou 17; mezedhes €3.50-13; ☺ 12.30pm-midnight; ✹ ☎ ✹) Rustic, colourful and lively, this is a fantastic place to while away the evening over mezedhes (appetisers) like flavoursome grilled mushrooms with mountain herbs, warm homemade dolmadhes with yoghurt, or mussels steamed with sage. The fried filo-coated feta with marmalade is divine, as is the sheep's-milk ice cream. Comfort food at its finest.

All ingredients are sourced from small farms around Greece.

koo koo　　　　　　CAFE **€**
(Map p302; ☎ 28310 26380; Plateia Martyron; dishes €4-6; ☺ 7am-11pm; ✹ ✹ ✹) The place to head to if you need respite from traditional Greek food, this contemporary cafe does a menu of all-day brunch fare. Expect the likes of smashed avocado on toast, crispy chicken waffles, pizza by the slice and a heap of tasty burgers. There's a welcome choice of healthy and vegetarian options, too, along with top-notch coffees, smoothies and teas.

Mojo Burgers　　　　　　AMERICAN **€**
(Map p302; ☎ 28310 50550, 6987328252; www.facebook.com/mojoburgers; Damvergi 38; meals €2.40-11; ☺ noon-midnight daily Apr-Oct, Tue-Sun Nov-Mar) With a divey graffitied interior and a large menu, Mojo's delivers some of the best burgers and hot dogs this side of the Atlantic. Try the Alabama Mama, with crispy pork, coleslaw and pickles, or a classic flame-grilled cheeseburger. Slap on some tasty extras like jalapeños or caramelised

onions for good measure. Good selection of local beers, too, and it delivers.

Gaias Gefseis
BAKERY €

(Map p302; ☑ 28311 00428; Ethnikis Antistaseos 15; pastries €0.50-2.50; ⊗ 7am-10pm) For *loukoumadhes* (doughnut-like concoctions drizzled with honey and cinnamon), follow your nose to Gaias Gefseis. This bakery creates some of the city's best traditional cakes and biscuits, as well as homemade sheep's-milk gelato. If your sweet tooth needs a break, there's a mammoth supply of savoury breads; try one stuffed with feta and olives.

Veneto
CRETAN €€

(Map p302; ☑ 28310 56634; www.veneto.gr; Epimenidou 4; mains €15-20; ⊗ 6-11pm May-Oct; 🛜) In a 14th-century manor house that doubles as a **boutique hotel** (s €70-95, d €95-130, ste €114-148), Veneto oozes historic charm from every nook and cranny. The kitchen adds a contemporary streak to traditional Cretan recipes, with results like fish with fennel and lime or meatballs with basil sauce. The owner is a wine buff and will happily help you pick a bottle to complement your meal.

The impressive cellar is housed in what was once the monks' quarters.

Avli
CRETAN €€

(Map p302; ☑ 28310 58250; www.avli.gr; Xanthoudidou 22; mains €12-20; ⊗ 12.30-11pm; ✳🛜) This well-established Venetian villa serves creative Cretan food with a side of romance. Farm-fresh fare steers the menu, resulting in dishes with bold flavour pairings such as *creatotouria* (ravioli filled with lamb, cheese,

---

MEET RETHYMNO'S LAST FILO MASTER

Established in 1948, **Yiorgos Hatziparaskos** (Map p302; ☑ 28310 29488; Vernardou 30; pastries €2-4; ⊗ 8am-9.30pm) is one of the last traditional filo masters in all of Greece. Assisted by his wife, Katerina, and son, Paraskevas, today he still makes superfine pastry by hand in his workshop. Watch the spectacle and try some of the best baklava and *kataïfi* ('angel hair' pastry) you will ever eat.

The highlight is when they whirl the dough into a giant bubble before stretching it over a huge table.

---

mint and lime) or *fouriariko* (slow-cooked organic goat with honey and thyme). Be sure to reserve a table in the bewitching garden courtyard filled with flowers and palms.

 Drinking & Nightlife

Rethymno's young and restless are mostly drawn to the cafe-bars along Eleftheriou Venizelou. The area around the Rimondi Fountain and Plateia Petihaki is popular with tourists. Wander the side streets to find quieter places.

★ Monitor
BAR

(Map p302; ☑ 6974130764; www.facebook.com/monitorartcafe; Vernardou 21-23; ⊗ 10am-late) A gathering spot for Rethymno's slightly older indie crowd, this relaxed, unpretentious bar is decked out in arthouse-film posters and modern-art installations. Its atmospheric old-town setting makes it a wonderful spot for a relaxed coffee, beer or old-fashioned cocktail and a good burger. Check the Facebook page for upcoming bands, DJs and events.

Bricks Beerhouse
CRAFT BEER

(Map p302; ☑ 6945297481; www.bricksbeerhouse.gr; Eleftheriou Venizelou 41; ⊗ 10am-1am mid-Apr–Oct, from 6pm Nov–mid-Apr) While Cretans are still developing a thirst for craft beer, Bricks is doing its best to convert them with its selection of 30 ales produced by Greek microbreweries, including a few local ones. You can also try a gin distilled in Irakalio that uses Cretan botanicals.

Chaplin's
BAR

(Map p302; ☑ 28310 24566; Eleftheriou Venizelou 52; ⊗ 9am-4am) Rethymno's most raucous drinking spot is this smoke-filled rock bar that's been banging out tunes since the 1970s. It attracts a boozy crowd of black-clad students and older rockers propped at the bar sinking shots between beers. While the music is mainstream rock, the DJs (from 8pm) are pretty good with requests.

Brew Your Mind
COFFEE

(Map p302; ☑ 28313 01940; www.facebook.com/brewyourmind1; Arkadiou 251; ⊗ 8am-10pm; 🛜) Wake up and smell the coffee at this hip microroaster that offers a pleasing array of speciality beans. Whether you're into V60, Aeropress, Chemex, syphon, cold brew, flat whites or your traditional Greek double, the baristas here have the full arsenal at their disposal to nail your next caffeine hit.

ℹ Information

You'll find a **tourist information office** (Map p302; www.rethymno.guide; Rethymno Old Port; ⊙9am-2.30pm Mon-Fri) at the Venetian Harbour, and a smaller **kiosk** (Map p302; www. rethymno.guide; Plateia Martyron; ⊙ 9am-2.30pm Mon-Fri) just south of Porta Guora. Both offer local maps and regional information and their website is also useful.

General Hospital of Rethymno (⌨ 28313 42100; www.rethymnohospital.gr; Triandalydou 17; ⊙24hr) Has 24-hour accident and emergency care.

Tourist Police (⌨ 28310 28156, emergency 171; Sofokli Venizelou 37; ⊙on call 24hr) At Rethymno's marina, next to the beach.

ℹ Getting There & Away

KTEL Bus Station (⌨ 28310 22785, 28310 22212; Kefalogiannidon; ☎) The bus station is at the western edge of the centre. Services are reduced at weekends and outside high season.

Seajets (⌨ 21041 21001; www.seajets.gr) Ferries from Rethymno's marina depart on Tuesday and Saturday at 8am for Santorini (€69, 2¼ hours), Ios (€70, 3½ hours), Naxos (€78, four hours) and Mykonos (€74, five hours). A car is an additional €60 to €65.

West of Rethymno

Argyroupoli

POP 450

Located 25km southwest of Rethymno, Argyroupoli is built on the ruins of the ancient city of Lappa, one of the most important Roman cities in western Crete, though very few remnants of it survive. Argyroupoli's network of atmospheric cobblestone alleyways lined with Venetian-era stone houses and Byzantine churches makes it a lovely place to stroll. As it's in the foothills of the Lefka Ori (White Mountains), the town is a useful gateway to some fine hiking trails.

At the bottom of the town is a watery oasis formed by springs from the Lefka Ori that keep the temperature markedly cooler here than on the coast, making it a good place to escape the summer heat. Running through aqueducts, washing down walls, seeping from stones and pouring from spigots, the gushing springs supply water for the entire city of Rethymno.

◉ Sights

Necropolis, Ancient Lappa's cemetery, lies north of the town and is reached via a signed 1.5km footpath from the main square. Hundreds of tombs have been cut into the rock cliffs here, especially around the Chapel of the Five Virgins. The path leads on to a plane tree that is said to be 2000 years old.

✖ Eating

Garden Arkoudenas (O Kipos Tis Arkoudenas; ⌨ 28310 61607; Episkopi; mains €10-18; ⊙1pm-late) is one of the most enjoyable places to experience traditional Cretan cuisine and hospitality is this vibrant taverna set among fruit trees and adjoining farmland. Gregarious host Georgios (who appears in Yotam Ottolenghi's *Mediterranean Feast* documentary) will take you through the day's specials, cooked by his mother using superb organic produce sourced from their farm and the mountains.

ℹ Getting There & Away

From Monday to Friday three daily buses ply the route from Rethymno to Argyroupoli. Before you head out, be sure to check that there is in fact a return bus to Rethymno (€3.60, 40 minutes); generally, the last bus back goes at 3.30pm.

Agreco Farm

Agreco Farm (⌨ 28310 72129; www.agreco. gr; Adelianos Kampos; tour & lunch or dinner from €38; ⊙11am-10pm May-Oct) is embedded in rolling hills near the village of Adele, about 13km southeast of Rethymno. Agreco Farm is a replica of a 17th-century estate and a showcase of centuries-old, organic and ecofriendly farming methods. It uses mostly traditional machinery, including a donkey-driven olive press, a watermill and a wine press. Call ahead to ensure it's open.

You'll also find small shops selling local produce and artwork, plus a mini-zoo featuring *kri-kri* (Cretan goats), wild boar and bantam chickens.

The farm is usually open from May to October, but private events, such as weddings or baptisms, often keep it closed to the public. Normally, farm tours culminate in a 30-course Cretan feast in the taverna. Most of the dishes are prepared with produce, dairy and meat grown on the farm.

If you're more the hands-on type, enquire in advance for upcoming **farm days**, when visitors are invited to participate in traditional agricultural activities. Depending on the time of year, you could find yourself shearing a sheep, milking a goat, making cheese, pressing grapes with your feet or baking bread using hand-picked, freshly stoneground flour; see the website for the schedule. This is followed by a buffet-style Harvest Festival Lunch. Reservations are essential for the farm tour and the Sunday experience.

If you're just stopping by during the day, you can do an independent **tour** (€5) and enjoy a drink in the *kafeneio* (coffeehouse).

East of Rethymno

Moni Arkadiou

Moni Arkadiou (Arkadi Monastery; ☑ 28310 83136; Arkadi; €3; ☉ 9am-8pm Jun-Sep, to 7pm Apr, May & Oct, to 5pm Nov, to 4pm Dec-Mar), a 16th-century Arkadi Monastery, 23km southeast of Rethymno, has deep significance for Cretans. As the site where hundreds of cornered locals massacred both themselves and invading Turks, it's a stark and potent symbol of resistance and considered a catalyst in the island's struggle towards freedom from Turkish occupation.

Arkadiou's impressive Venetian church (1587) has a striking Renaissance facade topped by an ornate triple-belled tower. The grounds include a small museum and the old wine cellar where the gunpowder was stored.

In November 1866, massive Ottoman forces arrived to crush island-wide revolts. Hundreds of Cretan men, women and children fled their villages to find shelter at Arkadiou. However, far from being a safe haven, the monastery was soon besieged by 2000 Turkish soldiers. Rather than surrender, the entrapped locals blew up stored gunpowder kegs, killing everyone, Turks included. One small girl miraculously survived and lived to a ripe old age in a village nearby. A bust of this woman and another of the abbot who lit the gunpowder are outside the monastery not far from the old windmill – now an **ossuary** with skulls and bones of the 1866 victims neatly arranged in a glass cabinet.

Four to five buses arrive here each weekday (two to three at weekends) from Rethymno (€3.10, 40 minutes), leaving you about 90 minutes for your visit before returning.

Ancient Eleutherna

The archaeological site of **Ancient Eleutherna** (☑ 28340 92501; http://en.mae.com.gr/archaeological-site; Eleutherna; necropolis adult/senior/student €4/2/free, with museum €6/3/free, acropolis free; ☉ necropolis 10am-6pm May-Oct, acropolis 24hr year-round) is a Dorian-built settlement that was among the most important in the 8th and 7th centuries BC, and also experienced heydays in Hellenistic and Roman times. Excavations have been ongoing since 1985 and archaeologists continue to make new finds all the time; many are showcased at the impressive museum nearby. The 2010 discovery of the gold-adorned remains of a woman in a 2700-year-old double tomb made international news.

The **museum** (http://en.mae.com.gr/museum.html; Milopotamos; adult/senior/student €4/2/free, combined necropolis ticket €6/3/free, Sun free; ☉ 10am-6pm Wed-Mon) is a must-see for anyone visiting the ruins of Eleutherna is the accompanying modern museum that contextualises the ancient city through the exhibition of treasures unearthed at the site over the past 30 years. Located 3km from the ruins, and set over three rooms, the beautifully curated collection covers artefacts ranging from the early Iron Age and Minoan periods to Hellenic, Roman and Byzantine eras.

Its showpiece is the bronze shield with a protruding lion's head, unearthed from the Tomb of the Warriors and dating to the 8th century BC; it sits alongside a polished, gleaming replica of how it would have originally looked. Other artefacts excavated from the necropolis include beautiful ceramic vases and ornaments, detailed gold pendants and marble statuettes, all with exquisite artisanship and much that has retained its colour.

Margarites   Μαργαρίτες

Tiny Margarites, 26km southeast of Rethymno, is famous for its pottery, a tradition that can be traced back to Minoan times. The village has only one road, and no bank or post office, but it has more than 20 ceramics stores and studios. Most studios source their clay by hand (the area is known for its clay), and offer unique, bright and good-quality usable pieces. This is the perfect place to pick up a keepsake.

If possible, try to avoid mornings and lunchtime, when droves of tour buses flood the town. By afternoon all is calm, and you can explore the atmospheric alleyways, wander through the studios and enjoy wonderful valley views from the eucalyptus-lined taverna terraces on the main square.

Melidoni Cave

About 2km outside the village of Melidoni is the stunning cathedral-like **Melidoni Cave** (Gerontospilios; www.melidoni.gr; adult/child under 12yr €4/free; ☉ 9am-8pm May-Sep, to 7pm Apr, Oct & Nov), an evocative underworld of stalactites and stalagmites. A place of worship since Neolithic times, it also carries heavy historical significance as the site of a massacre in 1824 during the Turkish occupation. Here 370 villagers and 30 soldiers sought refuge from the Ottoman army; after a three-month siege, the Turks lit a fire and asphyxiated the people inside, including 340 women and children.

Wear decent walking shoes, as the cave is poorly lit and the ground uneven and slippery in places. You'll need to descend 70 steps into the cave. Also bring a sweater: at 24m below ground, the temperature never gets above 18°C.

If you're out this way to the cave, tack on a visit to the nearby **Paraschakis Olive Oil Factory** (☑ 28340 22039, 6973863551; www.paraschakis.gr; Melidoni Geropotamou; ☉ 9am-6pm Mon-Sat Apr-Nov) **FREE** for a lowdown on the production process. Its welcoming American-Greek owner, Joanna, will guide you through the evolution of olive-oil pressing, from donkey-driven methods to the current-day machinery. The factory is part of a local co-op used by farmers to convert their yearly harvest into liquid gold.

Panormo   Πάνορμο

POP 880

Panormo, about 22km east of Rethymno, is one of the few relatively unspoilt beach towns on the northern coast. Despite a couple of big hotel complexes, it retains an unhurried, authentic village feel and makes for a quieter alternative to the overcrowded scene immediately east of Rethymno and at nearby Bali. In summer, concerts and other events are held in a carob mill turned cultural centre.

☉ Sights

Klados Winery   WINERY
(☑ 28340 51589, 6973654840; www.kladoswinery.gr; tasting 5/7 wines €3/4; ☉ 10am-6pm Mon-Fri, to 3pm Sat Apr-Oct, other times by appointment) While Iraklio gets all the plaudits as Crete's main wine producer, Rethymno has the honour of being the first place in Greece to be named a 'European City of Wine', in 2018. It's fitting recognition for this hard-working family, who've run their winery since 1997 and are known primarily for Vidiano, a dry white produced from a grape grown only in the immediate area.

Castel Milopotamo   VIEWPOINT
For wonderful views overlooking Panormo's port, head up the hill to a *tiny* segment of stone wall that remains from a 13th-century fortress. It's believed to have been built by the Genoese during their fleeting rule in 1206 before the Venetians took over.

Panormo Beach   BEACH
There's no one main beach in Panormo but a series of small, attractive coves with brown sand and a brilliant turquoise sea. The tiny swoop of sand at the harbour with its calm waters is perfect for families.

🛏 Sleeping & Eating

The touristy harbour tavernas serve standard Greek and international dishes as well as fresh fish. More traditional places can be found a block or two inland. If you have a car, try to make it out to Dalabelos Estate for lunch, a wonderful culinary experience.

Captain's House   GUESTHOUSE €
(☑ 28103 80833; www.captainshouse.gr; apt €40-60; ☉ Apr-Oct; ❄ 🛜) In a prime waterfront location, the Captain's modern and spacious split-level apartments are an excellent choice – all are different, but each is spacious and comfortable, and catches the sea breeze. They're equipped with satellite TV, fast wi-fi and kitchenette, and some feature sea views. Staff members are friendly, and a welcoming gift of fruit and wine is a lovely touch.

★ Idili   GUESTHOUSE €€
(☑ 6970994408, 28340 20240; www.idili.gr; apt €65-95; ❄ 🛜) If cookie-cutter rooms don't do it for you, you'll love the three traditionally furnished apartments in this protected stone house, which has seen incarnations as

courthouse, carpenter's workshop and residence. Arches, wooden ceilings and sleeping lofts endow each unit with charm and uniqueness, while the fireplace and veranda are delightful places to unwind. The flowering garden offers a shady retreat.

★ **George & Georgia's**　CRETAN €
(To Steki tou Sifaki; ☑ 28340 51230; mains €7-12; ☺ 12.30-4pm & 7pm-late; ☑) Husband-and-wife team George and Georgia serve up satisfying homestyle Cretan food at this cheerful, hopping place. Expect scrumptious oven-roasted dishes and flavoursome grilled fish, along with a great selection of veggie options. Find it between the waterfront and the main road, near the post office.

Angira　SEAFOOD €€
(mains €7-15; ☺ noon-11pm Apr-Oct) Seafood doesn't get any fresher than at this place right at the harbour. Choose from marinated anchovies, shrimp salad or grilled fish, or a wonderful slow-cooked lamb in wine sauce.

❶ Getting There & Away

In high season, hourly buses go from Rethymno to Panormo (€2.60, 25 minutes). Buses stop on the main road just outside town. For car hire, try **Rent-A-Car** (www.bestcars-rental.gr; ☺ 9am-2pm & 5-8pm), with branches opposite the carob factory and the Grecotel Club Marine Palace.

OFF THE BEATEN TRACK

DALABELOS ESTATE

Hemmed in by vines, olives and fruit trees, these 10 traditional-style **houses** (☑ 28340 22155; www.dalabelos.gr; Aggeliana; d/ste from €80/100; ❄ ☎ ☒) have a view over rolling hills to the sea. The modern rooms have stone fireplaces, private terraces, outdoor hot tubs and beautiful bathrooms. The infinity pool and restaurant are first class, plus there are seasonal activities from olive harvesting to raki distilling, as well as hands-on Cretan cooking classes.

It's located inland, 5km south of Panormo, so it helps to have your own transport, but otherwise there are free mountain bikes. The husband-and-wife owners are exceptionally hospitable and proud Cretans, with unsurpassed passion for local food and culture. In high season there's a minimum three-night stay.

A **taxi** (☑ 28340 23000) is available for drop-offs at Rethymno (€28) or Bali (€20).

Anogia　Ανώγεια

POP 2500

Perched beside Mt Psiloritis, 37km southwest of Iraklio, Anogia is a wonderful spot to slow things down and glimpse authentic rural Cretan life. It's the perfect base for excursions up to the Nida Plateau (1400m) and Zeus' cave.

Here locals cling to time-honoured traditions, and it's the norm to see men gossiping in the *kafeneia* (coffeehouses), flicking *komboloïa* (worry beads) in their hand, and dressed in traditional black shirts with *vraka* (baggy pants) tucked into black boots. Elderly women, meanwhile, keep busy selling traditional woven blankets and embroidered textiles. The town's turbulent history – in WWII and under Ottoman rule – has instilled a legacy of rebelliousness and a desire to express an undiluted Cretan character.

The town's also famous for its stirring music and has spawned many of Crete's best-known musicians, including Nikos Xylouris.

🛏 Sleeping & Eating

Hotel Aristea　HOTEL €
(☑ 6972410486, 28340 31459; www.hotelaristea.gr; Michaeli Stavrakaki; d/apt from €35/85; ℗ ☎) Run by the chatty and charming Aristea, this small inn offers sweeping valley views from balconies attached to five fairly basic but spotless and comfortable enough rooms. The four split-level apartments in a next-door annexe are more modern and have kitchen and a wood-burning fireplace for those chilly mountain nights. There's also a common kitchen with full cooking facilities.

Taverna Aetos　CRETAN €
(☑ 28340 31262; 13is Avgoustou 1944 17; grills €7-9; ☺ noon-11pm) This traditional taverna in the upper village has a giant charcoal grill out the front and mountain views out the back. On offer are such regional specialities as *ofto* (a flame-cooked lamb or goat), and spaghetti cooked in stock with cheese.

Arodamos　CRETAN €
(☑ 28340 31100; www.arodamos.gr; Tylisos-Ano gia Rd; mains €6-10.50; ☺ 10am-10pm; ☎) This restaurant in a modern stone house in the upper village is highly rated for its hearty mountain fare and gracious hospitality. Local specialities include the flame-teased

lamb or goat *(ofto)* and the deceptively simple but tasty dish of spaghetti cooked in stock and topped with *anthotiros* (white cheese). If you're ordering mezedhes, be sure to get the *dakos* (Cretan rusks).

ⓘ Getting There & Away

From Monday to Saturday there are three daily buses from Iraklio (€4.10, one hour), and one on Sunday. From Rethymno (€6, 1¼ hours) two buses depart daily Monday to Friday.

Mt Psiloritis

At 2456m, Mt Psiloritis, also known as Mt Ida, is Crete's highest mountain. At its eastern base is the Nida Plateau (1400m), a wide, fertile expanse reached via a paved 21km-long road from Anogia. It passes several round stone *mitata* (traditional shepherds' huts used for cheesemaking and shelter) as well as the turnoff to the highly regarded (but rarely open) Skinakas Observatory.

From the Nida Plateau it's a short walk to the Ideon Cave (1538m). Also on the plateau is Andartis, an impressive landscape sculpture honouring the WWII Cretan resistance.

◎ Sights

Although just a huge and fairly featureless hole in the ground, Ideon Cave (P) FREE has sacred importance in mythology as the place where Zeus was reared by his mother, Rhea, to save him from the clutches of his child-devouring father, Cronos. (Some also believe it's where he died and is buried.) Ideon is on Mt Psiloritis about 15km from Anogia; it's a 1km uphill walk along a rocky path from the parking lot to the entrance.

Ideon was a place of worship from the late 4th millennium BC onward, and many artefacts, including gold jewellery and bronze shields, statuettes and other offerings to Zeus, have been unearthed here. The rail track used for these archaeological digs is still here.

In winter (and sometimes as late as May) the cave entrance can be blocked by snow, in which case it's easy enough to climb over the fence. However, for safety reasons, avoid clambering on the snow.

ⓘ Getting There & Away

To reach Mt Psiloritis, you really need your own wheels. The views en route are stunning.

Buses run from Rethymno to Anogia (€6, 1¼ hours, twice daily on weekdays).

OFF THE BEATEN TRACK

ENAGRON

Enagron Ecotourism Village (☑ 28340 61611; www.enagron.gr; Axos Mylopotamou; studios/apt incl breakfast from €87/108; ☺ restaurant 2-4pm & 7-10pm; P ❋ 🔊 ≋) is a working farm that offers an immersion in the traditional Cretan way of life. Its attractive villas, laid out like a small village, have elegantly rustic rooms featuring beamed ceilings, stone walls and fireplaces as well as kitchenettes. Three-night minimum stay. The restaurant serves Cretan dishes prepared with farm-foraged ingredients, and there's a delightful program of daily activities (included in rates).

Activities range from guided hikes to the mountains and villages, cooking classes and cheese- and bread-making workshops to birdwatching and botanical walks, plus donkey rides for the kids. The farm also provides excellent hiking maps if you want to go solo, and offers free bike hire and recommended cycling trails. Be sure to allow time to laze by the luxurious infinity pool.

Nonguests are welcome to visit the farm and its small museum, and its restaurant is highly recommended. Book ahead.

South of Rethymno

Spili   Σπίλι

POP 630

Spili is a incredibly pretty mountain village and shutterbug favourite thanks to its cobbled streets, big old plane trees and flower-festooned whitewashed houses. Most people just stop for lunch on a coast-to-coast trip, but it's well worth staying a day or two to explore the trails weaving through the local mountains. The rugged Kourtaliotiko Gorge, which culminates at the famous palm grove of Preveli Beach (p312), starts not far south of town.

◎ Sights

On the western outskirts of town the Maravel Garden (☑ 28320 22056; www.maravelspili. gr; ☺ 8am-8pm Mar-Nov) FREE is a botanical

CLIMBING MT PSILORITIS

The classic route to the summit of Mt Psiloritis follows the east–west E4 European Path from the Nida Plateau and in summer can be done in a round trip of about seven hours. While you don't need to be an alpine mountaineer, it's a long slog and the views from the summit may be marred by haze or cloud cover. En route, occasional *mitata* (round, stone shepherds' huts) provide shelter should the weather turn inclement, while at the summit there's a small, twin-domed chapel. The best map is the Anavasi 1:30,000 *Psiloritis (Mt Ida)*. For trekking conditions and general advice, get in touch with the **visitor centre** (AKOMM; ☑ 28340 31402; www.psiloritisgeopark.gr; ⊙ 8am-4pm Mon-Fri) in Anogia prior to departure.

If you're planning on tackling Psiloritis from a destination other than Anogia, visit www.psiloritisgeopark.gr for the comprehensive online Psiloritis Tourist Guide. Be sure to bring a warm jacket, even if the weather's fine, as conditions can change quickly.

Backcountry skiing is possible at Mt Psiloritis from December to March; contact the **Cretan Ski School** (www.facebook.com/skiincrete) for equipment hire, lessons and guided trips.

gardens filled with an aromatic variety of plant species from Crete and across the globe. You're free to wander and check out the herbs and medicinal plants staff use to distil essential oils and produce the organic products sold in the shop. The cafe has a deck overlooking the gardens and does a menu of light meals, homemade ice cream, herbal teas and superfood smoothies.

Call in advance for tours (€5), but usually they're for groups only. The garden's **Maravel Shop** (☑ 28320 22056; www.shop.maravels pili.gr; ⊙ 9am-9pm) in town has a larger stock of its products.

🛏 Sleeping & Eating

★ Hotel Heracles   PENSION €
(☑ 28320 22111, 6973667495; www.heracles-hotel. eu; s/d/tr/q €35/40/45/50; ❇ 🅿 🛜) These five balconied rooms are quiet, spotless and simply furnished, but it's the charming and softly spoken Heracles himself who makes the place so special. Intimately familiar with the area, he's happy to put you on to the right hiking trail, birdwatching site or hidden beach. Optional breakfasts (from €4.50) feature local eggs and an array of homemade marmalades.

★ Taverna Sideratico   CRETAN €
(☑ 28320 22916; mains €8; ⊙ noon-10pm Apr-Nov; 🅿) In an appealing location away from Spili's touristy centre, this delightful taverna sits on the main road 500m south of town. There's no menu, so you'll be guided through its mouthwatering array of *mayirefta* prepared by chef-owner-farmer Nico, who sources all ingredients from the

immediate area. As well as slow-cooked meat dishes, its vegetarian meals are outstanding.

❶ Getting There & Away

Spili is on the Rethymno–Agia Galini bus route (€3.80, 30 minutes), which has up to five services daily.

Plakias   Πλακιάς

POP 300

Set beside a sweeping sandy crescent and accessed via two scenic gorges – Kotsifou and Kourtaliotiko – Plakias gets swarmed with package tourists in summer (when it can be very windy) but otherwise remains a laidback indie travellers' favourite. While the village itself isn't particularly pretty, it's an excellent launch pad for regional excursions and hikes through olive groves, along seaside cliffs and to some sparkling hidden beaches.

◉ Sights & Activities

There are well-worn walking paths to the scenic villages of Selia, Moni Finika and Lefkogia, and a lovely walk along the Kourtaliotiko Gorge to Moni Preveli. An easy 30-minute uphill path to Myrthios begins just before the youth hostel.

Several diving operators run certification courses, as well as shore and boat dives to nearby rocky bays, caves and canyons.

Captain Lefteris Boat Cruises   BOATING
(☑ 28320 31971, 6936806635; www.lbferries.gr; tours €15-39) In summer Baradakis Lefteris (owner-chef of the Smerna Bar) and his son Nikos run entertaining boat trips to nearby

beaches such as Preveli (adult/child €15/8), Loutro (€39/20), and Agios Pavlos and Triopetra (€30/15). They also offer boat hire (€120 per day, excluding fuel).

Elena Tours TOURS
(☑ 6936371451, 28320 20465; tours from €45; ⊙ 9.30am-1.30pm & 6-9pm) Hop in Elena's minibus for an excursion into the less touristy side of the area. Hike through gorges, take boats to unheard-of beaches, visit ancient churches and meet locals in quaint villages. Each tour includes a maximum of eight people. The office is located in the centre of Plakias, just over the bridge.

🛏 Sleeping

★ Plakias Youth Hostel HOSTEL €
(☑ 28320 32118; www.yhplakias.com; dm €10-12; ⊙ mid-Mar–Nov; ℗ @ 🛜) 🌊 This charismatic pad and 'Hoscar' winner for best Greek hostel is set in an olive grove about 500m from the beach. Serene and laid-back, it fosters an atmosphere of inclusiveness and good cheer that appeals to people of all ages and nationalities. There are six eight-bed dorms with fans, communal facilities, an outdoor kitchen and an honour-system fridge with cheap beers.

Gio-Ma PENSION €
(☑ 28320 31942, 694737793; www.gioma.gr; r from €40; ❄🛜) Located at the quiet end of town and fronted by a flower-filled balcony, the spacious self-contained rooms here are clean and comfortable, and feature fabulous sea views. Snag one of the upper units for postcard-perfect photos. The owners also run the waterfront taverna across the street.

Plakias Suites APARTMENT €€
(☑ 28320 31680, 6975811559; www.plakiassuites.com; d €75-140; ⊙ Mar–mid-Nov; ℗ ❄🛜) This stylish outpost has six two- and three-room apartments with contemporary aesthetics and zeitgeist-compatible touches such as large flat-screen TVs, supremely comfortable mattresses, a chic kitchen and a private balcony or patio. Staying here puts you within a whisker of the best stretch of local beach, albeit about 1km from the village centre.

🍽 Eating & Drinking

Tasomanolis SEAFOOD €€
(☑ 6979887749, 28320 31229; www.tasomanolis.gr; mains €7-16; ⊙ noon-11pm; 🛜🍴) Tasos and his Belgian wife, Lisa, preside over this colourful nautical-themed family taverna

towards the far end of town. Park yourself on the patio to tuck into classic Greek grills and inspired daily specials like anchovy bruschetta, ouzo shrimp or the daily catch with wild greens. Children's menu available.

Enquire about their **boat tours** (☑ 28320 31229; www.plakiasboattours.gr; cruises from €15).

Taverna Christos CRETAN €€
(☑ 28320 31472; mains €6-17; ⊙ noon-late; 🛜) This established taverna has a romantic tamarisk-shaded terrace right next to the crashing waves, and lots of interesting dishes that you won't find everywhere, including home-smoked sea bass, black spaghetti with calamari, and lamb *avgolemono* with fresh pasta. Finish off with the orange pie.

Cozy Backyard BAR
(⊙ 5pm-late Apr-Oct) Down a side street off the main drag is this much-loved drinking hole with an intimate bar fronted by a patio under a palm tree. Jovial staff sling drinks – including the signature Cretan Cocktail, a fruity amaretto number topped with a mini Greek flag – to a tipsy crowd of holidaymakers.

ℹ Information

Plakias has numerous ATMs along the waterfront and about town.

ℹ Getting There & Away

There are up to five buses daily to Rethymno (€5, one hour) and four to Preveli (€1.80, 30 minutes).

Around Plakias

POP 100

The postcard-pretty village of Myrthios, draped across the hillside above Plakias, makes for a quieter and more traditional alternative to staying beachside. You might also be lured by great food and good deals on boutique accommodation.

★ Taverna Panorama CRETAN €€
(☑ 28320 31450; mains €6-16; ⊙ 11am-11pm Apr–mid-Nov; 🛜) One of the oldest restaurants in the area, Panorama could not be more aptly named: on the shaded terrace, intoxicating views stretch towards the Libyan Sea. Women from the village prepare Cretan soul food here with passion and know-how, using impeccably fresh ingredients from the owner's farm. If there's freshly baked apple pie, don't miss it!

East of Plakias

A smooth, curving ribbon of road winds from the bottom of Kourtaliotiko Gorge towards the southern coast, soaring up to the historic Moni Preveli and plunging down to palm-studded Preveli Beach. Although home to two of the region's biggest draws, Preveli retains a feeling of remoteness.

Moni Preveli   MONASTERY

(Μονή Πρεβέλης; ☑ 28320 31246; www.preveli.org; Koxaron-Moni Preveli Rd; €3; ☺9am-6.30pm Apr, May, Sep & Oct, 9am-1.30pm & 3.30-7pm Jun-Aug; P) Historic Moni Preveli cuts an imposing silhouette high above the Libyan Sea. Like most Cretan monasteries, it was a centre of resistance during the Turkish occupation and also played a key role in WWII, hiding trapped Allied soldiers from the Nazis until they could escape to Egypt by submarine. A small museum features exquisite icons, richly embroidered vestments and two silver candelabra presented by grateful soldiers after the war.

Preveli Beach   BEACH

(Παραλία Πρεβέλης) Also known as Palm Beach, Preveli is one of Crete's most celebrated strands. At the mouth of the Kourtaliotiko Gorge, where the river Megalopotamos empties into the Libyan Sea, the palm-lined riverbanks have freshwater pools good for a dip. The beach is backed by rugged cliffs and punctuated by a heart-shaped boulder at the water's edge. A steep path leads down to the beach (10 minutes) from a car park (€2), 1km before Moni Preveli.

TRIOPETRA   ΤΡΙΟΠΕΤΡΑ

Triopetra is one for those who want to avoid the package-tourist beach-resort scene and instead keep their holiday blissfully simple. On a good day, this long, brown-sand beach is a real crowd-pleaser, featuring magnificent crystal-clear waters. However, it's often blighted by winds – the only thing keeping it from appearing in any top-100 lists. Instead, the attraction here is more the mellow pace of life.

It's named after the three giant rocks jutting out of the sea. Other than a few tavernas and pensions scattered about, there's not much else out this way.

Pavlos' Place   PENSION €

(☑ 6945998101; www.triopetra.com.gr; d €40-45; ☺taverna 8am-4pm & 6-10pm Apr-Oct; ✳🛜) Right above Little Triopetra Beach, dreamy Pavlos is the perfect chill spot and a popular yoga retreat. Rooms are down to earth (no TV), with kitchenettes, and balconies that catch the sea breeze. The attached taverna does homegrown fare (mains €8 to €12). Wifi is intermittent and available in public areas only – great for that digital detox.

AGIOS PAVLOS   ΑΓΙΟΣ ΠΑΥΛΟΣ

Cradled by cliffs, Agios Pavlos is little more than a couple of small tavernas with rooms and a beach bar all set simply around a picture-perfect crescent with dark, coarse sand and the distinctive silhouette of Paximadia Island looming offshore. Its beauty and tranquillity have made it a popular destination for yoga retreats. A steep staircase at the bay's western end leads up Cape Melissa to some intricately pleated multi-hued rock formations.

Agios Pavlos Hotel   HOTEL €

(☑ 28320 71104; www.agiospavloshotel.gr; s €25-30, d €35-45, apt €45-60; ☺Apr-Oct; P✳🛜) Hugging a rugged and remote sandy bay, this place offers small but updated rooms, some with gorgeous bay views, below a traditional taverna (☑ 28320 71104; mains €6-13; ☺8am-late Apr-Oct; 🛜). Alternatively, there are larger apartments with kitchens and balconies in a modern building about 1km uphill. At research time luxurious villas built into the natural landscape were under construction; these will have sea views and saltwater plunge pools.

AGIA GALINI   ΑΓΙΑ ΓΑΛΗΝΗ

One of southern Crete's most touristy seaside towns, the picturesque erstwhile fishing village of Agia Galini serves as a handy base for exploring miles of remote beaches, mountain villages and nearby Minoan sights. Despite the sparkling Libyan Sea setting, the town itself is blighted by package tourism and overdevelopment, which has diluted much of its original charm.

With ageing hotels and restaurants clinging densely to a steep hillside and hemmed in by cliffs, small beaches and a fishing harbour, the town can feel claustrophobic in high season. However, with its concentration of lively tavernas and pubs, the evenings bring a fun holiday atmosphere. While the town's pebbly beach is nothing special, the remote beaches west of here are lovely. Agia Galini all but shuts down in winter.

🛏 Sleeping & Eating

Glaros Hotel   HOTEL €€
(☑ 28320 91151; www.glaros-agiagalini.com; incl breakfast d €50-85, tr/q €91/101; 🌡 🛜 🌡) These well-maintained rooms have a modern edge in a town full of ho-hum hotels. Some rooms have balconies overlooking the pool, and there's a stylish common area and a decent buffet breakfast. Excellent, friendly service seals the deal. It's at the back of town, straight up from the harbour.

Faros Fish Tavern   SEAFOOD €€
(☑ 6944773702; mains €7-13; ⊙ 6-11pm) This no-frills family-run fish taverna is usually packed to the gills, and for good reason: the owner himself drops his nets into the Med, so you know that what's on the plate tonight was still swimming in the sea that morning. It's in the first lane coming from the port.

La Mar   CAFE
(☑ 28320 91018; ⊙ 8.30am-late Apr-Oct) Classy La Mar is the standout among the port-side terrace cafes, with tasteful decor and an interesting menu of cocktails. You can opt for a Martini shaken with a local twist, infused with *malotira* (mountain tea) or olive oil, or a G&T with local gin. Otherwise, pop in for a vegan burger or other Western fare.

ℹ Getting There & Away

In high season there are up to seven buses daily to Iraklio (€8.70, two hours), up to five to Rethymno (€6.80, 1½ hours) and to Phaestos (€2.30, 30 to 45 minutes), and around five buses to Matala (€3.60, 45 minutes), with a change in Tymbaki. Buses stop down in the village near the port.

If enough people have booked, **Galini Express** (☑ 6936923848; www.galiniexpress.com) offers direct buses to the airport in Iraklio (from €20) and Hania (from €25).

In 2019 **Anendyk** (www.anendyk.gr) began trialling a ferry service linking Agia Galini with Gavdos Island (two hours, one way/return €30/55) departing on Tuesday, Friday, Saturday and Sunday; check the website for the latest.

HANIA PROVINCE

The west of Crete stands apart in so many ways. A land of mountains, grandiose legends and memorials to battles past, it is presided over by the romantic port city of Hania, once Venice's jewel of a capital and now filled with boutique hotels, interesting shops and some of Greece's best restaurants. The region also has the grandest gorge in Europe, impressive west-coast beaches, Europe's southernmost possession (tranquil Gavdos, an island nearer to Africa than to Greece), and mountain villages that are a step back in time. The steep mountains that ripple west and into the southern sea guarantee the region generally remains untouched by the excesses of tourism. If you want to see beautiful and traditional Crete, Hania and the west is the place.

Hania   Χανιά
POP 54,000
Hania (also spelled Chania) is Crete's most evocative city, with its Venetian quarter criss-crossed by narrow lanes and culminating at a magnificent harbour. Remnants of Venetian and Turkish architecture abound, with old townhouses now transformed into restaurants and boutique hotels.

Although all this beauty means the old town is deluged with tourists in summer, it's still a great place to unwind. The Venetian Harbour is ideal for a stroll and a drink. Thanks to an active modern centre, the city retains its charm in winter. Indie boutiques and a lane (Skrydlof) dedicated to leather products provide good shopping, and creative restaurants means you'll eat very well.

◉ Sights

From Plateia 1866, the Venetian Harbour is a short walk north up Halidon. Zambeliou, once Hania's main thoroughfare, is lined with craft shops, small hotels and tavernas. The slightly bohemian Splantzia quarter, running from Plateia 1821 between Daskalogianni and Halidon, brims with atmospheric restaurants and cafes, boutique hotels and traditional shopping. The headland near the lighthouse separates the Venetian Harbour from the crowded town beach in the modern Nea Hora quarter.

★ Venetian Harbour   HISTORIC SITE
(Map p314) **FREE** There are few places where Hania's historic charm and grandeur are more palpable than in the old Venetian Harbour. It's lined by pastel-coloured buildings that punctuate a maze of narrow lanes lined with shops and tavernas. The eastern side is dominated by the domed Mosque of Kioutsouk Hasan (p316), now an exhibition hall, while a few steps further east the impressively restored **Grand Arsenal** (Map p314; ☑ 28210 34200; Plateia Katehaki; ⊙ varies

Hania

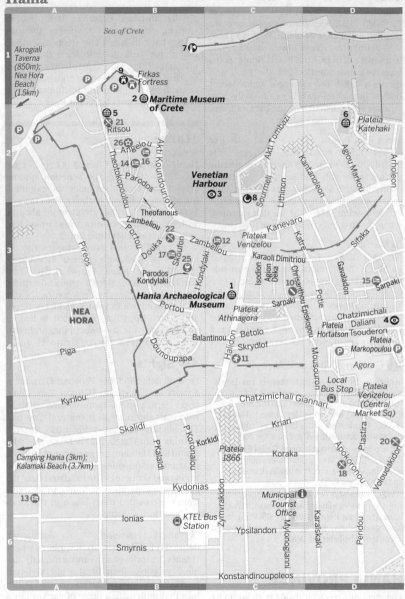

CRETE HANIA

by exhibit) **FREE** houses the Centre of Mediterranean Architecture.

At sunset, join locals and tourists on a stroll out to the **lighthouse** (Map p314) **FREE** that stands sentinel over the harbour entrance.

★**Hania
Archaeological Museum** MUSEUM
(Map p314; ☎28210 90334; http://chaniamuseum.culture.gr; Halidon 28; adult/concession/child €4/2/free; ◑8.30am-8pm Wed-Mon Apr-Oct, to 4pm Wed-Mon Nov-Mar) The setting alone in the beautifully restored 16th-century Venetian

CRETE HANIA

gold jewellery, clay tablets with Linear A and Linear B script, and a marble sculpture of the head of Roman emperor Hadrian.

Downstairs is a private collection of Minoan pottery, jewellery and clay models. Also particularly impressive are the statue of Diana and, in the pretty courtyard, a marble fountain decorated with lions' heads, a vestige of the Venetian tradition. A Turkish fountain is a relic from the building's days as a mosque.

The church itself was a mosque under the Turks, a movie theatre in 1913, and a munitions depot for the Germans during WWII. At the time of research there were plans to move the museum to a new location sometime in 2020; check ahead before visiting.

Church of San Francisco is reason to visit this fine collection of artefacts from Neolithic to Roman times. Late-Minoan clay baths used as coffins catch the eye, along with a large glass case with an entire herd of clay bulls (used to worship Poseidon). Other standouts include Roman floor mosaics, Hellenistic

★ **Maritime Museum of Crete** MUSEUM
(Map p314; ☑ 28210 91875; www.mar-mus-crete.gr; Akti Koundourioti; adult/concession €3/2; ⊙ 9am-5pm May-Oct, to 3.30pm Nov-Apr) Part of the hulking Venetian-built Firkas Fortress at the western port entrance, this museum celebrates Crete's nautical tradition with model ships, naval instruments, paintings, photographs, maps and memorabilia. One room is dedicated to historical sea battles, while upstairs there's thorough documentation of the WWII-era Battle of Crete. You might be lucky enough to see artists working on new model ships in the ship workroom.

Firkas Fortress FORTRESS
(Map p314; ⊙ 8am-2pm Mon-Fri) The Firkas Fortress at the western tip of the harbour heads the best-preserved section of the massive fortifications that were built by the Venetians to protect the city from marauding pirates and invading Turks. The Turks invaded anyway, in 1645, and turned the fortress into a barracks and a prison. Today, parts of it house the Maritime Museum of Crete. There's a great view of the harbour from the top.

Mosque of Kioutsouk Hasan MOSQUE
(Mosque of the Janissaries; Map p314) One of the prettiest and most dominant vestiges of the Turkish era is this dusky-pink multidomed former mosque on the eastern side of the Venetian Harbour. It was built in 1645,

making it the oldest Ottoman building in town. It's sometimes open for temporary art exhibits.

Byzantine & Post-Byzantine Collection MUSEUM
(Map p314; ☑ 28210 96046; Theotokopoulou 78; adult/concession/child €2/1/free; ⊙ 8am-4pm Wed-Mon) In the impressively restored Venetian Church of San Salvatore, this small but fascinating collection of artefacts, icons, jewellery and coins spans the period from AD 62 to 1913. Highlights include a segment of a mosaic floor from an early-Christian basilica, an icon of St George slaying the dragon, and a panel recently attributed to El Greco.

The building has a mixed bag of interesting architectural features from its various occupiers. A combined ticket (€6) also gives you entry to the archaeological museums of Hania (p314) and Kissamos (p321).

Venetian Fortifications FORTRESS
(Map p314) Part of a defensive system begun in 1538 by Michele Sanmichele, who also designed Iraklio's defences, Hania's massive fortifications remain impressive. Best preserved is the western wall, running from the Firkas Fortress to the Siavo Bastion. Entrance to the fortress is via the gates next to the Maritime Museum. The bastion offers good views of the old town.

⛱ Beaches

The town beach 2km west of the Venetian Harbour at Nea Hora (Akti Papanikoli) is crowded but convenient if you just want to cool off and get some rays. Koum Kapi is less used (and less clean). For better swimming, keep heading west to the beaches (in order) of Hrysi Akti (Nea Kydonia), Agioi Apostoli and Kalamaki, which are all served by local buses heading towards Platanias.

🏃 Activities

Trekking Plan OUTDOORS
(Map p314; ☑ 28210 27040, 6932417040; www.cycling.gr; Halidon 85; ⊙ 9am-2pm & 6-8.30pm, closed Sun Nov-Apr) Trekking Plan (operating out of the Attios travel agency) arranges hikes to Agia Irini, Samaria and Imbros Gorges; climbs of Mt Gingilos; canyoning, rappelling and rock climbing; and kayaking and mountain-biking tours. There are ski tours in winter.

WORTH A TRIP

MANOUSAKIS WINERY

This pretty winery (☑ 28210 78787; www.manousakiswinery.com; Vatolakkos; wine tasting from €10; ⊙ 11am-5pm Apr, to 10pm May–mid-Nov, by appointment rest of year) has been a family-run business for over 25 years. Located in the village of Vatolakkos, 16km southwest of the centre of Hania, it is well worth a visit. Taste the Nostos wines (the rosé is made blending the *Romeiko* grape, which is indigenous to Hania), take a free 15-minute tour of the winery production, or simply settle in for lunch or dinner with a bottle on the tree-shaded terrace set among olive groves and citrus trees.

A bus from Hania stops at the main square in Vatolakkos, an eight-minute walk from the winery.

Blue Adventures Diving
DIVING

(Map p314; ☑28210 40608; www.blueadven
tures.gr; Chrysanthou Episkopou 39; 2 dives incl
gear €90, snorkelling tour €50; ⊘9am-9pm Mon-
Sat May-Oct) This established outfit offers
a host of dive options, including discover
courses (€85), PADI open-water certification (€460), and diving trips around
Hania, including beginner dives in PADI
training standards. There are also snorkelling trips.

🛏 Sleeping

★ Cocoon City Hostel
HOSTEL €

(Map p314; ☑28210 76100; www.cocooncityhos
tel.com; Kydonias 145; dm from €18, d with/with-
out bathroom from €40/35; ❄🛜) Within easy
reach of the bus station and the old town,
this modern, spick-and-span hostel has
four- and six-bed mixed dorms that come
with their own light, charging point and
under-bed storage. Private rooms share a
bathroom, except one that comes with its
own (though its proximity to the lobby cafe-bar means some noise). Helpful staff can
arrange excursions to Samaria Gorge.

Pension Theresa
PENSION €

(Map p314; ☑28210 92798; www.pensiontheresa.
gr; Angelou 8; s €25-30, d €40-70; ❄🛜) This
creaky old Venetian house with a long,
steep, winding staircase and antique furniture delivers eight snug rooms with character aplenty. The location is excellent, the
ambience is rustic and convivial, and there
are fab views from the rooftop terrace, plus
a communal kitchen stocked with basic
breakfast items. There's an annexe nearby
with apartments suitable for families.

Delightful hosts Maria and Victor are on
hand to help at any time.

★ Ionas Hotel
HOTEL €€

(Map p314; ☑28210 55090; www.ionashotel.
com; cnr Sarpaki & Sorvolou; s/d/ste incl breakfast from €85/100/120; ❄🛜) In the quieter
Splantzia quarter, Ionas is housed in a
historic building with contemporary interior design and friendly owners. The
nine charming rooms are kitted out with
all mod cons (including a spa bath in one)
and share a rooftop terrace. Original features include a Venetian archway in the
entrance and walls from the mid-16th
century.

Ifigenia
Rooms & Studios
GUESTHOUSE €€

(Map p314; ☑28210 94357; www.ifigeniastudi-
os.gr; Gamba 23; r €50-130; ❄🛜) This network of refurbished buildings around
the Venetian Harbour has a bed for
every budget, from basic rooms to luxurious bi-level suites with Jacuzzis and
sea views. Most of the 25 units brim with
such old-timey touches as wrought-iron
canopy beds and beamed ceilings. The pricier ones have kitchens and can sleep four.

Bellmondo
HOTEL €€

(Map p314; ☑28210 36217; www.belmondo-
hotel.com; Zambeliou 10; s/d/tr incl breakfast
from €73/90/105; ❄🛜) With Turkish and
Venetian features, including part of an old
hammam (Turkish baths) in one room, the
Bellmondo is furnished with simple wooden
pieces and offers friendly service. The nicest
rooms have balconies (for about €25 more
than the standard rate) and harbour views.

★ Serenissima
BOUTIQUE HOTEL €€€

(Map p314; ☑28210 86386; www.serenissima.gr;
Skoufon 4; d incl breakfast from €170; ❄🛜) This
tranquil Venetian townhouse, renovated to
impeccable standards, packs plenty of design cachet into its historic walls. The elegant rooms feature the gamut of mod cons,
along with period touches such as stone
walls, wooden beams and candlelit niches.
Rates include an à la carte breakfast

🍴 Eating

★ Kouzina EPE
CRETAN €

(Map p314; ☑28210 42391; www.facebook.com/
kouzinaepe; Daskalogianni 25; dishes €5-10;
⊘noon-7.30pm Mon-Sat; 🛜🍴) This cheery
lunch spot gets contemporary designer flair
from the cement floor and hip lighting. It
wins the area's 'local favourite' hands down,
by serving a mix of modern à la carte options
and great-value, delicious blackboard-listed
mayirefta (ready-cooked meals); you can
inspect what you're about to eat in the open
kitchen. Good veg options, too.

Bougatsa Iordanis
CRETAN €

(Map p314; ☑28210 88855; www.iordanis.gr;
Apokoronou 24; bougatsa €3; ⊘6am-2pm) Locals
start salivating at the mention of this bakery
dedicated since 1924 to making the finest
bougatsa. The flaky treat, filled with sweet or
savoury cheese, is cooked fresh in enormous
slabs, carved into bite-sized pieces and served
on simple aluminium trays. Pair it with a

. Heraklion Archaeological Museum (p285)

he museum in Crete's capital, Iraklio, showcases xhibits spanning 5500 years in a restored auhaus building.

. Mosque of Kioutsouk Hasan p316)

ne of the prettiest vestiges of the Turkish era is his dusky-pink multidomed former mosque on the astern side of the Venetian Harbour.

. Dikteon Cave (p339)

ccording to legend, Rhea hid in this cave to give irth to Zeus, far from the clutches of his offspring- obbling father, Cronos.

. Lasithi windmills (p339)

Vindmills upon a hill sparkle against a light blue ummer sky

double Greek coffee and you're set for the morning. There's nothing else on the menu!

Pulse VEGAN €
(Map p314; Theotokopoulou 70; mains €9.50; ⊙noon-midnight daily May-Oct, noon-9pm Mon-Sat Nov-Mar; 🖉) Settle in at an outdoor table with sea views for some fantastic vegan dishes at meat-free Pulse, located at the western end of Firkas Fortress. The mezes boards are great for snacking on, as are the potato cakes with chilli jam; mains include a tasty cheeseburger and a beef-free red-wine casserole. The *mousakas* is an absolute highlight.

Oasis FAST FOOD €
(Map p314; Vouloudakidon 2; souvlaki €2; ⊙9am-10pm) Locals swear by the undeniably tasty *gyros* (meat slivers cooked on a vertical rotisserie) and souvlaki at tiny, old-style Oasis. There are a few seats inside, but it's mostly a takeaway joint.

★ To Maridaki SEAFOOD €€
(Map p314; 🖉28210 08880; www.tomaridaki.gr; Daskalogianni 33; dishes €6-13; ⊙noon-midnight Mon-Sat) This modern seafood *mezedhopoleio* (restaurant specialising in mezedhes) is often packed to the gills with chatty locals and tourists. Dishes straddle the line between tradition and innovation with to-die-for mussels *saganaki*, charcoal-grilled fresh fish, and delicious house white wine. The complimentary panna cotta is a worthy finish.

Tamam Restaurant MEDITERRANEAN €€
(Map p314; 🖉28210 96080; www.tamamrestaurant.com; Zambeliou 49; mains €7-14; ⊙noon-midnight; 🖃🖉) This stylish, convivial taverna, part of which is in a converted Turkish bathhouse, has captured people's attention since 1982 with strong-flavoured Cretan dishes that often incorporate Middle Eastern spices and touches. The boneless lamb in tomato sauce and yoghurt is a winner. Tables spill onto the narrow alleyway.

★ Thalassino Ageri SEAFOOD €€€
(🖉28210 51136; www.thalasino-ageri.gr; Vivilaki 35; fish per kg €55-65; ⊙6.30pm-midnight Mon-Sat, 12.30pm-midnight Sun Apr & May, from 7pm daily Jun-Oct) This solitary fish taverna among the vestiges of Hania's old tanneries in Halepa, 2km east of the centre, is one of Crete's top restaurants. Take in the sunset from the superb waterside setting and peruse the changing menu, dictated by the day's catch, which is cooked over charcoal. The fried calamari melts in your mouth.

🍷 Drinking & Nightlife

The cafe-bars around the Venetian Harbour are nice places to sit, but they charge top euro. For a more local vibe, head to Plateia 1821 in the Splantzia quarter, the interior streets near Potie, or to alt-flavoured Sarpidona at the eastern end of the harbour.

★ Monogram COFFEE
(Map p314; 🖉28215 07046; www.facebook.com/monogramchania; Daskalogianni 5; ⊙8am-9pm) Soak up the sun at a street-side table with music wafting from this hip corner coffee spot. Beans are sourced from around the globe, including Guatemala and Ethiopia, then roasted locally in Iraklio. It also has a large range of teas you'd be hard-pressed to find elsewhere in Greece, and a few tempting cakes.

★ Sinagogi BAR
(Map p314; 🖉28210 95242; Parodos Kondylaki 15; ⊙noon-5am May-Oct; 🖎) Housed in a roofless Venetian building on a small lane next to the synagogue, this popular summer-only lounge bar with eclectic decor is a laid-back place to take it all in. After dark it's bathed in a romantic glow while DJs play soft electro and staff whip up mojitos and daiquiris.

☆ Entertainment

Established in 1978, **Fagotto Jazz Bar** (Map p314; 🖉28210 71877; Angelou 16; ⊙8.30am-2pm & 9pm-late) is a Hania institution in a Venetian building that offers smooth jazz and blues, and occasionally live bands or DJs, in an intimate setting in a narrow lane close to the Maritime Museum. The action picks up after 10pm. It opens in the mornings as a cafe and does great breakfasts, too.

🛍 Shopping

Hania offers top shopping, especially in the backstreets. Theotokopoulou is lined with souvenir and handicraft shops. Skrydlof offers a vast array of local and imported sandals, belts and bags. Find some of the most authentic crafts in the Splantzia quarter, along Chatzimichali Daliani and Daskalogianni. The central *agora* (market hall) is touristy but still worth a wander.

ℹ Information

Free wi-fi is widely available in public spaces, including the harbour, around the central market and at Plateia 1866, as well as at most hotels, restaurants, cafes and bars.

Banks cluster around Plateia Markopoulou in the new city, but there are also ATMs in the old town on Halidon.

Alpha Bank (cnr Halidon & Skalidi; ◉ 8am-6pm Mon-Fri, 10am-5pm Sat, ATM 24hr)

National Bank of Greece (cnr Tzanakaki & Giannari; ◉ 8am-2pm)

Municipal Tourist Office (Map p314; ✆ 28213 36155; Kydonias 29; ◉ 9am-3pm Mon-Fri) Modest selection of brochures, maps and transport timetables.

Tourist Police (✆ 171, 28210 25931; ◉ 24hr) The tourist police can assist with legal matters in multiple languages, including English, French and German.

❶ Getting There & Away

AIR

Hania's **airport** (✆ 28210 83800; www.chania-airport.com) is 14km east of town on the Akrotiri Peninsula, and is served year-round from Athens and Thessaloniki and seasonally from throughout Europe. Carriers include Aegean Airlines, Olympic Air, easyJet and Ryanair. A taxi from the airport to anywhere in Hania costs €25. Public buses into town stop right outside the terminal (€2.50, 30 minutes) and run between 5.30am and 11pm daily.

BOAT

Hania's port is at Souda, 7km southeast of town (and the site of a NATO base). The port is linked to town by bus (€2, or €2.50 if paying onboard) and taxi (€10). Hania buses meet each boat, as do buses to Rethymno.

Anek Lines (www.anek.gr) runs an overnight ferry between Piraeus and Hania (from €38 per person, nine hours). Buy tickets online or at the port; reserve ahead for cars.

BUS

Hania's **KTEL bus station** (Map p314; ✆ info 28210 93052, tickets 28210 93306; www.e-ktel.com; Kelaidi 73-77; ☎) has an information kiosk with helpful staff and timetables, a cafeteria, a minimarket and a left-luggage service. Check the excellent website for the current schedule.

❶ Getting Around

Local buses are operated by **Chania Urban Buses** (✆ 28210 98115; http://chaniabus.gr). Zone A/B tickets cost €1.20/1.70 if bought from a kiosk or vending machine or €2/2.50 from the driver.

A handily central **bus stop** (Map p314) for Souda port, Halepa, Nea Hora and other local destinations is on Giannari, near the *agora*.

Taxi (✆ 28210 98700; www.chaniataxi.gr) Hania-based taxi company.

Kissamos   Κίσσαμος

POP 4275

Kissamos is not a place given entirely over to tourism and exudes an unpolished, almost gritty, air compared to other north-coast towns. It's a good base for day-tripping to Balos in the Gramvousa Peninsula by cruise boat and it has an archaeological museum to keep history buffs interested. There are two beaches in town, separated by a waterfront promenade: the sandy Mavros Molos in the west and the pebbly Telonio to the east.

The largest town and capital of Kissamos province, it is referred to interchangeably as Kissamos and as Kastelli (though the official name is the former).

◉ Sights

In an imposing two-level Venetian-Turkish building on the main square, the **Archaeological Museum of Kissamos** (✆ 28220 83308; http://odysseus.culture.gr; Plateia Tzanakaki; adult/child €2/free; ◉ 8.30am-6pm Wed-Mon) presents locally excavated treasure, including statues, jewellery, coins and a large mosaic floor from a Kissamos villa. Most items are from the Hellenistic and Roman eras, though there are also some Minoan objects. There are exhibits from Falasarna, Polyrrinia and Nopigia, too.

⏢ Sleeping

Stavroula Palace   HOTEL €€
(✆ 28220 23620; s/d/tr incl breakfast €50/65/80; ✳☎❄) Run by the warm and gracious Stavroula and her family, this cheery and good-value waterfront hotel has breezy, modern rooms with balconies fronting a large swimming pool and an immaculately kept garden where breakfast is served. Children's recreation area, too.

Christina Beach Hotel   APARTMENT €€
(✆ 28220 83333; www.christina-beach.gr; studios from €40; ℗✳@☎❄) This smart studio complex on the western side of Kissamos represents the upper end of accommodation in town. Right across from the water, the modern studios are large and airy, and the sandy beach is right nearby, or you can just lounge by the inviting pool.

CRETAN BREWERY

Established in 2007, this **brewery** (☑ 28240 31002; www.cretanbeer.gr; Zounaki; guided tour €3; ◷ 10am-8pm Apr-Nov) makes Charma, the first beer to be produced in Hania. You can sample the excellent brews at the slick operation here, set up by a local. There's a covered terrace where you can enjoy the range of beers, from a blond lager to an excellent pale ale, along with seasonal brews, or opt for a tasting flight of five beers (€5). There's good beer-soaking pub grub on the menu and you can join a guided tour of the brewery; book ahead.

It's located in Zounaki village, around 25km west of the centre of Hania. The attached shop is the only place in Crete where you can buy the beer to take away.

✖ Eating & Drinking

Taverna Sunset TAVERNA €€
(☑ 28220 83478; Paraliaki; mains €7-14; ◷ noon-midnight) Locals mix with in-the-know visitors at this quintessential family taverna presided over by Giannis, who's usually ensconced behind the grill coaxing meat and fish into succulent perfection. It's right on the waterfront, so you can feel the breezes coming from offshore.

★ Babel Cafe Bar BAR
(☑ 28220 22045; ◷ 8am-late; 🛜) Not only a good choice for a quick breakfast or snack, this smart modern waterfront cafe-bar is a great place for coffee and gets lively at night with young locals. It has one of the most extensive beer and cocktail lists in town, and it's worth swinging by simply for the amazing bay views from its bustling patio.

ℹ Getting There & Away

KTEL Bus Station (☑ 28210 93052; www.e-ktel.com; Kampouri)

Triton Ferries (☑ 28210 75444; www.tritonferries.gr) Triton has three ferries a week to Kythira (€15, four hours) and one to Gythio (€25, seven hours).

Around Kissamos

Balos

The rugged Gramvousa Peninsula cradles the lagoon-like sandy beach of Balos, whose shallow, shimmering turquoise waters draw huge crowds in summer. This remote stretch features on many tourist brochures for Crete, and when it's at its best it's a heavenly scene, with lapping waters shimmering with darting fish. If the tide is out, the wind is whipping up or it's overrun by visitors off the cruise ferry, it can be something of a letdown.

Balos can be accessed by a very rough, 12km dirt road, precarious at times, that begins at the end of the main street of Kalyviani village. While some cars do make the drive, a 4WD is really necessary (and note that most car-hire companies won't cover you for damage sustained on the drive to Balos). The views from the car park when you arrive are sensational. From here there's a 1km walking path down to the beach. The other option is to visit Balos on a **cruise** (☑ 28220 24344; www.cretandailycruises.com; adult/child €27/13; ◷ late Apr-Oct) from Kissamos, which stops first for around 90 minutes at the peninsula's offshore island Imeri Gramvousa, overlooking Balos, where you can make the sweaty climb to the ruins of a humongous Venetian fortress built to keep pirates at bay.

Note: there's no shade at Balos, but you can hire a sun-lounger and an umbrella. Toilet facilities are basic.

Falasarna Φαλάσαρνα

This broad sweep of beach has magical-looking pink-cream sands and teal waters and is known for its stunning sunsets. Along with superb water clarity, Falasarna has wonderfully big waves: long rollers coming from the open Mediterranean. It gets busy from mid-July to mid-August, primarily with day trippers from Hania and Kissamos.

Spread your towel on the Big Beach (Megali Paralia) at the southern end or pick a spot in one of the coves separated by rocky spits further north.

Bus schedules vary seasonally (check www.e-ktel.com). In summer at least three daily buses make the trip out to Falasarna from Hania (€8.30, 1¾ hours) via Kissamos (Kasteli; €3.80, 40 minutes).

Imbros Gorge

Half the length of the more famous Samaria Gorge, 8km-long Imbros Gorge (€2; ⊙year-round) is no less beautiful and a lot less busy. Most people start in the mountain village of Imbros and hike down to the southern coastal village of Komitades. Going the other way is a bit more of a workout, as you'll be walking up a gentle grade.

A taxi between the two villages (about €20 to €25) can be arranged by tavernas at either end. The hike takes you past 300m-high walls buttressed by cypresses, holm oaks, fig and almond trees, and redolent sage. Landmarks include a giant arch at the 2km mark (coming from the south) or the 6km mark (coming from the north) and the narrowest point of the ravine (near the 4.5km mark coming from Imbros), which is under 2m wide. The track is easy to follow, as it traces the stream bed past rockslides and caves. Sturdy shoes are essential. Allow two to three hours.

Southern Coast

Hania' s rocky southern coast is punctuated by laid-back beach communities and secluded coves reachable only by boat. Samaria Gorge spills out into the village of Agia Roumeli. Along with the impenetrable geography, strong summer winds keep the area happily safe from mass tourism.

Hora Sfakion   Χώρα Σφακίων

POP 212

The more bullet holes you see in the road signs along the way, the closer you are to Hora Sfakion, long renowned in Cretan history for its streak of rebellion against foreign occupiers. But don't worry: the tiny fishing village is today an amiable and somewhat scenic place that caters well to visitors, many of whom are Samaria Gorge hikers stumbling off the Agia Roumeli boat on their way back to Hania. Most pause just long enough to catch the next bus out, but there's sufficient appeal here to tempt you to stay, from boat trips to nearby isolated beaches to hiking the Aradena Gorge.

◉ Sights & Activities

Sweetwater Beach   BEACH
(Glyka Nera) West of Hora Sfakion, lovely Sweetwater Beach is accessible by a small daily ferry, by taxi boat (one way/return €25/50) or on foot via a stony and partly vertiginous 3.5km coastal path starting at the first hairpin turn of the Anopoli road. A small cafe rents umbrellas and sun chairs.

Notos Mare Marine Adventures   DIVING
(☑28210 08536, 6947270106; www.notosmare.com; New Harbour; 1/2 dives €49/85; ⊙8am-9pm Apr-Oct) In addition to PADI certification and dives for beginners and advanced divers, this long-running professional outfit also rents boats, organises charter boat and fishing trips, and operates taxi boats 24/7 to secluded beaches along the south coast, including Sweetwater Beach, Mareme and Loutro.

🛏 Sleeping & Eating

There are tavernas lined up along the harbour, but most are fairly touristy affairs. For stunning views, check out **Three Brothers** (☑28250 91040; www.three-brothers-chora-sfakion-crete.com; Vrissi Beach; mains €7.50-18; ⊙9am-midnight May-Oct; 🐀), set on a hill overlooking the sea backed by cliffs. Be sure to try the local *Sfakiani pita* – this thin, circular pancake filled with sweet *myzithra* (sheep's-milk cheese) and flecked with honey makes a great breakfast when served with a bit of Greek yogurt on the side.

CRETE IMBROS GORGE

OFF THE BEATEN TRACK

GAVDOS ISLAND

In the Libyan Sea, 65km from Paleohora and 45km from Hora Sfakion, Gavdos is Europe's most southerly point and as much a state of mind as it is an island. It's a blissful spot with only a few rooms, tavernas and unspoilt beaches, some accessible only by foot or boat. There's little to do here except swim, walk and relax. Gavdos attracts campers, nudists and free spirits happy to trade the trappings of civilisation for an unsullied nature experience.

The island is surprisingly green, with almost 65% covered in low-lying pine and cedar trees and vegetation. Most of the electricity is supplied by generators, which are often turned off at night and in the middle of the day. Note that the Anendyk ferry schedule does not make it possible to visit Gavdos on a day trip, but you can arrange a day trip with Hora Sfakion-based Gavdos Cruises (p325).

DON'T MISS

SAMARIA GORGE

Hiking the 16km-long **Samaria Gorge** (☎28210 45570; www.samaria.gr; Omalos; adult/child €5/free; ⏱7.30am-4pm May–mid-Oct), one of Europe's longest canyons, is high on the list of must-dos for many visitors to Crete. There's an undeniable raw beauty to the canyon, with its soaring cliffs and needlenose passageways. The hike begins at an elevation of 1230m just south of Omalos at Xyloskalo and ends in the coastal village of Agia Roumeli. It's also possible to do it the 'lazy way': hiking a shorter distance by starting at Agia Roumeli. The only way out of Agia Roumeli is by taking the boat to Sougia or Hora Sfakion, which are served by bus and taxi back to Hania.

The best time for the Samaria trek is in April and May, when wildflowers brighten the trail. Keep your eyes peeled for the endemic *kri-kri*, a shy endangered wild goat.

Hiking the Gorge

From the trailhead at Xyloskalo, a steep, serpentine stone path descends some 600m into the canyon to arrive at the simple, cypress-framed **Chapel of Agios Nikolaos**.

Beyond here the gorge is wide and open and not particularly scenic for the next 6km until you reach the abandoned settlement of Samaria. This is the main rest stop, with toilets, water and benches. Just south of the village is a 14th-century chapel dedicated to **St Maria of Egypt**, after whom the gorge is named.

Further on, the gorge narrows and becomes more dramatic until, at 11km, the walls are only 3.5m apart and you'll find the famous **Sideroportes** (Iron Gates), where a rickety wooden pathway leads hikers the 20m or so across the water.

The gorge ends at the 13km mark just north of the almost abandoned village of **Palea Agia Roumeli** (Old Agia Roumeli). From here it's a further 3km to the seaside village of **Agia Roumeli**, whose fine pebble beach and sparkling water are a most welcome sight. Few people miss taking a refreshing dip or at least bathing their aching feet before they fill up at one of the seaside tavernas.

The entire trek takes about four hours (for sprinters) to six hours (for strollers). This is a rocky trail and suitable footwear is essential.

Sleeping & Eating

It is forbidden to camp (or indeed spend the night) in the gorge. Stay at Omalos at the northern end, or Agia Roumeli in the south.

There are tavernas in Omalos, including one right by the gorge entrance. When the gorge is open, stands sell souvenirs, snacks, bottled water and the like. Agia Roumeli has several tavernas. There's also a snack stall at the national-park exit selling beer, coffee and other refreshments.

Getting There & Away

Most people hike Samaria one way, going north–south on a day trip that can be arranged from every sizeable town and resort in Crete. Confirm whether tour prices include gorge admission (€5) and the boat ride from Agia Roumeli to Sougia or Hora Sfakion.

With some planning, it's possible to do the trek on your own. There are early-morning public buses to Omalos from Hania (€7.50, one hour), Sougia (€5.30, one hour) and Paleohora (€7, one hour), once or twice daily in high season. Check www.e-ktel.com for the schedule, which changes seasonally. Taxis are another option.

At the end of the trail, in Agia Roumeli, ferries operated by **Anendyk** (☎28250 91251; www.anendyk.gr) depart for Sougia (€11) and Hora Sfakion (€12.50) at 5.30pm and take 40 minutes. These are usually met by public buses back to Hania from Hora Sfakion at 6.30pm and Sougia at 6.15pm; some buses from Sougia go to Omalos.

Xenia Hotel (☑ 28250 91490; www.sfakia-xenia-hotel.gr; Old Harbour; d incl breakfast €58; P ❄ 🛜) is well positioned overlooking the water, this hotel has been around since the early 1960s and has seen a number of upgrades, with another renovation underway at the time of writing.

ℹ Getting There & Away

KTEL buses (☑ 28210 93052; www.e-ktel.com) leave from the square up the hill above the municipal car park. Schedules change seasonally; check online. In summer there are three daily services to/from Hania (€8.30, 1¾ hours) and to/from Frangokastello (€2.30, 30 minutes).

ℹ Getting Around

Hora Sfakion is the eastern terminus for the south-coast **Anendyk** (⊙ 8am-4pm Mon-Fri 28250 91221; www.anendyk.gr; New Harbour) ferry route.

Ferries run to Paleohora (€20.70), Loutro (€6, 20 minutes), Agia Roumeli (€12.50, one hour) and Sougia (€16.20). Boats make extended stops in Agia Roumeli to accommodate Samaria Gorge hikers. Ferries may be cancelled in bad weather, so be careful not to get stuck in Agia Roumeli or Loutro. There are also two to three boats per week to/from Gavdos Island via Loutro and Agia Roumeli (€21.20, four hours). Some ferries carry vehicles (to Sougia with car one way/return €29/50, to Paleohora €36.40, reservation required). There are also ferries direct to Gavdos Island from Hora Sfakion from July to early September (€21.20, 2½ hours).

Schedules vary seasonally, so always check ahead. Often boats only run as far as Agia Roumeli, where you must change for another ferry to Sougia and Paleohora.

Day trippers to Gavdos Island can take the Gavdos Cruises (☑ 6981920076; www.gavdos-cruises.jimdo.com; adult/child return €40/20) fast boat departing at 10.10am and returning from Gavdos at 5pm. The journey takes one hour.

There's a daily small ferry (☑ 6978645212; New Harbour) to Sweetwater Beach (May to October; per person return €8). A boat taxi for up to six people costs €25 to Sweetwater and €40 to Loutro.

Loutro   Λουτρό
POP 56

The pint-sized fishing village of Loutro is a tranquil crescent of flower-festooned white-and-blue buildings hugging a narrow pebbly beach between Agia Roumeli and Hora Sfakion. It's only accessible by boat and on foot and is the departure point for coastal walks to isolated beaches, such as Finix, Marmara and Sweetwater.

🛏 Sleeping & Eating

Blue House   PENSION €
(☑ 28250 91035; www.thebluehouse.gr; d incl breakfast €50-65; ❄ 🛜) Midway along the white buildings lining the port, the Blue House has spacious, well-appointed rooms with big verandas overlooking the water. The nicest rooms are in the refurbished top-floor section. The taverna downstairs serves excellent *mayirefta* (ready-cooked meals; mains €6 to €9), including delicious *bourekia* baked with zucchini, potato and goat's cheese.

Ilios   SEAFOOD €€
(☑ 28250 91160; www.iliosloutro.gr; mains €5-15; ⊙ 8am-11pm mid-Apr–Oct; 🛜) Ilios is the best spot in town for fish and seafood, though it offers a full range of Cretan classics and breakfast, too. Rooms are also available.

ℹ Information

There's no bank, ATM or post office, and many places do not accept credit cards. Bring plenty of cash. The nearest ATM is in Hora Sfakion.

Sougia   Σούγια
POP 136

Sougia, 67km south of Hania and on the Hora Sfakion–Paleohora ferry route, is one of the most chilled-out and refreshingly undeveloped southern beach resorts. Cafes, bars and tavernas line a tamarisk-shaded waterfront promenade along a grey pebble-and-sand beach. Most pensions and apartments enjoy a quieter inland setting roughly 100m to 200m from the beach. There is little to do other than relax or explore the local hiking trails, including the popular Agia Irini Gorge and Lissos beach and ruins.

🏃 Activities

Sougia has a pleasant 1km-long grey sand-and-pebble beach, but its drop-off is steep, so it's not ideal for families with small children.

Pretty **Agia Irini Gorge** (€2; ⊙ year-round) starts around 13km north of Sougia near the village of Agia Irini. The well-maintained, well-signposted 7.5km trail (with a 500m elevation drop) follows the riverbed, is shaded by oleander, pines and other greenery, and passes caves hidden in the gorge walls. Allow around three hours to complete it.

It makes for a lovely, less crowded alternative to Samaria Gorge. The trail includes a few steep sections but is mostly relatively easy, with a few river crossings. There are rest stops with benches and toilets along the way, but be sure to take plenty of drinking water with you. You'll emerge at a taverna where you can call a taxi (€15) or continue on foot for another 4.5km via a quiet and paved road to Sougia.

🛌 Sleeping & Eating

Aretousa Studios & Rooms APARTMENT €
(☑ 28230 51178; studios €55-65; ☺ Apr-Oct; ℗ ✳ ☎) This lovely pension on the road to Hania, 200m from the sea, has bright and comfortably furnished studios with tile floors and balconies. There's a tranquil garden, friendly service and even a kids' playground out the back.

Polyfimos TAVERNA €
(☑ 28230 51343; www.polifimos.gr; Main Rd; mains €5-11; ☺ 1pm-midnight Apr-Oct) Hidden in a pretty grapevine-shrouded courtyard off the Hania road, this charismatic restaurant specialises in traditional charcoal-grilled local meats, fresh fish of the day, hearty stews such as rabbit *stifadho* (cooked with onions in a tomato puree) and lamb *tsigariasto*. It's run by ex-hippie Yiannis, who also makes his own oil, wine and raki.

OFF THE BEATEN TRACK

MARVELLOUS MILIA

The isolated mountain resort village of Milia (☑ 28210 46774; www.milia.gr; Vlatos; cottages incl breakfast from €85; ☺ year-round; ℗ ☎) ia one of Crete's ecotourism trailblazers. Inspired by a back-to-nature philosophy, 16 abandoned stone farmhouses were transformed into ecocottages sleeping one to four, with only solar energy for basic needs. Milia is one of the most peaceful places to stay in Crete, but it's also worth visiting just to dine at the superb **organic restaurant** (☑ 28210 46774; www.milia.gr; Vlatos; mains €9-13; ☺ 1-8pm; ℗ ☎).

Milia makes a great base for those who wish to unwind and see the Innahorion region. The cottages have antique beds, rustic furnishings, and fireplaces or wood-burning stoves. Since it's all solar powered, it's best to shelve the laptop and hairdryer. To reach Milia, follow the signposted turnoff north of the village of Vlatos. The narrow access road becomes a drivable 3km dirt road.

⭐ **Omikron** INTERNATIONAL €€
(☑ 28230 51492; Beach Rd; mains €7-12; ☺ 8am-late Apr-Oct; ☎ ✎) At this elegantly rustic beachfront spot with crushed pebbles underfoot, Jean-Luc Delfosse has forged his own culinary path in a refreshing change from taverna staples. From mushroom crêpes to *Flammekuche* (Alsatian-style pizza), seafood pasta to pepper steak – it's all fresh, creative and delicious.

ℹ Information

There is one ATM in Sougia.

ℹ Getting There & Away

At least one daily bus operates between Sougia and Hania (€7.80, 1¾ hours), with a stop in Agia Irini to drop off gorge hikers. The bus departing Sougia at 6.15pm waits for the Agia Roumeli boat. In summer there are also daily buses to Omalos (for Samaria Gorge; €5.30, one hour).

Local taxi drivers, including **Selino Taxi** (☑ 6940859860; www.taxi-selino.com) and **Sougia Taxi** (☑ 6970344422; www.sougiataxi. com), have a central kiosk on the waterfront.

Paleohora   Παλαιόχωρα

POP 1900

Appealing, laid-back and full of character, Paleohora lies on a narrow peninsula flanked by a long, curving, tamarisk-shaded sandy beach (Pahia Ammos) and a pebbly beach (Halikia). Shallow waters and general quietude make the village a good choice for families with small children. The most picturesque part of Paleohora is the maze of narrow streets below the castle. Tavernas spill out onto the pavement and occasional cultural happenings inject a lively ambience. In spring and autumn Paleohora attracts many walkers.

🛌 Sleeping

Joanna's Place APARTMENT €
(☑ 6978583503, 28230 41801; www.joanna-place. com; studios €50-60, 2-bed apt €100-110; ☺ Apr-Nov; ℗ ✳ ☎) This modern beige building sits in a quiet spot across from a small stone beach at the southeastern tip of the peninsula. The 16 spacious and spotless studios are outfitted with functional locally made furniture, and there's a kitchenette for preparing breakfast to enjoy on your balcony. There's also a two-bedroom apartment that will suit families.

PALEOHORA–SOUGIA COASTAL WALK

Following a portion of the E4 European Path, this hike connects two charming coastal towns via a 13km path that runs mostly along the coast and then heads inland from Lissos to Sougia.

From Paleohora, follow signs to the camp sites to the northeast and turn right at the sign for Anydri. After a couple of kilometres the path climbs steeply for a beautiful view back to Paleohora. You'll pass **Anydri Beach** and several inviting **coves** where people may be getting an all-over tan. Take a dip, because the path soon turns inland to pass over **Cape Flomes**. You'll walk along a plateau carpeted with brush that leads towards the coast and some breathtaking views over the Libyan Sea. About 10km into the hike you'll reach the Dorian site of **Lissos**, from where the path weaves through a pine forest before spilling out at Sougia.

Allow five to six hours for the nearly shadeless walk and take plenty of water, a hat and sunblock. From June to August it's best to start at sunrise in order to get to Sougia before the heat of the day. The boat back to Paleohora runs at around 6pm (check the schedule at www.anendyk.gr).

Villa Anna PENSION €
(📞 28103 46428; www.villaanna-paleochora.com; apt €50-75; ❄️📶) Run by the warm and welcoming Anna and set in a lovely shady garden bordered by tall poplars, these family-friendly apartments sleep up to five. There are cots, and swings and a sandpit in the garden, and the grounds are fenced.

✖️ Eating & Drinking

⭐ **To Skolio** CRETAN €
(📞 28230 83001; Anydri; dishes €5-13; ⊙ coffee from 9am, food noon-11pm daily Easter-Oct; 📶) Whether gorge walker or hire-car driver, do not miss the chance to dine at wonderful To Skolio, about 5km east of Paleohora. The converted red-and-white schoolhouse has cheerily painted tables on a tree-shaded cliff-side terrace with views out to sea. The daily-changing chalkboard menu of mezedhes (small dishes) incorporates the best local produce.

Third Eye VEGETARIAN €
(📞 6986793504, 28230 41234; https://third eye-paleochora.info; mains €6-9; ⊙1-10pm; 📶🍴) A local institution and community gathering spot since 1990, the Third Eye knew what to do with beetroot, quinoa and hummus long before meatless fare went mainstream. The globally inspired menu features delicious salads, rotating mains, and snacks such as a juicy portobello burger and caramelised-onion *fava* dip with bread. Sit on the streetside patio or in the tranquil garden.

⭐ **Monika's Garden Wine Bar** WINE BAR
(📞 28230 41150; www.facebook.com/monikas-garden; Kondekaki; ⊙6pm-1am Apr-Oct) One of the best spots for a drink in town, this attractive, modern wine bar with a delightful garden courtyard features more than 40 top-quality wines by the glass, all from Crete. Drop in for a tipple paired with snacks such as cheese platters and traditional *kalitsounia* (filled pastries).

ℹ️ Information

There's a couple of ATMs on the main drag, Eleftheriou Venizelou.

ℹ️ Getting There & Away

KTEL (📞 28230 41914; www.e-ktel.com; Eleftherios Venizelos) runs four daily buses to Hania (€8.30, 1¾ hours) and one bus daily except Sunday at 6.15am to Omalos (€7, one hour) for Samaria Gorge. Buses also stop in Sougia and, on request, at the Agia Irini Gorge trailhead. There are also Elafonisi-bound buses (€5.50, one hour).
Paleochora Taxi (📞 6979594667, 28230 41128; www.paleochora-taxi.com; ⊙7.30am-10pm) This professional outfit runs shuttle buses to the trailheads for Agia Irini (€19 per person) and Samaria Gorges (€25 per person including the boat ticket for the return) three times a week, departing at 7.30am.

Elafonisi Ελαφονήσι

Tucked into Crete's southwestern corner, **Elafonisi** (2 sunbeds & umbrella €9, umbrella only €3) is a symphony of fine pink-white sand, turquoise water and gentle rose dunes looks like a magical dreamscape. As the water swirls across the sands, rainbows shimmer across its surface. Off Elafonisi's long, wide strand lies Elafonisi Islet, occasionally connected by a thin, sandy isthmus, which creates a lovely double beach; otherwise, it's easily reached by wading through 50m of knee-deep water.

Elafonisi Islet is marked by low dunes and a string of semisecluded coves that attract a sprinkling of naturists. Walk the length of the beach and up to its high point for mind-blowing views of the beaches, sea and raw mountainscape. The area is part of EU environmental-protection program Natura 2000.

Alas, this natural gem is less than idyllic in high summer, when hundreds of umbrellas and sunbeds clog the sand (dash out to the island, where you can find peace). The invasion puts enormous pressure on this delicate ecosystem and on the minimal infrastructure, especially the toilets (€0.50). Come early or late in the day; better yet, stay overnight to truly sample Elafonisi's magic. Outside high season, when there's no public transport to the beach and very few tours, you may have it all to yourself. There are a few snack bars and stores at the beach entrance.

Elafonisi is about 75km southwest of Hania town – reckon on 1½ to two hours for the nonstop drive.

From Paleohora, one boat (€10, one hour) and one bus (€5.50, one hour) make a daily trip out here from June to September. There's also one daily bus from Hania (€11, 2¼ hours) via Kissamos (Kastelli; €6.90, 1¼ hours) from June to September.

LASITHI PROVINCE

Crete's easternmost region is home to the island's top resorts: Agios Nikolaos smoulders with cosmopolitan cool, while just around the bay, Elounda tiptoes between luxe and relaxed. Paradoxically, this is also the wildest region, with the richest biodiversity and the least trampled ranges; it's so rugged in places that you half expect Pan to emerge, pipes in hand, from the meadows.

For the wanderer in search of adventure and gastro delights, Lasithi ticks all the boxes: cyclists head up to misty Lasithi Plateau, trekkers tackle dramatic canyons such as the famous Zakros Gorge, and foodies enjoy some of Crete's finest tavernas and restaurants. Then there are attractions like the historic monastery of Toplou, Vaï's palm-lined beach, and scores of towns and villages that maintain a rich undertow of Cretan history and spirit. And let's not forget Lasithi's rich ancient history, with Minoan and Dorian sites to explore in numerous places.

Agios Nikolaos
Άγιος Νικόλαος

POP 12,000

Lasithi's capital, Agios Nikolaos has an enviable location on hilly terrain overlooking the sensuously curving Bay of Mirabello. There's a strong local character to Agios Nikolaos that imbues it with charismatic, low-key flair. A narrow channel separates the small harbour from the circular Voulismeni Lake, whose shore is lined with cafes and restaurants.

In the daytime the city beaches, while not particularly large or pretty, lend themselves to a few hours of relaxing and taking a dip in the sea. There's also some decent shopping in the pedestrianised lane above the lake.

Agios Nikolaos truly comes into its own at night, when a lively ambience descends on the lake, harbour and beaches, and loungebars fill with stylish young Greeks and holidaymakers from the nearby resorts.

Beaches

The most central beaches are sandy **Ammos** (Map p330) and **Kytroplatia** (Map p330), but both are small and get crowded. Let your feet take you 1km north and south respectively to tree-backed **Ammoudi** and **Almyros** for longer stretches of finer sand to spread your towel. Drawing mostly a local crowd is small, pebbly **Gargadoros**, just before Almyros. All beaches have umbrellas and sun chairs for rent.

🏃 Activities

Sail Crete   BOATING
(☑ 6937605600, 28410 24376; www.sailcrete.com; Minos Beach Art Hotel, Agios Nikolaos-Vrouchas Rd; half/full day incl snacks & drinks €900/1300) This sailing-charter outfit arranges private half- and full-day cruises to Spinalonga Island and beyond aboard the *General,* a handsome 14m catamaran, and the 12m *Jaquelina* yacht. Boats depart from the Pelagos Dive Centre (p329) at Minos Beach Art Hotel. Bring a swimsuit and towels for a cooling dip during the cruise.

Creta's Happy Divers   DIVING
(☑ 28410 82546; www.happydivers.gr; Akti Koundourou 23; boat dive €50) In business since 1989, Happy Divers has a wealth of experience and knows local sites inside out. Rates include all equipment. Also offers PADI certification courses from open water to dive master.

SPINALONGA ISLAND

Spinalonga Island (Νήσος Σπιναλόγκα; ☑ 28410 22462; adult/concession €8/4; ☺ 9am-6pm) became a leper colony in 1903 and catapulted into pop-cultural consciousness thanks to Victoria Hislop's 2005 bestselling novel *The Island* and the subsequent Greek TV series spin-off *To Nisi*. Boats departing from Elounda, Plaka and Agios Nikolaos drop visitors at Dante's Gate, the 20m-long tunnel through which patients arrived. From here, a 1km trail takes you past such 'sights' (mostly ruined) as a church, the disinfection room, the hospital and the cemetery.

Before it became a leper colony the island was a stronghold of the Venetians, who built a massive fortress in 1579 to protect the bays of Elounda and Mirabello. In 1715 the island fell under Ottoman control. Spinalonga's isolated location off the northern tip of the Spinalonga Peninsula made it a good leprosy quarantine zone. Also known as Hansen's Disease, the condition causes skin lesions, nerve damage and muscle weakness and has been around since ancient times. As many as 1000 Greeks were quarantined on Spinalonga, initially in squalid and miserable conditions. This changed in 1936 with the arrival of Epaminondas Remoundakis, a law student who contracted leprosy at the age of 21, and who fought passionately for better medical care and infrastructure on the island. A cure for leprosy was finally discovered in 1948 and the last person left Spinalonga in 1957.

Thanks to Hislop's tale about her own family's connection to the island, interest in Spinalonga has skyrocketed and you're unlikely to feel lonely during your visit.

Ferries operated by local boat cooperatives depart half-hourly from Elounda (€12) and Plaka (€8), giving you as much time on the island as you need. From Agios Nikolaos, Nostos Cruises runs one daily excursion boat.

Nostos Cruises BOATING
(Map p330; ☑ 28410 22819; www.nostoscruises.com; Rousou Koundourou 30; trips to Spinalonga with/without barbecue €25/16; ☺ 8am-9pm) Nostos Cruises runs 4½-hour boat trips to Spinalonga Island (p329), including a swim at Kolokytha Beach, from the harbour in Agios Nikolaos on large vessels with two bars and a restaurant. Another version of this trip includes a barbecue on the beach. Fishing trips are also possible.

Pelagos Dive Centre DIVING
(☑ 28410 24376, 6937605600; http://dive-crete.com; Minos Beach Art Hotel, Agios Nikolaos-Vrouchas Rd; dives incl equipment from €60, night dives €80; ☺ Apr-Nov) Just north of town, this well-established PADI centre offers dives at all levels as well as PADI courses and introductory dives for kids. It's part of the Minos Beach Art Hotel but has its own entrance in the northern section of the compound. Boat hire is also available.

🛏 Sleeping

Pension Mylos PENSION €
(Map p330; ☑ 28410 23783; http://pensionmylos.com; Sarolidi 24; s/d/tr €47/55/67; ☺ ❄ 🛜 🐾) At these prices, you know you're not getting the Ritz, but behind the faded facade lie surpris-ingly welcoming, though wee, rooms with bedside lamps, shiny en suites, seaward balconies and quality mattresses. The charming owner truly delivers on her tagline of 'home from home'. Fridge, TV and coffee-making service, too. Wi-fi in public areas only.

Pergola Hotel HOTEL €
(Map p330; ☑ 28410 28152; http://pergola-hotel.agios-nikolaos-crete.hotel-crete.net; Sarolidi 20; s/d/apt €32/38/65; ☺ Apr-Oct; ❄ ❄ 🛜) Though not of recent vintage, this low-key guesthouse is an excellent base of operation whose owners get an A+ for charm. Lovingly spruced-up units range from singles to family apartments with kitchen; the nicest sport four-poster beds and balconies from where you can wave at passing ships. Optional breakfast is €5.

Hotel Creta APARTMENT €€
(Map p330; ☑ 28410 28893; www.agiosnikolaos-hotels.gr; Sarolidi 22; apt €70-90; ☺ late Apr-Sep; ❄ ❄ 🛜) These 23 breezy and good-value self-catering studios and apartments sleeping two to four are in a quiet location, yet just a few minutes' walk from the harbour. All have balconies, but only units on the upper floors face the sparkling bay. There's a lift, as well as limited parking in the surrounding streets. Optional breakfast is €8.

Agios Nikolaos

Agios Nikolaos

🏃 Activities, Courses & Tours
1 Ammos Beach	A4
2 Kytroplatia Beach	D3
3 Nostos Cruises	D2

🛏 Sleeping
4 Hotel Creta	D3
5 Pension Mylos	D3
6 Pergola Hotel	D3

🍴 Eating
7 Ble Katsarolakia	C2
8 Creta Embassy	C2
9 Pelagos	C2
10 Portes	A4

🍸 Drinking & Nightlife
11 Arodo Cafe	B1
12 Bajamar	D2
13 Yanni's Rock Bar	D2

Minos Beach Art Hotel RESORT €€€
(📞 28410 22345; www.minosbeach.com; Agios Nikolaos-Vrouchas Rd; r incl breakfast from €500; ☺ Apr-Oct; 🅿 ✴ 🐾 🏊) Privacy, luxury and tranquillity are taken seriously in this sprawling resort in a superb waterfront location just north of town. Gardens dotted with conversation-sparking art lead to white-cube bungalows and villas kitted out in comfy but minimalist style. Some have private pools; the most coveted front the sea. Four restaurants, three bars, a gym and a spa invite lingering.

🍴 Eating

Creta Embassy GREEK €
(Map p330; 📞 28410 83153; www.cretaembassy. com; Kondylaki; mains €7-10; ☺ noon-late; ✴) Eclectic curios, wooden furniture and a fairytale garden make this traditional restaurant a few steps from the lake as welcoming as a hug from an old friend. Lamb *kleftiko* (slow oven-baked), veal with lemon, casseroles, and calamari with mouthwatering olives are among the menu stars.

★ **Pelagos** SEAFOOD €€
(Map p330; ☑28410 25737; Stratigou Koraka 11; mains €9-25; ☺noon-midnight Apr-Oct; 🐾) Pelagos is not for the indecisive. First you must choose whether to sit in the elegantly rustic historic house or in the romantic garden with colourful furniture and wall fountain. Tough one but perhaps not as tough as deciding whether to feast on fresh fish, grilled meats, inventive salads or homemade pastas. If in doubt, go for the seafood pasta.

Portes CRETAN €€
(Map p330; ☑28410 28489; Anapafseos 2; mezedhes €2.50-7.50; ☺12.30pm-1am; ▩) Conversation flows as freely as the excellent house wine at this garage-sized taverna, where wooden doors, all evocatively weathered and cheerfully painted, form part of the charming backdrop to home-cooked mezedhes (appetisers or small plates). Menu stars include a soulful rabbit *stifadho* (stew cooked with onions in a tomato puree) with plums and figs, and chicken with peppers and feta.

Ble Katsarolakia GREEK €€
(Map p330; ☑28410 21955; www.blekatsarolakia. gr; Akti Koundourou 8; mains €7-16; ☺noon-1am; ▩🐾✎) Enjoying great views of the harbour, this effervescent restaurant, with its modern decor of exposed stone, turquoise walls and white-wood floors, offers a contemporary take on Greek cuisine, serving up tzatziki, halloumi, souvlaki, octopus and much more. It's packed with young Greeks and deservedly so. Take the lift to the top floor.

🍸 **Drinking & Nightlife**

The buzziest party strip is along car-free Akti Koundourou east of the harbour, whose see-and-be-seen lounge bars are busy from midmorning until the wee hours. Akti Koundourou continues north of the harbour, where a few grittier watering holes lure more low-key punters.

Toedeledokie BAR
(☑28410 25537; www.toedeledokiecafe-bar.com; Akti Koundourou 19; ☺9am-late; 🐾) Dutch for 'cheerio', Toedeledokie is the brainchild of Dutch artist Lucia, who supplies killer coffee, creamy milkshakes and creative toasties all day long below cheerful umbrellas on the waterfront terrace. At night, make new friends over cold beers and finely crafted cocktails and see if you can coax Lucia into divulging tips on the area's 'secret' destinations.

Bajamar BAR
(Map p330; ☑6973366035; Sarolidi 1; ☺9am-2am or later) The most stylish among the harbour-front bars, Bajamar is a mellow daytime port of call for coffee, juices and snacks but is buzziest after 11pm, when the cocktails are flowing and a DJ showers shiny happy people with a high-energy mix of Latin, funk and house.

Arodo Cafe BAR
(Map p330; ☑28410 89895; www.facebook.com/pg/arodocoffeebeerwine; Akti Koundourou 6; ☺11am-2am; 🐾) This alt-flavoured lair buzzes with the conversation of earnest boho locals and offers a cocktail of cool tunes, a sea-facing terrace, and an eclectic selection of beer and wine. Located at the corner of Kantanoleontos. The entrance is up the steep stairs. Also serves breakfast and snacks.

Yanni's Rock Bar BAR
(Map p330; Akti Koundourou 1; ☺10pm-5am) The clientele is chatty, the rock music thunderous and the beer ice cold at this funky haunt that's rocked the waterfront since 1983, making it the town's oldest music bar. Its walls peppered with old Brando and Stallone photos, Yanni's oozes atmosphere from every nook and cranny and is a night owl's delight.

ℹ **Information**

General Hospital (☑28413 43000; cnr Knosou & Paleologou; ☺24hr) OK for broken bones and X-rays, but for anything more serious you'll need to head to Iraklio.

Municipal Tourist Office (Map p330; ☑28410 22357; www.agiosnikolaoscrete.com; Akti Koundourou 21; ☺9am-5pm Mon-Sat Apr-Nov, extended hours Jul & Aug; 🐾) Has helpful staff, free maps of the city and surrounds, and free bike rentals.

Tourist Police (☑28410 91409, emergency 171; Erythrou Stavrou 49)

ℹ **Getting There & Away**

Bus Station (☑28410 22234; Epimenidou 59) From the main bus station, about 1.5km north of the city centre, buses leave for Ierapetra (€4.10, one hour, nine daily), Iraklio (€7.70, 1½ hours, 22 daily), Kritsa (€1.80, 30 minutes, six daily), Sitia (€8.30, 1½ hours, six daily) and other destinations.

The most central **taxi rank** (Map p330; Paleologou) is behind the tourist office down by the lake. Typical fares are €14 for Elounda, €21 for Plaka, €14 for Kritsa and €20 for Ancient Lato. There are additional ranks on Plateia Venizelou and at the main bus station.

CRETE AGIOS NIKOLAOS

Around Agios Nikolaos

Elounda   Ελούντα

POP 2200

Although surrounded by some of Crete's most luxurious resorts, Elounda retains a charming down-to-earth feel. Salty fishing craft bob in its little harbour, where you can board a boat to Spinalonga, a former leper colony and the area's biggest tourist attraction. Attractive shops, bars and tavernas wrap around the harbour and continue north along the sandy municipal beach and south along a paved waterfront promenade. Offshore lies the rugged Spinalonga Peninsula, linked to the mainland by a narrow causeway and home to ancient ruins, beaches and hiking trails.

🏃 Activities

The crystalline sea around Elounda offers excellent diving, with around 20 sites ready to be explored. Make finny friends on expeditions run by the **Blue Dolphin Diving Centre** (☑6955897711, 28410 41802; www.dive-bluedolphin.com; Ellinika; dive incl equipment €55, open-water course €390), professional and experienced PADI centre based at the Hotel Aquila Elounda Village in Ellinika, about 3.5km south of Elounda.

🛌 Sleeping

Dolphins Apartments   APARTMENT €
(☑28410 41641; http://dolphins.elounda-crete. hotel-crete.net; Papandreou 51; apt €50; [P][❄][🛜]) These six one-bedroom apartments with pleasingly rustic furniture and tile floors pack a lot of features into a compact frame, including a kitchenette with microwave and a furnished balcony (with neat dolphin motif) overlooking the sea. It's a five-minute stroll into town along the waterfront promenade.

Corali Studios & Portobello Apartments   APARTMENT €
(☑28410 41712; www.coralistudios.com; Akti Poseidonos; apt €45-75; [P][❄][🛜][🏊]) Immaculately kept Corali and Portobello sit side by side amid flower-festooned gardens and overlooking the beach. The 35 stucco-walled studios and apartments come with balcony, kitchenette and wooden furniture painted cheerful shades of blue. All except the economy units have a sea view. Catch some rays by the good-size pool with snack bar.

Elounda Heights   HOTEL €€
(☑6932385337; www.eloundaheights.com; Emmanouil Pouli; apt €85-115; ⊘late Apr-Oct; [P][❄][🛜][🏊]) This hilltop hideaway run by a charming family is a class act all around. Swoon-worthy bay views unfold from your sunny studio or apartment with terrace, thoughtfully equipped kitchenette and crisp decor picking up the shades of the sea. A garden bursting with roses and oleander wraps around the units and the pool, where days start with a lavish breakfast.

Home-cooked dinners are available in the main house. No children permitted.

🍴 Eating & Drinking

Hope   CRETAN €€
(To Rakadiko Tou Kamari; ☑6972295150; Mavrikiano; mains €6-18; ⊘noon-11.30pm) Clinging to a steep hillside in the ancient hamlet of Mavrikiano above Elounda, Hope has been a local fixture since 1938. The terrace where fishermen once gathered nightly to suss out the next day's weather is now packed with people getting giddy on wine, raki, homemade mezedhes, succulent lamb chops and the stupendous bay view.

It's run by a charismatic couple, Dimitris and Amalia, with respect for the past *and* modern nutritional needs. If you're driving, the turnoff is about 600m north of Elounda's main square.

Okeanis   MEDITERRANEAN €€
(☑28410 44404; Akti Poseidonos 7; mains €8.50-14; ⊘11.30am-4pm & 6-11pm Apr-Oct) At Okeanis, the decor, menu and service blend as perfectly as the rich oven-baked lamb with garlic and sweet wine that's a top menu pick, alongside chef Adonis' handmade stuffed ravioli and tortellini. It's all served in an elegant yet relaxed loft-style al fresco space with white furniture and leafy plants.

Ergospasio   GREEK €€€
(☑28410 42082; www.facebook.com/pg/ergospasio; Akti Olountos 5; mains €15-23; ⊘noon-midnight Apr-Oct) A design feast in a converted carob factory with rave-worthy food to match. Count the fish in the sea from tables lined up along – and above – the waterfront while savouring market-fresh and skilfully executed Greek faves. If you're here for dinner, try lamb or chicken slow-roasted in the custom-designed *antikristo* spit grill. Also a great anytime spot for coffee or cocktails.

★ **Beeraki** PUB

(☑ 28410 42785; Mavrikiano; ⊙ 11am-midnight or later May-Oct) Well worth the uphill walk to the ancient village of Mavrikiano, this adorable drinking den does a roaring trade in bottled craft beers, quality local wines and expertly prepared cocktails. There's a small menu of elevated pub grub to keep your brain balanced so that you can enjoy the panoramic sea views just a little longer.

ℹ Getting There & Away

Up to 14 buses daily shuttle between Agios Nikolaos and Elounda (€1.90, 20 minutes). The **bus stop** (Plateia Elountas) is on the main square, where you can buy tickets at the kiosk next to Nikos Taverna.

The **taxi stand** (☑ 28410 41151; Plateia Elounda) is also on the square. The fare to Agios Nikolaos is €14 and to Plaka €8.

Cars, motorcycles and scooters can be hired at **Olous Travel** (☑ 28410 41324; www.olous-travel.gr; Plateia Elountas; ⊙ 9am-11pm) and **Elounda Travel** (☑ 28410 41800; www.eloundatravel.gr; Sfakianaki 3; car per day/week from €45/160; ⊙ 8am-9pm), both with offices on, you guessed it, the main square, which also serves as a (fee-based) car park.

Plaka Πλάκα

POP 100

Wind-pounded Plaka, 5km north of Elounda, is a bijou village of attractive boutiques, a narrow pebble beach and a string of cosy tavernas hugging the waterfront. It's also the best jumping-off point for Spinalonga Island (p329). A boat co-op makes the 10-minute trip to the island twice hourly.

Kritsa Κριτσά

POP 2000

Clinging to the craggy foothills of the Dikti range, Kritsa is one of the oldest and prettiest mountain villages in eastern Crete. The upper village with its web of narrow, car-free lanes is especially atmospheric. Along the main strip, Kritsotopoulas, you'll find charming cafes, shops slinging local products and surprisingly sophisticated boutiques. Away from the village, rugged Kritsa Gorge, the romantic ruins of Ancient Lato and the church of Panagia Kera, with its stunning Byzantine frescoes, are all worth your attention.

Note that in season Kritsa is often clogged with tour buses and day trippers, so come early or late in the day to avoid the worst crowds.

◉ Sights

★ **Church of Panagia Kera** CHURCH

(☑ 28410 51806; Eparchiotiki Odos Agios Nikolaos-Prinas; adult/concession €2/1; ⊙ 8.30am-4pm Wed-Mon; ℗) This tiny triple-aisled church on the main road shelters Crete's best-preserved Byzantine frescoes. The oldest in the central nave (13th century) depict scenes surrounding the life of Christ, including the Ascension in the apse, the four Gospel scenes (Presentation, Baptism, Raising of Lazarus and Entry into Jerusalem) in the dome and a superb Last Supper. The south aisle is dedicated to St Anne, mother of Mary, with depictions including her marriage and Mary's birth. The north aisle focuses on St Anthony.

The church is about 1km south of Krista – look for the parking area opposite the Paradise restaurant. After your visit, you can sit in the garden cafe and ponder it all.

★ **Ancient Lato** ARCHAEOLOGICAL SITE

(Λατώ; ☑ 28410 22462; http://odysseus.culture.gr; adult/concession €2/1; ⊙ 8.30am-4pm Wed-Mon) The fortified hilltop city state of Lato is one of Crete's best-preserved non-Minoan ancient sites and worth the trip for the rural serenity and stunning views down to the Bay of Mirabello alone. Founded by the Dorians in the 7th century BC, Lato reached its heyday in the 3rd century BC but was gradually abandoned. By the 2nd century AD its administrative centre had moved to its port in present-day Agios Nikolaos.

About 100m past the ticket gate, you enter the site via the **city gate**, from where a long, stepped street leads up to the **agora** (marketplace) past a wall with two towers, residences, and buildings that housed shops and workshops. At the top of the steps, as you approach the *agora*, you'll first come upon vestiges of a **stoa** (colonnaded portico). Immediately behind it is a rectangular temple where numerous 6th-century-BC figurines were unearthed. The deep hole to the left of the temple was Lato's public **cistern**. Behind it, a monumental staircase leads up to the **prytaneion** (administrative centre). At its centre, a hearth that burnt 24/7 was surrounded by stepped benches where the city leaders held their meetings.

South of the *agora*, climb up the slope to a terrace with another **sanctuary** fronted by a three-stepped **altar**. Views of the entire site are fabulous from here. Down below to your right (east) you can spot a **theatral area** that could seat about 350 spectators on stone benches cut into the rock and on an exedra (open portico with seats).

Nearchus, an admiral under Alexander the Great, is believed to hail from Lato, whose name derives from the goddess Leto. Legend has it that Leto's union with Zeus produced Artemis and Apollo.

There are no buses to Lato. The nearest stop is in Kritsa, from where it's a 3km walk north. The site is off the Kritsa–Lakonion Rd.

🏃 Activities

Kritsa Gorge, signposted off the road to Ancient Lato, is one of eastern Crete's most enchanting canyons. Flanked by steep cliffs, it follows a riverbed dotted with oak and olive trees and resplendent with spring wildflowers. Sturdy shoes and reasonable fitness are essential, since the trail is stony and requires occasional bouldering and the handling of metal rails and a rope.

There are two routes. The shorter one (about 5km) follows the canyon for about 2km before heading uphill; turn right and follow the trail paralleling the gorge below back to the parking area. The longer one (about 11km) continues to the village of Tapes. Along the way you will encounter fences put there by shepherds to keep the goat herd together. Be sure to close their gates again after passing through.

The hike can be done year-round except after heavy rain. Check in Kritsa before setting out.

🍽 Eating

Taverna Platanos (📞28410 51230; Kritsotopoulas; mains €6.50-9.50; ⏱10am-9pm) is a taverna-*kafeneio* (coffeehouse) halfway along Kritzotopoula, Platanos has a pleasant setting under a giant 200-year-old plane tree and vine canopy. The tasty menu revolves around grills, *mousakas* and *stifadho*.

ℹ Getting There & Away

Up to four buses on weekdays and three at weekends travel from Agios Nikolaos to Kritsa (€1.80). The **bus stop** (Olouf Palme) is in the centre of town. A taxi costs €14.

Mohlos Μόχλος
POP 100

At the end of a narrow road winding past massive open-cast quarries, tranquil Mohlos is an off-the-radar gem along Crete's north-

ern shore. In this pint-sized fishing village time moves as gently as the waves lapping the pebble-and-grey-sand beach. There's little to do but relax, soak up the peacefulness and enjoy a leisurely meal in one of the excellent waterfront cafes and tavernas.

In ancient times Mohlos was a thriving Early Minoan community, traces of which have been excavated on the small island that's now 200m offshore. If you want to visit, ask around in the village for someone to take you there in a boat. Swimmers should be wary of strong currents.

The oldest among several waterfront tavernas, **Ta Kochilia** (📞28430 94432; mains €5.50-17; ⏱10.30am-midnight; 🛜) has cooked up a storm for nearly a century and is still an excellent port of call for fanciers of fish and traditional Cretan dishes like spinach pies, lamb with artichokes, and oven-baked feta. Well-curated wine list, to boot. The restaurant section around the corner catches the evening sun.

ℹ Getting There & Away

There's no public transport to Mohlos. Buses between Sitia and Agios Nikolaos can drop you at the Mohlos turnoff, from where you'll need to hitch or walk the 6km down to the village.

Sitia Σητεία
POP 9900

Though not conventionally pretty, Sitia exudes an attractive vibe that stems from not having sold its soul to mass tourism. It's a slow-paced, friendly place where agriculture is the mainstay of the local economy.

In the tranquil old town above the fishing harbour, whitewashed buildings tumble down a hillside laced by steep staircases and accented by a ruined Venetian castle. Down below, tavernas and cafes line the bustling waterfront and wide promenade along Karamanli. A long, sandy beach skirts the bay to the east.

Many visitors use Sitia as launch pad for explorations of Vaï, Moni Toplou, Zakros and other remote destinations further east, although it's well worth spending a day or two in town.

👁 Sights

The **Sitia Archaeological Museum** (📞28430 23917; Piskokefalou; adult/concession €2/1; ⏱8.30am-4pm Wed-Mon) is a compact showcase of archaeological finds from eastern Crete spanning the arc from Neolithic to Roman times, with an emphasis on Minoan artefacts. Pride of place goes to the *Palekastro Kouros* – a statue carved from hippopotamus tusks that was once fully covered in gold leaf. Standout finds from the palace at Zakros include a wine press, a bronze saw and cult objects scorched by the fire that destroyed the palace.

🛏 Sleeping

Hotel El Greco
HOTEL €

(☑ 28430 23133; www.elgreco-sitia.gr; Arkadiou 13; d €50; ❄ 🛜 🛁) This old-school hotel has smart and impeccably clean rooms with tiled floors, nice but dated furniture, plasma TV, fridge and balcony (most with sea views). It's a good city hotel and a convenient base for short stays. A quality breakfast costs €5 per person.

★ Nereids Apartments
APARTMENT €€

(☑ 6944909834, 28430 26027; https://nereids.gr; Sitia-Palekastro Rd; studios €70-90; ☉ May-Oct; 🅿 ❄) One of the nicest properties in Sitia, this bungalow complex with studios and family apartments sits right across from the beach in a colourful garden brimming with jasmine and geranium. The nicest units have verandas facing the sea, although those at the back are quieter. The stylish lounge-bar serves breakfast, a mean burger, crisp salads and good cocktails.

🍴 Eating & Drinking

★ Mitsakakis
CAFE €

(☑ 28430 20200; Karamanli 6; galaktoboureko €2.70; ☉ 8am-midnight; ❄ 🛜 ♿) This cafe and pastry shop is a Sitian institution (open since 1965) and famous for its incredible sugar-rush-inducing *galaktoboureko* (custard-filled pastry), *loukoumadhes* (ball-shaped doughnuts) and *kataïfi* (angel-hair pastry). Sit on the seaside terrace or in the old-school cafe.

★ Rakadiko Oinodeion
CRETAN €

(☑ 28430 26166; El Venizelou 157; mezedhes €3.50-8, mains €7.50-13; ☉ 6pm-1am; ❄ 🛜) Tops among the waterfront tavernas, this rustic family place offers a recognisable array of Greek dishes, but it's the local seasonal specials that truly shine. Among these, anything with rabbit or goat gets top marks and is best paired with the local wine. Many ingredients, including the oil, bread and raki, are produced by the Garefalakis family itself.

Nouvelle Boutique
CAFE

(☑ 6972825942; El Venizelou 161; ☉ 9am-late; 🛜) This comfy-chic local fave with huge backlit bar and stone-walled interior is a top after-dark spot, when a youthful crowd invades for funky sounds, sweet and strong drinks, dancing and the occasional band. Also a nice place for a daytime chill session, with some of the best cappuccino in town.

ℹ Getting There & Away

AIR

Small **Sitia Municipal Airport** (JSH; ☑ 28430 24424) is about 1km north of the town centre and handles domestic flights to Athens, Alexandroupoli, Iraklio, Kassos and Rhodes as well as seasonal charter flights from Germany and Scandinavia. A taxi into town costs €6 to €8.

BOAT

Ferries dock about 1km north of the town centre. **Anek/Aegeon Pelagos Sea Lines** (☑ Hania 28210 24000; www.anek.gr) has service to Anafi (€20, eight hours), Chalki (€20, 8½ hours), Diafani (€18, six hours), Iraklio (€16, three hours), Karpathos (€19, 4½ hours), Kasos (€12, 2¾ hours), Milos (€26, 14¼ hours), Piraeus (€44, 21½ hours), Rhodes (€28, 10½ hours) and Santorini (€28, 10 hours) on a seasonally changing schedule. Prices quoted are for deckchair seating.

BUS

Connections from Sitia's **bus station** (☑ 28430 22272, 28102 46530; http://ktelherlas.gr; Sitia-Palekastro Rd; 🛜) include four buses daily to Ierapetra (€6.90, 1¾ hours), five buses to Iraklio (€16, three hours), and six to Agios Nikolaos (€8.30, 1¾ hours). Two buses leave for Zakros on Monday, Tuesday and Friday (€4.50, one hour). No services on Sunday.

Around Sitia

Moni Toplou

In splendid isolation on a windswept plateau, 15th-century fortified **Moni Toplou** (Μονή Τοπλού; ☑ 28430 61226; Toplou; €3; ☉ 8am-6pm Apr-Oct) is one of the most historically significant monasteries in Crete. Its defences were tested by everyone from pirates to crusading knights to the Turks. The church brims with superb icons, although the main magnet is the intricate *Lord Thou Art Great* icon by celebrated Cretan artist Ioannis Kornaros. It depicts scenes from the Old and New Testaments, including Noah's Ark, Jonah and the Whale, and Moses parting the Red Sea.

The name Toplou is derived from the Turkish word for cannon, which is what the monks used to defend themselves against pirates during Venetian times. The monastery was also repeatedly active in the cause of Cretan independence. Under the Turkish occupation a secret school operated on the premises, while during WWII resistance leaders ran an underground radio transmitter here. A small exhibit in the museum recalls this period with rifles, helmets and a field telephone. The adjacent main room displays engravings and icons.

Today the monastery is not only an attraction for fans of history, religion, art and architecture but also the largest landowner in the area and an active producer of award-winning wine and olive oil, which you can sample in a nearby tasting room (open 10.30am to 5pm Monday to Saturday).

Moni Toplou is about 15km east of Sitia. Buses can drop you at the junction of the Sitia–Palekastro road, from where you'll need to hitch or walk for 3.5km.

Vaï

The beach at Vaï (parking €2.50), 24km northeast of Sitia, is famous for its large grove of *Phoenix theophrasti* (Cretan date) palms. With calm, clear waters, it's one of the island's most popular strands and its tightly spaced rows of umbrellas and sunbeds often fill by 10am in July and August. Jet skis kick into gear shortly thereafter. Snack bars and a reasonably priced taverna provide refreshments. Two buses daily make the trip from Sitia (€3.30, one hour) between May and October.

Palekastro   Παλαίκαστρο

POP 1100

Palekastro (pah-leh-kas-tro) is an unpretentious farming village underpinned by low-key tourism. It lies in a rocky landscape interspersed with fields close to the beaches at Kouremenos (with Crete's best windsurfing), Hiona and Vaï. In the village you'll find an ATM, a petrol station and small markets.

About 1km east of town, about 150m south of Hiona Beach, is the archaeological site of Roussolakkos, where archaeologists are digging up a Minoan town and hoping for evidence of a major Minoan palace. This is where the *Palekastro Kouros* ivory figurine – now residing in the Archaeological Museum in Sitia – was found.

Eating

There are a number of earthy tavernas around the town square as well as two excellent fish restaurants overlooking Hiona Beach.

The **Hiona Taverna** (☑ 28430 61228; Hiona Beach; mains €15-25; ⊙ noon-11pm Apr-Oct; 🛜) is one of two top-ranked tavernas at the northern end of Hiona Beach, this more upscale contender in a stone house is usually filled with patrons lusting after the fresh fish and seafood, including a rich bouillabaisse-style soup called *kakavia*. Book ahead for a romantic table on the cliffs.

🛈 Getting There & Away

There are four buses per day from Sitia to Palekastro (€2.80, one hour). Buses stop in the central square.

Zakros & Kato Zakros
Ζάκρος & Κάτω Ζάκρος
POP 800

Zakros, 45km southeast of Sitia, is the starting point for the trail through Zakros Gorge. The small town has lodging, minimarkets, an ATM and a gas station but is otherwise a mere prelude to the coastal village of Kato Zakros. The 7km drive down a winding road is spectacular and delivers mesmerising views after every bend.

Shortly before reaching the village, you can see the huge jaw of Zakros Gorge breaching the cliffs in the distance. Look closely and you might also spot the ruins of the Minoan palace just up from Kato Zakros' pebbly, narrow beach and row of tavernas. Add to all this the isolated tranquillity and sense of peace, and you have the perfect recipe for escapism.

⊙ Sights & Activities

★**Zakros Palace**   ARCHAEOLOGICAL SITE
(☑ 28410 22462; Kato Zakros; adult/concession €6/3; ⊙ 8am-8pm May-Sep, to 3pm Oct-Apr) Ancient Zakros, the smallest of Crete's four Minoan palatial complexes, sat next to a harbour and was likely engaged in sea trade with the Middle East, as suggested by excavated elephant tusks and oxhide ingots. Like Knossos, Phaestos and Malia, Zakros centred on a courtyard flanked by royal apartments, shrines, ceremonial halls, storerooms and workshops. While the ruins are sparse, the remote setting makes it an attractive site to nose around. Information panels help spur your imagination.

★ Zakros Gorge HIKING

(Gorge of the Dead) Zakros Gorge is also known as the Gorge of the Dead because the Minoans used to bury their dead in the caves dotting the canyon walls. This easy-to-moderate walk starts just below Zakros village and follows a dry riverbed through a narrow and soaring canyon with a riot of vegetation and wild herbs before emerging close to Zakros Palace (p336) near the taverna-flanked beach of Kato Zakros.

There are two trailheads on the road to Kato Zakros. Budget about two hours to hike down from 'Entrance A' and 1½ hours from 'Entrance B'. There may still be water in the gorge until May – check locally. A taxi back to Zakros costs about €12.

The hike is part of the 12,000km-long E4 European Path, which kicks off in Tarifa (Spain) and ends in Larnaca (Cyprus).

🛏 Sleeping & Eating

Katerina Apartments APARTMENT €

(📱 6974656617, 28430 26893; www.kato-zakros.gr/_en/katerina.php; Kato Zakros; apt €50-70; ☉ Apr-Sep; 🅿 ⊕ 🛜) These four stone-built studios and maisonettes sleep up to four and enjoy a lovely garden setting in the hillside at Kato Zakros. The 800m walk to the beach takes you past the trailhead for Zakros Gorge (p337) and the Minoan palace ruins (p336). Units welcome you with family-style hominess, accented by the occasional lace doily, and a small jug of homemade raki.

★ Stella's Traditional Apartments APARTMENT €€

(📱 6976719461, 28430 23739; www.stelapts.com; Kato Zakros; studios €80-90; ☉ mid-Mar–mid-Nov; 🅿 ⊕ 🛜) Close to the mouth of Zakros Gorge, these charming self-contained studios are in a lovely garden setting and decorated with distinctive wooden furniture and other artefacts made by joint owner Elias Pagianidis. Perks range from hammocks under the trees to barbecues and an external kitchen with an honesty system for supplies. Rates include free breakfast provisions.

Elias and his wife, Stella, have excellent knowledge and experience of hiking trails in the area.

Akrogiali Taverna CRETAN €€

(📱 28430 26893; Kato Zakros; mains €6-19; ☉ 8am-midnight; 🛜) The food gods have been smiling upon Kato Zakros' oldest taverna, which does a brisk trade in fresh-off-the-boat fish and Cretan classics, all prepared with locally sourced ingredients, including oil made from the owner's trees. The cheerful blue-and-white furniture and the beachfront setting add two more notches to its appeal.

ℹ Getting There & Away

Buses from a central **stop** (📱 28102 45020; http://ktelherlas.gr; Eleftherias) link Zakros and Sitia twice on Monday, Tuesday and Friday (€4.50, one hour), continuing down to Kato Zakros in summer (June to September). A taxi from Sitia to Zakros costs about €50, while the fare between Zakros and Kato Zakros is €12. In summer there's usually one afternoon bus leaving Kato Zakros for Sitia Monday to Friday.

Ierapetra Ιεράπετρα

POP 16,150

Ierapetra is a laid-back seafront town and the commercial centre of southeastern Crete's substantial greenhouse-based agribusiness. Hot and dusty in summer, it offers a low-key, authentic Cretan experience and is also the jumping-off point for the semitropical Chrissi Island (p338) (also called Gaïdouronisi or Hrysi).

The city's grey-sand beaches are backed by tavernas and cafes where the nightlife is busy in summer. Though few visible signs remain, Ierapetra has an impressive history, with interludes as a Roman port and as a Venetian stronghold, as attested to by the harbour fortress. The narrow alleyways of the old quarter (Kato Mera) flash back to the Ottoman period.

👁 Sights & Activities

Ierapetra is the launch pad for day trips to Chrissi Island also known as Gaïdouronisi or Hrysi Island). There are usually a couple of departures in the morning that give you 4½ hours on the island before returning to Ierapetra in the late afternoon (€25).

Old Quarter AREA

(Kato Mera) Inland from the fortress is the labyrinthine old quarter, where you'll see a Turkish fountain, the restored **mosque** (Plateia Tzami) with its minaret, **Napoleon's house** and several churches, including **Agios Ioannis** (Katsanevaki) and **Agios Georgios** (Agiou Georgiou).

CHRISSI ISLAND

Ierapetra is the launch pad for boat trips to uninhabited **Chrissi Island** (Gaïdouronisi/Hrysi Island; ☑ 28420 20008; boat trip adult/child €25/12; ☺ mid-May–Oct). It is famous for its golden beaches, clear water shimmering in myriad shades of blue, cedar forest, traces of Minoan ruins, and Belegrina, a beach covered with a mountain of shells. There are usually a couple of morning boat departures that give you 4½ hours on the island. Tickets are sold online and by agents around town. Bring a picnic or buy refreshments on board. One company that will take you there is **Cretan Daily Cruises** (28420 20008, www. cretandailycruises.com boat trip adult/ child €25/12, mid-May–Oct)); their vessels carry 200-400 passengers.

Kales Fortress   FORTRESS

(Stratigou Samouil 10; ☺ 8am-3pm Tue-Sun) FREE Overlooking the fishing harbour, the crenellated Venetian fort dates from the 17th century but was built atop an older defensive structure reputedly built by Genoese pirates in the 13th century and destroyed by an earthquake and the Turks. There's not much to see inside, but it's fun to climb up to the ramparts and the single tower for grand views of the bay and the mountains.

🛏 Sleeping & Eating

★ Cretan Villa Hotel   HOTEL €

(☑ 28420 28522, 6973037671; www.cretan-villa.com; Lakerda 16; d €45-56; ❄ 🐾) A heavy wooden door gives way to a vine-shaded courtyard at this restful, friendly space that's a happy coupling of historic touches and mod cons. Beautiful rooms havestone walls, elegantly rustic furniture, stone-tiled showers, wood-beamed ceilings, small fridges and satellite TV. A central city hotel with country flair.

Coral Boutique Hotel   HOTEL €€

(☑ 28420 20444, 6977232766; www.coralhotel crete.gr; Plateia Eleftherias 19; d €57-86) A recent facelift has turned this breezy city hotel into a cocoon of relaxed sophistication, with ultra-comfy mattresses, an easy-on-the-eye palette of white and aqua tones, and accommodating staff. Breakfast is €7.50 extra but worth it.

Special   FAST FOOD €

(☑ 28420 27835; cnr Metaxaki 1 & Kothri; dishes €3.50-8; ☺ 10.30am-12.30am; ❄ 🐾) Special jazzes up Ierapetra's dining scene with quality fast food served in an upbeat, contemporary setting. The menu is a reminder of the simple goodness of charcoal-grilled souvlakia or well-prepared rotisserie *gyros* (chicken or pork), although the burgers, salads and sausages hold their own. Portions are big enough to share, and there's a kids' menu to boot.

★ Vira Potzi   CRETAN €€

(☑ 28420 28254; www.facebook.com/virapotzi; Stratigou Samouil 82; mains €7-14; ☺ noon-midnight Tue-Sun; ❄ 🐾 🐾) Next to the Kales Fortress (p338), this next-gen Cretan seaside tavern has an enticing menu packed with culinary twists such as grilled calamari with zucchini sticks and *fava* (bean dip) or the crowd-pleasing shrimp orzo-pasta pilaf. A classy place with nary a plastic picture menu in sight.

🍷 Drinking & Nightlife

Ierapetra has the most lively after-dark scene in the region. The waterfront tavernas often bustle until the wee hours, and if you want to bust a move on the dance floor, look for the latest music lairs in the streets behind the beachfront drag Stratigou Stamouil.

ℹ Getting There & Away

Ierapetra Bus Station (☑ 28420 28237; www. ktelherlas.gr; Lasthenous 28) KTEL operates up to eight buses per day to Iraklio (€12, 2½ hours) via Agios Nikolaos (€4.10, one hour), four to Sitia (€6.90, 1½ hours) and five to Myrtos (€2.40, 30 minutes).

Central Taxi Stand (☑ 28420 26600; cnr Kothri & Plateia Kanoupaki) The central taxi stand with fixed fares posted on a board is outside the town hall. Sample fares: Iraklio (€128), Agios Nikolaos (€50), Sitia (€83) and Myrtos (€20).

Myrtos   Μύρτος

POP 600

Tiny Myrtos, 14km west of Ierapetra, is a positively delightful lived-in community: cheerful, trim and fringed by an apron of grey pebble-and-sand beach and bright-blue water. It's also an excellent base for mountain and canyon hikes and even has a couple of minor Minoan sites. All these assets attract a devoted clientele that also cherishes its slow boho pulse, flower-festooned guesthouses, and cluster of tavernas in the village and along its languid seafront. In short, it's a traveller's jewel, the perfect antidote to noise, haste and mass tourism.

🛏 Sleeping & Eating

★ Big Blue
APARTMENT €€

(📞 28420 51094; www.big-blue.gr; studios €56-98; ❄ 📶) Modern amenities meet traditional Greece in these breezy sea-facing and self-catering studios decorated with plenty of style and imagination. Apartment 'Blue Eye', for instance, has a neat display of evil eyes (for good luck); in fact, every room is different. Private decks have expansive views, and the fragrant front garden is a good spot for sundowners.

O Platanos
CRETAN €€

(mains €7-13.50; ⏱ 11am-late Apr-Oct; 📶 🍴) Beneath a giant plane tree on the main street, Platanos is a focus of village social life and has live music on many summer evenings. Feast on reliable Cretan staples such as rabbit *stifadho* (stew cooked with onions in a tomato puree), or try such homey specials as the 'pita pizza' or grandma's meatballs with yoghurt sauce.

La Sera
MEDITERRANEAN €€

(📞 28420 51261; mains €8-16; ⏱ 5pm-midnight Apr-Oct; 📶) Soft lighting, fine wine and delicious food are the hallmarks of a romantic night out in this al fresco–only lair wedged into an alley off the main drag. The compact menu includes farm-fresh salads, grilled seafood, and tender lamb chops from the local butcher, alongside wine from the renowned Lyrarakis winery (p296) in Alagni.

ℹ Getting There & Away

There are five buses daily from Ierapetra (€2.40, 30 minutes). A taxi costs about €20.

Lasithi Plateau

The tranquil Lasithi Plateau, 900m above sea level (bring a sweater even in summer), is a windswept expanse of green fields interspersed with almond trees and orchards. Offering a sense of secluded rural Crete, it's really more a plain than a plateau, sitting as it does in a huge depression amid the rock-studded mountains of the Dikti range. It's sparsely inhabited, with just a few villages dotted along the periphery. Most people visit on a day trip to Psychro, the gateway to the Dikteon Cave, where – so the myth goes – Zeus was born and hidden as an infant to protect him from his voracious father.

Lasithi must have been a stunning sight in the 17th century, when it was dotted with some 20,000 **windmills** with white-canvas sails, put up by the Venetians for irrigation purposes. The skeletal few that remain are an iconic (and much-photographed) sight.

According to legend, Rhea hid in the **Dikteon Cave** (Cave of Psychro; 📞 28410 22462; http://odysseus.culture.gr; Psychro; adult/concession €6/3; ⏱ 8am-8pm Apr-Oct, to 3pm Nov-Mar) to give birth to Zeus, far from the clutches of his offspring-gobbling father, Cronos. A slick and vertiginous staircase corkscrews into the damp dark, passing overhanging stalactites, ethereal formations and a lake. From Psychro it's a steep 800m walk to the cave entrance, via a rocky but shaded natural trail or the sunny paved path starting near the car park.

The most famous formation is a stalactite nicknamed 'the mantle of Zeus' in a chamber on the right-hand side off the larger hall. Offerings found in the cave, including daggers, arrowheads, figures and double axes, indicate that it was a place of cult worship from Minoan to Roman times. Key items are now on display at the Archaeological Museum (p285) in Iraklio.

ℹ Getting There & Away

The Lasithi Plateau is not served by public buses. A taxi to Tzermiado or Psychro costs about €60 from Iraklio and €50 from Agios Nikolaos. To cut costs, take a bus to Malia and a taxi from there (about €25).

Dodecanese

Best Places to Eat

➜ Yevsea (p384)

➜ To Tsipouradiko Mas (p412)

➜ Taverna Mylos (p407)

➜ Marco Polo Cafe (p351)

➜ Bakaliko with Tsipouro (p409)

➜ Tholos (p376)

Best Places to Stay

➜ Mediterraneo (p373)

➜ Thea Apartments (p376)

➜ Kallichoron Art Boutique Hotel (p397)

➜ Aretanassa Hotel (p362)

➜ To Archontiko Angelou (p409)

➜ Marco Polo Mansion (p350)

Why Go?

Ever pined for the old Greece, where timeless islands beckon modern-day adventurers just as they did Odysseus and Alexander? Enter the far-flung Dodecanese archipelago, curving through the southeastern Aegean parallel to the ever-visible shoreline of Turkey. The footprints of everyone from Greeks and Romans to crusading medieval knights, and Byzantine and Ottoman potentates to 20th-century Italian bureaucrats, are found here. Beyond better-known Rhodes and Kos, enigmatic islands beg to be explored.

Hikers and naturalists flock to Tilos, while climbers scale the limestone cliffs in Kalymnos. Aesthetes adore the neoclassical mansions of Symi, Halki and Kastellorizo, and kitesurfers blow in to Karpathos for its legendary winds. Elsewhere around the Dodecanese, divers can explore underwater caves and ancient wrecks, archaeologists and history buffs let their imaginations loose on a bevy of ancient sites, while sybarites worship Helios on myriad beaches, far from the package crowds.

When to Go
Rhodes

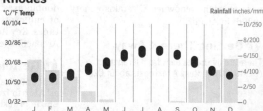

May Prices are low, few tourists are around and the sea is warming up.

Jul & Aug Hot weather, but peak season for accommodation and visitors – book ahead.

Sep & Oct Great time to come: low prices, warm seas and perfect hiking weather.

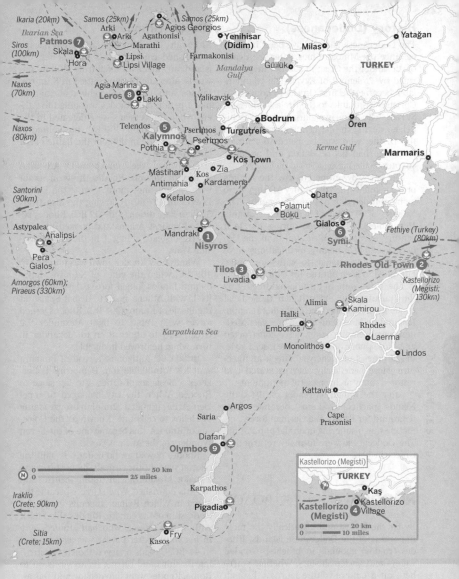

Dodecanese Highlights

1 **Nisyros** (p384) Entering its fabled volcano, home to an imprisoned Titan.

2 **Rhodes Old Town** (p345) Wandering beneath Byzantine arches and along ancient cobbled alleyways.

3 **Tilos** (p381) Hiking or birdwatching on this postcard-perfect island.

4 **Kastellorizo** (p371) Gasping in awe at the colour in the most dramatic of blue caves in the Mediterranean.

5 **Kalymnos** (p403) Testing your mettle diving for wrecks or climbing limestone cliffs.

6 **Symi** (p374) Feeling your pulse quicken as your boat pulls into the gorgeous Italianate harbour.

7 **Patmos** (p413) Making a pilgrimage to where St John experienced his 'Revelations'.

8 **Leros** (p408) Visiting Greece's most 'modern' town of Lakki.

9 **Olymbos** (p368) Following the winding road up to this timeless mountaintop village on Karpathos.

History (Dodecanese)

The Dodecanese islands have been inhabited since pre-Minoan times. After the death of Alexander the Great in 323 BC, they were ruled by Ptolemy I of Egypt. The islanders later became the first Greeks to convert to Christianity, thanks to the tireless efforts of St Paul, who made two journeys to the archipelago during the 1st century, and St John the Divine, who was banished to Patmos, where he had his revelation and added a chapter to the Bible.

The early Byzantine era saw the islands prosper, but by the 7th century AD they were being plundered by a string of invaders. The Knights of St John of Jerusalem (Knights Hospitaller), who arrived during the 14th century, eventually ruled almost all the Dodecanese. Their mighty fortifications have proved strong enough to withstand time, but failed to keep out the Turks in 1522.

The Turks were in turn ousted in 1912 by the Italians, who made Italian the official language and banned the Orthodox religion. Inspired by Mussolini's vision of a vast Mediterranean empire, they also constructed grandiose public buildings in the fascist style, the antithesis of archetypal Greek architecture. More beneficially, they excavated and restored many archaeological monuments.

After the Italian surrender of 1943, the islands (particularly Leros) became a battleground for British and German forces, inflicting much suffering upon the population. The Dodecanese were formally returned to Greece in 1947.

RHODES ΡΟΔΟΣ

POP 115,500

By far the largest and historically the most important of the Dodecanese islands, Rhodes (ro-dos) abounds in beaches, wooded valleys and ancient history. Whether you're here on a culture-vulture journey through past civilisations, or simply for some laid-back beach time, buzzing nightlife, or diving in crystal-clear waters, it's all here. The atmospheric Old Town of Rhodes is a maze of cobbled streets that will spirit you back to the days of the Byzantine Empire and beyond. Further south is the picture-perfect town of Lindos. While both Lindos and Rhodes Old Town get very crowded in summer, Rhodes is large enough to allow plenty of room to breathe that pure Aegean air.

History (Rhodes)

Although the Minoans and Mycenaeans established early outposts on Rhodes, the island only made itself felt from 1100 BC onwards, after the Dorians settled in Kamiros, Ialysos and Lindos. Switching allegiances like a pendulum, Rhodes was allied to Athens when the Persians were defeated in the Battle of Marathon (490 BC), but shifted to the Persian side in time for the Battle of Salamis (480 BC).

Following the unexpected Athenian victory at Salamis, Rhodes threw in its lot with Athens once more, joining the Delian League in 477 BC. Following the disastrous Sicilian Expedition (416–412 BC), Rhodes revolted against Athens and hooked up with Sparta instead, aiding it in the Peloponnesian Wars.

What's now Rhodes Town was founded in 408 BC, when the cities of Kamiros, Ialysos and Lindos joined forces. After aligning itself with Athens again to defeat Sparta at the Battle of Knidos (394 BC), Rhodes joined forces with Persia to fight Alexander the Great, only to attach itself to Alexander in turn when he proved invincible.

In 305 BC Antigonus, a rival of Ptolemy, sent his formidable son, Demetrius Poliorketes – Besieger of Cities – to lay siege to Rhodes. When the city managed to repel Demetrius, it built a 32m-high bronze statue of Helios to celebrate. Known as the Colossus of Rhodes, this became one of the Seven Wonders of the Ancient World.

Rhodes now knew no bounds. It built the biggest navy in the Aegean, its port became a major Mediterranean trading centre, and the arts flourished. When Greece became the arena in which Roman generals fought for leadership of the empire, Rhodes allied itself with Julius Caesar, who had studied here in his youth. After Caesar was assassinated in 44 BC, Cassius besieged the city, destroying its ships and carting its artworks off to Rome. Rhodes went into decline and was assimilated into the Roman Empire in AD 70.

In due course, Rhodes joined the Byzantine province of the Dodecanese and was granted independence when the Crusaders seized Constantinople. Later, the Genoese gained control. Next to arrive, in 1309, were the Knights of St John, who ruled Rhodes for 213 years. They in turn were ousted after two mighty sieges by the Ottomans, who were themselves kicked out by the Italians nearly four centuries later. In 1947, after 35

Rhodes

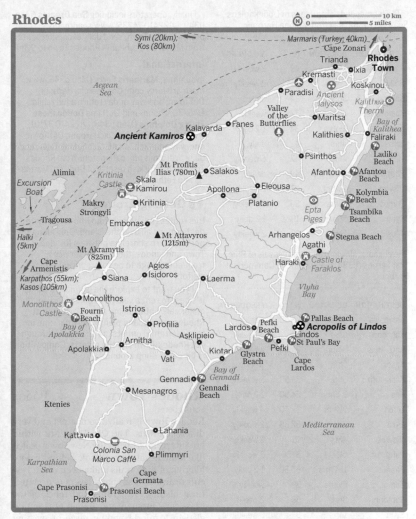

0 ___ 10 km
0 ___ 5 miles

Symi (20km);
Kos (80km)

Marmaris (Turkey; 40km)

Cape Zonari

Trianda · Ixia

Rhodes Town

Kremasti · Koskinou

Paradisi · *Ancient Ialysos* · Kalithea Thermi

Aegean Sea

Valley of the Butterflies · Maritsa · *Bay of Kalithea* · Faliraki

Kalavarda · Fanes · Kalithies · Ladiko Beach

Ancient Kamiros · Psinthos · Afantou · Afantou Beach

Mt Profitis Ilias (780m) · Salakos · Kolymbia Beach

Alimia · *Kritinia Castle* · Skala Kamirou · Apollona · Eleousa · Tsambika Beach

Excursion Boat · Makry Strongyli · Kritinia · Platanio · *Epta Piges*

Halki (5km) · Tragousa · Embonas · Arhangeios · Stegna Beach

· Mt Attavyros (1215m) · Agathi

Mt Akramytis (825m) · Haraki · *Castle of Faraklos*

Cape Armenistis · *Karpathos (55km); Kasos (105km)* · Siana · Agios Isidoros · Laerma · *Vlyha Bay*

Monolithos Castle · Monolithos · Istrios · *Mediterranean Sea*

Fourni Beach · Profilia · Lardos · Pefki Beach · Pallas Beach · **Acropolis of Lindos**

Bay of Apolakkia · Asklipieio · Lindos · St Paul's Bay

Apolakkia · Arnitha · Kiotari · Glystra Beach · Pefki · Cape Lardos

Vati · Gennadi · *Bay of Gennadi*

Ktenies · Mesanagros · Gennadi Beach

Kattavia · Lahania · *Karpathian Sea*

Colonia San Marco Caffé · Plimmyri

Cape Prasonisi · Prasonisi Beach

Prasonisi · Cape Germata

years of Italian occupation, Rhodes finally became part of Greece, along with the other Dodecanese islands.

ⓘ Getting There & Away

AIR

Diagoras Airport (RHO; Map p343; ☏ 22410 88700; www.rho-airport.gr) is near Paradisi on the west coast, 14km southwest of Rhodes Town.

Aegean Airlines (☏ 22410 98345; https://en.aegeanair.com; Diagoras Airport) flies to Athens, Iraklio, Kastellorizo and Thessaloniki.

Olympic Air (☏ 21035 50500; www.olympicair. com) offers frequent flights to and from Athens,

where you can connect to destinations throughout Greece, and also flies to Kastellorizo.

Sky Express (☏ 22410 88700; www.skyexpress. gr) offers direct flights to Iraklio on Crete, and island-hopping routes including Astypalea with stops on Leros, Kalymnos, and Kos; Kasos via Karpathos; and Limnos via Mytilini, Chios and Samos.

BOAT
Domestic

Rhodes Town is the main port in the Dodecanese. Three interisland ferry companies operate from immediately outside the walls of the Old Town.

The high-speed catamarans of Dodekanisos Seaways (p362) sail from Kolona Harbour.

DESTINATION	DURATION	FARE (€)	FREQUENCY
Agathonisi	5½hrs	49	2 weekly
Halki	1¼hrs	18	2 weekly
Kalymnos	3hrs	34	daily
Kastellorizo	2¼hrs	37	weekly
Kos	2½hrs	34	1-2 daily
Leros	4hrs	42	daily
Lipsi	4hrs	47	6 weekly
Patmos	5hrs	49	daily
Nisyros	2¾hrs	27	2 weekly
Samos	10hrs	59	2 weekly
Symi	50mins	19	1-2 daily
Tilos	2hrs	27	2 weekly

The cheaper, slower traditional vessels of Blue Star Ferries (p364) leave from the Commercial Harbour.

DESTINATION	DURATION	FARE (€)	FREQUENCY
Astypalea	9hrs	28.50	weekly
Kalymnos	5hrs	24	5 weekly
Karpathos	3¾hrs	24.50	weekly
Kasos	5hrs	29.50	weekly
Kastellorizo	3hrs	29.50	2 weekly
Kos	3-5hrs	24.50	1-2 daily
Leros	5½hrs	32.50	4 weekly
Lipsi	7½hrs	32.50	2 weekly
Nisyros	4hrs	16	2 weekly
Patmos	6½hrs	37.50	5 weekly
Piraeus	11-17hrs	65.50	1-2 daily
Samos	6½hrs	39	weekly
Santorini	8hrs	39	2 weekly
Symi	1hr	9	3 weekly
Syros	9hrs	49	3 weekly
Tilos	2¼hrs	16	2 weekly

Two weekly Anek Lines (p362) ferries from the Commercial Harbour call at Halki (2 hours, €8), Diafani on Karpathos (4¼ hours, €19), Karpathos Town (5¾ hours, €21), Kasos (8 hours, €25), Anafi (13 hours, €29), Santorini (15 hours, €29), Milos (19½ hours, €39) and Piraeus (25 hours, €47).

In addition, regular ferries link the tiny port at Skala Kamirou, 45km southwest of Rhodes Town and served by hour-long connecting buses, with the island of Halki. They're operated by Nissos Halki (p362) and Nikos Express (p362).

Finally, operators including **Sea Dreams** (Map p349; ☑ 22410 74235; www.seadreams.gr; Lambraki 46, New Town) send daily excursion boats from Mandraki Harbour in Rhodes Town to Symi

International

In summer, **Marmaris Ferry** (Map p346; www.marmarisferry.com; Commercial Harbour, Old Town; one-way or day return adult/child €45/30; ☉ Jun–mid-Oct) and **Dodecanese Flying Dolphins** (Map p346; ☑ 22410 37101; www.12fd.gr; Commercial Harbour, Old Town; one-way adult/child €40/25; ☉ May-Oct) send daily hydrofoils and catamarans from Rhodes Town to the Turkish resorts of Bodrum, Marmaris and Fethiye.

ⓘ Getting Around

Bus routes radiate out from Rhodes Town to destinations all over the island. Only along the northeastern shoreline between Rhodes Town and Lindos, though, are services frequent enough to be truly convenient for visitors.

If you want to explore the island as a whole, it's best to rent a vehicle of some kind. All the major car-rental chains are represented at Rhodes airport, and plenty more car- and motorcycle-rental outlets are scattered throughout Rhodes Town and the resorts. Competition is fierce, so shop around.

Rhodes Town Ρόδος

POP 90,000

Rhodes Town is really two distinct and very different towns. The **Old Town** lies within but utterly apart from the New Town, sealed like a medieval time capsule behind a double ring of high walls and a deep moat. Few cities can boast so many layers of architectural history, with ruins and relics of the Classical, Ottoman and Italian eras entangled in a mind-boggling maze of twisting lanes.

In season, the Old Town receives a huge daily influx of day trippers and, especially, passengers from giant cruise ships. Even then, you can escape the crowds by heading away from the busy commercial streets into its hauntingly pretty cobbled alleyways. Staying a night or two, and losing yourself in the labyrinth after dark, is an experience no traveller should miss.

The **New Town**, meanwhile, is a modern Mediterranean resort, with decent beaches, upscale shops, lively nightlife and waterfront bars servicing the package crowd.

⊙ Sights

⊙ Old Town

A glorious mixture of Byzantine, Turkish and Italian architecture, erected on top of far more ancient and largely unidentifiable remains, the Old Town is a world of its own. In theory, it consists of three separate sections, though casual visitors seldom notice the transition from one to the next. To the north, sturdy stone mansions known as inns line the arrow-straight streets of the **Knights' Quarter**. These strikingly austere edifices, built to house knights from specific countries, were laid out by the medieval Knights of St John. South of that, the **Hora**, also known as the **Turkish Quarter**, occupies the central bulk of the Old Town. This tangle of cobbled alleyways is now the main commercial hub, packed with restaurants and shops interspersed between derelict mosques and Muslim monuments, and, regrettably, bursting with visitors every day in summer. The **Jewish Quarter** in the southeast, which lost most of its inhabitants during WWII, is now a sleepy residential district.

Visitors can walk atop the central stretch of the imposing 12m-thick ramparts that still protect the landward side of the Old Town, and descend at various points into the wide, deep moat that encircles them, filled with lush gardens and perfect for a relaxed stroll.

Of the nine gateways to the Old Town, the busiest and most dramatic are the northernmost two, closest to the New Town. **Liberty Gate**, the nearest to Mandraki Harbour and the taxi rank, leads to a small bridge and the main tourist areas, while the atmospheric **D'Amboise Gate**, further inland, crosses an especially attractive section of the moat en route to the Palace of the Grand Master.

★**Archaeological Museum**   MUSEUM
(Map p346; ☑ 22413 65257; Plateia Mousiou; adult/child €8/free, combination ticket incl Grand Master's Palace, Panagia tou Kastrou & Decorative Arts Collection €10; ⊗ 8am-8pm daily Apr-Oct, to 3pm Tue-Sun Nov-Mar) A weathered, sun-kissed stone lion, visible from the street, invites visitors into the magnificent 15th-century Knights' Hospital that holds Rhodes' superb archaeology museum. Exhibits range through several upstairs galleries, and across beautiful gardens to an annexe that's open shorter hours in summer (9am to 4.50pm). Highlights include the exquisite *Aphrodite Bathing* marble statue from the 1st century BC, a pavilion displaying wall-mounted mosaics, and a reconstructed burial site from 1630 BC that held a helmeted warrior alongside his horse.

Ancient treasures unearthed all over Rhodes, including some wonderful ceramics and a sleek carved dolphin, trace 7000 years of local history. The annexe is especially strong on the Mycenean era, at its peak in the 14th and 13th centuries BC.

Palace of the Grand Master   HISTORIC BUILDING
(Map p346; ☑ 22413 65270; Ippoton; adult/child €6/free, combination ticket incl Archaeological Museum, Decorative Arts Collection & Panagia tou Kastrou €10; ⊗ 8am-8pm Apr-Oct, to 3pm Nov-Mar) From the outside, this magnificent castle-like palace looks much as it did when erected by the 14th-century Knights

---

THE COLOSSUS OF RHODES

A giant bronze statue of the sun god Helios, the Colossus of Rhodes was erected to celebrate the end of an unsuccessful siege of Rhodes. It took 12 years to build, was completed in 292 BC, and stood for less than a century, before being toppled by an earthquake in 227 BC.

The statue was considered one of the Seven Wonders of the Ancient World. In legend, its two legs straddled the entrance to what's now Mandraki Harbour, tall enough for high-masted triremes to pass underneath. Historians suggest that given the higher sea levels back then, however, it may have stood further up the hill, on the site of the modern Palace of the Grand Master.

After remaining in ruins on the waterfront for almost 1000 years, the Colossus was broken into pieces and sold by invading Arabs to a Syrian Jew in 654 AD. He supposedly transported it abroad on the backs of 900 camels. There has long been talk of recreating a colossal statue of Helios at Mandraki Harbour, but that looks no closer to happening than ever.

Rhodes Old Town

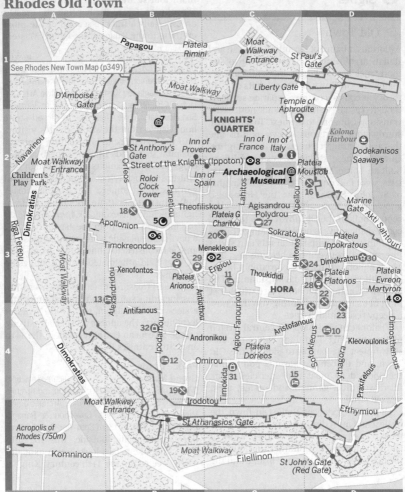

See Rhodes New Town Map (p349)

DODECANESE RHODES TOWN

Hospitaller. During the 19th century, however, it was devastated by an explosion, so the interior is now an Italian reconstruction, completed in the '18th year of the Fascist Era' (1940). Dreary chambers upstairs hold haphazard looted artworks, so the most interesting sections are the twin historical museums downstairs, one devoted to ancient Rhodes and the other to the island's medieval history.

The ancient section holds some lovely pottery from the 6th century BC, along with all sorts of everyday domestic objects and even glassware.

Street of the Knights HISTORIC SITE

(Map p346; Ippoton; ⊙24hr) Austere and somewhat forbidding, the Street of the Knights (Ippoton) was home from the 14th century to the Knights Hospitaller who ruled Rhodes. The knights were divided into seven 'tongues', or languages, according to their birthplace – England, France, Germany, Italy, Aragon, Auvergne and Provence – each responsible for a specific section of the fortifications. As wall displays explain, the street holds an 'inn', or palace, for each tongue. Its modern appearance, though, owes much to Italian restorations during the 1930s.

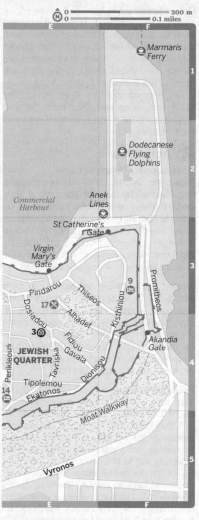

Jewish Quarter AREA

(Map p346) The Jewish Quarter, an enclave of narrow lanes in the Old Town's south-eastern corner, centres on Plateia Evreon Martyron (Square of the Jewish Martyrs). Now all too quiet and dilapidated, it was home a century ago to a population of 5500. Half fled in the 1930s, while 1673 Jews were deported to Auschwitz in 1944; only 151 survived.

The **Jewish Museum of Rhodes** (Map p346; ☎22410 22364; www.rhodesjewish museum.org; Dosiadou & Simiou; incl synagogue €4; ☺10am-3pm Sun-Fri Apr-Oct), entered via the 1577 **Kahal Shalom Synagogue** (Map p346; ☎22410 22364; www.jewishrhodes.org; Dosiadou & Simiou; incl museum €4; ☺10am-3pm Sun-Fri Apr-Oct) – the oldest synagogue in Greece – tells the full story.

DODECANESE RHODES TOWN

Hora
AREA

(Turkish Quarter; Map p346) The Old Town's central commercial and residential district, south of the Street of the Knights, is known as the Hora. Having acquired its current appearance following the Ottoman takeover of 1522, it's also called the Turkish Quarter. The most important of many churches that became mosques is the colourful, pink-domed **Mosque of Süleyman** (Map p346; Sokratous), at the top of Sokratous. Across the street, the **Muslim Library** (Map p346; Sokratous; ⊘9.30am-3pm Mon-Sat May-Oct) `FREE`, founded in 1793 by Turkish Rhodian Ahmed Hasuf, houses Persian and Arabic manuscripts plus handwritten Korans.

⊙ New Town

The so-called New Town of Rhodes has existed for 500 years, since Ottoman conquerors drove the local Greek population to build new homes outside the city walls. Almost nothing in the area, north of the Old Town and centred on Mandraki Harbour and the casino, though, holds any historic interest. Instead the New Town is a busy modern resort, alive with guesthouses and restaurants, from gleaming hotel monoliths to tiny tavernas, along with banks, boutiques and all the businesses that keep Rhodes ticking along.

A continuous strip of beach, starting north of Mandraki Harbour, stretches around the island's northernmost point and down the west side of the New Town. The best spots are on the east side, known as **Elli Beach**, where there's better sand, more facilities, and, usually, calmer water.

Modern Greek Art Museum
GALLERY

(Nestoridio Melathro; Map p349; ☑22410 43780; www.mgamuseum.gr; Plateia Haritou; adult/child €3/free, all four sections €8; ⊘8am-3pm Tue-Sat) The main gallery of the four-part Modern Greek Art Museum, near the New Town's northern tip, holds paintings, engravings and sculptures by some of Greece's greatest 20th-century artists. The real highlight is the top floor, devoted thanks to a bequest from his widow to the remarkable paintings of Valias Semertzidis (1911–83), whose work ranged from depictions of wartime struggle and hardship to Rhodian landscapes.

Acropolis of Rhodes
ARCHAEOLOGICAL SITE

(⊘24hr) `FREE` Now known as the Acropolis of Rhodes, the site of the ancient Hellenistic city of Rhodes stretches up the slopes of Monte Smith, 1km west of the Old Town.

Only a few of ruins have been restored, including an elongated, tree-lined stadium from the 2nd century BC. Steps climb from a theatre, used for lectures by the Rhodes School of Rhetoric (whose students included Cicero and Julius Caesar), to the stark columns of the Temple of Pythian Apollo.

Get here on city bus 6, or by walking along Komninon and Diagoridon from St Athanasius Gate at the southwest corner of the Old Town.

🏃 Activities

Waterhoppers Diving School
DIVING

(Map p349; ☑22410 38146; www.waterhoppers.com; Mandraki Harbour) Operating out of Mandraki Harbour and several other bases on Rhodes, Waterhoppers offers an 'experience scuba' one-day program (€93.50) and various diving courses, including two- and three-day PADI open-water certifications. Advanced divers can join night, wreck and cave dives.

Trident Scuba Diving School
DIVING

(Map p349; ☑22410 29160; www.tridentdiving-school.com; Mandraki Harbour; ⊕) Trident offers daily excursions to dive spots around the north of the island, plus beginner classes and two- and three-day PADI-certified courses. For more details, look for its boat, *Armonia*, on Mandraki Harbour.

Poseidon Submarine
BOATING

(Map p349; ☑6945370301; www.poseidonsub-marine.com; Mandraki Harbour; adult/child €15/5; ⊘9.30am-9.30pm mid-Apr–Oct; ⊕) Despite appearances, the bright-red *Poseidon* is not a submarine, but a glass-bottomed boat. After puttering out to the point where the Colossus of Rhodes (p345) supposedly stood, for fine views back to the Old Town, it returns to Mandraki Harbour, where a diver feeds fish outside the underwater windows. It's fun for kids, with turtle sightings a possibility. Cheaper tickets online. Boats leave every hour and the trip lasts 45 minutes.

🛏 Sleeping

Although the New Town holds plenty of modern hotels, as well as a good hostel, the most memorable and romantic places to stay are the various inns and B&Bs tucked into the Old Town's back alleys. In summer it's essential to reserve ahead; most budget options close altogether in winter. Be warned, too, that most Old Town hotels aren't accessible by taxi, so you'll have to haul your luggage along the narrow, cobbled lanes.

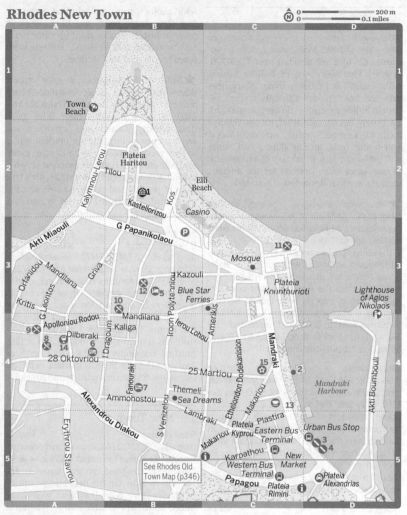

Rhodes New Town

Rhodes New Town

◎ Sights
1 Modern Greek Art Museum.................. B2

✪ Activities, Courses & Tours
2 Poseidon Submarine............................ C4
3 Trident Scuba Diving School............... D5
4 Waterhoppers Diving School D5

🛏 Sleeping
5 Florida Hotel....................................... B3
6 Hotel Anastasia.................................. A4
7 Stay Hostel B4

✴ Eating
8 Kerasma A4
9 Koozina A4
10 Koykos B3
11 Meltemi C3
12 Niohori B3

◉ Drinking & Nightlife
13 Aktaion Cafe....................................... C4
14 Christos Garden A4

✪ Entertainment
15 9D: Throne of Helios C4

🛏 Old Town

⭐ S Nikolis Hotel   HISTORIC HOTEL €€
(Map p346; 📞22410 34561; www.s-nikolis.gr; Ipodamou 61; r/ste incl breakfast from €120/220;
😊✳🛜) The life's work of builder Sotiris
Nikolis and his Danish partner Marianne,
this fine hotel ranges through several restored buildings and a flowery courtyard.
Its dozen stylish split-level rooms feature
medieval-accented quilts on dark-wood
four-poster beds, marble floors, and stone
and oxblood walls. Breakfast in the on-site
Arxaia Agora cafe – named for the ancient
marketplace that lies below – is superb.

⭐ Marco Polo Mansion   BOUTIQUE HOTEL €€
(Map p346; 📞22410 25562; www.marcopolo-
mansion.gr; Agiou Fanouriou 40; d incl breakfast
€80-160, apt €130-180; 🕙Apr-Oct; ✳🛜) This
15th-century pasha's house lovingly recreates
an Ottoman ambience with verve and style.
Some rooms are in the mansion itself, the
rest open onto the stunning garden courtyard where a superb breakfast is served.
With its stained-glass windows, dark-wood
furniture, wooden floors and raised beds, it's
like a journey back in time. Managers Efi and
Spiros are hospitality personified.

The Andreas   HOTEL €€
(Map p346; 📞22410 34156; www.hotelandreas.
com; Omirou 28d; ste incl breakfast €100, both stes
€160; 🕙Jul-Sep; ✳🖥🛜) This former pasha's
house holds just two suites, each with two
bedrooms. Best is the Tower Suite where you
wake in your traditional raised bed to a view
of the Aegean, while the Terrace Suite has its
own private sun terrace. The gardens and
shared roof terrace are lovely spots to make
conversation. Four-night minimum stay.

Hotel Cava d'Oro   B&B €€
(Map p346; 📞22410 36980; www.cavadoro.com;
Kisthiniou 15; s/d/tr incl breakfast €110/130/160;
🅿✳🛜) This small family-run hotel, set in a
medieval storage building, offers characterful
rooms of varying sizes, with canopied beds,
exposed stone walls and high arching ceilings.
Breakfast is served in a cool garden courtyard,
and guests can even walk on a short stretch
of ramparts. Unusually for the Old Town, it's
possible to drive right to the front door.

St Michel Hotel   HERITAGE HOTEL €€
(Map p346; 📞22410 25111; www.saintmichel.
gr; Perikleous 68; s/d/ste €70/90/130; ✳🛜)
This 700-year-old building has half-a-
dozen rooms, some large, some cramped,
with choice furniture including wrought-
iron four-poster beds, and tiled floors. A
sense of history exudes from its stone walls
and wood-beamed ceilings. The superior
room has its own roof terrace.

⭐ Spirit of the Knights   BOUTIQUE HOTEL €€€
(Map p346; 📞22410 39765; www.rhodesluxury-
hotel.com; Alexandridou 14; s/d incl breakfast from
€180/200; 😊✳🛜) With their thick rugs,
dark woods, stained-glass windows and
sense of tranquillity, the six opulent suites
in this gorgeous boutique hotel ooze medieval atmosphere. Perfectly isolated down a
side alley near the Old Town walls, it's a true
work of passion and vision. As well as a fragrant garden courtyard to read in and take
breakfast, there's also a library.

In Camera Art
Boutique Hotel   BOUTIQUE HOTEL €€€
(Map p346; 📞22410 77277; www.incamera.gr;
Sofokleous 35; r/ste incl breakfast from €175/250;
😊✳🛜) This stunning design hotel, owned
by a Greek photographer whose equipment
is on show throughout, looks out on ancient
ruins. It holds eight very different suites and
two rooms. The three-level 'Forms of Light'
suite has stained-glass windows, beautifully
finished bedrooms and two roof terraces.
Two rooms have private gardens with Jacuzzis, the rest share a garden and breakfast
cafe.

🛏 New Town

Stay Hostel   HOSTEL €
(Map p349; 📞22410 24024; www.stayrhodes.com;
Fanouraki 19-21, New Town; dm/r €22/69; 😊✳🛜)
This nicely equipped modern hostel in the
New Town is by far the best budget option
in Rhodes Town. As well as clean, well-maintained dorms and double rooms, where the
staff even leave little gifts for guests, it has a
shared kitchen downstairs, a lounge bar, a
cinema room and a small rooftop gym.

Hotel Anastasia   PENSION €€
(Map p349; 📞22410 28007; www.anastasia-hotel.
com; 28 Oktovriou 46, New Town; s/d/tr incl breakfast €59/70/94; ✳🖥🛜) The New Town's
friendliest and most peaceful lodgings, in
a handsome villa set well back from the
busy road. The ochre-coloured rooms have
wooden shutters, tiled floors and traditional
furnishings; two at the front have small private balconies, oddly accessed via their bathrooms. Breakfast is served in the lush garden.

Florida Hotel   HOTEL €€

(Map p349; ☑ 22410 22111; www.florida-rhodes. com; Amarandou 5, New Town; s/d/tr €43/78/97; ⊜✳🛜) This small, simple, modern hotel is set in a quiet little pedestrian street that's a short walk from the beach near the New Town's northern tip. The crisp, clean, white-washed rooms have kitchenettes and air-con, and each has its own flower-bedecked terrace or balcony. Yvonne, the helpful owner, provides her own hand-drawn local maps.

🍴 Eating

🍴 Old Town

To Marouli   VEGETARIAN €

(Map p346; ☑ 22413 04394; Platonos 22; mains €8-12; ⊘ noon-10pm Mon-Sat, 1-7pm Sun; ✳🛜🖊) 🖊 'Marouli' means lettuce, and you can expect greens galore in this standout vegetarian restaurant. The pasta, which like the owner comes from Italy, is delicious. But then again, it's hard to choose between the vegan Thai pineapple and fried rice, or the fine salads – not to mention the 'Junk Food' such as onion rings.

Old Town Corner Bakery   BAKERY €

(Map p346; ☑ 22410 38494; Omirou 88; snacks €2-6; ⊘ 7am-7pm Mon-Sat, 8am-3pm Sun; 🛜) With jazz and the scent of aromatic arabica coffee drifting through this tiny bakery cafe, and out to a handful of tables on the street, this is an Old Town residents' favourite, just inside St Athanasios' Gate. As well as amazing pastries – dawn-fresh croissants sell out very quickly – it serves club sandwiches, apple pie and a host of healthy juices.

To Megiston   TAVERNA €

(Map p346; ☑ 22410 29127; Sofokleous 9; mains €6-23; ⊘ 10am-1.30am; ✳) Look no further for the classic Greek-holiday taverna experience: welcoming, witty waiters; retsina flowing freely; and all the classics prepared just right. People-watch al fresco, as sightseers swoon at the Ibrahim Pasha mosque opposite, and feast on the likes of *spetsofaï* (sausage stewed with chicken and peppers), lamb *kleftiko* (slow oven-baked), and succulent little Symi shrimp.

⭐ Marco Polo Cafe   MEDITERRANEAN €€

(Map p346; ☑ 22410 25562; www.marcopolomansion.gr; Agiou Fanouriou 40-42; mains €15-25; ⊘ 7-11pm Apr-Oct; 🛜) 🖊 Despite being barely visible, or even signed, from the street, this irresistible dinner-only restaurant is filled nightly, with diners savouring exquisite culinary creations like sea-bream fillets on a 'risotto' of local wheat, pork loin with figs, or octopus sous vide with cream of beetroot. Linger over a romantic meal in the delightful lemon-fragrant garden courtyard.

Pizanias   SEAFOOD €€

(The Sea Star; Map p346; ☑ 22410 22117; Sofokleous 24; mains €10-17; ⊘ noon-midnight Mar-Oct; 🛜🖐) This atmospheric restaurant, opening onto one of the Old Town's most attractive, peaceful squares, is celebrated for its fresh seafood – from boned, slow-grilled sea bream to jumbo prawns or squid stuffed with cheese. Dine beneath a canopy of trees, with the night sky shining through.

Taverna Kostas   GREEK €€

(Map p346; ☑ 22410 26217; Pythagora 62; mains €9-22; ⊘ 10am-late; ✳) Run by grandfather Kostas, this friendly Old Town taverna spreads from a simple limewashed dining room into a bright rear conservatory. Come for Greek standards done well – like dolmadhes (stuffed vine leaves) with a hint of cumin – and a succulent octopus salad.

Romios Restaurant   GREEK €€

(Map p346; ☑ 22410 25549; www.romios-rhodes. gr; Sofokleous 15; mains €9-20; ⊘ noon-midnight; ✳🛜) Don't be misled by the enchanted-grotto setting of canopied couches, birdcage nooks and fairy lights. Romios (not to be confused with run-of-the-mill Romeo's, also in the Old Town) is very serious about its food, serving a classic Rhodian menu of local delicacies such as pork in chestnut sauce, veal with olives, and delicious octopus cooked with orange.

Petaladika   GREEK €€

(Map p346; ☑ 22410 27359; Menakleous 8; mains €6-20; ⊘ noon-late; ✳) Petaladika might look like just another tourist trap, tucked into a corner just off the main Old Town drag, but with its fresh white-wood interior, and chic tables and chairs out front, it's a good option. Try the deep-fried baby squid, zucchini balls and freshly grilled fish.

Mama Sofia   TAVERNA €€

(Map p346; ☑ 22410 24469; www.mamasofia.gr; Orfeos 28; mains €14-28; ⊘ 9am-late; ✳🛜🖐) A spit away from the Roloi clock tower, facing the Mosque of Süleyman, Mama's has been feeding travellers quality Greek cuisine for generations. The presentation and homely service is first class, and you can expect all the usual suspects from souvlakia to octopus, *stifadho* (meat, game or seafood stewed with tomatoes) and *kleftiko* (slow oven-baked lamb or goat).

Dinoris Fish Restaurant   SEAFOOD €€€
(Map p346; ☑ 22410 25824; www.dinoris.com; Plateia Mousiou 14; mains €20-30; ⊗ noon-midnight; ✴ 🛜 🚶) Tucked just inside the walls, across from the Archaeological Museum, Dinoris is among the Old Town's fanciest and more expensive options, with romantic trimmings like lemon-painted walls, candelabra, linen tablecloths and gleaming glassware. The menu is drenched with an oceanic array of mussels, risotto, fish soup, lobster and octopus. Some prices are per kilo; check costs before you eat.

Hatzikelis   SEAFOOD €€€
(Map p346; ☑ 22410 27215; www.hatzikelistavern. com; Alhadef 9; mains €9-45; ⊗ noon-midnight; ✴ 🛜 🚶) Smart Hatzikelis has a romantic setting near the harbour, beside a ruined basilica. Lunchtime sees bargain deals to lure in day trippers; in the evening it sells the concept of choosing a whole fish, making a soup with the head and assorted shellfish, and serving the rest as a main course. With ingredients sold by weight, dinner can work out expensive.

🍴 New Town

Koykos   GREEK €
(Map p349; ☑ 22410 73022; www.koukosrodos. com; Mandilana 20-22, New Town; mains €3-27; ⊗ 24hr; 🛜 🚶) This inviting complex of historic homes, on a pedestrian shopping street, consists of several antique-filled rooms – cuckoo clocks feature strongly – along with pavement patio seating and a bougainvillea-draped courtyard. Best known for fabulous pies (from around €2.30), it also serves classic mezedhes (small plates), plus meat and fish dishes, and a simple coffee or sandwich.

Niohori   TAVERNA €
(Map p349; ☑ 22410 35116; I Kazouli 29, New Town; mains €7-12; ⊗ 1-11pm Mon-Sat, 5-11pm Sun) It's all about the meat at this simple backstreet taverna; the owner is a butcher, with a shop across the street. Sit outside rather than the dazzling-white interior, or in the covered courtyard (really it's a garage), and tuck into steak, meatballs or veal liver with oil and oregano, occasionally seasoned with organ music from the nearby church.

★ Meltemi   SEAFOOD €€
(Map p349; ☑ 22410 30480; Kountourioti 8; mains €9-22.50; ⊗ 10am-late; 🅿 ✴ 🚶) If you want to eat on the waterfront, Rhodes Town holds no better option than Meltemi, nestled into the sands of Elli Beach, just beyond Mandraki Harbour. The building itself may be drab, but the terrace views are magnificent, while the menu bursts with the tastes of the sea: octopus, jumbo prawns, lobster and calamari, all delivered with gusto.

Kerasma   GREEK €€
(Map p349; ☑ 22413 02410; www.kerasmarestaurant.com; George Leontos 4-6, New Town; mains €14-32; ⊗ 12.15-11.30pm Mon-Sat, 6-11.30pm Sun; ✴ 🛜) The pick of several contemporary-styled restaurants on the New Town's fanciest dining street, Kerasma gives Greek classics a fusion twist, with dishes like grilled octopus dipped in honey with *fava*, and beef fillet with green pepper and white chocolate. An impressive cellar holds over 60 Greek wines.

Koozina   GREEK €€
(Map p349; ☑ 6943451450; George Leontos 19, New Town; mains €12-27; ⊗ 1-11.30pm) The New Town sees a lot of Scandinavian visitors, and with its wooden floors and tin watering cans artfully hanging from its white walls, this open-sided place has a real sense of 'Scandi' chic. The owner prides herself on fresh-made dishes like ravioli stuffed with shrimps and scallops, and lamb shank cooked in beer.

🍷 Drinking & Nightlife

The Old Town is surprisingly short of bars. The most popular drinking venues are the broad terraces of its many tavernas, though Sofokleous holds some laid-back options, and music-oriented bars circle Plateia Arionos.

The New Town has a more active nightlife scene. Orfanidou is an out-and-out 'bar street' – read 'drunk street' – while I Dragoumi too is lined with pubs. Classier bars and cafes line the streets parallel to Mandraki Harbour.

🍸 Old Town

★ Raxati Cafe   BAR
(Map p346; ☑ 22410 36365; Sofokleous 1-3; ⊗ 10am-late; 🛜) This high-ceilinged, free-spirited bar and coffeehouse, close to the attractive Ibrahim Pasha mosque, is as pretty as it is friendly. Inside, the stone walls are peppered with vintage ad posters, and the backlit bar glitters with glass spirit bottles. Snacks, cocktails, easy tunes and good conversation.

Rogmi Tou Chronou BAR
(Map p346; ☑22410 25202; Plateia Arionos 4; ⏱7pm-4am; 🛜) If Dracula developed a taste for rock music and opened a bar it might look something like this. Imagine purple velvet drapes, a handsomely crafted wooden bar lit with spirits, stained-glass windows, and the odd candle. Tables out on the square are perfect for a relaxed early-evening drink, while there's live rock later on Fridays and Saturdays.

Mevlana CAFE
(Map p346; ☑6942210846; Sokratous 76; ⏱10am-midnight; 🛜) Shoppers on the Old Town's most commercialised street tend to double-take when they spot this venerable Turkish-styled cafe, with its pebble-mosaic floor, carved wooden panels, laid-back atmosphere and hookah-smoking clientele reclining on cushions. Expect a hearty welcome if you drop in for coffee or cocktails, iced tea or ice cream, juice or beer; apart from desserts, though, there's no food.

Macao Bar BAR
(Map p346; ☑6936400305; www.macaobar.gr/en; Pleteia Arionos; ⏱7pm-5am; 🛜) Uber-stylish Macao bar, hidden away in the heart of the Old Town, has a moody, low-lit ambience, polished concrete floors and the occasional guest DJ spinning the decks to a well-heeled crowd of fashionistas. Be sure to try the herb-flavoured cocktails (€10).

🍸 New Town

Aktaion Cafe CAFE
(Map p349; ☑22410 76856; www.aktaion-rodos.gr; Pleteia Eleftheria, New Town; ⏱8am-midnight; 🛜♿) The New Town's busy central rendezvous sprawls across a large open-air terrace beneath the shade of a spreading plane tree, across the street from Mandraki Harbour. Locals and day trippers alike watch the world go by, relaxing over drinks and snacks, while children head straight to the adjoining enclosed playground.

Christos Garden BAR
(Map p349; ☑22410 32144; Griva 102, New Town; ⏱10pm-late; 🛜) With its grotto-like bar and pebble-mosaic courtyard, Christos offers New Town visitors a tranquil escape. During the day it doubles as an art gallery; after dark the fairy lights twinkle. Perfect for a cocktail.

☆ Entertainment

9D: Throne of Helios FILM
(Map p349; ☑22410 76850; www.throneofhelios.com; 25 Martiou 2, New Town; adult/child €13/9; ⏱10am-11pm; 🛜♿) This entertaining 20-minute movie takes viewers back to the very birth of Rhodes, its 3D effects complemented by a further six dimensions (!) including shaking chairs, falling rain, snow and bubbles. The historic content is good, while amazing visuals recreate the construction of the Colossus, the creation of the medieval citadel, and more.

There's no great reason for adults to stay on for the wordless short 3D cartoon that follows the main film, but young kids will enjoy the even more vigorous special effects.

Cafe Chantant LIVE MUSIC
(Map p346; ☑22410 32277; Dimokratou 3; ⏱11pm-late Fri & Sat) Locals flock to sit at the long wooden tables here and listen to live traditional Greek music while drinking ouzo or beer. It's dark inside and you won't find snacks or nibbles, but the atmosphere is warm-hearted and friendly and the band is always lively.

🛍 Shopping

As well as a *lot* of souvenir tat, the Old Town holds plenty of shops that sell quality keepsakes: Moorish lamps, icons, classical busts, leather sandals, belts and bags, silver jewellery, olive-wood chopping boards, Rhodian wine, and thyme honey. The New Town is more prosaic, with its grocery shops, general stores and clutch of big-name fashion and style brands.

Rhodes Handmade Gallery ARTS & CRAFTS
(Map p346; ☑22414 22242; Omirou 45; ⏱9am-9pm) Best viewed by night, this Aladdin's cave of a shop conjures up thoughts of the *Arabian Nights,* with its shiny brass lamps, ornate antique rings and Eastern mosaic lights glowing like clusters of fireflies.

So Greek FOOD & DRINKS
(Map p346; ☑22410 36870; https://sogreek.business.site; Ipodamou 40-42; ⏱9am-10pm Mon-Sat) 🥖 The perfect pit stop for choice gifts, So Greek sells nicely packaged Greek wine, olive oil and a wide range of homemade honey, natural cosmetics and herbs and spices.

ℹ Information

EMERGENCY & IMPORTANT NUMBERS

Emergencies & Ambulance (☑166)
Port Police (☑22410 27634; Mandraki Harbour, New Town)
Tourist Police (☑22410 27423; New Town; ⊘24hr)

MEDICAL SERVICES

Euromedica General Hospital (☑22410 45000; www.euromedica-rhodes.gr; Koskinou) Large private health facility, in Koskinou, 9km south of the Old Town, with a 24-hour emergency department and English-speaking staff.
General Hospital Rhodes (☑22413 60000; Andreas Papandreou; ⊘24hr) This public hospital, 5km southwest of the Old Town, has been hit hard by cuts in government funding. Staff shortages can result in long waits for treatment.
Rhodes Medical Care (☑22410 38008; www. rmc.gr; Krito Bldg, Ioannou Metaxa 3, New Town) Private clinic that will treat any emergency provided you have health insurance. Excellent staff and facilities.

MONEY

You'll find plenty of ATMs throughout Rhodes Town, with useful ATM-equipped branches of Alpha Bank next door to the Old Town tourist office (p354) and on Plateia Kypriou in the New Town. The National Bank of Greece has a conveniently located office in the **New Town** (Plateia Kyprou), as well as a branch on Plateia Mousiou in the Old Town.

TOURIST INFORMATION

EOT (Greek Tourist Information Office; Map p349; ☑22410 44335; www.ando.gr/eot; cnr Makariou & Papagou, New Town; ⊘8.30am-2.45pm Mon-Fri) National tourism information, with brochures, maps and transport details.
Rhodes Tourism Office – New Town (Map p349; ☑22410 35495; www.rhodes.gr; Plateia Rimini, New Town; ⊘7.30am-3pm Mon-Fri) Conveniently poised between Mandraki Harbour and the Old Town, with public toilets alongside, this efficient office has helpful staff.
Rhodes Tourism Office – Old Town (Map p346; ☑22410 35945; www.rhodes.gr; cnr Platonos & Ippoton; ⊘7am-3pm Mon-Fri) Rhodes Town's most useful tourist office, housed in an ancient building at the foot of the Street of the Knights, supplies excellent street maps, some good handouts on the whole island, and various commercial brochures.

ℹ Getting Around

BICYCLE

Bicycles can be rented from **Margaritis** (☑22410 37420; www.margaritisrentals.gr; I Kazouli 17, New Town; ⊘8am-9pm) in the New Town.

BOAT

Excursion boats based on the quayside at Mandraki Harbour offer day trips to towns and beaches along Rhodes' east coast, including Faliraki and Lindos.

BUS

Local buses within Rhodes Town leave from the **urban bus stop** (Map p349, New Town) on Mandraki Harbour. The most useful route for visitors is bus 6, which goes to the Acropolis. Buy tickets on board.

Regular buses serve the entire island on weekdays, with fewer services on Saturday and only a few on Sunday. Two bus terminals, at either end of the same short street in the New Town, serve half the island each. Schedules are posted beside the ticket kiosks at each terminal, and also online. All tickets cost €0.20 extra when bought from the driver as you board the bus.

Eastern Bus Terminal (Map p349; ☑22410 27706; www.ktelrodou.gr; Averof, New Town) Services to Faliraki (€2.40), Tsambika Beach (€3.90), Haraki (€4.90), Lindos (€5.50), Lahania (€7.80), Kattavia (€9) and Prasonisi (€10.40).

Western Bus Terminal (Map p349; ☑22410 26300; www.desroda.gr; Averof, New Town) Very frequent buses run down the coast to the airport (€2.40). Although fewer services continue any further, daily excursion buses head to Ancient Ialysos (Mon-Sat; €5.20), Ancient Kamiros (€5.20) and the Valley of the Butterflies (€5) while buses timed to coincide with ferry sailings connect Rhodes Town with Skala Kamirou (€4.50). Buses to Monolithos (€5) run on Monday and Friday only. One slight anomaly is that the Western Terminal also offers regular service to Kalithea Thermi (€2.40).

CAR & MOTORCYCLE

If you're based in Rhodes Old Town, it's worth remembering that you can't drive into the Old Town, let alone park there, so it makes sense to rent a car only for the actual day(s) you're going to use it.
Drive Rent A Car (☑22410 68243; www. driverentacar.gr; 1st Km Tsairi-Airport; ⊘8am-9pm) Sturdier, newer scooters and cars.
Margaritis (p354) Reliable cars, scooters and bicycles in the New Town.
Orion Rent a Car (☑22410 22137; www.orion-carrental.com; Leontos 38, New Town) A wide range of small and luxury cars.

TAXI

As the narrow lanes of the Old Town are largely pedestrianised, taxis cannot drive to most destinations within the walls; expect to be dropped at the gate nearest your destination. A few upscale hotels will pick up guests in golf buggies.

Rhodes Town's main **taxi rank** (Map p349; Papagou, Old Town) is on the northern edge of the Old Town, just east of Plateia Rimini; a board displays set fares for specific destinations. Meters charge slightly less for journeys in Rhodes Town than for the rest of the island. Rates double between midnight and 5am.

You can also phone for a **taxi** (☑ in Rhodes Town 22410 69800, outside Rhodes Town 22410 69600; www.rhodes-taxi.gr).

Northeastern Rhodes

Most of Rhodes' sandiest beaches lie along the island's northeastern coast, between Rhodes Town and Lindos. As a result, this stretch is punctuated by a long succession of resorts, filled with package holidaymakers in summer and holding endless strips of tourist bars.

One of Rhodes' loveliest (and busiest) beaches, **Ladiko Beach** (P🚻) consists of two back-to-back coves, just past Faliraki, 16km south of Rhodes Town. The first and larger of the two is composed of sand and gravel, while the even prettier bay beyond, consisting of pebbles and also known as **Anthony Quinn Beach**, is better for swimming. Quinn, the star of *Zorba the Greek*, bought the beach from the Greek government in the 1960s, but according to his family the authorities failed to honour the sale.

Two more fine beaches, **Kolymbia** and **Tsambika**, stand either side of the massive Tsambika promontory 10km further south. Both are sandy but get crowded in summer. Not far beyond, the coast road curves inland, but a short detour seawards brings you to the low-key little resort of Stegna, arrayed along sandy, idyllic **Stegna Beach**. The spotless little **Pirofani Fish Taverna** (☑ 6972165186; Stegna; mains €7-17; ⊙10am-11pm; P🛜🚻) here makes a good lunchtime stop.

The headland that marks the start of the final curve towards Lindos, 40km south of Rhodes Town, is topped by the ruins of the 15th-century **Castle of Faraklos**. Once a prison for recalcitrant knights, this was the last stronghold on the island to fall to the Turks and now offers fabulous views. A footpath climbs from the appealing little resort of **Haraki**, immediately south, where the neat horseshoe bay is lined by a pebbly beach.

◎ Sights

Kalithea Thermi ARCHITECTURE
(Map p343; ☑22410 37090; www.kallithea springs.gr; Kalithea; €3; ⊙8am-8pm Apr-Oct, to 5pm Nov-Mar; 🚻) Italian architect Pietro Lombardi constructed this opulent art deco spa, on the site of ancient thermal springs, in 1929. Its dazzling white-domed pavilions, pebble-mosaic courtyards and sweeping sea-view colonnades have appeared in movies such as *Zorba the Greek* and *The Guns of Navarone*. In peak season its small sandy bathing beach and cafe get impossibly crowded.

Epta Piges SPRING
(Seven Springs; Map p343; Kolymbia; ⊙24hr; P🚻) Seven natural springs at this beauty spot, in the hills 4km inland from Kolymbia, feed a river that's channelled into a narrow tunnel, exactly the size of an adult. Thrill-seeking visitors can walk a few hundred metres in pitch darkness, ankle-deep in fast-flowing water, to reach the shaded lake at the far end. There's also a taverna and the House of the Python gift shop, so called because it is indeed home to a colossal live snake.

❶ Getting There & Away

Frequent buses from Rhodes Town's Eastern Bus Terminal (p354) ply the main road, connecting the best-known beaches. If you're happy to hike, you can walk down to much emptier strands at several points along the way.

Lindos Λίνδος

POP 1100

With its timeless Acropolis atop a cypress-silvered hill, and sugar-cube houses tumbling towards an aquamarine bay, your first glimpse of the ancient village of Lindos is guaranteed to take your breath away.

Close up, things can feel very different. Lindos has become a major tourist destination, its approaches plagued by circling traffic and its narrow lanes jammed solid with sightseers. Come out of season, though, or stay the night and venture out before the day trippers arrive, and you can still experience the old Lindos, a warren of alleyways where the mansions of long-vanished sea captains hold tavernas, bars and cool cafes. Coax your calves up to the Acropolis, and you'll encounter one of the finest views in Greece.

Lindos has been enjoying its wonderful setting for 3000 years, since the Dorians first settled beside this excellent harbour. Since then it has been successively overlaid with Byzantine, Frankish and Turkish structures.

◉ Sights & Activities

★ Acropolis of Lindos
ARCHAEOLOGICAL SITE
(Map p343; ☑ 22440 31258; adult/concession/ child €12/6/free; ⊘ 8am-7.40pm Apr-Oct, to 3pm Tue-Sun Nov-Mar) A short, steep-stepped footpath climbs the rocky 116m-high headland above the village to reach Lindos' beautifully preserved Acropolis. First fortified in the 6th century BC, the clifftop is now enclosed by battlements constructed by the Knights of St John. Once within the walls, you're confronted by ancient remains that include the Temple to Athena Lindia and a 20-columned Hellenistic stoa. Silhouetted against the blue sky, the stark pillars are dazzling, while the long-range coastal views are out of this world.

Be sure to pack a hat and some water, as there's no shade at the top, and take care to protect young kids from the many dangerous drop-offs.

Donkey rides follow a longer pathway to the Acropolis from the village entrance (€8), an option that spares you a mere three minutes of exposed walking on the hillside. Animal-rights groups strongly urge visitors to consider how the donkeys are treated before deciding to ride.

★ Lepia Dive
DIVING
(☑ 6937417970; www.lepiadive.com; Pefkos; ⊛) Options with this brilliantly inclusive dive company include reef, wreck and cave dives, plus PADI courses for kids, beginners and advanced divers. The centre is adapted for wheelchairs, and offers expertly designed dives for people with additional needs, certified by Disabled Divers International. Free pickup.

🏖 Beaches

Lindos Main Beach
BEACH
The larger of Lindos' two superb beaches stretches north along the innermost shoreline of the bay, north of the village. Known logically enough as Main Beach, it's sandy and shelves softly into the sea, making it a perfect swimming spot for kids. In summer it gets very crowded. There's free parking on the hillside just above.

Pallas Beach
BEACH
Tucked just below Lindos village, pocket-sized, taverna-fringed Pallas Beach is reached by a footpath that drops down near the start of the mule trail up to the Acropolis, and can also be accessed directly from Main Beach by a narrow coastal path. Don't

swim near the jetty here, which is home to sea urchins, but if it gets too crowded you can launch yourself from the rocks beyond.

St Paul's Bay
BEACH
A short walk from the southern end of Lindos village, St Paul's Bay is an all-but-circular inlet that's only open to the Aegean via a slender gap in the rocks. Its tiny sheltered beach, caressed by turquoise waters, is a supremely tranquil place to swim, but does get very crowded in peak season.

Local tradition has it that St Paul sought refuge here in 57AD, when his ship was fleeing a storm at sea.

🛌 Sleeping

Accommodation in Lindos is very limited, so be sure to book in advance. And check carefully, as most hotels that include 'Lindos' in their names and/or addresses are in fact located not in the village centre, but along the coast nearby.

F Charm Hotel
BOUTIQUE HOTEL €€
(☑ 6944339937, 22440 32080; www.lindosfinestaying.com; Lindos VIllage; r incl breakfast from €140; ❋❀) This enclosed courtyard accommodation, next to the police station at the south end of the village, holds half-a-dozen heavenly white rooms plus two family-sized suites. All have shabby-chic distressed furniture, wood-beamed ceilings and traditional raised-platform beds with Cocomat mattresses, plus fridge and kitchenette.

Anastasia Studios
APARTMENT €€
(☑ 22440 31212; www.lindos-studios.gr; Lindos Village; d & tr €60; ℗❋❀) Focused around a geranium-filled courtyard, just in from the car park at Lindos' southern end, these six split-level apartments enjoy soaring Acropolis views. Each has a tiled floor, sofa bed, well-equipped kitchen and separate bedroom, while room 6 has its own private balcony.

★ Melenos Lindos
BOUTIQUE HOTEL €€€
(☑ 22440 32222; www.melenoslindos.com; Lindos Village; ste incl breakfast from €335; ❋@❀) ✎ This Moorish-style palace, on the mule trail above Pallas Beach, has bougainvillea walkways, pebble-mosaic floors, verandas festooned in lanterns and bauble lights that cast a glow on Ottoman furniture. Staff glide discreetly around as you soak up the stunning bay view. Rooms are lovingly re-created in traditional Lyndian style, with raised beds, wooden ceilings and private balconies, and there's a superb restaurant (p357).

DODECANESE LINDOS

🍴 Eating & Drinking

Most Lindos tavernas serve their customers on roof terraces high above the central tangle of lanes. Although these give fabulous views up to the Acropolis – illuminated at night – and over the bay, you can't necessarily tell whether there's anyone in your chosen venue until you've already committed to eat there.

Village Cafe
BAKERY €

(📋 22440 31559; www.villagecafelindos.com; Lindos Village; mains €8-20; ⊙ 8am-6.30pm Mon-Sat, to 5.30pm Sun; ⚹ 🛜 🚼) Near the start of the donkey path up to the Acropolis, this white-washed bakery-cafe consists of an enticing vine-covered pebble-mosaic courtyard, shaded over to keep things cool. Drop in for hot or frozen coffee, juice or ice cream, and a mouthwatering array of breakfasts, cheese-cakes, pies, salads, wraps and sandwiches. Don't miss the delectable *bougatsa* (vanilla custard pie).

⭐ Kalypso
TAVERNA €€

(📋 22440 32135; www.kalypsolindos.com; Lindos VIllage; mains €10-24; ⊙ 11am-midnight; ⚹ 🛜) This former sea captain's residence with its beautiful stone relief is perfect for lunch or dinner on the roof terrace or inside. Sea bass, octopus, *makarounes* (homemade pasta served with fresh onions and melted local cheese) and grilled lamb chops are but a few of the delights. Try the 'Kalypso bread' with feta and tomato.

Melenos
MEDITERRANEAN €€€

(📋 22440 32222; www.melenoslindos.com; Lindos VIllage; mains €22-32; ⊙ 8am-11pm; 🛜) This gorgeous terrace restaurant of the Melenos luxury hotel (p356) is set high above Pallas Beach on the donkey path up to the Acropolis. Standout dishes include salmon marinated in ouzo, steamed sea bass, goats' meat pasta and steak with baby vegetables in red-wine sauce. Round things off with a sumptuous dessert.

Ambrosia
MEDITERRANEAN €€€

(📋 22440 31804; Lindos Village; mains €14-42; ⊙ lunch & dinner; ⚹ 🍴) Lindos' smartest stand-alone restaurant doesn't have a roof garden – its dozen linen-clad tables are in the pristine white interior visible from the lanes – so the food has to be special. And it is, whether you opt for the raw sea-bream appetiser, squid-ink pasta or lamb shank. Owner George welcomes each diner with a little glass of sparkling wine.

Captain's House
CAFE

(📋 22440 31235; Lindos Village; snacks €5; ⊙ 8am-midnight; 🛜) Soaked in Lyndian atmosphere, this nautically themed, 16th-century sea captain's house is perfect for a juice or coffee on your way down from the Acropolis. Grab a pew in the pebble-mosaic courtyard and admire the fabulous carved reliefs, or peer into the ground floor, restored with period furniture to display the lifestyle of its original owners.

ℹ️ Information

Lindos Tourist Office (📋 22440 31900; Main Sq, Lindos Village; ⊙ 9am-3pm) Small information kiosk at the main village entrance.

Island Of The Sun Travel (📋 22440 31264; Lindos Village; ⊙ 9am-11pm) Local excursions, rental cars and accommodation.

ℹ️ Getting There & Away

Frequent buses connect the main square with the Eastern Bus Terminal (p354) in Rhodes Town, with services every half-hour at peak times (€5.50). That journey costs €65 by taxi, while a taxi to or from the airport costs €75.

Southeastern Rhodes

Immediately south of Lindos, resorts such as Pefki have been burgeoning in recent years. The further you continue down the east coast, however, traffic diminishes, villages seem to have a slower pace, and the landscape takes on an ever more windswept appearance.

Just 2km south of Lindos, sandy **Pefki Beach** is deservedly popular. If it's too crowded, try Glystra Beach, just down the road and a great spot for swimming.

Sleepy **Gennadi** consists of a cluster of coffeehouses, tavernas and whitewashed buildings, not far inland from the main road. In the opposite direction, the local beach is a long straight strand of sand and pebbles, which continues pretty much uninterrupted for the 11km south to **Plimmyri**. Watch for a signposted turning to Lahania, 2km inland; once there, head downhill into the centre to find an old village of winding alleyways and traditional buildings.

Beyond the signposted side road to Plimmyri, the main road heads west, leaving the coast and skirting Rhodes' southern tip. Don't miss the lonesome Colonia San Marco Caffé (p358), 5km along. It holds a little espresso cafe displaying memorabilia from its days as an Italian colonial outpost. Another 3km on, sleepy **Kattavia** livens up at lunchtime, when neighbouring tavernas jostle to feed circle-island day trippers.

A windswept road heads off south from Kattavia, snaking for 10km – and passing a monstrous new diesel-fuelled power plant – to reach remote **Cape Prasonisi**, the island's southernmost point. Joined to Rhodes by a tenuously narrow sandy isthmus in summer, it's cut off completely when water levels rise in winter. The Aegean Sea meets the Mediterranean here, creating ideal wind and wave conditions for kitesurfers and windsurfers. Outfitters help with everything from rental equipment and lessons to overnight accommodation in surfer-dude-style hostels, but it all closes down in winter.

🏃 Activities

Pro Center Christof Kirschner (☑ 22400 91045; www.prasonisi.com; Prasonisi Beach; ☉May-Oct; ♿) offers services for windsurfers include equipment rental (from €30 per hour) and two-hour classes (from €75).

🛏 Sleeping

Four comfortable and spacious apartments, perfect for a relaxing rural holiday, make up **Four Elements** (☑ 6939450014, 22440 46001; www.bnbthefourelements.com; Lahania; apt incl breakfast €115-180; 🅿❄@🛜🐾). All have full kitchens – one is adapted for wheelchair users – and there's a divine pool, outdoor barbecue and garden. Rates include buffet breakfast; minimum stay two nights. The friendly Belgian owners run the on-site Fifth Element cafe-bar.

🍴 Eating & Drinking

Taverna Platanos   TAVERNA €
(☑ 6944199991; www.lachaniaplatanostaverna.com; Lahania; mains €6-13.50; ☉11am-late; 🅿❄🛜)
It's worth braving Lahania's ultranarrow lanes to reach this classic village taverna, tucked behind Agios Georgios church and famed throughout the island. With its traditional decor and flower-filled patio, it's a great place to take a break. Lamb baked with lemon costs €13.50, while hearty beef or goat stews are €10.50, and salads and dips less than half that.

Mama's Kitchen   GREEK €
(☑ 22440 43547; mains €7-13; ☉breakfast, lunch & dinner; 🅿❄) In this lively and always-busy taverna in the heart of Gennadi, you can check out the murals depicting ancient myths while feasting on Olympian portions of grilled meat like lamb and beef, or child-friendly pizzas.

★**Colonia San Marco Caffé**   CAFE
(Map p343; ☑ 22440 91483; Kattavia; ☉8am-midnight; 🛜) This lonesome relic, 3km east of Kattavia, resembles something from a spaghetti western. Constructed in 1926 as the centrepiece of an Italian agricultural colony, it originally held a school and still holds a church. It's now home to a welcoming espresso cafe that, as well as selling snacks and local produce, displays memorabilia from its intriguing past.

ℹ Getting There & Away

If you don't have a rental car, local buses make a decent fallback. Regular buses (www.ktelrodou.gr) connect Rhodes Town with Pefki, Kiotari and Gennadi between around 6am and 9pm, but far fewer services continue to Lahania and Cape Prasonisi.

To get here direct from the airport by taxi costs around €120 and takes 1½ hours.

Western Rhodes & the Interior

Western Rhodes is redolent with the scent of pine, its hillsides shimmering with forests. More exposed than the east side, it's also windier – a boon for kitesurfers and windsurfers – so the sea tends to be rough and the beaches mostly pebbled. If you're cycling, or have a scooter or car, the hilly roads that cross the interior are well worth exploring for their wonderful scenery.

For sightseers, the most significant potential stopoffs along the west coast are the ruined ancient cities of Ialysos (p359) and, especially, Kamiros (p359). Once you get past the airport, settlements are few and far between. **Skala Kamirou**, 45km southwest of Rhodes Town, is a small port served by direct ferries to the nearby island of Halki. A couple of tavernas sit by the harbour, and connecting buses link it with Rhodes Town.

The ruins of 16th-century **Kritinia Castle** stand proudly on a headland immediately south of Skala Kamirou. Detour off the main road for awe-inspiring views along the coast and across to Halki, in a magical setting where you half expect to encounter Romeo or Rapunzel.

Continuing south, the road turns sublimely scenic. Vast mountainous vistas open up as you approach **Siana**, a picturesque village below Mt Akramytis (825m), and the village of **Monolithos**, 5km beyond. A spectacularly sited 15th-century castle (p359) stands 2km west, perched on a sheer-sided pinnacle. Thanks to a gap in the walls, there's free, unrestricted access; at sunset especially, the views are superb. Continue another 5km down a precipitous, winding road to reach the attractive, if gravelly, Fourni Beach ([P]).

◉ Sights

★ Ancient Kamiros
ARCHAEOLOGICAL SITE

(Map p343; ☑ 22410 40037; www.gtp.gr/archaeo logicalsiteofkameiros; €6; ⊗ 8am-7.40pm May-Oct, 8.30am-3pm Nov-Apr; ⊞) Cradled in a natural hillside amphitheatre 1km up from the sea, the remarkably complete ruins of ancient Kamiros stand 34km southwest of Rhodes Town. Founded in the 10th century BC, and mentioned by Homer, Kamiros reached its peak during the 7th century BC, but was devastated by earthquakes in 226 BC and 142 BC. Visitors enjoy a real feeling of walking the streets of an ancient city, complete with baths, temples, private homes and public squares.

Monolithos Castle
CASTLE

(Map p343; ⊗ 24hr; [P] ⊞) [FREE] Monolithos' 15th-century castle crowns an isolated pinnacle 2km west of the village towards Fourni Beach. Beside a cafe at a curve in the road, a short footpath climbs to the hole in the battlements that allows visitors unrestricted access. Only the inland side is walled; the far side is defended by sheer colossal cliffs. A little whitewashed chapel marks the summit, while another stands in ruins just below. Come if you can at sunset, when the views are magnificent.

Valley of the Butterflies
FOREST

(Petaloudes; Map p343; ☑ 22410 82822; €5; ⊗ 9am-5pm; [P] ⊞) The so-called Valley of the Butterflies, 7km up from the west coast, and 32km southwest of Rhodes Town, is a major day-trip destination for package tourists. A narrow wooded cleft in the mountains, threaded with attractive footpaths, it comes alive in summer – typically between around 10 June and 20 September – with colourful butterflies, drawn by the resin exuded by storax trees. That's by far the best time to visit, though the trails remain busy for most of the year.

Ancient Ialysos
ARCHAEOLOGICAL SITE

(Map p343; ☑ 22410 92202; www.gtp.gr/acropol isofialysos; €6; ⊗ 8am-7.40pm May-Oct, 8.30am-3pm Nov-Apr; ⊞) Ancient Ialysos was one of three cities that joined to create the new city of Rhodes in 408 BC. Its flat hilltop site, 12km southwest of Rhodes Town, can be reached by a signposted drive or a demanding but enjoyable 5km hike from nearby Ialysos, but there's surprisingly little to see. A paved walkway, lined by trees, climbs the final 100m to the Byzantine Monastery of Filcrimos that now occupies the summit, alongside the ruins of a small Athena temple.

🛏 Sleeping & Eating

Hotel Thomas
HOTEL €

(☑ 22460 61291; Monolithos; r €44; [P] ✳ 🛜) This good-value, long-standing village hotel, with very welcoming owners, sits 150m down the hillside from the southwestern end of Monolithos (turn opposite the Limeri restaurant). Its good-sized, tiled-floor rooms have tiny kitchenettes, and long-range views over the olive groves to the sea. A simple breakfast costs €5.

Limeri
GREEK €

(☑ 22460 61227; www.limeri.gr; Monolithos; mains €6.50-13; ⊗ breakfast, lunch & dinner; [P] ✳ 🛜) This large restaurant, beside the road as it heads out of Monolithos towards the castle, serves high-quality local food on a spacious terrace or in its cosy indoor dining room. The dolmadhes are excellent, while the hearty oven-baked lamb or goat is succulent and juicy. It also offers classy rooms (€50) and two-bedroom suites (€75).

To Stolidi Tis Psinthou
TAVERNA €€

(☑ 22410 50009; Psinthos; mains €9-13.50; ⊗ lunch & dinner; [P] ✳) The pick of several appealing lunch spots in the lively main square of Psinthos, 16km southeast of the Valley of the Butterflies. The wooden-beamed interior holds a colourful array of vintage bric-a-brac, and the excellent food comes in huge portions. Be sure to try high-cal, local speciality *kapamas* – meat, rice, potatoes and herbs all baked together – and the chickpea croquettes.

❶ Getting There & Away

All buses along the west coast depart from the Western Bus Terminal (p354) in Rhodes Town. Every morning, separate excursion buses serve Ialysos (Mon-Sat), Kamiros and the Valley of the Butterflies. In addition, connecting buses carry ferry passengers between Skala Kamirou and Rhodes Town, and there's also a bus service to Monolithos, on Monday and Friday only.

MATT MUNRO/LONELY PLANET ©

1. Kalymnos (p339)
A woman sells a selection of sponges on the rugged and dramatic island of Kalymos.

2. Monastery of St John (p413), Kalymnos
This sumptuously frescoed chapel is fronted by marble columns taken from an ancient temple.

3. Mandraki (p382), Nisyros
Stroll through this peaceful, almost traffic-free town.

4. Symi (p374)
The island abounds with Italian-influenced architecture.

HALKI ΧΑΛΚΗ

POP 310

Thanks to the gorgeous Italianate mansions that surround its harbour, the former sponge-diving island of Halki makes an irresistible first impression. Stepping off the ferry, you enter a composite of all that's best about Greece: an old fisherman shelling prawns under a fig tree, an Orthodox priest flitting down a narrow alley, brightly painted boats bobbing along the quay. There's little to do except relax and indulge in the sleepy splendour, venturing out to tempting little beaches lapped by aquamarine waters and, in cooler months, hiking along the island's spectacular high-mountain spine to visit the island's monastery and admire the views.

ⓘ Getting There & Away

The **Dodekanisos Seaways** (Map p346; ☏ 22410 70590; www.12ne.gr/en; Kolona Harbour, Old Town) catamaran stops at Halki's port in Emborios on Tuesday and Thursday as it heads from Rhodes via Halki (€18, 80 minutes) to Tilos (€13, 40 minutes), Nisyros (€24, 1½ hour), Kos (€24, 1½ hour) and Kalymnos (€35, three hours) in the morning, and back to Rhodes in the evening. On those days, you can visit the island as a day trip from Rhodes. Anek Prevalis (of **Anek Lines** (Map p346; ☏ 22410 35066; www.anek.gr/en; 5 Akti Sahtouri)) runs three days a week linking Santorini, Anafi, Kasos, Karpathos (Pigadia and Diafani) and finally, Rhodes. Once a week it heads between Halki and Iraklio on Crete (€22, 11½ hours).

Three boats, **Nissos Halki** (Velis Lines; Map p343; ☏ 6946519817, 6934117388; Skala Kamirou; ⊙ 2-3 daily Tue-Sun), **Nikos Express** (☏ 6946826905; nikos_express@hotmail.com; Skala Kamirou; ⊙ 1-2 daily Wed-Sun) and **Fedon** (☏ 22460 45110), link Halki daily with the tiny port of Skala Kamirou on the west coast of Rhodes; there's an hour-long connecting bus service with Rhodes Old Town.

ⓘ Getting Around

In summer, regular minibuses connect Emborios with Pondamos, Ftenagia and Kania beaches (€2 each way), while on Friday evenings there's also a round trip to Moni Agiou Ioanni monastery (€5). A summer-only excursion boat heads to the uninhabited island of Alimia (around €30).

Emborios Εμπορειός

POP 300

Halki's one tiny town curves luxuriantly around a sheltered turquoise bay. The waterfront is a broad expanse of flagstones, almost entirely pedestrianised, populated by as many cats as humans and lined with enticing tavernas and cafes. Climbing in tiers up a low ridge, the cream, ochre, stone and rose-hued homes of 19th-century fisherfolk and sea captains form a magnificent backdrop. There's no town beach, but here and there ladders enable swimmers to enter the water.

◉ Sights

The neoclassical mansions of Emborios are a visual feast. A few have crumbled into complete ruination, but most have been restored and many now serve as rental properties.

The impressive central **clock tower** was donated by the expat Halki community in Florida; the clock itself hasn't worked for over 20 years. Nearby, the **Church of Agios Nikolaos** has the tallest belfry in the Dodecanese, incorporating stones from an ancient temple of Apollo, and has a picturesque mosaic-pebbled courtyard.

The **Traditional House of Chalki** (☏ 22460 45284; €2.50; ⊙ 11am-3pm & 6-8pm) is perched on the hillside, not far up from the harbour (signed to the right off the road to Pondamos Beach), the Traditional House of Chalki – an alternative transliteration of Halki – is a two-storey family home, built a century ago. It's now meticulously preserved as a museum, displaying authentic furniture, tableware and costumes, old photos – and even the underwear of the owner's grandmother, neatly framed.

⎚ Sleeping

Captain's House PENSION €
(☏ 22460 45201, 6932511762; capt50@otenet.gr; d €45; ❊ 🕾) Attractive white-painted 19th-century house just up from the sea, near the church, featuring antique clocks and model schooners. Two lovely rooms have high ceilings, wood floors, air-con and good bathrooms, and the relaxing garden courtyard holds a sun terrace with great harbour views. Excellent value for money.

★ **Aretanassa Hotel** HOTEL €€
(☏ 22460 70927; www.facebook.com/aretanassa.hotel; Harbour; incl breakfast d €105-122, tr €127; ❊ 🕾 ≋) This wine-coloured former sponge

factory (donated to the municipality by the owner) has 19 gloriously sunny, sea-facing rooms with powder-blue walls, large beds and spotless tiled floors. Nearly all rooms have balconies. There's a lovely restaurant and bar, and a sun terrace over your own azure Mediterranean swimming pool. There's also a lift and access for those with additional needs.

✖ Eating

Magefseis GREEK €

(☎ 22460 45065; mains €7-11; ⊙ breakfast, lunch & dinner; 🖋) 🍃 Don't be misled by the commercial-looking, photo-filled menu. This place has a unique take, from the jovial owner, Christos, to the fresh (and yes, it is fresh) seafood that comes off the boats. The rest of the huge menu spans grills to the standard cooked favourites (*mousakas* etc), but you can't go wrong. Portions are not huge, but adequate.

Dimitri's Bakery BAKERY €

(snacks €1.50-3; ⊙ 6am-3pm) Generations of Halki residents and visitors have stocked up on Dimitri's delicious sweet and savoury pies and pastries, available from early morning. Cheese pies. Spinach pies. Apple pies. Croissants. You get the doughy, mouthwatering picture. Don't miss the *tsoureki*, the sweet bread.

Black Sea TAVERNA €€

(☎ 22460 45021; mains €8-15; ⊙ lunch & dinner; ❄🖋) 🍃 Sitting peacefully on the south side of the harbour, metres from bobbing boats, this blue-hued haunt is run by a charming Georgian family. It's great for fresh fish, from octopus and little shrimp to grilled bream, but the vegetable dishes, including fried mushrooms, are also delicious. Has a slightly gourmet touch that some others lack.

ℹ Information

The only ATM, which is located under the **post office** (⊙ 9am-2.45pm Mon-Fri) is often out of action, so bring plenty of spare cash.

Zifos Travel (☎ 22460 45028; www.zifos travel.gr; ⊙ 10am-8pm) The best source of help with boat tickets and currency exchange.

ℹ Getting There & Away

All boats arrive at the island's harbour in Emborios. From here, it's an easy walk to your hotel (albeit with steps); for around €5, a baggage cart meets boats and will transport your luggage.

Around Halki

A broad concrete road crosses the low hill above Emborios Harbour to reach Pondamos Beach (p363), the most popular of Halki's handful of tiny shingle beaches, after 500m. Beyond that, it climbs to the abandoned village of Horio, 3km along, then continues west to the hilltop monastery of Agiou Ioanni. That's a total one-way hike of 8km, recommended in the cooler months only.

Two more pebble beaches, both equipped with decent tavernas and served by buses in summer, lie within walking distance of Emborios. Ftenagia Beach is beyond the headland 500m south of the harbour, while Kania Beach is an enjoyable but unshaded 2.5km hike north, signposted off the main road halfway to Pondamos.

◉ Sights & Activities

Horio ARCHAEOLOGICAL SITE

A stiff switchback climb along the road from Pondamos Beach leads up through Halki's fertile central valley to Horio. This picturesque ruin was originally the island's main village, hidden away to escape the eyes of roving pirates. A freshly cobbled footpath heads up to the battlements of the Knights of St John Castle that once protected it. Pass through its forbidding gateway to see a restored chapel and amazing long-range views.

Chalki Dive Center DIVING

(☎ 6943117220; www.chalkidive.com; Kania Beach) This new PADI-certified diving operation, the only one on Halki, gives divers the chance to explore the waters off Kania Beach. And believe us, you'll want to don the tanks and masks when you see the crystal 'H-two-Oh!' here. Prices start from €40 for advanced certified divers, to €50 for beginners. Children over eight years can dive, too (€50).

🏖 Beaches

Pondamos Beach BEACH

Pretty little Pondamos Beach is lapped by the turquoise waters of a crescent bay 15 minutes' walk up and over the hill west of Emborios. The only way to get a comfortable shaded spot is to rent a sunbed alongside Nick's Taverna (☎ 22460 45295; Pondamos Beach; mains €6-15; ⊙ breakfast & lunch, dinner Fri only; 🖋), where separate sections serve good seafood meals, and drinks and snacks.

DODECANESE AROUND HALKI

KARPATHOS
ΚΑΡΠΑΘΟΣ

POP 6200

Celebrated for its wild mountains and blue coves, this long craggy island is among the least commercialised in Greece (although that is changing). Legend has it Prometheus and his Titans were born here, and with its cloud-wrapped villages and rugged beauty, there's still something undeniably primal in the air. Homer mentions it in the the *Iliad*. It's a lovely spot.

Popular with adrenaline junkies, southern Karpathos is in the spotlight each summer when it hosts an international kitesurfing competition. Meanwhile, the fierce wind that lifts the spray from the turquoise waves blows its way to the mountainous north, battering pine trees and howling past sugar-cube houses. Karpathian women at this end of the island still wear traditional garb, especially in the time-forgotten village eyrie of Olymbos, perched atop a perilous mountain ridge.

ⓘ Getting There & Away

AIR

The airport at the very southern tip of Karpathos is linked by Olympic Air (p343) which has daily flights to Athens (€75, one hour). Sky Express (p343) has daily links between Karpathos and Rhodes (€68, 40 minutes), plus Kasos (€56, 15 minutes). It also heads to Iraklio, Crete, via Rhodes (€162, two hours).

BOAT

The island's main port, Pigadia, is served by Blue Star Ferries and Anek Lines (which stops at Diafani). **Blue Star** (Map p349; ☑ 22410 22461; www.bluestarferries.com; Amerikis 111, New Town; ☺ 9am-8pm) has a weekly connection to/from Rhodes, Symi, Kos, Kalymnos, Leros and Patmos. Anek Lines (p362) ferries head once a week to/from Milos (€38, 20¼ hours), Santorini (€27, 15¼ hours), Anafi (€17, 13¼ hours), Iraklio (€19, 8¼ hours), Sitia (€19, 4¾ hours) and Kasos (€8, 1¾ hours) before ending up at Karpathos en route to Rhodes.

Local passenger ferry, the **Kasos Princess** (☑ 6977911209; one way €10; 1½ hours), also offers day excursions to Kasos three times a week; one-way trips are permitted (but check first as regulations change).

ⓘ Getting Around

TO/FROM THE AIRPORT

The airport is 14km southwest of Pigadia. A taxi will cost around €25. From Monday to Friday there is a daily bus departure to the airport from Pigadia (€3), but don't count on getting from the airport (at the time of research it departed at 7am). Given the size of the island it makes sense to rent a car. Many car-rental chains are based at the airport plus there are a couple of excellent in-town options that will arrange pickup.

BOAT

Day trips head from Pigadia up to Diafani, where they connect with buses to Olymbos, or continue north to remote beaches.

BUS

KTEL runs buses all over the island from the bus station (p368) in Pigadia, just up from the harbour. In summer, there's a daily departure to/from Apella Beach and around four weekly services to Finiki. There's a daily summer service to southern beaches though these change seasonally; check the return times before you head off. Between two and four buses a week go all the way north to Olymbos.

CAR

All major car-rental chains have outlets at the airport, and there are local agencies mainly based in Pigadia, but also in resort towns. A recommended operator is **Euromoto** (☑ 22450 23238, 6970130912; www.euromoto.com; scooter/car from €15/45) run by English-speaking George; it has four offices around the island.

TAXI

Taxi prices are posted at Pigadia's central **taxi rank** (☑ 22450 22705; Dimokratias). Fares are prohibitively high, with trips to Lefkos costing €60 and Olymbos €85.

Pigadia   Πηγάδια

POP 1690

Karpathos' capital and main ferry port, Pigadia sprawls beside a long bay in the island's southeast. Decent beaches stretch away to the north, backed by large resorts. The town lacks the photogenic good looks and geometrically pleasing whitewashed houses of other island capitals. But it makes up for this. For here, it's about the people. It's proudly, determinedly Greek. Give it a little time and wander its harbour and among waterfront bars and backstreet bakeries. Chat to the locals who frequently invite you to sit by them for a coffee. This place will grow on you.

🛏 Sleeping

Budget options are concentrated in the hillside streets that rise from central Pigadia, while newer and more luxurious options are resort style; these spread northwards around the curve of the bay.

Rose's Studios
APARTMENT €

(✆ 22450 22284; www.rosesstudios.com; r €35; ❄) For ultrasimple, but good-value budget lodgings, it's well worth trudging 300m up from the port to reach these eight dated, but functional, rooms. They have clean bathrooms, large sea-view balconies and decent fittings, including minimal kitchenettes. It's an extra €5 per day for air conditioning.

Nereides Hotel
HOTEL €€

(✆ 22450 23347; www.nereideshotel.gr; Nereidon; d incl breakfast €130; P❄❄🏊) This charming little hotel has been open since 2011 and everything from the paintwork to its up-to-the-minute bathrooms still gleams like new. It offers 30 stylish rooms with sea-view balconies, plus a good pool and snack bar. It's on the town's western edge and, although 10 minutes' walk from the beach, it's a good 15 minutes plus to the harbour.

Atlantis Hotel
HOTEL €€

(✆ 22450 22777; www.atlantishotelkarpathos.gr; incl breakfast s €65-75, d €75-88; ❄❄🏊) Long-established, family-run hotel across from the Italian-era public building just above the west end of the harbour. The pleasant, no-frills rooms are nicely maintained, though the hot water can be a bit temperamental. Although cheaper, those facing the decent-sized pool are pleasant; the lower ones have their own mini terrace. Decent breakfast.

✗ Eating

Both the quay and the pedestrian streets just behind it are lined with seafood tavernas, all-purpose brasseries, cafes and cocktail bars. Look out, too, for the Italian gelaterias on Apodimon Karpathion, parallel to the harbour.

Pantheon Cafe
CAFE €

(✆ 22450 22502; Papathanassiou; snacks €5-12; ⊙ 8am-late; ❄❄) The pick of the best-of-both-worlds cafes along this pedestrian street, with a fine old wood-panelled interior decorated in *kafeneio* style of old, and a rear balcony terrace, perched high above the harbour with fabulous views. Sure, you can get a full English breakfast (€11) but it's the salads that really hit the spot. Go for the Karpathian (€9, with cucumber, olives and local bread).

★ To Ellenikon
TAVERNA €€

(✆ 22450 23932; Apodimon Karpathion; mains €8-20; ⊙ lunch & dinner; ❄❄✍) If you're looking for typical Karpathian food cooked the way it should be then 'the Greek' is your place. Try

saganaki (fried cheese), meatballs, shrimp and calamari, served within the wood-accented traditional interior or outside on the narrow terrace. Also offers hefty, more 'international' dishes should you want a change. Owner, Christos, meets and greets and works the floor.

WORTH A TRIP

APELLA BEACH

However determined you may be to reach Olymbos, allow time to take the precipitous spur road that drops seawards from the east-coast highway 17km north of Pigadia. Here you'll find award-winning **Apella Beach** (Map p365); backed by a cascading hillside of wildflowers, with towering cliffs to both north and south, it is the finest beach in the Dodecanese. It's often described as 'sandy', though it was pebbly when we were there. Nevertheless, it's gorgeous. There's a good taverna at road's end, just above the beach.

Odyssey GREEK €€

(22450 23506; www.facebook.com/OdysseyRes taurantKarpathos; Harbour; mains €7-13.50) Owner Pascales comes from the region of Macedonia, so don't expect things to be served the same way here, despite their having the same menu listings. Your culinary odyssey will include delicious dolmadhes (with lemon and oil), eggplant salad that's grilled (not boiled), and pastas and grilled meats with different herbs. Mains are served with vegetables – a welcome treat.

Drinking & Nightlife

★**Caffe Karpathos** CAFE

(Angolo Italiano; 21022 87383; www.cafekarpa thos.com; Apodimon Karpathion; ⊙7am-late; 🛜) The oldest cafe on the island was once a magnet for Italians (thus the fabulous coffee served in the original Bialetti espresso pots). These days travellers and locals alike nestle into wicker chairs, with a fabulous brew or cocktail in hand, and philosophise with Michalis, the multilingual owner. Simply relax and chat, Greek style. It's a thrill in itself.

Enplo COCKTAIL BAR

(cocktails €6; ⊙8am-late; 🛜) This chilled spot on the quay offers good happy hour cocktails (from €8). Its impressive snack menu has six vegan options.

Information

Both the **National Bank of Greece** on Apodimon Karpathion, and **Alpha Bank**, a block higher on Dimokratias, have ATMs.

Possi Travel (22450 23342; 28 Oktovriou; ⊙8am-1pm & 5-8pm) The main travel agency

for ferry and air tickets. The helpful staff speak excellent English.

Tourist Office (www.karpathos.org; ⊙Jul & Aug) Summer-only kiosk, in the middle of the seafront.

Getting There & Away

Local passenger ferry, the Kasos Princess (p364), offers day excursions to Kasos three times a week; one-way trips are permitted (but check first as regulations change).

Pigadia's bus station (p368), just up from the harbour, is served by KTEL buses, which travel infrequently to various destinations across the island. You can obtain printed schedules from the station's tiny office.

There's a taxi (p364) stand up the hill from the harbourfront; a sign shows destinations and costs.

Southern Karpathos

Thanks to their sandy beaches, several appealing villages in the southern half of Karpathos have reinvented themselves as small-scale resorts. Peaceful villages nestle amid the hills inland, an area that's criss-crossed by scenic walking tracks. Here, too, you can have a surfing lesson on the island's only surf beach, Agios Nikolaos, near Arkasa.

Menetes

Buffeted by mountain gales, the tiny village of Menetes sits high in the cliffs just above Pigadia. Climb to the church at its highest point before exploring its narrow white-washed streets.

To gain entry to the anceint chapel that houses the two-roomed **Folklore Museum** (6985847672; Menetes; ⊙9am-1pm & 5-8pm) **FREE**, you need to call ahead to Irini, custodian of the keys. Having unlocked it, she'll talk you through its haphazard treasures and point you towards the tunnels in the hillside nearby, used by German troops in WWII. Donations welcomed.

Sit under the shade of the lemon tree at **Dionysos Fiesta** (22450 81269; Menetes; mains €6-10; ⊙breakfast, lunch & dinner; ❄🛜) and enjoy the likes of lemon chicken, artichoke omelettes and succulent Karpathian sausages. Run by the ultrafriendly Irini, and set in a restored traditional house, in the twisting village lanes just up from the main road, this relaxed and welcoming taverna spreads onto a raised garden terrace.

Arkasa

Arkasa, on the southwest coast 9km from Menetes, is one of the oldest settlements on Karpathos. The original village centre, just up from the water, is now complemented by a burgeoning beach resort below. A waterside track leads 500m to the remains of the 5th-century **Basilica of Agia Sophia**, where two chapels stand amid mosaic fragments and columns, and to an ancient acropolis on the headland beyond.

The best beach hereabouts, sandy **Agios Nikolaos Beach** is accessible from the village, but you'll need to drive there.

🛏 Sleeping

★**Glaros Studios** APARTMENT €€
(✆22450 61015; www.glarosstudios-karpathos. com; Agios Nikolaos Beach, Arkasa; apt €80; P 🛜) This well-managed, garden-set complex of five studios pretty much has Agios Nikolaos Beach to itself. There are spotless white studios, decorated in traditional Karpathian style with raised platform beds and small kitchenettes, plus a relaxed and good-value adjoining restaurant.

Eleni Studios APARTMENT €€
(✆22450 61248; www.elenikarpathos.gr; Arkasa; studio €70, apt from €90; P ✳🛜🞮) On the road to Finiki and fronting the beach, Eleni Studios has fully equipped and very tidy powder-blue apartments with appealing bedrooms, built around a relaxing garden. There's an on-site bar, too, for sunset drinks and breakfast (extra cost), and a very tempting pool. Great sea views.

Finiki

Arrayed along a neat little south-facing crescent bay, picturesque Finiki stands just 2km north of Arkasa. White-and-blue houses, interspersed with a peppering of tavernas, front its sleepy harbour and small grey-sand beach. The best local swimming is at **Agios Georgios Beach**, a short way south towards Arkasa.

🛏 Sleeping & Eating

★**Arhontiko Finikes** APARTMENT €
(✆22450 61473; www.hotelarhontiko.gr; Finiki; apt from €50) Clean, ultraspacious apartments with the most lovely view of the water. You can choose between contemporary decor or traditional Karpathian-style fit-outs, com-

plete with a platform bed to sleep in, and wooden shelving on the walls (there's even willow pattern plates in some). There's no full-time reception; instead, the friendly Australian-Greek owners cater to your needs as required.

Marina Taverna TAVERNA €€
(✆22450 61100; Finiki; mains €7-16; ☉breakfast, lunch & dinner; 🛜) One of the few places open all year, this laid-back taverna features an expansive terrace that surveys the gentle turquoise bay just metres from the waterfront. Enjoy inexpensive breakfasts, snack lunches and an enjoyable seafood-accented evening menu featuring squid, crab and grilled meats.

Lefkos

The largest and most attractive of the low-key west-coast resorts, Lefkos is 20km north of Finiki and a 5km detour down from the main road. Lefkos is here for a very good reason – its curving sandy beach is absolutely delightful. This is the kind of place where two weeks can vanish in gentle wanderings between beach and brunch.

🛏 Sleeping & Eating

★**Hotel Lefkorama** HOTEL €€
(✆6909091840, 22450 71173; www.lefkorama.gr; d/apt €95/58; P ✳🛜) This gorgeous hotel may not be on the beach, but sits instead in its own patch of peaceful olive-groved paradise. Recently renovated fresh white rooms pop with colour accents. Delightful English-speaking Sofia serves up amazing breakfasts in the lovely garden sunroom. It's a 2km walk from Potali Bay, and 2.5km from Lefkos Beach, and has a handy taverna 20m up the road.

It's also near interesting ruins of a Roman cistern (as Sofia says, 'sure, it ain't the Parthenon, but very interesting all the same!'). Prices are significantly less outside of high season.

Le Grand Bleu HOTEL €€
(✆22450 71009; www.karpathos-legrandbleu. com; Lefkos; studio/apt €88/125; ✳🛜) Very nicely equipped studios and two-bedroom apartments beside the graceful main beach, kitted out with crisp fresh linen, tasteful art and sumptuous balconies with cushioned armchairs. The kitchen of the highly recommended on-site taverna closes at 10pm to let guests sleep. A gorgeous spot.

DON'T MISS

OLYMBOS

Few moments can beat rounding a curve in the mountain road to receive your first glimpse of this mist-blown eyrie of pastel-coloured houses. Olymbos clings precariously to the summit of Mt Profitis Ilias (716m), as if flung there by a Titan's hand. Thread your way along its wind-tunnel alleys, passing old ladies in vividly coloured traditional dress, and you may feel as though you've strayed onto a film set. Some locals even speak with a dialect that still contains traces of ancient Dorian Greek.

It's considered to be the most traditional of all places in Greece; some of Olymbos' local ladies still wear their stunning hand-spun jackets and floral headgear. And the views – 'jaw-dropping' just doesn't cover it – will leave you spellbound as the earth plunges dramatically metres from your feet. Try to arrive in late afternoon or early morning to have the place to yourself.

The most memorable way of reaching Olymbos is by taking a private tour boat/water taxi to Diafani from Pigadia, then catching the connecting prearranged bus. The schedules vary according to the various taxi boats running from Pigadia's harbour, but most leave at around 8.30am and cost about €25.

There's also around three weekly summer bus services from Pigadia, departing at 8.45am or 9.15am and returning at 3.45pm. You can drive the spectacular, if winding, route (take it very slowly and keep your eyes on the road and *not* the views, however spectacular they are). Taxis from Pigadia cost €85.

Hotel Aphrodite (☑22450 51307; www.discoverolympos.com; d/tr €45/50; ☎) This hotel is located just beyond the central square at the far end of Olymbos. Its four rooms have seen better days (nothing has been done to them for years), but they are simple spaces with a fridge and kettle and above all – literally – they have astonishing west-facing sea views. The owners run the recommended Parthenon restaurant nearby, topped by a roof terrace.

Hotel Olymbos (☑22450 51009; r incl breakfast €45) Hidden away beneath the owners' excellent street-level restaurant, these two rooms have raised beds and traditional furnishings. Tread carefully; the walls are festooned in the traditional manner – with delicate decorated plates.

O Mylos (☑22450 51333; mains €7-14; ⊗lunch & dinner) This wonderful spot, beside a traditional (and working) windmill, serves Karpathian dishes, some of which are cooked in a traditional oven. This means while you wrap your teeth around some of the island's best home-baked bread, or tuck into a goat stew, you can gaze across at one of Greece's finest views.

Dramountana　　　　　　TAVERNA €€
(☑22450 71373; Lefkos; mains €8-15; ⊗8am-late) Part of a cluster of five almost-identical cafes-tavernas with waterside tables at the northern end of Lefkos Harbour, this all-day cafe serves everything from fresh juices and coffee to grilled squid, lamb and souvlakia.

❶ Getting There & Away

The airport is situated in the far south of the island. Finiki, Lefkos, Menetes and Arkasa are served by KTEL buses to/from Pigadia **bus terminus** (☑22450 22338; M Mattheou) with one to three buses per day, except Sundays (check this, however, as summer services do change).

Diafani　Διαφάνι
POP 250

Diafani is an intimate, wind-blasted huddle of white houses fronted by cobalt-blue water, with a mountain backdrop. Bar the crash of the waves and old men playing backgammon, nothing else stirs. Most travellers simply pass through Diafani, so if you stay you'll likely have the beaches and trails to yourself. There's no post office or petrol station, but there is an ATM (but no bank).

🏃 Activities

Hiking

Hiking trails from Diafani are waymarked with red or blue markers or stone cairns. The most popular route heads inland, straight up the valley to Olymbos. That takes around two hours – though inevitably some prefer to catch a bus uphill and walk back down. Alternatively, a 4km track (50 minutes) leads north along the coast, through the pines, to Vananda Beach, which has a seasonal taverna.

A more strenuous three-hour walk takes you 11km northwest to the Hellenistic site of Vroukounda, passing the agricultural village of Avlona along the way. There are no facilities, so carry food and water with you.

Anyone planning serious walking should get hold of the 1:60,000 *Karpathos-Kasos* map, published by Terrain Maps (www.terrainmaps.gr) and available in Pigadia. Note: conditions change regularly on these paths and each season they can get a little straggly. Check with locals before you head out.

Boat Trips

Boat excursions head north daily from Diafani to inaccessible beaches on Karpathos and the nearby island of Saria.

🛏 Sleeping & Eating

Balaskas Hotel　　　　　　　　HOTEL €
(📞 22450 51320; www.balaskashotel.com; d €40-45; ❄🏠) The choice here is of either 'economy' rooms (essentially pension-style minimalism with white walls and wood beds) or 'standard', which feature more colour and flair, with romantic mozzie nets and wrought-iron beds. Some have kitchenettes, all have fridges. It's a five- to 10-minute walk from the seafront.

★ Corali　　　　　　　　　　TAVERNA €
(📞 22450 51332; mains €7-12; ⊙ lunch & dinner) Run by Popi and Mihalis, this is *the* spot for fresh, tasty traditional fare. These spontaneous creatives whip up the likes of delicious *stifadho* (meat or seafood cooked with onions in a tomato puree) or eggplant. The salads are tops; vegetables are sourced locally. Service is slow but the quality of the food and *filoxenia* (hospitality) make up for it.

ℹ Getting There & Away

Anek (p362) ferries call in at Diafani's small jetty twice a week en route to/from Pigadia, Halki and Rhodes, and three times weekly en route to/from Pigadia and Kasos (€4, one hour). One of these continues to, or returns from, Crete (€19, eight hours) while two other services head to/from Santorini (€27, 15½ hours). There are also day trips by boat to Pigadia in summer, as well as assorted excursions (from €10 per person).

Tourist coaches carry day trippers from the jetty up to Olymbos. Unfortunately for both locals and tourists, there's only one weekly bus to/from Pigadia, but in summer services can increase (via Olymbos).

KASOS　　　　ΚΑΣΟΣ

POP 800

Kasos, the southernmost Dodecanese island, looks like the Greece that time forgot. Deceptively inviting in summer, it can feel very isolated in winter, when it's battered by severe winds and imprisoned by huge turquoise waves. Most of its visitors are rare seabirds; most of the human returnees are Kasiots on fleeting visits. Come here, though, and you may well succumb to its tumbledown charm.

ℹ Getting There & Away

There are daily flights (except Sundays) to/from Karpathos (€60, 10 minutes) and Rhodes (€75, one hour) with Sky Express (p343).

There's a once-a-week Blue Star Ferries (p364) service en route between Rhodes and Piraeus (via Milos (€35, 18 hours), Santorini (€27, 13½ hours) and Anafi (€23, 11½ hours); another goes to Karpathos (€8, 1½ hours) and Halki (€16, 5¾ hours). Anek Lines (p362) heads twice a week to/from Crete (€20, 6¼ hours). An excellent alternative to the ferries is the *Kasos Princess*, both an excursion boat (p370) and ferry alternative. In summer it runs daily except for Thursdays and Sundays (check ahead as schedules can change).

Fry　　　　Φρυ

POP 350

The capital, Fry (pronounced 'free'), is on the north coast. The broad gentle valley behind it is the only fertile land on Kasos, so the only other villages are dotted across the surrounding hillside. Although Fry is more of a working port than a tourist destination, the tiny old harbour at its core, known as Bouka, is impossibly photogenic. Shabby, if pretty, white houses with navy-blue trim line the quay, a few cafes sit waiting for customers, grizzled fishermen patiently mend their nets, and the white-and-pastel-blue church of Agios Spyridon surveys the scene.

Kasos

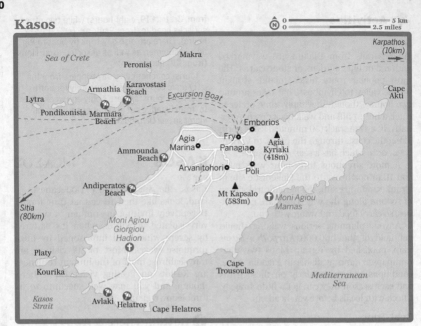

Even as late as June, though, Fry still has the feel of a ghost town.

The nearest beach is 10 minutes' walk east along the shoreline, in the tiny satellite port of **Emborios**. There are patches of gravel amid the sand, but the sea is clear and sheltered, so it's a good place for a quick dip.

◉ Sights & Activities

Archaeological Museum   MUSEUM
(☉9am-3pm Jul-Sep) FREE Housed in a grand 19th-century villa above the harbour, this seasonal museum displays objects pulled from ancient shipwrecks, assorted Greek oil lamps and Hellenistic finds, including inscribed stone slabs.

Excursion Boat   BOATING
(Kasos Princess; ☑22450 41047, 6977911209; ☷) When they can round up 10 or more passengers, two boats, *Athina* and *Kasos Princess,* offer summer excursions on Monday, Wednesday and Saturday (€15) to the uninhabited islet of Armathia, which has superb sandy beaches. The *Kasos Princess* also runs full-day trips to Pigadia on Karpathos, daily except Thursday and Sunday (€10 one way), plus it heads to Sitia, Crete, every Friday (€15 one way). Check ahead as schedules may change.

🛏 Sleeping & Eating

Amfi Rooms   APARTMENT €€
(☑6972140910, 22450 41175; r €70; P❋☎) Set 1km up on the hill behind Fry, with a glorious view, these dark wooded and stone studios comprise a spacious all-in-one traditional raised bed, kitchenette and living area, plus a washing machine. Mosquito netting covers the windows. The owner runs **Mylos** (☑22450 41825; Plateia Iroön Kasou; mains €6.50-11; ☉lunch & dinner; ☎☑) taverna and will arrange to pick you up from the airport.

Giaeli   GREEK €
(☑22450 41779; mains €5-9; ☉noon-late) The best spot to eat in Fry (and one of the best on the island), Giaeli (meaning 'traditional song') has raised the island's cuisine bar. This is traditional food but with a big difference: a gourmet twist and lovely presentation. The setting is gorgeous – in a pretty historic building or outside by the water – in the middle of Bouka Harbour.

Owner Maria also runs the gourmet canteen at Helatros Beach that's been celebrated by locals and tourists alike.

Taverna Emborios   TAVERNA €
(☑22450 41586; Emborios Beach; mains €8-10; ☉lunch & dinner Jun-Sep; ☎) Crisp, beautifully neat beachfront restaurant (open high sea-

son only), 10 minutes' walk from Fry. The friendly owner, who lived in New York for many years, serves up wonderful local specialities, including delicious octopus, tiny home-grown olives and his own salty preserved fish. One of the best on the island.

★ **Meltemi** MEZEDHES €€
(mezedhes €6-11; ⊙ 7.30pm-late) Open all year, this atmospheric spot – whose traditional artefacts accessorise a handsome wood-and-tile interior – is an *ouzerie* come *mezedhopoleio* (place that serves mezedhes, or appetisers). The enthusiastic owner will efficiently cook everything on the spot, from scrambled eggs with spicy sausage, to *fava* and meats. But the highlights are the seafood nibbles: cuttlefish, stingray and octopus. Located 80m behind the harbour.

❶ Information

Both the Commercial Bank on the main road leading off the port, and Alpha to the right of the port facing town, have ATMs.
Kasos Maritime & Travel Agency (☑ 22450 41495; www.kasos-island.gr; Plateia Iroön Kasou) For all travel tickets.

❶ Getting There & Away

The island's airport is 1km west of Fry. Either walk for 15 minutes along the coast road – yes, it's exposed, but you won't half feel pleased with yourself – or call a taxi. A small island bus runs from Monday to Friday; it's meant for the locals but tourists can take it, too, though keep in mind that for many elderly, it's their only means of transport. Cars and scooters can be hired from **Oasis Rent-a-Car** (☑ 6974594486, 22450 41746; from €30).

Around Kasos

None of the beaches on Kasos offer shade. The best is the isolated pebbled cove of **Helatros**, near Moni Agiou Georgiou Hadion, 11km southwest of Fry, but you'll need your own transport to reach it. In the summer months it has a fabulous food canteen run by the owner of Giaeli (p370). Otherwise, there's no facilities. There's another tiny but decent beach, **Avlaki**, in walking distance.

Agia Marina, 1km southwest of Fry, is a pretty village with a gleaming white-and-blue church that celebrates a festival on 17 July. You can grab a coffee or a meal at the friendly **To Steki** (☑ 22450 41885; Agia Marina; mains €2.50-10; ⊙ 10am-late). Beyond it, the road continues to verdant **Arvanitohori**,

with abundant fig and pomegranate trees and one of the island's most gorgeous *kafeneio*. It is also home to some prettily renovated houses. **Panagia**, 1km southeast of Fry, has an unusual series of six linked red-roofed, Byzantine churches; these are locked, but well worth seeing for the setting alone. **Poli**, 3km southeast of Fry, is the former capital, built on the ancient acropolis but there's not much here to see. For the most extraordinary views, head to **Agia Kyriaki**, east of Poli, as well as **Moni Agiou Mamas**, where a festival is held every 2 September. This area gives you a good idea of how harsh and barren the landscape is and evokes the sense of how people survived off the land in former times.

KASTELLORIZO
ΚΑΣΤΕΛΛΟΡΙΖΟ

POP 275

So close to the Turkish coast – Kaş is just 2km away – that you can almost taste the East, the tiny, far-flung island of Kastellorizo is insanely pretty. Sailing into its one village (of the same name), past the ruined castle, minaret and pastel-painted neoclassical houses huddled around the turquoise bay, is soul enriching. 'Megisti', as Kastellorizo was once called (meaning 'great'), is the largest of a small archipelago at around only 10 sq km. And while it may lack powder-fine beaches, there are bathing platforms with ladders into the ocean and satellite idylls you can reach by boat.

It's easy to get stuck on the harbour – it is a magnet indeed. However, venture up 400 zigzagging steps behind the village, and you'll be rewarded with a plateau, on which is a former monastery and the *paleokastro*, old town and fortress. Plus it has the most dramatic blue cave in the Med.

OFF THE BEATEN TRACK

BLUE CAVE MAGIC

Located on Kastellorizo's remote south-east shore, the extraordinary **Blue Cave** (water taxi per person €10) is famous for its mirror-like blue water. To get there, you must take one of around four competing water taxis in Kastellorizo. It's a 45-minute experience including the 15-minute journey there (and back) plus around 15 minutes in the cave itself, which is free to enter. Boats will not enter if conditions are not right. The entrance – a distance of around two metres – is so low that you must lie down in the boat.

History

Home to the best harbour between Beirut and Piraeus, Kastellorizo was successively a prosperous trading port for the Dorians, Romans, Crusaders, Egyptians, Turks and Venetians. Under Ottoman control, from 1552 onwards, it had the largest merchant fleet in the Dodecanese. A 1913 revolt against the Turks briefly resulted in it becoming a French naval base, and it subsequently passed into the hands of the Italians. The island progressively lost all strategic and economic importance, especially after the 1923 Greece–Turkey population exchange. Many islanders emigrated to Australia, where around 30,000 continue to live.

After Kastellorizo suffered bombardment during WWII, English commanders ordered the few remaining inhabitants to abandon the island. Most fled to Cyprus, Palestine and Egypt and those that later returned found their houses in ruins. While the island has never regained its previous population levels – the village alone was once home to 10,000 people – more recent returnees have finally restored almost all the waterfront buildings, and Kastellorizo is looking better than it has for a century.

The island has found itself in recent years in the migration path of thousands of fleeing refugees, though numbers have recently fallen to only a few; given their grandparents' experiences as refugees, the islanders acted, not surprisingly, with great compassion.

ⓘ Getting There & Away

AIR

Olympic Air (p343) flies six times weekly (four in low season) from Rhodes to Kastellorizo (one way €80, 40 minutes).

BOAT

A very limited ferry service arrives and leaves from Kastellorizo Village's harbour. Blue Star Ferries (p364) calls in twice a week to and from Piraeus via Rhodes (€23, three to four hours). Once a week in summer, Dodekanisos Seaways (p362) sails from Rhodes to Kastellorizo and back (one way €39, 2½ hours); used as a day trip, it gives you four hours on the island.

ⓘ Getting Around

The main destinations for boat trips are Kaş in Turkey and the spectacular Blue Cave (€10). Try **Antonis Sea Taxi** (6977776927). Given the limited road network (which heads to the airport only), most people get around using the island's one taxi. Hiking is a popular alternative.

Kastellorizo Village
Καστελλόριζο

POP 250

This village is the only settlement on the island. Its harbour is its lifeblood and where the limited action gathers: mounds of yellow nets, stretching cats, youths on mobile phones and sleepy fishermen sit outside *kafeneia*, backdropped by smartly shuttered, brightly coloured mansions. Make sure you explore the labyrinthine cobbled backstreets behind. An amazing 80% of the villagers are returned Aussie expats, which adds a definite upbeat energy to the community.

⊙ Sights

Reach the hilltop settlement of Horafia, and Mandraki Bay beyond, by climbing the broad steps east of the harbour.

A coastal pathway around the headland below passes precarious steps that climb to a rock-hewn Lycian tomb from the 4th century BC, which has an impressive Doric facade. There are several such tombs along Turkey's Anatolian coast, but they are very rare in Greece.

It's also possible to walk the 1km up to Paleokastro, the island's ancient capital. Follow the concrete steps that start just past a soldier's sentry box on the airport road. The old city's Hellenistic walls enclose a tower, a water cistern and three churches.

Alternatively, for a longer hike, you can walk up the 400 steps behind town (ask where they begin) and head to a monastery and other paths. The basic *Walking Map* by Pantazis C Houlis is available at some souvenir shops for €2. But the best way to get the local flavour is to head on a guided walk with the folk from Visit Kastellorizo (p373).

Archaeological Museum
MUSEUM

(📞22460 49283; €2; ⊙8.30am-4pm Wed-Mon; 📵) Holds an interesting assortment of ancient finds, costumes and photos relating to Kastellorizo. Labels are limited but it gives a reasonable sense of the island's past.

Megisti Museum
MUSEUM

(€2; ⊙8.30am-4pm Tue-Sun; 📵) In a former mosque near the ferry jetty, this museum devotes itself largely to display panels telling the island's fascinating story.

Knights of St John Castle
ARCHAEOLOGICAL SITE

(⊙24hr) FREE At the top of the hill, a rickety stairway leads to the ruins of the Knights of St John Castle, which gave the island its name – thanks to the red cliff on which it stood, this was the 'Castello Rosso'. It offers splendid views of Turkey.

🛏 Sleeping

★Mediterraneo
PENSION €€

(📞22460 49007; www.mediterraneo-kastelorizo.com; s/d/ste €70/80/180; ⊙May-Oct; 🌦🛜) If Picasso was a hotel, he'd be the Mediterraneo. With its lime, mango and Smurf-blue exterior, this revamped mansion has romantic rooms tastefully scattered with art and some with traditional raised-platform beds. Take breakfast on the terrace amid a confection of fruit and homemade jams, read in the shaded arbour, or flop on loungers by the sea.

The best suite takes up the whole of the ground floor and has its own Bedouin-style sunbathing area yards from the water.

Poseidon
HOTEL €€

(📞6956617585, 22460 49212; www.kastelorizo-poseidon.gr; Plateia Australias; apt/ste €125/150; 🌦🛜) Set in four faux-neoclassical villas, near the western corner of the harbour, Poseidon offers comfortably finished studios and apartments with grey shabby-chic furniture offset by sugar-white walls and contemporary accessories. Apart from the decent breakfast near reception, it's largely DIY here. Given its location – close to the harbour action – it can be slightly noisy if there's music.

Megisti Hotel
HOTEL €€€

(📞22460 49220; www.megistihotel.gr; d/ste incl breakfast €174/262; 🌦@🛜🏊) On the harbour's western extremity, it's impossible to miss the most imposing hotel on the island. Megisti's four suites and 15 stylish rooms have rain showers, tiled floors, standard lamps, safety deposit boxes and private bal-

conies. Outside on the chequerboard waterfront terrace, you can climb easily into the sea from Megisti's iron-hoop steps (like a giant swimming pool).

🍴 Eating & Drinking

★Radio Cafe
CAFE €

(📞22460 49029; mains €6-9; ⊙9am-late; 🌦🛜) This cool high-ceilinged cafe, run by Elma and Vaggelis, is close to the jetty, has art-spattered walls, outside tables and both Greek- and English-style breakfasts – from yogurt with honey and fruit salad, to fried eggs and bacon. By night it morphs into a relaxing bar. The name is a nod to the antique radios Vaggelis repairs to working condition.

★Alexandra's
TAVERNA €€

(📞22460 49019; mains €8.50-17; ⊙lunch & dinner; 🌦🛜) 🌿 With bouzouki music and salt breeze wafting over its thyme-topped tables, the friendliest of Kastellorizo's quayside restaurants also serves the best food. Everything from the squid-ink risotto and calamari stuffed with feta is made in-house. Mezedhes are full of vim and superfresh. Treat yourself to lamb on the spit or whatever goat dish is being offered.

Faros Bar
BAR

(mains €4.50-6; ⊙9am-late; 🛜) Occupying an enviable location in the former lighthouse, beyond the ferry jetty and beside the mosque, this bar offers a wonderful opportunity to swim in turquoise shallows before taking breakfast and drinking in wide-screen views of Turkey. It even has its own quayside loungers. Salads and snacks, plus cocktails, are the go here.

ℹ WALKING WITH LOCALS

Enthusiastic locals run **Visit Kastellorizo** (📞6971589790, 6977092616; www.facebook.com/visit kastellorizo; per person approx €20) and they couldn't be more passionate about their island. They take the visitor away from the tourist-focused harbour on excellent walks. On the town walk they reveal intricate details about Kastellorizo, from historic customs and current insights, to photogenic viewpoints. The tour ends at the museum. The other option is the mountain walk, which covers the ecology, nature and either the monastery or *paleokastro* (or both).

ⓘ Getting There & Away

Kastellorizo's tiny airport is up on the central plateau, 2.5km above the village. There's no bus, so you'll have to take the island's only taxi (p372) to and from the harbour (€5).

Ferries somehow manoeuvre themselves miraculously into Kastellorizo's small harbour.

SYMI   ΣΥΜΗ

POP 2610

Beautiful Symi is guaranteed to evoke oohs and aahs from ferry passengers before they even get off the boat. The first sight of Gialos Harbour, framed against an amphitheatre of pastel-coloured houses rising on all sides, is unforgettable. It's all thanks to the Italians, who ruled the island almost a century ago and established the neoclassical architectural style that Symi has followed ever since.

Although Symi is far from small, it's mostly barren and the only settlements are Gialos, the old village of Horio, which sprawls over the hilly ridge behind, and Pedi, down in the valley beyond. One road runs all the way to the monastery at Panormitis, near Symi's southern tip. The rest of the island is largely deserted, but it's surrounded by blue coves and small beaches.

Culturally, it's a little light on (beyond a couple of museums). But nobody seems to worry; there's enough here.

History

Symi has long traditions of both sponge diving and shipbuilding and is mentioned in the *Iliad* as sending three ships to assist Agamemnon's siege of Troy. In ancient legend, Glaucus, one of the island's sons, was the master builder of *Argo*, the ship that would take Jason and his compadres to distant Colchis in search of the Golden Fleece. During Ottoman times it was granted the right to fish for sponges in Turkish waters. In return, Symi supplied the sultan with first-class boat builders. This exchange enriched the island – gracious mansions were built and culture and education flourished. By the early 20th century, the population was 22,500 and Symi was launching around 500 ships a year. But the Italian occupation, the advent of the steamship and the decline of the sponge industry put an end to prosperity, obliging Symi to reinvent itself as a tourist destination.

ⓘ Getting There & Away

Dodekanisos Seaways (p362) runs catamarans to and from Rhodes at least once daily (€19, 50 minutes) and also offers frequent sailings northwest, to Kos and beyond. Blue Star Ferries (p364) calls in three times weekly heading towards Rhodes (€9, one hour), and one also en route for Tilos (€10, 30 minutes), Nisyros (€13.50, 2½ hours), Kos (€14.50, four hours), Kalymnos (€20, five hours) and Piraeus (16¼ hours, €56.50). Symi fills up every morning with day trippers from Rhodes, with several Rhodes-based excursion boats complementing the high-speed catamaran.

Look out for summer day trips from Gialos to Datça in Turkey (around €45, including Turkish port taxes).

ⓘ Getting Around

BOAT

Water taxis (☑ 22460 71423) from various companies line up along the inner side of Gialos Harbour (plus one in Pedi) and run regular trips to the island's beaches. Most head either north to Nimborios (€8) or south to Agia Marina, Agios Nikolaos, Nanou and Marathounda (€7 to €15). In high season there's at least one departure an hour, from 9am onwards, with the last boat back usually at 5pm or 6pm.

Larger boats offer day trips further afield to remote west-coast beaches, the monastery at Panormitis, or complete island-circuit tours (up to €40) that include a barbecue lunch.

BUS & TAXI

The island **bus** makes hourly runs between the south side of Gialos harbour and Pedi Beach, via Horio (flat fare €1.70).

Taxis (☑ 6987569469, 6974623492) depart from a rank 100m west of the bus stop. These can be pricey and have set rates between them (although run independently), and can take you to anywhere on the island where there are roads, including Panormitis, the monastery, Pedi Beach and Marathounda Beach.

Symi Tours (p376) runs twice daily trips to Panormitis Monastery.

The island's bus company, **Lakis Travel** (☑ 6945316248, 22460 71695; www.lakistravel. gr), can also take you around the island, and stops at viewpoints along the way. It will also do port transfers; these are often cheaper than the taxis.

CAR

Nearly all of the travel agencies also rent cars, though there are a couple of car rental operators. These are all based in Gialos, including **Glaros** (☑ 22460 71926, 6948362079; www. glarosrentacar.gr; scooter/car from €25/45 (high season); ⊙ 9am-9pm), which rents cars and scooters.

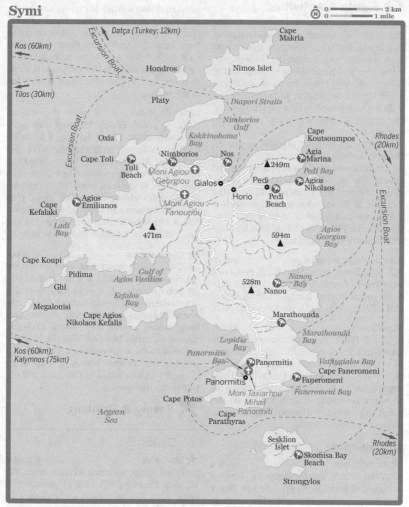

Gialos   Γιαλός

POP 2200

Your first view of Gialos is unforgettable, with its neoclassical biscuit- and ochre-hued buildings gathered aristocratically around what is perhaps the world's prettiest harbour. Fishing boats bob in water so perfectly clear they look as if they're floating on thin air, sponge salesmen hawk their weird-shaped treasures of the deep, while a few world-class boutique hotels and restaurants invite the attention of the occasional Hollywood star arriving on a superyacht.

Sit at one of the many tavernas and cafes along the quayside, making sure you try the island's celebrated shrimps. Wander away from the sea to find backstreets spilling with fruit stores, ice-cream parlours and aromatic bakeries. Head north along the seafront from the **clock tower**, away from the centre, and you're immediately in smaller **Harani Bay**. Traditionally a base for shipbuilding, it still holds assorted beached boats, along with its own crop of bars and tavernas.

The closest beach to Gialos, **Nos**, is around the headland, 500m north from the clock tower. Access to the narrow strip of gravel is controlled by a taverna and bar, though it's a great spot for a swim.

◉ Sights & Activities

Horio
VILLAGE

Climbing calf-crunching, knee-knobbling Kali Strata, the broad stair path that sets off from the alleyways behind the harbour, will bring you in a mere 500-or-so steps to the hilltop village of Horio. En route you'll pass a bewitching succession of majestic villas built for long-gone Symi sea captains – some are utterly dilapidated, others restored to splendour.

Constructed to deter marauding pirates, Horio is an absolute warren of a place. All its tavernas and bars, though, are clustered around the top of Kali Strata. Most of the houses beyond are in ruins, and so is the **Knights of St John Kastro** at the very top, thanks to an explosion of German munitions during WWII. The island's Archaeological Museum is up here, too.

Archaeological Museum
MUSEUM

(€2; ⊙8.30am-4pm Wed-Mon) **FREE** Reopened after years of restoration, this compact museum contains some fabulous archaeological and folkloric finds, and is worth checking out.

Symi Tours
BOATING

(🖰22460 71307; www.symitours.com; boat trip €40) Symi Tours organises daily excursions in the *Poseidon* to explore Symi's beautiful coves, bays and secluded beaches. Daily departures from Gialos Harbour leave at 10.30am, returning at 5pm. Find it on the south side of Gialos Harbour. The price includes a barbecue lunch.

🛏 Sleeping

★Hotel Fiona
HOTEL €

(🖰22460 72088; www.fionahotel.com; Horio; r incl breakfast from €55; ❄�'🡒) Offering Symi's best-value accommodation, this simple but charming family-run hotel perches on the edge of Horio. Its simple but attractive rooms, kitted out with blue and white furniture, have balconies that have truly astonishing views across the harbour. There's a pleasant breakfast area downstairs and a peaceful courtyard. Simple, if adequate, buffet breakfast.

The delightful owners are elderly, so it's a little get-on-with-it-yourself experience. Turn left at the top of Kali Strata.

★Thea Apartments
APARTMENT €€

(🖰22460 72559; www.symi-thea.gr; d/f incl breakfast €135/220) This tasteful spot oozes style. The owner's grandmother's house has been converted into studios (with sink and fridge, but no stove). Blonde-wood floors, tasteful faux-antique bedheads and yellow and olive hues combine well throughout these airy rooms. Each has a front-facing balcony. It's up the stairs directly behind the taxi rank. A simple but delicious breakfast is provided in the room.

Albatros Hotel
HOTEL €€

(🖰22460 71707, 6984107939; www.albatrosymi.gr; d incl breakfast €70; ⊙Apr-Nov; ❄🡒) With its cloud blue and aqua exterior, small and appealing Albatros has a sunny breakfast room and four whitewashed bedrooms with tiled floors, traditional wood ceilings and little balconies giving side-on sea views, plus great mattresses and memory-foam pillows. Just a block back from the harbour in the heart of Gialos, it's clean and welcoming.

★Old Markets
BOUTIQUE HOTEL €€€

(🖰22460 71440; www.theoldmarkets.com; r/ste incl breakfast €240/495; ❄🡒🡒) Symi's finest hotel stands a few steps up Kali Strata (it's unsigned). The old market space has seven stunningly individual rooms and three suites, housed over several adjoining mansions, with fabulous views across the harbour to the coloured houses beyond. All rooms enjoy a pillow library and use of an honesty bar, plus a roof terrace, pool and optional spa treatments.

🍴 Eating & Drinking

🍴 Gialos

★Meraklis
SEAFOOD €

(🖰22460 71003; www.omeraklis.com; mains €8-13; ⊙10.30am-late; 🡒) This old-school taverna, with Santorini-blue walls decked in vintage diving photos and antique mirrors, is as pretty as it is friendly. Sure, it is a tourist magnet, but it has good souvlakia, meatballs and roast lamb, not to mention fresh octopus, sea bream and Symi shrimp. Why not try the lot, with a mixed seafood plate for two (€35)? It's hidden in a backstreet, a block behind the waterfront.

★Tholos
TAVERNA €€

(🖰22460 72033; Harani Bay; mains €9-15; ⊙lunch & dinner May-Oct) The name on locals' lips is Tholos and there's no more romantic restaurant in the Dodecanese than this lovely taverna, poised at the tip of Harani Bay, along the quay from Gialos. The sunset views from its waterfront tables are stupendous, and so too is the food, which includes local meats prepared to the restaurant's own recipes, such as beef in lemon sauce, as well as fresh fish.

★ **Tsati**   BAR

(☑ 22460 72498; www.facebook.com/tsatibar; Harani Bay; ☉ 11am-late; 🛜) This ultrawelcoming quayside bar, 100m along Harani Bay beyond the clock tower, has tables on a tree-shaded terrace, plus it offers stone benches carved into the sea wall. Cushioned and whitewashed, they're perfect for a sunset cocktail, served with free snacks.

✗ Horio

Taverna Giorgos & Maria   TAVERNA €

(☑ 22460 71984; Horio; mains €8-13; ☉ lunch & dinner; 🛜) This ultratraditional spot, at the top of the Kali Strata (steps to Hora), is especially fun in summer, when bouzouki music pipes across its breezy pebble-mosaic veranda, and the locals and tourists mingle over an ouzo. It's not fancy, but the changing menu will have everything from Symi shrimp and grilled bream, to braised rabbit and pork casserole. Live music from 9pm on Friday and Saturday.

Secret Garden   BAR

(☑ 22460 72153; Hora; mains €5-12) 🌱 What does an owner do when his wife needs him at home if he's working too long elsewhere? Open up a business in his home (and garden), of course. This quirky spot, a bar and eatery, is housed in the owner's house. He's converted it into a fun bar-cum-restaurant. The family cooks up great meze plates, plus there's live music. Good vegetarian options, too.

ⓘ Information

Both the National Bank and Alpha Bank have ATM-equipped branches on the northern side of the harbour.

ⓘ Getting There & Away

Catamarans arrive at a smaller port nearer to Gialos, while Blue Star Ferries dock at the larger port, named 'new port', around 500m northeast of town. Here, you'll find car rental agencies.

The town's public bus (p374) runs hourly between the south side of Gialos Harbour and Pedi Beach (flat fare €1.70).

Taxis (p374) depart from a rank 100m west of the bus stop and can take you to anywhere on the island where there are roads, including the major sites and beaches.

MONI TAXIARHOU MIHAIL PANORMITI

Near Symi's southern tip, beyond the scented pine forests of the high interior, spectacular Panormitis Bay is home to the large monastery **Moni Taxiarhou Mihail Panormiti** (☑ 22460 72414; Panormitis; museum €1.50; ☉ dawn-dusk). Monasteries have stood here since the 5th century but the present building dates from the 18th century. The principal church contains an intricately carved wooden iconostasis, frescoes and an icon of St Michael, protector of sailors and patron saint of Symi.

Pilgrims who ask the saint for a favour leave an offering; you'll see piles of these, plus prayers in bottles that have been dropped off boats and found their own way here. The large complex comprises an ecclesiastical museum and a folkloric museum, a bakery with excellent bread, a restaurant and a cafe. Visitors should dress modestly. Buses come here from Gialos, and some ferries and daily excursion boats call in, too.

Around Symi

Apart from the monastery at Panormitis (which has two small museums), the only tourist destinations on Symi are the beaches scattered along its coastline.

Nimborios

Nimborios is a narrow, pebble beach 3km west of Gialos, reached by walking or driving all the way around the harbour and simply continuing along the exposed but beautiful shorefront road beyond. It's a peaceful spot, with an excellent little taverna that allows its customers to spend the day on sunloungers beneath the tamarisk trees alongside.

Niriides Apartments (☑ 22460 71784; www.niriideshotel.com; apt incl breakfast €140) sits by peaceful Symi Bay. Pleasant, traditional decor with kitchenettes, fridges and balconies with sea views. There's a snack bar to take breakfast at and also a library. The owners speak good English.

Pedi

Once a village, now more of a yachting marina and low-key resort, Pedi stretches along the inner end of a large bay east of Gialos, immediately below Horio. The gentle valley behind it has always been the agricultural heartland of Symi.

Two beaches, to either side of the mouth of the bay, can be reached on foot from Pedi or water taxi from Gialos; both have appealing tavernas. Agia Marina to the north is a lagoon-like little bay, facing a delightful chapel-topped islet across turquoise waters, which gets very crowded in summer. Agios Nikolaos, on the south side, is broader and sandier, with decent tree cover and idyllic swimming.

The pleasant, simple cool-tiled rooms of the Pedi Beach Hotel (☑22460 71981; www.pedibeachhotel.gr; Pedi; r from €117; ✴)are fresher than a tube of toothpaste with their aqua-marine-striped beds and cobalt-blue curtains, and unblemished sea-view balconies. Popular with overseas groups.

Nanou & Marathounda

Two large bays south of Pedi, Nanou and Marathounda, hold large beaches and tavernas and make great destinations for water-taxi day trips. Goat-roamed Marathounda, backed by a lush valley and also accessible via a rough road, is especially recommended.

The Marathounda Taverna (☑22460 71425; Marathounda; mains €10-12; ⊙10am-late) is a quintessential beach taverna (a boat shed in historic times), where the island's wild goats – responsible for the delicious homemade cheese and, whisper it, the goat stew, too – sometimes nuzzle up to the tables. Be sure to sample the Symi shrimp and grilled fish, along with herbs and vegetables.

TILOS ΤΗΛΟΣ
POP 550

With its russet gold mountains, lack of people, and wildflowers blooming at every turn, Tilos has a charm that will salve your busy mind like no other island. If you're looking for a green adventure on a lost idyll, this is the place, for you can hike through meadows, mountains and valleys on shepherds' paths before flopping onto one of Tilos' many deserted beaches. And while its azure waters play host to monk seals and sea turtles, the island has a beguiling biodiversity, drawing birdwatchers and wildlife buffs from across the globe.

Best still? Locals are proud of their island and, as such, want to ensure their guests enjoy it, too. Repeat visitors, many of whom have been coming for over 30 years, are testament to the fact that *filoxenia* (hospitality) is as strong here as anywhere in Greece; this tiny place has a very big heart.

❶ Getting There & Away

Tilos has no airport and only a minimal ferry service. The Dodekanisos Seaways (p362) catamaran stops at Tilos twice weekly, to/from Rhodes (€27, 2½ hours) and Halki (€13, 40 minutes). Check the schedules: if it heads to Nisyros, Kos and Kalymnos in the morning, and back to Rhodes in the evening, on those days, you can visit the island as a day trip from Rhodes or Halki. In addition, from Tilos, Blue Star Ferries (p364) sails twice each week to Piraeus via Nisyros, Kos and Kalymnos, and twice to Rhodes, one of which stops at Symi (€16, between two and three hours).

❶ Getting Around

Five buses each day connect Livadia with Megalo Horio, Eristos Beach and Agios Antonios (€1.70). There is no taxi, but you can rent a car or scooter from Drive Rent A Car (☑6946944883, 22460 44173; www.drivetilos.gr; ⊙9am-6pm) or Stefanakis Travel (p380).

Livadia Λιβαδειά
POP 470

Livadia is a photogenic jumble of whitewashed houses huddled around the northern end of Agios Stefanos Bay. Little happens here – a cat yawns, a fisherman falls asleep over his glass of ouzo... And that's precisely its charm: tranquillity. A narrow girdle of pebbled beach, perfect for sun worshipping, stretches some 2km from the village down the turquoise-laced bay, while the village's central square is hugged by cafes, old-time tavernas and Italian-era municipal buildings.

◉ Sights

When pirates prowled the Dodecanese, the medieval settlement of Mikro Horio (Map p379; ⊙24hr) was Tilos' main population centre. Its last inhabitants only left after WWII and it now stands empty, 45 minutes' walk up from Livadia. In various states of ruin – one house opens as a music bar in summer – it's a fascinating place to wander. Linger until the light fades and it turns downright eerie. If

Tilos

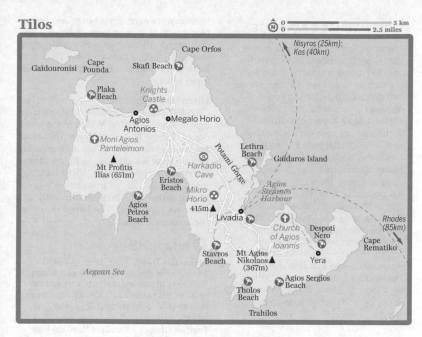

you can stay awake long enough, visit Mikro Horio nightclub (p380), in the middle of the village.

🛏 Sleeping

★ Apollo Studios
APARTMENT €

(☑ 22460 44379, 6942061912; www.apollostudios.gr; studio €50-80; ✳🔊) 🌿 Fresh, well-appointed studios, run by a lovely young couple and set a few streets back from the harbour, with spotless kitchenettes, modern bathrooms, private balconies and a great communal roof terrace. It also has roomy apartments with tiled floors and sofa beds – ask for number 3 (it has a massive terrace).

Hotel Irini
HOTEL €

(☑ 22460 44293; www.ilidirock.gr; r incl breakfast from €55; ✳🔊🏊) Irini has stunning white rooms with flat-screen TVs, shabby chic furniture, colourful quilts, tasteful ceramics, fridges and pool-facing balconies. Behind are great mountain views to admire over breakfast. Some of the rooms are slightly squishy, but there is a terrace and pool to make up for it.

★ Eleni Beach Hotel
HOTEL €€

(☑ 22460 44062; www.elenihoteltilos.gr; d incl breakfast from €80, studio €85; ✳🔊) Eleni has 35 studios and rooms, some with balconies,

all with sea views. Expect comfy, spotlessly fresh interiors surrounded by a garden abloom with flowers. You'll find it 10 minutes' walk from the jetty southeast along the promenade. Rates also include a sun lounger on the beach. Breakfast is not included in rates for studios, which have kitchenettes.

Ilidi Rock Hotel
HOTEL €€

(☑ 22460 44293; www.ilidirock.gr; studio/apt €95/137; ✳@🔊) The 'glitziest' hotel in Tilos cascades down the cliff to two tiny aquamarine-laced inlets, so the rooms' views are indeed ravishing. The fully equipped studios and apartments are stylishly minimalist; all have private balconies and four-poster beds The downsides (upsides for some) are the many stairs, breakfast is not included, plus 'favourite' rooms tend to get booked out by regulars.

🍴 Eating & Drinking

★ Omonoia Cafe
CAFE €

(☑ 22460 44287; breakfast €3-6, mains €8-13; ⊙8am-late; ☑) Shaded by a mature fig tree on Livadia's main square, just up from the quay, this much-loved all-day cafe is ideal for breakfast, light lunch or dinner. Its delightful elderly owners and family prepare everything from grilled meats and seafood to simple juices and salads, but you'll proba-

BIRDWATCHER'S PARADISE

The landscape of Tilos is much gentler than other Dodecanese islands. Rather than forbidding mountains, the interior is characterised by fertile valleys carved into agricultural terraces. It's criss-crossed by trails laid out by farmers that now serve as perfect footpaths. With small-scale ancient fortifications and medieval chapels scattered in profusion, Tilos makes a wonderful hiking destination.

What's more, thanks to the island's low population – and long-standing ban on hunting – it's also a favourite haunt for rare birds. More than 150 species have been recorded. Some are residential, some migratory. An estimated 46 species are threatened. As you hike, keep your eyes peeled for the Bonelli's eagle, Eleonora's falcon, long-legged buzzard, Sardinian warbler, scops owl and Mediterranean black shag.

bly lose your heart – and your waistline – to their sponge cake.

To Mikro Kafé   CAFE €
(☑6932086094; snacks €5-7, mains €7-15; ☺noon-midnight July-Oct, 6pm-late Nov-Jun; ✿✿☞) Micro in size it may be, but there's nothing diminutive about this cosy nook's appeal. With its exposed stone walls and nautically themed decoration, Micro offers porthole windows, board games and little corners to play in while you nurse a sun-downer on the beach-view patio (there's also a roof terrace). Offers salads, seafood, pies and sandwiches.

Faros Taverna   TAVERNA €€
(☑22460 44068; mains €7-12; ☺breakfast, lunch & dinner) Friendly Roula runs a tip-top taverna here that sits out on the eastern end of the beach, a half hour walk from Livadi. Expect fresh seafood and changing traditional Greek dishes (all excellent). But in truth, you'd be happy eating sand, such is the gorgeous setting, under a shady, bougainvillea-covered terrace with a view of miles of ocean and coast.

Gorgona   GREEK €€
(☑22460 70755; mains €7.50-15; ☺lunch & dinner; ☞✿) ✎ Enjoying sweeping views of Agios Stefanos Bay, this highly regarded

rooftop restaurant serves olives and vegetables grown at its own farm. Following special recipes from the owner's grandmother, there's a wealth of choice from Tilos goat, lamb chops and pasta, to shrimps and octopus salad.

Mikro Horio Nightclub   BAR
(☑22460 44204, 6932086094; Mikro Horio Village; ☺11pm-late Jul-Sep; ☞) Set in the abandoned village of Mikro Horio, this place has a delightful veranda bar with amazing views of the village that is lit up atmospherically for the patrons. Night owls can make the most of the free shuttle bus (10 minutes) that runs from Livadia until 1am (later on Saturdays). The longer you stay, the louder the music.

ⓘ Information

Stefanakis Travel (Tilos Travel; ☑22460 44360; www.tilos-travel.com; ☺9am-10pm) Sells ferry tickets and rents out cars and motorbikes. Also sells tickets for one-day cruises to Symi (€17) and Nisyros (€18) on the larger ferries.

Tourism Office (☺9am-2pm May-Oct) High season only, located on the beachfront centre; might have a few brochures, if you're lucky.

Megalo Horio

Megalo Horio, the tiny 'capital' of Tilos, is a hillside village where the narrow streets hold sun-blasted cubic houses and teem with battle-scarred cats. There's not much here but views and a couple of eateries, but it's a good base for walks. Ask about its small museum (☺9am-2pm Jun-Sep) FREE that displays dwarf elephants; at the time of research, the collection was relocating to a new, modern premises by Harkadio Cave, several kilometres away.

A taxing one-hour hike from the north end of Megalo Horio takes you to the Knights Castle, passing the island's most ancient settlement en route.

🛏 Sleeping & Eating

Miliou Studios   APARTMENT €
(☑6932086094, 22460 44204; www.milios-studios.gr; Megalo Horio; d/tr €40/50; ✿☞) ✎ Located in the centre of sleepy Megalo Horio, Miliou has comfortable rooms and self-catering studios with sweeping views of Eristos Bay far below. There's a supermarket close by, and free barbecue facilities in the

lush grounds, plus you can also pick herbs (and veggies, if there are any) for your own use from Miliou's organic garden.

Kastro Cafe
TAVERNA €

(☎22460 44232; Megalo Horio; mains €8-13; ☺lunch & dinner) The best taverna in the village, tucked into a fairly residential area, but with a glorious hillside terrace commanding a fabulous panorama of the bay. Everything on the menu is good, from the organic spit-roasted goat and locally raised pork, to the fresh little dolmadhes and tiny red shrimps.

Northwest Tilos

The northwestern end of Tilos is home to several attractive beaches. The best for swimming is long, broad **Eristos Beach**, lapped by sapphire-hued waters, 2.5km south of Megalo Horio. Generally deserted but for the odd local person line-fishing, its greyish sands are fringed by tamarisk trees.

The quiet settlement of **Agios Antonios**, in the large bay 1.5km northwest of Megalo Horio, is a narrow strip of shingle with a taverna at either end. Much prettier **Plaka Beach**, in a cove another 3km west, is completely undeveloped. The water is slightly warmer, there's shade in the afternoon and, once you wade in a little, the rock shelves are good for snorkelling.

Beyond Plaka, the coast road climbs the sheer hillside, skirting 3km of alarming drop-offs to reach cliff-edge **Agios Panteleimon monastery** (☎22420 31676).

🛏 Sleeping & Eating

Nitsa Apartments
APARTMENT €

(☎22460 44093; www.nitsa-tilosapartments.com; Eristos Beach; apt from €50) This modern studio block, 200m inland from Eristos Beach, holds simple, nondescript two-bedroom self-catering apartments. It's attached to the all-day En Plo (p381) snack bar, which can be a good (or bad) thing if you like to indulge.

Eristos Beach Hotel
HOTEL €€

(☎22460 44025; www.eristosbeachhotel. gr; Eristos Beach; d/apt incl breakfast €60/90; ⛆❄🛜🏊) Just off the beach, this large hotel is set in lush gardens crowded with hibiscus, orchids and lemon trees. Fresh rooms with tiled floors have balconies that look out to the sea beyond, while larger studios have kitchenettes and sleep four. There's also a lovely swimming pool and kids' pool, plus a restaurant and a bar.

En Plo
TAVERNA €€

(☎22460 44176; Eristos Beach; mains €8-13; ☺lunch & dinner; 🛜🚻) About 200m behind the beach, this taverna has slow-cooked food like goat stew, and regulars like squid *saganaki* (stuffed with fried cheese), souvlakia and superfresh vegetables. You can enjoy your meals under the vine-shaded canopy in a pleasant garden. While it seems to have a popular following, in our opinion the price-to-quality ratio is a little out.

TRAIL BLAZING ON TILOS

Walking is the reason many people, especially repeat visitors, come to Tilos. There are around 54km of trails in Tilos, with varying degrees of marking. Keen walkers should get their hands on the outstanding guide, *Exploring Tilos: a Walkers' Guide to the Island* by Jim Osborne (available online and in some local shops). It outlines in great detail every trail, and is a delight to follow, given the accuracy of visual cues and grading of each walk, from easy to difficult.

One well-maintained and very scenic 3km walk leads north from Livadia to Lethra Beach, an undeveloped pebble-and-sand cove with limited shade. Follow the tarmac behind the Ilidi Rock Hotel, at the northwestern end of the port, to find the start of the trail. Returning via the picturesque Potami Gorge brings you to the main island highway. (Note, however, at the time of research, part of the trail had been destroyed due to winter storms; check with other walkers before heading out.)

A longer walk leads to the small abandoned settlement of Yera and its accompanying beach at Despoti Nero. Simply follow the road south from Livadia around the bay and keep going beyond the Church of Agios Ioannis at the far eastern end. Allow half a day for the full 6km round trip.

NISYROS   ΝΙΣΥΡΟΣ

POP 950

Thanks to its lack of beaches, Nisyros is very much off the tourist radar – apart from the day trippers from nearby Kos who come to witness the magnificent volcano. Yet for those seeking an island of natural beauty, goats wandering meadows stippled with beehives, soaring mountain views over terraced fields and wildlflowers, intimate Nisyros is just the ticket. Then there's hidden Byzantine churches, an extraordinary ancient wall and gourmet offerings.

The main settlement, Mandraki, is a sleepy little fishing village garlanded with cafes, while hilltop villages Nikea and Emborios are stunning. Hike among the wildflowers, head into volcano craters, or immerse yourself in agrotourism. Those who chance a visit often return, again and again.

ⓘ Information

Visit www.nisyros.gr for information on sights, history and local services.

ⓘ Getting There & Away

Catamarans run by Dodekanisos Seaways (p362) call in at Nisyros on Tuesday and Thursday, heading to and from Kos (€10, one to 1½ hours) and Rhodes (€27, 2¾ hours). Blue Star Ferries (p364) also stops once to twice a week in each direction, en route to either Kos (€16, 50 minutes), Kalymnos (€9.50, two to three hours), Astypalea (€12.50, 5½ hours) and Piraeus (€56.50, 13½ hours), or Tilos (€14, 40 minutes), Symi (€13.50, 2½ hours) and Rhodes (€16, three hours).

There are also links with Kos five times a week. The Panagia Spiliani (p382) sails to either Kos Town or Kardamena (around €8), while the smaller *Agios Konstantinos* runs to and from Kardamena (€8).

ⓘ Getting Around

BOAT

Summer-only excursion boats leave Mandraki Harbour for the pumice-stone, sandy beach islet of Giali (€10), returning at around 6pm.

BUS

Public buses do a circuit around the island three times daily in summer, but you'll need to be clever to co-ordinate visits; catch them at the port (€2.50).

Alternatively, **Enetikon Travel** (☏ 22420 31180; www.enetikon.com; ⊙ 9.30am-2pm & 6.30-9pm) runs many daily bus tours. These are largely for groups (day visitors from Kos) but independent travellers can go with a day's notice. You visit the volcano (€8), allowing around 40 minutes at the crater. Catch them outside the office at Mandraki port.

CAR & MOTORCYCLE

In Mandraki, **Diakomihalis Travel** (☏ 22420 31459; www.visitnisyros.gr; ⊙ 9am-2pm & 5-9pm) offers good-value car rental and Manos (p384), just near the quay, has a wealth of scooters and cars.

TAXI

A taxi from Mandraki to the volcano costs around €25 return; call **Irini** (☏ 22420 31474).

Mandraki   Μανδράκι

POP 660

This pretty whitewashed and pastel-coloured town stretches languidly along the northern shore of Nisyros, lapped by gentle waters and lined with cafes and tavernas. Perched over the cliff is a castle and monastery. Behind these, and just out of sight, is the incredibly well-preserved ancient city wall. Mandraki is almost completely pedestrianised, so its maze of winding backstreets and garden plots are tranquil and timeless, with a fertile valley sloping up towards the rim of the volcano behind. The ferry jetty is 500m northeast of Mandraki proper. Simply walk straight along the coast to reach the centre.

◉ Sights

The major landmark is at the far western end, where the ruins of a 14th-century **Knights Castle** tower atop a cliff face. Its lower levels are occupied by an equally old monastery, **Moni Panagias Spilianis** (Virgin of the Cave; €2; ⊙ 10.30am-3pm), accessed by climbing a short but steep stairway.

With Nisyros being very short on beaches, local kids are glad of tiny but sandy **Mandraki Beach**, at the eastern end of town. It's a popular swimming spot, despite being sometimes covered in seaweed. There's also an exposed black-stone beach to the west, **Hohlaki**, reached by following a paved footpath around the headland below the monastery.

★ **Archaeological Museum**   MUSEUM
(Map p383; ☏ 22420 31588; €4; ⊙ 8.30am-3pm Sun & Mon; ♿) This showpiece modern museum, on Mandraki's main pedestrian street, displays a fascinating collection of Hellenistic and Roman pottery and sculpture, as well as earlier artefacts made of obsidian quar-

Nisyros

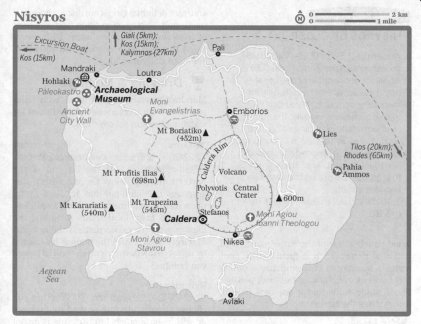

ried on neighbouring Giali. The exhibits are displayed in chronological order and will help you get your head around the different historical periods, from Neolithic to Hellenic, and much more. Don't miss it.

Ancient City Wall
ARCHAEOLOGICAL SITE

(Map p383; ⊘24hr) FREE Dating from the 4th century BC, the ancient walls above Nisyros, accessed from the path behind the monastery and medieval castle, are one of the Aegean's best surviving fortifications from the Classical period. The massive Cyclopic stones are remarkable, as is the one standing gateway. You can climb the steps and stand on the wall itself (be aware: no barriers), a superb sunset lookout.

Paleokastro
ARCHAEOLOGICAL SITE

(Map p383; ⊘24hr) FREE Best reached by a lovely 20-minute hike through the fields, along a trail that starts southwest of the monastery, this astonishing Mycenaean-era acropolis was founded 3000 years ago. Its restored cyclopean walls are a little newer, from the 4th century BC – what looks like modern graffiti is in fact ancient dedications. Pass through the forbidding gateway and you can climb atop the massive blocks of volcanic rock for breathtaking views. Good explanatory signs in English are scattered throughout.

🛏 Sleeping

Hotel Porfyris
HOTEL €

(☎22420 31376; www.porfyrishotel.gr; s/d incl breakfast €50/60; ❀🞥🞣) The only hotel in Mandraki town itself stands proudly on the hillside, set above a citrus orchard five minutes' walk from the sea. If you're arriving from the ferry, fork left at Piccolo Bar. Beyond the elegant marble lobby, expect simple, cosy en-suite rooms with comfy beds and terrace or balcony. There's also a welcome pool. Simple, but adequate, breakfast.

Anthousa Houses
BUNGALOW €€

(☎6972947320, 6976322131; house €120) Three gorgeous traditional homes have been renovated in stunning style. Fine accents, including flagstone floors, jute rugs and polished concrete, give these a designer edge like no other, and the shabby chic furniture fills spacious areas. Quirky nooks and crannies within the sides of rock accommodate a kitchen and bathroom. The bungalows are arranged around a lush garden.

Ta Liotridia
B&B €€

(☎22420 31580; www.nisyros-taliotridia.com/html/guesten.html; r incl breakfast from €140; ❀🞣) Two large and lovely B&B rooms (sleeping up to four) at the heart of the waterfront, on the upper floor of a smart

NISYROS UP CLOSE

Anaema (6972947320, 22420 31459; www.anaema.gr; per person from €30) is a brilliant cooperative of passionate island guides who offer culturally immersive experiences. If you don't want to go it alone, you can hike the volcano (and learn fabulous things along the way), as well as partake in everything from cookery to embroidery classes and much more. Owner Haris is trying to promote tourism on the island and knows his stuff.

It's based out of Diakomihalis Travel (p382).

wood-panelled bar of the same name (read, potential noise). Each is furnished in comfortable traditional style and has a double bed in an alcove, another box bed, polished floors, stone walls and a sea-view balcony (room 2 has the largest).

✖️ Eating

Irini   TAVERNA €

(22420 31365; Plateia Ilikiomenis; mains €9-13; ☺lunch & dinner; ❄🛜✏🚹) Sitting in the corner of a pebble-mosaic square in the shade of mature fig trees, with Irini Mark II diagonally opposite, Irini dishes up a mouthwatering menu of traditional fare like dolmadhes, goat in tomato sauce, souvlakia and *saganaki*. Try the heavenly baklava for dessert.

★ Yevsea   SEAFOOD €€

(Gefsea; Chevsea; 22420 31066; €9.50-12; ☺lunch & dinner) Meaning 'taste', this lovely, waterfront place is set to put Nisyros on the culinary map. Run by a passionate young duo, both *Masterchef* Greece contestants (one from Nisyros whose father is a fisherman), Yevsea serves up exceptional seafood and meat dishes featuring the masterful use of local ingredients (try the unique fish soup). Whatever you do, don't miss eating here.

Loles Kores   INTERNATIONAL €€

(Crazy Woman; 22420 31024; www.loleskores. com; mains €9-16; ☺lunch & dinner) ✐ This place is deceptive: you enter off the principal lane via basement stairs (with tasteful decorations of olde-world Greece), before entering a pretty, vine-covered rear terrace. The nicknamed 'Crazy Woman' conjures up

gourmet delights: Greek cuisine with a gourmet touch. There's everything from the likes of *giouvarlakia* (lemon soup with meatballs) to salad with herring and pistachio. Fabulous daily specials.

Drinking & Nightlife

Mandraki's waterfront is lined with cafes and bars, with terraces perfectly aligned for watching the sun set over Kos.

★ Oxos   CAFE

(22420 31873; www.facebook.com/oxos; ☺9am-midnight; 🛜) At the far end of the harbour, nestled below the monastery, this gorgeous cafe-cum-bar has it all: a pretty plaza setting with tamarisk trees, a sea view, shade and tasty local treats including the likes of *pitia* (chickpea patties) and *horiatiki* (Greek salad). And the bonus? It's backed by tiny Agios Nikolaos church (pop in before you imbibe!)

Rythmos Bar   BAR

(22420 31463; ☺9am-late; 🛜) Whether you choose a seat on its sun-soaked roof terrace or within its modish interior, this is a cool spot for a midday frappé or sunset glass of vino. Curiously it draws in the old boys as well as a young crowd – and it still works! One of the few places that's open all year.

ℹ️ Information

Alpha Bank has an ATM at the harbour and a bank (no ATM) in Mandraki, and there's another ATM at the **post office** (☺7am-2.30pm Mon-Fri).

ℹ️ Getting There & Away

Mandraki is your first stop for all arrivals and departures to the island. The port, 500m northeast of town, is easily walkable. There's no public transport from here, but you can rent a car from **Manos Rentals** (22420 31029; www. nisyros-rentacar.gr; ☺24hr), whose office is at the port.

Around Nisyros

The Volcano

Nisyros sits on a volcanic fault line that curves around the southern Aegean. While 25,000 years have passed since the volcano that formed it last erupted, it's officially classified as dormant rather than extinct. Its summit originally stood around 850m tall, but three violent eruptions 30,000 to 40,000 years ago blew off the top 100m and caused the centre to collapse. White-and-orange pumice stones can still be seen on the northern, eastern and southern flanks of the island, while a large lava flow covers the entire southwest around Nikea.

The islanders call the volcano Polyvotis. Legend has it that during the battle between the gods and Titans, Poseidon ripped a chunk off Kos and used it to trap the giant Polyvotis deep beneath. That rock became Nisyros and the roar of the volcano is Polyvotis' angered voice.

Visitors keen to experience the power of the volcano head by bus, car or on foot into the island's hollow caldera, a vast and otherworldly plain that was home to thousands of ancient farmers. Ruined agricultural terraces climb the walls, while cows graze amid sci-fi-set rocks.

The southern end encloses several distinct craters (Map p383; adult/child €3/free; ⊙8.30am-8pm; P). Get there before 11am and you may have the place to yourself. A path descends into the largest crater, Stefanos, where you can examine the multi-coloured 100°C fumaroles, sometimes listen to their hissing and smell the sulphurous vapours. The surface is soft and hot, making sturdy footwear essential. Don't stray too far out, as the ground is unstable and can collapse (at the time of research, the centre was roped off).

An obvious track leads to the smaller and wilder crater of Polyvotis nearby. You can't enter the caldera itself, and the fumaroles are around the edge here, so take great care.

Emborios

The village of Emborios is perched high on the jagged northern rim of the caldera, 9km up from Mandraki, and has some lovely stone houses, two restaurants and some very appealing accommodation. Many of the houses, formerly ruins, have been renovated by foreigners in recent years. These cling to the steep flanks of the rocky ridge. Apart from a few yawning cats, only around nine people live here permanently.

🛏 Sleeping & Eating

★Melanopetra   APARTMENT €€€
(☑6978060289; www.melanopetra.gr; Emborios; apt €150; ❄️🛜) With its ubiquitous white and bare-wood floors flooded in natural

light, Melanopetra is pure zen minimalism. Two apartments with gorgeous bedrooms and kitchens enjoy dual views of both the caldera and Aegean on the other side. It's as if the rooms have been carved from the mountain itself with rough adobe walls and contemporary fittings.

Balcony Restaurant   GREEK €
(☑22420 31607; www.balkoni-nisiros.com; Emborios; mains €7; ⊙9am-10pm Mon-Sat; ❄️🛜🍴) The streetside terrace, facing Emborios' church, has a namesake balcony at the rear with an unforgettable panorama of the vast hollow crater. The owners are renowned for their produce – fresh ingredients for local meat, and some vegetable, dishes. It was here, too, in WWII where a Greek naval captain was shot; the original shattered mirror is still on display.

Apiria Taverna   TAVERNA €€
(☑22420 31377; Emborios; mains €9-12; ⊙lunch & dinner; ❄️🛜🍽) Opening off a tiny alcove behind the church, this friendly taverna has tasteful burgundy-and-mustard walls and a few sheltered outdoor tables. It serves Nisyrian dishes, including *pitia* and lamb, pork and vegetable specialities. It's one of the few places open all year. Oh, and be sure to check out the air holes in the wall... natural heating from the volcano.

Nikea

The village of Nikea is 4km south along the crater's edge. No vehicles can penetrate this tight warren of dazzling white houses, so every visitor experiences the thrill of walking along the narrow lane from road's end to reach the tiny central square. Less a square than a circle, actually, it's among the most jaw-droppingly beautiful spots in the Dodecanese, with geometric pebble-mosaic designs in the middle and the village church standing above.

Throughout Nikea, signposted overlooks command astonishing views of the volcano, laid out far below. The challenging trail down into the crater drops from behind the Volcanological Museum (☑22420 31400; Plateia Nikolaou Hartofyli, Nikea; €4; ⊙8am-1.30pm Mon-Sat; 🍴) which is set beside the end of the road, this kid-friendly modern museum does a good job of explaining the history and mythology of the volcano and its impact on the island. There's also an interesting documentary worth a watch.

Located in Nikea's pretty central square, Porta (☑ 22420 31835; Nikea; snacks €5-8; ☺ 9am-late; ☎) is a wonderfully relaxing place to enjoy a cool drink, toasted sandwich, juice or beer.

Pali

This wind-buffeted seaside village sits 5km east of Mandraki, just beyond the turnoff to the volcano. Now primarily a yachting marina, it has a handful of tavernas among the sun-beaten buildings on the quay.

The coast road continues another 5km to Lies, Nisyros' most usable beach. Walking 1km along a precarious track from here brings you to Pahia Ammos, a shadeless expanse of coarse volcanic sand.

🛏 Sleeping & Eating

Mammis' Apartments
APARTMENT €€

(☑ 22420 31453; www.mammis.com; Pali; d €60; ❄☎) Set 100m up from the marina in gardens that are a riot of flowers, this peaceful complex holds 10 simple studios with kitchenettes, separate sofa beds for kids, and private balconies with sea views.

Captain's House
TAVERNA €

(☑ 22420 31016; Pali; mains €7-10; ☺ 8am-midnight; ❄☎) So close to the water that you can taste the salt, this taverna attracts yachties and wizened fishermen alike with a menu that's packed to the gills with seafood options including octopus, plus local bites including *fava* and cheeses. The owner is very knowledgeable about the island.

KOS
ΚΩΣ

POP 33,400

Fringed by the finest beaches in the Dodecanese, dwarfed beneath mighty crags, and blessed with lush valleys, Kos is an island of endless treasures. Visitors soon become blasé at sidestepping the millennia-old Corinthian columns that poke through the rampant wildflowers – even in Kos Town, the lively capital, ancient Greek ruins are scattered everywhere you turn, and a mighty medieval castle still watches over the harbour.

Visitors to Kos naturally tend to focus their attention on its beaches. Beyond those near Kos Town, there are three main resort areas. Kardamena, on the south coast, is very much dominated by package tourism, but Mastihari, on the north coast, and Kamari, in the far southwest, are more appealing. Away from the resorts, the island retains considerable wilderness, with the rugged Dikeos mountains soaring to almost 850m just a few kilometres west of Kos Town.

History

So many people lived on this fertile island in Mycenaean times that Kos was rich enough to send 30 ships to the Trojan War. In 477 BC, after suffering an earthquake and subjugation to the Persians, it joined the Delian League and again flourished. Hippocrates (460–377 BC), the Greek physician known as the founder of medicine, was born and lived on the island. After his death, the Sanctuary of Asclepius and a medical school were built, which perpetuated his teachings and made Kos famous throughout the Greek world.

That Ptolemy II of Egypt was also born on Kos secured the island the protection of Egypt. It became a prosperous trading centre, but fell under Roman domination in 130 BC and was administered by Rhodes from the 1st century AD onwards. Kos has shared the same ups and downs of fortune ever since, including conquest and/or occupation by the Knights, the Ottomans and the Italians and, much like Rhodes, its economy is now heavily dependent on tourism.

ℹ Getting There & Away

AIR

Kos' **airport** (KGS; Map p388; ☑ 22420 56000; www.kosairportguide.com) is located in the middle of the island, 24km southwest of Kos Town. Aegean Airlines (https://en.aegeanair.com), Olympic Air (p343) and Sky Express (p343) offer up to four daily flights to Athens (from €60, 55 minutes). Regular flights head to Rhodes (from €100, 30 minutes) and Leros (€110, 55 minutes). Flights to some other islands, such as Naxos, go via Athens.

BOAT
Domestic

The island's main ferry port is in Kos Town, in front of the castle. Dodekanisos Seaways (p362) runs catamarans up and down the archipelago: southeast to Rhodes via Nisyros (€16, one hour, two weekly); Tilos (€22, 1½ hours, two weekly); Halki (€26, 2½ hours, two weekly) and Symi (€26, 1½ hours, two weekly), and elsewhere to Pythagorio on Samos (€44, four hours, three weekly), Kalymnos (€16, 35 minutes, daily), Leros (€23, 1½ hours, daily) and Patmos (€31, 2½ hours, daily). Blue Star Ferries (p364) also sails to Rhodes (€24.50, three to five hours, daily), as well as west to Astypalea (€17, 1½ hours, once weekly) and Piraeus (€45 to €56, 10 to 12 hours, daily).

In summer, the smaller and slower **Panagia Spiliani** (Map p390; ☑ 22420 31015; www. visitnisyros.gr/en; Harbour), a passenger-car ferry, also runs trips between Kos and Nisyros and from Kardamena in high season.

Elsewhere on the island, regular daily ferries also connect Mastihari with Kalymnos (€6, 50 minutes); see www.anekalymnou.gr and www. anemferries.gr. **Leros Express** (☑ 6936141900, 22470 24000; www.lerosseaways.com) also does twice weekly circuits between Leros, Kalymnos and Kos.

International

High-speed catamarans connect Kos Town with both Bodrum (two daily) and Turgutreis in Turkey (one daily). Both journeys take 30 minutes to one hour. Tickets cost €17 each way, with same-day returns €15 and longer-stay returns €30. For schedules and bookings, visit www.exas.com.

ⓘ Getting Around

TO/FROM THE AIRPORT

The airport is served by several daily KTEL (p387) buses to and from Kos Town's bus station (€3.20). It is so far from Kos Town that if you're planning to rent a car anyway, it's worth doing so when you first arrive. A recommended car hire office just outside the airport is **Auto Bank Car Rental** (☑ 22420 23397; www.autobank-kos. com).

A taxi to Kos Town costs around €37.

Ferries arrive and depart from the main port in front of Kos Town's castle.

BICYCLE

Cycling is very popular, so you'll be tripping over bicycles for hire. Prices range from as little as €5 per day for a boneshaker, up to €20 for a decent mountain bike. In Kos Town, **Escape Rentals** (☑ 22420 29620, 6937175860; escape.rental@ mail.gr; Vasileos Georgiou 12; bike from €5) offers a good range of bikes, including electric bikes, and reasonable rates.

Kos Mountainbike Activities (☑ 6944150129; www.kosbikeactivities.com; Psalidi; mountain bike per day €25; ⊙ 9am-12.30pm & 5.30-7.30pm) offers bike rentals and guided tours.

BOAT

The massive line of boats moored in Kos Town offer excursions around Kos and to nearby islands. A 'three island' day trip to Kalymnos, Pserimos and Platy costs around €30, including lunch, while you can find day trips to Bodrum for as little as €15.

BUS

The island's main bus station is located well back from the waterfront in Kos Town. It is the base for **KTEL** (Map p390; ☑ 22420 22292; www.ktel-kos.gr; Kleopatras 7; ⊙ information office 8am-9pm Mon-Sat Apr-Oct, to 3pm Mon-Fri Nov-Mar), which has services to all parts of the island, including the airport and south-coast beaches.

Kos Town   Κως
POP 17,890

A handsome harbour community, fronted by a superb medieval castle and somehow squeezed amid a mind-blowing array of ancient ruins from the Greek, Roman and Byzantine eras, Kos Town is the island's capital, main ferry port and only sizeable town. While some central streets tend to be overrun by partying tourists, most remain attractive. The square houses a fabulous museum and features some extraordinary architecture. The port is lined by cafes and tavernas and its unbroken row of excursion boats, fishing vessels and fancy yachts bob and bristle against each other along the waterfront.

Popular beaches stretch in either direction from the harbour. Long, sandy **Kritika Beach**, in easy walking distance of the town centre, is lined with hotels and restaurants. Southeast of the harbour the thin strip of sand known as **Kos Town Beach** is dotted with parasols in summer and offers deep water for swimming.

◉ Sights

Castle of the Knights   CASTLE
(Map p390; ☑ 22420 27927; Harbour) Due to damage caused by an earthquake in 2017, Kos' magnificent 15th-century castle is currently closed. Nevertheless, given its extraordinary location at the harbour entrance, it is interesting to view from the outside.

Plateia Platanou   SQUARE
(Map p390) The warm, graceful charm and sedate pace of Kos Town is experienced at its best in this lovely cobblestone square, immediately south of the castle. Sitting in a cafe here, you can pay your respects to **Hippocrates' plane tree** (Map p390). Hippocrates himself is said to have taught his pupils in its shade. The ancient sarcophagus beneath it was converted into a fountain by the Ottomans, while the 18th-century

Kos

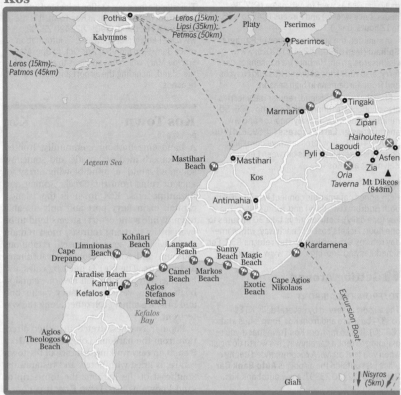

Mosque of Gazi Hassan Pasha (Map p390), now sadly in disrepair, stands opposite.

Western

Excavation Site
ARCHAEOLOGICAL SITE
(Map p390; ☉ dawn-dusk) FREE This open archaeological site, south of the centre, holds ancient ruins uncovered by an earthquake in 1933. Its real treasures are the mosaics of the House of Europa. The house was an opulent 2nd-century villa and the mosaics depict the abduction of Europa by Zeus in the form of a bull. Nearby, there's a section of the Decumanus Maximus, the Roman city's main thoroughfare. The site also holds the Nymphaeum, a columned structure that was actually a public toilet.

There's also the Xysto, a cluster of Doric columns, and the Temple of Dionysos, dating from the 2nd century BC. Across the street stands the Odeion, an impressive 2nd-century Roman theatre, which was built on the site of an even older Greek predecessor, and once seated around 750 spectators. In summer, performances are sometimes held here. Just east of here is the cleverly reconstructed Casa Romana.

Ancient Agora
ARCHAEOLOGICAL SITE
(Map p390; ☉ dawn-dusk) FREE Exposed by a devastating earthquake in 1933, Kos' ancient centre – an important market, political and social hub – occupies a large area south of the castle. Back in the 4th century BC, this was the first town ever laid out in blocks, and you can still discern the original town plan. Landmarks include a massive columned stoa, the ruins of a Shrine of Aphrodite, 2nd-century BC Temple of Hercules, and 5th-century Christian basilica. The site is fenced, but usually open all day.

Archaeological Museum
MUSEUM
(Map p390; Plateia Eleftherias; adult/child €6/free; ☉ 8am-8pm Sun & Mon) Housed in a superb example of an Italian-era building, located in

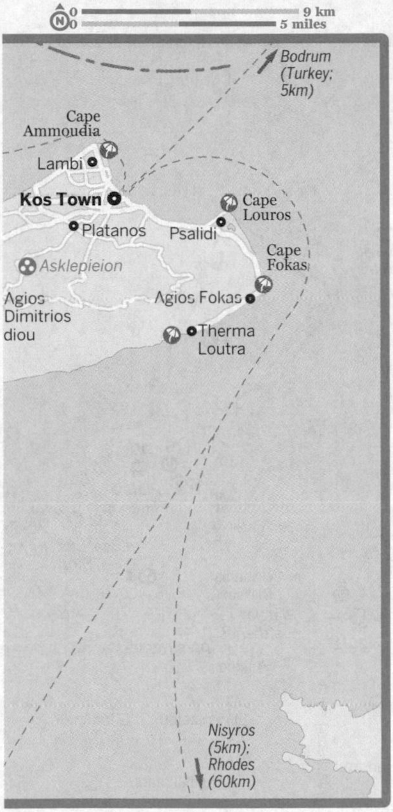
0
9 km
0
5 miles
Bodrum
(Turkey;
5km)
Cape
Ammoudia
Lambi
Kos Town
Cape
Louros
Platanos
Psalidi
Cape
Fokas
Asklepieion
Agios
Dimitrios
diou
Agios Fokas
Therma
Loutra
Nisyros
(5km);
Rhodes
(60km)

the central square, the small, but excellent archaeological museum possesses a wealth of sculptures from the Hellenistic to late Roman eras, with a statue of Hippocrates and a 3rd-century-AD mosaic as the star attractions. There are information panels for many of the rooms.

Casa Romana ARCHAEOLOGICAL SITE
(The Roman House; Map p390; ☎22420 23234; adult €6; ⏰8am-7.30pm Wed-Mon) Reopened to the public in 2015 after years of restoration, Casa Romana is believed to have been constructed during Hellenistic times and remodelled until the 3rd century AD. In 1940, and again only recently, it was restored. The surviving structure of the house was rebuilt; it provides enormous insight into how a wealthy Koan official and his family lived. Although not advertised, listening devices have invaluable recorded information and relate to numbered exhibits.

Beaches

The nearest beach to Kos Town, crowded **Lambi Beach** begins just 2km northwest and has its own strip of hotels and restaurants. Further west along the coast, a long stretch of pale sand is fringed by two more resorts – **Tingaki**, 10km from Kos Town, and the slightly less crowded **Marmari Beach** beyond. You can ride your bike to all of these. Windsurfing is popular at all three beaches, while the island of Pserimos is only a few kilometres offshore and served by excursion boats from Marmari in summer.

Heading south from Kos Town along Vasileos Georgiou, on the other hand, brings you to the three busy beaches of **Psalidi** (3km from Kos Town), **Agios Fokas** (8km), and **Therma Loutra** (12km). At Therma Loutra, hot mineral springs warm the sea but thousands flock here (hint: it gets packed here so go around 6am and have the place to yourself).

Sleeping

Accommodation here runs the gamut from basic guesthouse to upscale hotel. Regardless of whether you're aiming for a beach base, it's well worth spending a couple of nights in this interesting town. For those who don't need sand, Kos makes a good base.

★ **Hotel Afendoulis** HOTEL €
(Map p390; ☎22420 25321; www.afendoulishotel.com; Evripilou 1; s/d/tr from €35/50/60; ⏰Mar-Nov; ❄@🛜) Nothing is too much trouble at the delightful Afendoulis, where Alexis and his family run the most hospitable 'ship' in the Dodecanese. Sure, there may be plusher hotels in Kos, but none with the soul of this place. Expect clean rooms with small balconies, a homely lounge area (the focus of chatter and inspiration), and memorable breakfasts with homemade jams.

Kosta Palace HOTEL €€
(Map p390; ☎22420 22855; www.kosta-palace.com; cnr Akti Kountourioti & Averof; s/d/apt €80/85/135; ❄@🛜🏊) This massive harbour-front edifice, facing the castle across the port, holds 173 rooms, some with kitchenettes and private balconies. Apartments have separate rooms. There are also pools for kids and adults and a snack bar on the roof. While it's clean and functional (and good value if you nab a deal), it can be rather impersonal.

Kos Town

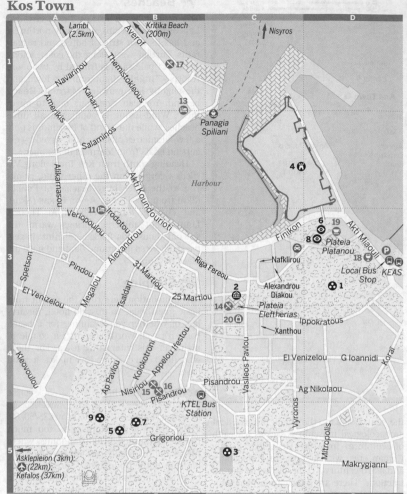

Hotel Sonia   HOTEL €€
(Map p390; ☎22420 28798; www.hotelsonia.
gr; Irodotou 9; d/tr/f incl breakfast €80/95/140;
❄☎) A block from the waterfront on a
peaceful backstreet, this small hotel offers
14 sparkling rooms with tiled floors, fridges and smart bathrooms. Rooms 4 and 5
have the best sea views; around five rooms
have balconies. If you want to, you can have
breakfast outside in the rear garden. There's
a decent book exchange.

Kos Aktis Art Hotel   HOTEL €€€
(Map p390; ☎22420 47200; www.kosaktis.gr;
Vasileos Georgiou 7; s/d/tr from €200/260/350;

❄☎) Aktis' beautiful hotels are scattered
across the Dodecanese and its representa-
tive here in Kos is stunning. Bedrooms are
minimalist affairs of glass, light and wood.
The view of the Aegean and, by night, Bodrum glittering like a giant chandelier, is romantic. There's a gym, fine restaurant and
bar. Prices vary significantly according to
supply and demand and season.

✗ Eating

★ Pote Tin Kyriaki   TAVERNA €
(Map p390; ☎6930352099; Pisandrou 9; mezedhes €2.50-8; ⊙7pm-2am Mon-Sat) Named 'Nev-

DODECANESE KOS TOWN

marmarites – translated as 'crumpets', but more like sourdough flatbread – with sweet or savoury toppings, but it also serves pies, juices, coffee and gigantic breakfasts (for two €20).

Elia   GREEK €€
(Map p390; ☏22420 22133; www.elia-kos.gr; Appelou Ifestou 27; mains €9-16; ☺12.30pm-late; ❄❄❄❄) 🍴 With its traditional wood-beamed ceiling and partly exposed stone walls covered in murals of the gods of the pantheon, Elia is earthy and friendly, and its massive menu is fit for a hard-to-please local deity or adventurous traveller. The Mediterranean dishes span traditional Greek, such as pork and lamb stews, to marinaded chicken and vegetarian mezedhes. All fresh. All good.

Ta Votsalakia   SEAFOOD €€
(Map p390; ☏22420 26555; Averof 10; mains €9-12, fish per kg €50; ☺1pm-midnight) 🍴 A lovely surprise awaits after the nondescript entrance of Ta Votsalakia. Pass the bustling kitchen and you'll be on the beach, almost netting your lunch yourself. The catch of

er on Sunday' to reflect its opening hours (yes, that's its day of rest), this traditional rough-and-ready *ouzerie* serves delicious specialities such as stuffed zucchini flowers, dolmadhes and steamed mussels. Come late, and you'll be cheek by jowl with the locals.

Aegli   CAFE €
(Map p390; ☏22420 30016; www.aiglikos.gr; Plateia Eleftherias; snacks €4-7; ☺breakfast, lunch & dinner) Stretching from beneath the arches of a municipal building onto the main square, this bakery-cafe is run by a cooperative supporting low-income women and employs only female staff. The speciality is

DON'T MISS

ASKLEPIEION

Asklepieion (Map p388; 22420 28763; adult/child €8/free; 8am-7.30pm daily Apr-Oct, to 2.30pm Sun & Mon Nov-Mar) is the island's most important ancient site stands on a pine-covered hill 3km southwest of Kos Town, commanding lovely views across towards Turkey. A religious sanctuary devoted to Asclepius, the god of healing, it was also a healing centre and a school of medicine. It was founded in the 3rd century BC, according to legend by Hippocrates himself, the Kos-born 'father' of modern medicine. He was already dead by then, though, and the training here simply followed his teachings.

Until the sanatorium was destroyed by an earthquake in AD 554, people came from far and wide for treatment.

The ruins occupy three levels, with the **propylaeum** (approach to the main gate), Roman-era **public baths** and remains of guest rooms on the first level. The second holds an **altar of Kyparissios Apollo**, with the 1st-century-BC **Temple to Apollo** to the east and the first **Temple of Asclepius**, built in the 4th century BC, to the west. The remains of its successor, the once-magnificent 2nd-century-BC **Temple of Asclepius**, are on the third level. Climb a little further, to the cool pine woods above, for the best views of all.

A small **museum** on the path down preserves ancient inscriptions. Bus 3 runs hourly from Kos Town to the site. It's also a pleasant, if uphill, bike ride.

the day is the thing to go for, but after this, choose from shrimps, mussels and seafood spaghetti. And much more. Vegetarians can munch on good mezedhes. In-the-know locals head here.

Taverna Lithino GREEK €€
(22420 24693; www.lithino.com; Archiepiskopou Gerasimou St; mains €9-14; lunch & dinner;) This incongruous place, behind the marina on a slightly 'busy' (for Kos) road, is worth the pilgrimage. Quality – not gourmet – Greek fare is the objective here. This means great grills, homemade mezedhes don't miss the meatballs) and even vegetarian dishes. There's a front and rear terrace; the latter is around a mulberry tree trunk. Friendly and family run.

Drinking & Nightlife

Kos Town has a very lively party scene, focused a block south of the harbour and along the waterfront on Kritika Beach. Locals congregate on weekends to drink coffee and gossip in the cafes on Plateia Eleftherias (Freedom Sq).

Kaseta BAR
(Map p390; 22420 22352; www.kaseta-kos.gr; Akti Miaouli 4; 8am-1am) For locals, this is the place to be, and to be seen. Prices are hefty (coffee is slightly more, given its location overlooking the harbour). But it's where you come to linger for a coffee by day, or a cocktail by night.

Law Court Cafe CAFE
(Map p390; Plateia Platanou; 7.30am-late) Despite being set on Kos Town's prettiest square, facing Hippocrates' plane tree (p387), this timeless little cafe feels remote from the tourist scene. Instead, as the name suggests, it's where local lawyers and businesspeople meet to discuss the order of the day, while savouring their morning espressos.

Shopping

For local products, the market has a fabulous selection. The Old Town is full of tourist paraphernalia; for high-street-style shops, head to the eastern end of Ioannidi and the pedestrian streets south of Ippokratous.

Fragrant with spices, **Dimotiki Agora** (Map p390; 22420 22900; Plateia Eleftherias; 8am-late) is a lively open-arched market that has a cornucopia of locally made honeys, natural soaps, bonbons, sandalwood spoons, mythological curios and Kalymnian sponges.

Getting Around

BICYCLE

Cycle lanes thread all through Kos Town, with the busiest route running along the waterfront to connect the town with Lambi to the north and Psalidi to the south. Many hotels have bikes for guests, or you can rent one from Escape Rentals (p387) or Kos Mountainbike Activities (p387).

BUS

Local buses, run by **KEAS** (Map p390; ☑ 22420 26276; fare €1.10-1.60), operate within Kos Town, the most useful being route 3 to Asklepieion; the **bus stop** (Map p390) is on Akti Miaouli.

Buses to the rest of the island, including the airport, depart from the KTEL bus station (p387). Note that Kefalos-bound buses also stop at the big roundabout near the airport entrance.

TAXI

Taxis (Map p390; ☑ 22420 22777, 22420 23333) congregate on the south side of the port.

TOURIST TRAIN

One way to get your bearings in summer is to take a 20-minute city tour on the **tourist train** (☑ 22420 26276; €5), which departs frequently from Akti Koundourioti on the harbourfront.

Around Kos

Mountain Villages

The villages scattered on the green northern slopes of the Dikeos mountains make ideal destinations for day trips.

Your first stop should be **Agios Dimitrios**, an abandoned village whose population left during WWII. Here, there is a stunning cafe Haihoutes (p393) and a gorgeous village church.

Then head to the mountain village of **Zia**, 14km southwest of Kos Town. Formerly one of Kos' prettiest villages, it's now essentially a one-street theme park. The views down to the sea are as wonderful as ever, but coachloads of tourists are deposited every few minutes to stroll along its swathe of souvenir shops and competing tavernas.

If you continue further on, you'll reach the villages of **Asfendiou** and **Lagoudi**, where you'll be rewarded with great views and incredible churches, and most likely have them to yourself. Continuing around 5km further west you'll reach the less commercialised village of **Pyli**. But just before the village a left turn leads to the extensive remains of its medieval predecessor, **Old Pyli**, scattered amid the towering rocks and pine trees of a high and very magical hillside. The summit here is crowned by the stark ruins of **Pyli Castle** and the whole place is so wild you half expect Pan, god of the wild and shepherds, to pop up. A well-marked trail climbs from the roadside parking area, forking left to the castle and right to the old village, where the only building still in use is the Oria Tavern (p393) hidden in the woods.

Buses connect Kos Town with Pyli itself (€2.10, two to four daily), but not Old Pyli.

Eating

★ Oria Taverna   GREEK €

(Map p388; ☑ 6974408843; Old Pyli; mains €7-12; ⊙ 9am-9pm; Ⓟ) ✎ You'll be rewarded by making the effort to get to this idyllic taverna, only accessible by a 15-minute walk up a track. Here you'll face the 1000-year-old Pyli Castle and enjoy the best rural view on Kos over great snacks and cooling drinks. But you can't beat a sunset dinner, tucking into the seasonal, locally sourced dishes of the day.

Watermill   CAFE €

(☑ 6947412440; Zia; snacks €4-8; ⊙ breakfast, lunch & dinner; 🛜 👪) ✎ With its vine-covered arbour and relaxing patio giving stunning mountain views, this former watermill is colourful and attractive, if ultrapopular. The menu includes burgers, crêpes and fruit salad. It's worth the brief climb up the hill just to sate your thirst with its delicious homemade lemonade.

I Palia Pyli   GREEK €€

(Old Spring Water; Pyli; mains €7.50-11.50; ⊙ 9am-11pm) This is one of the most understated

---

LOCAL KNOWLEDGE

COFFEE IN GHOSTLY HAIHOUTES

The tiny and -oh-so tasteful cafe **Haihoutes** (Map p388; ☑ 6932637905; snacks €5-12) is set in a ghost village of the same name (it was once a thriving village of 450 people) and has been restored and stands, along with the village church, as ongoing testament to its history. With stylish olive-green chairs and traditional tables, you can kick back with a coffee and think you were in a *kafeneio* (traditional cafe) from decades ago.

Come evening it turns into a cafe-bar, and there's sometimes live music, everything from island music to *rembetika* (blues). Be sure to check out the attached 'museum', a replica of a traditional home, plus the photos in the wee church showing life as it once was. Note: there's limited telephone reception.

spots on the island. Sure, it isn't fancy, just a couple of tables out on a veranda, under a ficus tree and overlooking an historic spring on a tiny square in the village of Pyli. But it has been serving up fabulous home cooking since 1950. Try the zucchini balls, meatballs and mezedhes.

Mastihari

Hardly more than a village, this delightful old-fashioned beach resort holds everything you need for a straightforward family holiday. There's a lovely broad strip of powder-fine sand scattered with tamarisk trees, a clutch of whitewashed rental studios and small hotels, and a row of appetising waterfront tavernas and bars. There's no historic core and nothing of any architectural interest, but as a place to spend a day or a week in the sun, Mastihari has it all. You won't have it to yourself (large resorts have been constructed behind), but it's less in-your-face than some of the island's other resort villages.

Mastihari's tiny port is served by frequent **Anek** (Anekalymnou; ☑ 22420 29900; www. anekalymnou.gr) and Anem (www.anemferries.gr) ferries to Pothia on Kalymnos, as well as excursion boats to the islet of Pserimos in summer.

🛏 Sleeping & Eating

Studios Diana   APARTMENT €
(☑ 22420 59116; Mastihari; apt €40) A fabulous budget option, with clean and basic studios, all opening onto the sea, with private balconies and very tiny kitchens. Turning on the air-con costs €5 extra. Not surprisingly, Studios Diana has its regulars.

Katerina & Efi   APARTMENT €
(☑ 6937529385; efikaterina@hotmail.com; Mastihari; d/f from €45/70; ❄🐱🗢) This well-run budget choice, with a spiffy blue-and-white exterior, is located so close to the beach that if it were any nearer you'd have sand in your bed. The tidy rooms and kitchenettes make it great for a longer stay; it's family and pet friendly, too. Even those with a village-facing view are pleasant and sport larger terraces.

★ O Makis   SEAFOOD €
(☑ 6948668417; Mastihari; mains €6-8, fish per kg around €40) Ask any local where to eat? O Makis, of course. Don't expect linen and haute cuisine. Think better: a genuine experience. Grilled fish and seafood platters cooked by the delightful Makis, a salt-of-the-earth, friendly character that makes you grateful to be in Greece. Go with a flexible attitude and enjoy the seafood, grills or whatever is recommended.

Kali Kardia   SEAFOOD €€
(☑ 22420 59289; Mastihari; mains €7-16; ⊘ breakfast, lunch & dinner) Atmospheric taverna near the harbour (that claims to be the oldest; see the lovely black-and-white photos), with tables out on the footpath and a wooden interior that's patronised by older folk staring out to sea. Piping aromas of squid, shrimp and souvlakia emerge from the kitchen, and large mixed platters for two cost €30.

Kamari & Kefalos Bay
Καμάρι & Κέφαλος

Enormous Kefalos Bay, a 12km stretch of high-quality sand, lines the southwest shoreline of Kos. For most of its length the beach itself is continuous, but the main road runs along a crest around 500m inland, so each separate section served by signposted tracks has its own name. Backed by scrubby green hills and lapped by warm water, these are the finest and emptiest beaches on the island. Kamari, at the western extremity of this black-pebbled beach, is a low-key resort with plenty of cafes, tavernas and accommodation, as well as decent water sports. High above Kamari, perched on a bluff, the touristy village of Kefalos has a few spots to eat and stay. If you're determined to escape the crowds, continue on to the island's southern peninsula beyond.

🏖 Beaches

The most popular stretch of sand is **Paradise Beach**, while the least developed is **Magic Beach**. **Exotic Beach** nearby is the nudist option. **Langada Beach** (which you may also see referred to as Banana Beach) makes a good compromise. Sadly, **Agios Stefanos Beach**, at the far western end, has been ruined by a massive resort behind. Nevertheless, this small beachfront promontory has the photogenic islet of **Kastri**, on which is a tiny church, offshore though within swimming distance.

On the west coast, **Agios Theologos Beach** is backed by meadow bluffs carpeted in olive groves, and feels far removed from the resort bustle.

🛏 Sleeping & Eating

Affordable studios and apartments are the order of the day, with an emphasis on package holiday accommodation in Kamari.

Albatross Studios   APARTMENT €€
(☑22420 71981; thealbatrossteam@gmail.com; Kamari Beach; d/apt/f €65/80/120; 🅿✳🛜🎬) Eleven simple, spotless and identical kitchenette studios, so freshly maintained they might have been built yesterday. All have sea views, there's a swimming pool (with small pool bar), and the beach is just across the road, with the jetty a short walk away. Airport pickup for stays of three nights or more. Excellent value; prices are significantly reduced outside high season.

★**Restaurant**
Agios Theologos   TAVERNA €€
(☑6974503556; Agios Theologos Beach; mains €10-17; ⏱lunch & dinner, Sun only Feb-Apr; ✳🛜) Set in dreamy sand dunes above Agios Theologos Beach, this much-loved seasonal taverna enjoys the best sunsets in Kos. It offers everything from zesty homemade cheese, courtesy of its inquisitive goats, at its most flavoursome fried, to fresh grilled bream. There are fantastic mezedhes, too. Pure romance.

Mylotopi   GREEK €€
(☑22420 73000; Kefalos; snacks €4-8, mains €8-12; ⏱9am-2pm) Mylotopi's complex comprises a bar, cafe and restaurant that has been reconstructed on a former village site (with restored windmill, thus its name). This smart stone structure sprawls across various outdoor terraces, while the interior – true to its provenance – maintains cosy nooks. It's the perfect spot to enjoy anything from a coffee and cocktail to a snack or heavier meal.

🛈 Getting There & Away

Buses to and from Kos Town (€4.80, three to six daily) stop nearby at Kamari Beach.

ASTYPALEA
ΑΣΤΥΠΑΛΑΙΑ

POP 1300
Swathed in silky aquamarine waters, farflung, butterfly-shaped Astypalea is richly rewarding for walkers, campers and history buffs. For any island hunter, this is the ulti-mate escape, with mountainous meadows straight from the pages of Homer, and rugged beaches fringed in vivid blue water. Chance of sighting a mermaid: fair to middling.

The island's main settlements, the merged villages of Pera Gialos and the hilltop Hora, are a tumble of bleached-white houses cascading down from a medieval fortress to a harbour, the former port. Although boutique hotels have been sprouting here in recent years, the tourist infrastructure – and ferry service – remains minimal, and most visitors are Greek, with the rest largely French and Italian. Fed up with the package crowds, Irish bars and fish and chips? You've come to the right place.

🛈 Getting There & Away

AIR
Sky Express (p343) services Astypalea with several flights a week from Leros (€80, 25 minutes), Kalymnos (€62, 1¾ hours) and Kos (€74, 1¾ hours). There are also daily flights from Athens (€121, one hour). Astypalea Tours (p397) in Pera Gialos also books flights.

BOAT
Only two ferry operators serve Astypalea.

In summer, Blue Star Ferries (p364) boats arrive at the 'new port', which is rather isolated at Agios Andreas, 6.5km north of Pera Gialos. A bus is scheduled to meet each boat, as are the island's two taxis. Astypalea Tours (p397) will transfer you for €5. Outside high season, however, inconveniently, the ferry arrives in the dead of night, so book your transfer ahead if your accommodation doesn't meet you.

One ferry arrives around four times weekly, having sailed from Piraeus (€38.50, 9¾ hours) via Paros (€37, 5¼ hours) and Naxos (€20, four hours), and sets off back along the same route. The other stops once per week between Piraeus and Rhodes, calling also at Kalymnos (€14.50, two hours), Kos (€17, three hours), Tilos (€15.50, six hours) and Nisyros (€12.50, five hours).

Nisos Kalymnos (www.anekalymnou.gr) connects Pera Gialos' small harbour (sometimes referred to as the Skala Port) twice weekly with Kalymnos.

🛈 Getting Around

Astypalea's airport is on the flat, narrow 'neck' of the island, 8km northeast of Pera Gialos. Buses connect with flights in summer, while taking either of the island's two **taxis** (☑6976256461, 6975706365) to Pera Gialos costs around €12. From June to September, Astypalea Tours (p397) offers both airport and port shuttles (around €5 per person).

Astypalea

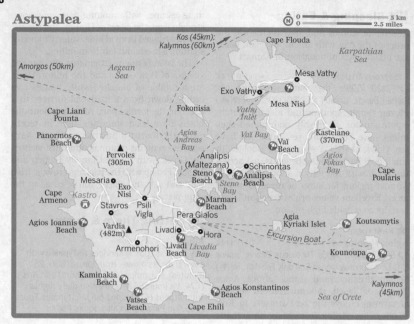

Summer buses also link Pera Gialos with Hora and Livadi to the west, and Analipsi/Maltezana to the east, stopping at beaches en route (€2).

There are several recommended vehicle-rental agencies, including **Vergoulis** (☑ 22430 61351; www.vergoulis.com; per day scooters from €18, cars €45-70; ☺ 9am-9pm) and **AstyCar** (☑ 22430 62265; www.astycar.gr; scooter/car from €32/55), both based in Pera Gialos.

Pera Gialos & Hora
Πέρα Γιαλός & Χώρα

POP 1036

Astypalea's main town, Pera Gialos, lies on the southern shore of the island's western half, curving around an attractive bay that's too shallow for large interisland ferries. This compact village holds a small sand-and-pebble beach that's popular with locals. Bars and tavernas punctuate the quay, which is the preserve of old sea dogs in low season, but surprisingly lively on summer evenings.

Visitors delight in the beauty of the old settlement of Hora looming above, its white houses spilling down the hillside beneath its impressive *kastro* (castle). For the original inhabitants of Hora, however, the upward migration was prompted by the threats of marauding pirates. These days Hora is a delightful maze to explore. Stroll around

the hushed tangle of streets and climb up to the fort. You can then relax in the clutch of inviting *kafeneia* and tavernas alongside the restored windmills that mark the village entrance.

◉ Sights & Activities

Kastro   CASTLE

(Hora; ☺ dawn-dusk) **FREE** Astypalea's imposing castle was built by the Venetian Quirini family early in the 15th century. For the next 300 years, up to 4000 people lived within this ever-expanding precinct, sheltered from pirate attacks. Its last inhabitants left in 1956, after an earthquake caused the stone houses integrated into its walls to collapse. The only entrance is through a gateway that burrows beneath the **Church of the Virgin of the Castle**; the magical **Church of Agios Georgios** lies beyond.

Archaeological Museum   MUSEUM

(☑ 22430 61500; Pera Gialos; €2; ☺ 9am-5pm Wed-Mon Jun-Sep) Pera Gialos' small archaeological museum, set back from the sea at the start of the road up to Hora, holds treasures found across the island, from earliest times up to the Middle Ages. Highlights include grave offerings from two Mycenaean chamber tombs and a little bronze Roman statue of Aphrodite.

Thalassopouli BOATING

(☑6974436338; Pera Gialos; per person €18; ☉Jun-Sep; 🖮) Run by Captain Yiannis, *Thalassopouli* leaves Pera Gialos at 11am and returns you glowing and salty at 6pm after a day's swimming around uninhabited neighbouring islands such as Kounoupa, with its golden isthmus of sand, and Koutsomytis, outlined in purest aquamarine. Take plenty of sunscreen.

🛏 Sleeping

Reservations are essential in July and August. The finer boutique options are in Hora but there are some smart small resorts elsewhere, too.

Gyrouli Studios APARTMENT €

(☑6946583570, 22430 61267; www.gyroulistudios.gr; Pera Gialos; from €60) These spotless studios, with kitchenettes and kind owners, are located in an ideal spot: between Hora and Pera Gialos (not too far up, nor down). Some studios are in an older style, while the newer, more modern ones would suit fussier travellers. But, hey, the view is the same. Low season prices significantly lower.

Studios Kilindra BOUTIQUE HOTEL €€

(☑22430 61131; www.astipalea.com.gr; Hora; studio/apt/ste incl breakfast €150/160/220; ❄@🛜🛋) 🅿 Just below the *kastro*, this enchanting boutique hotel has a swish pool with a terrace overlooking the mouthwash-green bay. The lobby is scattered with eclectic antiques as well as a grand piano, while studios and larger maisonettes fuse the contemporary with the traditional, featuring split-level floors, raised beds, sofas and kitchenettes. Massage, acupuncture and herbal treatments are also available.

★Kallichoron Art Boutique Hotel BOUTIQUE HOTEL €€€

(☑22430 61935; www.kallichoron.gr; Hora; d incl breakfast from €150; ❄🛜🛋) 🅿 Eleven gorgeous rooms and two maisonettes make up Kallichoron. The bright and beautifully decorated rooms have a terrace and face directly across to Hora. The hotel has received national awards for its environmentally friendly practices and, despite the fact the rooms have small kitchenettes, it serves up scrumptious breakfasts. These 'Grandma's breakfasts' comprise more local produce than a national providore.

Mooch on the terrace and stare at Hora. Or lie back and view the local artwork. Dreamy stuff.

🍴 Eating

Agoni Grammi TAVERNA €

(☑22430 62102; Hora; mains €8-15; ☉lunch & dinner, closed Mar) It's the outdoor terrace that first catches the eye here, close to Hora's landmark windmills, but the modern whitewashed interior with its lovely open kitchen is equally appealing. As well as handmade pasta, this smart spot, one of the island's favourites, is also renowned for its fish soup and sea urchin dish.

Maïstrali TAVERNA €

(☑22430 61691; Pera Gialos; mains €8.50-13; ☉10am-late; ❄🛜🛋) Tucked one street back from the harbour, near the stairway to heaven (well, Hora, anyway), this long-standing restaurant dishes up everything from zucchini balls, lamb chops and eggplant salad, to grilled shrimp *saganaki*. It's one of the few eateries open all year.

★Barbarossa TAVERNA €€

(☑22430 61577; Hora; mains €12-15; ☉lunch & dinner; ❄🛜🛋) 🅿 You can't miss this friendly taverna, serving food with soul along the main approach to Hora, with a buzzing terrace near the town hall. Menu highlights like pork fillet with prunes, mussels and grilled shrimps ensure you won't be disappointed. A favourite choice in Hora.

ℹ Information

Alpha Bank (☑22430 61402; Pera Gialos; ☉8am-2pm Mon-Fri) The island's only bank, with an ATM, is on the waterfront.

Astypalea Tours (☑22430 61571; www.astypaleatours.gr; Pera Gialos; ☉10am-1.30pm & 5.30-8.30pm) Extremely helpful. Can book air and ferry tickets, plus boat excursions to the small islands of Kounoupa, Koutsomytis and Agia Kiriaki.

Municipal Tourist Office (☑22430 61412; www.visitastypalea.com; Hora; ☉6-9pm Jun-Sep) In a restored windmill, this is a high-season operation only, and can provide basic information about the island. Opening hours can be irregular, depending on staff availability.

ℹ Getting There & Away

Local buses link Pera Gialos with Hora, Maltezana, Livadi and Agios Andreas (€2). Taxis (p395) to/from Pera Gialos or Hora and the airport cost around €12. In the summer months, Astypalea Tours (p397) offers shuttles to the airport and port (around €5 per person).

Nisos Kalymnos (www.anekalymnou.gr) connects Pera Gialos' small harbour (sometimes referred to as the Skala Port) twice weekly with Kalymnos, but major boats dock at Agios Andreas, 6.5km north of Pera Gialos.

Livadi

Livadi Beach, Astypalea's most popular, stands at the mouth of a lush valley in the first bay south of Hora. An easy 20-minute walk down from the old town, it's also served by local buses. In summer it's effectively transformed into a buzzing little resort, with a string of hip restaurants and bars lining the waterfront.

🛏 Sleeping & Eating

Mouras Studios APARTMENT €€
(☑ 22430 61227; www.mourastudios.gr; Livadi; studio from €80; ⊗ May–mid-Oct; ❄ 🛜) Radiating off a beachfront courtyard, these seven stunning whitewashed studios vary in size, but all have a stylish grey-and-white decor, kitchenettes and private balconies. Full-on sea views cost a few euros extra. (Note, don't confuse this with the Mouras Resort, though it is all part of the same family.)

Astropelos GREEK €€
(☑ 22430 61473; www.astropelos.com; Livadi; mains €10-20; ⊗ breakfast, lunch & dinner; ❄ 🛜 🅿) There's a whiff of expensive suncream about this place. But it's first-class dining by the beach, on a decked veranda with chic white tables and a gourmet menu that includes octopus salad and lobster. Vegan and vegetarian options available, too, plus daily specials. And lounge chairs under the shade of tamarisk trees to view Hora on the hilltop horizon.

Gerani TAVERNA €€
(☑ 22430 61484; www.astypalaiagerani.gr; Livadi; mains €8-12; 🅿) An ultrafriendly, English-speaking Greek couple run this lovely spot, nestled off the main drag – look for the hanging boat and the flower boxes. It serves delicious no-nonsense, traditional Greek food. Forget the menu (although extensive) and go for the daily specials, the likes of fish soup, or ravioli stuffed with the traditional *chlori* cheese and local saffron.

West of Pera Gialos

West of Pera Gialos, you swiftly hit the Astypalea outback – gnarled, bare rolling hills, perfect for a Cyclops. There's scarcely a sealed road to speak of but, depending on the conditions (the roads are graded in preparation for summer), it's just about possible to drive. Note, however, that car rental agencies might prohibit this, except if you have a SUV or jeep. If you can, cross the western massif by heading directly inland from Hora and, from the point where the road finally peters out after 8km, where the **Kastro** ruins and **Moni Agiou Ioanni** stand proudly cheek by jowl above the shoreline, energetic walkers can hike down to **Agios Ioannis Beach**. Alternatively, follow the track that branches northwards shortly before road's end and you'll probably have **Panormos Beach** to yourself.

The rough track that winds along the southern coast west of Livadi, on the other hand, leads through mountainous meadows to several remote beaches. First along the way, reached on a brief detour (most of this on sealed road), is the pretty, tree-shaded **Agios Konstantinos Beach** on the south side of Livadi Bay. It's back to a dirt track to reach **Kaminakia Beach** in the far west, where the track reaches its terminus. Book-ended by granite boulders, Kaminakia is Astypalea's best altar to sun worshipping, with water so clear you can see the pebbles through the turquoise. Both beaches hold excellent seasonal tavernas.

In July and August, boats head out for the day from Pera Gialos to the remote western beaches of **Agios Ioannis**, **Kaminakia** and **Vatses**, as well as to the islets of **Koutsomytis** (with ethereal, emerald-green water) and **Kounoupa**. Contact Astypalea Tours (p397) for details.

🍴 Eating

Sti Linda GREEK €
From the Stavros junction a rough track winds upwards to the shepherd's hut on the mountain spine and then an *extremely* rough track winds downwards to Kaminakia Beach, lapped by stunning turquoise water. Here you're also rewarded with a visit to **Sti Linda** (☑ 6932610050; mains €5-10; ⊗ Jul-Sep) 🅿 , a good seasonal restaurant, which rustles up hearty fish soups, oven-baked goat and homemade bread. Make it a day trip.

East of Pera Gialos

The slender isthmus that links Astypalea's two 'wings' holds some of the island's most popular beaches. Each of the three bays at **Marmari**, just 2km northeast of Pera Gialos, has its own pebble-and-sand beach, right beside the road. **Steno Beach**, another 2km along, is sandy, shady and conveniently shallow for kids. The name means 'narrow', with the isthmus being a mere 100m wide near this spot.

The only resort area away from Pera Gialos, **Analipsi** is pleasantly laid-back and spreads through a fertile valley alongside the airport, 8km northeast of Pera Gialos. Also known as Maltezana, having once been the lair of Maltese pirates, it's grown recently thanks to long **Analipsi Beach** to the southeast, which offers sand, pebbles, shade and clean, shallow water. Nearby the remains of the Tallaras Roman baths still hold some mosaics.

Almost no one lives on Astypalea's eastern half. The only settlement is the remote hamlet of **Mesa Vathy**, tucked into the shelter of an enormous bottleneck bay and home to barely half-a-dozen families. A summer yacht harbour, it doesn't have a decent beach.

🛌 Sleeping & Eating

Villa Barbara APARTMENT €
(☑ 22430 61448, 6930778530; www.villabarbara. gr; Analipsi; s/d from €45/50; ❄) Set in flowering gardens, these 12 fresh blue-and-white studios have tiled floors and balconies with sea views. The ocean is less than 100m away.

★ Galini Cafe CAFE €
(☑ 22430 61201; Exo Vathy; mains €4-8; ⊙ Jun-Oct) At remote Exo Vathy hamlet you can dine at the ultracasual, fishermen-packed Galini Cafe, which offers meat and fish grills and the odd oven-baked special. You're pretty much told to grab your plates and 'come and get it' (in the Greek equivalent). It hasn't changed for decades; worth coming here for the salt-of-the-earth experience alone.

★ Astakoukos SEAFOOD €€
(☑ 22430 64014; Sxoinontas Beach, Analipsi; mains €7-14; ⊙ breakfast, lunch & dinner; 📶🅿) While the name means 'the little lobster', there's nothing diminutive about the quality here. Hospitable John will sit you under the shaded pergola and serve up everything from his award-winning lobster and spaghetti to goat *stifhado* (goat stew with a lemon sauce). Or you can relax on the Sxoinontas Beach and order simpler snacks and refreshments. Pretty. And perfect.

KALYMNOS ΚΑΛΥΜΝΟΣ

POP 16,000

Rugged Kalymnos is characterised by its dramatic mountains that draw hardy climbers from all over the world. Its western flank is particularly spectacular with skeletal crags towering above dazzling blue waters. Surprisingly for its rocky landscape, it cradles a couple of pretty, fertile valleys with bee boxes and olive groves. The enticing, car-free islet of Telendos is immediately offshore, a mere 10 minutes in a water taxi.

While its sponge-fishing heyday is long past, Kalymnos remains inextricably entwined with the sea, particularly in its capital and main ferry port, Pothia, where statues of Poseidon and an historic diver survey the harbour.

In recent years, the island's activities have expanded from climbing alone. Add to this diving, plus hiking and a host of interesting little museums and cultural experiences, and you begin to see why Kalymnos is now on the Greek islands must-visit list.

ℹ Getting There & Away

AIR
Kalymnos' airport, 6km northwest of Pothia, is served by daily Sky Express (p343) flights to and from Athens (€133, one hour), Leros (€75, 15 minutes) and Kos (€75, 20 minutes). Connecting buses meet flights in summer.

BOAT
Kalymnos' main ferry port, Pothia, is linked by daily Dodekanisos Seaways (p362) catamarans running the route between Samos (€39, 3¼ hours), Ikaria (€32, 2¾ hours), Patmos (€28, 1¾ hours), Lipsi (€22, 1¼ hours), Leros (€20, 45 minutes), Kalymnos and Kos (€16, 35 minutes). A second route runs between Rhodes, Symi, Kos, Kalymnos, Leros, Lipsi and Patmos.
Blue Star Ferries (p364) connects Pothia with Piraeus (€54, 10¾ hours), plus Kos (€7.50, 45 minutes) and Rhodes (€53 to €65, 11 to 18 hours) five times weekly, and once weekly with Astypalea (€20, 3½ hours) and Symi (€29, two hours).
Anek (www.anekalymnou.gr) runs the passenger-only *Kalymnos Star* and *Kalymnos Dolphin* between Mastihari on the north shore of Kos (six daily, 45 minutes). **Anem** (www. anemferries.gr) offers the same trip three times a day. Several excursion boats offer day trips from Kos Town to Pothia.
In addition, the little resort of Myrties on Kalymnos' west coast is connected twice weekly with Agia Marina on Leros by Leros Express (p387).

Kalymnos

Leros (2km)
Kalpi
Aegean Sea
Cape Diapori
Leros (7km);
Lipsi (30km);
Patmos (40km)
Koukoula (365m)
Patella (435m)
Cape Hondri Myti
Kalolimnos
Arginonda
470m
Emborios
Paleonisos
Cape Pounda
Kalavros
Skalia
Paleonisos Bay
Arginonda Bay
Paradise Beach
Cape Aspro
Telendos Islet
Basilica of Agios Vasilios
Arginonda
Pezonda Bay
Drasonda Beach
Excursion Boat
Basilica of Palaiopanayia
Telendos
Armeos
Stimenia
Mt Pirnari (425m)
Almyres Beach
Hohlakas Beach
Masouri
Metohi
Mt Kyra Psili (650m)
Cape Atsipas
Myrties
Platys Gialos
Panormos Valley
Mt Profitis Ilias (725m)
Platanos
Agia Kyriaki
Linaria
Elies
Rina
Kandouni
Hora
Pera Kastro
Vathys
Cape Trahilos
Argos
Pothia
Mt Vokari (330m)
Akti Bay
Akti
Saronisi
Leros (10km);
Patmos (40km);
Samos (90km)
Pithari Bay
Vothyni
St Savvas
Cape Hali
Pserimos (6km)
Kefalas Cave
St Valsamidis
Therma
Astypalea (70km)
Agios Andreas
Vlihadia
Excursion Boat
Cape Kefalas
Cape Agios Georgios
Nera
Kos (10km)

ℹ Getting Around

BOAT

In summer, excursion boats run from Pothia to Kefalas Cave (around €20), the island of Pserimos and other beaches. Frequent **water taxis** (one way €2; ⊘ 8am-midnight) also connect Myrties with Telendos Islet year-round.

BUS

Buses from Pothia Harbour serve a number of the island's villages. See www.kalymnos-isl.gr.

CAR & MOTORCYCLE

Vehicle-hire companies along the harbour in Pothia include **Auto Market** (☑ 6972834628, 22430 24202; www.kalymnoscars.gr) and **Suzuki Rentals** (☑ 6937980591; www.kipreosrentals.gr). Expect to pay €20 to €40 per day for a car, and €12 to €15 for a scooter.

TAXI

Shared taxis, based at Pothia's **taxi stand** (☑ 22430 50300; Plateia Kyprou), cost little more than buses. Private taxis cost around €10 to Myrties, €10 to the airport, €17 to Vathys and €30 to Emborios.

Pothia   Πόθια

POP 12,300

Kalymnos' capital, Pothia has a low-slung harbourfront of cream and white facades and backs up the hill in a labyrinth of streets, beneath hulking mountains. If arriving by boat, this is most likely your first taste of the island. You may find some Kalymnians a little gruff, but don't be offended – these rugged islanders have been known throughout history for their toughness and terse manner. Pothia is not a resort, and makes no attempt to be one, though for the curious traveller there's an excellent archaeological museum and a tourist office. Wander the quayside peppered with old Venetian-style mansions and sea-god statues, past nut-brown fishermen and ex-divers in *kafeneia* and bars, nursing retsinas and ragged lungs.

⊙ Sights & Activities

In summer boats run from Pothia to Kefalas Cave (around €20), where an impressive 103m corridor is filled with stalactites and stalagmites; and the island of Pserimos, with its big, sandy beach and tavernas. Head to the harbour to see where else they go.

Archaeological Museum   MUSEUM
(☑ 22430 23113; adult/child €4/2; ⊙ 8.30am-4pm Wed-Mon) Kalymnos' modern Archaeological Museum is tricky to find, hidden in the backstreets behind the eastern end of Pothia's waterfront. It's worth the effort to enjoy beautifully displayed ancient artefacts dating as far back as 5300 BC. There's some remarkable glassware and gold jewellery, but the highlight is an exquisite, larger-than-life bronze statue of a woman from the 2nd century BC. Swathed in a chiton (tunic), she was discovered underwater off Kalymnos in 1994.

Nautical & Folklore Museum   MUSEUM
(☑ 22430 51361; €3; ⊙ 9am-5pm mid-Jun–mid-Sep) On the central waterfront, this is more of a collection than a museum. The nautical section focuses on sponge fishing, displaying mighty stone weights used by ancient divers and haunting photos of their 20th-century counterparts wearing early-model diving suits. Many divers suffered terrible injuries before the bends (decompression sickness) was understood. The folklore section holds a few costumes and furniture.

🛏 Sleeping

Archontiko Hotel   PENSION €
(☑ 6942838524, 22430 51344; www.apxontiko-ho tel.com; s/d €35/50; ❄ 🛜) Overlooking the harbour, five minutes' walk from the ferry, this central, custard-coloured mansion is one of the most handsome in town. The Danish manager has done a great job with 'old bones': the rooms are light and airy and oh so white. It's in the middle of the waterfront; look up for the sign. Great budget option.

Evanik Hotel   HOTEL €
(☑ 22430 22057; www.evanik-hotel.gr; s/d/tr incl breakfast €35/45/60; ❄ 🛜) Beyond its smart lobby, this modern hotel, a few blocks up from the harbour and lacking views, holds 28 plush rooms of varying size, with tiled floors, Ikea-style furniture, reading lamps and immaculate en-suite bathrooms. Downstairs there's a pleasant breakfast area. Ask for a quieter room at the back.

★ Villa Melina   HOTEL €€
(☑ 22430 22682; www.villa-melina.com; d/tr incl breakfast €65/70; ❄ 🛜 🏊) Set in a colourful walled garden, this rose-pink 1930s villa exudes old-world charm, its wood-panelled rooms featuring stucco ceilings, lilac walls, mahogany armoires and huge beds. Don't expect luxury – it's all slightly faded – but the delightful, kind and gentle owner Antonios and his cats provide a homey welcome, the bathrooms are spotless, and the large, sparkling swimming pool irresistible.

For families there are also four cosy apartments (€75) in the garden.

🍴 Eating

Stukas Taverna   GREEK €
(☑ 6932248357; mains €6-12; ⊙ lunch & dinner; 🛜 ☑) Run by friendly Greek-Australians, tiny Stukas has checked cloths and a wharfside terrace, serving hearty fare. Three-course set menus cost €10 for vegetarians and around €12 for fish- or meat eaters. Towards the far eastern end of the harbour, heading away from the ferry dock.

Barba Yiannis   GREEK €
(mains €8-12; ⊙ breakfast, lunch & dinner) Enjoying harbour views from its pretty decked terrace, Yiannis is a reliable spot to head for traditional Greek dishes such as *stifadho* and souvlakia. There's also swordfish, shrimp *saganaki* and calamari, or whatever fish might be going that day. Another plus? It serves breakfast from 8.30am.

★ Mamouzelos   SEAFOOD €€
(☑ 22430 47809; mains €12-15, fish per kg €50; ⊙ lunch & dinner) Without doubt, the best seafood-only taverna on the island. Prices here are slightly higher than your regular taverna, but you get what you pay for: the freshest of fresh fish thanks to the fishermen who save their quality catches for this place. Come with time to spare, grab a seat on the veranda. At the eastern end of the harbour.

ℹ Information

Municipal Tourist Information (☑ 22430 29299; www.kalymnos-isl.gr; ⊙ 8am-3pm Mon-Fri) Has basic, if well-organised, info for buses and ferries, climbing and diving, festivals and general island practicalities. At the entrance to the ferry dock.

Tezaris Tours (☑ 22430 22800; www.tezaris tours.gr; Agios Nikolaos) Arranges ferry and air tickets plus does two-hour trips of the island in minibuses.

VATHYS & RINA

Follow the barren coast road northeast from Pothia, instead of heading straight over to the west coast, and, after winding for 13km along the cliffs, it enters a long, lush, east-facing valley that was historically the agricultural heartland of Kalymnos. Narrow roads here thread between citrus orchards, bordered by high stone walls known as *koumoula*.

The valley takes its name from the inland settlement of **Vathys**, but the attraction for visitors is the little harbour of **Rina**. From the sea, it's accessed by a slender twisting inlet that's more like a fjord than anything you'd expect to find on a Greek island. In summer, large excursion boats bring troupes of day trippers here from Kos for lunch, keeping a clutch of competitive quayside tavernas busy, but it's a lovely spot at quieter times. Easy walks lead to 1500-year-old chapels on the hillside to either side of the bay. This is the place to hire a kayak or stand-up paddleboard and enjoy the tranquil waters. Grab your gear from **Kalymnos Kayak Centre** (☑ 6972261181, 22430 31132; www.waternative.co/kalymnoskayak; Rina; kayak or SUP per hour €10) at the end of the harbour.

Inland, beyond Vathys, a windswept road switchbacks up and over the mountains to reach the island's northwest coast, providing a speedier way to reach Emborios from Pothia than the built-up route through Myrties and Masouri.

❶ Getting There & Away

Ferries arrive in Pothia Harbour southeast of town.

Buses serve Myrties, Masouri and Armeos (€1.50, nine daily), Emborios (€2, two daily) and Vathys (€2, three daily). Check timetables at www.kalymnos-isl.gr. You'll find the **bus stop** (Plateia Kyprou) a few blocks back from the waterfront, next to the taxi stand (p400). Private taxis cost around €10 to Myrties, €10 to the airport, €17 to Vathys and €30 to Emborios.

Western Kalymnos

The best of Kalymnos is concentrated on its west side. Here you'll find clusters of tamarisk-shaded beaches and the bluest of blue bays. Here, too, are the three resort villages of Myrties, Masouri and the less-developed Armeos, although all have morphed into one long strip of tavernas and cafes. This is the island's best-known area for climbing – famous for the Grande Grotta – attracting a seasoned crowd of global climbers that mostly congregate in Masouri, with organised climbing along the nearby cliffs. The magical islet of Telendos, opposite languid Myrties, is also home to some great climbing routes. Of the beaches here, Masouri Beach is the largest and gets crowded in summer.

The former capital of Kalymnos, **Hora** (Horio), stands atop the brow of the low ridge behind Pothia, around 4km up from the sea. A steep, stony and unshaded old stairway that's a little hard to find climbs up from its eastern edge to the pirate-proof village of **Pera Kastro**, which was inhabited until the 18th century. Beyond its for-bidding walls and stern gateway, it now lies almost entirely in ruins and is overgrown with wildflowers, but amid the wreckage it's well worth seeking out nine tiny 15th-century churches that still hold stunning frescoes.

A tree-lined road drops for 2km beyond Hora to reach the pretty villages of Kandouni, Linaria and Elies within the valley of **Panormos**. Two neighbouring beaches are within walking distance: Linaria and the more attractive cove of Kandouni, surrounded by mountains and holding a small sandy beach with cafes, bars and hotels.

Directly facing Telendos Islet, across 800m of generally placid sea, **Myrties** and **Masouri** have attractive beaches, with the strand at Masouri being larger and sandier. Beyond the Telendos ferry quay in Myrties, the west-coast road is a one-way loop. To continue any further north, you have to double back and follow a largely empty stretch higher up the hillside. Only if you're heading south do you see the main commercial strip that connects the two resorts in a seamless row of restaurants, rental studios, bars, souvenir shops and minimarkets, one block up from sea level.

North of Masouri, the road becomes two-way once more and swiftly leads into **Armeos**, perched above the coast without a beach. Smarter and newer than its neighbours, it consists almost entirely of larger hotels and apartment complexes targeted at climbers.

North of Armeos, Kalymnos' west-coast road leaves civilisation behind. Its final stretch, skirting the deep inlet that cradles tiny **Arginonda**, is utterly magnificent, cut into the flanks of mighty cliffs and bordered with flowering oleander. It comes to an end 20km from Pothia at sleepy little **Emborios**, where sugar-white houses cluster around a long, narrow pebble beach.

For a pretty detour (and a local secret – few outsiders visit here), turn east after Skalia, to **Paleonisos**, and follow the winding road down to a gorgeous little cove. Here, there are several cantinas and water so calm it's like a massive swimming pool.

Southwest of Pothia, head over the steep headland to **St Savvas**, for some of the best views around. Behind here, the pretty **Vlihadia** is home to a lovely little beach strip, a couple of tavernas, and a quirky ocean-focused museum.

◎ Sights & Activities

★ St Valsamidis
MUSEUM
(Sea World Museum; Map p400; ☑ 22430 50662; www.valsamidis-museum.gr; Vlihadia; ⊙ 9am-5pm) This unorthodox collection is the life's work of a local Kalymnian man, Stavros Valsamidis, who for 48 years undertook private dives, and amassed items from the ocean floor. The 17,000 objects span from archaeological amphorae (all registered), shells, corals and WWII artefacts. Prized possessions include items from the Middle East that had clearly been pillaged by pirates. Stavros is no longer alive but these days, his son promotes what Kalymnians relate to best: the sea.

Head to the cafe-bar to the left of the museum and ask for the keys if it's not open.

Kalymnos Experience
OUTDOORS
(☑ 6946302515; www.kalymnosexperience.gr; Arginonda; ⊙ 8.30am-2pm & 5.30-10pm) ⚓ A group of passionate, young Kalymnians recently created Kalymnos Experience to offer alternative local experiences, some of which are difficult to do on your own. Options include nature walks, yoga, rock climbing, and scuba diving, to herb walks in the mountains (ending with a practical lab to prepare your own concoctions!). There's a weekly schedule or they'll arrange... almost anything!

🛏 Sleeping

Acroyali
APARTMENT €
(☑ 22430 47521, 6938913210; www.acroyali-kalymnos.gr; Myrties; apt €60-70; ❄ 🎇) Run by a lookalike of the late Leonard Cohen, Michalis, and right on the beach, Acroyali

has six mint-fresh apartments spread over two floors with large balconies. Apartments feature rustic furniture, comfy lounge, small kitchen with plenty of room to eat at the dining table, and a separate bedroom. The garden fronts onto the beach.

Myrties Boutique Apartments
APARTMENT €€
(☑ 6986285888; www.myrtiesboutiqueapart-ments.gr; Myrties; apt €105; ❄ 🎇) Two colourful and comfortable rental studios, a couple of minutes' walk up from the beach, each with two rooms, sleeping up to five guests and equipped with kitchenette and broad sea-view patio. They're cleaned daily and linen includes robes and beach towels.

🍴 Eating & Drinking

Fatolitis Snack Bar
CAFE €
(☑ 22430 47615; Masouri; snacks €3-7; ⊙ 7am-late; 🎇) A favourite with the après-climbing gang, this lively roadside cafe has a vine-shaded terrace and cosy interior spattered with rock posters. The menu isn't great, but it's carb-focused, with the likes of waffles, omelettes and toasties. No one cares much; they're too busy swapping stories over breakfast, lunch or an evening beer.

★ Aegean Tavern
GREEK €€
(☑ 22430 47146; www.aegeancuisine.org/Aigaiope lagitiko; Masouri; mains €11-19) As American trained, owner-chef George states of his produce, 'we have only the best of the best'. This means 100% Greek produce and traditional Greek cuisine. It's an upmarket experience in a stylish airy building that juts over the water, overlooking Telendos Islet. But local folk come here for the daily seafood catch that's fresh and beautifully prepared.

★ Azul Bar
BAR
(☑ 22430 48269; www.facebook.com/azulkalym nos; Armeos; ⊙ 5pm-late) This rather surreal space celebrates art, wine and food. It's part home (it was a former house built in the early 1970s), part gallery, and part garden. And it's fully fun, with a quirky interior decor of clocks, books and artefacts. It has a fabulous Greek wine list, plus gourmet international treats (tapas, veggie burgers and more).

ℹ Getting There & Away

Buses serve Myrties, Masouri and Armeos (€1.50, nine daily). Two daily buses connect Emborios with Pothia.

Telendos Islet
Νήσος Τέλενδος

The bewitching islet of Telendos looms from the Aegean just off the west coast of Kalymnos. Crowned by a mountainous ridge that soars 450m high, it's thought to have been set adrift from the rest of Kalymnos by an earthquake in AD 554. It now makes a wonderful, vehicle-free destination for a day trip or longer stay.

Daily life on Telendos focuses on the short line of tavernas, cafes and whitewashed guesthouses that stretches along the pretty waterfront to either side of the jetty. Head right to reach the ruins of the early Christian basilica of **Agios Vasilios** and a footpath that climbs to the similarly dilapidated basilica of **Palaiopanayia**. Head left, on the other hand, and you can either cross a slender ridge, rich in colourful oleander, to access windswept, fine-pebbled **Hohlakas Beach** or explore the islet's low-lying southern promontory, which holds some tiny early-Christian tombs now inhabited by goats, and a gloriously tranquil little swimming cove.

The cliffs along the northern flanks of Telendos hold several hugely popular rock-climbing routes (p404), which can be accessed by walking for an hour or so along a rough, exposed footpath.

🛏 Sleeping & Eating

Hotel Porto Potha HOTEL €
(📞 22430 47321, 6948884886; www.telendoshotel.gr; d incl breakfast €55; ❄ 🛜 🏊) Telendos' only hotel is located a five-minute walk out of the village heading north – look out for the smart sugar-cube complex up on the hill. Inside, rooms are adequate, and there's a large lobby where guests come to relax and watch TV over a drink. There are additional separate apartments (same price but excludes breakfast).

⭐ On The Rocks PENSION €€
(📞 6932978142, 22430 48260; www.telendos.org; r incl breakfast €70; ❄ @ 🛜) Behind its seafront garden cafe-bar-restaurant that's strung with nautical knick-knacks, this welcoming complex is a haven for active climbers and indolent beach bunnies alike. The spacious stu-

---

CLIMBING, HIKING & DIVING IN PARADISE

Steep crags, stark cliffs and daredevil overhangs have turned Kalymnos into Greece's premier destination for rock climbers. It now has more than 80 designated climbing sites, holding over 3500 marked routes. Most are located above the island's west-coast road, especially around and north of Armeos – white roadside markers identify the precise spots – though several of the finest ascend the flanks of **Telendos** Islet, just across the water.

Climbing season runs from March to mid-November, with the busiest period from mid-September until the end of October. An annual climbing festival takes place during the first 10 days of October.

The man largely responsible for the boom is Aris Theodoropoulos, who along with Katie Roussos writes the astonishingly detailed and comprehensive *Kalymnos Rock Climbing Guidebook* and maintains the useful www.climbkalymnos.com website, which includes a climbers' forum.

Kalymnos is also increasingly popular with hikers. Established routes are detailed on the excellent 1:25,000 *Kalymnos* map published by Terrain Maps (www.terrainmaps.gr). Serious hikers may want to undertake all or part of the highly demanding, multiday **Kalymnos Trail**, a 100km route that circles the island and also goes around Telendos for good measure. Shorter walks head to churches and monasteries, plus you can reach the castle at Hora. Less experienced climbers can make enquiries through Kalymnos Experience (p403).

Kalymnos is also becoming known as a diving island. For the beginner looking to qualify as a PADI open-water diver, as well as for the seasoned diver, there are plenty of hidden treasures in Poseidon's realm awaiting your inspection, including wreck dives, sea caves and diving with dolphins. There are several main outfits:

Diver's Island (📞 22430 48287; www.diversisland-kalymnos.gr; Kalydna Hotel, Elies; 🚗)

Kalymnos Diving (📞 6942062215; www.scubakalymnos.com; Agios Nikolaos, Pothia; ⏱ 8am-7pm)

Kalymnos Diving Club (📞 6974646413; www.kalymnosdiving.com)

dios have kitchenettes, private balconies and washing machines. It's run by a friendly Greek Australian, and is 200m right from the jetty.

To Kapsouli TAVERNA €
(☑ 22430 47363; mains €8-15; ☺ 8am-late) This claims to have been the first taverna on the island (1974) and nothing much has changed. Sitting at the waterfront tables of this impossibly picturesque little taverna, you can watch fishermen cleaning fish on the quay, straight from their boats, then dine on the freshest meat or seafood, scrutinised by a posse of purring pussycats.

Restaurant-Cafe Rita TAVERNA €
(☑ 22430 47914; www.telendos-rita.com; mains €8-16; ☺ breakfast, lunch & dinner; ☎) Welcoming Rita, Petroula and Yiannis serve up a chat and reaonable meals: succulent souvlakia, lamb in lemon and garlic and hearty lamb *stifadho*; there's a great octopus version, too. They also have a secondhand bookshop and sell crafts, as well as a few chalk-blue rooms (€30) to stay in.

❶ Getting There & Away

Telendos is easily reached on a 10-minute water taxi (p400) from Myrties. Note: you can't take a motorbike onto the island. It's walking path territory only.

LEROS ΛΕΡΟΣ
POP 8210

Leros is said to have been the original home of Artemis the Huntress. There's certainly something alluringly untamed and beautiful about the island, which is scattered with stunning Orthodox churches, dazzling blue coves and whitewashed villages. The capital, Platanos, with its stark windmills and ancient fortress towering above, makes a striking centrepiece, while down below, the busy little harbour of Agia Marina pulses with enterprise. Leros is less about chasing activities and more about worshipping Helios, seeking out your favourite beach, sampling the delectable cuisine at a sun-kissed taverna and allowing the magic of the place to slowly unfold.

❶ Information

There's no tourist office on the island. For information on local history and facilities, visit www.leros.org.uk or www.lerosisland.com, both private sites.

❶ Getting There & Away

AIR

Leros **airport** (Map p406; ☑ 22470 22777) is at the northern end of the island about 6km from Agia Marina. It's serviced by Olympic Air (p343), which offers daily flights to Athens (€80, one hour) and, in high season, thrice-weekly flights to Rhodes (€110, 1¾ hours), Kos (€177, 55 minutes) and Kastellorizo (€124, 2¾ hours).

BOAT

High-speed catamarans operated by Dodekanisos Seaways (p362) call at Leros daily as they ply their way to and from Kos, Kalymnos, Patmos, Samos, Rhodes and other nearby islands. Generally they stop at Agia Marina on Leros' east coast, but when there's bad weather they may stop at Lakki on the west coast, so always check the relevant port when you buy tickets, and double-check on the day you're due to depart and be prepared for a last-minute taxi dash across the island.

Blue Star Ferries (p364) makes late-night stops at Lakki two to three times weekly, heading towards Rhodes via Kos and Kalymnos, and towards Piraeus via Patmos and Lipsi.

Patmos Star (☑ 22470 32500; www.patmos-star.com) sails between Agia Marina and the islands of Lipsi and Patmos with varying frequency, increasing to daily in peak season.

Nisos Kalymnos (www.anekalymnou.gr) connects Lakki with Kalymnos to the south, and Lipsi, Patmos and assorted islets to the north, four times weekly.

Leros Express (p387) connects Agia Marina twice weekly with Lipsi, Agathonisi, Arki and Pythagorio (Samos). It also runs between Kalymnos and Kos.

❶ Getting Around

A **taxi** (☑ 6972014531, 6938918123) to Agia Marina from the airport will cost around €20 to €22.

Between June and September a green-and-beige-striped bus travels the full length of Leros between three and six times daily (€2 flat fare), including calling at the airport. It will usually stop anywhere if you flag it down.

Taxis (p405) are available for trips around the island, plus airport drop-off and pickup (€20 to €22).

Outlets in all resort areas rent cars, scooters and bikes; **Motoland** (☑ Alinda 22470 24584, Pandeli 22470 26400; www.motoland.gr; Panteli Beach Hotel; ☺ 9am-7pm) in Alinda and Pandeli is recommended.

The Agios Georgios (p407) excursion boat makes assorted day trips in summer, around the island and north to islets such as Arki and Marathi, typically costing around €25.

Leros

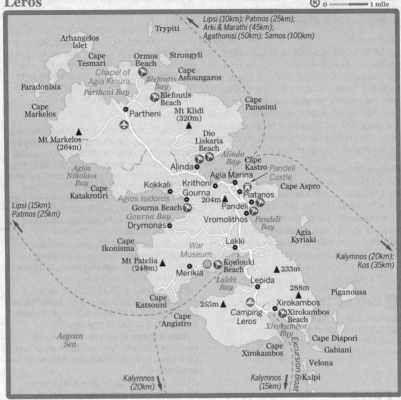

Lipsi (10km); Patmos (25km);
Arki & Marathi (45km);
Agathonisi (50km); Samos (100km)

Platanos & Agia Marina
Πλάτανος & Αγια Μαρίνα

POP 3000

Arriving at the bijou port of Agia Marina, with its yawning cats, mounds of yellow fishing nets and cluster of tavernas is a delight; the biscuit- and wine-coloured Italianate buildings are as if drawn from an artist's palette. And rising behind them are the white sugar-cube houses of Platanos, a 10-minute uphill walk. Stately mansions still pepper the slopes and the row of renovated windmills that marches up towards its imposing clifftop castle makes a magnificent spectacle.

Heading right from the ferry quay, following the shoreline for a couple of kilometres, will take you to Krithoni and Alinda.

Sights & Activities

Pandeli Castle
CASTLE

(Map p406; ☑22470 23211; €1; ⊙8.30am-12.30pm & 4-8pm; 🚶) A steep, stony stepped path zigzags up from Platanos to reach the hilltop ruins of Pandeli Castle. The castle's oldest, innermost sections date back 1000 years, but the outer ramparts were added by the Knights of St John during the 14th and 15th centuries. Few structures now survive, but the 360-degree views from the walls are breathtaking. You can also drive here, along an exposed road that winds up from Pandeli past the windmills, where you'll find a cafe (p408) in summertime.

Archaeological Museum
MUSEUM

(☑22470 24775; Agia Marina; €3; ⊙9am-2.30pm Tue-Sun Jul-Sep; 🚶) A 19th-century building on the edge of Agia Marina, at the start of the climb up to Platanos, holds Leros' small Archaeological Museum. Well-chosen artefacts collected on and around the island trace its varied history and include ancient masks and Byzantine mosaics.

Agios Georgios
BOATING

(☎6945551731, 22470 23060; agiosgeorgiosnl54@gmail.com; cruise incl food & drink €30; ⊙ departs 11am) Captain Manolis and his boat leave from Agia Marina Harbour, taking in the islands of Arki, Marathi, Arhangelos, Tiganakia, Lipsi and Aspronisia, allowing you to stop and swim in the best spots (three islands per day; changes daily). Wonderful Greek cuisine served, too. Returns at 7pm.

🛌 Sleeping

There's no accommodation in Agia Marina, and very little in Platanos. The closest and appealing alternative options are in Pandeli to the south, and Krithoni and Alinda to the north.

On Platanos, **Maison des Couleurs** (☎22470 23341; www.maisondescouleurs.com; Platanos; r incl breakfast from €130; 🐕) is a delightfully peaceful little boutique hotel set in a nostalgic wine-coloured villa that holds five spacious, high-ceilinged, antique-furnished rooms. Breakfast – and dinner, on request – is served on an idyllic flower-filled terrace. Look for a steep flight of yellow steps just west of the bus stop and taxi rank in Platanos.

🍴 Eating & Drinking

Some of the island's best eating is in Agia Marina and Platanos, whose excellent restaurants are putting the island well and truly on the foodie radar.

★ To Paradosiakon
BAKERY €

(Agia Marina; snacks €2.50-5; ⊙7.30am-late; 🌐🐕) 🍴 This patisserie and ice-cream bar, housed in an historic Italianate mansion on the waterfront, provides a sweet-toothed experience like no other. The knowledgeable owner Haris is an alchemist confectioner. He uses his grandmother's recipes to create traditional items, including *pastavouropita* (yogurt cake) and *pougakia* (almond and mandarin pastries). Don't miss the triple-layered chocolate gateau, spinach pie and homemade ice cream.

★ Taverna Mylos
SEAFOOD €€

(☎22470 24894; www.mylosexperience.gr; Agia Marina; mains €12-18; ⊙1pm-late; 🌐🐕📶) 🍴 If there's one reason to visit Leros, it's to eat here, one of the best restaurants in the Dodecanese. Run by two passionate and knowl-

HIDDEN OUZERIA

To enjoy a local secret, head to **O Zotos** (☎22470 24546; www.osotos-leros.gr; Drymonas), a wonderful *ouzerie* for a glass of ouzo and accompanying snack, whatever is available that day. Tapas-style plates of fresh seafood, including mussels and much (much) more. Don't miss the stuffed calamari if it's on offer.

edgeable brothers, this charming place is up there on the world's gastronomic scale. It features classic recipes with a modern twist: octopus carpaccio, peppery basil squid, and fabulous seafood pasta. And the setting? Sublime.

The wine list is one of Greece's best. It's beside an old windmill just north of the ferry dock and lapped by turquoise waves.

Faros Bar
BAR

(Agia Marina; ⊙7pm-late; 🐕) Tumbledown Faros Bar is partly hollowed into a cave beneath the lighthouse at the promontory beyond the ferry dock. With wall-mounted accordions and dim-lit ambience, it's great fun. Come evening, you can sit by the open windows and watch quicksilver fish swimming in the aquamarine water. Live music and DJs at weekends.

❶ Getting There & Away

One local bus (€2 flat fare) runs from Agia Marina to Krithoni and Alinda, Platanos, Lakki, Xirokambos and Vromolithos. Taxis stop at the rank just before To Paradosiakon (p407) in Agia Marina. Car hire signs line the marina.

Pandeli

The village of Pandeli, arrayed around a crescent bay 800m south of Platanos, is pretty, if crowded in summer. Overlooked by a clutch of hilltop windmills, its white houses tumble down the valley towards the sand-and-shingle beach and bobbing fishing boats in the harbour. There are some great tavernas by the water, too.

🛌 Sleeping

Studios Happiness
APARTMENT €

(☎22470 23498; www.studios-happiness-leros.com; Pandeli; d/studio/apt from €45/55/70; 🌐🐕) Very friendly family-run place, perched in colourful gardens beside the road down into

Pandeli, 50m up from the beach. Its vibrant white-and-blue studios have kitchenettes, twin beds and private balconies with great sea views. The rooms vary in size and are spotless throughout.

Panteli Beach Hotel APARTMENT €€
(✆22470 26400; www.panteli-beach.gr; Pandeli; studio/apt €100/140; P❄🐾🛜) Pretty, very comfortable complex, arrayed around an open courtyard right in front of the beach. All 14 studios have fresh white walls, safety deposit boxes, nice duvets and sparkling kitchenettes, and the attached Sorokos beach bar offers all-day sunloungers. Handily, the owner rents scooters and cars, plus it's open all year.

✖ Eating & Drinking

★ **El Greco** SEAFOOD €€
(✆22470 25066; www.elgrecoleros.gr; Pandeli; mains €8-12; ⏱lunch & dinner; ❄🛜) Offering tables right on the beach or on a thatch-roofed terrace, this stylish taverna prepares up-to-the-minute versions of traditional seafood cuisine. Locals rave about this spot for its quality and genial service. Their recommendations? The grilled octopus, the sardines, and the lip-smacking salted mackerel served on buttered toast.

Taverna Psaropoula TAVERNA €€
(✆22470 25200; Pandeli; mains €9-15; ⏱lunch & dinner) Bluer than a sea nymph's iris, this beachside favourite packs them in thanks to well-executed sea bass with ginger and basil (a favourite), calamari, tasty mezedhes and much more. It's open all year.

★ **The View** BAR
(✆6906454664; Apitiki, Pandeli; ⏱7pm-late Jun-Oct) An ethereal spot for a sunset drink, this place occupies one of the six windmills that sit high above Pandeli. It has a well-stocked bar...and, of course, The View. Service is a little slow and the food definitely isn't the magnet.

Vromolithos

Accessible only by walking or driving over the headland immediately south of Pandeli – there's no coastal footpath – Vromolithos consists of a long, narrow beach caressed by waters of a perfect shade of Aegean blue, scattered with turquoise. Forget the ugly village, this is all about the water.

✖ Eating & Drinking

★ **Dimitris O Karaflas** GREEK €€
(✆22470 25626; Marcopoulo, Vromolithos; mains €10-15; ⏱noon-4pm & 6pm-late; 🛜) The sign says 'O Karaflas', but everyone knows this hilltop eyrie (enjoying one of the best views in the Dodecanese) as 'Bald Dimitri's', after its owner, the head chef. Greek music washes over the terrace, where diners feast on an array of sea-urchin spaghetti, hearty island sausages, octopus carpaccio, steamed mussels, pork with green apples and plums, and substantial helpings of calamari.

Cafe Del Mar BAR
(✆22470 24766; Vromolithos; ⏱9am-late; 🛜) This superfriendly hillside lounge bar just above the north end of the beach has paradisiacal sea views, chilled pine-shaded patios, white sofas and deckchairs, plus cool tunes and DJs spinning the decks by night. Service can be a bit so-so (it gets busy) but call in any time for drinks and snacks. And don't miss a sunset mojito.

Lakki

Between 1912 and 1948, when the west-coast port of Lakki was a significant Italian naval base, the town was transformed beyond recognition by the construction of grandiose administrative and military buildings and homes for officers. The result is extraordinary. The prevalent architectural style, now classified as streamline moderne, started out resembling art deco and ended up distinctly more fascist. It's worth wandering the streets to view houses (those you might consider contemporary are actually from that period). Otherwise, it's a marina. It's best as a visit, not as a base.

◉ Sights

Who remembers now that a major WWII battle was fought on this remote little island? After British troops forced the Italians to surrender in September 1943, a massive German air onslaught recaptured the island in the Battle of Leros. A network of tunnels dug by the Italians beneath the woods west of Lakki now serves as a **war museum** (Map p406; ✆22470 22109; Merikia; €3; ⏱9.30am-1.30pm), housing countless relics of the conflict. There's an explanatory video.

✖ Eating

★ **Bakaliko with Tsipouro**   GREEK €
(Groceries with Spirits; www.bakalikoleros.com;
Lakki; mains €5-8; ⊘ 8am-10pm) Don't be fooled
by the unassuming exterior, fronted with
red and green wooden chairs and tables.
Formerly a grocery store (that was housed
across the road), this extraordinary spot is
still chock-a-block with delicious food items
– from cheeses to meats and useful DIY eats
– plus, it serves hearty plates of traditional
cuisine for a song. Dishes change daily.

Petrino   GREEK €€
(Lakki; mains €10; ⊘ 7am-11pm; 🖶 🛜) 🍴 Hands
down the most succulent meat on the island is to be found at smart Petrino. Aside
from delicious steaks there's octopus salad,
stewed rabbit, and beef in lemon sauce. Like
the architecture of Lakki, there's nothing ordinary about this place.

Xirokambos

At the southern end of Leros, Xirokambos
Bay holds a pebble-and-sand beach with
some good spots for snorkelling. As well
as a few village houses, it's home to a good
beach taverna and is served by small excursion boats from Kalymnos. Up the hill, 1km
inland towards Lakki, a signposted path
climbs to the ruined **Paleokastro** fortress,
which offers tremendous views.

🛏 Sleeping & Eating

Camping Leros   CAMPGROUND €
(Map p406; ☑ 6944238490, 22470 23372; www.
campingleros.com; Xirokambos; camp sites adult/
tent €8/4; ⊘ Jun-Sep) Set 500m up from the
beach, and 3km south of Lakki, the island's
lovely campground stands in a 400-year-old
olive grove and holds a welcoming cafe that
puts on evening barbecues. There are plenty
of pitches shaded by said olive trees. It's also
a centre for scuba diving, and owner Panos
offers CMAS-certified week-long open-water
courses (€500).

To Aloni   TAVERNA €
(☑ 22470 26048; Xirokambos; mains €9-15;
⊘ lunch & dinner; 🅿 🖶 🛜 🚼) You can't miss this
prominent taverna literally so close to the
sea it adds a little salt seasoning to your octopus croquettes, shrimp *saganaki*, swordfish,
lobster, or liver in wine sauce. Dine at tables
al fresco or within its pleasant interior. Great
desserts, too, if you have room.

Krithoni & Alinda
Κριθώνι & Αλιντα

POP 750

Starting just beyond the first headland
north of Agia Marina, the twin resorts of
Krithoni and Alinda sit next to each other
on Alinda Bay, running parallel to the beach
and bordered by *kafeneia* and restaurants.
Leros' longest beach is at Alinda – although
narrow, it's shaded and sandy with clean,
shallow water. Set just back from the sea, a
poignant war cemetery holds British casualties from the 1943 Battle of Leros.

For the best sun-worshipping in these
parts, continue through Krithoni and Alinda
to **Dio Liskaria Beach** (a few minutes' scooter ride). Bookended by rocks and with its own
taverna, it's lapped by aquamarine waves.

⊙ Sights

Housed in an incongruous castellated villa
on the seafront, the **Historic & Folklore
Museum** (☑ 22470 24775; Alinda; €3; ⊘ 9am-
1pm & 6-8pm Tue-Sun) covers several aspects of
local history. The upstairs rooms are given
over largely to weapons, helmets and photos
relating to WWII, while downstairs you'll
find displays of traditional costumes and an
emotive gallery devoted to artworks created
by political prisoners incarcerated on the island during the colonels' dictatorship of the
1960s and 1970s.

🛏 Sleeping

★ **To Archontiko Angelou**   HOTEL €€
(☑ 6944908182, 22470 22749; www.hotel-ange
lou-leros.com; Alinda; r incl breakfast from €95;
🅿 🛜) 🍴 Spilling with oleander and jaca-
randa, this incurably romantic, 19th-century
rose-coloured villa, five minutes' walk from
the beach, is like stepping into a vintage
Italian film, with wooden floors, Viennese
frescoes, antique beds and old-world-style
rooms. Breakfast on the sun-dappled terrace
is divine: a mouthwatering array of homemade bread, cheeses and gourmet treats.
One of the finest hotels in the Dodecanese.

To Archontiko Angelou is big on healthy
(and very good) eating, including vegetarian,
vegan, dairy- and gluten-free dining as well.

Hotel Alinda   HOTEL €€
(☑ 22470 23266; www.alindahotel-leros.gr; Alinda; s/d incl breakfast €40/60; 🖶 🛜) The very
pleasant rooms in this beachfront hotel
have private balconies, some of which look

out across the leafy rear garden and others, over the coast road to the bay. They vary in size, but all are spotless with comfy beds and tea-making facilities. The charming owners also run a good on-site Greek restaurant.

History buffs will enjoy the fact that it's the oldest hotel on Leros, yet it maintains a beautifully preserved old-school, 'modern' style.

Nefeli Hotel   APARTMENT €€
(☑ 22470 24611; www.nefelihotels.com; Krithoni; studio/apt incl breakfast from €90/125; P ❄ 🕿) Run by friendly Eva, Nefeli has lovely sugar-white apartments with vividly coloured lavender and pink trim. These are beautifully finished spaces with stone floors, gleaming kitchens, moulded-stone couches and swallow-you-up beds. All have private balconies and there's a tempting cafe in the herb-scented courtyard. It's 10 minutes' walk beyond the northern edge of Agia Marina.

✕ Eating & Drinking

Prima Plora   SEAFOOD €€
(☑ 22470 26122; Alinda; mains €8-12; ◷ lunch & dinner) While Leros offers more gourmet dining options elsewhere, this casual eatery in Alinda, with large indoor and gorgeous outdoor areas on the beach, will satisfy hungry souls craving seafood and Greek mezedhes. The very garlicky carrot salad with a Thai zing is recommended.

Nemesis Cafe   BAR
(☑ 22470 22070; Krithoni; ◷ 10am-late; 🕿) There's piping jazz and happy vibes at this well-stocked waterfront bar with a nautical theme. Perfect spot for a sundowner.

❶ Getting There & Away

The island's bus (€2 flat fare) passes through Alinda and travels the island, including to Xirokambos, Lakki and Agia Marina.

PATMOS   ΠΑΤΜΟΣ

POP 3040

Patmos has a bewitchingly spiritual feel about it. That's not surprising given that it was here, in a cave, that exiled St John received the apocalyptic visions that formed sinister Revelations in the Bible. Pilgrims from around the world visit St John's cave and the island's monasteries, especially in the whitewashed, labyrinthine sanctity of hilltop Hora. Other visitors, too, from movie stars to holidaymakers, head to this hour-glass-shaped island for its beautiful villages, including the picturesque harbour community of Skala, plus barely disturbed bays lined with sand and pebble beaches, and gorgeous pine- and heather-coated hillsides. The lack of an airport has protected the island from mass tourism; there is a calmness here that is reflected in the locals, who are as hospitable and friendly as they come.

History

St John the Divine was banished to Patmos by the pagan Roman Emperor Domitian in AD 95. Living as a hermit in a cave above what's now Skala, St John heard the voice of God issuing from a cleft in the rock and transcribed his terrifying visions as the Book of Revelation where he 'saw a beast rise up out of the sea, having seven heads and 10 horns...'. From these events Patmos became known as the 'Holy Island' or, less appealingly, 'the island of the Apocalypse'.

Around 1000 years later, in 1088, the Byzantine Emperor Alexis I Komninos gave the Blessed Christodoulos permission to erect a monastery in John's memory. Pirate raids necessitated powerful fortifications, so the monastery took the form of a mighty hilltop castle. In the centuries that followed, Patmos became a semi-autonomous monastic state and achieved such wealth and influence that it was able to resist Turkish oppression.

❶ Information

Both www.patmos-island.com and www.patmosweb.gr provide copious information. You can also pick up a free copy of the pocket-sized *Patmos Guide* and the larger *Patmostimes Guide* in shops and hotels.

The Municipal Tourist Office (p413) has useful tips on things to see and do on the island.

❶ Getting There & Away

All Patmos ferries dock in Skala. Almost daily Dodekanisos Seaways (p362) catamarans connect Patmos with Lipsi (€13.50, 1½ hours), Leros (€17, two hours), Kalymnos (€28, three hours), Kos (€15.50 to €20.50, three to four hours), Rhodes (€49, 5½ hours) and other islands to the south. Once a week there is a service between Arki (€14, 20 minutes) and Agathonisi (€16, one hour).

Blue Star Ferries (p364) also calls in several times each week, heading south through the Dodecanese chain towards Rhodes, or towards Piraeus.

The **Nisos Kalymnos** (www.anekalymnou.gr) connects Patmos with Kalymnos, Lipsi and Leros

Patmos

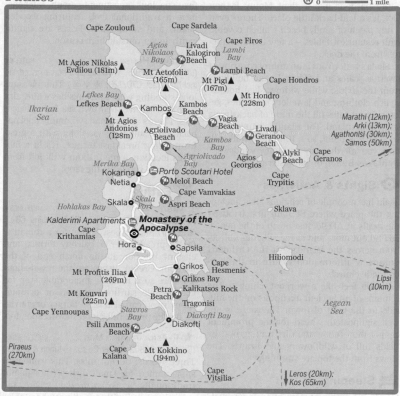

to the south, and the islets to the north, three to four times weekly.

The Patmos Star (p405) sails between Patmos and Lipsi (€8.50) and Leros (€12), daily in peak season and less frequently otherwise.

❶ Getting Around

BOAT

Patmos Daily Cruises (☑ 22470 31425, 6977035231; www.patmosdailycruises.com; incl wine, water & watermelon €25; ☺ departs 10am) offers summer boat excursions to beaches around the island, including Psili Ammos, and also to nearby islets.

BUS

Buses (flat fare €2) connect Skala with Hora around seven times daily, and with Grikos and Kambos four times daily, and more frequently in July and August. See www.patmosbus.gr.

CAR & MOTORCYCLE

The main seafront street in Skala holds several car- and motorcycle-hire outlets, including **TG**

Patmos Rentals (☑ 22470 32066; www.tgpat mosrentals.com). **Avis** (☑ 22470 33025, 22470 31900; ☺ 9am-9pm) cars can be rented through Astoria Travel. Demand often exceeds supply in high season, so book ahead if possible. The best scooter shop, **Moto Rent Faros** (☑ 22470 34400; www.patmos-motorentfaros.com; ☺ 8am-8.30pm), is behind the harbour on the road to Hora, and has quick, regularly serviced bikes (plus cars).

TAXI

You can catch a **taxi** (☑ 22470 31225) from Skala's taxi rank, opposite the police station. Fares are around €6.50 to Grikos, €8.50 to Kampos Beach, and €12 to Lambi Beach. Add an extra €2 if you book ahead.

Skala   Σκάλα

POP 3000

Skala, Patmos' photogenic ferry port, is set on a huge bay on the eastern shore of the island. Apart from those moments when mighty cruise ships suddenly obliterate the entire harbour like a giant Monty Python foot, it's a laid-back little place. There's even a tiny patch of sandy beach – albeit covered with restaurant tables – a few hundred metres from the dock.

Skala's waterfront is an unbroken string of tavernas, cafes and fading Italian buildings from the 1930s, while whitewashed houses, stylish clothing and jewellery boutiques, geletaria, and cafes fill the maze of backstreets stretching inland. The island is barely 700m wide at this point, so a 10-minute walk will take you all the way to stony, windswept Hohlakas Beach on its western side.

◉ Sights & Activities

Skala has a couple of religious sites, including the place where St John first baptised the locals in AD 96, just north of the beach. To find out more and to see religious objects from across the island, visit the Orthodox Culture & Information Centre in the harbourside church.

If you feel like a workout, climb to the remains of an ancient acropolis on the hillside to the west of town. The route is not well signposted – head for the prominent chapel then follow the dirt trail across the fields full of wildflowers and lizards. The views from the top are stunning.

⌂ Sleeping

Hotel and studio owners often meet boats at the port, but it's best to call ahead and arrange a pickup to avoid the scrum. Outside of high season (August) expect dramatically reduced rates.

★ Byzance Hotel HOTEL €€
(☑ 22470 31052; www.byzancehotel.gr; d/tr from €70/90, studio/apt from €80/110; ❋ 🛜) This lovely, freshly renovated hotel offers light and airy rooms, each decorated in chic style. There are also studios and apartments (with kitchenettes). A pleasant roof terrace offers excellent views and breakfast is in a charming, more traditional-style dining room. Its location, a block back from the waterfront, is superb, a stone's throw from the ferry. Fabulous value.

Kalderimi Apartments BOUTIQUE HOTEL €€
(Map p411; ☑ 22470 33008, 6972008757; www.kalderimi.com; apt incl breakfast €120; ⊙ late May–early Oct; ❋ 🛜) This inland whitewashed place south of Skala on a road just past the football stadium is pure tranquillity, with a shaded courtyard overflowing with palms,

bougainvillea and Moorish lanterns. The five spacious apartments (with kitchens) have a traditional feel, featuring wooden beams and stone walls. Prices are significantly lower outside high season.

Captain's House HOTEL €€
(☑ 22470 31793; www.captains-house.gr; d/ste incl breakfast €70/120; ❋ 🛜 ⛱) This pleasant long-standing wharfside digs has white, airy rooms; five have their own sea-facing balconies. There's also a small swimming pool out back with sunloungers, along with a great front-facing breakfast terrace. It's in a fabulous location, a mere 100m walk left from the quay as you leave the ferry.

✕ Eating

Tzivaeri MEZEDHES €
(☑ 22470 31170; mezedhes €6-15, mains €8-17; ⊙ dinner) Skala's best option for a romantic feast spreads over a balcony terrace and elegant interior at the north end of the harbour. Cretan dishes are the raved-about 'go' here so it makes a memorable stop for Cretan-style sardines, shrimp or octopus, though you can also get a burger or souvlaki. It's the prime full-moon viewing spot, too.

★ To Tsipouradiko Mas MEZEDHES €€
(☑ 22470 32803; tapas €6-15; ⊙ lunch & dinner) Three words: do not miss. This wonderful spot, named for small dishes (though not traditionally a *tsipouradiko*, where the spirit is served with appetisers), has tables on the beach, a can-do attitude, and some of the island's best cuisine. The caramelised octopus with *fava* is worth coming for alone. We won't say more so as not to spoil the surprise.

Pantelis TAVERNA €€
(☑ 22470 31230; mains €8-16; ⊙ lunch & dinner) Pantelis is one of Patmos' oldest tavernas, as the blue-and-white decor and vinyl-covered menus attest. But locals and visitors alike pack around tables on the narrow pedestrian street that runs parallel to the port. You can get standard Greek staples, but you can also be adventurous with the likes of smoky sea-urchin salad or the *fouskes* (sea figs – definitely an acquired taste).

Chiliomodi TAVERNA €€
(☑ 22470 34179; mains €12; ⊙ lunch & dinner) Chiliomodi has been keeping locals and travellers happy for nearly three decades and, thanks to the fisherman-owner, is synonymous with the freshest of fresh mouth-

watering sea bream, salted cod and various mezedhes to name a few. Its entrance is 50m along the road to Hora.

 Drinking & Nightlife

★ **Art Café**   BAR
(☑ 22470 33092; ⊙ 7pm-late; ☎) Escape the harbour hubbub by climbing to a fabulous panoramic roof terrace then blissing out over sunset cocktails (€7 to €9) amid plump pillows and white-cushioned benches. The friendly German owner also serves great homemade hummus and there's often live music in the indoor lounge below.

Arion   BAR
(☑ 22470 31595; snacks €3-6; ⊙ 7.30am-late; ☎) Over 100 years old, this venerable, high-raftered, wood-panelled bar, at the heart of the waterfront, is a major local landmark and rendezvous point. Travellers generally prefer to sit outside, watching the world and the waves go by as they hook up to the wi-fi. Snacks include toasties and crêpes.

Meltemi   CAFE
(☑ 22470 31839; ⊙ 9am-late; ☎) Irresistible beach bar at the far end of the harbour that curves 400m north from the ferry dock. Sit on the sand savouring a cocktail as the sun sinks into the sea, or come earlier for breakfast, a midday sandwich, fruit salad or milkshake under the shade of a tamarisk tree.

ⓘ **Information**

Apollon Travel (☑ 22470 31324; www.apol lontravel.gr; ⊙ 8am-11pm) and **Astoria Travel** (☑ 22470 31205; www.astoriatravel.com; ⊙ 9am-late), both centrally located on the waterfront, are the best outlets for ferry tickets, along with tours, plus other practical aspects of visiting Patmos.

Municipal Tourist Office (☑ 22470 31666; ⊙ 9.30am-2pm Mon-Fri, 6-9pm daily except Wed & Sun) Shares the same building as the post office and police station.

ⓘ **Getting There & Away**

Buses leave almost hourly for Hora between around 8am and 9pm, while less regular buses service Grikos and Kambos (flat fare €2). See www.patmosbus.gr for seasonal schedules.

Hora   Χώρα
POP 800

With gorgeous views of the island from its hilltop eyrie, enchanting Hora is more than just a whitewashed mountain settlement. As you wander its incense-scented warren of 17th-century houses, wind gusting through the alleys, the Boschian forms of St John's demons scuttling behind in your imagination, it's easy to see why Hora draws people back again and again. Allegedly there are more monasteries per square metre here than anywhere else in the world. Aside from the sanctity of the place there are some boutiques selling fine clothes and jewellery, and a couple of interesting galleries and upscale bars.

◉ **Sights**

★ **Monastery of
the Apocalypse**   MONASTERY
(Cave of the Apocalypse; Map p411; ☑ 22470 31398; €2; ⊙ 8am-1.30pm daily, plus 4-7pm Tue & Sat, 4-6pm Sun) Nestled amid the pines halfway to Hora, the Monastery of the Apocalypse focuses on the cave where St John lived as a hermit and received his revelation. Pilgrims and less-than-devout cruise passengers alike stream into the chapel built over the recess to see the rocky pillar where the saint rested his head, the handhold with which he'd haul himself up from his prayers and the stone slab that served as his writing desk.

★ **Monastery of
St John the Theologian**   MONASTERY
(☑ 22470 31223; €4; ⊙ 8am-1.30pm daily, plus 4-7pm Tue & Sat, 4-6pm Sun) As this immense 11th-century monastery-cum-fortress remains active, only a small portion is open to visitors. The entrance courtyard leads to a sumptuously frescoed chapel, fronted by marble columns taken from an ancient temple. Don't expect to attend a service; daily worship is at 3am! The museum of church treasures upstairs displays the original edict establishing the monastery, signed by the Byzantine emperor in 1088.

**Holy Monastery of
Zoödohos Pigi**   CONVENT
(☑ 22470 31991; ⊙ 9am-1pm daily) **FREE** The Orthodox convent known as the Holy Monastery of Zoödohos Pigi is tucked away in the back alleys of Hora. You can't go beyond its pretty little courtyard, where a small church holds remarkable 17th-century frescoes. One of the 40 resident nuns will cheerfully point out Jesus on Judgement Day dispatching assorted bishops and clerics down a river of fire that flows into the maw of the beast.

🛏 Sleeping & Eating

There is one restaurant in Hora's central square, while tavernas on the approach to St John's Monastery offer spectacular views.

Archontariki   B&B €€€
(☑ 22470 29368; www.archontariki-patmos.gr; ste €200; ⊙ Easter–Oct; ❉ 🤶) Hidden in a little alley near the Zoödohos Pigi monastery, these heavenly suites in a 400-year-old home are equipped with every convenience, traditional furnishings and plenty of plush touches. Relaxing under the fruit trees in the cool, quiet garden courtyard, you'll never want to leave. Suites 'Wisdom' and 'Joy' are spacious, while 'Love' and 'Hope' are smaller, traditional split-level affairs.

★ Pantheon   GREEK €
(☑ 22470 31226; mains €7-14; ⊙ 5pm-midnight; ❉ 🍴) Look for the octopus drying outside – hence its local moniker 'the octopus place'. This whitewashed belle with Aegean-blue chairs and soaring village views offers pure Greek fare at its best, including seafood, meatballs, and homemade sweets. Located in the 'restaurant strip', on the approach to the Monastery of St John the Theologian.

Jimmy's Balcony   GREEK €
(☑ 22470 32115; mains €9-15; ⊙ 10am-11pm; 🤶🍴) Perched above the road, on the principal lane through the village to the Monastery of the Apocalypse, the shaded terrace of this welcoming all-day cafe-restaurant commands regal views across Skala to the islands to the north. Drop in for a cooling drink, or to enjoy its decent salads, *mousakas* and veggie dishes.

Vaggelis   TAVERNA €€
(☑ 22470 31967; Plateia Agias Lesvias; mains €9-15; ⊙ lunch & dinner; ❉ 🤶) With chi-chi chairs and tables, Vaggelis sits in one of the most intimate squares in the world. At the time of research it was changing ownership back to the original management; the menu is to be tested. Regardless of the cuisine, the setting is gorgeous: sit in the atmospheric square itself, or for jaw-dropping views, under the carob tree in the garden out back.

ℹ Getting There & Away

While Hora is easily reached by road, it's much more atmospheric to hike up through the woods. Following the Byzantine footpath, signposted off the road roughly 10 minutes up from Skala, takes around 40 sweaty minutes. Allow extra time to stop off at the Monastery of the Apocalypse en route. A public bus heads to Hora around seven times daily (€2 flat fare); see www.patmosbus.gr.

North of Skala

The most popular and readily accessible beach in northern Patmos is wide, sandy **Kambos Beach**, which lies 5km northeast of Skala, just downhill from the village of Kambos. Crowded with local families in summer, it's a perfect spot for kids, with safe swimming and plenty of water-based activities.

Remoter and, with luck, quieter beaches can be reached by driving a little further. Fork inland (left) immediately after Kambos Beach and you'll soon find yourself winding down green slopes to **Lambi Beach**, an impressive expanse of multicoloured pebbles on the north shore. Stick to the coast road east of Kambos Beach, on the other hand,

---

ST JOHN THE DIVINE & THE APOCALYPSE

A great deal of confusion and uncertainty surrounds the Book of Revelation. But don't worry, it's not the end of the world. Well, maybe some of it is – the bits about the Four Horsemen of the Apocalypse, the Battle of Armageddon and the final defeat of Satan, say – but biblical scholars broadly agree that Revelation should in fact be read as a denunciation of the era in which its author lived.

St John experienced his Revelation on Patmos at the end of the 1st century AD, making it too late for him to have been either John the Evangelist, the author of the Gospel according to St John, or John the Apostle, or John the Baptist. Instead he was simply a wandering Jewish/Christian prophet of whom very little is known, though he has acquired the titles of John the Divine, John the Revelator, John the Theologian and, most simply of all, John of Patmos. His actual Revelation took the form of a letter to seven Christian churches in Asia Minor, condemning the Roman subjugation under which they then suffered and predicting an imminent apocalypse in which the Roman Empire would be swept away.

to reach **Vagia Beach**, a sheltered little cove that offers good snorkelling in the island's coldest though highest-visibility water, and beyond it the pebbled, tamarisk-shaded and stunningly turquoise-laced **Livadi Geranou Beach**, where a tiny whitewashed chapel beckons from the islet just offshore.

🏃 Activities

For over 35 years, friendly Andreas, the owner of **Kambos Beach Watersports** (☑ 6972123541; www.patmoswatersports.com; ⊕), has rented out water-sports gear. You can go wakeboarding (€50 per hour) and waterskiing (€50 for 15 minutes), set loose on a pedalo or kayak (€5 for 30 minutes), get your abs going on a stand-up paddleboard or for the less athletically inclined, simply rent a sunlounger (€15 per day).

🛌 Sleeping & Eating

Porto Scoutari Hotel   HOTEL €€
(Map p411; ☑ 22470 33123; www.portoscoutari. com; d incl breakfast €100-250; P❄🛰🏊) Focused around a lavish swimming pool and spa centre, this was the first luxe hotel on the island and in many ways is still among the most unique, if just *ever*-so-slightly tired. It surveys the Aegean from a rural spot, 600m from Meloi Beach and 3km north of Skala. Enjoy palace-sized rooms with stylish antiques, spotless bathrooms, private balconies and antique beds plus, above all, stunning sea views. Check for amazing low-season rates.

George's Place   CAFE €
(☑ 22470 31881; Kambos Beach; snacks €7-12; ⊕ breakfast & lunch; P❄🛰⊕) 🌿 Superchilled, long-standing beach bar, accessed straight off Kambos Beach sand, with an enticingly shaded, sun-dappled terrace facing the peacock-blue bay. Easy tunes, wi-fi, toilets that can double as changing rooms, and a simple menu of salads, homemade pies, chocolate cake, milkshakes and pastries keep the regulars happy.

Livadi Geranou Taverna   TAVERNA €
(☑ 22470 32046; Livadi Geranou Beach; mains €9-12; ⊕ 10am-late) With its flower-bedecked terrace perched on the heather-clad hillside at road's end, a few metres above the beach, this blue-trimmed taverna draws the crowds with its heavenly sea views. Feast on a seafood spread of whitebait and octopus, or opt for a simple platter of meatballs or souvlakia.

Cafe Vagia   CAFE €
(Vagia; mains €3-6; ⊕ 9am-7pm) Located a few hundred metres above Vagia Beach, this friendly little cafe, set in garden surrounds and run by the lovely Eftichia, is great for homemade pies, salads and cakes, and a pick-me-up coffee after a morning's sun worshipping.

Lambi Fish Tavern   TAVERNA €
(☑ 22470 31490; Lambi Beach; mains €8.50-16; ⊕ lunch & dinner; P❄⊕) Idyllic 'so-this-is-island-Greece' setting with tree-shaded tables propped up amid the beach pebbles and the waves almost lapping at your feet. The reliable no-frills local menu includes salted mackerel, stuffed vine leaves, and octopus cooked in wine.

Leonidas   TAVERNA €€
(Lambi; mains €12-15; ⊕ lunch & dinner Jun-Sep; P❄🌿) 🌿 Sitting on the crest of the hill overlooking Lambi Beach, Leonidas has a flower-filled terrace with food to match the serene view. Dine on souvlakia, *stifadho* and calf's liver, as well as the catch of the day. It's open for a blink-or-you'll-miss them two or three high season months.

South of Skala

The southern half of Patmos is scattered with small, tree-filled valleys and picturesque beaches. The first settlement south of Skala is tiny, peaceful **Sapsila**. **Grikos**, 1km further along over the hill, has a sandy(ish) beach that holds a handful of tavernas and is dominated by a plush resort hotel. St John is believed to have baptised islanders here during the 1st century AD, at a spot now marked by the chapel of **Agios Ioannis Theologos**.

South again, **Petra Beach** is peaceful and has plenty of shade, while a spit leads out to the startling **Kalikatsos Rock**. Both a rough coastal track from the beach and a longer paved road from Hora continue as far as **Diakofti**, the island's southernmost community. From there, a demanding half-hour hiking trail scrambles over the rocky hillside to reach the fine, tree-shaded stretch of sand known as **Psili Ammos Beach**, which holds a seasonal taverna. It's bewitchingly pretty and utterly isolated; if you've got kids with you, it's safer for you to hire a boat from Skala to get here.

ISLAND ESCAPES

Three quiet, tiny islands – Agathonisi, Arki and Marathi – are not exactly on the radar of many travellers. Yet arriving at these places is pure magic. With small permanent populations, there's little to do but read, swim and explore the caves where islanders once hid from pirates... and then do it again! As for other visitors? Expect an eclectic mix of yachties, artists and the occasional backpacker.

On **Agathonisi**, the port village of **Agios Georgios**, the island's primary settlement, holds a few tavernas and simple sugar-cube pensions. There are some lovely little beaches, including **Spilia Beach**, 900m southwest beyond the headland, and Gaïdouravlakos, where water from one of the island's few springs meets the sea. There's also **Tsangari Beach**, **Tholos Beach** and **Poros Beach**, the only sandy option. You can trek 1.5km uphill to **Megalo Horio**, site of several summer festivals, close to the eponymous church.

Elsewhere, Arki (with around 50 inhabitants) and Marathi, just north of Patmos and Lipsi and the largest of Arki's satellite islets, are the most peaceful islets in the Dodecanese chain.

On **Arki**, you can poke around the **Church of Metamorfosis** that stands on a hill behind the settlement, or laze on several sandy coves that can be reached along a path skirting the north side of the bay. **Marathi** has a superb sandy beach. The old settlement, with an immaculate little church, stands on a hill above the harbour. While only several people remain on Marathi year-round, local families return each summer to reopen tavernas. If you decide to stay, take your luck at the few informal *domatia* (rooms) attached to the tavernas.

Ferries stop once a week at Arki, but not Marathi, as they sail up and down the island chain, calling at Patmos, Leros, Lipsi and Agathonisi, Samos (and back). Dodekanisos Seaways (p362) catamarans do the circuit between Arki and Patmos (€14, 20 minutes), Leros (€17, 1¼ hours), Lipsi (€13.50, 50 minutes) and Agathonisi (€14, 30 minutes). **Nisos Kalymnos** (www.anekalymnou.gr) starts from Kalymnos, three to four times weekly. Leros Express (p387) heads to Arki twice a week (via Patmos or Lipsi). In summer, Lipsi-based excursion boats and Patmos-based caïques offer frequent day trips (around €25) to Arki and Marathi. For Marathi, a local caïque runs from Arki several times a week.

🛏 Sleeping & Eating

Mathios Studios
APARTMENT €€

(☎22470 32583; www.studiosmathios.gr; Sapsila; studio/apt €75/90; ❄@🛜) Located 2.5km south of Skala in sleepy Sapsila, Mathios has five studios and two apartments. All are equipped with kitchenettes. The style is very rustic-chic complemented by quirky driftwood sculptures scattered about the grounds, and the balconies afford views of the sparkling blue bay below. The owners do their best to make you feel at home.

Patmos Aktis Suites
DESIGN HOTEL €€€

(☎22470 32800; www.patmosaktis.gr/en; Grikos Bay; r from €260; P❄🛜≋) Sitting incongruously upon Grikos Beach, Patmos' ultraluxe design hotel leaps from a David Hockney painting with its sleek geometric aesthetic and cube-white suites. Expect rain showers and private terraces leading to a swimming pool metres from your bed. A high-end restaurant serves up contemporary Greek food, plus facilities range from massage treatments in the sumptuous spa to a gym and boutique.

★ Ktima Petra
TAVERNA €€

(☎22470 33207; Petra Beach; mains €6.50-12; ⏰lunch & dinner; 🚗) 🌱 For one of Patmos' wholesome and genuine foodie experiences, don't miss Ktima Petra. The setting – under a shaded terrace overlooking a vegetable garden – is idyllic. The restaurant, run by two hard-working brothers, sources its vegetables from their own adjoining plots which results in fabulous fresh and hearty traditional Greek cuisine. It's also walkable from the nearby Grikos Beach.

Benetos
MEDITERRANEAN €€

(☎22470 33089; www.benetosrestaurant.com; Sapsila; mains €10-28; ⏰7.30pm-late Tue-Sun Jun-Sep; 🚗) 🌱 Dropping down to the sea from the coast road, a couple of kilometres southeast of Skala, this romantic boutique restaurant and tapas bar is set on a working farm. The menu draws its inspiration from all over the Mediterranean, with dishes such as stuffed zucchini blossoms with turmeric sauce, octopus confit with eggplant salad. It's only open for several months, however.

LIPSI ΛΕΙΨΟΙ

POP 800

Lipsi might be tiny, at just 8km in length, but it has a powerful impact on the traveller, with its low-slung harbour bunched with crayon-yellow nets and the whitewashed, church-crowned village of Lipsi climbing the slope behind. If rugged hills, serene blue coves and deserted beaches are what you seek, you may have just found heaven. Check, too, the local speciality, *myzithra* cheese, made from goat's milk and seawater, and pick up a jar of distinctive thyme honey. The island even has its own winery, so enjoy a tipple.

❶ Getting There & Away

Lipsi has frequent connections with its neighbours. Dodekanisos Seaways (p362) catamarans head north to Arki (€13.50, 50 minutes), Agathonisi (€13.50, 1½ hours) and Samos (€32, two hours), and south to Patmos (€13.50, 30 minutes), Leros (€15, 30 minutes to 1½ hours), Kos (€29, two to three hours) and other islands. Twice a week, Blue Star Ferries (p364) heads to Patmos (€6.50, 30 minutes) and Leros (€7, 40 minutes). The **Nisos Kalymnos** (www.anekalymnou.gr) runs to Patmos, Leros and the islets to the north four times weekly, while the Patmos Star (p405) sails to both Patmos and Leros, daily in summer. Leros Express (p387) sails from Leros to Lipsi, Patmos, Arki, Agathonisi and Samos, plus has twice weekly trips to Kalymnos and Kos.

A small **office** (☑ 22470 41141; ⊗ 9.30am-3.30pm) on the ferry jetty sells all boat tickets.

❶ Getting Around

Ferries arrive at Lipsi's small port in front of the town. Frequent buses connect Lipsi Village with the main island beaches in summer. There is also one **taxi** (☑ 6942409679, 6942428223). Hire scooters and bicycles in Lipsi Village from **George Rental** (☑ 6942409679; www.motorentlipsi.com; bike/scooter/car per day from €7/12/35).

Lipsi Village Λειψοί

POP 800

Lipsi Village is a cosy place, with an atmospheric old town of blue-shuttered houses radiating up the hill in a tangle of alleyways. The harbour is the hub of the action and there's everything you need here, from an ATM and a great bakery, to delectable seafood restaurants. Be sure to visit the beautiful blue-domed church of Agios Ioannis Theologos with its panoramic harbour-view terrace. The closest beach to the village, Liendou Beach is a couple of minutes' walk north of the ferry port over a small headland. It's a narrow strip of sand, washed by calm, shallow water.

🏃 Activities

Sailing since 1980, *Rena,* a traditional wooden caïque, offers summer excursions from Lipsi's smaller jetty to islets Aspronisia, Makronisi (with their sapphire waters and weird rock formations), and Tiganakia, Marathi and Arki, for a picnic and swim. Organised by **Rena Five Island Cruise** (☑ 6947339141; www.facebook.com/pg/Rena5IslandCruise; adult/child €28/14; ⊗ Jun-Oct; 👪).

🛏 Sleeping

⭐ **Michalis Studios** APARTMENT €
(☑ 22470 41266, 6977906978; www.lipsimichalis.eu; studio €60-65) One of the best budget deals around, each of these simple, spacious studios comes with a kitchenette and small balcony. Rooms don't have direct sea views, but instead, face over a field and small church, and it's convenient to everything. As the island's former postmaster, the delightful and big-hearted owner, Michalis, knows everyone and everything about the island. Italian speaking, too. It's conveniently located next to the town's popular bakery-cafe. Prices are significantly reduced outside high season.

⭐ **Nefeli Hotel** APARTMENT €€
(☑ 22470 41120; www.lipsinefelihotel.com; studio/apt incl breakfast €90/160; P ❄ 🤖) This stylish, welcoming boutique hotel sits in splendid isolation above lovely Kambos Beach, 10 minutes' walk northwest of the village. The apartments are spacious, with comfy beds, kitchenettes, sofa beds and private sea-view patios. Prepare to be lulled to sleep by the call of owls. There's also an opulent bar, lounge and dining area, bedecked in a variety of purples.

Angela Studios APARTMENT €€
(☑ 6983666611, 22470 41177; www.lipsiangela.eu; Waterfront; studio/apt from €70/80; ❄🤖) Angela's individual studios have wrought-iron beds, sparkling kitchenettes with fridge and microwave. Add to this balconies with sea views and a delicious little cafe and you need look no further. Close to the ferry dock.

🍴 Eating

Kairis Lipsi Bakery Shop BAKERY €
(☑ 22470 41050; sweets €1-3; ⊗ 24hr; ❄🤖👪) Chances are you'll find yourself here, at this lively bakery-gelateria-cafe, on the western side of the waterfront; it's the social hub of the island and stays open all night. It's a veritable treasure trove of fresh-baked cookies, savoury items, alcohol and some very fancy Greek sweets including baklava. Fight your way through the locals for a seat.

Lipsi

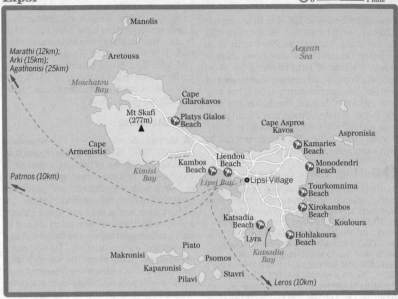

0 — 2 km
0 — 1 mile

Manolis

Aretousa

Marathi (12km);
Arki (15km);
Agathonisi (25km)

Moschatou
Bay

Aegean
Sea

Cape
Glarokavos

Mt Skafi
(277m) ▲

Platys Gialos
Beach

Cape Aspros
Kavos

Aspronisia

Cape
Armenistis

Kimisi
Bay

Kambos
Beach

Liendou
Beach

Kamaries
Beach

Monodendri
Beach

Patmos (10km)

Lipsi Bay

● Lipsi Village

Tourkomnima
Beach

Xirokambos
Beach

Kouloura

Katsadia
Beach

Lyra

Hohlakoura
Beach

Katsadia
Bay

Piato

Psomos

Makronisi

Kaparonisi

Pilavi

Stavri

Leros (10km)

★ **Kalypso**　　　SEAFOOD €€

(☑ 22470 41241; mains €8-12; ⊘ lunch & dinner; ❋ ☎) ✐ Chef/owner Nicolas cooks up a culinary storm at this gorgeous spot. He uses only organic vegetables (from his own farm or personally sourced elsewhere), plus fresh fish and meat. The picks are the fish soup and the *katsikaki* (stuffed goat). Blue and olive-green chairs dot the shaded terrace and there's a pleasant indoor area, too.

★ **Manolis Tastes**　　　TAVERNA €€

(☑ 22470 41065; www.manolistastes.com; mains €8-15; ⊘ noon-4pm & 5.30pm-late; ☎) ✐ In a handsome 19th-century neoclassical building (and former Italian Police station), Manolis Tastes has a roof terrace and upstairs lounge, and fine dining in a cream-and-wood interior. The real draw is Chef Manolis, his culinary flair recognised internationally. Mussels with ouzo, and pork with mustard and honey, are just a few of the splendid dishes served here. A must visit.

Yiannis　　　TAVERNA €€

(☑ 22470 41395; mains €10-14; ⊘ lunch & dinner May-Oct; ❋ ☎) This popular taverna, adorned with cobalt-and-white trim, sits to the west of the marina jetty with seating on a raised terrace next to a tiny vineyard (look out for the mural of the windmill). Try the stewed goat in red sauce and thin-sliced swordfish carpaccio.

Around Lipsi

Lipsi is remarkably green for a Dodecanese island. Walking to its farther-flung beaches leads you through countryside dotted with olive groves and cypress trees. In summer, a minibus also services the main beaches. Just 1km north of Lipsi Village, around the headland beyond Liendou Beach, Kambos Beach is narrower but sandier than its neighbour and somewhat shaded by tamarisk trees. The water is also deeper and rockier underfoot.

Fork inland at Kambos and a delightful 2.5km hike over the low-lying spine of the island will lead you to the shallow and child-friendly **Platys Gialos Beach**. Ringing with goat bells and shelving gently into crystal-clear water, it's home to an excellent summer-only, daytime **taverna** (☑ 6944963303; grills €10-12; ⊘ 8am-6pm).

Just 2km south of Lipsi Village, sandy **Katsadia Beach** is wilder, especially if it's windy. There's a certain amount of shade and another good summer-only **taverna** (☑ 22470 41041; www.dilaila.gr/en; mains €9; ⊘ 9.30am-10pm Jun-Sep; P ☎ ✐ ⊞), which stays open late as a bar. The beaches at Lipsi's eastern end are harder to reach, with the roads being too rough for taxis or buses. In summer, there is a boat that can drop you off here, too.

Northeastern Aegean Islands

Best Places to Eat

➡ Marymary (p429)

➡ Ouzeri To 11 (p465)

➡ Kazaviti Restaurant (p477)

➡ Kechribari Ouzerie (p446)

➡ Tavern at the End of the World (p439)

➡ Misirlou (p458)

Best Places to Stay

➡ Ikaria Utopia – Cusco Studios (p426)

➡ Homeric Poems (p445)

➡ Evgenikon (p447)

➡ A for Art (p476)

➡ Mastiha House (p451)

➡ Surf Club Keros (p470)

Why Go?

Clinging to the Turkish coast and influenced by Asia Minor in many ways, this is a bunch of radically idiosyncratic islands with landscapes and local cultures so distinct, even the smallest ones feel like proto-nations. In fact, many of them enjoyed quasi-independence at various points in time and remember it fondly.

Eccentric Ikaria is marked by jagged landscapes, pristine beaches and a famously long-lived, left-leaning population. Nearby Chios provides fertile ground for the planet's only gum-producing mastic trees. Other islands range from rambling Lesvos – producer of half the world's ouzo – to midsized islands such as semitropical Samos and workaday Limnos, and bright specks in the sea such as Inousses and Psara. Samothraki is home to the ancient Sanctuary of the Great Gods, while well-watered Thasos seems an extension of the mainland.

Lesvos, Chios and Samos offer easy connections to historical Hellenic sites and Turkey's coastal resorts.

When to Go
Vathy (Samos)

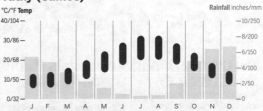

Apr & May Wild red poppies adorn the back roads; Greek Easter livens up every village.

Jul & Aug Beach bars and village councils (in Ikaria's case) throw wild parties for revellers.

Oct & Nov Summer crowds evaporate, and hearty soups return to the tavernas.

Northeastern Aegean Islands Highlights

① **Hristos Rahes** (p427) Refuelling with postmidnight coffee and spoon sweets in Hristos Rahes on Ikaria.

② **Panagia Kakaviotissa** (p468) Trekking through unearthly terrain towards a mountaintop cave chapel.

③ **Potami Beach** (p440) Finding a secret taverna above wooded waterfalls after lazing on a picture-perfect marble gravel beach.

④ **Teriade Museum** (p454) Discovering an unexpected treasure trove of top-notch 20th-century art.

⑤ **Molly's Bar** (p458) Watching yachts sailing through a turquoise bay in Molyvos.

⑥ **Mastiha House** (p451) Lodging in castle-like apartments in Pyrgi, a village that's a piece of decorative art.

⑦ **Sanctuary of the Great Gods** (p472) Contemplating the secretive cult of ancient gods who preceded the Olympians.

⑧ **Mineral Baths of Eftalou** (p456) Daydreaming in an ancient thermal pool on Lesvos.

ⓘ TURKISH CONNECTIONS

Visiting Turkey's Aegean coastal resorts and historical sites from Samos, Chios and Lesvos is easy. Visas aren't usually necessary for day trips. While boat itineraries, prices and even companies change often, the following explains how things generally work.

From **Samos**, the *Kuşadası Express* leaves daily from either Vathy or Pythagorio for the 80-minute trip to **Kuşadası** (one way/return €40/60), a coastal resort near **ancient Ephesus** (Efes). Daily excursions run from May through to October, with the option to also visit Ephesus. For tickets and information in Vathy, contact **By Ship Travel** (✆22730 27337; www.byshiptravel.gr; Sofouli 5; ⊗6am-10pm) opposite the old ferry terminal. In Pythagorio, contact **By Ship Travel** (✆22730 62285; Lykourgou Logotheti; ⊗6am-10pm May-Sep) at the main junction entering town. Additionally, a Turkish boat connects from Karlovasi in northern Samos to **Sığacık** (one way/return €30/40, five weekly), which is between Kuşadası and the airport at İzmir. None of these ferries has space for cars.

From **Chios**, daily departures year-round connect Chios Town with **Çeşme**, a port near İzmir; services are most frequent in summer and some carry vehicles on board. Boats depart morning and evening for the 40-minute journey (one way/return €20/30). Tour agencies on the seafront also sell package day trips to İzmir. Get information and tickets from **Sunrise Tours** (✆22710 41390; www.sunrisetours.gr; Kanari 28; ⊗8.30am-10pm).

From **Lesvos**, boats operated by Turkish company Turyol leave Mytilini Town for **Ayvalık** twice daily in summer and daily in winter (one way/return €15/25, 1½ hours). Thursday departures are especially popular for market day in Ayvalık. Vehicles are carried on board. Most Mytilini Town travel agencies sell Turkish tours; try **Mitilene Tours** (✆22510 54261; www.mitilenetours.gr; Pavlou Kountourioti 87; ⊗24hr) or **Tsolos Travel** (✆22510 25346; www.flytsolos.com; 1944 Christougennon 10; ⊗9am-2.15pm & 6.15-9.15pm).

ⓘ Getting There & Away

Chios (p443), Lesvos (p452) and Samos (p432) all have international airports that receive flights from a variety of European destinations. Limnos (p463) and Ikaria (p422) are served by domestic airlines.

The island group can be accessed by ferry from the mainland ports of Piraeus and Kavala. There is also a service connecting Limnos to the port of Lavrio.

IKARIA IKAPIA

If Greek islands were humans, then magical Ikaria would be the weirdest and most charismatic. Its outlandish terrain, largely untamed by agriculture, comprises dramatic forested gorges, rocky moonscapes and hidden beaches with aquamarine waters. Ikaria's independent spirit, unique culture (characterised by dwellings pretending to be rocks), nocturnal lifestyle and rave-like *panigyria* village festivals grew out of centuries of isolated life under the constant threat of pirates and foreign invaders.

Supposedly named after mythical Icarus, who is said to have crashed here after flying with wax wings too close to the sun, Ikaria is also honoured as the birthplace of Dionysos, god of wine. Villages here famously throw wild parties with loads of food, wine and tra-

ditional dance. The island becomes packed with Athenians and foreign visitors at the height of August's *panigyria*, but come any time to enjoy Ikaria's serenity and the locals' sybaritic attitude to life.

🏃 Activities

With its solitude and rugged natural beauty, Ikaria is perfect for mountain walks. The most popular starting point is Hristos Rahes, where shops sell a walking map. For inexpensive guided treks all over the island, approach **Discover Ikaria** (✆6907547342, 6974042417; www.discoverikaria.com; Hristos Rahes) or **Ikarian Footprints** (✆6974042417; https://ikarianfootprints.com).

The one-day circular walk along dirt roads from **Kambos**, south through **Dafni**, the remains of the 10th-century Byzantine **Castle of Koskinas**, and picturesque **Frandato** and **Maratho** villages is doable as an independent walk, and not too hard on the bones.

When you reach **Pigi**, look for the Frandato sign; continue past it for the unusual little Byzantine **Chapel of Theoskepasti**, tucked into overhanging granite. You must clamber up to reach it, and duck to get inside. The rows of old monks' skulls have been retired, but the chapel makes for an unusual visit, along with nearby **Moni Theoktistis**, with frescoes dating from 1686.

Ikaria & the Fourni Islands

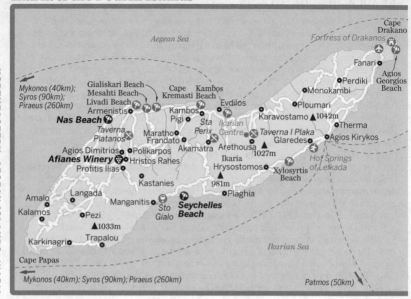

ℹ️ Information

Visit Ikaria (www.visitikaria.gr/en) is a very useful online guide.

ℹ️ Getting There & Away

AIR

Ikaria Airport (Map p422; 📞 22750 32216; Faros) is served by **Olympic Air** (www.olympic air.com), **Aegean Airlines** (www.aegeanair. com) and **Astra Airlines** (www.astra-airlines. gr). Tickets are available at agencies in Agios Kirykos and Evdilos, and at the **airport** (Map p422; 📞 22750 32216; Faros).

BOAT

Ikaria finds itself at a crossing of busy routes leading to the mainland ports of Piraeus (via Cyclades) and Kavala in the north as well as to the Dodecanese Islands. Its two ports, Evdilos and Agios Kirykos, are quite far apart; make sure you know which one you need on the way in and out to avoid losing way more than your boat fare on taxis.

From Evdilos, there are daily services to Karlovasi, Samos (€13.50, one hour).

Nyssos Mykonos calls at Evdilos six times a week on the way to Piraeus (€31.50, 6½ hours) via the Cycladic islands of Mykonos (€20, two hours) and Syros (€23, three hours).

Once a week, the same boat leaves for Kavala (€48, 16 hours) via Chios (€18.50, 5½ hours) and Lesvos (€24, eight hours). Another weekly boat does the same route out of Agios Kirykos.

From Agios Kirykos, boats or hydrofoils run to Fourni (€7 to €14, one hour) five times a week. At least four boats or hydrofoils a week go to Patmos (€10.50 to €22, one to 1½ hours) continuing to other Dodecanese islands.

Get tickets in Agios Kirykos at **Ikariada Travel** (📞 22750 23322; ⏰ 8.30am-5pm & 7-9pm) or **Dolihi Tours Travel Agency** (📞 22750 23230; dolichi@otenet.gr; ⏰ 9am-3pm & 6-9pm). In Evdilos, try **Ikaria Holiday** (📞 22750 71077, 6972221066; ⏰ 10am-10pm).

ℹ️ Getting Around

BOAT

In summer, a daily caïque (little boat; water taxi) goes from Agios Kirykos to Therma (€3). Another boat on Ikaria's south coast links Manganitis with the idyllic Seychelles Beach (p429), 2.5km away, for swimming and sunbathing.

BUS

In summer months, a daily bus makes the winding route from Agios Kirykos to Hristos Rahes, via Evdilos and Armenistis. It also calls at the Ikaria Airport (p422) on the way. Getting on it can be a challenge. A local bus makes the 10-minute trip to Therma every half-hour.

CAR & MOTORCYCLE

It's a good idea to hire a car or scooter for travel beyond the main towns. Hitchhiking is very common and considered safe by locals, but we don't recommend it.

For cars, try Dolihi Tours Travel Agency (p422) or Ikariada Travel (p422) in Agios Kirykos; **Mav Cars** (☑ 22750 31036, 6932908944; mav-cars@hol.gr; harbour; ☺ 9am-10pm) in Evdilos; and **Aventura** (☑ 22750 31140, 6972284054; aventura@otenet.gr; ☺ 9am-9pm) in Evdilos and Armenistis. Most car-hire offices can arrange for airport pick-up or drop-off, too, generally at no extra charge.

Agios Kirykos
Άγιος Κήρυκος

POP 1880

Ikaria's capital is an easy-going and dependable Greek port, with clustered old streets, hotels and domatia, tasty restaurants and a lively waterfront cafe scene. Although beaches are nicer in Ikaria's north, the area's renowned hot radioactive springs, scattered along the coast, attract aching bodies from around Europe. The main cluster is located 2km east at Therma, which also has a nice pebble beach.

Activities

Those with aching bodies and perfectly healthy pleasure seekers from all over Europe flock to hot radioactive springs in the vicinity of Agios Kirykos. Some of the springs discharge hot water into the sea, providing for a unique bathing experience. Most are located in Therma, 2km from Agios Kirykos.

★ **Spilio Hot Springs** HOT SPRINGS
(Therma) **FREE** The best hot springs experience on Ikaria, if not in all the Aegean, is to enter the sea on the beach in Therma and swim for some 30m towards a large cave on the southern side of the bay; you'll start feeling flows of hot radon-rich water long before reaching it. Inside, there's an improvised mini-arena made of large stones.

Spilio Baths HOT SPRINGS
(To Spilio; ☑ 22750 24048; Therma; hammam €3, Jacuzzi pool €4.50; ☺ 9am-4pm) This steamy gem is an authentic thermal sauna and bath that draws on a hot underground spring. Showers and lockers are included, but bring a towel. It's past the kiosk at the end of the waterfront, to the right as you face the sea.

Hot Springs of Lefkada HOT SPRINGS
(Map p422) **FREE** These hot sea-springs, 2.5km southwest of Agios Kirykos, are therapeutic, relaxing and free. Although it's a designated radioactive saltwater spring, in truth it's just a beautiful spot on the beach, identifiable by an irregular circle of rocks. You'll know you're in the right spot when you feel the now-it's-hot, now-it's-not intermingling of spring and seawater.

Festivals & Events

The **Ikaria International Chess Tournament** (☑ 6978197617; http://ikariachess.blogspot.com; ☺ Jul) is a traditional annual event and draws chess players of all types from around Europe and beyond. The tournament celebrated its 40th anniversary in 2017 and retains a distinctly local flavour. This battle of wits takes place in mid-July, lasting about a week.

Sleeping

Agios Kirykos has a number of fairly good hotels, but you'll find even better ones at nearby Therma, next to the beach and hot springs.

★ **Pension Plumeria Flowery** PENSION €
(☑ 22750 22742, 6945139021; www.therma-ikaria.com; Therma; r incl breakfast €50; ✳ ☎) Big-hearted women run these immaculate rooms – with names such as Bougainvillea, Anemone and Hyacinth – in the centre of Therma. In addition to being as helpful as anyone possibly can be, they make great cakes for breakfast.

LOCAL KNOWLEDGE

PANIGYRIA

Pagan god Dionysos may no longer reign over Ikaria's vineyards, but his legacy lives on in Christianised form in the summertime *panigyria*, all-night festival celebrations held on saints' days across the island. There's no better way to dive head first into Greek island culture than drinking, dancing and feasting while honouring a village's patron saint. Bring your wallet: *panigyria* are important fundraisers for the local community. Use this fact to explain any overindulgence as well-intended philanthropy.

Panigyria occur across the island on the following dates:

Kambos 5 May

Armenistis 40 days after Orthodox Easter

Agios Isidoros (Pezi) 24 June

Agios Giannis (Hristos Rahes) 24 June

Platani 29 June

Karavostamo 1 July

Agios Kirykos & Ikarian Independence Day 17 July

Arethousa 17 July

Agios Panteleinonas (Fidos) 27 July

Hristos Rahes & Dafni 6 August

Akamatra 15 August

Evdilos 15–20 August

Agios Sofia & Monokambi 17 September

Pyrgos Traditional Village   VILLA €€
(☑ 6970028000, 22750 22105; www.pyrgos-ika-ria.com; r from €80; P ❄ 🛜 ≋) Perched high above Agios Kirykos, this cluster of nine villas, styled as traditional stone houses, is as luxurious as it gets on this side of the island. The rooms are huge, stylishly designed and equipped with kitchenettes, even though breakfasts can be ordered. Going up from the waterfront can be a challenge after a few evening drinks; take a taxi.

✖ Eating

The port is filled with tavernas, but some of the best eateries hide in the little lanes behind the waterfront.

★ **Filoti**   TAVERNA €
(mains €6-11; ⊘ lunch & dinner) This tasty eatery 30m from the square, up the first alleyway, offers Agios Kirykos' best-value meals, including tasty grills, salads and excellent pizza.

★ **Tzivaeri**   FAST FOOD €
(☑ 22750 22850; snacks €2-4; ⊘ lunch & dinner) Best souvlaki and *gyros* (meat slithers cooked on a vertical rotisserie, eaten with pitta bread) at the port. Look for the umbrellas; it's next to Taverna Klimataria (p424).

Taverna Klimataria   TAVERNA €
(mains €6-8; ⊘ lunch & dinner Apr-Oct) An inviting backstreet taverna, behind the National Bank, with a lovely shaded courtyard. Strong on grilled meats with generous salads.

Taverna Arodou   TAVERNA €€
(☑ 22750 22700; Xilosirtis; €6-12; ⊘ 2pm-midnight Tue-Sun; P 🛜) An excellent traditional seaside eatery overlooking the sea in the village of Xilosirtis, 5km southwest of Agios Kirykos. Strong on fresh veggies, salads and Ikarian *soufiko* (layers of baked vegetables and potatoes) on top of traditional taverna fare. They also make their own ice cream.

🍷 Drinking & Nightlife

Ambariza Bistro   CAFE
(☑ 22750 31721; ⊘ 9am-late) A convivial little cafe-cum-bar with some tables in a romantic bougainvillea-filled lane behind the National Bank. In addition to coffee and alcohol, it serves great desserts and breakfasts.

Akti Café-Bar   BAR
(☑ 6945250954; ⊘ all day) Snappy bar at **Hotel Akti** (☑ 22750 23905; www.pensionakti.gr; r from €50; ❄ 🛜), with sturdy mixed drinks and decent snacks. At night you can see the twinkling lights of Fourni on the horizon.

Information

Dolihi Tours Travel Agency (p422) Full-service agency, next to Alpha Bank.

Naftiliako Praktoreio (22750 22426) Behind the waterfront, in the first alleyway, this helpful hole-in-the-wall specialises in ferry tickets to Fourni and Patmos, and has local tips.

Ikariada Travel (p422) Full-service waterfront travel agency next to Diagonios souvlaki shop.

Getting There & Away

Agios Kirykos is one of two major ports on the island, with ferry connections (p422) to Piraeus (Athens), other northeastern Aegean Islands and also the Dodecanese.

In summer, one or even two daily buses could be running to Evdilos and Armenistis, but don't count on that too much as it will still be a challenge getting on them.

Evdilos Εύδηλος

POP 460

Ikaria's second port, Evdilos skirts a small bay and rises in tiers up a hillside. It features stately old houses on winding streets, and a relaxed, appealing waterfront. Evdilos is 41km northwest of Agios Kirykos, to which it's connected by Ikaria's two main roads. The memorable trip takes in high mountain ridges, striking sea views and slate-roof villages.

Sleeping

Hotel Atheras HOTEL €

(22750 31434; www.atherashotel.gr; s/d/tr from €55/60/70; P ❄ 📶 🏊) The friendly, modern Atheras has an almost Cycladic feel due to its bright-white decor contrasting with the blue Aegean beyond. There's an outdoor bar by the pool. The hotel is in the backstreets, 200m from the port.

Kerame Studios APARTMENT €€

(22750 32600; www.keramehotel.gr; s/d/tr €60/70/80; P ❄ 📶 🏊) These studio apartments, located 1km before Evdilos, feature kitchens and spacious decks with views. Prices are as variable as the quarters. A breakfast cafe is built into a windmill. Kerame is the sister establishment of Hotel Atheras.

Eating

★ **Sta Perix** GREEK €

(Map p422; 22750 31056; mains €5-11; lunch & dinner) Classy eatery in Akamatra, 6km south of Evdilos, well regarded for its traditional Ikarian recipes, a variety of local cheeses and its own wine.

RakoStroto TAVERNA €

(22750 32266; mains €6-10; dinner) Up on the hill, at the bend in the street that connects with the main road to Kambos, this summer-only taverna occupies a kind of natural balcony with bay views. Competently made grills and vegetable dishes are served, and musicians come for impromptu concerts.

Drinking & Nightlife

★ **Slowdown Brewery** CRAFT BEER

(22750 32463; www.facebook.com/SlowDownBrewing; 5pm-late) Its own beer production was still in the works at the time of research, but you can try seven kinds of craft beer from different parts of Greece, including the excellent Ikariotissa red ale produced on the island. They serve mouth-watering snacks, including succulent mini-burgers, which are 'mini' only from the American perspective.

The place is out of town, on the main road leading towards Kambos.

Café-Bar Rififi CAFE

(22750 33060; Plateia Evdilou; all day; 📶) This snappy portside bar, with great pitta snacks, draught beer and good coffee, owes its name to the bank next door, with which it shares an interior wall. *Rififi* in Greek is a nickname for a bank robber, and the servers are happy to point out where the serious money is stashed.

Information

Ikaria Holiday (p422) Helpful full-service travel office, on the waterfront.

Getting There & Away

Evdilos is Ikaria's second port. **Hellenic Seaways** (https://hellenicseaways.gr) ferries connect it to other northeastern Aegean Islands and Piraeus.

One or two daily buses may or may not be running the route between Agios Kirykos and Hristos Rahes.

Aventura (p423) and Mav Cars (p423) rent cars and motorbikes.

Kambos Κάμπος

POP 250

Kambos, 3km west of Evdilos, was once mighty Oinoe (derived from the Greek word for wine), Ikaria's capital. Traces of this ancient glory remain, compliments of a ruined

WORTH A TRIP

COAST OF DIONYSOS

Dionysos, god of wine and merrymaking, may not have envisaged that planeloads of guests heading for *panigyria* festivals would be landing practically on the roof of his Ikarian cave dwelling. The island's – thankfully not so busy – airstrip is right next to the god's legendary lair and some spectacular scenery around the village of **Fanari**. One may only speculate what it means in terms of his relations with the island's other ancient celeb, Icarus, whose statue stands inside the airport terminal.

Lying in the lowlands next to a good pebble beach, Fanari is the starting point for a fairly easy circular trek that takes in some quirky attractions, in addition to breathtaking views of the sea and surrounding islands. You need no more than a couple of hours to do the entire route and take a dip in the sea.

On the eastern side of the village, a dirt track starts climbing up the hill before reaching a fork with a sign pointing towards the **Fortress of Drakanos** (Map p422; ⊙8am-3pm Tue-Sat) FREE: follow it to reach the 2500-year-old archaeological site with a name and outlook straight out of *Game of Thrones*. When Greek air-force jets fly overhead in regular drills, you may get a distinct feel that you have indeed found yourself in the land of dragons. On the way to the fortress, you may also choose to detour to the smallish **Agios Georgios chapel** next to the secluded beach of the same name.

From Drakanos, a well-marked trail leads through shrub-covered terrain to **Iero Beach**, a pleasant cove with crystal-clear water and a **cave**, where Dionysos cavorted with maenads and satyrs during his lifelong vacation, or so the legend says. A dirt track running along the airport fence will bring you back to Fanari, where **Evon's Rooms** (☑22750 32580, 6977139208; www.evonsrooms.com; Faros; studios/ste from €50/80; P❄@🖂) is a welcoming place to overnight or spend your entire holiday on Ikaria.

Byzantine palace, Ikaria's oldest **church** and a small **museum** (☑22750 32935; ⊙8.30am-3pm Wed) FREE. Kambos' other main attractions are its sand-and-pebble beach and scenic hill walks. It's a very quiet place with a couple of outstanding accommodation options and some veritable tavernas, while the far more diverse nightlife scene of Evdilos is reachable on foot.

🛏 Sleeping

⭐ **Ikaria Utopia –**
Cusco Studios   APARTMENT €
(☑6973848812, 22750 31381; http://ikariautopia.com; apt €30-55; P❄🖂) For musician and philosopher Christos, who runs this cluster of large and stylishly furnished apartments with huge terraces, this place seems to be an artistic as much as a business project. Perched on a hill, high above the beach, this windswept spot is a true bohemian haunt ideal for creative types in search of seclusion and inspiration. To reach it, take a side road that branches off the main one by **Sourta-Ferta** (☑22750 31651; snacks €1.50-4; ⊙lunch & dinner) cafe.

Rooms Dionysos   PENSION €
(☑6944153437, 22750 31688; www.ikaria-dionysos rooms.com; d/tr/q from €25/35/45; P🖂) The

many happy guests who return every year attest to the magical atmosphere of this pension run by the charismatic Vasilis 'Dionysos' Kambouris, his Australian-born wife, Demetra, and Italian-speaking brother Yiannis. Rooms are simple, with private bathrooms; rooftop beds are a summer steal at €10. There's a communal kitchen, a book exchange and you'll get great tips on exploring Ikaria.

🍴 Eating

Popi's   TAVERNA €
(Fytema Beach; mains €5-8.50; ⊙dinner) Very traditional setting on the road halfway between Kambos and Evdilos. Excellent taverna fare, cooked and happily served by Popi.

Kalypso   GREEK €€
(☑22750 31387; Kambos; €7-15; ⊙24hr, summer only) A summer-only affair run by a Greek-Belgian couple, Kalypso is renowned for its cooking – it's all about fish here – as much as for its festive atmosphere. It's located on the beach, halfway between Kambos and Evdilos.

ℹ Getting There & Away

The 2.7km to/from Evdilos can be easily done on foot, but if you have luggage, get a taxi.

Hristos Rahes
Χριστός Ραχών

POP 300

At night the heart of Ikaria beats in the cool highlands above Armenistis, where a cluster of picturesque villages, collectively known as Rahes (the main village is Hristos Rahes), come to life after dark, with children playing in the streets and adults drinking coffee or ouzo. These nocturnal habits hark back to the times when, fearing pirates based on nearby Fourni, Ikaria pretended to be an uninhabited island. An occasional roof covered with stone slabs is another vestige of that epoch, when people tried to camouflage their dwellings as piles of rocks. By day, Rahes villages serve as departure points for many exciting hikes through Ikaria's highlands, covered in pine forest and fruit orchards.

◉ Sights

Crowning the hill above Hristos Rahes, **Afianes Winery** (Map p422; ☑ 6977893731, 22750 40008; http://afianeswines.gr/en; ⊙ noon-8pm) **FREE** is a small family-run winery has won several recent awards in Europe. In addition to the offered tastings and small personal tours of the operation, an exhibition room features vintage winemaking equipment, gourd vessels and 19th-century wedding dresses.

⌂ Sleeping & Eating

Estia　　　　　　　　　　GUESTHOUSE €€
(☑ 22750 41007, 6979835757; evgeniaporis@gmail.com; r from €65; ❄ 🛜) Up the road from Hristos Rahes, this place offers simply but tastefully decorated rooms, with fully equipped kitchens and balconies that face the sea and the cascade of Rahes villages descending to Armenistis.

★ **Taverna Platanos**　　　　　　TAVERNA €
(Map p422; ☑ 22750 42395; Agios Dimitrios; mains €5-9.50; ⊙ 10am-2am) Nestled under the shade of a rambling plane tree, a 500m stroll from Hristos Rahes, Platanos offers authentic Ikarian dishes, including *soufiko,* a summer favourite of stewed veggies, generally featuring whatever is picked fresh that morning. Great grills, hearty salads and local wine round out the table.

★ **CousinA**　　　　　　　　　GREEK €
(☑ 22750 41374; mains €6-11; ⊙ lunch & dinner) A short walk from the main square, this tiny but outstanding eatery ventures well beyond the Ikarian mainstream, upgrading traditional Greek food to the level that would earn the acclaim of world food critics. It serves a superb aubergine salad with walnuts and *dakos* (Cretan rusks), an Ikarian version of bruschetta.

Argios Restaurant & Bar　　　　GREEK €
(☑ 6973669492, 22750 41564; Profitis Ilias; mains €6-10; ⊙ lunch & dinner) Located on the 'roof' of Ikaria, up high in Profitis Ilias, a 10-minute drive from Hristos Rahes, this large terrace serves a menu that is vaguely Greek, with some international guest dishes, such as hummus with goji berries. Live and DJ music events are held in summer – look for announcements around the island.

🍷 Drinking & Nightlife

In the main square, **Rahati** (☑ 22750 41512; ⊙ 9am-late) serves exquisite traditional Greek desserts, as well as perhaps the best coffee on the island. Lovely chatty women rule the house.

🛍 Shopping

The **Women's Cooperative** (☑ 22750 41076; ⊙ all day) is a wonderful market-deli-bakery in the heart of Hristos Rahes that sells jams, herbs and sweet treats made on the premises.

ℹ Getting There & Away

A daily bus service may or may not run to Evdilos. You may take a taxi down to Evdilos for €10, but your best bet really is to have a rented car. Many people hitchhike from Hristos Rahes and Armenistis. Hitching is never entirely safe, and we don't recommend it. Travellers who hitch should understand that they are taking a small but potentially serious risk.

Armenistis　　Αρμενιστής

POP 80

Armenistis, 15km west of Evdilos, is Ikaria's humble version of a resort. It boasts two long sandy beaches separated by a narrow headland; a fishing harbour; and a web of hilly streets to explore on foot. Cafes and tavernas line the beach. Moderate nightlife livens up Armenistis in summer with a mix of locals and Greek and foreign tourists.

◉ Sights & Activities

★ **Nas Beach**　　　　　　　　BEACH
(Map p422) Westward 3.5km from Armenistis lies the pebbled beach of Nas, lying below the road and the few tavernas. A nudist-friendly

beach, it has an impressive location at the mouth of a forested river, behind the trace ruins of an ancient **Temple of Artemis**, easily viewed from Artemis Studios.

Livadi Beach BEACH
Beside Armenistis, a little mountain river brings some fine sand to form this picture-perfect beach. Beware the strong currents and – occasionally – high waves that make it suitable for surfing, or at least body surfing.

Mesahti Beach BEACH
This is the kind of beach that makes it onto travel magazine covers. Mesahti is Ikaria's longest and arguably best organised, with gentle yellow sand, a picturesque estuary, sunbeds and a beach bar.

🛏 Sleeping

There are some truly wonderful places to stay in Ikaria's main tourist spot; if you plan to visit in high season, be aware that they get fully booked very early.

Artemis Studios PENSION €
(🖉 22750 71475; www.artemis-studio.gr; Nas; d from €40; P 🕸) This popular family-run place perched on the edge of the spectacular Chalari canyon above Nas Beach (p427) comes with its own taverna and an interesting pottery shop. Resident artists stay and work here throughout summer. Breakfast is €6 extra.

Pension Astaxi PENSION €
(🖉 22750 71318, 6982446227; www.island-ikaria.com/hotels/PensionAstaxi.asp; d/tr incl breakfast from €35/50; P @ 🛜) This excellent, attractive budget gem is tucked back 30m from the main road, just above the Carte Postal cafe and Taverna Baido. The gracious owner, Maria, has created a relaxing and welcoming lodging, with a dozen brightly outfitted rooms with fans and balcony views to the sea.

Atsachas Rooms HOTEL €
(🖉 22750 71226; www.atsachas.gr; btw Mesahti & Livadi beaches; d €40-60; 🕸🛜) On a headland between Mesahti (p428) and Livadi (p428) beaches, this hotel has clean, well-furnished rooms, some with fully equipped kitchens. Most have breezy sea-view balconies. The cafe spills onto a flowery garden, where a stairway descends to a nice stretch of beach.

Hotel Daidalos HOTEL €
(🖉 22750 71390; www.daidaloshotel.gr; s/d incl breakfast from €40/50; ⊙May-Oct; P 🕸🛜🏊) You can't miss the blue-and-white island

colour scheme at this attractive, well-managed 25-room hotel. Rooms are large and cheerful, most with sea views, and there's a small bar off the lobby. It's 200m west of the small bridge as you enter Armenistis.

★ Koimite GUESTHOUSE €€
(🖉 6974893877, 22750 71545; www.ikariarooms.gr; Armenistis; d/q from €60/110; 🕸🛜) Cascading down a rocky cliff, these pastel-coloured rooms come with balconies so huge you might be tempted to sell tickets to watch the spectacular sunset. Some rooms are equipped with kitchenettes; others have fridges. There are kerosene heaters. Super-nice staff leave homemade cookies when they finish cleaning.

Erofili Beach Hotel HOTEL €€
(🖉 22750 71058; www.erofili.gr; d/tr incl breakfast from €95/110; P 🕸🛜🏊) Swank studio apartments and rooms, with a pool and amenities to spare. It's found just before the bridge.

🍴 Eating

★ Thea's Restaurant & Rooms TAVERNA €
(🖉 22750 71491, 6932154296; www.theasinn.com; Nas; mains €6-11; ⊙lunch & dinner; 🛜) There are a few fine tavernas in Nas, but Thea's excels, serving up outstanding mezedhes, meat grills and a perfect veggie *mousakas* (baked layers of aubergine or courgette, minced meat and potatoes topped with cheese sauce). Good barrel wine and local *tsipouro* (distilled spirit of grape must) firewater complete the deal. An outdoor patio overlooks the sea. Thea (aka Dorothy) also has five bright and cosy rooms (€35 including breakfast) above the restaurant.

Syntages tis Giagias DESSERTS €
(Grandma's Recipes; 🖉 22750 71150; desserts €2-3; ⊙lunch & dinner) Occupying a terrace on the 2nd floor of the main shopping compound in Armenistis, this small confectionery makes exemplary *galaktoboureko*, *kataïfi* (angel-hair pastry) and ice cream with local fruit flavours. Shelves are filled with jars containing spoon sweets, such as caramelised seasonal fruit and vegetables.

Taverna Symposio TAVERNA €
(🖉 6972264046; Gialiskari; mezedhes & mains €3-8.50; ⊙lunch & dinner) A small taverna in tiny Gialiskari, next to Armenistis, overlooking the marina. It's known for great mezedhes and *mayirefta* (ready-cooked) dishes, and has outstanding hospitality, even by already outstanding Greek standards.

THE WILD SOUTH

You can now drive on a fairly good paved coastal road all around the island, except for a 15km section between **Manganitis** and **Karkinagri**, located in Ikaria's southwestern corner. Both are serene end-of-the-universe places, with quaint fishing ports and a few tavernas, where hikers wind up after descending from the desolate moonlike plateau south of Hristos Rahes.

Connected by a paved road to Agios Kirykos and Evdilos, Manganitis draws crowds from elsewhere on the island every lunar month in summer when the popular **Sto Gialo** (Map p422; 22750 32636; www.stogialokaneifourtouna.gr; 10am-late) bar and restaurant holds its Full Moon Party; check out its website and advertisements around the island for other live and DJ music events. People also flock to the small and stunning **Seychelles Beach** (Map p422), 3km east of Manganitis. Its marble pebbles, emerald water and giant rocks polished by the waves make you feel you've been teleported into the middle of the Indian Ocean – hence the name. To access it, follow an unmarked path from the parking lot by the tunnel on the road to Manganitis, always leaning to the left side of the ravine.

Karkinagri is now connected by a brand-new road that gives mind-blowing vistas up to the tourist clusters of Nas and Armenistis in Ikaria's northwest. Life in Karkinagri revolves around the bamboo-roofed seafront patio of taverna **O Karakas** (mains €6-9; lunch & dinner, the best place on the island to try the local speciality *soufiko*, a tasty vegetable stew.

East from Karkinagri, the dirt track in the direction of Manganitis is OK for a good car until Trapalou, which has a nice beach. Beyond that, the road is fairly atrocious and often gets completely blocked by falling rocks. Check with locals about its current condition.

Taverna Baido　　　　TAVERNA €
(6982331539; mains €6-10; 1.30-11.30pm) Past the bridge towards Nas, this taverna is the work of Marianthi, who serves well-priced dishes using local products, fresh fish and wine. Exceptional *soutzoukakia* (meat rissoles in tomato sauce) and *taramasalata* (a thick pink or white purée of fish roe, potato, oil and lemon juice).

Pashalia Taverna　　　　TAVERNA €
(6975562415, 22750 71302; mains €4-7; lunch & dinner) Meat dishes such as *katsikaki* (kid goat) or veal in a clay pot are specialities at this taverna, the first along the Armenistis harbour road. The mezedhes are also popular.

Kelaris Taverna　　　　SEAFOOD €
(22750 71227; Gialiskari; mains €6-11; lunch & dinner) Kelaris serves its own fresh-caught fish, cooked over coals, along with midday *mayirefta* dishes from the oven. Look for the landmark church on the point, 1.5km east of Armenistis.

★ **Marymary**　　　　MEDITERRANEAN €€
(22750 71595; Armenistis; mains €8-12; noon-midnight;) Marrying traditional island cuisine with cosmopolitan culinary fashion, this upmarket eatery in the heart of Armenistis has a small army of devoted regulars raving about its *mayirefta* dishes, such as rooster with homemade pasta or clay-pot stews. The sea-view terrace is inviting for sundowners and a bottle or two of local wine.

🍷 Drinking & Nightlife

Mythos　　　　BAR
(10am-late) Cosy, atmospheric bar managed by Dimitiros and Mariza, who deliver good drinks, fresh juices and live music in the summer. Walk down the street descending to the sea to find it.

Carte Postale　　　　BAR
(22750 71031, 6981719567; 10am-2am) This hip cafe-bar, 100m west of Armenistis' church, sits high over the bay. It has a mellow ambience, signalled by an eclectic music mix, from world beat to Greek fusion. Snacks range from small pizzas and salads to breakfast omelettes and evening risotto, all managed by the welcoming Myrto; her father makes the olives.

ℹ Information

Aventura (22750 71117; aventura@otenet.gr; 9am-9pm) Full-service travel agency located by the patisserie just before the bridge. Offers car and motorbike rentals, and is one of the few places that hires out mountain bikes. Also does airport pick-ups and drop-offs.

Dolihi Tours & Lemy Rent-a-Car
(6983418878, Dolihi 22750 71122, Lemy 22750 23230; lemy@otenet.gr; 9am-9pm) Efficient travel agency and car hire office next to the village market. Rents cars and organises walking tours and 4WD safaris. Located 200m past the small bridge, towards Nas.

❶ Getting There & Away

As bus services are virtually nonexistent and taxi prices are unreasonable it makes sense to rent a car, especially if your arrival/departure points on the island are the airport or Agios Kirykos. The Lemy Rent-a-Car (p429) office is 200m past the small bridge, towards Nas.

A taxi ride to Evdilos should cost around €20, but prepare to pay up to €70 if you are heading to the other side of the island.

Hitchhiking is the most common method of getting to Nas and Hristos Rahes. Hitching is never entirely safe, and we don't recommend it. Travellers who hitch should understand that they are taking a small but potentially serious risk.

Karavostamo Καραβόσταμο

POP 550

Karavostamo, 6km east of Evdilos, is one of Ikaria's largest coastal villages. From the main road, the village cascades down winding paths scattered with flowering gardens, village churches, veggie patches, chickens and goats, finally reaching a cosy square and a small fishing harbour. Here you'll find little more than a bakery (p430), a small general store, and a few domatia, tavernas and coffeehouses where villagers congregate each evening to chat, argue, eat, play backgammon, drink and tell stories. To reach the square, take the signed road off the main road.

LOCAL KNOWLEDGE

A VILLAGE BAKERY

In Karavostamo, everything you need to know about island values can probably be found at the village bakery, where Stephanos Kranas bakes long loaves of bread in his wood oven, along with crunchy *paximadia* (rusks) and sweet *koulouria* (fresh pretzel-style bread).

The bakery makes deliveries each morning by motorbike to village homes. But villagers can also drop by, grab a loaf from the wicker basket on the counter and, if no one's around, leave money in a counter cup. If the bakery appears to be closed, they may simply go upstairs and knock on the owner's door to enquire if there's any bread. The system has worked for years, one reason perhaps why Ikarians don't get too excited about fluctuations in the global price of oil. Olive oil...maybe.

⛵ Courses

The **Ikarian Centre** (Map p422; ☑ 6979024066, 22750 61140; www.ikariancentre.com; Arethousa) is a small Greek-language school that runs intensive residential courses (usually from 10 to 20 days). It's in Arethousa, 3km up the hill from Karavostamo, where you're more likely to hear the sound of goat bells than motorbikes. The school combines an up-to-date curriculum with an unbeatable setting overlooking the Aegean, and attracts students from around Europe. There's plenty of fun to be had, too, including trips to local eateries and surrounding sights.

🛏 Sleeping & Eating

Despina Rooms   PENSION €

(☑ 6977080808, 21066 13999; www.roomsdespina. gr; r €40-60; P ❋ 🛜) Well-appointed two-storey studios in the heart of the village, with kitchens and laundry facilities. It's about 200m from the sea and village square.

Taverna I Plaka   TAVERNA €

(Map p422; ☑ 6972512551; Arethousa; mains €6-10; ⏱ lunch & dinner) Excellent traditional taverna in Arethousa, serving traditional Greek dishes from a terrace overlooking the sea.

❶ Getting There & Away

Karavostamo is a 10-minute taxi ride from Evdilos.

FOURNI ISLANDS
ΟΙ ΦΟΥΡΝΟΙ

POP 1320

The Fourni archipelago is one of Greece's great unknown island gems. Its low-lying vegetation clings to gracefully rounded hills that overlap, forming intricate bays of sandy beaches and little ports. This former pirates' lair is especially beautiful at dusk, when the setting sun turns the terrain shades of pink, violet and black.

A clue to the area's swashbuckling past can be found in the name of the archipelago's capital, Fourni Korseon. The Corsairs were French privateers with a reputation for audacity, and their name became applied generically to all pirates and rogues then roaming the eastern Aegean.

Nowadays, Fourni Korseon offers most of the area's accommodation and services, plus several beaches. Other settlements include little Hrysomilia and Kamari to the north, plus another fishing hamlet on the islet of Thymena.

THE REFUGEE CRISIS

In 2015 the northeastern Aegean Islands hit the headlines when thousands of refugees landed on the islands' beaches, fleeing war and violence. The world watched as empathetic and concerned locals assisted the traumatised people, including children. Since then, many more refugees have arrived at Lesvos, Samos, Chios and Kos. Though refugee numbers are now at a trickle, there is a backlog in processing. While their applications for asylum are being validated and processed, the refugees are housed in several camps around the islands.

As a result of media coverage of the situation, tourism on several of the islands, particularly Lesvos and Samos, has suffered greatly. This is particularly difficult for the local people. Travellers take note: tourist infrastructure here is as strong as ever. The islands all offer wonderful accommodation, eating and cultural experiences. While it's important to stay attuned to the world news and keep alert to safety issues when planning any trip, do not overlook these wonderful islands. The world has seen how welcoming the big-hearted locals are to outsiders; deep-rooted *filoxenia* (hospitality) prevails here.

A few volunteer organisations operate on the islands trying to improve the plight of refugees in the squalid camps. **Indigo Volunteers** (https://indigovolunteers.org) is an international organisation that vets volunteers before placing them with local volunteer groups. Below are the organisations operating on some of the islands:

Samos Volunteers (https://samosvolunteers.org)

Lighthouse Relief (Lesvos; https://www.lighthouserelief.org)

◉ Sights & Activities

Kampi   BEACH
(Map p422) A short trek from the main village, this charming little bay with turquoise water has a tiny fishing port and a nice pebbly beach. A beach bar and a taverna come to life in summer. Follow a stone-paved path above the church in Fourni Korseon until you reach the windmills, then descend to the sea.

Kamari   BEACH
(Map p422) A picturesque medium-sized cove protected from high waves in any weather, ideal for both swimming and snorkelling. A popular taverna is nearby in the village.

🛏 Sleeping

★ Archipelagos Hotel   HOTEL €
(☑ 22750 51250, 6973494967; www.archipelago shotel.gr; Fourni Korseon; d incl breakfast from €50; [P][❄][🌐][📶]) This elegant and welcoming small hotel on the harbour's northern edge comprises Fourni's most sophisticated lodgings. From the patio restaurant, set under stone arches bursting with geraniums and roses, to the well-appointed rooms and cafe-bar, the Archipelagos combines traditional architecture with modern luxuries.

Patras Rooms & Apartments   APARTMENT €
(☑ 22750 51268, 22750 51355; www.fourni-patras rooms.gr; Fourni Korseon; r/ste/apt from €30/55/60; [❄][📶]) Under the same management as To Arhontiko (p431) cafe, this merry colony of brightly coloured and individually designed studios and apartments nestles on the slope right above the port. Near the cafe, there is also a cluster of rooms that are plain, but good value for money.

Toula Studios   PENSION €
(☑ 22750 51332, 6976537948; info@fournitoulas tudio.gr; Fourni Korseon; d with/without sea view €60/50; [❄][📶]) Look for the Aegean-blue balconies at this friendly seafront standby near shops and tavernas. It has clean and simple self-catering rooms with overhead fans. The rooms, 10 of which have sea views, surround a large courtyard.

Studios Nektaria   APARTMENT €
(☑ 6973097365, 22750 25134; studiosnektaria@ yahoo.gr; tr from €35; [❄][📶]) On the harbour's far side, this is a Fourni bargain, with small, clean rooms, three of which have shaded balconies overlooking the small beach that skirts the southern end of the bay.

✕ Eating

To Arhontiko   DESSERTS €
(Fourni Korseon; desserts €2-4; ⊙ breakfast, lunch & dinner; [📶]) Oranges are the reason why this

seafront place is a must-visit, but To Arhontiko makes a whole range of great desserts. Come here after you've finished your lobster in a nearby taverna.

Psarotaverna O Miltos
SEAFOOD €

(☑ 22750 51407; Fourni Korseon; mains €7-10; ☺ lunch & dinner; ☞) Fourni lobster and fresh fish are expertly prepared at this iconic waterfront taverna. Excellent mezedhes and traditional salads; fish and lobster are fairly priced by the kilo.

Taverna Almyra
TAVERNA €

(Map p422; Kamari; mains €5-9) Up in the little village of Kamari, 9km from the harbour, this relaxing waterfront taverna has subtle charm, and plenty of fresh fish and lobster.

Psarotaverna Nikos
SEAFOOD €

(Fourni Korseon; mains €7-10; ☺ lunch & dinner; ☞) This is a very reliable seafood option, next door to sibling restaurant O Miltos. Look for daily specials on the chalkboard.

🛍 Shopping

The wonderfully designed **Ka_ndilos** (☑ 22750 51581; Fourni Korseon; ☺ morning & evening) is packed with multisized jars, sells unusual homemade preserves – spoon sweets, made of all kinds of fruit and vegetables, as well as marinated products. Everything is grown here on the island and preserved the way locals do for themselves. On the main street.

ℹ Information

Fourni Fishermen & Friends (www.fourni.com) The online guide to Fourni.

ℹ Getting There & Away

Lying on major routes linking northeastern Aegean Islands to mainland ports near Athens and in northern Greece, Fourni is best connected to Agios Kirykos on Ikaria by both ferry and hydrofoil (€7 to €14, one hour, four to five weekly).

Fourni can be visited on a day trip twice a week from Samos, when *Dodekanisos Pride* calls in on the way from Pythagorio in the morning and returns by the same route in the early evening (€40 return, one hour). The same catamaran connects the archipelago with Patmos (€25, 1½ hours) and other Dodecanese islands down south.

Fourni Travel (☑ 6975576584, 22750 51019; Fourni Korseon; ☺ 10am-2pm & 6-9pm Mon-Sat, 11.30am-7pm Sun) provides information and sells tickets. **Dodecanese Seaways** (www.12ne.gr) provides faster and more expensive catamaran services.

ℹ Getting Around

Gleaming new sealed roads, all 20km of them, connect Fourni Korseon with Hrysomilia and Kamari. Everyone seems to walk everywhere in Fourni, and then walk some more.

Rental cars are a recent addition to the Fourni transport scene. Hire a small car or scooter at **Escape Car & Bike Rental** (☑ 22750 51514; www.fourni-rentals.com; Fourni Korseon; ☺ 8.30am-9.30pm) on the waterfront.

There's also the island's lone **taxi** (☑ 6970879102), commanded by the ebullient Georgos.

Hitching is common and considered quite safe; however, travellers who hitch should understand that they are taking a small but potentially serious risk.

Alternatively, weekly caïques serve Hrysomilia, while another two to three go daily to Thymena.

SAMOS
ΣΑΜΟΣ

POP 33,000

Lying just off the Turkish coast, Samos is one of the northeastern Aegean Islands' best-known destinations. Yet beyond its low-key resorts and the lively capital, Vathy, there are numerous off-the-beaten-track beaches and quiet spots in the cool, forested inland mountains where traditional life continues.

Famous for its deliciously sweet local wine, Samos is also historically significant. It was the legendary birthplace of Hera, and the sprawling ruins of her ancient sanctuary, the Heraion (p438), are impressive. Both the great mathematician Pythagoras and the hedonistic father of atomic theory, the 4th-century-BC philosopher Epicurus, were born here. Samos' scientific genius is also affirmed by the astonishing 524 BC Evpalinos Tunnel (p437), a spectacular feat of ancient engineering that stretches for more than 1km deep underground.

ℹ Getting There & Away

AIR

Samos' airport is 4km west of Pythagorio. **Aegean Airlines** (https://en.aegeanair.com), **Astra Airlines** (www.astra-airlines.gr), **Olympic Air** (www.olympicair.com) and **Sky Express** (www.skyexpress.gr) all serve Samos and have offices at the airport.

BOAT

Samos is home to three ports – Vathy (aka Samos), Pythagorio and Karlovasi. They provide connections to Athens and Kavala on the mainland as well as to other island groups. Karlovasi is convenient for Piraeus and Cycladic islands, while Vathy is best for Kavala and the northeastern Aegean Islands. Catamarans and regular boats out of Pythagorio are the most convenient option for the Dodecanese island group.

From Vathy, there are four boats a week to Piraeus (€41, 14 hours) via Ikaria (€10.50, three hours) and Fourni (€13.50, two hours) and two boats weekly to Kavala (€42, 18 hours) via Chios (€14, three hours), Lesvos (€19.50, seven hours) and Limnos (€31, 13 hours). On Fridays, *Blue Star 1* departs for the Dodecanese islands Kos (€37, 3½ hours) and Rhodes (€39, 6½ hours).

From Karlovasi, five boats a week travel to Piraeus (€51, eight hours) via the Cycladic islands of Mykonos (€40.50, 3½ hours) and Syros (€43.50, 4½ hours).

Originating from Pythagorio, boats and catamarans call at smaller Dodecanese islands of Agathonisi (from €8.50, 1½ hours) and Arki (from €8.50, 2½ hours) on the way to Patmos (from €9.50, 3½ hours) and Leros (from €13, six hours). The *Dodekanisos Pride* fast boat runs twice a week to Rhodes (€59, seven hours) via Fourni (€20, one hour) and Ikaria's Agios Kirykos (€25, 1½ hours) via almost every Dodecanese island.

Tickets are available from By Ship Travel (p421), which runs offices in all three ports.

❶ Getting Around

From Vathy's **bus station** (☑ 22730 27262; Themistokleous Sofouli), frequent daily buses serve Kokkari (20 minutes), Pythagorio (25 minutes), Agios Konstantinos (40 minutes), Karlovasi (one hour), the Ireon (25 minutes), Mytilinii (20 minutes) and Portrokali (20 minutes). Tickets cost €1.50 to €4 depending on distance.

From Pythagorio, five daily buses reach the Ireon (15 minutes), while four serve Mytilinii (20 minutes) and Marathokampos (one hour). Buy tickets on the buses. Services are reduced on weekends. Tickets cost €1.50 to €7 depending on distance.

In Vathy, **Pegasus Rent-a-Car** (☑ 6978536440, 22730 24470; www.samos-car-rental.com; Themistokleous Sofouli 5) has good rates on car, 4WD and motorcycle hire.

In Pythagorio, try **John's Rentals** (☑ 22730 61405, 6977253931; www.johns-rent-a-car.gr; Lykourgou Logotheti) on the main road near the waterfront.

TO/FROM THE AIRPORT
Buses between Vathy and the airport run eight times daily, with reduced schedules during weekends. Taxis from the airport cost €25 to Vathy, or €10 to Pythagorio, from where there are local buses to Vathy.

A MATTER OF MEASUREMENTS

While the obsession with the 'proper pint' may seem modern, the Ancient Greeks also fixated on measuring their alcohol. Pythagoras, a great Samian mathematician (and, presumably, drinker), created an invention that ensured party hosts and publicans could not be deceived by guests aspiring to inebriation. His creation was dubbed the *Dikiakoupa tou Pythagora* (Just Cup of Pythagoras). This mysterious, multiholed drinking vessel holds its contents perfectly, unless filled past the engraved line, at which point the glass drains completely from the bottom, punishing the glutton! Today, faithful reproductions, made of colourful glazed ceramic, are sold in Samos gift shops, and are tangible reminders of the Apollon Mean: 'Everything in moderation'.

Vathy   Βαθύ

POP 1900

The island's capital, Vathy (also called Samos) enjoys a striking setting within the fold of a deep bay, where its curving waterfront is lined with bars, cafes and restaurants. The historical quarter of Ano Vathy, filled with steep narrow streets and red-tiled 19th-century hillside houses, brims with atmosphere. The town centre boasts two engaging museums and a striking century-old church.

Vathy has two pebble beaches, the best being **Gagos Beach**, about 500m north from the old quay. Along the way you'll pass a string of cool bars clinging to the town's northeastern cliff.

◎ Sights

Vathy's attractions include the **Ano Vathy** old quarter (inland 1km via Sofouli), relaxing municipal gardens, Roditzes and Gagos Beaches, a first-rate archaeological museum (p435) and the splendid church of **Agios Spyridonas** (Map p436; Plateia Dimarheiou; ◷8-11am & 6.30-7.30pm).

★**Livadaki Beach**   BEACH
(Map p434) Follow the north-coast road out of Vathy for 10km and look for a signposted dirt road to the left leading to Livadaki Beach. Here, tropical azure waters lap against soft

Samos

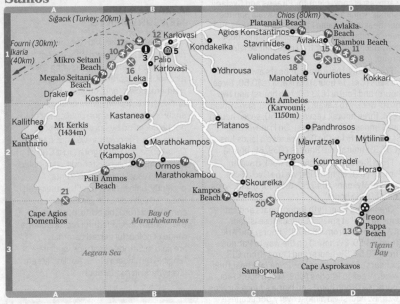

Samos

sand in a long-sheltered cove with facing islets. The water is warm and very shallow for a long way out, and Livadaki's mellow summer beach parties easily spill into it.

The excellent beach bar serves snacks and drinks. For a classic taverna, get back on the main road and drive down to the hamlet of **Agia Paraskevi**, where you can enjoy a meditative lunch or dinner with the backdrop of multicoloured boats moored in a picturesque bay.

Museum of Samos Wines
WINERY

(Map p434; ☑ 22730 87510, ext 548; www.samos wine.gr; €2; ☉ 10am-5.30pm May-Oct; 🅿) Look for this handsome stone building opposite the new ferry quay to find one of Samos' best vintners. Winery tours usually take place when you show up, and conveniently include a free tasting, with several reasonably priced wines for sale.

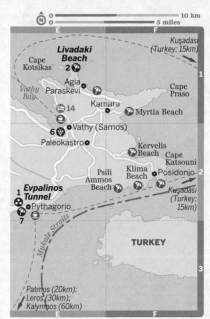

Ino Village Hotel & Restaurant

HOTEL €€

(Map p434; ☑22730 23241; www.inovillageho tel.com; Kalami; d incl breakfast €60-125; P❋⊛☎🏊) With its courtyard pool flanked by ivy-clad, balconied white buildings, Ino Village, just 500m above Vathy, feels remote and elegant. While this mini-resort is sometimes booked by small tour groups, and can therefore feel a little impersonal, walk-in travellers are still welcome. The hotel also boasts the popular Elea restaurant and cocktail bar, which serves fine Samian wines.

Hotel Aeolis

HOTEL €€

(Map p436; ☑22730 28904; www.aeolis.gr; Themistokleous Sofouli 33; s/d incl breakfast €50/60; ❋☎🏊) This central waterfront hotel attracts Athenians and foreign travellers alike, drawn by its two pools, Jacuzzi, taverna and bar. Rooms are ample and modern, all with balconies. Breakfast is advertised as American (read: more generous).

Archaeological Museum

MUSEUM

(Map p436; ☑22730 27469; adult/concession €4/2, 1st Sun of month Nov-Mar free; ⊘8.30am-4pm Wed-Mon) Housed in two adjacent buildings, this handsome complex displays the contents of the Heraion (p438) near Pythagorio (from Polycrates' rule in the 6th century BC). The most famous item is the imposing *kouros* (male statue of the Archaic period). At a height of 5.5m, it's the largest-known standing *kouros*. The museum is next to the town hall. The collection is rounded out by many other statues, most also from the Heraion, as well as bronze sculptures, *stelae* (pillars), pottery and pieces that are unusually made of wood and are still intact.

🛌 Sleeping

Pension Dreams

PENSION €

(Map p436; ☑6976425195, 22730 24350; Areos 9; d €35-40, tr €45-50; P❋☎) This small, quiet and central pension, 100m up from the waterfront, claims a hilltop view of the harbour. All seven rooms are bright and very well kept, some with large balconies and garden views. The energetic owner, Kostas, speaks English and French.

🍴 Eating

★ My Falasophy

MIDDLE EASTERN €

(Map p436; ☑22734 00835; Plateia Pythagorou; mains €4-6.5; ⊘noon-11pm) A guest from the Levant, this little fast-food joint in the main square serves large portions of artfully prepared hummus and falafel, as well as great salads. Healthy food is complemented by freshly squeezed tropical juices.

Pera Vrehi

GREEK €

(Map p436; ☑22730 27965; Logotheti; salads & snacks €4-7; ⊘6pm-2am; ☎🍴) Known to expat regulars as 'the salad place', Pera Vrehi serves large bowls of inventive salad arrangements with largely local ingredients, as well as an assortment of Greek mezedhes, such as fava-bean puree with marinated shallots. The menu is well balanced between vegetarian and carnivore food.

Garden Taverna

CAFE €€

(Map p436; ☑22730 24033; Manolis Kalomiris; mains €7-16; ⊘10am-midnight) Serves good Greek standards in a lovely garden setting. It's up to the left behind the main square.

🍸 Drinking & Nightlife

Nightlife in Vathy is more Hellenic than in the island's tourist clusters, where the scene is dominated by northern European tourists. While most cafes and bars cling to the water-

Vathy (Samos)

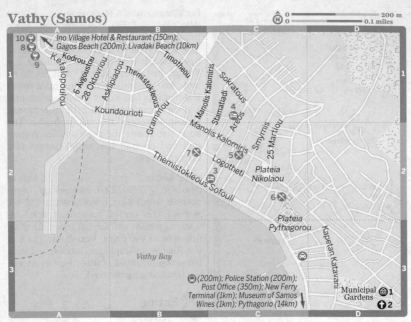

Ino Village Hotel & Restaurant (150m);
Gagos Beach (200m); Livadaki Beach (10km)

Vathy Bay

(200m); Police Station (200m);
Post Office (350m); New Ferry
Terminal (1km); Museum of Samos
Wines (1km); Pythagorio (14km)

Municipal Gardens

Vathy (Samos)

front, the coolest ones hang over the water along Kefalopoulou, 100m beyond the quay. Music and dancing is usually in full swing by midnight.

Joy CAFE
(Map p436; ☎22730 89770; Themistokleous Sofouli; ⊙8am-midnight) The best of the waterfront cafes, serving good coffee, fresh juices and crêpes in the morning, and sandwiches, burgers, beer and wine by evening.

Mezza Volta BAR
(Map p436; Kefalopoulou; ⊙9pm-dawn) Very popular beach bar, near the twin standbys of **Ble** (Map p436; Kefalopoulou 7; ⊙11am-4am) and **Escape** (Map p436; ☎22730 28345; Kefalopoulou 9; ⊙10pm-6am), with good iced drinks and snacks into the wee hours.

ℹ Getting There & Away

Vathy's large port handles boats to Turkey as well as domestic ferries, which connect Samos to other northeastern Aegean Islands, the Dodecanese and Piraeus. The bus station (p433) and nearby **taxi rank** (Map p436; ☎22730 28404) serve as a departure point to destinations all around the island.

Pythagorio Πυθαγόρειο

POP 1330

On the southeastern coast, pretty Pythagorio – named after mathematician and philosopher Pythagoras, who was born here – has a yacht-lined harbour, and Samos' main archaeological sites, including Heraion (p438) and the extraordinary Evpalinos Tunnel. All boats departing south from Samos leave from here, including those for day trips to Samiopoula.

◉ Sights

★ **Evpalinos Tunnel** ARCHAEOLOGICAL SITE
(Map p434; ☑ 22730 61400; www.eupalinos-tunnel.
gr; adult/child €8/4; ☺ 8.30am-3.30pm Wed-Mon
May-Sep) In a word: extraordinary. In 524 BC,
when Pythagorio (then called Samos) was
the island's capital and a bustling metropolis of 80,000, securing sources for drinking
water became crucial. To solve the problem,
ruler Polycrates ordered labourers to dig
into a mountainside according to the exact-
ing plan of his ingenious engineer, Evpalinos. Many workers died during the dangerous dig, but the result was the 1034m-long
Evpalinos Tunnel. In medieval times, locals
used it to hide from pirates.

The Evpalinos Tunnel is actually two tunnels: a service tunnel and a lower water con-
duit visible from the walkway. You enter the
tunnel on narrow stairs, and it's single file
from there. The first few metres are pretty
tight. There are three options: a 185m section (and return), a longer version and the
full 1km (you can walk back outside); guided tours take place every 20 minutes from
8.40am. Located just north of Pythagorio.

★ **Archaeological
Museum of Pythagorio** MUSEUM
(☑ 22730 62813; Polykratous; adult/concession
€4/2; ☺ 8.30am-4pm Tue-Sun) One of the best
museums on the islands. The exhibits in this
smart space include beautifully displayed
finds from Pythagorio, plus striking pottery
pieces spanning the 9th century BC through
to Greece's golden age. Museum labels are in
Greek and English.

Pythagorio Town Beach BEACH
(Map p434) A short walk west of Pythagorio
brings you to this pristine beach with umbrellas and toilets. There's decent swimming, but pack your own food and drinks.

Castle of Lykourgos Logothetis CASTLE
(☺ grounds 24hr) Samians took the lead locally in the 1821 War of Independence, and
this castle, built in 1824 by resistance leader
Logothetis, is the major relic of that turbulent time. It's situated on a hill at the southern end of Metamorfosis Sotiros, near the
car park. The city walls once extended from
here to the Evpalinos Tunnel.

Moni Panagias Spilianis MONASTERY
(Monastery of the Virgin of the Grotto; ☑ 22730
61361; ☺ 9am-8pm) FREE About 1.5km northwest of Pythagorio, the road forks right, past
traces of an ancient theatre, before reaching
this grotto monastery. The walk meanders
up through old olive groves; it's a welcome
respite from the summer heat and gives
clear views to the Turkish coast.

🏃 Activities

Try scuba diving with **Samos Dive Center**
(☑ 6972997645; www.samosdiving.com; Konstantinou Kanari 1). Professional instructors
lead dives in search of moray eels, octo-
puses, lobsters and other critters lurking in
sponge-covered crevices. A two-dive half-day
for beginners costs around €50; a full-day
dive, including open-water options, starts at
around €85. Snorkelling (€20) is also offered.

🛏️ Sleeping

Belvedere GUESTHOUSE €
(☑ 22730 61218; www.belvedere-samos.com; Ai-
sopou 6; d €30-45; ❄🛜) Manolis runs this
immaculate, nicely furnished guesthouse
in a quiet area not far from the main street
and the seafront. All rooms come with
balconies and a sea view. No breakfast on
offer, but there is a common kitchen for
self-caterers.

Pension Despina PENSION €
(☑ 6936930381, 22730 61677; A Nikolaou; studio/
apt €35/40; ❄🛜) An impeccably well-kept
quiet pension on the small and central
Plateia Irinis, the Despina offers attractive
rooms and studios (some with kitchenettes)
with overhead fans and balconies, plus a
relaxing back garden. Owner Athina is very
friendly. Find it on Facebook.

Samaina Hotel HOTEL €€
(☑ 22730 61024, 6936078159; Damous; d incl
breakfast from €80; ❄🛜) In a radical departure from the standard white-and-blue colour scheme, this hotel opts for a palette of
autumn foliage both inside and out. Rooms
feature many wooden surfaces and fittings.
All come with balconies and at least some
kind of sea view.

Polyxeni Hotel HOTEL €€
(☑ 22730 61590; www.polyxenihotel.com; s/d incl
breakfast from €65/72; ❄🛜) This reasonable
seafront lodging is bang in the middle of
the port hubbub. The several balconied harbour-view rooms are fitted with overhead
fans and double-glazed windows. The gar-
den-view rooms are the quieter ones to go
for if bar and cafe noise (from below) isn't
for you. Nothing special, but a decent, central bed-for-the-night choice.

✗ Eating

Pythagorio has the most sophisticated dining scene in Samos. Be sure to head beyond the eastern side of the wharf where several attractive waterfront tavernas are out of sight.

★ To Tigani tis Platias   TAVERNA €

(☑ 6971673770; Plateia Irinis; mains €7.50-10; ⊙ 11am-midnight; 🗟 ✍) Beautiful Greek standards, popular with both locals and visitors. It's especially great for veggie choices, such as baked feta, *gigantes* (white beans) and courgette balls, all a cut above average. Meat grills here are also superb, and there's a shady setting, cheerful service and good wine.

Two Spoons   DESSERTS €

(☑ 22730 62336; www.facebook.com/TwOSpOOns; Melissou; desserts €5-12; ⊙ 9am-1am; 🗟) Make sure you run a marathon before coming to this place, because you'll be hard pressed to prevent yourself from gorging on profiteroles, millefeuille and pavlova. Milkshakes are also on offer and – unusually for these coffee lands – a good selection of teas. With a garden setting by the sea, this place is the definition of guilty pleasure.

Kafeneio To Mouragio   CAFE €

(☑ 22730 62390; waterfront; mezedhes €3-6; ⊙ 8am-midnight; 🗟) The warm ambience and predominantly Greek clientele hint at the fact that this place delivers the goods, with snacks such as chickpea croquettes and assorted mezedhes. Enjoy coffee in the morning and, later, iced ouzo, wine and beer. Customers are welcome to leave their luggage for free.

🍷 Drinking & Nightlife

Iera Odos Art Cafe   BAR

(☑ 22730 61091; Lykourgou Logotheti; ⊙ 5pm-3am) Lush, decadent luxury is not what you'd expect in this corner of the Aegean, but here you are, amidst velvet cushions and lavish chandeliers, with a cocktail glass in your hand. There's also a terrace and a garden of 'magic crystals' where you can savour your drink in fresh air.

Katoi   BAR

(Lykourgou Logotheti) In the main street, this smallish modern place combines the virtues of a deli and an *ouzerie* (place that sells ouzo and like snacks). Ouzo and *tsipouro* are served with local cheeses and ham (€5 for the combo), which are also available for sale from the shop inside. Fresh juices also available.

Notos   BAR

(☑ 22730 62351; Tarsanas Beach; ⊙ noon-late; 🗟) From the main road, turn right (south) at the port to find this popular late-night music bar and taverna, opposite a public car park. Live music most Tuesdays and Saturdays.

ℹ Information

By Ship Travel (p421) Helpful full-service travel agency, offering car hire, accommodation, air and ferry tickets. At the junction entering town.

ℹ Getting There & Away

There are five buses daily to Vathy (25 minutes) and five buses daily to Ireon (15 minutes) for Heraion (p438). A taxi between Pythagorio and the airport (4km west of town) costs €10; it's €25 to/from Vathy. **Taxis** (☑ 22730 61450) also ply the route between Pythagorio and Vathy (useful for ferry arrivals and departures) for around €20.

Around Pythagorio

Heraion   ARCHAEOLOGICAL SITE

(Map p434; adult/child €6/3; ⊙ 8am-4pm Wed-Mon) It's hard to fully grasp the former magnificence of this ancient sanctuary of the goddess Hera, 4km west of Pythagorio, from these scattered ruins. The 'Sacred Way', once flanked by thousands of marble statues, led from the city to this World Heritage–listed site, built at Hera's legendary birthplace. However, enough survives to provide a glimpse of a sanctuary that was four times larger than the Parthenon.

Built in the 6th century BC, the Heraion was constructed over an earlier Mycenaean temple. Plundering and earthquakes have left only one column standing, though extensive foundations remain. Other remains include a stoa (long colonnaded building), a 5th-century Christian basilica, and the headless, and unsettling, statues of a family, the Geneleos Group. Archaeologists continue to unearth treasures.

★ Hotel Restaurant Cohyli   HOTEL €

(Map p434; ☑ 6977809389, 22730 95282; www.hotel-cohyli.com; Ireon; r incl breakfast from €43; 🅿 ❄ 🗟) You'll sleep and eat well at this welcoming hotel-taverna gem. Rooms are cosy and clean, and equipped with fridges and fans. When you're hungry, just relocate to the shaded courtyard next door to sample excellent mezedhes, *saganaki* (fried cheese), fresh fish and breakfast with 'sunshine eggs'. There's a small beach across the road, and live acoustic music many summer evenings.

WORTH A TRIP

SOUTHERN SAMOS

Driving west of Pythagorio, you enter a sparsely populated, beautiful mountainous terrain, dotted with just a few quaint fishing ports and the single fully fledged beach resort of Votsalakia. Up in the mountains, road signs point to beekeepers' huts, where the superlative but inexpensive Samian honey is on sale. But before you leave the coastal plain, make a detour to the celebrated archaeological site of the I Ieraion (p438), where ancient Samiots worshipped the goddess Hera.

Further west, the road starts climbing into the highlands, where mass tourism has had hardly any effect on the traditional life of mountain villages. Stop at the village of Spatharei for sweeping sea views and lunch at the quirky **Shall We Go to Anna's?** (Map p434; ☑ 22730 42141; Spatharei; €7-10; ⊙ 9.30am-late), and look out for roadside kiosks selling honey and other local products as you drive further on beyond **Pyrgos**.

After **Ormos Marathokambou**, the road starts to descend to a cluster of tourist villages, the most crowded of them being **Votsalakia** (often called Kampos), with its long, sandy beach. To escape the midsummer mob, head 3km further west to the more tranquil **Psili Ammos Beach** or **Limnionas**; stay the night in domatia here and sample the fresh fish at the beach tavernas. The latter can be combined with some great snorkelling if you venture west of Limnionas towards **Tavern at the End of the World** (Map p434; ☑ 6977664437; Limnionas; €8-15; ⊙ 10am-8pm mid-May–Sep; ☎), an aptly far-flung establishment.

Past Kampos, the rugged western route, undeveloped and tranquil, skirts **Mt Kerkis** (1434m) until reaching the villages of **Kallithea** and **Drakeï**, where the road abruptly ends. A walking trail is the only link between this point and **Potami** on the north coast.

Hikers keen on exploring the flanks of Mt Kerkis, or even reaching its peak, should ask in Votsalakia for the trailhead, which passes the convent of Evangelistrias on the way.

Northern Samos

Northern Samos is a wonderful mix of stunning sea and mountain scenery, marble gravel beaches and quirky villages favoured as a base by local and foreign artisans. The relatively remote (hence uncrowded) Potami Beach (p440) is the area's crown jewel, especially as it is a short trek away from waterfalls and pools of cool crystal water beneath the thick canopy of a broadleaf forest. Two more excellent secluded beaches can be reached by trekking from Potami.

Kokkari & Mountain Villages

From Vathy, the coast road west passes a number of beaches and resorts. The first, **Kokkari** (10km from Vathy), was once a fishing village, but is now a rather crowded resort. Windsurfers test the waves from its long pebble beach in summer, and the nearby beaches of **Limanaki** (Map p434), Tsamadou (p440), **Tsambou** and **Livadhaki** draw swimmers and sunbathers.

Continuing west, the landscape becomes more forested and mountainous. Take the left-hand turn-off after 5km to reach the lovely mountain village of **Vourliotes**. The village's multicoloured, shuttered houses cluster around a *plateia* (square). Walkers can enjoy an 8km loop trail between Vourliotes and Kokkari through olive groves and lofty woodlands – it's one of those magical *monopati* (footpath) routes where you hardly realise you've been climbing. Find the free walking map in Vourliotes.

Back on the coast road, look for the signposted turn-off for another fragrant village, **Manolates**, 5km further up the lower slopes of Mt Ambelos (Karvouni; 1150m). Set amid thick pine and deciduous forests, and boasting gorgeous traditional houses, Manolates is nearly encircled by mountains and offers a cooler alternative to the sweltering coast. The village is home to a fledgling artisan community, and has some excellent jewellery and souvenir shops.

Good tavernas are plentiful and, despite the more touristy patina of Manolates, both it and Vourliotes are worth visiting for a glimpse of old Samos.

Around Karlovasi

The coast road continues west from Vathy through flowery **Agios Konstantinos** before coming to workaday **Karlovasi**, Samos' third port, home to several hotels and tavernas. **Rhenia Tours** (☑22730 62280; Karlovasi; ☺May-Oct) is good for ferry tickets and reliable information. The town's blue-collar history is on display at the **Karlovasi Folk Art Museum** (Map p434; ☑22730 62286; Karlovasi; ☺9am-1pm Tue-Sun) FREE. Once in the port, wander around and admire multiple **street art** (Karlovasi Port Area; Map p434) objects – the legacy of a 2017 project to enliven this slightly dilapidated area. The old village, **Palio Karlovasi**, above the port is well worth the short drive up the hill. From the small car park, a 500m walk brings you to the chapel of **Agia Triada**, which has panoramic views.

Just 3km beyond Karlovasi lies the sand-and-pebble Potami Beach. It's complemented by nearby **forest waterfalls**; head west 50m from the beach and look for the signpost on the left. Entering the forest you'll first encounter the centuries-old **Metamorfosis Sotiros chapel**, where the devout light candles. Continuing about 1.5km through the wooded trail along the river brings you to a river channel, where you must wade or swim before enjoying a splash under the 2m-high waterfalls. Wooden stairs going up from the canyon will bring you to the excellent Archontissa Potami Adventure Cafe. After Potami, the coastal road becomes a dirt track and a popular trail veers off towards the scenic beaches **Mikro Seitani** and **Megalo Seitani**.

🏃 Activities

★ Potami Beach
BEACH
(Map p434) This long, tranquil beach of marble gravel and crystal-clear water in the mouth of a mountain river is one of the island's most attractive; its beach bar is one of the best, too. Trekking up the river, you'll reach a chain of waterfalls and pools, as well as a taverna hidden in the woods.

Megalo Seitani Trek
TREKKING
(Map p434) This medium-difficulty trail branches off the main road about 1km west of Potami Beach. It follows a rugged pine-covered coastline towards the charming little cove of Micro Seitani and then continues to the long sandy beach of Megalo Seitani. It takes around two hours to reach the latter, with sweeping vistas at every step. Take water and snacks.

Tsamadou
BEACH
(Map p434) Flanked by dramatic limestone cliffs, this attractive beach is famed for its clear water and a remarkable view – with

Chios and bits of the Turkish coast covering the entire horizon, it seems as if you're inside a Santorini-like giant volcanic caldera.

🛌 Sleeping

Pension Mary's House
PENSION €
(Map p434; ☑22730 93291; www.marys-house-samos.com; Vourliotes; d/tr €60/70; ❉ 🕸) Superb location in the village, with amazing balcony views, decent furnishings, and a lovely garden and orchard setting. Follow the painted wooden signs 200m from the village square.

Hesperia Hotel
APARTMENT €
(Map p434; ☑22730 30706; www.hesperiahotel.gr; Karlovasi; studios/apt from €45/60; P ❉ 🕸) Run by a friendly family, these spotless apartments across from the beach get rave reviews from loyal returning guests. It's close to the ferry port.

Kalidon Beach Hotel
HOTEL €€
(☑22730 92605; http://kalidon.gr/beach; Kokkari; d incl breakfast from €85; ❉ 🕸) A comfortable, friendly hotel with rooms set away from Kokkari's main road. Breakfasts are served on a terrace and the beach is seconds away.

Virginia Apartments
APARTMENT €€
(☑22730 92274, 210 777 5239; www.virginia.gr; apt from €130; ❉ 🕸) On Tarsanas Beach in Kokkari, these three elegant and tastefully furnished two-room apartments are completely outfitted with modern amenities, and balcony views of the small harbour and the Aegean beyond.

Kokkari Beach Hotel
HOTEL €€
(☑22730 92263; www.kokkaribeach.com; Kokkari; s/d/tr incl breakfast €70/80/90; P ❉ 🕸 ⛱) This striking upmarket establishment, 1km west of the bus stop, is set back from the road in a pastel-green-and-blue building, just opposite the beach. The airy and cool rooms are equally colourful.

🍴 Eating

Archontissa Potami Adventure Cafe
GREEK €
(Map p434; www.facebook.com/pg/ArchontissaPotamiWaterfalls; Potami; mains €8-10; ☺lunch & dinner) Its called Adventure for good reason: trekking along the creek before climbing wooden stairs on a near-vertical slope is indeed just that. But this canopy-level terrace is good enough reason to do the Potami waterfall hike. It has great food (try the goat ribs) and a fridge full of very cold drinks that you will desperately need.

Loukas Taverna
TAVERNA €

(Map p434; Manolates; mains €5-8; ☺ lunch & dinner) Upon entering Manolates you'll see signs, one after the other, pointing the way to this traditional eatery above the village. Proud owner Manolis serves up excellent and hearty taverna standards along with his own wines – red, white and sweet.

Café Bar Cavos
CAFE €

(☑ 22730 92426; Kokkari; mains €6-12; ☺ 9am-midnight; ☎) An efficient and comfortable Kokkari harbour bar, serving good breakfasts, afternoon snacks, fresh juices and evening cocktails. Decent prices, plus free wifi and satellite TV for big sports events. Ask about Uli's homemade cake of the day.

Kallisti Taverna
TAVERNA €

(Map p434; ☑ 22730 94661; Manolates; mains €6-9; ☺ 10am-11pm) This intriguing taverna on the square has numerous excellent dishes and unusual desserts.

★ Hippy's Restaurant Café
TAVERNA €€

(Map p434; ☑ 22730 33796, 6976770021; Potami Beach; mains €7-15; ☺ 9.30am-9pm; P ☎) This cool open-air cafe-bar is a family affair, combining Greek and South Seas decor with jazz, reggae, classical, trip-hop and ambient sounds. Good omelettes, pasta, grilled fresh fish and skewers are served, as well as owner Apolstolis' naturally fermented wine and assorted drinks and juices. The place has a relaxing, rambling end-of-the-road feel.

AAA Restaurant
GREEK €€

(☑ 22730 94472; www.aaasamos.com; Agios Konstantinos; mains €8-14; ☺ 2pm-11pm; ☎) Having relocated from Manolates to the main coastal road right at the turn to the village, this large restaurant offers a refined and somewhat urban take on traditional Greek cuisine. Try the slowly cooked *kleftiko* lamb.

Sophia's Place
MEZEDHES €€

(☑ 22730 92561; Kokkari; mains €6.50-14; ☺ 11am-11pm) Excellent tiny three-table gem, with superb small plates and charming service from Sophia and friends.

O Tarsanas Restaurant
TAVERNA €€

(☑ 22730 92337; Kokkari; mains €8-15; ☺ 5pm-midnight; ☎) Named for Kokkari's old boat-building area, this authentic old-style Greek taverna – nothing more, nothing less – does great pizzas and *mousakas*. Welcoming owner Kyriakos rolls out luscious dolmadhes and pours his own homemade wine.

Pera Vrysi
TAVERNA €€

(Map p434; Vourliotes; mains €6.50-14; ☺ 10am-midnight Tue-Sun) This old-style Samian taverna by the spring at Vourliotes' entrance offers exceptional village cuisine in ample portions, and homemade barrel wine.

🛍 Shopping

Kerannymi
JEWELLERY

(Map p434; ☑ 22730 94801; www.facebook.com/pg/kerannymi; Manolates; ☺ 9am-6pm) A duo or – as they call it – an alloy of female artists, Alek Lindus and Maria Karavatou produce mesmerisingly beautiful, prehistoric-looking jewellery that fuses silver with various mineral and organic materials. You can find them at work in their shop in the village square.

Genesis Pottery Shop
CERAMICS

(Map p434; Manolates; ☺ varies) Come to watch Giorgos spinning his wheel and making beauty out of mud. The main shop is in the main street between the car park and main square.

ℹ Getting There & Away

Karlovasi is the island's second port with connections to Ikaria, Fourni, other northeastern Aegean Islands and Turkey. Ferry tickets are available from local branches of **By Ship Travel** (☑ 22730 35252; Karlovasi; ☺ 8am-9.30pm) or Rhenia Tours (p440). Daily buses ply the route between Vathy and Karlovasi (one hour), stopping at Kokkari (20 minutes).

CHIOS
ΧΙΟΣ

POP 51,930

While no Greek island is like another, Chios has one of the most distinctive faces, thanks to the unique fortress-like architecture of its villages that makes them look so different from their sugar-cube cousins on other islands. That style stems from the island's history as the ancestral home of shipping barons and the world's only commercial producer of mastic. Many of these unusual heritage buildings now serve as hotels, bringing Chios into the top league of unusual accommodation.

The island's terrain ranges from lonesome mountain crags in the north, to the citrus-grove estates of Kampos near the island's port capital in the centre, to the fertile Mastihohoria in the south, where generations of mastic growers have turned their villages into decorative art gems.

The intriguing, little-visited satellite islands of Psara and Inousses share Chios' legacy of maritime greatness.

Chios

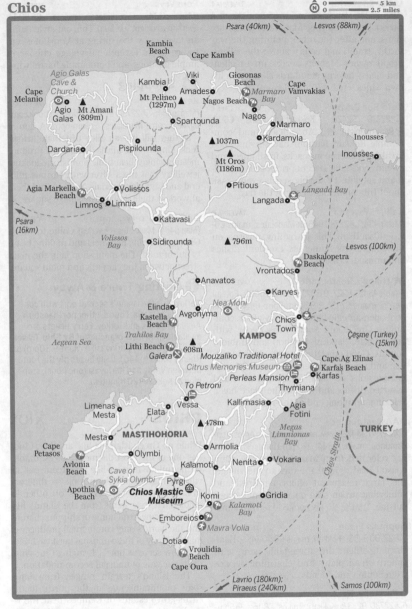

History

As with neighbours Samos and Lesvos, geographic proximity to Turkey has brought Chios both great success and great tragedy. Under the Ottomans, Chios' monopolistic production of mastic – the sultan's favourite gum – brought Chians wealth and privilege.

However, during the 1821–29 War of Independence, thousands of Chians were slaughtered by Ottoman troops.

In 1922, a military campaign launched from Chios to reclaim lands with Greek-majority populations in Asia Minor ended disastrously, as waves of refugees from Asia Minor flooded

Chios and neighbouring islands. The following year saw the 'population exchange', in which two million ethnic Greeks and Turks were forced to return to their homelands.

ⓘ Information

Check out www.chios.gr/en, a very comprehensive online guide to Chios run by the local branch of the Department of Tourism.

ⓘ Getting There & Away

Chios is connected by air and also enjoys regular boat connections throughout the northeastern Aegean Islands. Between them, the ports of Chios Town in the east and Volissos in the northwest offer regular ferries to the satellite islands of Psara and Inousses, and to the lively Turkish coastal resorts just across the water.

AIR

During summer, **Aegean Air** (www.aegeanair.com), **Sky Express** (www.skyexpress.gr) and **Astra Airlines** (www.astra-airlines.gr) serve Athens and surrounding islands.

The airport is 4km from Chios Town. It is served by three buses a day departing from the **local bus station** (Map p444; ☑ 22710 22079; https://chioscitybus.gr; Plateia Vounaki; 1.50); an airport taxi costs €8.

BOAT

There are always a couple of boats moored and being loaded in the busy Chios port, which in addition to island and Greek mainland connections, links Chios with the Turkish port of Çeşme.

Up to three boats daily sail east for Piraeus (€34.50, eight to 18 hours) or north for Lesvos (€21, 2¾ hours). There are four boats a week heading for ports in Samos (€14, 3¼ hours) and Ikaria (€18.50, 5½ to 7½ hours). Kavala (€35.50, 10¼ hours) on the Macedonian mainland is served by three boats a week, going via Limnos (€24.50, seven hours).

Smaller daily local ferries provide connection with nearby islands of Inousses and Psara (€6, three hours). Additionally, *Nissos Samos* calls at these two on the way to Piraeus on Tuesdays.

Once a week, the smallish port of Chios Mesta wakes up to greet *Express Pegasus* heading for Sigri (€21, 2½ hours) on Lesvos and Agios Efstratios (€25, five hours).

In addition to regular ferry service to nearby Inousses, daily **water taxis** (☑ 6944168104, 6945361281; Langada) travel between Langada and Inousses (€65; shared between up to eight passengers).

Buy ferry tickets in Chios Town from Sunrise Tours (p421) or **Michalakis Travel** (☑ 22710 40070; Kanari 9; ☺ 8am-10.30pm).

ⓘ Getting Around

BUS

Chios Town's waterfront **long-distance bus station** (Map p444; ☑ 22710 27507; Neorion) is well organised, and has a cafe and coin lockers. On working days, green buses depart from here to Pyrgi (€3.10, three daily), Mesta (€4.30, three daily), Lithi Beach (€3.60, two daily), Kardamyla (€3.60, two daily) and Langada (€2, two daily). There are three buses a week serving Volissos (€4.90).

Blue city buses on Plateia Vounaki (Vounakiou Sq) also serve nearby Karfas Beach (€1.50, four daily), just south of Chios Town, and Vrontados (€1.50, six daily), just north of town. Schedules are posted at both the local bus station (p443) and the long-distance bus station.

CAR & MOTORCYCLE

Smack in the middle of the waterfront promenade, the slick **Travelshop** (☑ 22710 81500, 6934517141; www.travel-shop.gr; Leoforos Egeou 56; ☺ 8am-9pm) has a good choice of budget vehicles, jeeps and convertibles.

TAXI

Taxis are plentiful in Chios Town; red taxis serve Chios Town only, and grey taxis are good for the rest of the island. Sample costs from Chios Town: Chios Airport (€8), Emporios (€40), Langada (€20), Mesta (€45) and Pyrgi (€30).

Chios Town   Χίος

POP 23,710

On the central east coast, Chios' main port and capital is home to almost half the island's inhabitants. Unlike smaller island capitals, it has a distinct urban feel. Behind the busy port area lies a quieter, intriguing old quarter, where some traditional Turkish houses and an old *hammam* (Turkish bathhouse (p445)) stand enclosed by the walls of a Genoese castle. There's also a busy market area behind the waterfront, and spacious public gardens (Vounaki) where an open-air cinema operates on summer evenings. The nearest decent beach is popular **Karfas**, 6km south.

◉ Sights

★**Korais Library &**
Philip Argenti Museum   MUSEUM

(Map p444; ☑ 22710 44246; www.koraeslibrary.gr; Korai 3; €2; ☺ 7am-3pm Mon-Sat) On the upper floor of the Korais Library, the Philip Argenti Museum contains a 19th-century birthing chair, along with shepherds' tools, embroidery, traditional costumes and portraits of the wealthy Argenti family. The place is a

Chios Town

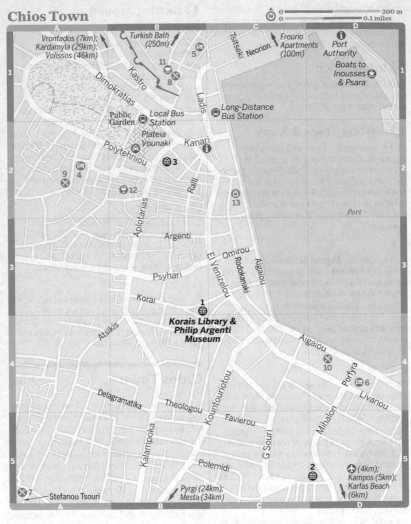

NORTHEASTERN AEGEAN ISLANDS CHIOS TOWN

Chios Town

touching tribute to Greek cultural renaissance figure Adamantios Korais, who set up the library in 1792 and replenished it after the massacre of Chios. Philip Argenti was a French-born benefactor and researcher of Chian history. The library holds medicinal texts from the 15th century.

Turkish Bath
HISTORIC BUILDING

(☑ 22710 44238; Navarchou Nikodimou 1; ☉ 8.30am-4pm Wed-Mon) **FREE** With its bubble-like cupolas pierced to let in gentle shafts of light, this classic early-18th-century *hammam* was built as a charitable institution by the Ottomans for the Turkish population of the *kastro* (castle). After the Turks were expelled in 1922, the building fell into disrepair, but was restored as a museum in 2011. Sadly, it no longer performs its original function.

Archaeological Museum
MUSEUM

(Map p444; ☑ 22710 44239; Mihalon 10; €2; ☉ 8.30am-4pm Wed-Mon) Along with prehistoric and Archaic treasures from the excavations of the British School at Emporios, this collection includes impressive Neolithic and Classical finds (coins, sculptures and pottery) from Agios Galas and Fana.

Byzantine Museum
MUSEUM

(Map p444; ☑ 22710 26866; Plateia Vounaki; €4; ☉ 8.30am-4pm Wed-Mon) Housed in a 19th-century Ottoman mosque, the Medjitie Djami, this museum contains relics from the Byzantine, post-Byzantine, Genoese and Islamic periods, including old cannons, fine icons, and Jewish, Muslim and Armenian tombstones.

🛏 Sleeping

There's a good selection of hotels in Chios Town, but those on the waterfront can be noisy. The *kastro* area is the quietest part of the centre.

Porta di Marina
APARTMENT €

(Map p444; ☑ 6948077911; Zachariou 4-6; apt €60; ❈ ☎) What were once the actual gates of the Genovese-built castle now contain two large and fully equipped apartments, complete with a washing machine and a bathtub – a delight for those who have been on the road for some time. The place is a short walk from the port, but very quiet at night.

Frourio Apartments
APARTMENT €

(☑ 22710 42476, 6945408464; www.chiosfrourio.gr; Kalothetou 10; s/d/tr/q from €50/60/70/80; ❈ ☎) After the hustle and bustle of traffic-filled Chios Town, it is a pleasure to find yourself in the serene neighbourhood inside the *kastro*, where the greatest noise is produced by singing canaries and church bells. There's enough equipment in the large modern apartments to sustain a nuclear winter. Crucially, that includes a washing machine.

Rooms Alex
PENSION €

(Map p444; ☑ 6979535256; roomsalex@hotmail.gr; Livanou 29; r €30) Host and former sea captain Alex Stoupas' handmade model ships decorate each of the simple but clean rooms here. The *kapetanios* (captain) is '100% helpful', as he'll happily tell you; he picks up guests from the ferry and speaks English, French and Spanish.

★ Homeric Poems
APARTMENT €€

(Map p444; ☑ 6907339239; Kontoleontos 3; d/tr €80/90; ❈ ☎) Two studios in a late-19th-century captain's house are furnished as a fancy boutique hotel, with comfy beds, couches and too many multicoloured pillows to count. Bric-a-brac and myriad jars filled with fragrances make the place feel like a curiosity shop from a children's movie and the magician-like owner, Angelika, adds to the effect.

🍴 Eating

Although filled with Turkish day-trippers, waterfront tavernas are not necessarily tourist traps. Better places hide away from the main action. A little square at the beginning of Frourio inside the *kastro* is a particularly nice and peaceful spot to enjoy a meal.

Pastards
ITALIAN €

(Map p444; ☑ 22710 81466; Livanou 13; mains €7-10; ☉ 1pm-1am; ☎) In a welcome departure from the island-taverna routine, this place serves homemade pastas, risottos and risonis, all with a strong locavore element, featuring items such as various types of Greek cheese and *loukanika* (pork sausages). Chios beer and good local wine are also on offer.

Kafenes
TAVERNA €

(Map p444; ☑ 22710 42242; Agiou Georgiou Frouriou 12; mains €5-8; ☉ 10am-midnight; ☎) In a cute little square within the castle walls, this welcoming and efficient taverna receives a batch of fresh catch from the port in the morning and proceeds from there. Try the salted lakedra fish, the owner's speciality.

Hotzas Taverna
TAVERNA €

(Map p444; ☑ 22710 42787; Kondyli 3; mains €5.50-9; ☉ 7pm-midnight; ☎ ☑) This comfortable, attractive taverna above Chios Town serves fine Greek standards with a twist, such as lamb kebab with yoghurt and rocket; white beans with tomato and mandarin; and dolmadhes with lemon. There's a variety of great veggie dishes, including risotto. Everything is *herisia* (handmade), from the pasta to the dessert.

⭐**Kechribari Ouzerie**　　　GREEK €€
(Map p444; ☑6942425459; Agion Anargyron 7; set meal €15; ◷12.30-5pm) This cosy gem of an *ouzerie* offers a variety of small plates in addition to excellent fish, mussels, baked potatoes and grilled meats. The choice is between two set menus featuring meat or fish; beyond that, you don't know exactly what you'll get. But indeed that's part of the appeal. It's a 10-minute walk up from the waterfront.

Drinking & Nightlife

Civitas Dimitris Cafe　　　CAFE
(Map p444; ☑22710 81565; Frourio 1; ◷8.30am till late; 🛜) Owner Dimitris is good to have a chat with and get travel tips from. He makes fresh orange juice from blood oranges and flavours Greek coffee with mastic. Fresh lemonades and an interesting selection of Greek wines are also on offer, as is the 'mastic submarine' – a typical Chios sweet.

Kubrick　　　BAR
(Map p444; ☑22711 02744; Anelastou 14; ◷8am-4am; 🛜) It's kind of apt that a favourite bohemian hang-out in this citrus region is themed around the director of *A Clockwork Orange*. Looking sombrely from a mural on the side of a stylish wooden bar, a bearded Stanley Kubrick observes Vergina (Macedonian craft beer) taps and the island's cool kids passing their time in mellow conversations over cocktails and coffee.

🛍 Shopping

Mastihashop　　　COSMETICS
(Map p444; ☑22710 81600; www.mastihashop. com; Aigaiou 36; ◷8.30am-10pm) Efficient and attractive shop with a range of mastic-based products such as lotions, toothpastes, soaps and condiments. Ask for a sample of pure mastic to chew on.

ℹ Information

Chios Tourist Office (Map p444; ☑22713 51726; www.chios.gr; Kanari 18; ◷7am-3pm & 6-10pm) Island transport and accommodation info, plus an assortment of brochures advertising local travel-related businesses.

　Port Authority (Map p444; ☑22710 44432; Neorion)

ℹ Getting There & Away

Chios Town is the island's main transport hub (p443), where boats arrive and planes land. Buses depart for destinations around the island from the long-distance bus station (p443) near the port. The local bus station (p443) in Plateia Vounaki serves destinations in the large suburban area of Kampos. Taxis are available for hire at the **taxi rank** (Map p444; ☑22710 41111; Plateia Vounaki) nearby.

Northern Chios

Northern Chios is rocky and sparsely populated, compared with the agricultural south. A string of fishing villages, with picturesque ports and fish tavernas, lines the northeastern coast. On the western side, the scenic Volissos and Avgonyma peer into the deep blue of the Aegean from their mountaintop positions. Avgonyma's abandoned village (p447) and the sombre Nea monastery (p447) serve as reminders of the 1822 massacre – the greatest catastrophe the island has ever experienced.

👁 Sights

Roughly 4km north of Chios Town, **Vrontados** is the site of Homer's legendary stone chair, the **Daskalopetra** (in Greek, 'teacher's stone'), a rock pinnacle near the sea that's an obvious choice for holding class.

Further north, **Langada** is a relaxed cove of pine trees, homes, domatia and tavernas, and a launching point for water taxis to nearby Inousses.

The main villages of **Marmaro** and **Kardamyla** follow as you head north, containing the ancestral homes of many wealthy ship-owning families. At **Nagos**, the road continues northwest, skirting **Mt Pelineo** (1297m), then winding its way through **Kambia**, high on a ridge overlooking the sea. In the northwest, wild camping is allowed around **Agio Galas**, also home to Agio Galas Cave (p447), the island's largest, if not the most impressive.

A road leading west from Chios Town will bring you to **Avgonyma**, a scenic mountaintop village and convenient base for exploring desolate historic sites – including the 'ghost village' of Anavatos (p447), and the tragic Nea Moni (p447) monastery – that witnessed some of the most catastrophic events in the island's history.

North of Avgonyma lies **Volissos**, Homer's legendary birthplace, now crowned with the

WORTH A TRIP

INOUSSES, THE TYCOON HIDEAWAY

Just northeast of Chios Town, serene Inousses is the ancestral home of nearly a third of Greece's shipping barons (the *arhontes*), whose wealthy descendants return here annually for summer vacations from their homes overseas. Their desire to keep the island for themselves partly explains the scarcity of accommodation on the island.

Inousses was settled in 1750 by ship-owning families from Kardamyla in northeastern Chios, some of whom amassed huge fortunes during the 19th and early 20th centuries. Traces of this history linger in Inousses' grand mansions and the ornate family tombs of the **Mausoleum of Inousses** (Nekrotafion Inousson; Inousses), high above the sea in the leafy courtyard of **Agia Paraskevi Church**.

Although Inousses is little visited, it does get lively in summer, with an open-air cinema, friendly residents and a buzzing night-time waterfront. The island's port attests to its seafaring identity. Arriving by ferry, you'll see a small, green, sculpted mermaid watching over the harbour. In the port, the striking statue of Mitera Inoussiotissa (Mother of Inoussa), a village woman waving goodbye to seafaring men, is incredibly photogenic at sunset.

The island's main attraction, the **Nautical Museum of Inousses** (☎22710 55182, 6973412474; Stefanou Tsouri 20; €2; ⊙9am-1pm) showcases the collection of local shipping magnate Antonis Lemos. Many of the models on display (some intentionally half-completed then set flush against a mirror so that you 'see' the whole vessel) were made by French prisoners of war during the Napoleonic Wars. There's also a swashbuckling collection of 18th-century muskets and sabres, a WWII-era US Navy diving helmet, a hand crank from a 19th-century lighthouse, and paintings of Nazi submarines attacking Greek sailing vessels.

Inconveniently for travellers (but conveniently for locals), the daily Inousses ferry (€5, one hour) leaves Chios Town in the afternoon and returns early next morning. You can construct a day trip with the help of a large ferry, *Nissos Samos,* that calls at both islands in the evening once a week.

In July and August, agencies such as Sunrise Tours (p421) run day trips to Inousses out of Chios Town (€20 to €50), which is how most people come to the island. Otherwise you can use water taxis (p443) out of Langada or consider staying overnight. The latter is easier said than done: the only reliable accommodation option is – quite aptly – a luxurious shipowner's villa and three cheaper flats that go under the collective brand of **Evgenikon** (www.evgenikon.com; Inousses; villa €150 plus €50 cleaning fee; ☎). You'll have to commit to a three-night stay.

---

impressive ruins of its hilltop Genoese fort. Down below, the tiny port of **Limnia** is flanked by a couple of pretty coves with pebble beaches. It has a few tavernas and domatia.

Driving 5km northeast will get you to **Moni Agias Markellas**, named for Chios' patron saint. From Volissos the coastal road continues south until **Elinda**, then heads eastward towards Chios Town.

Anavatos   VILLAGE
At the end of a silent stretch of road that branches off the main road near Avgonyma, this solemn site serves as a reminder of the island's brutal history. The abandoned village of grey-stone houses and narrow stepped pathways is perched on a precipitous cliff over which villagers hurled themselves to avoid capture during Turkish reprisals in 1822. Nowadays, it's referred to as the 'ghost village'.

Agio Galas Cave & Church   CAVE
(Map p442; ☎22740 22004; admission €5) Only a small section of the island's largest cave is accessible, but the main reason to drive all the way to the northern tip of Chios is the 12th-century cave church of Agio Galas just above the official cave entrance. Local woodcarvers populated the exquisite wooden altar with whimsical creatures barely compatible with Christian doctrine – mermaids, dragons and a character reminiscent of Dionysos, all of them looking heavily pregnant, even the dragons.

There are no specific hours, but the family that operates it is always around.

Nea Moni   MONASTERY
(New Monastery; Map p442; ⊙9am-1pm & 4-7pm) FREE At the island's centre, Nea Moni is a World Heritage–listed 11th-century Byzantine monastery. Once one of Greece's richest

WORTH A TRIP

PSARA, ISLAND OF HEROES

Celebrated Psara is one of maritime Greece's true oddities. A tiny speck in the sea 16km northwest of Chios, this island of scrub vegetation, wandering goats and weird red-rock formations has one settlement (also called Psara), a remote monastery and pristine beaches.

Psara looms inordinately large in modern lore. The Psariot clans became wealthy through shipping, and their participation in the 1821–29 War of Independence is etched into modern Greek history, particularly the daring exploits of Konstantinos Kanaris (1793–1877), whose heroic stature propelled him, six times, to the position of prime minister.

Kanaris' most famous operation occurred on the night of 6 June 1822. In revenge for Turkish massacres on Chios, the Psariots destroyed the Turkish admiral's flagship while the unsuspecting enemy was holding a postmassacre celebration. Kanaris' forces detonated the ship's powder keg, blowing up 2000 sailors and the admiral himself. However, as on Chios, their involvement sparked a brutal Ottoman reprisal, assisted by Egyptian and French mercenaries, that decimated the island in 1824.

Psara village is tucked within a long bay on the island's southwest. When you disembark the ferry, you can't miss the jagged **Mavri Rachi**, or 'Black Shoulder', the rock from which thousands of Psariots are said to have hurled themselves during the 1824 Ottoman assault.

In the centre of Psara village is the **Monument to Konstantinos Kanaris**, where Greeks honour their national hero; he's actually buried in Athens while his heart is kept in the Naval Museum in Piraeus. The hyperphotogenic wall of a ruined Ottoman-era mansion on the waterfront looks like a stone version of Edvard Munch's *The Scream*, or a web-chat emoticon.

Psara's main cultural attraction, the **Monastery of Kimisis Theotokou**, 12km north of town, is a smallish chapel surrounded by protective walls; it contains rare hieratic scripts from Mt Athos and a sacred icon that is paraded through the village on the night of 4 August. In all, there are 67 chapels across the island, each cared for by a local family.

There are only a couple of domatia on the island, the better one being **Studios Psara** (☏ 22740 61386; Psara; studios €50; ❄ ☎) at the back of the village. For a truly romantic sunset dinner, head to the old quarantine building on the far side of the quay, which now houses the excellent **Spitalia** (☏ 22740 61377; Katsounis Beach, Psara; €7-12; ☉ lunch & dinner).

The incongruous *Psara Glory* leaves Chios Town in the late afternoon on working days and returns early next morning (€12 return, three hours). The larger *Express Pegasus* frequently calls at Psara on the way to Limnos and the mainland port of Lavrio, or as it returns to Chios.

monasteries, it attracted pre-eminent Byzantine artists to create the mosaics in its *katholikon* (principal church). Disastrously, during the Greek War of Independence (1821–29), the Turks torched the monastery and massacred its monks. Their skulls are now kept in a glass cabinet inside a chapel to the left of the main entrance.

Another catastrophe occurred in 1881 when an earthquake demolished the *katholikon* dome. Nea Moni is now a convent.

🛏 Sleeping

Avgonyma is perhaps the most romantic place to overnight in northern Chios. You'll find domatia in Volissos, Langada and Kardamyla.

Spitakia   APARTMENT €
(☏ 22710 81200; missetzi@spitakia.gr; Avgonyma; r from €45; ℗ ❄ ☎) These traditional studios and cottages, spread across a striking village of medieval stone houses surrounded by olive and pine forests, feature modern kitchenettes and sublime sea views.

Zorbas Apartments   PENSION €
(☏ 6936775999, 22740 21436; www.chioszorbas.gr; Limnia; d/q €50/60; ❄ ☎) Well-furnished, if slightly fading, sea-facing apartments are equipped with kitchenettes and are spacious enough to keep an elephant inside – especially the two-storey quadruples intended for families. Excellent breakfasts cost an extra €8 per person, and the owner, Yannis Zorbas, leads undemanding hikes to Volissos castle and adjacent beaches.

Eating

⭐ Taverna Fabrika
TAVERNA €

(☎ 6976255829, 22740 22045; fabrika_chios@yahoo.com; mains €6-8.50; ⊙ lunch & dinner; ℗) This cheerful traditional eatery nestled in the trees of Volissos occupies a century-old olive-and-flour mill, where some of the vintage equipment is displayed. Serves excellent grills, *mayirefta* and good barrel wine and desserts. Above the taverna are six handsome rooms, with fireplaces and wi-fi (triples €50).

El Sueño
GREEK €

(☎ 22740 22122; Limnos Beach; €7-11; ⊙ 10am-11pm) Veering from the taverna mainstream, this beach cafe features a good variety of salads and unusual appetisers, such as spicy mussels with beer and ginger, as well as standard Greek seafood and meat dishes.

⭐ Pyrgos
TAVERNA €€

(☎ 22710 42175; www.chiospyrgosrooms.gr; Avgonyma; mains €8-15; ⊙ breakfast, lunch & dinner) Excellent setting, service and food. This traditional hilltop stone taverna serves up superb mezedhes plus spit-roasted lamb and pork. Upstairs are five classy rooms (from €40) with names such as Mary, Irene and Ben.

ⓘ Getting There & Away

Don't rely on buses for any travel beyond Langada. Services are extremely infrequent. The best way to enjoy this part of the island is by car or bike.

Southern Chios

Southern Chios' mastic- and citrus-growing villages are easily the most important reason to visit the island. Though it does grow elsewhere in the Aegean, the mastic tree of Chios has for centuries been the sole commercial producer of mastic gum. The tree thrives in a fertile, reddish territory known as the Mastihohoria (mastic villages). This region of rolling hills, criss-crossed with elaborate stone walls running through olive and mastic groves, is highly atmospheric. The stunning medieval villages, each uniquely designed, were built as fortresses protecting farmers from invaders and pirates. There is more defensive architecture in the maze-like suburbs on the southern outskirts of Chios Town, where rich citrus growers have been building their summer residences amidst orange-tree orchards since the 14th century. A few of these mansions have now been converted into atmospheric hotels.

⊙ Sights

⊙ Mastihohoria

As you drive south out of Chios Town, you'll immediately find yourself in the barely navigable stone-wall maze of **Kampos**. Behind those forbidding walls hide lush citrus orchards and lavish mansion houses where wealthy Genoese and Greek merchant families summered from the 14th century onwards. Some of them are now converted into atmospheric boutique hotels, while others are crumbling. The nearby **Karfas Beach**, also the nearest to Chios Town, is OK for a swim, but has a bit of a dreary urban feel.

The sun-dried hills further south are covered in mastic plantations, which gave the island its fame and determined its at-times tragic plight. The sad and dramatic story of mastic production in Chios is recognised in the Chios Mastic Museum, halfway between Pyrgi and **Emborios**, which was the Mastihohoria's port back when mastic producers were high rollers.

Today Emborios is much quieter, though it does have Mavra Volia Beach (p450), named for its black volcanic pebbles. Domatia and tavernas are available, and the archaeological ruins of an early Bronze Age temple to Athena are signed nearby. About 3.5km north, **Komi** is a larger but fairly laid-back tourist village that comes with a long sandy beach and a good restaurant scene, which only springs to life in the summer months.

The west-coast workaday port of **Limenas Mesta** (also called Limenas) is home to a couple of decent port tavernas and is a short drive from Mesta (p450). It sees an occasional ferry heading for Sigri in Lesvos and Agios Efstratios. Around 3km southeast of Mesta, **Olymbi** is a mastic-producing village characterised by its defensive architecture, similar to that of Mesta. A well-maintained 3km trail connects Olymbi and Mesta. A side trip takes you 5km south to the splendid Cave of Sykia Olymbi (p450), signposted as 'Olympi Cave'.

Some 10km north of Pyrgi, **Vessa** is another fortress village that hasn't really found itself on the tourist trail, although it has a couple of well-appointed domatia. Another 7km north, the port of **Lithi** has a nice sandy beach with sunbeds and several quality tavernas.

⭐ Chios Mastic Museum
MUSEUM

(Map p442; ☎ 22710 72212; www.piop.gr; Rachi Site; regular/concession €4/2; ⊙ 10am-6pm Wed-Mon, to 5pm winter) Brave new architecture arrives in Chios in the form of this airy hilltop structure that casts a curious glance on mastic gardens and ancient stone houses in the valley below, like a prodigious urban teenager on a visit to the land of their ancestors. The state-of-the-art museum narrates the sad and moving story of mastic production through a succession of images and sounds, including heartbreaking songs about mastic 'tears', which is what the farmers dubbed the fruits of their toil.

The museum has its own mastic garden and a good souvenir shop. It's located halfway between Pyrgi and Mavro Volia Beach.

Citrus Memories Museum   MUSEUM
(Map p442; ☑ 22710 31513; www.citrus-chios.gr; Kampos; ☉ 10am-9pm Jun-Sep, to 6pm Oct-May) FREE This museum has attractive and well-signed historical displays of Kampos-area citrus, the Chian mandarin in particular. Also has a shaded courtyard cafe with – *voila!* – fresh orange juice.

Cave of Sykia Olymbi   CAVE
(Map p442; ☑ 22710 93364; €5; ☉ 11am-6pm May-Nov) This 150-million-year-old cavern was discovered accidentally in 1985. It's 57m deep and filled with multicoloured stalactites and other rock formations that have whimsical names such as the Pipe Organ, Cacti and Jellyfish.

The cave is illuminated with floodlights, and connected via a series of platforms and staircases – be prepared for some climbing. A steady temperature of 18°C is maintained, and humidity is a moist 95%. Guided tours are mandatory and run every 30 minutes.

◉ Pyrgi & Mesta

The Ottoman rulers' penchant for mastic made the Mastihohoria (mastic villages) wealthy for centuries. Some architectural wonders remain in the Pyrgi and Mesta.

The Mastihohoria's largest village, **Pyrgi** (24km southwest of Chios Town) looks like a magic jewellery box, with its facades decorated in intricate grey-and-white patterns, some geometric and others based on flowers, leaves and animals. The technique, called *xysta,* uses equal amounts of cement, volcanic sand and lime as well as bent forks and a fine eye.

Pyrgi's central square is flanked by tavernas, shops and the little 12th-century **Church of Agios Apostolos** (Pyrgi; ☉ 8am-3pm Tue-Sun). East of the square, note the house with a plaque attesting to its former occupant – one Christopher Columbus, who

was also a fan of mastic gum, though he apparently preferred it as a sealant in boat construction. Should you wish to stay, the castle-like apartments at Mastiha House offer fantastic value for money.

Mesta, 9.5km from Pyrgi, is a truly memorable village, and one of Greece's most unusual. Its appealing stone alleyways, intertwined with flowers and intricate balconies, are completely enclosed by thick defensive walls – the work of Chios' former Genoese rulers, who built this fortress town in the 14th century to keep out pirates and would-be invaders. It's an ingenious example of medieval defensive architecture, featuring a double set of walls, four gates and a pentagonal structure, with the larger of the impressive **Churches of the Taxiarhes** (Mesta) at the centre. Mesta's rooftops are interconnected, and if you have the right guide you can actually walk across the entire town this way. You can have one of Mesta's stone houses for yourself for a few nights: Medieval Castle Suites is one of several operators. To remind yourself that the residents of these fortified villages are actually farmers, drop by Despina Karavella to stock up on fruit and vegetable preserves, as well as homemade booze.

A car-free village, this is a relaxing and romantic place where children can run around safely. Mesta also makes a good base for hill-walking, exploring southern beaches and caves, and participating in cultural and ecotourism activities.

🏃 Activities & Tours

Mavra Volia   BEACH
(Map p442; Emborios) Shaped as a perfect crescent, the island's most celebrated beach is made of stark black pebbles, giving it a darkly mysterious look. There are no facilities, except a kiosk selling drinks. A couple of ancient ruins in the vicinity draw archaeology buffs.

★ Masticulture
Ecotourism Activities   ECOTOUR
(☑ 22710 76084, 6976113007; www.masticulture. com; tours from €18) ⬤ To participate in traditional cultural activities such as Chian farming, contact Vassilis and Roula, who provide unique ecotourism opportunities that introduce visitors to the local community, its history and culture. Activities include mastic-cultivation tours, stargazing, and bicycle and sea-kayak outings. They can help find area accommodation and offer tips for visiting nearby Psara Island.

🛏 Sleeping

⭐**Mastiha House** PENSION €

(📞6944604870, 22710 72900; www.mastiha house.gr; Pyrgi; d/tr €54/67; ❄🛜) Kaliopi, a fluent English-speaker, runs these tastefully designed, luxurious castle-like apartments. All have sky-high ceilings, balconies facing a narrow street of Pyrgi's trademark painted stone houses, and kitchenettes – crucially equipped with a blender for making frappés.

To Petroni GUESTHOUSE €

(Map p442; 📞22710 73320; Vessa; r from €40; ❄🛜) Ultimate rural getaway in a traditional house resembling a castle tower, with vaulted ceilings and Gothic windows in well-appointed rooms. Breakfast (€6) is served in the garden. The village taverna is nearby, and the popular Lithi Beach is a short drive away.

⭐**Medieval Castle Suites** ACCOMMODATION SERVICES €€

(📞22710 76025; www.medievalcastlesuites.com; Mesta; d/tr from €95/120; ❄🛜) Castle Suites is a collection of 20 rooms spread throughout the village, all with traditional stone touches and modern bathrooms; a few have fireplaces and even computers. Rooms vary considerably in size and proximity to the square.

Mouzaliko Traditional Hotel GUESTHOUSE €€

(Map p442; 📞6974057299, 22710 31624; http:// mouzalikohotel.gr; Zanis & Marias Chalkousi 52, Kampos; r incl breakfast €50-80; ❄🛜) If you wonder what might be hiding behind the tall stone walls of Kampos, here's your chance to find out. Rooms in this typically introverted stone mansion all face the handsome courtyard, where the Greek–Quebecoise owners serve hearty breakfasts with honey buns. A citrus version of a Chekhovian cherry orchard, also inside the enclosure, adds to the idyll.

Perleas Mansion HISTORIC HOTEL €€

(Map p442; 📞22710 32217; www.perleas.gr; Vitiadou, Kampos; s/d/tr incl breakfast from €103/ 117/144; P❄🛜) The restored Perleas Mansion offers seven elegant well-appointed apartments, and a restaurant serving traditional Greek cuisine. The relaxing estate, built in 1640, exemplifies high Genoese architecture.

🍴 Eating

The **Galera** beach taverna (Map p442; 📞22710 73285; Lithi; €5-10; ⏰9am-midnight; 🛜) in Lithi marries Greek and Italian rural standards, with seafood spaghetti a definite highlight. Pizza made with Greek salad ingredients is also pretty delightful.

🛍 Shopping

Drop by **Despina Karavella** (📞22710 76065, 6977353451; Mesta; ⏰9am-7pm), a gem of a shop in Mesta, to taste homemade sweet wine and *tsipouro* or stock up on spoon sweet preserves made from citrus types you've likely never heard of. A couple of suites upstairs go for €50 to €60 per night.

ℹ Getting There & Away

From Mesta and Pyrgi there are three buses daily to Chios Town. English-speaking Dimitris Kokkinos provides a **taxi** (📞6972543543) service. Sample fares from Mesta: Chios Town (€45), Olymbi (€5) and Pyrgi (€20).

LESVOS ΛΕΣΒΟΣ

POP 86,436

Greece's third-largest island (and one of the best organised), Lesvos is marked by long sweeps of rugged desert-like western plains that give way to sandy beaches and salt marshes in the centre. To the east are thickly forested mountains and dense olive groves – around 11 million olive trees are cultivated here.

The port and capital, Mytilini Town, is a lively place year-round, filled with exemplary *ouzeries* and reasonable accommodation, while the north-coast town of Molyvos (aka Mithymna) is an aesthetic treat, with old stone houses clustered on winding lanes overlooking the sea. The island's therapeutic hot springs gush with some of the warmest mineral waters in Europe.

Despite its undeniable tourist appeal, Lesvos' chief livelihood is agriculture. Its olive oil is highly regarded, and the island's farmers produce around half the ouzo sold worldwide.

History

Lesvos' great cultural legacy stretches from the 7th-century-BC musical composer Terpander to 20th-century figures such as Nobel Prize–winning poet Odysseus Elytis and primitive painter Theophilos. Ancient philosophers Aristotle and Epicurus also led a philosophical academy here. Most famous, however, is Sappho, one of Ancient Greece's greatest poets. Her sensuous, passionate poetry has fuelled a modern-day following and draws lesbians from around the world to the village of Skala Eresou, where she was born (c 630 BC).

Lesvos (Mytilini)

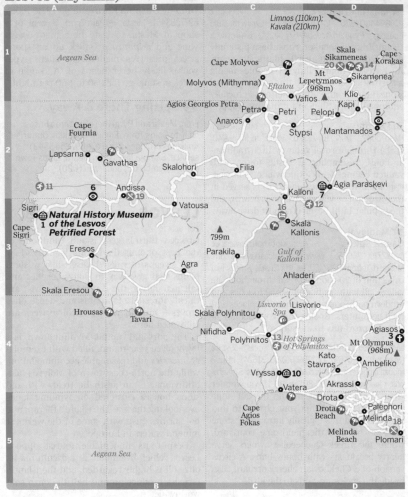

ℹ Getting There & Away

AIR

The **airport** (Mitiline Airport; Map p452; ☎ 22510 61212, 22510 38700; www.mjt-airport.gr/en) is 8km south of Mytilini Town. A taxi to town costs €10 and a bus €1.60.

Aegean Airlines (https://en.aegeanair.com), **Olympic Air** (www.olympicair.com), **Sky Express** (www.skyexpress.gr), **Astra Airlines** (www.astra-airlines.gr) and **Air Minoan** (www.minoanair.com/en) all have offices at the airport. Mytilini Town travel agents also sell tickets.

BOAT

Mytilini is a busy port with frequent connections to the Greek mainland as well as Ayvalyk in Turkey.

Up to three boats daily head for Piraeus (€38.50, 11¼ hours) via Chios (€21, 3¼ hours). Services to Kavala (€30.50, seven hours) via Limnos (€21, four hours) run three days a week. Four boats a week depart for ports located on Samos (€19.50, 5¼ hours) and Ikaria (€24, eight hours).

The smallish southern port of Sigri, 27km from Skala Eresou, comes to life once a week, when *Nissos Chios* sets off for Piraeus (€20, 7½ hours) via the equally obscure port of Mesta on Chios (€21, 2½ hours).

In Mytilini Town, buy ferry tickets from Mitilene Tours (p421) and Tsolos Travel (p421).

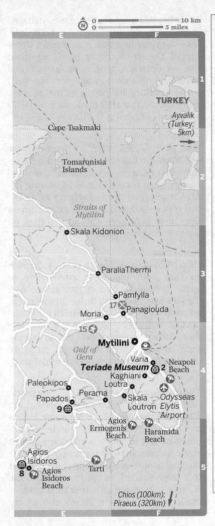

Lesvos (Mytilini)

ℹ Getting Around

BUS

Mytilini Town's **long-distance bus station** (KTEL; ☎ 22510 28873; www.ktel-lesvou.gr; El Venizelou) is near Agias Irinis Park. From here buses depart for Molyvos, Eresou and other popular destinations around the island. Services are typically reduced to one per day on Saturdays and there are none at all on Sundays. Uniquely for this island group, the local branch of the national bus operator runs a website where you can check routes and schedules, at www.ktel-lesvou.gr.

Destinations include: Agiasos (€3.20, 45 minutes, three daily), Molyvos via Petra (€7.50, 1½ hours, two daily), Plomari (€5, 1¼ hours, three daily), Sigri (€11.40, 2½ hours, two weekly), Skala Eresou via Eresos (€11.20, 2½ hours, two daily) and Vatera via Polyhnitos (€6.80, 1½ hours, two daily).

CAR & MOTORCYCLE

Local companies **Discover Rent-a-Car** (☎ 22510 20391, 6936057676; www.discover1.gr; Aristarhou 1; ⊗ 8am-10pm) and **Billy's Rentals** (☎ 22510 20006, 6944759716; www.billys-rent acar.com; Pavlou Kountourioti 87; ⊗ 7.30am-10pm) have newish cars and flexible service. Billy's also has motorbikes. In Molyvos, hire vehicles from **Kosmos Rent-a-Car** (☎ 22530 71710; www.lesvosrentals.com; ⊗ 8am-8.30pm).

Mytilini Town

POP 29,650

Lesvos' port and capital, Mytilini is a lively student town with great eating and drinking options, plus eclectic churches and grand 19th-century mansions and museums. Its remarkable, world-class Teriade Museum boasts paintings by Picasso, Chagall and Matisse, along with home-grown painter Theophilos. The island is known in equal parts for its poets and painters and for its olive oil and ouzo.

Ferries dock at the northeastern end of the curving waterfront thoroughfare, Pavlou Kountourioti, where most of the action is centred. Handmade ceramics, jewellery and traditional products are sold on and around the main shopping street Ermou, and there are many fine *ouzeries* and student-filled bars to enjoy.

◉ Sights & Activities

The small olive-groved peninsula south of Mytilini has several attractions. Following the coast road 7km south, opposite the airport (p452) you'll find the long, pebbled **Neapoli Beach**; it hosts a few chilled-out beach bars, popular with students, and usually pulsates with reggae and Greek sounds.

Around 9km further south, the peninsula wraps around to the popular sand-and-pebble **Agios Ermogenis Beach**, and **Haramida Beach**, which has toilets and showers under pine trees on the bluff above the beach.

★ Teriade Museum   MUSEUM

(Map p452; ☑ 22510 23372; http://museumteriade. gr; Varia; €3; ⊗ 9am-2pm Tue-Sun) Extraordinary. It's worth coming to Lesvos for this alone – the museum and its astonishing collection of paintings by artists including Picasso, Chagall, Miró, Le Corbusier and Matisse. The museum honours the Lesvos-born artist and critic Stratis Eleftheriadis, who brought the work of primitive painter Theophilos to international attention. Located in Varia, 4km south of Mytilini.

Fortress   FORTRESS

(Kastro; Map p455; €2; ⊗ 8.30am-4pm Wed-Mon) Mytilini's imposing early-Byzantine fortress was renovated in the 14th century by Genoese overlord Francisco Gatelouzo, and then the Turks enlarged it again. Flanked by pine trees, it's popular for a stroll, with some good views included.

Theophilos Museum   MUSEUM

(Map p452; ☑ 22510 41644; Varia; €3; ⊗ 8.30am-2.30pm Mon-Fri) On the same site as the Teriade Museum, this humble structure contains 86 paintings by the primitive painter Theophilos, who remains a folk hero among Greek literati. During his life he barely scratched out an existence, moving frequently and painting coffeehouse walls for his daily bread, depicting the people he met at work and at play. A year after his death in 1934, his work was exhibited at the Louvre.

Archaeological Museum   MUSEUM

(Map p455; ☑ 22510 40223; 8 Noemvriou; €4; ⊗ 8.30am-4pm Wed-Mon) This handsome refurbished museum, about 500m above the eastern quay, portrays island life during Roman times, from the 2nd century BC to the 3rd century AD, and features extraordinary floor mosaics. You can walk around these on a protective glass surface.

Yeni Tzami   MOSQUE

(Map p455) This early-19th-century Turkish mosque, with crumbling atmosphere to spare, is near the end of Ermou, where a Turkish market used to thrive. In front of it, a little boat with a Smyrna (Greek for Izmir) port of registration sign is a touching memorial to millions who were forced to leave their homes for good in the epic exchange of populations between Greece and Turkey in 1923.

Therma Spa   HOT SPRINGS

(Map p452; http://thermaspalesvos.com/en; Km 7 Mytilini–Kalloni Rd; €8; ⊗ 9am-9pm) Hikers and cyclists can give their muscles a well-deserved rest at this renovated spa, which now combines an old Ottoman-styled indoor thermal pool with a new open-air pool next to a large sundeck facing the Bay of Gera. A range of massage and other treatments is available (€20 to €40). There's also an on-site cafe.

🛏 Sleeping

Mytilini is filled with hotels that will suit any budget.

★ Theofilos Paradise
Boutique Hotel   BOUTIQUE HOTEL €€

(Map p455; ☑ 22510 43300; www.theofilospara dise.gr; Skra 7; s/d incl breakfast from €84/112, ste from €130; 🅿 ❈ @ ᠅ ≋) This smartly restored 100-year-old mansion is elegant and good value, with modern amenities and a traditional *hammam*. The 22 swanky rooms (plus two luxe suites) are spread among three adjacent buildings surrounding an inviting courtyard.

Mytilini Town

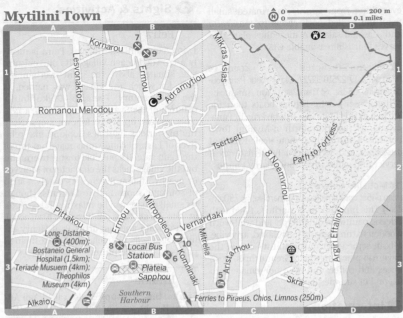

Mytilini Town

◎ Sights
1 Archaeological Museum C3
2 Fortress D1
3 Yeni Tzami B1

◎ Sleeping
4 Hotel Lesvion A3
5 Theofilos Paradise Boutique Hotel C3

◎ Eating
6 Cafe P B3
7 O Ermis B1
8 Taverna Kalnterimi B3
9 To Kastro B1

◎ Drinking & Nightlife
10 Mousiko Kafenio B3

Hotel Lesvion   HOTEL €€
(Map p455; ☑ 22510 28177; www.lesvion.gr; Pavlou Kountourioti 27a; s/d incl breakfast €47/67; ❋ ❧) The modern and well-positioned Lesvion, smack on the harbour, has reasonable service and attractive spacious rooms, some with excellent port-view balconies. A breakfast bar overlooks the harbour.

✕ Eating & Drinking

To Kastro   GREEK €
(Map p455; ☑ 6974925921; Ermou 326; mains €6-10; ◷ 10am-2am) Owner George spent a large part of his life in the Netherlands and, more importantly, he's also a magician. He'll probably show you a trick or two while serving excellent mezedhes and mouth-watering meatballs.

Cafe P   CAFE €
(Map p455; ☑ 22510 55594; Samou 2; mains €3-7; ◷ 11am-3am; ❧) This hip back-alley bistro

draws a crowd mostly from the university for its unusual and well-priced small plates, slight menu, eclectic music mix and all-round chilled atmosphere. Sauteed shrimps, served with a draught beer, cost around €8. Cheap daily specials, too. It's about 50m in from Plateia Sapphou (Sappho Sq). Look for a sign with the single Greek letter 'Π'.

O Ermis   TAVERNA €
(Map p455; cnr Kornarou & Ermou; mezedhes €5-9; ◷ 10am-midnight) This no-frills taverna began life in 1800 as a cafe in the Turkish quarter, as its traditional decor reveals in faded bits and pieces. It offers good Macedonian and Limnos wines, along with generous plates of Greek kitchen standbys.

Taverna Kalnterimi   TAVERNA €
(Map p455; ☑ 22510 46577; cnr Ermou & Thasou; mains €7-10; ◷ 11am-midnight; ❧) This reliable cafe between Ermou and the waterfront has

everything from *gavros* (marinated small fish) and grilled pork chops to *mayirefta* and seasonal salads. A mezedhes plate that serves four is a reasonable €15.

★ **Taverna Efkaliptos** SEAFOOD €€
(Map p452; ☑ 22510 32727; Old Harbour, Panagiouda; mains €8-18; ⊙ 11am-2am) You might be sitting closer to the fishing boats than the kitchen at this first-class fish taverna in Panagiouda; it's just 4km north of Mytilini Town but has a distinctly remote feel. Excellent mezedhes and well-priced fresh fish, great service and white wine from nearby Limnos.

★ **Mousiko Kafenio** CAFE
(Map p455; cnr Komninaki & Vernardaki; ⊙ 7.30am-2am) This hip student favourite is filled with eclectic paintings, old mirrors and well-worn wooden fixtures, giving it a relaxed, arty vibe. Mix in some great music and it's one of the most fun places in town. Great drinks, fresh juices and coffee, and even homemade iced tea on hot summer days.

❶ Information

Mitilene Tours (p421) Full-service agency on the east side of the port. Helps with accommodation, car rentals, and trips and tours to Turkey.

Tsolos Travel (p421) Full-service agency on the south side of the port. Sells ferry tickets to Turkey.

Zoumboulis Tours (☑ 22510 37755; Pavlou Kountourioti 69; ⊙ 8am-8pm) Sells ferry and air tickets, and runs boat trips to Turkey.

❶ Getting There & Away

The airport (p452) is 8km south along the coast.

Mytilini is the island's main port, with connections to other northeastern Aegean Islands and Piraeus (Athens).

Mytilini's **local bus station** (KTEL; Map p455; ☑ 22510 46436; Pavlou Kountourioti), near Plateia Sapphou, serves in-town destinations and nearby Loutra, Skala Loutron and Tahiarhis.

The long-distance bus station (p453) is beside Irinis Park, near the domed church.

The **taxi rank** (Map p455) is on the western side of Plateia Sapphou.

Northern Lesvos

Home to rolling hills covered in pine and olive trees, peaceful beaches and the aesthetically harmonious town of Molyvos (also called Mithymna), northern Lesvos offers both solitude and low-key resort action. Traditional seaside hot springs and intriguing Byzantine monasteries round out the region's offerings.

◉ Sights & Activities

◉ Petra

Lying 5km south of Molyvos, Petra is mostly a crowded beach village. Its one cultural site, situated above the giant overhanging rock for which the village was named, is the 18th-century **Panagia Glykofilousa** (Church of the Sweet-Kissing Virgin), accessible on foot up 114 rock-hewn steps. Note the mysterious figurines, looking like relatives of Easter Island stone heads, on top of the main gate. It's possible to stay overnight, but the village lacks the character of Molyvos or nearby Eftalou Beach – it's barely a strip of souvenir shops and restaurants, though its small square can be relaxing. Take a look at the **First Kiss Gallery** (⊙ 10am-noon), where local Canadian artist Paul Henry exhibits and sells his melancholic sea-themed papier-mâché sculptures.

◉ Eftalou

Eftalou Beach (Map p452; also called Agii Anargyri Beach), 2km northeast of Petra, is the place for solitude seekers. Backed by a cliff, the serene, narrow pebbled beach has pristine waters and also boasts the charming Mineral Baths of Eftalou. Beyond the baths, the beachfront **Hrysi Akti** (Map p452; ☑ 22530 71879; Eftalou Beach; s/d €30/35; ❋ 🔊) offers simple rooms with bathrooms in an idyllic pebbled cove, complete with the friendly owners' small restaurant overlooking the sea.

The vintage Ottoman bathhouse **Mineral Baths of Eftalou** (Map p452; ☑ 22530 71245; Eftalou Beach; group/private bathhouse €4/6; ⊙ 10am-6pm) is a traditional bathhouse on the beach at Eftalou, with clear, cathartic 46.5°C (and higher!) water temperatures. It is filled with mesmerising shafts of light piercing through the perforated cupola; an adjacent 20th-century bathhouse has private bathtubs. The springs are said to treat various ailments, from arthritis to hypertension.

◉ Skala Sikameneas & Around

From Eftalou (p456), a coastal road continues for 9.5km to Skala Sikameneas, an exceedingly pretty fishing port with some domatia and two popular tavernas, including I Mouria tou Mirivili (p457). Both eating options specialise in *astakomakaronadha* (fresh lobster with pasta). If these are overrun by day-trippers from Molyvos, take a walk to To Kyma, also on the seafront, some 800m west of the port. Just before the taverna, a signposted trail begins the ascent to the port's parent village of Sikamenea, connecting to a circular trekking route that will take you to the nearby village of Lepetymnos and back to Sikamenea in about three hours.

The nearest beach, Kagia (Map p452), is a short walk away from the port. Follow the trail cutting through the headland on the eastern side of the port. A large shady garden of Poseidon (Kagia Beach; Map p452; ☑ 22530 55370; Paralia Kagias; €7-13; ⊙ lunch & dinner) taverna provides escape from blistering midday sun. If you wish to stay at Skala Sikameneas, Gorgona (Map p452; ☑ 22530 55301; www.gorgona hotel.gr; Skala Sikameneas; d from €46; ❋ 🖤) is a good option right by the port.

At Sikamenea, the main road from Molyvos turns south towards Mantamados, home to Moni Taxiarhon monastery. Further south, Agia Paraskevi houses the excellent Museum of Industrial Olive Oil Production (Map p452; ☑ 22530 32300; www.piop.gr; Agia Paraskevi; regular/concession €4/2; ⊙ 10am-6pm Wed-Mon Mar-Oct, to 5pm Nov-Feb).

Around 36km north of Mytilini Town, near Mantamados village, stands one of Lesvos' most important pilgrimage sites. An axis of Orthodoxy, myth and militarism, the grand 17th-century Moni Taxiarhon (Map p452; ⊙ 8am-dusk) **FREE** says much about the blatant lack of separation between State and Church in Greece – note the fighter plane parked out the front, reminding the faithful that the Archangel Michael is the patron saint of the Hellenic Air Force.

🍴 Eating

To Kyma GREEK €
(Map p452; ☑ 22530 55302; Skala Sikameneas; €7-10; ⊙ 8am-late; 🖤) Some 800m along the beach from Skala Sikameneas, this friendly taverna serves freshly caught fish, grilled meat and excellent vegetables. Nice spot for sunset watching.

Restaurant Hrysi Akti TAVERNA €
(Map p452; ☑ 22530 71947; Eftalou Beach; mains from €5-8; ⊙ 8am-late; 🖤) Excellent taverna fare, fresh fish and tasty grills overlooking the beach; part of the Hrysi Akti domatia.

I Mouria tou Mirivili TAVERNA €€
(Map p452; ☑ 22530 55319; Skala Sikameneas; €8-16; ⊙ 10am-midnight; 🖤) People flock here for lobster spaghetti, but this vast taverna with tables in the shade of a mulberry tree offers an extensive list of seafood delicacies as well as great veggie snacks.

ℹ Getting There & Away

Two to three daily buses connect Molyvos with Mytilini Town (€7.50, 1½ hours). A bus runs six times a day between Petra, Molyvos and Eftalou.

Molyvos Μόλυμβος

POP 1500

Molyvos, also known as Mithymna, is a well-preserved Ottoman-era town of narrow cobbled lanes and stone houses with jutting wooden balconies wreathed in flowers, overlooking a sparkling pebble beach below. Its grand 14th-century Byzantine castle, some good nearby beaches and its north-central island location make it a great launch pad from which to explore Lesvos.

◉ Sights & Activities

Beach-lovers can take an excursion boat for Skala Sikameneas village (10km) and nearby Eftalou (from €20, 10.30am daily). It's also possible to hike one way and catch the excursion boat back to Molyvos. Sunset cruises are available. Enquire at the portside Faonas Travel Agency (☑ 22530 71630; tekes@ otenet.gr), inside the Sea Horse Hotel (p458), or Lesvorama (☑ 22530 72291; www.lesvorama. gr; ⊙ 9am-10pm) on the main road.

Byzantine-Genoese Castle CASTLE
(☑ 22530 71803; €2; ⊙ 8.30am-4pm Wed-Mon) This handsome 14th-century castle stands guard above Molyvos. A steep climb is repaid by sweeping views over the town and sea – even across to Turkey, shimmering on the horizon. In summer the castle hosts several festivals.

Stratis Boat Trips BOATING
(☑ 6974837055; www.facebook.com/stratkab; cruises per 2/4 people €50/80) Friendly bike-riding Stratis Kapanas captains the *Escape,* a caïque that makes for a sweet three-hour coastal cruise for up to four people, with stops for lunch and swimming. Look for his boat in front of the Sea Horse Hotel (p458) and Grand Bleu restaurant at the Old Port.

🛏 Sleeping

⭐ Nadia Apartments & Studios PENSION €
(☑ 2253071345; www.apartmentsnadia-molivos.com; studio/apt €38/53; ❋ 🖤) On the road to Sikamenea and a short walk from the Old Town, these large motel-styled rooms surrounding an expansive shady courtyard are owned by the organised Nadia. Her trademark cakes are complimentary. It's open all year.

Molyvos Queen Apartments
APARTMENT €

(☑ 22530 71452; www.molyvos-queen.gr; d/tr €40/50; ❄ 🛜) Fully equipped apartments perch on the hill that offer all the mod cons, plus sea and castle views. It's located at the top of the village on the way to the castle (p457).

Lela's Studios
APARTMENT €

(☑ 6942928224, 22530 71285; www.eftalou olivegrove.com/lelas_studios.htm; studios from €40; ❄ 🛜) Two handsome studios are set in a courtyard of roses and geraniums. Each comes with a fully outfitted kitchen and sunset sea views from a relaxing stone veranda. It's located above the junction of the main road and Agora.

Marina's House
PENSION €

(☑ 22530 71470; dimouks@yahoo.com; r €45; ❄ 🛜) Look for the geraniums climbing the steps of this well-managed pension 50m from the port. Rooms are spotless, bright and have small sea-facing balconies over the main road. Marina's husband, Kostas, paints icons for village shops.

Sea Horse Hotel
HOTEL €€

(☑ 22530 71630; www.seahorse-hotel.com; s/d incl breakfast from €60/65; P ❄ 🛜) In the heart of the port area, you'll find these modern and comfortable rooms, all with balconies overlooking the harbour, along with the family's restaurant and travel agency. Three family-friendly studios have kitchenettes and partial sea views.

Amfitriti Hotel
HOTEL €€

(☑ 22530 71741; www.amfitriti-hotel.com; s/d/tr from €45/65/80; P ❄ 🛜 🖵) Just 50m from the beach, this well-managed traditional stone hotel has modern tiled rooms and a large garden pool. Staff is friendly and helpful, and the hotel's quiet location is a plus.

Eating

⭐ Misirlou
INTERNATIONAL €

(☑ 22530 72388; Molyvos Harbour; mains €6-11; ☉ 1pm-midnight; 🛜) A new American-run place above the marina, Misirlou serves delicious tortilla wraps, burgers and pizzas – all using fresh local produce. In the evening, it turns into a stylish cocktail bar with an exemplary musical soundtrack.

⭐ Betty's
TAVERNA €

(☑ 22530 71421; 17 Noemvriou; mains €8; ☉ 9am-3pm & 6pm-late) This restored Turkish pasha's residence on the upper street, overlooking the harbour, offers a tasty variety of excellent *mayirefta* dishes such as *mousakas* (meat or veggie), baked fish and lamb souvlaki, plus tasty breakfast specials. Betty also has two spacious and well-appointed studio apartments occupying a quiet and shady corner near the restaurant.

Alonia
TAVERNA €

(mains €5-10; ☉ lunch & dinner) Locals swear by this unpretentious spot just outside of town, on the road to Eftalou Beach. It has a convivial atmosphere and serves up fresh fish, Greek salads and local wine.

Maistrali
TAVERNA €€

(☑ 22530 72160; Molyvos Harbour; mains €6-15; ☉ lunch & dinner) You can't eat much closer to the water than at this cosy traditional taverna at the harbour, below Molly's Bar (p458). Roula is the owner, cook and server of well-prepared Greek standards such as *mayirefta*, along with good draught wine.

🍷 Drinking & Nightlife

⭐ Molly's Bar
BAR

(☑ 22530 71772; ☉ 6pm-late; 🛜) With its painted blue stars, beaded curtains and bottles of Guinness, this whimsical British-run bar on the harbour waterfront's far eastern side is always in shipshape condition. Molly's caters to a lively local, international and expat crowd. The small balcony is perfect at sunset.

ℹ Information

Molyvos Tourism Association (☑ 22510 71990; www.theotheraegean.com; Agora; ☉ 8am-3pm) Tourist office on upper Agora, near the pharmacy.

ℹ Getting There & Away

At least one to two buses daily connect Molyvos with Mytilini Town (€7.50, 1½ hours).

Western Lesvos

Western Lesvos was formed by massive, primeval volcanic eruptions that fossilised trees and all other living things, making it an intriguing site for prehistoric-treasure hunters. Its striking bare landscape, broken only by craggy boulders and the occasional olive tree, is dramatically different from that of the rest of Lesvos. Heading far to the southwest, however, a grassier landscape emerges, leading to the coastal village of Skala Eresou, birthplace of one of Greece's most famous lyric poets, Sappho, who was dubbed the 10th Muse by Plato.

⊙ Sights

Heading west from Skala Kallonis towards Sigri, a stark and ancient volcanic landscape awaits, home to the scattered remains of a **petrified forest**. A fascinating and rare monument of geological heritage, the forest is a product of intense volcanic activity in the northern Aegean during the Miocene period. Sadly, the main visitors' area in the centre of this Unesco-nominated geopark was off limits at the time of research, due to acute underfunding. Check its current status with the museum (p459) in Sigri, which has a little patch of the forest in its premises.

Sleepy **Sigri** is a fishing port, with narrow streets lined with pretty whitewashed houses descending towards an impressive Ottoman **castle**. The village has beautiful sea views, especially at sunset. The excellent sand and gravel **Faneromeni Beach** (Map p452) is 4km from the village.

Coming back from Sigri, stop for lunch or coffee at **Andissa**, a jovial, rustic village of narrow streets kept cool by the two enormous plane trees that stand over its square. Listen to the banter of old-timers over a Greek coffee or frappé. Don't leave before trying the spoon sweets at To Kati Allo.

★**Natural History Museum
of the Lesvos Petrified Forest** MUSEUM
(Map p452; ☑22530 54434; www.lesvosmuseum. gr; Sigri; €5; ☉9am-5pm Jul-Sep, 8.30am-4.30pm Oct-Jun; P) This fascinating state-of-the-art museum chronicles what a volcano can do at a moment's notice – in this case 20 million years ago. Don't miss the interesting film and short verbal presentation. Well-signed exhibits and – crucially – the museum's own patch of the petrified forest transport visitors to when violent volcanic explosions discharged rapid flows of extremely hot ash and rock, covering the dense forest of western Lesvos, including trees, branches, root systems, leaves and fruits.

What followed – hot fluids rich in pyrite, rising from molten magma – perfectly fossilised plant fibres. This process involved the molecule-by-molecule replacement of organic plant matter with inorganic matter. Today's petrified forest reveals structural characteristics of plants, root systems and tree trunks exactly as they existed 20 million years ago. Among the star attractions are the giant trunks of petrified sequoia trees and tiny fossils of pistachio nuts and olive leaves.

Moni Ypsilou MONASTERY
(Moni Agiou Ioannou Theologou; Map p452; ☉dawn-dusk) **FREE** About 9km west of Andissa, the Byzantine Moni Ypsilou stands atop a solitary peak surrounded by volcanic plains. Founded in the 8th century, this storied place includes a flowering arched courtyard and a small but spectacular museum with antique icons and Byzantine manuscripts. From the top of the monastery walls, you can gaze out over the desolate ochre plains stretched out against the sea.

🛏 Sleeping & Eating

Pasiphae Hotel HOTEL €
(Map p452; ☑22530 23212; www.pasiphae.gr; Skala Kallonis; s/d incl breakfast from €40/45;

NORTHEASTERN AEGEAN ISLANDS WESTERN LESVOS

WORTH A TRIP

BIRDWATCHING

Just south of agricultural Kalloni, coastal **Skala Kallonis** turns from sleepy fishing village to birdwatching mecca every spring and autumn. During the spring migration, unrivalled across Europe, Lesvos' wetland reserves become home to more than 130 species of bird, from flamingos and raptors to woodpeckers and marsh sandpipers. It's a spectacular show that has grabbed the attention of European birdwatchers, who flock to the island during the peak viewing season of mid-April to mid-May, and again from mid-September to October. Skala Kallonis shares the enthusiasm, with the Pasiphae Hotel serving as an unofficial centre, where birdwatchers gather to compare notes (or brag) at the lobby bar. Bring your binoculars.

Nonexperts may find it worth stopping by a **watchtower** (Map p452) just off the Mytilini road on the outskirts of Kalloni to admire the flocks of flamingos that populate salt pans in springtime.

If you can't tell the difference between a blue-eyed hawker dragonfly and a crested grebe, pick up Steve Dudley's *A Birdwatching Guide to Lesvos*. Steve leads birdwatching tours around the island. There are also 50 species of butterfly and dragonfly flitting about, as well as marsh frogs filling the air with their croaky crooning.

P ✳ @ 🛜 🛁) A well-managed and welcoming hotel in a shady setting at Skala Kallonis, about 300m from the sea and village square. It's a favourite for returning visitors, including the birdwatchers who gather at the lobby bar to compare notes in spring and autumn. Managed by the informative Vasillis Vogiatzis, with exceptional service and spotless rooms.

To Kati Allo
CAFE €

(Something Different; Map p452; Andissa; spoon sweets €1-2, mains €6-10; ⊙ 7am-1am) Sweet in every sense of the word, this cafe in the main square of Andissa is a wonderful place to stop for a cup of Greek coffee with a spoon sweet – a piece of caramelised seasonal fruit or vegetables, from figs to cherry tomatoes and even aubergines. Traditional taverna food is also on offer.

🚍 Getting There & Away

One or two daily buses connect Skala Eresou and Sigri with Mytilini, but if you want to explore this remote part of the island, it's better to rent a car.

Skala Eresou · Σκάλα Ερεσού

POP 1560

Skala Eresou is part traditional fishing village, part laid-back bohemian beach town, and part lesbian mecca, especially during September when a lively two-week festival honours the great lyrical poet Sappho, born here in 630 BC. The small seaside community has an easy-going, end-of-the-road ambience, with little cafes and tavernas hugging the shore and wispy tamarisk trees swaying in the breeze.

◎ Sights & Activities

Near the town market, the remains of the early-Christian **Basilica of Agios Andreas** include partially intact 5th-century mosaics.

Eresos Archaeological Museum
MUSEUM

(€2; ⊙ 8.30am-3pm Tue-Sun) This is a modest museum, but the outside (and fenced) mosaics are of great interest. It is located on a quiet street in the southeastern part of the village, two blocks away from the sea.

Skala Eresou Circular Trail
TREKKING

A well-signposted 14km trail skirts the alluvial plain around Skala Eresou, climbing up to the top of Vigla hill by the quay, where the ancient acropolis of Skala Eresou once stood.

✨ Festivals & Events

The **International Eressos Women's Festival** (🖉 22530 52130; www.womensfestival.eu; tickets €30-65; ⊙ Sep) is an international event with a local atmosphere, and involves two weeks of partying. Activities range from live music, open-air cinema, Greek dancing and poetry to beach volleyball, water sports, yoga and meditation, all in a gay-friendly atmosphere under the sun and stars.

Highlights include an LGBT film festival, live Greek, Turkish and Mediterranean folk music, 4WD safaris, an alternative fashion show (with festival participants), photography workshops and tattooing demonstrations. Live performances cover comedy and spoken word to burlesque and rock 'n' roll.

🛏 Sleeping

★ Heliotopos
APARTMENT €

(🖉 6948510527; www.heliotoposeressos.gr; d/q €40/70; P ✳ 🛜) A leisurely 15-minute walk from the village, this lodging – set in a garden of palm trees – features five studios and three two-bedroom apartments, all with full kitchens. Free bikes are available for pedalling around.

★ Hotel Kyma
GUESTHOUSE €

(🖉 22530 53555; d €45; ✳ 🛜) You can almost plunge into the deep blue sea from your private balcony at this lovely guesthouse perched above the narrow beach at the eastern edge of Skala Eresou. Rooms are simple yet stylish, and sunset views are to die for.

Aumkara Apartments
APARTMENT €

(🖉 22530 53190, 6948131032; www.aumkara.eu; d/tr/q from €40/50/60; P ✳ 🛜) Smart spotless apartments near the village centre, managed by the welcoming Maria. Self-caterers will like the handy kitchenettes. Rooms range from small studios to two-bedroom apartments. About 50m from the beach.

Hotel Gallini
HOTEL €

(🖉 22530 53138; www.hotel-galinos.gr; Alkaiou; s/d incl breakfast from €40/50; P ✳ 🛜) This budget gem, about 80m back from the waterfront, has tile floors and small balconies overlooking the hillside. Breakfast, with homemade jams and cheeses, is served on the flowery veranda.

Sappho the Eresia
HOTEL €€

(Sappho Hotel; 🖉 22530 53233; www.sapphohotel.com; waterfront; s/d/tr €45/70/85; P ✳ 🛜) The friendly 18-room Sappho is what passes for a big hotel in laid-back Skala Eresou. Its modest position on the quieter west end of the beach is appealing, as are its overhead fans and an easy-going cafe-bar. The best rooms overlook the sea and the island of Psara. Breakfast is available for €8.

✖ Eating

★ **Soulatso**　　　　　　　　SEAFOOD €
(fish €6-12; ⊙ lunch & dinner) This busy beach-front *ouzerie*-taverna along the boardwalk has a large outdoor patio and specialises in fresh fish, reasonably priced by the kilo; it's also known for its excellent mezedhes. Good service, ample portions and worthy wines.

Aigaio　　　　　　　　TAVERNA €€
(Aegean; boardwalk; mains €7-13; ⊙ lunch & dinner; 🛜) Owner Theodoris spends most mornings fishing to provide the evening's fresh fish. Aigaio also serves very good *mayirefta* dishes and good grills, with traditional Greek music in the background.

🍷 Drinking & Nightlife

★ **Parasol**　　　　　　　　BAR
(☑ 22530 52050; ⊙ 9am-2am) With its orange lanterns and super-eclectic music mix, little Parasol on the waterfront does cocktails to match its South Seas decor. As the day rolls on, Christos and Anastasia's made-to-order breakfasts and cappuccinos give way to lunch specials, juices, noodles and handmade pizza.

Notia Jazz Bar　　　　　　　BAR
(Plateia Anthis) Come for the drinks and stay for the tunes at this hip music bar. There's live jazz on summer weekends. Cocktails, Greek wine and draught beer are always on offer.

❶ Information

The full-service **Sappho Travel** (☑ 22530 52130; www.sapphotravel.com; main square; ⊙ 9am-2.30pm, 6-10pm) arranges car hire and accommodation, and provides information about the International Eressos Women's Festival.

❶ Getting There & Away

One or two buses run daily between Skala Eresou and Mytilini Town (€11.20, 2½ hours).

Southern Lesvos

Interspersed groves of olive and pine trees mark southern Lesvos, from the flanks of Mt Olympus (968m), the area's highest peak, right down to the sea, where the best beaches lie. This is a hot, intensely agricultural place where the vital olive oil, wine and ouzo industries overshadow tourism.

SAPPHO

The classical Greek poet Sappho is renowned for her lyrical verse. Her words speak of passion and love for both sexes, but her emotion is balanced by clarity of language and a simple style. Though only fragments of her work remain, we do know that she married, had a daughter and was exiled for a period to Sicily, most likely for her political affiliation. Her surviving poems and love songs seem to have been addressed to an inner circle of female devotees. She was certainly an early advocate for women's voices, and hers continues to resonate.

◉ Sights

Just south of the Mytilini–Polyhnitos road, **Agiasos** is the first point of interest. On the northern side of Mt Olympus, it's a quirky, well-kept, traditional hamlet of narrow cobbled streets where fishers sell their morning catch from the back of old pick-up trucks; village elders sip Greek coffee in the local *kafeneia* (coffee houses); and cheese-makers and ceramic artisans hawk their wares. It's a relaxing, leafy place, and boasts the exceptional Church of the Panagia Vrefokratousa.

Upon reaching Polyhnitos, famous for its hot springs, the road turns directly south towards **Vatera beach** – a 10km-long stretch of sand that remains a low-key getaway destination with a couple of tavernas and a few domatias. Another road from Mytilini skirts the western shore of the Gulf of Gera before turning to **Papados,** home to the Vrana Olive-Press Museum. It continues to **Plomari**, the centre of Lesvos' ouzo industry. It's an attractive, busy, seaside village with a large palm-lined square and waterfront tavernas.

The popular beach settlement of **Agios Isidoros**, 3km east, absorbs most of Plomari's summertime guests. **Tarti**, a bit further east, is less crowded. West of Plomari, **Melinda** is a tranquil fishing village with a beach, tavernas and domatia.

Church of the Panagia Vrefokratousa　　　CHURCH
(Map p452; Agiasos) A pilgrimage site of national importance, this elegant walled-off church contains a namesake icon depicting the Virgin, which is believed to make miracles. Indeed, the recovery of a Turkish governor in 1701, attributed to the icon, relieved

the village from hefty Ottoman taxes for almost a century. On 15 August every year, the icon is taken from the church and carried around the village in a colourful procession attended by thousands of religious pilgrims.

Vrana Olive-Press Museum MUSEUM

(Map p452; ☑ 22510 82007; Papados; €1; ⊙ 9am-7pm Tue-Sun) Located in the village of Papados, between Mytilini and south-coast Plomari, this little museum showcases 19th-century steam-powered presses and vintage paintings of a bygone era. It also occupies a bit of Greek literary history – it was built by Nicholas Vranas, grandfather of Greek Nobel Prize–winning poet Odysseus Elytis.

Varvagianni Ouzo Museum MUSEUM

(Map p452; ☑ 22520 32741; www.barbayanni-ouzo. com; Plomari; ⊙ 9am-4pm Mon-Fri Apr-Oct, 10am-2pm Mon-Fri Nov-Mar, by appointment Sat & Sun) FREE Plomari is ouzo central for Greece. This museum, where the family has made ouzo for five generations, gives you the chance to tour its copper distillery and compare different ouzo tastes. When sampling ouzo, look for '100%' written on the label, indicating the quality of the distillate.

Vrisa Natural History Museum MUSEUM

(Map p452; ☑ 22520 61890; Vrisa; €1; ⊙ 9am-9pm Jun-Sep, 9.30am-3.30pm Wed-Sun Oct-May) Associated with the Museum of Palaeontology and Geology at the University of Athens, the museum displays impressive and well-signed prehistoric fossil remains from the area.

🏃 Activities

Hikers here can enjoy southern Lesvos' **olive trails**, which comprise paths and old local roads threading inland from Plomari and Melinda. The **Melinda–Paleohori trail** (1.2km, 30 minutes) follows the Selandas River for 200m before ascending to Paleohori, passing a spring with potable water along the way. The trail ends at the village's olive press.

Another appealing trail from Melinda leads to **Panagia Kryfti**, a cave church near a **hot spring** (built for two), and the nearby **Drota Beach**; or take the **Paleohori–Rahidi trail** (1km, 30 minutes), which is paved with white stone and passes springs and vineyards. Rahidi, which was only connected to electricity in 2001, has charming old houses and a coffeehouse.

Agricultural **Polyhnitos**, 10km north of Vatera on the road to Mytilini Town, is known for its two nearby hot springs, among the hottest in Europe. The more popular of the two,

the **Hot Springs of Polyhnitos** (Polyhnitos Spa; Map p452; ☑ 22520 41229, 6977592991; €4; ⊙ 2-8pm Mon-Sat, 11am-8pm Sun) are just 1.5km east of the village and has has some of Europe's warmest bath temperatures at 40°C (104°F). Rheumatism, arthritis, skin diseases and gynaecological problems are treated here, or visitors can simply enjoy a relaxing soak. While there, marvel at the psychedelically orange bed of the iron-rich stream that originates from the springs. A circular trail originating from here winds through olive groves and the lands of **Damandri monastery** with a few heritage religious buildings along the way.

🛌 Sleeping

Pano Sto Kyma PENSION €

(Map p452; ☑ 6942906124, 22520 33160; www. panostokyma.gr; Agios Isidoros; studios from €42; ❄ ⚛) Eleven sparkling-clean rooms come with wooden furniture painted in the lightest shade of blue – the same colour as the sea, just 30m from the front door. No breakfast is served, but village cafes open early and rooms come with kitchenettes.

Irini Studios APARTMENT €

(Map p452; ☑ 22520 33406; Plomari; d €45; 🅿 ❄ ⚛) A comfortable budget option across the road from Varvagianni Ouzo Museum and equidistant from the centre of Plomari and Agios Isidoros Beach; you need about 30 minutes to reach either on foot. A complimentary bottle of ouzo will greet you upon checking in.

🍴 Eating

★ **Sunset** GREEK €€

(Map p452; ☑ 22520 32740; Agios Isidoros; mains €8-16; ⊙ noon-1am) Perched above the main road, this is a fully fledged restaurant, with attentive service and a very competent chef-manager, Dimitris, whose advice about what's best on the day should be taken seriously. Beautiful sunsets are free of charge.

To Ammoudeli GREEK €€

(Map p452; Plomari seafront; mains €7-15; ⊙ noon-late) A friendly taverna perched dramatically on the edge of a near-vertical cliff. Specialities include octopus cooked in red wine, and their trademark salad with spinach, cheese and sun-dried tomatoes.

ℹ️ Getting There & Away

Buses link Plomari with Mytilini Town (€5, 1¼ hours, three daily), and Vatera with Mytilini Town (€6.80, 1½ hours, three daily).

LIMNOS ΛΗΜΝΟΣ

POP 16,700

Alone in the far northern corner of the Aegean Sea, save for neighbouring Agios Efstratios, Limnos rewards those who visit with pristine scenery unspoiled by mass tourism, superb sandy beaches, a celebrated winemaking culture and a scenic capital in the shadow of a grand Venetian castle.Its rugged and treeless western part is reminiscent of the islands much further south, while the gentle agricultural lowlands of the east feel like a piece of Macedonia thrown into the sea. There are a few notable ancient ruins to admire, more than a few flamingos to count during winter migration and a windsurfers' haunt on a distant beach (p469) for gliding on the waves.

History

Limnos is perhaps best known as being the command post of the Hellenic Air Force – the island is in an ideal position for monitoring the Straits of the Dardanelles. For this very reason the island was used as the operational base for the failed Gallipoli campaign in WWI. A moving military cemetery (p469) for fallen ANZAC (Australian and New Zealand Army Corps) soldiers remains near Moudros, where the Allied ships were based.

ⓘ Getting There & Away

AIR

The airport is 22km east of Myrina, and has offices for **Aegean Air** (www.aegeanair.com), **Sky Express** (www.skyexpress.gr) and **Astra Airlines** (www.astra-airlines.gr). Taxis to/from Myrina cost about €25.

BOAT

Limnos is the last port of call for ferries to Kavala (€16 to €27, six weekly, 4½ hours) and the first one on their way to Lesvos (€16 to €27, three weekly, six hours) and other northeastern Aegean Islands (and the last one on the way back). A helpful shortcut to Athens, four ferries a week travel to Lavrio (€31 to €38, nine hours).

Limnos provides a lifeline to its tiny neighbour, Agios Efstratios, with one or two services on working days and Saturdays (€8, 1½ hours).

Ferries depart the New Port in Myrina. Buy tickets at **Atzamis Travel** (☑ 22540 25690; atzamisk@otenet.gr; waterfront; ⊙ 8am-10pm), **Petrides Travel** (☑ 22540 22039; www.petrides travel.gr; Kyda-Karatza 116; ⊙ 8am-11pm) or **Aegean Travel** (☑ 22540 25936; www.aegeantravel. eu; waterfront), all in Myrina.

For all things Agios Efstratios, enquire at **Karaiskaki Travel** (☑ 22540 22900, 22540 22460; hrissa5a@otenet.gr; waterfront; ⊙ varies) in Myrina.

ⓘ Getting Around

BUS

Limnos' bus service has one purpose: to bring villagers to town for their morning shopping and to get them home by lunch. From Myrina, buses serve Moudros, via the airport (€3, 30 minutes, five daily), with the last return bus leaving at 12.15pm. However, buses do not coordinate with flight departures. For other destinations around the island, buses are not particularly useful.

Myrina's **bus station** (☑ 22540 22464; Plateia Eleftheriou Venizelou) displays no schedules – you'll have to deal with staffers who speak next to no English.

CAR & MOTORCYCLE

Petrides Travel (p463) and Aegean Travel (p463), both located near the waterfront in Myrina, rent cars from €30 per day. Motorcycle-hire outlets are on Kyda-Karatza.

Myrina Μύρινα

POP 5710

Backed by volcanic rock and a craggy Venetian castle, Limnos' capital has a lively, youthful vibe with a distinct Hellenic flavour (most visitors are continental Greeks). Occupying a neck of land abutting the castle rock, it has two waterfronts that are still known as 'Greek' and 'Turkish', the legacy of a community divide that existed before the exchange of population in 1923.

Filled with restaurants and cafes, Myrina enjoys a good fusion of traditional and progressive food culture influenced by mainland urban trends. In summer, waterfront bars stay packed with students until the wee hours. Above the town, on the castle's overgrown slopes, it's a different story: here, shy, fleet-footed deer dart about after dark, and even venture down to the *agora* (market) on winter nights.

⊙ Sights

Beaches include the wide and sandy **Rea Maditos**, and the superior **Romeïkos Gialos**, beyond the harbour; further on, the beach becomes Riha Nera, named for its gently shelving sea floor. Waterfront cafes and restaurants stay open late through summer. Five minutes south, on the road towards Thanos Beach, **Platy Beach** is a shallow, sandy crescent with cantinas, tavernas and a few lodgings.

★ Castle of Myrina CASTLE

FREE Myrina's lonely hilltop *kastro* dates from the 13th century and occupies a headland that divides the town from its popular beach. The ruins of the Venetian-built

Limnos

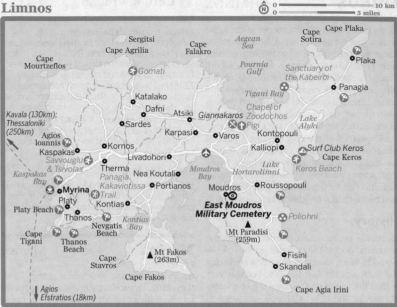

fortress are imposing but deserted, apart from the deer that roam here. It's worth the 20- to 25-minute walk up the hill for the sea views alone, which extend to Mt Athos and, come evening, the twinkling cafe lights below.

Archaeological Museum   MUSEUM
(☏ 22540 22990; Romeïkos Gialos; €2; ⊙ 8.30am-4pm Wed-Mon) Myrina's fine neoclassical museum overlooks Romeïkos Gialos Beach and contains 8th- and 7th-century-BC finds from Limnos' three major sites: Poliohni, the Sanctuary of the Kabeiroi and Hephaistia. Worth seeing are the earthenware lamp statuettes of sirens, along with details of the mandated Greek–Turkish population exchange of 1923.

🏃 Activities

From June to September, travel agencies organise round-the-island sightseeing tours by boat (half-/full day €20/25) and bus (full day €20). Boat tours stop for lunch and swimming, and take in the archaeological sites, usually ending at sunset. Bus tours can also visit the military cemeteries at Moudros (p469) and Portianos. Contact Petrides Travel (p463) or Atzamis Travel (p463).

This excellent sandy beach, **Riha Nera** is flanked by impressive rock formations is within walking distance from the centre of Myrina; inevitably, it gets crowded in high season. The sea is shallow, which is great for children. The beach is fully organised, with umbrellas, showers and several beach cafes.

🛏 Sleeping

Vicky Studios   APARTMENT €
(☏ 22540 22137; www.vickystudios.com; Maroulas 5; studios from €30; P ❄ 🤶) This immaculate and friendly budget gem is a five-minute walk from shops and the beach at Riha Nera. Rooms face a lovely garden and feature kitchenettes, desks and fridges. Also has accommodation in Platy.

To Arhontiko   BOUTIQUE HOTEL €
(☏ 22540 29800; www.arxontikohotel.gr; cnr Sahtouri & Filellinon; r incl breakfast from €50; ❄ 🤶) This restored mansion (Myrina's first hotel) dating from 1851 impresses with swanky boutique rooms, fireplaces, helpful staff, a cosy bar, classic charm throughout and a classic Greek breakfast to last the day. It's on a quiet alleyway near the *plateia* of Romeïkos Gialos.

Studios Efterpi   APARTMENT €€
(☏ 6984337698, 22540 22458; www.efterpilemnos. gr; studios from €65; ❄ 🤶) Top of the hill in every sense, these tastefully furnished studios with well-equipped kitchenettes come with balconies offering views of Myrina's red-tiled

roofs and the castle rock in the distance. It's a bit of a walk from the centre of Myrina, but not far from Riha Nera beach. To find Efterpi, walk up the lane that branches off Agiou Panteleimonos by Katsoula supermarket.

✖ Eating & Drinking

For a small town, Myrina has a rather energetic restaurant scene, with good eateries at the port and more at Romeïkos Gialos, on the other side beyond the harbour.

★ Ouzeri To 11   SEAFOOD €

(Glinou 6; seafood mezedhes €6-12; ⊙noon-4pm & 8pm-midnight Wed-Mon) This unassuming little *ouzerie* by the bus depot is the local favourite for seafood. From *kydonia* (mussels with garlic and Venus clams) to sea urchins and more, 'To *En*-dheka' (as it's pronounced) serves all the stranger stuff, along with plenty of ouzo to help you forget what you're eating.

Grammóphōno   GREEK €

(☑22541 11841; Plateia Eleftheriou Venizelou 3; mains €6-10; ⊙10am-1am; 🐾) The traffic circle may not be the most appealing location, but this place is special thanks to its creative take on traditional taverna fare. It prides itself on various types of smoked meats, but it also has more unusual stuff.

Sinialo   GREEK €

(☑6947328729; Glinou; mains €6.50-9; ⊙lunch & dinner; 🐾) A noncanonical taverna that strives to surprise you with foods that traditional establishments wouldn't feature. Shrimps in ouzo and milk sauce, fried baby octopus, croquettes with homemade cured meat, and many other unusual offerings are served in the romantic setting of a side-street patio.

O Platanos Restaurant   TAVERNA €

(Kyda-Karatza; mains €5-8; ⊙11am-11pm) Homemade pasta, good Limni wine and excellent *mayirefta* dishes with an emphasis on meat are served at this iconic place under two majestic plane trees, along the main street.

Kosmos   TAVERNA €€

(Romeïkos Gialos; mains €6.50-14; ⊙10.30am-1am) A waterfront favourite known for well-prepared fresh fish at decent per-kilo prices. It also has postcard-worthy sunset views across the sea to Mt Athos.

Karagiozis   BAR

(Romeïkos Gialos; ⊙9am-5am) On a leafy terrace near the sea, Karagiozis morphs from snazzy frappé-cafe by day to a drink-till-you-drop bar under the stars. Sturdy, fair-priced drinks.

🛍 Shopping

To Kelari (☑22540 23261; waterfront; ⊙8am-1.30pm & 6-9pm) is the kind of liquor shop you might have seen in pirate movies, with well-aged bottles covered in dust and spiderwebs, and an idiosyncratic bearded owner who makes excellent dry red, as well as *tsipouro*, at his small winery near Myrina.

ℹ Information

Aegean Travel (p463) Arranges car hire and island excursions.

Atzamis Travel (p463) Arranges ferry and air tickets, accommodation, excursions and bicycle rentals. Can arrange visits to the wetlands on Limnos' east coast.

Karaiskaki Travel (p463) Formerly known as Myrina Travel, specialises in trips to Agios Efstratios island.

Petrides Travel (p463) Helpful and informed staff arranges island sightseeing tours, boat trips, car hire, transfers and accommodation.

Pravlis Travel (☑22540 24617; www.pravlis.gr; ⊙8am-3pm & 5.30-10pm) Efficient and helpful full-service agency at the port.

ℹ Getting There & Away

Ferries arrive at the New Port on the other side of the harbour from Myrina's waterfront. Local buses depart for Moudros, the airport (p463) (22km east of Myrina) and other destinations around the island from the bus station (p463) on Plateia Eleftheriou Venizelou in the middle of town, where you will also find a **taxi rank** (☑22540 23820; Plateia Eleftheriou Venizelou).

Western Limnos

A densely populated area around Myrina boasts a few nice beaches and plenty of accommodation – especially at **Platy**, a scenic bay 2km south of the capital. The island's main road heads southeast, passing villages with quirky museums, wineries and interesting historical sites. A side road leads to the starting point of a trail, which runs through otherworldly terrain to the famous cave church of Panagia Kakaviotissa.

North of Myrina, the road left after Kaspakas village accesses the appealing Agios Ioannis Beach, set nicely beneath an overhanging volcanic slab. Hidden away in the mountainous hinterland, a cluster of villages around Sardes serves as a convenient pit stop on the way to the seldom visited sand dunes of Gomati Bay on the northern coast.

1. Mineral Baths of Eftalou (p456), Lesvos

A vintage Ottoman bathhouse fed by a natural spring.

2. Teriade Museum (p454), Mytilini Town, Lesvos

A surprising collection of artworks by masters such as Picasso and Matisse.

3. Pyrgi, Chios (p583)

Artists in this village use cement, volcanic sand, lime and bent forks to create intricate facades.

4. Sanctuary of the Great Gods, Samothraki (p472)

Top-secret ceremonies took place at this Thracian temple to the fertility deities.

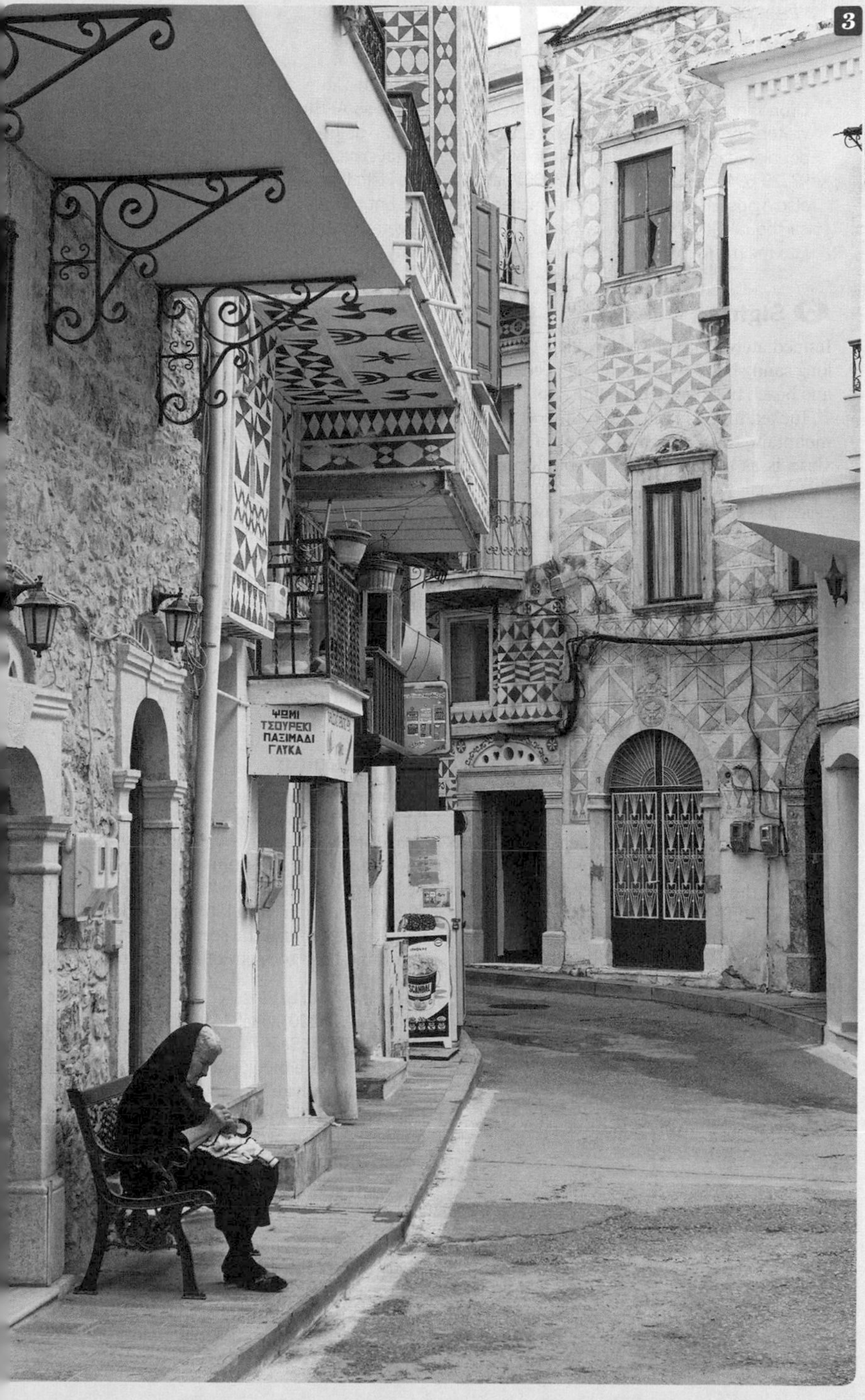

PICTURE PARTNERS/ALAMY ©

AGIOS EFSTRATIOS

You can't get any further from holidaying crowds than this little speck of land between Limnos and continental Greece. Abbreviated by locals as 'Aï-Stratis', the island attracts visitors for its isolation, beaches, relaxing hill walks and quiet beauty. The sparsely populated island has only a couple of domatia and tavernas, including **Ai Strati** (22540 93329, 6945563325; balaskajulia2000@yahoo.gr; Agios Efstratios; r €30-40). The main village, also Agios Efstratios, is often just called 'the village'. Entirely rebuilt after a catastrophic 1968 earthquake that virtually flattened it, it is a serene getaway and offers a chance to plunge into the microcosm of a close-knit island community.

Sights

Immediately south of Myrina, Platy (p465) is a long sandy beach with plenty of decent hotels and beach bars, but few restaurants.

Tucked into a giant rock cavity on top of a mountain, the **Church of Panagia Kakaviotissa** is as striking as the moonlike scenery that you'll pass through on a short trek to reach it. Further along the southwest coast, Kontias is a charming village of windmills and stone houses, and home to the celebrated **Kontias Gallery of Modern Balkan Art**. Closed at the time of research, it might be open when you visit; ask locally.

From Kontias, the main road continues east to the village of **Portianou**. The chair Winston Churchill sat on while commanding the Allied offensive at Gallipoli is the most venerated item at the village's lovely **Folklore Museum** (22543 50000; www.lao grafiko-limnos.gr; Portianou; 10am-2pm). Victims of Churchill's strategic gaffes lie at **Portianos Military Cemetery** nearby. The **Old Russian Cemetery** at Cape Punda (4km away) is the final resting place for more than 300 White Russians; they were interned on the islands by Allied troops, living in terrible conditions and dying of hunger and disease.

The road north passes near **Savvouglu & Tsivolas** winery, where you can taste the island's trademark Alexandrian muscat, before reaching a cluster of mountain villages around **Sardes**, which boasts the outstanding **Manetella Taverna**. Beyond them lies a desolate coast famous for its dunes, an unusual sight for Greek islands.

Activities

Panagia Kakaviotissa Trail TREKKING
(Map p464) A short trail leading to a locally famous cave chapel runs through a moonlike landscape of conical mountains and rock formations. You may drive to the parking lot at the start of the trail or trek 5.5km from Myrina.

Gomati BEACH
(Map p464) Tucked in the most remote corner of northwest Limnos, Gomati could be a wonderful set for a film about life on Mars thanks to its pinkish sand dunes and overall otherworldly feel. A beach bar operates here at the height of summer.

Savvouglu & Tsivolas WINE
(Limnos Organic Wines; Map p464; http://limnos organicwines.gr; 11am-2pm Mon-Fri, by appointment afternoons & weekends) FREE Limnos is full of wineries but this is one of the easiest to access. Off the road to Moudros, it specialises in Alexandrian muscat (white) and the local *kalabaki* red. But what earned it international acclaim is its Rodon rosé. Come for a brief tour of the facilities and an informal tasting session.

Sleeping

Panorama Plati GUESTHOUSE €
(22540 24118, 6947718755; www.panoramaplati. com; Platy Beach; studios from €40;) Standing on a hillock, 500m away from Platy Beach (p465), these tidy and well-equipped studios, complete with kitchens, indeed offer panoramic views of the scenic bay below. The charming host goes out of her way to help.

Paradise Apartments APARTMENT €
(22540 26200, 6945443455; www.paradise limnos.gr; Platy Beach; r from €60;) A gleaming white block with blue doors greets you upon arrival. It's set back 150m from the beach (p465), with palm trees and rose bushes, and has welcoming owners. Rooms are bright and spotless, all with kitchenettes.

Villa Victoria APARTMENT €€
(6942906120, 22540 29077; www.villa-victoria.gr; Platy Beach; d/apt €80/100;) These attractive stone buildings are just metres from the beach, set on a rambling kid-friendly green with a pool. Rooms have smart wood-and-stone motifs, with kitchenettes. Several two-storey apartments can sleep four.

✖ Eating

★ Mantella Taverna   TAVERNA €
(☎ 22540 61349; Sardes; mains €5-9.50; ☺ lunch & dinner) A popular well-managed taverna, 20 minutes' drive from Myrina in the village of Sardes, just north of Therma. Traditional country dishes include rooster, goat and pork stews, along with excellent local cheeses and crisp Limni wines. Although listed as a main course, the sweet *moustoukoulika* pasta makes a great calorie-bomb dessert.

O Sozos   TAVERNA €
(Platy; mains €6.50-8.50; ☺ lunch & dinner) In the main square of Platy, 2km east of Myrina, O Sozos excels in traditional Greek fare. Specialities include *kokkaras flomaria* (rooster served with pasta), lamb and dolmadhes.

❶ Getting There & Away

Western Limnos is best explored by car or a bike. Platy Beach is accessible on foot from Myrina.

Eastern Limnos

Eastern Limnos' flat plateaus are dotted with wheat fields, small vineyards and sheep. Limnos' second-largest town, Moudros, occupies the eastern side of muddy Moudros Bay, famous for its role as the principal base for the ill-fated Gallipoli campaign in 1915.

The rugged northeastern coast is sparsely populated, which was not the case in Trojan War times when Lemnians founded what's believed to be Europe's first constituted democracy. Three large, scenic archaeological sites in the area are related to that golden age of Limnos. Far more recently, steady winds have turned Keros Beach into a magnet for wind- and kitesurfers. The region also hosts the Greek Air Force's central command, meaning large parts are off limits to tourists.

◉ Sights & Activities

★ East Moudros
Military Cemetery   CEMETERY
(Map p464; near Moudros) FREE As if taken from the middle of England, this grassy patch is dotted with memorials to 800 ANZAC and other British Empire soldiers who died of wounds in a nearby military hospital and were laid to rest here, when Limnos served as the headquarters of the ill-fated Gallipoli operation during WWI. In 1921 the island also served as an internment camp for thousands of White Russians, escaping the Red Terror; around 20 of them are also buried here.

The site is located right outside Moudros, on the road to Roussopoli and Poliohni.

Chapel of Zoodochos Pigi   CHURCH
(Map p464; Kotsinas) This late-Byzantine church built on a hill next to a holy-water spring wouldn't be such an outstanding attraction if not for its scenic observation point with a striking statue of Maroula, a fierce sword-wielding female figure looking defiantly in the direction of nearby Turkey. A local heroine, Maroula is said to have taken her dying father's sword during the battle with the Ottomans in 1478. The site is a short walk from the beach in Kotsinas.

Sanctuary of
the Kabeiroi   ARCHAEOLOGICAL SITE
(Ta Kaviria; Map p464; €2; ☺ 8.30am-4pm Wed-Mon) A beautifully desolate clifftop site, the Sanctuary of the Kabeiroi lies at the northern tip of remote Tigani Bay. The worship of the Kabeiroi gods here actually predates that which took place on nearby Samothraki. The major attraction is a Hellenistic sanctuary with 11 partial columns. A trail leads down the cliff to the legendary Cave of Philoctetes, supposedly where the eponymous Trojan War hero was abandoned while his gangrenous, snake-bitten leg healed. A marked path from the site leads to the sea cave.

Poliohni   ARCHAEOLOGICAL SITE
(Map p464; €2; ☺ 8.30am-4pm Wed-Mon) On the southeast coast, Poliohni is considered the first prehistoric settlement in the Aegean and – allegedly – the first example of constituted democracy in the whole of Europe. It has the remains of four ancient settlements, the most significant being a pre-Mycenaean city that predated Troy VI (1800–1275 BC). The site, with its tiny museum, is fascinating, but remains are few.

Keros Beach   BEACH
(Map p464) This long sandy beach, 32km from Myrina, is high up in kitesurfers' pantheon of beaches thanks to steady northern winds and shallow waters, which are ideal for learning the craft. There are several restaurants and accommodation options in the vicinity.

⌖ Sleeping

Moudros has a couple of decent domatia. Elsewhere, **Varos Village** (☎ 22540 31728; www.varosvillage.com; Varos; ste & houses from €140; ❈ ☎ ⊠) stands out as one of the most luxurious accommodation options in the area and on the island. Keros Beach boasts a luxurious tent camp for wind- and kitesurfers.

Surf Club Keros TENTED CAMP €
(Map p464; ☑ 6980776064; www.surfclubkeros.
com; Keros Beach, Kalliopi; tents standard/luxury
from €40/90; ❋ ☎) Sleep in luxurious safari
tents, eat in a restaurant that gets most of
its supplies from a nearby village and – most
crucially – surf! That's the concept of this hedonistic tent resort doubling as a kitesurfing
school. Seaborne stand-up paddleboard yoga
classes sound especially intriguing.

✗ Eating

There are some nice fish tavernas in Moudros,
but the best one is found at Kotsinas on the
northern coast. Popular with visiting Greeks
and airbase personnel, the upmarket seafront
taverna **Giannakaros** (Map p464; ☑ 22540
41744; Limanaki Kotsina, Kotsinas; mains €6-14; ☺ 1-
11pm, to 12.30am Sat & Sun) is heaving at weekends when it roasts a whole lamb or goat.
Seafood dishes are excellent any day.

❶ Getting There & Away

Buses connect Moudros and Myrina (€3.30, 30
minutes, five daily). For other destinations, you'll
need a car or a bike.

SAMOTHRAKI
ΣΑΜΟΘΡΑΚΗ

POP 2860

Emerging from obscurity as it's discovered by
island hoppers, Samothraki sits alone in the
northeastern corner of the Aegean, accessible only from the mainland port of Alexandroupoli. This lush, forested island boasts one
of the most important archaeological sites in
Greece: the ancient Thracian Sanctuary of the
Great Gods (p472). Also here stands the Aegean's loftiest peak, Mt Fengari (1611m), from
where, according to Homer, Poseidon, god of
the sea, watched the Trojan War unfold.

Samothraki's mountainous interior, filled
with massive gnarled oak and plane trees, is
ideal for hiking and mountain biking, and the
island's waterfalls, plunging into deep, glassy
pools, provide cool relief on hot summer days.
Remote southeastern beaches are pristine,
while the north offers hot baths (p473) at
Loutra (Therma). Inland from the main fishing port of sleepy Kamariotissa lies the former
capital, Hora, bursting with flowers and handsome homes, all overlooking the distant sea.

❶ Information

A very comprehensive guide to the island can be
found at www.insamothraki.com.

❶ Getting There & Away

SAOS Lines (www.saos.gr) ferries connect
Samothraki with Alexandroupoli – twice daily
in summer, less frequently out of season, and
varying in price (from €10 to €15.60, two hours).
Rates for cars are prohibitively high at €58 (€38
on subsidised routes) and there is often not
enough space. Purchase tickets at the port kiosk.

❶ Getting Around

From Kamariotissa, there are six buses daily to
Hora and Palepoli, five to Profitis Ilias via Alonia
and Lakkoma, and two to Loutra.
Kyrkos Rent-a-Car (☑ 6972839231, 25510
41620; Kamariotissa) rents cars and small
Jeeps in Kamariotissa.

There are only a couple of cabbies on the
island; you can find their numbers displayed on
the noticeboard by the bus stop in Kamariotissa.
The longest trips cost under €20.

Kamariotissa & Around
Καμαριώτισσα

POP 960

Samothraki's port, largest town and transport
hub, Kamariotissa is home to the island's
main services. A nearby pebble beach has bars
and decent swimming. While most visitors
don't linger here, it's a likeable and attractive
port filled with flowers and fish tavernas.

🛌 Sleeping

Most domatia and hotels are out of town and,
unlike on many Greek isles, you won't find locals hawking rooms to arriving ferry passengers. Rooms are available at Lakkoma Beach.

Niki Beach Hotel HOTEL €
(☑ 25510 41545; www.nikibeach.gr; Kamariotissa;
s/d/tr incl breakfast €35/55/105; ❋ ☎ ☒) This
handsome, well-managed hotel with large
modern rooms is just opposite the town
beach. Balconies face the sea, while flowers and poplar trees fill an interior garden.
Owners Elena and Vasillis manage to give it
a boutique feel, despite the 37 rooms.

★ **Hotel Samothraki Village** HOTEL €€
(Map p471; ☑ 6982303396, 25510 42300; www.
samothrakivillage.gr; Paleopoli; s/d/tr €65/70/90;
❋ ☎ ☒) Located 4km east of Kamariotissa
on the coast road, and 1km before the Sanctuary of the Great Gods (p472), this excellent
lodging consists of spacious modern rooms
with sea-view balconies. There are two outdoor pools, a mini-playground for kids, a fitness centre and a *hammam*. Book ahead for
free port pick-up.

Samothraki

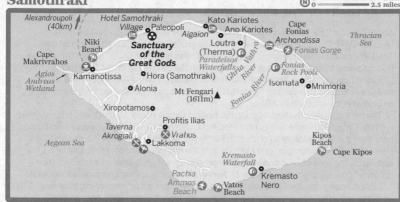

Eating & Drinking

Tavernas line the waterfront in Kamariotissa. The island's best tavernas are found south of the town.

Fournello ITALIAN €
(Kamariotissa; mains €5-10; ⊘ lunch & dinner) Fournello makes for a nice change of pace, serving good pizza and spaghetti. It's one of the few places where you can dine by the sea. Close to Niki Beach Hotel.

Vrahos TAVERNA €
(Map p471; ☑ 25510 95264; Profitis Ilias; mains €4.50-9; ⊘ lunch & dinner) This popular grill house in Profitis Ilias heaves during the weekends when a whole goat or sheep is grilled.

★I Synantisi TAVERNA €€
(☑ 25510 41308; Kamariotissa; fish €6-12; ⊘ lunch & dinner) Excellent fresh fish and *gavros* – the owner is a spear diver – as well as fine meat dishes. The place is cosy and welcoming, with a small open kitchen.

Taverna Akrogiali TAVERNA €€
(Map p471; ☑ 25510 95123; Lakkoma Beach; mains €6-15; ⊘ lunch & dinner) A short distance from Lakkoma Beach, this is a pretty terrace filled with rose bushes and geraniums. It's a prime spot to sample Aegean fish, from ubiquitous mackerel to far less obvious breeds.

Karnagio CAFE
(Kamariotissa waterfront) Snappy cafe for coffee and cheese pies by day, and a chill *ouzerie* for *tsipouro* and small plates at sunset.

❶ Getting There & Away

Ferries depart for the mainland from the port at Kamariotissa, as do buses for Hora and Loutra.

Hora (Samothraki)
Χώρα (Σαμοθράκη)
POP 700

Set within a natural fortress of two sheer cliffs, and with a commanding view of the sea, Hora (also called Samothraki) was the obvious choice for the island's capital. In the 10th century the Byzantines built a castle on its northwestern peak, though today's substantial remains mostly date from the 15th-century Genoese rule.

Marked by twisting and colourful cobbled streets wreathed in flowers, and vintage traditional houses with terracotta roofs, Hora is perfect for enjoying a leisurely lunch or coffee, and on summer evenings there's easy-going nightlife in the small lanes and rooftop bars.

◉ Sights

Freshly converted into a fully fledged tourist sight complete with English-language signs, the picturesque **Kastro** (⊘ 11am-2pm Wed & Fri-Sun) **FREE** was built in 1431–33 by Genovese noble Palamede Gattilusio, who received the island in exchange for assisting the Byzantine emperor in a fratricidal war. In addition to sweeping views, the ruins feature a large stone cistern used for collecting rainwater, and a murder hole for people whose company the Italian gentleman did not enjoy.

The castle used to house a police station, which was only demolished in 2015.

Both the nobleman's and the emperor's coats of arms appear on a marble plaque at the castle entrance.

DON'T MISS

SANCTUARY OF THE GREAT GODS

About 6km northeast of Kamariotissa, **Sanctuary of the Great Gods** (Map p471; ☑25510 41474; €6; ⊙8am-3pm) is one of Greece's most mysterious archaeological sites. The Thracians built this temple to their fertility deities around 1000 BC. By the 5th century BC, the secret rites and sacrifices associated with the cult had attracted famous pilgrims, including Egyptian queen Arsinou, Philip II of Macedon (father of Alexander the Great) and Greek historian Herodotus. Remarkably, the sanctuary operated until paganism was forbidden in the 4th century AD.

The principal deity, the fertility goddess Alceros Cybele (Great Mother), was later merged with the Olympian female deities Demeter, Aphrodite and Hecate. Other deities worshipped here were the Great Mother's consort, the virile young Kadmilos (god of the phallus), later integrated with the Olympian god Hermes; and the demonic Kabeiroi twins, Dardanos and Aeton, the sons of Zeus and Leda. Samothraki's great gods were venerated for their immense power – in comparison, the bickering Olympian gods were considered frivolous.

Little is known about what actually transpired here, though archaeological evidence points to two initiations, a lower and a higher. In the first, the great gods were invoked to grant the initiate a spiritual rebirth; in the second, the candidate was absolved of transgressions. This second confessional rite took place at the sacred **Hieron**, whose remaining columns are easily the most photographed ruin of the sanctuary.

We do know that the rituals at the sanctuary were open to all – men, women, citizens, servants and slaves – and since death was the penalty for revealing the secrets of the sanctuary, the main requirements seem to have been showing up and keeping quiet.

The **Archaeological Museum** at the Sanctuary of the Great Gods provides a helpful overview of the entire site. Pick up the free museum map before exploring the area. Museum exhibits include a striking marble frieze of dancing women, terracotta figurines and amphorae, jewellery, and clay lamps indicative of the nocturnal nature of the rituals. A plaster cast stands in for the celebrated **Winged Victory of Samothrace** (now in the Louvre), looted in 1863 by French diplomat and amateur archaeologist Charles Champoiseau.

About 75m south of the museum stands the **Arisinoeion** (rotunda), a gift from Queen Arisinou of Egypt. The sanctuary's original rock altar was discovered nearby. Adjacent are the rectangular **Anaktoron**, where lower initiations took place; the **Temenos**, a hall where a celebratory feast was held; and the Hieron, site of higher initiations.

Opposite the Hieron stand remnants of a **theatre**. Nearby, a path ascends to the **Nike monument** (*nike* means 'victory' in Greek), where once stood the magnificent *Winged Victory of Samothrace*, which faced northward overlooking the sea – appropriate since it was likely dedicated to the gods following a victorious naval battle.

🛏 Sleeping

Hora has several domatia, but Hotel Axieros, in the heart of the village, is one of the best for value.

The **Hotel Axieros** (☑25510 41416, 25510 41294; www.axieros.gr; d/tr/q from €50/60/65; ❉🛜) is friendly and welcoming, with handsomely furnished traditional rooms featuring well-equipped kitchenettes and views of the village.

🍴 Eating & Drinking

Cafes and tavernas are found high on the main street, where there's a small fountain with mountain-spring water.

O Lefkos Pyrgos   SWEETS €
(desserts €4-6; ⊙9am-late Jul & Aug) Open only in summer, Lefkos Pyrgos is an excellent, inventive and all-natural sweets shop run by master confectioners Georgios and Dafni. Try lemonade with honey and cinnamon, or Greek yoghurt with bitter almond, along with exotic teas, coffees and mixed drinks.

Trapeza me Thea   CAFE
(⊙all day) Ex-urbanites Elias and Theodora have taken over Hora's old bank building and transformed it into a wonderful coffee shop. Take a seat on the balcony overlooking the valley below and enjoy your coffee with 'submarine' (sweet mastic paste submerged in water) or a spoon sweet. The former bank director's desk has been turned into a bar.

Meltemi BAR
(☎25510 41071; ⊗8am-late) Opposite the fountain, this cool bar is managed by the gracious Panayioti, and has great views from a rooftop garden that's popular from morning until late.

ⓘ Getting There & Away

There are six buses daily to/from Kamariotissa (20 minutes).

Loutra Λουτρά
POP 100

Loutra (also called Therma), 14km east of Kamariotissa near the coast, is Samothraki's most popular place to stay. This relaxing village of plane and horse-chestnut trees, dense greenery and gurgling creeks comes to life at night when people of all ages gather in its outdoor cafes.

◉ Sights & Activities

Paradeisos Waterfalls WATERFALL
(Map p471) About 500m past Kafeneio Ta Therma, a lush wooded path (100m) leads to a series of rock pools and waterfalls, the most impressive being 30m in height. This is gorgeous, *Lord of the Rings*–like terrain, where gnarled 600-year-old plane trees covered in moss loom out of fog over a forest floor of giant ferns and brackish boulders. Have an ice-cold dip on a hot summer's day.

Pachia Ammos Beach BEACH
(Map p471) A horseshoe-shaped sand cove with a beach bar and sunbeds, this is the best beach on the southern tip of the island. You'll need to arrange your own transport in order to get here.

Thermal Baths BATHHOUSE
(☎25513 50800; €4-6; ⊗7-10am & 6-9pm Jun-Sep) Warm, therapeutic, mineral-rich springs, reportedly able to cure everything from skin problems to infertility. The prominent white building by the bus stop houses the official bath, though there is free bathing at two small outdoor baths 75m up the hill.

🛏 Sleeping

Aigaion PENSION €
(Map p471; ☎6986931337; Ano Karyotes; d from €40; ❋🐾) Set at the back of a shady garden, away from the main road, this family hotel has undergone a thorough renovation. Some of the old features, have been left intact, giving the place a nostalgic 1970s feel. All rooms come with balconies facing the sea and there is a common kitchen for self-caterers.

Mariva Bungalows BUNGALOW €
(☎25510 98230; www.mariva.gr; d incl breakfast €50; P❋🐾) These secluded vine-covered stone bungalows, with breezy modern rooms, sit on a lush hillside near a waterfall. To reach them, turn from the coast road inland towards Loutra and follow the signs.

Hotel Orfeas HOTEL €
(☎25510 42213, 25510 98233; http://samothraki orpheus.com; d/tr incl breakfast from €50/60; ❋🐾) The Orfeas is simple, comfortable and friendly, its best rooms have balconies overlooking the stream. The gracious owner, Christos, offers tips on exploring the hills around Loutra.

★Archondissa BOUTIQUE HOTEL €€
(Map p471; ☎6942210527, 25510 98098; www.ar chondissa.gr; d/tr €80/95; ❋🐾) This Cycladic-styled sugar-cube cluster, located 3km east of Loutra, contains brightly coloured apartments with kilim rugs and ergonomic kitchenettes camouflaged as wardrobes. The sea is 30m away across a pretty flower garden.

🍷 Drinking & Nightlife

Run by the jovial Iordanis Iordaninis for more than 20 years, **Kafeneio Ta Therma** (☎6984994856; mains €3-5; ⊗8am-2am) is the centre of the action in Loutra, with live music, impromptu vendors and artists in the surrounding open areas.

ⓘ Getting There & Away

There are four buses daily between Kamariotissa and Loutra.

WORTH A TRIP

FONIAS RIVER

Heading east from Loutra on the northeast coast takes you to the Fonias River and the famous **Fonias Rock Pools**. The walk (Map p471) starts at the bridge 4.7km east of Loutra, by the (summer-only) ticket booths. The first 40 minutes are along an easy, well-marked track leading to a large and swimmable rock pool fed by a dramatic 12m-high waterfall. The river is known as the 'Murderer', and in winter rain can transform the waters into a raging torrent. The real danger, however, is getting lost – though there are six waterfalls, marked paths are few.

THASOS ΘΑΣΟΣ

POP 13,770

One of Greece's greenest and most gentle islands, Thasos lies 10km from mainland Kavala. Its climate and vegetation make it seem like the island is an extension of northern Greece, yet it boasts enviable sandy beaches and a forested mountain interior. Quite inexpensive by Greek-island standards, it's popular with families and students from Bulgaria and the ex-Yugoslav republics. Frequent ferries from the mainland allow independent travellers to get here quickly, and the excellent bus network makes getting around easy.

The island's main draws are its natural beauty, beaches, inland villages and historical attractions. The excellent archaeological museum (p475) in the capital, Thasos (Limenas), is complemented by the Byzantine Moni Arhangelou (p478), with its stunning clifftop setting, and the Ancient Greek temple at Alyki (p478) on the southeast coast.

History

Over its long history, Thasos has benefited from its natural wealth. The Parians, who founded the ancient city of Thasos (Limenas) in 700 BC, struck gold at Mt Pangaion, creating an export trade lucrative enough to subsidise a naval fleet. While the gold is long gone, Thasos' white Parian marble is still being exploited, though scarring a mountainside in the process.

Activities

The **Victoria** (☑ 6977012769; ☉ Jul & Aug) excursion boat makes full-day trips around Thasos (Limenas), with stops for swimming and lunch. It departs the Old Harbour in Limenas at 10am. Water taxis run regularly to Hrysi Ammoudia (Golden Beach) and Makryammos Beach from the Old Harbour. Excursion boats of varying sizes and alcohol content also set sail regularly from the coastal resorts. Enquire at **Visit North Greece** (p476) or **Billias Travel Service** (p476) in Thasos (Limenas).

Information

Go Thasos (www.go-thassos.gr; ☉ 9am-2pm Mon-Fri) runs a comprehensive online guide to the island and a useful information office in Thasos (Limenas).

Getting There & Away

Thasos is only accessible from the mainland ports of Keramoti and Kavala. Ferries run between Keramoti and Limenas every 30 to 45 minutes (adult/car €4/18, 40 minutes), and six a day between Kavala and Skala Prinou (adult/car €5/19, 1¼ hours). Get ferry schedules at the **ticket booths** (☑ 25930 22318) in Thasos (Limenas) and the **port authority** (☑ 25930 71390; Skala Prinou).

Getting Around

BICYCLE

Basic bikes can be hired in Thasos (Limenas). Top-of-the-line models and detailed route information are available in Potos, on the southwest coast, from Velo Bike Rental (p477).

BUS

Frequent buses serve the entire island coast as well as inland villages. Buses meet arriving ferries at Skala Prinou and Thasos (Limenas), the island's transport hub. The two port towns are connected by eight daily buses (€2.10, 20 minutes).

Frequent buses run throughout the day from Thasos (Limenas) to west-coast villages such as Limenaria (€5), Potos (€5.30) and Theologos (€6.70). Buses from Limenas also reach the east-coast destinations of Hrysi Ammoudia (Golden Beach; €2.20), Skala Potamia (€1.90) via Panagia (€1.80) and Potamia (€1.80), some of them continuing to Paradise Beach (€2.80) and Alyki (€4.10).

A full circular tour (about 100km) of the island runs six to eight times daily (€10.60, 3½ hours) – three clockwise and three anticlockwise. This round-the-island ticket is valid all day, so you can jump on and off without paying extra. The **bus station** (☑ 25930 22162) on the Thasos (Limenas) waterfront provides timetables.

Services are reduced during weekends.

CAR & MOTORCYCLE

Potos Car Rentals (☑ 25930 52071; www.rentacarpotos.gr; Hotel Potos, Potos) is reliable and reasonable. **Avis Rent-a-Car** (☑ 25930 22535; www.avis.gr) is in Thasos (Limenas), Potamia and Skala Prinou.

Crazy Rollers (☑ 6978937536; crazyrollers@gmail.com; ☉ 9am-1pm & 5-9pm) in Thasos (Limenas) and **Moto Zagos** (☑ 25930 53340; www.motozagos.gr; Limenaria) motorbikes and bicycles.

TAXI

The Thasos (Limenas) **taxi rank** (☑ 6944170373, 25930 22394; waterfront) is on the waterfront, next to the main bus stop (p474). Sample destinations and fares: Skala Prinou €20, Panagia €12, Skala Potamia €20, Alyki €40 and Potos €50.

Thasos

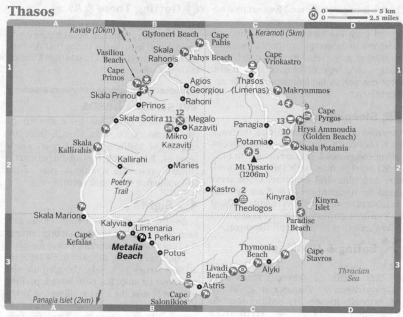

0 — 5 km
0 — 2.5 miles

Thasos

In Potos, there's a taxi rank with listed prices beside the bus stop on the main road.

Limenas   Λιμένας
POP 2610

Thasos (also called Limenas) has the island's main services and year-round activity. It sports a picturesque fishing harbour, a sandy beach, shopping, a few ancient ruins and an archaeological museum.

If you're exploring the eastern side of town, note the signpost for historical sites, beginning a five-minute walk up a shaded trail to the lovely chapel of Agioi Apostoli, where there are views over the seafront.

◉ Sights

★ Archaeological Museum   MUSEUM
(☏ 25930 22180; €2; ⊕ 8am-8pm Wed-Mon) Looking like an alien creature from the sci-fi movie *Avatar*, a 5m-tall 6th-century-BC *kouros* carrying a ram greets visitors at this large, modern archaeological museum. Statues and other artefacts from the Classical and Roman periods are on display. The museum is located about 100m from the Old Harbour's waterfront.

Ancient Agora   RUINS
Next to the archaeological museum stand the foundation ruins of the ancient *agora*, the commercial centre in ancient times. About 100m east of the *agora*, the ancient

theatre is occasionally used for performances of ancient dramas and comedies; it's signposted from the harbour. A path connects the *agora* to the acropolis, where substantial remains of a medieval fortress stand, with commanding views of the coast. Carved rock steps descend to the foundations of the ancient town.

🛏 Sleeping

Dreamed up in a psychedelic haze, the fanciful **A for Art** (📞 25930 58405; www.aforarthotel. gr; cnr Theogenous & 18 Oktovriou; d from €120; ❄🛜) hotel is filled with Dalí-esque furniture and whimsical sculpture. If you don't mind the decadent decor, it is a very comfortable place to spend a few nights, and has an excellent garden bar where you can meet fellow travellers (and a purple flamingo).

🍴 Eating & Drinking

⭐ **Masabuka**   GRILL €
(📞 25930 23651; 18 Oktovriou; mains €2-4; ⏱ 4pm-midnight; 🛜) Visitors rave about this exceptionally friendly 21st-century souvlaki joint, where meat skewers are served with a variety of mouth-watering dips. It's located in the pedestrianised street connecting the centre with the harbour area.

Simi   TAVERNA €€
(📞 25930 22517; Old Harbour; mains €7-12; ⏱ 9.30am-midnight; 🛜🚼) Locals agree that this year-round eatery at the Old Harbour serves Limenas' best fish, along with fine fish soup, *stifadho* (meat, game or seafood cooked with onions in a tomato puree) and grilled sardines. There's a kids' menu, good wines and spicy mezedhes, including hot peppers that can change your life.

⭐ **Karnagio**   BAR
(📞 25930 23170; ⏱ 8am-2am) Stroll past the Old Harbour for a quiet sunset drink at Karnagio, where outdoor seating straddles a rocky promontory. You can also clamber up the rocks to a small, candlelit chapel.

ℹ Information

Go Thasos (p474)
Billias Travel Service (📞 25930 24003; Pavlou Mela 6) Full-service travel agency.
Visit North Greece (📞 25106 20566, 6942524337; www.visitnorthgreece.com; Pavlou Mela 17; ⏱ 9am-9pm) Well-managed tour operator offering hiking, walking and cycling excursions, along with 4WD safaris and sailing trips. The helpful owners, Chrisoula and Stelios, also handle transfers and suggest accommodation.

ℹ Getting There & Away

Ferries from Keramoti on the mainland arrive at the New Port at Limenas. Buses around the island depart from the bus station (p474), where you can also purchase bus tickets from Keramoti to Thessaloniki.

Western Thasos

Thasos' west coast has been assailed by package tours for years, though there are still a few idyllic spots and quiet sandy beaches. Better still, the inland mountain villages preserve a traditional pace of life and some fine stone architecture.

◎ Sights

Following the coast west from Thasos (Limenas), two sandy beaches emerge: decent **Glyfoneri** and the superior **Pahys Beach**.

Continuing west, the port of **Skala Prinou** has ferries to Kavala, though little else to warrant a stop. But 6km inland, past the town of Prinos, the hillside villages of **Mikro Kazaviti** and **Megalo Kazaviti** (aka the **Prinou villages**) offer a lush break from the touristed coast, with undeniable character and a few places to stay and eat, including Menir Luxury Apartments. An easy-to-follow trail network branches off from the pretty square in Megalo Kazaviti, with a sign marking the routes.

The next real point of interest, the whimsical fishing port of **Skala Marion**, lies further south. Its few canopied tavernas overlooking the sea are faithfully populated by village elders shuffling backgammon chips while children scamper about. The village has a few domatia and a bakery on the northern jetty. On the village's feast day (24 June), church services are followed by folk dancing around the square.

The coast road south passes more beaches until reaching **Limenaria**, Thasos' second-largest town, which is followed quickly by **Pefkari** and **Potos**, two fishing villages turned package resorts, both with long sandy beaches lined with cafes and tavernas.

From the Theologos–Potos corner of the main road, head southeast round the coast for views of the stunning bays. The last southwestern settlement, **Astris**, has a good beach with tavernas and the **Astris Sun Hotel** (Map p475; 📞 25930 51281; www.astrissun hotel.gr; Astris; r from €76; ❄🚗).

Easily accessible on foot from Limenaria, the pretty cove of Metalia Beach (Map p475) features an elegiac retro-industrial sight in the form of a mining factory built by German entrepreneur Speidel in 1900. The ruins form an amphitheatre around the beach, with a colonial-styled administrative building, sadly abandoned, towering above the headland.

🏃 Activities

Despite its touristy feel, Thasos' west coast offers worthwhile outdoor activities such as scuba diving, mountain biking and bird-watching. There are walking trails above the coast.

★**Velo Bike Rental** CYCLING
(☑ 25930 52459, 6946955704; www.velobikerental.com; Potos) Hires out bikes year-round and also runs guided biking and hiking tours to Mt Ypsario. Inspired owner Yiannis Reizis also organises a number of international cycling events and races on the island.

Thassos Horse Club HORSE RIDING
(Map p475; ☑ 6999391777; www.thassoshorseclub.snadno.eu; Skala Prinou) Runs riding lessons and tailor-made horseback trips out of Skala Prinou.

Panagia Islet BIRDWATCHING
(☑ 6973209576; www.gothassos.com; trips €25) The rocky, uninhabited Panagia Islet, southwest of Potos, is home to Greece's largest shag colony. Local environmentalist Yiannis Markianos at Aldebran Pension arranges birdwatching boat trips in spring and autumn, weather permitting.

Diving Club Vasiliadis DIVING
(☑ 6944542974; www.scuba-vas.gr; ⊘ 9am-2pm & 5-8pm) Diving for beginners and open-water divers is offered in Potos by Vasilis Vasiliadis, including trips to Alyki's submerged ancient marble quarry. A one-day course for beginners costs €50.

🛏 Sleeping

Potos has some decent hotels, but Limenaria is simply a nicer place to stay.

★**Aldebran Pension** PENSION €
(☑ 25930 52494, 6973209576; www.gothassos.com; Potos; d from €55; ❋ 🛜) Well-informed and attentive owners Elke and Yiannis make Aldebran the best value in southern Thasos. Along with a leafy courtyard and table tennis, it boasts modern baths, a well-equipped communal kitchen and all-day coffee and tea. Resident ornithologist Yiannis offers birdwatching tours for guests in spring and autumn, and offers info on local hiking trails and more.

Villa Ioanna APARTMENT €€
(☑ 6974466730; https://villa-ioanna.com; Potos; d/tr from €64/74; Ⓟ❋🛜) This gentrified version of domatia has a fancy hotel quality, with an elegant subdued design that involves many wooden surfaces, ropes and bamboo stems. Comfy beds come with aromatic Coco-Mat mattresses, and are topped with an array of pillows. There are kitchenettes in each room, with complimentary coffee capsules and other breakfast supplies.

Hotel Menel – The Tree House DESIGN HOTEL €€
(☑ 6944578954, 25930 51396; www.dhotels.gr; Limenaria; d incl breakfast from €85; ❋🛜) This funky edifice stands out among Limenaria's seafront hotels thanks to its Scandinavian ecodesign, with a wooden facade and 16 airy modern rooms, all with sea-view balconies. A great rooftop terrace with sunbeds is a bonus.

Menir Luxury Apartments APARTMENT €€
(Map p475; ☑ 25930 58270; www.menir-thassos.gr; Mikro Kazaviti; r incl breakfast from €90; ❋🛜) Some of the most handsome and spacious digs in this rustic area. There are five apartments, two with spa and all with fireplaces, open year-round.

🍴 Eating

The margin between a decent taverna and a tourist trap is blurred in Potos and Limenaria, but you'll definitely not go hungry.

★**Armeno** TAVERNA €
(Skala Marion; mains €5-9; ⊘ 7am-1am) Well-regarded waterfront taverna, where you can have a look at the day's catch of fish. The organic produce here is from the gardens of the friendly Filakताki family, who also rent rooms (☑ 6977413789, 25930 52634; r from €35; ❋🛜) and can help with local information. Located in offbeat Skala Marion.

Kazaviti Restaurant GREEK €€
(Map p475; ☑ 6972053342; Megalo Kazaviti; €7-13; ⊘ 8am-11pm; 🛜) Set in the shade of plane trees on the beautiful square of its namesake village, this restaurant makes a conscious effort to surprise those used to (and possibly slightly tired of) the usual island taverna routine. Bean soup, lamb's head soup, liver, lamb in a pot and sundried octopus are some of the unusual and delicious menu options.

INLAND VILLAGES

Two interior villages warrant a day trip inland. About 6km from Skala Marion, forested **Maries** rewards visitors with cool highland air and a handsome monastery, Agios Taxiarchis.

Thasos' medieval and Ottoman capital, **Theologos**, is only accessible from Potos, where the road leads inland to the forested hamlet of 400 souls, notable for its whitewashed slate-roofed houses. Find the 1803 Church of Agios Dimitrios, distinguished by its grand slate roof, exquisite polished wood interior and white-plastered clock tower. An interesting local **folklore museum** (Map p475; Theologos; €2; ⊙10am-4pm) occupies the house of the island's 19th-century president. Relax at one of the local cafes or tavernas to soak it all up.

O Georgios   TAVERNA €€
(Potos; mains €6.50-13; ⊙lunch & dinner; 🛜) This traditional Greek grill house, set in a pebbled rose garden, is a local favourite away from Potos' more touristy main road. It offers friendly service and generous portions.

Psarotaverna To Limani   SEAFOOD €€
(Limenaria; mains €6.50-25; ⊙lunch & dinner) Limenaria's best seafood is served at this waterfront restaurant opposite the National Bank of Greece. Prices can be steep.

❶ Getting There & Away

Frequent daily buses serve Potos (€5.30) and Limenaria (€5) from Limenas.

Eastern Thasos

Thasos' east-coast beaches are beautiful in summer and less crowded than the more developed west coast. The dramatic coastal landscape features thick forests that run from mountains to sea. There are fewer organised activities here, but the warm, shallow waters are excellent for families.

Tiny Alyki may be the most overlooked spot on the southeast coast. The village is great for unwinding, with a few shops, domatia and tavernas, and there are two fine sandy beach coves, separated by a small olive grove dotted with ancient ruins comprising the archaeological site of Alyki.

⊙ Sights

Panagia and Potamia are 4km west of the east coast's most popular beaches: sand-duned **Hrysi Ammoudia (Golden Beach)**, tucked inside a long, curving bay; and gentle **Skala Potamia**, on its southern end. Both have accommodation, restaurants and a bit of nightlife.

Further south from Skala Potamia is the deservedly popular, family-friendly Paradise Beach, 2km after tiny Kinyra village.

You'll need stamina to reach the secluded Marble Beach, located at the bottom of a giant marble quarry, 6km south of Limenas, but it is one of the island's most memorable sights.

★**Archaeological Site of Alyki**   ARCHAEOLOGICAL SITE
(Alyki) FREE Alluring and easily accessible, the island's crown gem includes the considerable and photogenic remains of an ancient temple where the gods were once invoked to protect sailors. Enter the site through the back door by following a beautiful trail that skirts the headland, passing a partially submerged marble quarry that remained operational from the 7th century BC to the 6th century AD. The path starts at the far end of the beach lined by tavernas.

Moni Arhangelou   MONASTERY
(Map p475; ⊙9am-2pm & 5pm-sunset) FREE West from Alyki, past Thymonia Beach, is the clifftop Moni Arhangelou, an Athonite dependency and working convent, notable for its 400-year-old church (with some ungainly modern touches) and stellar sea views. Those improperly attired will get shawled up for entry by the friendly nuns. Archangel Michael, whose name the monastery bears, is venerated as the patron of the Greek armed forces; don't be surprised to see a room filled with sabres and uniforms attached to the main church.

From their island retreat, the nuns can observe Mt Athos, a forbidden place for women. The sacred mountain looms across the straits on Halkidiki Peninsula. About 1.5km west of the monastery, a small dirt road heads 1km to Livadi Beach, one of Thasos' most beautiful, with aquamarine waters ringed by cliffs and forests and just a few umbrellas set in the sand.

Panagia   VILLAGE
This inland village just south of Limenas is nothing if not photogenic. Its characteristic architecture includes stone-and-slate rooftops

and the elegant blue-and-white domed and icon-rich **Church of the Kimisis tou Theotokou** (Church of the Dormition of the Virgin). To reach this peaceful quarter, follow the sound of rushing spring water upwards along a stone path heading inland.

🏃 Activities

Paradise Beach   BEACH
(Map p475) Zanzibar-quality whitish sand, a shallow seabed and lush greenery in the background give this beautiful beach a tropical feel. There are two beach bars with sunbeds, but no showers. The beach used to attract nudists, but these days it's overrun by holidaying families from Eastern Europe. Located 2km after tiny Kinyra village.

Marble Beach   BEACH
(Map p475) This hard-to-reach beach at the bottom of a giant quarry is entirely made of marble crumbs, making the whole place so ethereally white it feels like literal paradise. In the middle of the beach, a pine tree growing out of a marble slab makes it extremely photogenic. There's a beach bar, sunbeds and a shower. Marble Beach is located 6km south of Limenas. Don't trust your navigator if you drive; follow graffiti signs on the main road to find the correct turn.

Mt Ypsario   HIKING
(Map p475) Potamia makes a good jumping-off point for climbing Thasos' highest peak, Mt Ypsario (1206m). A tractor trail west from Potamia continues to the valley's end, after which arrows and cairns point the way up a steep path. The three-hour Ypsario hike is classified as moderately difficult.

🛌 Sleeping

Studios Vaso   APARTMENT €
(📞6946524706, 25102 33507; gemitzi.alexandra@vaso-studios.gr; Alyki; r from €55; P🌸) Heading just east of Alyki's bus stop on the main road, look for the big burst of flowers and a sign pointing up the drive to this charming set of nine self-catering domatia, run by the welcoming Vaso Gemetzi and daughter Aleka. There's a leafy courtyard. Kids stay free.

Thassos Inn   HOTEL €
(📞25930 61612; www.thassosinn.gr; Panagia; d from €45; P🛜) Just follow the sound of rushing spring water to this rambling hotel by the church for great views of Panagia's slate-roofed houses. The welcoming owners, Toula and Tasos, can also advise hikers who want to stay close to the Mt Ypsario trailhead.

★**Hotel Kamelia**   HOTEL €€
(Map p475; 📞25930 61463, 6948898767; www.hotel-kamelia.gr; Skala Potamia; s/d incl breakfast from €80/90; P🌸🛜) This beachfront gem is the best in town – understated, with cool jazz in the garden bar and friendly service throughout. The gracious owners, Eleni, Stavros and family, serve a fine Greek breakfast overlooking the sea and provide plenty of tips about the area. It's 500m north of the busier main beach, over a very small bridge.

Hotel Dionysos   HOTEL €€
(Map p475; 📞25930 61822; www.hotel-dionysos-thassos.com; Hrysi Ammoudia; s/d/tr incl breakfast from €50/70/85; P🌸🛜🏊) This rambling and comfortable hilltop retreat overlooking Hrysi Ammoudia (Golden Beach) owes its appeal to energetic owners Sakis and Mary, who also ferry their guests by minivan to the beach and offer good taverna standards throughout the day from their kitchen.

🍴 Eating & Drinking

Arhontissa Alyki   GREEK €
(📞25930 32098; Alyki; mains €6-11; ⏱7am-11.30pm) The friendly Anastasios Kuzis and family run this tranquil taverna with great sea views. It serves excellent fare, with fresh fish and mezedhes among the star offerings. Find it east of the village car park, signposted up a steep drive.

Taverna Grill Elena   TAVERNA €
(📞25930 61709; Panagia; mains €6.50-12; ⏱noon-midnight) This classic taverna under a shady patio off the square, run by Georgios and Elena, specialises in spit-roasted lamb and goat. Before you get to the *kokoretsi* on the spit, sample the *bougloundi* (baked feta with tomatoes and chilli) appetiser.

Limanaki   CAFE
(Map p475; 📞6949551875; Hrysi Ammoudia; ⏱lunch & dinner) The words 'hip' and '*ouzerie*' seldom go together, but the understated stylishness of this terrace-bar at the northern edge of Hrysi Ammoudia (Golden Beach) succeeds. It's a pleasant place to unwind after some beach fun, with a glass of *tsipouro* and a plate of mezedhes, or simply a cup of Greek coffee.

ℹ️ Getting There & Away

Hrysi Ammoudia (Golden Beach; €2.20) and the villages above it are served by frequent buses from Limenas. There is also a daily service from Limenas to Alyki (€4.10).

Evia & the Sporades

Best Places to Eat

➡ Marmita (p489)

➡ To Rodi (p494)

➡ Taverna Mouries (p507)

➡ Astrofegia (p501)

➡ Cavo d'Oro (p486)

➡ O Pappous Kai Ego (p505)

Best Places to Stay

➡ Atrium Hotel (p491)

➡ Angelo's Apartments & Suites (p499)

➡ Nefeli Hotel (p505)

➡ Perigiali Hotel (p505)

➡ Konstantina Studios (p500)

➡ Eleonas (p484)

Why Go?

Evia, Greece's second-largest island, is hidden in plain view, separated from the mainland by the narrow Evripos Channel at Halkida. Away from this workaday hub, the pace slows as the island morphs into hilltop monasteries, hidden bays, small farms and vineyards, rugged gorges, sky-reaching peaks and curious goats.

Most visitors use Evia as a jumping-off point for the gorgeous, mountainous Sporades ('scattered ones'), which feel like extensions of the forested Pelion Peninsula – and they were joined in prehistoric times. Skiathos, the most developed, has some of the sandiest, most beautiful beaches in the Aegean. Low-key Skopelos kicks back with a sparkling-white old town, rich musical traditions and pristine pebble beaches, while secluded Alonnisos anchors a spectacular national marine park and a romantically ruined old capital. Skyros is known for its culinary and artistic heritage dating from Byzantine times, when pirates patrolled these islands.

When to Go
Skiathos Town

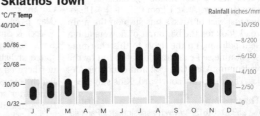

Feb–Apr Carnival season keeps things warm before spring and Easter festivities arrive.

Jun & Sep Perfect temperatures, clear skies and fewer crowds – ideal for hiking and swimming.

Jul & Aug Peak sun and beach fun (but higher prices – book ahead!)

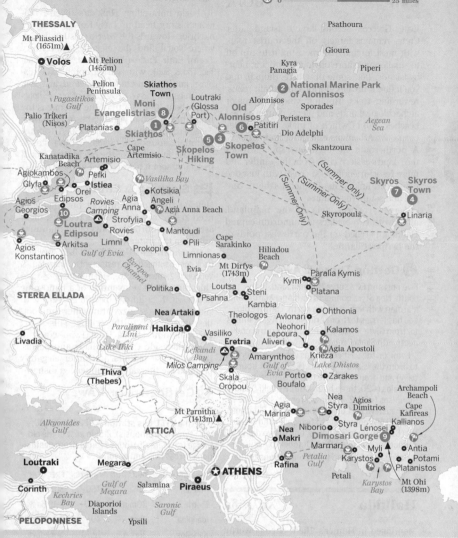

Evia & the Sporades Highlights

1 Skiathos beaches (p490) Lazing on white-sand beaches.

2 National Marine Park of Alonnisos (p500) Sailing between untouched islands and spotting dolphins.

3 Skopelos Town (p492) Drinking, dining and shopping waterside.

4 Skyros Town (p503) Delving into Skyros' unique architecture and art traditions below the Venetian fortress.

5 Skopelos hiking (p496) Meandering around glittering pebble bays and pine-sprinkled capes.

6 Old Alonnisos (p499) Wandering the alleys of this bucolic hilltop village.

7 Skyrian horses (p507) Meeting rare, gentle Skyrian horses at conservation centres.

8 Moni Evangelistrias (p490) Sampling monks' wine on Skiathos.

9 Dimosari Gorge (p486) Hiking this lush ravine in south Evia, then cooling off in the sea.

10 Loutra Edipsou (p485) Swimming year-round at a thermal-fed, north-Evia bay.

EVIA EYBOIA

POP 212,000

Evia, Greece's second-largest island after Crete, remains largely off the tourist map, with most foreign visitors using it to nip off to smaller and more obviously enticing nearby islands. Take some time here, though, and you'll find it unveils glorious mountain roads, rewarding treks, rippling vineyards, major archaeological finds and plenty of uncrowded beaches – all of which of make it a popular escape for Athenians and other mainlanders. A north–south mountainous spine divides the island's eastern cliffs from the gentler and more resort-friendly west coast, with just one main road linking its distinct northern, central and southern sections.

Ferries connect Evia to the mainland, along with two bridges at humdrum capital Halkida, perched on the narrowest point of the Evripos Channel.

ℹ Getting There & Away

Five ports on Evia serve the mainland. In the south, Nea Styra connects with Agia Marina and Marmari with Rafina. In the north, Loutra Edipsou has ferries to/from Arkitsa and Agiokambos to/from Glyfa, while in central Evia Eretria connects with Skala Oropou.

Kymi, on the east coast, has year-round ferries to/from the island of Skyros (€12.10, 1¾ hours, daily) and, from mid-June to mid-September, Skopelos (€20, three hours, three weekly) and Alonnisos (€20, 2¼ hours, three weekly). The northeastern port of Mantoudi serves Skiathos (€19.80, 2½ hours, one to two daily) and Skopelos (€19.80, 1½ to 3½ hours, one to two daily). All services are reduced from October to April.

Halkida has bus and train connections to the mainland.

Halkida Χαλκίδα

POP 59,100

Mentioned in Homer's 'Iliad', once-powerful Halkida (also Halkis or Chalkis) spawned several colonies around the Mediterranean. The name derives from the bronze that was manufactured here in antiquity (*halkos* means bronze in Greek). Today there's little to detain travellers, but Evia's capital is a lively commercial centre, and the main gateway to the island, with good restaurants and accommodation. As evening approaches, the scenic waterfront promenade extending from the old bridge comes to life beside the narrow Evripos Channel, which reverses direction several times a day.

◉ Sights

To begin unravelling Halkida's diverse religious history, head up busy Kotsou from the old bridge towards the *kastro* (castle) district, where you'll find the elegant 15th-century **Tzami Emir Zade** (Plateia Tzami; ⊙10am-2pm Tue, Thu & Sun), with cartographic Evia displays, an Ottoman-era fountain and, just east, a 19th-century **synagogue** (Kotsou; ⊙hours vary). About 100m south of the mosque is the Byzantine church of **Agia Paraskevi** (Tzavara; ⊙dawn-dusk), founded around 1250. A Roman-Venetian **aqueduct** (Stiron; ⊙24hr) stands 2km east, just north of the bus station (you'll inevitably spot it as you come into town).

🛏 Sleeping & Eating

Halkida isn't a tourist hotspot, but you might need to stay over for practical reasons; there are a few comfortable budget and midrange hotels on the waterfront.

Pantheon 1900 (☑22210 23123; www.facebook.com/pantheon1900restaurant; Kriezotou & Voudouri 22; mains €8-16; ⊙8am-1am; 🛜☑) is a chic, moodily lit reinvention of a handsome neoclassical building by the water, with snappy service, a buzzy atmosphere and bottles towering up to the ceiling. This smart bar-restaurant stocks local Evia wines to enjoy alongside creative salads and pastas, Italian cheese platters and other elegantly prepped Mediterranean-influenced dishes.

ℹ Getting There & Away

BUS

From the **KTEL bus station** (☑22210 20400; cnr Styron & Arethousis), 2.5km east of the old bridge (taxi fare €5), buses run to/from destinations across Evia and beyond.

DESTINATION	DURATION	FARE (€)	FREQUENCY
Athens	1hr	7.50	30mins
Eretria	30mins	2.20	8-10 daily
Ioannina	7hrs	40	4 weekly
Karystos	3hrs	12.70	weekdays
Kymi & Paralia Kymis	2hrs	9.20	8-10 daily
Limni	2hrs	8.60	2-3 daily
Loutra Edipsou	3½hrs	13	daily
Mantoudi	2hrs	6	2-3 daily
Steni	45mins	3.30	4 daily
Thessaloniki	6hrs	40	daily

TRAIN

Trains connect Halkida with Athens (€6.50, two hours, 12 daily); for Thessaloniki, change at Inoi.

Eretria   Ερέτρια

POP 4160

Eretria, 20km southeast of Halkida, is the first place of interest on Evia for travellers coming from the mainland. It has a small fishing harbour and a touristy boardwalk of lively tavernas, open-air cafes and beach bars; it's also home to some of Evia's most important archaeological remains.

◉ Sights & Activities

Ancient Eretria   ARCHAEOLOGICAL SITE
(◉ 8am-4pm Wed-Mon) FREE Ancient Eretria, a major maritime power with an eminent school of philosophy, was destroyed in 87 BC by the Roman commander Sylla. Its fascinating ruins lie scattered around town; pick up a map at the Archaeological Museum. Southwest of the ancient hilltop **acropolis** are the remains of a 5th-century-BC **theatre** and a 4th-century-BC temple; the most fascinating site is the **House of Mosaics** (370 BC), with pebble mosaics depicting mythological scenes.

Archaeological Museum of Eretria   MUSEUM
(⌨ 22290 62206; Archaiou Theatrou & Isidos; €2; ◉ 8.30am-4pm Wed-Mon) This captivating museum displays the archaeological riches unearthed here since the 19th century, with information detailed in Greek and French. The signature pieces are the 4th-century-BC terracotta depiction of the mythical Medusa, whose tresses were turned into live serpents by the goddess Athena as revenge for Medusa's dalliance with Poseidon, and the 10th-century-BC clay Centaur of Lefkandi, found broken in two.

Evia Adventure Tours   ADVENTURE SPORTS
(⌨ 6973856793; www.eviatours.com; Grand Bleu Beach Resort; ◉ 9am-noon & 5-7pm Sun-Thu, 9am-noon Fri & Sat Apr-Oct) An excellent, professional adventure-activity company offering cycling trips, winery tours (p487), guided hikes (including Dimosari Gorge (p486) and Mt Ohi (p486) in the south) and other cultural and adventure activities across Evia. The team also offers bike hire in Eretria (per day €10 to €55) and guided bike tours of Ancient Eretria (€40).

🛏 Sleeping & Eating

Diamanto Rooms   PENSION €
(⌨ 22290 62214; diamantorooms@gmail.com; Varvaki 2; s/d €35/45; ❄🛜) Ten sparkling, colourful, old-fashioned budget rooms with balconies, fridges, extra blankets, a shared kitchen and a plant-wreathed entranceway, all expertly managed by friendly owner Athina. Ask for a sea-view room.

Villa Belmar   APARTMENT €€
(⌨ 6971588424,6980003512; www.villabelmar.gr; 22 Aristonikou Eratonimou; studio €57-69, 1-bedroom, apt €87-119; ◉ Easter-Sep; P❄🛜) Handily positioned southwest of the port, these seven stylish studios and one- to three-bedroom apartments, with a private waterfront deck and direct sea access, are managed by welcoming sisters Lina and Renia. Each rustically modern apartment has its own balcony, with views out to sea or of the palm-dotted gardens.

La Cubana   GREEK €
(⌨ 22290 61665; www.facebook.com/lacubana restauramt; ArheouTheatrou44; mains €6-12; ◉ noon-midnight Apr-Oct, Fri-Sun only Nov-Mar; 🛜🍴) Dine on the waterfront terrace or in the elegant interior at this smart Greek-Cuban-owned seaside restaurant, known for its well-priced fresh fish, late-night grills, tasty seafood appetisers and good service. Veggie choices include feta-stuffed peppers and giant salads.

ℹ Information

Info Center Evia (⌨ 22290 65909; www.info centerevia.gr; ◉ 10am-2pm Mon-Fri)

ℹ Getting There & Away

Ferries (www.ferrieseretriaoropos.gr) travel between Eretria and mainland Skala Oropou (€2, 25 minutes) half-hourly from 8.30am to 8.30pm or 9.30pm; buy tickets at the dock kiosks.

From the **KTEL bus stop** (Filosofou Menedimou), 400m northwest of the ferry dock, buses run to/from Halkida (€2.20, 30 minutes, 10 to 14 daily) and Athens (€9.70, 1½ hours, nine daily).

Steni   Στενή

POP 400

The bucolic mountain village of Steni, with its gurgling springs and shady plane and chestnut trees, 30km northeast of Halkida, is the starting point for several hiking and cycling trips, including the popular trek up Evia's tallest peak, Mt Dirfys. From Steni, a scenic twisting mountain road continues to **Hiliadou Beach** and Kymi on the east coast.

🏃 Activities

Usually snow-dusted through spring, Mt Dirfys is Evia's highest mountain (1743m). From the 1120m-high **Dirfys Refuge**

(☑22210 25230; www.eoschalkidas.gr; per person €12) – accessible via a winding 9km road northeast from Steni, the last 2km by dirt track – it's a steep 7km to the summit and back. Experienced hikers should allow about six hours return. A couple of trails head uphill from Steni to the refuge.

For refuge bookings and information on current hiking conditions, contact the helpful EOS-affiliated **Halkida Alpine Club** (☑22210 25279, 22210 25230; www.eoschalkidas.gr; Angeli Gouviou 22; ◷6.30-9.30pm Tue & Wed). The Anavasi Topo 25 map, *Dirfys 5.11 1:25,000* is a handy resource.

🛏 Sleeping & Eating

⭐ **Mousiko Pandoxeio** BOUTIQUE HOTEL €€
(☑6932344755, 22280 51202; www.mousikopandoxeio.gr; incl breakfast d €75, ste €120, q €90-105; [P][❄][📶]) One of Evia's most wonderfully original hotels, the 'music lodge' conceals 10 individually designed, boutique-inspired, music-themed rooms, including two suites with hot tubs and family pads for three to five. All are styled with custom-made music-inspired headboards and many have log fires. Owner and composer Tassos Ioannides performs regularly.

Taverna Kissos TAVERNA €€
(☑22280 51226; mains €8-14; ◷noon-late May-Sep, reduced hours Oct-Apr; [P][📶]) One of a cluster of attractive brook-side eateries, this gentle wood-lined place serves hearty meat grills, roast mushrooms, *tyropita* (cheese pie), *mayirefta* (ready-cooked meals) and generous salads of locally grown greens. Grab a table on the terrace, with river and village views.

> ### ⓘ KYMI FERRIES
>
> A prosperous agricultural centre surrounded by vineyards and fruit orchards, the workaday east-coast town of Kymi perks up at dusk when its main square springs to life. The port of Paralia Kymis, 3.5km east, has a string of waterside tavernas and cafes. It is the departure point for ferries to Skyros, Alonnisos and Skopelos. Skyros Shipping Co (p492) ferries run to/from Skyros year-round (€12.10, 1¾ hours, daily) and, from mid-June to mid-September, to/from Skopelos (€20, three hours, three weekly) and Alonnisos (€20, 2¼ hours, three weekly). Buses to/from Halkida (€9.20, two hours, eight to 10 daily) meet ferry departures and arrivals.

ⓘ Getting There & Away

Steni has buses to/from Halkida (€3.30, 45 minutes, four daily).

Northern Evia

From Halkida a road threads 50km north into the mountainous, forested interior of northern Evia via the Derveni Gorge to the village of Prokopi. The town's inhabitants are descended from refugees who came from Turkey's Prokopion in 1923 and established the pilgrimage church of **St John the Russian** (Prokopi; ◷dawn-dusk).

At Strofylia, just north of Prokopi, the road forks northeast to the brown-sand beach resort of **Agia Anna** or southwest to picturesque Limni. North from Limni lie the olive-growing town of **Rovies** (with its crumbling medieval tower) and the well-known thermal resort of Loutra Edipsou. Northeast from Loutra Edipsou, on Evia's northernmost coast, are a string of beach-holiday spots favoured by Greeks, including **Pefki**.

Limni   Λίμνη

POP 1640

An attractive amphitheatre-like maze of whitewashed, rust-roofed houses and narrow lanes spilling on to a cosy harbour, the laid-back coastal town of Limni retains a small-island charm that makes it one of Evia's most appealing resorts. Slim silver-pebble beaches extend to the north and south, and there's an important 16th-century convent, Galataki, nearby. The town itself centres on its cafe- and taverna-speckled waterfront, with views across to the mainland.

◎ Sights

Moni Agios Nikolaos Galataki (☑22270 31489; ◷9am-noon & 5-8pm) is one of the island's oldest convents, now home to six welcoming nuns. The splendidly positioned 16th-century Galataki convent lies 9km southeast of Limni. It is accessed via a narrow road that hugs a shimmering shoreline (with plenty of stops for a swim) before climbing steeply (the last sections unpaved) to hillsides that were badly damaged by fires at research time. The fine *Entry of the Righteous into Paradise* fresco adorns its main church.

🛏 Sleeping & Eating

⭐ **Eleonas** AGROTURISMO €€
(☑6936887902, 22270 71619; www.eleonashotel.com; Rovies; d €60-80, ste €70-90; ◷Mar-Oct; [P][📶]) 🍴 Hidden amid a sea of olive trees,

SPA ESCAPE

The sedate spa resort of **Loutra Edipsou** is the most visited spot in northern Evia, with grandiose wellness-focused hotels sprinkled along its waterfront, which gazes south towards the mainland. The therapeutic sulphur waters here bubble up at up to 80°C and have been celebrated since antiquity, though it wasn't until the mid-20th century that they enjoyed peak popularity. Famous swimmers have included Aristotle, Strabo, Plutarch, Plinius, Sylla and Churchill. Today, the town continues to draw a stream of mostly mature medical tourists, and is known for hosting the country's most up-to-date hydrotherapy and physiotherapy centres.

The showstopper property is the fabulous **Thermae Sylla** ([✆]22260 60100; www.thermaesylla.gr; Posidonos 2; massage or treatment €60-140; ⊙9am-8pm) spa hotel, but there are also smaller, more affordable guesthouses and hotels, many of them with their own spas and pools.

There are several low-key waterfront eateries worth a try for mezedhes (appetisers) and skewered grills washed down with local wines. Loutra Edipsou has a refined and relaxed atmosphere, so nightlife usually consists of a poolside glass of wine before bed, though the waterfront has a few cafe-bars.

12km northwest of Limni, Eleonas delights with its 10 rustic-modern balconied rooms (some with bunks) and sweeping views. Knowledgeable owner Marina (who weaves the beautiful carpets) welcomes guests with fresh lemonade and breakfasts of home-baked bread, own-grown organic olive oil and other Evia goodies. Home-cooked dinners (€18.50), yoga, hiking trips and more available.

Graegos Studios APARTMENT €€
([✆]22270 31117; www.graegos.com; Posidonos; apt €50-70; [P][❀][☎]) A lemon-yellow home opening through a geranium-studded courtyard, year-round Greek-German-owned Graegos has three comfortable and sprucely maintained apartments with modern kitchenettes, as well as a simple private room, at the south end of town. The front two studios have big verandas and sea views.

To Astron TAVERNA €
([✆]22270 31487; dishes €4-12; ⊙noon-5pm & 7pm-midnight daily May-Sep, Sat & Sun only Oct-Apr) The family team catches and cooks its own fresh fish at this beautifully located seafood-starring taverna, with check-cloth tables dotted around a shady roadside terrace, 3.5km southeast of Limni en route to the Galataki convent. Mezedhes (appetisers) run from tzatziki and *taramasalata* (fish-roe puree) to potato salad, and there are plenty of meat-rich mains, too.

❶ Getting There & Away

There are two to three daily buses between Halkida and Limni (€8.60, two hours).

Southern Evia

Around 35km east of Eretria, the road branches south at Lepoura and the north's rich vegetation gives way to sparse, rugged southern mountains. You'll pass **Lake Dhistos** and plenty of wind farms, and catch views of both coasts as the island narrows and the road climbs spectacularly to run along clifftops before descending to Karystos. The latter is the south's attractive main seaside resort, with excellent hiking, and there are interesting sights in **Myli**, a well-watered village 4km inland, too. With your own transport you can explore the pristine, isolated **Cavo d'Oro** villages east of Karystos in the southern foothills of Mt Ohi, including pretty **Platanistos** (with its waterfall and stone bridges), **Potami** (with a beach and camping) and the whistling village of Antia.

Karystos   Κάρυστος
POP 5110

Set below Mt Ohi (1398m) on wide Karystos Bay, and flanked by two sandy silver-brown beaches, this low-key coastal resort is southern Evia's main hub, where friendly locals enjoy life at a pace that makes you forget how close you are to Athens. Mentioned in Homer's 'Iliad', Karystos was a powerful city-state during the Peloponnesian War. Today, there's little evidence of its former status, and the down-to-earth grid-design town is the starting point for stunning treks up Mt Ohi and down Dimosari Gorge, as well as a popular weekend getaway for Athenians.

LOCAL KNOWLEDGE

THE WHISTLING VILLAGE OF ANTIA

Around 35km northeast of Karystos, the 'whistling village' of Antia (pop 37) is famous for its linguistically talented villagers who speak in *sfyria*. One of a small global group of whistling languages, this one was devised during Byzantine times to warn of danger and invasion from pirates, with each tone corresponding to a letter of the alphabet. Until the early 1980s the language was still widely used, but today it's mostly the old-timers who communicate in whistles. That said, efforts are under way to save the language from extinction. Stay tuned.

The lively Plateia Amalias faces the harbour, which glitters come evening with lights and bobbing boats. A few white-sand-and-pebble beaches trickle southeast and southwest around the bay.

⊙ Sights & Activities

Archaeological Museum of Karystos   MUSEUM
(☏ 22240 29218; Kriezotou; €2; ⊘ 8am-4pm Wed-Mon) Karystos' small, insightful museum, opposite the Bourtzi (Waterfront), highlights the region's long history and ancient power. Displays, with multilingual booklets, range from tiny Neolithic clay lamps found on Mt Ohi to relics from the area's Roman quarries and a 4th-century-AD marble Aphrodite.

★ Dimosari Gorge   HIKING
This beautiful, well-maintained 10km trail descends northwards from the Petrokanalo mountain shoulder (950m) through Lenosei village to the sand-and-pebble beach of Kallianos. Much of the hike follows a cobbled path, splashing through shady creeks, ponds, giant ferns and forest. Allow four hours (including a swim!). South Evia Tours (☏ 22240 26200; www.eviatravel.gr; Plateia Amalias; ⊘ 9am-10pm) and Evia Adventure Tours (p483) arrange transport and guides.

Mt Ohi   HIKING
The summit of Mt Ohi (Profitis Ilias; 1398m), Evia's third-highest peak, is crowned by mysterious ancient *drakospita* (dragon houses): Stonehenge-like 7th-century-BC dwellings or temples, hewn from rocks weighing several tonnes and joined without mortar. From Myli, it's a 7.6km hike to the summit (three

to four hours). The dragon houses' position near marble quarries suggests that they were guard posts; another theory holds that they honoured mythological deities that roamed Mt Ohi, in particular the goddess Hera.

It's possible to stay overnight at the 1000m-high refuge then hike up Mt Ohi to catch sunrise (30 minutes); contact South Evia Tours or Evia Adventure Tours (p483) for details.

🛏 Sleeping & Eating

Karystion   HOTEL €€
(☏ 22240 22391; www.karystion.gr; Kriezotou 3; incl breakfast s €36-97, d €44-105; 🅿 ❄ 🛜) With helpful multilingual staff, the in-demand Karystion sits above the beach just east of the Bourtzi castle. The modern, uncluttered, well-appointed rooms (some smarter than others) have balconies that look out on to a pine-dotted headland. Stairs lead to a small sandy beach, while perfect local-produce breakfasts are served on the shady terrace.

Montofoli Estate   VILLA €€€
(☏ 6937282347, 22240 23951; www.montofoliwines.com; villas €180-330; 🅿 ❄ 🛜 🏊) On the historical Montofoli Estate, whose origins date to the Frankish era, these four character-rich, all-different villas comprise some of Evia's most inspiring accommodation. Vines and citrus trees scent the grounds, overlooked by a sea-view pool and the three main villas, which were part of a Venetian-era mansion (tiled floors, twisting staircases). The colourful Amfithea villa flaunts more contemporary style.

★ Cavo d'Oro   TAVERNA €
(☏ 22240 22326; mains €5-8; ⊘ 9am-late Apr-Nov; 🛜) Join the locals at this cheery alleyway restaurant just back from the central waterfront for beautifully home-cooked Greek mainstays such as octopus in red wine sauce, creamy *spanakorizo* (spinach and rice), grilled halloumi with tomato jam, and country salads featuring local produce and olive oil. Genial owner Kyriakos is a regular at the wine festival held in August and September, bouzouki in hand.

ℹ Getting There & Away

BOAT
There are regular ferries from Marmari (12km northwest of Karystos) to Rafina on the mainland (€9, one hour, two to six daily), and from Nea Styra (35km northwest of Karystos) to Agia Marina (€3, 45 minutes, around seven daily).

Buy tickets from dock kiosks, South Evia Tours or online.

BUS

From Karystos' **KTEL bus stop** (☑ 22240 26303; Ellinon Amerikis) opposite Agios Nikolaos church, buses run to Halkida (€12.70, three hours, 5.30am Monday to Friday) and Marmari (€2, 15 minutes, two to three daily). For Athens (€20.20, five hours), connect in Halkida.

SKIATHOS   ΣΚΙΑΘΟΣ

POP 6090

Blessed with some of the Aegean's most exquisite sandy white beaches, backed by rippling hills carpeted in scented pines and olive trees, Skiathos is the most developed of the Sporades. The beautiful beach-fringed south coast is filled with walled-in holiday villas, hotels and apartments, and from June to September, when the island fills up with sun-seeking Greeks and northern Europeans, prices soar and rooms dwindle. Seek out Skiathos' elegant monasteries, hidden-away churches and hillside hiking paths, however, and you'll still catch a glimpse of its soul.

Skiathos Town, on the southeast coast, is the attractive main port with a small cobbled old town of narrow whitewashed alleys. The only other settlement is tiny south-coast Troulos, 8km southwest.

ⓘ Getting There & Away

AIR

Skiathos airport (Map p489; ☑ 24270 22229) is 2km northeast of Skiathos Town. There are regular flights to/from Athens with **Olympic Air** (www.olympicair.com) and **Sky Express**

(www.skyexpress.gr), as well as numerous summer charter flights to/from northern Europe.

There's no public transport to/from the airport. Taxis charge €12 to Skiathos Town. Luggage permitting, some people even walk into town.

BOAT

Skiathos' main port is Skiathos Town, which has links to Agios Konstantinos (June to September only) and Volos on the mainland, as well as to Skopelos, Alonnisos and, during summer months, Mantoudi (Evia, via Skopelos). The main companies are **Hellenic Seaways** (https://hellenicseaways.gr), **Anes Ferries** (www.anes.gr), **Blue Star Ferries** (www.bluestarferries.com) and **Aegean Flying Dolphins** (www.aegeanflyingdolphins.gr); services are scaled down between October and April. Tickets can be purchased from **Skiathos OE** (☑ 24270 22209; www.skiathosoe.com; Papadiamanti) and other offices along the waterfront.

SeaCab (☑ 6934343287; www.seacab.gr; per person €25; ⊙ May-Sep) runs hourly speedboats linking Skiathos with Skopelos (Glossa/ Loutraki 10am to 8pm, Skopelos Town 9.30am to 7.30pm) from May until early October.

ⓘ Getting Around

BUS

Buses run between Skiathos Town and Koukounaries Beach (€2, 30 minutes) every 15 minutes from 7am to 11pm in July and August, with slightly reduced services the rest of the year (timetables are posted at stops); they stop at 26 numbered beach-access points along the south coast.

CAR & MOTORCYCLE

Reliable motorbike- and car-hire outlets include **Creator Tours** (Europcar; ☑ 69332382332, 24270 22385; www.creatortours.com; New Port; ⊙ 9am-9pm May-Oct, reduced hours Nov-Apr) (with a Europcar concession) and **Heliotropio**

WORTH A TRIP

EVIA WINERIES

Evia's increasingly popular wines highlight unique local grapes, some of which have been rescued from the brink of extinction, and several island vineyards have thrown open their doors to visitors for tours and tastings. Based in Eretria, Evia Adventure Tours (p483) runs winery-hopping excursions (from €35), while in the far south Karystos hosts a fun-filled summer wine festival.

Lukas Winery (☑ 22290 68222; www.facebook.com/lykoswinery; Malakonta; tours €9-18; ⊙ 10am-5pm)

Avantis Wine Estate (☑ 22210 55350; www.avantiswines.gr; Mytikas; tours & tastings €8-20; ⊙ 10am-5pm Mon-Fri, 11am-4pm Sat, 11am-3pm Sun)

Vriniotis Winery (☑ 22260 32429, 6944694082; www.vriniotiswinery.gr; Gialtra; tours €6; ⊙ 10am-2pm & 4-8pm Jun-Sep, by appointment Oct-May) ✿

Montofoli Estate (free Sat Jul-Sep; by appointment €8-12; ⊙ tours 7pm Sat Jul-Sep or by appointment)

Tourism & Travel (Aegean Car and Moto Rental; 24270 22024; www.heliotropio.gr; New Port; 9am-9pm May-Oct, reduced hours Nov-Mar), both in Skiathos Town's new port.

Skiathos Town   Σκιάθος

POP 4880

Extending gently across low-rise hills on the southeast coast, Skiathos Town is the island's hub and ferry harbour, with hotels, galleries, travel agents, tavernas, boutiques and bars strung along the waterfront and the cobbled pedestrian thoroughfare Papadiamanti. Away from the main drag, though, things quieten down quickly: the pedestrianised hillside old town – branching off near **Tris Ierarches** (Plateia Trion Ierarhon; dawn-dusk) church above the scenic old port, opposite pine-dusted **Bourtzi** islet – retains much of its charm and local flavour, with slim whitewashed streets, tiny squares and sky-blue doors.

Sights & Activities

Skiathitiko Spiti   MUSEUM
(24270 21334; skiathitikospiti@gmail.com; Polytechniou; €2; 10am-2pm & 6-11.30pm May-Oct) Bursting with generations' worth of Skiathos heirlooms, this handsome, stone-walled traditional early-20th-century home has been lovingly transformed into a fascinating two-floor museum by the knowledge-able Papadopoulis family, who show visitors around personally and offer a glass of wine in the back garden. It's in the old town, just south of Papadiamanti.

Papadiamantis House Museum   MUSEUM
(www.papadiamantis.net; Plateia Papadiamanti; €1.50; 9.30am-1.30pm & 5-8pm Tue-Sun Jun-Sep, 10am-1.30pm Tue-Sun May & Oct) Skiathos was the birthplace of famous 19th-century Greek novelist and short-story writer Alexandros Papadiamantis, who is looked on as the father of modern Greek literature, and whose writings draw upon the hard lives of the islanders he grew up with - many are inspired by or set in the old capital, Kastro (p490). His plain, whitewashed, wood-floor 1860 house is now a small and charming museum with books, paintings and photos of the author and his family.

★ **Argo III Yacht**   BOATING
(6932325167; www.argosailing.com; New Port; per person €85; Apr-Oct) For a splendid sail-ing tour of the island waters between Skiathos and Alonnisos (lunch included!), climb aboard the *Argo III*, managed by husband-and-wife team George and Dina.

Octopus Diving Centre   DIVING
(6944168958, 24270 24549; www.odc-skiathos.com; Hotel Alkyon, New Port; s dive €50; mid-Jun–Sep) This popular husband-and-wife diving team runs a range of dives and courses, including beginner dives (€60) and PADI open-water certification (€400), as well as half-day snorkelling trips (€20). Based on their boat opposite the taxi rank, or at Hotel Alkyon.

Sleeping

Skiathos House   GUESTHOUSE €
(6972887900, 24270 22733; www.skiathoshouse.gr; off Papadiamanti; r €40-50; Apr-Oct;) Comfortable, outstanding-value modern rooms, studios and apartments fill this lovingly restored townhouse, with a palm-shaded back garden and super-central location. Rooms come with kettles, hairdryers and simple pine furnishings; most have little balconies. Welcoming Athenian proprietor Denis is full of island tips, and has umbrellas and beach towels for guests. It's behind the post office, one street from upper Papadiamanti.

Mouria Hotel   HOTEL €€
(24270 21193; www.mouriahotelskiathos.com; Papadiamanti; d incl breakfast €60-90; Easter–mid-Oct;) Set back around a flower-filled courtyard, the handsome, super-central, ef-ficiently run Mouria hides just behind the National Bank. There's a shared kitchen – though a full breakfast awaits – plus 12 bright, modern, blue-and-white rooms (with hairdryers and, for most, wooden balconies) and vintage photos all around.

The reliably good terrace **taverna** (24270 23069; mains €8-14; 6pm-late mid-May–mid-Oct;) was once a regular haunt of novelist Alexandros Papadiamantis.

Bourtzi Boutique Hotel   BOUTIQUE HOTEL €€€
(24270 21304; www.hotelbourtzi.gr; Moraitou 8, cnr Papadiamanti; r incl breakfast €110-260; May-Oct;) All straight lines and creative touches, the swish Bourtzi brings a splash of boutique flair to down-to-earth Skiathos Town, on upper Papa-diamanti. Stripped-back contemporary rooms rise around an inviting pool; some

Skiathos

are decorated in upbeat statement colours. Warmly attentive staff deliver welcome cocktails, and there's a stylish bar.

🍴 Eating & Drinking

Skiathos Town is full of overpriced tourist-oriented eateries serving *etsi-ketsi* (so-so) food, but there are a few good exceptions, especially in the narrow lanes around the old port and along the waterfront past the new harbour (near the dance-until-dawn clubs).

The drink-till-you-drop scene heats up after midnight along the seafront club strip beyond the new port; most places open only from June or July to September. Late-night bars cluster on Plateia Papadiamanti, Polytechniou and Papadiamanti in town. For the beach-bar buzz, head out of town, especially to Koukounaries Beach (p490).

★ **Kabourelias**   TAVERNA €

(☑ 24270 21112; Old Port; mains €7-15; ⏱ 11am-midnight; 🛜) Poke your nose into the open kitchen

to glimpse the day's catch at this beloved, efficient, well-established old-port taverna with blue-cloth tables across from the water. Grilled octopus, *taramasalata* and halloumi dressed with lemon grace the standout mezedhes selection; perfect fish grills and house wines complete the picture, all at deliciously down-to-earth prices. And it's open all year!

O Batis   TAVERNA €

(☑ 6974380129, 24270 22288; Old Port; mains €4-13; ⏱ 9am-midnight May-Sep, reduced hours Oct-Apr) This popular, long-established fish taverna on the path above the old port is a local standby for reliable and well-priced fresh fish, *gavros* (a marinated small fish) and fine mezedhes. Cosy atmosphere, warm welcome, fresh Greek ingredients and a good selection of island wines, year-round.

★ **Marmita**   MEDITERRANEAN €€

(☑ 24270 21701; www.marmitaskiathos.com; 30 Evangelistrias; mains €11-18; ⏱ 6.30-11pm late Apr-Oct; 🍴) Twirls of greenery and soothing background music mingle with cheese-grater lamps, olive-oil baskets and candlelit tables in this tranquil, standout courtyard restaurant off upper Papadiamanti. From avocado-chicory salads, vegan *mousakas* (baked layers of aubergine or courgettes and potatoes) and mushroom-stuffed ravioli to succulent grilled meats and sea bass *en papillote*, Marmita's Greek-Mediterranean flavours are elegantly creative delights. Bread arrives in wooden boxes, and there are good Greek wines.

Ergon
DELI €€

(☑ 24270 21441; www.ergonfoods.com; Papadiamanti; breakfasts €4.50-9, mains €11-19; ☺9am-midnight May–mid-Oct; ☎🅿) Skiathos' upper-Papadiamanti outpost of Thessaloniki-born local-produce powerhouse Ergon is a firm favourite for third-wave coffee and internationally inspired breakfasts given a Greek twist – poached eggs with Greek yoghurt, omelettes stuffed with local cheeses, Skopelos cheese pies. It's a sleekly designed deli space where polished wood and varnished concrete offset shelves crammed with Greek wines, olive oil, ouzo and other goodies.

Taverna Akrogiali
TAVERNA €€

(Map p489; ☑ 24270 21330; kostasgeorgoulas9@gmail.com; Paraliakos; mains €9-15; ☺noon-midnight May-Oct) In an enviable seafront perch, 300m east of the new port, Akrogiali is the town's fresh-seafood favourite. The rustic blue-and-white-themed deck, decorated with bougainvillea and potted flowers, extends out over the water, while tempting classic Greek creations include stuffed tomatoes, grilled octopus and fried feta dressed with honey and sesame.

🛍 Shopping

★ Galerie Varsakis
ANTIQUES

(☑ 24270 22255; www.facebook.com/galerie varsakis; Plateia Trion Ierarhon; ☺9.30am-2pm & 6-11pm Mon-Sat, 6.30-11pm Sun Apr-Oct). Crammed with handmade jewellery and unusual antiques, such as 19th-century spinning sticks made by grooms for their intended brides, this collection rivals the best Greek folklore museums. Upstairs is a dazzling display of owner Harris Varsakis' paintings, in oil on gold leaf, begun in the 1970s and depicting Greek myths and predatory contemporary politicians.

ℹ Information

Tourist Information Kiosk (☑ 24270 23172; New Port; ☺Jul & Aug) By the ferry dock.

Around Skiathos

🏖 Beaches

With 65 beaches, beach-hopping on Skiathos can become a full-time occupation. Buses (€1.60 to €2) ply the beach-bejewelled south coast, stopping at 26 numbered beach-access points; the final stop is protected **Koukounaries** (Map p489) in the southwest, from where you can access several other lovely beaches (though the popular twin **Banana** beaches were mostly off-limits at research time due to construction work). Most south-coast beaches have sunbeds (€8), tavernas and beach bars. The northwest coast's beaches are less crowded and more unspoilt, though subject to summer *meltemi* (dry northerly winds). There are also alluring beaches on outlying islets such as **Tsougria**, which you can reach by taxi boat from Skiathos Town.

◉ Sights

★ Moni Evangelistrias
MONASTERY

(Map p489; museum €2; ☺9am-dusk Apr-Oct, reduced hours Nov-Mar) Centred on a triple-domed church, this historic 18th-century monastery was a hilltop refuge for freedom fighters during the War of Independence, and the Greek flag was first raised here in 1807. Today, several monks do the chores, which include wine-, marmalade- and olive-oil-making. The gift shop's vintage olive and wine presses recall an earlier era, while the museum displays antique furniture and documents from the Balkan Wars; a cafe sits beside the vineyard. It's 5km north of Skiathos Town.

★ Kastro
RUINS

(Map p489; ☺24hr) **FREE** Perched dramatically on the island's rocky northernmost headland, 9km north of Skiathos Town, Kastro was the fortified pirate-proof capital from 1540 until it was abandoned in 1829. At its peak it held 20 churches and 500 homes; now, among the restored ruins, you'll find an old cannon, a Turkish-era mosque, several water tanks and four churches (including 17th-century Christos, home to several fine frescoes). Drive or walk down the steep sealed track, or join a boat trip from Skiathos Town.

🏃 Activities

Boat Trips

From around May to October, excursion boats make half- and full-day trips around the island (€18 to €25), usually taking in Kastro, **Lalaria Beach** (Map p489), Trypia Petra (Punctured Rock) and the two *spilies* (caves) of Skotini (Dark Cave) and Galazia (Blue Cave), plus a swim stop; many continue to Skopelos and, in some cases, Alonnisos. Check the individual boat signboards at the old port.

You can also hop on taxi boats from the old port to Koukounaries, Achladies Bay and Kanapitsa, as well as the offshore island of Tsougria. Boats for private day trips are moored along the town's new port.

Diving & Snorkelling

The small islets off Skiathos' south shore make for great diving and snorkelling. Local dive schools offer beginner introductory dives (€60), open-water courses (€400) and dive trips for those already certified (€50), as well as snorkelling trips (from €20). Reputable local dive schools include Koukounaries-based **Skiathos Diving Center** (Map p489; ☑6977081444; www.skiathosdiving.gr; Koukounaries Beach; single dive €50; ⊘9am-7pm mid-Apr–Oct), **Dolphin Diving** (Map p489; ☑6944999181; www.ddiving.gr; Hotel Nostos, Tzaneria Beach; single dive €50; ⊘May-Oct), 5.5km southwest of Skiathos Town, and Theofanis and Eva of PADI-affiliated Octopus Diving Centre (p488) in Skiathos Town.

Hiking

Hiking on Skiathos gets you to places most visitors never reach. At the time of writing, 25 routes have been mapped, numbered and signposted. Long-time local resident **Ortwin Widmann** (☑6972705416; www.hikingskiathos.com; per person €18; ⊘May, Jun, Sep & Oct), whose excellent *Skiathos: Hiking in the Aegean Paradise* (available at local shops) outlines all walks, offers guided hikes (€18 per person).

A particularly popular hike is the demanding 12km, four-hour loop (Route 18) from Moni Evangelistrias to Cape Kastro, returning via Agios Apostolis.

🛏 Sleeping & Eating

Achladies Apartments　　　　APARTMENT €€
(Map p489; ☑6944232655, 24270 22486; www.achladiesapartments.com; Achladies Bay; d €65-80, tr €80-90, q €85-95; ⊘May-Sep; P🛜) Behind lime-green doors 3.5km southwest of Skiathos Town, this welcoming gem features comfortable, unfussy self-catering kitchenette rooms with balconies and ceiling fans, plus an eco-friendly tortoise sanctuary and a lovingly kept garden winding down to a sandy beach.

★ **Atrium Hotel**　　　　LUXURY HOTEL €€€
(Map p489; ☑24270 49345; www.atriumhotel.gr; Paraskevi Beach; d/ste incl breakfast from €150/160;

⊘May-Sep; P❄🛜♨) A fusion of monastery-inspired architecture and soothing contemporary design makes the hillside Atrium one of Skiathos' most seductive hideaways. Stone walls and hot-pink bursts of bougainvillea blend with stylishly updated white-and-wood rooms flaunting sea-view balconies and, for some, private pools or hot tubs. A taverna overlooks the pool; lavish Greek-produce breakfasts start the day.

Exantas　　　　GREEK €€
(Map p489; ☑24270 24035; www.facebook.com/exantasbarrestaurant; Megali Ammos Beach; mains €10-18; ⊘9am-11pm May-Oct; 🛜) A gorgeous rustic-chic terrace perched right above Megali Ammos' silvery sands is the setting for elegant Exantas' creative, contemporary Greek cuisine. From courgette-pesto pasta and spring rolls with watermelon dip to glammed-up *gyros* (meat slithers cooked on a vertical rotisserie), grilled Alonnisos tuna and cheese from Tinos, dishes are expertly executed and highlight local ingredients. Excellent Greek wines and cocktails round things off.

Taverna Agnadio　　　　TAVERNA €€
(Map p489; ☑24270 22016; www.facebook.com/agnadioskiathos; mains €8-15; ⊘6-11pm mid-May–Sep) Enjoying horizon-reaching views

---

ANIMAL WELFARE GROUPS

Like many other Greek Islands, the Sporades have large populations of stray cats and dogs. Several locally based charitable organisations run sterilisation, neutering, feeding and rehoming programmes. On Skiathos, the **Skiathos Cat Welfare Association** (www.skiathos-cats.org) accepts donations and has openings for volunteers with particular skills, as does the **Skiathos Dog Shelter** (www.skiathosdogshelter.com), which also welcomes visitors at its site just south of **Moni Panagias Kounistras** (Map p489; by donation; ⊘dawn-dusk), 4km northwest of Troulous. On Skopelos, **Straycare Skopelos** (straycare@yahoo.com) accepts donations and can find tasks for travellers interested in helping out.

Note: Lonely Planet does not endorse any organisation that we do not work with directly. Travellers should investigate any volunteering option thoroughly before committing to a project.

from its lovely hillside perch, 1.5km north of Skiathos Town, deservedly popular Agnadio turns out elegantly prepped fresh seafood, grilled meats and classic island mezedhes like fried feta with sesame seeds, all accompanied by excellent wines.

SKOPELOS ΣΚΟΠΕΛΟΣ

POP 4960

Pine forests, olive groves, rippling vineyards and orchards of plums and almonds (many of which find their way into local cuisine) carpet the handsome island of Skopelos, which is notably wilder, artier and more laid-back than neighbouring Skiathos. Though famed for its starring role in the 2008 film *Mamma Mia!*, Skopelos has managed to hang on to its low-key charm. The island's sheltered southeast coast harbours a string of beautiful sand-and-pebble beaches, while the northwest coast's high jagged cliffs are exposed to the elements.

There are two settlements: the wonderfully attractive main port of Skopelos Town, on the southeast coast, and the equally delightful northwest village of Glossa, 2km north of Loutraki, the island's second port.

❶ Getting There & Away

Skopelos has two ports, Skopelos Town and Glossa/Loutraki (p495). Between them they serve Volos and Agios Konstantinos on the mainland, and the islands of Skiathos, Alonnisos and Evia (Mantoudi). From mid-June to mid-September, **Skyros Shipping Co** (☑ 22220 93465, 22220 91789; www.sne.gr; Plateia; ☺ 9am-1pm & 6-9pm) also links Skopelos Town with Kymi (Evia) and Skyros. Tickets are available online or from **Madro Travel** (☑ 24240 22300, 24240 22145; Waterfront; ☺ 9am-10pm Jun-Sep, reduced hours Oct-May) and **Dolphin Tours** (☑ 24240 23060, 6948485567; www.dolphinofskopelos.com; Waterfront; ☺ 6.30-7am, 9am-4.30pm & 6-8pm Mon-Fri, 9.30am-3pm Sat, 9.30am-3pm & 5-9pm Sun) in Skopelos Town or from **Nikos Triantafillou Agency** (☑ 6932913748, 24240 33435; www.praktoreioglossas.gr; Loutraki; ☺ 7am-8.30pm) in Loutraki/Glossa.

The main companies are **Hellenic Seaways** (https://hellenicseaways.gr), **Anes Ferries** (www.anes.gr), **Blue Star Ferries** (www.bluestarferries.com) and **Aegean Flying Dolphins** (www.aegeanflyingdolphins.gr). Most services are reduced between November and April.

SeaCab (p487) runs hourly speedboats linking Glossa/Loutraki (10am to 8pm) and Skopelos Town (9.30am to 7.30pm) with Skiathos, from May to early October.

❶ Getting Around

BUS

In summer there are five to 10 **buses** (Waterfront) per day from Skopelos Town to Glossa/Loutraki (€5.60, 55 minutes) and Neo Klima (Elios; €4, 45 minutes); and several more that go to Panormos (€3.50, 25 minutes), Milia (€4, 35 minutes), Agnontas (€2, 15 minutes) and Stafylos (€1.70, 15 minutes). Outside season services trickle down to two daily.

CAR & MOTORCYCLE

Reliable vehicle-hire operators include **Magic Cars** (☑ 6973790936, 24240 23250; www.magiccars.gr; Potoki; ☺ 7am-11.30pm), Dolphin of Skopelos and **Thalpos Holidays** (☑ 24240 29036; www.holidayislands.com; ☺ 9am-5pm Mon-Sat mid-Apr–mid-Oct).

TAXI

Taxis wait by the bus stop in Skopelos Town, charging €9 to/from Stafylos, €14 to/from Agnontas and €35 to/from Glossa.

Skopelos Town Σκόπελος

POP 3090

Skopelos Town cascades down a hillside to a semicircular southeast-coast bay in picturesque tiers of centuries-old chapels and dazzling-white houses and mansions with flower-adorned balconies and bright-blue or deep-red shutters. It's flanked at its northwest end by a ruined 13th-century Venetian kastro and a cluster of four gleaming whitewashed churches. Two quays border the town's lively cafe- and boutique-lined waterfront: the old quay wraps around the northwest end of the harbour, while the new quay at the southeastern end is used by all ferries and hydrofoils.

Strolling around town and lazing at the waterside cafes might be your chief occupations here, though there are also two small museums as well as several intriguing monasteries (p496) just outside town.

◉ Sights

Vakratsa Mansion MUSEUM

(Old Skopelitian Mansion Museum; ☑ 24240 23494; €3; ☺ 10am-2pm & 6-9pm May-Sep, but hours vary) Housed in a doctor's 18th-century mansion, Vakratsa displays medical instruments, books, clothes and furniture of the era and is well worth seeing for the window it offers on to middle-class Greek life in the 19th century. It's near the middle of the waterfront, 100m inland from the Ploumisti (p495) shop, behind a tall white wall.

Skopelos

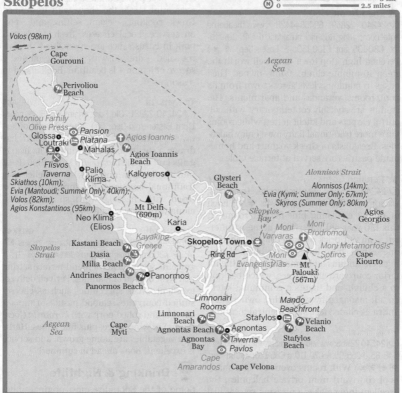

Folklore Museum
MUSEUM

(☑ 24240 23494; Hatzistamati; €3; ☺ 10am-2pm & 7-10pm Mon-Fri Jun-Sep, but hours vary) Occupying a restored 18th-century mansion, this handsome museum features a Skopelean wedding room, complete with traditional costumes and bridal bed, as well as collections of embroidery, woodcarving and other local crafts. It's just inland from the mid-waterfront and signposted.

🏃 Activities

From May to September, day-long **boat trips** (adult/child around €55/35) depart from the waterfront by 10am, taking in the neighbouring National Marine Park of Alonnisos (p500), with lunch and a swim. There's a chance of spotting dolphins along the way. For bookings, contact Madro Travel, Thalpos Holidays or Dolphin of Skopelos. Several agencies in Skopelos Town, including Dolphin Tours, offer *Mamma Mia!* tours to film locations around the island (per person €30).

SporadesSUP
WATER SPORTS

(☑ 6940448002; www.sporadessup.com; Water front; group class €25, 1hr rental €15, sunset tour €45; ☺ Jun-Sep) Fantastic paddleboarding excursions, including 2½-hour sunset jaunts, as well as classes and board hire. The same on-the-ball team runs **Skopelos Dive Center** (☑ 6940448000; www.sporadesdiving.gr; single dive €50-60; ☺ May-Sep), with its own cool cafe, as well as excellent **Ikion Diving** (☑ 24240 65158, 6984181598; www.ikiondiving.gr; Steni Vala; single dive €50-60; ☺ May-Sep) over on Alonnisos.

Skopelos Cycling
CYCLING

(☑ 6947023145; www.facebook.com/skopelos. cycling; Old Olive Oil Factory; per 24hr €10-25; ☺ 9am-2pm & 6-10pm Mon-Sat) High-quality trekking, mountain and e-bikes are available from Panos Provias at Skopelos Cycling, who provides detailed maps and route advice, as well as original guided bike tours, including 'moon rides' (€30) and a prebreakfast e-bike trip up Mt Delphi (€50).

🛏 Sleeping

⭐Thea Home Hotel PENSION €

(📞24240 22859, 6945344428; www.theahome
hotel.com; Ring Rd; incl breakfast d €45-80, studio €80-135, apt €100-150; ☺ Easter-Sep; 🛜🦽)
Perched high atop town (and well worth the
steep 10-minute climb), family-owned Thea
basks in fabulous views across town from its
pool, rooms, verandas and apartments. The
studios are stylishly contemporary, with colourful carpets and kitchenettes, while rooms
have more traditional flair; most enjoy balconies. Breakfasts of Greek yoghurt and homemade pastries are served at terrace tables.

⭐Pension Sotos PENSION €

(📞24240 22549; www.skopelostravel.net/sotos;
Waterfront; d €30-50, tr & q €30-45; ✳🛜) Each
of the 12 charming pine-floored rooms at
this 150-year-old waterfront home is different – an old brick oven becomes a shelf in
one, others have lovely wood-beamed ceilings. Geraniums and lemon trees dot the interior courtyard and terrace, which back on
to a church, and there's a communal kitch-
en, all managed by welcoming owner Alexandra. Secluded feel, super-central location.

Ionia Hotel HOTEL €€

(📞24240 22568; www.ioniahotel.gr; incl breakfast s
€48-85, d €55-95, tr €70-110, q €85-120; ☺ Jun-Sep;
🅿✳🛜🦽) With rooms overlooking a shady
pool courtyard from private balconies, the
excellent Ionia makes a pleasing retreat just
five minutes' walk inland from the waterfront. It's a traditional building, spread over
four floors, and Skopelos-inspired murals
adorn most rooms, which are done out with
a spruce rustic feel.

✗ Eating

Juices & Books CAFE €

(www.facebook.com/juicesandbooks; Waterfront;
dishes €4; ☺8am-1am Jul & Aug, 9am-2pm & 6pm-
late May, Jun & Sep; 🅙) 🖊 A fabulous midsea-
front breakfast spot and bookshop, Juices &
Books rustles up inventive toasted sandwiches, home-baked cakes, Greek-yoghurt smoothies and organic coffees (dairy-free options
available!), all served on stylish wooden trays
and infused with Skopelos ingredients. Italian-
Greek owners Tiziana and Pad put an emphasis on protecting the local environment.

⭐To Rodi GREEK €€

(📞24240 24601; Chimou; mains €11-14; ☺7pm-mid-
night May-Oct, Fri-Sun only Nov-Apr; 🅙) Sprinkled with overflowing geranium pots, in the

shade of a pomegranate tree, this courtyard
restaurant steals the show with its refined
Greek cooking, elegant setting and spot-
on service. Local cheeses, fresh salads and
pork in citrus sauce are specialities; the carrot salad – dressed with just olive oil and a
sqeeze of lemon – is beautiful. Book ahead in
season.

Ta Kymata TAVERNA €€

(📞24240 22381; Old Port; mains €7-15; ☺noon-
11pm Easter–mid-Dec; 🅙) The island's oldest
tavern, at the north end of the old port, has
drawn a steady local following for its hearty
grills and classic *mayirefta* since 1896. Peek
into the kitchen and pick from deliciously
traditional creations like shrimp *saganaki*
(fried with cheese), swordfish and lobster,
along with tasty veggie options.

To Perivoli GREEK €€

(📞24240 23758; off Plateia Platanos; mains €7-
14; ☺7.30pm-midnight approx Jun-Aug) 🖊 In a
graceful, secluded garden-and-terrace setting
just west of Plateia Platanos, Perivoli delivers
excellent Greek specialities such as cheese-
stuffed courgette, seafood pasta, shrimp *saganaki* and rolled pork with *koromila* (local
plums) in wine sauce, plus fine wines. Herbs
and vegetables are home-grown, and service
is excellent. Book ahead in summer!

🍷 Drinking & Nightlife

Some of the Sporades' most original, independent bars (both traditional and contemporary) are hidden around Skopelos Town's
alleys. There are also some fun small clubs
and venues staging earthy local live music,
especially *rembetika* (blues songs).

⭐Hidden Door COCKTAIL BAR

(Paraporti; 📞6978252848; Chimou; ☺7pm-late
May-Sep) Tucked into a moodily converted
100-year-old house where a side (hidden)
door once led to the kitchen, mellow yet
hugely popular Paraporti mixes Athens-
worthy cocktails (€11) served at candlelit
tables. It's on a lane 300m inland from the
waterfront, opposite To Rodi restaurant.

Vrachos BAR

(www.facebook.com/vrachoscocktailbar; Old Port;
☺10am-late May-Sep) Climb the twisting whitewashed stairs just left of the town hall to find
this soothing, fabulously positioned cafe-bar
spread across a tree-studded terrace next to
one of the island's most ancient churches. Go
for the homemade rose lemonade or one of
the original cocktails (€8 to €12).

★**Ouzerie Anatoli** TRADITIONAL MUSIC
(Kastro; ⊘8pm-2am approx Jun-Sep) Wait until
at least 11pm, then head to this breezy outdoor *ouzerie* (place that serves ouzo and
light snacks), high above the north corner of
the waterfront atop the *kastro,* to hear traditional *rembetika* sung by Georgos Xindaris,
Skopelos' own exponent of the Greek blues
and a bouzouki master.

🔒 Shopping

The waterfront hosts some wonderful shops
selling quality ceramics, paintings, handmade
jewellery and breezy island-style fashion.

★**Ploumisti** ARTS & CRAFTS
(📞24240 22059; Waterfront; ⊘10am-2pm &
6-9.30pm Easter-Sep) Owners Kostas and Voula
Kalafatis have been running this wonderful shop for 40 years, stocking linen shirts
and scarves, paintings, rugs and ceramics,
as well as their own handmade jewellery.
Kostas is a master of *rembetika* and often
plays at venues around town, as well as at
the Skopelos Rembetika Festival (www.
rembetikoskopelosfestival.com; ⊘mid-Jul).

Rodios Pottery CERAMICS
(📞24240 23605; Potoki; ⊘10.30am-2pm &
6-8.30pm May-Oct) Known for its black-clay
pieces made in ancient Greek style, Rodios
is one of Skopelos' original and best-known
pottery-making families in business since
1900. It's across from the main car park; the
workshop, opposite, is open year-round.

❶ Getting There & Away

BOAT

Ferries run to Alonnisos (€6, 30 minutes, one to
two daily), Evia (Kymi; €20, three hours, three
weekly), Skiathos (via Glossa; €6.50, one hour,
daily), Skyros (€20, six hours, three weekly)
and Volos (most via Glossa; €30, 4¼ hours, two
daily).

Hydrofoil services go to Alonnisos (€9, 20
minutes, two daily), Skiathos (via Glossa; €18,
45 minutes, two daily) and Volos (€35, 2½
hours, two daily).

BUS

From the bus stop (p114), just outside the ferry
dock, in summer there are five to 10 buses per
day to Glossa/Loutraki (€5.60, 55 minutes) and
Neo Klima (Elios; €4, 45 minutes); and several
more that go to Panormos (€3.50, 25 minutes),
Milia (€4, 35 minutes), Agnontas (€2, 15 minutes) and Stafylos (€1.70, 15 minutes). Outside
season services trickle down to two daily buses.

Glossa & Loutraki
Γλώσσα & Λουτράκι
POP 990

Clinging to a steep far-northwest-coast hillside, Glossa, Skopelos' sleepy second settlement, is a whitewashed cluster of typically
Greek homes and slim alleys fanning out from
a small church square, with a few shops, cafes
and restaurants. A 2km road winds down to
the laid-back port of Loutraki ('Glossa' in ferry timetables); a shorter *kalderimi* (cobble-
stoned path) also connects both villages.

⊙ Sights

Around 800m east of Glossa, signposted just
beyond a petrol station, the Antoniou Family Olive Press (Map p493; 📞24240 33517;
www.skopelosoliveoil.gr; ⊘10.30am-3pm & 5-7pm)
FREE, a 130-year-old, third-generation family-
owned mill, produces fine extra virgin olive
oil that is harvested traditionally. Visitors
are welcome to tour the modern facilities
(with audio guides), taste products and, of
course, stock up in the shop. Call ahead.

🛏 Sleeping & Eating

Pansion Platana PENSION €
(Map p493; 📞6973646702; pansionplatana@
hotmail.com; Glossa; r €35-55; ⊘May-Oct; 🅿🛜)
Just 700m east of Glossa (before you reach
the petrol station), this cosy and impeccable
guesthouse surrounded by greenery has jolly-
coloured rooms with overhead fans, kitchenettes and balcony views down to the port of
Loutraki. Welcoming Greek-Australian owner
Eleni provides tea and tips.

★**Flisvos Taverna** TAVERNA €€
(Map p493; 📞24240 33856, 6974718287; www.
facebook.com/flisvosrestaurant.loutraki.skopelos;
Loutraki; mains €8-15; ⊘noon-11pm late Apr-early
Oct) Turquoise tablecloths match the waves
washing directly below the fabulous seafront
terrace at friendly Flisvos, whose simple, superb Greek cooking excels. Appetisers such
as tzatziki, *taramasalata*, feta-courgette
fritters or halloumi with a squeeze of lemon
are standouts, and there's excellent fresh fish
plus traditional standards like *mousakas*
and *stifadho* (meat, game or seafood cooked
with onions in a tomato puree).

❶ Getting There & Away

There are also hydrofoils to Alonnisos (€11.50, one
hour, two daily), Skiathos (€11, 15 minutes, two
daily) and Volos (€32.50, two hours, two daily).

EVIA & THE SPORADES GLOSSA & LOUTRAKI

Ferry services from Loutraki/Glossa:

DESTINATION	DURATION	FARE (€)	FREQUENCY
Agios Konstantinos (summer only)	4¼hrs	29.90	daily
Alonnisos	1½hrs	9	1-2 daily
Evia (Mantoudi)	1½hrs	19.80	daily
Skiathos	30mins	5.30	1-2 daily
Volos	3¼hrs	26.50	1-2 daily

Around Skopelos

◎ Sights

There are more than 40 churches and monasteries sprinkled around Skopelos. Several of the most important monasteries can be visited on a scenic drive or day-long trek eastwards up Mt Palouki from Skopelos Town.

The monastery road forks 2km east of Skopelos Town. Continue straight then climb 2km east on a dirt track to reach **Moni Evangelistrias** (Map p493; ⊙9.30am-1pm & 4-8pm May-Oct), or take the right fork southwest to find **Moni Metamorfosis Sotiros** (Map p493; ⊙9am-2pm & 5-8pm approx Jun-Oct) (1.7km), **Moni Varvaras** (Map p493; ⊙9am-2pm & 5-8pm approx Jun-Oct) (4km) and **Moni Prodromou** (Map p493; ⊙8am-2pm & 4-8pm) (4.2km); at research time this road was paved until just beyond Sotiros, before becoming a (drivable) dirt track up to Prodromou. If you're **hiking**, it's about 1¾ hours' climb from Skopelos Town to Prodromou (6.2km), with the trail criss-crossing the main road.

The small, impossibly scenic cragtop chapel of **Agios Ioannis** (Map p493; ⊙dawn-dusk), surrounded by the shimmering Aegean 5.5km east of Glossa, is famous for having played the wedding venue in the 2008 Skopelos-starring movie *Mamma Mia!* Around 200 steps climb up the cliffs. There's a small grey-pebble beach below.

🏖 Beaches

Most of Skopelos' best beaches lie on the sheltered southwest and west coasts; a good way to reach them is by hiring a bike from Skopelos Cycling (p493).

Velanio Beach   BEACH
(Map p493) From the eastern end of **Stafylos Beach** (Map p493), 5km south of Skopelos Town, a path leads over a small headland to quieter silver-sand Velanio, the island's official nudist beach and coincidentally a great snorkelling spot, with a few sunbeds and a mellow beach bar.

Agnontas Beach   BEACH
(Map p493) Pines tumble down to almost kiss the turquoise water at the lovely little southwest-coast fishing port of Agnontas, 4km west of Stafylos, which has a tiny pebble-and-sand beach overlooked by a cluster of good seafront tavernas.

Cape Amarandos   NATURAL FEATURE
(Map p493) You could easily lose an entire day picnicking and hidden-cove swimming at spectacular Cape Amarandos. It's just south of Agnontas: take the turn 75m east of town to follow a steep dust-and-rock track (4WD recommended), off which there are plenty of private rocky beach stops backed by a sea of cascading pines. Some *Mamma Mia!* opening scenes were filmed here. At a sharp left turn 1.3km south of the original turn-off, you'll see a dramatic cleft in the rocks; follow the faint path here along the cliff to the water's edge, where a sea cave and pine shade provide a wonderfully spectacular stop.

Kastani Beach   BEACH
(Map p493) It's easy to see the temptations of Skopelos' famous 'Mamma Mia! beach': a pine-adorned, silver-sand-and-pebble stretch at the end of a steep track 13km west of Skopelos Town, with glittering aqua-coloured water, excellent swimming and a string of sun loungers (€7). These days it's overlooked by a large beach bar (May to early October).

🏃 Activities & Tours

Skopelos' pine-sprinkled hills and pebble beaches make for wonderful hiking, especially in spring and autumn. One of the most popular hikes is the 6.2km, 1¾-hour (one way) route up the slopes of Mt Palouki (567m), taking in some of the island's most fascinating monasteries. There are also good hikes in the island's north, including the two-hour trail (about 5km) from Glossa to Agios Ioannis.

★ Skopelos Walks   WALKING
(📱6945249328; www.skopelos-walks.com; guided hikes €20-40) 🌿 If you can't tell a twin-tailed pasha butterfly from a leopard orchid, join one of island resident Heather Parsons' guided walks. Her four-hour Coast to Coast walk follows a centuries-old *kalderimi* path across the island, ending at a beach taverna,

with wonderful views to Alonnisos and Evia along the way. Her book *Skopelos Trails* contains graded trail descriptions.

Heather and a loyal band of volunteers continue to clear, signpost and GPS the trails across the island. She also offers *Mamma Mia!* jeep tours to most of the movie's filming locations and guided walks around Skopelos Town, and can arrange mountain biking.

Kayaking Greece KAYAKING
(Map p493; ☑ 6983211298, 24240 33805; www.kayakinggreece.com; Milia Beach; ☺ May-Oct) This well-managed and experienced kayaking outfit offers everything from full-day trips (€65) and simple sunset outings (€35) to six-day adventures (€590) and customised island expeditions.

Sleeping & Eating

Limnonari Rooms GUESTHOUSE €
(Map p493; ☑ 6946464515, 24240 23046; www.skopelos.net/limnonarirooms; Limnonari Beach; r €45-65; ☺ Mar-Nov; [P][※][☎]) Cosy, colourful decor combines with views across beautiful Limnonari Bay and its secluded white sands at this appealing, efficiently run 10-room guesthouse, 1.5km northwest of Agnontas. Most rooms have private balconies, original artwork and fridges. The family's garden taverna serves vegetarian *mousakas,* fish and meat grills, and homemade olives and feta, or help yourself to the shared kitchen and barbecue.

★**Mando Beachfront** APARTMENT €€
(Map p493; ☑ 6936131316, 24240 23917; www.mandobeachfront.com; Stafylos; incl breakfast d €60-115, tr €75-130, villa €225-300; [P][※][☎]) ✪ Nestled above a sparkling cove on Stafylos Bay, 4.5km south of Skopelos Town, this homey, well-managed hit offers charmingly rustic rooms opening on to sea-view balconies, alongside luxe suites and villas. The outdoor communal kitchen gives way to a path down over the rocks and a platform for jumping straight in the sea, and breakfasts revolve around home-grown produce.

Taverna Pavlos TAVERNA €€
(Map p493; ☑ 24240 22409, 6948720954; www.facebook.com/pavlosagnodasskopelos; Agnontas; mains €9-15; ☺ noon-10pm May-Oct, Fri-Sun only Nov-Apr) Islanders think nothing of driving over to Agnontas for beautifully prepared fresh fish and excellent mezedhes at this cheerful and beautifully positioned shaded taverna overlooking the sea. Octopus *stifadho,* crunchy salads and *fava* (yellow split-pea dip) are among the star offerings, and the setting is dreamy.

ALONNISOS ΑΛΟΝΝΗΣΟΣ
POP 3500

The wildest, most distant and least touristed of the inhabited Sporades, Alonnisos rises from the sea in a mountain of greenery, with stands of Aleppo pine, kermes oak, mastic and arbutus bushes, vineyards and olive and fruit trees, all threaded with perfumed patches of untamed herbs. The west and north coasts are steep and rocky, while the east is speckled with seductive aquamarine bays and pebble-and-sand beaches, all of it protected by the pristine 2260-sq-km National Marine Park of Alonnisos (p500).

The original (now-restored) hilltop capital, Old Alonnisos, was rocked by an earthquake in 1965, after which locals relocated to Patitiri, now the quaint main port and island hub. The mellow village of Steni Vala (p501), 11km northeast of Patitiri, is the only other real settlement. Things amp up a few gears in July and August, while many locals decamp to Athens for the surprisingly harsh winter season.

Getting There & Away

Alonnisos' main port of Patitiri has links to mainland Volos; to nearby Skopelos and Skiathos; and, from mid-June to mid-September, to Skyros and Kymi (Evia). Services are reduced from around October to April. Tickets can be purchased online or in Patitiri from **Alkyon Travel** (☑ 22350 32444; http://alkyontravel.gr; Waterfront; ☺ 6am-8pm Apr-Oct), **Albedo Travel** (☑ 24240 65804; www.alonissosholidays.com; Waterfront; ☺ 9.30am-2pm & 5.30-8.30pm late Apr–mid-Oct) and **Alonnisos Travel** (☑ 24240 65188, 24240 66000; www.alonnisostravel.gr; Waterfront; ☺ 8.30am-10.30pm Apr-Oct).

Getting Around

Albedo Travel and Alonnisos Travel in Patitiri are reliable car-hire outlets.

Patitiri Πατητήρι
POP 1630

Alonnisos' main town and port, Patitiri (meaning 'wine press') sits between two sandstone cliffs peppered with pine trees, at the southern end of the island's east coast. With cafes, shops, travel agents and tavernas strung out along a seafront promenade, it's a modern but not *especially* charming place, though the natural setting is alluring and there's a small pebble beach. Two roads lead inland from the waterfront quay; the main road is at the eastern end of the harbour. There are no road signs: people simply refer to the left-hand or right-hand road.

Alonnisos

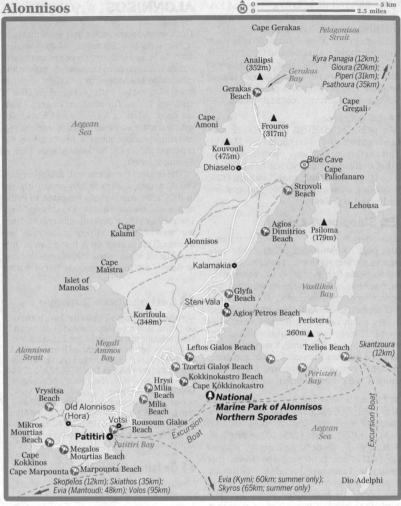

0 — 5 km
0 — 2.5 miles

Cape Gerakas

Pelagonisos Strait

Analipsi (352m) ▲

Kyra Panagia (12km);
Gioura (20km);
Piperi (31km);
Psathoura (35km);

Gerakas Bay

Gerakas Beach

Cape Gregali

Cape Amoni

Frouros (317m) ▲

Kouvouli (475m) ▲

Dhiaselo

Blue Cave

Cape Paliofanaro

Strovoli Beach

Lehousa

Aegean Sea

Cape Kalami

Alonnisos

Agios Dimitrios Beach

Psiloma (179m)

Cape Maistra

Kalamakia

Islet of Manolas

Vasilikos Bay

Glyfa Beach

Steni Vala

Agios Petros Beach

Korifoula (348m) ▲

Peristera

260m ▲

Tzelios Beach

Skantzoura (12km)

Alonnisos Strait

Megali Ammos Bay

Leftos Gialos Beach

Peristeri Bay

Tzortzi Gialos Beach

Kokkinokastro Beach

Cape Kókkinokastro

Hrysi Milia Beach

Milia Beach

⊙ National Marine Park of Alonnisos Northern Sporades

Vrysitsa Beach

Old Alonnisos (Hora)

Votsi

Rousoum Gialos Beach

Excursion Boat

Aegean Sea

Excursion Boat

Mikros Mourtias Beach

Patitiri

Patitiri Bay

Cape Kokkinos

Megalos Mourtias Beach

Cape Marpounta

Marpounta Beach

Skopelos (12km); Skiathos (35km);
Evia (Mantoudi; 48km); Volos (95km)

Evia (Kymi; 60km; summer only);
Skyros (65km; summer only)

Dio Adelphi

⊙ Sights

★ Alonnisos Museum
MUSEUM

(☑ 24240 66250; www.alonissosmuseum.com; adult/child €4/free; ⊙ 11am-7pm May & Sep, to 8pm Jun-Aug) Patitiri's excellent town museum takes in antique nautical maps, traditional island costumes, an impressive collection of pirates' weapons and boarding equipment, and an absorbing display on wartime resistance, all with detailed multilingual info booklets. Downstairs there's a recreated farmhouse interior and artefacts relating to traditional local crafts and industries, from mining to olive-oil production. It's signposted above Bar St at the southwest end of town.

MOM
MUSEUM

(☑ 24240 66350; www.mom.gr; Waterfront; ⊙ 10am-10pm Jun-Sep) 🎫 FREE Don't miss this superb 1st-floor waterfront info centre all about the rare, protected Mediterranean monk seal (p501). It has good displays, videos with English subtitles and helpful multilingual staff on hand, and the team is campaigning to reduce plastics across the local environment.

🏃 Activities & Tours

Popular excursions around the island and marine park (p500) depart from Patitiri's harbour. Knowledgeable islander **Pakis**

Athanasiou (📱 6978386588), who helped establish the marine park, captains the *Gorgona,* whose full-day marine-park trips (€40) visit the Blue Cave on Alonnisos' northeast coast and the islets of Kyra Panagia and Peristera in the marine park, with lunch, swimming breaks and a 16th-century monastery visit; book through Albedo Travel (p497). Alonnisos Travel (p497) offers similar trips (€45) aboard the *Planitis,* and there are also speedboat marine-park excursions (€50).

🛏 Sleeping

Patitiri has a selection of warmly hospitable hotels and pensions, as well as a campground and some surprisingly chic boutique-style picks. Book ahead in July and August.

Ilias Studios   APARTMENT €
(📱 24240 65451; www.ilias-studios.gr; Pelasgon 27; apt €40-50; ⏱ May-Sep; ✱ 🛜) Just 200m inland from the port, owners Ilias and Magdalini provide a warm welcome at this quiet, spruce blue-and-white building down a flower-fringed path. Rooms are bright and spotless, in simple contemporary style, with kitchenettes and balconies.

⭐ Angelo's
Apartments & Suites   APARTMENT €€
(📱 6973955267, 24240 65705; www.angelos alonissos.com; apt €40-180; ⏱ Easter-early Oct) The fabulous work of an Athenian designer, this collection of contemporary, all-different apartments is spread across two buildings, one just inland from the port and the other atop town. Soothing, creative styling marries custom-made furniture (like swing chairs) with rope, bamboo, driftwood and glassed-in showers, plus attention to detail from efficient owner Angelo.

⭐ Hotel Liadromia   HOTEL €€
(📱 24240 65521; www.liadromia.gr; d €50-80, studio €70-110; 🅿 ✱ 🛜) From hand-embroidered curtains to vintage furnishings, there's character to spare at Patitiri's welcoming, impeccably maintained original hotel, perched above the eastern harbour. Gracious owner Mary is full of tips and takes obvious delight in making it all work. Rooms (with balconies) are gradually being upgraded to a fresh rustic-chic look, and home-cooked breakfasts (€7.50) are served upstairs with sea views.

🍴 Eating

⭐ Archipelagos   TAVERNA €
(📱 24240 65031; mains €7-11; ⏱ noon-late Apr-Dec) At this outstanding and very Greek harbourfront taverna, locals gather to order round after round of fine mezedhes, always-fresh grilled fish, lovely fresh salads (try, say, the cabbage, carrot and lemon) and local firewater favourite *tsipouro* (distilled spirit of grape must) as the night rolls on.

To Kamaki Ouzerie   TAVERNA €€
(mains €5-15; ⏱ noon-1am mid-May–mid-Oct, Fri-Sun only mid-Jan–mid-May; 🛜 📱) This down-to-earth long-time local favourite, next to the National Bank tempts with its cheerful welcome and well-priced fresh fish, tasty vegetarian plates and excellent mezedhes. Weekends often see family bouzouki sessions take over.

ℹ Getting There & Away
BOAT
Ferries run to Kymi (summer only; €20, 2½ hours, three weekly) and Mantoudi (€19.80, 2¾ hours, two weekly) on Evia; Glossa (€9, 1½ hours, one daily) and Skopelos Town (€5.30, 45 minutes, two to three daily) on Skopelos; Skiathos (€9.50, two hours, two daily); Skyros (summer only; €20, 5¼ hours, three weekly) and Volos (€30, five hours, two daily).

There are also hydrofoil services to Skiathos (€15 to €18, 1½ hours, two daily), Skopelos Town (€9.50, 20 minutes, two daily), Glossa (€11.50, one hour, two daily) and Volos (€35, 3¼ hours, two daily)

BUS
Buses run to/from Old Alonnisos (€1.70, 10 minutes) at least hourly June to September from the harbourfront bus stop, or you can hike up (2.5km, 40 minutes). Summer **beach buses** (📱 6979269099, 24240 65389; return €5-10; ⏱ Jun-Sep) leave Patitiri around 10am, returning around 4pm and serving a different point to the north each day.

TAXI
Taxis gather on the harbourfront; it's €8 to €10 to Old Alonnisos and €18 to Steni Vala.

Old Alonnisos
Παλιά Αλόννησος
POP 208

Clinging to the island's southwesternmost tip, Old Alonnisos (also Palia Alonnisos or Hora) is an enchanting hilltop village of panoramic coastal views, traditionally built homes, swirling vines and flowers, and

DON'T MISS

NATIONAL MARINE PARK OF ALONNISOS NORTHERN SPORADES

In a country not particularly noted for ecological foresight, Europe's largest marine park (2260 sq km) is a welcome innovation. **National Marine Park of Alonnisos Northern Sporades** (Map p498; www.alonissos-park.gr; ⊙ May-Oct) was created in 1992, its prime aim is to protect the endangered Mediterranean monk seal and several rare seabirds. In summer, boats from Alonnisos (p498) and Skopelos run full-day trips through the pristine park, whose sea floors are carpeted in oxygen-producing posidonia. The shy monk seal is rarely seen, but you may spot dolphins (three species), turtles, Eleonora's falcons or migrating whales.

The marine park is divided into two zones, A and B. Alonnisos lies within Zone B, along with the islets of **Peristera** and **Dio Adelphi**. Access to Zone A is more restricted, with boats allowed no closer than 400m to most islets; one exception is the island of **Kyra Panagia**, whose beautifully renovated monastery dating from 1200 is visited on most boat trips. Rocky **Piperi** islet is protected by a 5km radius due to its importance for monk-seal reproduction and raptor populations.

winding, stepped, cobbled alleys branching out from a central church square. It was abandoned for Patitiri after a devastating 1965 earthquake, but has since been sensitively restored. Local families decamp here for the short summer season, when restaurants, bars, shops and hotels create a low-key buzz; at other times it's almost eerily peaceful.

◎ Sights

Church of the Birth of Christ   CHURCH
(Plateia Hristou; ⊙ hours vary) A 17th-century rough-hewn, slate-roof stone church, with its origins in the 12th century, sits on the village square; inside you'll see a tiny wooden gallery and an ornate screen depicting the lives of the Apostles.

Megalos Mourtias Beach   BEACH
(Map p498) East of Old Alonnisos, a steep road leads 2km downhill to popular Megalos Mourtias, a beautiful enclosed curve of pebbles with a couple of restaurants and apartments, a few sun loungers and umbrellas, and great views of Evia.

Mikros Mourtias Beach   BEACH
(Map p498) A 2km dirt track and a well-kept footpath lead south and downhill from the village to reach this peaceful, secluded sand-and-pebble beach, which has a wild feel (no tavernas!) and a bit of a nudist scene.

⎶ Sleeping

Old Alonnisos makes a perfect spot for a secluded stay for a night or two, with a smattering of apartments and pensions offering the chance to stay in beautiful old stone buildings. Book ahead for July and August.

Chiliadromia Studios   APARTMENT €
(☑ 6974532931, 24240 65814; www.chiliadromia.gr; Plateia Hristou; studio from €55; ⊙ late May–Sep; ✳ 🛜) Tucked into the heart of the old village, these homey studios are a wonderful budget find, featuring small balconies, comfortable beds, well-equipped kitchens and calming modern-rustic decor. The popular cafe, **Piperi** (☑ 24240 66384; www.facebook.com/piperibar; ⊙ 8.30am-2.30pm & 6pm-late mid-May–Oct) is, downstairs.

★ **Konstantina Studios**   APARTMENT €€
(☑ 24240 65900, 24240 66165; www.konstantinastudios.gr; d/ste/apt incl breakfast from €107/120/130; 🅿 ✳ 🛜) Among Alonnisos' most inspiring accommodation, these tranquil boutique studios amid gardens in the lower village are styled in calming pastels, with murals, fluffy bathrobes, fully equipped kitchens and balcony views of the southwest coast. Resourceful owner Konstantina collects guests from ferries, arranges hiking and yoga, and whips up wonderful breakfasts with homemade jams, omelettes and baked treats.

Elma's Houses   APARTMENT €€
(☑ 6945466776, 24240 66108; www.elmashouses.com; studio €60-85, apt €80-120; ⊙ May-Oct; ✳ 🛜) Two traditional village houses for up to four, overlooking a flower-filled courtyard, have been charmingly restored by architect-owner Elma, with full kitchen, comfy beds and updated bathrooms. Interiors are all rugged whitewashed walls, wood-beamed ceilings and twisting staircases, while the two kitchen-equipped studios have a balcony or terrace. It's at the south/upper end of town.

✗ Eating

★ Hayiati   CAFE €
(📞 24240 66244; www.facebook.com/melpomeni.
vas;   snacks €6-10;   ⏱ 10.30am-late May-Sep)
Gracious *glykopoleio* (sweets shop) by day
and piano bar by night (mid-June to early
September only), Hayiati delivers sweeping
coastal views from its descending outdoor
terraces at the south/upper end of town.
Morning goodies include fresh juices and
made-to-order *tyropita*; later, it's sandwiches, home-baked cakes and Greek
wines.

★ Astrofegia   GREEK €€
(📞 24240 65182; www.facebook.com/astrofegia.
alonissos; mains €9-15; ⏱ 7pm-midnight Jun-Sep;
🖋) There's a stunning village view from this
outdoor-dining delight, with its red-check
tablecloths, friendly family welcome and
wandering grape vines. Choose from good
house wines and expertly prepared Greek
standards with a touch of creativity: rare
veggie *mousakas*, white-wine-roasted lamb,
seafood souvlakia. Or go straight for the
galaktoboureko (custard slice). It's up an
alley from the village entrance.

Demi's   INTERNATIONAL €€
(📞 24240 65164; www.facebook.com/restaurants.
in.alonissos; mains €8-12; ⏱ 1-11pm, closed Mon
& Tue Nov-Apr; 🖋) Well-known internationally trained island chef Demi Karanasta-
sis turns his talents to a punchy, creative
Greek-international menu at this welcoming, shaded terrace restaurant near the
village entrance.

Around Alonnisos

Alonnisos' main road travels 20km northeast from Patitiri to **Gerakas Bay** (Map p498)
at the end of the island. Several minor roads
descend off it to small fishing bays and some
lovely secluded beaches.

⊙ Sights

Kokkinokastro Beach   BEACH
The gorgeous golden-white pebble-and-sand
arc hugging red-tinged Cape Kokkinokastro,
6km northeast of Patitiri, was the site of the
ancient, now-submerged city of Ikos, whose
ruined fortified wall you can still make out.
Expect a few sun loungers and umbrellas and
a summer beach bar beside the aqua waves.

Leftos Gialos Beach   BEACH
Washed by deep-turquoise water, this
white-pebble beach 7km northeast of Patitiri
is graced by a couple of lively summer tavernas and a sprinkling of sun loungers, and
framed by headlands thick with pine forests.

Steni Vala   VILLAGE
The island's third settlement, 11km northeast
of Patitiri, is an attractive little fishing village
and deep-water yacht port, backed by excellent seafront tavernas and rooms for rent.

Agios Dimitrios Beach   BEACH
Triangular Agios Dimitrios, 5.5km northeast
of Steni Vala, is one of the island's most beloved beaches, with a seasonal truck-canteen and
domatia sitting opposite a stretch of white
pebbles and a few sunbeds. The uninhabited
island of Peristera is just across the water.

MONKS OF THE SEA

Once populating hundreds of colonies in the Black Sea, the Mediterranean Sea and along
Africa's Atlantic coast, the Mediterranean monk seal has been reduced to approximately
just 500 individuals. Half of these live in the seas around Greece; others roam the waters
off the Turkish and Moroccan Atlantic coasts.

One of the earth's rarest mammals, the Mediterranean monk seal is now among
the 20 most endangered species worldwide. Major threats include decreasing food
supplies, destruction of habitat and low pup-survival rates (driven by seals now resting
in dangerous caves rather than on beaches). Thankfully, the once-common killings by
fishers – who saw the seal as a pest that tore holes in nets and robbed their catch –
have diminished with the recognition that protecting the seal also promotes recovery
of fish stocks. Conservation efforts are rising and, in 2015, the IUCN downgraded the
Mediterranean monk seal from Critically Endangered to Endangered, but there's a long
way to go yet.

The seals typically eat around 35kg of fish every day, with males weighing 400kg to
500kg and females 200kg to 300kg, and live around 40 years.

For more information about monk seals and to see infrared film of their impossibly
adorable pups, visit the MOM (p498) information centre in Patitiri.

🏃 Activities

Hiking opportunities abound on Alonnisos and 14 official trails have been waymarked. Popular hikes are highlighted on the Terrain, Road Cartography and Anavasi maps of Alonnisos, and in local hiking guides such as Bente Keller's *Alonnisos on Foot*. There's also basic information at www.alonissos.gr.

A few ancient sailing vessels have been discovered at the bottom of the shallow sea around Alonnisos and efforts are under way to open these sites to guided dives. Among them is the 5th-century Peristera shipwreck that is expected to open for dives in 2020. Divers might also spot dolphins, octopus and more. **Triton Dive Center** (⏺24240 65804; www.bestdivingingreece.com; Albedo Travel, Waterfront; 2-dive trip €90; ⏰May-Sep) and Ikion Diving (p493) are respected dive schools.

🛏 Sleeping & Eating

4 Epoches   HOTEL €€
(⏺24240 66101; www.4epochesalonnisos.com; Steni Vala; s €42-96, d €50-100, tr €70-120; ⏰May-Sep; 🅿❄🛜🏊) Just back from Steni Vala's waterfront, this smart, efficiently operated hotel has 22 whitewashed, modern-design rooms and kitchen-equipped studios set around a cool-blue pool garden with a few palms. All rooms have terraces, while those on top floors are graced with wood-beamed ceilings. There's a roof garden plus a bar.

⭐ Ilya Suites   APARTMENT €€€
(⏺6938327401; www.ilyasuites.gr; Glyfa Beach; ste €80-180, villa €200-300; ⏰May-Sep; 🅿❄🛜) Rose bushes, lavender and olive trees trickle down to a pebbly beach from these four low-key luxe suites and four-person villa, just north of Steni Vala, with sparkling views of Peristera island. From the bold white-on-white design, beamed ceilings and sleek kitchens to the sea-facing terraces and scented gardens, everything feels soothingly elegant and peaceful. Yoga, hiking and diving arranged.

Six new botanical-themed suites are due by the time you read this.

Dendrolimano   GREEK €€
(⏺24240 65252; Votsi; mains €10-20; ⏰6pm-late May-Oct; 🍴) With a lovely hillside terrace under the pines overlooking Votsi's azure bay, Dendrolimano is known for its creatively presented Greek-Italian cuisine given an original contemporary twist – watermelon salad and squid-ink pasta with Alonnisos tuna, for example. Good wines, glorious setting.

SKYROS   ΣΚΥΡΟΣ

POP 3000

The largest of the Sporades, low-key Skyros has a more Cycladic feel than its richly forested siblings and often seems like two entirely separate islands: small shimmering bays, rolling farmland and swaths of pines (plus an airforce base) speckle the north, while the south features arid hills and a rocky shoreline. In Greek mythology, Skyros was the hiding place of the young Achilles, who is thought to have ridden a Skyrian horse (p507) into Troy: these endangered small-bodied horses can still be seen in the wild, if you're lucky.

These days, the island has a subtly fashionable yet off-radar vibe, largely thanks to the alternative arts and wellness courses run by the British-owned **Skyros Centre** (⏺in UK 44(0)1983 865566; www.skyros.com; off Agoras; 7-day course incl meals & accommodation from £725; ⏰Jun-Sep), but it's also increasingly popular among holidaying Greeks from Athens and Thessaloniki, as well as birdwatchers seeking the slender Eleonora's falcon. Skyros Town, perched almost magically on its high rock, is the easy-going capital.

ℹ Getting There & Away

AIR

From Skyros **airport** (Map p503), 11km northwest of Skyros Town, **Olympic Air** (www.olympic air.com) flies to/from Athens and **Sky Express** (www.skyexpress.gr) to/from Thessaloniki, both several times weekly. Buses to/from Skyros Town meet flights (€2.80); taxis charge €20.

BOAT

Skyros' port is Linaria, on the west coast. Skyros Shipping Co has year-round ferries to/from Kymi on Evia (€12.10, 1¾ hours, daily); from mid-June to mid-September there are also services to/from Skopelos (€20, six hours, three weekly) and Alonnisos (€20, 5¼ hours, three weekly) .

Buy tickets online, from Skyros Shipping Co (p492) or **Skyros Travel** (⏺6944884588, 22220 91600; www.skyrostravel.com; Agoras; ⏰9.30am-1.30pm & 6.30-9.30pm) in Skyros Town, or from harbour ticket kiosks in Linaria or Kymi. Skyros Travel also arranges transfers to/from Athens, via Kymi.

ℹ Getting Around

BICYCLE

Vagios Rent a Moto-Car (⏺6986051760; www.facebook.com/rentamotocarskyros; off Agoras; ⏰9am-9pm) near the bus stop in Skyros Town and **Anemos Rent a Car -Bicycle** (⏺22220 93705, 6980038667; www.anemos-skyros.gr; Molos; ⏰9am-2pm & 5-9pm) in Molos rent out bikes (€10 per day).

BUS

Buses link up with ferry arrivals/departures, running between Linaria and Skyros Town, Magazia and Molos (€2); and with flights, connecting Skyros Town and the airport (€2.80).

CAR & MOTORCYCLE

Cars and motorbikes are available in Skyros Town from **Martina's Rental** (☏ 6974752380, 22220 92022; www.skyroscar.gr; Machairas; ☺ 9am-2pm & 6-9pm), Skyros Travel and Vagios Rent a Moto-Car, or in Magazia from **Europcar Skyros** (☏ 22220 92092; www.europcar.com; Magazia; ☺ 8.30am-8.30pm) and in Molos from Anemos Rent a Car-Bicycle.

Skyros Town Σκύρος

POP 1660

Draped over a high rocky bluff, Skyros' capital is topped by a Byzantine-Venetian **fortress** and laced with labyrinthine, smooth cobblestone streets that invite wandering, but were in fact designed to keep out the elements (as well as pirates).

A lively jumble of tavernas, bars, low-key boutiques and artisan workshops flanked by winding alleyways make up the main thoroughfare, Agoras. About 100m uphill and north from Plateia (the main square), Agoras forks left and zigzags to two small museums adjacent to Plateia Rupert Brooke (marked by a bronze nude in honour of the English poet), from where a wide stone path descends 1km to Magazia Beach (Map p503).

◉ Sights & Tours

★ Manos & Anastasia Faltaïts Museum   MUSEUM

(☏ 22220 91232; www.faltaits.gr; Plateia Rupert Brooke; €4, with tour €7; ☺ 10am-2pm & 6-9pm Jun-Sep, 10am-2pm Oct-May) Spread across the Faltaïts family's 19th-century mansion, this not-to-be-missed gem unravels the island's mythology and folklore in a multilevel

DON'T MISS

SKYROS' ARTISANS & ARTISTIC HOMES

Skyros has a flourishing community of working artists, from potters and painters to sculptors, embroiderers and jewellers. The island artistry dates from Byzantine times when passing pirates collaborated with rogue residents, whose houses became virtual galleries for stolen booty looted from merchant ships. Today, items adorn almost every Skyrian house, shown to best advantage on locally carved wooden shelves, and the island's artisans keep traditional crafts alive. The best places to see Skyrian domestic interiors are Skyros Town's Manos & Anastasia Faltaïts Museum (p503) and Archaeological Museum, which contain atmospheric recreated homesteads and traditional 18th- and 19th-century local outfits. A key feature of the Skyrian home is the *boulmes*, a dramatic carved screen often decorated with the Byzantine two-headed eagle, cockerels and pomegranates. Stone hearths are embellished with embroidery, and shelves display glass and clayware. The *krevatsoula* is a low wooden bed with fabric drapes and embroidered cushions, which might depict gorgons, ships or weddings, and small wooden chairs and shelves are carved with more emblems and patterns. Many homes feature a *sfa* (a wood-carved sleeping loft), and the overall effect is rich and sophisticated.

To see the legacy of Skyrian traditions, check out the Skyros Town workshops and showrooms of ceramicists **Stamatis Ftoulis** (☑ 22220 91559; Agoras; ⊙ 10am-1.30pm & 7.30-9.30pm Mon-Sat May-Oct) and **Olga Zachariaki** (☑ 6989992838; Plateia; ⊙ 10am-2pm & 7pm-midnight); embroiderer **Amerissa Panagiotou** (☑ 6973397693; Agoras; ⊙ 10am-2pm & 6.30-midnight May-Oct); and woodcarvers **Stamatiou Andreou** (☑ 22220 92827; Agoras; ⊙ 10am-2pm & 5-9pm May-Oct), **Yiannis Andreou** (☑ 6945229135; andreouyiannis@hotmail.com; Agoras; ⊙ 10am-2pm & 5-9pm May-Oct) and **Yiannis Trachanas** (☑ 6937215622; off Agoras; ⊙ 10.30am-2pm & 7pm-midnight May-Oct). There's more fine woodcarving, plus a Skyrian homestead, at **Woodcarving by Lefteris & Emmanouela** (Map p503; ☑ 22220 91106; www.thesiswood.com; Lino; ⊙ 10am-2pm & 7-9pm), 1km south of town. Chrysanthi Zygogianni at Feel Ingreece can fill you in on the local scene.

labyrinth of Skyrian costumes, embroidery, antique furniture, ceramics, daggers, cooking pots, historical documents and vintage photographs. There's also a collection of writings by prominent journalist Konstantinos Faltaïts, the father of artist Manos who founded the museum and whose colourful and sensual paintings are displayed throughout.

Monastery of Agios Georgios MONASTERY
(Kastro; ⊙ 10am-1pm & 6-8pm) Founded in 962, the working Byzantine Monastery of St George (whose bells might wake you early if you're staying in town) crowns Skyros Town, within the lower walls of the Byzantine-Venetian fortress (p503). You can visit its 17th-century chapel, which features an ornate gilded screen and faded 18th-century frescoes.

Archaeological Museum MUSEUM
(☑ 22220 91327; Plateia Rupert Brooke; €2; ⊙ 8.30am-4pm Wed-Mon) Along with Mycenaean pottery and jewellery found near Magazia, vessels unearthed in Skyros Town and artefacts from the Bronze Age excavation at Palamari (p507) – look especially for the two-handled ceramic cups and the head

of an imported early Cycladic idol – this attractive courtyard museum contains a traditional Skyrian house interior, transported in its entirety from the benefactor's home.

★ **Feel Ingreece** CULTURAL
(☑ 22220 93100; www.feelingreece.gr; off Agoras; ⊙ 9.30am-2pm & 6.30-11pm) ✎ Knowledgeable owner Chrysanthi Zygogianni is dedicated to helping sustain Skyrian culture, with a focus on local arts and the natural environment. The team arranges hikes (with a chance of glimpsing wild Skyrian horses, €10 per person); birdwatching trips; pottery, woodcarving, cooking, embroidery and Greek dance lessons; yoga; diving; and boat trips (€50 per person) around the island's south.

⚑ Festivals & Events

The Skyros Carnival, a wild pre-Lenten festival, which takes place on the last four weekends before Lent and Orthodox Easter, young men don goat masks, hairy jackets and dozens of copper goat bells. They then clank and dance through Skyros Town, each with a male partner dressed up as a Skyrian bride but also wearing a goat mask.

🛏 Sleeping

Nicolas Pension PENSION €
(📞 22220 91778; www.nicolaspension.gr; Playia; d €40-60, tr €55-75, q €65-85; 🅿 ❄ 🛜) On a quiet road on the southwest edge of town (off the Atsitsas road), this friendly pension is just a five-minute walk to busy Agoras. Upper-floor doubles have balconies and *kastro* views, while lower rooms (for three to four) open on to a shaded garden; some have traditional wood-carved sleeping lofts and all are full of rustic charm, with kitchenettes.

★ Nefeli Hotel HOTEL €€
(📞 22220 91964; www.skyros-nefeli.gr; d incl breakfast €89-122; 🅿 ❄ 🛜 🏊) With sleekly styled or updated-Skyrian balconied rooms strung around an enormous saltwater pool looking out on the distant hilltop castle (p503), this welcoming favourite on the southwest edge of town has a laid-back minimalist feel and a seductive boutique touch. A separate building has seven classically wood-carved, three-storey apartments.

🍴 Eating

★ O Pappous Kai Ego TAVERNA €
(📞 22220 93200; Agoras; mains €6-9; ⊙ 6pm-late daily Jun-Sep, Fri & Sat only May & Oct; 🛜 ✏) One generation of exquisite family recipes follows another at small, charming and elegant 'my grandfather and me'. It's known for its Skyrian dolmadhes, made with a touch of goat milk; other mezedhes, like potato salad and *fava*, are divine too. The raised terrace overlooks upper Agoras, while the interiors burst with flower baskets and dangling plants.

Taverna Maryeti GREEK €
(📞 6972320265, 22220 91311; Agoras; mains €6-9; ⊙ noon-late Jun-Sep, from 7pm Oct & Feb-May; 🛜 ✏) The local in-town favourite for grilled fish, goat in lemon sauce, great meat grills and marvellous mezedhes. Wines and service are excellent. Look for the snug flagstone terrace and green doors on mid-Agoras.

ℹ Information

Skyros Travel (p502) Helpful full-service agency for accommodation; transfers and onward travel; car and motorbike hire; boat excursions around Skyros; cooking classes; diving; hiking; and more.

ℹ Getting There & Away

Buses bring you into town from Linaria (€2, 15 minutes) and the airport (€2.80, 20 minutes); taxis cost €15/20. The **bus stop** (Agoras) is at the lower/southwestern end of Agoras.

Magazia & Molos
Μαγαζιά & Μώλος

POP 400

Skirting the southern end of a long, sandy grey-brown beach (p503) beneath Skyros Town, the low-key resort of Magazia is a compact whitewashed maze of winding cobbled alleys adorned with bursts of jasmine, bougainvillea and oleander. Towards the northern end of the beach and now blending with Magazia, once-sleepy **Molos** (Map p503) has its own share of tavernas, bars and accommodation, along with a landmark windmill (these days a bar; p506) and rock-hewn church (p506). The beaches get lively (by Skyros standards) in summer.

🛏 Sleeping

Magazia and Molos are wonderful places to stay, with an ever-expanding choice of laid-back beachside apartments, hotels and guesthouses to suit all budgets, many of them styled with Skyrian charm.

★ Antigoni Studios APARTMENT €
(📞 6945100230, 22220 91319; www.antigonistudios.com; Magazia; studio €55-115, 1-bedroom apt €80-150; 🅿 ❄ 🛜) A subtle boho-stylish look (jazzy throws, concrete-washed bathrooms) runs through this outstanding beach-facing pick, washed in soothing blues and whites. The 20 spacious, elegantly furnished, kitchen-equipped studios (for two to five) are just a three-minute walk to the sea, at the southern end of Magazia. Owner Katerina is full of island tips, and some rooms are adorned with Skyrian embroidery.

★ Perigiali Hotel HOTEL €€
(📞 22220 92075, 6974471053; www.perigiali.com; Magazia; incl breakfast d €60-160, q €90-200; 🅿 ❄ 🛜 🏊) Skyros embroidery and watercolours decorate cosy, bright, whitewashed rooms at leafy Perigiali, which feels deliciously secluded despite being only 60m inland from southern Magazia Beach (p503). The lovingly designed Skyrian-style rooms and apartments, with family-sized options, overlook gardens of pear and apricot trees and a saltwater pool. Breakfast is a feast of local goodies, and owner Amalia is full of advice.

Ammos Hotel HOTEL €€€
(📞 6974354181, 22220 91234; www.skyrosammoshotel.com; Magazia; incl breakfast d €72-200, q €126-235; ⊙ Easter-Oct; ❄ 🛜 🏊) Set around gardens and a pool, boutique-feel Ammos has an

inviting, low-key vibe to match its smartly updated cream-hued rooms, which feature, for some, private cabana-style terraces. Made-to-order Skyrian breakfasts start the day, and there's a summer pool bar and restaurant (mains €16) plus yoga and massage, all amid sparkling-white walls.

✖ Eating & Drinking

★ Stefanos Taverna
TAVERNA €

(☑ 22220 91272, 6974350372; Magazia; mains €6.50-10; ⊘ 9.30am-midnight Mar-Oct; 🕿 ☝) Kick back on the breezy beachside terrace at the southern end of Magazia and choose from juicy grills, baked dishes such as *yemista* (stuffed tomatoes), seriously good *saganaki* (fried cheese) drizzled with lemon, and locally sourced wild greens and fresh fish. Service is warm and efficient, and it's open early(ish) for breakfast omelettes and coffee.

★ Oi Istories Tou Barba
TAVERNA €

(☑ 22220 91453; Magazia; mains €6-10; ⊘ noon-late Feb-Nov; 🕿 ☝) Pale-blue tables and fabulous panoramas of Skyros Town mark this popular, welcoming terrace taverna overlooking the northern end of Magazia Beach (p503). Settle in for delicious fisherman's spaghetti, excellent mezedhes, lightly creative salads, fresh seafood, all in a bubbly atmosphere.

Anemomylos
BAR

(☑ 22220 93656; www.anemomulos.gr; Pouria; ⊘ 9am-3am Jun-Sep, reduced hours Oct-May; 🕿) Perched on the seafront by the rock-cut church of Agios Nikolaos (Map p503; ⊘ dawn-dusk), this chicly converted old windmill is perfect for sundowners, with wines, cocktails and light meals. Tables dot a beachside terrace and the surrounding rocks, from where you can gaze out on distant Skyros Town.

❶ Getting There & Away

Buses link Magazia and Molos with Linaria (€2, 15 minutes) and the airport (€2.80, 20 minutes), coinciding with flights and ferries; taxis charge €15 or €20 respectively.

Linaria   Λιναριά
POP 300

Skyros' mellow, fairly modern port Linaria is tucked into a small aqua bay filled with bobbing fishing boats and a few low-key tavernas and *ouzeries*, 10km southwest of Skyros Town. Things perk up briefly whenever the *Achilleas* ferry comes in and visitors flood the harbour, which is overlooked by a whitewashed blue-trim church.

◎ Sights

Pefkos Beach (Map p503) is a beautiful horseshoe-shaped beach of golden-brown sand graces deep-set Pefkos Bay, a 6km drive northwest of Linaria and home to the popular Stamatia's Taverna.

🛏 Sleeping

Lykomides
HOTEL €

(☑ 22220 93249, 6972694434; www.lykomides.gr; r €35-65, apt €70-120; ❋ 🕿) Opposite the ferry dock and efficiently managed by the hospitable Soula Pappa, traditional-style Lykomides has 13 spotless, neutral-toned, delicately updated doubles and triples with balconies overlooking the water. There's also a modern, all-white, kitchen-equipped apartment for up to five people.

Pegasus Studios & Apartments
APARTMENT €

(Map p503; ☑ 22220 91600, 6944884588; www.skyros-pegasus.gr; Acherounes; 1-bedroom apt €55-75, 2-bedroom apt €80-110; 🅿 🕿) Just back from Acherounes beach, 1.5km north of Linaria, this cluster of comfortable, uncluttered apartments with kitchens and balconies sits amid palms, vines and grassy gardens. Rooms sleep two to five, some split-level or in classic wood-carved Skyrian style, and kayaking and cooking classes are available. It's all under the watch of Skyros expert Lefteris Trakos.

✖ Eating

★ Marigo
TAVERNA €

(☑ 22220 96010; akamatra_makis@yahoo.gr; mains €7-12; ⊘ 8am-late Jun-Sep, 11am-late Apr, May & Oct, 11am-late Fri-Sun Nov-Mar; 🕿) Dressed in soothing greys, with fresh flowers, dangling baskets and modern-rustic style, Linaria's most elegant portside restaurant specialises in deliciously fresh seafood, home-cooked desserts and Skyrian specialities.

Stamatia's Taverna
TAVERNA €

(Map p503; ☑ 6972558232; www.facebook.com/stamatiaskyros; Pefkos Bay; mains €7-11; ⊘ noon-midnight Jun-Sep) Basking in views across sparkling pine-lined Pefkos Bay, with whitewashed wooden tables and a terrace enclosed by stone benches with cushions, always-a-hit Stamatia's rustles up superb daily specials, chilled *tsipouro*, fine mezedhes and plenty of grilled fresh fish and meat. It's a 6km drive northwest of Linaria.

THE SKYRIAN HORSE: AN ENDANGERED BREED

The endangered small-bodied Skyrian horse (*Equus Cabalus Skyriano*) is valued for its intelligence, beauty and gentleness. Though common across Greece in ancient times – the horses on the Parthenon frieze are thought to be Skyrian, and Skyrian horses are said to have pulled Achilles' legendary chariot – today there are fewer than 300 of these diminutive creatures worldwide, with a small minority living on the southern slopes of Mt Kochilas on Skyros. The major challenges the horses have faced are interbreeding with donkeys and severe loss of habitat due to goat and sheep breeding.

Several Skyrians are working hard to conserve this endangered species. Amanda Simpson and Stathis Katsarelias started the **Skyros Island Horse Trust** (Map p503; 6986051678; www.skyrosislandhorsetrust.com; Trachi; ⊙by appointment) in 2006 with just three horses. Their ranch in Trachi, 10km northwest of Skyros Town, has now grown into a home for 36 horses, as they seek to re-establish a herd of pure-bred Skyrian horses and raise awareness about the species' plight. Visitors are welcome at the ranch by appointment. Look for the hand-painted sign and fairground horse on the main road, just southeast of the airport.

You can also see Skyrian horses at **Mouries Farm** (Map p503; 6947465900; www.skyrianhorses.org; Flea; by donation; ⊙10am-1pm & 6-9pm Jul & Aug, hours vary Jun & Sep, by appointment Oct-May) , opposite the excellent Taverna Mouries. Run by Marion Auffray and Manolis Trachanas, the farm is engaged in both pure-breeding and increasing awareness about the horses, with a herd of 45. It also runs a volunteer programme and offers horse rides (€5) and horse-riding lessons (€25) for children only; call ahead.

For information on breeding efforts, other Skyros farms and Skyrian horses all over Greece, check out the **Skyrian Horse Society** (www.skyrianhorsesociety.gr).

ℹ️ Getting There & Away

Buses (€2, 15 minutes) to/from Skyros Town, Magazia and Molos connect with all arriving and departing ferries.

Skyros Shipping Co (p492) ferries run to/from Kymi on Evia year-round (€12.10, 1¾ hours, daily) and, from mid-June to mid-September, to/from Skopelos (€20, six hours, three weekly) and Alonnisos (€20, 5¼ hours, three weekly).

Around Skyros

◉ Sights

Palamari　　　　　　ARCHAEOLOGICAL SITE
(Map p503; ⊙7am-3pm Mon-Fri) At the fascinating Palamari Bronze Age excavation paths weave through what was once a powerfully fortified coastal settlement near the heart of early Mediterranean trade routes. The visitor centre provides an excellent introduction, and you can see more findings at Skyros Town's Archaeological Museum (p504). The site is signposted down a track off the main Skyros Town–airport road, northwest of the town.

Rupert Brooke's Grave　　　　HISTORIC SITE
(Map p503; Tris Boukes Bay) The well-tended marble grave of English poet Rupert Brooke lies in a quiet roadside olive grove just inland from Tris Boukes Bay, 11km southeast of Kalamitsa.

Paneri Winery　　　　　　WINERY
(6974230437; Trachi; ⊙by appointment) **FREE** Call ahead to visit this ambitious family-owned vineyard near the airport (with a winery in the works), which produces six wines including semisweets. The exact location is provided once you make an appointment. On Instagram @paneri_winery.

✖️ Eating

★ Taverna Mouries　　　　TAVERNA €
(22220 93555; Flea; mains €7-11; ⊙noon-late May-Oct;) Super-sized, deliciously traditional island cooking rooted in home-grown organic produce is the star at sprawling Mouries, whose soothing terrace sits beneath mulberry trees, 6.5km south of Skyros Town.

Asimenos　　　　　　　SEAFOOD €€
(Map p503; 22220 93007; www.facebook.com/asimenosfishtavern; Aspous; mains €6-12; ⊙noon-midnight May-Sep) Look for the turquoise-shutter sign and lightly stylish roof terrace, 3.5km south of Skyros Town, to find this sensational seafood taverna. The owners have their own fishing boat, so the super-fresh catch of the day is the thing here, and there are plenty of salads, wines, mezedhes and local cheeses to feast on, too.

Ionian Islands

POP 207,855

Best Places to Eat

➜ Old Perithia Taverna (p517)

➜ Ladokolla Stin Plagia (p538)

➜ Thymari (p529)

➜ Skandeia (p554)

➜ O Platanos (p554)

Best Places to Stay

➜ Perantzada 1811 (p542)

➜ Museum Hotel George Molfetas (p537)

➜ Locandieta Guest House (p516)

➜ Hotel Margarita (p551)

➜ Boschetto Hotel (p529)

Why Go?

With their cooler climate, abundant olive and cypress trees, and forested mountains, the Ionians are a lighter, greener variation on the Greek template. Venetian, French and British occupiers have all helped to shape the islands' architecture, culture and (excellent) cuisine, and contributed to the unique feel of Ionian life.

Though the islands form a chain along the west coast of mainland Greece, each has its own distinct landscape and history. Corfu Town holds Parisian-style arcades, Venetian alleyways and Italian-inspired delicacies. Lefkada boasts some of Greece's finest turquoise-lapped beaches, while Kefallonia is adorned with vineyards and soaring mountains. Paxi's Italianate harbour villages are postcard pretty, and soulful Ithaki preserves wild terrain and a sense of myth. Zakynthos has sea caves and waters teeming with turtles, and Kythira offers alluring off-the-beaten-track walks. Whether it's your first or 50th visit, the Ionians hold something new for adventure-seekers, food-lovers, culture vultures and beach bums alike.

When to Go
Corfu Town

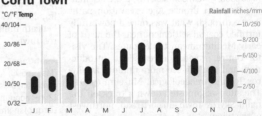

May Life is still quiet while the wildflowers are in bloom everywhere.	**Jul** Escape the heat elsewhere in Greece by heading to the country's coolest islands.	**Sep** Leaves change colour, and the *robola* grapes are harvested in Kefallonia.

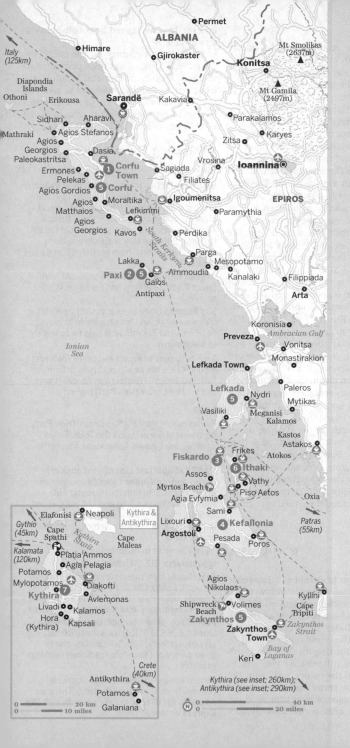

Ionian Islands Highlights

❶ Corfu Town (p512) Exploring world-class museums, fortresses and restaurants, as well as Venetian, French and British architecture.

❷ Paxi (p523) Hopping from one gorgeous harbour to another on this tiny pastoral island.

❸ Fiskardo (p539) Savouring the flavours in the waterfront restaurants of Kefallonia's best-preserved historic village.

❹ Kefallonia (p532) Diving and kayaking in the myriad magnificent bays that pepper the island's coastline and hiking through gorgeous forests in the hills.

❺ Beaches (p531) Ranking your favourite strips of sand, from the busiest on Corfu and Zakynthos to the quieter joys of Paxi and Lefkada's west coast.

❻ Ithaki (p541) Walking in the footsteps of epic poet Homer.

❼ Kythira (p549) Discovering tiny villages, waterfalls and remote coves.

History

The origin of the name 'Ionian' is obscure but may derive from the goddess Io. A paramour of Zeus, she passed through what's now known as the Ionian Sea while fleeing the wrath of Hera.

According to the writings of Homer, the Ionian Islands were important during Mycenaean times, but to date only tombs, not villages or palaces, have been identified. By the 8th century BC the islands belonged to mighty city state Corinth, but Corfu staged a successful revolt a century later. The Peloponnesian Wars (431–404 BC) left Corfu as little more than a staging post for whoever happened to be controlling Greece.

By the end of the 3rd century BC, the Romans ruled the Ionians. Antony and Cleopatra dined on Paxi the night before the Battle of Actium (31 BC), and the emperor Nero holidayed on Corfu in the 1st century AD. Later, the islands suffered waves of invaders: the Byzantine Empire, Venice, Napoleon (in 1797), Russia (from 1799 to 1807), and then Napoleon again.

In 1815 the Ionians became a British protectorate. Although the British improved infrastructure, developed agriculture and industry, and even taught the Corfiots cricket, nationalists campaigned against their oppressive rule, and by 1864 Britain had relinquished the islands to Greece.

WWII was rough on the Ionians, under occupation first by the Italians and then by the Germans. Further mass emigration followed devastating earthquakes in 1948 and 1953. But by the 1960s foreign holidaymakers were visiting in increasing numbers, and tourism has flourished ever since.

CORFU   ΚΕΡΚΥΡΑ

POP 102,070

From the writings of Gerald and Lawrence Durrell to the place where the shipwrecked Odysseus was soothed and sent on his way home, Corfu has been portrayed as an idyll for centuries. Today this reputation has led to parts of the island being defiled by mass tourism, but despite this, the Corfu of literature does still exist. All you need to do is sail around the corner, walk over the next headland or potter about the rugged interior and a place of bountiful produce, cypress-studded hills, vertiginous villages,

and sandy coves lapped by cobalt-blue waters awaits.

Since the 8th century BC the island the Greeks call Kerkyra has been prized for its untamed beauty and strategic location. Ancient armies fought to possess it, while in the early days of modern Greece it was a beacon of learning. Corfiots remain proud of their intellectual and artistic roots.

❶ Getting There & Away

AIR

Both **easyJet** (www.easyjet.com) and **Ryanair** (www.ryanair.com) offer direct flights in summer between Corfu and the UK, and several other European destinations, while **British Airways** (www.ba.com) also flies from the UK to Corfu. Between May and October, many charter flights come from northern Europe and the UK.

Aegean Airlines (https://en.aegeanair.com) Direct flights to Athens and European destinations.

Sky Express (www.skyexpress.gr) Operates a thrice-weekly island-hopping route to Preveza, Kefallonia and Zakynthos. It flies twice weekly to Thessaloniki.

Taxis between the airport and Corfu Town cost around €10, while local bus 15 runs to both Plateia G Theotoki (Plateia San Rocco) in town and the Neo Limani (New Port) beyond.

BOAT

Ferries depart from the Neo Limani (New Port), northwest of Corfu Town's Old Town. Ticket agencies line Ethnikis Antistaseos, facing the Neo Limani.

ANEK/Superfast Lines (www.anek.gr) ferries and/or **Minoan Lines** (www.minoan. gr) connect Corfu with Bari (around €60, eight hours, two weekly) and Ancona (around €85, 14½ hours, one to two daily) in Italy, and Igoumenitsa, where you can pick up other connections.

Ferry services from Corfu Town:

Igoumenitsa €12, 1¼ hours, hourly

Paxi (Gaïos; high-speed service) with **Ilida** (☑ Corfu 26610 49800, Paxi 26620 32401; Ethnikis Antistaseos 1); €25, 55 to 90 minutes, three to eight daily, mid-March to mid-October

Paxi (Gaïos; slower service) on the **Kamelia Lines** (☑ 26620 32131; www.kamelialines. gr) *Despina* ferry; €20, 90 minutes, one to three daily, April to October; advance bookings essential

Ferries also sail to **Igoumenitsa** from Lefkimmi (€8, one hour 10 minutes, six daily). There are no ferries sail directly to Zakynthos; fly with **Sky Express** instead.

Corfu

0 / 10 km
0 / 5 miles

Diapondia (Islands (15km))
Cape Drastis
Peroulades
Astrakeri
Lagos Beach
Sidhari
Karoussades
Roda
Aharavi
Old Perithia
Almyros Beach
Cape Agia Ekaterinis
Folklore Museum
Pelekito
Kassiopi
Avlaki
Kavo Barbaro
Avlaki Bay
North Kerkyra Straits
Agios Stefanos
Kefali
Arillas
Afionas
Agios Georgios
Makrades
Krini
Moni Theotokou
Troumbeta
Pagi
Ano Korakiana
Doukades
Lakones
Paleokastritsa
Sgombou
Liapades Bay
Dasia
Kommeno
Gouvia
Danilia
Giannades
Ropa Valley
Kontokali
Evropouli
Potamas
Agios Afra
Ioannis
Ermones
Vatos
Myrtiotissa Beach
Glyfada Beach
Kontogialos Beach
Pelekas
Yialiskari Beach
Kouramades
Achilleion Palace
Agios Gordios
Benitses
Strinylas
Spartylas
Barbati
Pyrgi
Ipsos
Edem Beach Nightclub
Grecotel Corfu Imperial
Gouvia Bay
Vidos Island
Cape Sidero
Corfu Town (Kerkyra)
Kanali
Kombitsi
Ambelonas
Perama
Kinopiastes
Achillion
Kanoni Peninsula
Nisaki
Kalami
Mt Pantokrator (906m)
Agios Stefanos
Kalamos

Brindisi (Italy; 125km);
Bari (Italy; 200km);
Venice (Italy; 625km)
Saranda (Albania; 10km)

ALBANIA

GREECE

Igoumenitsa (5km)

Paxi (25km)

Paramonas
Prasoudi
Agios Matthaios
Moraïtika
Strongyli
Gardiki
Alonaki
Halikounas Beach
Lake Korission
Boukari
Messonghi
Petriti
Lefkimmi Bay
Cape Lefkimmi
Ionian Sea
Marathias
Agios Georgios
Lefkimmi
South Kerkyra Straits
Vitalades
Kavos Beach
Kritika
Paleohori
Spartera
Asprokavos
Kavos
Cape Asprokavos

Some international ferries from Corfu also call in at Igoumenitsa (on the Greek mainland) and Kefallonia. For schedules, see https://travel.viva.gr. If you're heading to Patra, you must catch the ferry to Igoumenitsa first and then get a connecting bus.

BUS

Green Buses (www.greenbuses.gr) goes to Athens (€48.40, 8½ hours, three daily; one via Lefkimmi), Thessaloniki (€38.50, eight hours, twice daily) and Larissa (€30.40, 5½ hours, daily except Sunday). You can also just take one of the many daily ferries to the mainland and catch the bus of your choice from there.

❶ Getting Around

BUS

Long-distance Green Buses radiate from Corfu Town's **long-distance bus station** (26610 28900; https://greenbuses.gr; Lefkimmis 13) in the New Town. Fares cost €1.50 to €4.80; services are reduced on Saturday, and may be nonexistent on Sundays and holidays.

CAR & MOTORCYCLE

Car- and motorbike-hire outlets (Alamo, Hertz, Europcar etc) abound at the airport, in Corfu Town and at the resorts. Prices start at around €50 per day.

Corfu Town   Κέρκυρα

POP 30,000

Imbued with Venetian grace and elegance, historic Corfu Town (also known as Kerkyra) stands halfway down the island's east coast. The name Corfu, meaning 'peaks', refers to its twin hills, each topped by a massive fortress built to withstand Ottoman sieges. Sitting between the two, the Old Town is a tight-packed warren of winding lanes, some bursting with fine restaurants, lively bars and intriguing shops, others timeless back alleys where washing lines stretch from balcony to balcony. It also holds some majestic architecture, including the splendid Liston arcade, and high-class museums, along with no fewer than 39 churches.

During the day, cruise passengers and day-trippers bustle through the streets; come evening, the bustle continues around the bar areas. When it comes to drinking, dining and dancing, this is the hottest spot in the Ionian Islands.

◉ Sights

The Old Town's most eye-catching feature is the grand French-built Liston (Map p514) arcade, facing the Old Fort across the lawns of the Spianada (Map p514) and lined with packed cafes. At its northern end, the neoclassical Palace of St Michael & St George contains the excellent Corfu Museum of Asian Art. Head inland and you can lose yourself for a happy hour or two amid the maze-like alleyways, seeking out sumptuous Orthodox churches or cosy cafes as the mood takes you.

Continue southwest, skirting the mighty Neo Frourio (New Fort), to reach the New Town, busy with everyday shops and services and centring on Plateia G Theotoki (also known as Plateia San Rocco). To the south, around the curving Bay of Garitsa, the ruin-strewn Mon Repos Estate marks the site of the ancient settlement of Palaeopolis.

Palace of
St Michael & St George   PALACE

(Map p514; adult/concession/child €6/3/free; ⊗8am-8pm Apr-Oct, 9am-4pm Tue-Sun Nov-Mar) Beyond the northern end of the Spianada, the smart Regency-style Palace of St Michael and St George was built by the British from 1819 onwards, to house the high commissioner and the Ionian Parliament. It's now home to the prestigious Corfu Museum of

Asian Art (the entry fee covers both this museum and the palace). Two municipal art galleries, I (entry €3) and II (Map p514; ☑26610 48690; Palace of St Michael & St George; ⊗10am-4pm Tue-Sun) FREE, are housed in one annexe, and its small formal gardens make a pleasant refuge.

★ Corfu Museum of Asian Art   MUSEUM

(Map p514; ☑26610 30443; www.matk.gr; Palace of St Michael & St George; adult/concession/child incl palace entry €6/3/free; ⊗8am-8pm Apr-Oct, 9am-4pm Tue-Sun Nov-Mar) Home to stunning artefacts ranging from prehistoric bronzes to works in onyx and ivory, this excellent museum occupies the central portions of the Palace of St Michael and St George. One gallery provides a chronological overview of Chinese ceramics, and showcases remarkable jade carvings and snuff bottles. The India section opens with Alexander the Great, 'When Greece Met India', and displays fascinating Graeco-Buddhist figures, including a blue-grey schist Buddha. A Japanese section incorporates magnificent samurai armour and Noh masks.

Municipal Art Gallery I   GALLERY

(Map p514; ☑26610 48690; www.artcorfu.com; Palace of St Michael & St George; adult/child €3/free; ⊗10am-4pm Tue-Sun) Make the effort to find this gallery – it's entered from the exterior on the eastern side of the Palace of St Michael and St George. You'll be rewarded with a handful of high-quality Byzantine icons, including 16th-century works by the Cretan Damaskinos, plus a more extensive array of canvases by Corfiot painters. Look out for the work of Italian-influenced 19th-century father-and-son artists Spyridon and Pavos Prossalendis.

★ Palaio Frourio   FORTRESS

(Old Fort; Map p514; ☑26610 48310; adult/concession/child €6/3/free; ⊗8am-8pm Apr-Oct, 8.30am-3pm Nov-Mar) The rocky headland that juts east from Corfu Town is topped by the Venetian-built 14th-century Palaio Frourio. Before that, already enclosed within massive stone walls, it cradled the entire Byzantine city. A solitary bridge crosses its seawater moat.

Only parts of this huge site, which also holds later structures from the British era, are accessible to visitors; wander up to the lighthouse on the larger of the two hills for superb views.

A **gatehouse** contains the small Byzantine Collection of Corfu, while the temple-like **Church of St George** stands on a large terrace to the south.

Note that in season the queues for entry can be very long.

Corfu Living History   HOUSE
(Casa Parlante; Map p514; ☑ 26610 49190; www.casaparlante.gr; N Theotoki 16; adult/child €7/5; ☺ 10am-6pm) This town house has been remodelled to illustrate the daily lives of a fictitious merchant family from the mid-19th century. Enthusiastic guides make the whole experience fun and informative, while in each room waxworks undertake small, endlessly repeated movements. The tour is enlivened by the free glass of 19th-century-style rose liquor visitors get to try.

Vidos Island   ISLAND
(Map p511) Hourly boats from the Old Port make the 10-minute crossing to tiny, thickly wooded Vidos Island (€4 return), immediately offshore. The island is the final resting place of thousands of Serbian soldiers killed during WWII. There's a monument to them here and also some abandoned buildings once used by the scouts. There's a taverna at the jetty, but the big attraction is to walk the 600m across the island to reach a couple of attractive beaches.

Archaeological Museum   MUSEUM
(☑ 26610 30680; www.amcorfu.gr; Vraïla 1; adult/concession/child €6/3/free; ☺ 8am-8pm Thu-Tue) Built in the 1960s, Corfu Town's Archaeological Museum has finally reopened after nearly a decade of renovations. The result of this work is a modern and well-lit museum (although some of the English labelling is a bit hit and miss) housing some 16,000 pieces found around Corfu. The highlight of the fine collection is a massive gorgon pediment (590–580 BC) from the **Temple of Artemis** on the nearby Kanoni Peninsula.

Neo Frourio   FORTRESS
(New Fort; Map p514; ☺ 9am-3.30pm) **FREE** The forbidding Neo Frourio is in fact only a little younger than the Old Fort across town. Surrounded by massive walls that crown the low hill at the western edge of the Old Town, it too dates from the Venetian era. Climbing the stairway at the western end of Solomou brings you to the entrance, where dank tunnels and passages lead through the walls. The ramparts beyond enjoy wonderful views.

Antivouniotissa Museum   MUSEUM
(Byzantine Museum; Map p514; ☑ 26610 38313; www.antivouniotissamuseum.gr; adult/concession/child €4/2/free; ☺ 8am-3pm Tue-Sun) Home to an outstanding collection of Byzantine and post-Byzantine icons and artefacts, the exquisite, timber-roofed Church of Our Lady of Antivouniotissa has a double role as church and museum. It stands atop a short, broad stairway that climbs from shore-front Arseniou, and frames views out towards wooded Vidos Island.

Church of Agios Spyridon   CHURCH
(Map p514; Agios Spyridonos; ☺ 8am-9pm) Pilgrims and day-trippers alike throng this Old Town landmark. As well as magnificent frescoes, the small 16th-century basilica holds the remains of Corfu's patron saint, Spyridon, a 4th-century Cypriot shepherd. His body, brought here from Constantinople in 1453, lies in an elaborate silver casket, and is paraded through the town on festival days.

Mon Repos Estate   PARK
(Kanoni Peninsula; ☺ 8am-3pm Tue-Sun) **FREE** This park-like wooded estate 2km around the bay south of the Old Town was the site of Corfu's most important ancient settlement, Palaeopolis. More recently, in 1921, the secluded neoclassical villa that now holds the **Museum of Palaeopolis** (☑ 26610 32783; Mon Repos, Kanoni Peninsula; adult/concession €4/2; ☺ 8am-3pm Tue-Sun) was the birthplace of Prince Philip of Greece, who went on to marry Britain's Princess Elizabeth (now the current Queen). Footpaths lead through the woods to ancient ruins, including those of a Doric temple atop a small coastal cliff.

It takes half an hour to walk to Mon Repos from town, or you can catch bus 2a from the Spianada (€1.20, every 20 minutes). Bring a picnic and plenty of water; there are no shops nearby.

★ Achilleion Palace   HISTORIC BUILDING
(Map p511; ☑ 26610 56245; www.achilleion-corfu.gr; Gastouri; adult/concession €8/6; ☺ 8am-8pm Apr-Nov, to 4pm Dec-Mar) Set atop a steep coastal hill 12km south of Corfu Town, the Achilleion Palace was built during the 1890s as the summer palace of Austria's empress Elisabeth, the niece of King Otto of Greece. The palace's two principal features are its intricately decorated central staircase, rising in geometrical flights, and

Corfu Old Town

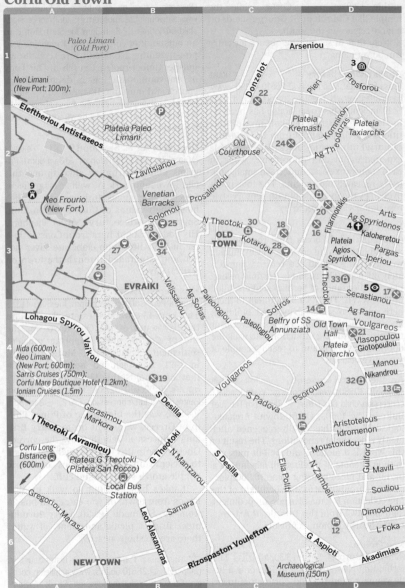

its sweeping garden terraces, which command eye-popping views.

There's surprisingly little to see inside, other than mementos of Elisabeth, who was assassinated in Genoa in 1898, and of the German kaiser Wilhelm II, who bought the palace in 1907 and added its namesake statue of Achilles Triumphant.

It's well worth getting an audio guide; the descriptions of various statues, paintings and background are excellent for context. Audio guides are free, but you'll

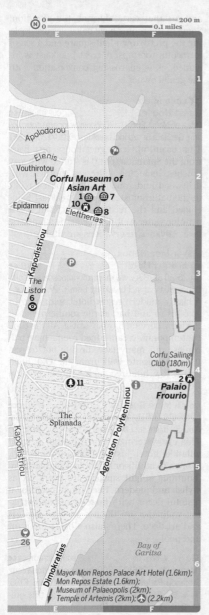

Corfu Old Town

◎ Top Sights

◎ Sights

⬛ Sleeping

✖ Eating

🍷 Drinking & Nightlife

🛍 Shopping

👉 Tours

★ Corfu Walking Tours   WALKING
(📞 6932894466, 6945894450; www.corfuwalking
tours.com; €64-78) Walking tours with expert
guides, covering the Old Town (€64, three
hours) or further afield, including popular
options oriented towards eating or wine
tasting (from €68), and customised hiking
trips.

Corfu Walks & Hikes   HIKING
(www.walking-corfu.blogspot.co.uk) Guided hiking expeditions exploring the wilder parts

---

need to hand over official government ID
of some kind. You can use the guides for up
to 50 minutes only.

Bus N-10 runs to the Achilleion from
Corfu Town (€1.70, 20 minutes).

of Corfu, including up to the top of Mt Pantokrator and along the hills around Paleokastritsa, with an eye to the island's flora and fauna.

Ionian Cruises
CRUISE

(☑26610 38690; www.ionian-cruises.com; Ethnikis Antistaseos 4; ☺7am-8pm) Day cruises from the New Port to the mainland and Sivota Islands (€27), south to Paxi and Antipaxi (€28) or across to Albania (€53).

Sarris Cruises
CRUISE

(☑26610 25317; www.sarriscruises.gr; Mouriki 1) Day trips from the New Port include an excursion to the ancient World Heritage–listed ruins at Butrinti in Albania (€59; passports required), and a boat trip taking in Paxi, the Blue Caves and Antipaxi (€40) – go on a calm day. Transfers included.

Trailriders
HORSE RIDING

(☑69466 53317; www.trailriderscorfu.com; Ano Korakiana; ☺10am-noon & 4-6pm Mon-Fri) Horse riding through the olive groves around the village of Ano Korakiana, 18km northwest of Corfu Town. Book in advance.

🛏 Sleeping

As many island visitors head straight to the beaches and resorts, Corfu Town holds fewer accommodation options than you might expect. Those that do exist tend to be relatively pricey, even in low season.

★ Bella Venezia
BOUTIQUE HOTEL €€

(Map p514; ☑26610 46500; www.bellavenezia hotel.com; N Zambeli 4; d incl breakfast from €130; ❄🤖) Enter this historic neoclassical villa, set in a peaceful central street, and you'll be seduced by its charm. It features an elegant lobby with candelabras, velvet chairs and a piano. The plush, high-ceilinged rooms (some with balconies) have fine city or garden views, while the garden breakfast area is delightful. The cheaper loft rooms have horizontal windows but no outlook.

Staff are friendly and warm, and provide fabulous service. This place will 'make' your stay in Corfu.

★ Puppet Guest House
GUESTHOUSE €€

(Map p514; ☑26610 40707; www.facebook.com/Puppet.corfu; Evaggelistrias 1; d incl breakfast €125; ❄🤖) Above a slightly eccentric bar full of string puppets, this wonderful guesthouse has big, bright rooms and fairy-tale decor

and art that certainly grab the attention! Some of the rooms have balconies overlooking the pretty town-hall square and a sea of terracotta rooftops. A great breakfast is included, as is engrossing conversation with the genial owner.

★ Locandieta Guest House
GUESTHOUSE €€

(Map p514; ☑26610 39035; www.locorfu.com; Ioanni Gennata 8; s/d incl breakfast €100/120; ❄🤖) This beautiful, cosy guesthouse just back from the Spianada (p512) is stuffed with arty touches, including staircases adorned with driftwood and rough-textured beach rocks in the bathrooms. A superb breakfast is included and the reception area even has a genuine water well. The owner is a fantastic host. Advance reservations are vital.

Mayor Mon Repos Palace Art Hotel
HOTEL €€

(☑26610 32783; www.mayormonrepospalace.com; Dimokratias; d incl breakfast from €127; ❄🤖) A classy, modern resort hotel, with its own spa, bistro and bar, at the southern end of the long, curving Bay of Garitsa. All the cool, contemporary cream-toned rooms have balconies, and many face directly out to sea. It's a 20-minute walk from the Old Town and a few hundred metres north of Mon Repos (p513).

Corfu Mare Boutique Hotel
HOTEL €€€

(☑26610 31011; www.corfumare.gr; Nikolau Zervou 5; d/ste incl breakfast €286/470; ❄🤖) This eye-wateringly expensive but palatial villa-like hotel, just up from the New Port, is open to adults only. While it's larger than 'boutique' might suggest, it's every bit as stylish and modern. Each room has its own tasteful decor, with huge prints and striking wallpaper on themes such as pop art and art deco. There's also a bar, restaurant and pool.

Siorra Vittoria
BOUTIQUE HOTEL €€€

(Map p514; ☑26610 36300; www.siorravittoria.com; Stefanou Padova 36; d incl breakfast from €185; 🅿❄🤖) Expect luxury and style at this quiet 19th-century Old Town mansion, where restored traditional architecture meets modern amenities; marble bathrooms, crisp linens and genteel service make for a relaxed stay. Breakfast is served in your room or beneath an ancient magnolia in the peaceful garden.

OLD PERITHIA

Falling away from the northern slope of Mt Pantokrator is a rugged land of tumbling valleys, beautiful cypress forests and mountain meadows where the only noise is goat bells. It's a magical part of the island that's well worth sacrificing some beach time to explore.

The remote village of Old Perithia is an ideal place to make for in the hills. Not so long ago lack of work and opportunities meant that this village of ramshackle stone houses was almost abandoned. Today, thanks to tourism and locals being able to work from home, the village is slowly coming back to life. Several buildings have been reconstructed and there are a couple of wonderful tavernas. The **Old Perithia Taverna** (✆26630 98055; Old Perithia; mains €5-10; ⏱11am-8pm), which has been a family-run restaurant for 150 years, has shelves full of dusty farming implements and sepia-coloured family photographs. Almost anything you eat here is outstanding, but the courgette nuggets followed by rabbit stew washed down with rough homemade red wine might turn out to be the best meal you eat in Corfu.

When you've finished eating, lace up your hiking boots and set off along any of the many country tracks and walking trails that spiral away from the village. Note that trail information and signposting are very limited, so unless you're on a walking tour you'll probably have to make it up as you go along.

✖ Eating

Corfiot cuisine shows the delicious influence of many cultures, especially Italian. Solid, but few outstanding, restaurants and tavernas are scattered throughout the Old Town.

★**Pane & Souvlaki**　　　　GRILL €
(Map p514; ✆26610 20100; www.panesouvlaki. com; Guilford 77; mains €6-13.50; ⏱noon-1am) Arguably the Old Town's best-value budget option (the locals rave), with outdoor tables on the town-hall square, this quick-fire restaurant does exactly what its name suggests, serving up three skewers of chicken or pork with chunky chips, dipping sauce and warm pitta in individual metal trays. The salads and burgers are good, too.

Chrisomalis　　　　TAVERNA €
(Map p514; ✆26610 30342; N Theotoki 6; mains €7-13; ⏱noon-midnight) Going strong since 1904, this traditional little taverna was a haunt of the Durrell family and actor Anthony Quinn, and there are old pictures on the wall of Gerald and Lawrence Durrell with the owner. Follow your nose to the traditional grill for souvlaki, pork chops and swordfish. Warm service and pavement tables make it ideal for people-watching.

Oinos kai Geuseis　　　　MEDITERRANEAN €€
(Map p514; ✆26610 8335; Mitropoleos 22; tapas €4-8; ⏱6pm-midnight) Sip a glass of wine and look forward to tucking into tasty treats such as shrimps with feta or fried fish marinated in sweet and sour sauce at this ex-

citing new bar-restaurant serving what the owners describe as Greek 'tapas'. Ideal place for an *apéro* with friends.

Salto Wine Bar　　　　MEDITERRANEAN €€
(Map p514; ✆26613 02325; www.saltowinebar. gr; Donzelot 23; mains €9-18; ⏱6.30pm-12.30am Mon-Sat, 12.30-4.30pm & 6.30pm-12.30am Sun; ✴) This small, bright and modern wine bar and bistro down on the waterfront is causing waves among foodies in Corfu. With a menu strong on Italian influences and grilled meats, the place was a favourite for the cast and crew of hit UK TV series *The Durrells*.

Estiatorio Bellissimo　　　　MEDITERRANEAN €€
(Map p514; ✆26610 41112; Plateia Limonia; mains €8-18; ⏱10am-midnight) The Old Town holds few nicer spots for an al-fresco evening than this casual but stylish restaurant that spreads across a peaceful pedestrian square. It's renowned for its pizzas but also excels in Corfiot specialities such as *pastitsadha kokora* – chicken in red sauce, 'with a lot of cheese' – plus crêpes and salads.

Anthos　　　　SEAFOOD €€
(Map p514; ✆26610 32252; www.facebook.com/ anthosrestaurant; Maniarizi-Arlioti 15; mains €10-21; ⏱noon-midnight Mon-Sat, 6pm-midnight Sun; ✆) Much-loved little back-alley restaurant with a handful of outdoor tables. Most diners are here for the seafood, savouring dishes such as squid carpaccio, octopus with *fava*-bean mousse, and grilled sea bass, but it also serves standard Greek meat favourites.

To Tavernaki tis Marinas TAVERNA €€
(Map p514; 26611 00792; Velissariou 35; mains €8-15; noon-11.30pm) The stone walls, hardwood floors and cheerful staff lift the ambience of this taverna. Check the daily specials, or choose anything from *mousakas* (baked layers of aubergine or courgette, minced meat and potatoes topped with cheese sauce), sardines-in-the-oven or steak. Accompany it all with a dram of ouzo or *tsipouro* (a distilled spirit similar to raki).

★**Fishalida** SEAFOOD €€€
(Map p514; 26614 01213; Spirou Vlaikou 1; mains €12-20; 11am-midnight;) Right next to the market and a fishmongers, this is an easy-going, youthful place to eat inventive and truly superb seafood such as prawn tortellini with wild-mushroom sauce or the unexpectedly delightful octopus with hummus. There's a light-filled interior or you can eat outside at one of the couple of tables. Advance bookings almost essential.

★**Venetian Well** INTERNATIONAL €€€
(Map p514; 26615 50955; www.venetianwell.gr; Plateia Kremasti; mains €16-24; 7-11.30pm Mon-Sat;) Corfu Town's finest special-occasion restaurant has a beautifully faded square to itself, hidden away near the cathedral and complete with a genuine Venetian well. The exquisite contemporary approach to cuisine adorns local meats, fish and vegetables with all sorts of foams, mousses and gels; even if you can't always tell what you're eating, it's invariably delicious.

Drinking & Nightlife

Perhaps the best place to kick-start the evening is on the stylish Liston arcade; after that, the choices are legion.

For dance venues, head after 11pm to Corfu's disco strip, starting west beyond the New Port, along Ethnikis Antistaseos; take a taxi, as it's a busy, unlit road without walkways. A €10 or so admission fee usually includes one drink.

★**Firi Firi – The Beer House** BAR
(Map p514; 26610 33953; www.facebook.com/FiriFiriCorfu; Solomou 1; 6pm-2am Tue-Sun;) Sample local and imported beers, either inside the custard-coloured villa at the foot of the steps leading up to the Neo Frourio (p513) or at the terraced tables beside the neighbouring church; if you find it hard to leave, it grills up some decent dishes, too.

★**Antonis Toursas Juice Bar** JUICE BAR
(Map p514; 26610 22550; Solomou 28; juices €2.50-3; 8am-10pm) Brilliant little juice bar that has boxes of fruit piled up outside like a fruit shop (which it also is). Pick your five a day and get them blended straight up into a juice to enjoy at the small bar.

★**Mikro Café** BAR
(Map p514; 26610 31009; N Theotoki 42; 9am-midnight) You can smell the coffee beans roasting from 25m down the street, and whether your favoured beverage comes from these beans or is something a little more alcoholic, the Old Town holds no finer spot for drinking and people-watching than the delightful, multilevel, vine-shaded terrace of the convivial 'little cafe'.

54 Dreamy Nights CLUB
(6940645436; www.54dreamynights.com; Ethnikis Antistaseos 54; 10pm-late;) Gleaming, bright-white nightspot, west along the New Port, with a minimalist aesthetic, spectacular night shows and a retractable roof. Open-air DJ parties and live gigs by big-name Greek music stars attract up to 3000 clubbers.

Polytechno BAR
(Map p514; 26610 27794; www.facebook.com/pg/polytechnocorfu; Sholemvorgou 39; 8.30pm-late;) Bar and venue for performance art and experimental music. In-the-know patrons reach it by turning left along the hillside footpath at the top of the steps up from Solomou, below the Neo Frourio (p513).

Cavalieri Hotel Rooftop Bar BAR
(Map p514; 26610 39041; www.cavalieri-hotel.com; Kapodistriou 4; 6.30pm-late) Rather wonderful rooftop bar that makes an ideal venue for mellow predinner drinks, with stunning views across the Spianada (p512) to the Palaio Frourio (p512). There's the hope that you'll stay for an Italian-flavoured meal, but you don't have to.

Shopping

The Old Town is crammed with shopping opportunities. The heaviest concentration of souvenir shops, which sell everything from 'evil eye' amulets and olive-wood carvings to pashminas and perfume, is along narrow Filarmonikis between the two main churches, while N Theotoki is good for idiosyncratic boutiques.

★**Corfu Gallery** ART
(Map p514; ✐26610 25796; www.corfugallery.com;
N Theotoki 72; ☺10am-11pm) Fabulous sculptures, paintings and objets d'art are sold at
this gallery. The pieces are uniformly expensive, but you're welcome to just browse.

★**Sweet'n'Spicy Bahar** SPICES
(Map p514; ✐26610 33848; www.sweetnspicy.gr;
Agias Sofias 12; ☺9.45am-2pm) Gloriously aromatic spice and condiment shop, run by an
ever-so-enthusiastic Greek-Canadian-Leba-
nese woman with a palpable love for devis-
ing her own enticing mixes of Greek and
imported spices.

Icon Gallery ARTS & CRAFTS
(Map p514; ✐26614 00928; www.iconcraft.gr; Guilford 52; ☺10am-10.30pm Mon-Sat; ☎) True to
its name, this hole-in-the-wall boutique sells
stunning icons, handmade by an artists' co-
op, as well as fine heraldic art and antiques.
Some of the icons have a distinctly modern
twist – Adam being titillated by a not-very-
shy Eve, for example – that the Church sure-
ly wouldn't approve of!

Corfu Sandals SHOES
(Map p514; ✐26610 47301; www.facebook.com/
corfusandals; Philhellinon 9; ☺9am-11pm) This
standout shoe store, on the narrow lane
that holds Corfu Town's heaviest (and tack-
iest) concentration of souvenir shops, sells
well-priced handmade leather sandals in all
styles and sizes, many with ergonomic bubble soles. To find it, look out for the sandals
that only a giant could wear.

Papagiorgis FOOD & DRINKS
(Map p514; ✐26610 39474; www.papagiorgis.
gr; N Theotoki 32; ☺9am-midnight) Irresistible old-fashioned patisserie that's an Old
Town landmark thanks to its 40 flavours of
ice cream, plus a mouth-watering array of
homemade tarts, biscuits and honey.

🛈 Information

Corfu General Hospital (✐26613 60400;
www.gnkerkyras.gr; Kontokali) About 8km west
of the town centre.

Municipal Tourist Kiosk (Map p514; www.
corfu.gr; Spianada; ☺8am-4pm Mon-Fri Mar-
Nov) Helps with accommodation, transport and
things to do around Corfu.

Tourist Police (✐26610 29169; I Andreadi 1)
In the New Town, off Plateia G Theotoki (Plateia
San Rocco).

TRAVEL AGENCIES

All Ways Travel (✐26610 33955; www.allways
travel.com.gr; Plateia G Theotoki 34) Helpful
English-speaking staff in the New Town's main
square.

Aperghi Travel (✐26610 48713; www.aperghi
travel.gr; I Polyla 1) Handles tours and accommodation, especially for walkers on the Corfu
Trail (www.thecorfutrail.com).

Pachis Travel (✐26610 28298; www.pachis
travel.com; Guilford 7; ☺9.30am-3pm &
6-8.30pm Mon-Fri, 9.30am-2pm Sat) Busy little
agency that's useful for hotels, ferry and plane
tickets, and excursions to Paxi.

🛈 Getting There & Away

Corfu Town is at the centre of an efficient network of local buses, and you can get pretty much
anywhere on the island from the long-distance
bus station (p511) in the New Town.

🛈 Getting Around

Local blue buses depart from the **local bus
station** (Map p514; ✐26610 31595; www.
astikoktelkerkyras.gr; Plateia G Theotoki) in the
Old Town. Journeys cost €1.20 or €1.70. Buy
tickets at the booth on Plateia G Theotoki or on
the bus itself. All trips are less than 30 minutes.
Service is reduced at weekends.

Most Corfu Town rental companies are based
along the northern waterfront.

Budget (✐26610 24404; www.budget.gr;
Eleftheriou Antistaseos 6)

Sunrise (✐26610 44325; www.corfusunrise.
com; Ethnikis Antistaseos 16)

Top Cars (✐26610 35237; www.carrental
corfu.com; Donzelot 25)

Northern Corfu

Immediately north of Corfu Town, the coastline consists of an all-but-continuous strip
of busy beach resorts, including Gouvia,
Dasia, Ipsos and Pyrgi. These offer all you
need for a family holiday but are otherwise
unremarkable.

Continue north, though, and it's like
heading 50 years back in time to the days before mass tourism struck parts of Corfu. The
coastal road begins to wind and undulate
around the massif formed by the island's
highest peak, Mt Pantokrator (906m), and
the scenery becomes ever more attractive,
with olive groves dipping down to sapphire
waters and hidden coves. Many of the pretty
little inlets that punctuate the seafront here
hold a delightful village or at least a taverna.

IONIAN ISLANDS NORTHERN CORFU

COASTAL WALK: AGIOS STEFANOS TO AVLAKI

Large parts of Corfu's coastline have been scarred by mass tourism, but fortunately there still exist some beaches without a single hotel, taverna or sunlounger. Some of the most untouched shores in all of the Ionians can be found in the very far northeast of Corfu, and only those prepared to go to the effort of walking there will get to enjoy them. Indeed, outside high summer there's a very good chance you'll have some of these beaches all to yourself. A 6.5km coastal path heads from the port village of Agios Stefanos to the long windsurfing beach of Avlaki. The walk takes 1½ hours, but bring a picnic and allow a full day so that you can enjoy the beaches.

The trail is well signposted and begins from the Eucalyptus Bar at the northern edge of Agios Stefanos. The trail follows the bay along the beach and then crosses multiple headlands and seven beaches, including **Vromolimni** and **Akoli**, both backed by small lakes. It's also worth making a short detour off the main trail to the gorgeous pebble beach of **Arias**, which is hemmed in by thick forest. From the turn-off for the Arias detour, the main trail then crosses straight over the peninsula to further beaches before arriving in Avlaki. However, a minor trail veers through dank, tangled forest to the headland of **Kavo Barbaro**, which has wanderlust-tingling views to Albania. There's a small cove beach here, as well as great snorkelling.

Unfortunately, even in this apparently untouched area the impact of humans is only too apparent in the piles of plastic waste washed up at the beaches' high-tide line. Unless you've prearranged return transport, once you reach Avlaki you'll have to retrace your steps to Agios Stefanos or take a short cut following the road over the hill (4km; one hour).

◉ Sights

An enjoyable mishmash of everything from accordions and olive presses to puppets and phones, the cavernous private **Folklore Museum** (Map p511; ☑ 26630 63052; www.museum-acharavi.webs.com; Aharavi; adult/child €3/1.50; ⊙10am-2pm Mon-Sat) is a fun place to learn about Corfu's traditional way of life. It doubles as a craft shop.

⊨ Sleeping

Northern Corfu (and the northeast in particular) is the most enticing and attractive part of the island because it's the least developed. Thus accommodation is quite limited, so you should book as far ahead as possible. Accommodation in the north is generally of a high standard.

★**Manessis Apartments** APARTMENT €€
(☑ 6973918416; Kassiopi; 4-person apt €110; ❋☎) Lovely, refurbished, bougainvillea-draped two-bedroom apartments, with sea-facing balconies, set in flower-filled gardens towards the far end of Kassiopi's picturesque harbour. The friendly and super-helpful Greek-Irish owners make sure everything goes smoothly. It's hard to find better.

Theofilos Studios & Apartments APARTMENT €€
(☑ 26630 81261; www.theofiloskassiopi.com; Kassiopi; d €80; ❋☎) A block back from Kassiopi's northern beach, but still with memorable sea views, this is a super-friendly place to stay, with fairly plain but comfortable apartments (kitchenettes are very basic), and an owner who'll happily divulge tips and suggestions for things to do. There's an impressive swimming pool.

Melina Bay Hotel BOUTIQUE HOTEL €€
(☑ 26630 81030; http://melinabay.com; Kassiopi; s/d/tr €90/90/114; ❋☎) Gleaming modern hotel immediately below the castle and with a drop-dead-stunning view of Kassiopi's harbourfront. The small rooms have a sailing-ship theme and excellent amenities. Book ahead.

Grecotel Corfu Imperial RESORT €€€
(Map p511; ☑ 26610 88400; www.corfuimperial.com; Kommeno; d incl breakfast from €470; ⊙May-Oct; ❋☎❊) One of the most lavish hotels in Greece, this place occupies a regal waterfront position at the western tip of the curving peninsula that defines Kommeno Bay. Ultraluxurious rooms are set in pastel-toned sea-view villas, plus there are three fine-dining restaurants and a spa. Normally there's a two-night minimum stay in summer; rates drop considerably in low season.

✗ Eating & Drinking

White House   MEDITERRANEAN €€
(☑ 26630 91040; www.corfu-kalami.gr; Kalami; mains €10-23; ⊙9am-midnight) Almost a site of pilgrimage for fans of the Durrell family, this utterly ravishing waterfront restaurant in the former home of writer Lawrence Durrell has tables quayside – many diners arrive by motorboat – as well as on a vine-shaded terrace. The appetisers are predominantly Greek, the mains Italian. The food is decent but, as is to be expected, a bit overpriced.

Cavo Barbaro   SEAFOOD €€
(☑ 26630 81905; Avlaki; mains €10-22; ⊙9.30am-11.30pm) With widescreen views of the beach, and sea breezes wafting through the garden, this pretty and very spacious restaurant makes a charming spot for a leisurely meal of octopus, calamari, *saganaki* (fried cheese), *mousakas* or swordfish.

To Fagopotion   TAVERNA €€
(☑ 26630 82020; Agios Stefanos; €11-19; ⊙noon-1am) Of the procession of similar tavernas that serve up seafront dining at Agios Stefanos, Fagopotion, presided over by the genial Christos, has to be the best for its inventive Greek seafood and meat cuisine.

Edem Beach Nightclub   CLUB
(Map p511; ☑ 26610 93013; www.edemclub.com; Dasia; ⊙11am-5am) Head for a sunset chillout at one of Greece's top beach bars before the party starts at around 11pm. To get here from Corfu Town, catch bus 7 (€1.70, 30 minutes) from Plateia G Theotoki.

❶ Information

San Stefano Travel (☑ 26630 51771, 26630 81335; www.san-stefano.gr; Agios Stefanos) offers all travel services, including boat rental and excursions to the Diapondia Islands and other nearby islands.

❶ Getting There & Away

Green Buses (www.greenbuses.gr) runs frequent services from Corfu Town, both anticlockwise around the northwestern coast as far as Kassiopi, and straight to Roda and its neighbouring resorts on the north coast.

To explore the region at all thoroughly, however, you'll need your own transport.

Western Corfu

Corfu's western shoreline boasts some of the island's most spectacular scenery, its prettiest villages and its finest beaches. No coastal road connects the many sandy coves that nibble into the towering cliffs along its central stretch, so sightseers must choose their targets wisely. Paleokastritsa in the north has a great beach, a beautiful monastery and fine hiking; Pelekas is a delightful hilltop village; and Agios Gordios in the south is a backpackers' haven with a long, sandy beach.

Paleokastritsa & North

The popular resort area of **Paleokastritsa**, 23km northwest of Corfu Town, stretches for nearly 3km through a series of small, picturesque bays. Craggy mountains swathed in cypress and olive trees tower above. The real treat comes at the resort's end, where an exquisite little beach is said to be where the weary Odysseus washed ashore. Boat trips from the jetty include **Paradise Sunset** (☑ 6972276442; Paleokastritsa; per person €10-20) cruises to nearby grottoes.

Set amid splendid gardens on the rocky promontory above, an easy 10-minute walk from the beach, **Moni Theotokou monastery** (Map p511; Paleokastritsa; ⊙7am-1pm & 3-8pm) 𝗙𝗥𝗘𝗘 dates to the 13th century. It's home to an interesting little **museum** (Paleokastritsa; ⊙Apr-Oct) 𝗙𝗥𝗘𝗘 and a shop selling olive oils and herbs.

A circuitous hike or drive west from Paleokastritsa will take you along a high, winding road through the unspoilt villages of **Lakones** and **Krini**. A minor track that drops west of Krini dead-ends far above the waves at a mighty isolated crag, where a broad stone stairway climbs to the impregnable Byzantine fortress of **Angelokastro**. Though its ramparts remain largely intact, luxuriant wildflowers now fill its interior; the views back to Paleokastritsa are unforgettable.

Further north, the coastline becomes much flatter, and the low-key resorts of **Agios Georgios** and **Arillas** line their own long beaches.

IONIAN ISLANDS WESTERN CORFU

LOCAL KNOWLEDGE

THE DURRELLS

British writers Gerald and Lawrence Durrell lived on Corfu for the four years preceding WWII. Gerald, then a child but later a prominent naturalist, chronicled his eccentric family's island idyll in several charming and hilarious books, the most famous of which is *My Family and Other Animals*. The three houses where they lived and which featured in this book are all north of Corfu Town and are not open to visitors. The White House (p521) at Kalami, however, which was home to Lawrence and his wife Nancy while he wrote his lyrical nonfiction account of Corfu, *Prospero's Cell*, is now a lovely restaurant.

As for the hit UK TV series *The Durrells*, its principal shooting location is Danilia, a restored, once-abandoned village that is only accessible to guests of the Grecotel Corfu Imperial (p520) resort on the coast.

South of Paleokastritsa

South of Paleokastritsa, the pebbly beach at **Ermones** has become overdeveloped but retains a certain attraction. Sleepy little **Pelekas**, atop wooded cliffs 6km southeast, is an attractive confection of biscuit-cream-hued buildings. **Kalimera Bakery** (Pelekas; pastries from €2; ⊙ 7am-late) sells fresh pastries, while the frog-green **Witch House** (☑ 6974525376; Pelekas; ⊙ 10am-10pm), almost opposite, is perfect for offbeat gifts. Kaiser Wilhelm rode his horse to get 360-degree island views from the peak immediately above the village, now known as the **Kaiser's Throne**.

Sandy beaches within easy reach of Pelekas include **Kontogialos** (also called Pelekas) and **Glyfada**, both now fully fledged resorts with large hotels and other accommodation. Writer Lawrence Durrell hailed **Myrtiotissa Beach** (Map p511), further east, as arguably the best in the world. Now dominated by nudists, it remains relatively pristine because it's so hard to reach – it requires a long slog down a steep and only partly surfaced road (drivers should park on the hilltop).

The rambling old vineyard estate at **Ambelonas** (☑ 6932158888; http://ambelonas-corfu.gr; ⊙ 7-11pm Wed-Fri Jun-Oct, 1-6pm Sun

Dec-May), 5km east of Pelekas (and only 8km west of Corfu Town), produces enticing wares ranging from wine and vinegar to olive oil and sweets.

Continuing south, the resort of **Agios Gordios** is set below a stupendous verdant hillside, with a long sand-and-pebble beach that can accommodate any crowd. Another 12km south, just off the main road, the Byzantine **Gardiki Castle** makes an impressive spectacle but is largely ruined. Beyond it lies vast **Lake Korission**, which is a good birdwatching site. It's separated from the sea by a narrow spit that's fronted by long, sandy and often wind-blasted **Halikounas Beach**.

🛏 Sleeping

Sunrock HOSTEL €
(☑ 26610 94637; www.sunrockhostel.com; Kontogialos Beach; incl breakfast & dinner dm €25, r with/without bathroom €85/55; ⊛ 🛜) 🏄 Run by the charming Magdalena, this complex, 30m from the sea, has dorms and doubles. It's faded on the outside, perhaps, but inside it's fresh and friendly. There's a great balcony for soaking up the sun, and a large bar full of travellers. Best of all, though, are the home-cooked, delicious meals made using produce from the owner's organic farm.

⭐**Levant Hotel** HOTEL €€
(☑ 26610 94230; www.levantcorfu.com; Pelekas; s/d incl breakfast €80/100; ⊙ May–mid-Oct; 🅿 ⊛ 🛜 🏊) Creamy neoclassical Levant sits high up with the gods at the top of a hill just below the Kaiser's Throne peak. It has pastel-blue rooms, wooden floors, belle époque lights and balconies, and a general feeling of countryside charm. Rounding things off is a refined restaurant serving shrimp, risotto and *stifadho* (stew) on a terrace with sublime sunset views.

⭐**Hotel Zefiros** HOTEL €€
(☑ 26630 41244; www.zefiroscorfuhotel.gr; Paleokastritsa; d/tr/q from €95/120/140; ⊛ 🛜) Set slightly askew of Paleokastritsa's pretty main beach, with a cool olive-grey terrace cafe at lobby level, wine-coloured Zefiros offers bright and breezy rooms with flowery stencils and balconies. The top floor has the finest views. Prices are reduced significantly outside high season.

Rolling Stone PENSION €€
(☑ 26610 94942; www.pelekasbeach.com; Kontogialos Beach; r/apt €70/95; ⊛ 🛜) The most

bohemian and backpacker-friendly place to stay on Kontogialos (Pelekas) Beach has two fresh, simple family apartments with bathrooms and kitchenettes, plus two ample-sized and spotless rooms. People gather to chat on the large, shaded terrace out the front, which has a small bar and a communal semioutdoor kitchen. It's a steep two-minute walk to the beach.

Kallisto Resort
APARTMENT €€€

(📞 6977443555; www.corfuresorts.gr; Kontogialos Beach; apt from €170, villas €240-480; 🅿 ❋ 🗲) Exuberant terraced gardens cascading down the hillside at the northern end of Kontogialos Beach hold apartments and villas (sleeping two to 12) that are the last word in Corfu luxury. When you're not lounging around your palatial apartment or soaking up the sea views from your terrace, take your pick from the two sparkling pools.

✕ Eating

While the resorts have plenty of restaurants, it's worth hunting out locally popular tavernas in inland villages such as Pelekas, or the various panoramic-view options perched along the high road between Lakones and Krini.

Ella Restaurant
TAVERNA €

(📞 6980696364; www.eliamirtiotissa.com; Myrtiotissa; mains €7-14; ⊙ noon-late May-Oct) An irresistible taverna, perched above the track down to breathtaking Myrtiotissa Beach, serving an enticing menu of Corfiot specialities and much-needed cold drinks. Many of the ingredients used in the meals come from the owner's own farm.

To Stavrodromi
TAVERNA €

(📞 26610 94274; www.tostavrodromi.com; Pelekas; mains €7-12; ⊙ 6-11pm) A homey dinner-only joint at the main crossroads just east of Pelekas. Delicious local specialities include Corfu's finest *kontosouvli* (spit-roast pork with paprika and onions), as well as rabbit *stifadho* and pepper steak.

★ Alonaki Bay
TAVERNA €€

(📞 26610 75872; Alonaki; mains €10-15; ⊙ 9.30am-midnight; 🛜) Follow the dirt roads out to the headland northwest of Lake Korission to find this simple, family-run taverna, perched on dramatic cliffs. It serves a small menu of home-cooked meat and *mayirefta* (ready-cooked meals), and also offers clean rooms (€50) and apartments (€55), overlooking the garden.

Nereids
TAVERNA €€

(📞 26630 41013; Paleokastritsa; mains €12-19; ⊙ 11am-midnight) Just below a huge curve in the road as you enter Paleokastritsa, this romantic spot is best experienced at night, when its terrace of ornamental rock pools and urns is softly lit. The dolmadhes (vine leaves stuffed with rice, and somctimes meat), meatballs in tomato sauce, *kleftiko* (slow-cooked meat) and *stifadho* are particularly recommended.

❶ Getting There & Away

Green Buses (www.greenbuses.gr) provides a handy way to get to and from Corfu Town if you're based in, say, Paleokastritsa or Agios Gordios, but to reach outlying sights and beaches you'll need to rent a vehicle.

PAXI ΠΑΞΟΙ
POP 2300

Measuring a mere 13km from tip to toe, and spared overdevelopment by its lack of an airport, Paxi packs a lot of punch into its tiny frame. Facilities are concentrated in three delightful harbour villages tucked into its eastern shores – Lakka, Loggos and the ferry port of Gaïos. Each has its own crop of tasteful little hotels, rental apartments and seafront tavernas, and its own devoted fans.

All villages make wonderful bases for exploring the rolling hills and centuries-old olive groves of the interior, and the wilder scenery of the west coast. Unspoilt coves can be reached by motorboat, while former mule trails lead to sheer limestone cliffs that plunge into the azure sea. Great hikes lead out to majestic **Tripitos Arch** (Map p524) in the south, and down to **Erimitis Beach** (Map p524), beneath a vast wall of crumbling rock, in the west.

❶ Information

Helpful travel agencies include **New Plans** (Bouas Tours; 📞 6980344759; www.newplans. gr; ⊙ 9am-8pm) in Gaïos and **Sun & Sea** (📞 26620 31162; www.paxossunandsea.com; ⊙ 8.30am-2.30pm & 5.30-11pm) in Lakka.

❶ Getting There & Away

BOAT

Busy passenger-only Ilida (p510) hydrofoils link Paxi's ferry port at Gaïos with Corfu Town (€25, 55 to 90 minutes, three to eight daily,

Paxi & Antipaxi

Corfu (10km)
Igoumenitsa (25km)

Harami Beach
Lakka
Torri E Merli
Monodendri Beach
Loggos
Paxi
Levrecchio Beach
Magazia
Erimitis Beach
Fontana
Panagia Islet
Agios Nikolaos Islet
Achai Bay
Bogdanatika
Gaïos
Avlaki
Ozias
Paxos Beach Hotel
Agrilas Bay
Vellianitatika
Tripitos Arch
Mogonisi
Agrapidia Bay
Vrika Beach
Voutoumi Beach
Vigla
Antipaxi
Ionian Sea
South Kerkyra Straits

IONIAN ISLANDS GAÏOS

mid-March to mid-October) and occasionally with Igoumenitsa on the Greek mainland. A slower but cheaper service on the Corfu Town route (€20, 90 minutes, one to three daily, April to October) is provided by Kamelia Lines (p510), while car ferries also link Paxi with Igoumenitsa (passenger/vehicle €11/42.30, one to three daily, April to October). Buy ferry tickets from New Plans (p523).

Fast water taxis are available on demand; Corfu to Paxi costs €330 with **Paxos Sea Taxi** (☑ 26620 32444, 6932232072; www.paxos seataxi.com).

Regular excursion boats run from Gaïos to Antipaxi (€10 return) in summer from June onwards.

ⓘ Getting Around

Buses link Gaïos and Lakka via Loggos twice daily except Sunday (€2.50); they're not convenient for day trips.

Taxis between Gaïos and Lakka or Loggos cost around €15; Gaïos' taxi rank is by the inland car park.

Many agencies rent small boats (from €50 to €100, depending on engine capacity).

Daily car rental with **Alfa Hire** (☑ 26620 32505; www.alfacarhirepaxos.com) starts at €35 in high season.

Gaïos   Γαϊος

POP 500

Gaïos is a supremely peaceful harbour village. Arrayed in a lazy, gentle curve along a narrow, fjord-like channel, it's caressed by beautiful teal water and faces the wooded islet of Agios Nikolaos. A long row of rose- and biscuit-hued neoclassical villas lines the waterfront promenade, many of them housing cafes and tavernas, while yachts and excursion boats bob quayside.

🛏 Sleeping

Gaïos has hotels and studios to suit all budgets; owners usually offer ferry transfers.

Paxos Beach Hotel   HOTEL €€
(Map p524; ☑ 26620 32211; www.paxosbeach hotel.gr; incl breakfast d €105-180, ste €200-280; ❄🛜🏊) Nestling into a tiny cove a pleasant 1.5km walk southeast along the waterfront from Gaïos, this family-run hotel has its own beach, plus a jetty, a swimming pool, a tennis court and a seaside restaurant. With rooms in separate villas on the terraced hillside, you can expect a lot of steps. Ferry transfers and rental boats available.

Water Planet Rooms   APARTMENT €€
(☑ 6972111995; www.waterplanet.gr; d €60; ❄🛜) As much a homestay as a guesthouse, Water Planet is run by friendly and very helpful owners, with assistance from their entertaining little son. Rooms are pleasingly decorated in a sea-faring style, and there's a copious breakfast. Expect that a lot of fuss will be made of you. The owners run the adjoining dive shop.

Theklis-Clara Studios   PENSION €€
(☑ 6972923838, 26620 32313; www.theklis-studios .com; studios €110; ❄) Lovely Thekli, a freediver with her own boat, rents out four beautiful two-person studios, furnished with shabby-chic flair, in a handsome house 100m up from the quayside. All have well-equipped kitchenettes and bathrooms, and balconies with serene sea views. Ferry transfers possible on request.

🍴 Eating

★**Carnayo**   MEDITERRANEAN €€
(☑ 26620 32376; www.carnayopaxos.gr; mains €10-22; ⏱ noon-4pm & 7-11pm Tue-Sun) Paxi's finest restaurant, 400m up from central Gaïos, serves local food that's head and shoulders above what's on offer at the harbourfront

tavernas, for similar prices. The mixed plate of starters alone is worth a visit; mains range from slow-roasted pork to homemade burgers and crispy-skin bream. Sit in the refined dining room or the romantically lit garden courtyard.

Dodos
TAVERNA €€

(📞 26620 32265; http://dodos-paxos.blogspot. co.uk; mains €7-15; ⊙ noon-midnight) Presided over by the genial Dodo, this friendly little taverna is hidden in a quirky secret garden (follow the signs from the southern end of the waterfront), with seating that will remind you of rainbows. Come for traditional dishes such as lamb cooked with honey or pork stuffed with cheese, and linger for live music. Also rents simple **studios** (from €60).

ⓘ Information

Gaïos has no tourist office, but travel agencies, such as New Plans (p523) and **Paxos Magic Holidays** (📞 26620 32269; www.paxosmagic. com), organise excursions, book tickets and arrange accommodation.

ⓘ Getting There & Away

Paxi's ferry port is 1km north along the paved, level waterfront from Gaïos' central square, and has connections to Corfu Town and Igoumenitsa. Excursion boats dock along the quayside in the heart of town. A water taxi from Corfu to Paxi costs €330.

ⓘ Getting Around

You can rent a car from Alfa Hire from €35 a day.

Loggos
Λόγγος

Bookended by white cliffs and the hulk of an old olive-oil factory, breathtaking little Loggos, 6km northwest of Gaïos, consists of a cluster of pretty Venetian houses huddled around a tiny bay of crystal-clear water. Bars and restaurants overlook the sea, while wooded slopes climb steeply above. Just to the south are a couple of pebble beaches backed by olive groves and with beautiful swimming and reasonable snorkelling. All these things make Loggos probably the most enticing of all Paxi's villages.

🏃 Activities

Paxos Thalassa Travel (📞 26620 31662; www. paxos-thalassatravel.com) is a fantastic travel agency offering kayak hire, guided walks, snorkelling trips, sundowner boat trips and much more.

🛏 Sleeping & Eating

There are no hotels in Loggos, but there's a limited number of studio and apartment rentals. In most cases it's safer to book these in advance through an agency.

The chefs at **Vasilis** (📞 26620 31587; www. vassilisrestaurant.com; mains €13-20; ⊙ noon-midnight), a low-slung terracotta cottage on the paved harbourfront, are by far the most creative in town. Well-turned-out local specialities include pan-fried cuttlefish, sea urchin, *bourdeto* (fresh fish cooked in tomato and paprika sauce) and a delicious slow-cooked rabbit in yoghurt sauce. Reserve in summer.

IONIAN ISLANDS LOGGOS

WORTH A TRIP

ANTIPAXI

The ravishing and barely inhabited little island of Antipaxi is a favourite day-trip destination from Paxi, just 2km north, and Corfu. While very few visitors stay overnight, the two superb beach coves near the island's northern tip are thronged every day in summer with boats large and small. Sandy **Vrika Beach**, the closest to Paxi, and longer but stonier **Voutoumi Beach** further south are among the best beaches in the Ionian Islands, and they hold a couple of tavernas each. Both lie cradled beneath densely wooded slopes and shelter dazzlingly clear waters.

Footpaths from both beaches and from the island's totally undeveloped harbour, 600m south of Voutoumi, climb to Antipaxi's central spine, where the 'village' of **Vigla** consists of a few scattered villas and no centre or commercial activity. Keep walking to reach the wilder and beachless western coast within a few minutes, or head for the lighthouse at the island's southernmost tip; take plenty of water and allow at least 1½ hours each way.

Between June and September boats to Antipaxi typically leave Gaïos on Paxi (return €10) at 10am and return around 4.30pm, with increased services in July and August. Ionian Cruises (p516) and other operators offer day trips to Paxi and Antipaxi from Corfu Town.

ⓘ Getting There & Away

Ideally you'd make your way to and from Loggos by yacht, but alternatively you can hire one of the motorboats of various shapes and sizes that you'll see lined up in the harbour; contact Paxos Thalassa Travel (p525).

A bus travels between Gaïos and Lakka via Loggos twice daily. Its main function is to get children to and from school.

Lakka   Λάκκα

So languid it seems forever on the point of slipping into the yacht-flecked waters, Lakka is sure to slow your pulse and make you smile. Wander the quayside to savour the tempting aromas and gentle music that waft from the tavernas, or venture westward around the bay to reach sandy **Harami Beach**, or the **lighthouse** atop the headland beyond.

🏃 Activities

With clear visibility and diverse habitats, Paxos offers some great diving. **Paxos Oasi Sub** (☑ 26620 33493; www.paxosoasisub.com) offers try dives (€80), snorkelling safaris (€45) and PADI open-water courses (€550).

🛏 Sleeping & Eating

Accommodation options in and around Lakka range from luxury hotels to inexpensive rental studios.

Yorgos Studios — APARTMENT €€
(☑ 26620 31807; www.routsis-holidays.com; d €80; ❄🛜) Immaculate, comfy and colourful two-person studios, next door to and run by travel agency Routsis Holidays, which represents several other local studios and apartments.

⭐ **Torri E Merli** — BOUTIQUE HOTEL €€€
(Map p524; ☑ 26212 34123; www.torriemerli.com; ste from €420; ☺May-Oct; 🅿❄🛜🏊) Constructed in 1750, its towers designed to repel pirates, this beautiful boutique property complements its original Venetian elements with contemporary decor – exposed-stone walls, white-wood floors – to create what's arguably the Ionians' loveliest hotel. Set in the olive groves 800m south of Lakka, it holds just seven suites, along with a restaurant and a kidney-shaped pool.

Arriva Fish Restaurant — SEAFOOD €€
(☑ 26620 33041; mains €10-17; ☺11am-11pm) Waterfront taverna with little tables perched on the very brink of the quayside. Check out the blackboard for an amazing list of freshly caught fish and seafood, from lobster to scorpionfish, prepared every imaginable way – grilled, barbecued, or in risotto or pasta dishes. The cuttlefish with scallops is delectable.

ⓘ Information

Helpful **Routsis Holidays** (☑ 26620 31807; www.routsis-holidays.com) rents out well-appointed apartments and villas to suit all budgets, and arranges transport and excursions. Harbourside Sun & Sea (p523) also offers accommodation, as well as boat rental (from €50).

ⓘ Getting There & Away

The twice-daily bus connection between Lakka and Gaïos via Loggos is designed to get local kids to and from school, and is not convenient for visitors. A rental car is much more practical.

LEFKADA   ΛΕΥΚΑΔΑ

POP 22,650

Despite being connected to the mainland by a narrow causeway, making it one of the few Greek islands that you can drive to, much of Lefkada remains surprisingly unaffected by tourism.

Laid-back Lefkada Town is a charming place to spend a day or two, while the soaring mountains of the interior still conceal timeless villages and wild olive groves, and the rugged west coast holds some amazing beaches, albeit in some cases badly damaged by recent earthquakes. Only along the east coast are there some overdeveloped enclaves; if you continue all the way south you'll find stunning little bays and inlets, as well as windy conditions that attract kitesurfers and windsurfers from all over the world.

Lefkada was originally a peninsula, not a true island. Corinthian colonisers cut a canal through the narrow isthmus that joined it to the rest of Greece in the 8th century BC.

ⓘ Getting There & Away

AIR

Lefkada's closest airport is near Preveza (Aktion; PVK), on the mainland 20km north. **Sky Express** (www.skyexpress.gr) connects it with Corfu (€73, 30 minutes), Kefallonia (€67, 30 minutes), Zakynthos (€73, 1½ hours) and Sitia

Lefkada & Meganisi

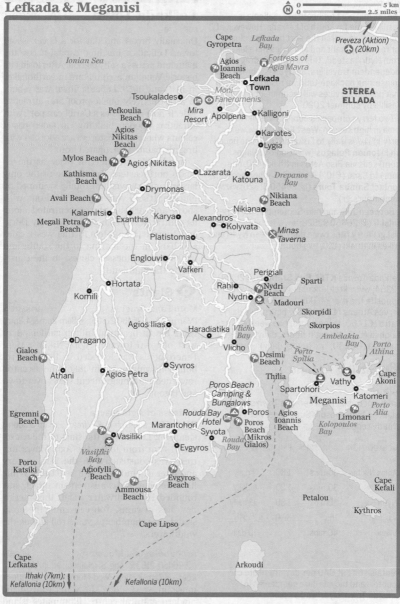

(Crete; €117, 1½ hours, June to September only). **Olympic Air** (www.olympicair.com) flies from Preveza to Athens, with connections throughout Greece. In summer, **easyJet** (www.easyjet.com) flies to Preveza from the UK, as do charter flights from all over northern Europe.

There's no direct bus between Lefkada Town and Preveza airport, but buses connect Lefkada Town with Preveza itself (€2.90, 30 minutes, six daily), from where you can take a taxi to the airport (€15).

Taxis from the airport to Lefkada Town cost from €40.

BOAT

The normal port for boats to Kefallonia is Vasiliki in the far south of Lefkada. However, at the time of research the port here was closed for redevelopment and all ferries were leaving from Nydri instead. This is a bit of a drag for independent travellers, as Nydri is a brash and uninspiring package-tourism resort. It's hoped that normal services will recommence from Vasiliki by summer 2020.

Two ferry companies connect Vasiliki to Kefallonia in high season; **West Ferry** (www.west ferry.gr) runs daily to Fiskardo (€10, one hour), while **Ionion Pelagos** (www.ionionpelagos .com) sails via Piso Aetos in Ithaki (€10, one hour) to Sami (€10, 1¾ hours). For bookings contact **Samba Tours** (☑ 26450 31520; www. sambatours.gr).

Between July and mid-September, the **Meganisi II** (☑ 26450 92528; www.ferryboatmega nisi.gr) ferry runs twice daily between Nydri and Frikes in Ithaki (€10, two hours).

BUS

Lefkada Town's **KTEL Bus Station** (☑ 26450 22364; www.ktel-lefkadas.gr; Ant Tzeveleki), opposite the marina 1km from the centre, serves Athens (€33.90, 5½ hours, five daily), Patra (€17.60, three hours, two weekly), Thessaloniki (€35.40, eight hours, daily) and Igoumenitsa (€13.30, two hours, daily).

❶ Getting Around

BUS

Frequent buses from Lefkada Town serve the island in high season; Sunday services are greatly reduced.

DESTINATION	DURATION	FARE (€)	FREQUENCY
Agios Nikitas	30mins	1.80	3 daily
Karya	30mins	1.80	6 daily
Nydri	30mins	1.80	13 daily
Vasiliki	1hr	3.70	3 daily
Vlicho	40mins	2	10 daily

CAR

Rentals start at €40 per day; there are car-, scooter- and bicycle-hire companies in Lefkada Town, Nydri and Vasiliki.

It's possible to pick up a hire car at Preveza's Aktion Airport and return it in Nydri if you're catching a ferry south (or vice versa).

Lefkada Town   Λευκάδα
POP 8670

Unusually broad and flat for a Greek-island town, Lefkada's bustling capital faces the mainland across a salty lagoon. After losing its historic Venetian architecture in earthquakes in 1948 and 1953, Lefkada Town was rebuilt in a distinctively quake-proof and attractive style. It now resembles a Caribbean port, with attractive wooden buildings in faded pastel colours whose upper storeys are adorned with brightly painted corrugated iron.

A relaxed and cheerful place at the island's northeastern tip, it's one of the only larger Ionian towns not totally swamped by tourism. It's all very logically laid out, with shops and restaurants concentrated along its central pedestrian street (initially Dorpfeld, then Ioannou Mela further west); cafes and bars on the marina to the south; and banks and businesses closest to the causeway to the mainland.

◉ Sights

Moni Faneromenis   MONASTERY
(Map p527; ☑ 26450 21305; ⊘ 8am-2pm & 4-8pm) **FREE** Set in beautiful hilltop gardens 3km west of town towards Agios Nikitas, Moni Faneromenis was founded in 1634 and rebuilt following a fire in 1886. The ascent is rewarded with magnificent views over town and lagoon.

Fortress of Agia Mavra   FORTRESS
(Map p527; adult/child €2/free; ⊘ 8am-3.30pm) Guarding Lefkada at the start of the causeway, 1.4km from town, the Agia Mavra fortress was constructed in the 14th century and later expanded by the Venetians. While its lichen-covered walls remain intact, surrounded by a saltwater moat, the interior now lies in ruins. You can enter the occasional bare chamber as you stroll among the wildflowers.

Archaeological Museum   MUSEUM
(☑ 26450 21635; Ang Sikelianou; adult/child €2/ free; ⊘ 8am-3.30pm Wed-Mon) This excellent museum, west along the waterfront in the modern cultural centre, illuminates island history from the Palaeolithic era to the Romans. Prize exhibits include terracotta ensembles from the 6th century BC depicting a flute player surrounded by dancing nymphs, seen as evidence that a Pan cult once flourished on Lefkada.

MEGANISI

The elongated island of Meganisi, off Lefkada's southeastern corner, is an easy boat ride from Nydri, on Lefkada's east coast. Most people visit on a day trip, but with its verdant hills still thick with woodland, and turquoise bays fringed by pebbled beaches with a minimum of development, the island's well worth a longer, more relaxed stay. From the ferry dock at **Porto Spilia**, climb the steep road or stairway to reach the narrow lanes and bougainvillea-bedecked houses of **Spartohori**, on the plateau above. The next inlet to the east holds pretty **Vathy**, Meganisi's second harbour, 1km below the village of **Katomeri**.

Ferries from Nydri sail to both Porto Spilia and Vathy (per person/car €1.90/12.90, 25 to 40 minutes, three to four daily); buy tickets from Borsalino Travel (p530). Local buses connect Spartohori and Vathy five to seven times daily, via Katomeri, but bringing your own vehicle is recommended.

🛏 Sleeping

Several good-value hotels are located at the eastern end of Lefkada Town, just a few steps from the causeway.

⭐**Boschetto Hotel**　　BOUTIQUE HOTEL €€

(☑ 26450 20244; www.boschettohotel.com; Dorpfeld 1; d incl breakfast from €95; ❋ 🛜) This attractive century-old building on the seafront square holds four large, tasteful rooms and a single suite, all with wooden floors, fine linen, cosy armchairs, attractively weatherworn wooden desks, and balconies looking across the cafe below to the bright-blue waters of the lagoon. The included breakfast is top notch.

Pirofani Boutique　　HOTEL €€

(☑ 26450 25844; www.pirofanilefkada.com; Dorpfeld 10; d €120; ❋ 🛜) Very friendly and central family-run hotel that has slightly over-the-top decoration, with a few too many gold flurries, but immaculate bathrooms. The location – on the main old-town street – can't be beaten.

🍴 Eating & Drinking

⭐**Thymari**　　MEDITERRANEAN €€

(☑ 26450 22266; www.thymari-lefkada.gr; 19 Pinelopis St; mains €15-20; ⊘ 7-11pm May-Oct) With tables laid out on a large, sunny terrace surrounded by flowers on a quiet neighbourhood alleyway, this is a delightful place to eat truly outstanding modern Mediterranean cuisine. Expect innovative dishes such as 'deconstructed' lasagne, and don't miss out on tasting the various olive oils. Excellent wine list.

All the tables are outside, so it's not the place to head to on a wet day!

Nissi　　MEDITERRANEAN €€

(☑ 26454 00725; www.facebook.com/nissilefkada; Plateia Ethnikis Antistaseos; mains €8-16; ⊘ 1pm-12.30am; ❋ 🛜) Memorably good Greek–Italian restaurant, as popular with locals as with tourists, with stylish, comfortable seating on the central inland square. The jet-black squid-ink risotto (€11.50), with octopus and huge grilled prawns, is an astonishing bargain.

⭐**Gogos Gefsis**　　BAR

(☑ 26453 00509; Ioannou Mela 149; ⊘ 10am-2am; 🛜) Very friendly bar cafe on the main pedestrian street, with pavement tables plus a quirky interior kitted out like a vintage grocery. The Greek sign is fiendishly hard to read; look for the hammer-and-sickle flag flying above. While it sells a short menu of grilled snacks and cheesy shrimp, just buying a beer gets you a free hot snack.

ℹ Getting Around

Rental outlets in Lefkada Town include **Green Motion** (☑ 26450 23581; www.greenmotion.gr; Panagou 16) for cars and **Santas** (☑ 26450 25250; www.ilovesantas.gr) for scooters and bikes.

Eastern Lefkada

Lefkada's east coast has experienced the island's heaviest tourist development. Head south, however, to find the unspoilt strand at lovely **Poros Beach** (also known as Mikros Gialos) and the relaxed and very sheltered harbour at fjord-like **Syvota**, where yachts now bob alongside the fishing boats (although there's no beach here). **Nydri** has seen the most development; what was once a gorgeous fishing village is now a crowded strip of kiss-me-quick tourist shops, without a decent beach.

📇 Sleeping

Poros Beach Camping & Bungalows
CAMPGROUND €

(Map p527; ☑26450 95452; www.porosbeach. com.gr; Poros Beach; sites adult/car/tent €10/3/5, r/studios €70/80; ☺May-Sep; 🅿❄@🛜🏊) A short walk up from perfect Poros Beach, this well-equipped campsite has a great pool, shaded olive-grove tent sites, a nice bar and a restaurant stretching across a huge wooden deck. It also offers attractive double rooms and studios – some family size.

Rouda Bay Hotel
HOTEL €€

(Map p527; ☑6932567502, 26450 95634; http:// roudabay.gr; Poros Beach; d from €80; ❄🛜) Comfortable, high-standard, modern rooms and studios, right in the middle of gorgeous Poros Beach. All are capable of accommodating a family of four, and there's also a good waterfront restaurant.

🍴 Eating

⭐Sivota Bakery
CAFE €

(☑6972432497; Syvota; mains €6-12; ☺7am-1am) With its harbourfront walls hung with antique bikes and carriage lamps, this cool arbour is much more cafe than bakery, serving pizzas, waffles, cocktails and wine among many other items. However, it's the breakfasts, which range from full English to a delicious melange of yoghurt, honey, fruit and granola, that are the real stars of the show.

Taberna Ionion
TAVERNA €€

(☑26650 93506; Syvota; mains €9-14; ☺11am-midnight) On the quieter, eastern side of the port, this long-standing family-run place is a little less hectic than others, which means that staff members can pay that little extra bit of attention to diners. Expect good seafood eaten under the shade of a 'living' roof of plants.

Stavros
TAVERNA €€

(☑26450 31181; http://tavernastavros.gr; Syvota; mains €9-16; ☺8am-midnight Easter-Oct) The pick of several similarly tempting and colourful seafood tavernas along the pretty quayside, Stavros, which has been going strong since the mid-1970s, offers a full menu of freshly caught fish along with local delicacies such as fish soup and leg of lamb in honey.

Minas Taverna
TAVERNA €€

(Map p527; ☑26450 71480; Nikiana; mains €8-18; ☺5pm-midnight, reduced hours in low season) Top-notch taverna with a sea-view terrace shaded by vines and a menu that serves up everything from seafood pasta to rice cooked in squid ink to grilled meat and fish. It's above the main road 5km north of Nydri, just south of Nikiana.

ℹ️ Information

Borsalino Travel (☑26450 92528; www. borsalinotravel.gr; Nydri) For all travel arrangements, including accommodation and car rental as well as ferry and excursion tickets.

ℹ️ Getting There & Away

Frequent buses link Nydri with Lefkada Town (€1.80, 30 minutes, 13 daily), but only a few continue any further south.

Vasiliki
Βασιλική

POP 395

This friendly harbour village, complete with stony beach, is one of the top places to learn windsurfing in Greece. This is thanks to a summer-only local thermal wind known to windsurfers as – of all things – Eric! This wind means it's not an ideal place for sunbathers, but a tasty clutch of eucalyptus-shaded tavernas fringing the waterfront, a number of boutique shops and an exceptional place to stay all mean that even nonwindsurfers will find something to like about Vasiliki.

🤾 Activities

Caïques take visitors to nearby beaches and coves. The big attraction for boating day trips is Egremni Beach, especially since earthquake damage means it's no longer accessible by road. Helpful Samba Tours (p528) sells tickets for excursion boats, including to Egremni, and arranges bicycle hire. Along the quayside, flags indicate water-sports outfits; some have their own hotels for clients.

Club Vassiliki
WATER SPORTS

(☑26450 31588; www.clubvass.com) Long-established club specialising in learn-to-windsurf packages that include flights and accommodation. Also offers board hire, private lessons and a wide range of other activities from diving to mountain biking.

It's marketed very much at a UK audience and even has a dedicated UK phone number for queries: 0844 463 0191.

Nautilus Diving Club
DIVING

(☑6936181775; www.underwater.gr; ☺May-early Oct) Very well-run dive and water-sports centre. Offers single dives (€60) and PADI open-water courses (€430), plus sea-kayak hire (per hour/half-day €15/40) and snorkelling safaris (€55), which get great feedback and take explorers of the deep blue to a hidden beach that even locals describe as being 'like the Caribbean'.

🛏 Sleeping & Eating

⭐ Pension Holidays   HOTEL €€
(☑ 26450 31426; d/apt €65/70; ❄ 🖥) This guesthouse has it all: immaculate, tastefully furnished double rooms and simply furnished, great-value kitchenette apartments, all with sea views and run by a family with big smiles. It's perfectly located in a quiet spot that's just around the corner beyond the main bay. One of the best guesthouses in all of the Ionian Islands.

Vasiliki Blue   APARTMENT €€
(☑ 26450 31602; www.vasilikiblue.gr; d €75; ❄ 🖥) Bright, scrupulously clean kitchenette apartments, perched on the hillside a few metres up from the harbour, with sea-view balconies draped in bougainvillea.

Vagelaras   TAVERNA €€
(☑ 26450 31224; mains €7-16; ⊙ 8am-midnight; 🖥) Sitting at the end of the harbour, just short of the ferry dock, this century-old taverna serves great salads, mezedhes, pasta and fresh seafood at waterfront tables.

ℹ Information

Samba Tours (p528) sells tickets for ferries and boat excursions, including to Egremni Beach. Also arranges car and bicycle hire and accommodation, and offers all-round assistance.

ℹ Getting There & Away

Three daily buses (€3.70, one hour) connect Vasiliki with Lefkada Town in high season.

Western Lefkada

On Lefkada's west coast, steep mountain slopes covered in olive trees drop dramatically to dazzling-white beaches that have long been regarded as some of the best in Greece. Tourism development remains fairly minimal and the few villages that cling precariously to this vertiginous landscape retain a slow, traditional vibe. The best-known beaches were, sadly, seriously damaged by a 2015 earthquake and can be hard to reach, but others remain intact and there's still plenty of scope for exploration.

⊙ Sights

The one resort on the west coast, the ever-expanding village of Agios Nikitas, stands 13km southwest of Lefkada Town along the coastal road. A short street of inviting tavernas leads down to a curving white-sand beach lapped by aquamarine water. Head across the headland to the west, following the footpath from the Poseidon taverna, and you'll come to broad, straight and utterly delightful Mylos Beach (Map p527). White-pebbled Pefkoulia Beach (Map p527) is a five-minute drive north, and similar Kathisma Beach (Map p527) is the same distance south.

Further south, beyond the village of Athani, where stalls sell olive oil, honey and wine, two of Lefkada's most famous beaches, Egremni Beach (Map p527) and Porto Katsiki (Map p527), were devastated by the 2015 earthquake. Both were submerged in debris as the white cliffs that tower above them came crumbling down, though geologists believe that they will eventually be washed clean and restored to their former glory. Porto Katsiki is in slightly better shape, and remains accessible by car, but both the 720-step stairway that led to Egremni and the road by which it was reached were obliterated and are unlikely to be rebuilt. Now the only way to see what's left of Egremni, and to bathe in its magical turquoise waters, is to take a boat excursion from ports elsewhere on the island, such as Vasiliki.

🛏 Sleeping

If you fancy basing yourself on the west coast, little Agios Nikitas has everything you need. There are also a few options in the village of Kalamitsi, a little way to the south.

⭐ Mira Resort   APARTMENT €€
(Map p527; ☑ 26450 24967, SMS only 6977075881; www.miraresort.com; Tsoukalades; maisonettes incl breakfast from €145; ⊙ May-Oct; P ❄ 🖥 ☀) Perfectly positioned on the mountainside 6km southwest of Lefkada Town, with panoramic views of the glittering sea, Mira has cosy and immaculate maisonettes, plus a large pool and a cafe-bar.

Hotel Agatha   HOTEL €€
(☑ 6948620615; www.agatha-hotel.com; Agios Nikitas; studios/apt €90/100; ❄ 🖥) Beside the coastal road, a few minutes' walk up from the eastern end of the beach at Agios Nikitas, Agatha offers lovely, cool kitchenette studios and two-room apartments that are flooded with sunlight and set within pretty gardens ringing with birdsong. Number 1 is the pick.

Olive Tree Hotel
HOTEL €€

(☑ 26450 97453; www.olivetreehotel.gr; Agios Nikitas; s/d/studios incl breakfast €80/90/100; ☺ May-Sep; ❄ ☎) Brushed in the colours of olive oil, this modest hotel just above the village centre is managed by friendly Greek-Canadians. Each room has its own terrace, with side-on sea views, and there's a good buffet breakfast.

✖ Eating

In addition to the abundant eating options in Agios Nikitas, the road south – around Athani in particular – is scattered with attractive village restaurants.

★ Cape of Lefkatas
TAVERNA €

(☑ 26450 33149; www.lefkatas.gr; Athani; mains €7-13; ☺ 1-11pm May-Sep; ☎) ✎ This delightful terrace restaurant in Athani village has inspiring views down the mountainside to the sea beyond. Join the locals sitting in the shade of a cedar tree to enjoy superb seafood, including a risotto (€13) that's so thick in creatures of the deep that it wouldn't be a surprise to find Neptune himself hidden among the rice!

T'Agnantio
TAVERNA €

(☑ 26450 97383; www.tagnantio.gr; Agios Nikitas; mains €7-15; ☺ noon-midnight Easter-Oct) The vine-shaded terrace of Agios Nikitas' finest taverna sits in a quiet, tucked-away spot slightly up from the beach and offers sweeping views out to sea. Feast on seafood – including swordfish, shrimp and octopus – as well as souvlaki, meatballs and local cheese.

❶ Getting There & Away

Buses from Lefkada Town run to Agios Nikitas (€1.80, 30 minutes, three daily) and Kathisma Beach, and also as far south as Athani.

Central Lefkada

Replete with traditional farming villages, lush green peaks, fragrant pine trees, olive groves and vineyards, Lefkada's dramatic central spine is hugely rewarding to explore.

◉ Sights

The small village of Karya has a pretty central square with plane trees and tavernas, but it attracts crowds in high season. It's famous for its embroidery, introduced during the 19th century by a remarkable one-handed local woman, Maria Koutsochero. A small museum (€2.50) showcases the embroidery and traditional village life. Opening hours are flexible.

✦ Activities

The island's highest village, Englouvi, is renowned for honey and lentils. Book ahead for a herbal walk (☑ 6934287446; www.lefkas.cc; Kolyvata) near quaint Alexandros that aims to show how easy it can be to live off the land.

There's some great walking in Lefkada's mountainous centre, but route information is hard to come by. Follow your nose down dirt roads and along goat trails.

⌖ Sleeping & Eating

Unless you find a rental villa in some far-flung village, the hills of the interior are more of a day-trip destination than an overnight stop.

★ Maria's Tavern
TAVERNA €

(☑ 6984056686, 26450 41228; www.facebook. com/MariasTavern; Kolyvata; mains €6-9; ☺ 12.30-11.30pm Apr-Oct) In the hamlet of Kolyvata, which enjoys idyllic views over the hills, the gregarious Kiria Maria opens her home to culinary adventurers. Using whatever's ready in her garden, she serves fresh, perfectly cooked treats. Call ahead to check she's there. Kolyvata is signposted between Alexandros and Nikiana.

❶ Getting There & Away

Although frequent buses can get you to Karya, for example, you'll see much more if you rent your own vehicle.

KEFALLONIA
ΚΕΦΑΛΛΟΝΙΑ

POP 35,800

Perhaps the most enticing of all the Ionian islands, magical Kefallonia is a place where it's easy to lose yourself, amid air thick with oleander and the sound of goat bells. The largest, and perhaps the most varied, of the islands, there's space to breathe here, and its convoluted coastline conceals all sorts of captivating coves and beach-lined bays lapped by gin-clear waters teeming with colourful fish. Despite the devastating earthquake of 1953 that razed much of the island's historic Venetian architecture, ravishing harbourfront villages such as Fiskardo and Assos still show off Italianate good looks, while the lush and mountainous interior, dotted with wild meadows, Mediterranean oak forests and vineyards, invites endless exploration.

Kefallonia & Ithaki

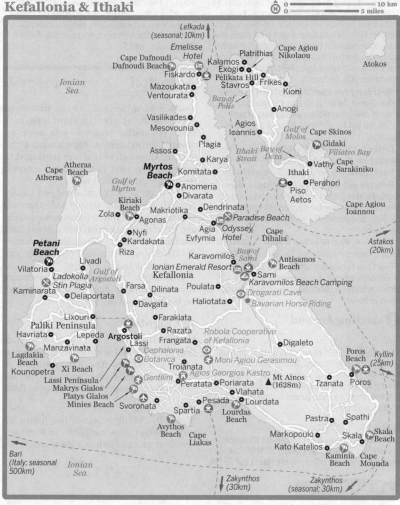

Getting There & Away

AIR

The **airport** (Map p533; ☎ 26710 29900; http://kefaloniaairport.info) is 9km south of Argostoli. From May to September, **easyJet** (www.easyjet.com) flies from London and other cities, and many charter flights come from northern Europe and the UK. In addition, **Olympic Air** (www.olympicair.com) serves Athens, and **Sky Express** (www.skyexpress.gr) serves Corfu, Preveza and Zakynthos.

There's no airport bus; taxis to Argostoli cost around €20.

BUS

Three daily buses from the **KTEL Bus Station** (☎ 26710 22281; www.ktelkefalonias.gr; A Tritsi 5) in Argostoli use the ferry from Poros to make the journey to Athens (€33, seven hours, three daily).

BOAT

Up to five daily **Ionian Group** (www.ioniangroup.com) ferries connect Poros with Kyllini in the Peloponnese in summer (€9, 1½ hours), where you can catch onward ferries to Zakynthos.

Ionian Pelagos (www.ionionpelagos.com) runs up to three ferries a day between Sami and Piso Aetos in Ithaki (€4, 30 minutes), with one or two continuing to Astakos in the Peloponnese (total trip from Sami €11, three hours). It connects Sami to Vasiliki in Lefkada twice weekly in summer (€9, 1¾ hours); and also runs twice daily in summer between the remote and not readily accessible port of Pesada in southern Kefallonia and similarly isolated Agios Nikolaos in northern Zakynthos (€8, 1½ hours).

West Ferry (www.westferry.gr) runs between Fiskardo and Vasiliki (Lefkada; €9, one hour, two to three daily); buy tickets at **Nautilus Travel** (☑ 26740 41440; ◷ 9am-1.30pm & 5-9pm) in Fiskardo.

Ertsos (☑ 26710 27301; www.ertsostravelkefalonia.com; Antoni Tritsi; ◷ 9am-9pm) in Argostoli sells tickets for services to Ithaki and Kyllini.

Between mid-July and mid-September, **Ventouris Ferries** (http://ventourisferries.com) offers a once-weekly connection between Sami, Zakynthos, Igoumenitsa on the mainland, and Bari, Italy.

Buy tickets from **Blue Sea Travel** (☑ 26740 23007; www.samistar.com; Posidonos 16, Sami).

From July to mid-September **Red Star Ferries** (www.ionianislands.it) runs weekly services between Sami and Brindisi (Italy). The crossing takes 16 hours.

❶ Getting Around

BUS

KTEL buses (p533) connect Argostoli with all the island's major towns. In addition, one or two daily services run along the east coast, linking Katelios with Skala, Poros, Sami, Agia Evfymia and Fiskardo. Buses run on Sunday in high season only.

CAR & MOTORCYCLE

Car- and motorbike-hire companies fill major resorts, while **Europcar** (☑ 26710 41008; www.europcar.com; ◷ 7.30am-9pm), **Hertz** (☑ 26714

40040) and other operators have offices at the airport. Sami-based **Kefalonia2Ride** (☑ 26740 22970; www.kefalonia2ride.rentals; Maiouli 29, Sami; ◷ 9.30am-9pm) offers scooters (from €22 per day) and ATVs.

Argostoli   Αργοστόλι

POP 9750

Shielded from the open sea, its waterfront stretching along the landward side of a short peninsula, Argostoli was once renowned for its elegant Venetian-era architecture. Almost all of that was destroyed by earthquake in 1953, but Argostoli is now a lively, forward-looking town.

The main focus of activity is just inland, centred on charming, freshly pedestrianised Plateia Valianou, where locals come to chat and eat at the many restaurants. In summer, musicians stroll the streets singing *kantades* (traditional songs accompanied by guitar and mandolin).

Lithostroto, the pedestrian shopping street immediately south, is lined with stylish boutiques and cafes.

❍ Sights

Makrys Gialos   BEACH
(Map p533) Blessed with enticing turquoise water, and located just 3km southwest of Argostoli, Makrys Gialos tends to be packed to the gills in summer with holidaying Brits.

Platys Gialos   BEACH
(Map p533) This little 'pocket' beach, just beyond Makrys Gialos, has plenty of shade and very clear water, as well as a few places to eat.

LOCAL KNOWLEDGE

IONIAN ON THE VINE

The Ionian Islands would not be the same without wine, and Kefallonia is especially famed for its vintages. The most notable derive from the unique *robola* grape (VQRPD; Vin de Qualité Produit dans une Région Déterminée), thought to have been introduced by the Venetians, while other varieties include *mavrodaphni* (AOC; Appellation d'Origine Contrôlée) and *muscat* (AOC).

Nestled at the heart of the verdant Omala Valley, in the hilly country southeast of Argostoli, the winery of the **Robola Cooperative of Kefallonia** (Map p533; ☑ 26710 86301; www.robola.gr; Omala; ◷ 9am-9pm daily Jul & Aug, to 6pm May, Jun, Sep & Oct, to 3pm Mon-Fri Nov-Apr) transforms grapes from 300 independent growers into a dry white wine of subtle yet lively flavour. Visitors can take an interesting guided tour and enjoy an all-important tasting afterwards. Smaller yet similarly distinguished **Gentilini** (Map p533; ☑ 26710 41618; www.gentilini.gr; Minies; tastings & tour from €5; ◷ 11am-8pm), 5km south of Argostoli on the airport road, has a charming setting and produces a range of superb wines, including the scintillating Classico. It also offers short tours and tastings.

Cephalonia Botanica
GARDENS

(Map p533; ☑ 26710 24866; www.focas-cosmeta tos.gr; ☺ 9am-2pm) **FREE** This lovely botanical garden, designed for the study, preservation and display of the island's plants and herbs, is located 2km south of central Argostoli. It also holds a small artificial lake. Last admission is 45 minutes before closing.

Korgialenio
History & Folklore Museum
MUSEUM

(Map p535; ☑ 26710 28835; Ilia Zervou 12; €3; ☺ 9am-2pm Mon-Sat) Dedicated to preserving Kefallonian art and culture, this fine museum houses icons, furniture, clothes and artwork from the homes of gentry and farm workers.

🛏 Sleeping

Camping Argostoli
CAMPGROUND €

(☑ 26710 23487; www.camping-argostoli.gr; sites adult/car/tent €7/3/5.50; ☺ May-Sep; 🅿) This pleasant, peaceful and hugely welcoming family-run campsite, 2km beyond Argostoli near the lighthouse at the northernmost point of the peninsula, can hardly have changed in years – and it's all the better for it. It also has its own tavern.

Vivian Villa
APARTMENT €

(Map p535; ☑ 26710 23396; www.kefalonia-vivian villa.gr; Deladetsima 11; d/studios €55/60; 🕸🛜) Tasteful guesthouse on a quiet inland street, overlooking a garden fragrant with thyme and basil. As well as hotel-style rooms, some with balconies, it offers larger apartments with well-stocked kitchenettes and separate bedrooms for the kids. Don't be surprised if the warm-hearted owner plies you with homemade cakes and lemonade.

Mouikis Hotel
HOTEL €€

(Map p535; ☑ 26710 23032; http://mouikis.com. gr; Vyronos 3; d incl breakfast from €99; 🕸🛜) Clean, modern hotel, near the market at the southern end of the town centre, with smart, mauve-coloured rooms. Most of the small but very well-equipped rooms have balconies; some have sea views. Rates include a substantial buffet breakfast.

🍴 Eating

⭐ Tzivras
GREEK €

(Map p535; ☑ 26710 24259; Vandorou 1; mains €7-9; ☺ 1-5pm) Slightly grungy and brilliantly atmospheric, this veteran restaurant a block inland from the waterfront market is where

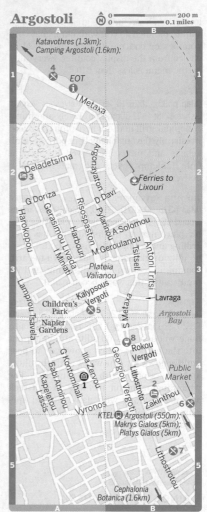

IONIAN ISLANDS ARGOSTOLI

locals lunch on hearty, great-value baked standards, such as veal with okra, goat with potatoes or cod pie. Choose your meal of choice from the display counter. Everything on the menu is less than €10.

★ **Ladokolla** GRILL €

(Map p535; ☑26710 25522; Kalypsous Vergoti; dishes €2-8; ☉12.30pm-2am) Lively and hugely popular grill house, where piping-hot and irresistibly flavourful chicken, pork or lamb kebabs and pittas are served up straight onto tabletop covers (no plates). It also delivers.

Taverna Patsouras TAVERNA €

(Map p535; ☑26711 02960; Antoni Tritsi; mains around €8; ☉noon-11pm) Since 1963 this simple place next to the fish market has been grilling and frying delicious seafood. There's no glitz or glamour; it's just down-to-earth cooking in a down-to-earth setting, and it's pretty out of this world because of it.

Kiani Akti SEAFOOD €€

(Map p535; ☑26710 26680; Antoni Tritsi; mains €8-20; ☉1pm-2am; ☎) This restaurant has a huge wooden deck on stilts stretching out into the harbour, which allows you to peer guiltily down into the water at the brothers and sisters of the fish on your plate. The wide-ranging menu includes tasty Greek appetisers, along with daily seafood specials and meaty classics. You can also just drop in for a drink.

🍷 Drinking & Nightlife

Cafes line Plateia Valianou and Lithostroto, and are buzzing by late evening. **Bass Club** (Map p535; ☑26710 25020; www.bassclub.gr; cnr S Metaxa & Vergoti; ☉noon-7am; ☎) draws a younger set, while club-restaurant **Katavothres** (☑26710 22221; www.katavothres.gr; Mikeli Davi 10; ☉noon-midnight Mon-Thu & Sun, 24hr Fri & Sat; ☎) at the tip of the peninsula combines strange geological formations with iconic futuristic furnishings, and hosts big-name DJs.

ℹ Information

EOT (Greek National Tourist Organisation; Map p535; ☑26710 22248; ☉7am-2.30pm Mon-Fri)

ℹ Getting There & Away

BUS

The KTEL Bus Station (p533) on Argostoli's southern waterfront is the epicentre of the island's public-transport network, with services to the following destinations: Fiskardo (€6.40, two daily), Lassi Peninsula (€1.50, seven daily), Poros (€4.50, three daily), Skala (€4.50, two daily), Sami (€4, four daily). Buses run on Sunday in high season only.

BOAT

The main ferry quay is at the northern end of the waterfront, close to the EOT information office. Car **ferries** (Map p535; person/car €2.80/4) connect Argostoli with Lixouri on the Paliki Peninsula (per person/car €2.80/4, 30 minutes, 7am to 10.30pm). Between May and September they run half-hourly from noon to 5.30pm and hourly at other times. From October to April they run a little less frequently. Ertsos (p534) sells tickets for services to Ithaki and Kyllini.

AINOS NATIONAL PARK

Standing proud over the island is the lumbering hulk of **Mt Ainos** (1628m), most of which falls within Ainos National Park. The mountain's upper reaches are dominated by ancient, gnarled Greek fir and black pine, through which afternoon mist and cloud frequently swirl. In winter the mountain can be blanketed by snow, and at any time of year the views from close to the top (the actual summit has a crown of radio masts) are astounding.

Visitor facilities are fairly undeveloped, but five **walking trails** have been established. The trails themselves are well signposted and very clear, though the trailheads are a little less obvious (a road runs right through the middle of the park and up to the summit; to find the trailheads, keep an eye out for information panels). The two most popular trails go up to the summit from opposite sides of the mountain and then loop back around to their respective starting points. Each is around 6.5km and easy, with a fairly gentle ascent. Unfortunately, in both cases the return route is back along the road, so it's best to ignore this and just retrace your steps along the footpath in the forest. Allow 1½ hours, excluding stops. Another, much more challenging, route heads to the summit from the village of Digaleto, on the road between Sami and Poros. It's a 13km return walk with an altitude gain of 1096m. If walking isn't your thing, you can drive pretty much all the way to the summit.

ℹ Getting Around

First Class Travel (☎ 26710 20026; www.first classtravel.gr; D Davi) Car hire from €25 a day.

Around Argostoli

◉ Sights

Moni Agiou Gerasimou MONASTERY
(Map p533; ☎ 26710 86045; Omala; ⊘ 9am-1pm & 3.30-8pm) **FREE** Dedicated to Kefallonia's patron saint, Moni Agiou Gerasimou is maintained by nuns. The large complex contains pretty gardens, a big, modern church and a small chapel, which encloses the cave to which St Gerasimos withdrew to escape the rigours of monastic life. Its interiors are filled with soot-stained frescoes and the air is heavy with incense. If you're lucky your visit will coincide with the haunting praying and singing of nuns clad head to toe in black.

The monastery is located in the Omala Valley. Take the stated opening hours with a heavenly pinch of salt.

Agios Georgios Kastro FORTRESS
(Castle of St George; Map p533; Peratata; ⊘ 8.30am-4pm Wed-Mon) **FREE** This 16th-century Venetian castle enjoys stellar views from atop a conspicuous pyramid-shaped hill 7km southeast of Argostoli. Kefallonia's capital for 200 years, it's now in ruins, and approached via a short pedestrian street from the adjoining village. Strolling around the unshaded, wildflower-strewn site takes around 20 minutes; relax afterwards over a coffee or snack in the gardens of the neighbouring Kastro Cafe or a full meal at nearby Il Borgo (☎ 26710 69800; Peratata; mains €9-15; ⊘ noon-midnight; ❀).

🛏 Sleeping & Eating

★ Museum Hotel George Molfetas BOUTIQUE HOTEL €€€
(☎ 26710 84630; www.kefaloniamuseumhotel. com; Marinaki, Faraklata; r €120-180; ☎) One-of-a-kind boutique guesthouse with six rooms that are a monument to the art, antiques and general bric-a-brac one family can gather, and it's all been put together with the eye of a natural artist. The garden courtyard is a masterpiece of earthy oranges and big flowers, and owner Katerina is a born raconteur.

★ Gentilini Retreat BOUTIQUE HOTEL €€€
(☎ 26710 26632; www.gentiliniretreat.gr; Mitakata; d from €142) Lose yourself among swathes of olive trees at this dreamy six-room boutique guesthouse set within gentle farming countryside at the base of Mt Ainos. The individually styled rooms are redolent of country living and you get the chance to learn about Kefallonian olive-oil production while staying here.

Run by the Gentilini Winery (p534), but not on the same site, it's the perfect retreat for those after total peace.

Kastro Cafe CAFE €
(☎ 26710 69367; Peratata; mains €6-10; ⊘ 10am-7pm; ❀) Relaxed garden cafe, just before the gateway to Agios Georgios Kastro, that's a wonderfully peaceful spot for coffee, cake, cold drinks or lunchtime snacks.

Paliki Peninsula
Χερσόνησος Παλική

Anchored by the bustling gulf-side town of Lixouri, the Paliki Peninsula is an underexplored region of spectral white, cream and red clay cliffs, verdant farmland and vineyards, and hilltop villages. And beaches – oh, what beaches these are! From dreamy, perfect Petani Beach in the northwest to red-sand Xi Beach in the south, there's a place to plonk a towel for everyone. Between Petani and Kounopetra in the far west, overlooking stark cliffs, azure seas and robust vineyards, the Moni Kipouria monastery was built by a lone, solitude-loving monk.

The highlight of the Paliki Peninsula is breathtaking Petani Beach (Map p533), a spectacular strand of white sand and pebble that's enough to entice a jaded mermaid. In fact, it's so blissful that it's fair to call it one of the best beaches in all of Greece. Although it gets busy in summer, development remains happily minimal. Walk to the far-northern end for a little peace in high season.

🛏 Sleeping

Perdikis Travel (☎ 2671091097; ptravel1@otenet .gr; Lixouri), on Lixouri's southern seafront, can help with accommodation and all travel arrangements. There's plenty of accommodation around Xi and a scattering elsewhere.

★ Ksouras APARTMENT €€
(☎ 26710 97458; www.facebook.com/ksouras; Petani; d €85; P❀🖾) Very pleasant rooms are on offer inside this bright-blue villa immediately above the owners' beachfront taverna. It's a sublimely tranquil spot in the evenings, when the sunset is in full swing. The taverna is open for all meals, and serves excellent and inexpensive Greek classics.

★ **Petani Bay Hotel** HOTEL €€€
(☑ 26710 97701; www.petanibayhotel.gr; Petani; d incl breakfast €210-330; [P][❄][❢][⊞]) Boasting one of the finest infinity pools in Greece, this adults-only boutique eyrie overlooks the cobalt-blue bay far below. There are just 13 romantic suites, with marble floors, wood-blade fans and kitchenettes. It's all about peace here; the only sound is the bleating of goats and the chink of chilled wine glasses.

✖ Eating

Lixouri's waterfront promenade, especially around the main square, is lined with lively cafes and restaurants. There are also good tavernas at Xi Beach and Petani Beach.

Mavroeidis BAKERY €
(☑ 26710 91246; Lixouri; baked goods from €1.50; ☉ 8am-late; [❄][❢]) For over a hundred years, this large bakery-cafe in the heart of Lixouri, with outdoor tables at the inland end of the main pedestrian square, has been baking a panoply of sweet delights. Buying a coffee gets you a free taster of the island's best *amygdalopita* (sweet almond cake).

★ **Ladokolla Stin Plagia** TAVERNA €€
(Map p533; ☑ 26710 97493; Damoulianata; mains €10-22; ☉ 11am-midnight; [❄]) High in the hills in the whitewashed and near-silent village of Damoulianata is this superb, family-run restaurant (the chefs are twin brothers). The menu changes according to what was available in the market or garden that day, but it's especially renowned for its meat pies and its pork cooked in honey, orange and beer.

❶ Getting There & Away

It's easy to access the peninsula on the ferry (p536) from Argostoli to Lixouri (per person/car €2.80/4, 30 minutes, 7am to 10.30pm). Between May and September they run half-hourly from noon to 5.30pm and hourly at other times. From October to April they run a little less frequently.

Sami & Around Σάμη

POP 1030

Cheerful Sami, Kefallonia's main port, stands 25km northeast of Argostoli on the other side of the island. Nestled in a bright bay and flanked by steep hills, it consists of a waterside strip that stares across to Ithaki and is loaded with tourist-oriented cafes. Nearby monasteries, castle ruins and natural features, including the much-hyped

Drogarati Cave, offer enticements to linger. Quieter alternative bases with better beaches, such as **Karavomilos** and **Agia Evfymia**, line the bay as you head further north.

Agia Evfymia in particular is an attractive little port town, with some pretty cove beaches where the water glows and the snorkelling is great. On the flip side, the main road runs right past these beaches and the winds, funnelled between the mountains that stand behind the town, can be strong.

◉ Sights

A popular stop for round-island coach tours, **Drogarati Cave** (Map p533; ☑ 26740 23302; adult/child €5/3; ☉ 10am-5pm Jun-Sep, shorter hours in low season) is a natural cavern hollowed into the hillside 4km south of Sami. A short, steep stairway drops from the ticket booth; once you're down, it takes 10 minutes at most to walk around the single large subterranean chamber, festooned with dripping stalactites. A couple of tavernas stand alongside.

🛏 Sleeping & Eating

Karavomilos Beach Camping CAMPGROUND €
(Map p533; ☑ 26740 22480; www.camping-karavomilos.gr; Sami-Karavomilos Rd; adult/car/tent €9/3.50/6.50; ☉ Apr–mid-Oct; [❢][⊞]) Large family-oriented campground just 800m west of central Sami, with well-shaded sites stretching back from a decent pebble beach. Good facilities include excellent washrooms, a swimming pool, a cafe and a shop.

Odyssey Hotel HOTEL €€€
(Map p533; ☑ 26740 61089; www.hotelodyssey.gr; Agia Evfymia; d from €216; [P][❄][❢][⊞]) Plush resort hotel just around the corner north of the harbour, with very comfortable balcony suites looking across to Ithaki, as well as a spa, gym, restaurant and two bars. Three-night minimum stay in high season.

Ionian Emerald Resort HOTEL €€€
(Map p533; ☑ 26740 22708; www.ionianemerald.gr; Karavomilos; d incl breakfast from €160; [❄][❢][⊞]) Lavish luxury hotel with a spa and gym to complement its spacious pool area. Rooms are creamy cool, with contemporary styling, lush linens and picture windows; some are two-bedroom 'maisonettes'.

★ **Paradise Beach** TAVERNA €€
(Map p533; ☑ 26740 61392; www.paradise beachtaverna.com; Agia Evfymia; mains €7-22; ☉ noon-11pm Apr-Oct; [❢]) This much-loved taverna has a dreamy vine-shaded terrace over-

DON'T MISS

KEFALLONIA'S GREAT OUTDOORS

Kefallonia offers abundant and wonderful hiking, as detailed in many commercial maps and on noticeboards around the island. One gorgeous loop encompasses Agios Georgios Kastro, Moni Agiou Gerasimou, *robola*-producing vineyards and the south coast. If you fancy getting off the beaten path, it's well worth enlisting an experienced local to guide you.

Sea Kayaking Kefallonia (☑ 6934010400; www.seakayakingkefalonia-greece.com; day trips from €65) Offers a full range of day-long kayak tours, with lunch and snorkelling gear included (€65), plus some adventurous multiday excursions that see you paddling to out-of-the-way coves and beaches, and hopping between islands. It also does certified courses.

Outdoor Kefallonia (☑ 6979987611; http://outdoorkefalonia.com) Offers all manner of trips throughout the island, from coasteering (€45), hiking (€60) and canyoning (€60) to sea kayaking (€65) and 4WD safaris (from €50).

Bavarian Horse Riding (Map p533; ☑ 6977533203; www.kephalonia.com; Koulourata; 1-8hr €25-130) Ride sturdy Bavarian horses through the Kefallonian countryside. Day trips range from one to eight hours, with your choice of route. A longer trek leads across Mt Ainos and down to the sea, where you can take the horses for a swim. Multiday itineraries also possible.

---

looking a little beach. Thanks to its locally reared meat – in dishes such as exceptionally tender lamb chops, Kefallonian meat pie or braised rabbit – and seafood delights, it's an island institution and people even visit Kefallonia solely to eat here.

ℹ Information

Blue Sea Travel (p534) offers day trips to Ithaki as well as general travel services.

ℹ Getting There & Away

BOAT

Ionian Pelagos (www.ionionpelagos.com) runs up to three daily services from Sami to Piso Aetos in Ithaki (€4, 30 minutes), of which one or two continue to Astakos in the Peloponnese (€11, three hours); and two weekly sailings run in high season to Vasiliki on Lefkada (€9, 1¾ hours).

Between mid-July and mid-September, some **Ventouris Ferries** (http://ventourisferries.com) head north from Sami to Bari in Italy (€66, 18 hours) and south to Zakynthos (1½ hours).

BUS

KTEL (www.ktelkefalonias.gr) buses link Sami with Argostoli (€4, two to three daily), and also with Poros, Agia Evfymia and Fiskardo (€4.70, one hour, one or two daily). Argostoli buses usually meet ferries.

CAR

Hire cars through **Karavomilos Car Rental** (☑ 26740 23769; http://karavomylosrentacar.gr; Sami) and scooters from Kefalonia2Ride (p534).

Fiskardo   Φισκάρδο

POP 295

One of the prettiest towns in the Ionians, the little port of Fiskardo curves serenely beside coral-blue waters, gazing out towards Ithaki. Thanks to its colourful crop of Venetian villas, spared from earthquake damage because they rest on a sturdy bed of flat rock, Fiskardo is the island's most exclusive resort, home to upmarket restaurants and choice accommodation. There's no real dock or jetty here; ferries from Lefkada arrive unceremoniously at the northern end, while yachts jostle for space along the rest of the harbour. While it can get very crowded in summer, it has a cosmopolitan buzz unmatched elsewhere on the island.

◉ Sights & Activities

There are two small pebble beaches in Fiskardo. The best is just over the headland to the east. It's backed by Venetian-style houses and olive trees, and is as nice a town beach as you could hope for. The other is just next to where the ferries dock and almost within the town centre itself, but it's only a so-so beach. Much better beaches can be found further north, where the gorgeous sand at Emblissi is shaded by olive trees, and to the south, where Foki Bay is home to an attractive taverna.

One of the more secluded beaches is Dafnoudi, which is around a 5km drive northwest of Fiskardo. The tiny white-pebble beach is hemmed in by forest-covered cliffs and there are absolutely no facilities or development of any type (and long may that continue!). To make the journey to Dafnoudi even more enjoyable, leave the car in Fiskardo and walk. Using well-marked trails through forest and abandoned farmland, it's an easy 3.5km (45-minute) one-way walk.

There are also other options for some reasonable low-level **walking** around Fiskardo. An information panel in the car park just above town gives basic route suggestions and descriptions for three well-marked short trips.

Offering trips to caves, wrecks, reefs and a downed Bristol Beaufort WWII bomber, **Fiskardo Divers** (☑6970206172; www.fiskardo -divers.com; 3hr beginner courses €55, 4-day PADI open-water courses €430; ⊙ 9.30am-2pm & 5-7pm Mon-Sat, from 10.30am Sun) has won awards for its eco-credentials. It also offers beginner courses. The waterfront shop displays marine skeletons, including a monk seal, a loggerhead turtle and a shark.

🛌 Sleeping

As well as holding hotels to suit all budgets, Fiskardo and the adjacent bays are peppered with rental villas and apartments. Several are available via **Ionian Villas** (www. ionian-villas.co.uk).

Regina Studios　　　　APARTMENT €
(☑26740 41125; www.regina-studios.gr; d/tr from €55/75; ❄️📶) A pink villa, beside the village car park up the steps from the waterfront, Regina offers great-value 'en-suite' economy rooms, larger studios with sea-view balconies and shared kitchens, and larger two-bedroom apartments.

MYRTOS BEACH

From the road that zigzags down to it, you'll understand why **Myrtos Beach** (Map p533) is touted as one of the most breathtaking beaches in all of Greece. From afar it's certainly a stunning sight, with electric-blue waters offset by what appears to be searing-white 'sand' (in reality it's white pebbles). Unfortunately, a scrappy car park rather spoils the idyll. Even so, it's a beautiful spot and once you're in the sea it's heavenly.

The closest village is Divarata, which has a couple of tavernas, including Alexandros (☑26740 61777; https:// alexandrosrestaurant-myrtos.gr; Divarata; mains €7-9; ⊙noon-midnight).

Villa Romantza　　　　PENSION €€
(☑26740 41322; www.villa-romantza.gr; r/studio/ apt €60/80/100; ❄️📶) Excellent budget option, near the central car park, where simple, spacious and well-maintained rooms, studios and apartments share a communal terrace; some have two bedrooms and kitchenettes.

Emelisse Hotel　　　　RESORT €€€
(Map p533; ☑26740 41200; www.emelisseresort. com; Emblissi Bay; d incl breakfast from €263; ⊙mid-Apr–mid-Oct; 🅿️❄️@📶🏊) This luxury hotel is set in magnificent seclusion on a headland overlooking superb Emblissi Beach, 1.5km north of Fiskardo along the winding coastal road. Its beautifully appointed rooms are laid out on immaculately groomed terraces, leading down to a lavish swimming pool and a restaurant with fantastic views to Lefkada, Ithaki and beyond.

Fiscardonna Luxury Suites　　　BOUTIQUE HOTEL €€€
(☑26740 41289; www.fiscardonna.com; d incl breakfast €120-250; ❄️📶) One of the few hotels in town, this five-room boutique choice, in a lovingly restored building dating to 1840, mixes the old with utterly modern technological marvels (you're unlikely to have seen door-key swipes quite like these). The result doesn't quite gel, but it's very comfortable all the same. It's in a quiet side alley just back from the waterfront.

🍴 Eating & Drinking

Café Tselenti　　　　MEDITERRANEAN €€
(☑26740 41344; mains €8-26; ⊙8am-midnight May-Oct) Owned by the Tselenti family since 1893, this popular restaurant serves Italian-influenced dishes such as a terrific linguine with prawns, mussels and crayfish, as well as local specialities such as lamb shank, beef *stifadho* and grilled swordfish. It has a romantic terrace on the village square as well as quayside tables. If you just want a quick snack, it also does pitta *gyros* (meat slivers cooked on a vertical rotisserie; €3).

Tassia　　　　TAVERNA €€
(☑2674041205; www.tassia.gr; mains €9-19; ⊙noon-2am May-Oct) Step straight off your yacht and into a waterside seat at this taverna run by well-known Kefallonian chef Tassia, who delights diners with her homemade pies, mezedhes and courgette croquettes. Try the 'fisherman's pasta', incorporating finely chopped squid, octopus, mussels and prawns in a magical combination with a dash of cognac.

WORTH A TRIP

ASSOS

It's almost hard to believe that a place as picture-perfect as Assos (population 88) can really exist. The pint-sized village is a confection of Italianate cream- and ochre-coloured houses, with a pretty crescent-shaped cove that's protected by a wooded peninsula. The fortress atop the headland makes a great hike (3.6km return), while the bay is eminently swimmable, and the water's so clear that you hardly need to put on a snorkel and mask in order to ogle the fish.

A mouth-watering array of tasty tavernas, such as **Molos** (26740 51220; Assos; mains €7-14; 9.30am-late;) or **Platanos** (26740 51143; Assos; mains €7-15; 9am-midnight Easter-Oct;), plus a pace so slow you can palpably feel your pulse dropping, are compelling reasons to visit. **Apartment Linardos** (26740 51563; www.linardosapartments. gr; Assos; d/tr/q €80/90/120; May-Sep;) and **Vassilis Retreat** (26740 51174; www. vassilis-retreat.gr; Assos; apt €100;) are both great places to stay.

Want a local secret? There's a **hidden beach** around the other side of the headland from the jetty at the northern end of the village, but it can only be reached by boat or a 15-minute swim!

★ **Irida**   INTERNATIONAL €€€
(26740 41343; mains €9-35; 9am-late;) Whether you dine in the shadowy boho interior or out on the waterfront, there's something for everyone at this 200-year-old salt store. Dishes include stuffed aubergine, and the much pricier lobster risotto or spaghetti, and it's all scrupulously prepared and presented.

Le Passage   CAFE
(26740 41505; 9am-midnight;) Cool, very mellow quayside cafe festooned with little white lamps, and with a soothing soft-grey palette and cosy cushioned banquettes beside the water. Come early for simple breakfasts, at any hour for espresso with a smile, or in the evening for classy cocktails.

ⓘ Information

Nautilus Travel (p534) and **Pama Travel** (26740 41033; www.pamatravel.com; 9am-2pm & 5.30-9pm) can make travel and ferry arrangements.

ⓘ Getting There & Away

BOAT

Two or three surprisingly large **West Ferry** (www. westferry.gr) boats arrive from and return daily to the big package-tourism resort of Nydri on the east coast of Lefkada. Buy tickets from Nautilus Travel (p534).

In the past these ferries used to sail to Vasiliki in southern Lefkada instead of Nydri, which was generally more useful for independent travellers, but at the time of research the port was undergoing reconstruction and was closed to the ferries. It's hoped that this service will restart in time for the 2020 summer season. Be sure to check which port in Lefkada you'll be heading to!

BUS

KTEL (www.ktelkefalonias.gr) buses connect Fiskardo with Argostoli (€6.40, 1¾ hours, two daily), and with Sami via Agia Evfymia (€4.70, one hour, one or two daily).

ITHAKI   IΘAKH

POP 3230

Every bit as rugged, romantic and epic as its role in Homeric legend would suggest, Ithaki is something special. The hilly, sea-girt homeland to which Odysseus struggled to return for 10 heroic years continues to charm and seduce travellers with its ancient ruins, breathtaking harbour villages and wilderness walks. Squeezed between Kefallonia and the mainland, it's the kind of island where time seems to slow down and cares slip away.

Cut almost in two by the huge gulf that shields Vathy, its main town, Ithaki effectively consists of two separate islands linked by a narrow isthmus. Vathy is the only significant settlement, but the mighty northern massif has lovely villages such as Stavros and Anogi.

Ithaki doesn't go in for beaches the way the other Ionian islands do. It's true that there are lots of little cove beaches, but most of these are impossible to reach without a boat.

ⓘ Getting There & Away

Ionian Pelagos (www.ionionpelagos.com) runs two or three times daily in high season between Piso Aetos and Sami (Kefallonia; €4, 30 minutes), and once or twice from Piso Aetos to Astakos (on the mainland; €10, two hours 20 minutes).

Between July and mid-September, **Meganisi II** (26740 33120; www.ferryboatmeganisi.gr)

runs twice daily between Frikes and Nydri on Lefkada (€8, one hour).

Buy tickets from **El Greco Tours** (✆26740 30000; www.elgrecotours.gr; ⏰9am-8pm) or **Ithaca Tours** (✆26740 33336; www.ithacatours.gr; ⏰9am-1pm & 2-7pm) in Vathy.

In the past **West Ferry** (www.westferry.gr) has connected Frikes with Fiskardo (Kefallonia) and Vasiliki (Lefkada), but the service has not run in recent years – but it's worth checking the website to see whether it has resumed.

ⓘ Getting Around

Piso Aetos, the port on Ithaki's west coast, has no settlement. **Taxis** (✆6945700214, 6946552397) often meet boats, as does the municipal bus in high season. Bus services are very limited, though, with just two services a day running between Vathy, Stavros and Kioni, and so it's well worth renting a car – easiest in Vathy – for at least one day of your stay.

Vathy   Βαθύ

POP 1820

Set around a superbly sheltered natural harbour, and fringed with sky-blue and ochre villas holding lively bars and restaurants, pretty Vathy is Ithaki's main commercial hub. The quayside buzzes with activity as small local fishing boats pootle out to sea and yachts throw anchor in the bay, while narrow lanes wriggle away inland.

◎ Sights & Activities

Other than a couple of moderately interesting museums, Vathy holds few sights to see, but there's some wonderful walking nearby. Follow the line of the harbour all the way east, until the road finally peters out, and a spectacular coastal footpath leads in another half-hour to the whitewashed waterfront chapel of **Agios Andreas**. Alternatively, stay on the road as it climbs away at the eastern end of the harbour; cross the brow of the hill, and you'll come to a succession of increasingly idyllic, secluded beaches – first Mnimata, then Skinos and, finally, after a total of 4km, the magnificent white sands of **Gidaki** (Map p533).

Albatross (✆6973467977) and **Mana Korina** (✆6976654351) offer boat excursions from Vathy in high season to outlying beaches and unpopulated islets. **Odyssey Diving & Sea Kayaking** (✆6948182655; www.outdoorithaca.com; ⏰9am-8pm mid-Apr–mid-Oct) is a very professional outfit offering an exciting array of kayaking, diving and snorkelling trips.

🛏 Sleeping

★**Perantzada 1811**   BOUTIQUE HOTEL €€
(✆26740 33496; www.perantzadahotel.com; Odyssea Androutsou; d/q incl breakfast from €110/345; ⏰Easter–mid-Oct; ❄🌐⛱) Centred on a 19th-century neoclassical villa hovering above the harbour, this self-styled 'art hotel' holds large, balconied rooms as minimal as white clouds, replete with granite-and-wood bathrooms. Cheaper rooms lack sea views and share balconies, while larger suites in the new wing have baths you could free-dive in. The breakfast buffet is pure decadence, and there's an enticing infinity pool.

Hotel Familia   BOUTIQUE HOTEL €€
(✆26740 33366; www.hotel-familia.com; Odysseos 60; s/d incl breakfast from €110/125; ❄🌐) Converted from an old olive press, juxtaposing chic slate with soft tapestries and gentle lighting, this charming family-run and family-friendly boutique hotel has real wow factor. Superb value. Note that, although it's only 50m from the southwestern corner of the harbour, there are no sea views, and only one room has a courtyard.

Korina Gallery Hotel   BOUTIQUE HOTEL €€
(✆26740 33383; www.korinahotel.com; Telemachou 4; d from €70; ❄🌐⛱) This small hotel a short walk uphill from the town centre aims for an elegant, stately look, but it doesn't quite pull it off. Even so, the spacious rooms with full-length wooden shutters and paintings with filigree frames are an excellent option, with plenty of character.

🍴 Eating

★**Trehantiri**   TAVERNA €
(✆26740 33444; http://trehantiri.ithakionline.com; mains €7-12; ⏰11am-11pm; ❄🌐) Traditional taverna with blue tables set up off the square in the heart of town. Every day the kitchen cooks up something different, from goat stew to stuffed tomatoes, *saganaki* to *kleftiko* (slow oven-baked lamb or goat). Most of the ingredients are organically sourced. Look out for *savoro* (marinated local fish).

O Batis   SEAFOOD €€
(✆26740 33010; mains €8-18, lunch menu €15; ⏰11am-1am; ❄🌐) Vathy's top pick for ultra-fresh seafood sits amid similar-looking places along the harbour. Tourists flock to the waterfront tables, while local fishers, who've had quite enough sea views for one day, prefer the no-frills interior. It's one of the few places that do a set lunchtime menu (€15), which will net you a whole grilled fish plus salad and wine or beer.

Sirenes
GREEK €€

(☑ 26740 33001; http://sirines.eu; mains €8-15; ☺ noon-midnight; ❄ 🛜) A smart restaurant a block back from the waterfront, with a cool front terrace and a swanky bar in its elegant wood-panelled dining room. Distinctive local dishes include lamb cooked in a clay pot and slow-cooked rabbit, plus there's fresh seafood.

ℹ Information

El Greco Tours Ferries, car rental and accommodation.

Ithaca Tours Ferries, water taxis and accommodation, plus boat tours and rentals.

ℹ Getting There & Away

Rent cars from **AGS** (☑ 26740 32702; www.agscars.com), on the western harbourfront, and bikes or scooters from **Alpha Bike & Car Hire** (☑ 26740 33240; www.alphacarsgreece.com; ☺ 9am-1pm & 5-7pm), behind Alpha Bank.

Ithaki's one bus runs twice daily between Vathy and Kioni, via Stavros and Frikes, on weekdays only (€4). Its limited schedule is not suited to day-trippers, however.

Around Ithaki

Cross the slender isthmus to reach Ithaki's northern half and you face an immediate choice of onward routes, along either flank of the island's towering (809m) central spine. Following the eastern road brings you after 5.5km to the somewhat dilapidated hilltop monastery of **Katharon**, which commands astonishing views back down to Vathy. Another 4km along this fabulously scenic mountain road, you'll reach sleepy **Anogi**, once the island's capital. Ask in the village *kafeneio* (coffee house) for the keys to the restored church of **Agia Panagia**, which holds incredible Byzantine frescoes.

Further north again, the east- and westcoast roads rejoin at the larger village of **Stavros**, above the Bay of Polis. A lovely rural walk up the nearby hillside leads to a site long known as the **School of Homer** (Stavros) but suggested by recent archaeological digs to be the long-lost palace of Odysseus himself. It's all in ruins, and smaller than you might expect, but wonderfully evocative nonetheless. Artefacts associated with the legendary hero are on show in Stavros' oneroom **archaeological museum** (☑ 26740 31305; ☺ 8.30am-3.30pm Wed-Mon) FREE.

Dropping back seawards northeast of Stavros takes you to the tiny ferry port of **Frikes**, clasped between windswept cliffs and home

HIKING AROUND ANOGI

The highest village in Ithaki, Anogi is a beautiful, time-dusted place centred on its church and *kafeneio* (coffeehouse). The village is the starting point for a number of excellent walks. The easiest is the 6.5km, roughly two-hour return walk to the monastery of **Kathara**. An even better walk is the 11.5km, 4½-hour **Travel in Time** hike, which winds all the way downhill to Kioni before climbing 520m back up to Anogi via a different route. Along the way hikers take in historic sites, churches and chapels, wild oak forests and soaring coastal cliffs, and get a chance to cool off with a swim on the way. For this walk, follow signs for route 12 to Kioni and then signs for route 12A back to Anogi.

to a cluster of waterfront restaurants and bars. The beautiful and sinuous coastal road beyond ends at pretty little **Kioni**, a hamlet of mustard-and-cream Venetian houses tumbling down to an irresistibly bijou harbour.

👉 Tours

Charming expat artist Ester runs **Island Walks** (☑ 6944990458; www.islandwalks.com; walks €15-18) offering guided walks of varying lengths all over the island. Her most popular route, the three-hour Homer Walk, winds up the hillside near Stavros to the ruins where the real Odysseus may have lived 2800 years ago, and also takes in the village museum.

🛏 Sleeping

Hotel Nostos
HOTEL €€

(☑ 26740 31644; www.hotelnostos-ithaki.gr; Frikes; s/d/f €100/135/165; ☺ mid-Apr-Oct; ❄ 🛜 🏊) The only real hotel in the northern part of Ithaki, the large, pink family-run Nostos has delightful airy rooms richly shaded in blues and with impressive photo art on the walls. The beds are unusually comfortable, the bathrooms decent and it's all set around a very inviting swimming pool. Attentive service rounds out the deal. It's located a short way out of Frikes on the road to Stavros, but still within easy walking distance of the sea.

Kioni Apartments
APARTMENT €€

(☑ 26740 31144; www.ithacagreece.eu; Kioni; apt €110; ☺ May-Oct; ❄ 🛜) A handsome Italianate building in the corner of the harbour, drowning in bougainvillea and housing welcoming apartments with wooden ceilings and large balconies. Stylish but homey, central but quiet. In a word: perfect. There's a four-day minimum stay.

Eating

Rementzo TAVERNA €
(📞26740 31719; www.ithacagreece.com/Rementzo/rementzo.html; Frikes; mains €8-15; ⊗9am-midnight; 🏵🛜) Right on the harbour in Frikes, this is a great place to sample traditional cuisine such as *stifadho* or fresh bream and dried apricots, as well as local speciality *savoro* (fish with vinegar, currants and garlic).

★Yefuri TAVERNA €€
(📞26740 31131; www.facebook.com/Yefuri; Platrithias; mains €7-17; ⊗6-11pm Tue-Sat, 11am-2pm Sun; 🏵🛜) This eclectic, very popular little restaurant, 2km north of Stavros, is renowned island-wide for its fresh produce and rotating Italian-influenced menu, which ranges from eggs Benedict for Sunday brunch to stir-fried chicken and roast pork for dinner.

Ithaki Restaurant GREEK €€
(📞26740 31081; Stavros; mains €8-15; ⊗11am-10pm) The best restaurant in Stavros wins big points for its expansive terrace with sunset views. The food is equally memorable: expect succulent meaty specialities such as local sausages, charcoal-grilled veal or pork, and lamb souvlaki.

ZAKYNTHOS ΖΑΚΥΝΘΟΣ

POP 40,760

Zakynthos, also known by its Italian name Zante, is an island of two stories. The southern and southeastern shorelines are dominated by heavy – and often low-quality – package tourism, although even here there are some attractive lower-key bases hiding just out of sight of the larger, run-of-the-mill resorts; examples include Keri and Limni Keriou in the remoter southwest. Once you leave the south behind, however, and set off to explore the rest of the island, you'll discover a different place altogether. It's one where plenty of forested wilderness and traditional rural villages remain, but it's the spectacular scenery of the rugged west coast, where mighty limestone cliffs plummet down to unreal turquoise waters, that's the true highlight.

ⓘ Information

Isala Travel (📞26953 01600; www.facebook.com/pg/isalatravel; Lomvardou 30) in Zakynthos Town sells ferry tickets and offers boat excursions, vehicle hire and a wide range of island activities.

ⓘ Getting There & Away

AIR

Between May and September numerous charter flights connect Zakynthos with northern Europe and the UK.

Zakynthos Airport (Map p545; 📞26950 29500; www.zakynthos-airport.com) is 5km southwest of Zakynthos Town.

Olympic Air (www.olympicair.com) Flies to Athens.

Sky Express (www.skyexpress.gr) Flies to Corfu via Kefallonia and Preveza.

Taxis between the airport and Zakynthos Town cost around €15.

BOAT

Ionian Group (www.ionian-group.com) runs between three and five ferries daily, depending on the season, between Zakynthos Town and Kyllini in the Peloponnese (€9.10, one hour). Occasional international ferries call in on the way to/from Igoumenitsa (on the mainland), Sami (Kefallonia), and Bari and Brindisi (Italy).

From the isolated northern port of Agios Nikolaos, **Ionian Pelagos** (www.ionionpelagos.com) ferries sail to Pesada in southern Kefallonia twice daily from mid-May to October (€8, 1½ hours); Chionis Tours (p546) sells tickets. Neither port has good bus connections, however, so most travellers find it easier and cheaper to cross to mainland Kyllini from Zakynthos Town and catch another ferry from there to Kefallonia.

Ventouris Ferries (http://ventourisferries.com) connects Zakynthos Town with Bari (Italy) in high season, with a stop in Sami (Kefallonia) en route.

BUS

The **KTEL Bus Station** (📞26950 22255; www.ktel-zakynthos.gr) is on the hillside bypass in Zakynthos Town, 500m up from the waterfront and 15 minutes' walk southwest of Plateia Solomou. Long-distance routes include Athens (€28.60, six hours, four daily), Patra (€8.70, 3½ hours, four daily) and Thessaloniki (€54.40, 10 hours, two weekly). Budget an additional €9 for the ferry to Kyllini.

ⓘ Getting Around

Zakynthos Town is the centre of an extensive local bus network.

Rental cars (from €40 per day in high season) and motorcycles are available at the airport and in larger resorts.

Zakynthos

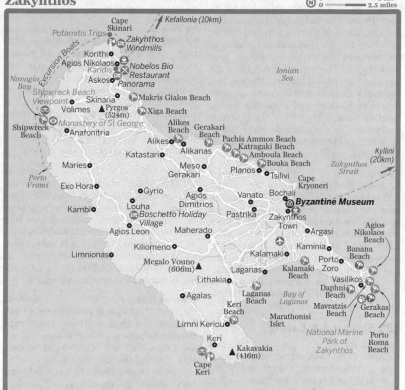

Europcar (☑ 26950 43313; www.europcar
-greece.com; Zakynthos Airport) At the airport;
office is open for all incoming flights.

Hertz (☑ 26950 24287; www.hertz.gr; Zakynthos Airport) Airport office open for all incoming flights and also in Zakynthos Town (p546).

Zakynthos Town Ζάκυνθος

POP 16,810

Sandwiched between steep wooded slopes
topped by a ruined Venetian fortress and
a huge harbour cradled between two long
jetties, Zakynthos Town is the pulsing capital of the island. Famous for its glorious
ensemble of Italianate architecture until
an earthquake struck in 1953, it was subsequently reconstructed in fine style, with
arcaded streets and gracious neoclassical
public buildings. Recent years have seen
the restoration of its showpiece waterfront
square, the dazzling Plateia Solomou. The
hubbub of everyday life centres on the pedestrianised streets behind it, leading to
smaller Plateia Agiou Markou.

You wouldn't base your whole holiday
around the town's scruffy beach, but if you
need to cool off with a swim, follow locals to
the pebble beach a few minutes' walk north
of the centre.

◎ Sights & Activities

★ **Byzantine Museum**   MUSEUM
(Map p545; ☑ 26950 42714; Plateia Solomou;
adult/child €4/free; ⊙ 8am-3pm Tue-Sat) This
magnificent museum of ecclesiastical art
is housed in a beautifully restored building on the central waterfront plaza. Almost
everything here was rescued – by volunteer
sailors! – in the immediate aftermath of the
1953 earthquake, with displays including entire church interiors, and frescoes arranged
in a replica of the 16th-century monastery
of St Andreas.

Church of St Dionysios
CHURCH

(museum adult/child €1/free; ⊙9am-1pm & 4.30-9pm) Devoted to Zakynthos' patron saint, the Church of St Dionysios (1948; rebuilt following the 1953 earthquake) stands at the southern end of the waterfront, near the ferry jetty. Its interior holds opulent gilt work and impressive frescoes. The contrast between visiting tourists in shorts and praying elderly locals dressed all in black is quite startling. Around the back of the church is a museum. Exhibits include ecclesiastical trappings and vestments, including those of Dionysios himself.

Kastro
FORTRESS

(☑26950 48099; adult/child €4/free; ⊙8am-2.30pm Mon & Wed-Sat) A ruined Venetian fortress sits atop the wooded slope that looms over the town centre. Reached by a steep but enjoyable 15-minute hike or a circuitous 2.5km drive, it's now essentially a peaceful forest park, enclosed within sturdy ramparts and affording tremendous views. Tumbledown churches lie scattered through the woods, along with a 19th-century British-made football pitch and a cafe.

🛏 Sleeping & Eating

Palatino Hotel
HOTEL €€

(☑26950 27780; www.palatinohotel.gr; Kolokotronis 10; d incl breakfast €70-120; ❄🅰) The best-value hotel in town, the Palatino offers functional but comfortable rooms, and staff members take enormous pride in how clean everything is. Its real selling point, though, is that it's just a couple of minutes' walk from the town centre but set on a quiet side street just back from the beach. A handful of rooms have sea views.

To Kantouni
TAVERNA €

(☑26950 42550; Logotheton 15; mains €6-9; ⊙11am-6pm) No-frills, traditional home-style cooking is the order of the day at this small backstreet taverna that has a loyal local following. With checked tablecloths, strings of garlic hanging from the ceiling, and walls covered in replica 1930s posters, it could pass for a French bistro.

Stathmos
TAVERNA €

(☑2695 024040; Filita 42; mains €6-9; ⊙9am-11pm) A spit-and-sawdust kind of place attracting a diverse crowd of locals and in-the-know tourists, Stathmos has a list of daily specials written on a blackboard as well as a good range of island classics. The house special is rabbit stew.

★ Prosilio
MEDITERRANEAN €€

(☑26950 22040; www.prosiliozakynthos.gr; A Latta 15; mains €9-19; ⊙6pm-late Tue-Sat summer, Fri & Sat winter; ❄🅰) Gourmet dinner-only restaurant, with a boutique interior and a romantic garden courtyard. The hushed atmosphere may be unusual, but the service is relaxed and friendly, and if you love Greek food you're sure to relish inventive dishes such as Greek blue-crab risotto. The wine list abounds in well-priced local choices.

★ Malanos
TAVERNA €€

(☑26950 45936; www.malanos.gr; Agiou Athanasiou, Keri; mains €9-15; ⊙noon-4pm & 7.30pm-late) This much-loved family-run taverna, set amid fields on the southern outskirts of town 2km from the centre, is renowned island wide for its huge portions of rich local favourites such as rooster, rabbit and wild boar, served at simple, plaid-clothed tables. For an authentic Greek dining experience it's unbeatable.

Ammos Taverna
TAVERNA €€

(☑26950 23753; Agiou Dionisiou 46; mains €8-15; ⊙1-11pm) In a small, tree-lined square right down at the far southern end of town and well away from the worst of the tourist hubbub, this nautical-themed, family-run taverna claims to be the oldest in the neighbourhood. Enjoy the expertly grilled sardines and other fish while watching the huge ferries pull into port.

ℹ Information

Chionis Tours (☑26950 48996; Lomvardou 8; ⊙7am-11.30pm) Useful agency for ferry tickets and other travel arrangements.

Isala Travel (p544) Ferry tickets, boat excursions, vehicle hire and a wide range of island activities. Also rents out luxury boats.

ℹ Getting There & Away

BUS

Frequent buses (€1.80) link the KTEL bus station (p544) with the resorts of Alikes, Tsilivi, Argasi, Laganas and Kalamaki. Fewer services run to inland villages.

CAR

A rental car is essential to explore the island in any depth. **Hertz** (☑26950 45706; www.hertz.gr; Lomvardou 38; ⊙8am-2pm & 5.30-9pm) has locations in town and at the airport (p545).

Around Zakynthos

◉ Sights & Activities

◉ Southern Coast

The **Vasilikos Peninsula**, poking south from the island's southeastern corner, is a little less developed than many other parts of the southern coast, though long, narrow **Banana Beach** (Map p545) on its northern side is awash with crowds, water sports and parasols. A little further along and things start to mellow out a bit. Take a side road heading west from the village of Vasilikos to find the 80-hectare **Logothetis Organic Farm** (☑ 26950 35106; www.oliveoilfarmshop. com; Vasilikos; ⊙10am-9pm) **FREE**. It produces purely organic olive oils (some flavoured with orange, lemon and other fruits) as well as olive-oil products. You can do an olive-oil tasting and watch the process of extraction. It also has accommodation (p548). Keep going right to the tip of the peninsula to reach **Gerakas Beach** (Map p545); a strand of fine sand that faces the Bay of Laganas, it's the best beach in the south. It's also a crucial turtle-nesting site, so visitor numbers are restricted, and all access is forbidden between dusk and dawn from May to October. Conservation advice is displayed near the access path and at the small **Mediterranean Marine Life Centre** (Gerakas Beach; ⊙9am-8pm) **FREE** next to the car park, where you can learn about the problems turtles face and perhaps see some at the in-house rescue and rehabilitation centre.

◉ Southwestern Coast

Beyond **Laganas** the rugged terrain of the far southwest starts to unfold. Follow a tiny road from the quiet village of **Keri** to reach lighthouse-topped **Cape Keri** and a high viewpoint surveying the endless cliffs that stretch away up the west coast; a converted van sells snacks. To access the parking and viewpoint here, you're expected to buy at least a drink at the van.

There's no shoreline road north, but a happily confusing tangle of highland routes threads through the wooded hill country parallel to the coast. Here and there, spur roads drop to coves such as **Limnionas** or climb to the clifftops, as at **Kambi**. Detouring inland brings you to villages such as **Kiliomeno**, where the Church of St Nikolaos features an unusual roofless campanile,

and gorgeous **Louha**, a tiny, silent-at-noon village that tumbles down a valley surrounded by woodlands and pastures. There's nothing much to do here, but there are some enjoyable signed walks in the surrounding countryside and a small cafe selling snacks at the edge of the village.

◉ Northwestern Coast

The most dramatic sight along the west coast is magnificent **Shipwreck Beach** (Map p545). A favourite of Instagrammers travelling through the Greek islands, the beach is home to a stranded cargo ship that ran aground in the 1960s. The beach itself is only accessible on boat trips – in summer the waters immediately offshore are chock-a-block with sightseeing cruises – but you can admire it from above, and get that all-important selfie, from a precarious lookout platform signposted between Anafonitria and Volimes. Do be careful here, though, if you're travelling with children or it's a windy day. There are no guardrails and the sheer cliff is quite unstable – it would be very easy to get blown off, and people have fallen here.

In an evocative clifftop site just south of the Shipwreck Beach turn-off, the **Monastery of St George** (Map p545) **FREE** is well worth a visit on the way to the beach. The interior is covered in faded frescoes, and the strange tower at the centre of the complex was used by monks as a defence from pirate and Turkish attack: the monks hid inside and threw boiling olive oil over their attackers. (Today the only Turkish thing about the monastery are the free Turkish delights that are made by one of the monks and given to visitors!)

Locals sell honey and seasonal products pretty much everywhere, but **Volimes**, just north of the monastery and the beach, is the major sales centre for traditional products such as olive oil, tablecloths and rugs.

◉ East & North Coast

The resorts immediately north of Zakynthos Town are generally humdrum, but the further north you go the more dramatic the scenery becomes. The road narrows at the little ferry village of **Agios Nikolaos**, which holds a nice crop of restaurants and accommodation and has a small harbour beach as well as some pretty rocky platforms to swim off. It's a world away from the mega-resorts of the south. A nice walk (or drive) from here will bring you to the majestic headland of **Cape Skinari**, which marks the island's northern tip.

TURTLE TALK

The Ionian Islands are home to one of Europe's most endangered marine species, the loggerhead turtle (*Caretta caretta*). Zakynthos hosts the largest density of loggerhead nests, with up to 1300 recorded in some years along the Bay of Laganas, an area protected as the National Marine Park of Zakynthos.

Unfortunately, the extended tracts of clean, flat sand on which the turtles lay their eggs are also the favoured habitat of basking beach-lovers. Strict regulations are supposed to limit building, boating, fishing and water sports in designated zones, but these rules are not always obeyed. During breeding season (from May to October), nesting beaches are barred to visitors between dusk and dawn; from July onwards, as the eggs start to hatch, conservation agencies place frames with warning notes over buried nests. Many eggs are still destroyed by visitors, however, and countless hatchlings don't reach the water, having been disoriented by sunbeds, noise and lights.

Volunteers from Archelon (www.archelon.gr) and the park run education and volunteer programs, including a visitor centre at Gerakas Beach. To avoid harming nesting sites, don't use umbrellas on dry sand (use the wet part of the beach instead) and don't take boat trips in the Bay of Laganas, which have been known to torment and even kill turtles.

 Tours

Boat trips, run by **Karidis** (Map p545; ☑6977275463; Agios Nikolaos) and **Potamitis Trips** (Map p545; ☑26950 31132; www.potamitisbros.gr; Cape Skinari; ☺9am-9pm Apr-Oct), head from both Agios Nikolaos and Cape Skinari to the **Blue Caves** and Shipwreck Beach (p547); smaller vessels can enter these sea-level caverns between roughly 9am and 2pm.

Sleeping

The huge curve of the Bay of Laganas, along the south coast, is lined with hotels catering to package holidaymakers, while the beach resorts immediately northwest of Zakynthos Town are a bit more sedate. More upmarket options are hidden away on the Vasilikos Peninsula in the southeast, and in Agios Nikolaos in the north.

Panorama APARTMENT €
(Map p545; ☑26950 31013; studios €50; P ✳ ☎) Excellent studios with sea views and basic kitchenettes occupy a lovely garden set back from the main road. Managed by a friendly English-speaking family, the place is a 700m uphill walk south of Agios Nikolaos.

Logothetis Organic Farm Houses COTTAGE €€
(☑26950 35106; www.logothetisfarm.gr; Vasilikos; cottages from €80) Deep within an 80-hectare olive grove, the cottages here offer utter tranquillity. Horses and goats wander freely, and horse riding and learning about olive-oil production are possible. It's perfect for families, as cottages sleep two to seven.

Joanna's Stone Villas APARTMENT €€
(☑26953 06787; www.joannasvillas.com; Vasilikos; d/q €124/152; ✳ ☎ ☒) Set among the olive trees a short way inland from the island's southeastern corner, these impressive apartments, maisonettes and entire villas have commanding views down to the coast, and lots of space. All have kitchens and share separate kids' and adults' pools. There's normally a three-day minimum stay.

Zakynthos Windmills APARTMENT €€
(Map p545; ☑26950 31132; www.potamitisbros.gr; Cape Skinari; apt from €60, windmills from €130; ✳ ☎) Two converted windmills – one dazzling white, the other with exposed-stone walls, each sleeping two guests – plus two- and four-person rooms and apartments occupy an old stone house with a fantastic clifftop location in Cape Skinari. Although there's a novelty factor to sleeping in a windmill, the rooms, which have boutique flourishes, are actually more comfortable.

There's a taverna alongside, and steps lead to a lovely swimming area.

★**Boschetto Holiday Village** VILLA €€€
(Map p545; ☑6973743071; www.boschettovillage.gr; Agios Leon; villas €240; ✳ ☎ ☒) Fancy your own luxury stone cottage surrounded by oaks and olives that's tucked away from the rat race at the end of a long, dusty track? This place should do nicely. Each of the six villas has three bedrooms, two bathrooms, a fully fitted kitchen and a sunny terrace with private pool. Perfect for families and long country walks. It's not far from Louha village in the ravishing hilly interior of the island.

Eating

Allegro
GREEK €

(📞6979261627; Keri; mains €8-12; ⏱10am-11pm May-Oct; ❄🛜) Don't expect to get much of a say in what you eat at this delightful, very welcoming taverna-cafe on Keri's village square. The chatty woman who runs it will likely take one look at you and decide what you're going to like. Fortunately, she's normally right! Whatever you have, it'll be good, home-cooked local food.

Cross Tavern
TAVERNA €€

(Stavros; 📞6973334560, 26950 48481; Kambi; mains €7-16; ⏱10am-midnight; ❄🛜) Perched above the west-coast cliffs at the end of the road that climbs beyond Kambi, and marked by a huge white Christian cross, this top-notch taverna extends over terraces, so diners can enjoy views so stunning they'll understand why someone built such a big cross here. The menu covers all bases, from omelettes to baked standards and grilled fish.

Nobelos Bio Restaurant
MEDITERRANEAN €€€

(Map p545; 📞26950 31400; www.nobelos.gr; Agios Nikolaos; mains €22-30; ⏱7am-midnight; ❄🛜) This exquisitely romantic restaurant is built into and around the rocks beside the private beach of its namesake boutique hotel. The irresistible setting is the main reason to come here, along with the sunset cocktail menu, but the Italian-Greek food is reliably good, with lots of seafood pasta options and meaty stews.

KYTHIRA   ΚΥΘΗΡΑ

POP 3973

Poised between the Aegean and Ionian Seas, the gloriously time-forgotten island of Kythira lies just 12km off the southern tip of the Peloponnese's Lakonian Peninsula. Despite its distinctly Cycladic sugar-cube architecture, both historic and modern, Kythira is officially regarded as belonging to the Ionian Islands.

With its population of fewer than 4000 spread between 40 villages, Kythira feels for much of the year like a ghost land; it's an unspoilt dreamscape of lush valleys, abrupt overgrown gorges, and flower-speckled cliffs tumbling into the vivid blue sea. The lucky few who do make it here are invariably charmed by the island's spell and never want to leave. Do yourself a favour: however long you think you might need here, double it!

ℹ Information

For more information on Kythira, visit www.kythera.gr, www.kythira.info or www.visitkythera.com. The free annual English-language Kythera is distributed in travel agencies, hotels and shops.

Kythira is doing admirable work to promote its **hiking trails**, with signposts added to many routes. Invaluable information, including trail guides and maps, can be found at www.kytherahiking.com, while Frank van Weerde's Kythira on Foot: 32 Carefully Selected Walking Routes (€10) is widely available.

ℹ Getting There & Away

AIR

Kythira Airport (Map p550; 📞27360 33297), 10km southeast of Potamos, is connected to Athens in summer by both **Olympic Air** (www.olympicair.com; around €65, 50 minutes, one daily) and **Sky Express** (www.skyexpress.gr; €88, 50 minutes, twice daily except Tuesday and Wednesday). **Ellinair** (http://en.ellinair.com) flies to Kythira from Thessaloniki (€89, 75 minutes, twice weekly). There are far fewer flights in low season.

BOAT

Kythira's ferry port is at sleepy little Diakofti, halfway up the east coast. Buy tickets at the port just before departure, or via Kithira Travel, with offices in **Hora (Kythira)** (📞27360 31390; www.kithiratravel.gr; ⏱9am-2pm & 6-8pm Mon-Fri, 9am-2pm Sat) and in **Potamos** (📞27360 31848; https://kithiratravel.gr).

Boats from Neapoli in the Peloponnese come to Diakofti twice daily in summer, and once daily otherwise (€12.50, 1¼ hours); two each week continue to the more remote island of Antikythira.

LANE Lines operates an intricate, seasonally changing schedule of ferries that connect Diakofti with Piraeus (€27, 6½ hours), Antikythira (€9.50), Kissamos (Kastelli, Crete; €22, 2½ to four hours) and Gythio (Peloponnese; €12.50, 2½ hours); in summer there are usually two weekly services to and from each of those destinations.

ℹ Getting Around

Occasional buses operate in August. **Taxis** (📞6944305433, 6977991799) are pricey and charge around €30 between Hora (Kythira) and the airport. Your best bet is to hire a car; either pick one up at the airport or have it dropped off at your hotel. Prices start at €30 per day.

Drakakis Tours (📞27360 31160; www.drakakistours.gr; Livadi; ⏱9am-1pm & 4-8pm Mon-Sat) Rental cars, vans and 4WDs, with airport pick-up; airport transfers; buses to Athens (€45, one to two weekly) and sightseeing tours.

Panayotis Rent A Car (📞6944263757; www.panayotis-rent-a-car.gr; car/scooter per day from €30/15) A fleet of 120 cars – including 4WDs, small cars, motorbikes and scooters. Branches at the airport and across the island, including at Diakofti and Kapsali (call 27360 31600).

IONIAN ISLANDS KYTHIRA

Kythira & Antikythira

0 — 5 km
0 — 2.5 miles

Gythio
(55km)

Neapoli
(25km)

Diakofti (50km)

Crete
(55km)

Cape Spathi

Kythira
Strait

Potamos

Harhaliana

Galaniana

Antikythira

0 — 2 km
0 — 1 mile

Antikythira

Platia Ammos

Fourni
Beach

Karavas

Myrtoön
Sea

Piraeus
(230km)

Gerakari

Agia Pelagia

Agios Nikolaos

Petrouni

Lagada
Beach

Stavli

Trifyllianika

Potamos

Antikythira
(50km; see inset);
Crete (100km)

Katsoulianika

Hristoforianika

Lykodimou
Beach

Logothetianika

Lianianika

Ionian
Sea

Pitsinades

Vamvakaradika

458m

Makronisi
Island

Aroniadika

Kastrisianika

Frilingianika

490m

Diakofti

Mitata

Kythira

389m

Kato
Hora

Mylopotamos

Viaradika

Avlemonas

Cape
Limnionas

507m

Skandeia

Paleopoli
Beach

Cape
Modoni

Fratsia

Kaladi
Beach

Pitsinianika

Karvounades

Kalokerines

Goudianika

Alexandrades

Tsikalaria

Travasarianika

Kombonada
Beach

Sea of
Crete

Fatsadika

Skoulianika

410m

Katouni Bridge

Livadi

Kato Livadi

Kominianika

Katelouzianika

Fyri Ammos

Pourko

Strapodi

477m

Manitohori

Melidoni
Beach

Kalamos

Hora
(Kythira)

El Sol Hotel

Kastro

Kapsali

Vroulea

Cape
Trahilos

Cape
Kapello

Mediterranean
Sea

Avgo/Itra

Hora (Kythira)
Χώρα (Κύθηρα)

POP 270

Hora (also known as Kythira or Chora), the island's small capital, consists of a Cycladic-style cluster of white-and-blue cubes stretching south along a slender ridge towards a 14th-century Venetian *kastro* perched on a separate craggy hilltop. Most of the action centres on the open square at the town's northern end, while tasteful little shops, selling fine antiques and bespoke jewellery, line the way to the *kastro*.

◉ Sights

★ Kastro
FORTRESS

(Map p550; ☺ 8am-sunset) FREE Crowning the rocky headland that soars at the southern end of Hora, this tumble-down 14th-century fortress was built by Kythira's first Venetian governor. Within its ramparts the fort is now largely in ruins, but the site is stupendous, drenched in wildflowers and commanding stunning views down to Kapsali and out as far as Antikythira. Only the underwhelming **Coat of Arms Collection** (adult/child €2/1; ☺ 9am-2pm & 5-8pm Tue-Sun), in a former powder magazine, charges an admission fee.

As you leave, take a stroll along the adjoining eastern hillside, where several pretty little fresco-adorned chapels stand near the top of the footpath that leads to Kapsali.

Archaeological Museum of Kythira
MUSEUM

(☎ 27360 39012; adult/child €4/free; ☺ 8.30am-4pm Wed-Mon) Hora's impressive archaeological museum, beside the main road at the northern end of town, traces the history of 'this small island' in two rooms. Among artefacts from the ancient settlements of Palaiopolis and Palaiokastro, pride of place goes to the white-marble statue known as the Lion of Kythira.

⌂ Sleeping

Hora only has a handful of hotels, but it's the best place to stay if you're visiting Kythira in low season, and at any time of year it has a more local feeling than the nearby beach resort of Kapsali.

★ Hotel Margarita
PENSION €€

(☎ 27360 31711; www.hotel-margarita.com; s/d/tr incl breakfast €60/90/110; ☺ Easter-Oct; ❉ 🛜) Set in an impeccably restored, white-walled 19th-century villa just off the main alleyway

not far beyond the square, this charming French-run hotel offers 12 antique-furnished rooms accessed via a quirky old spiral staircase; note that bathrooms are very small. A wonderful terrace, used for the accomplished breakfast and afternoon drinks, affords fantastic *kastro* and sea views.

Nostos
PENSION €€

(☎ 27360 31056; www.nostos-kythera.gr; d from €80; ❉ 🛜) A delightfully old-fashioned five-room guesthouse right next to the church (the bells start ringing around 7.30am) and below the *kastro*. Each room is different, but the unifying features are oil paintings on the walls and lots of polished-wood furnishings. Bathrooms are small. Breakfast is served in a time-warp cafe across the alleyway.

Corte O
APARTMENT €€

(☎ 27360 39139; www.corteo.gr; r/2-bedroom apt incl breakfast 80/170; ☺ Apr-Oct; ❉ 🛜) Three beautiful two-bedroom apartments set in a late-18th-century house just steps from the *kastro*. All have modern, minimal decor and full kitchens, private terraces and sea or valley views; one can be divided to create two en-suite rooms.

✕ Eating

Hora is very short of dining options, though a couple of seasonal restaurants open in high summer. Nothing seems to have changed at **Zorba's**, (☎ 27360 31655; mains €9; ☺ 7pm-midnight Tue-Sun; ❉) a Hora institution for at least 60 years and it's now so retro that it could make the hipster generation giddy with excitement. Fortunately, though, the family who runs it isn't interested in such things and cares only about serving quality grilled meats, including the house special: Kythira sausages swaddled in local herbs. It's halfway down the main alleyway, not far off the square.

LOCAL KNOWLEDGE

THE BIRTH OF APHRODITE

Kythira was famous in antiquity as the birthplace of Aphrodite. As described by Hesiod and painted by Botticelli, the goddess of love, desire and beauty rose resplendent from the foam upon a giant scallop, possibly off the islet of Avgo (Egg) off Kapsali. Confusingly, she's also said to have re-emerged near Pafos in Cyprus, so the two places haggle over the title of Love Island...

IONIAN ISLANDS HORA (KYTHIRA)

WORTH A TRIP

MYLOPOTAMOS

The delightful village of Mylopotamos nestles in a small valley 13km north of Hora (Kythira). The tables of charming *kafeneio* (coffee house) O Platanos (p554) fill its tiny central square, which is flanked on one side by the walled channel of a babbling stream that's populated by tame ducks and geese. As it flows northwest towards the sea, the stream cuts ever deeper into the wooded hillside, along a gorge that once held 22 **watermills**. Only one now survives – Mylopotamos means 'Mill on the River' – but a ravishing little footpath still follows the stream, leading through luxuriant greenery to the aquamarine pool of the **Neraïda (Water Nymph) waterfall**.

A separate hike, signposted along the left-hand fork in the road north of the village square, takes 15 minutes to reach the older village of **Kato Hora**. Make your way behind a castellated 19th-century villa here and you'll find the extraordinary ruins of Mylopotamos' Venetian-era **kastro**, a magical warren of abandoned churches and fortified houses, liberally overgrown with colourful flowers.

🛍 Shopping

Every other shop in Hora seems to be a boutique selling designer jewellery and clothing.

Borse FASHION & ACCESSORIES
(Yafanda; https://borse.gr; ⏱9am-9pm) Intriguing one-room, one-woman workshop on the pedestrian alleyway south of the main square. All the colourful and very distinctive shoulder and clutch bags for sale are created on the loom in the middle of the room.

Aquarium JEWELLERY
(☑6977287741; ⏱10am-9pm) Exquisite one-off pieces of bespoke jewellery are available in this boutique, overseen by the eponymous fish tank. It's not always open and hours vary, but it's worth persevering; if you hang around long enough the owner might come out of the next-door house. It's on the street that leads down the hill to Hora's main square.

ℹ Information

Kithira Travel (p549) Helpful staff; sells flights and boat tickets.

Kapsali Καψάλι
POP 63

Down by the sea 2km east of Hora (Kythira), pretty little Kapsali was the island's main port during the Venetian era. These days, in summer at least, it's a bustling resort, with its two languidly curving bays lined by a necklace of tavernas, chic cafes and studios, and the sandy, ochre-coloured beach with its sheltered swimming. It's a superb spectacle when viewed from Hora's clifftop *kastro*.

Don't miss climbing up to the lighthouse- and church-topped low headland that separates the two bays. The views from the top are stunning. The rocky islet offshore is known by two names. **Avgo** (Egg), referring to its legendary role as the birthplace of Aphrodite, and **Itra** (Cooking Pot), referring to its resemblance when topped by clouds to a steaming cauldron.

🛏 Sleeping & Eating

There's a good selection of hotels and rental studios perched above the beach in Kapsali, but it all turns very quiet indeed in low season.

★El Sol Hotel HOTEL €€
(Map p550; ☑27360 31766; www.elsolhotels.gr; d incl breakfast €120, 5-person apt €170; 🅿❄☎☎) Striking white-cube apartments, perched high above the Hora–Kapsali road, with Olympian views of the sea and across to Hora's *kastro*. Immaculate, minimalist rooms have private terraces, and there's a terrific pool, plenty of sunloungers, and a breakfast room packed with board games for rainy days (but let's hope those don't happen).

Vassili Studios PENSION €€
(☑27360 31125; http://kithirabiz.com; d/tr incl breakfast from €65/75; 🅿❄☎) This tree-lined complex has a perfect setting overlooking Kapsali Beach. Rooms are light and welcoming, with wooden ceilings and floors, shabby-chic furniture and wrought-iron beds; the larger and more expensive options have bay views. It's about halfway between Kapsali and Hora.

Aphrodite Apartments APARTMENT €€
(☑27360 31328; www.hotel-afrodite.gr; d/tr/q from €60/75/80; ❄☎) On the coast road, barely a minute up from the beach, the gleaming white Aphrodite offers a choice

between simple but spacious tile-floor rooms or apartments with kitchenettes and balconies. For the best views, choose the top floor. Irene and Yiannis are great hosts.

Trattamento TAVERNA €€
(☑ 2736 037226; mains €9-12; ☺ noon-11pm) A newbie on the Kapsali dining scene, modern taverna Trattamento appeals as much to salt-crusted fishers as it does to holidaying city folk. The kitchen takes classic island dishes and serves them with contemporary zest. Try the cuttlefish in onion sauce.

▼ Drinking & Nightlife

In summer, when bars and music venues open up along the waterfront, Kapsali becomes the nightlife capital of Kythira.

Fox Anglais (☑ 27360 31458; ☺ noon-late Jun-Sep; ☎) is a veteran bar-club on the waterfront, with outdoor tables and a cosy interior, is the epicentre of Kythira's nightlife in summer, hosting acoustic music on the beach on Tuesday and DJs every other night.

❶ Getting There & Away

While you'll need to drive to reach Kapsali from elsewhere on the island, a very pleasant (and very steep) footpath connects the bay with the village of Hora (Kythira) high above.

Potamos Ποταμός

POP 395

The attractive hillside village of Potamos, at the heart of the island, serves as Kythira's social hub. Its flower-filled central square hosts a Sunday-morning **flea market** and is great for people-watching any day of the week.

Pyrgos House (☑ 6989863140; www.pyrgos house.com) is highly recommended for outdoor activities, including €15 guided walks of Hora's *kastro* (10am Wednesday), a honeybee excursion, grape gathering, olive-oil tasting and olive harvesting, cooking and dancing lessons, kayaking and exciting multiday walking holidays, among an apparently limitless array of options.

One of five tavernas that amiably share the main village square for al-fresco dining at cream-coloured tables and chairs, **Panaretos** (☑ 27360 34290; www.panaretos-kythira. gr; mains €7-14; ☺ 1pm-midnight daily Mar-Oct, Thu-Sun Nov-Feb; ☎) excels with dishes based on home-grown produce.

The high-ceilinged and shadowy interior of **Kafe Astikon** (☑ 27360 33141; www.astikon.

gr; ☺ 7am-late; ☎) oozes atmosphere with its coral-green walls and its long wooden benches arranged around a makeshift stage. It's a very charming old cafe–music bar near the main square. Expect live music (late) nightly in July and August, and impromptu jam sessions at other times. It also serves breakfast, pizza and pasta.

Agia Pelagia Αγία Πελαγία

POP 280

Kythira's northernmost resort, Agia Pelagia is a simple seafront village backed by swooping cliffs and wooded valleys. Vibrant azure waters lick against its sand-and-pebble beaches, while some magnificent volcanic beaches lie south beyond the headland. Red, pink and tawny along to **Lagada Beach**, they make a great target for coastal hikers.

🛏 Sleeping & Eating

Hotel Pelagia Aphrodite HOTEL €€
(☑ 27360 33926; www.pelagia-aphrodite.com; s/d/tr incl breakfast €90/100/140; ☺ Easter-Oct; ⓟ ❄ ☎) Right on the beach at the southern end of town, and run by returning Aussie-Kythirans, this lovely hotel has 13 terrific rooms with wooden ceilings and huge, sea-facing balconies. The older rooms, whitewashed and simple, are closest to the waves, and there's a pleasant breakfast room downstairs.

★ **Kaleris** GREEK €
(☑ 27360 33461; www.facebook.com/kaleris; mains €7-11; ☺ noon-midnight Apr-Oct; ☎) Renowned for its creative cuisine, romantic little Kaleris has a waterfront pavilion and tables on the beach itself, shaded by tamarisk trees. Trust the charismatic owner, Yiannis, to advise on handwritten daily specials such as yoghurt salad with smoked aubergine, filo parcels with feta drizzled with thyme-infused honey, braised lamb shank or grilled prawns.

Around Kythira

You'll need your own transport to explore the back roads that thread between Kythira's scattered villages, which pass orchards and vineyards, olive groves and stands of cypress.

In the south, the small **Museum of Byzantine & Post-Byzantine Art** (☑ 27360 31731; Kato Livadi; adult/child €2/1; ☺ 8.30am-3pm Tue-Sun) in Kato Livadi, 6km north of Hora, houses icons and frescoes salvaged from churches all over the island. Spanning a shallow stream bed just north, incongruous **Katouni Bridge** (Map p550), built by the British in the 19th century, is the largest stone bridge in Greece. Head southeast, following spectacular twisty roads, to reach the mauve-grey stone beach at **Fyri Ammos**.

Avlemonas, further up the coast, is a former fishing village turned exquisite resort. A spotless vision of blue and dazzling white, with footpaths leading across the rocks to ladders that drop into the limpid turquoise waters (good snorkelling), it's basically everything the Greek island experience is supposed to be. The closest beaches lie to the west: first comes broad, pebbled **Paleopoli Beach**, then **Kaladi Beach**, in a separate cove and accessed via a staircase.

Few traces survive of ancient **Paleopoli**, just inland, but you can spend an enjoyable hour hiking up and around the hill that once held the **Temple of Aphrodite**, marking the birthplace of the goddess of beauty. There's not a lot left of it today, but the quiet, barren wind- and sun-battered hilltop has its own special kind of romance.

Much more substantial ruins survive of Kythira's medieval capital, **Paliohora**, in the north. It's a magnificent spot, set on a craggy pinnacle at the confluence of two deep-cut gorges. In theory it was safely hidden from enemy ships, but it was destroyed by a Turkish fleet in 1537. Strewn with the tumbledown remains of chapels and mansions, the isolated hilltop can now be reached by driving a 4km dead-end road east of Potamos, the last 2km of which is unsurfaced, or following the delightful parallel hiking trail.

Kythira has a web of quiet country roads spinning out over the island, and one of the most enjoyable things to do here is to slowly drive around, going where whim and road take you (the island's so small that you won't be able to get *too* lost!). At the end of the road you might find yourself on a dramatic headland, at a tranquil beach, in a pretty village or at a half-forgotten church.

🛏 Sleeping & Eating

⭐**Maryianni** APARTMENT €€

(📞 27360 33316; www.maryianni.gr; Avlemonas; studios €125-170; 🅿 ❄ 🛜) Rather wonderful white-and-blue studios sleeping up to four are stacked Cycladic style above the Avlemonas shoreline, with kitchens and sumptuous sea-view terraces. Even the smaller options are well above average, with boutique flourishes such as terracotta tiles, wrought-iron beds, classical art and choice furniture.

⭐**O Platanos** TAVERNA €

(📞 2736033397; Mylopotamos; mains €5-12; ⏱ 1pm-midnight; 🛜) The family behind this charming restaurant say that if you're searching for modern food then you're in the wrong place, but if you prefer to savour hand-me-down recipes full of family secrets, pull up a chair here. And what recipes these are – the special is slow-cooked pork in honey that's laced with herbs and pretty much tastes of the island.

The setting is also delightful: a creaky old villa with a broad terrace shaded by plane trees and overlooking a babbling stream. Although it's open all afternoon and evening, no food is served between about 4pm and 8pm.

⭐**Filio** TAVERNA €

(📞 27360 31549; Kalamos; mains €8-12; ⏱ 4pm-midnight; 🛜) An acclaimed local taverna far off the beaten track, 1km beyond Kalamos en route to Fyri Ammos (look for signs), Filio offers island classics such as slow-cooked lamb in lemon sauce, aubergine stuffed with meat, and Kythiran sausages, served in a well-shaded terrace garden. The owners also rent out attractive **apartments** nearby.

Pierros GREEK €

(📞 27360 31014; mains €6-10; ⏱ 1-4pm & 7-11pm; ❄ 🛜) For almost a century this family-run favourite has been serving no-nonsense staples such as *mousakas* (layers of eggplant or zucchini, minced meat and potatoes topped with cheese sauce) and *pastitsio* (layers of macaroni and minced lamb). The main road through Livadi is hardly a beautiful setting, but locals drive here from across the island. For an authentic Greek experience, it's hard to beat.

O Manolis SEAFOOD €

(📞 27360 38230; www.manolis-kythira.gr; Diakofti; mains €8-12; ⏱ 1pm-midnight May-Sep; 🛜) Locals head to this seafood specialist, its tables propped in the sand just north of the causeway in Diakofti, to savour excellent grilled fish or Italian-influenced risotto and pasta.

⭐**Skandeia** TAVERNA €€

(Map p550; 📞 27360 33700; www.skandeia.gr; Paleopoli; mains €8-15; ⏱ 1-11pm; 🛜) A delightful family-run taverna just back from the eastern end of Paleopoli Beach, Skandeia places major emphasis on wholesome, freshly sourced local produce in preparing its definitive Greek cuisine, which ranges from lightly grilled red mullet to roasted aubergine with an aroma of wood smoke. Relax beneath the spreading elms and enjoy the Greek idyll.

Understand the Greek Islands

History

Over the centuries, the Greek islands have been the stepping stones between North Africa, Asia Minor and Europe, across which warriors, tradesmen, conquerors and even civilisations have hopped. Successive invaders have fought over and claimed the islands as prizes. Their strategic location, in a seafaring world, made many islands prosperous and autonomous trading centres. Some were run by foreign masters, as evidenced by the Venetian ports, Roman aqueducts and Frankish castles found on the islands today.

Cycladic Civilisation

The Cycladic civilisation – centred on the islands of the Cyclades – comprised a cluster of small fishing and farming communities with a sophisticated artistic temperament. Scholars divide the Cycladic civilisation into three periods: Early (3000–2000 BC), Middle (2000–1500 BC) and Late (1500–1100 BC).

The most striking legacy of this civilisation is the famous Cycladic figurines – carved statuettes from Parian marble. Other remains include bronze and obsidian tools and weapons, gold jewellery, and stone and clay vases and pots. Cycladic sculptors are also renowned for their impressive, life-sized *kouroi* (marble statues), carved during the Archaic period.

The Cycladic people were also accomplished sailors who developed prosperous maritime trade links with Crete, continental Greece, Asia Minor (the west of present-day Turkey), Europe and North Africa.

Top Ancient Sights

....

Acropolis (Athens)
....
Knossos (Crete)
....
Delos
....
Lindos Acropolis (Rhodes)
....
Ancient Thira (Santorini)

Minoan Civilisation

The Minoans – named after King Minos, the mythical ruler of Crete (and stepfather of the Minotaur) – built Europe's first advanced civilisation, drawing their inspiration from two great Middle Eastern civilisations: the Mesopotamian and the Egyptian.

The Minoan civilisation (3000–1100 BC) reached its peak during the Middle period; around 2000 BC the grand palace complexes of Knossos, Phaestos, Malia and Zakros were built, marking a sharp acceleration from Neolithic village life. Evidence uncovered in these palaces indicates

TIMELINE	7000–3000 BC	3000–1100 BC	2000 BC
	For 4000 years the early inhabitants of the Greek peninsula live a simple agrarian life, tending crops and animals. Communities with housing and planned streets appear around 3000 BC.	The discovery of how to blend copper and tin gives rise to the Bronze Age. Trade gains traction and sees the flourishing of the Cycladic, Minoan – and later, the Mycenaean – civilisations.	Minoan civilisation reaches its peak in Crete: architectural advances lead to the first palaces in Knossos, Phaestos, Malia and Zakros, while pottery-making improves and Crete's first script emerges.

a sophisticated society, with splendid architecture and wonderful, detailed frescoes, highly developed agriculture and an extensive irrigation system.

The advent of bronze enabled the Minoans to build great boats, which helped them establish a powerful *thalassocracy* (sea power) and prosperous maritime trade. They used tremendous skill to produce fine pottery and metalwork of great beauty, and exported their wares throughout Greece, Asia Minor, Europe and North Africa.

Scholars are still debating the sequence of events that led to the ultimate demise of the Minoans. Scientific evidence suggests they were weakened by a massive tsunami and ash fallout attributed to the eruption of a cataclysmic volcano on Santorini (Thira) around 1500 BC. Some argue that a second powerful quake a century later decimated the society, or perhaps it was the invading force of Mycenae. The decline of the Minoans certainly coincided with the rise of the Mycenaean civilisation on the mainland (1600–1100 BC).

Geometric Age

The Dorians were an ancient Hellenic people who settled in the Peloponnese by the 8th century BC. In the 11th or 12th century BC these warrior-like people fanned out to occupy much of the mainland, seizing control of the Mycenaean kingdoms and enslaving the inhabitants. The Dorians also spread their tentacles into the Greek islands, founding the cities of Kamiros, Ialysos and Lindos on Rhodes in about 1000 BC, while Ionians fleeing to the Cyclades from the Peloponnese established a religious sanctuary on Delos.

The following 400-year period is often referred to as Greece's 'dark age'. In the Dorians' favour, however, they introduced iron and developed a new intricate style of pottery, decorated with striking geometric designs. They also introduced the practice of polytheism, paving the way for Zeus and his pantheon of 12 principal deities.

Archaic Age

By about 800 BC, the Dorians had developed into a class of landholding aristocrats and Greece was becoming divided into a series of independent city-states. Led by Athens and Corinth (which took over Corfu in 734 BC), the city-states created a Magna Graecia (Greater Greece), with southern Italy as an important component. Most abolished monarchic rule and aristocratic monopoly, establishing a set of laws that redistributed wealth and allowed citizens to regain control over their lands.

During the so-called Archaic Age, from around 800 to 650 BC, Greek culture developed rapidly. Many advances in literature, sculpture, theatre, architecture and intellectual endeavour began; this revival overlapped

Learn about everything from mythology to ancient Greek art and architecture through the web portal www.ancientgreece.com, where you can also apply to assist on an archaeological dig.

In pre-Classical times, the Ionians were a Hellenic people who inhabited Attica and parts of Asia Minor. These people colonised the islands that later became known as the Ionian Islands.

c 1650 BC	1500–1200 BC	1200–1100 BC	800–650 BC
Santorini erupts with a cataclysmic volcanic explosion, causing a massive Mediterranean-wide tsunami that scholars suggest contributed to the destruction of the Minoan civilisation.	The authoritarian Mycenaean culture from the Peloponnese usurps much of the Cretan and Cycladic cultures. Goldsmithing is a predominant feature of Mycenaean life.	The Dorians overrun the Mycenaean cities in Crete. They reorganise the political system, dividing society into classes. A rudimentary democracy replaces monarchic government.	Independent city-states begin to emerge in the Archaic Age as the Dorians develop. Aristocrats rule these mini-states while tyrants occasionally take power by force. The Greek alphabet emerges.

with the Classical Age. Developments from this period include the Greek alphabet; the verses of Homer, including epics the 'Iliad' and the 'Odyssey'; the founding of the Olympic Games; and the creation of central sanctuaries such as Delphi.

Classical Age

From the 6th to 4th centuries BC, Greece continued its renaissance in cultural creativity. As many city-states enjoyed increased economic reform and political prosperity, literature and drama blossomed.

Athens' rapid growth meant heavy reliance on food imports from the Black Sea, while Persia's imperial expansions threatened coastal trade routes across Asia Minor. Athens' support for a rebellion in the Persian colonies of Asia Minor sparked the Persian Wars.

In 477 BC Athens founded the Delian League, a naval alliance that was based on Delos. It was formed to liberate the city-states still occupied by Persia, and to defend against further Persian attack. The alliance included many of the Aegean islands and some of the Ionian city-states in Asia Minor. Swearing allegiance to Athens and making an annual contribution to the treasury of ships (later contributing just money) were mandatory.

When Pericles became the leader of Athens in 461 BC, he moved the treasury from Delos to the Acropolis, using the funds to construct new buildings and grander temples to replace those destroyed by the Persians.

With the Aegean Sea safely under its wing, Athens looked westwards for more booty. One of the major triggers of the first Peloponnesian War (431–421 BC) that pitted Athens against Sparta was Athens' support for Corcyra (present-day Corfu) in a row with Corinth, the island's mother city. Athens finally surrendered to Sparta after a drawn-out series of pitched battles.

> Greek is Europe's oldest written language, second only to Chinese in the world. It is traceable back to the Linear B script of the Minoans and Mycenaeans.

Foreign Rule

Roman Era

While Alexander the Great was forging his vast empire in the east, the Romans had been expanding theirs to the west, and were keen to start making inroads into Greece. After several inconclusive clashes, they defeated Macedonia in 168 BC. By 146 BC the mainland became the Graeco-Roman province of Achaea. Crete fell in 67 BC, and the southern city of Gortyn became capital of the Roman province of Cyrenaica, which included a large chunk of North Africa. Rhodes held out until AD 70.

As the Romans revered Greek culture, Athens retained its status as a centre of learning. Indeed, the Romans adopted many aspects of Hellenic culture, spreading its unifying traditions throughout their empire. During

594 BC	477 BC	461–432 BC	334–323 BC
Solon, a ruling aristocrat in Athens, introduces rules of fair play to his citizenry. His radical rule-changing – in effect creating human and political rights – is credited as being the first step to real democracy.	Seeking security while building a de facto empire, the Athenians establish a political and military alliance called the Delian League. Many city-states and islands join the new club.	New Athenian leader Pericles shifts power from Delos to Athens, and uses the treasury wealth of the Delian League to fund massive works, including building the magnificent Parthenon.	Alexander the Great sets out to conquer the known world. The Thebans are first, followed by the Persians, the Egyptians and finally the peoples of today's Central Asia. He dies in 323 BC.

a succession of Roman emperors, namely Augustus, Nero and Hadrian, the whole empire experienced a period of relative peace, known as the Pax Romana, which was to last for almost 300 years.

Byzantine Empire & the Crusades

The Pax Romana began to crumble in AD 250 when the Goths invaded what is now Greece – the first of a succession of invaders.

In an effort to resolve the conflict in the region, in AD 324 the Roman Emperor Constantine I, a Christian convert, transferred the capital of the empire from Rome to Byzantium, a city on the western shore of the Bosphorus, which was renamed Constantinople (present-day İstanbul). While Rome went into terminal decline, the eastern capital began to grow in wealth and strength as a Christian state. In the ensuing centuries, Byzantine Greece faced continued pressure from Venetians, Franks, Normans, Slavs, Persians and Arabs; the Persians captured Rhodes in 620, but were replaced by the Saracens (Arabs) in 653. The Arabs also captured Crete in 824. Other islands in the Aegean remained under Byzantine control.

The Byzantine Empire began to fracture when the renegade Frankish leaders of the Fourth Crusade decided that Constantinople presented richer pickings than Jerusalem. Constantinople was sacked in 1204, and much of the Byzantine Empire was partitioned into fiefdoms ruled by self-styled 'Latin' (mostly Frankish or western-Germanic) princes. The Venetians, meanwhile, had also secured a foothold in Greece. Over the next few centuries they took over key mainland ports, the Cyclades, and Crete in 1210, becoming the most powerful traders in the Mediterranean.

Ottoman Rule

On 29 May 1453, Constantinople fell under Turkish Ottoman rule (referred to by Greeks as *turkokratia*). Once more Greece became a battleground, this time fought over by the Turks and Venetians. Eventually, with the exception of the Ionian Islands (where the Venetians retained control), Greece became part of the Ottoman Empire.

Ottoman power reached its zenith under Sultan Süleyman the Magnificent, who ruled from 1520 to 1566. His successor, Selim the Sot, added Cyprus to Ottoman dominion in 1570. Although they captured Crete in 1669 after a 25-year campaign, the ineffectual sultans that followed in the late 16th and 17th centuries saw the empire go into steady decline.

By the end of the 18th century, pockets of Turkish officials, aristocrats and influential Greeks had emerged as self-governing cliques that ruled over the provincial Greek peasants. But there also existed an ever-increasing group of Greeks, including many intellectual expatriates, who aspired to emancipation.

The intellectual vigour of Classical Greece has yet to be equalled – scarcely an idea is discussed today that was not already debated by that era's great minds, whether in the dramatic tragedies by Aeschylus, Euripides and Sophocles and political satire of Aristophanes, or the histories of Herodotus and Thucydides.

168 BC–AD 224	AD 63	250–394	529
Roman expansion includes Greek territory. First defeating Macedonia at Pydna in 168 BC, the Romans ultimately overtake the mainland and establish the Pax Romana. It lasts 300 years.	Christianity emerges after St Paul visits Crete and leaves his disciple, Titus, to convert the island. St Titus becomes Crete's first bishop.	The invasion of Greece by the Goths signals the decline of the Pax Romana, and in 324 the capital is moved to Constantinople. In 394 Christianity is declared the official religion.	Athens' cultural influence is dealt a fatal blow when Emperor Justinian outlaws the teaching of classical philosophy in favour of Christian theology, by now regarded as the ultimate intellectual endeavour.

Independence

In 1814 the first Greek independence party, the Filiki Eteria (Friendly Society), was founded and its message spread quickly. On 25 March 1821, the Greeks launched the War of Independence. Uprisings broke out almost simultaneously across most of Greece and the occupied islands. The fighting was savage and atrocities were committed on both sides; in the Peloponnese 12,000 Turkish inhabitants were killed after the capture of the city of Tripolitsa (present-day Tripoli), while the Turks retaliated with massacres in Asia Minor, most notoriously on the island of Chios.

The campaign escalated, and within a year the Greeks had won vital ground. They proclaimed independence on 13 January 1822 at Epidavros.

Soon after, regional wrangling twice escalated into civil war, in 1824 and 1825. The Ottomans took advantage and by 1827 the Turks (with Egyptian reinforcements) had regained control. Western powers intervened and a combined Russian, French and British naval fleet sunk the Turkish-Egyptian force in the Battle of Navarino in October 1827. Despite the long odds against him, Sultan Mahmud II proclaimed a holy war, prompting Russia to send troops into the Balkans to engage the Ottoman army. Fighting continued until 1829 when, with Russian troops at the gates of Constantinople, the sultan accepted Greek independence with the Treaty of Adrianople. Independence was formally recognised in 1830.

The Modern Greek Nation

In April 1827, Greece elected Corfiot Ioannis Kapodistrias as the first president of the republic. Nafplio, in the Peloponnese, became the capital. There was much dissension and Kapodistrias was assassinated in

> Alexander the Great is considered to be one of the best military leaders of all time. He was never beaten in battle and by the age of 30 reigned over one of the largest ancient empires, stretching from Greece to the Himalayas.

ALEXANDER THE GREAT

Alexander the Great is considered to be one of the best military leaders of all time. He was never beaten in battle and by the age of 30 reigned over one of the largest ancient empires, stretching from Greece to the Himalayas.

Following the assassination of his father Phillip II in 336 BC, 20-year-old Alexander became king. He wasted no time in gathering the troops and winning a few bloody battles with the Persians. Alexander then marched through Syria, Palestine and Egypt – where he was proclaimed pharaoh and founded the city of Alexandria. He continued his reign east into parts of what are now Uzbekistan, Afghanistan and northern India.

After Alexander's untimely death in 323 BC at the age of 33, his generals swooped like vultures on the empire and carved it up into independent kingdoms. The Dodecanese became part of the kingdom of Ptolemy I of Egypt, while the remainder of the Aegean islands became part of the League of Islands ruled by the Antigonids of Macedon.

1204	1453	1541	1669
Marauding Frankish crusaders sack Constantinople (modern-day İstanbul). Trading religious fervour for self interest, the Crusaders strike a blow that sets Constantinople on the road to a slow demise.	Greece becomes a dominion of the Ottoman Turks after they seize control of Constantinople, sounding the death knell for the Byzantine Empire.	Dominikos Theotokopoulos, later known as 'El Greco', is born in Candia (Crete); his subsequent creations in Italy and Spain are marked by both Cretan School influence and bold personal innovation.	Venetian-ruled Crete falls under Ottoman power after keeping the Turks at bay in a fierce 20-year siege (Spinalonga Island and Souda hold out until 1715).

1831. Amid the ensuing anarchy, Britain, France and Russia declared Greece a monarchy and set on the throne the non-Greek, 17-year-old Bavarian Prince Otto, in January 1833. The new kingdom (established by the London Convention of 1832) consisted of the Peloponnese, Sterea Ellada, the Cyclades and the Sporades. Otto ruled until he was deposed in 1862.

The Great Idea

Greece's foreign policy (dubbed the 'Great Idea') was to assert sovereignty over its dispersed Greek populations. Set against the background of the Crimean conflict, British and French interests were nervous at the prospect of a Greek alliance with Russia against the Ottomans.

British influence in the Ionian Islands had begun in 1815 (following a spell of political ping-pong between the Venetians, Russians and French). The British did improve the islands' infrastructure, and many locals adopted British customs (such as afternoon tea and cricket in Corfu). However, Greek independence put pressure on Britain to give sovereignty to the Greek nation, and in 1864 the British left. Meanwhile, Britain eased onto the Greek throne the young Danish Prince William, crowned King George I in 1863, whose reign lasted 50 years.

In 1881, Greece acquired Thessaly and part of Epiros as a result of a Russo-Turkish war. But Greece failed miserably when it tried to attack Turkey in an effort to reach *enosis* (union) with Crete (which had persistently agitated for liberation from the Ottomans). Timely diplomatic intervention by the Great Powers prevented the Turkish army from taking Athens.

Crete was placed under international administration, but the government of the island was gradually handed over to the Greeks. In 1905 the president of the Cretan assembly, Eleftherios Venizelos (later to become prime minister), announced Crete's union with Greece (although this was not recognised by international law until 1913).

The Balkan Wars

The declining Ottomans still retained Macedonia, prompting the Balkan Wars of 1912 and 1913. The outcome was the Treaty of Bucharest (August 1913), which greatly expanded Greek territory to take in the southern part of Macedonia (which included Thessaloniki, the vital cultural centre strategically positioned on the Balkan trade routes), part of Thrace, another chunk of Epiros and the northeastern Aegean Islands; the treaty also recognised the union with Crete.

The Histories, written by Herodotus in the 5th century BC, chronicles the conflicts between the Ancient Greek city-states and Persia. The work is considered to be the first narrative of historical events ever written.

The Venetian Empire by Jan Morris (1990) vividly describes the imperial influence of the Venetians across the Greek islands. This very readable account includes the social, cultural and architectural legacies still evident today.

HISTORY THE MODERN GREEK NATION

1821	1827–31	1833	1862–63
The War of Independence begins on the mainland on 25 March. Greece celebrates this date as its national day of independence.	Ioannis Kapodistrias is appointed prime minister of a fledgling government with its capital in the Peloponnesian town of Nafplio. Discontent ensues and Kapodistrias is assassinated.	The powers of the entente (Britain, France and Russia) decree that Greece should be a monarchy and dispatch Prince Otto of Bavaria to Greece to be the first appointed monarch in modern Greece.	The monarchy takes a nosedive and King Otto is deposed in a bloodless coup. The British return the Ionian Islands (a British protectorate since 1815) to Greece in an effort to quell Greece's expansionist urges.

WWI & Smyrna

During the First World War, the Allies (Britain, France and Russia) put increasing pressure on neutral Greece to join forces with them against Germany and Turkey, promising concessions in Asia Minor in return. Greek troops served with distinction on the Allied side, but when the war ended in 1918 the promised land in Asia Minor was not forthcoming. Prime Minister Venizelos then led a diplomatic campaign to further the 'Great Idea' and sent troops to Smyrna (present-day İzmir) in May 1919. With a seemingly viable hold in Asia Minor, by September 1921 Greece had advanced as far as Ankara. But by this stage foreign support for Venizelos had ebbed, and Turkish forces, commanded by Mustafa Kemal (later to become Atatürk), halted the offensive. The Greek army retreated and Smyrna fell in 1922, and tens of thousands of its Greek inhabitants were killed.

The outcome of these hostilities was the Treaty of Lausanne in July 1923, whereby Turkey recovered eastern Thrace and the islands of Imvros and Tenedos, while the Italians kept the Dodecanese (which they had temporarily acquired in 1912 and would hold until 1947).

The treaty also called for a population exchange between Greece and Turkey to prevent any future disputes. Almost 1.5 million Greeks left Turkey and almost 400,000 Turks left Greece. The exchange put a tremendous strain on the Greek economy and caused great bitterness and hardship for the individuals concerned. Many Greeks had to abandon a privileged life in Asia Minor for one of extreme poverty in emerging urban shanty towns in Athens and Thessaloniki.

WWII & the Civil War

During a tumultuous period, a republic was declared in 1924 amid a series of coups and counter-coups. Then in November 1935, King George II installed the right-wing General Ioannis Metaxas as prime minister. He assumed dictatorial powers under the pretext of preventing a communist-inspired republican coup. Metaxas' grandiose vision was to create a utopian Third Greek Civilisation, based on its glorious ancient and Byzantine past. He then exiled or imprisoned opponents, banned trade unions and the recently established Kommounistiko Komma Elladas (KKE, the Greek Communist Party), imposed press censorship, and created a secret police force and fascist-style youth movement. But Metaxas is best known for his reply of *ohi* (no) to Mussolini's ultimatum to allow Italian forces passage through Greece at the beginning of WWII. The Italians invaded anyway, but the Greeks drove them back into Albania.

Despite Allied help, when German troops invaded Greece on 6 April 1941, the whole country was rapidly overrun. The Germans used Crete as an air and naval base to attack British forces in the eastern Mediterranean.

Medieval & Venetian Sites

Rhodes Old Town (Rhodes)

Monastery of St John (Patmos)

Hania's Old Town (Crete)

Rethymno (Crete)

Corfu Old Town (Corfu)

Eugène Delacroix' oil canvas The Massacre at Chios (1824) was inspired by the events in Asia Minor during Greece's War of Independence in 1821. The painting hangs in the Louvre Museum in Paris.

1914	1919–23	1924–35	1940
The outbreak of WWI sees Greece initially neutral but eventually siding with the Western Allies against Germany and Turkey on the promise of land in Asia Minor.	Greece's 'Great Idea' attempts to unite the former Hellenic areas of Asia Minor. It fails and leads to a population exchange between Greece and Turkey in 1923, known as the 'Asia Minor catastrophe'.	Greece is proclaimed a republic and King George II leaves. The Great Depression counters the nation's return to stability. Monarchists and parliamentarians under Venizelos tussle for control of the country.	Greeks shout *Ohi!* (No!) to Italian fascists demanding surrender without a fight on 28 October. Officially referred to as Ohi Day, many Greeks use language that is rather more colourful for this day.

The civilian population suffered appallingly during the occupation, many dying of starvation. The Germans rounded up between 60,000 and 70,000 Greek Jews, at least 80% of the country's Jewish population, and transported them to death camps. Numerous resistance movements sprang up, eventually polarising into royalist and communist factions which fought one another with as much venom as they fought the Germans, often with devastating results for the civilian Greek population.

The German retreat from Greece began in October 1944. Meanwhile, the resistance groups continued to fight one another. A bloody civil war resulted, lasting until 1949. The civil war left Greece in chaos, politically frayed and economically shattered. More Greeks were killed in three years of bitter civil war than in WWII, and a quarter of a million people were left homeless. The sense of despair triggered a mass exodus. Villages – whole islands even – were abandoned as almost a million Greeks left in search of a better life elsewhere, primarily to countries such as Australia, Canada and the US.

One of the few movies to broach the sensitive subject of Greece's civil war, Pantelis Voulgaris' 2009 film *Psyhi Vathia* (Deep Soul) is set in the final period of the bitter battle.

Colonels, Monarchs & Democracy

Georgos Papandreou came to power in February 1964. He had founded the Centre Union (EK) and wasted no time in implementing a series of radical changes: he freed political prisoners and allowed exiles to come back to Greece, reduced income tax and the defence budget, and increased spending on social services and education. The political right in Greece was rattled by Papandreou's tolerance of the left, and a group

---

LASKARINA BOUBOULINA: A FEMALE FORCE

Women have played a strong role in Greek resistance movements throughout history. One national heroine was Laskarina Bouboulina (1771–1825), a celebrated seafarer who became a member of Filiki Eteria (Friendly Society), an organisation striving for independence against Ottoman rule.

Originally from Hydra, she settled in Spetses, from where she commissioned the construction of and then commanded, as admiral, several warships that were used in significant naval blockades (the most famous vessel being the *Agamemnon*). Bouboulina helped maintain the crews of her ships and a small army of soldiers, and supplied the revolutionaries with food, weapons and ammunition, using her ships for transportation. Her role in maritime operations significantly helped the independence movement. However, political factionalism within the government led to her postwar arrest and subsequent exile to Spetses, where she died.

Today, streets across Greece bear her name and there are statues dedicated to her and her great-granddaughter, Lela Karagianni – who fought with the resistance in WWII – in Spetses Town, where Bouboulina's home is now a private museum.

1941–44	1944–49	1967	1974
Germany invades and occupies Greece. Monarchists, republicans and communists form resistance groups that, despite infighting, drive out the Germans after three years.	The end of WWII sees Greece descend into civil war, pitching monarchists against communists. The monarchy is restored in 1946; however, many Greeks migrate in search of a better life.	Right- and left-wing factions continue to bicker, provoking a right-wing military coup d'état by army generals who establish a junta. They impose martial law and abolish many civil rights.	A botched plan to unite Cyprus with Greece prompts the invasion of Cyprus by Turkish troops and the military junta falls. It's a catalyst for the restoration of parliamentary democracy in Greece.

of army colonels led by Georgos Papadopoulos and Stylianos Patakos staged a coup on 21 April 1967. They established a military junta, with Papadopoulos as prime minister.

The colonels declared martial law, banned political parties and trade unions, imposed censorship, and imprisoned, tortured and exiled thousands of dissidents. In June 1972, Papadopoulos declared Greece a republic and appointed himself president.

On 17 November 1973, tanks stormed a building at the Athens Polytechnic (Technical University) to quell a student occupation calling for an uprising against the US-backed junta. While the number of casualties is still in dispute (more than 20 students were reportedly killed and hundreds injured), the act spelt the death knell for the junta.

Shortly after, the head of the military security police, Dimitrios Ioannidis, deposed Papadopoulos and tried to impose unity with Cyprus in a disastrous move that led to the partition in Cyprus and the collapse of the junta.

Konstandinos Karamanlis, prime minister from the 1950s, was invited to return to Greece from self-imposed exile in Paris. His New Democracy (ND) party won a large majority at the November 1974 elections against the newly formed Panhellenic Socialist Union (PASOK), led by Andreas Papandreou (son of Georgos). A plebiscite voted 69% against the restoration of the monarchy, and the ban on communist parties was lifted.

For an insight into the 1967 colonels' coup, read Andreas Papandreou's account in *Democracy at Gunpoint: The Greek Front* published in 1971.

The 1980s & 1990s

When Greece became the 10th member of the EU in 1981, it was the smallest and poorest country in the bloc. In October 1981 Andreas Papandreou's PASOK party was elected as Greece's first socialist government, ruling for almost two decades (except for 1990–93). PASOK promised ambitious social reform, to close the US air bases and to withdraw from NATO. US military presence was reduced, but unemployment was high and reforms in education and welfare were limited. Women's issues fared better: the dowry system was abolished, abortion legalised, and civil marriage and divorce were implemented. But by 1990, significant policy wrangling and economic upheaval wore thin with the electorate and it returned the ND to office, led by Konstandinos Mitsotakis.

Intent on addressing the country's economic problems – high inflation and high government spending – the government imposed austerity measures, including a wage freeze for civil servants and steep increases in public utility costs and basic services.

By late 1992 corruption allegations were being levelled against the government, and many Mitsotakis supporters abandoned ship; ND

1981	1981–90	1999	2001
Greece joins the EU, effectively removing protective trade barriers and opening up the Greek economy to the wider world for the first time. The economy grows smartly.	Greece acquires its first elected socialist government (PASOK) under the leadership of Andreas Papandreou. The honeymoon lasts nine years. The conservatives ultimately reassume power.	Turkey and Greece experience powerful earthquakes within weeks of each other that result in hundreds of deaths. The two nations pledge mutual aid and support, initiating a warming of diplomatic relations.	Greece joins the eurozone, with the drachma currency replaced by the euro.

lost its parliamentary majority, and an early election held in October returned PASOK to power.

Andreas Papandreou stepped down in early 1996 due to ill health and he died on 26 June, sparking a dramatic change of direction for PASOK. The party abandoned Papandreou's left-leaning politics and elected economist and lawyer Costas Simitis as the new prime minister. Simitis then won a comfortable majority at the October 1996 polls.

The 21st Century

The new millennium saw Greece join the eurozone in 2001, amid rumblings from existing members that it was not economically ready – its public borrowing was too high, as was its inflation level. In hindsight, many look back on that year and bemoan the miscalibration of the drachma against the euro, claiming Greece's currency was undervalued, and that, overnight, living became disproportionately more expensive. That said, billions of euros poured into large-scale infrastructure projects across Greece, including the redevelopment of Athens – spurred on largely by its hosting of the 2004 Summer Olympic Games. However, rising unemployment, ballooning public debt, slowing inflation and the

DIVIDED CYPRUS

Since the 1930s, Greek Cypriots (four-fifths of the island's population) had desired union with Greece, while Turkey had maintained its claim to the island ever since it became a British protectorate in 1878 (it became a British crown colony in 1925). Greece was in favour of a union, a notion strongly opposed by Britain and the US on strategic grounds.

In 1959, after extensive negotiations, Britain, Greece and Turkey agreed on a compromise solution whereby Cyprus would become an independent republic, with Greek Cypriot Archbishop Makarios as president and a Turk, Fazil Kükük, as vice president. In reality this did little to appease either side: right-wing Greek Cypriots rallied against the British, while Turkish Cypriots clamoured for partition of the island.

In July 1974, Greece's newly self-appointed prime minister Dimitrios Ioannidis tried to impose unity with Cyprus by attempting to topple the Makarios government. However, Makarios got wind of an assassination attempt and escaped. Consequently, mainland Turkey sent in troops until they occupied northern Cyprus, partitioning the island and displacing almost 200,000 Greek Cypriots, who fled their homes for the safety of the south (reportedly more than 1500 remain missing).

The Green Line separating Greece and Turkey in Cyprus is a demilitarised buffer zone where the clock stopped in 1974. Greeks still peer through the barbed-wire partition to the place they were born and banished from, and are unlikely to return to live. A divided Cyprus joined the European Union in 2004 after a failed referendum on unification, and international mediation continues.

2004	2007	2009	2009
Athens successfully hosts the 28th Summer Olympic Games. Greece also wins the European football championship.	Vast forest fires devastate much of the western Peloponnese as well as parts of Evia and Epiros, causing Greece's worst ecological disaster in decades. Thousands lose their homes and 66 people perish.	Greece raises concerns over Turkey's plan to explore for oil and gas off the coasts of Kastellorizo and Cyprus. Diplomatic tension mounts when locals spot Turkish jets flying low over several Greek islands.	Konstandinos Karamanlis calls for an early general election. Socialist PASOK, under George Papandreou, wins the October election with a landslide result against the conservatives.

squeezing of consumer credit took their toll. Public opinion soured further in 2007 when the conservative government (which had come to power in 2004) was widely criticised for its handling of severe summer fires, responsible for widespread destruction throughout Greece. Nevertheless, snap elections held in September 2007 returned the conservatives to power, albeit with a diminished majority.

In the following years, a series of massive general strikes and blockades highlighted mounting electoral discontent. Hundreds of thousands of people protested against proposed radical labour and pension reforms and privatisation plans that analysts claimed would help curb public debt. The backlash against the government reached a boiling point in December 2008, when urban rioting broke out across the country, led by youths outraged by the police shooting of a 15-year-old boy in Athens following an alleged exchange between police and a group of teenagers. Youths hurled stones and firebombs at riot police who responded with tear gas. Following a series of financial and corruption scandals a general election held in October 2009, midway through Karamanlis' term, saw PASOK (under George Papandreou) take back the reins in a landslide win against the conservatives.

The Crisis & Austerity

In 2009 a lethal cocktail of high public spending and widespread tax evasion, combined with the credit crunch of global recession, threatened to cripple Greece's economy. In 2010 Greece's fellow eurozone countries agreed to a €125 billion package (half of Greece's GDP) to get the country back on its feet, though with strict conditions – the ruling government, PASOK, still led by Georgios Papandreou, would have to impose austere measures of reform and reduce Greece's bloated deficit.

The austerity programme didn't work, Papandreou resigned in 2011 to be replaced as prime minister by Lucas Papademos – a former vice president of the European Central Bank – who lasted barely six months in the post. A second EU bailout of €130 billion brought further austerity requirements and Athens again saw major strikes aimed at the massive cuts – 22% off minimum wage, 15% off pensions and the axing of 15,000 public-sector jobs.

These were indeed brutal times for the average Greek, with wage cuts of around 30% and up to 17 'new' taxes crippling monthly income. While the EU and IMF initially predicted that Greece would return to growth in 2014, the inability for many Greeks to pay their taxes at the end of the year meant that growth was a mere 0.4%.

2010	2011	2012	2013
Greece is granted the biggest financial bailout in history as fellow EU countries commit a €125 billion package. Strict austerity measures by the Greek government to cut the bloated deficit are met with civil protest.	Despite loans, the economy continues to shrink with rising unemployment and riots in Athens. The EU and IMF rally to prevent a Greek default and avert a crisis across the eurozone.	Proposed government cuts include 22% off the minimum wage, 15% off pensions and 15,000 public-sector jobs.	Unemployment rises to 26.8% – the highest rate in the EU. Youth unemployment climbs to almost 60%.

Road to Recovery?

In January 2015, left-wing Syriza, led by Alexis Tsipras, won the general election with an antiausterity platform, the first-ever such victory for the radical left-wing party. To reach a majority, Syriza established a coalition with right-wing Independent Greeks (ANEL), unlikely bedfellows united by their mutual condemnation of the bailout program.

Initially, Tsipras stuck to his guns and June 2015 saw Greece become the first developed nation to go into arrears with the EU and IMF. Attempts to negotiate a new bailout and avoid default were unsuccessful as Tsipras took the offer back to Greece and held a referendum. Over 61% of voters were not willing to accept the bailout conditions.

The week that followed was one of turmoil. Greek banks closed and began running out of cash, and markets around the world fell as the EU produced a detailed plan for a possible Grexit – Greece's removal from the EU. At the 11th hour, Tsipras secured an €86 billion bailout loan – but the austerity measures attached were even more vigorous than those proposed before the referendum.

Continued political turmoil over the bailout led Tsipras to resign in August 2015 and return to the polls in September. This was Greece's fourth election in just over three years. The outcome was an unexpectedly large victory for Tsipras, just six seats short of an absolute majority. Nevertheless, voter turnout was 57%, the lowest recorded in Greece's history.

In August 2018 Greece finally exited the €86 billion bailout program. Under Tsipras' government unemployment had fallen, consumer spending had risen and poverty was on the decline. Even so, voters, exhausted with austerity, rejected Syriza, first in the local and European Parliament elections in May 2019, and then the general election in July. The centre-right New Democracy party, led by Kyriakos Mitsotakis, won by a landslide, giving it an outright majority of 158 seats in the Greek parliament.

Prince Philip, Duke of Edinburgh, was part of the Greek royal family – born on Corfu as Prince Philip of Greece and Denmark in 1921. Former king of Greece, Constantine, is Prince William's godfather and Prince Charles' third cousin. Constantine and his family were exiled in London for 46 years, returning to Athens in 2013.

HISTORY THE 21ST CENTURY

2015	2015	2017	2019
The New Democrat party is replaced by left-wing Syriza, led by 40-year-old Alexis Tsipras and an anti-austerity platform.	Unable to pay its debt, Greece faces the very real possibility of an exit from the eurozone and is forced to take on further debt with the strictest austerity measures yet.	The number of refugees reaches 62,000 (over half of them women and children), mainly from Syria, Afghanistan and Iraq. With borders to other European countries closed, they are trapped, mainly in island camps.	After the ruling Syriza party suffers devastating defeats in both European and local elections, it is trounced in the Greek general election in July by the centre-right New Democracy party, led by Kyriakos Mitsotakis.

Ancient Greek Culture

When the Roman Empire assimilated Greece it did so with considerable respect and idealism. The Romans in many ways based themselves on the Ancient Greeks, absorbing their deities (and renaming them), literature, myths, philosophy, fine arts and architecture. So what made the Ancient Greeks so special? From thespians to philosophers, from monster-slewing heroes to a goddess born of sea foam, the Ancient Greeks were captivating.

The Golden Age

Exploring the World of the Ancient Greeks (2010), by archaeologists John Camp and Elizabeth Fisher, is a broad and in-depth look at how the Greeks have left their imprint on politics, philosophy, theatre, art, medicine and architecture.

In the 5th century BC, Athens had a cultural renaissance that has never been equalled – in fact, such was the diversity of its achievements that modern classical scholars refer to it as 'the miracle'. The era started with a vastly outnumbered Greek army defeating the Persian horde in the battles of Marathon and Salamis, and ended with the beginning of the inevitable war between Athens and Sparta. It's often said that Athens' 'Golden Age' is the bedrock of Western civilisation, and had the Persians won, Europe today would have been a vastly different place. Like Paris in the 1930s, ancient Athens was a hotbed of talent. Any artist or writer worth their salt left their hometown and travelled to the great city of wisdom to share their thoughts and hear the great minds of the day express themselves.

Drama

The great dramatists such as Aeschylus, Aristophanes, Euripides and Sophocles redefined theatre from religious ritual to become a compelling form of entertainment. They were to be found at the Theatre of Dionysos at the foot of the Acropolis, and their comedies and tragedies reveal a great deal about the psyche of the Ancient Greeks.

Across the country, large open-air theatres were built on the sides of hills, designed to accommodate plays with increasingly sophisticated backdrops and props, choruses and themes, and to maximise sound so that even the people in the back row might hear the actors on stage. The dominant genres of theatre were tragedy and comedy. The first known actor was a man called Thespis, from whose name we derive the word 'thespian'.

The Greek tragedy *Medea*, by Euripides, is about the sun god Helios' granddaughter who takes revenge on her estranged husband Jason by killing his new wife and her own children. It was turned into a namesake TV film by Lars von Trier in 1988.

Philosophy

While the dramatists were cutting their thespian cloth, three philosophers were introducing new trains of thought rooted in rationality and logic. Posthumously considered to be Athens' greatest, most noble citizen, Socrates (469–399 BC) was forced to drink hemlock for allegedly corrupting the youth by asking probing, uncomfortable questions. However, before he died he established a school of hypothetical reductionism that is still used today. Two of Socrates' most famous quotes are: 'The only true wisdom consists of knowing that you know nothing' and 'The unexamined life is not worth living'.

Plato (427–347 BC), Socrates' star student, was responsible for documenting his teacher's thoughts, and without his work in books such as the *Symposium,* they would have been lost to us. Considered an idealist, Plato wrote *The Republic* as a warning to the city-state of Athens that unless its people respected law and leadership, and educated its youth sufficiently, it would be doomed.

Plato's student Aristotle (384–322 BC), at the end of the Golden Age, focused his gifts on astronomy, physics, zoology, ethics and politics. Aristotle was also the personal physician to Philip II, King of Macedon, and the tutor of Alexander the Great. The greatest gift of the Athenian philosophers to modern-day thought is their spirit of rational inquiry.

Sculpture

Classical sculpture began to gather pace in Greece in the 6th century BC with the renderings of nudes in marble. Most statues were created to revere a particular god or goddess and many were robed in grandiose garments. The statues of the preceding Archaic period, known as *kouroi,* had focused on symmetry and form, but in the early 5th century BC artists sought to create expression and animation. As temples demanded elaborate carvings, sculptors were called upon to create large reliefs upon them.

During the 5th century BC, the craft became yet more sophisticated, as sculptors were taught to successfully map a face and create a likeness of their subject in marble busts. Perhaps the most famous Greek sculptor was Pheidias (c 480–430 BC), whose reliefs upon the Parthenon depicting the Greek and Persian Wars – now known as the Parthenon Marbles – are celebrated as among the finest of the Golden Age.

No original works by the celebrated classical sculptor Pheidias survive, though copies were made by Roman sculptors. Pheidias' colossal chryselephantine (gold and ivory) statue of Zeus was one of the Wonders of the Ancient World.

Mythology

Ancient Greece revolved around careful worship of 12 central gods and goddesses, all of whom played a major role in the *mythos* (mythology), and none of whom can be commended for their behaviour. They frequently displayed pettiness, spitefulness, outright cruelty and low self-esteem that led to unworthy competitions with mortals that were always rigged in the gods' favour. Each city-state had its own patron god or goddess to appease and flatter, while on a personal level a farmer might make a sacrifice to the goddess Demeter to bless his crops, or a fisherman to Poseidon to bring him fish and safe passage on the waves.

ISLANDS IN MYTHOLOGY

Greece is steeped in mythology and its many islands provided dramatic settings for its legends and interactions between gods and mortals.

Myrina, Limnos Believed to have been founded by Myrina, queen of the Amazons.

Crete Zeus' mother allegedly gave birth to him in a cave to prevent him from being eaten by his father, Cronos. Crete was also home of the dreaded minotaur.

Lesvos When Orpheus was killed and dismembered by the Maenads, the waves brought his head here and it was buried near Antissa.

Kythira Aphrodite is said to have been born out of the waves surrounding Kythira.

Delos This island rose up from the waves when the goddess Leto was looking for a place to give birth to Apollo and Artemis.

Mykonos Zeus and the Titans battled it out on this island and Hercules slew the Giants here.

Rhodes The island given to Helios the sun god after Zeus' victory over the Giants.

TOP FIVE MYTHICAL CREATURES

Of the grotesque and fantastical creatures whose stories are dear to Greek hearts, these five are the most notorious.

Medusa The snake-headed one punished by the gods for her inflated vanity. Even dead, her blood is lethal.

Cyclops A one-eyed giant. Odysseus and his crew were trapped in the cave of one such cyclops, Polyphemus.

Cerberus The three-headed dog of hell, he guards the entrance to the underworld – under his watch no one gets in or out.

Minotaur This half-man, half-bull mutant leads a life of existential angst in the abysmal labyrinth, tempered only by the occasional morsel of human flesh.

Hydra Cut one of its nine heads off and another two will grow in its place. Heracles solved the problem by cauterising each stump with his burning brand.

The Ancient Pantheon

Here's a quick guide to the 12 central gods and goddesses of Greek mythology – their Roman names are in brackets.

Zeus (Jupiter) The fire-bolt-flinging king of the gods, ruler of Mt Olympus, lord of the skies and master of disguise in pursuit of mortal maidens. Wardrobe includes shower of gold, bull, eagle and swan.

Hera (Juno) Protector of women and family, the queen of heaven is both the embattled wife and sister of Zeus. She was the prototype of the jealous, domineering wife who took revenge on Zeus' illegitimate children.

Poseidon (Neptune) God of the seas, master of the mists and younger brother of Zeus. He dwelt in a glittering underwater palace.

Hades (Pluto) God of death and also brother of Zeus, he ruled the underworld, bringing in the newly dead with the help of his skeletal ferryman, Charon. Serious offenders were sent for torture in Tartarus, while heroes went to the Elysian Fields.

Athena (Minerva) Goddess of wisdom, war, science and guardian of Athens, born in full armour out of Zeus' forehead. The antithesis of Ares, Athena was deliberate and, where possible, diplomatic in the art of war. Heracles, Jason (of Jason and the Argonauts fame) and Perseus all benefited from her patronage.

Aphrodite (Venus) Goddess of love and beauty who was said to have been born of sea foam. When she wasn't cuckolding her husband, Hephaestus, she and her son Eros (Cupid) were enflaming hearts and causing trouble (cue the Trojan War).

Apollo God of music, the arts and fortune-telling, Apollo was also the god of light and an expert shot with a bow and arrow. It was his steady hand that guided Paris' arrow towards Achilles' only weak spot – his heel – thus killing him.

Artemis (Diana) The goddess of the hunt and twin sister of Apollo was, ironically, patron saint of wild animals. By turns spiteful and magnanimous, she was closely associated with the sinister Hecate, patroness of witchcraft.

Ares (Mars) God of war, bloodthirsty and lacking control. Zeus' least favourite of his progeny. Not surprisingly, Ares was worshipped by the bellicose Spartans.

Hermes (Mercury) Messenger of the gods, patron saint of travellers and the handsome one with a winged hat and sandals. He was always on hand to smooth over the affairs of Zeus, his father.

Hephaestus (Vulcan) God of artisanship, metallurgy and fire, this deformed and oft-derided son of Zeus made the world's first woman of clay, Pandora, as a punishment for man. Inside her box were the evils of mankind.

Hestia (Vesta) Goddess of the hearth, she protected state fires in city halls from which citizens of Greece could light their brands. She stayed unmarried and a virgin.

British actor and author Stephen Fry brings his inimitable wit to his retellings of key Greek myths and legends in *Mythos* (2017) and *Heroes* (2018).

The Heroes

Some of the greatest tales of all time – and some say the wellspring of story itself – are to be found in the Greek myths. Contemporary writers continue to reinterpret these stories and characters for books and films.

Heracles (Hercules)

The most celebrated, endearing hero of ancient Greece, the son of Zeus and the mortal Alcmene. After killing his family in a fit of madness induced by the jealous Hera (sister-wife of Zeus), Heracles seeks penance by performing 12 labours set by his enemy Eurystheus, King of Mycenae. These labours included cleaning the Augean Stables in one day; slaying the arrow-feathered Stymphalian Birds; capturing the Cretan Bull; stealing the man-eating Mares of Diomedes; obtaining the Girdle of Hippolyta and the oxen of Geryon; and stealing the Apples of the Hesperides.

Theseus

The Athenian hero volunteered himself as one of seven men and maidens in the annual sacrifice to the Minotaur, the crazed half-bull, half-man offspring of King Minos of Crete. Once inside its forbidding labyrinth (from which none had returned), Theseus, aided by Princess Ariadne (who had a crush on him induced by Aphrodite's dart), loosened a spool of thread to find his way out once he'd killed the monster.

Icarus

Along with Daedalus (his father), Icarus flew off the cliffs of Crete pursued by King Minos and his troops, using wings made of feathers and wax. His father instructed him to fly away from the midday sun, but Icarus became carried away with the exhilaration of flying...the wax melted, the feathers separated and the bird-boy fell to his death.

Perseus

Perseus' impossible task was to kill the gorgon, Medusa. With a head of snakes Medusa could turn a man to stone with a single glance. Armed with an invisibility cap and a pair of flying sandals from Hermes, Perseus used his reflective shield to avoid Medusa's stare. He cut off her head and secreted it in a bag, but it was shortly unsheathed to save Andromeda, a princess bound to a rock and about to be sacrificed to a sea monster. Medusa's head turned the sea monster to stone and Perseus got the girl.

Oedipus

Oedipus was the Ancient Greeks' gift to the Freudian school of psychology. Having been abandoned at birth, Oedipus learned from the Delphic oracle that he would one day slay his father and marry his mother. On the journey back to his birthplace, Thiva (Thebes), he killed a rude stranger and then discovered the city was plagued by a murderous Sphinx (a winged lion with a woman's head). The creature gave unsuspecting travellers and citizens a riddle: if they couldn't answer it, they were dashed on the rocks. Oedipus succeeded in solving the riddle, felled the Sphinx and so gained the queen of Thiva's hand in marriage. On discovering the stranger he'd killed was his father and that his new wife was in fact his mother, Oedipus ripped out his eyes and exiled himself.

Marcel Camus' film *Black Orpheus* (1959) won an Oscar for its reimagining of the Orpheus and Eurydice tale, set in a favela in 1950s Brazil to a bossa nova soundtrack. The lovers flee a hitman and Orfeu's vindictive fiancée.

From the Greek stories of Oedipus and the castration of Uranus by Cronos, Sigmund Freud drew the conclusion that myths often reflect strong, taboo desires that are otherwise unable to be expressed in society.

ANCIENT GREEK CULTURE MYTHOLOGY

The Islanders

The Greek islands are more low-key and relaxed than the mainland, and people generally lead a more traditional lifestyle. Periods of isolation, varying geography and the influence of foreign cultures throughout history have led to strong regional identities, both between and within island groups.

Island Life

Living on a Greek island may be the stuff of fantasies, but even the most idyllic islands have their challenges. Island life is predominantly seasonal, revolving largely around agriculture, stock breeding, fishing and tourism. From May to September, visitors far outnumber the local population on many islands.

The majority of islanders are self-employed and run family businesses. Stores close during the heat of the day, and then reopen until around 11pm – which is when locals generally head out to dinner with family or their *parea* (company of friends).

Regardless of the long working hours, Greeks are inherently social and enjoy a rich communal life. Shopkeepers sit outside their stores chatting to each other until customers arrive, and in villages you will see people sitting outside their homes watching the goings on. In the evenings, the seafront promenades and town squares are bustling with people of all ages taking their *volta* (evening walk), dressed up and refreshed from an afternoon siesta (albeit a dying institution).

Island Pursuits

The island of Ikaria has one of the highest life expectancy rates in Europe, with one in three islanders living into their 90s. The islanders' longevity is ascribed to long afternoon naps, lots of mountain tea and beans, little coffee and meat, and healthy sex lives into their 80s.

Traditional agrarian life on many islands has given way to tourism-related pursuits, though they often coexist, with families running hotels and tavernas during summer and focusing on agricultural activities in the winter.

Tourism has brought prosperity to many islands, and larger ones including Crete, Rhodes and Corfu have thriving and sophisticated urban centres. Islands with flourishing agricultural industries, such as Lesvos and Chios, are less affected by tourism. Overall, better transport, technology, telecommunications and infrastructure have made life easier and far less isolated for islanders.

Major social and economic disparities still exist, however, even within islands and island groups. Cosmopolitan Mykonos, for example, is a far cry from smaller, remote islands where many people live frugally in a time warp of traditional island life.

Winter can be especially tough for people living on isolated islands without airports or regular ferry services. On some islands, people move back to Athens after the tourist season, while on larger islands, some locals move from the beach resorts back to mountain villages and larger towns with schools and services. While many young people once left for work and educational opportunities on the mainland, some are now returning to their family homes due to high unemployment. Others are looking for work abroad.

The islanders have been feeling the crunch of Greece's economic woes, with domestic tourism declining as Greeks curtail holidays and eating out, and international tourism has been impacted by the media's recurring portrayal of a country in crisis.

Regional Identity

In a country where regional identities remain deep-rooted, Greek islanders often identify with their island (and their village) first – as Cretans, Ithacans or Kastellorizians etc – and as Greeks second. Islanders living in Athens or abroad invariably maintain a strong connection to their ancestral towns and villages, and regularly return during holidays.

Customs, traditions and even the characteristics of the people vary from island to island, influenced by their particular history and topography, which is reflected in everything from the cuisine and architecture to music and dance.

In the Ionians, Corfu escaped Turkish rule and has a more Italian, French and British influence, and its people retain an aristocratic air. The Cretans are renowned for their independent streak and hospitality, and have perhaps the most enduring and distinctive folk culture and traditions, as well as their own dialect.

In villages such as Olymbos in far-eastern Karpathos, many women still wear traditional dress, including headscarves and goatskin boots. Sifnos is renowned for its unique pottery tradition; on Chios the mastic tree has spawned its own industry; Lesvos is the home of ouzo; while Kalymnos' sponge-diving industry shaped the island's identity as much as fishing and agriculture have forged those of others.

Greece is a largely urban society, with over 80% of its population living in cities, and around a third in the Greater Athens area alone. Less than 15% live on the islands, the most populous of which are Crete, Evia and Corfu.

Changing Faces

Greece has long been a magnet for foreigners seeking an idyllic island lifestyle and an escape from the rat race. Apart from those owning holiday houses, the small resident population of disparate *xenoi* (foreigners) has largely been made up of somewhat eccentric or retired Europeans, ex-hippies and artists, or people married to locals as a result of summer romances. In recent years, there has also been a steady stream of Americans, Australians and others with Greek heritage returning to their ancestral islands.

But Greece has also become home to many of the economic migrants who have settled here since the 1990s, when the country suddenly changed from a nation of emigration to one of immigration. Today it also struggles with an ever-growing number of asylum seekers.

Greece's own population only grows through immigration, with immigrants accounting for a quarter of the workforce. Economic decline, concerns about immigrant crime and urban degradation have fuelled xenophobia and extremism, sparking anti-immigrant rallies and growing hostility towards immigrants.

First published in 1885, James Theodore Bent's *The Cyclades, or Life Among the Insular Greeks* is a classic account of island life. John Freely's more recent *The Cyclades* (2006) is rich on history and insight.

Family Life

Greek society remains dominated by family and kinship. Extended family plays an important role, with grandparents often looking after grandchildren while parents work or socialise. Many working Athenians send their children to their grandparents on the islands for the summer.

Greeks attach great importance to education, determined to provide their children the opportunities many of them lacked. English and other languages are widely spoken. Over 37,000 Greeks were studying in foreign universities in 2017, making the country seventh in the world in proportion to its total population.

It's still uncommon for young people to move out of home before marrying, unless they leave to study or work, which is inevitable on most islands, where employment and educational opportunities are limited. While this is slowly changing among professionals, with people marrying later, low wages and persistent unemployment are also keeping young Greeks at home. Traditionally, parents strive to provide homes for their children when they get married, often building apartments for each child above their own.

Despite the machismo, Greece has very much a matriarchal society and the male-female dynamic throws up some interesting paradoxes. Men love to give the impression that they rule the roost but, in reality, it's the women who often run the show both at home and in family businesses. Greek women (at least the older generation) are famously houseproud and take pride in their culinary skills. It's still relatively rare for men to be involved in housework or cooking.

In conservative provincial towns and villages, many women maintain traditional roles, though women's agricultural cooperatives play a leading role in regional economies and in the preservation of cultural heritage. Things are far more liberal for women living in bigger towns.

The Greek Character

Greek islanders have by necessity been relatively autonomous, but they share with the mainland a common history that spans centuries, as well as typical traits of the Greek character.

Years of hardship and isolation have made islanders stoic and resourceful, but they are also friendly and laid-back. Like most Greeks, they are fiercely independent, patriotic and proud of their heritage. They pride themselves on their *filotimo* (dignity and sense of honour), and their *filoxenia* (hospitality), which you will find in even the poorest household.

Forthright and argumentative, most Greeks will freely state their opinions and talk about personal matters rather than engage in polite small talk. Few subjects are off limits, from your private life and why you don't have children, to how much you earn or what you paid for your house or shoes. Greeks are also notoriously late (turning up to an appointment on time is often referred to as 'being English').

Personal freedom and democratic rights are almost sacrosanct, and there is residual mistrust of authority and disrespect for the state. Rules and regulations are routinely ignored or seen as a challenge. Patronage and nepotism are rife, an enduring byproduct of having to rely on personal networks to survive during years of foreign masters and meddlers, civil war and political instability (though graft and corruption are its more extreme form). The notion of the greater good often plays second fiddle to personal interests, and there is little sense of collective responsibility.

While Greeks will mercilessly malign their own government and society, they are defensive about external criticism and can be fervently patriotic and nationalistic.

Faith & Identity

The Orthodox faith is the official religion of Greece and a key element of Greek identity and culture. During foreign occupations the church was the principal upholder of Greek culture, language and traditions. The church still exerts significant social, political and economic influence.

Religious rituals are a part of daily life on the islands. You will notice people making the sign of the cross when they pass a church; compliments to babies and adults are followed by the *ftou ftou* (spitting) gesture to ward off the evil eye. Many Greeks will go to a church when they have a problem, to light a candle or leave a *tama* (votive offering) for the relevant saint.

Most of Greece's shipping dynasties hail from the islands – more than a third from Chios and nearby Inousses, where they own many grand mansions. Shipping families also own the private islands of Spetsopoula (Niarchos) and Skorpios (where Aristotle Onassis married Jackie Kennedy).

During the annual sheep blessing in the Cretan village of Asi Gonia on 23 April, local shepherds bring their flock to be blessed at the church of Agios Yiorgos. Then they milk them and hand out fresh milk to everyone gathered.

The Greek year is centred on the saints' days and festivals of the church calendar (every other day seems to be dedicated to a saint or martyr). Name days (celebrating your namesake saint) are more important than birthdays, and baptisms are an important rite. Most people are named after a saint, as are boats, towns and mountain peaks.

The islands are dotted with hundreds of churches and private chapels built to protect their seafaring families. You will also see many iconostases (tiny chapels) on the roadside, which are either shrines to people who died in road accidents or dedications to saints. Island churches and monasteries are open to visitors, but you should always dress appropriately. Men should wear long trousers, and women should cover arms (and cleavage) and wear skirts that reach below the knees.

Most *panigyria* (festivals) on the islands revolve around annual patron saints' days or those of the local church or monastery. Harvest and other agricultural festivals also have a religious base or ritual. Easter is the biggest event of the year, celebrated everywhere with candlelit street processions, midnight fireworks and spit-roasted lamb, with some islands renowned for their particular Easter festivities.

Catholicism has been historically strong in the Cyclades, where Syros and Tinos have some entirely Catholic villages and parishes. A small Jewish community (around 40 people) lives in Rhodes, their roots dating back to the 2nd century AD.

Easter: Island-Style

Easter is a major event on all the islands, with many renowned for their unique Holy Week customs and celebrations – from the bonfires burning Judas effigies in southwestern Crete to the three-day procession of the icon of the Virgin Mary through almost every house and boat on Folcgandros.

The resurrection on Easter Saturday in the village of Vrontados on Chios is celebrated with gusto. During the village's famous *Rouketopolemos* (rocket war), two rival churches on hilltops about 400m apart fire around 60,000 rounds of firework rockets at each other, aiming for the bell towers.

In Corfu, Easter takes on a special grandeur, with evocative candlelit *epitafios* (funeral bier) processions through the streets, accompanied by bands and choirs. A peculiar tradition, dating back to the Venetians, is *botides* on Holy Saturday morning, when people in Corfu Town throw big ceramic pots out of their windows and balconies, smashing them onto the streets below.

Patmos is considered one of the holiest places to celebrate Easter, with many faithful converging for the religious holiday on the island where John is believed to have written the Book of Revelations. A cacophony of fireworks and countless lamb roasts and parties engulf the island.

The Arts

Greece is revered for its artistic and cultural legacy, and the arts remain a vibrant and evolving element of Greek culture, identity and self-expression. Despite, or because of, Greece's recent economic woes, it has seen a palpable burst of artistic activity and creativity. While savage cuts in meagre state-arts funding have some sectors reeling, an alternative cultural scene is fighting back with low-budget films, artist collectives, and small underground theatres and galleries popping up in the capital.

Visual Arts

Byzantine & Renaissance Art

Until the start of the 19th century, the primary art form in Greece was Byzantine religious painting. There was little secular artistic output under Ottoman rule, during which Greece essentially missed the Renaissance.

Byzantine church frescoes and icons depicted scenes from the life of Christ and figures of the saints. The 'Cretan school' of icon painting, influenced by the Italian Renaissance and artists fleeing to Crete after the fall of Constantinople, combined technical brilliance and dramatic richness. The most famous Cretan-born Renaissance painter is El Greco ('The Greek' in Spanish), née Dominikos Theotokopoulos (1541–1614). He got his grounding in the tradition of late-Byzantine fresco painting before moving to Spain in 1577, where he lived and worked until his death.

Modern Art

Modern Greek art evolved after Independence, when painting became more secular, focusing on portraits, nautical themes and the War of Independence. Major 19th-century painters included Dionysios Tsokos, Theodoros Vryzakis, Nikiforos Lytras and Nicholas Gyzis, a leading artist of the Munich School (where many Greek artists of the day studied).

During the 20th century Greek creatives drew inspiration from worldwide movements and developments in the art world, such as the expressionist George Bouzianis, the cubist Nikos Hatzikyriakos-Ghikas and surrealist and poet Nikos Engonopoulos. Other notable Greek 20th century artists include Konstantinos Parthenis, Fotis Kontoglou, Yiannis Tsarouhis, Panayiotis Tetsis, Yannis Moralis, Dimitris Mytaras and Yiannis Kounellis, a pioneer of the Arte Povera movement.

The National Sculpture & Art Gallery in Athens has the most extensive collection of Greek 20th-century art, with significant collections at the Modern Greek Art Museum on Rhodes and the Museum of Contemporary Art on Andros.

Greece's marble sculpture tradition endures on Tinos, birthplace of renowned sculptors Dimitrios Filippotis (1839–1919) and Yannoulis Halepas (1851–1938), as well as Costas Tsoclis (b 1930), whose work is showcased in the island's Costas Tsoclis Museum.

Athens' metro stations feature an impressive showcase of Greek art from prominent artists including Yannis Gaitis (1923-84; Larisa), the sculptor Giorgos Zongolopoulos (1903-2004; Syntagma) and Alekos Fassianos (b 1935; Metaxourgio), whose work fetches record prices for a living Greek artist.

Contemporary Art Scene

Contemporary Greek art has been gaining exposure in Greece and abroad, with a growing number of Greek artists participating in international art events. The Greek arts scene has become more vibrant, less isolated and more experimental, and Athens' street art is gaining recognition.

Many Greek artists have studied and made their homes and reputations abroad, but a new wave is returning or staying put, contributing to a fresh artistic energy. Watch for work by street artists, Cacao Rocks and INO, the collages of Chryssa Romanos, painter Lucas Samaras, kinetic artist Takis, and sculptor Stephen Antonakos whose works often incorporate neon.

Greeks have had unprecedented exposure to global art through major international exhibitions held in impressive new art venues, small private galleries and artist-run initiatives such as the annual Hydra School Project. Since 2007, Biennales in Athens have put the capital on the international contemporary-arts circuit.

Modern Greek Literature

Greek literature virtually ceased under Ottoman rule, and was then stifled by conflict over language – Ancient Greek versus the vernacular *dimotiki* (colloquial language). The compromise was *katharevousa*, a conservative form of ancient Greek. (*Dimotiki* was made the country's official language in 1976.)

One of the most important works of early Greek literature is the 17th-century 10,012-line epic poem 'Erotokritos', by Crete's Vitsenzos Kornaros. Its 15-syllable rhyming verses are still recited in Crete's famous *mantinadhes* (rhyming couplets) and put to music.

Greece's most celebrated (and translated) 20th-century novelist is Nikos Kazantzakis (1883–1957), whose novels are full of drama and larger-than-life characters, such as the magnificent title character in his 1946 work *Life and Times of Alexis Zorbas* (better known as *Zorba the Greek*). Another great novelist of the time, Stratis Myrivilis (1890–1969), wrote the classics *Vasilis Arvanitis* and *The Mermaid Madonna*.

Eminent 20th-century poets include Egypt-born Constantine Cavafy (1863–1933) and Nobel-prize laureates George Seferis (1900–71) and Odysseus Elytis (1911–96), awarded in 1963 and 1979 respectively.

Other local literary giants of the 20th century include Iakovos Kambanellis (1921–2011), Kostis Palamas (1859–1943), a poet who wrote the words to the *Olympic Hymn*, and poet-playwright Angelos Sikelianos (1884–1951).

British writer Patrick Michael Leigh Fermor (1915–2011) walked across Greece in his late teens, recounting the journey in *The Broken Road – Travels from Bulgaria to Mount Athos* (2013). His other classic Greek travelogues are *Mani: Travels in the Southern Peloponnese* (1958) and *Roumeli: Travels in Northern Greece* (2004).

Contemporary Writers

Greece has a prolific publishing industry but scant fiction is translated into English. Contemporary Greek writers who have made small inroads into foreign markets include Apostolos Doxiadis with his international bestseller *Uncle Petros and Goldbach's Conjecture* (2000) and award-winning children's writer Eugene Trivizas.

Greek publisher Kedros' modern-literature translation series includes Dido Sotiriou's *Farewell Anatolia* (1996), Maro Douka's *Fool's Gold* (1991) and Kostas Mourselas' bestselling *Red-Dyed Hair* (1996), which was made into a popular TV series.

The quirky, Rebus-like Inspector Haritos in Petros Markaris' popular crime series provides an enjoyable insight into crime and corruption in Athens. *Che Committed Suicide* (2010), *Basic Shareholder* (2009), *The Late Night News* (2005) and *Zone Defence* (2007) have been translated into English.

Carving a name for himself as the preeminent literary voice of contemporary Greece is Christos Ikonomou. In both his 2016 collection of short stories, *Something Will Happen, You'll See* (focusing on the lives of poor Athenians) and *Good Will Come from the Sea* (2019; four loosely connected tales set on an unnamed Greek island), the country's economic crisis provides the grim background.

Bypassing the translation issue and writing in English are Panos Karnezis whose books include *The Maze* (2004), *The Birthday Party* (2007) and *The Fugitives* (2015); and Soti Triantafyllou, author of *Poor Margo* (2001) *and Rare Earths* (2013). Other notable contemporary authors available in translation include Alexis Stamatis, who penned *Bar Flaubert* (2000) and *The Book of Rain* (2015), and Vangelis Hatziyannidis, writer of *Four Walls* (2006) and *Stolen Time* (2007).

Plays by Yiorgos Skourtis (b 1940) and Pavlos Matessis (1933–2013) have been translated and performed abroad.

Cinema

Learn all about the ancient Epirotic folk music of northwestern Greece and Albania in *Lament from Epirus* (2018), an inspired travelogue by Christopher King, a Grammy winning producer and avid record collector.

Greek movies have racked up multiple Academy Award nominations over the years, as well as two Palme d'Ors at Cannes for *Missing* (1982) and *Eternity and a Day* (1998) – the latter directed by Theo Angelopoulos (1935–2012), one of Greece's most critically acclaimed filmmakers.

The best known films about the country remain the 1964 Oscar-winner *Zorba the Greek* and *Never on a Sunday* (1960) for which Melina Mercouri won a Cannes festival award. Another classic is Nikos Koundouros' 1956 noir thriller *O Drakos* (*The Fiend of Athens*), regularly voted top Greek film of all time by the Hellenic Film Critics' Association.

In recent years, a new generation of filmmakers has been gaining international attention for what some critics have dubbed the 'weird wave' of Greek cinema. Examples including the award-winning films of Yorgos Lanthimos, some of which are in English (*Alps; The Lobster; The Killing of a Sacred Deer*) and Athina Rachel Tsangari (*Attenburg; Chevalier*).

Ektoras Kygizos' extraordinary *Boy Eating Bird Food* (2012) is an allegory for Greece's recent economic plight, and emblematic of the small, creative collaborations largely produced in the absence of state or industry funding.

Music

Traditional Folk Music

Byzantine music is mostly heard in Greek churches these days, though Byzantine choirs perform in concerts in Greece and abroad, and the music has influenced folk music.

Traditional folk music was shunned by the Greek bourgeoisie after Independence, when they looked to Europe – and classical music and opera – rather than their Eastern or 'peasant' roots.

Greece's regional folk music is generally divided into *nisiotika* (the lighter, upbeat music of the islands) and the more grounded *dimotika* of the mainland – where the *klarino* (clarinet) is prominent and lyrics refer to hard times, war and rural life. The spirited music of Crete, dominated by the Cretan *lyra* (a pear-shaped, three-string, bowed instrument) and lute, remains a dynamic musical tradition, with regular performances and recordings by new-generation exponents.

Laïka & Entehna

Laïka (popular or urban folk music) is Greece's most popular music. A mainstream offshoot of *rembetika* (blues), *laïka* emerged in the late 1950s and '60s, when clubs in Athens became bigger and glitzier, and the music more commercial. The bouzouki went electric and the sentimental tunes about love, loss, pain and emigration came to embody the nation's spirit. The late Stelios Kazantzidis was the big voice of this era, along with Grigoris Bithikotsis.

Classically trained composers Mikis Theodorakis and Manos Hatzidakis led a new style known as *entehni mousiki* ('artistic' music) also known as *entehna*. They drew on *rembetika* and used instruments such as the bouzouki in more symphonic arrangements, and created popular hits from the poetry of Seferis, Elytis, Ritsos and Kavadias.

Composer Yiannis Markopoulos later introduced rural folk music and traditional string instruments such as the *lyra, santouri* and *kanonaki* into the mainstream, and brought folk performers such as Crete's legendary Nikos Xylouris to the fore.

During the junta years the music of Theodorakis and Markopoulos became a form of political expression (Theodorakis' music was banned and the composer jailed). Today, headline *laïka* performers include Yiannis Ploutarhos, Antonis Remos and Thanos Petrelis.

Contemporary & Pop Music

While few Greek performers have made it big internationally – 1970s singers Nana Mouskouri and Demis Roussos remain the best known – Greece has a strong local music scene, from traditional and pop music to Greek rock, heavy metal, rap and electronic dance.

Some of the most interesting music emerging from Greece fuses elements of folk with Western influences. One of the most whimsical examples was Greece's tongue-in-cheek 2013 Eurovision contender, in which *rembetika* (blues) veteran Agathonas Iakovidis teamed up with the ska-Balkan rhythms of Thessaloniki's kilt-wearing Koza Mostra.

REMBETIKA: THE GREEK BLUES

Known as the Greek 'blues', *rembetika* emerged in Greece's urban underground and has strongly influenced the sound of Greek popular music.

Two styles make up what is broadly known as *rembetika*. *Smyrneika* or Cafe Aman music emerged in the mid- to late-19th century in the thriving port cities of Smyrna and Constantinople, which had large Greek populations, and in Thessaloniki, Volos, Syros and Athens. With a rich vocal style, haunting *amanedhes* (vocal improvisations) and occasional Turkish lyrics, its sound had more Eastern influence. Predominant instruments were the violin, *outi* (oud), guitar, mandolin, *kanonaki* and *santouri* (a flat multistringed instrument). The second style, dominated by the six-stringed bouzouki, evolved in Piraeus.

After the influx of refugees from Asia Minor in Piraeus following the 1922 population exchange (many also went to America, where *rembetika* was recorded in the 1920s), the two styles somewhat overlapped and *rembetika* became the music of the ghettos. Infused with defiance, nostalgia and lament, the songs reflected life's bleaker themes and *manges* (streetwise outcasts) who sang and danced in the *tekedhes* (hash dens that inspired many songs).

In the mid-1930s, the Metaxas dictatorship tried to wipe out the subculture through censorship, police harassment and raids on *tekedhes*. People were arrested for carrying a bouzouki. Many artists stopped performing and recording, though the music continued clandestinely. After WWII, a new wave of *rembetika* emerged that eliminated much of its seedy side.

Rembetika legends include Markos Vamvakaris, who became popular with the first bouzouki group in the early 1930s, composer Vasilis Tsitsanis, Apostolos Kaldaras, Yiannis Papaioannou, Giorgos Mitsakis and Apostolos Hatzihristou, and the songstresses Sotiria Bellou and Marika Ninou, whose life inspired Costas Ferris' 1983 film *Rembetiko*.

Interest in genuine *rembetika* was revived in the late 1970s to early 1980s – particularly among students and intellectuals – and it continues to be rediscovered by new generations.

Rembetika ensembles perform seated in a row and traditionally play acoustically. A characteristic feature is an improvised introduction called a *taxim*.

Big names in popular Greek music include Dionysis Savopoulos, dubbed the Bob Dylan of Greece, and seasoned performers George Dalaras and Haris Alexiou.

Standout contemporary performers include Cypriot-born Alkinoos Ioannides, folk singer Eleftheria Arvanitakiis, ethnic-jazz-fusion artists Kristi Stasinopoulou and the Cretan-inspired folk group Haïnides. Also check out Imam Baildi (www.imambaildi.com), a band who give old Greek music a modern makeover.

The local pop scene sees a steady stream of performers creating a uniquely Greek sound. Listen for Σtella (http://stellawithasigma.com), Sarah P (one half of the Athenian chillwave duo Keep Shelley), and Marina Satti (a young Greek-Sudanese singer who does a terrific dance cover of the *rembetika* 'Koupes').

Classical Music & Opera

Despite classical music and opera appealing to an (albeit growing) minority of Greeks, this field is where Greece has made the most significant international contribution, most notably composers Mikis Theodorakis and Manos Hatzidakis and opera diva Maria Callas.

Dimitris Mitropoulos led the New York Philharmonic in the 1950s, while distinguished composers include Stavros Xarhakos and the late Yannis Xenakis. Leading contemporary performers include pianist Dimitris Sgouros, tenor Mario Frangoulis and sopranos Elena Kelessidi and Irini Tsirakidou. Teodor Currentzis (b 1972) is a Greek conductor who is Artistic Director of Russia's Perm Tchaikovsky State Opera and Ballet Theatre.

The country's concert halls and major cultural festivals such as the Hellenic Festival offer rich international programs, while opera buffs have the Greek National Opera and Syros' Apollo Theatre.

Greek Dance

Greeks have danced since the dawn of Hellenism. Some folk dances derive from the ritual dances performed in ancient temples – ancient vases depict a version of the well-known *syrtos* folk dance. Dancing was later part of military education; in times of occupation it became an act of defiance and a covert way to keep fit.

Regional dances, like musical styles, vary across Greece. The slow and dignified *tsamikos* reflects the often cold and insular nature of mountain life, while the brighter islands gave rise to light, springy dances such as the *ballos* and the *syrtos*. The Pontian Greeks' vigorous and warlike dances such as the *kotsari* reflect years of altercations with their Turkish neighbours. Crete has its graceful *syrtos*, the fast and triumphant *maleviziotiko* and the dynamic *pentozali,* with its agility-testing high kicks and leaps. The so-called 'Zorba dance', or *syrtaki,* is a stylised dance for two or three dancers with arms linked on each other's shoulders, though the modern variation is danced in a long circle with an ever-quickening beat. Women and men traditionally danced separately and had their own dances, except in courtship dances such as the *sousta*.

Folk-dance groups throughout Greece preserve regional traditions. The best place to see folk dancing is at regional festivals and the Dora Stratou Dance Theatre in Athens.

Contemporary dance is gaining prominence in Greece, with leading local troupes taking their place among the international line-up at the Athens International Dance Festival.

Athens' live-music scene includes glitzy, cabaret-style venues known as *bouzoukia* notorious for flower-throwing (plate-smashing is rare these days), expensive displays of excess and exuberant *kefi* (good spirits). Second-rate *bouzoukia* clubs are referred to as *skyladhika* (doghouses) because the crooning singers resemble a whining dog.

Men dance the often spectacular solo *zeïmbekiko* – whirling, meditative improvisations with roots in *rembetika* (blues). Women do the sensuous *tsifteteli,* a svelte, sinewy show of femininity evolved from the Middle Eastern belly dance.

Architecture

Cast your eyes around most major cities and you'll find various reinterpretations of classical Greek architecture. The Renaissance was inspired by the ancient style, as was the neoclassical movement and the British Greek Revival. For those with an eye to the past, part of the allure of Greece is the sheer volume of its well-preserved buildings. Stand in the ruins of the Parthenon and with a little imagination it's easy to transport yourself back to classical 5th-century Greece.

Minoan Magnificence

Most of our knowledge of Greek architecture proper begins at around 2000 BC with the Minoans, who were based in Crete but whose influence spread throughout the Aegean to include the Cyclades. Minoan architects are famous for having constructed technologically advanced, labyrinthine palace complexes. The famous site at Knossos is one of the largest. Usually characterised as 'palaces', these sites were in fact multi-functional settlements that were the primary residences of royalty and priests, but housed some plebs too. Large Minoan villages, such as those of Gournia and Palekastro in Crete, also included internal networks of paved roads that extended throughout the countryside to link the settlements with the palaces. More Minoan palace-era sophistication exists in Crete at Phaestos, Malia and Ancient Zakros, and at the Minoan outpost of Ancient Akrotiri on the south of Santorini.

Several gigantic volcanic eruptions rocked the region in the mid-15th century BC, causing geological ripple effects that at the very least caused big chunks of palace to fall to the ground. The Minoans resolutely rebuilt on an even grander scale, only to have more natural disasters wipe the palaces out again. The latter effected an architectural chasm that was filled by the emerging Mycenaean rivals on mainland Greece.

According to myth, the man tasked with designing a maze to withhold the dreaded Minotaur was famous Athenian inventor Daedalus, father of Icarus. He also designed the Palace of Knossos for King Minos.

Grandeur of Knossos

First discovered by a Cretan, Milos Kalokirinos, in 1878, it wasn't until 1900 that the ruins of Knossos were unearthed by Englishman Sir Arthur Evans. The elaborate palace complex at Knossos was originally formed largely as an administrative settlement surrounding the main palace, which comprised the main buildings arranged around a large central courtyard (1250 sq metres). Over time the entire settlement was rebuilt and extended. Long, raised causeways formed main corridors; narrow labyrinthine chambers flanked the palace walls (this meandering floor plan, together with the graphic ritual importance of bulls, inspired the myth of the labyrinth and the Minotaur). The compound featured strategically placed interior light wells, sophisticated ventilation systems, aqueducts, freshwater irrigation wells and bathrooms with extensive plumbing and drainage systems. The ground levels consisted mostly of workshops, cylindrical grain silos and storage magazines.

Thanks to its restoration, today's Knossos is one of the easiest ruins for your imagination to take hold of.

The distinctive blue-and-white Cycladic-style architecture most associated with the Greek islands was pragmatic and functional. The cuboid flat-roofed houses, huddled together along labyrinthine alleys, were designed to guard against the elements: strong winds and pirates.

Classic Compositions

The classical age (5th to 4th centuries BC) is when most Greek architectural clichés converge. This is when temples became characterised by the famous orders of columns, particularly the Doric, Ionic and Corinthian.

In the meantime, the Greek colonies of the Asia Minor coast were creating their own Ionic order, designing a column base in several tiers and adding more flutes. This more graceful order's capital (the head) received an ornamented necking, and Iktinos fused elements of its design in the Parthenon. This order is used on the Acropolis' Temple of Athena Nike and the Erechtheion, where the famous Caryatids sculptures regally stand.

Towards the tail end of the classical period, the Corinthian column was in vogue. Featuring a single or double row of ornate leafy scrolls (usually the very sculptural acanthus), the order was subsequently adopted by the Romans and used only on Corinthian temples in Athens. The Temple of Olympian Zeus, completed during Emperor Hadrian's reign, is a grand, imposing structure.

The Greek theatre design is a hallmark of the classical period (an example is Odeon of Herodes Atticus in Athens) and had a round stage, radiating a semicircle of steeply banked stone benches that seated many thousands. Cleverly engineered acoustics meant every spectator could monitor every syllable uttered on the stage below. Many ancient Greek theatres are still used for summer festivals, music concerts and plays.

Hellenistic Citizens

In the twilight years of the classical age (from about the late 4th century BC), cosmopolitan folks started to weary of temples, casting their gaze towards a more decadent urban style. The Hellenistic architect was in hot demand for private homes and palace makeovers as wealthy citizens, dignitaries and political heavyweights lavishly remodelled their abodes in marble, and striking mosaics were displayed as status symbols. The best Hellenistic ancient-home displays are the grand houses at Delos.

Byzantine Zeal

Church-building was particularly expressive during the time of the Byzantine Empire in Greece (from around AD 700 to the early 13th century). The original Greek Byzantine model features a distinctive cross shape – essentially a central dome supported by four arches on piers and flanked by vaults, with smaller domes at the four corners and three apses to the east. Theologian architects opted for spectacular devotional mosaics and frescoes instead of carvings for the stylistic religious interiors.

THE COLUMNS OF ANCIENT GREECE

Columns are columns are columns, right? Recognising the differences between them is, in fact, the easiest way to differentiate between the three distinct architectural orders of Ancient Greece.

Doric The most simple of the three styles. The shaft (the main part of the column) is plain and has 20 sides, while the capital (the head) is formed in a simple circle. Also there's no base. An obvious example of this is the Parthenon.

Ionic Look out for the ridged flutes carved into the column from top to bottom. The capital is also distinctive for its scrolls, while the base looks like a stack of rings.

Corinthian The most decorative and popular of all three orders. The column is ridged; however, the distinctive feature is the capital's flowers and leaves, beneath a small scroll. The base is like that of the Ionic.

PROVINCIAL ORIGINALS

Considering the historical mishmash of cultural influences peppered across Greece, alongside a varying landscape, it's hardly surprising to find unique variations in architectural design.

Pyrgi See the medieval, labyrinthine, vaulted island village of Pyrgi in Chios, for its unique Genoese designs of intricate, geometric, grey-and-white facades.

Oia Squint at the volcanic rock–hewn clifftop village of Oia in Santorini, with its dazzlingly whitewashed island streetscapes and homes.

Lefkada Town Discover the strangely attractive wooden-framed houses of Lefkada Town: the lower floors are panelled in wood, while the upper floors are lined in painted sheet metal or corrugated iron.

In Athens, the very appealing 12th-century Church of Agios Eleftherios incorporates fragments of a classical frieze in Pentelic marble; the charming 11th-century Church of Kapnikarea sits stranded, smack-bang in the middle of downtown Athens – its interior flooring is of coloured marble, and the external brickwork, which alternates with stone, is set in patterns.

Venetian & Ottoman Influences

From the mid-14th century until the late 18th century, the Venetians held control of several parts of modern day Greece. They built the impenetrable 16th-century Koules fortress in Iraklio and, despite the devastating 1953 earthquake that razed much of Kefallonia's Venetian architecture, there are distinct traces of Italianate style in the seaside villages of Fiskardo and Assos.

Interestingly, remarkably few monuments are left to catalogue after four centuries of Ottoman Turkish rule (16th to 19th centuries). Though many mosques and their minarets have sadly crumbled or are in serious disrepair, some terrific Ottoman-Turkish examples still survive. These include the prominent pink-domed Mosque of Süleyman in Rhodes Old Town. The Fethiye Mosque and Turkish Baths are two of Athens' few surviving Ottoman reminders.

Neoclassical Splendour

Regarded by experts as the most beautiful neoclassical building worldwide, the 1885 Athens Academy reflects Greece's post-Independence yearnings for grand and geometric forms, and Hellenistic detail. Renowned Danish architect Theophile Hansen drew inspiration from the Erechtheion to design the Academy's Ionic-style column entrance (guarded over by Apollo and Athena); the great interior oblong hall is lined with marble seating, and Austrian painter Christian Griepenkerl was commissioned to decorate its elaborate ceiling and wall paintings. In a similar vein, the Doric columns of the Temple of Hephaestus influenced Theophile's solid-marble National Library, while Christian Hansen (Theophile's brother) was responsible for the handsome but more sedate Athens University, with its clean lines.

Meticulously restored neoclassical mansions house notable museums such as the acclaimed Benaki Museum in Athens.

Many provincial towns also display beautiful domestic adaptations of neoclassicism. In Symi, the harbour at Gialos is flanked by colourful neoclassical facades - still striking even if a little derelict.

The mother of all Doric structures is the 5th-century-BC Parthenon, the ultimate in ancient architectural bling. To this day, it's probably the most obsessively photographed and painted structure in all of Greece.

THE CAPTAIN'S HOUSE

During the 17th century, Greek ship captains grew increasingly prosperous. Many of them poured their newfound wealth into building lofty homes that towered over the traditional village houses. These captains' houses are now dotted throughout the islands and many have been given a new lease on life as boutique hotels or restaurants.

While the size of the house often reflected the wealth of a captain, some of the smallest of these 400-year-old homes are the most grand. Captain's houses didn't need to be large as they spent so much time at sea. Whitewashed walls stretch upward to the soaring resin ceiling, often intricately painted with elaborate, colourful patterns. The windows are sea-facing and placed very high, often with wooden lofts to reach them. This was to let the heat out in summer and also so the captain's wife could watch the sea for the arrival of her husband's ship. The traditional *pyliones* (stone doorways) are hand-carved with symbolic pictures. Corn means good harvest, birds mean peace, the cross brings safety and the sunflowers sunlight. The number of ropes carved around the perimeter of the door shows how many ships the captain had.

Some of the finest examples of these houses are found in Lindos, on Rhodes.

Modern & Contemporary Ideas

Recently, Athens has embraced a sophisticated, look-both-ways architectural aesthetic to showcase its vast collection of antiquities and archaeological heritage and to beautify landscapes for pedestrian zones to improve the urban environment. Examples include the well-designed facelift of the historic centre, including its spectacular floodlighting (designed by the renowned Pierre Bideau) of the ancient promenade, and the cutting-edge spaces emerging from once-drab and derelict industrial zones, such as the Technopolis gasworks arts complex in Gazi.

The predominant motif of late-20th-century urban Greek architecture is the *polykatoikia* (multiresidence) apartment block. In Athens alone around 35,000 five-storey cement blocks with awning-shaded balconies were erected between the 1950s and 1980s.

The Acropolis Museum, designed by Bernard Tschumi and opened in 2009, features an internal glass cella (inner room) mirroring the Parthenon with the same number of columns (clad in steel) and a glass floor overlooking excavated ruins in situ.

Built for the 2004 Olympics, the Athens Olympic Complex was designed by Spanish architect Santiago Calatrata. It has a striking, ultra-modern glass-and-steel roof, which is suspended by cables from large arches. The laminated glass, in the shape of two giant leaves, is capable of reflecting 90% of the sunlight.

Even more impressive is the Stavros Niarchos Foundation Cultural Center (SNFCC) which generates 100% of its energy needs from the 5400 photovoltaic panels on its roof in summer. Designed by Pritzker Prize–winning architect Renzo Piano, the SNFCC, which opened in 2016, houses the National Library of Greece and the National Opera amid a beautiful and sustainably designed park with both city and sea views.

French firm Architecture Studio designed the Onassis Cultural Centre, a performance and exhibition space that opened in 2010. The building's facade is wrapped in strips of marble across which images can be projected.

Nature & Wildlife

Greece is an ideal location for getting up close to nature. Hike through valleys and mountains covered with wildflowers, come eye to eye with a loggerhead turtle or simply stretch out on a beach. Environmental awareness is beginning to seep into the fabric of Greek society, leading to slow but positive change. However, problems such as deforestation and soil erosion date back thousands of years. Live cultivation, goats, construction and industry have all taken their toll.

Experiencing the Outdoors

Geography & Geology

No matter where you go in Greece, it's impossible to be much more than 100km from the sea. Rugged mountains and seemingly innumerable islands dominate the landscape, which was shaped by submerging seas, volcanic explosions and mineral-rich terrain.

The mainland covers 131,944 sq km, with an indented coastline stretching for 15,020km. Mountains rise over 2000m and occasionally tumble down into plains. Meanwhile, the Aegean and Ionian Seas link together the country's 1400 islands, with just 169 of them inhabited. These islands fill 400,000 sq km of territorial waters.

During the Triassic, Jurassic, Cretaceous and even later geological periods, Greece was a shallow, oxygen-rich sea. The continuous submerging of land created large tracts of limestone through the whole submarine land mass. Later, as the land emerged from the sea to form the backbone of the current topography, a distinctly eroded landscape with crystalline rocks and other valuable minerals began to appear, marking the spine that links the north and south of the mainland today. Limestone caves are a major feature of this karst landscape, shaped by the dissolution of a soluble layer of bedrock.

Volcanic activity regularly hits Greece. In 1999 a 5.9-magnitude earthquake near Athens killed nearly 150 people and left thousands homeless. Since 2006, the country has had seven quakes ranging from 6.4 to 6.9 in magnitude. None caused major damage. To check out Greece's explosive past, visit the craters of Santorini, Nisyros and Polyvotis.

Greece is short on rivers, with none that are navigable, although those that do exist have become popular locations for white-water rafting. The long plains of the river valleys, and those between the mountains and the coast, form Greece's only lowlands. The mountainous terrain, dry climate and poor soil leave farmers at a loss, and less than 25% of the land is cultivated. Greece is, however, rich in minerals, with reserves of oil, manganese, bauxite and lignite.

Around 1650 BC, the island of Santorini (Thira) experienced one of the largest volcanic events in Earth's recorded history, ejecting up to four times as much matter as the eruption of Krakatoa in 1883.

Wildflowers & Herbs

Greece is endowed with a variety of flora unrivalled in Europe. The wildflowers are spectacular, with more than 6000 species, including more than 200 varieties of orchid. They continue to thrive because most of the land is inadequate for intensive agriculture and has therefore escaped the ravages of chemical fertilisers.

One of the regions with the most wildflowers is the Lefka Ori (White Mountains) in Crete. Trees begin to blossom as early as the end of February in warmer areas and the wildflowers start to appear in March. During spring, hillsides are carpeted with flowers, which seem to sprout even from the rocks. By summer the flowers have disappeared from everywhere but the northern mountainous regions. Autumn brings a new period of blossoming.

Herbs grow wild throughout much of Greece and you'll see locals out picking fresh herbs for their kitchen. Locally grown herbs are also increasingly sold as souvenirs and are generally organic.

Herbs in Cooking is an illustrative book by Maria and Nikos Psilakis that can be used as both an identification guide and a cookbook for Greek dishes seasoned with local herbs.

Forests

The lush forests that once covered ancient Greece are increasingly rare. Having been decimated by thousands of years of clearing for grazing, boatbuilding and housing, they've more recently suffered from severe forest fires. Northern Greece is the only region that has retained significant areas of native forest – there are mountainsides covered with dense thickets of hop hornbeam (Ostrya carpinifolia), noted for its lavish display of white-clustered flowers. Another common species is the Cyprus plane (Platanus orientalis insularis), which thrives wherever there's ample water.

Watching for Wildlife

On the Ground

In areas widely inhabited by humans, you're unlikely to spot any wild animals other than the odd fox, weasel, hare or rabbit. The more remote mountain areas of Greece continue to support a wide range of wildlife, including wild dogs and shepherds' dogs, which often roam higher pastures on grazing mountains and should be given a wide berth.

The golden jackal is a strong candidate for Greece's most misunderstood mammal. Although its diet is 50% vegetarian (the other 50% is made up of carrion, reptiles and small mammals), it has traditionally

NATIONAL PARKS

National parks were first established in Greece in 1938 with the creation of Mt Olympus National Park. There are now 10 national parks and two marine parks, which aim to protect Greece's unique flora and fauna.

Facilities for visitors are often basic, abundant walking trails are not always maintained and the clutch of refuges is very simple. To most, the facilities matter little when compared to nature's magnificent backdrop. It's well worth experiencing the wild side of Greece in one of these settings.

The ones covered in this guide are:

National Marine Park of Alonnisos Northern Sporades (p500) Covers six islands and 22 islets in the Sporades and is home to monk seals, dolphins and rare birdlife.

Samaria Gorge (p324) Spectacular gorge in Crete and a refuge for the *kri-kri* (Cretan goat).

Cape Sounion (p147) A cape with panoramic views and home to the Temple of Poseidon.

National Marine Park of Zakynthos (NMPZ; ☏26950 29870; www.nmp-zak.org) An Ionian refuge for loggerhead turtles.

Ainos National Park The only island park, on Kefallonia (p532), the stand of forest here is home to a single species of endemic fir and small wild horses.

DON'T BE A BOAR

Greece's relationship with its wildlife has not been a happy one. Hunting wild animals is a popular Greek activity, as a means of providing food. This is particularly true in mountainous regions where the partisanship of hunters is legendary. Despite signs forbidding hunting, Greek hunters often shoot freely at any potential game. While this can include rare and endangered species, the main game is often wild boars, which have been around since antiquity. Considered destructive and cunning animals, wild boars have increased in number in recent decades, likely due to a lower number of predators. Many argue that hunting is an important means of culling them. There is also an increasing number of boar breeding farms, with boar showing up on many menus.

shouldered much of the blame for attacks on stock and has been hunted by farmers as a preventative measure. Near the brink of extinction, it was declared a protected species in 1990 and now survives only in small clusters on mainland Greece and Samos Island.

Originally brought to the island of Skyros in the 5th century BC by colonists, the diminutive Skryrian horses are an ancient breed that became wild once they had been replaced by agricultural mechanisation. You'll also see these horses featured in the Parthenon friezes. Around 190 survive on the island, approximately 70% of their global population. Mouries Farm is home to 45 Skyrian horses.

Greece has an active snake population and in spring and summer you will inevitably spot them on roads and pathways around the country. Fortunately the majority are harmless, though the viper and the coral snake can cause fatalities. Lizards are in abundance too.

In the Air

Birdwatchers hit the jackpot in Greece as much of the country is on north–south migratory paths.

Lesvos (Mytilini) in particular draws a regular following of birders from all over Europe, who come to spot some of more than 279 recorded species that stop at the island annually. Storks are more visible visitors, arriving in early spring from Africa and returning to the same nests year after year. These are built on electricity poles, chimney tops and church towers, and can weigh up to 50kg.

Over 350 pairs of the rare Eleonora's falcon (60% of the world's population) nest on the island of Piperi in the Sporades and on Tilos, which is also home to the very rare Bonelli's eagle and the shy, cormorant-like Mediterranean shag.

Under the Sea

One of Europe's most endangered marine mammals, the Mediterranean monk seal (*Monachus monachus*) ekes out an extremely precarious existence in Greece. Approximately 200 to 250 monk seals, about 50% of the world's population, are found in both the Ionian and Aegean Seas. Small colonies also live on the island of Alonnisos and there have been reported sightings on Tilos.

The waters around Zakynthos are home to the last large sea-turtle colony in Europe, that of the endangered loggerhead turtle (*Caretta caretta*). Loggerheads also nest in smaller numbers on Kefallonia and Crete. Greece's turtles have many hazards to dodge: entanglement in fishing nets and boat propellers, consumption of floating rubbish, and the destruction of their nesting beaches by sunloungers and beach umbrellas which threaten their eggs. It doesn't help that the turtles' nesting time coincides with the European summer-holiday season.

There is still the chance that you will spot dolphins from a ferry deck, though a number of the species, including common dolphins (*Delphinus*

Wildlife Websites

Pelicans and pygmy cormorants (www.spp.gr)

Birdlife (www. ornithologiki.gr)

Wildflowers (www. greekmountain flora.info)

Sea turtles (www. archelon.gr)

Loggerhead-turtle hatchlings use the journey from the nest to the sea to build up their strength. Helping the baby turtles to the sea can actually lower their chances of survival.

delphis) and Risso's dolphins (*Grampus griseus*) are now considered endangered. The main threats to dolphins are a diminished food supply and entanglement in fishing nets.

Environmental Issues

Illegal development of mainly coastal areas, and building in forested or protected areas, has gained momentum in Greece since the 1970s. Despite attempts at introducing laws, and protests by locals and environmental groups, corruption and the lack of an infrastructure to enforce the laws means little is done to abate the land-grab. The issue is complicated by population growth and increased urban sprawl. Developments often put a severe strain on water supplies and endangered wildlife. While a few developments have been torn down, in more cases illegal buildings are legalised as they offer much needed, affordable housing.

The lifting of the diesel ban in Athens in 2012 decreased air quality as people opted for cheaper transport. As heating oil tripled in price, people turned to burning wood, often treated, as well as garbage to keep warm. Wintertime particle pollution increased by 30% on some evenings, with lead and arsenic particles found in the air. Smog is a particular problem in Athens as the greater metropolitan area hosts over half of the country's industry, not to mention the lion's share of Greece's population. Athens has subsequently pledged to ban all diesel vehicles from its city centre by 2025.

Each year, forest fires rage across Greece, destroying many thousands of hectares, often in some of the country's most picturesque areas. During the summer of 2018 a series of wildfires across coastal areas of Attica, not far from Athens, claimed 102 lives, making it Greece's most deadly natural disaster.

The increasing scale of recent fires is blamed on rising Mediterranean temperatures and high winds. Many locals argue that the government is ill-prepared and that its attempts to address the annual fires are slow. Fearing they won't receive help, many locals refuse to leave areas being evacuated, preferring to take the risk and attempting to fight the flames themselves.

Greece's recycling rate is 17%, below the European Union average of 39%. In the main cities and towns, however, you will find recycling bins to dispose of paper, plastic, aluminium and other packaging.

Survival Guide

Directory A–Z

Accessible Travel

Access for travellers with disabilities has improved somewhat in recent years, though mostly in Athens where there are more accessible sights, hotels and restaurants. Much of the rest of Greece, with its abundance of stones, marble, slippery cobbles and stepped alleys, remains inaccessible or difficult for wheelchair users. People who have visual or hearing impairments are also rarely catered to.

Careful planning before you go can make a world of difference.

Travel Guide to Greece (www. greecetravel.com/handicapped) Links to local articles, resorts and tour groups catering to tourists with physical disabilities.

DR Yachting (www.disabled sailingholidays.com) Two-day to two-week sailing trips around the Greek islands in fully accessible yachts.

Sirens Resort (www.disableds -resort.gr) Family-friendly resort with accessible apartments, tours and ramps into the sea.

Download Lonely Planet's free Accessible Travel guides from http://lptravel.to/ AccessibleTravel.

Accommodation

Greece's plethora of accommodation means that, whatever your taste or budget, there is somewhere to suit your needs. All places to stay are subject to strict price controls set by the tourist police. It's difficult to generalise accommodation prices in Greece as rates depend entirely onseason and location. Don't expect to pay the same price for a double room on one of the islands as you would in central Greece or Athens.

When considering hotel prices, take note of the following points.

➡ Prices include community tax and VAT (value-added tax).

➡ An Overnight Stay Tax of between €0.50 and €4 depending on the star rating of your accommodation will also be added per night.

➡ A mandatory charge of 20% is levied for an additional bed (although this is often waived if the bed is for a child).

➡ During July and August accommodation owners will charge the maximum price, which can be as much as double the low-season price. In spring and autumn prices can drop by 20%.

➡ Also during high season there may be a two- or three-night minimum reservation policy, particularly at accommodation in the most popular islands and resorts.

➡ Rip-offs are rare; if you suspect that you have been exploited, make a report to the tourist police or the regular police, and they will act swiftly.

Camping

Camping is a decent option, especially in summer. There are almost 350 campgrounds in Greece, found on the majority of islands (with the notable exception of the Saronic Gulf Islands). Standard facilities include hot showers, kitchens, restaurants and minimarkets – and often a swimming pool.

Most camping grounds are open only between May and October, although always check ahead; in the north in particular, some don't open until June. The **Panhellenic Camping Association** (📞21036 21560; www.greece camping.gr) website lists all of its campgrounds and relevant details.

If you're camping in the height of summer, bring a silver fly sheet to reflect the heat off your tent (dark tents become sweat lodges). Between May and mid-September the weather is warm enough to sleep out under the stars. Many campgrounds have covered areas where tourists who don't have tents can sleep in summer; you can get by with a lightweight sleeping bag. It's a good idea to have a foam pad to lie on, a waterproof cover for your sleeping bag and plenty of bug repellent.

➡ Camping fees are highest from mid-June through to the end of August.

➡ Campgrounds charge €6 to €12 per adult and €3 to €5 for children aged four to 12. There's no charge for children under four.

➡ Tent sites cost from €5 per night.

➡ You can often rent tents for around €5.

➡ Caravan sites start at around €7; car costs are typically €4 to €5.

Domatia

Once upon a time, domatia (literally 'rooms') were little more than spare rooms in the family home; nowadays, many are purpose-built appendages with fully equipped kitchens. Standards of cleanliness are generally high.

Domatia remain a popular option for budget travellers. Expect to pay from €30 to €60 for a single, and €40 to €80 for a double, depending on whether bathrooms are shared or private, the season and how long you plan to stay. Domatia are found throughout the mainland (except in large cities) and on almost every island that has a permanent population. Many domatia are open only between April and October.

From June to September, domatia owners are out in force, touting for customers. They meet buses and boats, shouting 'room, room!' and often carry photographs of their rooms. In peak season it can prove a mistake not to take up an offer – but be wary of owners who are vague about the location of their accommodation.

Hostels

The Greek Youth Hostel Organisation (https://higreece.gr) covers 18 properties across the country including guesthouses and hotels as well as traditional hostels; you don't have to be a member to stay in them but HI membership will give you a 10% discount on rates.

There are many private hostels, too. Rates vary from around €10 to €20 for a bed in a dorm. Few have curfews.

Hotels & Pensions

Hotels in Greece are divided into five categories: one to five stars. Hotels are categorised according to the size of the rooms, whether or not they have a bar, and the ratio of bathrooms to beds, rather than standards of cleanliness, comfort of beds and friendliness of staff – all elements that may be of greater relevance to guests.

5 & 4 star Full amenities, private bathrooms and constant hot water.

3 star A snack bar and rooms with private bathrooms, but not necessarily constant hot water.

2 star Generally have shared bathrooms and they may have solar-heated water, meaning hot water is not guaranteed.

1 star Shared bathrooms and hot water may cost extra.

Mountain Refuges

Mountain refuges are dotted around the Greek mainland, Crete and Evia. They range from small huts with outdoor toilets and no cooking facilities to very comfortable modern lodges. They are run by the country's various mountaineering and skiing clubs. Prices start at around €10 per person, depending on the facilities.

The EOT (Greek National Tourist Organisation; www.visitgreece.gr) publication *Greece: Mountain Refuges & Ski Centres* has details about each refuge; copies are available at all EOT branches. Also see the online maps of the Balkan Mountaineering Union (www.mountain-huts.net).

Rental Accommodation

A practical way to save money and maximise comfort is to rent a furnished apartment or villa. Many are purpose-built for tourists, while others – villas in particular – may be

---

SLEEPING PRICE RANGES

The following price ranges refer to a double room with private bathroom in high season (May to August).

€ less than €60 (less than €90 in Athens)

€€ €60–150 (€90–185 in Athens)

€€€ more than €150 (more than €185 in Athens)

BOOK YOUR STAY ONLINE

For more accommodation reviews by Lonely Planet authors, check out http://lonelyplanet.com/hotels/. You'll find independent reviews, as well as recommendations on the best places to stay. Best of all, you can book online.

owners' homes that they are not using. Some owners insist on a minimum stay of a week.

Airbnb (www.airbnb.com) also has lots of rental properties listed in Greece and can be a great way to hunt down reasonable accommodation if you're planning to stay in one location for more than a couple of nights. Also check out sites such as www.mygreek-villa.com and www.prettygreekvillas.com.

Customs Regulations

There are no duty-free restrictions within the EU. Upon entering Greece from outside the EU, customs inspection is usually cursory for foreign tourists and a verbal declaration is generally all that is required. Random searches are still occasionally made for drugs. Import regulations for medicines are strict; if you are taking medication, make sure you get a statement from your doctor before you leave home. It is illegal, for instance, to take codeine into Greece without an accompanying doctor's certificate.

It is strictly forbidden in Greece to acquire and export antiquities without special permits issued by the Hellenic Ministry of Culture/General Directorate of Antiquities and Cultural Heritage (gda@culture.gr). Severe smuggling penalties might be incurred. It is an offence to remove even the smallest article from an archaeological site.

Discount Cards

Camping Card International (CCI; www.campingcardinter

national.com) Gives up to 25% savings in camping fees and third-party liability insurance while in the campground. Valid in over 2500 campsites across Europe.

European Youth Card (www.eyca.org) Available for anyone up to the age of 26 or 31, depending on the country. You don't have to be a resident of Europe. It provides discounts of up to 20% at sights, shops and for some transport. Available from the website or travel agencies in Athens and Thessaloniki for €14.

International Student Identity Card (ISIC; www.isic.org) Entitles the holder to half-price admission to museums and ancient sites, and discounts at some budget hotels and hostels. Available from travel agencies in Athens. Applicants require documents proving their student status, a passport photo and €15. Available to students aged 12 to 30.

Seniors cards Card-carrying EU pensioners can claim a range of benefits such as reduced admission to ancient sites and museums, and discounts on bus and train fares.

Embassies & Consulates

All foreign embassies in Greece are in Athens and its suburbs, with a few consulates in Thessaloniki.

Albanian Embassy (☏210 687 6200; Vekiareli 7, Filothei; ☒A7, 550 to Kollegio)

Australian Embassy (☏210 870 4000; http://greece.embassy.gov.au; Level 2, Chatzigianni Mexi 5, Hilton; Ⓜ Megaro Moussikis)

Bulgarian Embassy (☏210 674 8105; www.mfa.bg/embassies/greece; Stratigou Kallari 33a, Psyhiko; ☒550 to Ag Varvara)

Canadian Embassy (☏210 727 3400; www.greece.gc.ca; Ethnikis Antistaseos 48, Halandri; ☒10 to Serron)

Cypriot Embassy (☏210 373 4800; www.mfa.gov.cy; Xenofontos 2a, Syntagma; ☉8am-3.30pm Mon-Fri; Ⓑ Syntagma)

French Embassy (☏210 339 1000; https://gr.ambafrance.org; Leoforos Vasilissis Sofias 7, Kolonaki; Ⓜ Syntagma)

German Embassy (☏210 728 5111; www.athen.diplo.de; Karaoli-Dimitriou 3, Kolonaki; Ⓜ Evangelismos)

Irish Embassy (☏210 723 2771; www.dfa.ie/irish-embassy/greece; Leoforos Vasileos Konstantinou 7, Pangrati; ☉9am-1pm Mon-Fri; ☒2, 4, 10, 11 to Stadio, Ⓜ Akropoli, ☒Zappeio)

Italian Embassy (☏210 361 7260; www.ambatene.esteri.it; Sekeri 2, Kolonaki; Ⓜ Syntagma)

Netherlands Embassy (☏210 725 4900; www.nederlandwereldwijd.nl/landen/griekenland; Leoforos Vasileos Konstantinou 5, Pangrati; ☒2, 4, 10, 11 to Stadio, Ⓜ Akropoli, ☒Zappeio)

Turkish Embassy (☏210 726 3000; http://atina.be.mfa.gov.tr; Vasileos Georgiou B-8, Kolonaki; Ⓜ Syntagma) Has an additional branch in **Athens** (☏210 672 9830; http://atinapire.bk.mfa.gov.tr; Vasileos Pavlou 22, Psyhiko; ☒550 to Pharos) and one in **Thessaloniki** (☏2310 965 070; turkbaskon@kom.forthnet.gr; Agiou Dimitriou 151; ☉9am-5pm Mon-Fri).

UK Embassy (☏210 727 2600; www.gov.uk/world/organisations/british-embassy-athens; Ploutarhou 1, Kolonaki; Ⓜ Evangelismos)

US Embassy (☏210 721 2951; http://gr.usembassy.gov; Vasilissis Sofias 91, Ilissia; Ⓜ Megaro Mousikis) Also has a branch in **Thessaloniki** (☏2310 242 905; https://gr.usembassy.gov; 7th fl, Tsimiski 43).

Electricity

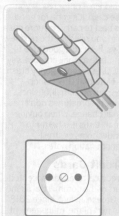

Type C
220V/50Hz

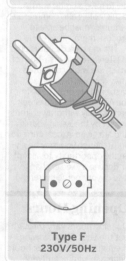

Type F
230V/50Hz

Health

Availability & Cost of Health Care

Although medical training is of a high standard in Greece, the public health service is badly underfunded. Hospitals can be overcrowded, hygiene is not always what it should be, and relatives are expected to bring in food for the patient – which can be a problem for a solo traveller. Conditions and treatment are much better in private hospitals, which are expensive. All this means that a good health-insurance policy is essential.

➡ If you need an ambulance in Greece call 166 or 112.

➡ There is at least one doctor on every island, and larger islands have hospitals.

➡ Pharmacies can dispense medicines that are available only on prescription in most European countries.

➡ Consult a pharmacist for minor ailments.

Insurance

If you're an EU citizen, a European Health Insurance Card (EHIC) covers you for most medical care but not emergency repatriation or nonemergencies. Citizens from other countries should find out if there is a reciprocal arrangement for free medical care between their country and Greece. If you do need health insurance, make sure you get a policy that covers you for the worst possible scenario, such as an accident requiring an emergency flight home. Find out in advance if your insurance plan will make payments directly to providers or reimburse you later for overseas health expenditures.

Worldwide travel insurance is available at www.lonelyplanet.com/travel-insurance. You can buy, extend and claim online anytime – even if you're already on the road.

Environmental Hazards

➡ The only dangerous snake in Greece is the viper (also known as the common European viper). To minimise the possibilities of being bitten, always wear boots, socks and long trousers when walking through undergrowth where snakes may be present.

➡ Mosquitoes can be an annoying problem, though there is no danger of contracting malaria. Electric mosquito-repellent devices are usually sufficient to keep the insects at bay at night. Choose accommodation that has fly screen on the windows wherever possible.

➡ The Asian tiger mosquito (*Aedes albopictus*) can be a voracious daytime biter and is known to carry several viruses, including Eastern equine encephalitis, which can affect the central nervous system and cause severe complications and death. Use protective sprays or lotion if you suspect you are being bitten during the day.

Tap Water

Tap water is drinkable and safe in most of Greece but not always in small villages and on some of the islands. Always ask locally if the water is safe, and if in doubt drink boiled or bought water. Even when water is safe, the substances and bacteria in it may be different from those you are used to, and occasionally can cause vomiting or diarrhoea. Bottled water is widely available, but think about environmental considerations when you opt for bottled over tap water.

Internet Access

Free wi-fi is available in most hotels, many cafes and some restaurants. A number of cities have free wi-fi zones in shopping and eating areas and plazas. Internet cafes have virtually disappeared – instead buy a local SIM with data to insert in your unlocked device. Some, but not all, hotels offer computers for guests to use.

Legal Matters

Arrests

It is a good idea to have your passport (or at least a copy and some ID) with you at all times in case you are stopped by the police and questioned. This is particularly true if you are travelling in border areas. Greek citizens are presumed always to have identification on them and the police presume foreign visitors do too. If you are arrested by police, insist on an interpreter (diermi_néas; say 'the-lo dhi-ermi-nea') and/or a lawyer (diki_góros; say 'the-lo dhi-ki-go-ro').

Drugs

Greek drug laws are among the strictest in Europe. Greek courts make no distinction between possession and pushing. Possession of even a small amount of marijuana is likely to land you in jail.

LGBT+ Travellers

Same-sex unions (but not marriages) were legally recognised in Greece in 2015 and attitudes to the LGBT+ community have grown more liberal across the country. However, the Orthodox Church plays a prominent role in shaping society's views on social issues, so you may find your sexuality being frowned upon by some locals – especially outside major cities.

Rest assured, Greece is an extremely popular destinations for LGBT+ travellers for a reason. Athens has a busy scene, but most LGBT+ travellers head for the islands. Mykonos has long been famous for its bars, beaches and general hedonism, while Skiathos also has its share of hang-outs. The island of Lesvos (Mytilini), birthplace of the lesbian poet Sappho, has become something of a place of pilgrimage for lesbians.

The Beloved Republic (http://thebelovedrepublic. com) is a company specialising in organising same-sex unions in Greece. For more info, see https://queerinthe world.com/gay-greece.

Maps

Unless you are going to hike or drive, the free maps given out by the EOT and larger hotels will probably suffice, although they are not 100% accurate.

Anavasi (www.mountains.gr) Athens-based company publishing maps with excellent coverage. Hikers should consider its *Topo* series, which has durable, waterproof paper and detailed walking trails for many of the Aegean islands.

Terrain (www.terrainmaps.gr) Maps published in Athens and offering equally good coverage. All maps can be bought online or at major bookstores in Greece.

Money

Debit and credit cards are accepted in cities, but elsewhere it's handy to have cash. Most towns have ATMs, but they may be out of order.

ATMs

There are ATMs in every town large enough to support a bank and in almost all the tourist areas. If you have MasterCard or Visa, there are plenty of places to withdraw money. Cirrus and Maestro withdrawals can be made in major towns and tourist areas.

Note that in small tourist villages, the only option may be a Euronet ATM (yellow and blue). These charge a €3.95 fee (compared to €2 to €3 at bank ATMs), and offer significantly worse exchange rates.

Be aware that many ATMs on the islands can lose their connection for a day or two at a time, making it impossible for anyone (locals included) to withdraw cash. It's useful to have a backup.

Automated foreign-exchange machines are common in major tourist areas. They take all major European currencies, Australian and US dollars and Japanese yen, and are useful in an emergency, although they charge a hefty commission.

Be warned that many card companies can put an automatic block on your card after your first withdrawal abroad, as an antifraud mechanism. To avoid this happening, inform your bank of your travel plans.

Cash

Nothing beats cash for convenience – or for risk. If you lose cash, it's gone for good. It's best to carry no more cash than you need for the next few days. It's also a good idea to set aside a small amount, say €100, as an emergency stash.

Note that Greek shopkeepers and small-business owners sometimes don't have small change. When buying small items it is better to tender coins or small-denomination notes.

Credit Cards

Credit cards are an accepted part of the commercial scene in Greece. In fact, since 2018 (as part of the 'management' of the financial crisis) Greeks aged below 65 and earning an income have been required by law to have a credit card. As a result, hotels and commercial ventures must be able to process them.

The main credit cards are MasterCard and Visa, both of which are widely accepted. They can also be used as cash cards to draw cash from the ATMs of affiliated Greek banks. Daily withdrawal limits are set by the issuing bank and are given in local currency only (though you may be given the opportunity to accept or decline a fixed exchange rate of your home currency).

Opening Hours

Opening hours vary throughout the year. The following are high-season hours; hours decrease significantly for shoulder and low seasons, and some places close completely. In tourist locations, some shops stay open longer year round.

Banks 8.30am–2.30pm Monday to Thursday, 8am–2pm Friday

Bars 8pm–late

Cafes 10am–midnight

Clubs 10pm–4am

Post Offices 7.30am–2pm Monday to Friday (rural); 7.30am–8pm Monday to Friday, 7.30am–2pm Saturday (urban)

Restaurants 11am–11pm
Shops 8am–2pm Monday, Wednesday and Saturday; 8am–2pm and 5pm–9pm Tuesday, Thursday and Friday

Photography

→ Digital memory cards are readily available from camera stores.

→ Never photograph a military installation; some are less than obvious and near to wildlife-viewing areas.

→ Flash photography is not allowed inside churches and it's considered taboo to photograph the main altar.

→ Greeks usually love having their photos taken, but always ask permission first.

→ At archaeological sites you will be stopped from using a tripod as it marks you as a 'professional'.

Public Holidays

New Year's Day 1 January

Epiphany 6 January

First Sunday in Lent February

Greek Independence Day 25 March

Good Friday 17 April 2020, 30 April 2021, 22 April 2022

Orthodox Easter Sunday 19 April 2020, 2 May 2021, 24 April 2022

May Day (Protomagia) 1 May

Whit Monday (Agiou Pnevmatos) 8 June 2020, 21 June 2021, 13 June 2022

Feast of the Dormition 15 August

Ohi Day 28 October

Christmas Day 25 December

St Stephen's Day 26 December

Safe Travel

Adulterated & Spiked Drinks

Adulterated drinks (known as *bombes*) are served in some bars and clubs in Athens and at resorts known for partying. These drinks are diluted with cheap illegal imports that leave you feeling worse for wear the next day.

At many of the party resorts catering to large budget-tour groups, spiked drinks are not uncommon; keep your hand over the top of your glass. More often than not, the perpetrators are foreign tourists rather than locals.

Tourist Police

The *touristikí astynomía* (tourist police) work in cooperation with the regular Greek police and are found in cities and popular tourist destinations. Each tourist police office has at least one member of staff who speaks English. Hotels, restaurants, travel agencies, tourist shops, tourist guides, waiters, taxi drivers and bus drivers all come under the jurisdiction of the tourist police. If you have a complaint about any of these, report it to the tourist police and they will investigate. If you need to report a theft or loss of passport, go to the tourist police first, and they will act as interpreters between you and the regular police.

Smoking

Smoking is banned inside public places, with the penalty being fines placed on the business owners. Greece is home to some of the heaviest smokers in Europe, so enforcement is a challenge. They are often imposed in only a nominal way in remote locations where proprietors fear they would lose business.

Taxes & Refunds

Greece has some of the highest tax rates in Europe, largely due to its economic struggles. Value-added tax (VAT) is 24% for most things, although hotel accommodation, food and medicine is 13%, and for books and newspapers it's 6%. VAT is included in the price unless otherwise stated.

Telephone

The Greek telephone service is maintained by the public corporation OTE (pronounced o-*teh*; Organismos Tilepikoinonion Ellados). You may still find some public phones in central locations in cities and villages, though as people now use mobile (cell) phones, these are becoming rarities.

Note that in Greece the area code must always be dialled when making a call (ie all Greek phone numbers are 10-digit).

Mobile Phones

Local SIM cards can be used in unlocked phones. Most other phones can be set to roaming. US and Canadian phones need to have a dual- or tri-band system.

There are several mobile service providers in Greece, among which Cosmote (www.cosmote.gr), Vodafone (www.vodafone.gr) and Wind (www.wind.gr) are the best known. Of these three, Cosmote tends to have the best coverage in remote areas. All offer 4G connectivity and pay-as-you-talk services for which you can buy a rechargeable SIM card and have your own Greek mobile number. If you're buying a package, be sure to triple-check the fine print. There are restrictions on deals such as 'free minutes' only being available to phones using the same provider.

The use of a mobile phone while driving in Greece is prohibited, but the use of a Bluetooth headset is allowed.

Phonecards & Public Phones

Public phones use OTE phonecards, known as *telekarta*, not coins. These cards are available at *periptera* (street kiosks), and some corner shops and tourist shops. Public phones are easy to operate. The 'i' at the top left of the push-button dialling panel brings up the operating instructions in English.

It's also possible to use payphones with discount-card

schemes. This involves dialling an access code and then punching in your card number. The OTE version of this card is known as 'Chronokarta'. The cards come with instructions in Greek and English, and the talk time is good compared with the standard phonecard rates.

Time

Greece is two hours ahead of GMT/UTC and three hours ahead on daylight-saving time – which begins on the last Sunday in March, when clocks are put forward one hour. Daylight saving ends on the last Sunday in October.

Toilets

➡ Nearly all places have Western-style toilets, including hotels and restaurants. Public toilets at transport terminals (bus and train) sometimes have Turkish squat-style toilets.

➡ Public toilets tend to be limited to airports and bus and train stations, with the very occasional one in tourist-heavy town centres. Cafes are the best option, but in tourist-heavy places, it's polite to buy something for the privilege.

➡ The Greek plumbing system can't handle toilet paper; apparently the pipes are too narrow and anything larger than a postage stamp seems to cause a problem. Toilet paper etc must be placed in the small bin provided next to every toilet.

Tourist Information

The Greek National Tourist Organisation (www.visitgreece.gr) is known as GNTO abroad and EOT within Greece. The quality of service from office to office varies dramatically; in some you'll get information aplenty and in others you'll be hard-pressed to find anyone behind the desk. Offices can be found in major tourist locations. In some regions tourist offices are run by the local government/municipality.

Visas

Countries whose nationals can stay in Greece for up to 90 days without a visa include Australia, Canada, EU countries, Iceland, Israel, Japan, New Zealand, Norway and the USA. Other countries included are the European principalities of Monaco and San Marino, and most South American countries. The list changes though – contact Greek embassies for the latest. The Greek Ministry of Foreign Affairs publishes an updated list of countries requiring visas (www.mfa.gr/en/visas).

If you wish to stay in Greece for longer than three months within a six-month period, you will probably need a national visa (type D) from the Greek embassy in your country of residence. You cannot apply for this in Greece.

Volunteering

Hellenic Wildlife Hospital (http://ekpazp.gr) Volunteers head to Aegina (particularly during winter) to this large wildlife rehabilitation centre.

Mouries Farm (Map 503; ☑6947465900; www.skyrian horses.org; Flea; by donation; ☉10am-1pm & 6-9pm Jul & Aug, hours vary Jun & Sep, by appointment Oct-May) 🐾 Help with the breeding and care of rare Skyrian horses.

Skyros Island Horse Trust (Map 503;☑6986051678; www.sky rosislandhorsetrust.com; Trachi; ☉by appointment) 🐾 A great project for volunteers to assist with programmes to preserve the endangered horses.

Sea Turtle Protection Society of Greece (☑210 523 1342; www.archelon.gr) Includes monitoring sea turtles in the Peloponnese.

Skopelos Walks (☑6945249328; www.skopelos-walks.com; guided hikes €20-40) 🐾 Takes volunteers to help with maintaining and opening up island trails.

WWOOF (World Wide Opportunities on Organic Farms; https://wwoof.gr) Offers opportunities for volunteers at one of over 100 farms in Greece.

Women Travellers

Many women travel alone in Greece. The crime rate remains relatively low and solo travel is probably safer than in most European countries. This does not mean that you should be lulled into complacency; bag snatching and sexual assault do occur, particularly at party resorts.

The majority of Greek men treat foreign women with respect. However, smooth-talking guys aren't in the least bashful about approaching women in the street. They can be very persistent, but they are usually a hassle rather than a threat.

Work

EU nationals don't need a work permit, but do need a residency permit and a Greek tax-file number to stay longer than three months. Nationals from other countries require a work permit.

Bar & Hostel Work

Bars of the Greek islands rely on foreign workers and there are thousands of summer jobs up for grabs every year. The pay is not fantastic, but you get to spend a summer on the islands. April and May are the times to go looking. Hostels and travellers' hotels are other places that regularly employ foreign workers.

English Tutoring

If you're looking for a permanent job, the most widely available option is teaching English. A TEFL (Teaching English as a Foreign Language) certificate or a university degree is an advantage but not essential. For jobs listings check sites such as www.gooverseas.com.

You can also find a job teaching English when you are in Greece – there are language schools everywhere. Strictly speaking, you need a licence to teach in them, but many will employ teachers without one. Check the noticeboards of popular bookshops to see if anyone is looking for private tutoring.

Transport

GETTING THERE & AWAY

Greece is easy to reach by air or sea – particularly in summer when it opens its arms (and schedules) wide. Getting to or from Greece overland takes more planning but isn't impossible. Flights, cars and tours can be booked online at lonelyplanet.com/bookings.

Entering the Region

Visitors to Greece with EU passports are rarely given more than a cursory glance, but customs and police may be interested in what you are carrying. EU citizens may also enter Greece on a national identity card.

Visitors from outside the EU may require a visa. Be sure to check with consular authorities before you arrive.

Air

Most visitors to Greece arrive by air, which tends to be the fastest and cheapest option, if not the most environmentally friendly.

Airports & Airlines

Greece has four main international airports that take chartered and scheduled flights; ones relevant to this guide are:

Eleftherios Venizelos International Airport (ATH; ☏210 353 0000; www.aia.gr) Athens' international airport is near Spata, 27km east of the capital. It has all the modern conveniences, including 24-hour luggage storage and a children's play area.

Nikos Kazantzakis Heraklion International Airport (HER; ☏2810 397800; www.ypa.gr) About 5km east of Iraklio (Crete). Has an ATM, duty-free shop and cafe-bar.

Diagoras Airport (RHO; ☏22410 88700; www.rho-airport.gr) On the island of Rhodes.

Other international airports across the country include Santorini (Thira), Karpathos, Samos, Skiathos, Kefallonia and Zakynthos. These airports are most often used for charter flights from the UK, Germany and Scandinavia.

Tickets

If you're coming from outside Europe, consider a cheap flight to a European hub (eg London) and then an onward ticket with a budget or charter airline such as **easyJet** (☏211 198 0013; www.easyjet.com), which offers some of the cheapest tickets between Greece and the rest of Europe. Some airlines also offer cheap deals to students. If you're planning to travel between June and September, it's wise to book ahead.

CLIMATE CHANGE & TRAVEL

Every form of transport that relies on carbon-based fuel generates CO_2, the main cause of human-induced climate change. Modern travel is dependent aeroplanes, which might use less fuel per kilometre per person than most cars but travel much greater distances. The altitude at which aircraft emit gases (including CO_2) and particles also contributes to their climate change impact. Many websites offer 'carbon calculators' that allow people to estimate the carbon emissions generated by their journey and, for those who wish to do so, to offset the impact of the greenhouse gases emitted with contributions to portfolios of climate-friendly initiatives throughout the world. Lonely Planet offsets the carbon footprint of all staff and author travel.

Land

International train travel, in particular, has become much more feasible in recent years, with speedier trains and better connections. You can now travel from London to Athens by train and ferry in less than two days. By choosing to travel on the ground instead of the air, you'll also be reducing your carbon footprint.

Border Crossings

Make sure you have all of your visas (p20) sorted out before attempting to cross land borders into or out of Greece. Before travelling, also check the status of borders with the relevant embassies.

OVERLAND FROM WESTERN EUROPE

Overland enthusiasts can reach Greece by rail or bus through the Balkan peninsula, passing through Croatia, Serbia and North Macedonia. Or head to the eastern coast of Italy and then take a ferry to Greece. For example from Bari in Italy there's an overnight boat to Patra in the Peloponnese from where you can take a combination of bus and trains to Athens in around three hours. Not only will you be doing your bit for the earth, but you'll see some gorgeous scenery from your window.

Train

Greece is part of the Eurail (www.eurail.com) network. Eurail passes can only be bought by residents of non-European countries; they should be purchased before arriving in Europe, but can be bought in Europe if your passport proves that you've been there for less than six months. Greece is also part of the Interrail Pass system (www.interrail.eu), available to those who have resided in Europe for six months or more, and the Rail Plus Balkan Flexipass (www.raileurope.com), which offers unlimited travel for five, 10 or 15 days within a month. See the websites for full details of passes and prices.

Sea

Ferries can get very crowded in summer. If you want to take a vehicle across, it's wise to make a reservation beforehand. Port tax for departures to Turkey is around €10.

Another way to visit Greece by sea is to join one of the many cruises that ply the Aegean.

GETTING AROUND

Air

The vast majority of domestic mainland flights are handled by the country's national carrier **Aegean Airlines** (A3; ☑801 112 0000; https://en.aegeanair.com) and its subsidiary, **Olympic Air** (☑801 801 0101, 21035 50500; www.olympicair.com). You'll find offices wherever there are flights, as well as in other major towns. There are also a number of smaller Greek carriers, including Thessaloniki-based **Astra Airlines** (☑23104 89391; www.astra-airlines.gr) and **Sky Express** (☑21521 56510; www. skyexpress.gr).

There are discounts for return tickets for travel between Monday and Thursday, and bigger discounts for trips that include a Saturday night away. Find full details and timetables on airline websites. Viva.gr (https:/travel.viva.gr) is a good

INTERNATIONAL FERRY ROUTES

The services indicated are for high season (July and August). For further information see www.openseas.gr.

DESTINATION	DEPARTURE POINT	ARRIVAL POINT	DURATION	FREQUENCY
Albania	Corfu	Saranda	30-70min	3 daily
Italy	Patra	Ancona	20-22hr	daily
Italy	Patra	Bari	16hr	daily
Italy	Igoumenitsa	Bari	9½-11½hr	2 daily
Italy	Patra	Brindisi	15hr	3 weekly
Italy	Patra	Venice	31-32hr	4-5 weekly
Turkey	Chios	Çeşme	20-30min	6 daily
Turkey	Kos	Bodrum	45min	daily
Turkey	Lesvos	Ayvalik	1½hr	daily
Turkey	Rhodes	Marmaris	50min	2 daily
Turkey	Samos	Kuşadası	1½hr	2 daily

website for finding cheap domestic flights as well as other travel and entertainment tickets.

The baggage allowance on domestic flights varies according to the airline and the category of ticket you've purchased, and can be scrutinised carefully at check-in. It's usually 20kg if the domestic flight is part of an international journey.

Bicycle

Cycling is gaining popularity as a way to tour Greece. You'll need strong leg muscles to tackle the mountains, or you can stick to some of the flatter coastal routes. Bike lanes are rare to nonexistent; helmets are not compulsory. The main dangers are the cars on the roads – locals and tourists alike. The island of Kos is about the most bicycle-friendly place in Greece, as is anywhere flat.

You can hire bicycles in most tourist places, but they are not as widely available as cars and motorcycles. Prices range from €10 to €15 per day, depending on the type and age of the bike.

Bicycles are carried free on ferries but cannot be taken on the fast ferries (catamarans and the like; there simply isn't room to store them).

You can buy decent mountain or touring bikes in Greece's major towns, though you may have a problem finding a ready buyer if you wish to on-sell it. Bike prices are much the same as across the rest of Europe: anywhere from €300 to €2000.

Boat

Greece has an extensive network of ferries – the only means of reaching many of the islands. Schedules are often subject to delays due to poor weather (note: this is a safety precaution) plus the occasional industrial action, and prices fluctuate regularly. Timetables are not announced until just prior to the season due to competition for route licences. In summer, ferries run regular services between all but the most out-of-the-way destinations; however, services seriously slow down in winter (and in some cases stop completely).

Domestic Ferry Operators

Ferry companies have local offices on many of the islands. The big companies compete for routes annually (and seem to merge and demerge regularly), so the following may have changed by the time you read this. A useful website to check is **Greek Ferries** (☑281 052 9000; www.greekferries.gr), which is also available as an app.

Aegean Flying Dolphins (www.aegeanflyingdolphins.gr) Hydrofoils between Athens, Aegina and the Sporades.

Aegean Speed Lines (www.aegeanspeedlines.gr) Super-speedy boats between Athens and the Cyclades.

Aegeon Pelagos (www.anek.gr) Subsidiary of ANEK Lines serving routes to Crete, the Cyclades and the Dodecanese.

ANEK Lines (www.anek.gr) Crete-based long-haul ferries.

ANEK/Superfast Ferries (www.superfast.com) Routes to/from Ancona, Bari, Corfu, Igoumenitsa, Patra and Venice.

ANES (www.anes.gr) Old-style ferries servicing Evia and the Sporades.

Blue Star Ferries (www.bluestarferries.com) Long-haul, high-speed ferries and Seajets catamarans between the mainland, the Cyclades, the northeastern Aegean Islands, the Sporades, Crete and the Dodecanese.

Dodekanisos Seaways (www.12ne.gr) Runs large, high-speed catamarans in the Dodecanese.

Fast Ferries (www.fastferries.com.gr) Comfortable ferries from Rafina to the Cyclades islands including Andros, Tinos, Naxos and Mykonos.

Glyfa Ferries (www.ferriesglyfa.gr) Comfortable short-haul ferry services between Glyfa on the mainland and Aglokambos in northern Evia.

Hellenic Seaways (https://hellenicseaways.gr) Offers catamarans from the mainland to the Cyclades and between the Sporades and Saronic islands.

Levante Ferries (www.levanteferries.com) Large ferries serving the Ionian Islands.

LANE Lines (www.ferries.gr/lane) Long-haul ferries serving the Ionians, Dodecanese and Crete.

Minoan Lines (www.minoan.gr) High-speed luxury ferries between Piraeus and Iraklio (Heraklion) among other destinations.

Patmos Star (www.patmos-star.com) Small, local ferry linking Patmos, Leros and Lipsi in the Dodecanese.

SAOS Lines (www.saos.gr) Big, slow boats between Samothraki and Alexandroupoli.

Seajets (www.seajets.gr) Catamarans calling at Athens, Crete, Santorini (Thira), Paros and many islands in between.

Skyros Shipping Company (www.sne.gr) Slow boats connecting Skyros to Kymi (Evia) and, mid-June to mid-September, to Alonnisos and Skopelos.

Zante Ferries (http://zanteferries.gr) Older ferries connecting the mainland (Piraeus) with the western Cyclades.

Bus

The bus network is comprehensive. All long-distance buses, on the mainland and the islands, are operated by regional collectives known as KTEL (www.ktelbus.com). Within towns and cities, different companies run inter urban services. The fares are fixed by the government; bus

Ferry Routes

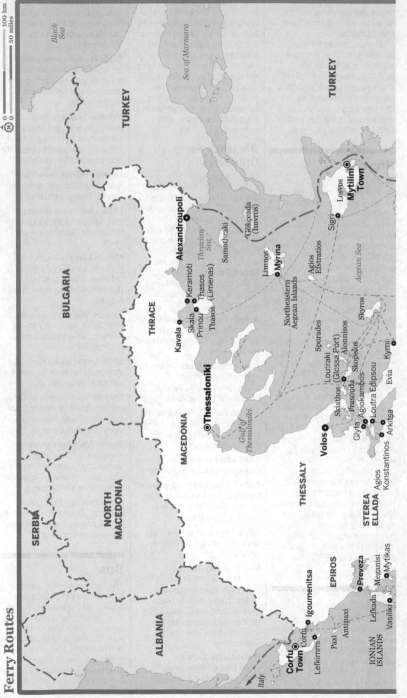

100 km
50 miles

Black
Sea

Sea of Marmara

TURKEY

TURKEY

Mytilini
Town

Lesvos

Sigri

Aegean Sea

Gökçeada
(İmvros)

Agios
Efstratios

Alexandroupoli

Thracian
Sea

Samothraki

Limnos

Myrina

Skala
Keramoti

Prinou
Thasos
(Limenas)
Thasos

Kavala

Northeastern
Aegean Islands

Skyros

THRACE

BULGARIA

Sporades

Lourraki

Skiathos (Glossa Port)

Alonnisos

Skopelos

Kymi

Evia

MACEDONIA

Thessaloniki

Gulf of
Thessaloniki

Volos

Skiathos

Prasouda

Agiokambos

Glyfa

Loutra Edipsou

Arkitsa

SERBIA

NORTH
MACEDONIA

THESSALY

STEREA
ELLADA

Agios
Konstantinos

ALBANIA

EPIROS

Preveza

Meganisi

Mytikas

Corfu
Town

Igoumenitsa

Corfu

Lefkimmi

Paxi

Antipaxi

Lefkada

Vasiliki

IONIAN
ISLANDS

Italy

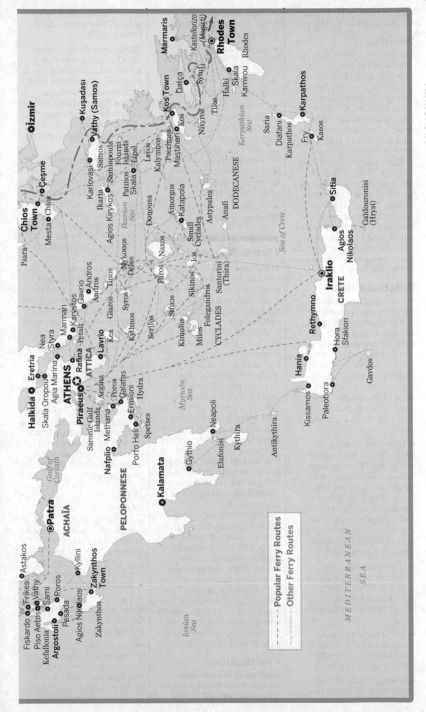

travel is reasonably priced. All have good safety records.

Services

Every prefecture on the mainland has a KTEL, which operates local services within it and to the main towns of other prefectures. The islands of Corfu, Kefallonia and Zakynthos can be reached directly from Athens by bus – often the fares include the price of the ferry ticket.

Most villages have a daily bus service of some sort, although remote areas may have only one or two buses a week. They operate for the benefit of people going to town to shop, rather than for tourists, and consequently leave the villages very early in the morning and return early in the afternoon.

Practicalities

➜ It is important to note that big cities like Athens and Iraklio may have more than one bus station, each serving different regions. Make sure you find the correct station for your destination. In small towns and villages the 'bus station' may be no more than a bus stop outside a *kafeneio* (coffee house) or taverna that doubles as a booking office.

➜ There is no central source of bus information, and each KTEL company runs its own website, with varying amounts of info. Frustratingly, KTEL bus timetables only give the end destination – check when you buy tickets at stations about intermediate town stops on a given route.

➜ In remote areas, the timetable may be in Greek only, but most booking offices have timetables in both Greek and Roman script.

➜ Arrive early as buses have been known to leave a few minutes before their scheduled departure.

➜ When you buy a ticket you may be allotted a seat

number, printed on the ticket. (In some cases locals ignore these.)

➜ You can board a bus without a ticket and pay on board, but on a popular route or during high season, you may have to stand.

➜ The KTEL buses are safe, modern and air-conditioned. In more remote, rural areas they may be older and less comfortable. Note that buses often have toilets on board that are not used; instead, on longer journeys, they must stop every 2½ hours.

➜ Smoking is prohibited on all buses in Greece.

Car & Motorcycle

In the past, Greece had a terrible reputation for road safety. In recent years, however, roads and highways have improved dramatically and European Commission statistics (2010–18) report a drop of 45% in fatalities. However, no one who has travelled on Greece's roads will be surprised to hear that the road toll of 69 deaths for every million inhabitants is still a lot higher than the EU average of 49. Overtaking is listed as the greatest cause, along with speed. Accidents can occur on single-lane roads when slower vehicles pull to the right on both sides and are overtaken at the same time, leading to head-on collisions.

Heart-stopping moments aside, your own car is a great way to explore off the beaten track. The road network has improved enormously in recent years, with a similar increase in tourist traffic, especially on the islands. This brings its own problems such as parking and congestion in island towns. There are regular (if costly) car-ferry services to almost all islands.

Practicalities

Automobile Associations
Nationwide roadside assistance is provided by **ELPA** (Elliniki

Leschi Aftokinitou kai Periigiseon;☏24hr roadside assistance 10400).

Entry EU-registered vehicles enter free for up to six months without road taxes being due. A green card (international third-party insurance) is required, along with proof of date of entry (ferry ticket or your passport stamp). Non-EU-registered vehicles may be logged in your passport.

Driving licences EU driving licences are valid in Greece. Rental agencies require the corresponding driving licence for every vehicle class (eg motorcycle/moped licence for motorbikes or mopeds). Greek law requires drivers from outside the EU to have an International Driving Permit (IDP). Rental agencies will request it, as may local authorities if you're stopped. IDPs can only be obtained in person and in the country where your driving licence was issued. Carry this alongside your regular licence.

Fuel Available widely throughout the country, though service stations may be closed on weekends and public holidays. On the islands, there may be only one petrol station; check where it is before you head out. Self-service and credit-card pumps are not the norm in Greece. Petrol in Greece is among the most expensive in Europe. Petrol types include *amolyvdi* (unleaded) and *petreleo kinisis* (diesel).

Hire

CAR
➜ All the big multinational companies are represented in Athens; most have branches in major towns and popular tourist destinations. The majority of islands have at least one outlet.

➜ Very often a car is quite scratched up when you get it. Be sure to take photos of all the damage.

➜ The minimum driving age in Greece is 18 years, but most car-hire firms require you to be at least 21 (or 23 for larger vehicles). In some cases, you pay extra if you're a younger driver.

➡ High-season weekly rates with unlimited mileage start at about €280 for the smallest models (eg a Fiat Seicento), dropping to about €150 per week in winter.

➡ You can often find great deals at local companies. Their advertised rates can be up to 50% cheaper than the multinationals and they are normally open to negotiation, especially if business is slow.

➡ On the islands, you can rent a car for the day for around €35 to €60, including all insurance and taxes.

➡ Always check what the insurance includes; there are often rough roads or dangerous routes that you can only tackle by renting a 4WD.

➡ It is not possible to take a car hired in Greece into another country without permission.

➡ Unless you pay with a credit card, most hire companies will require a minimum deposit of €120 per day.

➡ Some of the international car-rental agencies insist you prepay for a tank of gas. If you return the car with the tank full, you're entitled to a refund.

The major car-hire companies in Greece:

Avis (www.avis.gr)

Budget (www.budget.gr)

Europcar (www.europcar-greece.gr)

MOTORCYCLE

➡ Mopeds, motorcycles, scooters and quad bikes (ATVs) are available for hire wherever there are tourists to rent them. Most machines are newish and in good condition. Nonetheless, check the brakes at the earliest opportunity.

➡ You must produce a licence that shows proficiency to ride the category of bike you wish to rent; this applies to everything from 50cc up. British citizens must obtain a Category A1 licence from the Driver & Vehicle Licensing Agency (www.dft.gov.uk/dvla) in the UK (in most other EU countries separate licences are automatically issued.

➡ Rates start from about €20 per day for a moped or 50cc motorcycle, ranging to €35 per day for a 250cc motorcycle. Out of season these prices drop considerably, so use your bargaining skills.

➡ Most motorcycle hirers include third-party insurance in the price, but it's wise to check this. This insurance will not include medical expenses.

➡ Helmets are compulsory and rental agencies are obliged to offer one as part of the hire deal.

Road Conditions

➡ Main highways in Greece have been improving steadily over the years and are now all excellent.

➡ The old highways are now quite empty of big trucks, and much nicer for driving.

➡ Some main roads retain a two-lane/hard-shoulder format, which can be confusing and even downright dangerous.

➡ Roadworks can take years and years in Greece – especially on the islands.

➡ Many island roads aren't paved, which doesn't always show up clearly on GPS or online maps.

Road Hazards

➡ Slow drivers – many of them hesitant tourists – can cause serious traffic events on Greece's roads.

➡ Road surfaces can change rapidly when a section of road has succumbed to subsidence or weathering. Snow and ice can be a serious challenge in winter,

and drivers are advised to carry snow chains. In rural areas, keep a close eye out for animals on roads.

➡ Roads passing through mountainous areas are often littered with fallen rocks, which can cause extensive damage to a vehicle's underside or throw a motorbike rider.

➡ When driving on a single carriageway, slower vehicles, including older trucks, tend to pull over to the right into the 'safety' lane, allowing impatient drivers to pass around them.

Road Rules

➡ In Greece you drive on the right and overtake on the left.

➡ Outside built-up areas, unless signed otherwise, traffic on a main road has right of way at intersections. In towns, vehicles coming from the right have right of way. This includes roundabouts – even if you're in the roundabout, you must give way to drivers coming on to the roundabout to your right.

➡ Seatbelts must be worn in front seats, and in back seats if the car is fitted with them.

➡ Children under 12 years of age are not allowed in the front seat.

➡ You must carry a first-aid kit, fire extinguisher and warning triangle. It's forbidden to carry cans of petrol.

➡ Helmets are compulsory for motorcyclists.

➡ Outside residential areas the speed limit is 120km/h on highways, 90km/h on other roads and 50km/h in built-up areas. The speed limit for motorcycles is the same as cars. Drivers exceeding the speed limit by 20% are liable to receive a fine of €40 to €120; exceeding it by 30% costs €350 plus your licence will be suspended for 60 days.

➡ A blood-alcohol content of 0.05% can incur a fine, while over 0.08% is a criminal offence.

➡ If you are involved in an accident and no one is hurt, the police are not required to write a report, but it is advisable to go to a nearby police station and explain what happened as you may need a police report for insurance purposes.

Hitching

Hitching is never entirely safe, and we don't recommend it. For travellers who decide to hitch, some parts of Greece are much better than others. Getting out of major cities, particularly Athens, tends to be hard work. Hitching is much easier in remote areas and on islands with poor public transport. should understand that they

Local Transport

Bus

Most Greek towns are small enough to get around on foot. All the major towns have local buses.

Metro

Athens has a good underground system. Note that only Greek student cards are valid for a student ticket on the metro.

Taxi

Taxis are widely available in Greece, except on very small or remote islands. They are reasonably priced by European standards. City cabs are metered, with rates doubling between midnight and 5am. Additional costs are charged for trips from an airport or a bus, port or train station, as well as for each piece of luggage over 10kg. Before you get into the taxi, ask how much the price is likely to be. In some places, such as on islands, where they shuttle tourists between popular

> ### MOTORCYCLE WARNING
>
> If you plan to hire a motorcycle or moped, you require a motorcycle licence. Expect gravel roads, particularly on the islands; scooters are particularly prone to sliding on gravelly bends. If you plan to use a motorcycle or moped, check that your travel insurance covers you; many insurance companies don't cover motorcycle accidents.

locations, the price is set each season.

Some taxi drivers in Athens have been known to overcharge unwary travellers. If you have a complaint about a taxi driver, take the cab number and report your complaint to the tourist police. Useful taxi apps include Beat (www.thebeat.co/gr) and Taxiplon (www.taxiplon.gr).

Tours

Tours are worth considering if your time is very limited or if you prefer someone else do the planning. In Athens, you'll find countless day tours, with some agencies offering two- or three-day trips to nearby sights. For something on a larger scale, try Intrepid Travel (www.intrepidtravel.com; offices in Australia, the UK and the USA): it offers, for example, a 10-day sailing tour around the Cyclades, starting and ending in Santorini and including Naxos and Mykonos (€1198) including everything except meals and flights. Encounter Greece (www.encountergreece.com) also offers a plethora of tours.

More adventurous tours include guided activities such as hiking, climbing, white-water rafting, kayaking, canoeing and canyoning. Try the **Alpin Club** (www.alpinclub.gr) for kayaking, rafting, canyoning and mountain biking – just to name a few.

Train

Trains are operated by **OSE** (Organismos Sidirodromon

Ellados; ☎14511; www.trainose.gr). The railway network is extremely limited with many lines closed in recent years. You might use the train for routes between Athens and some of the nearby ports or for accessing Halkida on Evia.

Prices and schedules are very changeable – double-check on the OSE website. Information on departures from Athens or Thessaloniki are also available by calling ☎1440.

Classes

There are two types of service: regular (slow) trains that stop at all stations, and faster, modern intercity (IC) trains that link most major cities. Train fares have increased dramatically since the economic crisis; it used to be the country's cheapest form of transport, but is no longer.

Having said that, the IC trains that link the major Greek cities are an excellent way to travel and the trains are modern and comfortable, with a cafe-bar on board.

Train Passes

➡ Eurail, Interrail and Rail Plus Balkan Flexipass cards are valid in Greece, but they're generally not worth buying if Greece is the only place you plan to use them. Check if a supplement is required for IC journeys.

➡ Whatever pass you have, you must have a reservation to board the train.

➡ On presentation of ID or a passport, passengers over 65 years old are entitled to a 25% discount on all lines.

Language

The Greek language is believed to be one of the oldest European languages, with an oral tradition of 4000 years and a written tradition of approximately 3000 years. Due to its centuries of influence, Greek constitutes the origin of a large part of the vocabulary of many Indo-European languages (including English). It is the official language of Greece and co-official language of Cyprus (alongside Turkish), and is spoken by many migrant communities throughout the world.

The Greek alphabet is explained on the following page, but if you read the pronunciation guides given with each phrase in this chapter as if they were English, you'll be understood. Note that dh is pronounced as 'th' in 'there'; gh is a softer, slightly throaty version of 'g'; and kh is a throaty sound like the 'ch' in the Scottish 'loch'. All Greek words of two or more syllables have an acute accent ('), which indicates where the stress falls. In our pronunciation guides, stressed syllables are in italics.

In this chapter, masculine, feminine and neuter forms of words are included where necessary, separated with a slash and indicated with 'm', 'f' and 'n' respectively. Polite and informal options are indicated where relevant with 'pol' and 'inf'.

BASICS

Hello.	Γεια σας.	ya·sas (pol)
	Γεια σου.	ya·su (inf)
Goodbye.	Αντίο.	an·di·o

> ### WANT MORE?
>
> For in-depth language information and handy phrases, check out Lonely Planet's *Greek Phrasebook*. You'll find it at **shop.lonelyplanet.com**, or you can buy Lonely Planet's iPhone phrasebooks at the Apple App Store.

Yes./No.	Ναι./Οχι.	ne/o·hi
Please.	Παρακαλώ.	pa·ra·ka·lo
Thank you.	Ευχαριστώ.	ef·ha·ri·sto
You're welcome.	Παρακαλώ.	pa·ra·ka·lo
Excuse me.	Με συγχωρείτε.	me sing·kho·ri·te
Sorry.	Συγγνώμη.	sigh·no·mi

What's your name?
Πώς σας λένε; pos sas le·ne

My name is ...
Με λένε … me le·ne ...

Do you speak English?
Μιλάτε αγγλικά; mi·la·te an·gli·ka

I don't understand.
Δεν καταλαβαίνω. dhen ka·ta·la·ve·no

ACCOMMODATION

campsite	χώρος για κάμπινγκ	kho·ros yia kam·ping
hotel	ξενοδοχείο	kse·no·dho·khi·o
youth hostel	γιουθ χόστελ	yuth kho·stel
a ... room	ένα ... δωμάτιο	e·na ... dho·ma·ti·o
single	μονόκλινο	mo·no·kli·no
double	δίκλινο	dhi·kli·no
How much is it ...?	Πόσο κάνει ...;	po·so ka·ni ...
per night	τη βραδυά	ti·vra·dhya
per person	το άτομο	to a·to·mo
air-con	έρκοντίσιον	er·kon·di·si·on
bathroom	μπάνιο	ba·nio
fan	ανεμιστήρας	a·ne·mi·sti·ras
window	παράθυρο	pa·ra·thi·ro

DIRECTIONS

Where is ...?
Πού είναι …; pu *i*·ne …

What's the address?
Ποια είναι η διεύθυνση; pia *i*·ne i dhi·*ef*·thin·si

Can you show me (on the map)?
Μπορείς να μου δείξεις bo·*ris* na mu *dhik*·sis
(στο χάρτη); (sto *khar*·ti)

Turn left.
Στρίψτε αριστερά. *strips*·te a·ri·ste·*ra*

Turn right.
Στρίψτε δεξιά. *strips*·te dhe·*ksia*

at the next corner
στην επόμενη γωνία stin e·*po*·me·ni gho·*ni*·a

at the traffic lights
στα φώτα sta *fo*·ta

behind πίσω *pi*·so
far μακριά ma·kri·*a*
in front of μπροστά bro·*sta*
near (to) κοντά kon·*da*
next to δίπλα *dhi*·pla
opposite απέναντι a·*pe*·nan·di
straight ahead ολο ευθεία o·lo ef·*thi*·a

EATING & DRINKING

a table for ... Ενα τραπέζι *e*·na tra·*pe*·zi
για … ya …

(eight) o'clock στις (οχτώ) stis (okh·*to*)
(two) people (δύο) άτομα (*dhi*·o) a·to·ma

I don't eat ... Δεν τρώγω … dhen *tro*·gho …
fish ψάρι *psa*·ri
(red) meat (κόκκινο) (*ko*·ki·no)
κρέας *kre*·as
peanuts φυστίκια fi·*sti*·kia
poultry πουλερικά pu·le·ri·*ka*

What would you recommend?
Τι θα συνιστούσες; ti tha si·ni·*stu*·ses

What's in that dish?
Τι περιέχει αυτό το ti pe·ri·e·hi af·*to* to
φαγητό; fa·ghi·to

Cheers!
Εις υγείαν! is i·*yi*·an

That was delicious.
Ήταν νοστιμότατο! *i*·tan no·sti·*mo*·ta·to

Please bring the bill.
Το λογαριασμό, to lo·ghar·ya·*zmo*
παρακαλώ. pa·ra·ka·lo

GREEK ALPHABET

The Greek alphabet has 24 letters, shown below in their upper- and lower-case forms. Be aware that some letters look like English letters but are pronounced very differently, such as **B**, which is pronounced v; and **P**, pronounced r. As in English, how letters are pronounced is also influenced by the way they are combined, for example the **ou** combination is pronounced u as in 'put', and **oι** is pronounced ee as in 'feet'.

A α	a	as in 'father'		**Ξ ξ**	x	as in 'ox'
B β	v	as in 'vine'		**O o**	o	as in 'hot'
Γ γ	gh	a softer, throaty 'g', or		**Π π**	p	as in 'pup'
	y	as in 'yes'		**P ρ**	r	as in 'road',
Δ δ	dh	as in 'there'				slightly trilled
E ε	e	as in 'egg'		**Σ σ, ς**	s	as in 'sand'
Z ζ	z	as in 'zoo'		**T τ**	t	as in 'tap'
H η	i	as in 'feet'		**Y υ**	i	as in 'feet'
Θ θ	th	as in 'throw'		**Φ φ**	f	as in 'find'
I ι	i	as in 'feet'		**X χ**	kh	as the 'ch' in the
K κ	k	as in 'kite'				Scottish 'loch', or
Λ λ	l	as in 'leg'			h	like a rough 'h'
M μ	m	as in 'man'		**Ψ ψ**	ps	as in 'lapse'
N ν	n	as in 'net'		**Ω ω**	o	as in 'hot'

Note that the letter **Σ** has two forms for the lower case – **σ** and **ς**. The second one is used at the end of words. The Greek question mark is represented with the English equivalent of a semicolon (;).

Key Words

appetisers	ορεκτικά	o·rek·ti·ka
bar	μπαρ	bar
beef	βοδινό	vo·dhi·no
beer	μπύρα	bi·ra
bottle	μπουκάλι	bu·ka·li
bowl	μπωλ	bol
bread	ψωμί	pso·mi
breakfast	πρόγευμα	pro·yev·ma
cafe	καφετέρια	ka·fe·te·ri·a
cheese	τυρί	ti·ri
chicken	κοτόπουλο	ko·to·pu·lo
coffee	καφές	ka·fes
cold	κρύο	kri·o
cream	κρέμα	kre·ma
delicatessen	ντελικατέσεν	de·li·ka·te·sen
desserts	επιδόρπια	e·pi·dhor·pi·a
dinner	δείπνο	dhip·no
egg	αυγό	av·gho
fish	ψάρι	psa·ri
food	φαγητό	fa·yi·to
fork	πιρούνι	pi·ru·ni
fruit	φρούτα	fru·ta
glass	ποτήρι	po·ti·ri
grocery store	οπωροπωλείο	o·po·ro·po·li·o
herb	βότανο	vo·ta·no
high chair	καρέκλα για μωρά	ka·re·kla yia mo·ra
hot	ζεστός	ze·stos
juice	χυμός	hi·mos
knife	μαχαίρι	ma·he·ri
lamb	αρνί	ar·ni
lunch	μεσημεριανό φαγητό	me·si·me·ria·no fa·yi·to
main courses	κύρια φαγητά	ki·ri·a fa·yi·ta
market	αγορά	a·gho·ra
menu	μενού	me·nu
milk	γάλα	gha·la
nut	καρύδι	ka·ri·dhi
oil	λάδι	la·dhi
pepper	πιπέρι	pi·pe·ri
plate	πιάτο	pia·to
pork	χοιρινό	hi·ri·no
red wine	κόκκινο κρασί	ko·ki·no kra·si
restaurant	εστιατόριο	e·sti·a·to·ri·o
salt	αλάτι	a·la·ti
soft drink	αναψυκτικό	a·na·psik·ti·ko
spoon	κουτάλι	ku·ta·li
sugar	ζάχαρη	za·kha·ri
tea	τσάι	tsa·i
vegetable	λαχανικά	la·kha·ni·ka
vegetarian	χορτοφάγος	khor·to·fa·ghos
vinegar	ξύδι	ksi·dhi
water	νερό	ne·ro
white wine	άσπρο κρασί	a·spro kra·si
with/without	με/χωρίς	me/kho·ris

KEY PATTERNS

To get by in Greek, mix and match these simple patterns with words of your choice:

When's (the next bus)?
Πότε είναι (το επόμενο λεωφορείο); — po·te i·ne (to e·po·me·no le·o·fo·ri·o)

Where's (the station)?
Πού είναι (ο σταθμός); — pu i·ne (o stath·mos)

Do you have (a local map)?
Έχετε οδικό (τοπικό χάρτη); — e·he·te o·dhi·ko (to·pi·ko khar·ti)

Is there a (lift)?
Υπάρχει (ασανσέρ); — i·par·hi (a·san·ser)

Can I (try it on)?
Μπορώ να (το προβάρω); — bo·ro na (to pro·va·ro)

Could you (please help)?
Μπορείς να (βοηθήσεις, παρακαλώ); — bo·ris na (vo·i·thi·sis pa·ra·ka·lo)

Do I need (to book)?
Χρειάζεται (να κλείσω θέση); — khri·a·ze·te (na kli·so the·si)

I need (assistance).
Χρειάζομαι (βοήθεια). — khri·a·zo·me (vo·i·thi·a)

I'd like (to hire a car).
Θα ήθελα (να ενοικιάσω ένα αυτοκίνητο). — tha i·the·la (na e·ni·ki·a·so e·na af·to·ki·ni·to)

How much is it (per night)?
Πόσο είναι (για κάθε νύχτα); — po·so i·ne (yia ka·the nikh·ta)

EMERGENCIES

Help!	Βοήθεια!	vo·i·thya
Go away!	Φύγε!	fi·ye
I'm lost.	Έχω χαθεί.	e·kho kha·thi
Where's the toilet?	Πού είναι η τουαλέτα;	pu i·ne i tu·a·le·ta

Signs

ΕΙΣΟΔΟΣ	Entry
ΕΞΟΔΟΣ	Exit
ΠΛΗΡΟΦΟΡΙΕΣ	Information
ΑΝΟΙΧΤΟ	Open
ΚΛΕΙΣΤΟ	Closed
ΑΠΑΓΟΡΕΥΕΤΑΙ	Prohibited
ΑΣΤΥΝΟΜΙΑ	Police
ΓΥΝΑΙΚΩΝ	Toilets (Women)
ΑΝΔΡΩΝ	Toilets (Men)

Call ...! Φωνάξτε ...! fo·nak·ste ...
  a doctor ένα γιατρό e·na yi·a·tro
  the police την tin
    αστυνομία a·sti·no·mi·a

I'm ill. Είμαι άρρωστος. i·me a·ro·stos
I'm allergic to (antibiotics).
Είμαι αλλεργικός/ i·me a·ler·yi·kos/
αλλεργική a·ler·yi·ki (m/f)
(στα αντιβιωτικά) (sta an·di·vi·o·ti·ka)

SHOPPING & SERVICES

I'd like to buy ...
Θέλω ν' αγοράσω ... the·lo na·gho·ra·so ...
I'm just looking.
Απλώς κοιτάζω. ap·los ki·ta·zo
Can I see it?
Μπορώ να το δω; bo·ro na to dho
I don't like it.
Δεν μου αρέσει. dhen mu a·re·si
How much is it?
Πόσο κάνει; po·so ka·ni
It's too expensive.
Είναι πολύ ακριβό. i·ne po·li a·kri·vo
Can you lower the price?
Μπορείς να κατεβάσεις bo·ris na ka·te·va·sis
την τιμή; tin ti·mi

ATM	αυτόματη	af·to·ma·ti
	μηχανή	mi·kha·ni
	χρημάτων	khri·ma·ton
bank	τράπεζα	tra·pe·za
credit card	πιστωτική	pi·sto·ti·ki
	κάρτα	kar·ta
internet cafe	καφενείο	ka·fe·ni·o
	διαδικτύου	dhi·a·dhik·ti·u
mobile phone	κινητό	ki·ni·to
post office	ταχυδρομείο	ta·hi·dhro·mi·o
tourist office	τουριστικό	tu·ri·sti·ko
	γραφείο	ghra·fi·o

TIME & DATES

What time is it?
Τι ώρα είναι; ti o·ra i·ne
It's (two) o'clock.
Είναι (δύο) η ώρα. i·ne (dhi·o) i o·ra
It's half past (10).
(Δέκα) και μισή. (dhe·ka) ke mi·si

morning	πρωί	pro·i
(this)	(αυτό το)	(af·to to)
afternoon	απόγευμα	a·po·yev·ma
evening	βράδυ	vra·dhi
yesterday	χθες	hthes
today	σήμερα	si·me·ra
tomorrow	αύριο	av·ri·o
Monday	Δευτέρα	dhef·te·ra
Tuesday	Τρίτη	tri·ti
Wednesday	Τετάρτη	te·tar·ti
Thursday	Πέμπτη	pemp·ti
Friday	Παρασκευή	pa·ras·ke·vi
Saturday	Σάββατο	sa·va·to
Sunday	Κυριακή	ky·ri·a·ki
January	Ιανουάριος	ia·nu·ar·i·os
February	Φεβρουάριος	fev·ru·ar·i·os
March	Μάρτιος	mar·ti·os
April	Απρίλιος	a·pri·li·os
May	Μάιος	mai·os
June	Ιούνιος	i·u·ni·os
July	Ιούλιος	i·u·li·os
August	Αύγουστος	av·ghus·tos
September	Σεπτέμβριος	sep·tem·vri·os
October	Οκτώβριος	ok·to·vri·os
November	Νοέμβριος	no·em·vri·os
December	Δεκέμβριος	dhe·kem·vri·os

Question Words

How?	Πώς;	pos
What?	Τι;	ti
When?	Πότε;	po·te
Where?	Πού;	pu
Who?	Ποιος;	pi·os (m)
	Ποια;	pi·a (f)
	Ποιο;	pi·o (n)
Why?	Γιατί;	yi·a·ti

TRANSPORT

Public Transport

boat	πλοίο	pli·o
city bus	αστικό	a·sti·ko
intercity bus	λεωφορείο	le·o·fo·ri·o
plane	αεροπλάνο	ae·ro·pla·no
train	τρένο	tre·no

Where do I buy a ticket?
Πού αγοράζω εισιτήριο;   pu a·gho·ra·zo i·si·ti·ri·o
I want to go to ...
Θέλω να πάω στο/στη ...   the·lo na pao sto/sti...
What time does it leave?
Τι ώρα φεύγει;   ti o·ra fev·yi
Does it stop at (Iraklio)?
Σταματάει στο   sta·ma·ta·i sto
(Ηράκλειο);   (i·ra·kli·o)
I'd like to get off at (Iraklio).
Θα ήθελα να κατεβώ   tha i·the·la na ka·te·vo
στο (Ηράκλειο).   sto (i·ra·kli·o)

I'd like (a) ...	Θα ήθελα (ένα) ...	tha i·the·la (e·na) ...
1st class	πρώτη θέση	pro·ti the·si
2nd class	δεύτερη θέση	def·te·ri the·si
one-way ticket	απλό εισιτήριο	a·plo i·si·ti·ri·o
return ticket	εισιτήριο με επιστροφή	i·si·ti·ri·o me e·pi·stro·fi
cancelled	ακυρώθηκε	a·ki·ro·thi·ke
delayed	καθυστέρησε	ka·thi·ste·ri·se
platform	πλατφόρμα	plat·for·ma
ticket office	εκδοτήριο εισιτηρίων	ek·dho·ti·ri·o i·si·ti·ri·on
timetable	δρομολόγιο	dhro·mo·lo·gio
train station	σταθμός τρένου	stath·mos tre·nu

Driving & Cycling

I'd like to hire a ...	Θα ήθελα να νοικιάσω ...	tha i·the·la na ni·ki·a·so ...
4WD	ένα τέσσερα επί τέσσερα	e·na tes·se·ra e·pi tes·se·ra
bicycle	ένα ποδήλατο	e·na po·dhi·la·to
car	ένα αυτοκίνητο	e·na af·to·ki·ni·to
jeep	ένα τζιπ	e·na tzip
motorbike	μια μοτοσυκλέττα	mya mo·to·si·klet·ta

Do I need a helmet?

Numbers

1	ένας	e·nas (m)
	μία	mi·a (f)
	ένα	e·na (n)
2	δύο	dhi·o
3	τρεις	tris (m&f)
	τρία	tri·a (n)
4	τέσσερεις	te·se·ris (m&f)
	τέσσερα	te·se·ra (n)
5	πέντε	pen·de
6	έξη	e·xi
7	επτά	ep·ta
8	οχτώ	oh·to
9	εννέα	e·ne·a
10	δέκα	dhe·ka
20	είκοσι	ik·o·si
30	τριάντα	tri·an·da
40	σαράντα	sa·ran·da
50	πενήντα	pe·nin·da
60	εξήντα	ek·sin·da
70	εβδομήντα	ev·dho·min·da
80	ογδόντα	ogh·dhon·da
90	ενενήντα	e·ne·nin·da
100	εκατό	e·ka·to
1000	χίλιοι	hi·li·i (m)
	χίλιες	hi·li·ez (f)
	χίλια	hi·li·a (n)

Χρειάζομαι κράνος;   khri·a·zo·me kra·nos
Is this the road to ...?
Αυτός είναι ο   af·tos i·ne o
δρόμος για ... ;   dhro·mos ya ...
Where's a petrol station?
Πού είναι ένα πρατήριο   pu i·ne e·na pra·ti·ri·o
βενζίνας;   ven·zi·nas
(How long) Can I park here?
(Πόση ώρα) Μπορώ να   (po·si o·ra) bo·ro na
παρκάρω εδώ;   par·ka·ro e·dho
The car/motorbike has broken down (at ...).
Το αυτοκίνητο/   to af·to·ki·ni·to/
η μοτοσυκλέττα   i mo·to·si·klet·ta
χάλασε (στο ...).   kha·la·se (sto ...)
I need a mechanic.
Χρειάζομαι μηχανικό.   khri·a·zo·me mi·kha·ni·ko
I have a flat tyre.
Έπαθα λάστιχο.   e·pa·tha la·sti·cho
I've run out of petrol.
Έμεινα από βενζίνη.   e·mi·na a·po ven·zi·ni

Behind the Scenes

SEND US YOUR FEEDBACK

We love to hear from travellers – your comments keep us on our toes and help make our books better. Our well-travelled team reads every word on what you loved or loathed about this book. Although we cannot reply individually to your submissions, we always guarantee that your feedback goes straight to the appropriate authors, in time for the next edition. Each person who sends us information is thanked in the next edition – the most useful submissions are rewarded with a selection of digital PDF chapters.

Visit **lonelyplanet.com/contact** to submit your updates and suggestions or to ask for help. Our award-winning website also features inspirational travel stories, news and discussions.

Note: We may edit, reproduce and incorporate your comments in Lonely Planet products such as guidebooks, websites and digital products, so let us know if you don't want your comments reproduced or your name acknowledged. For a copy of our privacy policy visit lonelyplanet.com/privacy.

WRITER THANKS

Simon Richmond

Many thanks to the following: Steve Boyd, Valie Voutsa, Vangelis Koronakis, Yannis Bournias, Nikos Tsoniotis, Danae Zaoussis, Zora O'Neill, Harry and Jane Lushington, and Brana Vladisavljevic for hiring me for a great gig.

Kate Armstrong

I'd be a trillionaire for all the times I've uttered *efharisto poli* to the helpful Greeks who've opened their hearts. Especially Eleni and Yiannis (Kalymnos), Michalis of Michalis Studios (Lipsi), the Alexakis family (Alexakis Hotel; Kos), Michalis (Café Angolo Italiano; Karpathos), George (Euromoto; Karpathos), fabulous walkers Mike and John (Tilos), Tonia, Maria and Christina (Leros). Brana V, DE extraordinaire, you were the best of the LP best to work with. Finally, fellow Gemini Apostolos, without whom my Odyssey would have stalled in the Meltemi winds.

Stuart Butler

Thank you once again to my wife, Heather, and children, Jake and Grace, for putting up with me sauntering off to sunny Greece while they were stuck at home. And then I must thank them again for being the best travel partners I could ever want when they flew out to Corfu to join me towards the end of my research. Thank you also to Brana for giving me this dream gig in the first place.

Peter Dragicevich

It's always a complete delight to have company on the road, especially when it comes in the form of one of your very best friends. Thank you, David Mills, for being so diligent in assisting me in researching the Mykonos nightlife. Special thanks are also due to editor extraordinaire Brana Vladisavljevic for all of the support and opportunities you've given me over the years.

Trent Holden

First up, a huge thanks to the destination editor, Brana Vladisavljevic, not only for commissioning me on this title, but for all her work at Lonely Planet over the past 15 years. You will be missed! Also sending out my gratitude to the Cretan people who make this island so special with their humbling hospitality, good humour and willingness to help out at all times. Finally lots of love to my fiancée Kate Morgan, and to my family and friends.

Anna Kaminski

Huge thanks to Brana for entrusting me with half of the Cyclades, and to everyone who's helped me along the way. In particular: Alex in Halki (Naxos), Apostolos of Atlantis Oia in Santorini, the lifeguard who rescued me when I was swept out to sea on a paddleboard in Ios, Kostas in Folegandros, Alix and Semeli in Amorgos, Flora in Antiparos, plus all wine experts on Sikinos, Paros, Santorini and in Naxos who've contributed to my ongoing oenological education.

Vesna Maric

Many thanks to Brana Vladisavljevic, who commissioned the project – it was always an absolute joy to work with her. Thanks to Stathis Kampouridis for his generosity in Athens.

Kate Morgan

Huge thanks to amazing destination editor Brana for commissioning me to work on Crete, LP won't be the same without you. Thank you to Despina in Hania for all of your assistance, to the staff at the Hania tourist information office for your help and to all of the amazing Cretans I met along the way – your generosity and hospitality is unforgettable. And, as always, thank you to my fiancé Trent for being the best travel companion and for driving me all over Hania.

Isabella Noble

Efharisto to all the wonderful people who helped out on the road and back at home. Denis in Skiathos; Heather, Alexandra, Voula, Kostas, Valeria and Natasa in Skopelos; Mary, Pakis, Paul, Angela and Justine in Alonnisos; Lefteris, Katerina, Chrysanthi, Amanda and Nikos in Skyros; Marina, Giorgios and Steven in Evia. Back at home, thanks to Jack, Andrew, Papi and Sarah.

Leonid Ragozin

I would like to thank Christos of Ikaria Utopia for helping to get my head around new things on the island; Samos Volunteers for insights into the refugee situation; Manolis of Belvedere in Pythagorio for good tips about Samos; Paulette Roberge for opening the doors of her splendid Inousses villa; dozens of other friendly and hospitable people who shared ideas and pointed me in the right direction. I also feel very grateful to Greece for its very existence – it's a great and beloved country.

Kevin Raub

Thanks to Brana Vladisavljevic and all my fellow partners in crime at LP. On the road, Kjetil Jikiun, Giorges Kteniadakis, Andria Mitsakis, Iossif Serafimidis, Dr Emmanuel Prokopkis and the nurses at Pagni, Lydia and Nikos and the brews of Kykao and Solo.

Andrea Schulte-Peevers

Heartfelt thank yous to Kerstin Göllrich for her patience, curiosity, stamina and awesome driving skills; Johannes Bolz for literally going the extra mile for me in the Kritsa Gorge; Konstantinos and Natalie Zivas for wonderful insider tips on Elounda and the north coast, and father Vaggelis for his kitchen wizardry; Alaska Klaus for his insights into hiking the E4; Margarita Kurowska and Jutta Berger for keeping things under control on the home front; and David for being with me in spirit.

Greg Ward

Many thanks to all the wonderful people who helped me along the way, and who created so many happy memories. And thanks above all to my dear wife, Sam, for sharing such an amazing trip.

ACKNOWLEDGEMENTS

Climate map data adapted from Peel MC, Finlayson BL & McMahon TA (2007) 'Updated World Map of the Köppen-Geiger Climate Classification', *Hydrology and Earth Sciences*, 11, 1633–44.

Illustrations pp148–9 and pp336–7 by Javier Zarracina.

Cover photograph: Oia old town, Santorini; Dmitry Morgan/Shutterstock ©

THIS BOOK

This 11th edition of Lonely Planet's *Greek Islands* guidebook was researched and written by Simon Richmond, Kate Armstrong, Stuart Butler, Peter Dragicevich, Trent Holden, Anna Kaminski, Vesna Maric, Kate Morgan, Isabella Noble, Leonid Ragozin, Kevin Raub, Andrea Schulte-Peevers and Greg Ward. The previous edition was written by Korina Miller, Alexis Averbuck, Anna Kaminski, Craig McLachan, Zora O'Neill, Leonid Ragozin, Andrea Schulte-Peevers, Helena Smith, Greg Ward and Richard Waters.

This guidebook was produced by the following:
Destination Editor Brana Vladisavljevic
Senior Product Editors Elizabeth Jones, Kathryn Rowan
Regional Senior Cartographer Anthony Phelan
Product Editors Fergus O'Shea, Claire Rourke
Book Designers Mazzy Prinsep, Jessica Rose
Assisting Editors Katie O'Connell, Gabrielle Stefanos

Assisting Cartographer James Leversha
Assisting Book Designers Gwen Cotter, Wibowo Rusli
Cover Researcher Naomi Parker
Thanks to Ronan Abayawickrema, Imogen Bannister, Michael Bechlet, Hannah Cartmel, Fergal Condon, Gwen Cotter, Shona Gray, Ian Gretton, Karen Henderson, Sandie Kestell, Amy Lynch, Catherine Naghten, Genna Patterson, Martine Power, Gary Rafferty, Kirsten Rawlings, Shane Scanlan, Vicky Smith

Index

INDEX B-D

Map Legend

Sights

- Beach
- Bird Sanctuary
- Buddhist
- Castle/Palace
- Christian
- Confucian
- Hindu
- Islamic
- Jain
- Jewish
- Monument
- Museum/Gallery/Historic Building
- Ruin
- Shinto
- Sikh
- Taoist
- Winery/Vineyard
- Zoo/Wildlife Sanctuary
- Other Sight

Activities, Courses & Tours

- Bodysurfing
- Diving
- Canoeing/Kayaking
- Course/Tour
- Sento Hot Baths/Onsen
- Skiing
- Snorkelling
- Surfing
- Swimming/Pool
- Walking
- Windsurfing
- Other Activity

Sleeping

- Sleeping
- Camping
- Hut/Shelter

Eating

- Eating

Drinking & Nightlife

- Drinking & Nightlife
- Cafe

Entertainment

- Entertainment

Shopping

- Shopping

Information

- Bank
- Embassy/Consulate
- Hospital/Medical
- Internet
- Police
- Post Office
- Telephone
- Toilet
- Tourist Information
- Other Information

Geographic

- Beach
- Gate
- Hut/Shelter
- Lighthouse
- Lookout
- Mountain/Volcano
- Oasis
- Park
- Pass
- Picnic Area
- Waterfall

Population

- Capital (National)
- Capital (State/Province)
- City/Large Town
- Town/Village

Transport

- Airport
- Border crossing
- Bus
- Cable car/Funicular
- Cycling
- Ferry
- Metro station
- Monorail
- Parking
- Petrol station
- S-Bahn/Subway station
- Taxi
- T-bane/Tunnelbana station
- Train station/Railway
- Tram
- U-Bahn/Underground station
- Other Transport

Routes

- Tollway
- Freeway
- Primary
- Secondary
- Tertiary
- Lane
- Unsealed road
- Road under construction
- Plaza/Mall
- Steps
- Tunnel
- Pedestrian overpass
- Walking Tour
- Walking Tour detour
- Path/Walking Trail

Boundaries

- International
- State/Province
- Disputed
- Regional/Suburb
- Marine Park
- Cliff
- Wall

Hydrography

- River, Creek
- Intermittent River
- Canal
- Water
- Dry/Salt/Intermittent Lake
- Reef

Areas

- Airport/Runway
- Beach/Desert
- Cemetery (Christian)
- Cemetery (Other)
- Glacier
- Mudflat
- Park/Forest
- Sight (Building)
- Sportsground
- Swamp/Mangrove

Note: Not all symbols displayed above appear on the maps in this book

Kevin Raub

Crete Atlanta native Kevin started his career as a music journalist in New York, working for *Men's Journal* and *Rolling Stone* magazines. He ditched the rock 'n' roll lifestyle for travel writing and has written more than 95 Lonely Planet guides, focused mainly on Brazil, Chile, Colombia, USA, India, Italy and Portugal. Raub also contributes to a variety of travel magazines in both the USA and UK. Along the way, the self-confessed hophead is in constant search of wildly high IBUs in local beers. Find him at www.kevinraub.net or follow him on Twitter and Instagram (@RaubOnTheRoad).

Andrea Schulte-Peevers

Crete Born and raised in Germany and educated in London and at UCLA, Andrea has travelled the distance to the moon and back in her visits to some 75 countries. She has earned her living as a professional travel writer for over two decades and authored or contributed to nearly 100 Lonely Planet titles as well as to newspapers, magazines and websites around the world. She also works as a travel consultant, translator and editor. Andrea's destination expertise is especially strong when it comes to Germany, Dubai and the UAE, Crete and the Caribbean Islands. She makes her home in Berlin.

Greg Ward

Rhodes Since his youthful adventures on the hippy trail to India, and living in northern Spain, Greg has written guides to destinations all over the world. As well as covering the USA from the Southwest to Hawaii, he has ranged on recent assignments from Corsica to the Cotswolds, and Dallas to Delphi. Visit his website, www.gregward.info, to see his favourite photos and memories.

Trent Holden

Crete A Geelong-based writer, located just outside Melbourne, Trent has worked for Lonely Planet since 2005. He's covered 30-plus guidebooks across Asia, Africa and Australia. With a penchant for megacities, Trent's in his element when assigned to cover a nation's capital – the more chaotic the better – to unearth cool bars, art, street food and underground subculture. On the flipside he also writes books to idyllic tropical islands across Asia, in between going on safari to national parks in Africa and the subcontinent. When not travelling, Trent works as a freelance editor, reviewer and spends all his money catching live gigs. You can catch him on Twitter @hombreholden.

Anna Kaminski

Cyclades Originally from the Soviet Union, Anna grew up in Cambridge, UK. She graduated from the University of Warwick with a degree in Comparative American Studies, a background in the history, culture and literature of the Americas and the Caribbean, and an enduring love of Latin America. Her restless wanderings led her to settle briefly in Oaxaca and Bangkok and her flirtation with criminal law saw her volunteering as a lawyer's assistant in the courts, ghettos and prisons of Kingston, Jamaica. Anna has contributed to almost 30 Lonely Planet titles.

Vesna Maric

Around Athens, Saronic Gulf Islands Vesna has been a Lonely Planet author for nearly two decades, covering places as far and wide as Bolivia, Algeria, Sicily, Cyprus, Barcelona, London and Croatia, among others. Her latest work has been updating Florida, Greece and North Macedonia.

Kate Morgan

Crete Having worked for Lonely Planet for over a decade now, Kate has been fortunate enough to cover plenty of ground working as a travel writer on destinations such as Shanghai, Japan, India, Russia, Zimbabwe, the Philippines and Phuket. She has done stints living in London, Paris and Osaka but these days is based in one of her favourite regions in the world – Victoria, Australia. In between travelling the world and writing about it, Kate enjoys spending time at home working as a freelance editor.

Isabella Noble

Evia & Sporades English-Australian on paper but Spanish at heart, Isabella has been wandering the globe since her first round-the-world trip as a one-year-old. Having grown up in a whitewashed Andalucian village, she is a Spain specialist travel journalist, but also writes extensively about India, Thailand, the UK and beyond for Lonely Planet, the *Daily Telegraph* and others. Isabella has co-written Lonely Planet guides to Spain and Andalucía, and is a *Daily Telegraph* Spain expert. She has also contributed to Lonely Planet *India*, *South India*, *Thailand*, *Thailand's Islands & Beaches*, *Southeast Asia on a Shoestring* and *Great Britain*, and authored *Pocket Phuket*. Find Isabella on Twitter and Instagram (@isabellamnoble).

Leonid Ragozin

Northeastern Aegean Islands Leonid studied beach dynamics at the Moscow State University, but for want of decent beaches in Russia, he switched to journalism and spent 12 years voyaging through different parts of the BBC, with a break for a four-year stint as a foreign correspondent for the Russian Newsweek. Leonid is currently a freelance journalist focusing largely on the conflict between Russia and Ukraine (both his Lonely Planet destinations), which prompted him to leave Moscow and find a new home in Rīga.

OUR STORY

A beat-up old car, a few dollars in the pocket and a sense of adventure. In 1972 that's all Tony and Maureen Wheeler needed for the trip of a lifetime – across Europe and Asia overland to Australia. It took several months, and at the end – broke but inspired – they sat at their kitchen table writing and stapling together their first travel guide, *Across Asia on the Cheap*. Within a week they'd sold 1500 copies. Lonely Planet was born.

Today, Lonely Planet has offices in Franklin, London, Melbourne, Oakland, Dublin, Beijing and Delhi, with more than 600 staff and writers. We share Tony's belief that 'a great guidebook should do three things: inform, educate and amuse'.

OUR WRITERS

Simon Richmond

Athens Journalist and photographer Simon Richmond has specialised as a travel writer since the early 1990s and first worked for Lonely Planet in 1999 on their Central Asia guide. He's long since stopped counting the number of guidebooks he's researched and written for the company, but countries covered include Australia, China, Greece, India, Indonesia, Iran, Poland, Japan, Malaysia, Mongolia, Myanmar (Burma), Russia, Singapore, South Africa, South Korea and Turkey and the USA. For Lonely Planet's website he's penned features on topics from the world's best swimming pools to the joys of Urban Sketching – follow him on Instagram (simonrichmond) to see some of his photos and sketches. Simon also wrote the Plan Your Trip, Understand and Surival Guide chapters.

Kate Armstrong

Dodecanese Kate Armstrong has spent much of her adult life travelling and living around the world. A full-time freelance travel journalist, she has contributed to more than 50 Lonely Planet guides and trade publications and is regularly published in Australian and worldwide publications. She is the author of several books and children's educational titles.

Stuart Butler

Ionian Islands Stuart has been writing for Lonely Planet for a decade and during this time he's come eye to eye with gorillas in the Congolese jungles, met a man with horns on his head who could lie in fire, huffed and puffed over snow bound Himalayan mountain passes, interviewed a king who could turn into a tree, and had his fortune told by a parrot. Oh, and he's met more than his fair share of self-proclaimed gods. When not on the road for Lonely Planet he lives on the beautiful beaches of southwest France with his wife and two young children.

Peter Dragicevich

Cyclades After a successful career in niche newspaper and magazine publishing, both in his native New Zealand and in Australia, Peter finally gave in to Kiwi wanderlust, giving up staff jobs to chase his diverse roots around much of Europe. Over the last decade he's written literally dozens of guidebooks for Lonely Planet on an oddly disparate collection of countries, all of which he's come to love. He once again calls Auckland, New Zealand his home – although his current nomadic existence means he's often elsewhere.

OVER PAGE — MORE WRITERS

Published by Lonely Planet Global Limited
CRN 554153
11th edition – March 2020
ISBN 978 1 78701 574 6
© Lonely Planet 2020   Photographs © as indicated 2020
10 9 8 7 6 5 4 3 2 1
Printed in China